S0-AVT-299

t DISTRIBUTION

Areas in Both Tails Combined for Student's *t* Distribution.*

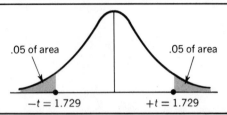

.05 of area   .05 of area

$-t = 1.729$ $+t = 1.729$

EXAMPLE: To find the value of *t* which corresponds to an area of .10 in both tails of the distribution combined, when there are 19 degrees of freedom, look under the .10 column, and proceed down to the 19 degrees of freedom row; the appropriate *t* value there is 1.729.

Degrees of freedom	Area in both tails combined			
	.10	.05	.02	.01
1	6.314	12.706	31.821	63.657
2	2.920	4.303	6.965	9.925
3	2.353	3.182	4.541	5.841
4	2.132	2.776	3.747	4.604
5	2.015	2.571	3.365	4.032
6	1.943	2.447	3.143	3.707
7	1.895	2.365	2.998	3.499
8	1.860	2.306	2.896	3.355
9	1.833	2.262	2.821	3.250
10	1.812	2.228	2.764	3.169
11	1.796	2.201	2.718	3.106
12	1.782	2.179	2.681	3.055
13	1.771	2.160	2.650	3.012
14	1.761	2.145	2.624	2.977
15	1.753	2.131	2.602	2.947
16	1.746	2.120	2.583	2.921
17	1.740	2.110	2.567	2.898
18	1.734	2.101	2.552	2.878
19	1.729	2.093	2.539	2.861
20	1.725	2.086	2.528	2.845
21	1.721	2.080	2.518	2.831
22	1.717	2.074	2.508	2.819
23	1.714	2.069	2.500	2.807
24	1.711	2.064	2.492	2.797
25	1.708	2.060	2.485	2.787
26	1.706	2.056	2.479	2.779
27	1.703	2.052	2.473	2.771
28	1.701	2.048	2.467	2.763
29	1.699	2.045	2.462	2.756
30	1.697	2.042	2.457	2.750
40	1.684	2.021	2.423	2.704
60	1.671	2.000	2.390	2.660
120	1.658	1.980	2.358	2.617
Normal Distribution	1.645	1.960	2.326	2.576

* Taken from Table III of Fisher and Yates, *Statistical Tables for Biological, Agricultural and Medical Research,* published by Longman Group Ltd., London (previously published by Oliver & Boyd, Edinburgh) and by permission of the authors and publishers.

Statistics
for
Management

FIFTH EDITION

Richard I. Levin ▪ David S. Rubin

The University of North Carolina
at Chapel Hill

The University of North Carolina
at Chapel Hill

Prentice Hall, Englewood Cliffs, New Jersey 07632

Library of Congress Cataloging-in Publication Data

Levin, Richard I.
　　Statistics for management / Richard I. Levin, David S. Rubin. —
5th ed.

　　Includes bibliographical references and index.
　　ISBN 0-13-851965-x
　　1. Social sciences—Statistical methods. 2. Commercial
statistics. 3. Management—Statistical methods. I. Rubin, David
S. II. Title.
HA29.L3887　1990
519.5—dc20

　　　　　　　　　　　　　　　　90-7712
　　　　　　　　　　　　　　　　CIP

Editorial/production supervision: *Keith Faivre*
Interior design: *Lorraine Mullaney*
Cover design: *Lorraine Mullaney/Christine Wolf*
Manufacturing buyers: *Trudy Pisciotti/Bob Anderson*
Photo research: *Ilene Cherna*
Photo editor: *Lorinda Morris-Nantz*

Cover photo: *Charles Bell: Marbles VII,* 1982. Oil on canvas. 60″ × 78¼″. Photograph courtesy of
Louis K. Meisel Gallery, New York.

Chapter opening photo credits:　**Chapter 1:**　Dick Luria/Photo Researchers　**Chapter 2:**　Carl Purcell/Photo Researchers
Chapter 3:　Van Bucher/Photo Researchers　**Chapter 4:**　Charles Bell, *Rol-A-Top,* 32½ × 40 inches, oil on canvas, 1981. Photo
courtesy Louis K. Meisel Gallery, New York　**Chapter 5:**　Dan McCoy/Rainbow　**Chapter 6:**　Danny Brass/Photo
Researchers　**Chapter 7:**　Thomas Hovland/Grant Heilman Photography　**Chapter 8:**　Tony Duffy/Woodfin Camp &
Associates　**Chapter 9:**　Charles Gupton/Stock, Boston　**Chapter 10:** Jack Fields/Photo Researchers　**Chapter 11:**　Bill
Anderson/Monkmeyer Press　**Chapter 12:**　Alan Pitcairn/Grant Heilman Photography　**Chapter 13:**　Michael Serraillier/
Rapho-Photo Researchers　**Chapter 14:**　Jon Feingersh/Stock, Boston　**Chapter 15:** Georgia/Grant Heilman Photography

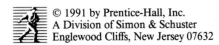

© 1991 by Prentice-Hall, Inc.
A Division of Simon & Schuster
Englewood Cliffs, New Jersey 07632

All rights reserved. No part of this book may be reproduced, in any form or by any means, without
permission in writing from the publisher.

Printed in the United States of America

10　9　8　7　6　5　4　3

ISBN 0-13-851965-X

Prentice-Hall International (UK) Limited, *London*
Prentice-Hall of Australia Pty. Limited, *Sydney*
Prentice-Hall Canada Inc., *Toronto*
Prentice-Hall Hispanoamericana, S.A., *Mexico*
Prentice-Hall of India Private Limited, *New Delhi*
Prentice-Hall of Japan, Inc., *Tokyo*
Simon & Schuster Asia Pte. Ltd., *Singapore*
Editora Prentice-Hall do Brasil, Ltda., *Rio de Janeiro*

Statistics
for
Management

Contents

3
Measures of Central Tendency and Dispersion in Frequency Distributions 62

4
Probability I: Introductory Ideas 134

5
Probability II: Distributions 190

9
Chi-Square and Analysis of Variance 414

10
Simple Regression and Correlation 478

11
Multiple Regression and Modeling Techniques 536

Preface

BUILDING ON A STRONG BASE

After four previous editions, preparing a new edition is always a very exciting time for us. We have a strong base of time-tested approaches and topics on which to build. And now, we have an opportunity to build onto this base and add new ideas, topics, teaching and learning aids, and approaches which we hope will make teaching and learning statistics more decision-focused, and thus more fun!

FOUR EDITIONS OF PROVEN APPROACHES

Each time we revise our book, we listen very carefully to what our adopters (and students) tell us. And each time, we incorporate their suggestions into the revision. This close relationship has already produced a textbook with these strong features:

Philosophy. Since our first edition, back in 1978, our philosophy has been to produce a book that minimizes the anxiety students typically associate with statistics. Our teaching colleagues and their students will quickly see that this fifth edition remains the most easily followed, easily understood, business statistics book written.

How We Explain Statistics. We begin with what the student already knows, and we extend this carefully, patiently, and intuitively to the introduction of statistical concepts. We use lots of commonsense analogies, examples, and anecdotes to reinforce this kind of learning. We don't leave out any steps when we explain ideas, and we never lapse into the dangerous phrase, "it can be shown." If we need to show it we show it; if we can't explain it so that everyone will understand it, then the topic must be too complex for a beginning book in business statistics.

The Topics We Cover. Before we began this revision, our research showed that our book already contained the most comprehensive set of topics to be found in any beginning business statistics text. The in-depth coverage of these topics has been extended even more in this new fifth edition.

Mathematical Complexity and Notation. Complex mathematical notation is necessary for mathematicians, but instructors who use this book quickly see that we never obscure the effective teaching of statistics with difficult-to-understand notation. Students have appreciated the fact that we use only the level of notation necessary to explain things effectively; and they also notice that the notation we do use is carefully explained and kept absolutely consistent throughout the entire book. Any equation that appears in the book has a unique equation number which identifies the chapter in which it was first introduced; and we use that same number whenever the equation reappears.

MAKING TEACHING AND LEARNING EASIER

Previous users of *Statistics For Management* and those teachers who adopt this edition will notice the extensive set of pedagogical aids built into the text, and the instruction manuals that accompany it. Each of these helping pedagogies makes learning statistics more effective, and, we hope, less painful. The list of such teaching-learning aids grows even more extensive with this edition; it includes:

- Chapter introductions built around a photographically-described decision environment in which a person must make a business decision. In each instance, the problem is worked out in detail later in the chapter. This, we believe, helps students see the significant usefulness of statistics in managerial decision-making.
- Each chapter contains a "conceptual case," which is a decision situation where we ask the student to focus on the problem and not the numbers. In each instance, the student is encouraged to think about (1) the data that ought to be collected to help make an effective decision, (2) the kind of statistical analysis that might be helpful to the decision maker, (3) what the decision maker would do with the solution if he or she could provide one, and (4) what kinds of improvement or savings would likely result from a successful application. This approach helps students learn that what you do with the answer is vastly more important than simply "cranking out" a solution.
- A comprehensive computer data base exercise is introduced early in the book, and this same company-based situation reappears in each chapter that follows. It is built around a young analyst who is attempting to use statistics effectively to make important decisions for her company. It details her tribulations and her successes and motivates students to appreciate both the potential of statistics in business and the problems associated with applying it.
- Each chapter ends with an annotated review of all of the equations that were introduced in that chapter. Each equation is assigned a unique identifying number, and the page on which the equation was first introduced is also cited. The information needs of the equation are briefly reviewed.
- A comprehensive glossary of terms appears at the end of each chapter. All statistical terms that were introduced in the chapter are listed alphabetically and defined. This provides a very effective way for students to review the particular language associated with the chapter.
- Each chapter ends with an extensive set of mixed review exercises. These cover all of the topics introduced in that chapter. We also provide exercises at the end of each section within a chapter. In this way, students can reinforce their learning of individual tools and constructs as they proceed through the chapter by using the

section-ending exercises; they can also hone their skills at choosing the particular tool appropriate for a specific situation by using the chapter-ending review.

■ A comprehensive flow chart is provided at the end of each chapter. This is designed to help students learn which statistical approach is appropriate for each individual decision environment. It motivates students to think of statistical analysis as a comprehensive approach to problem solving, and not just as a set of tools to use.

■ The book ends with an index of applications. Here we have listed every one of the more than 1000 exercises in the text, under one or more of nearly a hundred areas in business in which that exercise is being applied. Thus, if the teacher wants to illustrate a use of multiple regression in a marketing situation, he/she can find such exercises in a matter of a few seconds.

■ There are almost 1600 marginal notes designed to make studying more efficient. Students can see very quickly what is being discussed on any page of the text by using these.

■ The text contains over 1000 exercises, with answers provided for the even-numbered exercises at the back of the book.

■ Enhanced four-color art work makes it easier to explain and learn difficult concepts.

■ Sections titled "From the textbook to the real world" appear in selected chapters. In each case, we have brought to the book real examples of how statistical analysis was used to solve significant problems. We provide complete citations in each instance, so that further research into that particular situation can be done.

■ We provide with this book a comprehensive instructor's manual with worked out answers to all of the exercises in the text.

■ There is a student workbook and study guide to help students reinforce their understanding and application of statistical methods.

■ A test bank is provided for instructors.

Features New to the 5th Edition

■ Our previous adopters will notice the extended use of computer analysis in this edition. But this goes beyond just more computer "drill." Computer solutions appear as logical extensions of learned methods, and not as "black boxes." First we work an exercise using hand computation methods; then we introduce the computer as a way to handle complexity.

■ A fourth of the text exercises have been changed or significantly altered.

■ Many exercises are identified with icons, which indicate whether the exercise ought to be done with hand computation methods, with a computer, or a combination (some hand computation work, first to prepare or rearrange the data, and then use of the computer to complete the solution).

■ All of the "From the textbook to the real world" examples found in the fourth edition have been replaced with current, comprehensive, applications.

■ The teachability and learning ease of this 5th edition have been greatly enhanced with the use of a four-color format. This is the first time such a unique approach has been used in a business statistics textbook.

■ The basic descriptive statistics material has been covered in two shorter introductory chapters; this allows instruction to proceed efficiently and logically to the study of probabilities.

■ Each exercise in the text has been solved by three different "quality control persons." This insures a standard of accuracy never before available in a business statistics text.

THE TEAM

A very important change this time around is the addition of David Rubin's name on the cover as co-author. Dave has worked behind the scenes for several editions and now takes a much-deserved place on the marquee.

Writing a business statistics text or revising an existing one is not a job that two people can do by themselves. It takes a team of folks working together to produce a book that "works": Writers, reviewers, problem checkers, editors, users of previous editions, folks who write with suggestions, students who help us in many ways, and more people than we can possibly thank! Each of these leaves a mark on the finished work and we are only two such marks among many.

A few such folks need special mention. Our editor, Valerie Ashton, is always patient beyond words, supportive, market-sensitive, and a thoroughly nice person above all. She makes the entire process happen, and we know that.

Folks who reviewed this edition deserve special thanks. It is their comments and suggestions that shape our original ideas, and they keep us and our book focused on good classroom teaching. Reviewers for this edition were: Michael Abruzzese, Mark Bambach, R. Campapiano, John Daughtry, John P. Evans, Donald Goldschen, Joel Greenman, Thomas Hiestand, Michael Hu, J. Jarrett, Nathan Keith, William Koellner, I. Kwon, J. Michael McGuire, S. Mohaghegh, Gary Neff, E. N. Onunkwo, Ralph St. John, Diego Salazar, Marla Scafe, Alice Sineath, Faye Teer, E. G. Zapatero.

An extra special thanks should be extended to the "quality control" readers of this edition. Jackie Hoell of Virginia Polytechnic Institute coordinated this effort and was helped greatly by Annie Puciloski of Merrimack College and Barbara Russell of St. Bonaventure University.

We're also grateful to the literary executor of the late Sir Ronald Fisher, F.R.S., to Dr. Frank Yates, F.R.S., and to Longman Group, Ltd. London, for permission to reprint tables III and IV from their book, *Statistical Tables For Biological, Agricultural, and Medical Research,* (6th ed. 1974).

Our production editor, Keith Faivre, gets a special hand. He is the person who makes a book happen. He works with the printers, authors, copy editors, binders, and a hundred other folks who are involved in the process. He has been of great help and comfort for the last year and we are grateful!

Folks who have written with suggestions, students who have helped us in many ways (in particular, Hope Connell, Deena Dizengoff, Peter Krueger, Tim Nelson, Mark Pruett, and Chris Rump), and Lisa Levin, who produced the index, all get our thanks!

And finally, a very warm thanks to Barbara Hoopes for orchestrating Laurel McRae's move from Colorado to Florida.

All of these people came together and produced *Statistics For Management, 5th edition.* We are indebted to them for all that they did, and we are indebted to you, student and teacher, for giving all of us a chance to be a part of your classroom. We hope you like what we have written.

Dick Levin
Dave Rubin
Chapel Hill, NC

Statistics
for
Management

1

Introduction

This book was written for students taking statistics for the first time. A glance at this chapter should convince any concerned citizen and future manager that a working knowledge of basic statistics will be quite useful in coping with the complex problems of our society. Your first look will also convince you that this book is dedicated to helping you acquire that knowledge with virtually no previous formal mathematical training and with no pain at all.

1-1
Getting Started

Different meanings of statistics depending on use

The word *statistics* means different things to different people. To a football fan, statistics are the information about rushing yardage, passing yardage, and first downs, given at halftime. To the manager of a power generating station, statistics may be information about the quantity of pollutants being released into the atmosphere. To a school principal, statistics are information on absenteeism, test scores, and teacher salaries. To a medical researcher investigating the effects of a new drug, statistics are evidence of the success of research efforts. And to a college student, statistics are the grades made on all the quizzes in a course this semester.

Each of these people is using the word *statistics* correctly, yet each uses it in a slightly different way and for a somewhat different purpose. *Statistics* is a word that can refer to quantitative data (such as wheat yield per acre) or to a field of study (you may, for example, major in statistics). Benjamin Disraeli once made the statement,

How to lie with statistics

"There are three kinds of lies: lies, damned lies, and statistics." This rather severe castigation of statistics, made so many years ago, has come to be a rather apt description of many of the statistical deceptions we encounter in our everyday lives. Darrell Huff, in an enjoyable little book, *How to Lie with Statistics,* noted that "the crooks already know these tricks; honest men must learn them in self-defense." One goal of this book is to review some of the common ways statistics are used incorrectly, whether out of honest lack of knowledge or in an attempt to deceive the user. In either case, users of statistics who do not know how to cope with such deceptive practices cannot derive much real value from this discipline.

Today, statistics and statistical analysis are used in nearly every profession. For managers in particular, statistics have become a most valuable tool.

1-2
History

Origin of the word

The word *statistik* comes from the Italian word *statista* (meaning "statesman"). It was first used by Gottfried Achenwall (1719–1772), a professor at Marlborough and Göttingen. Dr. E. A. W. Zimmerman introduced the word *statistics* into England. Its use was popularized by Sir John Sinclair in his work, *Statistical Account of Scotland 1791–1799.* Long before the eighteenth century, however, people had been recording and using data.

Early government records

Official government statistics are as old as recorded history. The Old Testament contains several accounts of census taking. Governments of ancient Babylonia, Egypt, and Rome gathered detailed records of populations and resources. In the Middle Ages, governments began to register the ownership of land. In A.D. 762, Charlemagne asked for detailed descriptions of church-owned properties. Early in the ninth century, he completed a statistical enumeration of the serfs attached to the land. About 1086, William the Conqueror ordered the writing of the *Domesday Book,* a record of the ownership, extent, and value of the lands of England. This work was England's first statistical abstract.

An early prediction from statistics

Because of Henry VII's fear of the plague, England began to register its dead in 1532. About this same time, French law required the clergy to register baptisms, deaths, and marriages. During an outbreak of the plague in the late 1500s, the English government started publishing weekly death statistics. This practice continued, and by 1632 these *Bills of Mortality* listed births and deaths by sex. In 1662, Captain John

Graunt used thirty years of these Bills to make predictions about the number of persons who would die from various diseases and the proportion of male and female births that could be expected. Summarized in his work, *Natural and Political Observations . . . Made upon the Bills of Mortality,* Graunt's study was a pioneer effort in statistical analysis. For his achievement in using past records to predict future events, Graunt was made a member of the original Royal Society.

The history of the development of statistical theory and practice is a lengthy one. We have only begun to list the people who have made significant contributions to this field. Later we will encounter others whose names are now attached to specific laws and methods. Many people have brought to the study of statistics refinements or innovations that, taken together, form the theoretical basis of what we will study in this book.

1-3
Subdivisions Within Statistics

Managers apply some statistical technique to virtually every branch of public and private enterprise. These techniques are so diverse that statisticians commonly separate them into two broad categories: *descriptive statistics* and *inferential statistics.* Some examples will help us understand the difference between the two.

Descriptive statistics

Suppose a professor computes an average grade for one history class. Since statistics describe the performance of that one class but do not make a generalization about several classes, we can say that the professor is using *descriptive* statistics. Graphs, tables, and charts that display data so that they are easier to understand are all examples of descriptive statistics.

Inferential statistics

Now suppose that the history professor decides to use the average grade achieved by one history class to estimate the average grade achieved in all ten sections of the same history course. The process of estimating this average grade would be a problem in *inferential* statistics. Statisticians also refer to this category as *statistical inference.* Obviously, any conclusion the professor makes about the ten sections of the course will be based on a generalization that goes far beyond the data for the original history class; and the generalization may not be completely valid, so the professor must state how likely it is to be true. Similarly, statistical inference involves generalizations and statements about the *probability* of their validity.

Decision theory

The methods and techniques of statistical inference can also be used in a branch of statistics called *decision theory.* Knowledge of decision theory is very helpful for managers, because it is used to make decisions under conditions of uncertainty—when, for example, a manufacturer of stereo sets cannot specify precisely the demand for its products or when the chairperson of the English department at your school must schedule faculty teaching assignments without knowing precisely the student enrollment for next fall.

1-4
Strategy, Assumptions, and Approach

For students, not statisticians

This book is designed to help you get the feel of statistics—what it is, how and when to apply statistical techniques to decision-making situations, and how to interpret the results you get. Since we are not writing for professional statisticians, our writing is tailored to the backgrounds and needs of college students, who, as future citizens, probably accept the fact that statistics can be of considerable help to them in their future occupations but are very likely apprehensive about studying the subject.

We discard mathematical proofs in favor of intuitive ones. You will be guided through the learning process by reminders of what you already know, by examples with which you can identify, and by a step-by-step process instead of statements like, "it can be shown," or, "it therefore follows."

Symbols are simple and explained

As you thumb through this book and compare it with other basic business statistics textbooks, you will notice a minimum of mathematical notation. In the past, the complexity of the notation has intimidated many students, who got lost in the symbols even though they were motivated and intellectually capable of understanding the ideas. Each symbol and formula that is used is explained in detail, not only at the point at which it is introduced but also in a section at the end of the chapter.

No math beyond simple algebra required

If you felt reasonably comfortable when you finished your high school algebra course, you have enough background to understand *everything* in this book. Nothing beyond basic algebra is either assumed or used. Our goals are for you to be comfortable as you learn and for you to get a good intuitive grasp of statistical concepts and techniques. As a future manager, you will need to know when statistics can help your decision process and which tools to use. If you do need statistical help, you can find a statistical expert to handle the details.

Text problems cover a wide variety of situations

The problems used to introduce material in the chapters, the exercises at the end of each section within the chapter, and the chapter review exercises are drawn from a wide variety of situations you are already familiar with or are likely to confront quite soon. You will see problems involving all facets of the private sector of our economy: accounting, finance, individual and group behavior, marketing, and production. In addition, you will encounter managers in the public sphere coping with problems in public education, social services, the environment, consumer advocacy, and health systems.

Goals

In each problem situation, a manager is trying to use statistics creatively and productively. Helping you become comfortable doing exactly that is our goal.

1-5
Features In This Book That Make Learning Easier And How To Use Them

In our preface we mentioned briefly a number of learning aids that are a part of this book. Each of them has a particular role in helping you study and understand statistics, and if we spend a few minutes here discussing the most effective way to use some of these aids, you will not only learn more effectively, but will gain a greater understanding of how statistics is used to make managerial decisions.

Marginal Notes. Each of the more than 1500 marginal notes highlights the material in a paragraph or group of paragraphs. Because the notes briefly indicate the focus of the textual material, you can avoid having to read through pages of information to find what you need. Learn to read "down the left-hand column" as you work through the textbook; that way, you will get a good sense of the flow of topics and the meaning of what the text is explaining.

Glossary of Terms. Each chapter ends with a glossary of every new term introduced in that chapter. Having all of these new terms defined again in one convenient place can be a big help. As you work through a chapter, use the glossary to reinforce your understanding of what the terms mean. Doing this is easier than going back in the chapter trying to find the definition of a particular term. When you finish studying a chapter, use the glossary to make sure you understand what *each* term introduced in that chapter means.

Equation Review. Every equation introduced in a chapter is found in this section. All of them are explained again, and the page on which they were first introduced is given. Using this feature of the book is a very effective way to make sure you understand what each equation means and how it is used.

Chapter Concepts Test. Using these tests is a good way to see how well you understand the chapter material. As a part of your study, be sure to take these tests and then compare your answers with those in the back of the book. Doing this will point out areas in which you need more work, especially before quiz time.

Features that make learning easier

Conceptual Case. In each of these situations, a Northern White Metals Company employee, Dick Lennox, applies statistics to a managerial problem. The emphasis here is not on numbers; in fact, it's hard to find any numbers in these cases. As you read each of these cases, focus on what the problem is and what statistical approach might help find a solution; forget the numbers temporarily. In this way, you will develop a good appreciation for identifying problems and matching solution methods with problems, without being bogged down by numbers.

Flow Chart. The flow charts at the end of the chapters will enable you to develop a systematic approach to applying statistical methods to problems. Using them helps you understand where you begin, how you proceed, and where you wind-up; and if you get good at using them, you will not get lost in some of the more complex word problems instructors are fond of putting on tests.

From the Textbook to the Real World. Each of these will take you no more than two or three minutes to read, but doing so will show you how the concepts developed in this book are used to solve real-world problems. As you study each chapter, be sure to review the "From the Textbook to the Real World" example; see what the problem is, how statistics solves it, and what the solution adds in value. These situations also generate good classroom discussion questions.

Computer Data Base Exercise. This running case follows a young statistical analyst as she helps HH Industries use statistics to solve important problems. In each instance, the quantity of data makes it necessary for you to use your computer as a part of the analysis. Use this feature to become comfortable with the various statistical routines available for your machine, with the input formats they require, and with the output formats they provide. Doing this will make it easier for you to cope with the massive amounts of data you will confront in most real problems.

The authors' goals

Our own work experience has brought us into contact with thousands of situations where statistics helped decision makers. We participated personally in formulating and applying many of those solutions. It was stimulating, challenging, and in the end, very rewarding as we saw sensible application of these ideas produce value for organizations. Although very few of you will likely end up as statistical analysts, we believe very strongly that you too can learn, develop, and have fun studying statistics, and that's why we wrote this book. Good luck!

A water quality control engineer is responsible for the chlorination level of the water. It must be close to the level required by the department of health. To watch the chlorine without checking every gallon of water leaving the plant, the engineer samples several gallons each day, measures chlorine content, and draws a conclusion about the average chlorination level of water treated that day. The table below shows the chlorine levels of the 30 gallons selected as one day's sample. These levels are the raw data from which the engineer can draw conclusions about the entire population of that day's treatment.

**Chlorine Levels in Parts Per Million (ppm) in
30 Gallons of Treated Water**

16.2	15.4	16.0	16.6	15.9	15.8	16.0	16.8	16.9	16.8
15.7	16.4	15.2	15.8	15.9	16.1	15.6	15.9	15.6	16.0
16.4	15.8	15.7	16.2	15.6	15.9	16.3	16.3	16.0	16.3

Using the methods introduced in this chapter, we can help the water quality control engineer draw the proper conclusions.

2

Arranging Data to Convey Meaning: Tables and Graphs

■ OBJECTIVES

Chapters 2 and 3 will introduce the concepts and techniques of descriptive statistics. Chapter 2 examines two methods for describing a collection of items: tables and graphs. If you have ever heard a long-winded report droning about dues owed by all eighty club members, and you have wished for a quick graphic display to ease the pain, you already have an appreciation of what's to come in Chapter 2.

Data are collections of any number of related observations. We can collect the number of telephones that several workers install on a given day or that one worker installs per day over a period of several days, and we can call the results our data. A collection of data is called a *data set,* and a single observation a *data point.*

2-1

How Can We Arrange Data?

For data to be useful, our observations need to be organized so that we can pick out patterns and come to logical conclusions. This chapter introduces the techniques of arranging data in tabular and graphical forms. Chapter 3 will show how to use numbers to describe data.

COLLECTING DATA

Represent all groups

Statisticians select their observations so that all relevant groups are represented in the data. To determine the potential market for a new product, for example, analysts might study 100 consumers in a certain geographical area. The analysts must be certain that this group contains a variety of people representing variables such as income level, race, education, and neighborhood.

Find data by observation or from records

Data can come from actual observations or from records that are kept for normal purposes. For billing purposes and doctors' reports, a hospital, for example, will record the number of patients using the X-ray facilities. But this information can also be organized to produce data that statisticians can describe and interpret.

Use data about the past to make decisions about the future

Data can assist decision makers in educated guesses about the *causes* and therefore the probable *effects* of certain characteristics in given situations. Also, knowledge of trends from past experience can enable concerned citizens to be aware of potential outcomes and to plan in advance. Our marketing survey may reveal that the product is preferred by black housewives of suburban communities, average incomes, and average education. This product's advertising copy should address this target audience. And if hospital records show that more patients used the X-ray facilities in June than in January, the hospital personnel division should determine if this was accidental to this year or an indication of a trend, and perhaps it should adjust its hiring and vacation practices accordingly.

When data are arranged in compact, usable form, decision makers can take reliable information from the environment and use it to make intelligent decisions. Today, computers allow statisticians to collect enormous volumes of observations and compress them instantly into the tables, graphs, and numbers. These are all compact, usable forms—but are they reliable? Remember that the data that come out of a computer are only as accurate as the data that go in. As computer programmers say, "GIGO!" or "Garbage In, Garbage Out!" Managers must be very careful to be sure that the data they are using are based on correct assumptions and interpretations. Before relying on any interpreted data, from a computer or not, test the data by asking these questions:

Tests for data
1. Where did the data come from? Is the source biased; that is, is it likely to have an interest in supplying data points that will lead to one conclusion rather than another?
2. Do the data support or contradict other evidence we have?

3. Is evidence missing that might cause us to come to a different conclusion?
4. How many observations do we have? Do they represent all the groups we wish to study?
5. Is the conclusion logical? Have we made conclusions that the data do not support?

Study your answers to these questions. Are the data worth using? Or should we wait and collect more information before acting? If the hospital was caught short-handed because it hired too few nurses to staff the X-ray room, its administration relied on insufficient data. If the advertising agency targeted its copy only toward black suburban housewives when it could have tripled its sales by appealing to white suburban housewives too, it also relied on insufficient data. In both cases, testing available data would have helped managers make better decisions.

Double counting example

The effect of incomplete or biased data can be illustrated with this example. A national association of trucklines claimed in an advertisement that "75 percent of everything you use travels by truck." This might lead us to believe that cars, railroads, airplanes, ships, and other forms of transportation carry only 25 percent of what we use. Reaching such a conclusion is easy but not enlightening. Missing from the trucking assertion is the question of "double counting." What did they do when something was carried to your city by rail and delivered to your house by truck? Or how were packages treated if they went by airmail and then by scooter? When the double-counting issue (a very complex one to treat) is resolved, it turns out that trucks carry a much lower proportion of the goods you use than truckers claimed. Although trucks are involved in *delivering* a relatively high proportion of what you use, railroads and ships still carry more goods for more total miles.

DIFFERENCE BETWEEN SAMPLES AND POPULATIONS

Sample and population defined

Statisticians gather data from a sample. They use this information to make inferences about the population that the sample represents. Thus, *sample* and *population* are relative terms. A population is a whole, and a sample is a fraction or segment of that whole.

Function of samples

We will study samples in order to be able to describe populations. Our hospital may study a small, representative group of X-ray records rather than examining each record for the last fifty years. The Gallup Poll may interview a sample of only 2,500 adult Americans in order to predict the opinion of all adults living in the United States. Studying samples is obviously easier than studying whole populations, and it is reliable if carefully and properly done.

Function of populations

A *population* is a collection of all the elements we are studying and about which we are trying to draw conclusions. We must define this population so that it is clear whether or not an element is a member of the population. The population for our marketing study may be all women within a 15-mile radius of center-city Cincinnati who have annual family incomes between $10,000 and $25,000 and have completed at least eleven years of school. A woman living in downtown Cincinnati with a family income of $15,000 and a college degree would be a part of this population. A woman living in San Francisco, or with a family income of $7,000, or with five years of schooling would not qualify as a member of this population.

Need for a representative sample

A *sample* is a collection of some, but not all, of the elements of the population. The population of our marketing survey is *all* women who meet the qualifications listed above. Any group of women who meet these qualifications can be a sample, as long as the group is only a fraction of the whole population. A large helping of cherry filling with only a few crumbs of crust is a sample of pie, but it is not a representative sample because the proportion of the ingredients are not the same in the sample as they are in the whole.

A *representative sample* contains the relevant characteristics of the population *in the same proportion* as they are included in that population. If our population of women is one-third black, then a sample of the population that is representative in terms of race will also be one-third black. Specific methods for sampling will be covered in detail in Chapter 6.

FINDING A MEANINGFUL PATTERN IN THE DATA

Data come in a variety of forms

There are many ways to sort data. We can simply collect it and keep it in order. Or if the observations are measured in numbers, we can list the data points from the lowest to the highest in numerical value. But if the data are skilled workers (such as carpenters, masons, and ironworkers) required at construction sites, or the different types of automobiles manufactured by all automakers, or the various colors of sweaters manufactured by a given firm, we will need to organize them differently. We will need to present the data points in alphabetical order or by some other organizing principle. One useful way to organize data is to divide them into similar categories or classes and then count the number of observations that fall into each category. This method produces a *frequency distribution* and is discussed later in this chapter.

Why should we arrange data?

The purpose of organizing data is to enable us to see quickly some of the characteristics of the data we have collected. We look for things such as the range (the largest and smallest values), apparent patterns, what values the data may tend to group around, what values appear most often, and so on. The more information of this kind that we can learn from our sample, the better we can understand the population from which it came, and the better we can make decisions.

Exercises

2-1 When asked what they would use if they were marooned on an island with only one choice for a pain reliever, more doctors chose Bayer than Tylenol, Bufferin or Advil. Is this conclusion drawn from a sample or a population?

2-2 Twenty-five percent of the cars sold in the United States in 1989 were manufactured in Japan. Is this conclusion drawn from a sample or a population?

2-3 An electronics firm recently introduced a new amplifier, and warranty cards indicate that 10,000 of these have been sold so far. The president of the firm, very upset after reading three letters of complaint about the new amplifiers, informed the production manager that costly control measures would be implemented immediately to ensure that the defects would not appear again. Comment on the president's reaction from the standpoint of the five tests for data given on page 8.

2-4 "Germany will remain ever divided" stated Walter Ulbricht after the building of the Berlin Wall in 1961. However, during the fall of 1989, the communists of East Germany began allowing free travel between the east and west, thereby destroying the wall for all practical purposes. Give reasons for Ulbricht's incorrect prediction.

2-5 Discuss the data given in the chapter-opening problem in terms of the five tests for data.

2-2
Examples of Raw Data

Problem facing
admissions staff

Information before it is arranged and analyzed is called *raw data.* It is "raw" because it is unprocessed by statistical methods.

The chlorine data in the chapter-opening problem was one example of raw data. Consider a second. Suppose that the admissions staff of a university, concerned with the success of the students it selects for admission, wishes to compare the students' college performances with other achievements, such as high school grades, test scores,

TABLE 2-1 High School and College Grade-Point Averages of 20 College Seniors

H.S.	COLLEGE	H.S.	COLLEGE	H.S.	COLLEGE	H.S.	COLLEGE
3.6	2.5	3.5	3.6	3.4	3.6	2.2	2.8
2.6	2.7	3.5	3.8	2.9	3.0	3.4	3.4
2.7	2.2	2.2	3.5	3.9	4.0	3.6	3.0
3.7	3.2	3.9	3.7	3.2	3.5	2.6	1.9
4.0	3.8	4.0	3.9	2.1	2.5	2.4	3.2

and extracurricular activities. Rather than study every student from every year, the staff can draw a sample of the population of all the students in a given time period and study only that group, to conclude what characteristics appear to predict success. The staff can, for example, compare high school grades with college grade-point average (GPA) for students in the sample. The staff can assign each grade a numerical value. Then it can add the grades and divide by the total number of grades to get an average for each student. Table 2-1 shows a sample of this raw data in tabular form: 20 pairs of average grades in high school and college.

Bridge-building problem

When designing a bridge, engineers are concerned with the stress that a given material, such as concrete, will withstand. Rather than test every cubic inch of concrete to determine its stress capacity, the engineers can take a sample of the concrete, test it, and conclude how much stress, on the average, that kind of concrete can withstand. Table 2-2 summarizes the raw data gathered from a sample of 40 batches of concrete that will be used in constructing a bridge.

TABLE 2-2 Pounds of Pressure Per Square Inch That Concrete Can Withstand

2500.2	2497.8	2496.9	2500.8	2491.6	2503.7	2501.3	2500.0
2500.8	2502.5	2503.2	2496.9	2495.3	2497.1	2499.7	2505,0
2490.5	2504.1	2508.2	2500.8	2502.2	2508.1	2493.8	2497.8
2499.2	2498.3	2496.7	2490.4	2493.4	2500.7	2502.0	2502.5
2506.4	2499.9	2508.4	2502.3	2491.3	2509.5	2498.4	2498.1

Exercises

2-6 Look at the data in Table 2-1. Why do these data need further arranging? Can you form any conclusions from the data as they exist now?

2-7 The marketing manager of a large company receives a report each month on the sales activity of one of the company's products. The report is a listing of the sales of the product by state during the previous month. Is this an example of raw data?

2-8 The production manager in a large company receives a report each month from the quality control section. The report gives the reject rate for the production line (the number of rejects per 100 units produced), the machine causing the greatest number of rejects, and the average cost of repairing the rejected units. Is this an example of raw data?

2-3
Arranging Data Using the Data Array and the Frequency Distribution

Data array defined

The data array is one of the simplest ways to present data. It arranges values in ascending or descending order. Table 2-3 repeats the chlorine data from our chapter-opening problem, and Table 2-4 rearranges these numbers in a data array in ascending order.

Advantages of data arrays

Data arrays offer several advantages over raw data:

1. **We can quickly notice the lowest and highest values in the data.** In our chlorination example, the range is from 15.2 ppm to 16.9 ppm.

2. **We can easily divide the data into sections.** In Table 2-4, the first fifteen values (the lower half of the data) are between 15.2 and 16.0 ppm, and the last fifteen values (the upper half) are between 16.0 and 16.9 ppm. Similarly, the lowest third of the values range from 15.2 to 15.8 ppm, the middle third from 15.9 to 16.2 ppm, and the upper third from 16.2 to 16.9 ppm.

3. **We can see whether any values appear more than once in the array.** Equal values appear together. Table 2-4 shows that nine levels occurred more than once when the sample of 30 gallons of water was tested.

4. **We can observe the distance between succeeding values in the data.** In Table 2-4, 16.6 and 16.8 are succeeding values. The distance between them is .2 ppm (16.8 − 16.6).

Disadvantages of data arrays

In spite of these advantages, sometimes a data array isn't helpful. Since it lists every observation, it is a cumbersome form for displaying large quantities of data. We need

TABLE 2-3 Chlorine Levels in ppm of 30 Gallons of Treated Water

16.2	15.8	15.8	15.8	16.3	15.6
15.7	16.0	16.2	16.1	16.8	16.0
16.4	15.2	15.9	15.9	15.9	16.8
15.4	15.7	15.9	16.0	16.3	16.0
16.4	16.6	15.6	15.6	16.9	16.3

TABLE 2-4 Data Array of Chlorine Levels in ppm of 30 Gallons of Treated Water

15.2	15.7	15.9	16.0	16.2	16.4
15.4	15.7	15.9	16.0	16.3	16.6
15.6	15.8	15.9	16.0	16.3	16.8
15.6	15.8	15.9	16.1	16.3	16.8
15.6	15.8	16.0	16.2	16.4	16.9

to compress the information and still be able to use it for interpretation and decision making. How can we do this?

A BETTER WAY TO ARRANGE DATA: THE FREQUENCY DISTRIBUTION

Frequency distributions handle more data

One way we can compress data is to use a *frequency table* or a *frequency distribution.* To understand the difference between this and an array, take as an example the average inventory (in days) for 20 convenience stores:

In Tables 2-5 and 2-6, we have taken identical data concerning the average inventory and displayed them first as an array in ascending order and then as a frequency distribution. To obtain Table 2-6, we had to divide the data into groups of similar values. Then we recorded the number of data points that fell into each group. Notice

They lose some information

that we lose some information in constructing the frequency distribution. We no longer know, for example, that the value 5.5 appears four times or that the value 5.1

But they gain other information

does not appear at all. Yet we gain information concerning the *pattern* of average inventories. We can see from Table 2-6 that average inventory falls most often in the range from 3.8 to 4.3 days. It is unusual to find an average inventory in the range from 2.0 to 2.5 days or from 2.6 to 3.1 days. Inventories in the ranges of 4.4 to 4.9 days and 5.0 to 5.5 days are not prevalent but occur more frequently than some others. Thus, frequency distributions sacrifice some detail but offer us new insights into patterns of data.

Function of classes in a frequency distribution

A frequency distribution is a table that organizes data into *classes;* that is, into groups of values describing one characteristic of the data. "The average inventory" is one characteristic of the 20 convenience stores. In Table 2-5, this characteristic has eleven different values. But these same data could be divided into any number of classes. Table 2-6, for example, uses six. We could compress the data even further and use only the two classes "less than 3.8" and "greater than, or equal to 3.8." Or we could increase the number of classes by using smaller intervals, such as we have done in Table 2-7.

Why it is called a "frequency" distribution

A frequency distribution shows **the number of observations from the data set that fall into each of the classes.** If you can determine the frequency with which values occur in each class of a data set, you can construct a frequency distribution.

TABLE 2-5 Data Array of Average Inventory (in Days) for 20 Convenience Stores

| 2.0 | 3.4 | 3.8 | 4.1 | 4.1 | 4.3 | 4.7 | 4.9 | 5.5 | 5.5 |
| 3.4 | 3.8 | 4.0 | 4.1 | 4.2 | 4.7 | 4.8 | 4.9 | 5.5 | 5.5 |

TABLE 2-6 Frequency Distribution of Average Inventory (in Days) for 20 Convenience Stores (6 Classes)

CLASS (GROUP OF SIMILAR VALUES OF DATA POINTS)	FREQUENCY (NUMBER OF OBSERVATIONS IN EACH CLASS)
2.0 to 2.5	1
2.6 to 3.1	0
3.2 to 3.7	2
3.8 to 4.3	8
4.4 to 4.9	5
5.0 to 5.5	4

TABLE 2-7 Frequency Distribution of Average Inventory (in Days) for 20 Convenience Stores (12 Classes)

CLASS	FREQUENCY	CLASS	FREQUENCY
2.0 to 2.2	1	3.8 to 4.0	3
2.3 to 2.5	0	4.1 to 4.3	5
2.6 to 2.8	0	4.4 to 4.6	0
2.9 to 3.1	0	4.7 to 4.9	5
3.2 to 3.4	2	5.0 to 5.2	0
3.5 to 3.7	0	5.3 to 5.5	4

CHARACTERISTICS OF RELATIVE FREQUENCY DISTRIBUTIONS

Relative frequency distribution defined

So far, we have expressed the frequency with which values occur in each class as the total number of data points that fall within that class. We can also express the frequency of each value as a *fraction* or a *percentage* of the total number of observations. The frequency of an average inventory of 4.4 to 4.9 days, for example, is 5 in Table 2-6 but .25 in Table 2-8. To get this value of .25, we divided the frequency for that class (5) by the total number of observations in the data set (20). The answer can be expressed as a fraction (5/20), a decimal (.25), or a percentage (25%). A *relative frequency distribution* presents frequencies in terms of fractions or percentages.

TABLE 2-8 Relative Frequency Distribution of Average Inventory (in Days) for 20 Convenience Stores

CLASS	FREQUENCY	RELATIVE FREQUENCY: FRACTION OF OBSERVATIONS IN EACH CLASS
2.0 to 2.5	1	.05
2.6 to 3.1	0	.00
3.2 to 3.7	2	.10
3.8 to 4.3	8	.40
4.4 to 4.9	5	.25
5.0 to 5.5	4	.20
	20	1.00 sum of the relative frequencies of all classes

Notice in Table 2-8 that the sum of all the relative frequencies equals 1.00, or 100 percent. This is true because a relative frequency distribution pairs each class with its appropriate fraction or percentage of the total data. Therefore, the classes in any relative or simple frequency distribution are *all-inclusive.* All the data fit into one category or another. Also notice that the classes in Table 2-8 are *mutually exclusive;* that is, no data point falls into more than one category. Table 2-9 illustrates this concept by comparing mutually exclusive classes with ones that overlap. In frequency distributions, there are no overlapping classes.

Classes are all-inclusive

They are mutually exclusive

TABLE 2-9 Mutually Exclusive and Overlapping Classes

Mutually exclusive	1 to 4	5 to 8	9 to 12	13 to 16
Not mutually exclusive	1 to 4	3 to 6	5 to 8	7 to 10

TABLE 2-10 Occupations of Sample of 100 Graduates of Central College

OCCUPATIONAL CLASS	FREQUENCY DISTRIBUTION (1)	RELATIVE FREQUENCY DISTRIBUTION (1) ÷ 100
Actor	5	.05
Banker	8	.08
Businessperson	22	.22
Chemist	7	.07
Doctor	10	.10
Insurance representative	6	.06
Journalist	2	.02
Lawyer	14	.14
Teacher	9	.09
Other	17	.17
	100	**1.00**

Classes of qualitative data

Up to this point, our classes have consisted of numbers and have described some quantitative attribute of the items samples. We can also classify information according to qualitative characteristics, such as race, religion, and sex, which do not fall naturally into numerical categories. Like classes of quantitative attributes, these classes must be all-inclusive and mutually exclusive. Table 2-10 shows how to construct both simple and relative frequency distributions using the qualitative attribute of occupations.

Open-ended classes for lists that are not exhaustive

Although Table 2-10 does not list every occupation held by the graduates of Central College, it is still all-inclusive. Why? The class "other" covers all the observations that fail to fit one of the enumerated categories. We will use a word like this whenever our list does not specifically list all the possibilities. If, for example, our characteristic can occur in any month of the year, a complete list would include twelve categories. But if we wish to list only the eight months from January to August, we can use the term "other" to account for our observations during the four months of September, October, November, and December. Although our list does not specifically list all the possibilities, it is all-inclusive. This "other" is called an *open-ended class* when it allows either the upper or the lower end of a quantitative classification scheme to be limitless. The last class in Table 2-11 ("72 and older") is open-ended.

TABLE 2-11 Ages of Bunder County Residents

CLASS: AGE (1)	FREQUENCY (2)	RELATIVE FREQUENCY (2) ÷ 89,592
Birth to 7	8,873	.0990
8 to 15	9,246	.1032
16 to 23	12,060	.1346
24 to 31	11,949	.1334
32 to 39	9,853	.1100
40 to 47	8,439	.0942
48 to 55	8,267	.0923
56 to 63	7,430	.0829
64 to 71	7,283	.0813
72 and older	6,192	.0691
	89,592	**1.0000**

Classification schemes can be either quantitative or qualitative *and* either discrete or continuous. *Discrete* classes are separate entities that do not progress from one class to the next without a break. Such classes as the number of children in each family, the number of trucks owned by moving companies, or the occupations of Central College graduates are discrete. Discrete data are data that can take on only a limited number of values. Central College graduates can be classified as either doctors or chemists but not something in between. The closing price of AT&T stock can be 39¾, or your basketball team can have a center who is 7 feet 1½ inches tall.

Continuous data do progress from one class to the next without a break. They involve numerical measurement such as the weights of cans of tomatoes, the pounds of pressure on concrete, or the high school GPAs of college seniors. Continuous data can be expressed in either fractions or whole numbers.

Exercises

 2-9   Transmission Fix-It stores recorded the number of service tickets submitted by each of its 20 stores last month as follows:

823	648	321	634	752
669	427	555	904	586
722	360	468	847	641
217	588	349	308	766

The company believes that a store cannot really hope to break even financially with fewer than 475 service actions a month. It is also company policy to give a financial bonus to any store manager who generates more than 725 service actions a month. Arrange this data in a data array and indicate how many stores are not breaking even and how many are to get bonuses.

 2-10   Use the data from Transmission Fix-It in exercise 2-9. The company financial VP has set up what she calls "store watch list," that is, a list of the stores whose service activity is low enough to warrant additional attention from the home office. This category includes stores whose service activity is between 550 and 650 service actions a month. How many stores should be on that list based on last month's activity?

2-11   The number of hours taken by transmission mechanics to remove, repair, and replace transmissions in one of the Transmission Fix-It stores one day last week is recorded as follows:

4.3	2.7	3.8	2.2	3.4
3.1	4.5	2.6	5.5	3.2
6.6	2.0	4.4	2.1	3.3
6.3	6.7	5.9	4.1	3.7

Construct a frequency distribution with intervals of 1.0 hours from this data. What conclusions can you reach about the productivity of mechanics from this distribution? If Transmission Fix-It management believes that more than 6.0 hours is evidence of unsatisfactory performance, does it have a major or minor problem with performance in this particular store?

2-12 Here are the ages of 50 members of a county social service program:

83	51	66	61	82	65	54	56	92	60
65	87	68	64	51	70	75	66	74	68
44	55	78	69	98	67	82	77	79	62
38	88	76	99	84	47	60	42	66	74
91	71	83	80	68	65	51	56	73	55

Use this data to construct relative frequency distributions using seven equal intervals and thirteen equal intervals. State policies on social service programs require approximately 50 percent of the program participants to be older than 50.
(a) Is the program in compliance with the policy?
(b) Does your thirteen-interval relative frequency distribution help you answer part (a) better than your seven-interval distribution?
(c) Suppose the director of social services wanted to know the proportion of program participants between 45 – 80 years old. Could you estimate the answer for her better with a seven- or a thirteen-interval relative frequency distribution?

2-13 Arrange the data in Table 2-2 on page 11 in an array from highest to lowest.
(a) Suppose that state law requires bridge concrete to withstand at least 2,500 lbs./sq. in. How many samples would fail this test?
(b) How many samples could withstand a pressure of at least 2,497 lbs./sq. in. but could not withstand a pressure greater than 2,504 lbs./sq. in.?
(c) As you examine the array, you should notice that some samples can withstand identical amounts of pressure. List these pressures and the number of samples that can withstand each amount.

2-14 Using the data in Table 2-1 on page 11, arrange the data in an array from highest to lowest high school GPA. Now arrange the data in an array from highest to lowest college GPA. What can you conclude from the two arrays you have that you could not from the original data?

2-15 The Environmental Protection Agency took water samples from twelve different rivers and streams that feed into Lake Erie. These samples were tested in the EPA laboratory and rated as to the amount of solid pollution suspended in each sample. The results of the testing are given in the following table:

Sample	1	2	3	4	5	6
Pollution rating (ppm)	37.2	51.7	68.4	54.2	49.9	33.4
Sample	7	8	9	10	11	12
Pollution rating (ppm)	39.8	52.7	60.0	46.1	38.5	49.1

(a) Arrange the data into an array from highest to lowest.
(b) Determine the number of samples having a pollution content between 30.0 and 39.9, 40.0 and 49.9, 50.0 and 59.9, 60.0 and 69.9.
(c) If 45.0 is the number used by the EPA to indicate excessive pollution, how many samples would be rated as having excessive pollution?
(d) What is the largest distance between any two consecutive samples?

2-16 Suppose that the admissions staff mentioned in the discussion of Table 2-1 on page 11 wishes to examine the relationship between a student's differential on the college SAT examination (the difference between actual and expected score based on the student's high school GPA) and the spread between the student's high school and college GPA (the difference between the college and high school GPA). The admissions staff will use the following data:

H.S. GPA	COLLEGE GPA	SAT SCORE	H.S. GPA	COLLEGE GPA	SAT SCORE
3.6	2.5	1,100	3.4	3.6	1,180
2.6	2.7	940	2.9	3.0	1,010
2.7	2.2	950	3.9	4.0	1,330
3.7	3.2	1,160	3.2	3.5	1,150
4.0	3.8	1,340	2.1	2.5	940
3.5	3.6	1,180	2.2	2.8	960
3.5	3.8	1,250	3.4	3.4	1,170
2.2	3.5	1,040	3.6	3.0	1,100
3.9	3.7	1,310	2.6	1.9	860
4.0	3.9	1,330	2.4	3.2	1,070

In addition, the admissions staff has received the following information from the Educational Testing Service:

H.S. GPA	AVG. SAT SCORE	H.S. GPA	AVG. SAT SCORE
4.0	1,340	2.9	1,020
3.9	1,310	2.8	1,000
3.8	1,280	2.7	980
3.7	1,250	2.6	960
3.6	1,220	2.5	940
3.5	1,190	2.4	920
3.4	1,160	2.3	910
3.3	1,130	2.2	900
3.2	1,100	2.1	880
3.1	1,070	2.0	860
3.0	1,040		

(a) Arrange these data into an array of spreads from highest to lowest. (Consider an increase in college GPA over high school GPA as positive and a decrease in college GPA below high school GPA as negative.) Include with each spread the appropriate SAT differential. (Consider an SAT score below expected as negative and above expected as positive.)
(b) What is the most common spread?
(c) For this spread in part (b), what is the most common SAT differential?
(d) From the analysis you have done, what do you conclude?

2-4
Constructing a Frequency Distribution

Now that we have learned how to divide a sample into classes, we can take raw data and actually construct a frequency distribution. To solve the chlorination problem on the first page of the chapter, follow these three steps:

Classify the data

1. Decide on the type and number of classes for dividing the data. In this case, we have already chosen to classify the data by the quantitative measure of the number of ppm of chlorine in treated water rather than by a qualitative attribute like the color or odor of the water. Next, we need to decide how many different classes to use and the range (from where to where) each class should cover. The range must be divided by *equal* classes; that is, the width of the interval from the beginning of one class to the beginning of the next class needs to be the same for every class. If we choose a width of .5 ppm for each class in our water example, the classes will be those shown in Table 2-12.

Divide the range by equal classes

TABLE 2-12 Chlorine Levels
in Samples of Treated
Water With .5 ppm
Class Intervals

CLASS IN PPM	FREQUENCY
15.1–15.5	2
15.6–16.0	16
16.1–16.5	8
16.6–17.0	4
	30

Problems with unequal classes

If the classes were unequal and the width of the intervals differed among the classes, then we would have a distribution that is much more difficult to interpret than one with equal intervals. Imagine how hard it would be to interpret the data presented in Table 2-13!

Use 6 to 15 classes

The number of classes depends on the number of data points and the range of the data collected. The more data points or the wider the range of the data, the more classes it takes to divide the data. Of course, if we have only ten data points, it is senseless to have as many as ten classes. As a rule, statisticians rarely use fewer than six or more than fifteen classes.

Determine the width of the class intervals

Because we need to make the class intervals of equal size, the number of classes determines the width of each class. To find the intervals, we can use this equation:

$$\frac{\text{Width of}}{\text{class intervals}} = \frac{\text{Next unit value after largest value in data} - \text{Smallest value in data}}{\text{Total number of class intervals}} \qquad [2\text{-}1]$$

We must use the *next value of the same units* because we are measuring the *interval* between the first value of one class and the first value of the next class. In our water study, the last value is 16.9, so 17.0 is the next value. Since we are using six classes in this example, the width of each class will be:

$$\frac{\text{Next unit value after largest value in data} - \text{Smallest value in data}}{\text{Total number of class intervals}} \qquad [2\text{-}1]$$

$$= \frac{17.0 - 15.2}{6}$$

$$= \frac{1.8}{6}$$

$$= .3 \text{ ounces} \leftarrow \text{width of class intervals}$$

TABLE 2-13 Chlorine Levels in Samples of Treated Water
Using Unequal Class Intervals

CLASS	WIDTH OF CLASS INTERVALS	FREQUENCY
15.1–15.5	15.6 − 15.1 = .5	2
15.6–15.8	15.9 − 15.6 = .3	8
15.9–16.1	16.2 − 15.9 = .3	9
16.2–16.5	16.6 − 16.2 = .4	7
16.6–16.9	17.0 − 16.6 = .4	4
		30

TABLE 2-14 Chlorine Levels in Samples of Treated Water With .3 ppm Class Intervals

CLASS	FREQUENCY
15.2–15.4	2
15.5–15.7	5
15.8–16.0	11
16.1–16.3	6
16.4–16.6	3
16.7–16.9	3
	30

Examine the results

Step 1 is now complete. We have decided to classify the data by the quantitative measure of how many ppm of chlorine are in the treated water. We have chosen six classes to cover the range of 15.2 to 16.9 and, as a result, will use .3 ppm as the width of our class intervals.

Create the classes and count the frequencies

2. **Sort the data points into classes and count the number of points in each class.** This we have done in Table 2-14. Every data point fits into at least one class, and no data point fits into more than one class. Therefore, our classes are all-inclusive and mutually exclusive. Notice that the lower boundary of the first class corresponds with the smallest data point in our sample, and the upper boundary of the last class corresponds with the largest data point.

3. **Illustrate the data in a chart.** (See Fig. 2-1.)

These three steps enable us to arrange the data in both tabular and graphic form. In this case, our information is displayed in Table 2-14 and in Fig. 2-1. These two frequency distributions omit some of the detail contained in the raw data of Table 2-3, but they make it easier for us to notice patterns in the data. One obvious characteristic, for example, is that the class 15.8–16.0 contains the most elements; class 15.2–15.4, the fewest.

Notice any trends

Notice in Fig. 2-1 that the frequencies in the classes of .3 ppm widths follow a regular progression: The number of data points begins with 2 for the first class, builds to 5, reaches 11 in the third class, falls to 6, and tumbles to 3 in the fifth and sixth classes. We will find that the larger the width of the class intervals, the smoother this

FIGURE 2-1

Frequency distribution of chlorine levels in samples of treated water, using .3 ppm class intervals

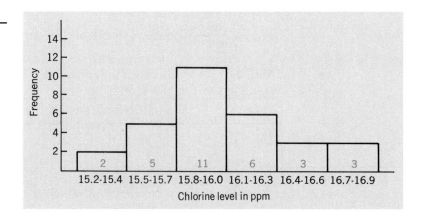

2 ARRANGING DATA TO CONVEY MEANING: TABLES AND GRAPHS

FIGURE 2-2

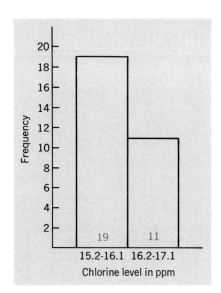

progression will be. However, if the classes are too wide, we lose so much information that the chart is almost meaningless. If, for example, we collapse Fig. 2-1 into only two categories, we obscure the pattern. This is evident in Fig. 2-2.

USING THE COMPUTER TO CONSTRUCT FREQUENCY DISTRIBUTIONS

Hand calculations are cumbersome

Throughout this text, we will be using simple examples to illustrate how to do many different kinds of statistical analyses. With such examples, you can learn what sort of calculations have to be done. We hope you will also be able to understand the concepts behind the calculations, so you will appreciate why these particular calculations are appropriate. However, the fact of the matter remains that hand calculations are cumbersome, tiresome, and error-prone. Many real problems have so much data that doing the calculations by hand is not feasible.

Software packages for statistical analysis

For this reason, most real-world statistical analysis is done on computers. You prepare the input data and interpret the results of the analysis and take appropriate actions, but *the machine* does all the "number crunching." There are many widely-used software packages for statistical analyses, including Minitab, SAS, SPSS, and SYSTAT.* It is not our intention to teach you how to use any of these to do your analyses, but we will be using Minitab, MYSTAT (a student version of SYSTAT), and the SAS System to illustrate typical sorts of outputs that these packages produce.

Using the grade data

Appendix 9 contains grade data for the 199 students who used this text in our course in 1989. In Fig. 2-3, we have used SAS to create a frequency distribution of the students' raw total scores in the course. Often you will also be interested in *bivariate frequency distributions,* in which the data are classified with respect to two different attributes. In Fig. 2-4, we have such a distribution showing the letter grades in each of the six sections of the class.

* Minitab is a registered trademark of Minitab, Inc., University Park, Pa. SAS is a registered trademark of SAS Institute, Inc., Cary, N.C. SPSS is a registered trademark of SPSS, Inc., Chicago, Il. SYSTAT is a registered trademark of SYSTAT, Inc., Evanston, Il.

FIGURE 2-3
Frequency distribution of raw total scores

SAS
1989 GRADES IN BUSINESS STATISTICS

TOTAL	FREQUENCY	CUM FREQ	PERCENT	CUM PERCENT
[20-30)	1	1	0.503	0.503
[30-40)	1	2	0.503	1.005
[40-50)	9	11	4.523	5.528
[50-60)	27	38	13.568	19.095
[60-70)	68	106	34.171	53.266
[70-80)	65	171	32.663	85.930
[80-90)	26	197	13.065	98.995
[90-100)	2	199	1.005	100.000

FIGURE 2-4
Bivariate frequency distribution showing grades in each section

SAS
1989 GRADES IN BUSINESS STATISTICS
TABLE OF GRADE BY SECTION

GRADE / FREQUENCY / PERCENT	SECTION 1	2	3	4	5	6	TOTAL
F	2	3	0	1	3	2	11
	1.01	1.51	0.00	0.50	1.51	1.01	5.53
D	3	6	5	2	4	6	26
	1.51	3.02	2.51	1.01	2.01	3.02	13.07
C-	2	2	1	2	7	4	18
	1.01	1.01	0.50	1.01	3.52	2.01	9.05
C	9	11	3	9	6	6	44
	4.52	5.53	1.51	4.52	3.02	3.02	22.11
C+	3	6	10	6	7	2	34
	1.51	3.02	5.03	3.02	3.52	1.01	17.09
B-	1	5	5	1	0	3	15
	0.50	2.51	2.51	0.50	0.00	1.51	7.54
B	2	5	3	2	2	3	17
	1.01	2.51	1.51	1.01	1.01	1.51	8.54
B+	1	1	1	2	1	1	7
	0.50	0.50	0.50	1.01	0.50	0.50	3.52
A-	2	2	8	1	3	0	16
	1.01	1.01	4.02	0.50	1.51	0.00	8.04
A	2	5	1	0	3	0	11
	1.01	2.51	0.50	0.00	1.51	0.00	5.53
TOTAL	27	46	37	26	36	27	199
	13.57	23.12	18.59	13.07	18.09	13.57	100.00

Appendix 10 contains earnings data for 224 companies whose 1989 last-quarter earnings were published in the *Wall Street Journal* during the week of February 12, 1990. In Fig. 2-5, we have used MYSTAT to create a frequency distribution of those last-quarter earnings. The headings over the boxed frequencies are the midpoints of the class intervals.

Because companies listed on the New York Stock Exchange (N) tend to have different financial characteristics from those listed on the American Stock Exchange (A), and since those, in turn, are different from companies listed "over-the-counter" (O), we also used MYSTAT to produce the bivariate distribution of the same earnings data in Fig. 2-6.

FIGURE 2-5

Frequency
distribution of 1989
last-quarter earnings

TABLE OF VALUES FOR GRPLQ89 (Grouped last-quarter 1989 earnings) FREQUENCIES					
-5.500	-3.750	-1.500	-0.750	-0.500	-0.250
1	2	1	2	9	17
0.000	0.250	0.500	0.750	1.000	1.250
75	54	28	12	11	7
1.500	2.000	2.250	4.750	5.250	TOTAL
1	1	1	1	1	224

TABLE OF GRPLQ89 (ROWS) BY EXCHANGE♦ (COLUMNS) FREQUENCIES				
	A	N	O	TOTAL
-5.500	0	1	0	1
-3.750	0	1	1	2
-1.500	0	0	1	1
-0.750	0	1	1	2
-0.500	3	1	5	9
-0.250	5	3	9	17
0.000	17	14	44	75
0.250	6	12	36	54
0.500	3	16	9	28
0.750	1	10	1	12
1.000	2	7	2	11
1.250	0	5	2	7
1.500	0	1	0	1
2.000	0	1	0	1
2.250	0	1	0	1
4.750	1	0	0	1
5.250	0	1	0	1
TOTAL	38	75	111	224

Exercises

 2-17 High Performance Bicycle Products Company in Chapel Hill, North Carolina, sampled its shipping records for a certain day with these results:

TIME FROM RECEIPT OF ORDER TO DELIVERY (IN DAYS)

4	12	8	14	11	6	7	13	13	11
11	20	5	19	10	15	24	7	29	6

Construct a frequency distribution for these data and a relative frequency distribution. Use intervals of 6 days.

(a) What statement can you make about the effectiveness of order processing from the frequency distribution?

(b) If the company wants to insure that half of its deliveries are made in 10 or fewer days, can you determine from the frequency distribution whether they have reached this goal?

(c) What does having a relative frequency distribution permit you to do with the data that is difficult to do with only a frequency distribution?

2-18 Refer to Table 2-2 on page 11 and construct a relative frequency distribution using intervals of 4.0 lbs./sq. in. What do you conclude from this distribution?

2-19 The Bureau of Labor Statistics has sampled 30 communities nationwide and compiled prices in each community at the beginning and end of August in order to find out approximately how the Consumer Price Index (CPI) has changed during August. The percentage changes in prices for the 30 communities is given below:

0.7	0.4	−0.3	0.2	−0.1	0.1	0.3	0.7	0.0	−0.4
0.1	0.5	0.2	0.3	1.0	−0.3	0.0	0.2	0.5	0.1
−0.5	−0.3	0.1	0.5	0.4	0.0	0.2	0.3	0.5	0.4

(a) Arrange the data in an array from lowest to highest.

(b) Using the following four equal-sized classes, create a frequency distribution: -0.5 to -0.2, -0.1 to 0.2, 0.3 to 0.6, 0.7 to 1.0.

(c) How many communities had prices that either did not change or that increased less than 1.0%?

(d) Are these data discrete or continuous?

2-20 Sarah Anne Rapp, the president of Baggit, Inc., has just obtained some raw data from a marketing survey that her company recently conducted. The survey was taken to determine the effectiveness of the new company slogan, "When you've given up on the rest, Baggit!" To determine the effect of the slogan on the sales of Luncheon Baggits, 20 people were asked how many boxes of Luncheon Baggits per month they bought before and after the slogan was used in the advertising campaign. The results were as follows:

BEFORE	AFTER	BEFORE	AFTER	BEFORE	AFTER	BEFORE	AFTER
4	3	2	1	5	6	8	10
4	6	6	9	2	7	1	3
1	5	6	7	6	8	4	3
3	7	5	8	8	4	5	7
5	5	3	6	3	5	2	2

(a) Create both frequency and relative frequency distributions for the before responses, using as classes 1 to 2, 3 to 4, 5 to 6, 7 to 8, and 9 to 10.

(b) Work part (a) for the "After" responses.

(c) Give the most basic reason why it makes sense to use the same classes for both the "Before" and "After" responses.

(d) For each pair of "Before/After" responses, subtract the "Before" response from the "After" response to get the number that we will call "Change" (example: $3 - 4 = 1$), and create frequency and relative frequency distributions for "Change" using classes -5 to -4, -3 to -2, -1 to 0, 1 to 2, 3 to 4 and 5 to 6.

(e) Based on your information collected above, state whether or not the new slogan has helped sales, and give one or two reasons to support your conclusion.

2-21 Here are the ages of 30 people who bought video recorders at Symphony Music Shop last week:

26	37	40	18	14	45	32	68	31	37
20	32	15	27	46	44	62	58	30	42
22	26	44	41	34	55	50	63	29	22

(a) From looking at the data just as they are, what conclusions can you come to quickly about Symphony's market?

(b) Construct a six-category closed classification. Does having this enable you to conclude anything more about Symphony's market?

2-22 Use the data from exercise 2-21.

(a) Construct a five-category open-ended classification. Does having this enable you to conclude anything more about Symphony's market?

(b) Now construct a relative frequency distribution to go with the five-category open-ended classification. Does having this provide Symphony with additional information useful in their marketing? Why?

2-23 John Lyon, owner of Fowler's Food Store in Chapel Hill, North Carolina, has arranged his customers' purchase amounts last week into this frequency distribution:

$ SPENT	FREQUENCY	$ SPENT	FREQUENCY	$ SPENT	FREQUENCY
0.00– 0.99	50	16.00–18.99	1,150	34.00–36.99	610
1.00– 3.99	240	19.00–21.99	980	37.00–39.99	420
4.00– 6.99	300	22.00–24.99	830	40.00–42.99	280
7.00– 9.99	460	25.00–27.99	780	43.00–45.99	100
10.00–12.99	900	28.00–30.99	760	46.00–48.99	90
13.00–15.99	1050	31.00–33.99	720		

John says that having seventeen intervals each defined by two numbers is cumbersome. Can you help him simplify the data he has without losing too much of its value?

2-24 Here are the class marks (midpoints of the intervals) for a distribution representing minutes it took the members of a university track team to complete a 5 mile cross-country run.

25   35   45

(a) Would you say that the team coach can get enough information from these class marks to help the team?

(b) If your answer to (a) is "no," how many intervals do seem appropriate?

2-25 Mr. Franks, a safety engineer for the Mars Point Nuclear Power Generating Station, has charted the peak reactor temperature each day for the past year and has prepared the following frequency distribution:

TEMPERATURES IN °C	FREQUENCY
Below 500	4
501–510	7
511–520	32
521–530	59
530–540	82
550–560	65
561–570	33
571–580	28
580–590	27
591–600	23
Total	**360**

List and explain any errors you can find in Mr. Franks's distribution.

2-26 Construct a discrete, closed classification for the possible responses to the "marital status" portion of an employment application. Also, construct a three-category, discrete, open-ended classification for the same responses.

2-27 Stock exchange listings usually contain the company name, the high and low bids, the closing price, and the change from the previous day's closing price. Here's an example:

NAME	HIGH BID	LOW BID	CLOSING	CHANGE
Systems Associates	11½	10⅞	11¼	+½

Is a distribution of all (a) stocks on the New York Stock Exchange by industry, (b) closing prices on a given day, (c) changes in prices on a given day
(1) Quantitative or qualitative?
(2) Continuous or discrete?
(3) Open-ended or closed?
Would your answer to (c) be different if the change were expressed simply as "higher," "lower," or "unchanged"?

2-28 The noise level in decibels of aircraft departing Westchester County Airport was rounded to the nearest decibel and grouped in a frequency distribution having class marks at 100 and 130. Under 100 decibels is not considered loud at all, while anything over 140 decibels is almost deafening. If Residents for a Quieter Neighborhood are gathering data for their lawsuit against the airport, is this distribution adequate for their purpose? (Class marks are the midpoints of their intervals.)

2-29 Use the data from exercise 2-28. If the lawyer defending the airport is collecting data preparatory to going to trial, would she approve of the class marks in exercise 2-28 for her purposes?

2-30 The president of Ocean Airlines is trying to estimate when the Civil Aeronautics Board (CAB) is most likely to rule on the company's application for a new route between Charlotte and Nashville. Assistants to the president have assembled the following waiting times for applications filed during the past year. The data are given in days from the date of application until a CAB ruling.

34	40	23	28	31	40	25	33	47	32
44	34	38	31	33	42	26	35	27	31
29	40	31	30	34	31	38	35	37	33
24	44	37	39	32	36	34	36	41	39
29	22	28	44	51	31	44	28	47	31

(a) Construct a frequency distribution using ten closed intervals, equally spaced. Which interval occurs most often?
(b) Construct a frequency distribution using five closed intervals, equally spaced. Which interval occurs most often?
(c) If the president of Ocean Airlines had a relative frequency distribution for either (a) or (b), would that help him estimate the answer he needs?

2-31 For the purpose of performance evaluation and quota adjustment, Ralph Williams monitored the auto sales of his 40 salespeople. Over a one-month period, they sold the following numbers of cars:

7	8	5	10	9	10	5	12	8	6
10	11	6	5	10	11	10	5	9	13
8	12	8	8	10	15	7	6	8	8
5	6	9	7	14	8	7	5	5	14

(a)   Based on frequency, what would be the desired class marks (midpoints of the intervals)?

(b)   Construct a frequency and relative frequency distribution having as many of these marks as possible. Make your intervals evenly spaced and at least two cars wide.

(c)   If sales fewer than seven cars a month is considered unacceptable performance, which of the two answers, (a) or (b), helps you more in identifying the unsatisfactory group of salespersons?

2-32   Kessler's Ice Cream Delight attempts to keep all of its 55 flavors of ice cream in stock at each of its stores. Their marketing-research director suggests that keeping better records for each store is the key to preventing stockouts. Don Martin, director of store operations, collects data to the nearest half gallon on the daily amount of each flavor of ice cream that is sold. No more than 20 gallons of any flavor is ever used on one day.

(a)   Is the flavor classification discrete or continuous? Open or closed?

(b)   Is the "amount of ice cream" classification discrete or continuous? Open or closed?

(c)   Are the data qualitative or quantitative?

(d)   What would you suggest Martin do to generate better data for market-research purposes?

2-33   Doug Atkinson is the owner and ticket collector for a ferry that transports people and cars from Long Island to Connecticut. Doug has data indicating the number of people, as well as the number of cars, that have ridden the ferry during the past two months. For example:

JULY 3   NUMBER OF PEOPLE, 173   NUMBER OF CARS, 32

might be a typical daily entry for Doug. Doug has set up six equally spaced classes to record the daily number of people, and the class marks are 84.5, 104.5, 124.5, 144.5, 164.5, and 184.5. Doug's six equally spaced classes for the daily number of cars have class marks of 26.5, 34.5, 42.5, 50.5, 58.5, and 66.5. (The class marks are the midpoints of the intervals.)

(a)   What are the upper and lower boundaries of the classes for the number of people?

(b)   What are the upper and lower boundaries of the classes for the number of cars?

2-5
Graphing Frequency Distributions

Identifying the horizontal and vertical axes

Figures 2-1 and 2-2 (on pages 20 and 21) are previews of what we are going to discuss now: how to present frequency distributions graphically. Graphs give data in a two-dimensional picture. On the *horizontal* axis, we can show the values of the variable (the characteristic we are measuring), such as the chlorine level in ppm. On the *vertical* axis, we mark the frequencies of the classes shown on the horizontal axis. Thus, the height of the boxes in Fig. 2-1 measures the number of observations in each of the classes marked on the horizontal axis.

Function of graphs

Graphs of frequency distributions and relative frequency distributions are useful because they emphasize and clarify patterns that are not so readily discernible in tables. They attract a reader's attention to patterns in the data. Graphs can also help us do problems concerning frequency distributions. They will enable us to estimate some values at a glance and will provide us with a pictorial check on the accuracy of our solutions.

HISTOGRAMS

Histograms described

Figures 2-1 and 2-2 (pp. 20, 21) are two examples of histograms. A *histogram* is a series of rectangles, each proportional in width to the range of values within a class and proportional in height to the number of items falling in the class. If the classes we

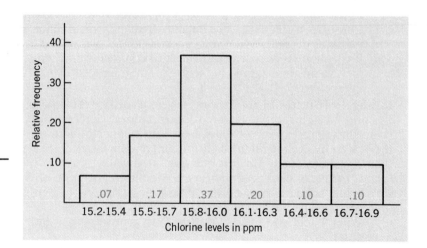

use in the frequency distribution are of equal width, then the vertical bars in the histogram are also of equal width. The height of the bar for each class corresponds to the number of items in the class. As a result, the area contained in each rectangle (width times height) is the same percentage of the area of all the rectangles as the relative frequency of that class is to all the observations made.

Function of a relative frequency histogram

A histogram that uses the relative frequency of data points in each of the classes rather than the actual number of points is called a *relative frequency histogram.* The relative frequency histogram has the same shape as an absolute frequency histogram made from the same data set. This is true because in both, the relative size of each rectangle is the frequency of that class compared to the total number of observations.

Recall that the relative frequency of any class is the number of observations in that class divided by the total number of observations made. The sum of all the relative frequencies for any data set is equal to 1.0. With this in mind, we can convert the histogram of Fig. 2-1 into a relative frequency histogram such as we find in Fig. 2-7. Notice that the only difference between these two is the left-hand vertical scale. Whereas the scale in Fig. 2-1 is the *absolute* number of observations in each class, the scale in Fig. 2-7 is the number of observations in each class as a *fraction* of the total number of observations.

Advantage of the relative frequency histogram

Being able to present data in terms of the relative rather than the absolute frequency of observations in each class is useful because, while the absolute numbers may change (as we test more gallons of water for example), the relationship among the classes may remain stable. Twenty percent of all the gallons of water may fall in the class "16.1 – 16.3 ppm" whether we test 30 gallons or 300 gallons. It is easy to compare the data from different sizes of samples when we use relative frequency histograms.

FREQUENCY POLYGONS

Use class marks on the horizontal axis

Although less widely used, frequency polygons are another way to portray graphically both simple and relative frequency distributions. To construct a frequency polygon, we mark the frequencies on the vertical axis and the values of the variable we are measuring on the horizontal axis, as we did with histograms. Next, we plot each class frequency by drawing a dot above its *class mark,* or midpoint, and connect the successive dots with a straight line to form a polygon (a many-sided figure).

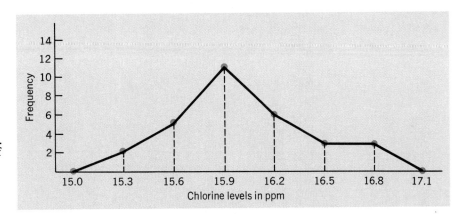

FIGURE 2-8

Frequency polygon of
chlorine levels in
samples of treated
water, using .3 ppm
class intervals

Add two classes

Figure 2-8 is a frequency polygon constructed from the data in Table 2-14 on page 20. If you compare this figure with Fig. 2-1, you will notice that classes have been added at *each end* of the scale of observed values. These two new classes contain zero observations but allow the polygon to reach the horizontal axis at both ends of the distribution.

Converting a frequency polygon to a histogram

How can we turn a frequency polygon into a histogram? A frequency polygon is simply a line graph that connects the midpoints of all the bars in a histogram. Therefore, we can reproduce the histogram by drawing vertical lines from the bounds of the classes (as marked on the horizontal axis) and connecting them with horizontal lines at the heights of the polygon at each class mark. We have done this with dotted lines in Fig. 2-9.

Constructing a relative frequency polygon

A frequency polygon that uses the relative frequency of data points in each of the classes rather than the actual number of points is called a *relative frequency polygon*. The relative frequency polygon has the same shape as the frequency polygon made from the same data set but a different scale of values on the vertical axis. Rather than the absolute number of observations, the scale is the number of observations in each class as a fraction of the total number of observations.

Advantages of histograms

Histograms and frequency polygons are similar. Why do we need both? The advantages of histograms are:

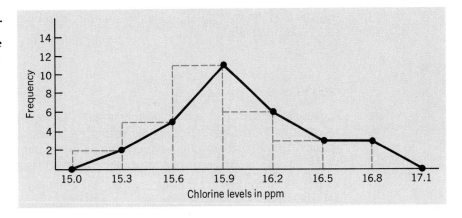

FIGURE 2-9

Histogram drawn
from the points of the
frequency polygon in
Fig. 2-8

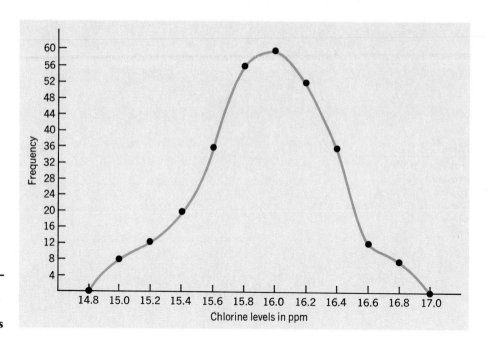

FIGURE 2-10

Frequency curve of the chlorine levels in 300 gallons of water, using .2 ppm intervals

1. The rectangle clearly shows each separate class in the distribution.
2. The area of each rectangle, relative to all the other rectangles, shows the proportion of the total number of observations that occur in that class.

Advantages of polygons

Frequency polygons, however, have certain advantages too.

1. The frequency polygon is simpler than its histogram counterpart.
2. It sketches an outline of the data pattern more clearly.
3. The polygon becomes increasingly smooth and curvelike as we increase the number of classes and the number of observations.

Creating a frequency curve

A polygon such as the one we have just described, smoothed by added classes and data points, is called a *frequency curve*. In Fig. 2-10, we have used our water example, but we have increased the number of observations to 300 and the number of classes to ten. Notice that we have connected the points with curved lines to approximate the way the polygon would look if we had an infinite number of data points and very small class intervals.

OGIVES

Cumulative frequency distribution defined

A cumulative frequency distribution enables us to see how many observations lie above or below certain values, rather than merely recording the number of items within intervals. If, for example, we wish to know how many gallons contain less than 17.0 ppm, we can use a table recording the cumulative "less-than" frequencies in our sample, such as Table 2-15.

Table of "less-than" frequencies

30   2 ARRANGING DATA TO CONVEY MEANING: TABLES AND GRAPHS

TABLE 2-15 Cumulative "Less-Than" Frequency Distribution of Chlorine Levels in ppm

CLASS	CUMULATIVE FREQUENCY
Less than 15.2	0
Less than 15.5	2
Less than 15.8	7
Less than 16.1	18
Less than 16.4	24
Less than 16.7	27
Less than 17.0	30

A "less-than" ogive

A graph of a cumulative frequency distribution is called an *ogive* (pronounced "**oh**-jive"). The ogive for the cumulative distribution in Table 2-15 is shown in Fig. 2-11. The plotted points represent the number of gallons having less chlorine than the ppm shown on the horizontal axis. Notice that the lower bound of the classes in the table becomes the upper bound of the cumulative distribution of the ogive.

Occasionally the information we are using is presented in terms of "more-than" frequencies. The appropriate ogive for such information would slope down and to the right instead of up and to the right as it did in Fig. 2-11.

Ogives of relative frequencies

We can construct an ogive of a relative frequency distribution in the same manner in which we drew the ogive of an absolute frequency distribution in Fig. 2-11. There will be one change—the vertical scale. As in Fig. 2-7, on page 28, this scale must mark the *fraction* of the total number of observations that fall into each class.

To construct a cumulative "less-than" ogive in terms of relative frequencies, we can refer to a relative frequency distribution (like Fig. 2-7) and set up a table using the data (like Table 2-16). Then we can convert the figures there to an ogive (as in Fig.

FIGURE 2-11

"Less-than" ogive of the distribution of chlorine levels in ppm for 30 gallons of treated water

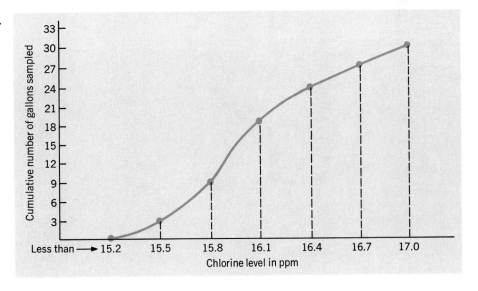

TABLE 2-16 Cumulative Relative Frequency Distribution of Chlorine Levels in ppm

CLASS	CUMULATIVE FREQUENCY	CUMULATIVE RELATIVE FREQUENCY
Less than 15.2	0	.00
Less than 15.5	2	.07
Less than 15.8	7	.23
Less than 16.1	18	.60
Less than 16.4	24	.80
Less than 16.7	27	.90
Less than 17.0	30	1.00

2-12). Notice that Figs. 2-11 and 2-12 are equivalent except for the left-hand vertical axis.

Approximating the data array

Suppose we now draw a line perpendicular to the vertical axis at the .50 mark to intersect our ogive. (We have done this in Fig. 2-13). In this way, we can read an approximate value for the chlorine level in the fifteenth gallon of an array of the 30 gallons. Thus, we are back to the first data arrangement discussed in this chapter. From the data array, we can construct frequency distributions. From frequency distributions, we can construct cumulative frequency distributions. From these, we can graph an ogive. And from this ogive, we can approximate the values we had in the data array. However, we cannot normally recover the *exact* original data from any of the graphic representations we have discussed.

USING THE COMPUTER TO GRAPH FREQUENCY DISTRIBUTIONS

Using SAS to produce histograms

Let's use SAS to produce some histograms of our grade data in Appendix 9. Figure 2-14 gives a histogram of the students' raw total scores. Notice that this histogram has horizontal bars instead of the vertical bars that we have drawn so far. In addition, to

FIGURE 2-12

"Less-than" ogive of the distribution of chlorine levels in ppm for 30 gallons of treated water, using relative frequencies

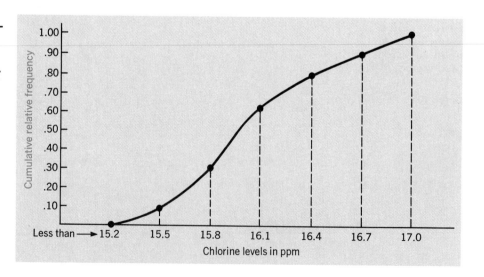

2 ARRANGING DATA TO CONVEY MEANING: TABLES AND GRAPHS

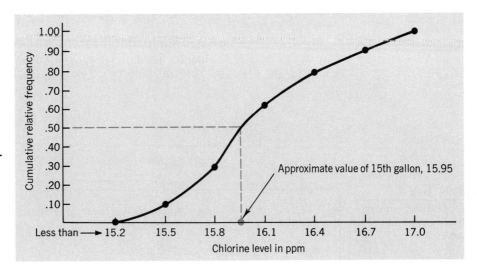

FIGURE 2-13

"Less-than" ogive of the distribution of chlorine levels in ppm for 30 gallons of treated water, indicating approximate middle value in original data array

the right of the bars, SAS gives the absolute frequencies, relative frequencies, and cumulative less-than frequencies (both absolute and relative).

In Fig. 2-4, we looked at a bivariate frequency distribution. We can also create histograms which contain information about two variables. Figure 2-15 is a vertical histogram of the students' letter grades in which each of the bars is divided into two segments showing the fractions of the students getting that grade who were in sections

FIGURE 2-14

Histogram and frequency distributions of raw total scores

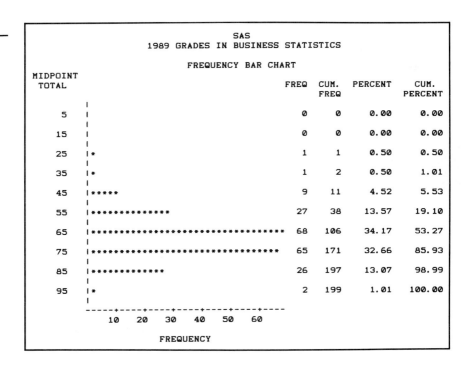

taught by professors and graduate teaching assistants (denoted by constructing the bars with P's and T's).

Using Minitab   In Fig. 2-16, we have used Minitab to produce a histogram of the 1989 last-quarter earnings of the 224 companies listed in Appendix 10. Fig. 2-17 gives separate histograms for the 111 OTC, 38 ASE, and 75 NYSE companies in the data set.

FIGURE 2-15

Histogram of grades showing type of instructor

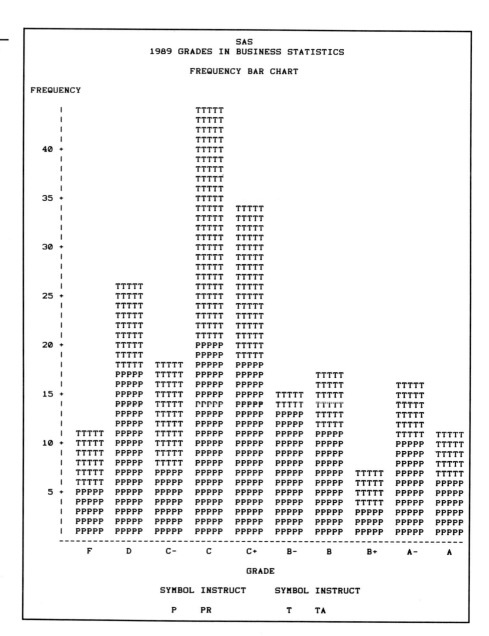

FIGURE 2-16

**Histogram of 1989
last-quarter earnings**

```
Histogram of LQ89    N = 224
Each * represents 5 obs.

Midpoint    Count
  -5.500        1   *
  -5.000        0
  -4.500        0
  -4.000        0
  -3.500        2   *
  -3.000        0
  -2.500        0
  -2.000        0
  -1.500        1   *
  -1.000        2   *
  -0.500       15   ***
   0.000      115   ***********************
   0.500       60   ************
   1.000       21   *****
   1.500        3   *
   2.000        1   *
   2.500        1   *
   3.000        0
   3.500        0
   4.000        0
   4.500        1   *
   5.000        1   *
```

FIGURE 2-17

**Separate histograms
by stock exchange of
1989 last-quarter
earnings**

```
Histogram of LQ89
EXCHANGE = 0   N = 111              EXCHANGE = 1   N = 38        EXCHANGE = 2   N = 75
Each * represents 2 obs.

Midpoint Count                                  Count                    Count
  -5.500   0                                      0                        1  *
  -5.000   0                                      0                        0
  -4.500   0                                      0                        0
  -4.000   0                                      0                        0
  -3.500   1  *                                   0                        1  *
  -3.000   0                                      0                        0
  -2.500   0                                      0                        0
  -2.000   0                                      0                        0
  -1.500   1  *                                   0                        0
  -1.000   1  *                                   0                        1  *
  -0.500   6  ***                                 7  *******               2  **
   0.000  72  ************************************ 21  *********************  22  **********************
   0.500  26  *************                        6  ******               28  ****************************
   1.000   4  **                                   3  ***                 14  **************
   1.500   0                                       0                        3  ***
   2.000   0                                       0                        1  *
   2.500   0                                       0                        1  *
   3.000   0                                       0                        0
   3.500   0                                       0                        0
   4.000   0                                       0                        0
   4.500   0                                       1  *                     0
   5.000   0                                       0                        1  *
```

Exercises

2-34 Here is a frequency distribution of the weight of 150 people who used a ski lift a certain day. Construct a histogram for this data.

CLASS	FREQUENCY	CLASS	FREQUENCY
75– 89	10	150–164	23
90–104	11	165–179	9
105–119	23	180–194	9
120–134	26	195–209	6
135–149	31	210–224	2

(a) What can you see from the histogram about the data that was not immediately apparent from the frequency distribution?

(b) If each ski lift chair holds two people but is limited in total safe weight capacity to 400 pounds, what can the operator do to maximize the people capacity of the ski lift without exceeding the safe weight capacity of a chair? Do the data support your proposal?

2-35 Here are data in feet on the lengths of a sample of 25 boats using the North Canal in New York State:

```
66   65   96   80   71
93   66   96   75   61
69   61   51   84   58
73   77   89   69   92
57   56   55   78   96
```

Construct an ogive that will help you answer these questions:

(a) Toll is collected on boats over 60-feet long. Roughly what portion of boats will pass through the canal toll-free?

(b) Toll is 50¢ a foot for boats over 60 feet in length. Roughly what portion of the time will the canal toll collector be collecting $12 or more?

2-36 Homer Willis, a fishing boat captain from Salter Path, North Carolina, believes that the breakeven catch on his boats is 5,000 pounds per trip. Here are data on a sample of catches on 20 fishing trips Homer's boats have made recently:

```
6500   6700   3400   3600   2000
7000   5600   4500   8000   5000
4600   8100   6500   9000   4200
4800   7000   7500   6000   5400
```

Construct an ogive that will help you answer these questions:

(a) Roughly what portion of the trips break even for Homer?

(b) What catch represents the approximate middle value in the data array for Homer's boats?

(c) What catch do Homer's boats exceed 80 percent of the time?

2-37 Central Carolina Hospital has the following data representing weight in pounds at birth of 200 premature babies.

CLASS	FREQUENCY	CLASS	FREQUENCY
0.5–0.9	10	2.5–2.9	29
1.0–1.4	19	3.0–3.4	34
1.5–1.9	24	3.5–3.9	40
2.0–2.4	27	4.0–4.4	17

Construct an ogive which will help you answer these questions:
(a) What was the approximate middle value in the original data set?
(b) If premature babies under 3.0 pounds are normally kept in an incubator for several days as a precaution, about what percentage of Central's premature babies will need an incubator?

 2-38 Prior to constructing a dam on the Colorado River, the U.S. Army Corps of Engineers performed a series of tests to measure the water flow past the proposed location of the dam. The results of the testing were used to construct the following frequency distribution:

RIVER FLOW (THOUSANDS OF GALLONS PER MINUTE)	FREQUENCY
1,001–1,050	7
1,051–1,100	21
1,101–1,150	32
1,151–1,200	49
1,201–1,250	58
1,251–1,300	41
1,301–1,350	27
1,351–1,400	11
Total	**246**

(a) Use the data given in the table to construct a "more-than" cumulative frequency distribution and ogive.
(b) Use the data given in the table to construct a "less-than" cumulative frequency distribution and ogive.
(c) Use your ogive to estimate what portion of the flow occurs at less than 1,300 thousands of gallons per minute.

2-39 Pamela Mason, a consultant for a small local brokerage firm, was attempting to design investment programs attractive to senior citizens. She knew that if potential customers could obtain a certain level of return, they would be willing to risk an investment, but below a certain level, they would be reluctant. From a group of 50 subjects, she obtained the following data regarding the various levels of return required for each respective subject to invest $1,000:

INDIFFERENCE POINT	FREQUENCY
$70–74	2
75–79	5
80–84	10
85–89	14
90–94	11
95–99	3
100–104	3
105–109	2
	50

(a) Construct "more-than" and "less-than" cumulative relative frequency distributions.
(b) Graph the 2 distributions in part (a) into relative frequency ogives.

2-40 At a newspaper office, the time required to set the entire front page in type was recorded for 50 days. The data, to the nearest tenth of a minute, are given below.

20.8	22.8	21.9	22.0	20.7	20.9	25.0	22.2	22.8	20.1
25.3	20.7	22.5	21.2	23.8	23.3	20.9	22.9	23.5	19.5
23.7	20.3	23.6	19.0	25.1	25.0	19.5	24.1	24.2	21.8
21.3	21.5	23.1	19.9	24.2	24.1	19.8	23.9	22.8	23.9
19.7	24.2	23.8	20.7	23.8	24.3	21.1	20.9	21.6	22.7

(a) Arrange the data in an array from lowest to highest.
(b) Construct a frequency distribution and a "less-than" cumulative frequency distribution from the data, using intervals of .8 minutes.
(c) Construct a frequency polygon from the data.
(d) Construct a "less-than" ogive from the data.
(e) From your ogive, estimate what percentage of the time the front page can be set in less than 24 minutes.

2-41 Jonathan Webb, insurance agent for the Safety Insurance Corporation, has data on the monthly dollar amount of insurance policies that he has sold over the past three years. He has arranged his data into the following frequency distribution:

MONTHLY SALES	FREQUENCY
$10,000–12,449	2
12,500–14,999	4
15,000–17,449	7
17,500–19,999	5
20,000–22,449	6
22,500–24,999	8
25,000–27,449	2
27,500–29,999	1

(a) Construct a relative frequency distribution.
(b) Construct, on the same graph, a relative frequency histogram and a relative frequency polygon.

2-42 The National Association of Real Estate Sellers has collected these data on a sample of 130 salespersons representing their total commission earnings annually:

EARNINGS	FREQUENCY
$5,000 or less	5
$5,001 –$10,000	9
$10,001 – $15,000	11
$15,001 – $20,000	33
$20,001 – $30,000	37
$30,001 – $40,000	19
$40,001 – $50,000	9
over $50,000	7

Construct an ogive that will help you answer these questions.
(a) About what portion of the salespersons earn more than $25,000?
(b) About what does the "middle" salesperson in the sample earn?
(c) Approximately how much could a real estate salesperson whose performance was about 25 percent from the top expect to earn annually?

2-43 The Smithsonian Museum of Natural History has data on the number of minutes people spend viewing a certain dinosaur exhibit. These data, rounded to the nearest minute, are:

MINUTES SPENT IN EXHIBIT	FREQUENCY
Less than 2	30
2– 3	40
4– 5	40
6– 7	90
8– 9	70
10–11	50
12–13	50
14–15	30
	400

(a) Construct a "less-than" cumulative frequency distribution.
(b) Construct an ogive based on part (a).
(c) Management has decided that an exhibit is a failure if 50 percent of the people spend less than 4 minutes in it. What is the percentage of the people observed spending less than 4 minutes? Also, management would like to know roughly how many minutes the 200th visitor spent in the exhibit, so give an approximate value for this.

2-6
Terms Introduced in Chapter 2

Continuous data Data that may progress from one class to the next without a break and may be expressed by either whole numbers or fractions.

Cumulative Frequency Distribution A tabular display of data showing how many observations lie above, or below, certain values.

Data A collection of any number of related observations on one or more variables.

Data Array The arrangement of raw data by observations in either ascending or descending order.

Data Point A single observation from a data set.

Data Set A collection of data.

Discrete Data Data that do not progress from one class to the next without a break; i.e., where classes represent distinct categories or counts and may be represented by whole numbers.

Frequency Curve A frequency polygon smoothed by adding classes and data points to a data set.

Frequency Distribution An organized display of data that shows the number of observations from the data set that fall into each of a set of mutually exclusive and collectively exhaustive classes.

Frequency Polygon A line graph connecting the midpoints of each class in a data set, plotted at a height corresponding to the frequency of the class.

Histogram A graph of a data set, composed of a series of rectangles, each proportional in width to the range of values in a class and proportional in height to the number of items falling in the class, or the fraction of items in the class.

Ogive A graph of a cumulative frequency distribution.

Open-Ended Class A class that allows either the upper or lower end of a quantitative classification scheme to be limitless.

Population A collection of all the elements we are studying and about which we are trying to draw conclusions.

Raw Data Information before it is arranged or analyzed by statistical methods.

Relative Frequency Distribution The display of a data set that shows the fraction or percentage of the total data set that falls into each of a set of mutually exclusive and collectively exhaustive classes.

Representative Sample A sample that contains the relevant characteristics of the population in the same proportion as they are included in that population.

Sample A collection of some, but not all, of the elements of the population under study, used to describe the population.

2-7
Equations Introduced in Chapter 2

[2-1] $$\text{Width of class intervals} = \frac{\text{Next unit value after largest value in data} - \text{Smallest value in data}}{\text{Total number of class intervals}}$$ *p. 19*

To arrange raw data, decide the number of classes into which you will divide the data (normally, between 6 and 15), and then use Equation 2-1 to determine the *width of class intervals of equal size.* This formula uses the next value of the same units because it measures the interval between the first value of one class and the first value of the next class.

2-8
Chapter Review Exercises

2-44   The following set of raw data gives income and education level for a sample of individuals. Would rearranging the data help us to draw some conclusions? Rearrange the data in a way that makes it more meaningful.

INCOME	EDUCATION	INCOME	EDUCATION	INCOME	EDUCATION
$17,000	High school	$ 21,200	B.S.	$17,200	2 yrs. college
20,800	B.S.	28,000	B.S.	19,600	B.A.
27,000	M.A.	30,200	High school	36,200	M.S.
70,000	M.D.	22,400	2 yrs. college	14,400	1 yr. college
29,000	Ph.D.	100,000	M.D.	18,400	2 yrs. college
14,400	10th grade	76,000	Law degree	34,400	B.A.
19,000	High school	44,000	Ph.D.	26,000	High school
23,200	M.A.	17,600	11th grade	52,000	Law degree
30,400	High school	25,800	High school	64,000	Ph.D.
25,600	B.A.	20,200	1 yr. college	32,800	B.S.

2-45   All 50 states send the following information to the Department of Labor: the average number of workers absent daily during the 13 weeks of a financial quarter, and the percentage of absentees for each state. Is this an example of raw data? Explain.

2-46   The Nebraska Department of Agriculture has these data representing weekly growth (in inches) on samples of newly planted spring corn:

| 0.4 | 1.9 | 1.5 | 0.9 | 0.3 | 1.6 | 0.4 | 1.5 | 1.2 | 0.8 |
| 0.9 | 0.7 | 0.9 | 0.7 | 0.9 | 1.5 | 0.5 | 1.5 | 1.7 | 1.8 |

(a)   Arrange the data in an array from highest to lowest.
(b)   Construct a relative frequency distribution using intervals of .25.
(c)   From what you have done so far, what conclusions can you come to about growth in this sample?
(d)   Construct an ogive which will help you determine what portion of the corn grew at more than 1.0 inch a week.
(e)   About what was the weekly growth rate of the middle item in the data array?

2-47 The National Safety Council randomly sampled the tread depth of 60 right front tires on passenger vehicles stopped at a rest area on an interstate highway. From their data, they constructed the following frequency distribution:

TREAD DEPTH (INCHES)	FREQUENCY	TREAD DEPTH (INCHES)	FREQUENCY
$^{16}/_{32}$ (new tire)	5	$^{4}/_{32}-^{6}/_{32}$	7
$^{13}/_{32}-^{15}/_{32}$	10	$^{1}/_{32}-^{3}/_{32}$	4
$^{10}/_{32}-^{12}/_{32}$	20	$^{0}/_{32}$ bald	2
$^{7}/_{32}-^{9}/_{32}$	12		

(a) Approximately what was the tread depth of the thirtieth tire in the data array?
(b) If tread depth less than $^{7}/_{32}$ inch is considered dangerous, approximately what proportion of the tires on the road are unsafe?

2-48 The High Point Fastener Company produces fifteen basic items. The company keeps records on the number of each item produced per month in order to examine the relative production levels. Records show the following numbers of each item were produced by the company for the last month of 20 operating days:

9,897	10,052	10,028	9,722	9,908
10,098	10,587	9,872	9,956	9,928
10,123	10,507	9,910	9,992	10,237

Construct an ogive which will help you answer these questions.
(a) On how many of their items did production exceed the breakeven point of 10,000 units?
(b) What production level did 75 percent of their items exceed for the month?
(c) What production level did 90 percent of their items exceed that month?

2-49 The administrator of a hospital has ordered a study of the amount of time a patient must wait before being treated by emergency room personnel. The following data were collected during a typical day:

WAITING TIME (MINUTES)

12	16	21	20	24	3	11	17	29	18
26	4	7	14	25	1	27	15	16	5

(a) Arrange the data in an array from lowest to highest. What comment can you make about patient waiting time from your data array?
(b) Now construct a frequency distribution using six classes. What additional interpretation can you give to the data from the frequency distribution?
(c) From an ogive, state how long 75 percent of the patients should expect to wait based on these data.

2-50 Of what additional value is a relative frequency distribution once you have already constructed a frequency distribution?

2-51 Below are the weights of an entire population of 100 NFL football players.

226	198	210	233	222	175	215	191	201	175
264	204	193	244	180	185	190	216	178	190
174	183	201	238	232	257	236	222	213	207
233	205	180	267	236	186	192	245	218	193
189	180	175	184	234	234	180	252	201	187
155	175	196	172	248	198	226	185	180	175
217	190	212	198	212	228	184	219	196	212
220	213	191	170	258	192	194	180	243	230
180	135	243	180	209	202	242	259	238	227
207	218	230	224	228	188	210	205	197	169

(a) Select two samples: one sample of the first ten elements, and another sample of the largest ten elements.

(b) Are the two samples equally representative of the population? If not, which sample is more representative, and why?

(c) Under what conditions would the sample of the largest ten elements be as representative as the sample of the first ten elements?

2-52 In the population under study, there are 2,000 women and 8,000 men. If we are to select a sample of 250 individuals from this population, how many should be women, to make our sample considered strictly representative?

2-53 The U.S. Department of Labor publishes several classifications of the unemployment rate, as well as the rate itself. Recently, the unemployment rate was 6.8 percent. The department reported the following educational categories:

LEVEL OF EDUCATION	RELATIVE FREQUENCY (% OF THOSE UNEMPLOYED)
Did not complete high school	.35
Received high school diploma	.31
Attended college but did not receive a degree	.16
Received a college degree	.09
Attended graduate school but did not receive a degree	.06
Received a graduate degree	.03
Total	**1.00**

Using these data, construct a relative frequency histogram.

2-54 Using the relative frequency distribution given in exercise 2-62, construct a relative frequency histogram and polygon. For the purposes of the present exercise, assume that the upper limit of the last class is $51.00.

2-55 Using the frequency distribution given in exercise 2-56 for miles per day of jogging, construct an ogive which will help you estimate what proportion of the joggers are averaging 4.0 or fewer miles daily.

2-56 A sports psychologist studying the effect of jogging on college students' grades collected data from a group of college joggers. Along with some other variables, he recorded the average number of miles run per day. He compiled his results into the following distribution:

MILES PER DAY	FREQUENCY
1.00–1.39	32
1.40–1.79	43
1.8C–2.19	81
2.20–2.59	122
2.60–2.99	131
3.00–3.39	130
3.40–3.79	111
3.80–4.19	95
4.20–4.59	82
4.60–4.99	47
5.00 and up	53
	927

(a) Construct an ogive which will tell you approximately how many miles a day the middle jogger runs.

(b) From the ogive you constructed in part (a), approximately what proportion of college joggers run at least 3.0 miles a day?

2-57 A behavioral researcher studying the success of college students in their careers conducts interviews with 100 Ivy League undergraduates, half men and half women, as the basis for the study. Comment on the adequacy of this survey.

 2-58 If the following age groups are included in the proportions indicated, how many of each age group should be included in a sample of 3,000 people to make the sample representative?

AGE GROUP	RELATIVE PROPORTION IN POPULATION
12–17	.17
18–23	.31
24–29	.27
30–35	.21
36+	.04

2-59 State University has three campuses, each with its own business school. Last year, State's business professors published numerous articles in prestigious professional journals, and the board of regents counted these articles as a measure of the productivity of each department.

JOURNAL NUMBER	NUMBER OF PUBLICATIONS	CAMPUS	JOURNAL NUMBER	NUMBER OF PUBLICATIONS	CAMPUS
9	3	North	14	20	South
12	6	North	10	18	South
3	12	South	3	12	West
15	8	West	5	6	North
2	9	West	7	5	North
5	15	South	7	15	West
1	2	North	6	2	North
15	5	West	2	3	West
12	3	North	9	1	North
11	4	North	11	8	North
7	9	North	14	10	West
6	10	West	8	17	South

(a) Construct a frequency distribution and a relative frequency distribution by journal.
(b) Construct a frequency distribution and a relative frequency distribution by university branch.
(c) Construct a frequency distribution and a relative frequency distribution by number of publications (using intervals of 3).
(d) Briefly interpret your results.

2-60 A questionnaire on attitudes about sex education in the schools is sent out to a random sample of 2,000 people; 880 are completed and returned to the researcher. Comment on the data available from these questionnaires in terms of the five tests for data.

2-61 With each appliance that Central Electric produces, the company includes a warranty card for the purchaser. In addition to validating the warranty and furnishing the company with the purchaser's name and address, the card also asks for certain other information that is used for marketing studies. For each of the numbered blanks on the card, determine the most likely characteristics of the categories that would be used by the company to record the information. In particular, would they be (1) quantitative or qualitative? (2) continuous or discrete? (3) open-ended or closed? Briefly state the reasoning behind your answers.

```
┌─────────────────────────────────────────────────────────────────────┐
│   Name_____          Marital Status_____ ③_____ │
│                                                                       │
│   Address_____          Where was appliance purchased?      │
│   City_____ State_____          _____④_____            │
│                                                                       │
│   Zip Code_____          Why was appliance purchased?         │
│   Age__①__  Yearly Income___②___          _____⑤_____           │
└─────────────────────────────────────────────────────────────────────┘
```

2-62 The following relative frequency distribution resulted from a study of the dollar amounts spent per visit by customers at a supermarket:

AMOUNT SPENT	RELATIVE FREQUENCY
$ 0–$ 5.99	1%
6.00–$10.99	3
11.00–$15.99	4
16.00–$20.99	6
21.00–$25.99	7
26.00–$30.99	9
31.00–$35.99	11
36.00–$40.99	19
41.00–$45.99	32
46.00 and above	8
Total	**100%**

Determine the class marks (midpoints) for each of the intervals.

2-63 The following responses were given by two groups of hospital patients, one receiving a new treatment, the other receiving a standard treatment for an illness. The question asked was, "What degree of discomfort are you experiencing?"

GROUP 1			GROUP 2		
Mild	Moderate	Severe	Moderate	Mild	Severe
None	Severe	Mild	Severe	None	Moderate
Moderate	Mild	Mild	Mild	Moderate	Moderate
Mild	Moderate	None	Moderate	Mild	Severe
Moderate	Mild	Mild	Severe	Moderate	Moderate
None	Moderate	Severe	Severe	Mild	Moderate

Suggest a better way to display these data. Explain why it is better.

2-64 The production manager of the Browner Typewriter Company posted final worker performance ratings based on total units produced, percentages of rejects, and total hours worked. Is this an example of raw data? Why, or why not? If not, what would the raw data be in this situation?

2-65 The head of a large business department wanted to classify the specialties of its 67 members. He asked Peter Wilson, a Ph.D. candidate, to get the information from the faculty members' publications. Peter compiled the following:

SPECIALTY	FACULTY MEMBERS PUBLISHING
Accounting only	1
Marketing only	5
Statistics only	4
Finance only	2
Accounting and marketing	7
Accounting and statistics	6
Accounting and finance	3
Marketing and finance	8
Statistics and finance	9
Statistics and marketing	21
No publications	1
	67

Construct a relative frequency distribution for the *types* of specialities. (*Hint:* The categories of your distribution will be mutually exclusive, but any individual may fall into several categories.)

2-66 The Ferebee Ergonomic Toy Company hired consultant Robin Clark to design a new management investment program. In order to estimate the various amounts managers would be willing to invest from their respective paychecks, Clark researched the second incomes of managers' families. His data reveal that no family has a second income over $35,000, and several families appear to have no second income. In a preliminary analysis, he decides to construct both frequency and relative frequency distributions for second income. He wants to use $5,000 intervals.
(a) Develop a continuous, closed distribution that meets his requirements.
(b) Develop a continuous distribution with six categories that meets his requirements and that is open at both ends. You may relax the requirement for $5,000 intervals for the open-ended categories.

2-67 The Kawahondi Computer Company compiled data regarding the number of interviews required for each of its 40 salespeople to make a sale. Following are a frequency distribution and a relative frequency distribution of the number of interviews required per salesperson per sale. Fill in the missing data.

NUMBER OF INTERVIEWS (CLASSES)	FREQUENCY	RELATIVE FREQUENCY
0–10	?	.075
11–20	1	?
21–30	4	?
31–40	?	?
41–50	2	?
51–60	?	.175
61–70	?	.225
71–80	5	?
81–90	?	.000
91–100	?	.025
	?	?

2-68 A. T. Cline, the mine superintendent of the Grover Coal Co., has recorded the amount of time per workshift that Section Crew #3 shuts down its machinery for on-the-spot adjustments, repairs, and moving. Here are the records for the crew's last 35 shifts:

60	72	126	110	91	115	112
80	66	101	75	93	129	105
113	121	93	87	119	111	97
102	116	114	107	113	119	100
110	99	139	108	128	84	99

(a)   Arrange the data in an array from highest to lowest.

(b)   If Cline believes that a "typical" amount of downtime per shift is 108 minutes, how many of Crew #3's last 35 shifts exceeded this limit? How many were under the limit?

(c)   Construct a relative frequency distribution with 10-minute intervals.

(d)   Looking at your frequency distribution, do you believe Cline should be concerned?

2-69   Cline has obtained information on Section Crew #3's coal production per shift for the same 35-shift period discussed in exercise 2-68. The values are in tons of coal mined per shift:

356	331	299	391	364	317	386
360	281	360	402	411	390	362
311	357	300	375	427	370	383
322	380	353	371	400	379	380
369	393	377	389	430	340	368

(a)   Construct a relative frequency distribution with six equal intervals.

(b)   If Cline considers 330 to 380 tons per shift to be an expected range of output, how many of the crew's shifts produced less than expected? How many did better than expected?

(c)   Does this information affect the conclusions you reached from the preceding problem on equipment downtime?

2-70   Virginia Suboleski is an aircraft maintenance supervisor. A recent delivery of bolts from a new supplier caught the eye of a clerk. Suboleski sent 25 of the bolts to a testing lab to determine the force necessary to break each of the bolts. In thousands of pounds of force, the results are:

147.8	137.4	125.2	141.1	145.7
119.9	133.3	142.3	138.7	125.7
142.0	130.8	129.8	141.2	134.9
125.0	128.9	142.0	118.6	133.0
151.1	125.7	126.3	140.9	138.2

(a)   Arrange the data into an array from highest to lowest.

(b)   What proportion of the bolts withstood at least 120,000 pounds of force? What proportion withstood at least 150,000 pounds?

(c)   If Suboleski knows that these bolts when installed on aircraft are subjected to up to 140,000 pounds of force, what proportion of the sample bolts would have failed in use? What should Suboleski recommend the company do about the new supplier?

2-71   The telephone system used by PHM, a mail-order company, keeps track of how many customers tried to call the toll-free ordering line but could not get through because all the firm's lines were busy. This number, called the phone overflow rate, is expressed as a percentage of the total number of calls taken in a given week. Mrs. Loy has used the overflow data for the last year to prepare the following frequency distribution:

OVERFLOW RATE	FREQUENCY
0.00– 2.50%	3
2.51– 5.00%	7
5.00– 7.50%	13
7.51–10.00%	10
10.00–12.50%	6
12.51–15.00%	4
17.51–20.00%	3
20.01–22.51%	2
22.51–25.50%	2
25.51 or greater	2
	52

List and explain errors you can find in Mrs. Loy's distribution.

2-72 Hanna Equipment Co. sells process equipment to agricultural companies in developing countries. A recent office fire burned two staff members and destroyed most of Hanna's business records. Karl Slayden has just been hired to help rebuild the company. He has found sales records for the last two months:

COUNTRY	# OF SALES	COUNTRY	# OF SALES	COUNTRY	# OF SALES
1	3	11	3	21	1
2	1	12	7	22	2
3	1	13	1	23	1
4	8	14	1	24	7
5	3	15	5	25	3
6	5	16	6	26	1
7	4	17	6	27	1
8	9	18	2	28	5
9	5	19	2		
10	1	20	1		

(a) Arrange the sales data in an array from highest to lowest.
(b) Construct two relative frequency distributions of number of sales—one with three classes and one with nine classes. Compare the two. If Slayden knows nothing about Hanna's sales patterns, think about the conclusions he might draw from each about country-to-country sales variability.

2-73 Jeanne Moreno is analyzing the waiting times for cars passing through a large expressway toll plaza which is severely clogged and accident-prone in the morning. Information was collected on the number of minutes that 3000 consecutive drivers waited in line at the toll gates:

MINUTES OF WAITING	FREQUENCY
less than 1	75
1– 2.99	183
3– 4.99	294
5– 6.99	350
7– 8.99	580
9–10.99	709
11–12.99	539
13–14.99	164
15–16.99	106
	3000

(a) Construct a "less-than" cumulative frequency and cumulative relative frequency distribution.

(b) Construct an ogive based on part (a). What percentage of the drivers had to wait more than 4 minutes in line? 8 minutes?

 2-74 Maribor Cement Company, of Montevideo, Uruguay, hired Delbert Olsen, an American manufacturing consultant, to help design and install various production reporting systems for its concrete roof tile factory. For example, today Maribor made 7000 tiles and had a breakage rate during production of 2 percent. To measure daily tile output and breakage rate, Olsen has set up equally spaced classes for each. The class marks (midpoints of the class intervals) for daily tile output are 4900, 5500, 6100, 6700, 7300, and 7900. The class marks for breakage rates are .70, 2.10, 3.50, 4.90, 6.30, and 7.70.

(a) What are the upper and lower boundaries of the classes for the daily tile output?

(b) What are the upper and lower boundaries of the classes for the breakage rate?

 2-75 BMT, Inc. manufactures performance equipment for cars used in various types of racing. It has gathered the following information on the number of models of engines in different size categories used in the racing markets it serves:

CLASS (ENGINE SIZE IN CUBIC INCHES)	FREQUENCY (# OF MODELS)
101–150	1
151–200	7
201–250	7
251–300	8
301–350	17
351–400	16
401–450	15
451–500	7

Construct a cumulative relative frequency distribution which will help you answer these questions:

(a) Seventy percent of the engine models available are larger than about what size?

(b) What was the approximate middle value in the original data set?

(c) If BMT has designed a fuel injection system which can be used on racing engines up to 400 cubic inches, about what percentage of the engine models available will not be able to use BMT's system?

2-76 A professor of organizational behavior has found a file of organization charts from various companies and institutions she has studied. She determines the following from the file:

# OF POSITIONS DENOTED ON ORGANIZATION CHARTS	FREQUENCY
1–10	20
11–20	18
21–30	11
31–40	8
41–50	3
51–60	1

Use this information to help you answer the following:

(a) Organization charts with more than 30 but less than 41 positions comprise what percentage of the total number of charts?

(b) The professor believes that people in organizations tend not to refer to organization charts if the charts denote ten or fewer positions. She also believes that charts with more than 30 positions often become outdated soon after issue. If she is right, then what proportion of the companies she has studied have correct charts that employees actually use?

2-77 Refer to the toll plaza problem in exercise 2-73. Jeanne Moreno's employer, the state Department of Transportation, recently worked with a nearby complex of steel mills, with 5000 employees, to modify the complex's shift changeover schedule so that shift changes do not coincide with the morning rush hour. Moreno wants an initial comparison to see if waiting times at the toll plaza appear to have dropped. Here are the waiting times observed for 3000 consecutive drivers after the mill schedule change:

MINUTES OF WAITING	FREQUENCY
less than 1	177
1– 2.99	238
3– 4.99	578
5– 6.99	800
7– 8.99	713
9–10.99	326
11–12.99	159
13–14.99	9
15–16.99	0
	3000

(a) Construct a "less-than" cumulative frequency and cumulative relative frequency distribution.

(b) Construct an ogive based on part (a). What percentage of the drivers had to wait more than 4 minutes in line? 8 minutes?

(c) Compare your results with your answers to exercise 2-73. Is there an obvious difference in waiting times?

2-9
Chapter Concepts Test

Answers are in the back of the book.

T F   1. In comparison to a data array, the frequency distribution has the advantage of representing data in compressed form.

T F   2. A "more-than" ogive is S-shaped and slopes downward and to the right.

T F   3. A histogram is a series of rectangles, each proportional in width to the number of items falling within a specific class of data.

T F   4. A single observation is called a data point, whereas a collection of data is known as a tabular.

T F   5. The classes in any relative frequency distribution are all-inclusive and mutually exclusive.

T F   6. When a sample contains the relevant characteristics of a certain population in the same proportion as they are included in that population, the sample is said to be a representative sample.

T F   7. A population is a collection of all the elements we are studying.

T F   8. If we were to connect the midpoints of the consecutive bars of a frequency histogram with a series of lines, we would be graphing a frequency polygon.

T F   9. Before information is arranged and analyzed, using statistical methods, it is known as preprocessed data.

T (F) 10. One disadvantage of the data array is that it does not allow us to easily find the highest and lowest values in the data set.

T (F) 11. Discrete data can be expressed only in whole numbers.

T (F) 12. As a general rule, statisticians regard a frequency distribution as incomplete if it has fewer than 20 classes.

(T) F 13. It is always possible to construct a histogram from a frequency polygon.

(T) F 14. The vertical scale of an ogive for a relative frequency distribution marks the fraction of the total number of observations that fall into each class.

T (F) 15. A data array is formed by arranging raw data in order of time of observation.

T (F) 16. A "less-than" ogive is S-shaped and slopes down and to the right.

(T) F 17. One advantage of a histogram in comparison with a frequency polygon is that it more clearly shows each separate class in the distribution.

T (F) 18. A baseball player's batting average is computed using a sample.

(T) F 19. A frequency distribution organizes data into groups of values describing one or more characteristics of the data.

T (F) 20. A series of rectangles, each proportional in width to the range of values within a class and proportional in height to the number of items falling in the class, is called a frequency polygon.

T (F) 21. The class widths of a frequency distribution are of equal size.

22. Which of the following represents the most accurate scheme of classifying data?
    (a) Quantitative methods.
    (b) Qualitative methods
    (c) A combination of quantitative and qualitative methods
    (d) A scheme can be determined only with specific information about the situation.

23. Which of the following is NOT an example of compressed data?
    (a) Frequency distribution   (c) Histogram
    (b) Data array   (d) Ogive

24. Which of the following statements about histogram rectangles is correct?
    (a) The rectangles are proportional in height to the number of items falling in the classes.
    (b) There are generally five rectangles in every histogram.
    (c) The area in a rectangle depends only upon the number of items in the class as compared to the number of items in all other classes.
    (d) All of these.
    (e) a and c but not b.

25. Why is it true that classes in frequency distributions are all-inclusive?
    (a) No data point falls into more than one class.
    (b) There are always more classes than data points.
    (c) All data fit into one class or another.
    (d) All of these.
    (e) a and c but not b.

26. When constructing a frequency distribution, the first step is:
    (a) Divide the data into at least five classes.
    (b) Sort the data points into classes and count the number of points in each class.
    (c) Decide on the type and number of classes for dividing the data.
    (d) None of these.

27. As the numbers of observations and classes increase, the shape of a frequency polygon:
    (a) Tends to become increasingly smooth.
    (b) Tends to become jagged.
    (c) Stays the same.
    (d) Varies only if data become more reliable.

28. Which of the following statements is true of cumulative frequency ogives for a particular set of data?

(a) Both "more-than" and "less-than" curves have the same slope.
(b) "More-than" curves slope up and to the right.
(c) "Less-than" curves slope down and to the right.
(d) "Less-than" curves slope up and to the right.

29. From an ogive constructed for a particular set of data:
(a) The original data can always be reconstructed exactly.
(b) The original data can always be approximated.
(c) The original data can never be approximated or reconstructed, but valid conclusions regarding the data can be drawn.
(d) None of these.
(e) a and b but not c.

30. In constructing a frequency distribution for a sample, the number of classes depends upon:
(a) Number of data points.　　　(c) Size of the population.　　(e) a and b but not c.
(b) Range of the data collected.　(d) All of these.

31. Which of the following statements is true?
(a) The size of a sample can never be as large as the size of the population from which it is taken.
(b) Classes describe only one characteristic of the data being organized.
(c) As a rule statisticians generally use between six and fifteen classes.
(d) All of these.
(e) b and c but not a.

32. As a general rule, statisticians tend to use which of the following number of classes when arranging data?
(a) Fewer than five.　　　(c) More than 30.　　　(e) None of these.
(b) Between one and five.　(d) Between 20 and 25.

33. Which of these is NOT a test for usability of data:
(a) Source　　　　　　　　　　(c) Missing evidence　　　　(e) None of these
(b) Contradiction of other evidence　(d) Number of observations

34. A relative frequency distribution presents frequencies in terms of:
(a) fractions　　　(c) percentages　　(e) both a and c.
(b) whole numbers　(d) all of the above

35. Graphs of frequency distributions are used since:
(a) they have a long history in practical applications
(b) they attract attention to data patterns
(c) they account for biased or incomplete data
(d) they allow for easy estimates of values
(e) both b and d.

36. Continuous data is differentiated from discrete data in that:
(a) discrete data classes are represented by fractions
(b) continuous data classes may be represented by fractions
(c) continuous data takes on only whole numbers
(d) discrete data can take on any real number

37. Double counting is a result of _____ or _____ data.

38. It is found that 50 of 1,000 customers in a survey contain the relevant characteristics of all customers in the survey. The 50 customers are a _____ sample.

39. The _____ and the _____ _____ are two methods of data arrangement.

40. A _____ is a collection of all the elements in a group. A collection of some, but not all, of these elements is a _____ .

41. Dividing data points into similar classes and counting the number of observations in each class will give a _____ distribution.

42. If data can take on only a limited number of values, the classes of these data are called _____ . Otherwise, the classes are called _____ .

43. A relative frequency distribution presents frequencies in terms of _____ or _____.

44. A graph of cumulative frequency distributions is called a _____.

45. If a collection of data is called a data set, a single observation would be called a _____.

2-10
Conceptual Case

(Northern White Metals Company)

It was early in the autumn of 1980 that Dick Lennox began the job search that would ultimately lead him to the Northern White Metals Company. Dick had started his career in business as a sales representative with a large, diversified industrial firm. Late in 1974, after several successful years of sales work, he was lured away from life in a large corporation by one of his better customers, a medium-sized, highly profitable, family-owned metal manufacturing company. He accepted a job as marketing manager, bringing with him some fresh ideas and an eagerness to succeed. By the end of his first year, the company posted a record sales increase. Dick worked long hours, traveling extensively throughout the Northeast and industrial Midwest. Sales continued to grow, and Dick continued to develop his management expertise.

One midsummer's day in 1980, the president of the firm called Dick into his office and proudly announced that his two sons would be joining the company. One was to be shop foreman in the stamping department. The other, a recent graduate of a reputable eastern business school, was to be brought in as assistant marketing manager and would work closely with Dick. The long-run career implications of this development were strikingly clear, and that night, Dick began to consider the possibility of moving on.

After several months and many interviews, Dick began to get discouraged. He had received several offers, some quite attractive, but nothing that really matched what he wanted to do. Then, through a chance meeting with an old friend and fellow salesman, Dick heard of a small firm in New England. The Northern White Metals Company was seeking a qualified applicant to serve as general manager.

Northern White Metals began in the late 1940s as New England Metals Supply, a distributor of nonferrous metals, primarily aluminum, copper, and brass. These were sold in a variety of forms, such as sheet, rod, cable, and pipe, for a variety of industrial applications. Growth was never dramatic, but the company prospered in the postwar period, and sales and earnings increased steadily. Manufacturing capacity was added in 1952 with the purchase of an old, empty textile mill and a mid-sized, 1,850-ton aluminum extrusion press. Within three years, the copper and brass business was sold off. NWMC was by then fully involved in manufacturing and fabricating extruded aluminum products, primarily for the building and construction industry.

The aluminum extrusion manufacturing process begins with the raw material, aluminum billet. This is essentially aluminum ingot in cylindrical form, the shape necessary for use in the extrusion press. The billet is softened by being passed by a conveyor through high-heat ovens. It is then fed into the press and pushed with tremendous pressure through heavy steel dies. The result is long sections of aluminum with the desired cross-sectional shape. These are then stretched to remove twists and slight bends in the metal, cut into desired lengths, hardened in tempering ovens, packed, and shipped.

NWMC quickly developed a reputation for quality work and timely delivery. To better serve an expanding customer base, the company added an anodizing department, where a durable finish could be added to the metal; a fabricating department, with special cutting, bending, milling, and assembly capabilities; and a small machine shop, which offered tool and die and special repair capabilities.

Prosperity in the 1950s and the high growth potential of aluminum fostered a proliferation of small and medium-sized fabricating companies. Few developed primary manufacturing facilities, though, since the higher capital investment made ventures into this area more difficult. With the rapid expansion of fabricating firms came an increasing intensity of competition. By the early 1960s, a recession and steep price declines pushed the industry into a profit squeeze from which many firms never recovered. NWMC operated its fabricating department unprofitably during this period, primarily to serve the overall needs of better customers. The extrusion department prospered, however, and served as a source of supply for many of the smaller fabricating firms that were forced to slash prices to preserve volume and utilize capacity.

The company performed well and, with the 1965 industry turnaround, had its most profitable year ever. Internal departments were expanded and NWMC flourished, securing a now smaller but very loyal group of customers. The 1970 downturn caused even this loyal group to shrink, though, as commercial construction slowed. Still, NWMC managed to remain profitable, and even grow a little, as new applications for extruded aluminum were sought in the rapidly emerging high-technology businesses.

The 1974 recession had a much more severe impact on the firm, however, as energy prices increased sharply. With its energy-intensive manufacturing process, NWMC's costs rose dramatically. The pressure on profits was severe. This, together with the sales decline that accompanied a depressed economy, left the company with its first unprofitable year ever.

Although general business conditions began to improve in 1975, NWMC never seemed to recover its previous position and exhibited a lackluster performance over the next five years. The president and principal owner of NWMC began to lose interest in the firm, and decided to contact a business broker about putting the company up for sale.

A prospect was found, and negotiations proceeded swiftly. NWMC was acquired with an exchange of common stock by Segue, Inc., a diversified architectural-products conglomerate that had long been interested in developing extrusion capability.

It was at this point that Dick Lennox first found out about NWMC. He arranged to meet with Segue management, and preliminary discussions ensued. A tour of the NWMC plant and offices followed and, although neither seemed particularly exciting, Dick thought there was potential in the operation. He was certainly enthusiastic about the prospect of stepping into a general manager's role.

That evening, Dick had dinner with the CEO of Segue. The man was an abrupt sort, but was relating the history and philosophy of his company with an almost reverential tone.

Suddenly he stopped. Looking directly at Dick with clear, penetrating eyes, he began to speak again.

"Lennox," he said with measured deliberation, "I want you to tell me why I should hire you."

Dick leaned forward and replied without hesitation.

"Two reasons, sir. I can increase sales, and I can increase profits."

Taken aback by the simplicity of the response, the CEO raised an eyebrow.

"Well, we shall see, young fellow," he chortled. He then snapped, "Report to Northern in three weeks, and be ready to go to work!"

The president of NWMC was to remain for an additional year and gradually turn over operating responsibility to Dick, his Segue-appointed successor. Running the company as it was did not seem to be exceptionally difficult, but sales gains and margin improvements would clearly be hardwon. It was to this task that Dick was to devote himself.

After three weeks of meeting the sales force, reviewing the production process, and getting to know the office staff, Dick was beginning to feel more comfortable in his new position. He also began to realize how formidable the challenge of his new position was. The company was in disarray, customer agreements were informal and subject to frequent changes, and the records systems were quite disorganized. Dick was in the process of addressing himself to these concerns when he received a late Friday afternoon call from corporate headquarters.

"Lennox," the CEO barked, "I want you in New York a week from Monday to make a presentation at the division presidents' meeting. We need a thorough analysis of sales and production cost trends at NWMC over the past three years and some kind of general suggestions about marketing and production plans for the coming year. Give us some thoughts on problem areas and potential problem areas—you know—the whole routine."

Dick swallowed hard as he hung up the phone. Back in his old job, he could have asked his M.B.A. assistant to punch up such information on the computer, draw up some projections, and there would be the report. Now he found himself staring at ten aging file cabinets packed with bills, orders, sales records, production records, and a plethora of other information.

Dick's task is to review a rather large body of data, select relevant information, and organize it into some meaningful and presentable form. How might he now proceed?

2-11
Computer Data Base Exercise

"Everybody, this is Laurel. Laurel McRae," Hal Rodgers, president of HH Industries, announced at the weekly staff meeting. "Laurel, this is Stan Hutchings, Vice President in charge of Sales; Peggy Noble, Manager of Accounting and Data Processing; Bob Ritchie,

Manager of Purchasing and Inventory Control; and Gary Russell, Operations Manager.

"You all know HH Industries is doing well," Hal continued. "The last three years have reflected market stability and promising growth in a number of areas. However, much of what we currently base our decisions on is our collective years of experience and gut feel. Laurel is an experienced data analyst and strategic planner and is joining our team to help us analyze, in a more quantitative, statistical fashion, where we are now and where we hope to be in a few years. We may be good, but I feel that with some sophisticated marketing and analysis strategies, we have a tremendous future ahead of us. Besides, maybe we can finally find a productive use for some of this paper we generate!"

The staff chuckled. If the company didn't prosper, it wasn't due to a lack of data. Since the introduction of a tailored data processing program in the previous fiscal year, a plethora of data, some useful and some merely confusing, had been available. Daily sales and margin (profit) figures were kept religiously, along with detailed inventory data and manifest (shipping) data. No one had quite figured out what to do with it all yet, though the president and his staff kept track of simple figures of merit.

Back in her office, Laurel contemplated her recent move to the Florida Suncoast headquarters of HH Industries from the Rocky Mountain home of her first position with Cold River Toy Company. She wasn't too sure about the president's use of "experienced," but she'd do her best. Her decision to leave the successful sled and toy manufacturer had been difficult, but she was confident that warehousing and distribution firms, like HH Industries, were a solid bet for the future. And Laurel had been impressed during the interview process with both Hal Rodgers and the company's positive, efficient atmosphere. Soon enough she'd know if she liked the hydraulics industry as much as she had liked toys.

"Get to know us," Hal had said. "My staff is completely available to you. Ask questions, get a look at the data we collect. I'm a little new at exactly where statistics will help us, but I have full confidence in you. You come very highly recommended, both as an analyst and as an innovative thinker."

"Well," Laurel thought, "here goes nothing." First stop, an afternoon with Stan Hutchings for some company background. Stan, she knew, had been with HH Industries longer than any other staff member and had an excellent intuitive feel for the hydraulics industry.

Days later, and after several such familiarization meetings, the data had already started to clutter her once empty desk. Laurel reflected on what she had learned. HH Industries had the typical profile of a family-owned business. Established more than

20 years before by the Douglas family, Handy Hydraulics (as it was then known) sprang up to fill a need perceived by its founders—a source of spare and repair parts to the rapidly growing mobile hydraulics industry. The booming population of the 1960s required the support of an increasing number of construction vehicles, garbage trucks, and other large pieces of equipment which, in turn, required spare and repair parts for a huge variety of hydraulic seals, pumps, cylinders, gauges, etc. As a distributor, Handy Hydraulics tracked down part sources and either resold directly, under the manufacturer's name, or packaged individual parts into repair kits for resale under its own name.

The first 5 years of business saw steady growth, though little actual marketing was done. Word-of-mouth and an important market niche provided a healthy atmosphere for the company. Early sales were almost exclusively within Florida and it wasn't until after the first catalog was produced in 1974 that business began to spread northward to Alabama and Georgia.

"Brute-force" marketing was the next step, and Laurel grimaced as she thought of the poor secretary who had had to distribute mailers to prospective customers gleaned from the yellow pages of all the communities, nationwide, of over 25,000 people. The philosophy was simple: Where there are large groups of people, there are garbage trucks and construction equipment which support these communities. And it worked. The late 1970s and the early 1980s saw burgeoning growth, as new customers appeared daily. Unfortunately, and yet typical of family-run companies, management just couldn't quite keep up.

By this time, numerous competitors had sprung up throughout the United States, some of whom had originally been customers of Handy Hydraulics. It became apparent that the company's goals of maintaining nationwide prominence could only be served by opening satellite warehouses elsewhere, from which the company's emphasis on next-day service could be continued, cost-effectively, to all areas of the country. To achieve this end, the Douglas family sold Handy Hydraulics to its present parent company, BMP Enterprises, and Mr. Douglas was given a 3-year contract to remain on as president. With additional capital provided by the investment firm, warehouses were opened in Arizona (1985) and Ohio (1986). However, the company was kept on tight reins by the original founder, with little thought given toward how best to manage the satellite warehouses. Similarly, no recognition was given to the importance of the changing business environment (increased competition, new technologies and management strategies available, etc.). The result was a business out of control, suffocating itself by once-proven, but now too inflexible, policies and procedures. Something had to give.

That something occurred when Mr. Douglas retired in 1988 and BMP Enterprises brought in Hal Rodgers to try to save Handy Hydraulics. A solid business executive with good intuition and even better "people skills," Hal inherited a company that was operating by the proverbial seat of its pants. While averaging over $900,000 in sales per quarter, outrageously high payroll and operating expenses were causing net losses.

Over the next 3 years, significant changes were introduced which succeeded in increasing sales while holding expenditures down. The payroll was trimmed to a bare minimum and a walk-in parts counter, once useful for public relations but now merely a costly burden, was closed. Toll-free customer order numbers were installed. The Ohio warehouse was closed down and, nearly 2 years later, a streamlined version was reopened in Pennsylvania. The company's catalog, previously consisting of two bulky 3-ring binders which had to be kept updated by continual mailings, was downsized to a "throwaway" version which more clearly and concisely represented the company's products. Finally, to publicize and celebrate the company's new image, the name was changed to HH Industries.

This was the organization which Laurel found herself contemplating. She summarized the current structure: three profit centers (Florida, Arizona and Pennsylvania); three product lines (seals and seal kits, finished hardware — cylinders, pumps, valves, etc. — and spare/repair parts). The company had 42 full-time and nine part-time employees, over 3000 active customer accounts, and approximately 15,000 line items of inventory. The corporate fiscal year ran from December to November, and quarterly sales figures now averaged close to $1.4 million. "Whew," Laurel muttered to herself. "Slightly different from toy manufacturing! But I'm getting paid to be a statistician and analyst, so let's see if I can sink my teeth into this monster."

Laurel extracted the most current year's worth of sales data (the third and fourth quarters of 1990, and the first and second quarters of 1991), both the number of orders per day and the dollar value of those orders (referred to as "sales"), by profit center. These are given in the following table. From what she had seen, the entire company's mood seemed to revolve around what was termed the "daily figure" — total corporate sales each day. Laurel's experience, however, told her to look a little deeper. She knew, for instance, that total sales dollars were the direct result of two factors: the number of orders per day and the average dollar value per order.

1. Construct histograms and relative frequency distributions of the company's daily *average order size* (total sales divided by total orders) for the last four quarters. For each chart, use interval widths of 20 and let the first interval run from 0 to 20.

2. Construct similar quarterly charts for the company's total *number of orders per day.* Use interval widths of ten, with the first interval running from 100 to 110.

3. What changing patterns are evident in the data from quarter to quarter? What are some possible explanations?

QRTR	ORDERS 1	SALES 1	ORDERS 2	SALES 2	ORDERS 3	SALES 3
3	120	19610	27	3125	0	0
3	132	21573	28	2027	0	0
3	130	17917	34	2980	0	0
3	120	17572	30	3701	0	0
3	115	15154	37	2724	0	0
3	126	22795	40	5767	0	0
3	140	19191	35	3691	0	0
3	136	13153	37	2556	0	0
3	126	14192	30	4686	0	0
3	115	18097	33	4228	0	0
3	121	20444	36	1005	0	0
3	129	19821	40	5609	0	0
3	151	18234	27	2461	0	0

QRTR	ORDERS 1	SALES 1	ORDERS 2	SALES 2	ORDERS 3	SALES 3
3	122	27417	37	6405	0	0
3	90	14540	42	3103	0	0
3	79	12764	46	3236	0	0
3	132	11114	31	7290	0	0
3	123	8712	42	2207	0	0
3	107	16059	24	4591	0	0
3	89	8366	33	4310	0	0
3	150	27419	45	4858	0	0
3	104	18988	45	2819	0	0
3	118	15394	35	1558	0	0
3	78	8369	32	3502	0	0
3	125	24230	45	3282	0	0
3	132	13633	50	4653	0	0
3	115	16311	46	3236	0	0
3	128	17494	28	1459	0	0
3	88	20221	36	3879	22	2103
3	81	9820	37	2600	27	3255
3	82	13674	32	2165	31	2169
3	92	12748	38	4661	22	2178
3	76	14311	36	3721	16	1618
3	86	19171	32	2255	33	2774
3	70	15606	38	4547	22	1849
3	73	15477	32	2966	36	3878
3	97	12962	27	3931	40	2631
3	90	11544	32	4082	22	1774
3	105	14710	27	2565	30	2447
3	96	12190	28	4061	27	3905
3	81	19646	42	3967	31	2478
3	96	15587	43	3590	37	4006
3	90	16264	34	4094	26	3234
3	92	13802	37	2542	21	2349
3	100	11483	44	1899	31	2810
3	82	7465	37	2852	28	2900
3	93	9445	34	4425	33	2797
3	88	18025	30	3583	23	2398
3	90	10723	40	6174	30	2176
3	103	16769	36	5529	34	4881
3	71	12381	29	2405	16	2050
3	99	24183	37	4000	33	4464
3	103	14691	15	3189	32	2868
3	86	18336	38	3461	28	3409
3	104	19426	32	2349	33	3017
3	96	15848	36	3744	27	2749
3	105	13368	46	8112	26	2058
3	86	15862	51	3568	33	2443
3	102	11856	45	2897	33	2542
3	77	19282	58	2853	27	2045
3	100	10906	51	5089	22	1363
3	97	9865	44	2077	34	3124
3	83	10661	49	3409	20	2865
4	119	26650	49	3491	25	3790
4	69	9310	48	3325	35	3118
4	73	6879	21	1417	33	2605
4	87	14674	44	1916	26	2789
4	72	15329	53	3760	30	2820
4	89	15073	57	7133	35	3102
4	95	10766	39	1782	29	3511

QRTR	ORDERS 1	SALES 1	ORDERS 2	SALES 2	ORDERS 3	SALES 3
4	85	9910	56	3990	23	2575
4	81	9600	44	2600	33	4637
4	71	13522	50	2620	27	2222
4	80	12551	44	6330	39	2988
4	111	14770	49	3942	41	4235
4	89	10826	48	3876	24	1350
4	68	11788	54	4670	31	1761
4	78	10484	63	4276	37	4333
4	95	14419	66	5382	33	3692
4	84	17298	50	3111	35	2323
4	93	11633	52	4630	30	3901
4	81	16741	38	3046	31	3223
4	77	15412	38	2805	22	1410
4	101	13145	55	4401	33	5864
4	99	13162	52	3624	26	2507
4	90	16018	45	4838	33	4908
4	78	15182	42	4846	33	2395
4	94	11619	53	3802	28	3066
4	91	9598	74	5268	24	3480
4	100	18481	54	2505	31	2422
4	93	11957	38	2065	31	4400
4	85	17568	48	3647	18	1992
4	79	11336	45	4057	33	2933
4	109	14584	52	4850	36	3737
4	73	12833	45	1961	32	4596
4	95	12754	49	2915	29	1927
4	85	13275	42	2457	28	2072
4	102	16297	54	3885	45	5422
4	102	12091	61	4964	34	5030
4	82	11473	53	3289	28	2857
4	103	17480	54	3174	32	3838
4	82	6076	42	2065	28	3271
4	102	14277	37	4981	26	4281
4	100	8544	63	4104	27	2062
4	111	17361	50	6852	31	3367
4	101	11880	43	2765	28	1474
4	137	17722	72	6762	40	6194
4	110	21066	55	2289	32	2597
4	101	15818	47	4677	38	2352
4	103	18211	40	1729	31	1576
4	91	11234	51	4475	23	2436
4	87	8535	51	4972	30	3339
4	98	11759	56	6222	32	2067
4	89	8806	50	4863	26	1825
4	87	6831	55	4068	27	2567
4	75	14679	50	3207	19	1242
4	91	11109	44	4731	37	7450
4	129	21011	52	4006	35	2351
4	95	15511	62	4922	36	2982
4	107	22138	54	5848	37	4755
4	77	9935	45	5764	28	2524
4	73	20894	34	2372	33	3447
4	89	10875	50	6348	33	2623
4	68	4216	34	2479	28	2400
4	106	14338	59	2630	36	3746
4	97	25821	45	2552	25	1741
4	91	11869	48	2948	25	2723

2-11 Computer Data Base Exercise

QRTR	ORDERS 1	SALES 1	ORDERS 2	SALES 2	ORDERS 3	SALES 3
1	110	32892	60	4487	30	3034
1	83	13066	46	4706	22	1491
1	105	18326	46	3327	18	1962
1	110	21758	57	5428	26	2797
1	109	18250	57	5651	23	1704
1	92	21057	46	3450	33	2808
1	84	13490	33	1903	23	2443
1	101	12889	50	3767	35	4176
1	111	11105	45	1741	25	2677
1	113	20343	55	3276	38	3568
1	78	12904	50	5007	22	2089
1	72	6490	38	4407	25	7743
1	89	11317	38	2011	28	2164
1	90	11827	46	4034	22	2683
1	82	14602	38	2173	41	3768
1	74	20086	34	1309	24	3394
1	70	7075	29	2050	23	2450
1	68	6877	30	2067	20	2105
1	89	12461	36	2767	24	1749
1	99	14245	35	1368	29	2262
1	61	8210	22	1244	23	1288
1	69	7527	56	2263	35	2437
1	99	18906	57	4482	31	3643
1	100	15753	51	5159	23	2255
1	84	17706	47	2565	31	3283
1	102	11364	45	5061	42	4308
1	101	17598	45	4009	31	2715
1	96	19154	62	6505	29	4106
1	84	10868	42	5359	42	3199
1	91	15668	53	4755	25	4734
1	99	14198	32	624	41	3949
1	97	15682	44	3111	26	1667
1	118	12885	53	5015	43	4664
1	92	17842	47	5265	29	1695
1	84	18017	47	1324	28	2618
1	104	15049	47	2588	52	5314
1	102	11574	56	3663	39	3263
1	105	28370	62	4395	36	2633
1	79	7634	44	3148	33	2230
1	72	6433	42	2841	33	6729
1	91	21444	41	2951	38	4154
1	100	14174	39	2590	38	3003
1	99	17898	55	6293	25	1463
1	100	17256	44	3756	46	3544
1	88	17487	46	3230	27	2268
1	85	15369	40	3120	29	3505
1	88	9390	54	3868	31	5238
1	91	10973	52	3522	31	1708
1	83	12239	50	3327	29	3067
1	81	13536	54	5644	20	1146
1	96	14434	47	8637	37	6088
1	99	16300	55	3535	21	2365
1	113	18644	65	4179	50	5416
1	94	11708	49	3697	35	2924
1	94	13076	47	3932	37	2450
1	114	18152	37	2154	29	2126
1	109	13236	55	8129	42	3818

QRTR	ORDERS 1	SALES 1	ORDERS 2	SALES 2	ORDERS 3	SALES 3
1	111	14449	50	3194	37	2653
1	96	17339	52	3732	29	3136
1	76	5100	47	3927	28	2873
1	127	29116	41	2789	40	5039
1	89	10860	50	4381	31	1733
2	90	13067	66	4133	47	3517
2	84	18381	43	5580	34	3007
2	89	13133	42	1997	27	3416
2	120	12961	38	5416	23	2302
2	92	14029	51	5569	38	2443
2	101	16651	59	3902	32	3152
2	91	9383	56	5832	37	2273
2	86	12240	45	2459	29	3869
2	84	9880	53	5694	38	3860
2	74	10869	62	8214	35	2218
2	85	9828	70	4490	36	1989
2	105	18997	55	3398	44	3472
2	81	6461	41	2396	30	3634
2	101	13193	58	4121	40	4598
2	101	17089	52	4511	43	2787
2	102	27159	39	3093	31	3633
2	88	15741	51	3736	37	2172
2	61	10252	29	1757	18	1313
2	92	8688	43	2831	37	3403
2	101	15644	53	5185	37	4183
2	101	10162	53	6660	31	2171
2	101	14009	49	4094	41	3752
2	78	9823	45	4105	24	1780
2	100	24296	50	6800	50	4275
2	80	19437	47	6205	26	2219
2	94	11885	54	4476	34	3578
2	80	9520	52	5675	44	3737
2	82	13839	46	4512	29	3440
2	94	15426	41	2766	37	3397
2	118	20349	51	3428	34	3638
2	98	11275	47	5887	46	3453
2	87	9351	55	3379	32	2144
2	102	10904	56	6889	29	1592
2	89	13265	41	3544	34	3048
2	87	9829	57	7184	45	3658
2	87	12359	60	6170	31	4111
2	89	4028	46	5006	29	3557
2	105	23923	79	6400	45	6369
2	93	19956	43	3044	38	3788
2	94	20218	45	3919	29	2349
2	97	15405	59	4780	34	2742
2	89	10705	46	6078	23	3345
2	103	11839	36	6736	33	2378
2	100	10964	40	4404	31	2946
2	95	10083	50	3755	35	4759
2	110	17461	43	5350	22	2963
2	91	11530	60	10255	29	2839
2	89	9839	38	2625	35	2453
2	98	11372	43	5742	34	4843
2	108	15980	34	1680	40	2602
2	94	13897	47	4639	45	3766
2	72	7580	40	4424	38	2213

QRTR	ORDERS 1	SALES 1	ORDERS 2	SALES 2	ORDERS 3	SALES 3
2	101	17713	45	4114	43	5755
2	104	17148	50	4870	37	4537
2	102	12122	46	4425	34	3172
2	90	11062	46	4721	31	2777
2	85	8476	49	3591	41	5074
2	109	14964	69	5035	36	3400
2	93	7098	48	4635	32	2384
2	102	15790	48	1944	39	3153
2	76	8359	47	4231	33	2518
2	84	10362	52	5515	33	3163
2	93	13176	48	4096	37	3745
2	109	16770	48	5832	48	8228

2-12
Flow Chart

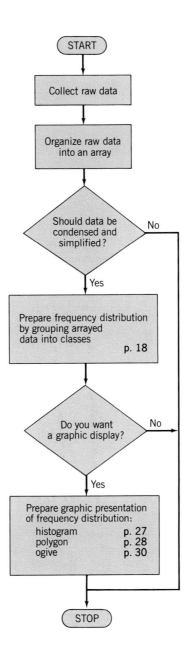

The vice-president of marketing of a fast food chain is studying the sales performance of the 100 stores in his eastern district and has compiled this frequency distribution of annual sales:

SALES (000s)	FREQUENCY	SALES (000s)	FREQUENCY
700– 799	4	1,300–1,399	13
800– 899	7	1,400–1,499	10
900– 999	8	1,500–1,599	9
1,000–1,099	10	1,600–1,699	7
1,100–1,199	12	1,700–1,799	2
1,200–1,299	17	1,800–1,899	1

The vice-president would like to compare the eastern district with the other three districts in the country. To do so, he will summarize the distribution, with an eye toward getting information about the central tendency of the data. This chapter also discusses how he can measure the variability in a distribution and thus get a much better feel for the data.

3

Measures of Central Tendency and Dispersion in Frequency Distributions

■ OBJECTIVES

Chapter 3 focuses on special ways to describe a collection of items, particularly the way observations tend to "bunch up" and "spread out." Here we shall encounter some familiar terms, such as the concept of an average or mean. We'll also study the median and the mode, all useful ways of measuring and locating data. If the basketball coach at your university reports the average height of her team as 5'11", she is really saying that there is a tendency for the heights of the players to bunch up around 5'11". In this chapter we'll also introduce you to the concept of dispersion, the tendency for observations to spread out. If the same basketball coach indicates that the range of heights on her team is only 3", she is saying that the heights of her players don't spread out much since the difference in heights from the tallest player to the shortest player is only 3". To measure how much observations spread out we'll use some new terms such as average deviation and standard deviation. Finally, we will look at *exploratory data analysis,* ways in which statisticians take a first cut at a mass of data to see what they are confronted with.

3-1
Summary Statistics

Summary statistics,
central tendency, and
dispersion

In Chapter 2 we constructed tables and graphs from raw data. The resulting "pictures" of frequency distributions illustrated trends and patterns in the data. In most cases, however, we need more exact measures. In these cases we can use single numbers called *summary statistics* to describe characteristics of a data set.

Two of these characteristics are particularly important to decision makers — *central tendency* and *dispersion*.

Middle of a data set

Central Tendency. Central tendency refers to the middle point of a distribution. Measures of central tendency are also called *measures of location*. In Fig. 3-1, the central location of curve B lies to the right of those of curve A and curve C. Notice that the central location of curve A is equal to that of curve C.

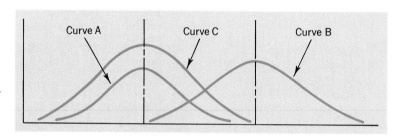

FIGURE 3-1

Comparison of central location of three curves

Spread of a data set

Dispersion. *Dispersion* refers to the spread of the data in a distribution — that is, the extent to which the observations are scattered. Notice that curve A in Fig. 3-2 has a wider spread, or dispersion, than curve B.

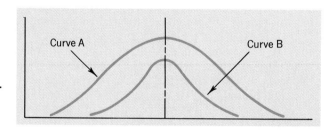

FIGURE 3-2

Comparison of dispersion of two curves

There are two other characteristics of data sets which provide useful information — *skewness* and *kurtosis*. While the derivation of specific statistics to measure these characteristics is beyond the scope of this book, a general understanding of what each means will be helpful.

Symmetry of a data set

Skewness. Curves representing the data points in the data set may be either symmetrical or skewed. *Symmetrical* curves, like the one in Fig. 3-3, are such that a vertical line drawn from the peak of the curve to the horizontal axis will divide the area of the curve into two equal parts. Each part is the mirror image of the other.

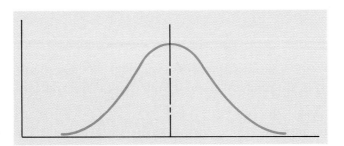

FIGURE 3-3
Symmetrical curve

Skewness of a data set

Curves A and B in Fig. 3-4 are *skewed* curves. They are skewed because values in their frequency distributions are concentrated at either the low end or the high end of the measuring scale on the horizontal axis. The values are not equally distributed. Curve A is skewed to the right (or *positively* skewed), because it tails off toward the high end of the scale. Curve B is just the opposite. It is skewed to the left (*negatively* skewed), because it tails off toward the low end of the scale.

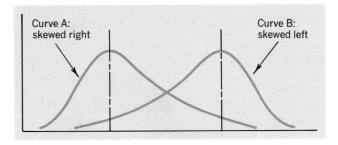

FIGURE 3-4
Comparison of two skewed curves

Curve A might represent the frequency distribution of the number of days' supply on hand in the wholesale fruit business. The curve would be skewed to the right, with many values at the low end and few at the high, because the inventory must turn over rapidly. Similarly, curve B could represent the frequency of the number of days a real-estate broker requires to sell a house. It would be skewed to the left, with many values at the high end and few at the low, because the inventory of houses turns over very slowly.

Peakedness of a data set

Kurtosis. When we measure the *kurtosis* of a distribution, we are measuring its peakedness. In Fig. 3-5, for example, curves A and B differ only by the fact that one is more peaked than the other. They have the same central location and dispersion, and both are symmetrical. Statisticians say that the two curves have different degrees of kurtosis.

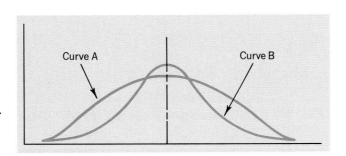

FIGURE 3-5
Two curves with the same central location but different kurtosis

Exercises

3-1 Draw three curves, all symmetrical but with different dispersions.

3-2 Draw 3 curves, all symmetrical and with the same dispersion, but with the following central locations:
(a) 0.0   (b) 1.0   (c) −1.0

3-3 Draw a curve that would be a good representation of the grades on a statistics test in a poorly prepared class; a well-prepared class.

3-4 For the following distributions, indicate which distribution:
(a) Has the larger average value.
(b) Is more likely to produce a small value than a large value.
(c) Is the better representation of the distribution of ages at a rock concert.
(d) Is the better representation of the distribution of the times you have to wait at a doctor's office.

For the next two distributions, indicate which distribution, if any:
(e) Has values most evenly distributed across the range of possible values.
(f) Is more likely to produce a value near 0.
(g) Has a greater likelihood of producing positive values than negative values.

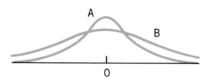

3-5 If the following two curves represent the distribution of scores for a group of students on two tests, which test appears to be more difficult for the students, A or B? Explain.

3-2
A Measure of Central Tendency: The Arithmetic Mean

Most of the time when we refer to the "average" of something, we are talking about the arithmetic mean. This is true in cases such as the average winter temperature in New York City, the average life of a flashlight battery, and the average corn yield from an acre of land.

TABLE 3-1 Downtime of Generators at Lake Ico Station

GENERATOR	1	2	3	4	5	6	7	8	9	10
DAYS OUT OF SERVICE	7	23	4	8	2	12	6	13	9	4

Table 3-1 presents data describing the number of days the generators at a power station on Lake Ico are out of service owing to regular maintenance or some malfunction. To find the arithmetic mean, we sum the values and divide by the number of observations:

$$\text{Arithmetic mean} = \frac{7 + 23 + 4 + 8 + 2 + 12 + 6 + 13 + 9 + 4}{10}$$

$$= \frac{88}{10}$$

$$= 8.8 \text{ days}$$

In this one-year period, the generators were out of service for an average of 8.8 days. With this figure, the power plant manager has a reasonable single measure of the behavior of *all* her generators.

CONVENTIONAL SYMBOLS

To write equations for these measures of frequency distributions, we need to learn the mathematical notations used by statisticians. A *sample* of a population consists of n observations (a lower-case n) with a mean of $\bar{x}$ (read x-bar). Remember that the measures we compute for a sample are called *statistics*.

The notation is different when we are computing measures for the entire *population;* that is, for the group containing every element we are describing. The mean of a population is symbolized by μ, which is the Greek letter *mu*. The number of elements in a population is denoted by the capital italic letter N. Generally in statistics, we use Roman letters to symbolize sample information and Greek letters to symbolize population information.

CALCULATING THE MEAN FROM UNGROUPED DATA

In the example, the average of 8.8 days would be μ (the population mean) if the population of generators is exactly ten. It would be $\bar{x}$ (the sample mean) if the ten generators are a sample drawn from a larger population of generators. To write the formulas for these two means, we combine our mathematical symbols and the steps we used to determine the arithmetic mean. If we add the values of the observations and divide this sum by the number of observations, we will get:

Population mean → Sum of values of all observations →

$$\mu = \frac{\Sigma x}{N}$$ [3-1]

← Number of elements in the population

and:

Sample mean → Sum of values of all observations →

$$\bar{x} = \frac{\Sigma x}{n}$$ [3-2]

← Number of elements in the sample

Since μ is the *population arithmetic mean,* we use N to indicate that we divide by the number of observations or elements in the population. Similarly, $\bar{x}$ is the *sample arithmetic mean,* and n is the number of observations in the sample. The Greek letter sigma, Σ, indicates that all the values of x are summed together.

Another example: Table 3-2 lists the percentile increase in SAT verbal scores shown by seven different students taking an SAT preparatory course.

TABLE 3-2 **Percentile Increase in SAT Verbal Scores**

STUDENT	1	2	3	4	5	6	7
INCREASE	9	7	7	6	4	4	2

We compute the mean of this sample of seven students as follows:

$$\bar{x} = \frac{\Sigma x}{n}$$ [3-2]

$$= \frac{9 + 7 + 7 + 6 + 4 + 4 + 2}{7}$$

$$= \frac{39}{7}$$

$$= 5.6 \text{ points per student} \leftarrow \text{sample mean}$$

Dealing with ungrouped data

Notice that to calculate this mean, we added every observation. Statisticians call this kind of data *ungrouped* data. The computations were not difficult, because our sample size was small. But suppose we are dealing with the weight of 5,000 head of cattle and prefer not to add each of our data points separately. Or suppose we have access to only the frequency distribution of the data, not to every individual observation. In these cases, we will need a different way to calculate the arithmetic mean.

CALCULATING THE MEAN FROM GROUPED DATA

Dealing with grouped data

A frequency distribution consists of data that are grouped by classes. Each value of an observation falls somewhere in one of the classes. Unlike the SAT example, we do not know the separate values of every observation. Suppose we have a frequency distribution (illustrated in Table 3-3) of average monthly checking-account balances of

TABLE 3-3 **Average Monthly Balances of 600 Customers**

CLASS (DOLLARS)	FREQUENCY
0– 49.99	78
50.00– 99.99	123
100.00–149.99	187
150.00–199.99	82
200.00–249.99	51
250.00–299.99	47
300.00–349.99	13
350.00–399.99	9
400.00–449.99	6
450.00–499.99	4
	600

600 customers at a branch bank. From the information in this table, we can easily

Estimating the mean

compute an *estimate* of the value of the mean of this grouped data. It is an estimate because we do not use all 600 data points in the sample. Had we used the original, ungrouped data, we could have calculated the actual value of the mean—but only after we had averaged the 600 separate values. For ease of calculation, we must give up accuracy.

Calculating the mean

To find the arithmetic mean of grouped data, we first calculate the midpoint of each class. To make midpoints come out in whole cents, we round up. Thus, for example, the midpoint for the first class becomes 25.00, rather than 24.995. Then we multiply each midpoint by the frequency of observations in that class, sum all these results, and divide the sum by the total number of observations in the sample. The formula looks like this:

$$\bar{x} = \frac{\Sigma(f \times x)}{n}$$

[3-3]

where:

- $\bar{x}$ is the sample mean
- Σ is the symbol meaning "the sum of"
- f is the frequency (number of observations) in each class
- x represents the midpoint for each class in the sample
- n is the number of observations in the sample

Table 3-4 illustrates how to calculate the arithmetic mean from our grouped data, using Equation 3-3.

In our sample of 600 customers, the average monthly checking-account balance is

We make an assumption

$142.25. This is our approximation from the frequency distribution. Notice that since we did not know every data point in the sample, we assumed that every value in

TABLE 3-4 Calculation of Arithmetic Sample Mean From Grouped Data in Table 3-3

CLASS (DOLLARS) (1)	MIDPOINTS (x) (2)		FREQUENCY (f) (3)		f × x (3) × (2)
0– 49.99	25.00	×	78	=	1,950
50.00– 99.99	75.00	×	123	=	9,225
100.00–149.99	125.00	×	187	=	23,375
150.00–199.99	175.00	×	82	=	14,350
200.00–249.99	225.00	×	51	=	11,475
250.00–299.99	275.00	×	47	=	12,925
300.00–349.99	325.00	×	13	=	4,225
350.00–399.99	375.00	×	9	=	3,375
400.00–449.99	425.00	×	6	=	2,550
450.00–499.99	475.00	×	4	=	1,900
			$\Sigma f = n = $ **600**		**85,350** ← $\Sigma(f \times x)$

$$\bar{x} = \frac{\Sigma(f \times x)}{n} \quad \text{[3-3]}$$

$$= \frac{85,350}{600}$$

$$= 142.25 \leftarrow \text{sample mean (dollars)}$$

a class was equal to its midpoint. Our results, then, can only approximate the actual average monthly balance.

CODING

Assigning codes to the midpoints

When we have to do the arithmetic by hand, we can further simplify our calculation of the mean from grouped data. Using a technique called *coding,* we eliminate the problem of large or inconvenient midpoints. Instead of using the actual midpoints to perform our calculations, we can assign small-value consecutive integers (whole numbers) called *codes* to each of the midpoints. The integer zero can be assigned anywhere, but to keep the integers small, we will assign zero to the midpoint in the *middle* (or the one nearest to the middle) of the frequency distribution. Then we can assign negative integers to values smaller than that midpoint and positive integers to those larger, as follows:

Class	1-5	6-10	11-15	16-20	21-25	26-30	31-35	36-40	41-45
Code (u)	−4	−3	−2	−1	0	1	2	3	4

$$\uparrow$$
$$x_0$$

Calculating the mean from grouped data, using codes

Symbolically, statisticians use x_0 to represent the midpoint that is assigned the code 0, and u for the coded midpoint. The following formula is used to determine the sample mean using codes:

$$\bar{x} = x_0 + w \frac{\Sigma(u \times f)}{n}$$ [3-4]

where:

- $\bar{x}$ = mean of sample
- x_0 = value of the midpoint assigned the code 0
- w = numerical width of the class interval
- u = code assigned to each class
- f = frequency or number of observations in each class
- n = total number of observations in the sample

Keep in mind that $\Sigma(u \times f)$ simply means that we (1) multiply u by f for every class in the frequency distribution, and (2) sum all of these products. Table 3-5 illustrates how to code the midpoints and find the sample mean of the annual snowfall (in inches) over 20 years in Harlan, Kentucky.

ADVANTAGES AND DISADVANTAGES OF THE ARITHMETIC MEAN

Advantages of the mean

The arithmetic mean, as a single number representing a whole data set, has important advantages. First, its concept is familiar to most people and intuitively clear. Second, every data set has a mean. It is a measure that can be calculated, and it is unique because every data set has one and only one mean. Finally, the mean is useful for

TABLE 3-5 Annual Snowfall in Harlan, Kentucky

CLASS (1)	MIDPOINT (x) (2)	CODE (u) (3)		FREQUENCY (f) (4)		u × f (3) × (4)
0– 7	3.5	−2	×	2	=	−4
8–15	11.5	−1	×	6	=	−6
16–23	19.5 ← x_0	0	×	3	=	0
24–31	27.5	1	×	5	=	5
32–39	35.5	2	×	2	=	4
40–47	43.5	3	×	2	=	6
				$\Sigma f = n = 20$		5 ← $\Sigma(u \times f)$

$$\bar{x} = x_0 + w \frac{\Sigma(u \times f)}{n} \qquad \text{[3-4]}$$

$$= 19.5 + (8)\left(\frac{5}{20}\right)$$

$$= 19.5 + 2$$

$$= 21.5 \leftarrow \text{average annual snowfall}$$

performing statistical procedures such as comparing the means from several data sets (a procedure we will carry out in Chapter 8).

Three disadvantages of the mean

Yet, like any statistical measure, the arithmetic mean has disadvantages of which we must be aware. **First,** although the mean is reliable in that it reflects all the values in the data set, it may also be affected by extreme values that are not representative of the rest of the data. Notice that if the seven members of a track team have times in a mile race shown in Table 3-6, the mean time is:

$$\mu = \frac{\Sigma x}{N} \qquad \text{[3-1]}$$

$$= \frac{4.2 + 4.3 + 4.7 + 4.8 + 5.0 + 5.1 + 9.0}{7}$$

$$= \frac{37.1}{7}$$

$$= 5.3 \text{ minutes} \leftarrow \text{population mean}$$

If we compute a mean time for the first six members, however, and exclude the 9.0 value, the answer is about 4.7 minutes. The one *extreme value* of 9.0 distorts the value we get for the mean. It would be more representative to calculate the mean *without* including such an extreme value.

A **second** problem with the mean is the same one we encountered with our 600 checking-account balances: It is tedious to compute the mean because we *do* use every data point in our calculation (unless, of course, we take the short-cut method of using grouped data to approximate the mean).

TABLE 3-6 Times for Track-Team Members in a One-Mile Race

MEMBER	1	2	3	4	5	6	7
TIME IN MINUTES	4.2	4.3	4.7	4.8	5.0	5.1	9.0

3-2 A Measure of Central Tendency: The Arithmetic Mean   **71**

TABLE 3-7 Times for Track-Team Members in a One-Mile Race

CLASS IN MINUTES	4.2–4.5	4.6–4.9	5.0–5.3	5.4 and above
FREQUENCY	2	2	2	1

The **third** disadvantage is that we are unable to compute the mean for a data set that has open-ended classes at either the high or low end of the scale. Suppose the data in Table 3-6 had been arranged in the frequency distribution shown in Table 3-7. We could not compute a mean value for this data because of the open-ended class of "5.4 and above." We have no way of knowing whether the value is 5.4, near to 5.4, or far above 5.4.

Exercises

3-6 Child-Care Community Nursery is eligible for a county social services grant as long as the average age of its children stays below 9. If these data represent the ages of all the children currently attending Child-Care, do they qualify for the grant?

$$8 \quad 5 \quad 9 \quad 10 \quad 9 \quad 12 \quad 7 \quad 12 \quad 13 \quad 7 \quad 8$$

3-7 Child-Care Community Nursery can continue to be supported by the county social services office as long as the average annual income of the families whose children attend the nursery is below $12,500. The family incomes of the attending children are:

$14,500	$15,600	$12,500	$8,600	$ 7,800
$ 6,500	$ 5,900	$10,200	$8,800	$14,300	$13,900

(a) Does Child-Care qualify now for county support?
(b) If the answer to (a) is no, by how much must the average family income fall for them to qualify?
(c) If the answer to (a) is yes, by how much can average family income rise and Child-Care still stay eligible?

3-8 These data represent the ages of patients admitted to a small hospital on February 28, 1990:

85	75	66	43	40
88	80	56	56	67
89	83	65	53	75
87	83	52	44	48

(a) Construct a frequency distribution with classes 40–49, 50–59, etc.
(b) Compute the sample mean from the frequency distribution.
(c) Compute the sample mean from the raw data.
(d) Compare (b) and (c) and comment on your answer.

3-9 The frequency distribution below represents the weights in pounds of a sample of packages carried last month by a small air freight company.

CLASS	FREQUENCY	CLASS	FREQUENCY
10.0–10.9	1	15.0–15.9	11
11.0–11.9	4	16.0–16.9	8
12.0–12.9	6	17.0–17.9	7
13.0–13.9	8	18.0–18.9	6
14.0–14.9	12	19.0–19.9	2

(a) Compute the sample mean using Equation 3-3.
(b) Compute the sample mean using the coding method (Equation 3-4) with 0 assigned to the fourth class.
(c) Repeat (b) with 0 assigned to the sixth class.
(d) Explain why your answers in (b) and (c) are the same.

 3-10 Davis Furniture Company has a revolving credit agreement with the First National Bank. The loan showed the following ending monthly balances last year:

Jan. $121,300	Apr. $72,800	July $58,700	Oct. $52,800
Feb. $112,300	May $72,800	Aug. $61,100	Nov. $49,200
Mar. $ 72,800	June $57,300	Sept. $50,400	Dec. $46,100

The company is eligible for a reduced rate of interest if its average monthly balance is over $65,000; does it qualify?

 3-11 A cosmetics manufacturer recently purchased a machine to fill 3-ounce cologne bottles. To test the accuracy of the machine's volume setting, eighteen trial bottles were run. The resulting volumes (in ounces) for the trials were as follows:

3.02 2.89 2.92 2.84 2.90 2.97 2.95 2.94 2.93
3.01 2.97 2.95 2.90 2.94 2.96 2.99 2.99 2.97

The company does not normally recalibrate the filling machine for this cologne if the average volume is within .04 of 3.00 ounces; should it recalibrate?

3-12 The production manager of Hinton Press is determining the average time needed to photograph one printing plate. Using a stopwatch and observing the platemakers, he collects the following times (in seconds):

20.4 20.0 22.2 23.8 21.3 25.1 21.2 22.9 28.2 24.3
22.0 24.7 25.7 24.9 22.7 24.4 24.3 23.6 23.2 21.0

An average per-plate time of less than 23.0 seconds indicates satisfactory productivity. Should the production manager be concerned?

 3-13 National Tire Company holds reserve funds in short-term marketable securities. The ending daily balance (in millions) of the marketable securities account for two weeks is shown below:

Week 1	$1.973	$1.970	$1.972	$1.975	$1.976
Week 2	1.969	1.892	1.893	1.887	1.895

What was the average (mean) amount invested in marketable securities during
(a) the first week?
(b) the second week?
(c) the two-week period?
(d) An average balance over the two weeks of more than $1.970 qualifies National for special interest rates. Does it qualify?

(e) If the answer to (d) is less than $1.970 million, by how much would the last day's invested amount have to rise to qualify the company for the special interest rates?

(f) If the answer to (d) is more than $1.970 million, how much could the company treasurer withdraw from reserve funds on the last day and still qualify for the special interest rates?

3-14 M. T. Smith travels the eastern United States for a textbook publisher. She is paid on a commission basis related to volume. Her quarterly earnings over the last 3 years are given below.

	1ST QUARTER	2ND QUARTER	3RD QUARTER	4TH QUARTER
Year 1	$10,000	$ 5,000	$25,000	$15,000
Year 2	20,000	10,000	20,000	10,000
Year 3	30,000	15,000	45,000	50,000

(a) Calculate separately M. T.'s average earnings in each of the 4 quarters.
(b) Calculate separately M. T.'s average quarterly earnings in each of the 3 years.
(c) Show that the mean of the four numbers you found in part (a) is equal to the mean of the three numbers you found in part (b). Furthermore, show that both these numbers equal the mean of all twelve numbers in the data table. (This is M. T.'s average quarterly income over 3 years.)

3-15 Lillian Tyson has been the chairperson of the county library committee for 10 years. She contends that during her tenure she has managed the bookmobile repair budget better than her predecessor. Here are data for bookmobile repair for 15 years:

YEAR	TOWN BUDGET	YEAR	TOWN BUDGET	YEAR	TOWN BUDGET
1989	$30,000	1984	$24,000	1979	$30,000
1988	28,000	1983	19,000	1978	20,000
1987	25,000	1982	21,000	1977	15,000
1986	27,000	1981	22,000	1976	10,000
1985	26,000	1980	24,000	1975	9,000

(a) Calculate the average annual budget for the last five years (1985–1989).
(b) Calculate the average annual budget for her first five years in office (1980–1984).
(c) Calculate the average annual budget for the 5 years before she was elected (1975–1979).
(d) Based on the answers you found for parts (a), (b), and (c), do you think that there has been a decreasing or increasing trend in the annual budget? Has she been saving the county money?

3-3
A Second Measure of Central Tendency: The Weighted Mean

A weighted mean

The weighted mean enables us to calculate an average that takes into account the importance of each value to the overall total. Consider, for example, the company in Table 3-8, which uses three grades of labor — unskilled, semiskilled, and skilled — to produce two end products. The company wants to know the average cost of labor per hour for each of the products.

TABLE 3-8 Labor Input in Manufacturing Process

| GRADE OF LABOR | HOURLY WAGE (x) | Labor hours per unit of output | |
		PRODUCT 1	PRODUCT 2
Unskilled	$5.00	1	4
Semiskilled	7.00	2	3
Skilled	9.00	5	3

A simple arithmetic average of the labor wage rates would be:

$$\bar{x} = \frac{\Sigma x}{n} \qquad\qquad [3\text{-}2]$$

$$= \frac{\$5 + \$7 + \$9}{3}$$

$$= \frac{\$21}{3}$$

$$= \$7.00/\text{hour}$$

In this case, the arithmetic mean is incorrect

Using this average rate, we would compute the labor cost of one unit of product 1 to be $7(1 + 2 + 5) = $56, and of one unit of product 2 to be $7(4 + 3 + 3) = $70. But these answers are incorrect.

To be correct, the answers must take into account the fact that different amounts of each grade of labor are used. We can determine the correct answers in the following manner. For product 1, the total labor cost per unit is ($5 × 1) + ($7 × 2) + ($9 × 5) = $64, and, since there are eight hours of labor input, the average labor cost per hour is $64/8 = $8.00 per hour. For product 2, the total labor cost per unit is ($5 × 4) + ($7 × 3) + ($9 × 3) = $68, for an average labor cost per hour of $68/10, or $6.80 per hour.

The correct answer is the weighted mean

Another way to calculate the correct average cost per hour for the two products is to take a *weighted average* of the cost of the three grades of labor. To do this, we weight the hourly wage for each grade by its proportion of the total labor required to produce the product. One unit of product 1, for example, requires eight hours of labor. Unskilled labor uses ⅛ of this time, semiskilled labor uses ⅔ of this time, and skilled labor requires ⅝ of this time. If we use these fractions as our weights, then one hour of labor for product 1 costs an average of:

$$\left(\frac{1}{8} \times \$5\right) + \left(\frac{2}{8} \times \$7\right) + \left(\frac{5}{8} \times \$9\right) = \$8.00/\text{hour}$$

Similarly, a unit of product 2 requires ten labor hours, of which ⁴⁄₁₀ is used for unskilled labor, ³⁄₁₀ for semiskilled labor, and ³⁄₁₀ for skilled labor. Using these fractions as weights, one hour of labor for product 2 costs:

$$\left(\frac{4}{10} \times \$5\right) + \left(\frac{3}{10} \times \$7\right) + \left(\frac{3}{10} \times \$9\right) = \$6.80/\text{hour}$$

Calculating the weighted mean

Thus, we see that the weighted averages give the correct values for the average hourly labor costs of the two products because **they take into account the fact that different amounts of each grade of labor are used in the products.**

Symbolically, the formula for calculating the weighted average is:

$$\bar{x}_w = \frac{\Sigma(w \times x)}{\Sigma w} \qquad [3\text{-}5]$$

where

- $\bar{x}_w$ = the symbol for the weighted mean*
- w = weight assigned to each observation (1/8, 2/8, and 5/8 for product 1 in our example)
- $\Sigma(w \times x)$ = sum of the weight of each element times that element
- Σw = sum of all of the weights

If we apply Equation 3-5 to product 1 in our labor-cost example, we find:

$$\bar{x}_w = \frac{\Sigma(w \times x)}{\Sigma w} \qquad [3\text{-}5]$$

$$= \frac{(1/8 \times \$5) + (2/8 \times \$7) + (5/8 \times \$9)}{1/8 + 2/8 + 5/8}$$

$$= \frac{\$8}{1}$$

$$= \$8.00/\text{hour}$$

The arithmetic mean of grouped data: the weighted mean

Notice that Equation 3-5 states more formally something we have done previously. When we calculated the arithmetic mean from grouped data (page 69), we actually found a weighted mean, using the midpoints for the x values and the frequencies of each class as the weights. We divided this product by the sum of all the frequencies, which is the same as dividing by the sum of all the weights.

In like manner, *any* mean computed from all the values in a data set according to Equation 3-1 or 3-2 is really a weighted average of the components of the data set. What those components are, of course, determines what the mean measures. In a factory, for example, we could determine the weighted mean of all the wages (skilled, semiskilled, and unskilled), or of the wages of men workers, women workers, or union and nonunion members.

* The symbol $\bar{x}_w$ is read *x-bar sub w*. The lower-case w is called a subscript and is a reminder that this is not an ordinary mean but one that is weighted according to the relative importance of the values of x.

Exercises

3-16 A professor has decided to use a weighted average in figuring final grades for his seminar students. The homework average will count for 20 percent of a student's grade; the midterm, 25 percent; the final, 35 percent; the term paper, 10 percent; and quizzes, 10 percent. From the data below, compute the final average for the five students in the seminar.

STUDENT	HOMEWORK	QUIZZES	PAPER	MIDTERM	FINAL
1	85	89	94	87	90
2	78	84	88	91	92
3	94	88	93	86	89
4	82	79	88	84	93
5	95	90	92	82	88

3-17 Dave's Giveaway Store advertises, "If our average prices are not equal or lower than everyone else's, you get it free." One of Dave's customers came into the store one day and threw on the counter bills of sale for six items she bought from a competitor for an average price less than Dave's. The items cost:

$1.29 $2.97 $3.49 $5.00 $7.50 $10.95

Dave's prices for the same six items are $1.35, $2.89, $3.19, $4.98, $7.59, and $11.50. Dave told the customer, "My ad refers to a weighted average price of these items. Our average is lower because our sales of these items have been":

7   9   12   8   6   3

Is Dave getting himself into or out of trouble with his contention about weighted averages?

3-18 Keyes Home Furnishings ran 6 local newspaper advertisements during December. The following frequency distribution resulted:

NUMBER OF TIMES SUBSCRIBER SAW AD DURING DECEMBER	0	1	2	3	4	5	6
Frequency	897	1,082	1,325	814	307	253	198

What is the average number of times a subscriber saw a Keyes advertisement during December?

3-19 Bennett Distribution Company, a subsidiary of a major appliance manufacturer, is forecasting regional sales for next year. The Atlantic branch, with current yearly sales of $193.8 million, is expected to achieve a sales growth of 7.25 percent; the Midwest branch, with current sales of $79.3 million, is expected to grow by 8.20 percent; and the Pacific branch, with sales of $57.5 million, is expected to increase sales by 7.15 percent. What is the average rate of sales growth forecasted for next year?

3-20 The U.S. Postal Service handles seven basic types of letters and cards: third class, second class, first class, air mail, special delivery, registered, and certified. The mail volume during 1977 is given in the following table:

TYPE OF MAILING	OUNCES DELIVERED (IN MILLIONS)	PRICE PER OUNCE
Third class	16,400	$.05
Second class	24,100	.08
First class	77,600	.13
Air mail	1,900	.17
Special delivery	1,300	.35
Registered	750	.40
Certified	800	.45

What was the average revenue per ounce for these services during the year?

3-21 Matthews, Young and Associates, a management consulting firm, has four types of professionals on its staff: managing consultants, senior associates, field staff, and office staff. Average rates charged to consulting clients for the work of each of these professional categories is $75/hour, $40/hour, $30/hour and $15/hour. Office records indicate the following number of hours billed last year in each category: 8,000, 14,000, 24,000, and 35,000. If Matthews, Young is trying to come up with an average billing rate for estimating client charges for next year, what would you suggest they do and what do you think an appropriate rate is?

3-4
A Third Measure of Central Tendency: The Geometric Mean

Finding the growth rate: the geometric mean

Sometimes when we are dealing with quantities that change over a period of time, we need to know an average rate of change, such as an average growth rate over a period of several years. In such cases, the simple arithmetic mean is inappropriate, because it gives the wrong answers. What we need to find is the *geometric mean,* called simply the G.M.

Consider, for example, the growth of a savings account. Suppose we deposit $100 initially and let it accrue interest at varying rates for five years. The growth is summarized in Table 3-9.

TABLE 3-9 Growth of $100 Deposit in a Savings Account

YEAR	INTEREST RATE	GROWTH FACTOR	SAVINGS AT END OF YEAR
1	7%	1.07	$107.00
2	8	1.08	115.56
3	10	1.10	127.12
4	12	1.12	142.37
5	18	1.18	168.00

The entry labeled "growth factor" is equal to:

$$1 + \frac{\text{interest rate}}{100}$$

The growth factor is the amount by which we multiply the savings at the beginning of the year to get the savings at the end of the year. The simple arithmetic mean growth factor would be $(1.07 + 1.08 + 1.10 + 1.12 + 1.18)/5 = 1.11,$ which corresponds to an average interest rate of 11 percent per year. If the bank gives interest at a constant

In this case, the arithmetic mean growth rate is incorrect

rate of 11 percent per year, however, a $100 deposit would grow in five years to:

$$\$100 \times 1.11 \times 1.11 \times 1.11 \times 1.11 \times 1.11 = \$168.51$$

Table 3-9 shows that the actual figure is only $168.00. Thus, the correct average growth factor must be slightly less than 1.11.

Calculating the geometric mean

To find the correct average growth factor, we can multiply together the five years' growth factors and then take the fifth root of the product—the number that, when multiplied by itself four times, is equal to the product we started with. The result is the *geometric mean growth rate,* which is the appropriate average to use here. The formula for finding the geometric mean of a series of numbers is:

Number of x values

$$\text{G.M.} = \sqrt[n]{\text{Product of all the } x \text{ values}} \qquad [3\text{-}6]$$

If we apply this equation to our savings-account problem, we can determine that 1.1093 is the correct average growth factor.

$$\text{G.M.} = \sqrt[n]{\text{Product of all the } x \text{ values}} \qquad [3\text{-}6]$$
$$= \sqrt[5]{1.07 \times 1.08 \times 1.10 \times 1.12 \times 1.18}$$
$$= \sqrt[5]{1.679965}$$
$$= 1.1093 \leftarrow \text{average growth factor}$$

Notice that the correct average interest rate of 10.93 percent per year obtained with the geometric mean is very close to the incorrect average rate of 11 percent obtained with the arithmetic mean. This happens because the interest rates are relatively small. Be careful, however, not to be tempted to use the arithmetic mean instead of the more complicated geometric mean. The following example demonstrates why.

In highly inflationary economies, banks must pay high interest rates to attract savings. Suppose that over five years in an unbelievably inflationary economy, banks pay interest at annual rates of 100, 200, 250, 300, and 400 percent, which correspond to growth factors of 2, 3, 3.5, 4, and 5. (We've calculated these growth factors just as we did in Table 3-9.)

In five years, an initial deposit of $100 would grow to $100 $\times$ 2 $\times$ 3 $\times$ 3.5 $\times$ 4 $\times$ 5 = $42,000. The arithmetic mean growth factor is (2 + 3 + 3.5 + 4 + 5)/5, or 3.5. This corresponds to an average interest rate of 250 percent. Yet if the banks actually gave interest at a constant rate of 250 percent per year, then $100 would grow to $52,521.88 in five years:

$$\$100 \times 3.5 \times 3.5 \times 3.5 \times 3.5 \times 3.5 = \$52,521.88$$

This answer exceeds the actual $42,000 by more than $10,500, a sizable error.

Let's use the formula for finding the geometric mean of a series of numbers to determine the correct growth factor:

$$
\begin{aligned}
\text{G.M.} &= \sqrt[n]{\text{Product of all the } x \text{ values}} \qquad\qquad [3\text{-}6] \\
&= \sqrt[5]{2 \times 3 \times 3.5 \times 4 \times 5} \\
&= \sqrt[5]{420} \\
&= 3.347 \leftarrow \text{average growth factor}
\end{aligned}
$$

This growth factor corresponds to an average interest rate of 235 percent per year. In this case, the use of the appropriate mean *does* make a significant difference.

Exercises

 3-22 Hayes Textiles has shown the following percentage increase in net worth over the last 5 years:

1986	1987	1988	1989	1990
5%	10.5%	9.0%	6.0%	7.5%

What is the average percentage increase in net worth over the 5-year period?

 3-23 The growth in bad debt expense for Johnston Office Supply Company over the last few years is given below. Calculate the average percentage increase in bad-debt expense over this time period. If this rate continues, estimate the percentage increase in bad debts for 1991.

1983	1984	1985	1986	1987	1988	1989
.11	.09	.075	.08	.095	.108	.120

 3-24 The Birch Company, a manufacturer of electrical circuit boards, has manufactured the following number of units over the past 5 years:

1986	1987	1988	1989	1990
12,500	13,250	14,310	15,741	17,630

Calculate the average percentage increase in units produced over this time period, and use this to estimate production for 1993.

3-25 Bob Headen is calculating the average growth factor for his stereo store over the last 6 years. Using a geometric mean, he comes up with an answer of 1.24. Individual growth factors for the first five years were 1.19, 1.35, 1.23, 1.19, and 1.30, but Bob lost the records for the sixth year, after he calculated the mean. What was it?

3-26 Over a 3-week period, a store owner purchased $120 worth of acrylic sheeting for new display cases in three equal purchases of $40 each. The first purchase was at $1.00 per square foot; the second, $1.10; and the third, $1.15. What was the average weekly rate of increase in the price per square foot paid for the sheeting?

3-27 Realistic Stereo Shops marks up its merchandise 35 percent above the cost of its latest additions to stock. Until 4 months ago, the Dynamic 400-S VHS recorder had been $300. During the last 4 months Realistic has received 4 monthly shipments of this recorder at these unit costs: $275, $250, $240, and $225. At what average rate per month has Realistic's retail price for this unit been decreasing during this 4 month period?

3-28 Industrial Suppliers, Inc., keeps records on the cost of processing a purchase order. Over the last 5 years this cost has behaved as follows: $55.00, $58.00, $61.00, $65.00, and $66.00. What has Industrial's average percentage increase been over this period? If this average rate stays the same for 3 more years, what will it cost Industrial to process a purchase order at that time?

3-29 A sociologist has been studying the yearly changes in the number of convicts assigned to the largest correctional facility in the state. His data are expressed in terms of the percentage increase in the number of prisoners (a negative number indicates a percentage decrease). The sociologist's most recent data are given below.

1985	1986	1987	1988	1989	1990
−4%	5%	10%	3%	6%	−5%

(a) Calculate the average percentage increase using only the 1986-through-1989 data.
(b) Rework part (a) using the data from all 6 years.
(c) A new penal code was passed in 1984. Previously, prison population grew at a rate of about 2 percent per year. What seems to be the effect of the new code?

3-5
A Fourth Measure of Central Tendency: The Median

Median defined

The median is a measure of central tendency different from any of the means we have discussed so far. The median is a single value from the data set that measures the central item in the data. This single item is the *middlemost* or *most central* item in the set of numbers. Half of the items lie above this point, and the other half lie below it.

CALCULATING THE MEDIAN FROM UNGROUPED DATA

Finding the median of ungrouped data

To find the median of a data set, first array the data in ascending or descending order. If the data set contains an *odd* number of items, the middle item of the array is the median. If there is an *even* number of items, the median is the average of the two middle items. In formal language, the median is:

$$\text{Median} = \text{the } \left(\frac{n+1}{2}\right) \text{th item in a data array} \qquad [3\text{-}7]$$

An odd number of items

Suppose we wish to find the median of seven items in a data array. According to Equation 3-7, the median is the $(7 + 1)/2 = $ 4th item in the array. If we apply this to our previous example of the times for seven members of a track team, we discover that the fourth element in the array is 4.8 minutes. This is the median time for the track team. Notice that unlike the arithmetic mean we calculated earlier, the median we calculated in Table 3-10 was *not* distorted by the presence of the last value (9.0). This value could have been 15.0 or even 45.0 minutes, and the median would have been the same!

The median is not distorted by extreme values

TABLE 3-10 **Times for Track-Team Members**

ITEM IN DATA ARRAY	1	2	3	4	5	6	7
TIME IN MINUTES	4.2	4.3	4.7	4.8	5.0	5.1	9.0

median

An even number of items

Now let's calculate the median for an array with an even number of items. Consider the data shown in Table 3-11 concerning the number of patients treated daily in the emergency room of a hospital. The data are arrayed in descending order. The median of this data set would be:

$$\text{Median} = \text{the } \left(\frac{n+1}{2}\right) \text{th item in a data array} \qquad [3\text{-}7]$$

$$= \frac{8+1}{2}$$

$$= 4.5\text{th item}$$

Since the median is the 4.5th element in the array, we need to average the fourth and fifth elements. The fourth element in Table 3-11 is 43, and the fifth is 35. The average of these two elements is equal to $(43 + 35)/2$, or 39. Therefore, 39 is the median number of patients treated in the emergency room per day during the 8-day period.

TABLE 3-11 **Patients Treated in Emergency Room on 8 Consecutive Days**

ITEM IN DATA ARRAY	1	2	3	4	5	6	7	8
NUMBER OF PATIENTS	86	52	49	43	35	31	30	11

median of 39

CALCULATING THE MEDIAN FROM GROUPED DATA

Finding the median of grouped data

Often, we have access to data only after it has been grouped in a frequency distribution. We do not, for example, know every observation that led to the construction of

TABLE 3-12 Average Monthly Balances
for 600 Customers

CLASS IN DOLLARS	FREQUENCY	
0– 49.99	78	
50.00– 99.99	123	
100.00–149.99	187	median class
150.00–199.99	82	
200.00–249.99	51	
250.00–299.99	47	
300.00–349.99	13	
350.00–399.99	9	
400.00–449.99	6	
450.00–499.99	4	
	600	

Table 3-12, the data on 600 bank customers originally introduced earlier. Instead, we have ten class intervals and a record of the frequency with which the observations appear in each of the intervals.

Locate the median class Nevertheless, we can compute the median checking-account balance of these 600 customers by determining which of the ten class intervals *contains* the median. To do this, we must add the frequencies in the frequency column in Table 3-12 until we reach the $(n + 1)/2$th item. Since there are 600 accounts, the value for $(n + 1)/2$ is 300.5 (the average of the 300th and 301st items). The problem is to find the class intervals containing the 300th and 301st elements. The cumulative frequency for the first two classes is only $78 + 123 = 201$. But when we move to the third class interval, 187 elements are added to 201 for a total of 388. Therefore, the 300th and 301st observations must be located in this third class (the interval from $100.00 to $149.99).

The *median class* for this data set contains 187 items. If we assume that these 187 items begin at $100.00 and are *evenly spaced over the entire class interval* from $100.00 to $149.99, then we can interpolate and find values for the 300th and 301st items. First, we determine that the 300th item is the 99th element in the median class:

$$300 - 201 \text{ [items in the first two classes]} = 99$$

and that the 301st item is the 100th element in the median class:

$$301 - 201 = 100$$

Then we can calculate the *width* of the 187 equal steps from $100.00 to $149.99, as follows:

First item of next class — First item of median class

$$\frac{\$150.00 - \$100.00}{187} = \$.267 \text{ in width}$$

Now, if there are 187 steps of $.267 each and if 98 steps will take us to the 99th item, then the 99th item is:

$$(\$.267 \times 98) + \$100 = \$126.17$$

and the 100th item is one additional step:

$$\$126.17 + \$.267 = \$126.44$$

Therefore, we can use $126.17 and $126.44 as the values of the 300th and 301st items, respectively.

The actual median for this data set is the value of the 300.5th item; that is, the average of the 300th and 301st items. This average is:

$$\frac{\$126.17 + \$126.44}{2} = \$126.30$$

This figure ($126.30) is the median monthly checking account balance, as estimated from the grouped data in Table 3-12.

In summary, we can calculate the median of grouped data as follows:

Steps for finding the median of grouped data

1. Use Equation 3-7 to determine which element in the distribution is centermost (in this case, the average of the 300th and 301st items).
2. Add the frequencies in each class to find the class that contains that centermost element (the third class, or $100.00 − $149.99).
3. Determine the number of elements in the class (187) and the location in the class of the median element (item 300 was the 99th element; item 301, the 100th element).
4. Learn the width of each step in the median class by dividing the class interval by the number of elements in the class (width = $.267).
5. Determine the number of steps from the lower bound of the median class to the appropriate item for the median (98 steps for the 99th element; 99 steps for the 100th element).
6. Calculate the estimated value of the median element by multiplying the number of steps to the median element times the width of each step and by adding the result to the lower bound of the median class ($100 + 98 × $.267 = $126.17; $126.17 + $.267 = $126.44).
7. If, as in our example, there is an even number of elements in the distribution, average the values of the median element calculated in step #6 ($126.30).

An easier method

To shorten this procedure, statisticians use an equation to determine the median of grouped data. For a sample, this equation would be:

Sample median

$$\tilde{m} = \left(\frac{(n + 1)/2 - (F + 1)}{f_m} \right) w + L_m \qquad [3\text{-}8]$$

where:

- $\tilde{m}$ = sample median
- n = total number of items in the distribution
- F = sum of all the class frequencies *up to,* but *not including,* the median class
- f_m = frequency of the median class
- w = class interval width
- L_m = lower limit of the median class interval

3-5 A Fourth Measure of Central Tendency: The Median **83**

If we use Equation 3-8 to compute the median of our sample of checking-account balances, then $n = 600$, $F = 201$, $f_m = 187$, $w = \$50$, and $L_m = \$100$.

$$\tilde{m} = \left(\frac{(n+1)/2 - (F+1)}{f_m} \right) w + L_m \qquad [3\text{-}8]$$

$$= \left(\frac{601/2 - 202}{187} \right) \$50 + \$100$$

$$= \left(\frac{300.5 - 202}{187} \right) \$50 + \$100$$

$$= \left(\frac{98.5}{187} \right) \$50 + \$100$$

$$= (.527)(\$50) + \$100$$

$$= 126.35 \leftarrow \text{estimated sample median}$$

The slight difference between this answer and our answer calculated the long way is due to rounding.

ADVANTAGES AND DISADVANTAGES OF THE MEDIAN

Advantages of the median

The median has several advantages over the mean. The most important, demonstrated in our track-team example in Table 3-10, is that extreme values do not affect the median as strongly as they do the mean. The median is easy to understand and can be calculated from any kind of data—even for grouped data with open-ended classes such as the frequency distribution in Table 3-7—*unless* the median falls into an open-ended class.

We can find the median even when our data are qualitative descriptions like color or sharpness, rather than numbers. Suppose, for example, we have five runs of a printing press, the results from which must be rated according to sharpness of the image. We can array the results from best to worst: extremely sharp, very sharp, sharp, slightly blurred, and very blurred. The median of the five ratings is the $(5 + 1)/2$, or third rating (sharp).

Disadvantages of the median

The median has some disadvantages as well. Certain statistical procedures that use the median are more complex than those that use the mean. Also, because the median is an average of position, we must array the data before we can perform any calculations. This is time-consuming for any data set with a large number of elements. Therefore, if we want to use a sample statistic as an estimate of a population parameter, the mean is easier to use than the median. Chapter 7 will discuss estimation in detail.

Exercises

 3-30 Meridian Trucking maintains mileage records on all of its rolling equipment. Here are weekly mileage records for its trucks.

810 450 756 789 210 657 589 488 876 689
1,450 560 469 890 987 559 788 943 447 775

(a) Calculate the median miles a truck traveled.
(b) Calculate the mean for the 20 trucks.
(c) Compare (a) and (b) and explain which one is a better measure of the central tendency of the data.

3-31 Swifty Markets compares prices charged for identical items in all of its food stores. Here are the prices charged by each store for a pound of bacon last week:

$$\$1.08 \quad .98 \quad 1.09 \quad 1.24 \quad 1.33 \quad 1.14 \quad 1.55 \quad 1.08 \quad 1.22 \quad 1.05$$

(a) Calculate the median price per pound.
(b) Calculate the mean price per pound.
(c) Which value is the better measure of the central tendency of these data?

3-32 For the frequency distribution below, determine:
(a) Which is the median class.
(b) Which number item represents the median item.
(c) The width of the equal steps in the median class.
(d) The estimated value of the median for this data.

CLASS	FREQUENCY	CLASS	FREQUENCY
100–149.5	12	300–349.5	72
150–199.5	14	350–399.5	63
200–249.5	27	400–449.5	36
250–299.5	58	450–499.5	18

3-33 The following data represent weights of gamefish caught on the charter boat "Slickdrifter":

CLASS	FREQUENCY
0– 24.9	5
25– 49.9	13
50– 74.9	16
75– 99.9	8
100–124.9	6

(a) Use Equation 3-8 to estimate the median weight of the fish caught.
(b) Use Equation 3-3 to compute the mean for these data.
(c) Compare (a) and (b) and comment on which is the better measure of the central tendency of these data.

3-34 The Chicago Transit Authority thinks that excessive speed on its buses increases maintenance cost. It believes that a reasonable median time from O'Hare Airport to the John Hancock Center should be about 30 minutes. From the sample data below (in minutes) can you help them determine whether the buses have been driven at excessive speeds? If you conclude from these data that they have, what explanation might you get from the bus drivers?

$$
\begin{array}{cccc}
17 & 32 & 21 & 22 \\
29 & 19 & 29 & 34 \\
33 & 22 & 28 & 33 \\
52 & 29 & 43 & 39 \\
44 & 34 & 30 & 41 \\
\end{array}
$$

3-35 Mark Merritt, manager of Quality Upholstery Company, is researching the amount of material used in the firm's upholstery jobs. The amount varies between jobs, owing to different furniture styles and sizes. Merritt gathers the following data (in yards) from the jobs completed last week. Calculate the median yardage used on a job last week.

5¼	6¼	6	7⅞	9¼	9½	10½
5⅜	6	6¼	8	9½	9⅞	10¼
5½	5⅞	6½	8¼	9⅜	10¼	10⅛
5⅞	5¾	7	8½	9⅛	10½	10⅛
6	5⅞	7½	9	9¼	9⅞	10

If there are 150 jobs scheduled in the next 3 weeks, use the median to predict how many yards of material will be required.

3-36 If insurance claims for automobile accidents follow the distribution given below, determine the median using the method outlined on page 83 in this chapter. Verify that you get the same answer using Equation 3-8.

AMOUNT OF CLAIM ($)	FREQUENCY	AMOUNT OF CLAIM ($)	FREQUENCY
less than 250	52	750–999.99	1,776
250–499.99	337	1000 and above	1,492
500–749.99	1,066		

3-37 A researcher got the following answers to a statement on an evaluation survey: strongly disagree, disagree, mildly disagree, agree somewhat, agree, strongly agree. Of the six answers, which is the median?

3-6
A Final Measure of Central Tendency: The Mode

Mode defined

The mode is a measure of central tendency that is different from the mean but somewhat like the median because it is not actually calculated by the ordinary processes of arithmetic. The mode is *that value that is repeated most often in the data set.*

Risks in using the mode of ungrouped data

As in every other aspect of life, chance can play a role in the arrangement of data. Sometimes chance causes a single unrepresentative item to be repeated often enough to be the most frequent value in the data set. For this reason, we rarely use the mode of ungrouped data as a measure of central tendency. Table 3-13, for example, shows the number of delivery trips per day made by a Redi-mix concrete plant. The modal value is 15 because it occurs more often than any other value (three times). A mode of 15 implies that the plant activity is higher than 6.7 (6.7 is the answer we'd get if we calculated the mean). The mode tells us that 15 is the most frequent number of trips, but it fails to let us know that most of the values are under 10.

TABLE 3-13 Delivery Trips Per Day in One 20-Day Period

TRIPS ARRAYED IN ASCENDING ORDER				
0	2	5	7	15
0	2	5	7	15 ← mode
1	4	6	8	15
1	4	6	12	19

TABLE 3-14 Frequency Distribution of Delivery Trips

CLASS IN NUMBER OF TRIPS	0–3	4–7	8–11	12 and more
FREQUENCY	6	8	1	5

↑
modal class

Finding the modal class of grouped data

Now let's group this data into a frequency distribution, as we have done in Table 3-14. If we select the class with the most observations, which we can call the *modal class*, we would choose "4–7" trips. This class is more representative of the activity of the plant than is the mode of 15 trips per day. For this reason, whenever we use the mode as a measure of the central tendency of a data set, we should calculate the mode from grouped data.

CALCULATING THE MODE FROM GROUPED DATA

When data are already grouped in a frequency distribution, we must assume that the mode is located in the class with the most items; that is, the class with the highest frequency. To determine a single value for the mode from this modal class, we use Equation 3-9:

Mode

$$Mo = L_{Mo} + \frac{d_1}{d_1 + d_2} w \qquad [3\text{-}9]$$

where:

- L_{Mo} = lower limit of the modal class
- d_1 = frequency of the modal class minus the frequency of the class *directly below it*
- d_2 = frequency of the modal class minus the frequency of the class *directly above it*
- w = width of the modal class interval

If we use Equation 3-9 to compute the mode of our checking-account balances, then $L_{Mo} = \$100$, $d_1 = 187 - 123 = 64$, $d_2 = 187 - 82 = 105$, and $w = \$50$.

$$Mo = L_{Mo} + \frac{d_1}{d_1 + d_2} w \qquad [3\text{-}9]$$

$$= \$100 + \frac{64}{64 + 105} \$50$$

$$= \$100 + (.38)(\$50)$$

$$= \$100 + \$19$$

$$= \$119.00 \leftarrow \text{Mode}$$

Our answer of $119 is the estimate of the mode.

TABLE 3-15 Billing Errors Per Day in 20-Day Period

ERRORS ARRAYED IN ASCENDING ORDER			
0	2	6	9
0	4	6	9
1	4 ← mode	7	10
1 ← mode	4	8	12
1	5	8	12

MULTIMODAL DISTRIBUTIONS

Bimodal distributions

What happens when we have two different values that *each* appears the greatest number of times of any values in the data set? Table 3-15 shows the billing errors for a 20-day period in a hospital office. Notice that both 1 and 4 appear the greatest number of times in the data set. They each appear three times. This distribution, then, has two modes and is called a *bimodal distribution.*

In Fig. 3-6, we have graphed the data in Table 3-15. Notice that there are *two* highest points on the graph. They occur at the values 1 and 4 billing errors. The distribution in Fig. 3-7 is also called bimodal, even though the two highest points are not equal. Clearly, these points stand out above the neighboring values in the frequency with which they are observed.

FIGURE 3-6
Data in Table 3-15, showing bimodal distribution

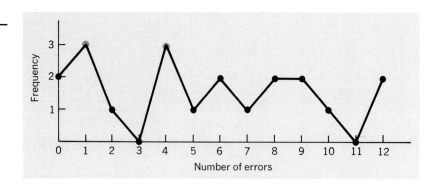

FIGURE 3-7
Bimodal distribution with two unequal modes

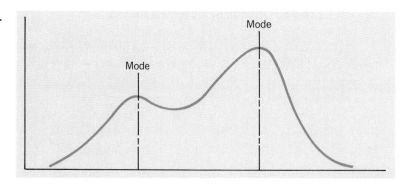

ADVANTAGES AND DISADVANTAGES OF THE MODE

Advantages of the mode

The mode, like the median, can be used as a central location for qualitative as well as quantitative data. If a printing press turns out five impressions, which we rate "very

3 CENTRAL TENDENCY AND DISPERSION IN FREQUENCY DISTRIBUTIONS

sharp," "sharp," "sharp," "sharp," and "blurred," then the modal value is "sharp." Similarly, we can talk about modal styles when, for example, furniture customers prefer Early American furniture to other styles.

Also like the median, **the mode is not unduly affected by extreme values.** Even if the high values are very high and the low values very low, we choose the most frequent value of the data set to be the modal value. We can use the mode no matter how large, how small, or how spread out the values in the data set happen to be.

A third advantage of the mode is that we can use it even when one or more of the classes are open-ended. Notice, for example, that Table 3-14 on page 87 contains the open-ended class "12 trips and more."

Disadvantages of the mode

Despite these advantages, the mode is not used as often to measure central tendency as are the mean and median. Too often, there is no modal value because the data set contains no values that occur more than once. Other times, every value is the mode, because every value occurs the same number of times. Clearly, the mode is a useless measure in these cases. Another disadvantage is that when data sets contain two, three, or many modes, they are difficult to interpret and compare.

COMPARING THE MEAN, MEDIAN, AND MODE

Mean, median, and mode are identical in a symmetrical distribution

When we work statistical problems, we must decide whether to use the mean, the median, or the mode as the measure of central tendency. Symmetrical distributions that contain only one mode always have the same value for the mean, the median, and the mode. In these cases, we need not choose the measure of central tendency, because the choice has been made for us.

In a positively skewed distribution (one skewed to the right), the values are concentrated at the left end of the horizontal axis. Here, the mode is at the highest point of the distribution; the median is to the right of that; and the mean is to the right of both the mode and the median. In a negatively skewed distribution, the values are concentrated at the right end of the horizontal axis. The mode is at the highest point of the distribution, and the median is to the left of that. The mean is to the left of both the mode and the median.

The median may be the best location measure in skewed distributions

When the population is skewed negatively or positively, the median is often the best measure of location, because it is always between the mean and the mode. The median is not as highly influenced by the frequency of occurrence of a single value as the mode is, nor is it pulled by extreme values as the mean is.

Otherwise, there are no universal guidelines for applying the mean, median, or mode as the measure of central tendency for different populations. Each case must be judged independently, according to the guidelines we have discussed.

Exercises

 3-38 Here are the ages in years of the cars worked on by the Village Autohaus last week:

$$5, 6, 3, 6, 11, 7, 9, 10, 2, 4, 10, 6, 2, 1, 5$$

(a) Compute the mode for this data set.
(b) Compute the mean of the data set.
(c) Compare (a) and (b) and comment on which is the better measure of the central tendency of the data.

3-39 The ages of residents of Twin Lakes Retirement Village are described by this distribution:

CLASS	FREQUENCY
47 – 51.9	4
52 – 56.9	9
57 – 61.9	13
62 – 66.9	42
67 – 71.9	39
72 – 76.9	20
77 – 81.9	9

Estimate the modal value of the distribution using Equation 3-9.

3-40 What are the modal values for the following distributions?

(a)
Hair color	Black	Brunette	Redhead	Blonde
Frequency	11	24	6	18

(b)
Blood type	AB	O	A	B
Frequency	4	12	35	16

(c)
Day of Birth	Mon.	Tues.	Wed.	Thurs.	Fri.	Sat.	Sun.
Frequency	22	10	32	17	13	32	14

3-41 The ages of a sample of the students attending Sandhills Community College this semester are:

```
19  17  15  20  23  41  33  21  18  20
18  33  32  29  24  19  18  20  17  22
55  19  22  25  28  30  44  19  20  39
```

(a) Construct a frequency distribution with intervals 15 – 19, 20 – 24, 25 – 29, 30 – 34, and 35 and older.
(b) Estimate the modal value using Equation 3-9.
(c) Now compute the mean of the raw data.
(d) Compare your answers in (b) and (c) and comment on which of the two is the better measure of the central tendency of these data and why.

3-42 Estimate the mode for the distribution given in exercise 3-36.

3-43 The number of solar heating systems available to the public is quite large, and their heat storage capacities are quite varied. Here is a distribution of heat storage capacity (in days) of 28 systems that were tested recently by University Laboratories, Inc.:

DAYS	FREQUENCY
0 – 0.99	2
1 – 1.99	4
2 – 2.99	6
3 – 3.99	7
4 – 4.99	5
5 – 5.99	3
6 – 6.99	1

University Laboratories, Inc., knows that its report on the tests will be widely circulated and

used as the basis for tax legislation on solar heat allowances. It therefore wants the measures it uses to be as reflective of the data as possible.
(a) Compute the mean of these data.
(b) Compute the mode for these data.
(c) Compute the median for these data.
(d) Select the answer among (a), (b), and (c) which best reflects the central tendency of the test data and justify your choice.

3-44 Ed Grant is the director of the Student Financial Aid Office at Wilderness College. He has used available data on the summer earnings of all students who have applied to his office for financial aid to develop the frequency distribution given below:

SUMMER EARNINGS	NUMBER OF STUDENTS
$ 0-$ 499	231
500- 999	304
1,000- 1,499	400
1,500- 1,999	296
2,000- 2,499	123
2,500- 2,999	68
3,000 or more	23

(a) Find the modal class for Ed's data.
(b) Use Equation 3-9 to find the mode for Ed's data.
(c) If student aid is restricted to those whose summer earnings were at least 10 percent lower than the modal summer earnings, how many of the applicants qualify?

3-7
Dispersion: Why It Is Important

Need to measure dispersion or variability

Early in this chapter in Fig. 3-2, we illustrated two sets of data with the same central location but with one more spread out than the other. This is true of the three distributions in Fig. 3-8. The mean of all three curves is the same, but curve A has less spread (or *variability*) than curve B, and curve B has less variability than curve C. If we measure only the mean of these three distributions, we will miss an important difference among the three curves. Likewise for any data, the mean, the median, and the mode tell us only part of what we need to know about the characteristics of the

FIGURE 3-8

Three curves with the same mean but different variabilities

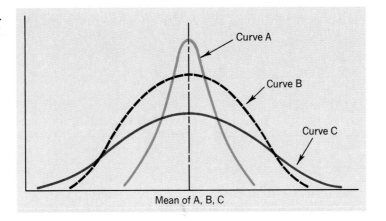

data. To increase our understanding of the pattern of the data, we must also measure its *dispersion*—its spread, or variability.

Uses of dispersion measures

Why is the dispersion of the distribution such an important characteristic to understand and measure? **First,** it gives us additional information that enables us to judge the reliability of our measure of the central tendency. If data are widely dispersed, such as those in curve C in Fig. 3-8, the central location is less representative of the data as a whole than it would be for data more closely centered around the mean, as in curve A. **Second,** because there are problems peculiar to widely dispersed data, we must be able to recognize that data are widely dispersed before we can tackle those problems. And, **third,** we may wish to compare dispersions of various samples. If a wide spread of values away from the center is undesirable or presents an unacceptable risk, we need to be able to recognize and avoid choosing those distributions with the greatest dispersion.

Financial use

Financial analysts are concerned about the dispersion of a firm's earnings. Widely dispersed earnings—those varying from extremely high to low or even negative levels—indicate a higher risk to stockholders and creditors than do earnings remaining relatively stable. Similarly, quality control experts analyze the dispersion of a product's quality levels. A drug that is average in purity but ranges from very pure to highly impure may endanger lives.

Quality control use

Exercises

3-45 A firm using two different methods to ship orders to its customers found the following distributions of delivery time for the two methods, based on past records. From available evidence, which shipment method would you recommend?

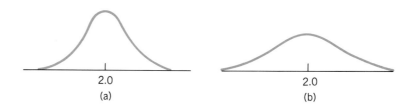

3-46 For which of the following distributions is the mean more representative of the data as a whole? Why?

3-47 To measure scholastic achievement, educators need to test students' levels of knowledge and ability. Taking students' individual differences into account, teachers can plan their curricula better. The curves below represent distributions based on previous scores of two different tests. Which would you select as the better for the teachers' purpose?

3-48   Which of the following is not one of the reasons for measuring the dispersion of a distribution?
(a)   It provides an indication of the reliability of the central tendency measure.
(b)   It enables us to compare several samples with similar averages.
(c)   It uses more data in describing a distribution.
(d)   It draws attention to problems associated with very small or very large variability in distributions.

3-49   Of the 3 curves shown in Fig. 3-8, choose one that would best describe the distribution of values for the ages of the following groups: members of Congress, newly elected members of the House of Representatives, the chairmen of major congressional committees. In making your choices, disregard the common mean of the curves in Fig. 3-8 and consider only the variability of the distributions. Briefly state your reasons for your choices.

3-50   How do you think the concept of variability might apply to an investigation by the Federal Trade Commission (FTC) into possible price fixing by a group of manufacturers?

3-51   Choose which of the three curves shown in Fig. 3-8 best describes the distribution of the following characteristics of various groups. Make your choices only on the basis of the variability of the distributions. Briefly state a reason for each choice.
(a)   The number of points scored by each player in a professional basketball league during an 80-game season
(b)   The salary of each of 100 people working at roughly equivalent jobs in the federal government
(c)   The grade-point average of each of the 15,000 students at a major state university
(d)   The salary of each of 100 people working at roughly equivalent jobs in a private corporation
(e)   The grade-point average of each student at a major state university who has been accepted for graduate school
(f)   The percentage of shots made by each player in a professional basketball league during an 80-game season

3-8
Ranges: Useful Measures of Dispersion

Three distance measures

Dispersion may be measured in terms of the difference between two values selected from the data set. In this section, we shall study three of these so-called *distance measures:* the range, the interfractile range, and the interquartile range.

RANGE

Defining and computing the range

The range is the difference between the highest and lowest observed values. In equation form, we can say:

$$\text{Range} = \frac{\text{Value of highest}}{\text{observation}} - \frac{\text{Value of lowest}}{\text{observation}} \qquad [3\text{-}10]$$

TABLE 3-16 Annual Payments from Blue Cross–Blue Shield (000s Omitted)

Cumberland	863	903	957	1,041	1,138	1,204	1,354	1,624	1,698	1,745	1,802	1,883
Valley Falls	490	540	560	570	590	600	610	620	630	660	670	690

Using this equation, we compare the ranges of annual payments from Blue Cross–Blue Shield received by the two hospitals illustrated in Table 3-16.

The range of annual payments to Cumberland is $1,883,000 − $863,000 = $1,020,000. For Valley Falls, the range is $690,000 − $490,000 = $200,000.

Characteristics of the range

The range is easy to understand and to find, but its usefulness as a measure of dispersion is limited. The range considers only the highest and lowest values of a distribution and fails to take account of any other observation in the data set. As a result, it ignores the nature of the variation among all the other observations, and it is heavily influenced by extreme values. Because it measures only two values, the range is likely to change drastically from one sample to the next in a given population, even though the values that fall between the highest and lowest values may be quite similar. Keep in mind, too, that open-ended distributions have no range, because no "highest" or "lowest" value exists in the open-ended class.

INTERFRACTILE RANGE

Fractiles

In a frequency distribution, a given fraction or proportion of the data lie at or below a *fractile*. The median, for example, is the .5 fractile, because half the data set is less than or equal to this value. You will notice that fractiles are similar to percentages. In any distribution, 25 percent of the data lie at or below the .25 fractile; likewise, 25 percent of the data lie at or below the 25th percentile. The *interfractile range* is a measure of the spread between two fractiles in a frequency distribution; that is, the difference between the values of two fractiles.

Meaning of the interfractile range

Calculating the interfractile range

Suppose we wish to find the interfractile range between the first and second *thirds* of Cumberland's receipts from Blue Cross–Blue Shield. We begin by dividing the observations into thirds, as we have done in Table 3-17. Each third contains four items ($\frac{1}{3}$ of the total of twelve items). Therefore, $33\frac{1}{3}$ percent of the items lie at $1,041,000 or below it, and $66\frac{2}{3}$ percent are equal to or less than $1,624,000. Now we can calculate the interfractile range between the $\frac{1}{3}$ and $\frac{2}{3}$ fractiles by subtracting the value $1,041,000 from the value $1,624,000. This difference of $583,000 is the spread between the top of the first third of the payments and the top of the second third.

TABLE 3-17 Blue Cross–Blue Shield Annual Payments to Cumberland Hospital (000s Omitted)

FIRST THIRD	SECOND THIRD	LAST THIRD
863	1,138	1,698
903	1,204	1,745
957	1,354	1,802
1,041 ← $\frac{1}{3}$ fractile	1,624 ← $\frac{2}{3}$ fractile	1,883

Fractiles have special names, depending on the number of equal parts into which they divide the data. Fractiles that divide the data into ten equal parts are called *deciles*. *Quartiles* divide the data into four equal parts. *Percentiles* divide the data into 100 equal parts.

INTERQUARTILE RANGE

The interquartile range measures approximately how far from the median we must go on either side before we can include one-half the values of the data set. To compute this range, we divide our data into four parts, each of which contains 25 percent of the items in the distribution. The *quartiles* are then the highest values in each of these four parts, and the *interquartile range* is the difference between the values of the first and third quartiles:

$$\text{Interquartile range} = Q_3 - Q_1 \qquad [3\text{-}11]$$

Figure 3-9 shows the concept of the interquartile range graphically. Notice in that figure that the widths of the four quartiles need *not* be the same.

FIGURE 3-9
Interquartile range

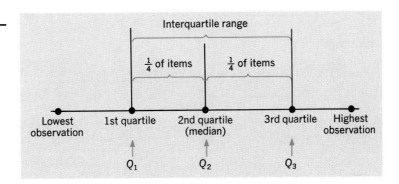

In Fig. 3-10, another illustration of quartiles, the quartiles divide the area under the distribution into four equal parts, each containing 25 percent of the area.

FIGURE 3-10
Quartiles

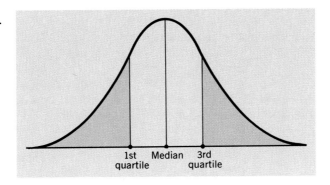

Exercises

 3-52 These are the total fares (in dollars) collected Tuesday by the 20 taxis belonging to City Transit, Ltd.

147	95	93	127	143	101	123	83	135	129
185	92	115	126	157	93	133	51	125	132

Compute the range of these data and comment on whether you think it is a useful measure of dispersion.

 3-53 Here are student scores on a history quiz. Find the score which represents the 80th percentile.

95	81	59	68	100	92	75	67	85	79
71	88	100	94	87	65	93	72	83	91

 3-54 For the following data, compute the interquartile range.

99	75	84	61	33	45	66	97	69	55
72	91	74	93	54	76	52	91	77	68

 3-55 For the sample below, compute the:
(a) Range
(b) Interfractile range between the 20th and 80th percentiles.
(c) Interquartile range

2,549	3,897	3,661	2,697	2,200	3,812	2,228	3,891	2,668	2,268
3,692	2,145	2,653	3,249	2,841	3,469	3,268	2,598	3,842	3,362

 3-56 Redi-Mix Incorporated kept the following record of time (to the nearest 100th of a minute) its trucks waited at the job to unload. Calculate the range and the interquartile range.

0.10	0.45	0.50	0.32	0.89	1.20	0.53	0.67	0.58	0.48
0.23	0.77	0.12	0.66	0.59	0.95	1.10	0.83	0.69	0.51

 3-57 Warlington Appliances has developed a new combination blender-crockpot. In a marketing demonstration, a price survey determined that most of those sampled would be willing to pay around $60, with a surprisingly small interquartile range of $14.00. In an attempt to replicate the results, the demonstration and accompanying survey were repeated. The marketing department hoped to find an even smaller interquartile range. The data are given below. Were their hopes confirmed?

52	35	48	46	43	40	61	49	57	58	65	46
72	69	38	37	55	52	50	31	41	60	45	41
55	38	51	49	46	43	64	52	60	61	68	49
69	66	35	34	52	49	47	28	38	57	42	38

 3-58 The Casual Life Insurance Company is considering purchasing a new fleet of company cars. The financial department's director, Tom Dawkins, sampled 40 employees to determine the number of miles each drove over a 1-year period. The results of the study are given below. Calculate the range and interquartile range.

3,600	4,200	4,700	4,900	5,300	5,700	6,700	7,300
7,700	8,100	8,300	8,400	8,700	8,700	8,900	9,300
9,500	9,500	9,700	10,000	10,300	10,500	10,700	10,800
11,000	11,300	11,300	11,800	12,100	12,700	12,900	13,100
13,500	13,800	14,600	14,900	16,300	17,200	18,500	20,300

3-59 The New Mexico State Highway Department is charged with maintaining all state roads in good condition. One measure of condition is the number of cracks present in each 100 feet of roadway. From the department's yearly sample, the following data were obtained:

4	7	8	9	9	10	11	12	12	13
13	13	13	14	14	14	15	15	16	16
16	16	16	17	17	17	18	18	19	19

Calculate the interfractile ranges between the 20th, 40th, 60th, and 80th percentiles.

3-60 Ted Nichol is a statistical analyst who reports directly to the highest levels of management at Research Incorporated. He helped design the company slogan: "If you can't find the answer, then RESEARCH!" Ted has just received some disturbing data—the monthly dollar volume of research contracts that the company has won for the past year. Ideally, these monthly numbers should be fairly stable, since too much fluctuation in the amount of work to be done can result in an inordinate amount of hiring and firing of employees. Ted's data (in thousands of dollars) follow:

253	104	633	57	500	201
43	380	467	162	220	302

Calculate the following:
(a) The interfractile range between the second and eighth deciles
(b) The median, Q_1, and Q_3
(c) The interquartile range.

3-9
Dispersion: Average Deviation Measures

Two measures of
average deviation

The most comprehensive descriptions of dispersion are those that deal with the average deviation from some measure of central tendency. Two of these measures are important to our study of statistics: the *variance* and the *standard deviation*. Both of these tell us an average distance of any observation in the data set from the mean of the distribution.

POPULATION VARIANCE

Variance

Every population has a variance, which is symbolized by σ^2 (sigma squared). To calculate the population variance, we divide the sum of the squared distances between the mean and each item in the population by the total number of items in the population. By squaring each distance, we make each number positive and, at the same time, assign more weight to the larger deviations.

The formula for calculating the variance is:

$$\sigma^2 = \frac{\Sigma(x-\mu)^2}{N} = \frac{\Sigma x^2}{N} - \mu^2 \qquad [3\text{-}12]$$

Formula for the variance of a population (margin note)

where:

- σ^2 = the population variance
- x = the item or observation
- μ = population mean
- N = total number of items in the population
- Σ = sum of all the values $(x-\mu)^2$, or all the values x^2

In Equation 3-12, the middle expression, $\dfrac{\Sigma(x-\mu)^2}{N}$, is the definition of σ^2. The last expression, $\dfrac{\Sigma x^2}{N} - \mu^2$, is *mathematically* equivalent to the definition but is often much more convenient to use if we must actually compute the value of σ^2, since it frees us from calculating the deviations from the mean. However, when the x values are large and the $x - \mu$ values are small, it may be more convenient to use the middle expression, $\dfrac{\Sigma(x-\mu)^2}{N}$, to compute σ^2. Before we can use this formula in an example, we need to discuss an important problem concerning the variance. In solving that problem, we will learn what the standard deviation is and how to calculate it. Then we can return to the variance itself.

Units in which the variance is expressed cause a problem (margin note)

Earlier, when we calculated the range, the answers were expressed in the same units as the data. (In our examples, the units were "thousands of dollars of payments.") For the variance, however, the units are the *squares of the units* of the data—for example, "squared dollars" or "dollars squared." Squared dollars or dollars squared are not intuitively clear or easily interpreted. For this reason, we have to make a significant change in the variance to compute a useful measure of deviation, one that does not give us a problem with units of measure and thus is less confusing. **This measure is called the standard deviation, and it is the square root of the variance.** The square root of 100 dollars squared is 10 dollars, because we take the square root of both the value and the units in which it is measured. The standard deviation, then, is in units that are the same as the original data.

POPULATION STANDARD DEVIATION

Relationship of standard deviation to the variance (margin note)

The population standard deviation, or σ, is simply the square root of the population variance. Since the variance is the average of the squared distances of the observations from the mean, **the standard deviation is the square root of the average of the squared distances of the observations from the mean.** While the variance is expressed in the square of the units used in the data, the standard deviation is in the same units as those used in the data. The formula for the standard deviation is:

$$\sigma = \sqrt{\sigma^2} = \sqrt{\frac{\Sigma(x-\mu)^2}{N}} = \sqrt{\frac{\Sigma x^2}{N} - \mu^2} \qquad [3\text{-}13]$$

3 CENTRAL TENDENCY AND DISPERSION IN FREQUENCY DISTRIBUTIONS

where

■ x = the observation
■ μ = the population mean
■ N = the total number of elements in the population
■ Σ = the sum of all the values $(x - \mu)^2$, or all the values x^2
■ σ = the population standard deviation
■ σ^2 = the population variance

Use the positive square root

The square root of a positive number may be either positive or negative, since $a^2 = (-a)^2$. When taking the square root of the variance to calculate the standard deviation, however, statisticians consider only the positive square root.

Computing the standard deviation

To calculate either the variance or the standard deviation, we construct a table, using every element of the population. If we have a population of fifteen vials of compound produced in one day and we test each vial to determine its purity, our data might look like Table 3-18. In Table 3-19, we show how to use these data to compute the mean (column 1 divided by N = 2.49/15), the deviation of each value from the mean (column 3), the square of the deviation of each value from the mean (column 4), and the sum of the squared deviations. From this, we can compute the variance, which is .0034 percent squared. (Table 3-19 also computes σ^2 using the second half of Equation 3-12, $\dfrac{\Sigma x^2}{N} - \mu^2$. Note that we get the same result but do a bit less work, since we do not have to compute the deviations from the mean.) Taking the square root of σ^2, we can compute the standard deviation, .058 percent.

TABLE 3-18 **Results of Purity Test on Compounds**

OBSERVED PERCENT OF IMPURITY				
.04	.14	.17	.19	.22
.06	.14	.17	.21	.24
.12	.15	.18	.21	.25

USES OF THE STANDARD DEVIATION

Chebyshev's theorem

The standard deviation enables us to determine, with a great deal of accuracy, where the values of a frequency distribution are located in relation to the mean. We can do this according to a theorem devised by the Russian mathematician, P. L. Chebyshev (1821–1894). Chebyshev's theorem says that no matter what the shape of the distribution, at least 75 percent of the values will fall within plus and minus 2 standard deviations from the mean of the distribution, and at least 89 percent of the values will lie within plus and minus 3 standard deviations from the mean.

We can measure with even more precision the percentage of items that fall within specific ranges under a symmetrical, bell-shaped curve like the one in Fig. 3-11. In these cases, we can say that:

1. About 68 percent of the values in the population will fall within plus and minus 1 standard deviation from the mean.

2. About 95 percent of the values will lie within plus and minus 2 standard deviations from the mean.
3. About 99 percent of the values will be in an interval ranging from 3 standard deviations below the mean to 3 standard deviations above the mean.

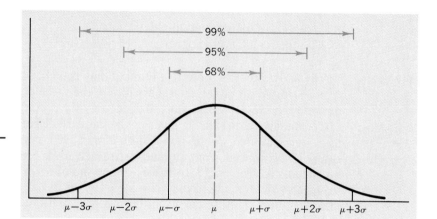

FIGURE 3-11

Location of observations around the mean of a bell-shaped frequency distribution

TABLE 3-19 Determination of the Variance and Standard Deviation of Percent Impurity of Compounds

OBSERVATION (x) (1)		MEAN $(\mu) = 2.49/15$ (2)		DEVIATION $(x - \mu)$ (3) = (1) − (2)	DEVIATION SQUARED $(x - \mu)^2$ (4) = [(1) − (2)]²	OBSERVATION SQUARED (x^2) (5) = (1)²
.04	—	.166	=	−.126	.016	.0016
.06	—	.166	=	−.106	.011	.0036
.12	—	.166	=	−.046	.002	.0144
.14	—	.166	=	−.026	.001	.0196
.14	—	.166	=	−.026	.001	.0196
.15	—	.166	=	−.016	.000	.0225
.17	—	.166	=	.004	.000	.0289
.17	—	.166	=	.004	.000	.0289
.18	—	.166	=	.014	.000	.0324
.19	—	.166	=	.024	.001	.0361
.21	—	.166	=	.044	.002	.0441
.21	—	.166	=	.044	.002	.0441
.22	—	.166	=	.054	.003	.0484
.24	—	.166	=	.074	.005	.0576
.25	—	.166	=	.084	.007	.0625
2.49 $\leftarrow \Sigma x$					**.051** $\leftarrow \Sigma(x - \mu)^2$	**.4643** $\leftarrow \Sigma x^2$

$\sigma^2 = \dfrac{\Sigma(x - \mu)^2}{N}$ [3-12]

$= \dfrac{.051}{15}$

$= .0034$ percent squared

$\sigma = \sqrt{\sigma^2}$ [3-13]
$= \sqrt{.0034}$
$= .058$ percent

←OR →

$\sigma^2 = \dfrac{\Sigma x^2}{N} - \mu^2$ [3-12]

$= \dfrac{.4643}{15} - (.166)^2$

$= .0034$ percent squared

In the light of Chebyshev's theorem, let's analyze the data in Table 3-19. There, the mean impurity of the fifteen vials of compound is .166 percent, and the standard deviation is .058 percent. Chebyshev's theorem tells us that at least 75 percent of the values (at least eleven of our fifteen items) are between $.166 - 2(.058) = .050$ and $.166 + 2(.058) = .282$. In fact, 93 percent of the values (fourteen of the fifteen values) are actually in that interval. Notice that the distribution is reasonably symmetrical and that 93 percent is close to the theoretical 95 percent for an interval of plus and minus 2 standard deviations from the mean of a bell-shaped curve.

The standard deviation is also useful in describing how far individual items in a distribution depart from the mean of the distribution. A measure called the *standard score* gives us the number of standard deviations a particular observation lies below or above the mean. If we let x symbolize the observation, the standard score computed from population data is:

$$\text{Population standard score} = \frac{x - \mu}{\sigma} \qquad [3\text{-}14]$$

where

- x = the observation from the population
- μ = the population mean
- σ = the population standard deviation

Suppose we observe a vial of compound that is .108 percent impure. Since our population has a mean of .166 and a standard deviation of .058, an observation of .108 would have a standard score of -1:

$$\text{Standard score} = \frac{x - \mu}{\sigma} \qquad [3\text{-}14]$$

$$= \frac{.108 - .166}{.058}$$

$$= -\frac{.058}{.058}$$

$$= -1$$

An observed impurity of .282 percent would have a standard score of $+2$:

$$\text{Standard score} = \frac{x - \mu}{\sigma} \qquad [3\text{-}14]$$

$$= \frac{.282 - .166}{.058}$$

$$= \frac{.116}{.058}$$

$$= 2$$

The standard score indicates that an impurity of .282 percent deviates from the mean by $2(.058) = .116$ units, which is equal to $+2$ in terms of units of standard deviations away from the mean.

CALCULATION OF VARIANCE AND STANDARD DEVIATION USING GROUPED DATA

Calculating the variance and standard deviation for grouped data

In our chapter-opening example, data on sales of 100 fast-food restaurants were already grouped in a frequency distribution. With such data we can use the following formulas to calculate the variance and the standard deviation:

$$\sigma^2 = \frac{\Sigma f(x - \mu)^2}{N} = \frac{\Sigma fx^2}{N} - \mu^2 \qquad [3\text{-}15]$$

and:

$$\sigma = \sqrt{\sigma^2} = \sqrt{\frac{\Sigma f(x - \mu)^2}{N}} = \sqrt{\frac{\Sigma fx^2}{N} - \mu^2} \qquad [3\text{-}16]$$

where:

- σ^2 = population variance
- σ = population standard deviation
- f = frequency of each of the classes
- x = midpoint for each class
- μ = population mean
- N = size of the population

Table 3-20 shows how to apply these equations to find the variance and standard deviation of the sales of 100 fast-food restaurants.

We leave it as an exercise for the curious reader to verify that the second half of Equation 3-15, $\frac{\Sigma fx^2}{N} - \mu^2$, will yield the same value of σ^2.

Switching to sample variance and sample standard deviation

Now we are ready to compute the sample statistics that are analogous to the population variance σ^2 and the population standard deviation σ. These are the sample variance s^2 and the sample standard deviation s. In the next section, you'll notice we are changing from Greek letters (which denote population parameters) to the Latin letters of sample statistics.

SAMPLE STANDARD DEVIATION

Computing the sample standard deviation

To compute the sample variance and the sample standard deviation, we use the same formulas as Equations 3-12 and 3-13, replacing μ with $\bar{x}$ and N with $n - 1$. The formulas look like this:

$$s^2 = \frac{\Sigma(x - \bar{x})^2}{n - 1} = \frac{\Sigma x^2}{n - 1} - \frac{n\bar{x}^2}{n - 1} \quad \times \text{Frequency} \qquad [3\text{-}17]$$

and

$$s = \sqrt{s^2} = \sqrt{\frac{\Sigma(x - \bar{x})^2}{n - 1}} = \sqrt{\frac{\Sigma x^2}{n - 1} - \frac{n\bar{x}^2}{n - 1}} \qquad [3\text{-}18]$$

where

- s^2 = sample variance
- s = sample standard deviation

TABLE 3-20 Determination of the Variance and Standard Deviation of Sales of 100 Fast-Food Restaurants in the Eastern District (000s Omitted)

CLASS	MIDPOINT (x) (1)	FREQUENCY (f) (2)	f × x (3) = (2) × (1)	MEAN (μ) (4)	x − μ (1) − (4)	(x − μ)² [(1) − (4)]²	f(x − μ)² (2) × [(1) − (4)]²
700– 799	750	4	3,000	1,250	−500	250,000	1,000,000
800– 899	850	7	5,950	1,250	−400	160,000	1,120,000
900– 999	950	8	7,600	1,250	−300	90,000	720,000
1,000–1,099	1,050	10	10,500	1,250	−200	40,000	400,000
1,100–1,199	1,150	12	13,800	1,250	−100	10,000	120,000
1,200–1,299	1,250	17	21,250	1,250	0	0	0
1,300–1,399	1,350	13	17,550	1,250	100	10,000	130,000
1,400–1,499	1,450	10	14,500	1,250	200	40,000	400,000
1,500–1,599	1,550	9	13,950	1,250	300	90,000	810,000
1,600–1,699	1,650	7	11,550	1,250	400	160,000	1,120,000
1,700–1,799	1,750	2	3,500	1,250	500	250,000	500,000
1,800–1,899	1,850	1	1,850	1,250	600	360,000	360,000
		100	**125,000**				**6,680,000**

$$\bar{x} = \frac{\Sigma(f \times x)}{n} \qquad [3\text{-}3]$$

$$= \frac{125,000}{100}$$

$$= 1,250 \text{ dollars} \leftarrow \text{mean}$$

$$\sigma^2 = \frac{\Sigma f(x - \mu)^2}{N} \qquad [3\text{-}15]$$

$$= \frac{6,680,000}{100}$$

$$= 66,800 \text{ (or } 66,800 \text{ dollars squared)} \leftarrow \text{variance}$$

$$\sigma = \sqrt{\sigma^2} \qquad [3\text{-}16]$$

$$= \sqrt{66,800}$$

$$= 258.5 \quad \text{standard deviation} = \$258,500$$

- x = value of each of the n observations
- $\bar{x}$ = mean of the sample
- $n - 1$ = number of observations in the sample minus 1

Use of $n - 1$ as the denominator

Why do we use $n - 1$ as the denominator instead of n? Statisticians can prove that if we take many samples from a given population, find the sample variance (s^2) for each sample, and average each of these together, then this average tends not to equal the population variance, σ^2, unless we use $n - 1$ as the denominator. In Chapter 7, we shall learn the statistical explanation of why this is true.

Calculating sample variance and standard deviation for hospital data

Equations 3-17 and 3-18 enable us to find the sample variance and the sample standard deviation of the annual Blue Cross–Blue Shield payments to Cumberland Hospital in Table 3-21; note that both halves of Equation 3-17 yield the same result.

Computing sample standard scores

Just as we used the population standard deviation to derive population standard scores, we may also use the sample deviation to compute sample standard scores. These sample standard scores tell us how many standard deviations a particular

TABLE 3-21 Determination of the Sample Variance and Standard Deviation of Annual Blue Cross – Blue Shield Payments to Cumberland Hospital (000s Omitted)

OBSERVATION (x) (1)	MEAN $(\bar{x})$ (2)	$x - \bar{x}$ (1) − (2)	$(x - \bar{x})^2$ [(1) − (2)]²	x^2 (1)²
863	1,351	−488	238,144	744,769
903	1,351	−448	200,704	815,409
957	1,351	−394	155,236	915,849
1,041	1,351	−310	96,100	1,083,681
1,138	1,351	−213	45,369	1,295,044
1,204	1,351	−147	21,609	1,449,616
1,354	1,351	3	9	1,833,316
1,624	1,351	273	74,529	2,637,376
1,698	1,351	347	120,409	2,883,204
1,745	1,351	394	155,236	3,045,025
1,802	1,351	451	203,401	3,247,204
1,883	1,351	532	283,024	3,545,689
		$\Sigma(x - \bar{x})^2 \rightarrow$ **1,593,770**	**23,496,182** $\leftarrow \Sigma x^2$

$$s^2 = \frac{\Sigma(x - \bar{x})^2}{n - 1} \qquad [3\text{-}17]$$

$$= \frac{1,593,770}{11}$$

$= 144,888$ (or \$144,888 million squared) ← sample variance

$$s = \sqrt{s^2} \qquad [3\text{-}18]$$

$$= \sqrt{144,888}$$

$= 380.64$ (that is, \$380,640) ← sample standard deviation

OR

$$s^2 = \frac{\Sigma x^2}{n - 1} - \frac{n\bar{x}^2}{n - 1} \qquad [3\text{-}17]$$

$$= \frac{23,496,182}{11} - \frac{12(1,351)^2}{11}$$

$$= \frac{1,593,770}{11}$$

$$= 144,888$$

sample observation lies below or above the sample mean. The appropriate formula is:

$$\text{Sample standard score} = \frac{x - \bar{x}}{s} \qquad [3\text{-}19]$$

where:

- $x =$ the observation from the sample
- $\bar{x} =$ the sample mean
- $s =$ the sample standard deviation

In the example we just did, we see that the observation 863 corresponds to a standard score of − 1.28:

$$\text{Sample standard score} = \frac{x - \bar{x}}{s} \qquad \text{[3-19]}$$

$$= \frac{863 - 1{,}351}{380.64}$$

$$= \frac{-488}{380.64}$$

$$= -1.28$$

This section has demonstrated why the standard deviation is the measure of dispersion used most often. We can use it to compare distributions and to compute standard scores, an important element of statistical inference to be discussed later. Like the variance, the standard deviation takes into account every observation in the data set. But the standard deviation has some disadvantages too. It is not as easy to calculate as the range, and it cannot be computed from open-ended distributions. In addition, extreme values in the data set distort the value of the standard deviation, although to a lesser extent than they do the range.

Exercises

3-61 Talent, Ltd., a Hollywood casting company, is selecting a group of extras for a movie. The ages of the first 20 men to be interviewed are:

| 50 | 56 | 55 | 49 | 52 | 57 | 56 | 57 | 56 | 59 |
| 54 | 55 | 61 | 60 | 51 | 59 | 62 | 52 | 54 | 49 |

The director of the movie wants men whose ages are fairly tightly grouped around 55 years. Being a statistics buff of sorts, the director suggests that a standard deviation of 3 years would be acceptable. Does this group of extras qualify?

3-62 These data are a sample of the daily production rate of fiberglass boats from Hydrosport, Ltd., a Miami manufacturer:

17 21 18 27 17 21 20 22 18 23

The company production manager feels that a standard deviation of more than three boats a day indicates unacceptable production rate variations. Should she be concerned about plant production rates?

3-63 In a set of 60 observations with a mean of 66.8, a variance of 12.60, and an unknown distribution shape:
(a) Between what values should at least 75 percent of the observations fall, according to Chebyshev's theorem?
(b) If the distribution is symmetrical and bell-shaped, approximately how many observations should be found in the interval 59.7 to 73.9?
(c) Find the standard scores for the following observations from the distribution: 61.45, 75.37, 84.65, and 51.50.

3-64 The number of checks cashed each day at the five branches of The Bank of Orange County during the past month had the following frequency distribution:

CLASS	FREQUENCY
0–199	10
200–399	13
400–599	17
600–799	42
800–999	18

Hank Spivey, director of operations for the bank, knows that a standard deviation in check cashing of more than 200 checks per day creates staffing and organizational problems at the branches because of the uneven workload. Should Hank worry about staffing next month?

3-65 The Federal Reserve Board has given permission to all member banks to raise interest rates ½ percent for all depositors. Old rates for passbook savings were 5¼%; for certificates of deposit (CDs): 1-year CD, 7½%; 18-month CD, 8¾%; 2-year CD, 9½%; 3-year CD, 10½%; 5-year CD, 11%. The president of the First State Bank wants to know what the characteristics of the new distribution of rates will be if the full ½ percent is added to all rates. How are the new characteristics related to the old ones?

3-66 The administrator of a Georgia hospital conducted a survey of the number of days 200 randomly chosen patients stayed in the hospital following an operation. The data are given below:

Hospital stay in days	1–3	4–6	7–9	10–12	13–15	16–18	19–21	22–24
Frequency	18	90	44	21	9	9	4	5

(a) Calculate the standard deviation and mean.
(b) According to Chebyshev's theorem, how many stays should be between 0 and 17 days? How many are actually in that interval?
(c) Since the distribution is roughly bell-shaped, how many stays can we expect between 0 and 17 days?

3-67 In an attempt to estimate potential future demand, the National Motor Company did a study asking married couples how many cars the energy-minded family should own in 1990. For each couple, National averaged the husband's and wife's responses to get the overall couple response. The answers were then tabulated in a frequency distribution.

Number of cars	0–.49	.50–.99	1.00–1.49	1.50–1.99	2.00–2.49	2.50–2.99
Frequency	2	14	23	7	4	2

(a) Calculate the variance and the standard deviation.
(b) Since the distribution is bell-shaped, how many of the observations should theoretically fall between .7 and 1.8? between .2 and 2.4? How many actually do fall in those intervals?

3-68 Nell Berman, owner of the Earthbred Bakery, said that the average weekly production level of her company was 11,398 loaves, with a variance of 49,729. If the data used to compute the results were collected for 32 weeks, during how many weeks was the production level below 11,175? above 11,844?

3-69 The Creative Illusion Advertising Company has three offices in three different cities. Wage rates differ from state to state. In the Washington, D.C., office, the average wage increase for the past year was $1,500, with a standard deviation of $400. In the New York office, the average raise was $3,760, with a standard deviation of $622. In Durham, N.C., the average increase was $850, with a standard deviation of $95. Three employees were interviewed. The Washington employee received a raise of $1,100; the New York employee, a raise of $3,200; and the Durham employee, a raise of $500. Which of the three had the smallest raise in relation to the mean and standard deviation of his office?

3-70　American Foods heavily markets three different products nationally. One of the underlying objectives of each of the product's advertisements is to make consumers recognize that American Foods makes the product. To measure how well each ad implants recognition, a group of consumers was asked to identify as quickly as possible the company responsible for a long list of products. The first American Foods product had an average latency of 2.5 seconds with a standard deviation of .004 seconds. The second had an average latency of 2.8 seconds, with a standard deviation of .006 seconds. The third had an average latency of 3.7 seconds with a standard deviation of .09 seconds. One particular subject had the following latencies: 2.495 for the first, 2.79 for the second, and 3.90 for the third. For which product was this subject furthest from average performance, in standard deviation units?

3-71　Sid Levinson is a doctor who specializes in the knowledge and effective use of pain-killing drugs for the seriously ill. In order to know approximately how many nurses and office personnel to employ, he has begun to keep track of the number of patients that he sees each week. Each week he records the number of seriously ill patients and the number of routine patients. Sid has reason to believe that the number of routine patients per week would look like a bell-shaped curve if he had enough data. (This is not true of seriously ill patients.) However, he has data for only the past 5 weeks.

Seriously ill patients	33	50	22	27	48
Routine patients	34	31	37	36	27

(a)　Calculate the mean and variance for the number of seriously ill patients per week. Use Chebyshev's theorem to find boundaries within which the "middle 75 percent" of numbers of seriously ill patients per week should fall.

(b)　Calculate the mean, variance, and standard deviation for the number of routine patients per week. Within what boundaries should the "middle 68 percent" of these weekly numbers fall?

3-72　The superintendent of any local school district has two major problems: A tough job dealing with the elected school board is the first, and the second is the need to always be prepared to look for a new job because of the first problem. Tom Langley, superintendent of School District 18, is no exception. He has learned the value of understanding all numbers in any budget and being able to use them to his advantage. This year, the school board has proposed a media research budget of $350,000. From past experience, Tom knows that actual spending always exceeds the budget proposal, and the amount by which it exceeds the proposal has a mean of $40,000 and variance of 100,000,000 dollars squared. Tom learned about Chebyshev's theorem in college, and he thinks that this might be useful in finding a range of values within which the actual expenditure would fall 75 percent of the time in years when the budget proposal is the same as this year. Do Tom a favor and find this range.

3-73　Bea Reele, a well-known clinical psychologist, keeps very accurate data on all her patients. From these data, she has developed four categories within which to place all her patients: child, young adult, adult, and elderly. For each category, she has computed the mean IQ and the variance of IQs within that category. These numbers are given in the table below. If on a certain day Bea saw four patients (one from each category), and the IQs of those patients were as follows: child, 90; young adult, 92; adult, 100; elderly, 98; then which of the patients had the IQ farthest above the mean, in standard deviation units, for that particular category?

CATEGORY	MEAN IQ	IQ VARIANCE
Child	110	81
Young adult	90	64
Adult	95	49
Elderly	90	121

3-10
Relative Dispersion: The Coefficient of Variation

Shortcomings of the standard deviation

The coefficient of variation, a relative measure

The standard deviation is an *absolute* measure of dispersion that expresses variation in the same units as the original data. The annual Blue Cross–Blue Shield payments to Cumberland Hospital (Table 3-21) have a standard deviation of $380,640. The annual Blue Cross–Blue Shield payments to Valley Falls Hospital (Table 3-16) have a standard deviation (which you can compute) of $57,390. Can we compare the values of these two standard deviations? Unfortunately, no.

The standard deviation cannot be the sole basis for comparing two distributions. If we have a standard deviation of 10 and a mean of 5, the values vary by an amount twice as large as the mean itself. If, on the other hand, we have a standard deviation of 10 and a mean of 5,000, the variation relative to the mean is insignificant. Therefore, we cannot know the dispersion of a set of data until we know the standard deviation, the mean, *and* how the standard deviation compares with the mean.

What we need is a *relative* measure that will give us a feel for the magnitude of the deviation relative to the magnitude of the mean. The *coefficient of variation* is one such relative measure of dispersion. It relates the standard deviation and the mean by expressing the standard deviation as a percentage of the mean. The unit of measure, then, is "percent" rather than the same units as the original data. For a population, the formula for the coefficient of variation is:

Standard deviation of the population

$$\text{Population coefficient of variation} = \frac{\sigma}{\mu}(100) \qquad [3\text{-}20]$$

Mean of the population

Using this formula in an example, we may suppose that each day, laboratory technician A completes 40 analyses with a standard deviation of 5. Technician B completes 160 analyses per day with a standard deviation of 15. Which employee shows less variability?

At first glance, it appears that technician B has three times more variation in the output rate than technician A. But B completes analyses at a rate four times faster than A. Taking all this information into account, we can compute the coefficient of variation for both technicians:

Computing the coefficient of variation

$$\text{Coefficient of variation} = \frac{\sigma}{\mu}(100) \qquad [3\text{-}20]$$

$$= \frac{5}{40}(100)$$

$$= 12.5\% \leftarrow \text{for technician A}$$

and

$$\text{Coefficient of variation} = \frac{15}{160}(100)$$

$$= 9.4\% \leftarrow \text{for technician B}$$

So we find that technician B, who has more *absolute* variation in output than technician A, has less *relative* variation, because the mean output for B is much greater than for A.

Using the computer to compute measures of central tendency and variability

For large data sets, we use the computer to calculate our measures of central tendency and variability. In Fig. 3-12, we have used the SAS system to compute some of these summary statistics for the grade data in Appendix 9. The statistics are shown for each section as well as for the course as a whole. In Fig. 3-13, we have used Minitab to calculate several measures of central tendency and variability for the earnings data in Appendix 10. The statistics are given for all 224 companies together, and they are

FIGURE 3-12

Output from SAS showing summary statistics for course grade data

```
                              SAS
                 1989 GRADES IN BUSINESS STATISTICS
            SUMMARY STATISTICS FOR ENTIRE COURSE AND BY SECTION

  VARIABLE      N      MEAN      STANDARD      VARIANCE       RANGE      C. V.
                                 DEVIATION

  EXAM1        199    50.221106    9.4885022    90.031674    52.000000    18.893
  EXAM2        199    56.894472   10.7126810   114.761535    57.000000    18.829
  HWK          199   108.597990   19.0127335   361.484036   122.000000    17.507
  FINAL        199    45.281407   10.0141923   100.284046    61.000000    22.115
  TOTAL        199    68.567959   11.2397325   126.331586    76.103163    16.392


  ------------------------------ SECTION=1 ----------------------------

  EXAM1         27    47.148148   10.8617314   117.977208    48.000000    23.037
  EXAM2         27    53.296296   13.5868002   184.601140    52.000000    25.493
  HWK           27   109.074074   20.5106463   420.686610   102.000000    18.804
  FINAL         27    45.740741   10.6792127   114.045584    50.000000    23.347
  TOTAL         27    67.103469   13.6211984   185.537045    65.043309    20.299


  ------------------------------ SECTION=2 ----------------------------

  EXAM1         46    50.826087   10.6129990   112.635749    43.0000000   20.881
  EXAM2         46    58.260870   10.8370451   117.441546    49.0000000   18.601
  HWK           46   112.521739   17.6417927   311.232850    79.0000000   15.679
  FINAL         46    44.760870   11.8999249   141.608213    61.0000000   26.586
  TOTAL         46    69.388850   12.4966506   156.166277    60.3211679   18.010


  ------------------------------ SECTION=3 ----------------------------

  EXAM1         37    53.189189    8.9809608    80.657658    33.0000000   16.885
  EXAM2         37    60.513514    7.6034408    57.812312    28.0000000   12.565
  HWK           37   111.783784   16.8030009   282.340841    96.0000000   15.032
  FINAL         37    49.081081    7.3650012    54.243243    29.0000000   15.006
  TOTAL         37    72.816098    8.8560862    78.430262    34.8340633   12.162


  ------------------------------ SECTION=4 ----------------------------

  EXAM1         26    50.769231    8.7466917    76.504615    37.0000000   17.228
  EXAM2         26    59.384615    6.4440790    41.526154    27.0000000   10.851
  HWK           26   104.576923   15.0417368   226.253846    65.0000000   14.383
  FINAL         26    44.923077    8.0643565    65.033846    31.0000000   17.951
  TOTAL         26    68.600037    8.0832528    65.338975    32.0038929   11.783


  ------------------------------ SECTION=5 ----------------------------

  EXAM1         36    49.472222    8.1643340    66.656349    37.000000    16.503
  EXAM2         36    55.944444   11.4391419   130.853968    47.000000    20.447
  HWK           36   107.361111   24.3359262   592.237302   120.000000    22.667
  FINAL         36    44.333333   10.3730420   107.600000    40.000000    23.398
  TOTAL         36    67.428710   11.8180624   139.666600    51.431630    17.527


  ------------------------------ SECTION=6 ----------------------------

  EXAM1         27    48.666667    8.4352739    71.153846    32.0000000   17.333
  EXAM2         27    52.074074   11.0902796   122.994302    35.0000000   21.297
  HWK           27   102.592593   17.0322302   290.096866    53.0000000   16.602
  FINAL         27    42.111111    9.4353400    89.025641    38.0000000   22.406
  TOTAL         27    64.300478    9.8485111    96.993170    35.9532847   15.316
```

EXCHANGE	N	MEAN	MEDIAN	TRMEAN	STDEV	MIN	MAX	Q1	Q3
	224	0.2105	0.1300	0.2139	0.8316	-5.4500	5.2300	-0.0075	0.4400
0	111	0.0766	0.1100	0.1070	0.5110	-3.7500	1.2200	-0.0200	0.2600
1	38	0.199	0.045	0.083	0.837	-0.560	4.740	-0.085	0.292
2	75	0.415	0.440	0.459	1.130	-5.450	5.230	0.070	0.810

also broken down by stock exchange (0 = OTC, 1 = ASE, 2 = NYSE). The statistic TRMEAN is a "trimmed mean," a mean calculated with the top 5% and bottom 5% of the data omitted. This helps to alleviate the distortion caused by those extreme values from which the ordinary arithmetic mean suffers.

Exercises

3-74 The weights of the Baltimore Bullets professional football team have a mean of 224 pounds with a standard deviation of 18 pounds, while the mean weight and standard deviation of their Sunday opponent, the Chicago Trailblazers, are 195 and 12, respectively. Which team exhibits the greater relative dispersion in weights of team members?

3-75 Bassart Electronics is considering employing one of two training programs. Two groups were trained for the same task. Group 1 was trained by program A; group 2, by program B. For the first group, it took an average of 32.11 hours to train each employee, with a variance of 68.09. For the second group, it took an average of 19.75 hours to train each employee, with a variance of 71.14. Which training program has less relative variability in its performance?

3-76 Students' ages in the regular daytime M.B.A. program and the evening program of Central University are described by these two samples:

Regular M.B.A.	23	29	27	22	24	21	25	26	27	24
Evening M.B.A.	27	34	30	29	28	30	34	35	28	29

If homogeneity of the class is a positive factor in learning, use a measure of relative variability to suggest which of the two groups will be easier to teach.

3-77 There are a number of possible measures of sales performance, including how consistent a salesperson is, in meeting established sales goals. The data below represent the percentage of goal met by each of three salespersons over the last 5 years.

Patricia	88	68	89	92	103
John	76	88	90	86	79
Frank	104	88	118	88	123

(a) Which salesperson is the most consistent?
(b) Comment on the adequacy of using a measure of consistency along with percentage of sales goal met to evaluate sales performance.
(c) Can you suggest an alternative measure of consistency more appropriate in this instance?

3-78 The board of directors of Gothic Products is considering acquiring one of two companies and is closely examining the management of each company in regard to their inclinations toward risk. During the past 5 years, the first company had an average return on investment of 28 percent, with a standard deviation of 5.3 percent. The second company had an average return of 37.8 percent, with a standard deviation of 4.8 percent. If we consider risk to be associated with greater relative dispersion, which of these 2 companies has pursued a riskier strategy?

3-79 A drug company that supplies hospitals with premeasured doses of certain medications uses different machines for medications requiring different dosage amounts. One machine, designed to produce doses of 100 cc, has as its mean dose 100 cc, with a standard deviation of 5.2 cc. Another machine produces premeasured amounts of 180 cc of medication and has a standard deviation of 8.6 cc. Which machine has the lower accuracy from the standpoint of relative dispersion?

3-80 Southeastern Stereos, a wholesaler, was contemplating becoming the supplier to three retailers, but inventory shortages have forced Southeastern to select only one. Southeastern's credit manager is evaluating the credit record of these three retailers. Over the past 5 years, these retailers' accounts receivable have been outstanding for the following average number of days. The credit manager feels that consistency, in addition to lowest average, is important. Based on relative dispersion, which retailer would make the best customer?

Lee	62.2	61.8	63.4	63.0	61.7
Forrest	62.5	61.9	62.8	63.0	60.7
Davis	62.0	61.9	63.0	63.9	61.5

3-81 Wyatt Seed Company sells three grades of Early White Sugar corn seed, distinguished according to the consistency of germination of the seeds. The state seed testing laboratory has a sample of each grade of seed and their test results on the number of seeds which germinated out of packages of 100 are as follows:

Grade I (Regular)	88	91	92	89	79
Grade II (Extra)	87	92	88	90	92
Grade III (Super)	90	89	79	93	88

Does Wyatt's grading of its seeds make sense?

3-82 Sunray Appliance Company has just completed a study of three possible assembly-line configurations for producing its best-selling two-slice toaster. Configuration I has yielded a mean time to construct a toaster of 34.8 minutes, with a standard deviation of 4.8 minutes. Configuration II has yielded a mean of 25.5 minutes, with a standard deviation of 7.5 minutes. Configuration III has yielded a mean of 37.5 minutes, with a standard deviation of 3.8 minutes. Which assembly-line configuration has the least relative variation in the time it takes to construct a toaster?

3-11
Exploratory Data Analysis

Assumptions necessary in classical analysis

Robust analysis methods

Chapters 2 and 3 have been concerned with the *presentation* of data: how to organize and summarize raw data so we can recognize important characteristics of the data. The rest of the book is devoted almost entirely to classical methods of statistical analysis of data that can be used once the data have been collected and organized. As we shall see when we discuss these methods, many of these classical analyses depend on assumptions that must be made about the data being analyzed.

Recent work, led principally by Prof. John W. Tukey of Princeton University and Bell Telephone Laboratories, has tried to develop methods for analyzing data that require very few prior assumptions. Statisticians call such methods *robust*. These techniques of *exploratory data analysis* (EDA) allow the statistician to examine the data and determine what further analyses may be appropriate.

Alternatives for doing exploratory analysis

Most widely used computer packages for doing statistical analysis have the ability to do EDA. Figure 3-14 gives the output when the SAS package is used to do an elementary exploratory analysis of the chlorine-level data from Chapter 2. We will briefly glance at this output; if you wish to learn more about EDA, the bibliography at the end of the book gives several references.

The first section of the output (headed "moments") gives the mean, standard deviation, and numerical measures of the skewness and kurtosis of the data. As we have already seen in Chapters 2 – 3, these quantities tell us about the *shape* of the data.

Quartiles, ranges, and percentiles

The next section of output (headed "quantiles") gives the quartiles and various ranges, as well as several percentiles that delineate the upper (99%, 95%, 90%) and

FIGURE 3-14

An exploratory analysis of the chlorine-level data from Chapter 2, using the SAS computer package

```
        ILLUSTRATING THE USE OF SAS FOR EXPLORATORY DATA ANALYSIS

                              UNIVARIATE

VARIABLE=PPM              CHLORINE LEVELS IN PPM
                               MOMENTS

            N              30          SUM WGTS          30
            MEAN      16.0367          SUM            481.1
            STD DEV  0.411459          VARIANCE    0.169299
            SKEWNESS 0.345475          KURTOSIS    -0.10233
            USS       7720.15          CSS          4.90967
            CV        2.56574          STD MEAN   0.0751219
            T:MEAN=0  213.475          PROB>|T|      0.0001
            SGN RANK    232.5          PROB>|S|      0.0001
            NUM ~= 0       30
            W:NORMAL 0.969853          PROB<W         0.571

                        QUANTILES(DEF=4)

            100% MAX     16.9          99%            16.9
             75% Q3      16.3          95%          16.845
             50% MED       16          90%           16.78
             25% Q1     15.775         10%            15.6
              0% MIN     15.2          5%            15.31
                                       1%             15.2

            RANGE         1.7
            Q3-Q1    0.524988
            MODE         15.9

                            EXTREMES

               LOWEST               HIGHEST
                15.2                  16.4
                15.4                  16.6
                15.6                  16.8
                15.6                  16.8
                15.6                  16.9

        STEM LEAF                    #          BOXPLOT

        168 000                      3             |
        166 0                        1             |
        164 00                       2             |
        162 00000                    5          +-----+
        160 00000                    5          *--+--*
        158 0000000                  7          |     |
        156 00000                    5          +-----+
        154 0                        1             |
        152 0                        1             |
        150
            ----+----+----+----+
            MULTIPLY STEM.LEAF BY 10**-01
```

lower (10%, 5%, 1%) tails of the data. Thus EDA not only identifies the center of the data; it also calls our attention to the noncentral, atypical values in the data. Often, closer examination of these "outliers" will show that they really don't belong in the data set. (Perhaps they were incorrectly recorded.) We've already seen how such outliers distort sample means.

Graphical plots of the data

SAS then gives several different plots of the data. "Stem and leaf displays" are like histograms, but they simultaneously display all the data values while grouping them. Thus they have the histogram's advantage of summarizing the data without having its disadvantage of losing detail. "Boxplots" give a graphical representation of the median (the middle horizontal line in Fig. 3-14), the quartiles (the top and bottom horizontal lines of the box in Fig. 3-14), and the extremes (the "whiskers" extending from the box). You might want to think of a boxplot as a skeletal frequency distribution.

Figs. 3-15 and 3-16 show some of the EDA which can be done with MYSTAT and Minitab, respectively. In Fig. 3-15, we have used MYSTAT to do a stem and leaf plot of the earnings data in Appendix 10. Notice how the outliers are singled out as the

FIGURE 3-15

MYSTAT stem and leaf plot of 1989 last-quarter earnings

```
STEM AND LEAF PLOT OF VARIABLE:      LQ89    , N =    224


MINIMUM IS:        -5.450
LOWER HINGE IS:        -0.005
MEDIAN IS:         0.130
UPPER HINGE IS:         0.440
MAXIMUM IS:         5.230


              -54    5
              -37    5
              -36    9
              -16    0
               -8    4
               -7    8
        ***OUTSIDE VALUES***
               -6    10
               -5    87655
               -4    1
               -3    831
               -2    998743320
               -1    876654221100
               -0  H 8887776655543322221
                0    0011122233333333444445566666677788888999
                1  M 000001122222333333344555555677899
                2    00002222345556777899
                3    0002233444555668
                4  H 001344445556889
                5    0222334678
                6    01446
                7    00236
                8    01458
                9    12357
               10    79
               11    00
        ***OUTSIDE VALUES***
               11    2347
               12    12
               13    05
               14    2
               19    0
               23    1
               47    4
               52    3
```

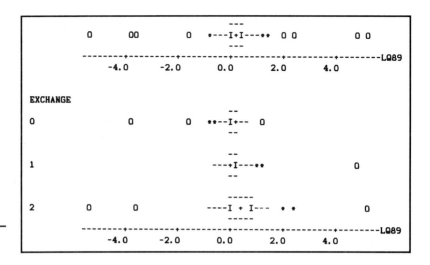

```
                O       OO        O     *---I+I---**  O O         O O
                                        ---
        --------+---------+---------+---------+---------+--------LQ89
              -4.0      -2.0       0.0       2.0       4.0


    EXCHANGE

                                        --
    0       O               O         O   **--I+--   O
                                        --


                                        --
    1                                  ---+I---**               O
                                        --


                                        -----
    2       O       O                  ----I + I---  * *         O
                                        -----
        --------+---------+---------+---------+---------+--------LQ89
              -4.0      -2.0       0.0       2.0       4.0
```

FIGURE 3-16

Minitab boxplots of the earnings data

OUTSIDE VALUES in the plot. The "hinges" are essentially the same as the quartiles of the distribution.

Fig. 3-16 shows boxplots of the earnings data as a whole and broken down by stock exchange. These were produced by Minitab. Once again EDA calls our attention to the outliers, the observations far from the center of the distribution. In the boxplots, these outlying observations are denoted by O's. Closer examination of the data set shows that for the two most extreme of the outliers, the companies discontinued some of their operations, in one case (Airgas, Inc.) receiving a large sum for the sale of those discontinued operations, and in the other (Monarch Capital Corp.) incurring a large cost for shutting down the discontinued operations. Because of these extraordinary factors, these two data points should probably be excluded from further analyses of the data set.

3-12
Terms Introduced in Chapter 3

Bimodal Distribution A distribution of data points in which two values occur more frequently than the rest of the values in the data set.

Chebyshev's Theorem No matter what the shape of a distribution, at least 75 percent of the values in the population will fall within 2 standard deviations of the mean, and at least 89 percent will fall within 3 standard deviations.

Coding A method of calculating the mean for grouped data by recoding values of class marks to more simple values.

Coefficient of Variation A relative measure of dispersion, comparable across distributions, which expresses the standard deviation as a percentage of the mean.

Deciles Fractiles that divide the data into ten equal parts.

Dispersion The spread or variability in a set of data.

Distance Measure A measure of dispersion in terms of the difference between two values in the data set.

Exploratory Data Analysis (EDA) Methods for analyzing data that require very few prior assumptions.

Fractile In a frequency distribution, the location of a value at, or above, a given fraction of the data.

Geometric Mean A measure of central tendency used to measure the average rate of change or growth for some quantity, computed by taking the nth root of the product of n values representing change.

Interfractile Range A measure of the spread between two fractiles in a distribution; i.e., the difference between the values of two fractiles.

Interquartile Range The difference between the values of the first and the third quartiles; this difference indicates the range of the middle half of the data set.

Kurtosis The degree of peakedness of a distribution of points.

Mean A central tendency measure representing the arithmetic average of a set of observations.

Measure of Central Tendency A measure indicating the value to be expected of a typical or middle data point.

Measure of Dispersion A measure describing how scattered or spread out the observations in a data set are.

Median The middle point of a data set, a measure of location that divides the data set into halves.

Median Class The class in a frequency distribution that contains the median value for a data set.

Mode The value most often repeated in the data set. It is represented by the highest point in the distribution curve of a data set.

Parameters Numerical values that describe the characteristics of a whole population, commonly represented by Greek letters.

Percentiles Fractiles that divide the data into 100 equal parts.

Quartiles Fractiles that divide the data into four equal parts.

Range The distance between the highest and lowest values in a data set.

Skewness The extent to which a distribution of data points is concentrated at one end or the other; the lack of symmetry.

Standard Deviation The positive square root of the variance; a measure of dispersion in the same units as the original data, rather than in the squared units of the variance.

Standard Score Expressing an observation in terms of standard deviation units above or below the mean; i.e., the transformation of an observation by subtracting the mean and dividing by the standard deviation.

Statistics Numerical measures describing the characteristics of a sample. Represented by Roman letters.

Summary Statistics Single numbers that describe certain characteristics of a data set.

Symmetrical A characteristic of a distribution in which each half is the mirror image of the other half.

Variance A measure of the average squared distance between the mean and each item in the population.

Weighted Mean An average calculated to take into account the importance of each value to the overall total; i.e., an average in which each observation value is weighted by some index of its importance.

3-13
Equations Introduced in Chapter 3

[3-1]
$$\mu = \frac{\Sigma x}{N}$$
p. 67

The *population arithmetic mean* is equal to the sum of the values of all the elements in the population (Σx) divided by the number of elements in the population (N).

[3-2]
$$\bar{x} = \frac{\Sigma x}{n}$$
p. 67

To derive the *sample arithmetic mean,* sum the values of all the elements in the sample (Σx) and divide by the number of elements in the sample (n).

[3-3]
$$\bar{x} = \frac{\Sigma(f \times x)}{n}$$
p. 69

To find the *sample arithmetic mean of grouped data*, calculate the midpoints (x) for each class in the sample. Then multiply each midpoint by the frequency (f) of observations in that class, sum (Σ) all these results, and divide by the total number of observations in the sample (n).

[3-4]

$$\bar{x} = x_0 + w\,\frac{\Sigma(u \times f)}{n}$$

p. 70

This formula enables us to calculate the *sample arithmetic mean of grouped data* using codes to eliminate dealing with large or inconvenient midpoints. Assign these codes (u) as follows: Give the value of zero to the middle midpoint (called x_0), positive consecutive integers to midpoints larger than x_0, and negative consecutive integers to smaller midpoints. Then, multiply the code assigned to each class (u) by the frequency (f) of observations in each class and sum (Σ) all of these products. Divide this result by the total number of observations in the sample (n), multiply by the numerical width of the class interval (w), and add the value of the midpoint assigned the code zero (x_0).

[3-5]

$$\bar{x}_w = \frac{\Sigma(w \times x)}{\Sigma w}$$

p. 76

The *weighted mean*, $\bar{x}_w$, is an average that takes into account how important each value is to the overall total. We can calculate this average by multiplying the weight, or proportion, of each element (w) by that element (x), summing the results (Σ), and dividing this amount by the sum of all the weights (Σw).

[3-6]

$$\text{G.M.} = \sqrt[n]{\text{Product of all the } x \text{ values}}$$

p. 78

The *geometric mean*, or G.M., is appropriate to use whenever we need to measure the average rate of change (the growth rate) over a period of time. In this equation, n is equal to the number of x values dealt with in the problem.

[3-7]

$$\text{Median} = \text{the } \left(\frac{n+1}{2}\right) \text{th item in a data array}$$

p. 81

where: $n = $ the number of items in the data array

The *median* is a single value that measures the central item in the data set. Half the items lie above the median, half below it. If the data set contains an odd number of items, the middle item of the array is the median. For an even number of items, the median is the average of the two middle items. Use this formula when the data are ungrouped.

[3-8]

$$\tilde{m} = \left(\frac{(n+1)/2 - (F+1)}{f_m}\right) w + L_m$$

p. 83

This formula enables us to find the *sample median of grouped data*. In it, n equals the total number of items in the distribution; F equals the sum of all the class frequencies up to, but not including, the median class; f_m is the frequency of observations in the median class; w is the class interval width; and L_m is the lower limit of the median class interval.

[3-9]

$$Mo = L_{Mo} + \frac{d_1}{d_1 + d_2}\,w$$

p. 87

The *mode* is that value most often repeated in the data set. To find the *mode of grouped data* (symbolized *Mo*), use this formula and let L_{Mo} = the lower limit of the modal class; d_1 = the frequency of the modal class minus the frequency of the class directly below it; d_2 = the frequency of the modal class minus the frequency of the class directly above it; and w = the width of the modal class interval.

[3-10]
$$\text{Range} = \frac{\text{Value of highest}}{\text{observation}} - \frac{\text{Value of lowest}}{\text{observation}}$$
p. 93

The *range* is the difference between the highest and lowest values in a frequency distribution.

[3-11]
$$\text{Interquartile range} = Q_3 - Q_1$$
p. 95

The *interquartile range* measures approximately how far from the median we must go on either side before we can include one-half the values of the data set. To compute this range, divide the data into four equal parts. The *quartiles* (Q) are the highest values in each of these four parts. The *interquartile range* is the difference between the values of the first and third quartiles (Q_1 and Q_3).

[3-12]
$$\sigma^2 = \frac{\Sigma(x-\mu)^2}{N} = \frac{\Sigma x^2}{N} - \mu^2$$
p. 98

This formula enables us to calculate the *population variance,* a measure of the average *squared* distance between the mean and each item in the population. The middle expression, $\frac{\Sigma(x-\mu)^2}{N}$, is the definition of σ^2. The last expression, $\frac{\Sigma x^2}{N} - \mu^2$, is mathematically equivalent to the definition but is often much more convenient to use, since it frees us from calculating the deviations from the mean.

[3-13]
$$\sigma = \sqrt{\sigma^2} = \sqrt{\frac{\Sigma(x-\mu)^2}{N}} = \sqrt{\frac{\Sigma x^2}{N} - \mu^2}$$
p. 98

The population standard deviation, σ, is the square root of the population variance. It is a more useful parameter than the variance, because it is expressed in the same units as the data (whereas the units of the variance are the squares of the units of the data). The standard deviation is always the *positive* square root of the variance.

[3-14]
$$\text{Population standard score} = \frac{x-\mu}{\sigma}$$
p. 101

The *standard score* of an observation is the number of standard deviations the observation lies below or above the mean of the distribution. The standard score enables us to make comparisons between distribution items that differ in order of magnitude or in the units employed. Use Equation 3-14 to find the standard score of an item in a *population.*

[3-15]
$$\sigma^2 = \frac{\Sigma f(x-\mu)^2}{N} = \frac{\Sigma fx^2}{N} - \mu^2$$
p. 102

This formula in either form enables us to calculate the *variance* of data already *grouped* in a frequency distribution. Here, f represents the frequency of the class, and x represents the midpoint.

[3-16]
$$\sigma = \sqrt{\sigma^2} = \sqrt{\frac{\Sigma f(x-\mu)^2}{N}} = \sqrt{\frac{\Sigma fx^2}{N} - \mu^2}$$
p. 102

Take the square root of the variance, and you have the *standard deviation using grouped data.*

[3-17]

$$s^2 = \frac{\Sigma(x - \bar{x})^2}{n-1} = \frac{\Sigma x^2}{n-1} - \frac{n\bar{x}^2}{n-1}$$

p. 102

To compute the *sample variance,* use the same formula as Equation 3-12, replacing μ with $\bar{x}$ and N with $n - 1$. Chapter 7 contains an explanation of why we use $n - 1$ rather than n to calculate the sample variance.

[3-18]

$$s = \sqrt{s^2} = \sqrt{\frac{\Sigma(x - \bar{x})^2}{n-1}} = \sqrt{\frac{\Sigma x^2}{n-1} - \frac{n\bar{x}^2}{n-1}}$$

p. 102

The *sample standard deviation* is the square root of the sample variance. It is similar to Equation 3-13, except that μ is replaced by the sample mean $\bar{x}$ and N is changed to $n - 1$.

[3-19]

$$\text{Sample standard score} = \frac{x - \bar{x}}{s}$$

p. 104

Use this equation to find the standard score of an item in a *sample.*

[3-20]

$$\text{Population coefficient of variation} = \frac{\sigma}{\mu}(100)$$

p. 108

The *coefficient of variation* is a relative measure of dispersion that enables us to compare two distributions. It relates the standard deviation and the mean by expressing the standard deviation as a percentage of the mean.

3-14
Chapter Review Exercises

 3-83 Johnson Machine Company has a contract with one of its customers to supply machined pump gears. One requirement is that the diameter of its gears be within specific limits. Here are the diameters (in inches) of a sample of 20 gears:

4.01	4.00	4.02	4.02	4.03	4.00	3.98	3.99	3.99	4.01
3.99	3.98	3.97	4.00	4.02	4.01	4.02	4.00	4.01	3.99

What can Johnson say to its customer about the diameters of 95 percent of the gears they are receiving?

3-84 How would you react to this statement from a football fan: "The Rockland Raiders average 3.6 yards a carry in their ground game. Since they need only 10 yards for a first down, and they have 4 plays to get it, they can't miss if they just stick to their ground game."

3-85 How would you reply to the following statement: "Variability is not an important factor, because even though the outcome is more uncertain, you still have an equal chance of falling either above or below the median. Therefore, on average, the outcome will be the same."

3-86 Following are three general sections of one year's defense budget, each of which was allocated the same amount of funding by Congress:
(a) Officer salaries (total)   (b) Aircraft maintenance   (c) Food purchases (total)
Considering the distribution of possible outcomes for the funds actually spent in each of these areas, match each section to one of the curves in Fig. 3-8. Support your answers.

3-87   Ed's Sports Equipment Company stocks two grades of fishing line. Data on each line are:

	MEAN TEST STRENGTH (LBS.)	STANDARD DEVIATION
Master	40	Exact value unknown, but estimated to be quite large
Super	30	Exact value unknown, but estimated to be quite small

If you are going fishing for bluefish, which have been averaging 25 pounds this season, with which line would you probably land more fish?

3-88   The VP of sales for Vanguard Products has been studying records regarding the performances of his sales reps. He has noticed that in the last 2 years, the average level of sales per sales rep has remained the same, while the distribution of the sales levels has widened. Salespeople's sales levels from this period have significantly larger variations from the mean than in any of the previous 2-year periods for which he has records. What conclusions might be drawn from these observations?

3-89   New cars sold in December at eight Ford dealers within 50 miles of Canton, Ohio, can be described by this data set:

$$200 \quad 156 \quad 231 \quad 222 \quad 96 \quad 289 \quad 126 \quad 308$$

(a) Compute the range, interquartile range, and standard deviation of these data.
(b) Which of the three measures you have computed in (a) best describes the variability of these data?

3-90   Two economists are studying fluctuations in the price of gold. One is examining the period of 1968–1972. The other is examining the period of 1975–1979. What differences would you expect to find in the variability of their data?

3-91   The Downhill Ski Boot Company runs two assembly lines in its plant. The production manager is interested in improving the consistency of the line with the greatest variation. Line number 1 produces a monthly average of 11,350 units, with a standard deviation of 1,050. Line number 2 produces a monthly average of 9,935, with a standard deviation of 1,010. Which line has the greater relative dispersion?

3-92   The Fish and Game station on Lake Wylie keeps records of fish caught on the lake and reports their findings to the National Fish and Game Service. The catch in pounds for the last 20 days was:

$$
\begin{array}{cccccccccc}
101 & 132 & 145 & 144 & 130 & 88 & 156 & 188 & 169 & 130 \\
90 & 140 & 130 & 139 & 99 & 100 & 208 & 192 & 165 & 216
\end{array}
$$

Calculate the range, variance, and standard deviation for these data. In this instance is the range a good measure of the variability? Why?

3-93   The owner of Records Anonymous, a large record retailer, employs two different formulas for predicting monthly sales. The first formula has an average miss of 700 records, with a standard deviation of 35 records. The second formula has an average miss of 300 records, with a standard deviation of 16. Which formula is relatively less accurate?

3-94   Using the following population data, calculate the interquartile range, variance, and standard deviation. What do your answers tell you about the cost behavior of heating fuel?

AVERAGE HEATING-FUEL COST PER GALLON
FOR EIGHT STATES

$$1.89 \quad 1.66 \quad 1.77 \quad 1.83 \quad 1.71 \quad 1.68 \quad 1.69 \quad 1.73$$

3-95 Below is the average number of New York City policemen and policewomen on duty each day between 8 and 12 P.M. in the borough of Manhattan:

Mon. 2,950	Wed. 2,900	Fri. 3,285	Sun. 2,975
Tues. 2,900	Thurs. 2,980	Sat.3,430	

(a) Would either the variance or the standard deviation be a good measure of the variability of these data?
(b) What is it in the staffing pattern that caused you to answer (a) the way you did?

3-96 A psychologist wrote a computer program to simulate the way a person responds to a standard IQ test. To test the program, he gave the computer fifteen different forms of a popular IQ test and computed its IQ from each form.

IQ VALUES

134	136	137	138	138
143	144	144	145	146
146	146	147	148	153

(a) Calculate the mean and standard deviation of the IQ scores.
(b) According to Chebyshev's theorem, how many of the values should be between 132.44 and 153.56? How many are actually in that interval?

3-97 On a particular day, a city sanitation department measured the garbage weight in tons collected by the department's 40 trucks. The data were arranged in the following array:

GARBAGE WEIGHT (TONS)

11.9	12.8	14.6	15.8	13.7	9.9	18.8	16.9	10.4	9.1
17.1	13.0	18.6	16.0	13.9	14.7	17.7	12.1	18.0	17.8
19.0	13.3	12.4	9.3	14.2	15.0	19.3	10.6	11.2	9.6
13.6	14.5	19.6	16.6	12.7	15.3	10.9	18.3	17.4	16.3

List the values in each decile. Eighty percent of trucks brought in fewer than _____ tons.

3-98 Baseball attendance at the Baltimore Eagles last ten home games looked like this:

20,100	24,500	31,600	28,400	49,500
19,350	25,600	30,600	11,300	28,560

(a) Compute the range, variance, and standard deviation for these data.
(b) Are any of your answers in (a) an accurate portrayal of the variability in the attendance data?
(c) What other measure of variability might be a better measure?
(d) Compute the value of the measure you suggest in (c).

3-99 Matthews-Young Associates, a Chapel Hill consulting firm, has these records indicating the number of days each of its eight staff consultants billed last year:

212	220	230	210	228	229	231	219	221	222

(a) Without computing the value of any of these measures, which of them would you guess would give you the most information about this distribution: range, standard deviation?

(b) Considering the difficulty and time of computing each of the measures you reviewed in part (a), which one would you suggest is best?

(c) What will cause you to change your mind about your choice?

3-100 MC Tern, operations manager at Piltdown Fabrication, has fourteen major types of metal-working equipment. Below are the number of days of downtime for each equipment group for last year.

EQUIPMENT GROUP	DAYS OUT OF SERVICE	EQUIPMENT GROUP	DAYS OUT OF SERVICE
1	2	8	8
2	19	9	29
3	14	10	6
4	21	11	0
5	5	12	4
6	7	13	4
7	11	14	10

(a) What was last year's mean downtime for the equipment groups?

(b) What was the median?

3-101 MC Tern (see exercise 3-100) has just been given the following additional information:

EQUIPMENT GROUP	PIECES OF MACHINERY	EQUIPMENT GROUP	PIECES OF MACHINERY
1	1	8	5
2	3	9	8
3	1	10	2
4	4	11	2
5	2	12	6
6	1	13	1
7	1	14	1

(a) What is the average downtime per piece of machinery?

(b) What are the average downtimes per piece of machinery for each group when classified by group?

(c) How many groups had a higher than average downtime per piece of machinery?

3-102 Compare and contrast the central position and skewness of the distributions of the readership volume in numbers of readers per issue for all nationally-distributed:

(a) monthly magazines in the U.S.

(b) weekly news magazines in the U.S.

(c) monthly medical journals in the U.S.

3-103 Compare and contrast the central tendency and skewness of the distributions of the amount of taxes paid (in dollars) for all:

(a) individuals filing federal returns in the U.S. where the top tax bracket is 28 percent.

(b) individuals paying state income taxes in North Carolina where the top tax bracket is 7 percent.

(c) individuals paying airport taxes (contained in the price of the airplane ticket) at JFK International Airport in New York City.

3-104 Allison Barrett does statistical analyses for an automobile racing team. Here are the fuel consumption figures in miles per gallon for the team's cars in recent races:

$$4.77 \quad 6.11 \quad 6.11 \quad 5.05 \quad 5.99 \quad 4.91 \quad 5.27 \quad 6.01$$
$$5.75 \quad 4.89 \quad 6.05 \quad 5.22 \quad 6.02 \quad 5.24 \quad 6.11 \quad 5.02$$

(a) Calculate the median fuel consumption.
(b) Calculate the mean fuel consumption.
(c) Group the data into five equally-sized classes. What is the fuel consumption value of the modal class?
(d) Which of the three measures of central tendency is best for Allison to use when she orders fuel? Explain.

3-105 Claire Chavez, an Internal Revenue Service analyst, has been asked to describe the "average" American taxpayer in terms of gross annual income. She has summary data grouping taxpayers into different income classes. Which measure of central tendency should she use?

3-106 Emmot Bulb Co. sells a grab bag of flower bulbs. The bags are sold by weight; thus the number of bulbs in each can vary depending on the varieties included. Below are the number of bulbs in each of 20 bags sampled:

$$21 \quad 33 \quad 37 \quad 56 \quad 47$$
$$36 \quad 23 \quad 26 \quad 33 \quad 37$$
$$25 \quad 33 \quad 32 \quad 47 \quad 34$$
$$26 \quad 37 \quad 37 \quad 43 \quad 45$$

(a) What are the mean and median number of bulbs per bag?
(b) Based on your answer, what can you conclude about the shape of the distribution of number of bulbs per bag?

3-107 An engineer tested nine samples of each of three designs of a certain bearing for a new electrical winch. The following data are the number of hours it took for each bearing to fail when the winch motor was run continuously at maximum output, with a load on the winch equivalent to 1.9 times the intended capacity.

DESIGN		
A	B	C
16	18	31
16	27	16
53	23	42
15	21	20
31	22	18
17	26	17
14	39	16
30	17	15
20	28	19

(a) Calculate the mean and median for each group.
(b) Based on your answer, which design is best and why?

3-108 Table Spice Co. is installing a screener in one stage of its new processing plant to separate leaves, dirt, and insect parts from a certain expensive spice seed which it receives in bulk from growers. The firm can use a coarse 3.5 millimeter mesh screen or a finer 3 millimeter mesh. The smaller mesh will remove more debris but also will remove more seeds. The larger mesh will pass more debris and remove fewer seeds. Table Spice has the following information from a sample of pieces of debris.

DEBRIS SIZE (IN MILLIMETERS)	FREQUENCY
less than 1.0	12
1.01–1.5	129
1.51–2.0	186
2.01–2.5	275
2.51–3.0	341
3.01–3.5	422
3.51–4.0	6287
4.01–4.5	8163
4.51–5.0	6212
5.01–5.5	2416
more than 5.5	1019

(a) What is the median debris size and the modal class size?
(b) Which screen would you use based on (a) if you wanted to remove at least half of the debris?

3-15
Chapter Concepts Test

Answers are in the back of the book.

T **F** 1. The value of every observation in the data set is taken into account when we calculate its median.

T F 2. When the population is either negatively or positively skewed, it is often preferable to use the median as the best measure of location, because it always lies between the mean and the mode.

T **F** 3. Measures of central tendency in a data set refer to the extent to which the observations are scattered.

T **F** 4. A measure of the peakedness of a distribution curve is its skewness.

T **F** 5. With ungrouped data, the mode is most frequently used as the measure of central tendency.

T F 6. If we arrange the observations in a data set from highest to lowest, the data point lying in the middle is the median of the data set.

T F 7. When working with grouped data, we may compute an approximate mean by assuming that each value in a given class is equal to its midpoint.

T **F** 8. The value most often repeated in a data set is called the arithmetic mean.

T F 9. If the curve of a certain distribution tails off toward the left end of the measuring scale on the horizontal axis, the distribution is said to be negatively skewed.

T **F** 10. After grouping a set of data into a number of classes, we may identify the median class as being the one that has the largest number of observations.

T F 11. A mean calculated from grouped data always gives a good estimate of the true value, although it is seldom exact.

T **F** 12. We can compute a mean for any data set, once we are given its frequency distribution.

T F 13. The mode is always found at the highest point of a graph of a data distribution.

T **F** 14. The number of elements in a population is denoted by *n*.

T **F** 15. For a data array with 50 observations, the median will be the value of the 25th observation in the array.

T **F** 16. Extreme values in a data set have a strong effect upon the median.

T **F** 17. The difference between the largest and smallest observations in a data set is called the geometric mean.

T F 18. The dispersion of a data set gives insight into the reliability of the measure of central tendency.

T F 19. The standard deviation is equal to the square root of the variance.

T **F** 20. The difference between the highest and lowest observations in a data set is called the quartile range.

T F 21. The interquartile range is based upon only two values taken from the data set.

T F 22. The standard deviation is measured in the same units as the observations in the data set.

T **F** 23. A fractile is a location in a frequency distribution that a given proportion (or fraction) of the data lies at or above.

T F 24. The variance, like the standard deviation, takes into account every observation in the data set.

T **F** 25. The coefficient of variation is an absolute measure of dispersion.

T F 26. The measure of dispersion most often used by statisticians is the standard deviation.

T **F** 27. One of the advantages of dispersion measures is that any statistic that measures absolute variation also measures relative variation.

T F 28. One disadvantage of using the range to measure dispersion is that it ignores the nature of the variations among most of the observations.

T F 29. The variance indicates the average distance of any observation in the data set from the mean.

T **F** 30. Every population has a variance, which is signified by s^2.

T F 31. According to Chebyshev's theorem, no more than 11 percent of the observations in a population can have population standard scores greater than 3 or less than -3.

T F 32. The interquartile range is a specific example of an interfractile range.

T **F** 33. It is possible to measure the range of an open-ended distribution.

T **F** 34. The interquartile range measures the average range of the lower fourth of a distribution.

35. When calculating the average rate of debt expansion for a company, the correct mean to use is the:
(a) arithmetic mean   (b) weighted mean   (c) geometric mean   (d) either a or c

36. The mode has all of the following disadvantages except:
(a) A data set may have no modal value.
(b) Every value in a data set may be a mode.
(c) A multimodal data set is difficult to analyze.
(d) The mode is unduly affected by extreme values.

37. What is the major assumption we make when computing a mean from grouped data?
(a) All values are discrete.
(b) Every value in a class is equal to the midpoint.
(c) No value occurs more than once.
(d) Each class contains exactly the same number of values.

38. Which of the following statements is NOT correct?
(a) Some data sets do not have means.
(b) Calculation of a mean is affected by extreme data values.
(c) A weighted mean should be used when it is necessary to take the importance of each value into account.
(d) All these statements are correct.

39. Which of the following is the first step in calculating the median of a data set?
(a) Average the middle two values of the data set.
(b) Array the data.
(c) Determine the relative weights of the data values in terms of importance.
(d) None of these.

40. Which of the following is NOT an advantage of using a median?
(a) Extreme values affect the median less strongly than they do the mean.
(b) A median can be calculated for qualitative descriptions.

(c) The median can be calculated for every set of data, even for all sets containing open-ended classes.

(d) The median is easy to understand.

(e) All these are advantages of using a median.

41. Why is it usually better to calculate a mode from grouped, rather than ungrouped, data?

(a) The ungrouped data tend to be bimodal.

(b) The mode for the grouped data will be the same, regardless of the skewness of the distribution.

(c) Extreme values have less effect on grouped data.

(d) The chance of an unrepresentative value being chosen as the mode is reduced.

42. In which of these cases would the mode be most useful as an indicator of central tendency?

(a) Every value in a data set occurs exactly once.

(b) All but three values in a data set occur once; three values occur 100 times each.

(c) All values in a data set occur 100 times each.

(d) Every observation in a data set has the same value.

43. Which of the following is an example of a parameter?

(a) $\bar{x}$ (c) μ (e) b and c, but not a

(b) n (d) All of these

44. Which of the following is NOT a measure of central tendency?

(a) Geometric mean.   (c) Mode.   (e) All these are measures of central

(b) Median.   (d) Arithmetic mean.   tendency.

45. When a distribution is symmetrical and has one mode, the highest point on the curve is referred to as the:

(a) Range   (c) Median   (e) All of these

(b) Mode   (d) Mean   (f) b, c, and d, but not a

46. When referring to a curve that tails off to the left end, you would call it:

(a) Symmetrical   (c) Positively skewed   (e) None of these

(b) Skewed right   (d) All of these

47. Disadvantages of using the range as a measure of dispersion include all of the following except:

(a) It is heavily influenced by extreme values.

(b) It can change drastically from one sample to the next.

(c) It is difficult to calculate.

(d) It is determined by only two points in the data set.

48. Why is it necessary to square the differences from the mean when computing the population variance?

(a) So that extreme values will not affect the calculation.

(b) Because it is possible that N could be very small.

(c) Some of the differences will be positive and some will be negative.

(d) None of these.

49. Assume that a population has $\mu = 100$, $\sigma = 10$. If a particular observation has a standard score of 1, it can be concluded that:

(a) Its value is 110.

(b) It lies between 90 and 110, but its exact value cannot be determined.

(c) Its value is greater than 110.

(d) Nothing can be determined without knowing N.

50. Assume that a population has $\mu = 100$, $\sigma = 10$, and $N = 1,000$. According to Chebyshev's theorem, which of the following situations is NOT possible?

(a) 150 values are greater than 130.

(b) 930 values lie between 100 and 108.

(c) 22 values lie between 120 and 125.

(d) 70 values are less than 90.

(e) All these situations are possible.

51. Which of the following is an example of a relative measure of dispersion?
    (a) Standard deviation   (c) Coefficient of variation   (e) a and b but not c
    (b) Variance   (d) All of these

52. Which of the following is true?
    (a) The variance can be calculated for grouped or ungrouped data.
    (b) The standard deviation can be calculated for grouped or ungrouped data.
    (c) The standard deviation can be calculated for grouped or ungrouped data, but the variance can be calculated only for ungrouped data.
    (d) a and b but not c

53. If one were to divide the standard deviation of a population by the mean of the same population and multiply this value by 100, one would have calculated the:
    (a) Population standard score   (d) Population coefficient of variation
    (b) Population variance   (e) None of these
    (c) Population standard deviation

54. How does the computation of a sample variance differ from the computation of a population variance?
    (a) μ is replaced by $\bar{x}$ (d) a and c but not b
    (b) N is replaced by $n - 1$ (e) a and b but not c
    (c) N is replaced by n

55. The square of the variance of a distribution is the:
    (a) Standard deviation   (c) Range   (e) a and d
    (b) Mean   (d) Absolute deviation   (f) None of these

56. Chebyshev's theorem says that 99 percent of the values will lie within plus and minus 3 standard deviations from the mean for:
    (a) Bell-shaped distributions   (d) All distributions
    (b) Positively skewed distributions   (e) No distributions
    (c) Left-tailed distributions

57. If a curve can be divided into two equal parts that are mirror images, it is _____. If it cannot be divided in this way, it is _____.

58. The symbol $\bar{x}$ denotes the mean of a _____. μ denotes the mean of a _____.

59. Assigning small-value consecutive integers to midpoints during calculation of the mean is called _____.

60. When dealing with quantities that change over a period of time, it is better to calculate a _____ mean than a _____ mean.

61. If two values in a group of data occur more often than any others, the distribution of the data is said to be _____.

62. The extent to which values in a distribution are grouped together is a measure of _____.

63. In a frequency distribution, the median is the .5 _____ because half of the data values are less than or equal to this value.

64. The difference between the values of the first and third quartiles is the _____ range.

65. The measure of the average squared distance between the mean and each item in the population is the _____. The positive square root of this value is the _____.

66. The expression of the standard deviation as a percentage of the mean is the _____.

67. The number of standard deviation units that an observation lies above or below the mean is called the _____.

68. Fractiles that divide the data into 100 equal parts are called _____.

69. Which of the following is an example of a distance measure?
    (a) Range   (c) Interquartile range   (e) a and b but not c
    (b) Interfractile range   (d) All of these
70. Which pair of phrases best completes this sentence? Fractiles that divide data into
    _____ equal parts are called _____.
    (a) 100 . . . . deciles   (c) 10 . . . . percentiles
    (b) 4 . . . . quartiles   (d) 16 . . . . octiles

3-16
Conceptual Case

(Northern White Metals Company)

Dick was truly impressed with the amount of information he, with the aid of two reluctant file clerks, had gleaned from the bulging file drawers. The purpose of these drawers had long been that of a repository for papers that seemed too important to discard, yet were of no immediate apparent use. Clearly, current invoices, orders, and other pertinent material had to be kept on hand, but Dick smiled as he tried to think of an occasion when an acknowledgement copy of a customer order dated May 12, 1954, might be needed.

A mandatory first step had been to clean out and update the record system, with all files more than 3 years old carted down to the basement for permanent storage. Unimportant material was discarded altogether. With much less clutter to deal with, Dick could organize the needed information into a form he felt was suitable for the presentation at Segue headquarters. Records were reviewed, and Dick developed a comprehensive analysis of sales volume, production volume, and raw-material price fluctuations and buying patterns.

Dick anxiously took the data he had accumulated and subsequently organized to the head draftsman, George Barbour, who had a strong artistic bent as well as considerable mechanical-drawing skill. An impressive series of tables and graphs was developed, and Dick felt the detail would make for a most effective presentation. George, on the other hand, was less convinced.

"Dick, from what I can tell, you've done quite a job in sizing up the company based on sales and production figures. As far as presentations go, though, I think you've got a real snoozer here," he offered cautiously.

"What makes you say that, George?" Dick asked, although he was beginning to see why as he perused the stack of information.

"Too complex, too much detail. Nothing really jumps out and says, 'Here's where we are,' in a nice concise way." George continued, "I don't know, it just seems by the time you make your point, everyone will be lost. This stuff is great supporting material, but it seems to me there should be some kind of summary measure in each of these areas that really lays out the situation."

Dick nodded, not unsurprised at George's concern or his perception. "I think you're right about this," he replied gratefully, "I'm going to review what we've got here and see what I can come up with."

Dick has identified three principal areas—sales volume, production volume, and raw-materials purchases—about which he will present some data and look at trends over the past three years. From this, a clearer picture should be gained about where the company is and how it got there. George has suggested that some summary measures of the rather large groupings of information Dick has developed might make his presentation more meaningful and more interesting. What might Dick do to more clearly depict sales, sales by customer class, sales by region, production volume, departmental breakdowns, and so forth, so that both he and corporate management might be better prepared to tackle the problem of charting NWMC's direction in the future?

With a detailed, and now clearly summarized, three-year history of NWMC in hand, Dick was confident that his presentation would be a resounding success. As he reviewed his notes and figures, however, a feeling of concern crept over him. "This presentation is by no means complete," he thought. "Some of the departments have very high average sales growth rates, but the monthly sales figures themselves tend to fluctuate wildly. Other departments exhibit a lower growth rate, but on a higher sales volume that seems to fluctuate very little."

Similar situations were observable in sales grouped by customer class. Looking at certain account groupings, Dick had noticed the rapid appreciation in the importance of high-technology engineering firms to NWMC. Once again, though, this high-growth area seemed to be characterized by wide variations in observed data. Furthermore, accounts receivable collections among this group tended to jump around quite a bit as well. Slow collections were always troubling, but were even more so in view of the wide swings in primary aluminum ingot prices that had occurred over the past few years.

"Clearly," Dick thought, "the strategic policy NWMC pursues regarding departments and customer classes to develop must consider how reliable these descriptive measures we've come up with really are. Before I put the wrap on this presentation, I need to develop some feel for the consistency and reliability of all these accumulated data." As he pondered what he hoped would be the final phase of his presentation plight, the telephone range.

"Lennox!" barked the by now familiar voice of the CEO, "we're looking forward to your pitch on Monday. Much of what you come up with is going to be used in the budget allocation for 1982. How's it coming?"

"In the process of wrapping it up, sir," Dick replied. "I'm looking at sales volume and I've analyzed the figures so we can get an idea of trends in a variety of areas of the firm's operations. I'm also reviewing production volume and purchasing, too. I've also done some calculations to make the rather large body of supportive data easier to interpret." He added, "I've noticed some interesting behavior in sales and cash-flow patterns. . . . "

"Good, good," the CEO responded, cutting Dick off. "Sounds like you're right on track."

Dick hung up the phone, reassured. "Now back to the business at hand," he thought.

It has occurred to Dick that his presentation, although currently broad in scope, will be incomplete without some further analysis. He has noticed that certain figures tend to fluctuate considerably more than others. Not wanting to make a hasty or erroneous recommendation, Dick has decided it would be useful to assess the variability of the data he is presenting. How should he go about doing this? What measures would be useful? How might they be interpreted and used in a planning function?

3-17
Computer Data Base Exercise

 From what Laurel could see, the trends identified in the histograms she had prepared earlier reflected several possibilities:

1. The numbers of customers buying from HH Industries are increasing, and their initial purchases are relatively small. With proper "nurturing," these customers should buy increasingly larger quantities as their confidence in the company's quality and service grows.

2. HH Industries' established customers are recognizing the expense of maintaining large inventories. Consequently, their orders will be more frequent and for smaller amounts than before.

3. Large construction or waste management firms which have traditionally maintained their own fleets of equipment may be tending more towards contracting for repairs with smaller service shops.

In addition, there might be a seasonal trend present, which would make sense since adverse winter weather might cause construction slowdowns. (This concept will be addressed in a later chapter.)

Stan Hutchings, VP of Sales, verified that these trends were all very real possibilities. "In fact," he acknowledged, "we can probably target some promotions to take advantage of this information. But even with the decreasing dollars-per-order figures, I'm pretty sure total sales are continuing to increase; at least that's what the 'daily figure' seems to indicate. After all, that's what really matters—the total sales!"

Back in her office, Laurel contemplated Stan's "total sales" philosophy. True, the company's total sales were important, but she knew that each profit center played a key role in the overall health of the corporation. She needed to know if all three locations were pulling their own weight. In addition, Laurel was curious as to whether the trends she had identified were reflected in each profit center, or whether the majority of sales being at the Florida headquarters obscured any important information from the Arizona and Pennsylvania warehouses.

1. Calculate the mean, median and mode for the quarterly data on number of orders and average order size from Chapter 2. Do these numbers support Laurel's intuitive findings from the histograms? Which measure of

central tendency seems most appropriate in this situation? Now calculate the company's total sales dollars for the last four quarters. Is Stan correct in his assumption that the total sales are doing well?

2. Calculate the mean number of daily orders and order size for Profit Center 3 (Pennsylvania) over the last four quarters. Does this warehouse exhibit trends similar to those of the entire company? Is Laurel's planned investigation of the performance of each profit center a good idea?

Laurel caught Hal in his office late Thursday afternoon and gave him a brief outline of her findings.

"This is all quite interesting," Hal responded. "I'd like to get opinions from the staff at Monday's meeting. Think you can have a short presentation worked up? It'd need to be heavy on the conclusions and light on the statistics for this crew!"

"Sure thing," Laurel agreed. "I still want to do some variability testing, then I'll be ready to put the whole picture together. See you back here on Monday."

3. Determine the interquartile ranges of the average order size in each quarter. Compare these to the total range in each case.

4. Using the raw data, calculate the quarterly sample variance and standard deviation values for both the number of orders and the average order size. Compute the coefficient of variation for each quarter.

5. (a) Using Chebyshev's theorem, determine the range of daily number of orders and average order size for the second quarter of 1989 that will include at least 75 percent of the data.
(b) Examine the histograms plotted for Chapter 2 and compare them to the Chebyshev ranges calculated above. How precise is Chebyshev's theorem in establishing the range in each case?

6. Looking at each warehouse separately, calculate the coefficient of variation for both the number of orders and average order size for the entire 12-month period. Are there significant differences between the relative dispersions experienced at each profit center?

7. How would you present your findings to the staff? What recommendations could you make about promotions, future data collection, etc?

3-18
Flow Charts

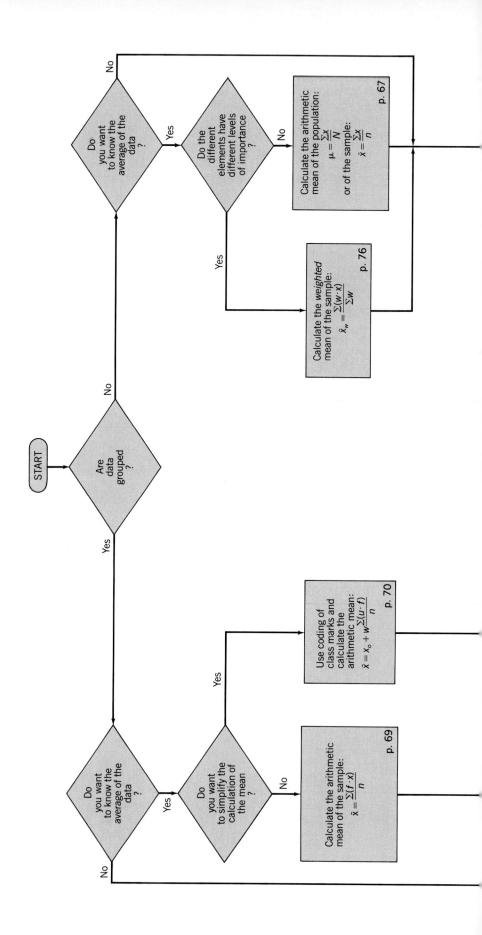

START

Are data grouped ?

No → Yes

No branch:

Do you want to know the average of the data ?

Yes →

Do the different elements have different levels of importance ?

No →

Calculate the arithmetic mean of the population:
$$\mu = \frac{\sum x}{N}$$
or of the sample:
$$\bar{x} = \frac{\sum x}{n}$$

p. 67

Yes →

Calculate the *weighted* mean of the sample:
$$\bar{x}_w = \frac{\sum(w \cdot x)}{\sum w}$$

p. 76

Yes branch:

Do you want to know the average of the data ?

Yes →

Do you want to simplify the calculation of the mean ?

Yes →

Use coding of class marks and calculate the arithmetic mean:
$$\bar{x} = x_o + w\frac{\sum(u \cdot f)}{n}$$

p. 70

No →

Calculate the arithmetic mean of the sample:
$$\bar{x} = \frac{\sum(f \cdot x)}{n}$$

p. 69

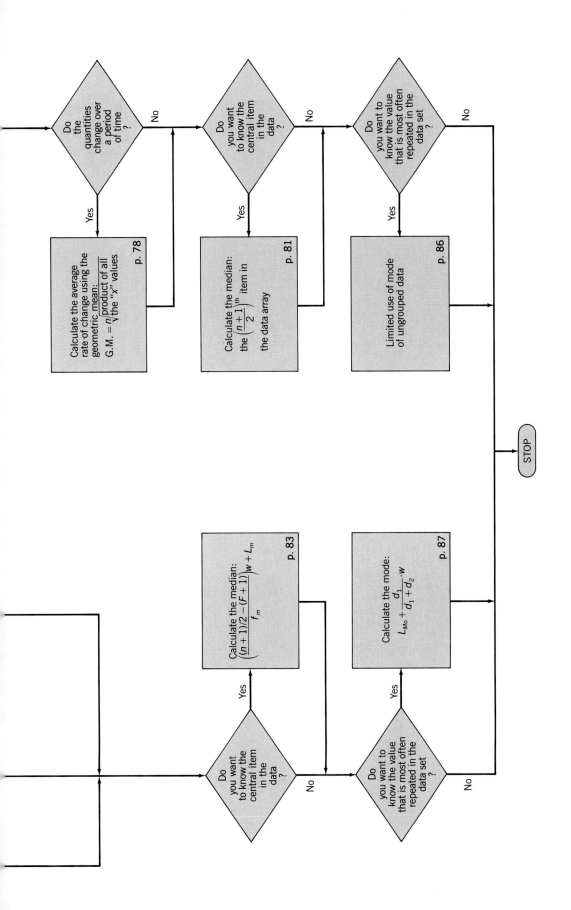

Do the quantities change over a period of time?

No

Yes

Calculate the average rate of change using the geometric mean:
$$G.M. = \sqrt[n]{\text{product of all the "}x\text{" values}}$$

p. 78

Do you want to know the central item in the data?

No

Yes

Calculate the median: the $\left(\frac{n+1}{2}\right)^{\text{th}}$ item in the data array

p. 81

Do you want to know the value that is most often repeated in the data set?

No

Yes

Limited use of mode of ungrouped data

p. 86

Calculate the median:
$$\left(\frac{(n+1)/2 - (F+1)}{f_m}\right)w + L_m$$

p. 83

Do you want to know the central item in the data?

Yes

No

Calculate the mode:
$$L_{Mo} + \frac{d_1}{d_1 + d_2} \cdot w$$

p. 87

Do you want to know the value that is most often repeated in the data set?

Yes

No

STOP

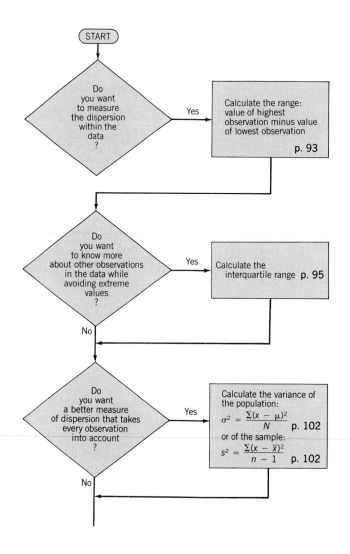

START

Do you want to measure the dispersion within the data ? — Yes → Calculate the range: value of highest observation minus value of lowest observation

p. 93

Do you want to know more about other observations in the data while avoiding extreme values ? — Yes → Calculate the interquartile range p. 95

No

Do you want a better measure of dispersion that takes every observation into account ? — Yes → Calculate the variance of the population:

$$\sigma^2 = \frac{\Sigma(x - \mu)^2}{N} \quad \text{p. 102}$$

or of the sample:

$$s^2 = \frac{\Sigma(x - \bar{x})^2}{n - 1} \quad \text{p. 102}$$

No

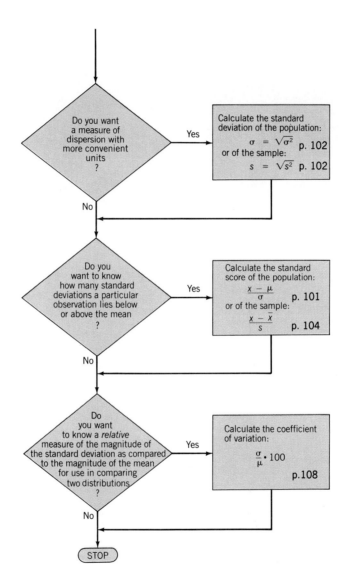

Gamblers have used odds to make bets during most of recorded history. But it wasn't until the seventeenth century that a French nobleman Antoine Gombauld (1607–1684) questioned the mathematical basis for success and failure at the dice tables. He asked the French mathematician Blaise Pascal (1623–1662), "What are the odds of rolling two sixes at least once in twenty-four rolls of a pair of dice?" Pascal solved the problem, having become as interested in the idea of probabilities as was Gombauld. They shared their ideas with the famous mathematician Pierre de Fermat (1601–1665), and the letters written by these three constitute the first academic journals in probability theory. We have no record of the degree of success enjoyed by these gentlemen at the dice tables, but we do know that their curiosity and research introduced many of the concepts we shall study in this chapter and the next.

4

Probability I: Introductory Ideas

■ OBJECTIVES

Chapter 4 introduces the basic concepts of probability (or chance). Together with Chapter 5 it provides a foundation for our study of statistical inference in later chapters. Here, we examine methods of calculating and using probabilities under various conditions. If you are one of 200 students in a class and it seems that the professor calls on you each time the class meets, you might accuse that professor of not calling on students at random. If, on the other hand, you are one student in a class of eight and you never prepare for class, assuming that the professor will not get around to you, then you may be the one who needs to examine probability ideas a bit more.

4-1

History and Relevance of Probability Theory

Early probability theorists

Jacob Bernoulli (1654–1705), Abraham de Moivre (1667–1754), the Reverend Thomas Bayes (1702–1761), and Joseph Lagrange (1736–1813) developed probability formulas and techniques. In the nineteenth century, Pierre Simon, Marquis de Laplace (1749–1827), unified all these early ideas and compiled the first general theory of probability.

Need for probability theory

Probability theory was successfully applied at the gambling tables and, more relevant to our study, eventually to other social and economic problems. The insurance industry, which emerged in the nineteenth century, required precise knowledge about the risk of loss in order to calculate premiums. Within 50 years, many learning centers were studying probability as a tool for understanding social phenomena. Today, the mathematical theory of probability is the basis for statistical applications in both social and decision-making research.

Examples of the use of probability theory

Probability is a part of our everyday lives. In personal and managerial decisions, we face uncertainty and use probability theory whether or not we admit the use of something so sophisticated. When we hear a weather forecast of a 70 percent chance of rain, we change our plans from a picnic to a pool game. Playing bridge, we make some probability estimate before attempting a finesse. Managers who deal with inventories of highly styled women's clothing must wonder about the chances that sales will reach or exceed a certain level, and the buyer who stocks up on skateboards considers the probability of the life of this particular fad. Before Muhammad Ali's highly publicized fight with Leon Spinks, Ali was reputed to have said, "I'll give you **odds** I'm still the greatest when it's over." And when you begin to study for the inevitable quiz attached to the use of this book, you may ask yourself, "What are the chances the professor will ask us to recall something about the history of probability theory?"

We live in a world in which we are unable to forecast the future with complete certainty. Our need to cope with uncertainty leads us to the study and use of probability theory. In many instances we, as concerned citizens, will have some knowledge about the possible outcomes of a decision. By organizing this information and considering it systematically, we will be able to recognize our assumptions, communicate our reasoning to others, and make a sounder decision than we could by using a shot-in-the-dark approach.

Exercises

4-1   The insurance industry uses probability theory to calculate premium rates, but life insurers know for certain that every policyholder is going to die. Does this mean that probability theory does not apply to the life insurance business? Explain.

4-2   "Use of this product may be hazardous to your health. This product contains saccharin which has been determined to cause cancer in laboratory animals." How might probability theory have played a part in this statement?

4-3 Is there really any such thing as an "uncalculated risk"? Explain.

4-4 A well-known soft drink company decides to alter the formula of its oldest and most popular product. How might probability theory be involved in such a decision?

4-2
Some Basic Concepts in Probability

In general, probability is the chance something will happen. Probabilities are expressed as fractions ($\frac{1}{6}$, $\frac{1}{2}$, $\frac{8}{9}$) or as decimals (.167, .500, .889) between zero and 1. Assigning a probability of zero means that something can never happen; a probability of 1 indicates that something will always happen.

An event

In probability theory, an *event* is one or more of the possible outcomes of doing something. If we toss a coin, getting a tail would be an *event,* and getting a head would be another event. Similarly, if we are drawing from a deck of cards, selecting the ace of spades would be an event. An example of an event closer to your life, perhaps, is being picked from a class of 100 students to answer a question. When we hear the frightening predictions of highway traffic deaths, we hope not to be one of those events.

An experiment

The activity that produces such an event is referred to in probability theory as an *experiment.* Using this formal language, we could ask the question, "In a coin-toss *experiment,* what is the probability of the event *head*?" And, of course, if it is a fair coin with an equal chance of coming down on either side (and no chance of landing on its edge), we would answer, "½" or ".5." The set of all possible outcomes of an

Sample space

experiment is called the *sample space* for the experiment. In the coin-toss experiment, the sample space is:

$$S = \{\text{head, tail}\}$$

In the card-drawing experiment, the sample space has fifty-two members: ace of hearts, deuce of hearts, and so on.

Most of us are less excited about coins or cards than we are interested in questions like, "What are the chances of making that plane connection?" or, "What are my chances of getting a second job interview?" In short, we are concerned with the chances that certain events will happen.

Mutually exclusive events

Events are said to be *mutually exclusive* if one and only one of them can take place at a time. Consider again our example of the coin. We have two possible outcomes, heads and tails. On any toss, either heads or tails may turn up, but not both. As a result, the events heads and tails on a single toss are said to be mutually exclusive. Similarly, you will either pass or fail this course or, before the course is over, you may drop it without a grade. Only one of those three outcomes can happen; they are said to be mutually exclusive events. The crucial question to ask in deciding whether events are really mutually exclusive is, "Can two or more of these events occur at one time?" If the answer is yes, the events are *not* mutually exclusive.

A collectively exhaustive list

When a list of the possible events that can result from an experiment includes every possible outcome, the list is said to be *collectively exhaustive.* In our coin example, the list "head and tail" is collectively exhaustive (unless, of course, the coin stands on its edge when we toss it). In a presidential campaign, the list of outcomes "Democratic candidate and Republican candidate" is *not* a collectively exhaustive list of outcomes, since an independent candidate or the candidate of another party could conceivably win.

Exercises

4-5   Give a collectively exhaustive list of the possible outcomes of tossing two dice.

4-6   Which of the following are pairs of mutually exclusive events in the drawing of a single card from a standard deck of fifty-two?
(a)   A heart and a queen   (c)   An even number and a spade
(b)   A club and a red card   (d)   An ace and an even number
Which of the following are mutually exclusive outcomes in the rolling of two dice?
(a)   A total of 5 and a five on one die
(b)   A total of 7 and an even number of points on both dice
(c)   A total of 8 and an odd number of points on both dice
(d)   A total of 9 points and a two on one die
(e)   A total of 10 points and a four on one die

4-7   A batter "takes" (does not swing at) each of the pitches he sees. Give the sample space of outcomes for the following experiments in terms of balls and strikes: the delivery of a) two pitches, b) three pitches.

4-8   Give the probability for each of the following totals in the rolling of two dice: 1, 2, 5, 6, 7, 10, 11.

4-9   In a recent meeting of union members supporting Joe Royal for union president, Royal's leading supporter said "chances are good" that Royal will defeat the single opponent facing him in the election.
(a)   What are the "events" that could take place with regard to the election?
(b)   Is your list collectively exhaustive? Are the events in your list mutually exclusive?
(c)   Disregarding the supporter's comments and knowing no additional information, what probabilities would you assign to each of your events?

4-10   Southern Bell is considering the distribution of funds for a campaign to increase long distance calls within North Carolina. The following table lists the markets that the company considers worthy of focused promotions:

MARKET SEGMENT	COST OF SPECIAL CAMPAIGN AIMED AT GROUP
Minorities	$350,000
Businesspeople	$550,000
Women	$250,000
Professionals and white collar workers	$200,000
Blue collar workers	$250,000

There is up to $800,000 available for these special campaigns.
(a)   Are the market segments listed in the table collectively exhaustive? Are they mutually exclusive?
(b)   Make a collectively exhaustive and mutually exclusive list of the possible events of the spending decision.
(c)   Suppose the company has decided to spend the entire $800,000 on special campaigns. Does this change your answer to part (b)? If so, what is your new answer?

4-3
Three Types of Probability

There are three basic ways of classifying probability. These three represent rather different conceptual approaches to the study of probability theory; in fact, experts disagree about which approach is the proper one to use. Let us begin by defining the:

1. Classical approach
2. Relative frequency approach
3. Subjective approach

CLASSICAL PROBABILITY

Classical probability defined

Classical probability defines the probability that an event will occur as:

$$\text{Probability of an event} = \frac{\substack{\text{Number of outcomes where} \\ \text{the event occurs}}}{\text{Total number of possible outcomes}} \qquad [4\text{-}1]$$

It must be emphasized that in order for Equation 4-1 to be valid, each of the possible outcomes must be equally likely. This is a rather complex way of defining something that may seem intuitively obvious to us, but we can use it to write our coin-toss and dice-rolling examples in symbolic form. First, we would state the question, "What is the probability of getting a head on one toss?" as:

$$P(\text{Head})$$

Then, using formal terms, we get:

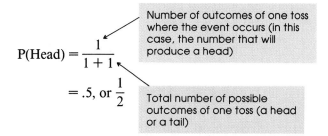

$$P(\text{Head}) = \frac{1}{1+1}$$

Number of outcomes of one toss where the event occurs (in this case, the number that will produce a head)

$$= .5, \text{ or } \frac{1}{2}$$

Total number of possible outcomes of one toss (a head or a tail)

And for the dice-rolling example:

$$P(5) = \frac{1}{1+1+1+1+1+1}$$

Number of outcomes of one roll of the die that will produce a 5

$$= \frac{1}{6}$$

Total number of possible outcomes of one roll of the die (getting a 1, a 2, a 3, a 4, a 5, or a 6)

Classical probability is often called *a priori* probability, because if we keep using orderly examples like fair coins, unbiased dice, and standard decks of cards, we can state the answer in advance (a priori) *without* tossing a coin, rolling a die, or drawing a card. We do not have to perform experiments to make our probability statements about fair coins, standard card decks, and unbiased dice. Instead, we can make statements based on logical reasoning before any experiments take place.

This approach to probability is useful when we deal with card games, dice games, coin tosses, and the like but has serious problems when we try to apply it to the less orderly decision problems we encounter in management. The classical approach to probability assumes a world that does not exist. It assumes away situations that are very unlikely but that could conceivably happen. Such occurrences as a coin landing on its edge, your classroom burning down during a discussion of probabilities, or your eating pizza while on a business trip at the North Pole are all extremely unlikely but not impossible. Nevertheless, the classical approach assumes them all away. Classical probability also assumes a kind of symmetry about the world, and that assumption can get us into trouble. Real-life situations, disorderly and unlikely as they often are, make it useful to define probabilities in other ways.

RELATIVE FREQUENCY OF OCCURRENCE

Suppose we begin asking ourselves complex questions such as, "What is the probability that I will live to be 85?" or, "What are the chances that I will blow one of my stereo speakers if I turn my 200-watt amplifier up to wide open?" or, "What is the probability that the location of a new paper plant on the river near our town will cause a substantial fish kill?" We quickly see that we may not be able to state in advance, without experimentation, what these probabilities are. Other approaches may be more useful.

In the 1800s, British statisticians, interested in a theoretical foundation for calculating risk of losses in life insurance and commercial insurance, began defining probabilities from statistical data collected on births and deaths. Today this approach is called *relative frequency of occurrence*. It defines probability as either:

1. The observed relative frequency of an event in a very large number of trials, or
2. The proportion of times that an event occurs in the long run when conditions are stable.

This method uses the relative frequencies of past occurrences as probabilities. We determine how often something has happened in the past and use that figure to predict the probability that it will happen again in the future. Let us look at an example. Suppose an insurance company knows from past actuarial data that of all males 40 years old, about 60 out of every 100,000 will die within a one-year period. Using this method, the company estimates the probability of death for that age group as:

$$\frac{60}{100,000}, \text{ or } .0006$$

A second characteristic of probabilities established by the relative frequency of occurrence method can be shown by tossing one of our fair coins 300 times. Figure 4-1 illustrates the outcomes of these 300 tosses. Here we can see that although the

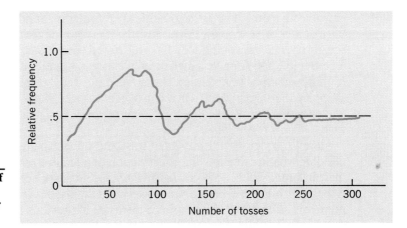

proportion of heads was far from .5 in the first 100 tosses, it seemed to stabilize and approach .5 as the number of tosses increased. In statistical language, we would say that the relative frequency becomes stable as the number of tosses becomes large (if we are tossing the coin under uniform conditions). Thus, when we use the relative frequency approach to establish probabilities, our probability figure will gain accuracy as we increase the number of observations. Of course, this improved accuracy is not free; although more tosses of our coin will produce a more accurate probability of heads occurring, we must bear both the time and the cost of additional observations.

A limitation of relative frequency

One difficulty with the relative frequency approach is that people often use it without evaluating a sufficient number of outcomes. If you heard someone say, "My aunt and uncle got the flu this year, and they are both over 65, so everyone in that age bracket will probably get the flu," you would know that your friend did not base his assumptions on enough evidence. He had insufficient data for establishing a relative frequency of occurrence probability.

But what about a different kind of estimate, one that seems not to be based on statistics at all? Suppose your school's basketball team lost the first ten games of the year. You were a loyal fan, however, and bet $100 that your team would beat Indiana's in the eleventh game. To everyone's surprise, you won your bet. We would have difficulty convincing you that you were statistically incorrect. And you would be right to be skeptical about our argument. Perhaps without knowing that you did so, you may have based your bet on the statistical foundation described in the next approach to establishing probabilities.

SUBJECTIVE PROBABILITIES

Subjective probability defined

Subjective probabilities are based on the beliefs of the person making the probability assessment. In fact, subjective probability can be defined as the probability assigned to an event by an individual, based on whatever evidence is available. This evidence may be in the form of relative frequency of past occurrences, or it may be just an educated guess. Probably the earliest subjective probability estimate of the likelihood of rain occurred when someone's Aunt Bess said, "My corns hurt; I think we're in for a downpour." Subjective assessments of probability permit the widest flexibility of the three concepts we have discussed. The decision maker can use whatever evidence is available and temper this with personal feelings about the situation.

Subjective probability assignments are frequently found when events occur only once or at most a very few times. Say that it is your job to interview and select a new social services caseworker. You have narrowed your choice to three people. Each has an attractive appearance, a high level of energy, abounding self-confidence, a record of past accomplishments, and a state of mind that seems to welcome challenges. What are the chances each will relate to clients successfully? Answering this question and choosing among the three will require you to assign a subjective probability to each person's potential.

Using the subjective approach

Here is one more illustration of this kind of probability assignment. A judge is deciding whether to allow the construction of a nuclear power plant on a site where there is some evidence of a geological fault. He must ask himself the question, "What is the probability of a major nuclear accident at this location?" The fact that there is no relative frequency of occurrence evidence of previous accidents at this location does not excuse him from making a decision. He must use his best judgment in trying to determine the subjective probabilities of a nuclear accident.

Since most higher level social and managerial decisions are concerned with specific, unique situations, rather than with a long series of identical situations, decision makers at this level make considerable use of subjective probabilities.

The subjective approach to assigning probabilities was introduced in 1926 by Frank Ramsey, in his book, *The Foundation of Mathematics and Other Logical Essays.* The concept was further developed by Bernard Koopman, Richard Good, and Leonard Savage, names that appear regularly in advanced work in this field. Professor Savage pointed out that two reasonable people faced with the same evidence could easily come up with quite different subjective probabilities for the same event. The two people who made opposing bets on the outcome of the Indiana basketball game would understand quite well what he meant.

Exercises

4-11 Union shop steward B. Lou Khollar, has drafted a set of wage and benefit demands to be presented to management. To get an idea of worker support for the package, he randomly polls the two largest groups of workers at his plant, the machinists (M) and the inspectors (I). He polls 30 of each group with the following results:

OPINION OF PACKAGE	M	I
Strongly support	9	10
Mildly support	11	3
Undecided	2	2
Mildly oppose	4	8
Strongly oppose	4	7
	30	**30**

(a) What is the probability that a machinist randomly selected from the polled group mildly supports the package?

(b) What is the probability that an inspector randomly selected from the polled group is undecided about the package?

(c) What is the probability that a worker (machinist or inspector) randomly selected from the polled group strongly or mildly supports the package?

(d) What types of probability estimates are these?

4-12 Determine the probabilities of the following events in drawing a card from a standard deck of 52 cards:

(a) A seven
(b) A black card
(c) An ace or a king
(d) A black two or a black three
(e) A red face card (king, queen, or jack)

What type of probability estimates are these?

4-13 Below is a frequency distribution of annual sales commissions from a survey of 300 media salespeople.

ANNUAL COMMISSION	FREQUENCY
$ 0– 4,999	15
5,000– 9,999	25
10,000–14,999	35
15,000–19,999	125
20,000–24,999	70
25,000+	30

Based on this information, what is the probability that a media salesperson makes a commission: (a) between $5000 and $10,000, b) less than $15,000, c) more than $20,000, d) between $15,000 and $20,000.

4-14 General Buck Turgidson is preparing to make his annual budget presentation to the U.S. Senate and is speculating about his chances of getting all or part of his requested budget approved. From his 20 years of experience in making these requests, he has deduced that his chances of getting between 50 and 74 percent of his budget approved are twice as good as those of getting between 75 and 99 percent approved, and two and one-half times as good as those of getting between 25 and 49 percent approved. Further, the general believes that there is no chance of less than 25 percent of his budget's being approved. Finally, the entire budget has been approved only once during the general's tenure, and the general does not expect this pattern to change. What are the probabilities of 0–24%, 25–49%, 50–74%, 75–99%, and 100% approval, according to the general?

4-15 The office manager of an insurance company has the following data on the functioning of the copiers in the office:

COPIER	DAYS FUNCTIONING	DAYS OUT OF SERVICE
1	209	51
2	217	43
3	258	2
4	229	31
5	247	13

What is the probability of a copier's being out of service, based on this data?

4-16 Classify the following probability estimates as to their type (classical, relative frequency, or subjective):

(a) The probability of scoring on a penalty shot in ice hockey is .47.
(b) The probability that the current mayor will resign is .85.

(c) The probability of rolling 2 sixes with 2 dice is 1/36.
(d) The probability that a president elected in a year ending in zero will die in office is 7/10.
(e) The probability that you will go to Europe this year is .14.

4-4
Probability Rules

Most managers who use probabilities are concerned with two conditions:

1. The case where one event *or* another will occur
2. The situation where two or more events will *both* occur

We are interested in the first case when we ask, "What is the probability that today's demand will exceed our inventory?" To illustrate the second situation, we could ask, "What is the probability that today's demand will exceed our inventory *and* that more than 10 percent of our sales force will not report for work?" In the sections to follow, we shall illustrate methods of determining answers to questions like these under a variety of conditions.

SOME COMMONLY USED SYMBOLS, DEFINITIONS, AND RULES

Symbol for a Marginal Probability. In probability theory, we use symbols to simplify the presentation of ideas. As we discussed earlier in this chapter, the probability of the event *A* would be expressed as:

$$P(A) \quad \text{the} \quad \boxed{\text{probability}} \quad \text{of} \quad \boxed{\text{event } A} \quad \text{happening}$$

Marginal or unconditional probability

A *single* probability means that only one event can take place. It is called a *marginal* or *unconditional probability.* To illustrate, let us suppose that 50 members of a school class drew tickets to see which student would get a free trip to the National Rock Festival. Any one of the students could calculate his or her chances of winning by the formulation:

$$P(\text{Winning}) = \frac{1}{50}$$
$$= .02$$

In this case, a student's chance is one in 50, because we are certain that the possible events are mutually exclusive; that is, only one student can win at a time.

Venn diagrams

There is a nice diagrammatic way to illustrate this example and other probability concepts. We use a pictorial representation called a *Venn diagram,* after the nineteenth-century English mathematician, John Venn. In these diagrams, the entire sample space is represented by a rectangle, and events are represented by parts of the rectangle. If two events *are* mutually exclusive, their parts of the rectangle will not overlap each other, as shown in Fig. 4-2(a). If two events are *not* mutually exclusive, their parts of the rectangle *will* overlap, as in Fig. 4-2(b).

Since probabilities behave a lot like areas, we shall let the rectangle have an area of 1 (because the probability of *something* happening is 1). Then the probability of an

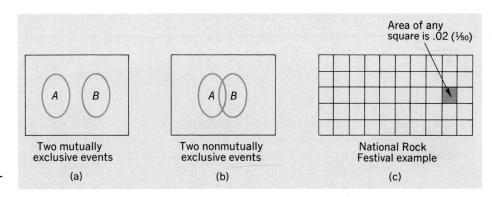

FIGURE 4-2
Some Venn diagrams

Two mutually exclusive events
(a)

Two nonmutually exclusive events
(b)

Area of any square is .02 (1/50)

National Rock Festival example
(c)

event is the area of *its* part of the rectangle. Figure 4-2(c) illustrates this for the National Rock Festival example. There the rectangle is divided into 50 equal, non-overlapping parts.

Probability of one or more mutually exclusive events

Addition Rule for Mutually Exclusive Events. Often, however, we are interested in the probability that one thing *or* another will occur. If these two events are mutually exclusive, we can express this probability using the addition rule for mutually exclusive events. This rule is expressed symbolically as:

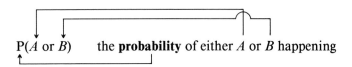

P(*A* or *B*)   the **probability** of either *A* or *B* happening

and is calculated as follows:

$$P(A \text{ or } B) = P(A) + P(B) \qquad [4\text{-}2]$$

This addition rule is illustrated by the Venn diagram in Fig. 4-3, where we note that the area in the two circles together (denoting the event *A or B*) is the sum of the areas of the two circles.

Now to use this formula in an example. Five equally capable students are waiting for a summer job interview with a company that has announced that it will hire only one of five by random drawing. The group consists of Bill, Helen, John, Sally, and Walter. If our question is, "What is the probability that John will be the candidate?" we can use Equation 4-1 and give the answer.

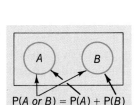

$P(A \text{ or } B) = P(A) + P(B)$

FIGURE 4-3
Venn diagram for the addition rule for mutually exclusive events

$$P(\text{John}) = \frac{1}{5}$$
$$= .2$$

If, however, we ask, "What is the probability that either John *or* Sally will be the candidate?" we would use Equation 4-2:

$$P(\text{John or Sally}) = P(\text{John}) + P(\text{Sally})$$
$$= \frac{1}{5} + \frac{1}{5}$$
$$= \frac{2}{5}$$
$$= .4$$

TABLE 4-1 Family-Size Data

Number of children	0	1	2	3	4	5	6 or more
Proportion of families having this many children	.05	.10	.30	.25	.15	.10	.05

Let's calculate the probability of two or more events happening once more. Table 4-1 contains data on the sizes of families in a certain town. We are interested in the question, "What is the probability that a family chosen at random from this town will have four or more children (that is, four, five, six or more children)?" Using Equation 4-2, we can calculate the answer as:

$$P(4, 5, 6 \text{ or more}) = P(4) + P(5) + P(6 \text{ or more})$$
$$= .15 + .10 + .05$$
$$= .30$$

A special case of Equation 4-2

There is an important special case of Equation 4-2. For any event A, either A happens or it doesn't. So the events A and *not A* are exclusive and exhaustive. Applying Equation 4-2 yields the result:

$$P(A) + P(not\ A) = 1$$

or equivalently:

$$P(A) = 1 - P(not\ A)$$

For example, referring back to Table 4-1, the probability of a family's having five or fewer children is most easily obtained by subtracting from 1 the probability of the family's having six or more children, and thus is seen to be .95.

Probability of one or more events *not* mutually exclusive

Addition Rule for Events That Are Not Mutually Exclusive. If two events are not mutually exclusive, it is possible for both events to occur. In these cases, our addition rule must be modified. For example, what is the probability of drawing either an ace *or* a heart from a deck of cards? Obviously, the events ace and heart can occur together because we could draw the ace of hearts. Thus, ace and heart are not mutually exclusive events. We must adjust our Equation 4-2 to avoid double counting; that is, we have to *reduce* the probability of drawing either an ace or a heart *by the chance* that we could draw both of them together. As a result, the correct equation for the probability of one or more of two events that are not mutually exclusive is:

Probability of A happening   Probability of A and B happening together

$$P(A \text{ or } B) = P(A) + P(B) - P(AB)$$ [4-3]

Probability of A or B happening when A and B are *not* mutually exclusive

Probability of B happening

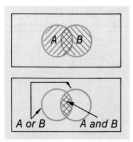

FIGURE 4-4

Venn diagram for the addition rule for two events not mutually exclusive

A Venn diagram illustrating Equation 4-3 is given in Fig. 4-4. There, the event *A or B* is outlined with a heavy line. The event *A and B* is the cross-hatched wedge in the middle. If we add the areas of circles *A* and *B*, we *double count* the area of the wedge, and so we must subtract it, to make sure it is counted only once.

Using Equation 4-3 to determine the probability of drawing either an ace *or* a heart, we can calculate:

$$P(\text{Ace or Heart}) = P(\text{Ace}) + P(\text{Heart}) - P(\text{Ace and Heart})$$

$$= \frac{4}{52} + \frac{13}{52} - \frac{1}{52}$$

$$= \frac{16}{52} \text{ or } \frac{4}{13}$$

Let's do a second example. The employees of a certain company have elected five of their number to represent them on the employee-management productivity council. Profiles of the five are as follows:

1. male   age 30
2. male   32
3. female   45
4. female   20
5. male   40

This group decides to elect a spokesperson by drawing a name from a hat. Our question is, "What is the probability the spokesperson will be *either* female *or* over 35?" Using Equation 4-3, we can set up the solution to our question like this:

$$P(\text{Female or Over 35}) = P(\text{Female}) + P(\text{Over 35}) - P(\text{Female and Over 35})$$

$$= \frac{2}{5} + \frac{2}{5} - \frac{1}{5}$$

$$= \frac{3}{5}$$

We can check our work by inspection and see that, of the five people in the group, three would fit the requirements of being either female or over 35.

Exercises

From the Venn diagrams below, which indicate the number of outcomes of an experiment corresponding to each event and the number of outcomes that do not correspond to either event, give the probabilities indicated:

4-17   Total Outcomes = 60

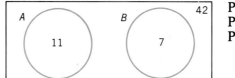

$P(A) =$
$P(B) =$
$P(A \text{ or } B) =$

4-18 Total Outcomes = 50

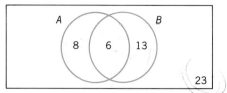

$P(A) =$
$P(B) =$
$P(A \text{ or } B) =$

4-19 An urn contains 75 marbles: 35 are blue, and 25 of these blue marbles are swirled. The rest of them are red, and 30 of the red ones are swirled. The marbles that are not swirled are clear. What is the probability of drawing:

(a) A blue marble from the urn?   (d) A red, clear marble?
(b) A clear marble from the urn?   (e) A swirled marble?
(c) A blue, swirled marble?

4-20 The Herr-McFee Company, which produces nuclear fuel rods, must X-ray and inspect each rod before shipping. Karen Wood, an inspector, has noted that for every 1,000 fuel rods she inspects, 10 have interior flaws, 8 have casing flaws, and 5 have both flaws. In her quarterly report, Karen must include the probability of flaws in fuel rods. What is this probability?

4-21 An inspector on the Alaskan Pipeline has the task of comparing the reliability of two pumping stations. Each station is susceptible to two kinds of failure: pump failure and leakage. When either (or both) occur, the station must be shut down. The data at hand indicate that the following probabilities prevail:

STATION	P(PUMP FAILURE)	P(LEAKAGE)	P(BOTH)
1	.07	.10	0
2	.09	.12	.06

Which station has the higher probability of being shut down?

4-22 The HAL Corporation wishes to improve the resistance of its personal computer to disk-drive and keyboard failures. At present, the design of the computer is such that disk-drive failures occur only one-third as often as keyboard failures. The probability of simultaneous disk-drive and keyboard failure is .05.

(a) If the computer is 80 percent resistant to disk-drive and/or keyboard failure, how low must the disk-drive failure probability be?
(b) If the keyboard is improved so that it fails only twice as often as the disk-drive (and the simultaneous failure probability is still .05), will the disk-drive failure probability from part (a) yield a resistance to disk-drive and/or keyboard failure higher or lower than 90 percent?

4-23 In this section, two expressions were developed for the probability of either of two events, A or B, occurring. Referring to Equations 4-2 and 4-3:

(a) What can you say about the probability of A and B occurring simultaneously when A and B are *mutually exclusive?*
(b) Develop an expression for the probability that at least one of three events, A, B, or C, could occur, i.e., P(A or B or C). Do *not* assume that A, B, and C are mutually exclusive of each other.
(c) Rewrite your expression for the case in which A and B are mutually exclusive, but A and C and B and C are not mutually exclusive.
(d) Rewrite your expression for the case in which A and B and A and C are mutually exclusive, but not B and C.
(e) Rewrite your expression for the case in which A, B, and C are mutually exclusive of the others.

Probabilities Under Conditions of Statistical Independence

Independence defined

When two events happen, the outcome of the first event may or may not have an effect on the outcome of the second event. That is, the events may be either dependent or independent. In this section, we examine events that are *statistically independent:* The occurrence of one event *has no effect* on the probability of the occurrence of any other event. There are three types of probabilities under statistical independence:

1. Marginal
2. Joint
3. Conditional

MARGINAL PROBABILITIES UNDER STATISTICAL INDEPENDENCE

Marginal probability of independent events

As we explained previously, a marginal or unconditional probability is the simple probability of the occurrence of an event. In a fair coin toss, $P(H) = .5$, and $P(T) = .5$; that is, the probability of heads equals .5, and the probability of tails equals .5. This is true for every toss, no matter how many tosses have been made or what their outcomes have been. Every toss stands alone and is in no way connected with any other toss. Thus the outcome of *each* toss of a fair coin is an event that is statistically independent of the outcomes of *every other* toss of the coin.

Imagine that we have a biased or unfair coin that has been altered in such a way that heads occurs .90 of the time and tails .10 of the time. On each individual toss, $P(H) = .90$, and $P(T) = .10$. The outcome of any particular toss is completely unrelated to the outcomes of the tosses that may precede or follow it. The outcomes of several tosses of *this* coin are statistically independent events, too, even though the coin is biased.

JOINT PROBABILITIES UNDER STATISTICAL INDEPENDENCE

Multiplication rule for joint, independent events

The probability of two or more independent events occurring together or in succession is the product of their marginal probabilities. Mathematically, this is stated:

$$P(AB) = P(A) \times P(B) \qquad [4\text{-}4]$$

where:

- $P(AB)$ = probability of events A and B occurring together or in succession; this is known as a *joint probability*
- $P(A)$ = marginal probability of event A occurring
- $P(B)$ = marginal probability of event B occurring

The fair coin example

In terms of the fair coin example, the probability of heads on two successive tosses is the probability of heads on the first toss (which we shall call H_1) times the probability of heads on the second toss (H_2). That is, $P(H_1 H_2) = P(H_1) \times P(H_2)$. We have shown that the events are statistically independent, because the probability of any outcome is not affected by any preceding outcome. Therefore, the probability of heads on any toss is .5, and $P(H_1H_2) = .5 \times .5 = .25$. Thus, the probability of heads on two successive tosses is .25.

Likewise, the probability of getting three heads on three successive tosses is $P(H_1H_2H_3) = .5 \times .5 \times .5 = .125$.

Assume next that we are going to toss an unfair coin that has $P(H) = .8$ and $P(T) = .2$. The events (outcomes) are independent, because the probabilities of all tosses are exactly the same—the individual tosses are completely separate and in no way affected by any other toss or outcome. Suppose our question is, "What is the probability of getting three heads on three successive tosses?" We use Equation 4-4 and discover that:

$$P(H_1H_2H_3) = P(H_1) \times P(H_2) \times P(H_3) = .8 \times .8 \times .8 = .512$$

Now let us ask the probability of getting three tails on three successive tosses:

$$P(T_1T_2T_3) = P(T_1) \times P(T_2) \times P(T_3) = .2 \times .2 \times .2 = .008$$

Note that these two probabilities do not add up to 1 because the events $H_1H_2H_3$ and $T_1T_2T_3$ do not constitute a collectively exhaustive list. They *are* mutually exclusive, because if one occurs, the other cannot.

Constructing a probability tree

We can make the probabilities of events even more explicit using a *probability tree*. Figure 4-5 is a probability tree showing the possible outcomes and their respective probabilities for one toss of a fair coin.

FIGURE 4-5

Probability tree of one toss

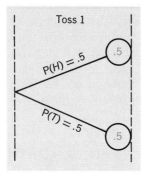

One toss, two possible outcomes

For toss 1 we have two possible outcomes, heads and tails, each with a probability of .5. Assume that the outcome of toss 1 is heads. We toss again. The second toss has two possible outcomes, heads and tails, each with a probability of .5. In Fig. 4-6 we add these two branches of the tree.

FIGURE 4-6

Probability tree of partial second toss

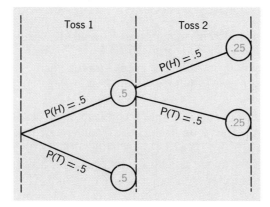

Next we consider the possibility that the outcome of toss 1 is tails. Then the second toss must stem from the lower branch representing toss 1. Thus in Fig. 4-7, we add two more branches to the tree. Notice that on two tosses, we have four possible outcomes: H_1H_2, H_1T_2, T_1H_2, and T_1T_2 (remember that the subscripts indicate the toss number and that T_2, for example, means tails on toss 2). Thus, after two tosses, we may arrive at any one of four possible points. Since we are going to toss three times, we must add more branches to the tree.

FIGURE 4-7

**Probability tree of
two tosses**

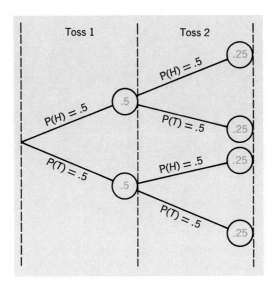

Three tosses, eight
possible outcomes

Assuming that we have had heads on the first two tosses, we are now ready to begin adding branches for the third toss. As before, the two possible outcomes are heads and tails, each with a probability of .5. The first step is shown in Fig. 4-8. The additional

FIGURE 4-8

**Probability tree of
partial third toss**

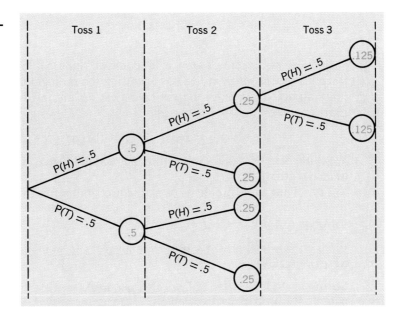

All tosses are
independent

branches are added in exactly the same manner. The completed probability tree is shown in Fig. 4-9. Notice that both heads and tails have a probability of .5 of occurring no matter how far from the origin (first toss) any particular toss may be. **This follows from our definition of independence: No event is affected by the events preceding or following it.**

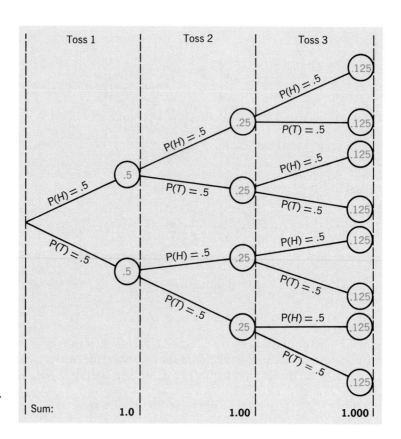

FIGURE 4-9
Completed
probability tree

Suppose we are going to toss a fair coin and want to know the probability that all three tosses will result in heads. Expressing the problem symbolically, we want to know $P(H_1H_2H_3)$. From the mathematical definition of the joint probability of independent events, we know that:

$$P(H_1H_2H_3) = P(H_1) \times P(H_2) \times P(H_3) = .5 \times .5 \times .5 = .125$$

We could have read this answer from the probability tree in Fig. 4-9 by following the branches giving $H_1H_2H_3$.

Try solving these problems using the probability tree in Fig. 4-9:

EXAMPLE 1

Outcomes in a
particular order

What is the probability of getting tails, heads, tails, *in that order* on three successive tosses of a fair coin?

Solution $P(T_1H_2T_3) = P(T_1) \times P(H_2) \times P(T_3) = .125$. Following the prescribed path on the probability tree will give us the same answer. ∎

EXAMPLE 2

What is the probability of getting tails, tails, heads *in that order* on three successive tosses of a fair coin?

Solution If we follow the branches giving tails on the first toss, tails on the second toss, and heads on the third toss, we arrive at the probability of .125. Thus, $P(T_1T_2H_3) = .125$.

It is important to notice that the probability of arriving at a given point by a given route is *not* the same as the probability of, say, heads on the third toss. $P(H_1T_2H_3) = .125$, but $P(H_3) = .5$. The first is a case of *joint probability;* that is, the probability of getting heads on the first toss, tails on the second, and heads on the third. The latter, by contrast, is simply the *marginal probability* of getting heads on a particular toss, in this instance toss 3.

Notice that the sum of the probabilities of all the possible outcomes for each toss is 1. This results from the fact that we have mutually exclusive and collectively exhaustive lists of outcomes. These are given in Table 4-2. ■

EXAMPLE 3

Outcomes in terms of "at least"

What is the probability of *at least* two heads on three tosses?

Solution Recalling that the probabilities of mutually exclusive events are additive, we can note the possible ways that at least two heads on three tosses can occur, and we can sum their individual probabilities. The outcomes satisfying the requirement are $H_1H_2H_3$, $H_1H_2T_3$, $H_1T_2H_3$, and $T_1H_2H_3$. Since each of these has an individual probability of .125, the sum is .5. Thus the probability of at least two heads on three tosses is .5. ■

EXAMPLE 4

What is the probability of *at least* one tail on three tosses?

Solution There is only one case in which no tails occur, namely, $H_1H_2H_3$. Therefore we can simply subtract for the answer:

$$1 - P(H_1H_2H_3) = 1 - .125 = .875$$

The probability of at least one tail occurring in three successive tosses is .875. ■

TABLE 4-2 Lists of Outcomes

1 TOSS		2 TOSSES		3 TOSSES	
Possible outcomes	Probability	Possible outcomes	Probability	Possible outcomes	Probability
H_1	.5	H_1H_2	.25	$H_1H_2H_3$	.125
T_1	.5	H_1T_2	.25	$H_1H_2T_3$	.125
	1.0	T_1H_2	.25	$H_1T_2H_3$	.125
		T_1T_2	.25	$H_1T_2T_3$	.125
			1.00	$T_1H_2H_3$	.125
				$T_1H_2T_3$	.125
				$T_1T_2H_3$	.125
				$T_1T_2T_3$	.125
					1.000

EXAMPLE 5

What is the probability of *at least* one head on two tosses?

Solution The possible ways a head may occur are H_1H_2, H_1T_2, T_1H_2. Each of these has a probability of .25. Therefore, the probability of at least one head on two tosses is .75. Alternatively, we could consider the case in which no head occurs—namely, T_1T_2—and subtract its probability from 1; that is:

$$1 - P(T_1T_2) = 1 - .25 = .75 \qquad \blacksquare$$

CONDITIONAL PROBABILITIES UNDER STATISTICAL INDEPENDENCE

Conditional probability

Thus far we have considered two types of probabilities, marginal (or unconditional) probability and joint probability. Symbolically, marginal probability is $P(A)$ and joint probability is $P(AB)$. Besides these two, there is one other type of probability, known as *conditional* probability. Symbolically, conditional probability is written:

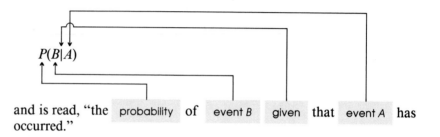

and is read, "the probability of event B given that event A has occurred."

Conditional probability is the probability that a second event (B) will occur *if* a first event (A) has already happened.

Conditional probability of independent events

For statistically independent events, the conditional probability of event B given that event A has occurred is simply the probability of event B:

$$P(B|A) = P(B) \qquad [4\text{-}5]$$

At first glance, this may seem contradictory. Remember, however, that by definition, independent events are those whose probabilities are in no way affected by the occurrence of each other. In fact, statistical independence is defined symbolically as the condition in which $P(B|A) = P(B)$.

We can understand conditional probability better by solving an illustrative problem. Our question is, "What is the probability that the second toss of a fair coin will result in heads, given that heads resulted on the first toss?" Symbolically, this is written as $P(H_2|H_1)$. Remember that for two independent events, the results of the first toss have absolutely no effect on the results of the second toss. Since the probabilities of heads and tails are identical for every toss, the probability of heads on the second toss is .5. Thus, we must say that $P(H_2|H_1) = .5$.

Table 4-3 summarizes the three types of probabilities and their mathematical formulas under conditions of statistical independence.

TABLE 4-3 Probabilities Under Statistical Independence

TYPE OF PROBABILITY	SYMBOL	FORMULA
Marginal	$P(A)$	$P(A)$
Joint	$P(AB)$	$P(A) \times P(B)$
Conditional	$P(B|A)$	$P(B)$

Exercises

4-24 What is the probability that a couple's second child will be:
  (a) A boy, given that their first child was a girl?
  (b) A girl, given that their first child was a girl?

4-25 In rolling two dice, what is the probability of rolling:
  (a) A total of 7 on the first roll, followed by a total of 11 on the second roll?
  (b) A total of 21 on the first two rolls combined?
  (c) A total of 6 on the first three rolls combined?

4-26 What is the probability that, in selecting two cards one at a time from a deck with replacement, the second card is:
  (a) A face card, given that the first card was red?
  (b) An ace, given that the first card was a face card?
  (c) A black jack, given that the first card was a red ace?

4-27 George, Richard, Paul, and John play the following game. Each man takes one of four balls numbered 1 through 4 from an urn. The man who draws ball 4 loses. The other three return their balls to the urn and draw again. This continues until there are only two balls left, at which point the man who draws ball 1 wins.
  (a) What is the probability that John does not lose in the first two draws?
  (b) What is the probability that Paul wins the game?

4-28 The health department routinely conducts two independent inspections of each restaurant, with the restaurant passing only if both inspectors pass it. Inspector A is very experienced, and, hence, passes only 2 percent of restaurants that actually do have health code violations. Inspector B is less experienced and passes 7 percent of restaurants with violations. What is the probability that:
  (a) Inspector A passes a restaurant, given that inspector B has found a violation?
  (b) Inspector B passes a restaurant with a violation, given that inspector A passes it?
  (c) A restaurant with a violation is passed by the health department.

4-29 The four floodgates of a small hydroelectric dam fail and are repaired independently of each other. From experience, it's known that each floodgate is out of order 4 percent of the time.
  (a) If floodgate 1 is out of order, what is the probability that floodgates 2 and 3 are out of order?
  (b) During a tour of the dam, you are told that the chances of all four floodgates being out of order are less than 1 in 5,000,000. Is this statement true?

4-30 Rob Rales is preparing a report that his employer, the Titre Corporation, will eventually deliver to the Federal Aviation Administration. First, the report must be approved by Rob's group leader, department head, and division chief (in that order). Rob knows from experience that the three managers act independently. Further, he knows that his group leader approves 85 percent of his reports, his department head approves 80 percent of the reports written by Rob that reach him, and his division chief approves 82 percent of Rob's work.

(a) What is the probability that the first version of Rob's report is submitted to the FAA?

(b) What is the probability that the first version of Rob's report is approved by his group leader and department head, but is not approved by his division chief?

4-31 Sol O'Tarry, a prison guard, has been reviewing the prison records on attempted escapes by inmates. He has data covering the last 45 years that the prison has been opened, arranged by seasons. The data are summarized in the table below:

ATTEMPTED ESCAPES	WINTER	SPRING	SUMMER	FALL
0	3	2	1	0
1–5	15	10	11	12
6–10	15	12	11	16
11–15	5	8	7	7
16–20	3	4	6	5
21–25	2	4	5	3
More than 26	2	5	4	2
	45	45	45	45

(a) What is the probability that in a year selected at random, the number of escapes was between sixteen and twenty during the winter?

(b) What is the probability that more than ten escapes were attempted during a randomly chosen summer season?

(c) What is the probability that between eleven and twenty escapes were attempted during a randomly chosen season? (*Hint:* Group the data together.)

4-32 Bill Borde, top advertising executive for Grapevine Concepts, has just launched a publicity campaign for a new restaurant in town, The Black Angus. Bill has just installed four billboards on a highway outside of town, and he knows from experience the probabilities that each will be noticed by a randomly chosen motorist. The probability of the first billboard's being noticed by a motorist is .75. The probability of the second's being noticed is .82, the third has a probability of .87 of being noticed, and the probability of the fourth sign's being noticed is .9. Assuming that the event that a motorist notices any particular billboard is independent of whether or not he notices the others, what is the probability that:

(a) All four billboards will be noticed by a randomly chosen motorist?

(b) The first and fourth, but not the second and third, billboards will be noticed?

(c) Exactly one of the billboards will be noticed?

(d) None of the billboards will be noticed?

(e) The third and fourth billboards won't be noticed?

4-6
Probabilities Under Conditions of Statistical Dependence

Dependence defined

Statistical dependence exists when the probability of some event is dependent upon or affected by the occurrence of some other event. Just as with independent events, the types of probabilities under statistical dependence are:

1. Conditional
2. Joint
3. Marginal

CONDITIONAL PROBABILITIES UNDER STATISTICAL DEPENDENCE

Conditional and joint probabilities under statistical dependence are more involved than marginal probabilities are. We shall discuss conditional probabilities first, because the concept of joint probabilities is best illustrated by using conditional probabilities as a basis.

Examples of conditional probability of dependent events

Assume that we have one box containing ten balls distributed as follows:

- Three are colored and dotted
- One is colored and striped
- Two are gray and dotted
- Four are gray and striped

The probability of drawing any one ball from this box is .1, since there are ten balls, each with equal probability of being drawn. The discussion of the following examples will be facilitated by reference to Table 4-4 and to Fig. 4-10, which shows the contents of the box in diagram form.

TABLE 4-4 Color and Configuration of 10 Balls

Event	Probability of event	
1	.1	
2	.1	colored and dotted
3	.1	
4	.1	colored and striped
5	.1	gray and dotted
6	.1	
7	.1	
8	.1	gray and striped
9	.1	
10	.1	

EXAMPLE 1

Suppose someone draws a colored ball from the box. What is the probability that it is dotted? What is the probability it is striped?

Solution This question can be expressed symbolically as $P(D|C)$, or, "What is the conditional probability that this ball is dotted, *given* that it is colored?"

FIGURE 4-10

Contents of the box

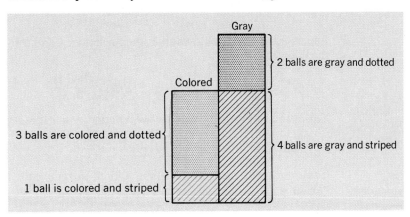

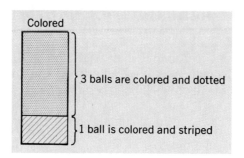

FIGURE 4-11

Probability of dotted and striped, given colored

Colored

3 balls are colored and dotted

1 ball is colored and striped

We have been told that the ball that was drawn is colored. Therefore, to calculate the probability that the ball is dotted, we will ignore *all* the gray balls and concern ourselves with colored only. In diagram form, we consider only what is shown in Fig. 4-11.

From the statement of the problem, we know that there are four colored balls, three of which are dotted and one of which is striped. Our problem is now to find the simple probabilities of dotted and striped. To do so, we divide the number of balls in each category by the total number of colored balls:

$$P(D|C) = \frac{3}{4} = .75$$

$$P(S|C) = \frac{1}{4} = .25$$

$$\overline{1.00}$$

In other words, three-fourths of the colored balls are dotted, and one-fourth of the colored balls are striped. Thus, the probability of dotted, given that the ball is colored, is .75. Likewise, the probability of striped, given that the ball is colored, is .25. ■

Now we can see how our reasoning will enable us to develop the formula for conditional probability under statistical dependence. We can first assure ourselves that these events *are* statistically dependent by observing that the color of the balls determines the probabilities that they are either striped or dotted. For example, a gray ball is more likely to be striped than a colored ball is. Since color affects the probability of striped or dotted, these two events are dependent.

Formula for conditional probability of dependent events

To calculate the probability of dotted given colored, P(D|C), we divided the probability of colored and dotted balls (3 out of 10, or .3) by the probability of colored balls (4 out of 10, or .4):

$$P(D|C) = \frac{P(DC)}{P(C)}$$

Expressed as a general formula using the letters *A* and *B* to represent the two events, the equation is:

$$P(B|A) = \frac{P(BA)}{P(A)}$$ [4-6]

This is the formula for *conditional probability under statistical dependence.*

EXAMPLE 2

Continuing with our example of the colored and gray balls, let's answer the questions, "What is P(D|G)?" and, "What is P(S|G)?"

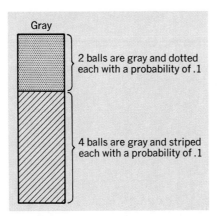

Gray

2 balls are gray and dotted each with a probability of .1

4 balls are gray and striped each with a probability of .1

FIGURE 4-12

Probability of dotted and striped, given gray

Solution

$$P(D|G) = \frac{P(DG)}{P(G)} = \frac{.2}{.6} = \frac{1}{3}$$

$$P(S|G) = \frac{P(SG)}{P(G)} = \frac{.4}{.6} = \frac{2}{3}$$

$$\overline{1.0}$$

The problem is shown diagrammatically in Fig. 4-12.

The total probability of gray is .6 (6 out of 10 balls). To determine the probability that the ball (which we know is gray) will be dotted, we divide the probability of gray and dotted (.2) by the probability of gray (.6), or .2/.6 = 1/3. Similarly, to determine the probability that the ball will be striped, we divide the probability of gray and striped (.4) by the probability of gray (.6), or .4/.6 = 2/3. ∎

EXAMPLE 3

Calculate $P(G|D)$ and $P(C|D)$.

Solution Figure 4-13 shows the contents of the box arranged according to the striped or dotted markings on the balls. Since we have been told that the ball that was drawn is dotted, we can disregard striped and consider only dotted.

FIGURE 4-13

Contents of the box arranged by configuration, striped and dotted

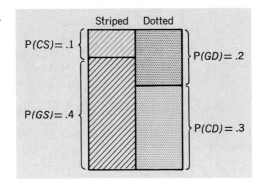

Striped   Dotted

$P(CS) = .1$

$P(GD) = .2$

$P(GS) = .4$

$P(CD) = .3$

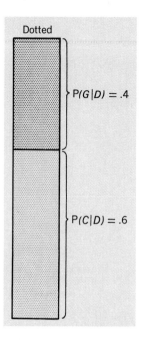

Dotted

$P(G|D) = .4$

$P(C|D) = .6$

FIGURE 4-14
**Probability of colored
and gray, given dotted**

Now see Figure 4-14, showing the probabilities of colored and gray, given dotted. Notice that the relative proportions of the two are as .4 is to .6. The calculations used to arrive at these proportions were:

$$P(G|D) = \frac{P(GD)}{P(D)} = \frac{.2}{.5} = \ .4$$

$$P(C|D) = \frac{P(CD)}{P(D)} = \frac{.3}{.5} = \ .6$$

$$\overline{1.0}$$ ■

EXAMPLE 4

Calculate $P(C|S)$ and $P(G|S)$.

Solution

$$P(C|S) = \frac{P(CS)}{P(S)} = \frac{.1}{.5} = \ .2$$

$$P(G|S) = \frac{P(GS)}{P(S)} = \frac{.4}{.5} = \ .8$$

$$\overline{1.0}$$ ■

JOINT PROBABILITIES UNDER STATISTICAL DEPENDENCE

We have shown that the formula for conditional probability under conditions of statistical dependence is:

$$P(B|A) = \frac{P(BA)}{P(A)}$$ [4-6]

If we solve this for P(*BA*) by cross multiplication, we have the formula for *joint probability under conditions of statistical dependence:*

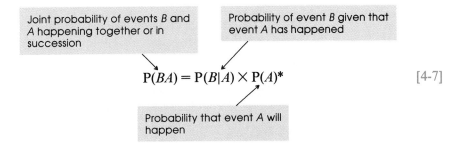

$$P(BA) = P(B|A) \times P(A)* \qquad [4\text{-}7]$$

Joint probability of events *B* and *A* happening together or in succession

Probability of event *B* given that event *A* has happened

Probability that event *A* will happen

Notice that this formula is *not* P(*BA*) = P(*B*) × P(*A*), as it would be under conditions of statistical independence.

Converting the general formula P(*BA*) = P(*B*|*A*) × P(*A*) to our example and to the terms of colored, gray, dotted, and striped, we have P(*CD*) = P(*C*|*D*) × P(*D*), or P(*CD*) = .6 × .5 = .3. Here, .6 is the probability of colored, given dotted (computed in example 3 above), and .5 is the probability of dotted (also computed in example 3).

P(*CD*) = .3 can be verified in Table 4-4, where we originally arrived at the probability by inspection: Three balls out of ten are colored and dotted.

Several examples   The following joint probabilities are computed in the same manner and can also be substantiated by reference to Table 4-4.

$$P(CS) = P(C|S) \times P(S) = .2 \times .5 = .1$$

$$P(GD) = P(G|D) \times P(D) = .4 \times .5 = .2$$

$$P(GS) = P(G|S) \times P(S) = .8 \times .5 = .4$$

MARGINAL PROBABILITIES UNDER STATISTICAL DEPENDENCE

Marginal probabilities under statistical dependence are computed by summing up the probabilities of all the joint events in which the simple event occurs. In the example above, we can compute the marginal probability of the event colored by summing the probabilities of the two joint events in which colored occurred:

$$P(C) = P(CD) + P(CS) = .3 + .1 = .4$$

Similarly, the marginal probability of the event gray can be computed by summing the probabilities of the two joint events in which gray occurred:

$$P(G) = P(GD) + P(GS) = .2 + .4 = .6$$

In like manner, we can compute the marginal probability of the event dotted by summing the probabilities of the two joint events in which dotted occurred:

$$P(D) = P(CD) + P(GD) = .3 + .2 = .5$$

---

* To find the joint probability of events *A* and *B*, you could also use the formula P(*BA*) = P(*AB*) = P(*A*|*B*) × P(*B*). This is because *BA* = *AB*.

And finally, the marginal probability of the event striped can be computed by summing the probabilities of the two joint events in which gray occurred:

$$P(S) = P(CS) + P(GS) = .1 + .4 = .5$$

These four marginal probabilities, $P(C) = .4$, $P(G) = .6$, $P(D) = .5$, and $P(S) = .5$, can be verified by inspection of Table 4-4 on page 157.

TABLE 4-5 Probabilities Under Statistical Independence and Dependence

TYPE OF PROBABILITY	SYMBOL	FORMULA UNDER STATISTICAL INDEPENDENCE	FORMULA UNDER STATISTICAL DEPENDENCE
Marginal	$P(A)$	$P(A)$	Sum of the probabilities of the joint events in which A occurs
Joint	$P(AB)$ or $P(BA)$	$P(A) \times P(B)$ $P(B) \times P(A)$	$P(A\vert B) \times P(B)$ $P(B\vert A) \times P(A)$
Conditional	$P(B\vert A)$	$P(B)$	$\dfrac{P(BA)}{P(A)}$
	or $P(A\vert B)$	$P(A)$	$\dfrac{P(AB)}{P(B)}$

We have now considered the three types of probability (conditional, joint, and marginal) under conditions of statistical dependence. Table 4-5 provides a resumé of our development of probabilities under both statistical independence and statistical dependence.

Exercises

4-33　At a soup kitchen, a social worker gathers the following data. Of those visiting the kitchen, 59 percent are men, 32 percent are alcoholics, and 21 percent are male alcoholics. What is the probability that a random male visitor to the kitchen is an alcoholic?

4-34　According to a survey, the probability that a family owns two cars if their annual income is greater than $35,000 is .75. Of the households surveyed, 60 percent had incomes over $35,000 and 52 percent had two cars. What is the probability that a family has two cars and an income over $35,000 a year?

4-35　Two events, A and B, are statistically dependent. $P(A) = .39$, $P(B) = .21$, and $P(A \text{ or } B) = .47$. Find the probability that:
(a)　Neither A nor B will occur.
(b)　Both A and B will occur.
(c)　B will occur, given that A has occurred.
(d)　A will occur, given that B has occurred.

4-36　Given that $P(A) = 3/14$, $P(B) = 1/6$, $P(C) = 1/3$, $P(A \text{ and } C) = 1/7$, and $P(B\vert C) = 5/21$, find the following probabilities: $P(A\vert C)$; $P(C\vert A)$; $P(B \text{ and } C)$; $P(C\vert B)$.

4-37　During a study of auto accidents, the Highway Safety Council found that 60 percent of all accidents occur at night, 52 percent are alcohol related, and 37 percent occur at night and are alcohol related.

(a) What is the probability that an accident was alcohol related, given that it occurred at night?

(b) What is the probability that an accident occurred at night, given that it was alcohol related?

4-38 If a hurricane forms in the eastern half of the Gulf of Mexico, there is a 76 percent chance that it will strike the western coast of Florida. From data gathered over the past 50 years, it has been determined that the probability of a hurricane's occurring in this area in any given year is .85.

(a) What is the probability that a hurricane will occur in the eastern Gulf of Mexico and strike Florida this year?

(b) If a hurricane in the eastern Gulf of Mexico is seeded (induced to rain by addition of chemicals from aircraft), its probability of striking Florida's west coast is reduced by one-fourth. If it is decided to seed any hurricane in the eastern gulf, what is the new value for the probability in part (a)?

4-39 Al Cascade, president of the Litre Corporation, is studying his company's chances of being awarded an important water purification system contract for the Tennessee Valley Authority. Accordingly, two events are of interest to him. First, Litre's major competitor, WTR, is conducting purification research, which it hopes to complete before the contract award deadline. Second, there are rumors of a TVA investigation of all recent contractors, of which Litre is one and WTR is not. If WTR finishes its research and there is no investigation, then Litre's probability of being awarded the contract is .67. If there is an investigation but WTR doesn't finish its research, the probability is .72. If both events occur, the probability is .58, and if neither occurs, the probability is .85. The occurrence of an investigation and WTR's completion of research in time are independent events.

(a) Suppose that Al knows that the probability of WTR's completing its research in time is .80. How low must the probability of an investigation be so that the probability of Litre's being awarded the contract is at least .65?

(b) Suppose that Al knows that the probability of an investigation is .70. How low must the probability of WTR's completing its research on time be so that the probability of Litre's being awarded the contract is at least .65?

(c) Suppose that the probability of an investigation is .75 and the probability of WTR's completing its research in time is .85. What is the probability of Litre's being awarded the contract?

4-40 Assume that for two events A and B, $P(A) = .65$, $P(B) = .80$, $P(A|B) = P(A)$, and $P(B|A) = .85$. Is this a consistent assignment of probabilities? Why or why not?

4-41 Friendly's Department Store has been the target of many shoplifters during the past month, but owing to increased security precautions, 250 shoplifters have been caught. Each shoplifter's sex is noted; also noted is whether the perpetrator was a first-time or repeat offender. The data are summarized in the table below.

SEX	FIRST-TIME OFFENDER	REPEAT OFFENDER
Male	60	70
Female	44	76
	104	146

Assuming that an apprehended shoplifter is chosen at random, find:

(a) The probability that the shoplifter is male.

(b) The probability that the shoplifter is a first-time offender, given that the shoplifter is male.

(c) The probability that the shoplifter is female, given that the shoplifter is a repeat offender.

(d) The probability that the shoplifter is female, given that the shoplifter is a first-time offender.

(e) The probability that the shoplifter is both male and a repeat offender.

4-42 The southeast regional manager of General Express, a private parcel delivery firm, is worried about the likelihood of strikes by some of his employees. He has learned that the probability of a strike by his pilots is .75 and the probability of a strike by his drivers is .65. Further, he knows that if the drivers strike, there is a 90 percent chance that the pilots will strike in sympathy.
(a)   What is the probability of both groups' striking?
(b)   If the pilots strike, what is the probability that the drivers will strike in sympathy?

4-7
Revising Prior Estimates of Probabilities: Bayes' Theorem

At the beginning of the baseball season, the fans of last year's pennant winner thought their team had a good chance of winning again. As the season progressed, however, injuries sidelined the shortstop and the team's chief rival drafted a terrific home run hitter. The team began to lose. Late in the season, the fans realized that they must alter their prior probabilities of winning.

A similar situation often occurs in business. If a manager of a boutique finds that most of the purple and chartreuse ski jackets that she thought would sell so well are hanging on the rack, she must revise her prior probabilities and order a different color combination or have a sale.

Posterior probabilities defined

In both these cases, certain probabilities were altered after the people involved got additional information. The new probabilities are known as revised, or *posterior,* probabilities. Because probabilities can be revised as more information is gained, probability theory is of great value in managerial decision making.

Bayes' theorem

The origin of the concept of obtaining posterior probabilities with limited information is attributable to the Reverend Thomas Bayes (1702–1761), and the basic formula for conditional probability under dependence:

$$P(B|A) = \frac{P(BA)}{P(A)}$$

[4-6]

is called *Bayes' theorem.*

Bayes, an Englishman, was a Presbyterian minister and a competent mathematician. He pondered how he might prove the existence of God by examining whatever evidence the world about him provided. Attempting to show "that the Principal End of the Divine Providence . . . is the Happiness of His Creatures," the Reverend Bayes used mathematics to study God. Unfortunately, the theological implications of his findings so alarmed the good Reverend Bayes that he refused to permit publication of his work during his lifetime. Nevertheless, his work outlived him, and modern decision theory is often called Bayesian decision theory in his honor.

Value of Bayes' theorem

Bayes' theorem offers a powerful statistical method of evaluating new information and revising our prior estimates (based upon limited information only) of the probability that things are in one state or another. **If correctly used, it makes it unnecessary to gather masses of data over long periods of time in order to make decisions based upon probabilities.**

CALCULATING POSTERIOR PROBABILITIES

Finding a new posterior estimate

Assume, as a first example of revising prior probabilities, that we have equal numbers of two types of deformed (biased or weighted) dice in a bowl. On half of them, ace (or

TABLE 4-6 Finding the Marginal Probability of Getting an Ace

ELEMENTARY EVENT	PROBABILITY OF ELEMENTARY EVENT	P(ACE|ELEMENTARY EVENT)	P(ACE, ELEMENTARY EVENT)*
Type 1	.5	.4	.4 × .5 = .20
Type 2	.5	.7	.7 × .5 = .35
	1.0		**P(ace) = .55**

* A comma is used to separate joint events. We can join individual letters to indicate joint events without confusion (*AB*, for example), but joining whole words in this way could produce strange looking events (aceelementaryevent) in this table, and they could be confusing.

Revising probabilities based on one outcome one dot) comes up 40 percent of the time; therefore, P(ace) = .4. On the other half, ace comes up 70 percent of the time, and P(ace) = .7. Let us call the former type 1 and the latter type 2. One die is drawn, rolled once, and comes up ace. What is the probability that it is a type 1 die? Knowing the bowl contains the same number of both types of dice, we might incorrectly answer that the probability is one-half; but we can do better than this. To answer the question correctly, we set up Table 4-6.

The sum of the probabilities of the elementary events (drawing either a type 1 or a type 2 die) is 1.0, because there are only two types of dice. The probability of each type is .5. The two types constitute a mutually exclusive and collectively exhaustive list.

The sum of P(ace|elementary event) does *not* equal 1.0. The figures .4 and .7 simply represent the conditional probabilities of getting an ace, given type 1 and type 2, respectively.

The fourth column shows the joint probability of ace and type 1 occurring together (.4 × .5 = .20), and the joint probability of ace and type 2 occurring together (.7 × .5 = .35). The sum of these joint probabilities (.55) is the marginal probability of getting an ace. Notice that in each case, the joint probability was obtained by using the formula:

$$P(AB) = P(A|B) \times P(B) \qquad [4\text{-}7]$$

To find the probability that the die we have drawn is type 1, we use the formula for conditional probability under statistical dependence:

$$P(B|A) = \frac{P(BA)}{P(A)} \qquad [4\text{-}6]$$

Converting to our problem, we have:

$$P(\text{type 1}|\text{ace}) = \frac{P(\text{type 1, ace})}{P(\text{ace})}$$

or:

$$P(\text{type 1}|\text{ace}) = \frac{.20}{.55} = .364$$

Thus, the probability that we have drawn a type 1 die is .364.

Let us compute the probability that the die is type 2:

$$P(\text{type 2}|\text{ace}) = \frac{P(\text{type 2, ace})}{P(\text{ace})} = \frac{.35}{.55} = .636$$

What have we accomplished with one additional piece of information made available to us? What inferences have we been able to draw from one roll of the die? Before we rolled this die, the best we could say was that there is a .5 chance it is a type 1 die and a .5 chance it is a type 2 die. However, after rolling the die, we have been able to *alter,* or revise, *our prior probability estimate.* Our new posterior estimate is that there is a higher probability (.636) that the die we have in our hand is a type 2 than that it is a type 1 (only .364).

POSTERIOR PROBABILITIES WITH MORE INFORMATION

We may feel that one roll of the die is not sufficient to indicate its characteristics (whether it is type 1 or type 2). In this case, we can obtain additional information by rolling the die again. (Obtaining more information in most decision-making situations, of course, is more complicated and time-consuming.) Assume that the same die is rolled a second time and again comes up ace. What is the further revised probability that the die is type 1? To determine this answer, see Table 4-7.

We have one new column in this table, P(2 aces|elementary event). This column gives the *joint* probability of two aces on two successive rolls if the die is type 1 and if it is type 2: P(2 aces|type 1) = .4 × .4 = .16, and P(2 aces|type 2) = .7 × .7 = .49. In the last column, we see the joint probabilities of two aces on two successive rolls and the elementary events (type 1 and type 2). That is, P(2 aces, type 1) equals P(2 aces|type 1) times the probability of type 1, or .16 × .5 = .080. And P(2 aces, type 2) equals P(2 aces|type 2) times the probability of type 2, or .49 × .5 = .245. The sum of these (.325) is the marginal probability of two aces on two successive rolls.

We are now ready to compute the probability that the die we have drawn is type 1, given an ace on each of two successive rolls. Using the same general formula as before, we convert to:

$$P(\text{type } 1|2 \text{ aces}) = \frac{P(\text{type } 1, 2 \text{ aces})}{P(2 \text{ aces})} = \frac{.080}{.325} = .246$$

Similarly,

$$P(\text{type } 2|2 \text{ aces}) = \frac{P(\text{type } 2, 2 \text{ aces})}{P(2 \text{ aces})} = \frac{.245}{.325} = .754$$

What have we accomplished with two rolls? When we first drew the die, all we knew was that there was a probability of .5 that it was type 1 and a probability of .5 that it was type 2. In other words, there was a 50-50 chance that it was either type 1 or

TABLE 4-7 Finding the Marginal Probability of Two Aces on Two Successive Rolls

ELEMENTARY EVENT	PROBABILITY OF ELEMENTARY EVENT	P(ACE| ELEMENTARY EVENT)	P(2 ACES| ELEMENTARY EVENT)	P(2 ACES, ELEMENTARY EVENT)
Type 1	.5	.4	.16	.16 × .5 = .080
Type 2	.5	.7	.49	.49 × .5 = .245
	1.0			**P(2 aces) = .325**

type 2. After rolling the die once and getting an ace, we revised these original probabilities to the following:

$$\text{Probability that it is type } 1 = .364$$

$$\text{Probability that it is type } 2 = .636$$

After the second roll (another ace), we revised the probabilities again:

$$\text{Probability that it is type } 1 = .246$$

$$\text{Probability that it is type } 2 = .754$$

Conclusion after two rolls   We have thus changed the original probabilities from .5 for each type to .246 for type 1 and .754 for type 2. This means that we can now assign a probability of .754 that if a die turns up ace on two successive rolls, it is type 2.

In both these experiments, we gained new information free of charge. We were able to roll the die twice, observe its behavior, and draw inferences from the behavior without any monetary cost. Obviously, there are few situations in which this is true, and managers must not only understand how to utilize new information to revise prior probabilities, but also be able to determine *how much that information is worth* to them before the fact. In many cases, the value of the information obtained may be considerably less than its cost.

A PROBLEM WITH THREE REVISIONS

Example of posterior probability based on three trials   Consider the problem of a Little League baseball team that has been using an automatic pitching machine. If the machine is correctly set up—that is, properly adjusted—it will pitch strikes 85 percent of the time. If it is incorrectly set up, it will pitch strikes only 35 percent of the time. Past experience indicates that 75 percent of the setups of the machine are correctly done. After the machine has been set up at batting practice one day, it throws three strikes on the first three pitches. What is the revised probability that the setup has been done correctly? Table 4-8 illustrates how we can answer this question.

We can interpret the numbered table headings in Table 4-8 as follows:

1. **P**(event) describes the individual probabilities of correct and incorrect. P(correct) = .75 is given in the problem. Thus we can compute:

$$\text{P(incorrect)} = 1.00 - \text{P(correct)} = 1.00 - .75 = .25$$

2. **P**(1 strike|event) represents the probability of a strike given that the setup is correct or incorrect. These probabilities are given in the problem.

TABLE 4-8 Posterior Probabilities With Joint Events

EVENT	P(EVENT) (1)	P(1 STRIKE| EVENT) (2)	P(3 STRIKES| EVENT) (3)	P(EVENT, 3 STRIKES) (4)
Correct	.75	.85	.6141	.6141 × .75 = .4606
Incorrect	.25	.35	.0429	.0429 × .25 = .0107
	1.00			**P(3 strikes) = .4713**

3. P(3 strikes|event) is the probability of getting three strikes on three successive pitches, given the event; that is, given correct or incorrect. The probabilities are computed as follows:

$$P(3\ strikes|correct) = .85 \times .85 \times .85 = .6141$$

$$P(3\ strikes|incorrect) = .35 \times .35 \times .35 = .0429$$

4. P(event, 3 strikes) is the probability of the joint occurrence of the event (correct or incorrect) and three strikes. We can compute the probability in the problem as follows:

$$P(correct,\ 3\ strikes) = .6141 \times .75 = .4606$$

$$P(incorrect,\ 3\ strikes) = .0429 \times .25 = .0107$$

Notice that if A = event and B = strikes, these last two probabilities conform to the general mathematical formula for joint probabilities under conditions of dependence: $P(AB) = P(BA) = P(B|A) \times P(A)$, Equation 4-7.

After finishing the computation in Table 4-8, we are ready to determine the revised probability that the machine is correctly set up. We use the general formula

$$P(A|B) = \frac{P(AB)}{P(B)}$$ [4-6]

and convert it to the terms and numbers in this problem:

$$P(correct|3\ strikes) = \frac{P(correct,\ 3\ strikes)}{P(3\ strikes)}$$

$$= \frac{.4606}{.4713} = .9773$$

The *posterior probability* that the machine is correctly set up is .9773, or 97.73 percent. We have thus revised our original probability of a correct setup from 75 to 97.73 percent, based on three strikes being thrown in three pitches.

POSTERIOR PROBABILITIES WITH INCONSISTENT OUTCOMES

An example with inconsistent outcomes

In each of our problems so far, the behavior of the experiment was consistent—the die came up ace on two successive rolls, and the automatic machine threw strikes on each of the first three pitches. In most situations, we would expect a less consistent

TABLE 4-9 Posterior Probabilities With Inconsistent Outcomes

EVENT	P(EVENT)	P(S|EVENT)	P(SBSSS|EVENT)	P(EVENT, SBSSS)
Correct	.75	.85	.85 × .15 × .85 × .85 × .85 = .07830	.07830 × .75 = .05873
Incorrect	.25	.35	.35 × .65 × .35 × .35 × .35 = .00975	.00975 × .25 = .00244
	1.00			**P(SBSSS) = .06117**

$$P(correct\ setup|SBSSS) = \frac{P(correct\ setup,\ SBSSS)}{P(SBSSS)}$$

$$= \frac{.05873}{.06117}$$

$$= .9601$$

distribution of outcomes. In the case of the pitching machine for example, we might find the five pitches to be: strike, ball, strike, strike, strike. Calculating our posterior probability that the machine is correctly set up in this case is really no more difficult than it was with a set of perfectly consistent outcomes. Using the notation S = strike and B = ball, we have solved this example in Table 4-9.

Exercises

4-43   Given: The probabilities of three events, A, B, and C, occurring are: $P(A) = .35$, $P(B) = .45$, and $P(C) = .2$. Assuming that A, B, or C has occurred, the probabilities of another event, X, occurring are: $P(X|A) = .8$, $P(X|B) = .65$, and $P(X|C) = .3$. Find $P(A|X)$; $P(B|X)$; $P(C|X)$.

4-44   Martin Coleman, credit manager for Beck's, knows that the company uses three methods to encourage collection of delinquent accounts. From past collection records, he learns that 70 percent of the accounts are called on personally, 20 percent are phoned, and 10 percent are sent a letter. The probability of collecting an overdue amount from an account with the three methods is .75, .60, and .65 respectively. Mr. Coleman has just received payment from a past-due account. What is the probability that this account:
   (a)   Was called on personally?
   (b)   Received a phone call?
   (c)   Received a letter?

4-45   A public-interest group was planning to make a court challenge to auto insurance rates in one of three cities: Atlanta, Baltimore, or Cleveland. The probability that it would choose Atlanta was .40; Baltimore, .35; Cleveland, .25. The group also knew that it had a 60 percent chance of a favorable ruling if it chose Baltimore, 45 percent if it chose Atlanta, and 35 percent if it chose Cleveland. If the group did receive a favorable ruling, which city did it most likely choose?

4-46   A doctor has decided to prescribe two new drugs to 200 heart patients, as follows: 50 get drug A, 50 get drug B, and 100 get both. Drug A reduces the probability of a heart attack by 35 percent, drug B reduces the probability by 20 percent, and the two drugs, when taken together, work independently. The 200 patients were chosen so that each has an 80 percent chance of having a heart attack. If a randomly selected patient has a heart attack, what is the probability that the patient was given both drugs?

4-47   An independent research group has been studying the chances that an accident at a nuclear power plant will result in radiation leakage. The group considers that the only possible types of accidents at a reactor are fire, material failure, and human error, and that two or more accidents never occur together. It has performed studies that indicate that if there were a fire, a radiation leak would occur 20 percent of the time; if there were a mechanical failure, a radiation leak would occur 50 percent of the time; and if there were a human error, a radiation leak would occur 10 percent of the time. Its studies have also shown that the probability of:

   ▪ A fire and a radiation leak occurring together is .0010.
   ▪ A mechanical failure and a radiation leak occurring together is .0015.
   ▪ A human error and a radiation leak occurring together is .0012.

   (a)   What are the respective probabilities of a fire, mechanical failure, and human error?
   (b)   What are the respective probabilities that a radiation leak was caused by a fire, mechanical failure, and human error?
   (c)   What is the probability of a radiation leak?

4-48   A physical therapist at Enormous State University knows that the football team will play 40 percent of its games on artificial turf this season. He also knows that a football player's chances of incurring a knee injury are 50 percent higher if he is playing on artificial turf instead of grass. If a player's probability of knee injury on artificial turf is .42, what is the probability that:
   (a)   A randomly selected football player incurs a knee injury?
   (b)   A randomly selected football player with a knee injury incurred the injury playing on grass?

4-49   The physical therapist from exercise 4-48 is also interested in studying the relation between foot injuries and position played. His data, gathered over a 3-year period, are summarized in the following table:

	OFFENSIVE LINE	DEFENSIVE LINE	OFFENSIVE BACKFIELD	DEFENSIVE BACKFIELD
Number of players	45	56	24	20
Number injured	32	38	11	9

Given that a randomly selected player incurred a foot injury, what is the probability that he plays in the (a) offensive line? (b) defensive line? (c) offensive backfield? (d) defensive backfield?

4-50   A state Democratic official has decided that changes in the state unemployment rate will have a major effect on her party's chance of gaining or losing seats in the state senate. She has determined that if unemployment rises by 2 percent or more, the respective probabilities of losing more than ten seats, losing six to ten seats, gaining or losing five or fewer seats, gaining six to ten seats, and gaining more than ten seats are .25, .35, .15, .15, and .10, respectively. If unemployment changes by less than 2 percent, the respective probabilities are .10, .10, .15, .35, and .30. If unemployment falls by 2 percent or more, the respective probabilities are .05, .10, .10, .40, and .35. Presently, this official believes that unemployment will rise by 2 percent or more with probability .25, change by less than 2 percent with probability .45, and fall by 2 percent or more with probability .30.
   (a)   If the Democrats gain seven seats, what is the probability that unemployment fell by 2 percent or more?
   (b)   If the Democrats lose one seat, what is the probability that unemployment changed by less than 2 percent?

4-51   T. C. Fox, marketing director for Metro-Goldmine Motion Pictures, believes that the studio's upcoming release has a 60 percent chance of being a hit, a 25 percent chance of being a moderate success, and a 15 percent chance of being a flop. To test the accuracy of his opinion, T. C. has scheduled two test screenings. After each screening, the audience rates the film on a scale of 1 to 10, 10 being best. From his long experience in the industry, T. C. knows that a hit picture will receive a rating of 7 or higher 60 percent of the time, a rating of 4, 5, or 6, 30 percent of the time, and a rating of 3 or lower, 10 percent of the time. For a moderately successful picture, the respective probabilities are .30, .45, and .25; for a flop, the respective probabilities are .15, .35, and .50.
   (a)   If the first test screening produces a score of 6, what is the probability that the film will be a hit?
   (b)   If the first test screening produces a score of 6 and the second screening yields a score of 2, what is the probability that the film will be a flop (assuming that the screening results are independent of each other)?

4-8
Terms Introduced in Chapter 4

A Priori Probability Probability estimate made prior to receiving new information.

Bayes' Theorem The formula for conditional probability under statistical dependence.

Classical Probability The number of outcomes favorable to the occurrence of an event divided by the total number of possible outcomes.

Collectively Exhaustive Events The list of events that represents all the possible outcomes of an experiment.

Conditional Probability The probability of one event occurring, given that another event has occurred.

Event One or more of the possible outcomes of doing something, or one of the possible outcomes which results from conducting an experiment.

Experiment The activity that results in, or produces, an event.

Joint Probability The probability of two events occurring together or in succession.

Marginal Probability The unconditional probability of one event occurring; the probability of a single event.

Mutually Exclusive Events Events that cannot happen together.

Posterior Probability A probability that has been revised after additional information was obtained.

Probability The chance that something will happen.

Probability Tree A graphical representation showing the possible outcomes of a series of experiments and their respective probabilities.

Relative Frequency of Occurrence The proportion of times that an event occurs in the long run when conditions are stable, or the observed relative frequency of an event in a very large number of trials.

Sample Space The set of all possible outcomes of an experiment.

Statistical Dependence The condition when the probability of some event is dependent upon, or affected by, the occurrence of some other event.

Statistical Independence The condition when the occurrence of one event has no effect upon the probability of occurrence of any other event.

Subjective Probability Probabilities based on the personal beliefs of the person making the probability estimate.

Venn Diagram A pictorial representation of probability concepts, in which the sample space is represented as a rectangle and the events in the sample space as portions of that rectangle.

4-9
Equations Introduced in Chapter 4

[4-1]
$$\text{Probability of an event} = \frac{\text{The number of outcomes where the event occurs}}{\text{The total number of possible outcomes}}$$

p. 139

This is the definition of the *classical* probability that an event will occur.

$$P(A) = \text{The probability of an event } A \text{ happening}$$

p. 144

A single probability refers to the probability of one particular event occurring, and it is called *marginal* probability.

$$P(A \text{ or } B) = \text{The probability of } either \, A \, or \, B \text{ happening}$$

p. 145

This notation represents the probability that one event *or* the other will occur.

[4-2] $$P(A \text{ or } B) = P(A) + P(B)$$ p. 145

The probability of either A or B happening when A and B are mutually exclusive equals the sum of the probability of event A happening and the probability of event B happening. This is the *addition rule for mutually exclusive events.*

[4-3] $$P(A \text{ or } B) = P(A) + P(B) - P(AB)$$ p. 146

The addition rule for events that are not mutually exclusive shows that the probability of A or B happening when A and B are not mutually exclusive is equal to the probability of event A happening plus the probability of event B happening minus the probability of A and B happening together, symbolized $P(AB)$.

[4-4] $$P(AB) = P(A) \times P(B)$$ p. 149

where:

$P(AB)$ = the joint probability of events A and B occurring together or in succession
$P(A)$ = the marginal probability of event A happening
$P(B)$ = the marginal probability of event B happening

The *joint* probability of two or more *independent* events occurring together or in succession is the product of their marginal probabilities.

$$P(B|A) = \text{The probability of event } B, \textit{given} \text{ that event } A \text{ has happened} \qquad \textit{p. 154}$$

This notation shows *conditional* probability, the probability that a second event (B) will occur if a first event (A) has already happened.

[4-5] $$P(B|A) = P(B)$$ p. 154

For *statistically independent* events, the *conditional* probability of event B, given that event A has occurred, is simply the probability of event B. Independent events are those whose probabilities are in no way affected by the occurrence of each other.

[4-6] $$P(B|A) = \frac{P(BA)}{P(A)}$$ p. 158

and

$$P(A|B) = \frac{P(AB)}{P(B)}$$

For statistically *dependent* events, the *conditional* probability of event B, given that event A has occurred, is equal to the joint probability of events A and B divided by the marginal probability of event A.

[4-7] $$P(AB) = P(A|B) \times P(B)$$ p. 161

and

$$P(BA) = P(B|A) \times P(A)$$

Under conditions of statistical *dependence,* the *joint* probability of events *A* and *B* happening together or in succession is equal to the probability of event *A*, given that event *B* has already happened, multiplied by the probability that event *B* will happen.

4-10
Chapter Review Exercises

4-52 Life insurance premiums are higher for older people, but auto insurance premiums are generally higher for younger people. What does this suggest about the risks and probabilities associated with these two areas of the insurance business?

4-53 "The chance of rain today is 80 percent." Which of the following best explains this statement?
   (a) It will rain 80 percent of the day today.
   (b) It will rain in 80 percent of the area of which this forecast applies today.
   (c) In the past, weather conditions of this sort have produced rain in this area 80 percent of the time.

4-54 "There is a .25 probability that a restaurant in the United States will go out of business this year." When researchers make such statements, how have they arrived at their conclusions?

4-55 Using probability theory, explain the success of gambling and poker establishments.

4-56 If we assume that a person is equally likely to be born on any day of the week, what are the probabilities of a certain baby being born:
   (a) On a Tuesday?
   (b) On a day beginning with the letter S?
   (c) Between Wednesday and Friday, inclusive?
   (d) What type of probability estimates are these?

4-57 Isaac T. Olduso, an engineer for Schlockheed Aircraft, disagrees with his supervisor about the likelihood of landing-gear failure on the company's new airliner. Isaac contends that the probability of landing-gear failure is .12, while his supervisor maintains that the probability is only .03. The two agree that if the landing gear fails, the airplane will crash with probability .55. Otherwise, the probability of a crash is only .06. A test flight is conducted, and the airplane crashes.
   (a) Using Isaac's figure, what is the probability that the airplane's landing gear failed?
   (b) Repeat part (a) using the supervisor's figure.

4-58 Congressman Bob Forehead has been thinking about the upcoming midterm elections, and has prepared the following list of possible developments in his career during the midterm elections:

   ▪ He wins his party's nomination for reelection.
   ▪ He returns to his law practice.
   ▪ He is nominated for Vice President.
   ▪ He loses his party's nomination for reelection.
   ▪ He wins reelection.

   (a) Is each item on this list an "event" in the category of "Midterm Election Career Developments?"
   (b) Are all of the items qualifying as "events" in part (a) mutually exclusive? If not, are any mutually exclusive?
   (c) Are the events on the list collectively exhaustive?

4-59 Which of the following pairs of events are mutually exclusive?
(a) A defense department contractor loses a major contract, and the same contractor increases its workforce by 50 percent.
(b) A man is older than his uncle, and he is younger than his cousins.
(c) A baseball team loses its last game, and it wins the World Series.
(d) A bank manager discovers that a teller has been embezzling, and she promotes the same teller.

4-60 The scheduling officer for a local police department is trying to decide whether to schedule additional patrol units in each of two neighborhoods. She knows that on any given day during the past year, the probabilities of major crimes and minor crimes being committed in the northern neighborhood were .478 and .602, respectively, and that the corresponding probabilities in the southern neighborhood were .350 and .523. Assume that major and minor crimes occur independently of each other and likewise that crimes in the two neighborhoods are independent of each other.
(a) What is the probability that no crime of either type will be committed in the northern neighborhood on a given day?
(b) What is the probability that a crime of either type will be committed in the southern neighborhood on a given day?
(c) What is the probability that no crime of either type will be committed in either neighborhood on a given day?

4-61 The Environmental Protection Agency is trying to assess the pollution effect of a paper mill that is to be built near Spokane, Washington. In studies of six similar plants built during the last year, the EPA determined the following pollution factors:

Plant	1	2	3	4	5	6
Sulfur dioxide emission in parts per million (ppm)	15	12	18	16	11	19

EPA defines excessive pollution as a sulfur dioxide emission of 18 ppm or greater.
(a) Calculate the probability that the new plant will be an excessive sulfur dioxide polluter.
(b) Classify this probability according to the three types discussed in the chapter: classical, relative frequency, and subjective.
(c) How would you judge the accuracy of your result?

4-62 The American Cancer Society is planning to mail out questionnaires concerning breast cancer. From past experience with questionnaires, the society knows that only 15 percent of the people receiving questionnaires will respond. It also knows that 1.3 percent of the questionnaires mailed out will have a mistake in address and never be delivered, that 2.8 percent will be lost or destroyed by the post office, that 19 percent will be mailed to people who have moved, and that only 48 percent of those who move leave a forwarding address.
(a) Do the percentages in the problem represent classical, relative frequency, or subjective probability estimates?
(b) What is the probability that the Society will receive a reply from a given questionnaire?

4-63 McCormick and Tryon, Inc., is a "shark watcher," hired by firms fearing takeover by larger companies. This firm has found that one of its clients, Pare and Oyd Co., is being considered for takeover by two firms. The first, Engulf and Devour, considered 20 such companies last year, and took over seven. The second, R. A. Venus Corp., considered fifteen such companies last year, and took over six. What is the probability of Pare and Oyd's being taken over this year, assuming that:
(a) The acquisition rates of both Engulf and Devour and R. A. Venus are the same this year as they were last year?
(b) This year's acquisition rates are independent of last year's?
In each case, assume that only one firm may take over Pare and Oyd.

4-64 As the administrator of a hospital, Cindy Turner wants to know what the probability is that a person checking into the hospital will require X-ray treatment and will also have hospital insurance that will cover the X-ray treatment. She knows that during the past 5 years, 23 percent of the people entering the hospital required X-rays and that during the same period, 72 percent of the people checking into the hospital had insurance that covered X-ray treatments. What is the correct probability? Do any additional assumptions need to be made?

4-65 An air traffic controller at Dulles Airport must obey regulations that require her to divert one of two airplanes if the probability of the aircrafts' colliding exceeds .025. The controller has two inbound aircraft scheduled to arrive 10 minutes apart on the same runway. She knows that Flight 100, scheduled to arrive first, has a history of being on time, 5 minutes late, and 10 minutes late 95, 3, and 2 percent of the time, respectively. Further, she knows that Flight 200, scheduled to arrive second, has a history of being on time, 5 minutes early, and 10 minutes early 97, 2, and 1 percent of the time, respectively. The flights' timings are independent of each other.
(a) Must the controller divert one of the planes, based on this information?
(b) If she finds out that Flight 100 will definitely be 5 minutes late, must the controller divert one of the airplanes?
(c) If the controller finds out that Flight 200 will definitely be 5 minutes early, must she divert one of the airplanes?

4-66 Thatcher Tennis Ball Co. imposes the following quality controls on its product. If a ball bounces too high or too low, or if it has a flaw in its cover, it is rejected. Currently, 12 percent of all balls produced bounce too high or too low, and 50 percent of these balls also have cover flaws. Overall, 10 percent of all balls produced have cover flaws. Out of a randomly selected lot of 1,000 balls how many will have:
(a) Bounce flaws?
(b) Cover flaws?
(c) Both flaws?
(d) Any flaws?

4-67 Which of the following pairs of events are statistically independent?
(a) The times until failure of a calculator and of a second calculator marketed by a different firm.
(b) The lifespans of the current U.S. president and the current U.S.S.R. premier.
(c) The amounts of settlements in asbestos poisoning cases in Maryland and New York.
(d) The takeover of a company and a rise in the price of its stock.
(e) The frequency of organ donation in a community and the predominant religious orientation of that community.

4-68 F. Liam Laytor, supervisor of customer relations for GLF Airlines, is studying his company's overbooking problem. He is concentrating on three late-night flights out of LaGuardia Airport in New York City. In the last year, 7, 8, and 5 percent of the passengers on the Atlanta, Kansas City, and Detroit flights, respectively, have been bumped. Further, 55, 20, and 25 percent of the late-night GLF passengers at LaGuardia take the Atlanta, Kansas City, and Detroit flights, respectively. What is the probability that a bumped passenger was scheduled to be on the:
(a) Atlanta Flight?
(b) Kansas City Flight?
(c) Detroit Flight?

4-69 An electronics manufacturer is considering expansion of its plant in the next 4 years. The decision will be influenced by increased production that will occur if either government or consumer sales increase. Specifically, the plant will be expanded if one of two events occurs: (1) consumer sales increase 50 percent over the present sales level, or (2) a major government contract is obtained. The company also believes that both these events will not happen in the same year. The planning director has obtained the following estimates:

1. The probability of consumer sales increasing by 50 percent within 1, 2, 3, and 4 years is .05, .08, .12, and .16, respectively.
2. The probability of obtaining a major government contract within 1, 2, 3, and 4 years is .08, .15, .25, and .32, respectively.

What is the probability that the plant will expand:
(a) Within the next year (in year 1)?
(b) Between 1 and 2 years from now (in year 2)?
(c) Between 2 and 3 years from now (in year 3)?
(d) Between 3 and 4 years from now (in year 4)?
(e) At all in the next 4 years (assume at most one expansion)?

4-70 Draw Venn diagrams to represent the following situations involving three events, A, B, and C, which are part of a sample space of events but do not include the whole sample space.
(a) Each pair of events (A and B, A and C, and B and C) may occur together, but all three may not occur together.
(b) A and B are mutually exclusive, but not A and C nor B and C.
(c) A, B, and C are all mutually exclusive of one another.
(d) A and B are mutually exclusive, B and C are mutually exclusive, but A and C are not mutually exclusive.

4-71 Cartoonist Barry Bludeau sends his comics to his publisher via the Union Postal Delivery. UPD uses two modes of transportation in Mr. Bludeau's part of the country, rail and truck. In the 20 years during which UPD has operated, only 2 percent of the mail carried by rail and only 3.5 percent of the mail carried by truck have been lost. The claims manager receives a call from Mr. Bludeau, who informs him that a package containing a week of comics has been lost. If UPD sends 60 percent of the mail in that area by rail, which mode of transportation was more likely used to carry the lost comics? How does the solution change if UPD loses only 2 percent of its mail, regardless of the mode of transportation?

4-72 Determine the probability that:
(a) Both engines on a small airline fail, given that each engine fails with probability .05 and that an engine is twice as likely to fail when it is the only engine working.
(b) An automobile is recalled for brake failure and has steering problems, given that 15 percent of that model were recalled for brake failure and 2 percent had steering problems.
(c) A citizen files his or her tax return and cheats on it, given that 70 percent of all citizens file returns and 25 percent of those who file, cheat.

4-73 Professor Pedro Agogh has ordered textbooks for his new course from Riley Publishing. Two-fifths of these books are printed at Riley's plant in New Jersey; the remaining three-fifths are printed at the Delaware plant. The New Jersey and Delaware plants have respective printing error probabilities of .075 and .053. If Dr. Agogh selects a copy from the shipments and finds that it has a printing error, which plant is more likely to have printed the book?

4-74 A senior North Carolina senator knows he will soon vote on a controversial bill. To learn his constituents' attitudes about the bill, he met with groups in three cities in his state. An aide jotted down the opinions of fifteen attendees at each meeting:

OPINION	CITY		
	Chapel Hill	Raleigh	Lumberton
Strongly oppose	2	2	4
Slightly oppose	2	4	3
Neutral	3	3	5
Slightly support	2	3	2
Strongly support	6	3	1
Total	15	15	15

(a) What is the probability that someone from Chapel Hill is neutral about the bill? Strongly opposed?

(b) What is the probability that someone in the three city groups strongly supports the bill?

(c) What is the probability that someone from the Raleigh or Lumberton groups is neutral or slightly opposed?

4-75 A produce shipper has 10,000 boxes of bananas from Ecuador and Honduras. An inspection has determined the following information:

	# OF BOXES	# OF BOXES WITH DAMAGED FRUIT	# OF BOXES WITH OVERRIPE FRUIT
Ecuadoran	6000	200	840
Honduran	4000	365	295

(a) What is the probability that a box selected at random will contain damaged fruit? Overripe fruit?

(b) What is the probability that a randomly-selected box is from Ecuador or Honduras?

(c) Given that a randomly-selected box contains overripe fruit, what is the probability that it came from Honduras?

(d) If damaged fruit and overripe fruit are mutually-exclusive, what is the probability that a box contains damaged or overripe fruit? What if they are not mutually-exclusive?

4-76 Marcia Lerner will graduate in three months with a master's degree in business administration. Her school's placement office indicates that the probability of receiving a job offer as the result of any given on-campus interview is about .07 and is statistically independent from interview to interview.

(a) What is the probability that Marcia will not get a job offer in any of her next 3 interviews?

(b) If she has three interviews per month, what is the probability that she will have at least one job offer by the time she finishes school?

(c) What is the probability that in her next five interviews she will get job offers on the third and fifth interviews only?

4-77 A standard set of pool balls contains fifteen balls numbered from one to fifteen. Pegleg Woodhull, the famous blind poolplayer, is playing a game of eight-ball, in which the eight-ball must be the last one hit into a pocket. He is allowed to touch the balls to determine their positions before taking a shot, but he does not know their numbers. Every shot Woodhull takes is successful.

(a) What is the probability that he hits the eight-ball into a pocket on his first shot, thus losing the game?

(b) What is the probability that the eight-ball is one of the first three balls he hits?

(c) What is the probability that Pegleg wins the game, that is, that the eight-ball is the last ball hit into a pocket?

4-78 BMT, Inc. is trying to decide which of two oil pumps to use in its new race car engine. One pump produces 75 pounds of pressure and the other 100. BMT knows the following probabilities associated with the pumps:

	PROBABILITY OF ENGINE FAILURE DUE TO	
	Seized bearings	Ruptured head gasket
pump A	.08	.03
pump B	.02	.11

(a) If seized bearings and ruptured head gaskets are mutually exclusive, which pump should BMT use?

(b) If BMT devises a greatly-improved "rupture-proof" head gasket, should they change their decision?

4-79 Sandy Irick is the public relations director for a large pharmaceutical firm which has been attacked in the popular press for distributing an allegedly unsafe vaccine. The vaccine protects against a virulent contagious disease which has a .04 probability of killing an infected person. 25 percent of the population has received the vaccine.

A researcher has told her the following: The probability of any unvaccinated individual acquiring the disease is .30. Once vaccinated, the probability of acquiring the disease through normal means is zero. However, 2 percent of vaccinated people will show symptoms of the disease, and 3 percent of that group will die from it. Of people who are vaccinated and show no symptoms from the vaccination, 0.05 percent will die. Irick must draw some conclusions from this data for a staff meeting in one hour and a news conference later in the day.

(a) If a person is vaccinated, what is the probability of dying from the vaccine? If he was not vaccinated, what is the probability of dying?

(b) What is the probability of a randomly-selected person dying from either the vaccine or the normally-contracted disease?

4-80 The press-room supervisor for a daily newspaper is being pressured to find ways to print the paper closer to distribution time, thus giving the editorial staff more leeway for last-minute changes. She has the option of running the presses at "normal" speed or at 110 percent of normal—"fast" speed. She estimates that they will run at the higher speed 60 percent of the time. The roll of paper (the newsprint "web") is twice as likely to tear at the higher speed, which would mean stopping the presses temporarily.

(a) If the web on a randomly-selected printing run has a probability of .112 of tearing, what is the probability that the web will not tear at normal speed?

(b) If the probability of tearing on fast speed is .20, what is the probability that a randomly-selected torn web occurred on normal speed?

4-81 Refer to exercise 4-80. The supervisor has noted that the web tore during each of the last four runs and that the speed of the press was not changed during these four runs. If the probabilities of tearing at fast and slow speeds were .14 and .07, respectively, what is the revised probability that the press was operating at fast speed during the last four runs?

4-11
Chapter Concepts Test

Answers are in the back of the book.

T F 1. In probability theory, the outcome from some experiment is known as an activity.

T F 2. The probability of two or more statistically independent events occurring together or in succession is equal to the sum of their marginal probabilities.

T F 3. Using Bayes' theorem, we may develop revised probabilities based upon new information; these revised probabilities are also known as posterior probabilities.

T F 4. In classical probability, we can determine a priori probabilities based upon logical reasoning before any experiments take place.

T F 5. The set of all possible outcomes of an experiment is called the sample space for the experiment.

T F 6. Under statistical dependence, a marginal probability may be computed for some simple event by taking the product of the probabilities of all joint events in which the simple event occurs.

T F 7. When a list of events resulting from some experiment includes all possible outcomes, the list is said to be collectively exclusive.

T	F	8.	An unconditional probability is also known as a marginal probability.
T	F	9.	A subjective probability may be nothing more than an educated guess.
T	F	10.	When the occurrence of some event has no effect upon the probability of occurrence of some other event, the two events are said to be statistically independent.
T	F	11.	When using the relative frequency approach, probability figures become less accurate for large numbers of observations.
T	F	12.	Symbolically, a marginal probability is denoted P(AB).
T	F	13.	If A and B are statistically dependent events, the probability of A and B occurring is P(A) $\times$ P(B).
T	F	14.	Classical probability assumes that each of the possible outcomes of an experiment is equally likely.
T	F	15.	One reason that decision makers at high levels often use subjective probabilities is that they are concerned with unique situations.
T	F	16.	In assessing the probability of some event, the relative frequency of occurrence approach gives the greatest flexibility.
T	F	17.	Bayes' theorem is the formula for conditional probability under statistical dependence.
T	F	18.	One disadvantage of the subjective approach to probability is that it assumes away unlikely events.
T	F	19.	The relative frequency approach to probability will provide correct statistical probabilities after 100 trials.
T	F	20.	When using a subjective approach to probability, two people with the same given information can produce different but equally correct answers.
T	F	21.	A and B are independent events if P($A|B$) = P(B).

22. If one event is unaffected by the outcome of another event, the two events are said to be:
   (a) Dependent (c) Mutually exclusive (e) Both b and c.
   (b) Independent (d) All of the above

23. If P(A or B) = P(A), then
   (a) A and B are mutually exclusive
   (b) The Venn diagram areas for A and B overlap
   (c) P(A) + P(B) is the joint probability of A and B
   (d) None of the above.

24. The simple probability of an occurrence of an event is called the
   (a) Bayesian probability (c) Marginal probability
   (b) Joint probability (d) Conditional probability

25. Why are the events of a coin toss mutually exclusive?
   (a) The outcome of any toss is not affected by the outcomes of those preceding it.
   (b) Both a head and a tail cannot turn up on any one toss.
   (c) The probability of getting a head and the probability of getting a tail are the same.
   (d) All of these.
   (e) a and b but not c.

26. If a Venn diagram were drawn for events A and B, which are mutually exclusive, which of the following would always be true of A and B?
   (a) Their parts of the rectangle will overlap.
   (b) Their parts of the rectangle will be equal in area.
   (c) Their parts of the rectangle will not overlap.
   (d) None of these.
   (e) b and c but not a.

27. What is the probability that a value chosen at random from a particular population is larger than the median of the population?
   (a) .25 (b) .5 (c) 1.0 (d) .67

28. Assume that a single fair die is rolled once. Which of the following is true?
   (a) The probability of rolling a number higher than one is 1 − P(one is rolled).

(b) The probability of rolling a three is $1 - P(1, 2, 4, 5,$ or 6 is rolled).
(c) The probability of rolling a 5 or 6 is higher than the probability of rolling a 3 or 4.
(d) All of these.
(e) a and b but not c.

29. If A and B are mutually exclusive events, then $P(A$ or $B) = P(A) + P(B)$. How does the calculation of $P(A$ or $B)$ change if A and B are *not* mutually exclusive?
(a) $P(AB)$ must be subtracted from $P(A) + P(B)$.
(b) $P(AB)$ must be added to $P(A) + P(B)$.
(c) $[P(A) + P(B)]$ must be multiplied by $P(AB)$.
(d) $[P(A) + P(B)]$ must be divided by $P(AB)$.
(e) None of these.

30. Leo C. Swartz, a taxi driver in Chicago, has found that the weather affects his customers' tipping. If it is raining, his customers usually tip poorly. When it is not raining, however, they usually tip well. Which of the following is true?
(a) Tips and weather are statistically independent.
(b) The weather conditions Leo cited are not mutually exclusive.
(c) P(good tip|rain) is larger than P(bad tip|rain).
(d) None of these.
(e) a and c but not b.

31. Assume that a die is rolled twice in succession and that you are asked to draw the probability tree showing all possible outcomes of the two rolls. How many branches will your tree have?
(a) 6   (b) 12   (c) 36   (d) 42   (e) 48

Questions 32–34 refer to the following situation: Ten numbered balls are placed in an urn. Numbers 1–4 are red and numbers 5–10 are blue.

32. What is the probability that a ball drawn at random from the urn is blue?
(a) .1   (b) .4   (c) .6   (d) 1.0
(e) Cannot be determined from the information given.

33. The probability of drawing the ball numbered 3, of course, is .1. A ball is drawn, and it is red. Which of the following is true?
(a) P(ball drawn is #3|ball drawn is red) = .1
(b) P(ball drawn is #3|ball drawn is red) < .1
(c) P(ball drawn is #3|ball drawn is red) > .1
(d) P(ball drawn is red|ball drawn is #3) = .25
(e) c and d only

34. In question 33, the probability of drawing the #3 ball was reconsidered after it was found that the ball drawn was red. The new probabilities we considered are called:
(a) Exhaustive   (b) A priori   (c) Marginal   (d) Subjective   (e) None of these

35. Symbolically, a marginal probability is:
(a) $P(AB)$ (b) $P(BA)$ (c) $P(B|A)$ (d) $P(ABC)$ (e) None of these

36. If we sum all the probabilities of the conditional events in which the event A occurs while under statistical dependence, the result is:
(a) The marginal probability of A
(b) The joint probability of A
(c) The conditional probability of A
(d) None of these

37. One of the possible outcomes of doing something is a _____. The activity that produced this outcome is a _____.

38. The set of all possible outcomes of an activity is the _____.

39. A pictorial representation of probability concepts, using symbols to represent outcomes, is a _____.

40. Events that cannot happen together are called _____.

41. The probability of one event occurring, given that another event has occurred, is called _____ probability.

42. In terms of its assumptions, the least restrictive approach to the study of probability is the _____.

43. _____ theorem is often used in management decisions, since it provides ways to easily update previous probability estimates based on new information.

44. A list is _____ if it includes all the possible outcomes that can result from an experiment.

45. Three different approaches to probability include the _____ approach, the _____ approach, and the _____ approach.

4-12
Conceptual Case

(Northern White Metals Company)

The 7:00 A.M. shuttle out of New York was crowded and noisier than usual, but Dick Lennox sat back in his seat, undisturbed and deep in thought. His presentation and status report on NWMC had been well received. Segue management had decided to increase substantially the capital resources available to Northern in the coming year. Sales and earnings gains were expected, and Dick had been granted considerable latitude in ensuring that they were realized. Sufficient funding and operating flexibility were all that was needed, he had asserted, to make NWMC a significant contributor to the Segue system.

Three principal objectives were established. First, sales dollars were to be increased through greater utilization of fabricating and anodizing departments by present customers. Sales growth would also come from increasing marketing efforts with the engineering and high-technology industries, although it was suspected that stiff competition would leave this area less profitable than traditional lines of business for some time yet. A second major objective was profit improvement through the introduction of production efficiencies. NWMC had an unusually high amount of waste material compared to finished products, and it was felt that some investment in better quality assurance procedures was sorely needed. Additionally, it was felt that inefficient scheduling led to shorter and more frequent production runs, resulting in higher costs and more unproductive time than was necessary.

The third objective Dick had defined was a review and possible restructuring of the company's credit policy. Current procedures had left Northern with an average collection period of more than 60 days. The company's terms were 1½ 10 net 20, and having receivables outstanding more than three times Northern's net limit was intolerable. Just thinking about the cash flow implications made Dick wince.

Back at the office and ready to formulate his "action plan," as he liked to call it, Dick was considering various ways of expanding sales. He felt he could either add additional sales representatives or simply require the current sales force to make more calls. Management had in the past frequently adjusted the size of the sales force both up and down, and had occasionally raised call quotas to burdensome levels. Dick felt the sales force had been poorly managed, but he still had no real feeling as to which choice would be the better one. Dick was also considering implementing a program suggested by one of his bright young salespeople, Bill Hamilton. Bill had proposed that the company engage in a direct-mail campaign to some of the newer high-tech firms with the hope of generating productive new leads for the sales reps. The program was a costly one, but Bill felt sure it would be well worth it. His excitement was infectious, but Dick knew better than to get caught up in the enthusiasm of impetuous youth. The firm had no data available on this kind of program, but Dick felt he could get his hands on some industry figures that might help him make a decision.

Production efficiency improvements, although complex, were less uncertain. Dick had assigned NWMC's chief foreman and expediter, Neill Jansen, a man with considerable operations experience, the task of coordinating production runs and improving scheduling procedures. He had made rapid progress in this area, but quality problems remained. Although many of the extruded aluminum shapes were quite simple, customer specifications were often very precise and there was generally little room for tolerance error. Tolerance tests were being conducted as the extruded metal came out of the press as well as just after the stretching procedure. Dick believed some further examination of past Q/A test data could provide some insight into where the problem might lie.

Some additional insight into the outstanding credit problem was necessary too. The major primary aluminum producers, NWMC's principal raw-material suppliers, were not nearly as flexible with their credit terms as Northern was. Pay early and collect late hardly seemed like an effective financial strategy to Dick. He was quite adamant, then, when he suggested to Northern's financial officer that an analysis of outstanding past-due accounts was warranted, and quickly too.

In deciding what actions to take to reach his established objectives, Dick once again recognizes the need for more information and analysis. In resolving the sales-force question, data regarding past actions may help Dick in his current situation. What kind of information might he gather, and how should it be used in helping him select the alternative most likely to lead to success? Company data are not available to assess the viability of a direct-mail marketing program. How might external information be applied in determining whether the benefits of the program justify the costs? Quality problems occur in two steps of the manufacturing process. How might Dick determine which is more likely the problem area in most situations? Finally, in resolving Northern's payables-receivables timing disparity and its detrimental effects on cash flow, how might the financial officer determine how likely past-due collections are at all? How likely within some acceptable time frame? How might Dick and the financial officer utilize this information in credit policy formulation?

4-13
Computer Data Base Exercise

 Gary Russell, Operations Manager, caught Laurel on the way out of the staff meeting. "That was pretty impressive," he said. "I don't have an awful lot of experience with statistics, but it seems like a pretty powerful analysis tool. You've only been here a short while, but it looks like you're already getting some insight into our business posture which will be really useful to us."

"Thanks," answered Laurel. "That was just some basic work. But you're right—you can do some amazing things if you know where to start! Let me know if there's anything in your area I can look into for you."

"Now that you mention it," Gary grinned, "I've been meaning to ask you about something. Let me give you a little background. When HH Industries made the decision to reopen a warehouse in the Northeast, after the Ohio disaster, we did a study in conjunction with UPS, the carrier we do most of our business with. Using about 6 months of shipping data, they ran some fancy computer program and determined the optimal location for our warehouse. It seemed like a sound methodology at the time, and there is no doubt that the warehouse is doing well, but I've got some of my own opinions about what was and what wasn't considered in the study. However, that's a story for another time. For now, I'm just interested in whether the warehouse is effectively reaching its targeted area or not. I've got some shipping data from the Pennsylvania warehouse, with packages categorized by destination zip code and weight. Think you could do anything with it?"

"I don't see why not," Laurel replied. "Aren't state zip codes arranged in some sort of consecutive order? That would help separate out particular geographic regions."

"Sure. The first three digits indicate the area, and each state has a specific range. I'll get you that breakout when I bring back the data."

Later, entering data at her terminal, Laurel wondered about the best way to attack the problem at hand. She knew that shipping costs were based on both package weight and destination. The most critical packages, from a cost standpoint, were those designated "Next Day Air." This was where costs could add up very quickly, especially for heavier packages, as charges were 5–10 times normal UPS rates.

The following chart contains the state zip code data for use in Laurel's analysis:

STATE	ZIP RANGE	STATE	ZIP RANGE
MA	010–026	DE	197–199
RI	027–029	DC	200–205
NH	030–038	MD	206–219
ME	039–049	VA	220–246
VT	050–059	WV	247–268
CT	060–069	NC	270–289
NJ	070–089	SC	290–299
NY	100–149	GA	300–319
PA	150–196	FL	320–346

Table continued

STATE	ZIP RANGE	STATE	ZIP RANGE
AL	350–369	NE	680–693
TN	370–385	LA	700–714
MS	386–397	AR	716–729
KY	400–427	OK	730–749
OH	430–458	TX	750–799
IN	460–479	CO	800–816
MI	480–499	WY	820–831
IA	500–528	ID	832–838
WI	530–549	UT	840–847
MN	550–567	AZ	850–865
SD	570–577	NM	870–884
ND	580–588	NV	889–899
MT	590–599	CA	900–961
IL	600–629	OR	970–979
MO	630–658	WA	980–994
KS	660–679		

With Gary's help, Laurel identified seven geographic regions for the purpose of the study. *New England* would contain MA, ME, RI, NH, VT, and CT. The *Northeast* would be made up of NJ, NY, PA, DE, DC, MD, VA, and WV. The *Southeast* would include NC, SC, GA, FL, AL, TN, and MS. KY, OH, IN and MI would be called the *Midwest. North Central* would indicate IA, WI, MN, SD, ND, IL, MO, KS, and NE. The *South Central* region would include LA, AR, OK, and TX. Finally, MT, CO, WY, ID, UT, AZ, NM, NV, CA, OR, and WA would be called the *West*. In addition, packages were categorized as being of normal weight (less than ten pounds) or heavy (weighing ten pounds or more).

1. Using the shipping data on pp. 184–188, find the relative frequency of packages shipped to the seven geographic regions.

2. The target area for the Pennsylvania warehouse comprises New England, the Northeast and the Midwest. What is the probability that a package shipped from this warehouse has a destination within the target area?

3. What is the probability of a package from the Pennsylvania warehouse being shipped by Next Day Air? What is the probability of a package being classified as heavy? What is the probability of a package being heavy or being shipped by Next Day Air?

4. What is the probability of a package being heavy and being shipped within the target area? What is the probability of a package being heavy and being shipped outside of the target area?

5. Given that destination and the chance of being shipped by Next Day Air are not in-dependent, what is the probability that, given a Next Day Air package, it is shipped within the target area?

6. If a package is sent outside of the target area, what is the chance that it is shipped by Next Day Air? What about if it is sent within the target area?

7. What can Laurel generally conclude about whether the Pennsylvania warehouse is being used effectively to reach its targeted area?

A flip side to the question, Laurel realized a couple of days later, was whether or not the central warehouse in Florida, which had shipped packages to the Northeast and Midwest before the Pennsylvania location came on-line, was now taking full advantage of this particular satellite warehouse. Though there were instances, she knew, where Pennsylvania's limited inventory prevented it from servicing *every* customer in its territory, a quick look at a random sample of Florida's shipping data would show whether or not things seemed to be in order. Laurel hunted Gary down, told him of her additional questions, and got some Florida shipping data from approximately the same time period as before. Then she headed back to her terminal.

Since the most expensive packages were those shipped by Next Day Air, she extracted those from the manifests and divided them into the seven geographic regions she had previously defined. Out of a total of 2,404 packages shipped, 500 fit into this category. The results are as follows:

New England	24
Northeast	42
Southeast	172
Midwest	32
North Central	63
South Central	110
West	57

8. What is the relative frequency of Next Day Air packages shipped from Florida to within the Pennsylvania warehouse's targeted area?

9. If the intended target area of the Florida warehouse is the Southeast and South Central areas, what is the probability of a Next Day Air package being shipped within that region?

10. Can Laurel give Gary any idea whether the Florida warehouse is being used efficiently, considering the location of the other two warehouses?

ZIP	WEIGHT	NEXT DAY	ZIP	WEIGHT	NEXT DAY	ZIP	WEIGHT	NEXT DAY
852	6	N	435	1	N	117	5	N
554	1	N	63	5	Y	159	16	N
272	8	N	478	2	N	402	2	N
465	4	N	32	4	Y	451	1	N
478	2	N	448	2	Y	146	3	N
61	1	N	11	1	Y	88	2	N
161	2	N	117	2	Y	191	2	N
197	2	N	232	2	N	447	2	N
462	2	N	448	3	N	130	1	N
23	6	Y	20	2	Y	145	1	N
212	1	N	18	1	Y	179	1	N
478	4	Y	487	1	N	440	1	N
117	2	N	440	3	Y	11	1	N
448	3	N	478	3	Y	18	1	N
620	1	Y	67	3	Y	487	4	Y
441	1	N	30	14	N	70	2	N
217	3	N	77	1	N	30	3	N
75	2	N	207	5	N	852	8	N
334	1	Y	441	1	N	173	5	N
226	2	N	489	2	N	452	1	N
31	2	N	927	2	Y	425	7	N
315	1	Y	460	6	N	463	9	N
477	1	N	120	7	N	23	1	Y
444	1	N	191	2	N	487	2	Y
184	3	N	172	1	N	409	2	Y
448	9	N	237	1	N	233	2	N
103	3	N	117	1	N	161	1	N
43	2	Y	440	1	N	454	3	N
130	1	Y	64	1	N	11	1	Y
440	6	N	463	2	N	247	2	Y
172	1	N	140	6	N	478	2	N
11	2	N	30	3	Y	477	2	N
440	2	Y	197	2	N	171	1	N
265	10	N	121	1	N	441	2	N
175	1	N	144	1	N	334	1	N
212	3	N	120	2	Y	166	1	N
70	4	Y	103	13	N	172	1	N
719	1	N	232	1	N	117	7	N
80	3	N	333	1	N	852	1	N
176	1	N	237	5	N	140	2	Y
454	2	N	112	5	Y	12	1	Y
121	3	N	334	1	N	161	2	Y
331	1	N	468	4	Y	140	6	N
303	1	N	12	2	Y	121	2	N
170	1	N	445	1	N	30	3	N
68	1	N	172	1	N	232	1	N
253	1	N	194	1	N	236	1	N
21	1	N	121	1	Y	194	1	N
477	7	Y	30	4	N	464	2	Y
20	1	N	465	2	N	448	3	N
252	2	N	850	1	Y	117	9	N
444	5	N	443	3	N	135	10	N
443	5	N	444	2	N	207	5	N
497	1	N	448	4	N	87	1	N
130	1	N	23	1	N	448	2	N

Table continued

ZIP	WEIGHT	NEXT DAY	ZIP	WEIGHT	NEXT DAY	ZIP	WEIGHT	NEXT DAY
130	22	N	440	2	N	441	1	N
700	1	N	478	3	N	486	2	Y
117	5	N	184	2	N	120	4	Y
145	2	N	68	1	N	443	1	N
479	6	Y	64	60	N	12	1	Y
172	1	N	212	1	N	293	2	Y
478	4	N	70	7	N	67	3	N
145	3	N	18	2	N	70	1	N
553	1	Y	497	2	N	482	1	N
77	1	N	117	2	N	441	2	N
175	2	N	478	2	N	957	3	N
30	8	N	77	3	N	409	1	Y
294	1	N	232	2	N	75	3	N
70	4	N	30	1	N	174	4	N
448	10	N	443	2	N	232	2	N
478	1	N	23	1	Y	212	3	N
180	33	N	159	7	N	448	7	Y
180	53	N	477	1	N	832	1	N
136	1	N	176	1	N	64	2	Y
625	1	N	75	3	N	160	3	N
153	7	Y	136	1	N	443	2	N
442	2	N	21	1	N	178	4	N
191	4	N	145	1	N	191	2	N
346	4	N	32	2	N	759	1	N
218	9	N	117	1	N	159	5	N
184	1	N	120	1	N	121	2	N
117	7	N	172	1	N	121	3	N
70	2	N	32	2	N	212	1	N
165	1	N	136	1	N	64	2	Y
70	1	N	448	2	N	370	1	Y
120	3	Y	100	7	N	487	2	N
32	3	Y	441	2	N	20	6	Y
128	3	Y	563	1	N	218	1	N
117	1	N	236	4	N	30	22	N
463	11	N	103	5	N	128	3	Y
130	3	N	232	1	N	441	2	N
145	2	N	194	4	N	145	6	N
136	4	N	432	4	Y	44	4	N
161	5	N	487	6	Y	446	4	N
41	1	N	18	1	Y	159	1	N
218	1	N	478	3	Y	871	1	N
487	1	Y	466	6	N	922	1	N
700	1	Y	477	2	Y	922	1	N
176	2	N	486	2	Y	117	2	N
448	2	N	425	50	N	140	2	N
30	3	N	443	2	N	64	3	N
18	1	Y	70	51	N	432	2	Y
176	2	N	175	2	N	448	1	N
448	2	N	172	6	N	120	1	N
174	4	N	163	7	N	245	12	N
117	4	N	448	3	N	14	1	N
852	6	N	159	5	N	64	2	N
30	1	Y	487	4	N	232	2	N
172	3	N	12	1	Y	236	11	N
87	2	N	30	8	N	218	1	N

Table continued

ZIP	WEIGHT	NEXT DAY	ZIP	WEIGHT	NEXT DAY	ZIP	WEIGHT	NEXT DAY
140	10	N	18	2	Y	145	5	N
442	4	N	302	6	Y	409	2	N
237	4	N	402	9	Y	232	3	N
140	5	N	130	8	N	440	4	N
217	2	N	463	9	N	130	4	N
245	2	N	87	2	N	121	1	Y
451	1	N	458	3	N	189	4	N
165	1	N	487	2	Y	179	4	N
265	4	N	197	1	N	159	8	N
31	4	N	87	1	N	478	8	N
32	2	Y	681	4	N	336	1	Y
11	2	Y	11	1	Y	113	1	N
265	2	N	448	2	N	12	2	Y
352	1	N	441	1	N	68	1	N
67	5	N	237	8	N	109	3	N
435	2	N	75	3	N	432	1	Y
478	3	N	207	4	N	30	2	N
121	1	N	478	1	N	329	1	N
30	4	N	131	2	N	67	1	N
30	1	Y	80	4	N	87	3	Y
448	2	Y	70	1	N	18	2	Y
448	3	N	120	1	Y	440	2	Y
172	1	N	32	3	Y	497	1	N
103	3	N	166	2	N	451	16	N
147	1	N	88	4	N	237	4	N
563	1	N	30	7	N	480	2	Y
322	2	N	446	6	N	159	1	N
140	27	N	478	3	N	41	3	Y
451	5	N	159	6	N	194	2	N
489	1	Y	681	1	N	12	1	Y
409	3	Y	463	1	Y	67	8	Y
144	1	N	477	4	N	163	1	N
150	1	Y	63	5	N	443	1	Y
117	1	N	444	3	N	445	1	N
135	1	N	161	1	Y	448	2	Y
346	1	Y	346	7	N	444	2	N
18	4	Y	440	1	Y	207	6	Y
18	3	Y	176	3	N	64	3	Y
21	1	Y	463	1	N	21	1	Y
320	2	N	284	1	N	154	4	N
23	1	Y	117	2	N	755	1	Y
218	1	N	87	1	N	436	2	N
441	7	N	443	4	N	146	1	N
463	6	N	145	1	N	442	1	N
30	5	N	117	2	Y	30	1	N
232	2	N	265	16	N	30	1	N
443	2	Y	336	1	N	159	1	N
436	1	Y	462	3	Y	218	1	N
64	2	Y	486	2	Y	117	7	N
440	4	Y	70	1	N	100	7	N
12	5	Y	462	9	N	435	1	N
338	1	N	21	5	N	140	8	N
704	1	Y	150	1	N	75	13	N
121	1	N	443	3	N	130	5	N
232	1	N	463	3	N	136	2	N

Table continued

ZIP	WEIGHT	NEXT DAY	ZIP	WEIGHT	NEXT DAY	ZIP	WEIGHT	NEXT DAY
70	2	Y	30	13	N	487	3	N
140	1	Y	449	1	N	165	3	N
44	4	N	174	7	N	444	4	N
172	5	N	196	4	N	117	1	N
30	9	N	161	4	Y	233	5	N
448	3	N	445	28	N	162	1	N
191	2	N	32	2	Y	77	6	N
265	2	N	448	4	N	324	1	N
220	2	N	338	1	N	184	5	N
479	3	N	479	2	N	448	1	N
70	3	N	489	1	Y	64	2	Y
346	8	Y	331	2	N	443	3	Y
478	9	N	600	2	Y	445	2	N
441	1	N	30	4	N	194	5	N
446	1	N	440	1	N	32	3	Y
207	2	N	191	1	N	64	4	N
30	5	N	60	1	N	64	12	Y
103	8	N	159	1	N	448	4	N
212	1	N	466	4	N	338	1	Y
218	1	N	178	5	N	441	1	N
463	3	N	236	2	N	184	1	N
17	12	N	232	2	N	445	6	N
336	1	Y	440	1	N	30	2	N
130	2	N	559	1	Y	232	4	N
208	2	N	448	3	N	628	2	N
163	1	N	478	4	N	128	3	N
232	1	N	70	2	N	462	6	N
146	3	N	237	2	N	323	1	Y
335	1	N	161	3	N	117	5	N
87	7	N	21	50	N	237	1	N
481	3	Y	70	30	N	109	3	N
218	1	N	117	2	N	463	1	N
161	2	N	478	3	N	448	4	N
197	1	Y	294	1	N	30	2	N
67	2	N	41	2	N	441	1	N
217	1	N	480	2	N	172	2	N
440	1	N	113	2	N	485	3	N
121	1	N	482	1	N	30	5	N
88	5	N	161	2	Y	20	2	N
435	1	N	480	1	Y	109	2	N
115	1	N	121	2	N	478	6	N
258	4	N	443	2	Y	207	50	Y
39	2	N	30	5	N	451	1	N
442	2	N	112	1	Y	442	4	Y
117	3	N	117	5	N	136	5	N
265	3	N	184	4	N	70	1	Y
70	1	N	463	9	N	40	1	N
463	2	Y	465	1	Y	446	7	N
247	1	N	70	2	N	237	1	N
150	2	N	159	7	N	723	2	N
232	3	N	486	4	Y	184	2	N
293	8	N	12	1	Y	487	3	N
20	8	Y	487	2	N	21	5	Y
30	6	N	310	1	N	32	1	Y
477	1	N	448	3	N	443	3	N

Table continued

ZIP	WEIGHT	NEXT DAY	ZIP	WEIGHT	NEXT DAY	ZIP	WEIGHT	NEXT DAY
70	1	N	446	4	N	30	1	N
245	4	N	194	4	N	184	2	N
109	5	N	70	1	Y	329	1	Y
478	3	N	117	3	N	87	2	Y
21	2	N	708	5	N	448	2	N
432	6	Y	554	1	N	497	3	N
30	7	N	448	1	Y	232	1	N
172	1	N	625	4	Y	30	2	N
88	1	N	145	1	N	440	2	N
217	1	N	478	4	N	153	2	Y
443	4	N	87	1	Y	331	1	N
463	3	N	212	5	N	462	5	Y
178	5	N	478	3	Y	402	21	N
477	8	N	436	1	Y	130	9	N
80	4	N	174	8	N	441	1	N
215	1	N	197	1	N	67	2	N
117	1	N	486	38	N	465	14	N
218	1	N	161	2	Y	70	2	N
454	1	Y	212	2	N	237	5	N
87	2	Y	121	4	N	161	5	N
453	2	Y	120	2	N	174	2	N
140	20	N	440	8	N	486	1	N
137	2	N	253	5	N	176	5	N
77	1	Y	30	5	N	20	2	N
153	12	Y	850	1	Y	70	4	N
445	4	N	304	1	N	448	5	N
402	7	N	982	2	N	435	1	Y
10	1	N	316	1	N	161	3	Y
441	1	N	478	1	N	191	2	N
233	2	N	64	1	N	799	2	Y
70	2	Y	80	1	N	175	3	N
232	1	N	130	1	N	12	2	Y
236	1	N	70	5	N	448	3	N
18	2	N	70	1	Y	30	7	N
21	5	Y	161	2	Y	207	6	N
443	1	N	128	1	Y	319	1	N
478	7	N	293	1	N	30	4	Y
21	5	N	64	1	Y			
478	3	Y	444	5	Y			

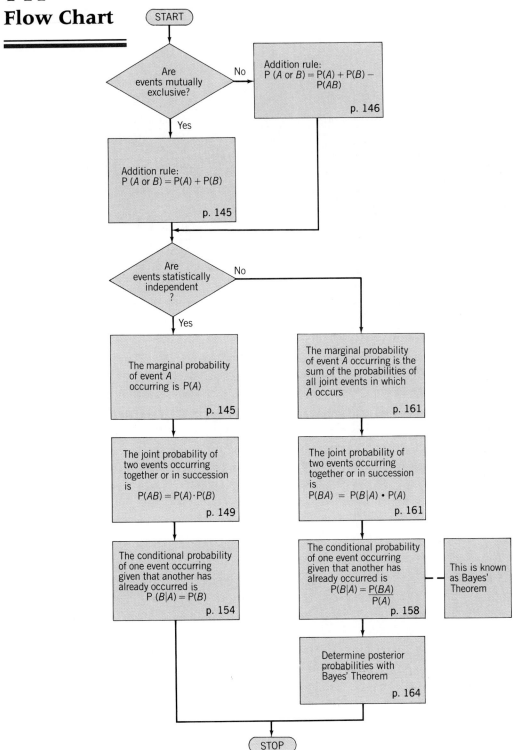

Modern filling machines are designed to work efficiently and with high reliability. Machines like the one pictured can fill tooth paste tubes to within .1 ounce of the desired level 80 percent of the time. A visitor to the plant, watching filled tubes being placed into cartons, asked, "What's the chance that exactly half the tubes in a carton selected at random will be filled to within .1 ounce of the desired level?" Although we cannot make an exact forecast, the ideas about probability distributions discussed in this chapter enable us to give a pretty good answer to the question.

5

Probability II: Distributions

■ **OBJECTIVES**

In Chapter 5, we are concerned with probability distributions; that is, the various ways data array themselves when we graph them. Here again we are laying the foundation for later work in statistical inference. You may have a notion about probability distributions if you have dealt with the bell-shaped curve in psychology or mathematics. Or if you are a male who wears a 16EE shoe or a female who wears size 3AAAA, you may have an intuitive idea about probability distributions. When you cannot be fitted, you probably wish the shoe-store manager would order a larger distribution of sizes; but a manager who thinks in terms of correct probability distributions will probably not order such unusual sizes and won't be able to accommodate people with very large or very small feet.

Most consequential managerial decisions are made under conditions of uncertainty, because decision makers seldom have complete information about what the future will bring. Also introduced in Chapter 5 is statistical decision theory, those methods that are useful when we must decide among alternatives despite uncertain conditions.

Introduction to Probability Distributions

Probability distributions and frequency distributions

In Chapter 2, we described frequency distributions as a useful way of summarizing variations in observed data. We prepared frequency distributions by listing all the possible outcomes of an experiment and then indicating the observed frequency of each possible outcome. *Probability distributions* are related to frequency distributions. **In fact, we can think of a probability distribution as a theoretical frequency distribution.** Now, what does that mean? A theoretical frequency distribution is a probability distribution that describes how outcomes are *expected* to vary. Since these distributions deal with expectations, they are useful models in making inferences and decisions under conditions of uncertainty. In later chapters, we will discuss the methods we use under these conditions.

EXAMPLES OF PROBABILITY DISTRIBUTIONS

Experiment using a fair coin

To begin our study of probability distributions, let's go back to the idea of a fair coin, which we introduced in Chapter 4. Suppose we toss a fair coin twice. Table 5-1 illustrates the possible outcomes from this two-toss experiment.

TABLE 5-1 Possible Outcomes from Two Tosses of a Fair Coin

FIRST TOSS	SECOND TOSS	NUMBER OF TAILS ON TWO TOSSES	PROBABILITY OF THE FOUR POSSIBLE OUTCOMES
T	T	2	$.5 \times .5 = .25$
T	H	1	$.5 \times .5 = .25$
H	H	0	$.5 \times .5 = .25$
H	T	1	$.5 \times .5 = .25$
			1.00

Now suppose that we are interested in formulating a probability distribution of the number of tails that could possibly result when we toss the coin twice. We would begin by noting any outcome that did *not* contain a tail. With a fair coin, that is only the third outcome in Table 5-1: *H, H*. Then we would note those outcomes containing only one tail (the second and fourth outcomes in Table 5-1), and finally we would note that the first outcome contains two tails. In Table 5-2 we rearrange the outcomes of Table 5-1 to emphasize the number of tails contained in each outcome. We must be careful to note at this point that Table 5-2 is *not* the actual outcome of tossing a fair

TABLE 5-2 Probability Distribution of Possible Number of Tails from Two Tosses of a Fair Coin

NUMBER OF TAILS T	TOSSES	PROBABILITY OF THIS OUTCOME P(T)
0	(H, H)	.25
1	(T, H) + (H, T)	.50
2	(T, T)	.25

FIGURE 5-1

Probability
distribution of the
number of tails in
two tosses of a
fair coin

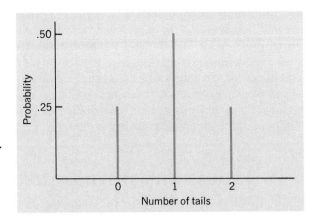

coin twice. Rather, it is a *theoretical* outcome; that is, it represents the way in which we would *expect* our two-toss experiment to behave over time.

We can illustrate in graphic form the probability distribution in Table 5-2. To do this, we graph the number of tails we might see on two tosses against the probability that this number would happen. We have shown this graph in Fig. 5-1.

Voting example

Consider another example. A political candidate for local office is considering the votes she can get in a coming election. Assume that votes can take on only four possible values. If the candidate's assessment is like this:

Number of votes	1,000	2,000	3,000	4,000	
Probability this will happen	.1	.3	.4	.2	**Total 1.0**

then the graph of the probability distribution representing her expectations will be like the one shown in Fig. 5-2.

Difference between
frequency distributions
and probability
distributions

Before we move on to other aspects of probability distributions, we should point out that a **frequency distribution is a listing of the observed frequencies of all the outcomes of an experiment that actually occurred when the experiment was done,**

FIGURE 5-2

Probability
distribution of
number of votes

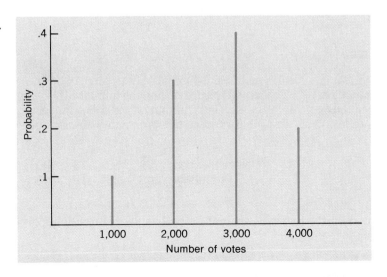

whereas a probability distribution is a listing of the probabilities of all the possible outcomes that *could* result if the experiment were done. Also, as we can see in the two examples we presented in Figs. 5-1 and 5-2, probability distributions can be based on theoretical considerations (the tosses of a coin) or on a subjective assessment of the likelihood of certain outcomes (the candidate's estimate). Probability distributions can also be based on experience. Insurance company actuaries determine insurance premiums, for example, by using long years of experience with death rates to establish probabilities of dying among various age groups.

TYPES OF PROBABILITY DISTRIBUTIONS

Discrete probability distributions

Probability distributions are classified as either *discrete* or *continuous*. A discrete probability is allowed to take on only a limited number of values. An example of a discrete probability distribution is shown in Fig. 5-2, where we expressed the candidate's ideas about the coming election. There, votes were allowed to take on only four possible values (1,000, 2,000, 3,000, or 4,000). Similarly, the probability that you were born in a given month is also discrete, since there are only twelve possible values (the twelve months of the year).

Continuous probability distributions

In a continuous probability distribution, on the other hand, the variable under consideration is allowed to take on any value within a given range. Suppose we were examining the level of effluent in a variety of streams, and we measured the level of effluent by parts of effluent per million parts of water. We would expect quite a continuous range of ppm (parts per million), all the way from very low levels in clear mountain streams to extremely high levels in polluted streams. In fact, it would be quite normal for the variable "parts per million" to take on an enormous number of values. We would call the distribution of this variable (ppm), a continuous distribution. Continuous distributions are convenient ways to represent discrete distributions that have many possible outcomes, all very close to each other.

Exercises

 5-1 The regional chairman of the Muscular Dystrophy Association is trying to estimate the amount that each caller will pledge during the annual MDA telethon. Using data gathered over the past 10 years, she has computed the following probabilities of various pledge amounts. Draw a graph illustrating this probability distribution.

Dollars pledged	25	50	75	100	125
Probability	.45	.25	.15	.10	.05

 5-2 Based on the following graph of a probability distribution, construct the table that corresponds to the graph.

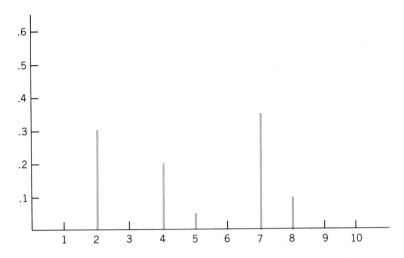

5-3 In the last chapter, we looked at the possible outcomes of tossing two dice, and we calculated some probabilities associated with various outcomes. Construct a table and a graph of the probability distribution representing the outcomes (in terms of total numbers of dots showing on both dice) for this experiment.

5-4 Which of the following statements regarding probability distributions are correct?
    (a) A probability distribution provides information about the long-run or expected frequency of each outcome of an experiment.
    (b) The graph of a probability distribution has the possible outcomes of an experiment marked on the horizontal axis.
    (c) A probability distribution lists the probabilities that each outcome is random.
    (d) A probability distribution is always constructed from a set of observed frequencies like a frequency distribution.
    (e) A probability distribution may be based on subjective estimates of the likelihood of certain outcomes.

5-5 Southport Autos offers a variety of luxury options on its cars. Because of the 6- to 8-week waiting period for customer orders, Ben Stoler, the dealer, stocks his cars with a variety of options. Currently, Mr. Stoler, who prides himself on being able to meet his customers' needs immediately, is worried because of an industrywide shortage of cars with V-8 engines. Stoler offers the following luxury combinations:

1. V-8 engine   electric sun roof   halogen headlights
2. Leather interior   power door locks   stereo cassette deck
3. Halogen headlights   V-8 engine   leather interior
4. Stereo cassette deck   V-8 engine   power door locks

Stoler thinks that combinations 2, 3, and 4 have an equal chance of being ordered, but that combination 1 is twice as likely to be ordered as any of these.
    (a) What is the probability that any one customer ordering a luxury car will order one with a V-8 engine?
    (b) Assume that two customers order luxury cars. Construct a table showing the probability distribution of the number of V-8 engines ordered.

5-6 Jim Rieck, a marketing analyst for Flatt and Mitney Aircraft, believes that the company's new Tigerhawk jet fighter has a 70 percent chance of being chosen to replace the U.S. Air Force's current jet fighter completely. However, there is one chance in five that the Air Force will buy only enough Tigerhawks to replace half of its 5,000 jet fighters. Finally, there is one chance in ten that the Air Force will replace all of its jet fighters with Tigerhawks and will buy enough Tigerhawks to expand its jet fighter fleet by 10 percent. Construct a table and draw a graph of the probability distribution of sales of Tigerhawks to the Air Force.

5-2
Random Variables

Random variable defined

A random variable is a variable that takes on different values as a result of the outcomes of a random experiment. A random variable can be either discrete or continuous. If a random variable is allowed to take on only a limited number of values, it is a *discrete random variable.* On the other hand, if it is allowed to assume any value within a given range, it is a *continuous random variable.*

Example of discrete random variables

You can think of a random variable as a value or magnitude that changes from occurrence to occurrence in no predictable sequence. A breast-cancer screening clinic, for example, has no way of knowing exactly how many women will be screened on any one day. So tomorrow's number of patients is a random variable. The values of a random variable are the numerical values corresponding to each possible outcome of the random experiment. If past daily records of the clinic indicate that the values of the random variable range from 100 to 115 patients daily, the random variable is a discrete random variable.

Creating a probability distribution

Table 5-3 illustrates the number of times each level has been reached during the last 100 days. Note that Table 5-3 gives a frequency distribution. To the extent that we believe that the experience of the past 100 days has been typical, we can use this historical record to assign a probability to each possible number of patients and find a probability distribution. We have accomplished this in Table 5-4, by *normalizing* the

TABLE 5-3 **Number of Women Screened Daily During 100 Days**

NUMBER SCREENED	NUMBER OF DAYS THIS LEVEL WAS OBSERVED
100	1
101	2
102	3
103	5
104	6
105	7
106	9
107	10
108	12
109	11
110	9
111	8
112	6
113	5
114	4
115	2
	100

TABLE 5-4 Probability Distribution for Number of Women Screened

NUMBER SCREENED (VALUE OF THE RANDOM VARIABLE)	PROBABILITY THAT THE RANDOM VARIABLE WILL TAKE ON THIS VALUE
100	.01
101	.02
102	.03
103	.05
104	.06
105	.07
106	.09
107	.10
108	.12
109	.11
110	.09
111	.08
112	.06
113	.05
114	.04
115	.02
	1.00

observed frequency distribution (in this case, dividing each value in the right-hand column of Table 5-3 by 100, the total number of days for which the record has been kept). The probability distribution for the random variable "daily number screened" is illustrated graphically in Fig. 5-3. Notice that the probability distribution for a random variable provides a probability for each possible value and that these probabilities must sum to 1. Table 5-4 shows that both these requirements have been met. Furthermore, both Table 5-4 and Fig. 5-3 give us information about the long-run frequency of occurrence of daily patient screenings we would expect to observe if this random "experiment" were repeated.

FIGURE 5-3

Probability distribution for the discrete random variable "daily number screened"

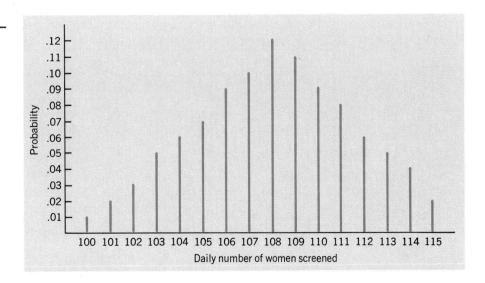

THE EXPECTED VALUE OF A RANDOM VARIABLE

Suppose you toss a coin ten times and get seven heads, like this:

HEADS	TAILS	TOTAL
7	3	10

Hmm, strange, you say. You then ask a friend to try tossing the coin 20 times; she gets fifteen heads and five tails. So now you have, in all, 22 heads and eight tails out of 30 tosses.

What did you expect? Was it something closer to fifteen heads and fifteen tails (half and half)? Now suppose you turn the tossing over to a machine and get 792 heads and 208 tails out of 1,000 tosses of the same coin. You might now be suspicious of the coin because it didn't live up to what you expected.

Expected value is a fundamental idea in the study of probability distributions. For many years, the concept has been put to considerable practical use by the insurance industry, and in the last 20 years, it has been widely used by many others who must make decisions under conditions of uncertainty.

Calculating expected value

To obtain the **expected value of a discrete random variable,** we multiply each value that the random variable can assume by the probability of occurrence of that value and then sum these products. Table 5-5 illustrates this procedure for our clinic problem. The total in Table 5-5 tells us that the expected value of the discrete random variable "number screened" is 108.02 women. What does this mean? It means that over a long period of time, the number of daily screenings should average about 108.02. Remember that an expected value of 108.02 does *not* mean that tomorrow exactly 108.02 women will visit the clinic.

TABLE 5-5 Calculating the Expected Value of the Discrete Random Variable "Daily Number Screened"

POSSIBLE VALUES OF THE RANDOM VARIABLE (1)	PROBABILITY THAT THE RANDOM VARIABLE WILL TAKE ON THESE VALUES (2)	(1) × (2)
100	.01	1.00
101	.02	2.02
102	.03	3.06
103	.05	5.15
104	.06	6.24
105	.07	7.35
106	.09	9.54
107	.10	10.70
108	.12	12.96
109	.11	11.99
110	.09	9.90
111	.08	8.88
112	.06	6.72
113	.05	5.65
114	.04	4.56
115	.02	2.30
	Expected value of the random variable "daily number screened" →	**108.02**

The clinic director would base her decisions on the expected value of daily screenings because the expected value is a *weighted average of the outcomes she expects in the future.* Expected value *weights* each possible outcome by the frequency with which it is expected to occur. Thus, more common occurrences are given more weight than are less common ones. As conditions change over time, the director would recompute the expected value of daily screenings and use this new figure as a basis for decision making.

Deriving expected value subjectively

In our clinic example, the director used past patients' records as the basis for calculating the expected value of daily screenings. The expected value can also be derived from the director's subjective assessments of the probability that the random variable will take on certain values. In that case, the expected value represents nothing more than her personal convictions about the possible outcome.

In this section, we have worked with the probability distribution of a random variable in tabular form (Table 5-5) and in graphic form (Fig. 5-3). In many situations, however, we will find it more convenient, in terms of the computations that must be done, to represent the probability distribution of a random variable in *algebraic* form. By doing this, we can make probability calculations by substituting numerical values directly into an algebraic formula. In the following sections, we shall illustrate situations in which this is appropriate and methods for accomplishing it.

Exercises

5-7 Construct a table for a probability distribution based on the frequency distribution given below.

Outcome	102	105	108	111	114	117
Frequency	10	20	45	15	20	15

(a) Draw a graph of the hypothetical probability distribution.
(b) Compute the expected value of the outcome.

5-8 From the following graph of a probability distribution:
(a) Construct a table of the probability distribution.
(b) Find the expected value of the random variable.

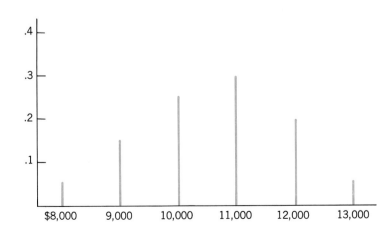

5-2 Random Variables**199**

5-9 Bob Walters, who frequently invests in the stock market, carefully studies any potential investment. He is currently examining the possibility of investing in the Trinity Power Company. Through studying past performance, Walters has broken the potential results of the investment into five possible outcomes with accompanying probabilities. The outcomes are annual rates of return on a single share of stock that currently costs $150. Find the expected value of the return on investing in a single share of Trinity Power.

Return on investment ($)	0.00	10.00	15.00	25.00	50.00
Probability	.20	.25	.30	.15	.10

If Walters purchases stock only if the expected rate of return exceeds 10 percent, will he purchase the stock, according to these data?

5-10 The only information available to you regarding the probability distribution of a set of outcomes is the following list of frequencies:

X	0	15	30	45	60	75
Frequency	25	125	75	175	75	25

(a) Construct a probability distribution for the set of outcomes.
(b) Find the expected value of an outcome.

5-11 Steven T. Opsine, supervisor of traffic signals for the Fairfax County division of the Virginia State Highway Administration, must decide whether to install a traffic light at the reportedly dangerous intersection of Dolley Madison Blvd. and Lewinsville Rd. Toward this end, Mr. Opsine has collected the following data on accidents at the intersection:

NUMBER OF ACCIDENTS

YEAR	J	F	M	A	M	J	J	A	S	O	N	D
1988	10	8	10	6	9	12	2	10	10	0	7	10
1989	12	9	7	8	4	3	7	14	8	8	8	4

S.H.A. policy is to install a traffic light at an intersection at which the monthly expected number of accidents is higher than seven. According to this criterion, should Mr. Opsine recommend that a traffic light be installed at this intersection?

5-12 Alan Sarkid is the president of the Dinsdale Insurance Company and is concerned about the high cost of claims that take a long time to settle. Consequently, he has asked his chief actuary, Dr. Ivan Acke, to analyze the distribution of time until settlement. Dr. Acke has presented him with the following graph:

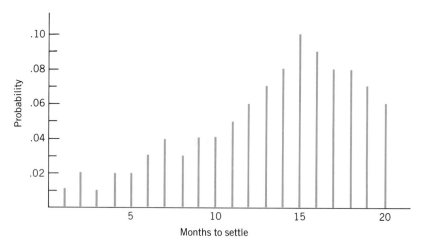

Dr. Acke also informed Mr. Sarkid of the expected amount of time to settle a claim. What is this figure?

5-13 The fire marshall of Baltimore County, Maryland, is compiling a report on single-family dwelling fires. He has the following data on the number of such fires from the last 2 years:

Number of Fires

YEAR	J	F	M	A	M	J	J	A	S	O	N	D
1989	25	30	15	10	10	5	2	2	1	4	8	10
1990	20	25	10	8	5	2	4	0	5	8	10	15

Based on these data:
(a) What is the expected number of single-family dwelling fires per month?
(b) What is the expected number of single-family dwelling fires per winter month (January, February, March)?

5-14 Ted Olson, the director of Overnight Delivery, Inc., has become concerned about the number of first-class letters lost by his firm. Since these letters are carried by both truck and airplane, Mr. Olson has broken down the lost letters for the last year into those lost from trucks and those lost from airplanes. His data are as follows:

Number lost from:	J	F	M	A	M	J	J	A	S	O	N	D
Truck	4	5	2	3	2	1	3	5	4	7	0	1
Airplane	5	6	0	2	1	3	4	2	4	7	4	0

Mr. Olson plans to investigate either the trucking or air division of the company, but not both. If he decides to investigate the division with the highest expected number of lost letters per month, which will he investigate?

5-3
Use of Expected Value in Decision Making

In the preceding section, we calculated the expected value of a random variable and noted that it can have significant value to decision makers. Now we need to take a moment to illustrate how decision makers combine the probabilities that a random variable will take on certain values with the monetary gain or loss that results when it does take on those values. Doing just this enables them to make intelligent decisions under uncertain conditions.

COMBINING PROBABILITIES AND MONETARY VALUES

Wholesaler problem Let us look at the case of a fruit and vegetable wholesaler who sells strawberries. This product has a very limited useful life. If not sold on the day of delivery, it is worthless. One case of strawberries costs $20, and the wholesaler receives $50 for it. The wholesaler cannot specify the number of cases customers will call for on any one day, but her analysis of past records has produced the information in Table 5-6.

TABLE 5-6 Sales During 100 Days

DAILY SALES	NUMBER OF DAYS SOLD	PROBABILITY OF EACH NUMBER BEING SOLD
10	15	.15
11	20	.20
12	40	.40
13	25	.25
	100	**1.00**

TABLE 5-7 Conditional Loss Table

POSSIBLE REQUESTS FOR STRAWBERRIES	Possible stock actions			
	10	11	12	13
10	$ 0	$20	$40	$60
11	30	0	20	40
12	60	30	0	20
13	90	60	30	0

TYPES OF LOSSES DEFINED

Obsolescence and opportunity losses

Two types of losses are incurred by the wholesaler: (1) *obsolescence losses,* caused by stocking too much fruit on any one day and having to throw it away the next day; and (2) *opportunity losses,* caused by being out of strawberries any time that customers call for them. (Customers will not wait beyond the day a case is requested.)

Table of conditional losses

Table 5-7 is a table of conditional losses. Each value in the table is conditional on a specific number of cases being stocked and a specific number being requested. The values in Table 5-7 include not only losses from decaying berries but also those losses resulting from lost revenue when the wholesaler is unable to supply the requests she receives for the berries.

Obsolescence losses

Neither of these two types of losses is incurred when the number of cases stocked on any one day is the same as the number of cases requested. When that happens, the wholesaler sells all she has stocked and incurs no losses. This situation is indicated by a colored zero in the appropriate column. Figures **above** any zero represent losses arising from spoiled berries. In each case here, the number of cases stocked is greater than the number requested. For example, if the wholesaler stocks twelve cases but receives requests for only ten cases, she loses $40 (or $20 per case for spoiled strawberries).

Opportunity losses

Values **below** the colored zeros represent opportunity losses resulting from requests that cannot be filled. If only ten cases are stocked on a day that eleven requests are received, the wholesaler suffers an opportunity loss of $30 for the case she cannot sell ($50 income per case that would have been received minus $20 cost equals $30).

CALCULATING EXPECTED LOSSES

Examining each possible stock action, we can compute the expected loss. We do this by weighting each of the four possible loss figures in each column of Table 5-7 by the probabilities from Table 5-6. For a stock action of ten cases, the expected loss is computed as in Table 5-8.

TABLE 5-8 Expected Loss from Stocking Ten Cases

POSSIBLE REQUESTS	CONDITIONAL LOSS		PROBABILITY OF THIS MANY REQUESTS		EXPECTED LOSS
10	$ 0	×	.15	=	$ .00
11	30	×	.20	=	6.00
12	60	×	.40	=	24.00
13	90	×	.25	=	22.50
			1.00		$52.50

Meaning of
expected loss

Optimal solution

The conditional losses in Table 5-8 are taken from the first column of Table 5-7 for a stock action of ten cases. The fourth column total in Table 5-8 shows us that if ten cases are stocked each day, over a long period of time the average or expected loss will be $52.50 a day. There is no guarantee that *tomorrow's* loss will be exactly $52.50.

Tables 5-9 through 5-11 show the computations of the expected loss resulting from decisions to stock eleven, twelve, and thirteen cases, respectively. **The optimal stock action is the one that will minimize expected losses.** This action calls for the stocking of twelve cases each day, at which point the expected loss is minimized at $17.50. We could just as easily have solved this problem by taking an alternative approach; that is, *maximizing expected gain* ($50 received per case less $20 cost per case) instead of minimizing expected loss. The answer, twelve cases, would have been the same.

In our brief treatment of expected value, we have made quite a few assumptions. To name only two, we've assumed that demand for the product can take on only four values, and that the berries are worth nothing one day later. Both these assumptions reduce the value of the answer we got. In Chapter 15, you will again encounter expected-value decision making, but there we will develop the ideas as a part of

TABLE 5-9 Expected Loss from Stocking Eleven Cases

POSSIBLE REQUESTS	CONDITIONAL LOSS		PROBABILITY OF THIS MANY REQUESTS		EXPECTED LOSS
10	$20	×	.15	=	$ 3.00
11	0	×	.20	=	.00
12	30	×	.40	=	12.00
13	60	×	.25	=	15.00
			1.00		$30.00

TABLE 5-10 Expected Loss from Stocking Twelve Cases

POSSIBLE REQUESTS	CONDITIONAL LOSS		PROBABILITY OF THIS MANY REQUESTS		EXPECTED LOSS
10	$40	×	.15	=	$ 6.00
11	20	×	.20	=	4.00
12	0	×	.40	=	.00
13	30	×	.25	=	7.50
			1.00	minimum → expected loss	$17.50

TABLE 5-11 Expected Loss from Stocking Thirteen Cases

POSSIBLE REQUESTS	CONDITIONAL LOSS		PROBABILITY OF THIS MANY REQUESTS		EXPECTED LOSS
10	$60	×	.15	=	$ 9.00
11	40	×	.20	=	8.00
12	20	×	.40	=	8.00
13	0	×	.25	=	.00
			1.00		$25.00

statistical decision theory (a broader use of statistical methods to make decisions), and we shall devote an entire chapter to expanding the basic ideas we have developed at this point.

Exercises

 5-15 Harry Byrd, the director of publications for the Baltimore Orioles, is trying to decide how many programs to print for the team's upcoming three-game series with the Oakland A's. Each program costs 25¢ to print and sells for $1.25. Any programs unsold at the end of the series must be discarded. Mr. Byrd has estimated the following probability distribution for program sales, using data from past program sales:

Programs sold	25,000	40,000	55,000	70,000
Probability	.10	.30	.45	.15

Mr. Byrd has decided to print either 25-, 40-, 55-, or 70-thousand programs. Which number of programs will minimize the team's expected losses?

5-16 Airport Rent-a-Car is a locally operated business in competition with several major firms. ARC is planning a new deal for prospective customers who want to rent a car for only one day and will return it to the airport. For $35, the company will rent a small economy car to a customer, whose only other expense is to fill the car with gas at day's end. ARC is planning to buy a number of small cars from the manufacturer at a reduced price of $6,300. The big question is how many to buy. Company executives have decided on the following distribution of demands per day for the service.

Number of cars rented	13	14	15	16	17	18
Probability	.08	.15	.22	.25	.21	.09

The company intends to offer the plan 6 days a week (312 days per year) and anticipates that its variable cost per car per day will be $2.50. After the end of one year, the company expects to sell the cars and recapture 50 percent of the original cost. Disregarding the time value of money and any noncash expenses, use the expected-loss method to determine the optimal number of cars for ARC to buy.

 5-17 Mario, owner of Mario's Pizza Emporium, has a difficult decision on his hands. He has found that he always sells between one and four of his famous "everything but the kitchen sink" pizzas per night. These pizzas take so long to prepare, however, that Mario prepares all of them in advance and stores them in the refrigerator. Because the ingredients go bad within one day, Mario always throws out any unsold pizzas at the end of each evening. The cost of preparing each pizza is $7, and Mario sells each one for $12. In addition to the usual costs, Mario also calculates that each "everything but" pizza which is ordered but which he cannot deliver due to insufficient stock costs him $5 in future business. What number of "everything but" pizzas should Mario stock each night in order to minimize expected loss if the number of pizzas ordered has the probability distribution given below?

Number of pizzas demanded	1	2	3	4
Probability	.40	.30	.20	.10

The Binomial Distribution

One widely used probability distribution of a discrete random variable is the binomial distribution. It describes a variety of processes of interest to managers. The binomial distribution describes discrete, not continuous, data, resulting from an experiment known as a *Bernoulli process*, after the seventeenth-century Swiss mathematician, Jacob Bernoulli. The tossing of a fair coin a fixed number of times is a Bernoulli process, and the outcomes of such tosses can be represented by the binomial probability distribution. The success or failure of interviewees on an aptitude test may also be described by a Bernoulli process. On the other hand, the frequency distribution of the lives of fluorescent lights in a factory would be measured on a continuous scale of hours and would not qualify as a binomial distribution.

USE OF THE BERNOULLI PROCESS

We can use the outcomes of a fixed number of tosses of a fair coin as an example of a Bernoulli process. We can describe this process as follows:

1. Each trial (each toss, in this case) has only *two* possible outcomes: heads or tails, yes or no, success or failure.
2. The probability of the outcome of any trial (toss) remains *fixed* over time. With a fair coin, the probability of heads remains .5 for each toss regardless of the number of times the coin is tossed.
3. The trials are *statistically independent;* that is to say, the outcome of one toss does not affect the outcome of any other toss.

Each Bernoulli process has its own characteristic probability. Take the situation in which historically seven-tenths of all persons who applied for a certain type of job passed the job test. We would say that the characteristic probability here is .7, but we could describe our testing results as Bernoulli only if we felt certain that the proportion of those passing the test (.7) remained constant over time. The other characteristics of the Bernoulli process would also have to be met, of course. Each test would have to have only two outcomes (success or failure), and the results of each test would have to be statistically independent.

In more formal language, the symbol p represents the probability of a success (in our example .7), and the symbol q, $(q = 1 - p)$, the probability of a failure (.3). To represent a certain number of successes, we will use the symbol r, and to symbolize the total number of trials, we use the symbol n. In the situations we will be discussing, the number of trials is fixed before the experiment is begun.

Using this language in a simple problem, we can calculate the chances of getting exactly two heads (in any order) on three tosses of a fair coin. Symbolically, we express the values as follows:

- p = Characteristic probability or probability of success = .5
- $q = 1 - p$ = Probability of failure = .5
- r = Number of successes desired = 2
- n = Number of trials undertaken = 3

We can solve the problem by using the *binomial formula:*

$$\text{Probability of } r \text{ successes in } n \text{ trials} = \frac{n!}{r!(n-r)!} p^r q^{n-r} \qquad [5\text{-}1]$$

Although this formula may look somewhat complicated, it can be used quite easily. The symbol ! means *factorial,* which is computed as follows: 3! means $3 \times 2 \times 1$, or 6. To calculate 5!, we multiply $5 \times 4 \times 3 \times 2 \times 1 = 120$. Mathematicians define 0! as equal to 1. Using the binomial formula to solve our problem, we discover:

$$
\begin{aligned}
\text{Probability of 2 successes in 3 trials} &= \frac{3!}{2!(3-2)!} (.5^2)(.5^1) \\
&= \frac{3 \times 2 \times 1}{(2 \times 1)(1 \times 1)} (.5^2)(.5^1) \\
&= \frac{6}{2} (.25)(.5) \\
&= .375
\end{aligned}
$$

Thus, there is a .375 probability of getting two heads on three tosses of a fair coin.

By now you've probably recognized that we can use the binomial distribution to determine the probabilities for the toothpaste tube problem we introduced at the beginning of this chapter. Recall that historically, eight-tenths of the tubes were correctly filled (successes). If we want to compute the probability of getting exactly three of six tubes (half a carton) correctly filled, we can define our symbols this way:

$$p = .8$$
$$q = .2$$
$$r = 3$$
$$n = 6$$

and then use the binomial formula as follows:

$$\text{Probability of } r \text{ successes in } n \text{ trials} = \frac{n!}{r!(n-r)!} p^r q^{n-r} \qquad [5\text{-}1]$$

$$
\begin{aligned}
\text{Probability of 3 out of 6} \atop \text{tubes correctly filled} &= \frac{6 \times 5 \times 4 \times 3 \times 2 \times 1}{(3 \times 2 \times 1)(3 \times 2 \times 1)} (.8^3)(.2^3) \\
&= \frac{720}{(6 \times 6)} (.512)(.008) \\
&= (20)(.512)(.008) \\
&= .08192
\end{aligned}
$$

Of course, we *could* have solved these two problems using the probability trees we developed in Chapter 4, but for larger problems, trees become quite cumbersome. In fact, using the binomial formula (Equation 5-1) is no easy task when we have to compute the value of something like 46 factorial. For this reason, binomial probability tables have been developed, and we shall use them shortly.

SOME GRAPHIC ILLUSTRATIONS
OF THE BINOMIAL DISTRIBUTION

To this point, we have dealt with the binomial distribution only in terms of the binomial formula, but the binomial, like any other distribution, can be expressed graphically as well.

To illustrate several of these distributions, consider a situation at Kerr Elementary School, where students are often late. Five students are in kindergarten. The principal has studied the situation over a period of time and has determined that there is a .4 chance of any one student being late and that students arrive independently of one another. How would we draw a binomial probability distribution illustrating the probabilities of 0, 1, 2, 3, 4, or 5 students being late simultaneously? To do this, we would need to use the binomial formula where

$$p = .4$$

$$q = .6$$

$$n = 5*$$

and to make a separate computation for each r, from 0 through 5. Remember that mathematically, any number to the zero power is defined as being equal to one. Beginning with our binomial formula:

$$\text{Probability of } r \text{ late arrivals out of } n \text{ students} = \frac{n!}{r!(n-r)!} \, p^r q^{n-r} \qquad [5\text{-}1]$$

Using the formula to derive the binomial probability distribution

For $r = 0$, we get:

$$P(0) = \frac{5!}{0!(5-0)!} \, (.4^0)(.6^5)$$

$$= \frac{5 \times 4 \times 3 \times 2 \times 1}{(1)(5 \times 4 \times 3 \times 2 \times 1)} \, (1)(.6^5)$$

$$= \frac{120}{120} \, (1)(.07776)$$

$$= (1)(1)(.07776)$$

$$= .07776$$

For $r = 1$, we get:

$$P(1) = \frac{5!}{1!(5-1)!} \, (.4^1)(.6^4)$$

$$= \frac{5 \times 4 \times 3 \times 2 \times 1}{(1)(4 \times 3 \times 2 \times 1)} \, (.4)(.6^4)$$

$$= \frac{120}{24} \, (.4)(.1296)$$

$$= (5)(.4)(.1296)$$

$$= .2592$$

---

* When we define n, we look at the number of students. The fact that there is a possibility that none will be late does not alter our choice of $n = 5$.

For $r = 2$, we get:

$$P(2) = \frac{5!}{2!(5-2)!}(.4^2)(.6^3)$$

$$= \frac{5 \times 4 \times 3 \times 2 \times 1}{(2 \times 1)(3 \times 2 \times 1)}(.4^2)(.6^3)$$

$$= \frac{120}{12}(.16)(.216)$$

$$= (10)(.03456)$$

$$= .3456$$

For $r = 3$, we get:

$$P(3) = \frac{5!}{3!(5-3)!}(.4^3)(.6^2)$$

$$= \frac{5 \times 4 \times 3 \times 2 \times 1}{(3 \times 2 \times 1)(2 \times 1)}(.4^3)(.6^2)$$

$$= (10)(.064)(.36)$$

$$= .2304$$

For $r = 4$, we get:

$$P(4) = \frac{5!}{4!(5-4)!}(.4^4)(.6^1)$$

$$= \frac{5 \times 4 \times 3 \times 2 \times 1}{(4 \times 3 \times 2 \times 1)(1)}(.4^4)(.6)$$

$$= (5)(.0256)(.6)$$

$$= .0768$$

Finally, for $r = 5$, we get:

$$P(5) = \frac{5!}{5!(5-5)!}(.4^5)(.6^0)$$

$$= \frac{5 \times 4 \times 3 \times 2 \times 1}{(5 \times 4 \times 3 \times 2 \times 1)(1)}(.4^5)(1)$$

$$= (1)(.01024)(1)$$

$$= .01024$$

The binomial distribution for this example is shown graphically in Fig. 5-4.

General appearance of binomial distributions

Without doing all the calculations involved, we can illustrate the general appearance of a family of binomial probability distributions. In Fig. 5-5, for example, each distribution represents $n = 5$. In each case, the p and q have been changed and are noted beside each distribution. From Fig. 5-5, we can make the following generalizations:

1. When p is small (.1), the binomial distribution is skewed to the right.
2. As p increases (to .3, for example), the skewness is less noticeable.
3. When $p = .5$, the binomial distribution is symmetrical.

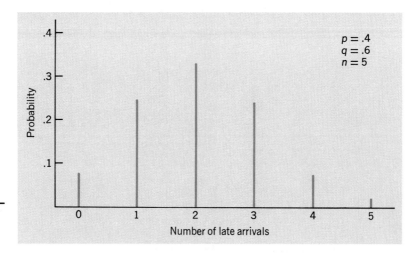

FIGURE 5-4

Binomial probability distribution of late arrivals

4. When p is larger than .5, the distribution is skewed to the left.
5. The probabilities for .3, for example, are the same as those for .7 except that the values of p and q are *reversed.* This is true for any pair of complementary p and q values (.3 and .7, .4 and .6, and .2 and .8).

Let us examine graphically what happens to the binomial distribution when p stays constant but n is increased. Figure 5-6 illustrates the general shape of a family of binomial distributions with a constant p of .4 and n's from 5 to 30. As n increases, the vertical lines not only become more numerous but also tend to bunch up together to form a *bell shape.* We shall have more to say about this bell shape shortly.

FIGURE 5-5

Family of binomial probability distributions with constant $n = 5$ and various p and q values

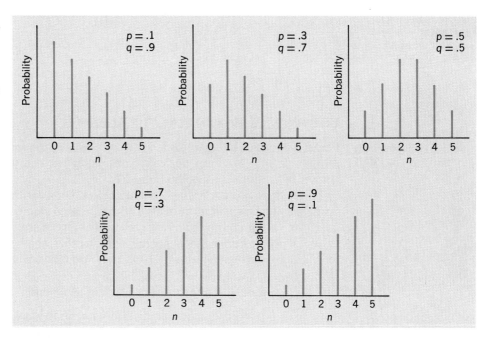

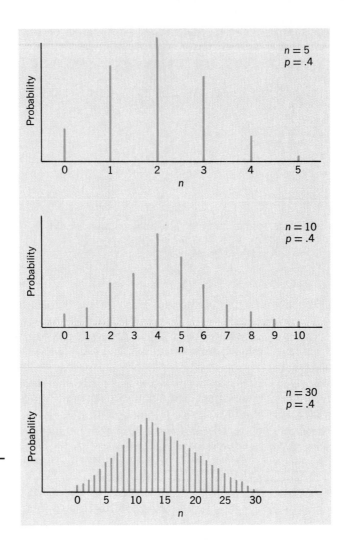

FIGURE 5-6

FIGURE 5-6
Family of binomial
probability
distributions with
constant $p = .4$ and
$n = 5, 10,$ and 30

USING THE BINOMIAL TABLES

Solving problems using
the binomial tables

Earlier we recognized that it is tedious to calculate probabilities using the binomial formula when n is a large number. Fortunately, we can use Appendix Table 3 to determine binomial probabilities quickly.

To illustrate the use of the binomial tables, consider this problem. What is the probability that eight or more of the fifteen registered Democrats on Prince Street will fail to vote in the coming primary if the probability of any individual's not voting is .30 and if people decide independently of each other whether or not to vote? First we represent the elements in this problem in binomial distribution notation:

$$n = 15 \quad \text{number of registered Democrats}$$

$$p = .30 \quad \text{probability that any one individual won't vote}$$

$$r = 8 \quad \text{number of individuals who will fail to vote}$$

5 PROBABILITY II: DISTRIBUTIONS

Then, since the problem involves fifteen trials, we must find the table corresponding to $n = 15$. Since the probability of an individual's not voting is .30, we must look through the $n = 15$ table until we find the column where $p = .30$. (This is denoted as 30.) We then move down that column until we are opposite the $r = 8$ row. The answer there is 0500, which can be interpreted as being a probability value of .0500. This represents the probability of eight or more nonvoters, since the tables are so constructed.

How to use the binomial table Our problem asked for the probability of eight or more nonvoters. If it had asked for the probability of more than eight nonvoters, we would have looked up the probability of nine or more nonvoters. Had the problem asked for the probability of exactly eight nonvoters we would have subtracted .0152 (the probability of nine or more nonvoters) from .0500 (the probability of eight or more nonvoters). The answer would be .0348 = the probability of exactly eight nonvoters. Finally, if the problem had asked for the probability of fewer than eight nonvoters, we would have subtracted .0500 (the probability of eight or more nonvoters) from 1.0, for an answer of .9500. (Note that Appendix Table 3 only goes up to $p = .50$. Instructions for using the table when p is larger than .50 are found on the first page of Appendix Table 3.)

MEASURES OF CENTRAL TENDENCY AND DISPERSION FOR THE BINOMIAL DISTRIBUTION

Computing the mean and the standard deviation Earlier in this chapter, we encountered the concept of the expected value or mean of a probability distribution. The binomial distribution has an expected value or mean (μ) and a standard deviation (σ), and we should be able to compute both these statistical measures. Intuitively, we can reason that if a certain machine produces good parts with a $p = .5$, then, over time, the mean of the distribution of the good parts in the output would be .5 times the total output. If there is a .5 chance of tossing a head with a fair coin, over a large number of tosses the mean of the binomial distribution of the number of heads would be .5 times the total number of tosses.

Symbolically, we can represent the mean of a binomial distribution as:

The mean
$$\mu = np \qquad\qquad [5\text{-}2]$$

where

- n = number of trials
- p = probability of success

And we can calculate the standard deviation of a binomial distribution by using the formula:

The standard deviation
$$\sigma = \sqrt{npq} \qquad\qquad [5\text{-}3]$$

where:

- n = number of trials
- p = probability of success
- q = probability of failure = $1 - p$

To see how to use Equations 5-2 and 5-3, take the case of a packaging machine that produces 20 percent defective packages. If we take a random sample of ten packages, we can compute the mean and the standard deviation of the binomial distribution of that process like this:

$$\mu = np \qquad\qquad\qquad [5\text{-}2]$$
$$= (10)(.2)$$
$$= 2 \leftarrow \text{mean}$$

$$\sigma = \sqrt{npq} \qquad\qquad\qquad [5\text{-}3]$$
$$= \sqrt{(10)(.2)(.8)}$$
$$= \sqrt{1.6}$$
$$= 1.265 \leftarrow \text{standard deviation}$$

MEETING THE CONDITIONS FOR USING THE BERNOULLI PROCESS

Problems in applying the binomial distribution to real-life situations

We need to be careful in the use of the binomial probability distribution to make certain that the three conditions necessary for a Bernoulli process introduced earlier are met, particularly conditions 2 and 3. Condition 2 requires the probability of the outcome of any trial to remain fixed over time. In many industrial processes, however, it is extremely difficult to guarantee that this is indeed the case. Each time an industrial machine produces a part, for instance, there is some infinitesimal wear on the machine. If this wear accumulates beyond a reasonable point, the proportion of acceptable parts produced by the machine will be altered, and condition 2 for the use of the binomial distribution may be violated. This problem is not present in a coin-toss experiment, but it is an integral consideration of all real applications of the binomial probability distribution.

Condition 3 requires that the trials of a Bernoulli process be statistically independent; that is, the outcome of one trial cannot affect in any way the outcome of any other trial. Here, too, we can encounter some problems in real applications. Consider an interviewing process in which high-potential candidates are being screened for top political positions. If the interviewer has talked with five unacceptable candidates in a row, he may not view the sixth with complete impartiality. The trials, therefore, might not be statistically independent.

Exercises

5-18   For a binomial distribution with $n = 7$ and $p = .2$, find:
(a) $P(r = 5)$ (b) $P(r > 2)$ (c) $P(r < 8)$ (d) $P(r \geqslant 4)$

5-19   For a binomial distribution with $n = 12$ and $p = .45$, use Appendix Table 3 to find:
(a) $P(r = 8)$ (b) $P(r > 4)$ (c) $P(r \leqslant 10)$

 5-20   Find the mean and standard deviation of the following binomial distributions:
(a) $n = 16, p = .40$ (d) $n = 350, p = .90$
(b) $n = 10, p = .75$ (e) $n = 78, p = .05$
(c) $n = 22, p = .15$

5 PROBABILITY II: DISTRIBUTIONS

5-21 For $n = 8$ trials, compute the probability that $r \geq 1$ for each of the following values of p:
  (a) $p = .1$ (b) $p = .3$ (c) $p = .6$ (d) $p = .4$

5-22 Harley Davidson, director of quality control for the Kyoto Motor Company, is conducting his monthly spot check of automatic transmissions. In this procedure, ten transmissions are removed from the pool of components and are checked for manufacturing defects. Historically, only 2 percent of the transmissions have such flaws. (Assume that flaws occur independently in different transmissions.)
  (a) What is the probability that Harley's sample contains more than two transmissions with manufacturing flaws? (Do not use the tables.)
  (b) What is the probability that none of the selected transmissions has any manufacturing flaws? (Do not use the tables.)

5-23 Diane Bruns is the mayor in a large city. Lately, she has become concerned about the possibility that a large number of people who are drawing unemployment checks are secretly employed. Her assistants estimate that 40 percent of unemployment beneficiaries fall into this category, but Ms. Bruns is not convinced. She asks one of her aides to conduct a quiet investigation of ten randomly selected unemployment beneficiaries.
  (a) If the mayor's assistants are correct, what is the probability that more than eight of the individuals investigated have jobs? (Do not use the tables.)
  (b) If the mayor's assistants are correct, what is the probability that only three of the investigated individuals have jobs? (Do not use the tables.)

5-24 A month later, Mayor Bruns (from exercise 5-23) picks up the morning edition of the city's leading newspaper, the *Sun-American,* and reads an exposé of unemployment fraud. In this article, the newspaper claims that, out of every fifteen unemployment beneficiaries, the probability that four or more have jobs is .9095, and the expected number of employed beneficiaries exceeds 7. You are a special assistant to Mayor Bruns who must respond to these claims at an afternoon press conference. She asks you to find the answers to the following two questions:
  (a) Are the claims of the *Sun-American* consistent with each other?
  (b) Does the first claim conflict with the opinion of the mayor's assistants?

5-25 The latest nationwide political poll indicates that for Americans who are randomly selected, the probability that they are conservative is .55, the probability that they are liberal is .30, and the probability that they are middle-of-the-road is .15. Assuming that these probabilities are accurate, answer the following questions pertaining to a randomly chosen group of ten Americans. (Do not use Appendix Table 3.)
  (a) What is the probability that four are liberal?
  (b) What is the probability that none are conservative?
  (c) What is the probability that two are middle-of-the-road?
  (d) What is the probability that at least eight are liberal?

5-26 Harry Ohme is in charge of the electronics section of a large department store. He has noticed that the probability that a customer who is just browsing will buy something is .3. Suppose that fifteen customers browse in the electronics section each hour. Use Appendix Table 3 in the back of the book to answer the following questions:
  (a) What is the probability that at least one browsing customer will buy something during a specified hour?
  (b) What is the probability that at least four browsing customers will buy something during a specified hour?
  (c) What is the probability that no browsing customers will buy anything during a specified hour?
  (d) What is the probability that no more than four browsing customers will buy something during a specified hour?

5-5
The Poisson Distribution

Examples of Poisson
distributions

There are many discrete probability distributions, but our discussion will focus on only two: the *binomial,* which we have just concluded, and the *Poisson,* which is the subject of this section. The Poisson distribution is named for Siméon Denis Poisson (1781 – 1840), a Frenchman who developed the distribution from studies during the latter part of his lifetime.

The Poisson distribution is used to describe a number of processes, including the distribution of telephone calls going through a switchboard system, the demand (needs) of patients for service at a health institution, the arrivals of trucks and cars at a tollbooth, and the number of accidents at an intersection. These examples all have a common element: They can be described by a discrete random variable that takes on integer (whole) values (0, 1, 2, 3, 4, 5, and so on). The number of patients who arrive at a physician's office in a given interval of time will be 0, 1, 2, 3, 4, 5, or some other whole number. Similarly, if you count the number of cars arriving at a tollbooth on the New Jersey Turnpike during some 10-minute period, the number will be 0, 1, 2, 3, 4, 5, and so on.

CHARACTERISTICS OF PROCESSES THAT PRODUCE A POISSON PROBABILITY DISTRIBUTION

Conditions leading to a
Poisson probability
distribution

The number of vehicles passing through a single turnpike tollbooth at rush hour serves as an illustration of Poisson probability distribution characteristics:

1. The average (mean) arrivals of vehicles per rush hour can be estimated from past traffic data.
2. If we divide the rush hour into periods (intervals) of one second each, we will find these statements to be true:
    (a) The probability that exactly one vehicle will arrive at the single booth per second is a very small number and is constant for every one-second interval.
    (b) The probability that two or more vehicles will arrive within a one-second interval is so small that we can assign it a zero value.
    (c) The number of vehicles that arrive in a given one-second interval is independent of the time at which that one-second interval occurs during the rush hour.
    (d) The number of arrivals in any one-second interval is not dependent on the number of arrivals in any other one-second interval.

Now, we can generalize from these four conditions described for our tollbooth example and apply them to other processes. If these new processes meet the same four conditions, then we can use a Poisson probability distribution to describe them.

CALCULATING PROBABILITIES USING THE POISSON DISTRIBUTION

The Poisson probability distribution, as we have shown, is concerned with certain processes that can be described by a discrete random variable. The letter X usually represents that discrete random variable, and X can take on integer values (0, 1, 2, 3, 4, 5, and so on). We use capital X to represent the random variable and lower case x to represent a specific value that capital X can take. The probability of exactly x occurrences in a Poisson distribution is calculated with the formula:

Poisson distribution formula

$$P(x) = \frac{\lambda^x \times e^{-\lambda}}{x!}$$ [5-4]

Look more closely at each part of this formula:

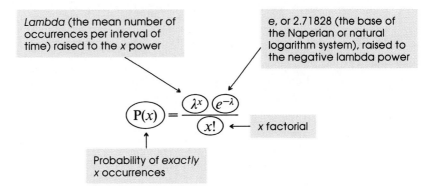

Lambda (the mean number of occurrences per interval of time) raised to the x power

e, or 2.71828 (the base of the Naperian or natural logarithm system), raised to the negative lambda power

x factorial

Probability of *exactly* x occurrences

Suppose that we are investigating the safety of a dangerous intersection. Past police records indicate a mean of five accidents per month at this intersection. The number of accidents is distributed according to a Poisson distribution, and the Highway Safety Division wants us to calculate the probability in any month of exactly 0, 1, 2, 3, or 4 accidents. We can use Appendix Table 4 to avoid having to calculate e's to negative powers. Applying the formula:

An example using the Poisson formula

$$P(x) = \frac{\lambda^x \times e^{-\lambda}}{x!}$$ [5-4]

we can calculate the probability of no accidents:

$$P(0) = \frac{(5^0)(e^{-5})}{0!}$$

$$= \frac{(1)(.00674)}{1}$$

$$= .00674$$

For exactly one accident:

$$P(1) = \frac{(5^1)(e^{-5})}{1!}$$

$$= \frac{(5)(.00674)}{1}$$

$$= .03370$$

For exactly two accidents:

$$P(2) = \frac{(5^2)(e^{-5})}{2!}$$

$$= \frac{(25)(.00674)}{2 \times 1}$$

$$= .08425$$

For exactly three accidents:

$$P(3) = \frac{(5^3)(e^{-5})}{3!}$$

$$= \frac{(125)(.00674)}{3 \times 2 \times 1}$$

$$= \frac{.8425}{6}$$

$$= .14042$$

Finally, for exactly four accidents:

$$P(4) = \frac{(5^4)(e^{-5})}{4!}$$

$$= \frac{(625)(.00674)}{4 \times 3 \times 2 \times 1}$$

$$= \frac{4.2125}{24}$$

$$= .17552$$

Using these results Our calculations will answer several questions. Perhaps we want to know the probability of 0, 1, or 2 accidents in any month. We find this by adding together the probabilities of exactly 0, 1, and 2 accidents like this:

$$P(0) = .00674$$
$$P(1) = .03370$$
$$P(2) = \underline{.08425}$$
$$P(0, 1, 2) = \textbf{.12469}$$

We will take action to improve the intersection if the probability of more than three accidents per month exceeds .65. Should we act? To solve this problem, we need to calculate the probability of having 0, 1, 2, or 3 accidents and then subtract the sum from 1.0 to get the probability for more than three accidents. We begin like this:

$$P(0) = .00674$$
$$P(1) = .03370$$
$$P(2) = .08425$$
$$P(3) = \underline{.14042}$$
$$P(3 \text{ or fewer}) = \textbf{.26511}$$

Because the Poisson probability of three or fewer accidents is .26511, the probability of more than three must be .73489 (1.00000 − .26511). Since .73489 exceeds .65, steps should be taken to improve the intersection.

Constructing a Poisson probability distribution We could continue calculating the probabilities for more than four accidents and eventually produce a Poisson probability distribution of the number of accidents per month at this intersection. Table 5-12 illustrates such a distribution. To produce this table, we have used Equation 5-4. Try doing the calculations yourself for the probabilities beyond exactly four accidents. Figure 5-7 illustrates graphically the Poisson probability distribution of the number of accidents.

TABLE 5-12 Poisson Probability Distribution of Accidents per Month

x = NUMBER OF ACCIDENTS	P(x) = PROBABILITY OF EXACTLY THAT NUMBER	
0	.00674	
1	.03370	
2	.08425	
3	.14042	
4	.17552	
5	.17552	
6	.14627	
7	.10448	
8	.06530	
9	.03628	
10	.01814	
11	.00824	
	.99486	← Probability of 0 through 11 accidents
12 or more	.00514	← Probability of 12 or more (1.0 − .99486)
	1.00000	

POISSON DISTRIBUTION AS AN APPROXIMATION OF THE BINOMIAL DISTRIBUTION

Using a modification of the Poisson formula to approximate binomial probabilities

Sometimes, if we wish to avoid the tedious job of calculating binomial probability distributions, we can use the Poisson instead. The Poisson distribution can be a reasonable approximation of the binomial, but only under certain conditions. These conditions are when *n* is large and *p* is small; that is, when the number of trials is large and the binomial probability of success is small. **The rule most often used by statisticians is that a Poisson is a good approximation of the binomial when *n* is equal to or greater than 20, and *p* is equal to or less than .05.** In cases that meet these conditions, we can substitute the mean of the binomial distribution (*np*) in place of the mean of

FIGURE 5-7

Poisson probability distribution of the number of accidents

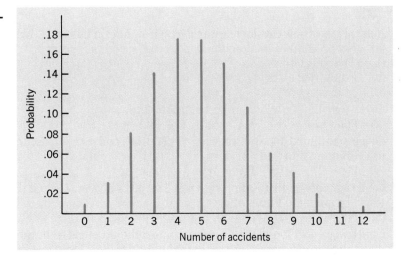

TABLE 5-13 Comparison of Poisson and Binomial Probability Approaches to the Kidney Dialysis Situation

POISSON APPROACH	BINOMIAL APPROACH
$P(x) = \dfrac{(np)^x \times e^{-np}}{x!}$ [5-5]	$P(r) = \dfrac{n!}{r!(n-r)!} p^r q^{n-r}$ [5-1]
$P(3) = \dfrac{(20 \times .02)^3 e^{-(20 \times .02)}}{3!}$	$P(3) = \dfrac{20!}{3!(20-3)!}(.02^3)(.98^{17})$
$= \dfrac{(.4^3)(e)^{-.4*}}{(3 \times 2 \times 1)}$	$= .0065$
$= \dfrac{(.064)(.67032)^*}{6}$	
$= .00715$	

* Use Appendix Table 4 to find the value of $(e)^{-.4}$.

the Poisson distribution (λ), so that the formula becomes:

$$P(x) = \frac{(np)^x \times e^{-np}}{x!} \qquad [5\text{-}5]$$

Comparing the Poisson and binomial formulas Let us use both the binomial probability formula (5-1) and the Poisson approximation formula (5-5) on the same problem to determine the extent to which the Poisson is a good approximation of the binomial. Say that we have a hospital with 20 kidney dialysis machines and that the chance of any one of them malfunctioning during any day is .02. What is the probability that exactly three machines will be out of service on the same day? Table 5-13 shows the answers to this question. As we can see, the difference between the two probability distributions is slight (only about a 10 percent error, in this example).

Exercises

5-27 If the prices of new cars increase an average of four times every 3 years, find the probability of:
  (a) No price hikes in a randomly selected period of 3 years
  (b) Two price hikes
  (c) Four price hikes
  (d) Five or more

5-28 Given $\lambda = 4.2$, for a Poisson distribution, find:
  (a) $P(X \le 2)$ (b) $P(X \ge 5)$ (c) $P(X = 8)$

5-29 Given a binomial distribution with $n = 30$ trials and $p = .04$, use the Poisson approximation to the binomial to find:
  (a) $P(r = 25)$ (b) $P(r = 3)$ (c) $P(r = 5)$

5-30 Given a binomial distribution with $n = 28$ trials and $p = .025$, use the Poisson approximation to the binomial to find:
  (a) $P(r \ge 3)$ (b) $P(r < 5)$ (c) $P(r = 9)$

5-31 Concert pianist Donna Prima has become quite upset at the number of coughs occurring in the audience just before she begins to play. On her latest tour, Donna estimates that on average eight coughs occur just before the start of her performance. Ms. Prima has sworn to her conductor that if she hears more than five coughs at tonight's performance, she will refuse to play. What is the probability that she will play tonight?

5-32 Guy Ford, production supervisor for the Winstead Company's Charlottesville plant, is worried about an elderly employee's ability to keep up the minimum work pace. In addition to the normal daily breaks, this employee stops for short rest periods an average of 4.1 times per hour. The rest period is a fairly consistent 3 minutes each time. Ford has decided that if the probability of the employee resting for 12 minutes (not including normal breaks) or more per hour is greater than .5, he will move the employee to a different job. Should he do so?

5-33 On average, five birds hit the Washington Monument and are killed each week. Bill Garcy, an official of the National Parks Service, has requested that Congress allocate funds for equipment to scare birds away from the monument. A Congressional subcommittee has replied funds cannot be allocated unless the probability of more than three birds' being killed in any week exceeds .7. Will the funds be allocated?

5-34 Southwestern Electronics has developed a new calculator that performs a series of functions not yet performed by any other calculator. The marketing department is planning to demonstrate this calculator to a group of potential customers, but it is worried about some initial problems, which have resulted in 4 percent of the new calculators developing mathematical inconsistencies. The marketing VP is planning on randomly selecting a group of calculators for this demonstration and is worried about the chances of selecting a calculator that could start malfunctioning. He believes that whether or not a calculator malfunctions is a Bernoulli process, and he is convinced that the probability of a malfunction is really about .04.
   (a) Assuming that the VP selects exactly 50 calculators to use in the demonstration, and using the Poisson distribution as an approximation of the binomial, what is the chance of getting at least three calculators that malfunction?
   (b) No calculators malfunctioning?

5-35 The Orange County Dispute Settlement Center handles various kinds of disputes, but most are marital disputes. In fact, 96 percent of the disputes handled by the DSC are of a marital nature.
   (a) What is the probability that, out of the 80 disputes handled by the DSC, exactly seven are non-marital?
   (b) None are non-marital?

5-36 The U.S. Bureau of Printing and Engraving is responsible for printing this country's paper money. The BPE has an impressively small frequency of printing error; only .5 percent of all bills are too flawed for circulation. What is the probability that, out of a batch of 1,000 bills,
   (a) None are too flawed for circulation?
   (b) Ten are too flawed for circulation?
   (c) Fifteen are too flawed for circulation?

5-6
The Normal Distribution: A Distribution of a Continuous Random Variable

Continuous distribution defined

So far in this chapter, we have been concerned with discrete probability distributions. In this section, we shall turn to cases in which the variable can take on *any* value within a given range and in which the probability distribution is continuous.

A very important continuous probability distribution is the *normal* distribution. Several mathematicians were instrumental in its development, among them the eighteenth-century mathematician-astronomer Karl Gauss. In honor of his work, the normal probability distribution is often called the Gaussian distribution.

Importance of the normal distribution

There are two basic reasons why the normal distribution occupies such a prominent place in statistics. First, it has some properties that make it applicable to a great

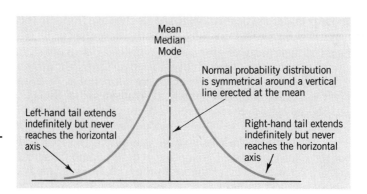

FIGURE 5-8

Frequency curve for
the normal
probability
distribution

many situations in which it is necessary to make inferences by taking samples. In Chapter 6, we will find that the normal distribution is a useful sampling distribution. Second, the normal distribution comes close to fitting the actual observed frequency distributions of many phenomena, including human characteristics (weights, heights, and IQs), outputs from physical processes (dimensions and yields), and other measures of interest to managers in both the public and private sectors.

CHARACTERISTICS OF THE NORMAL PROBABILITY DISTRIBUTION

The normal curve
described

Look for a moment at Fig. 5-8. This diagram suggests several important features of a normal probability distribution:

1. The curve has a single peak; thus, it is unimodal. It has the bell shape that we described earlier.
2. The mean of a normally distributed population lies at the center of its normal curve.
3. Because of the symmetry of the normal probability distribution, the median and the mode of the distribution are also at the center; thus, for a normal curve, the mean, median, and mode are the same value.

TABLE 5-14 Different Normal Probability Distributions

NATURE OF THE POPULATION	ITS MEAN	ITS STANDARD DEVIATION
Annual earnings of employees at one plant	$10,000/year	$1,000
Length of standard 8′ building lumber	8′	.5″
Air pollution in one community	2,500 particles per million	750 particles per million
Per capita income in a single developing country	$1,400	$300
Violent crimes per year in a given city	8,000	900

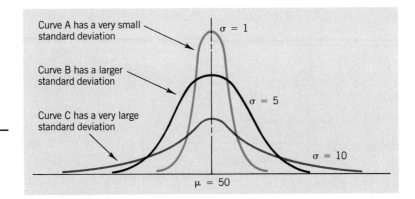

FIGURE 5-9

Normal probability distributions with identical means but different standard deviations

4. The two tails of the normal probability distribution extend indefinitely and never touch the horizontal axis. (Graphically, of course, this is impossible to show.)

Significance of the two parameters which describe a normal distribution

Most real-life populations do not extend forever in both directions; but for such populations, the normal distribution is a convenient approximation. There is no single normal curve, but rather a family of normal curves. To define a particular normal probability distribution, we need only two parameters: the mean (μ) and the standard deviation (σ). In Table 5-14, each of the populations is described only by the mean and the standard deviation, and each has a particular normal curve.

Figure 5-9 shows three normal probability distributions, each of which has the same mean but a different standard deviation. Although these curves differ in appearance, all three are "normal curves."

Figure 5-10 illustrates a "family" of normal curves, all with the same standard deviation but each with a different mean.

Finally, Fig. 5-11 shows three different normal probability distributions, each with a different mean *and* a different standard deviation. The normal probability distributions illustrated in Figs. 5-9, 5-10, and 5-11 demonstrate that the normal curve can describe a large number of populations, differentiated only by the mean and/or the standard deviation.

FIGURE 5-10

Normal probability distributions with different means but the same standard deviation

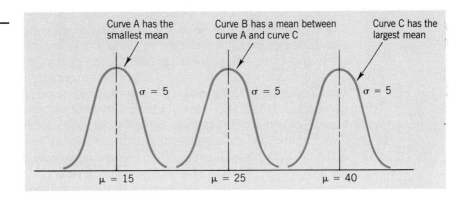

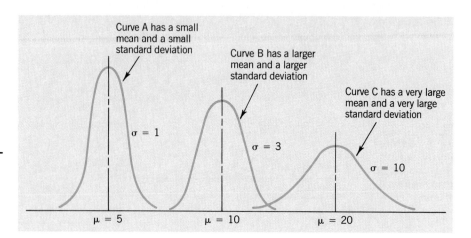

FIGURE 5-11

FIGURE 5-11

Three normal probability distributions, each with a different mean and a different standard deviation

Curve A has a small mean and a small standard deviation

Curve B has a larger mean and a larger standard deviation

Curve C has a very large mean and a very large standard deviation

$\sigma = 1$

$\sigma = 3$

$\sigma = 10$

$\mu = 5$ $\mu = 10$ $\mu = 20$

AREAS UNDER THE NORMAL CURVE

Measuring the area under a normal curve

No matter what the values of μ and σ are for a normal probability distribution, the total area under the normal curve is 1.00, so that we may think of areas under the curve as probabilities. Mathematically, it is true that:

1. Approximately 68 percent of all the values in a normally distributed population lie within 1 standard deviation (plus and minus) from the mean.
2. Approximately 95.5 percent of all the values in a normally distributed population lie within 2 standard deviations (plus and minus) from the mean.
3. Approximately 99.7 percent of all the values in a normally distributed population lie within 3 standard deviations (plus and minus) from the mean.

These three statements are shown graphically in Fig. 5-12.

Figure 5-12 shows three different ways of measuring the area under the normal curve. However, very few of the applications we shall make of the normal probability distribution involve intervals of *exactly* 1, 2, or 3 standard deviations (plus and minus) from the mean. What should we do about all these other cases? Fortunately, we can refer to statistical tables constructed for precisely these situations. They indicate portions of the area under the normal curve that are contained within any number of standard deviations (plus and minus) from the mean.

Standard normal probability distribution

It is not possible or necessary to have a different table for every possible normal curve. Instead, we can use a **standard normal probability distribution** to find areas under any normal curve. With this table, we can determine the area, or probability, that the normally distributed random variable will lie within certain distances from the mean. These distances are defined in terms of standard deviations.

We can better understand the concept of the standard normal probability distribution by examining the special relationship of the standard deviation to the normal curve. Look at Fig. 5-13. Here we have illustrated two normal probability distributions, each with a different mean and a different standard deviation. Both area *a* and area *b*, the shaded areas under the curves, contain the *same* proportion of the total area under the normal curve. Why? Because both these areas are defined as being the area between the mean and one standard deviation to the right of the mean. *All* intervals containing the same number of standard deviations from the mean will contain the same proportion of the total area under the curve for *any* normal proba-

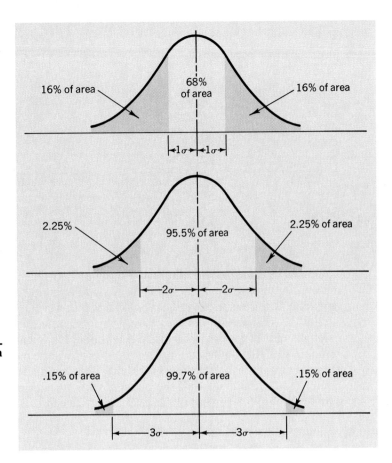

FIGURE 5-12

Relationship between the area under the curve for a normal probability distribution and the distance from the mean measured in standard deviations

bility distribution. This makes possible the use of only one standard normal probability distribution table.

Let's find out what proportion of the total area under the curve is represented by colored areas in Fig. 5-13. In Fig. 5-12, we saw that an interval of one standard deviation (plus *and* minus) from the mean contained about 68 percent of the total area under the curve. In Fig. 5-13, however, we are interested only in the area between the mean and one standard deviation to the *right* of the mean (plus, *not* plus and minus). This area must be half of 68 percent, or 34 percent, for both distributions.

Deriving the percentage of the total area under the curve

FIGURE 5-13

Two intervals, each one standard deviation to the right of the mean

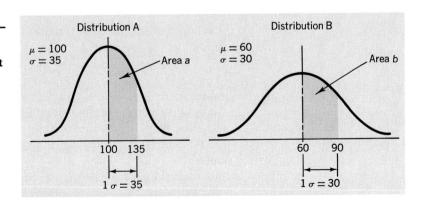

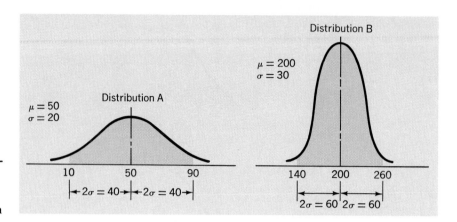

FIGURE 5-14

Two intervals, each
two standard
deviations plus and
minus from the mean

One more example will reinforce our point. Look at the two normal probability distributions in Fig. 5-14. Each of these has a different mean and a different standard deviation. The colored area under *both* curves, however, contains the same proportion of the total area under the curve. Why? Because the problem states that both colored areas fall within two standard deviations plus and minus from the mean. Two standard deviations plus and minus from the mean include the same proportion of the total area under any normal probability distribution. In this case, we can refer to Fig. 5-12 again and see that the colored areas in both distributions in Fig. 5-14 contain about 95.5 percent of the total area under the curve.

USING THE STANDARD NORMAL PROBABILITY DISTRIBUTION TABLE

Formula for measuring distances under the normal curve

Appendix Table 1 shows the area under the normal curve between the mean and any value of the normally distributed random variable. Notice in this table the location of the column labeled z. The value for z is derived from the formula:

$$z = \frac{x - \mu}{\sigma} \qquad [5\text{-}6]$$

where

- x = value of the random variable with which we are concerned
- μ = mean of the distribution of this random variable
- σ = standard deviation of this distribution
- z = number of standard deviations from x to the mean of this distribution

Why do we use z rather than "the number of standard deviations"? Normally distributed random variables take on many *different units* of measure: dollars, inches, parts per million, pounds, time. Since we shall use one table, Table 1 in the Appendix, we talk in terms of *standard units* (which really means standard deviations), and we denote them by the symbol z.

Using z values

We can illustrate this graphically. In Fig. 5-15, we see that the use of z is just a change of the scale of measurement on the horizontal axis.

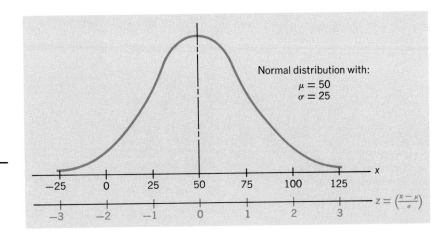

FIGURE 5-15

Normal distribution illustrating comparability of *z* values and standard deviations

Standard Normal Probability Distribution Table

Using the table to find probabilities (examples)

The Standard Normal Probability Distribution Table, Appendix Table 1, is organized in terms of standard units, or *z* values. It gives the values for only *half* the area under the normal curve, beginning with 0.0 at the mean. Since the normal probability distribution is symmetrical (return to Fig. 5-8 to review this point), the values true for one half of the curve are true for the other. We can use this one table for problems involving both sides of the normal curve. Working a few examples will help us to feel comfortable with the table.

We have a training program designed to upgrade the supervisory skills of production-line supervisors. Because the program is self-administered, supervisors require different numbers of hours to complete the program. A study of past participants indicates that the mean length of time spent on the program is 500 hours and that this normally distributed random variable has a standard deviation of 100 hours.

EXAMPLE 1

What is the probability that a participant selected at random will require more than 500 hours to complete the program?

Solution In Fig. 5-16, we see that half of the area under the curve is located on either side of the mean of 500 hours. Thus, we can deduce that the probability that the random variable will take on a value higher than 500 is the colored half, or .5. ■

FIGURE 5-16

Distribution of time required to complete the training program, with interval more than 500 hours in color

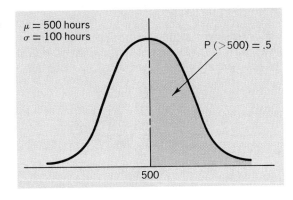

5-6 The Normal Distribution: A Distribution of a Continuous Random Variable

225

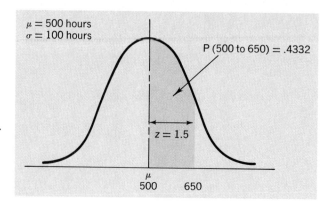

FIGURE 5-17

FIGURE 5-17

Distribution of time required to complete the training program, with interval 500 to 650 hours in color

EXAMPLE 2

What is the probability that a candidate selected at random will take between 500 and 650 hours to complete the training program?

Solution We have shown this situation graphically in Fig. 5-17. The probability that will answer this question is represented by the colored area between the mean (500 hours) and the x value in which we are interested (650 hours). Using Equation 5-6, we get a z value of:

$$z = \frac{x - \mu}{\sigma} \tag{5-6}$$

$$= \frac{650 - 500}{100}$$

$$= \frac{150}{100}$$

$$= 1.5 \text{ standard deviations}$$

If we look up $z = 1.5$ in Appendix Table 1, we find a probability of .4332. Thus, the chance that a candidate selected at random would require between 500 and 650 hours to complete the training program is slightly higher than .4. ∎

EXAMPLE 3

What is the probability that a candidate selected at random will take more than 700 hours to complete the program?

Solution This situation is different from our previous examples. Look at Fig. 5-18. We are interested in the colored area to the right of the value "700 hours." How can we solve this problem? We can begin by using Equation 5-6:

$$z = \frac{x - \mu}{\sigma} \tag{5-6}$$

$$= \frac{700 - 500}{100}$$

$$= \frac{200}{100}$$

$$= 2 \text{ standard deviations}$$

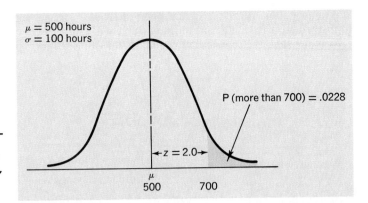

FIGURE 5-18

Distribution of time
required to complete
the training program,
with interval above
700 hours in color

Looking in Appendix Table 1 for a z value of 2.0, we find a probability of .4772. That represents the probability the program will require *between* 500 and 700 hours. However, we want the probability it will take *more* than 700 hours (the colored area in Fig. 5-18). Since the right half of the curve (between the mean and the right-hand tail) represents a probability of .5, we can get our answer (the area to the right of the 700-hour point) if we subtract .4772 from .5; $.5000 - .4772 = .0228$. Therefore, there are just over two chances in 100 that a participant chosen at random would take more than 700 hours to complete the course. ■

EXAMPLE 4

Suppose the training-program director wants to know the probability that a participant chosen at random would require between 550 and 650 hours to complete the required work.

Solution This probability is represented by the colored area in Fig. 5-19. This time, our answer will require two steps. First, we calculate a z value for the 650-hour point, as follows:

$$z = \frac{x - \mu}{\sigma} \qquad [5\text{-}6]$$

$$= \frac{650 - 500}{100}$$

$$= \frac{150}{100}$$

$$= 1.5 \text{ standard deviations}$$

FIGURE 5-19

Distribution of time
required to complete
the training program,
with interval
between 550 and 650
hours in color

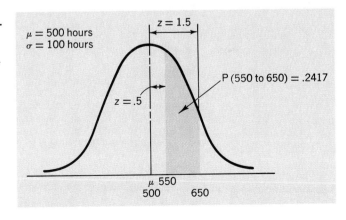

When we look up a z of 1.5 in Appendix Table 1, we see a probability value of .4332 (the probability that the random variable will fall between the mean and 650 hours). Now for step 2. We calculate a z value for our 550-hour point like this:

$$z = \frac{x - \mu}{\sigma} \qquad [5\text{-}6]$$

$$= \frac{550 - 500}{100}$$

$$= \frac{50}{100}$$

$$= .5 \text{ standard deviations}$$

In Appendix Table 1, the z value of .5 has a probability of .1915 (the chance that the random variable will fall between the mean and 550 hours). To answer our question, we must subtract as follows:

.4332   Probability that the random variable
           will lie between the mean and 650 hours
$-$.1915   Probability that the random variable
           will lie between the mean and 550 hours
.2417 $\leftarrow$ Probability that the random variable
           will lie between 550 and 650 hours

Thus, the chance of a candidate selected at random taking between 550 and 650 hours to complete the program is a bit less than one in four. ∎

EXAMPLE 5

What is the probability that a candidate selected at random will require less than 580 hours to complete the program?

Solution This situation is illustrated in Fig. 5-20. Using Equation 5-6 to get the appropriate z value for 580 hours, we have:

$$z = \frac{x - \mu}{\sigma} \qquad [5\text{-}6]$$

$$= \frac{580 - 500}{100}$$

$$= \frac{80}{100}$$

$$= .8 \text{ standard deviations}$$

FIGURE 5-20

Distribution of time required to complete the training program, with interval less than 580 hours in color

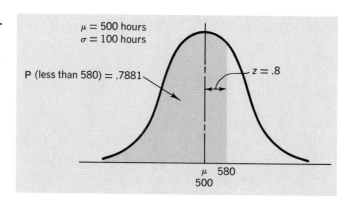

5 PROBABILITY II: DISTRIBUTIONS

Looking in Appendix Table 1 for a z value of .8, we find a probability of .2881 — the probability that the random variable will lie between the mean and 580 hours. We must add to this the probability that the random variable will be between the left-hand tail and the mean. Since the distribution is symmetrical with half the area on each side of the mean, we know this value must be .5. As a final step, then, we add the two probabilities:

.2881 Probability that the random variable
      will lie between the mean and 580 hours

$+$.5000 Probability that the random variable
      will lie between the left-hand tail and the
      mean

.7881 $\leftarrow$ Probability that the random variable
      will lie between the left-hand tail and 580
      hours

Thus, the chances of a candidate requiring less than 580 hours to complete the program are slightly higher than 75 percent. ∎

EXAMPLE 6

What is the probability that a candidate chosen at random will take between 420 and 570 hours to complete the program?

Solution Figure 5-21 illustrates the interval in question, from 420 to 570 hours. Again the solution requires two steps. First, we calculate a z value for the 570-hour point:

$$z = \frac{x - \mu}{\sigma}$$ [5-6]

$$= \frac{570 - 500}{100}$$

$$= \frac{70}{100}$$

$$= .7 \text{ standard deviations}$$

We look up the z value of .7 in Appendix Table 1 and find a probability value of .2580. Second, we calculate the z value for the 420-hour point:

FIGURE 5-21

Distribution of time required to complete the training program, with interval between 420 and 570 hours in color

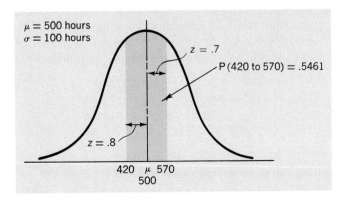

$$z = \frac{x - \mu}{\sigma} \qquad\qquad\qquad \text{[5-6]}$$

$$= \frac{420 - 500}{100}$$

$$= \frac{-80}{100}$$

$$= -.8 \text{ standard deviations}$$

Since the distribution is symmetrical, we can disregard the sign and look for a z value of .8. The probability associated with this z value is .2881. We find our answer by adding these two values as follows:

.2580   Probability that the random variable
         will lie between the mean and 570 hours
+.2881   Probability that the random variable
_____ will lie between the mean and 420 hours
.5461 ← Probability that the random variable
          will lie between 420 and 570 hours

Thus, there is slightly better than a 50 percent chance that a participant chosen at random will take between 420 and 570 hours to complete the training program. ∎

SHORTCOMINGS OF THE NORMAL PROBABILITY DISTRIBUTION

Theory and practice

Earlier in this section, we noted that the tails of the normal distribution approach but never touch the horizontal axis. This implies that there is *some* probability (although it may be very small) that the random variable can take on enormous values. It is possible for the right-hand tail of a normal curve to assign a minute probability of a person's weighing 2,000 pounds. Of course, no one would believe that such a person exists. (A weight of one ton or more would lie about 50 standard deviations to the right of the mean and would have a probability that began with 250 zeroes to the right of the decimal point!) **We do not lose much accuracy by ignoring values far out in the tails. But in exchange for the convenience of using this theoretical model, we must accept the fact that it can assign impossible empirical values.**

THE NORMAL DISTRIBUTION AS AN APPROXIMATION OF THE BINOMIAL DISTRIBUTION

Sometimes the normal is used to approximate the binomial

Although the normal distribution is continuous, it is interesting to note that it can sometimes be used to approximate discrete distributions. To see how we can use it to approximate the binomial distribution, suppose we would like to know the probability of getting five, six, seven, or eight heads in ten tosses of a fair coin. We could use Appendix Table 3 to find this probability, as follows:

$$\binom{\text{Probability of 5, 6,}}{\text{7, or 8 heads}} = \binom{\text{Probability of 5 or}}{\text{more heads}} - \binom{\text{Probability of 9 or}}{\text{more heads}}$$

$$= \qquad\quad .6230 \qquad\quad - \qquad\quad .0107$$

$$= \qquad\quad .6123$$

Two distributions with the same means and standard deviations

Figure 5-22 shows the binomial distribution for $n = 10$ and $p = \frac{1}{2}$ with a normal distribution superimposed on it with the *same* mean ($\mu = np = 10(\frac{1}{2}) = 5$) and the *same* standard deviation ($\sigma = \sqrt{npq} = \sqrt{10(\frac{1}{2})(\frac{1}{2})} = \sqrt{2.5} = 1.581$).

Look at the area under the normal curve between 5 + ½ and 5 − ½. We see that this area is *approximately* the same size as the area of the colored bar representing the binomial probability of getting five heads. The two ½s that we add to and subtract from 5 are called *continuity correction factors* and are used to improve the accuracy of the approximation.

Continuity correction factors

Using the continuity correction factors, we see that the binomial probability of 5, 6, 7, or 8 heads can be approximated by the area under the normal curve between 4.5 and 8.5. Compute that probability by finding the z values corresponding to 4.5 and 8.5.

$$\text{At } x = 4.5, \ z = \frac{x - \mu}{\sigma} \tag{5-6}$$

$$= \frac{4.5 - 5}{1.581}$$

$$= -0.32 \text{ standard deviations}$$

$$\text{At } x = 8.5, \ z = \frac{x - \mu}{\sigma} \tag{5-6}$$

$$= \frac{8.5 - 5}{1.581}$$

$$= 2.21 \text{ standard deviations}$$

Now, from Appendix Table 1, we find:

.1255	The probability that z will be between −0.32 and 0 (and correspondingly, that x will be between 4.5 and 5)
+.4864	The probability that z will be between 0 and 2.21 (and correspondingly, that x will be between 5 and 8.5)
.6119	The probability that x will be between 4.5 and 8.5

FIGURE 5-22

Binomial distribution with $n = 10$ and $p = ½$, with superimposed normal distribution with $\mu = 5$ and $\sigma = 1.581$

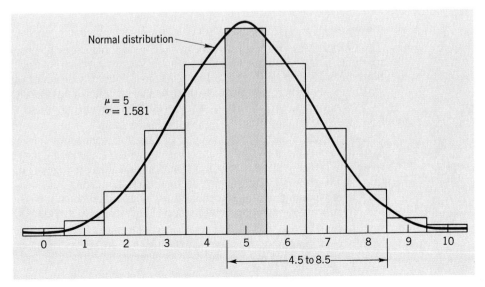

Normal distribution

$\mu = 5$
$\sigma = 1.581$

4.5 to 8.5

Comparing the binomial probability of .6123 (which we got from Appendix Table 3) with this normal approximation of .6119, we can see that the error in the approximation is less than $\frac{1}{10}$ of 1 percent.

The normal approximation to the binomial distribution is very convenient, since it enables us to solve the problem without extensive tables of the binomial distribution. (You might note that Appendix Table 3, which gives binomial probabilities for

values of n up to 15, is already thirteen pages long.) **We should note that some care needs to be taken in using this approximation, but it is quite good whenever both np and nq are at least 5.**

Exercises

5-37 Given that a random variable, X, has a normal distribution with mean 6.4 and standard deviation 2.7, find:
(a) $P(4.0 < x < 5.0)$ (c) $P(x < 7.2)$
(b) $P(x > 2.0)$ (d) $P((x < 3.0)$ or $(x > 9.0))$

5-38 Given that a random variable, X, has a binomial distribution with $n = 50$ trials and $p = .25$, use the normal approximation to the binomial to find:
(a) $P(x > 10)$ (b) $P(x < 18)$ (c) $P(x > 21)$ (d) $P(9 < x < 14)$

5-39 In a normal distribution with a standard deviation of 5.0, the probability that an observation selected at random exceeds 21 is .14.
(a) Find the mean of the distribution.
(b) Find the value below which 4 percent of the values in the distribution lie.

5-40 The manager of a small postal substation is trying to quantify the variation in the weekly demand for mailing tubes. She has decided to assume that this demand is normally distributed. She knows that on average 100 tubes are purchased weekly and that, 90 percent of the time, weekly demand is below 115.
(a) What is the standard deviation of this distribution?
(b) The manager wants to stock enough tubes each week so that the probability of running out of tubes is no higher than .05. What is the lowest such stock level?

5-41 Use the normal approximation to compute the following binomial probabilities:
(a) $n = 30$, $p = .35$, between ten and fifteen successes, inclusive
(b) $n = 42$, $p = .62$, thirty or more successes
(c) $n = 15$, $p = .30$, at most seven successes
(d) $n = 51$, $p = .42$, between seventeen and twenty-five successes, inclusive

5-42 The Gilbert Machinery Company has received a big order to produce electric motors for a manufacturing company. In order to fit in its bearing, the drive shaft of the motor must have a diameter of $5.1 \pm .05$ (inches). The company's purchasing agent realizes that there is a large stock of steel rods in inventory with a mean diameter of 5.07″, with a standard deviation of .07″. What is the probability of a steel rod from inventory fitting the bearing?

5-43 The manager of a Spiffy Lube auto lubrication shop is trying to revise his policy on ordering grease gun cartridges. Currently, he orders 110 cartridges per week, but he runs out of cartridges in 1 out of every 4 weeks. He knows that, on average, the shop uses 95 cartridges per week. He is also willing to assume that demand for cartridges is normally distributed.
(a) What is the standard deviation of this distribution?
(b) If the manager wants to order enough cartridges so that his probability of running out during any week is no greater than .2, how many cartridges should he order per week?

5-44 Jarrid Medical, Inc., is developing a compact kidney dialysis machine, but its chief engineer, Mike Crowe, is having trouble controlling the variability of the rate at which fluid moves through the device. Medical standards require that the hourly flow be 4 liters, plus or minus .1 liter, 80 percent of the time. Mr. Crowe, in testing the prototype, has found that, 68 percent of the time, the hourly flow is within .08 liters of 4.02 liters. Does the prototype satisfy the medical standards?

5-45 Sgt. Wellborn Fitte, the U.S. Army's quartermaster at Fort Riley, Kansas, prides himself on being able to find a uniform to fit virtually any recruit. Currently, Sgt. Fitte is revising his stock requirements for fatigue caps. Based on experience, Sgt. Fitte has decided that hat size among recruits varies in such a way that it can be approximated by a normal distribution with a mean of 7″. Recently, though, he has revised his estimate of the standard deviation from .75 to .875. Present stock policy is to have on hand hats in every size (increments of ⅛″) from 6¼″ to 7¾″. Assuming that a recruit is fit if his or her hat size is within this range, find the probability that a recruit is fit:
(a) Assuming the old estimate of the standard deviation.
(b) Assuming the new estimate of the standard deviation.

5-46 Glenn Howell, VP of personnel for the Standard Insurance Company, has developed a new training program that is entirely self-paced. New employees work various stages at their own pace; completion occurs when the material is learned. Howell's program has been especially effective in speeding up the training process, as an employee's salary during training is only 67 percent of that earned upon completion of the program. In the last several years, average completion of the program has been in 44 days, with a standard deviation of 12 days.
(a) What is the probability an employee will finish the program in between 33 and 42 days?
(b) What is the probability of finishing the program in fewer than 30 days?
(c) Fewer than 25 or more than 60 days?

5-47 On the basis of past experience, automobile inspectors in Pennsylvania have noticed that 5 percent of all cars coming in for their annual inspection fail to pass. Using the normal approximation to the binomial distribution, find the probability that between seven and eighteen of the next 200 cars to enter the Lancaster inspection station will fail the inspection.

5-48 Dennis Hogan is the supervisor for the Conowingo Hydroelectric Dam. Mr. Hogan knows that the dam's turbines generate electricity at the peak rate only when at least 1,000,000 gallons of water pass through the dam each day. He also knows, from experience, that the daily flow is normally distributed, with mean equal to the previous day's flow and a standard deviation of 200,000 gallons. Yesterday, 850,000 gallons flowed through the dam. What is the probability that the turbines will generate at peak rate today?

5-49 Maurine Lewis, an editor for a large publishing company, calculates that it requires 11 months on average to complete the publication process from manuscript to finished book, with a standard deviation of 2.4 months. She believes that the normal distribution well describes the distribution of publication times. Out of nineteen books she will handle this year, approximately how many will complete the process in less than a year?

5-50 The Quickie Sales Corporation has just been given two conflicting estimates of sales for the upcoming quarter. Estimate I says that sales (in millions of dollars) will be normally distributed with mean 325 and standard deviation of 60. Estimate II says that sales will be normally distributed with mean 300 and standard deviation of 50. The board of directors finds that each estimate appears to be equally believable *a priori*. In order to determine which estimate should be used for future predictions, the board of directors has decided to meet again at the end of the quarter to use updated sales information to make a statement about the credibility of each estimate.
(a) Assuming that Estimate I is accurate, what is the probability that Quickie will have quarterly sales in excess of $350 million?
(b) Rework part (a) assuming that Estimate II is correct.
(c) At the end of the quarter, the board of directors finds that Quickie Sales Corp. has had sales in excess of $350 million. Given this updated information, what is the probability that Estimate I was originally the accurate one? (*Hint:* Remember Bayes' theorem.)
(d) Rework part (c) for Estimate II.

5-51 The Nobb Door Company manufactures doors for recreational vehicles. It has two conflicting objectives: It wants to build doors as small as possible to save on material costs, but to preserve its good reputation with the public, it feels obligated to manufacture doors that are tall enough for 95 percent of the adult population in the United States to pass through without stooping. In order to determine the height at which to manufacture doors, Nobb is willing to assume that the height of adults in America is normally distributed with mean 73 inches and standard deviation 6 inches. How tall should Nobb's doors be?

5-7
Choosing the Correct Probability Distribution

If we plan to use a probability distribution to describe a situation, we must be careful to choose the right one. We need to be certain that we are not using the *Poisson* probability distribution when it is the *binomial* that more nearly describes the situation we are studying. Remember that the binomial distribution is applied when the number of trials is fixed before the experiment begins, and each trial is independent and can result in only two mutually exclusive outcomes (success/failure, either/or, yes/no). Like the binomial, the Poisson distribution applies when each trial is independent. But although the probabilities in a Poisson distribution approach zero after the first few values, the possible values are infinite. The results are not limited to two mutually exclusive outcomes. Under some conditions, the Poisson distribution can be used as an approximation of the binomial, but not always. All the assumptions that form the basis of a distribution must be met if our use of that distribution is to produce usable results.

Even though the normal probability distribution is the only continuous distribution we have discussed in this chapter, we should realize that there are other useful continuous distributions. In the chapters to come, we shall study three additional continuous distributions, each of interest to decision makers who solve problems using statistics.

Exercises

5-52 Which probability distribution is most likely the appropriate one to use for the following variables: binomial, Poisson, or normal?
(a) The lifespan of a female born in 1957.
(b) The number of autos passing through a toll booth.
(c) The number of defective radios in a lot of 100.
(d) The water level in a reservoir.

5-53 What characteristics of a situation help to determine which is the appropriate distribution to use?

5-54 Explain in your own words the difference between discrete and continuous random variables. What difference does such classification make in determining the probabilities of future events?

5-55 In practice, managers see many different types of distributions. Often, the nature of these distributions is not as apparent as are some of the examples provided in this book. What alternatives are open to students, teachers, and researchers who want to use probability distributions in their work but who are not sure exactly which distributions are appropriate for given situations?

5-8

Terms Introduced in Chapter 5

Bernoulli Process A process in which each trial has only two possible outcomes, the probability of the outcome of any trial remains fixed over time, and the trials are statistically independent.

Binomial Distribution A discrete distribution describing the results of an experiment known as a Bernoulli process.

Continuity Correction Factor Corrections used to improve the accuracy of the approximation of a binomial distribution by a normal distribution.

Continuous Probability Distribution A probability distribution in which the variable is allowed to take on any value within a given range.

Continuous Random Variable A random variable allowed to take on any value within a given range.

Discrete Probability Distribution A probability distribution in which the variable is allowed to take on only a limited number of values.

Discrete Random Variable A random variable that is allowed to take on only a limited number of values.

Expected Value A weighted average of the outcomes of an experiment.

Expected Value of a Random Variable The sum of the products of each value of the random variable with that value's probability of occurrence.

Normal Distribution A distribution of a continuous random variable with a single-peaked, bell-shaped curve. The mean lies at the center of the distribution, and the curve is symmetrical around a vertical line erected at the mean. The two tails extend indefinitely, never touching the horizontal axis.

Poisson Distribution A discrete distribution in which the probability of the occurrence of an event within a very small time period is a very small number, the probability that two or more such events will occur within the same time interval is effectively 0, and the probability of the occurrence of the event within one time period is independent of where that time period is.

Probability Distribution A list of the outcomes of an experiment with the probabilities we would expect to see associated with these outcomes.

Random Variable A variable that takes on different values as a result of the outcomes of a random experiment.

Standard Normal Probability Distribution A normal probability distribution, with mean $\mu = 0$ and standard deviation $\sigma = 1$.

5-9

Equations Introduced in Chapter 5

[5-1]
$$\text{Probability of } r \text{ successes in } n \text{ Bernoulli or binomial trials} = \frac{n}{r!(n-r)!} p^r q^{n-r} \qquad \text{p. 206}$$

where

$r =$ number of successes desired
$n =$ number of trials undertaken
$p =$ probability of success (characteristic probability)
$q =$ probability of failure ($q = 1 - p$)

This *binomial formula* enables us to calculate algebraically the probability of success. We can apply it to any Bernoulli process, where (1) each trial has only two possible outcomes—a success or a failure; (2) the probability of success remains the same trial after trial; and (3) the trials are statistically independent.

$$\mu = np$$

The *mean* of a *binomial distribution* is equal to the number of trials multiplied by the probability of success.

$$\sigma = \sqrt{npq}$$

The *standard deviation* of a *binomial distribution* is equal to the square root of the product of (1) the number of trials, (2) the probability of a success, and (3) the probability of a failure (found by taking $q = 1 - p$).

$$P(x) = \frac{\lambda^x \times e^{-\lambda}}{x!}$$

This formula enables us to calculate the probability of a discrete random variable occurring in a *Poisson distribution.* The formula states that the probability of *exactly x* occurrences is equal to λ, or lambda (the mean number of occurrences per interval of time in a Poisson distribution), raised to the *x*th power and multiplied by *e*, or 2.71828 (the base of the natural logarithm system), raised to the negative lambda power, and the product divided by *x* factorial. The table of values for $e^{-\lambda}$ is Appendix Table 4.

$$P(x) = \frac{(np)^x \times e^{-np}}{x!}$$

If we substitute in Equation 5-4 the mean of the binomial distribution (np) in place of the mean of the Poisson distribution (λ), we can use the Poisson probability distribution as a reasonable approximation of the binomial. The approximation is good when n is equal to or greater than 20 and p is equal to or less than .05.

$$z = \frac{x - \mu}{\sigma}$$

where:

x = value of the random variable with which we are concerned
μ = mean of the distribution of this random variable
σ = standard deviation of this distribution
z = number of standard deviations from x to the mean of this distribution

Once we have derived z using this formula, we can use the Standard Normal Probability Distribution Table (which gives the values for areas under half the normal curve, beginning with 0.0 at the mean) and determine the probability that the random variable with which we are concerned is within that distance from the mean of this distribution.

5-10
Chapter Review Exercises

5-56 In the past 20 years, on average only 3 percent of all checks written to the American Heart Association have bounced. This month, the A.H.A. received 200 checks. What is the probability that:

(a) Exactly ten of these checks bounced?

(b) Exactly five of these checks bounced?

5-57 An inspector for U.S. Department of Agriculture is about to visit a large meat-packing company. She knows that, on average, 2 percent of all sides of beef inspected by the USDA are contaminated. She also knows that if she finds that more than 5 percent of the meat-packing company's beef is contaminated, the company will be closed for at least 1 month. Out of curiosity, she wants to compute the probability that this company will be shut down as a result of her inspection. Should she assume here inspection of the company's sides of beef is a Bernoulli process? Why or why not?

5-58 The regional office of the Environmental Protection Agency annually hires second-year law students as summer interns to help the agency prepare court cases. The agency is under a budget and wishes to keep its costs at a minimum. However, hiring student interns is less costly than hiring full-time employees. Accordingly, the agency wishes to hire the maximum number of students without overstaffing. On the average, it takes two interns all summer to research a case. The interns turn their work over to staff attorneys, who prosecute the case in the fall when the circuit court convenes. The legal staff coordinator has to place his budget request in June of the preceding summer for the number of positions he wishes to maintain. It is therefore impossible for him to know with certainty how many cases will be researched in the following summer. The data from preceding summers are as follows:

YEAR	1981	1982	1983	1984	1985	1986	1987	1988	1989	1990
Number of cases	6	4	8	7	5	6	4	5	4	5

Using these data as his probability distribution for the number of cases, the legal staff coordinator wishes to hire enough interns to research the expected number of cases that will arise. How many intern positions should be requested in the budget?

5-59 Label the following probability distributions as discrete or continuous:

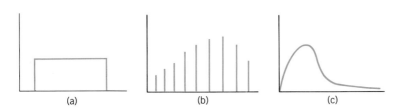

(a)   (b)   (c)

5-60 Which probability distribution would you use to find binomial probabilities in the following situations: binomial, Poisson, or normal?

(a) 112 trials, probability of success .06

(b) 15 trials, probability of success .4

(c) 650 trials, probability of success .02

(d) 59 trials, probability of success .1

5-61 Lauch Faircloth, a produce broker at the Pompano Beach, Florida, market, buys and resells vegetables. It is squash season now, and Lauch is currently buying squash at $8 a crate (350 crates per truckload). If he resells it by the next day, he gets $16 a crate. If he takes longer than a day his receipts drop to $7 a crate. Tomorrow's demand for squash is a random variable with demand for either 2, 3, 4, or 5 truckloads with probability .2, .25, .4, and .15, respectively. How much can Lauch expect to clear per day if he buys very sensibly?

5-62 Reginald Dunfey, president of British World Airlines, is fiercely proud of his company's on-time percentage; only 2 percent of all BWA flights arrive more than 10 minutes early or late. In his upcoming speech to the BWA board of directors, Mr. Dunfey wants to include the probability that none of the 200 flights scheduled for the following week will be more than 10 minutes early or late. What is this probability? What is the probability that exactly ten flights will be more than 10 minutes early or late?

5-63 Marvin Thornbury, an attorney working for the Legal Aid Society, estimates that, on average, seven of the daily arrivals to the L.A.S. office are people who were (in their opinion) unfairly evicted. Further, he estimates that, on average, five of the daily arrivals are people whose landlords have raised their rent illegally.
(a) What is the probability that six of the daily arrivals report an unfair eviction?
(b) What is the probability that eight daily arrivals have suffered an illegal rent increase?

5-64 The City Bank of Durham has recently begun a new credit program. Customers meeting certain credit requirements can obtain a credit card accepted by participating area merchants that carries a discount. Past numbers show that 25 percent of all applicants for this card are rejected. Given that credit acceptance or rejection is a Bernoulli process, out of fourteen applicants, what is the probability that:
(a) Exactly four will be rejected?   (c) Fewer than three?
(b) Exactly eight?   (d) More than five?

5-65 Anita Daybride is a Red Cross worker aiding earthquake victims in rural Colombia. Ms. Daybride knows that typhus is one of the most prevalent post-earthquake diseases: 44 percent of earthquake victims in rural areas contract the disease. If Anita treats thirteen earthquake victims, what is the probability that:
(a) Six or more have typhus?   (c) Nine or more?
(b) Seven or fewer?

5-66 On average, 12 percent of those enrolled in the Federal Aviation Administration's air traffic controller training program will have to repeat the course. If the current class size at the Leesburg, Virginia, training center is fifteen, what is the probability that:
(a) Fewer than six will have to repeat the course?
(b) Exactly ten will pass the course?
(c) More than twelve will pass the course?

5-67 The Virginia Department of Health and Welfare publishes a pamphlet, *A Guide to Selecting Your Doctor.* Free copies are available to individuals, institutions, and organizations that are willing to pay the postage. Most of the copies have gone to a small number of groups who, in turn, have disseminated the literature. Mailings for 5 years have been as follows:

| | YEAR | | | | |
	1986	1987	1988	1989	1990
Virginia Medical Association	7,000	3,000	—	2,000	4,000
Octogenarian Clubs	1,000	1,500	1,000	700	1,000
Virginia Federation of Women's Clubs	4,000	2,000	3,000	1,000	—
Medical College of Virginia	—	—	3,000	2,000	3,000
U.S. Department of Health, Education, and Welfare	1,000	—	1,000	—	1,000

In addition, an average of 2,000 copies per year were mailed or given to walk-in customers. Assistant secretary Susan Fleming, who has to estimate the number of pamphlets to print for 1991, knows that a revised edition of the pamphlet will be published in 1992. She feels that the demand in 1991 will most likely resemble that of 1988. She has, however, constructed this assessment of the probabilities:

| | YEAR | | | | |
	1986	1987	1988	1989	1990
Probability that 1991 will resemble this year	.10	.25	.45	.10	.10

(a) Construct a table of the probability distribution of demand for the pamphlet, and draw a graph representing that distribution.

(b) Assuming Fleming's assessment of the probabilities was correct, how many pamphlets should she order to be certain that there will be enough for 1991?

5-68 Production levels for Giles Fashion vary greatly according to consumer acceptance of the latest styles. Therefore, the company's weekly orders of wool cloth are difficult to predict in advance. On the basis of 5 years of data, the following probability distribution for the company's weekly demand for wool has been computed:

Amount of wool (lbs.)	2500	3500	4500	5500
Probability	.30	.45	.20	.05

From these data, the raw-materials purchaser computed the expected number of pounds required. Recently she noticed that the company's sales were lower in the last year than in years before. Extrapolating, she observed that the company will be lucky if its weekly demand averages 2,500 this year.
(a) What was the expected weekly demand for wool based on the distribution from past data?
(b) If each pound of wool generates $5 in revenue and costs $4 to purchase, ship, and handle, how much would Giles Fashion stand to gain or lose each week if it orders wool based on the past expected value and the company's demand is only 2,500?

5-69 Heidi Tanner is the manager of an exclusive shop that sells women's leather clothing and accessories. At the beginning of the fall/winter season, Ms. Tanner must decide how many full-length leather coats to order. These coats cost Ms. Tanner $100 each, and will sell for $200 each. Any coats left over at the end of the season will have to be sold at a 20 percent discount in order to make room for spring/summer inventory. From past experience, Heidi knows that demand for the coats has the following probability distribution:

Number of coats demanded	8	10	12	14	16
Probability	.10	.20	.25	.30	.15

She also knows that there is never any problem with selling all leftover coats at discount.
(a) If Heidi decides to order fourteen coats, what is her expected profit?
(b) How would the answer to part (a) change if the leftover coats were sold at a 40 percent discount?

5-70 The Executive Camera Company provides full expenses for its sales force. When attempting to budget automobile expenses for its employees, the financial department uses mileage figures to estimate gas, tire, and repair expenses. Salespeople average 5,650 miles a month, with a standard deviation of 120. In the interest of conservatism, the financial department wants its expense estimate and subsequent budget to be adequately high and, therefore, does not want to use the data from drivers who drove fewer than 5,500 miles. What percentage of drivers drove 5,500 miles or more?

5-71 Carolina Airlines flies a small number of routes in North and South Carolina. A flight carries an average of 30 passengers. In the summer, however, travel is heavier, and Carolina Airlines expects to average 45 passengers per flight in June.
(a) Does the airline's expectation provide any insight into expected value computation?
(b) Assume that the number of passengers is normally distributed with a given mean (30) and some standard deviation. The probability of having 45 passengers on a flight is very low. Does that fact cause Carolina Airlines not to expect them?

5-72 The purchasing agent in charge of procuring automobiles for the state of Minnesota's inter-agency motor pool was considering two different models. Both were 4-door, 4-cylinder cars with comparable service warranties. The decision was to choose the automobile that achieved the best mileage per gallon. The state had done some tests of its own, which produced the following results for the two automobiles in question:

	AVERAGE MPG	STANDARD DEVIATION
Automobile A	42	4
Automobile B	38	7

The purchasing agent was uncomfortable with the standard deviations, so she set her own decision criterion for the car that would be most likely to get more than 45 miles per gallon.
  (a) Using the data provided in combination with the purchasing agent's decision criterion, which car should she choose?
  (b) If the purchasing agent's criterion was to reject the automobile that most likely obtained less than 39 mpg, which car should she buy?

5-73 In its third year, the Liberty Football League averaged 16,050 fans per game, with a standard deviation of 2,500.
  (a) According to these data, what is the probability that the number of fans at any given game was greater than 20,000?
  (b) Fewer than 10,000?
  (c) Between 14,000 and 17,500?

5-74 Ted Hughes, the mayor of Chapelboro, wants to do something to reduce the number of accidents in the town involving motorists and bicyclists. Currently, the probability distribution of the number of such accidents per week is as follows:

Number of accidents	0	1	2	3	4	5
Probability	.05	.10	.20	.40	.15	.10

The mayor has two choices of action: He can install additional lighting on the town's streets or he can expand the number of bike lanes in the town. The respective revised probability distributions for the two options are as follows:

Number of accidents	0	1	2	3	4	5
Probability (lights)	.10	.20	.30	.25	.10	.05
Probability (lanes)	.20	.20	.20	.30	.05	.05

Which plan should the mayor approve if he wants to produce the largest possible reduction in:
  (a) Expected number of accidents per week?
  (b) Probability of more than three accidents per week?
  (c) Probability of three or more accidents per week?

5-75 Surveys by the Federal Deposit Insurance Corporation have shown that the life of a regular savings account maintained in one of its member banks averages 24 months, with a standard deviation of 7.5 months.
  (a) If a depositor opens an account at a bank that is a member of the FDIC, what is the probability that there will still be money in the account after 28 months?
  (b) What is the probability that the account will have been closed before one year?

5-76 Sensurex Productions, Incorporated, has recently patented and developed an ultrasensitive smoke detector for use in both residential and commercial buildings. Whenever a detectable amount of smoke is in the air, a wailing siren is set off. In recent tests conducted in a $20' \times 15' \times 8'$ room, the smoke levels that activated the smoke detector averaged 320 parts per million (ppm) of smoke in the room, with a standard deviation of 25 ppm.
  (a) If a cigarette introduces 82 ppm into the atmosphere of a $20' \times 15' \times 8'$ room, what is the probability that four people smoking cigarettes simultaneously will set off the alarm?
  (b) Three people?

5-77 Rework exercise 5-65 using the normal approximation. Compare the approximate and exact answers.

5-78 Try to use the normal approximation for exercise 5-66. Notice that np is only 1.8. Comment on the accuracy of the approximation.

5-79 Randall Finan supervises the packaging of college textbooks for Newsome-Cluett Publishers. He knows that the number of cardboard boxes he will need depends partly on the size of books. All Newsome-Cluett books use the same size paper but may have differing numbers of pages. After pulling shipment records for the last five years, Finan derived the following set of probabilities:

# of pages	100	300	500	700	900	1100
Probability	.05	.10	.25	.25	.20	.15

(a) If Finan bases his box purchase on an expected length of 600 pages, will he have enough boxes?
(b) If all 700 page books are edited down to 500 pages, what expected number of pages should he use?

5-80 D'Addario Rose Co. is planning rose production for Valentine's Day. Each rose costs $.35 to raise and sells wholesale for $.70. Any roses left over after Valentine's Day can be sold the next day for $.10 wholesale. D'Addario has the following probability distribution based on previous years:

Roses sold	15,000	20,000	25,000	30,000
Probability	.10	.30	.40	.20

How many roses should D'Addario produce in order to minimize the firm's expected losses?

5-81 A certain business school has 400 students in its MBA program. One hundred and sixteen of the students are married. Without using Appendix Table 3, determine
(a) The probability that exactly two of three randomly selected students are married.
(b) The probability that exactly four of thirteen students chosen at random are married.

5-82 Kenan Football Stadium has four light towers with 25 high-intensity floodlights mounted on each. Sometimes an entire light tower will go dark. Smitty Moyer, head of maintenance, wonders what the distribution of light tower failures is. He knows that any individual tower has a probability of .11 of failing during a football game and that the towers fail independently of one another.
   Construct a graph, like Fig. 5-4, of a binomial probability distribution showing the probabilities of exactly 0, 1, 2, 3, or 4 towers going dark during the same game.

5-83 Smitty Moyer (see exercise 5-82) knows that the probability that any one of the 25 individual floodlights in a light tower fails during a football game is .05. The light tower electrical systems have been modified so that an entire tower can no longer fail.
(a) Using both the binomial and the Poisson approximation, determine the probability that seven floodlights from a given tower will fail during the same game.
(b) Using both methods, determine the probability that two will fail.

5-84 Ansel Fearrington wants to borrow $75,000 from his bank for a new tractor for his farm. The loan officer doesn't have any data specifically on the bank's history of equipment loans, but he does tell Ansel that over the years the bank has received about 1460 loan applications per year and that the probability of approval was, on average, about .8.
(a) Ansel is curious about the average and standard deviation of the number of loans approved per year. Find these figures for him.
(b) Suppose after careful research that the loan officer tells Ansel the correct figures actually are 1327 applications per year with an approval probability of .77. What are the mean and standard deviation now?

5-85 Ansel Fearrington (see exercise 5-84) learns that the loan officer has been fired for failing to follow bank lending guidelines. The bank now announces that all financially sound loan applications will be approved. Ansel guesses that three out of every five applications are unsound.
 (a) If Ansel is right, what is the probability that exactly six of the next ten applications will be approved?
 (b) What is the probability that more than three will be approved?
 (c) What is the probability that more than two but fewer than six will be approved?

5-86 Krista Engel is campaign manager for a candidate for U.S. Senator. Staff consensus is that the candidate has the support of 40 percent of registered voters. A random sample of 300 registered voters shows that 34 percent would vote for Krista's candidate. If 40 percent of voters really are allied with her candidate, what is the probability that a sample of 300 voters would indicate 34 percent or fewer on her side? Is it likely that the 40 percent estimate is correct?

5-87 Krista Engel (see exercise 5-86) has learned that her candidate's major opponent, who has the support of 50 percent of registered voters, will likely lose the support of ¼ of those voters because of his recent support of clear-cutting of timber in national forests, a policy to which Krista's candidate is opposed.
 If Krista's candidate now has the support of 34 percent of registered voters, and all the dissatisifed voters then switch to Krista's candidate, what is the probability that a new survey of 250 registered voters would show her candidate to have the support of 51 percent to 55 percent of the voters?

5-11
Chapter Concepts Test

Answers are in the back of the book.

T F 1. The expected value of an experiment is obtained by computing the arithmetic average value over all possible outcomes of the experiment.

T F 2. The value of z for some point x lying in a normal distribution is the area between x and the mean of the distribution.

T F 3. The right and left tails of the normal distribution extend indefinitely, never touching the horizontal axis.

T F 4. For a normal distribution, the mean always lies between the mode and the median.

T F 5. All but about three-tenths of 1 percent of the area in a normal distribution lies within plus and minus 3 standard deviations from the mean.

T F 6. Developing a conditional loss table is cumbersome when there are many possible actions and outcomes, because the loss resulting from every action/outcome pair must be included in the table.

T F 7. The area under the curve of a normal distribution between the mean and a point 1.8 standard deviations above the mean is greater for a distribution having a mean of 100 than it is for a distribution having a mean of 0.

T F 8. The normal distribution may be used to approximate the binomial distribution when the number of trials, n, is equal to or greater than 60.

T F 9. The two types of losses we consider in solving an inventory-stocking problem are (a) opportunity losses and (b) activity losses.

T F 10. When the probability of success in a Bernoulli process is 50 percent ($p = .5$), its binomial distribution is symmetrical.

T F 11. A frequency distribution lists observed frequencies for an experiment that has already been

5 PROBABILITY II: DISTRIBUTIONS

performed; a probability distribution lists those outcomes that could result *if* the experiment were performed.

T F 12. The value of a random variable can usually be predicted in advance of a particular occurrence.

T F 13. Once the value of *p* has been decided for a Bernoulli process, the value of *q* is calculated as $(1 - p)$.

T F 14. If the expected number of arrivals in an office is calculated as five per hour, one can be reasonably confident that five people will arrive within the next hour.

T F 15. The binomial distribution is not really necessary, since its values can always be approximated by another distribution.

T F 16. The height of adult humans can be described by a Poisson distribution.

T F 17. Any action that minimizes expected loss will also minimize expected gain.

T F 18. After 20 trials of an experiment, a correctly shaped distribution curve is created.

T F 19. An example of an opportunity loss could be loss of sales due to the excess age of fruit on a grocery shelf.

T F 20. A distribution where the mean and median have different values cannot be a normal distribution.

T F 21. The mean of a binomial distribution is given by *np*.

22. If the expected daily profit of a lemonade stand is $13.45, then:
  (a) Tomorrow's profit will be $13.45.
  (b) Tomorrow's profit will be less than $13.45
  (c) Tomorrow's profit will be more than $13.45
  (d) Tomorrow's loss will be $13.45
  (e) None of the above

23. For a given binomial distribution with *n* fixed, if $p < .5$,
  (a) The Poisson distribution will provide a good approximation
  (b) The Poisson distribution will provide a bad approximation
  (c) The binomial distribution will be skewed left
  (d) The binomial distribution will be skewed right
  (e) The binomial distribution will be symmetric

24. Suppose we have a Poisson distribution with $\lambda = 2$. Then the probability of having exactly 10 occurrences is:
  (a) $\dfrac{2^{-10}e^{10}}{10!}$ (c) $\dfrac{10^2 e^{-10}}{10!}$

  (b) $\dfrac{2^{10}e^{-2}}{2!}$ (d) $\dfrac{2^{10}e^{-2}}{10!}$

25. Which of the following is a characteristic of a probability distribution for a random variable?
  (a) A probability is provided for every possible value.
  (b) The sum of all probabilities is 1.
  (c) No given probability occurs more than once.
  (d) All of these.
  (e) a and b but not c.

26. Which of the following could never be described by a binomial distribution?
  (a) The number of defective widgets produced by an assembly process.
  (b) The amount of water used daily by a single household.
  (c) The number of people in your class who can answer this question correctly.
  (d) All of these could always be described by a binomial distribution.

27. If $p = .4$ for a particular Bernoulli process, the calculation $\dfrac{7!}{3! \times 4!} (.4)^3 (.6)^4$ gives the probability of getting:
  (a) Exactly three successes in seven trials (d) Four or more successes in seven trials
  (b) Exactly four successes in seven trials (e) None of these
  (c) Three or more successes in seven trials

28. For binomial distributions with $p = .2$:
    (a) A distribution for $n = 2,000$ would more closely approximate the normal distribution than one for $n = 50$.
    (b) No matter what the value of n, the distribution is skewed to the right.
    (c) The graph of this distribution with $p = .2$ and $n = 100$ would be the exact reverse of the graph for the binomial distribution with $n = 100$ and $p = .8$.
    (d) All of these.
    (e) a and b but not c.

29. Which of the following is a necessary condition for use of a Poisson distribution?
    (a) Probability of one arrival per second is constant.
    (b) The number of arrivals in any 1-second interval is independent of arrivals in other intervals.
    (c) The probability of two or more arrivals in the same second is zero.
    (d) All of these.
    (e) b and c but not a.

30. In which of these cases would the Poisson distribution be a good approximation of the binomial?
    (a) $n = 40$, $p = .32$ (d) $n = 10$, $p = .03$
    (b) $n = 40$, $q = .79$ (e) All of these.
    (c) $n = 200$, $q = .98$

31. For a normal curve with $\mu = 55$ and $\sigma = 10$, how much area will be found under the curve to the right of the value 55?
    (a) 1.0   (d) .32
    (b) .68   (e) Cannot be determined from the information given.
    (c) .5

32. Suppose you are using a normal distribution to approximate a binomial distribution with $\mu = 5$, $\sigma = 2$ and wish to determine the probability of getting more than seven successes. From the normal table, you would determine the probability that z is greater than:
    (a) 0   (b) .5   (c) .75   (d) 1.0   (e) 1.25

33. For a normal curve with a mean of 120 and a standard deviation of 35, what proportion (in percent) of the area under the curve will lie between the values of 40 and 82.

34. Which of the following normal curves looks most like the curve for $\mu = 10$, $\sigma = 5$?
    (a) Curve for $\mu = 10$, $\sigma = 10$.   (c) Curve for $\mu = 20$, $\sigma = 5$.
    (b) Curve for $\mu = 20$, $\sigma = 10$.   (d) Curve for $\mu = 12$, $\sigma = 3$.

35. A binomial distribution may be approximated by a Poisson distribution if:
    (a) n is large and p is large   (c) n is small and p is small
    (b) n is small and p is large   (d) None of these

36. The standard deviation of a binomial distribution depends on:
    (a) Probability of success   (d) a and b but not c
    (b) Probability of failure   (e) b and c but not a
    (c) Number of trials   (f) a, b, and c.

37. The weighted average of the outcomes of an experiment is called the _____.

38. The distribution that deals only in successes and failures is the _____ distribution. It is usually used to describe a _____ process.

39. When approximating a binomial distribution by a normal distribution, a _____ correction factor should be used.

40. The mean of a binomial distribution, μ, can be calculated as _____, once n and p are known. The standard deviation, σ, is calculated as _____.

41. For a Poisson distribution, the symbol that represents the mean number of occurrences per interval of time is _____.

42. A list of the probabilities of outcomes that could result if an experiment were performed is called a _____.

43. The two parameters needed to describe a normal distribution are the _____ and the _____.

44. A _____ variable is a variable which assumes different values according to the results of an experiment.

45. _____ distributions can take on only a limited number of values, while _____ distributions can take on any value within a range.

5-12
Conceptual Case

(Northern White Metals Company)

Late in January, 1981, Dick Lennox made the decision to expand NWMC's sales force. The economy had rebounded from the brief 1980 recession, the prospects for a spring boom in commercial construction were strong, and continual gains were being posted in the high-tech applications area. NWMC aluminum was being increasingly accepted as both a structural material and exterior trim, largely through the efforts of Bill Hamilton, who had made microprocessor, computer, and instrumentation businesses his specialty.

Four experienced sales reps were hired to service the upsurge in building, and three new reps, all midyear graduates from a local engineering school, were taken on to service the burgeoning technology field. It was planned that growth in this industry would lead to growth for Northern, too.

And so it went, with all three new reps bringing in at first small, but soon larger and larger orders. Of the new salespeople, one, Lynn Martin, seemed to progress faster than the rest and was soon rivaling Bill as top producer in the special-applications area. By mid-May, the total order backlog had increased 20 percent, and Dick was quite pleased. An additional, somewhat unexpected benefit of increased sales in this area was a greater demand for services of the fabricating and anodizing departments. Capacity utilization in each of these had risen nearly 50 percent, since the newer applications frequently required cut, milled, finished material and not just raw extruded aluminum.

This growth spurt, though, carried with it some problems. Particularly troubled was the anodizing department. Anodizing involves putting a protective, often decorative, oxide film on the aluminum by an electrolytic process in which the metal serves as an anode. The metal is placed on special racks and dipped sequentially in large tanks containing concentrated solutions of acid, caustic soda, and a neutral rinse. There are six tanks in all, and the aluminum sections must spend a certain amount of time in each tank before being transferred to the next. When the metal is brought out of the sixth tank and dried, the process is complete. The process is a fairly delicate one, and it is important to maintain the proper pH levels, or acid and alkaline concentrations, in the different solutions.

Improper pH levels, either too acid or too alkaline, could result in a finish that is either too light or too heavy. If too light a finish is imparted, the entire cycle has to be repeated. If the finish is too heavy, or textured, the metal is suitable only for scrap.

In the past, the anodizing foreman could use a judgment born of years of experience and compensate for concentration deviations by using longer or shorter dipping periods. The significantly increased volume had begun to strain the process, though, and this system was no longer practicable. Mike Schutzer, the foreman, was growing increasingly frustrated, and he stopped in to talk with Dick one afternoon at quitting time.

"We've reached the limit!" he erupted with dismay.

"The limit of what?" Dick replied curiously. The growing bottleneck problem in anodizing had not yet been brought to his attention.

"The limit of reason," the foreman responded. "I can't go on juggling orders through the line anymore. Each pass-through changes the solution concentrations from the ideal levels. Either we have to monitor levels continuously to keep them at the ideal mark or risk turning out batch after batch of bad product."

Dick thought for a moment, then replied, "Mike, I think there's a compromise solution here. It's true that there is actually some acceptable range of concentrations around the ideal, isn't there?"

"Well, yes, I suppose there is," the foreman answered cautiously.

Dick was relieved to know that was true. The cost of maintaining a constant, unchanging pH would easily exceed the price addition of an anodized finish, of that he was sure.

"We both know how costly it is to maintain a fixed concentration," he continued, "so it seems to me we have a tradeoff point. We'll select a waste/reject level that will allow us to operate the process continuously while only requiring periodic concentration adjustments."

Clearly, increased demand has introduced an unforeseen problem into the anodizing department. Dick seems to have an idea about how to get operations under control, and fortunately, he has the support of his foreman. What information is now needed? Once acquired, how should the information be used to better manage the anodizing department?

5-13
Computer Data Base Exercise

Mary D'Angelo, Hal Rodgers' secretary, caught Laurel in the hall one Wednesday morning. "Could I stop in and see you for a few minutes? We've got a problem with our copy machines and Hal said you might be able to give me some advice."

"Sure thing," Laurel smiled. "Anytime this morning is fine." She knew the two copiers used by HH Industries were a source of frustration for the entire office staff. They had been purchased by the previous owner, Mr. Douglas, at a used-office-supply store during one of the business' leaner months. While somewhat reliable for the first year or two, the repairman had recently become a familiar fixture around the office.

Mary tapped on the door and came in when Laurel beckoned. "Hal's asked me to determine our best option for dealing with the copy machine situation," she explained. "You know how aggravating it can be when the workload picks up and one of the copiers is down! What I need from you are some details about how to go about evaluating the costs of our various alternatives. I know this isn't exactly marketing analysis, but . . . ."

Laurel laughed. "This will be a welcome change. Statistics doesn't always have to be boring, boardroom stuff! Do you keep track of the daily status of the machines?"

"I have to," Mary groaned. "It seems like one or the other is down at least once a week, and we have had to send some stuff out for reproduction recently, which is a real nuisance! I also have dated receipts for service calls during the last year or so. Will that help?"

"It sure will. Could you calculate the average service call costs for the cases when either one or both machines was down? That will help us with the evaluation. Meanwhile, I'll get started on the rest of this."

"Okay," Mary said. "I'll see you later this afternoon."

1. Using the data given in Table DB5-1 on page 248, what is the probability that a machine will be down on any given day?

2. With 250 work days per year, how many days per year would you expect one machine to be down? Two to be down?

Mary calculated the average service call costs: $68 for one machine, $100 for two. Figuring what copier "downtime" cost the company was a little more difficult. Laurel and Mary decided that a reasonable measure would be .05 per copy (the standard fee charged by local copy shops) times the number of copies lost, which was estimated at 150 per copier per day.

3. Calculate the expected yearly cost for the current situation.

Next, Mary outlined for Laurel the other alternatives. "HH Industries has been presented with two proposals. First, there's a company that will lease us two copiers for $350 per month. It has data to support its claim that the probability of a machine being down on any given day is .05. Furthermore, service calls are included in the contract price. Second, we have the opportunity to purchase a new state-of-the-art machine which would replace both our old copiers. The initial cost is $8,750, and it comes with a one-year guarantee under which service calls would be free. I've checked around and determined that we can expect about $175 per call after that. That sounds high, except when you consider that this machine is pretty reliable—only a .017 chance of it being down on any given day."

4. Using a 3-year period for comparison (and ignoring the time-value of money), which is the best alternative for HH Industries?

Hal addressed his staff at the next weekly meeting. "The last item on the agenda has to do with staffing. With phone-in orders being the lifeline of our business, it is imperative that we put as much effort as is needed toward serving our phone customers. It has been brought to my attention recently that our current staff may be inadequate in processing the volume of calls we're receiving. Based on some conversations with Stan and his people, it seems unreasonable to ask someone to deal with more than eight calls per hour. Beyond that, there's just too much pressure on our people to rush folks off the line, and we haven't built our reputation for personalized service just to see it destroyed when we start to grow. Laurel, I'd like you to get together with Stan and come up with some recommendations by next week's meeting. Any questions?"

Laurel jotted down a few notes. "Peggy's staff keeps the phone bills?" she asked.

Hall nodded and stood up, signalling the end of the meeting. "Have a good one, folks."

Laurel trotted off to find Peggy, from whom she got some recent phone bills, which itemized incoming calls. She spent some time coming up with a profile of an average month, then headed toward Stan's office.

"Is Hal's figure of eight calls per hour reasonable?" she asked the VP in charge of sales.

"You've got to remember that the majority of our calls are customers ordering parts directly out of the catalog," Stan answered. "Occasionally, there will be a guy who needs to describe a part he wants matched, which takes a little legwork on the part of the sales rep, but those are definitely in the minority. Then there are the ones who just want to request a catalog. I'd say that eight is a pretty solid figure, even including short breaks. Having a phone growing out of your ear all day can get kind of uncomfortable, and we don't want to be accused of slave labor!"

"Okay," Laurel smiled. "We'll go with eight. I'll let you know soon what I come up with so we can have something for Hal next week. Catch you later."

Back in her office, Laurel set up the data. "I'll have to assume Poisson arrivals for the time being," she mused. "I can check that out a little later."

5. Using the data given in Table DB5-2 on page 248, calculate the average number of calls received per hour.

6. If Laurel wants to be 98% sure that a sales rep only has to deal with eight calls an hour, how many reps should she and Stan recommend?

7. After a little more discussion, Laurel found out from Stan that he handles an average of two calls per hour (new customers, requests for new product lines, complaints, etc.). Does this change the recommendations from question 6?

The day after the phone-line study was completed, Stan caught Laurel as she was eating lunch on the picnic table outside in the shade. "Quite a change from the Rockies, isn't it?" he asked.

"I'm afraid so," Laurel smiled, "but it does have its advantages." She crinkled her slightly sunburned nose. "The whole toy company would envy this tan! Besides, I've got a winter vacation planned to take in some cross-country skiing with an old buddy of mine from out there. To tell you the truth, I'm looking forward to a little cool weather."

"I know what you mean," said Stan. "The only thing remotely cool here is air conditioning! By the way, if you've got a minute this afternoon, stick your head in my office. I've got a study in mind, but it's not urgent or anything."

"That's the kind I like!" said Laurel. "I'll see you in a while."

Later, Stan explained to Laurel that he was interested in working up what amounted to a "typical customer profile." "That early work you did on the daily number of orders and the average order size really got me to thinking. So I had Peggy run a sales report for our active customers, giving the last year of purchases for each." He pointed to a stack of green-bar computer paper almost two inches thick. "It would really help me use my advertising budget efficiently," he concluded. "Like I said—no big rush on this."

"Good thing," muttered Laurel on the way back to her office. "I'm not interested in spending my weekend doing data analysis!"

8. Using the data given in Table DB5-3 on pages 248–253, what distribution appears to describe the customers' purchases?

9. What are the mean, median, and standard deviation?

10. Suppose that the active customer accounts are normally distributed with μ and σ calculated in question 9. What proportion of customers would be expected to have accounts greater than $20,000? less than $10,000? What proportions actually do fall in these ranges?

TABLE DB5-1 Copy Machine Status

										1—UP, 0—DOWN																
Machine 1	1	1	1	0	1	1	1	1	1	1	1	1	1	1	0	1	1	0	1	1	1	1	1	1	1	1
Machine 2	1	1	1	1	1	1	1	1	1	0	1	1	1	1	1	1	1	1	1	1	1	1	1	1	1	0
Machine 1	1	1	1	1	1	1	0	1	1	1	1	1	1	1	1	1	1	1	1	0	1	1	1	0	1	
Machine 2	0	1	0	1	1	1	1	1	1	1	1	1	1	1	1	1	1	1	1	0	1	1	1	1	1	
Machine 1	0	1	1	1	1	1	0	1	1	1	1	1	1	1	1	1	1	1	1	0	1	1	1	1	1	
Machine 2	1	1	1	1	1	0	1	1	1	1	1	1	1	1	1	0	1	1	1	1	1	1	1	1	0	
Machine 1	1	1	1	1	1	1	1	1	1	1	0	1	1	0	1	1	1	1	1	1	1	1	1	1	1	
Machine 2	1	0	1	1	1	1	1	1	1	1	1	1	1	1	1	1	1	1	0	1	1	1	1	0	1	
Machine 1	1	1	1	1	1	1	1	0	1	1	1	1	1	1	1	1	1	1	0	1	1	1	1	1	1	
Machine 2	1	0	1	1	1	1	1	1	1	0	1	1	1	1	1	1	1	1	1	1	1	1	0	1		
Machine 1	1	1	1	0	1	1	1	1	1	1	1	1	1	0	1	1	0	1	1	1	1	1	1	1	1	
Machine 2	1	1	1	1	1	1	1	1	1	0	1	1	1	1	1	1	1	1	1	1	1	1	1	1	0	
Machine 1	1	1	0	1	1	1	0	1	1	1	1	1	1	1	1	0	1	1	1	1	1	1	1	1	0	1
Machine 2	1	1	1	1	1	1	1	1	1	1	0	1	1	1	1	1	1	1	0	1	1	1	1	1	1	
Machine 1	1	1	1	1	1	0	1	1	1	1	1	1	1	1	0	1	1	1	1	1	1	1	1	1	1	
Machine 2	1	0	1	1	1	1	1	1	1	1	1	1	1	1	1	1	1	0	1	1	1	1	1	0		
Machine 1	0	1	1	1	1	1	1	1	1	1	1	1	0	1	1	1	1	1	1	1	1	1	0	1		
Machine 2	1	1	1	0	1	1	1	1	1	0	1	1	1	1	1	1	1	0	1	1	1	1	1	1		
Machine 1	1	0	1	1	1	1	1	1	1	1	1	1	1	0	1	1	1	1	1	1	1	1	1			
Machine 2	1	1	1	1	1	1	0	1	0	1	1	1	1	1	1	1	1	1	1	1	1	1	0	1		

TABLE DB5-2 Phone Call Data

HOUR	NUMBER OF CALLS RECEIVED PER HOUR																			
8	10	16	9	12	13	8	20	16	9	13	18	14	16	10	13	10	23	23	13	18	24	11
9	24	29	38	26	26	28	28	24	35	26	32	33	10	26	21	21	34	22	24	16	19	37
10	28	27	29	20	35	31	38	31	28	19	27	31	38	26	29	19	26	29	29	25	22	27
11	26	24	38	41	41	36	38	23	31	33	31	30	46	20	39	28	27	29	27	26	23	37
12	18	23	31	26	23	20	29	30	17	17	26	30	28	32	19	20	25	31	23	12	25	18
1	23	23	36	25	31	37	33	36	31	27	35	28	25	25	25	35	35	34	35	25	36	36
2	48	41	43	34	36	39	40	36	44	41	47	48	42	40	32	46	39	36	37	15	41	30
3	46	46	31	46	33	27	32	38	40	21	34	33	31	37	38	46	42	31	23	18	32	29
4	21	23	13	20	16	29	20	14	26	12	12	18	23	23	15	29	24	18	21	15	20	17

TABLE DB5-3 Sales Report for Active Customers

CUSTOMER NUMBER	PURCHASES (IN $)	CUSTOMER NUMBER	PURCHASES (IN $)	CUSTOMER NUMBER	PURCHASES (IN $)	CUSTOMER NUMBER	PURCHASES (IN $)
1	19962	10	16052	19	17590	28	12308
2	15946	11	9353	20	19624	29	8996
3	8180	12	12644	21	10732	30	12415
4	10487	13	10671	22	4856	31	21375
5	18960	14	14533	23	11462	32	10413
6	17938	15	15953	24	17603	33	18231
7	13687	16	11729	25	22443	34	17049
8	9397	17	19578	26	19878	35	5238
9	8582	18	15901	27	18095	36	17160

5 PROBABILITY II: DISTRIBUTIONS

TABLE DB5-3 *(Continued)*

CUSTOMER NUMBER	PURCHASES (IN $)	CUSTOMER NUMBER	PURCHASES (IN $)	CUSTOMER NUMBER	PURCHASES (IN $)	CUSTOMER NUMBER	PURCHASES (IN $)
37	11331	92	12870	147	16502	202	8897
38	6965	93	11061	148	14550	203	17849
39	7633	94	15584	149	10254	204	9609
40	11224	95	3916	150	11633	205	12713
41	14647	96	7343	151	16673	206	7245
42	10521	97	11715	152	24020	207	13244
43	13185	98	10971	153	22980	208	15448
44	19318	99	4084	154	14622	209	16581
45	19854	100	10662	155	15524	210	7373
46	15892	101	21832	156	19114	211	15106
47	21836	102	12984	157	9329	212	20031
48	14625	103	17499	158	14034	213	15372
49	8024	104	13360	159	8912	214	19473
50	12001	105	10331	160	12227	215	9998
51	15835	106	5632	161	14745	216	22550
52	11361	107	10755	162	19250	217	18663
53	15226	108	16220	163	2826	218	13570
54	12162	109	7759	164	11228	219	15228
55	10958	110	6800	165	5316	220	19413
56	6164	111	14008	166	4500	221	17437
57	12754	112	16797	167	11259	222	21548
58	13410	113	3765	168	16400	223	1301
59	8337	114	13342	169	11994	224	12687
60	14773	115	17508	170	9533	225	11629
61	15033	116	17662	171	12611	226	14583
62	24219	117	16777	172	1088	227	13223
63	14931	118	8814	173	11389	228	8147
64	6736	119	8978	174	12482	229	17391
65	16800	120	11925	175	16763	230	10245
66	12498	121	9961	176	9701	231	13545
67	17632	122	13793	177	13009	232	6000
68	12359	123	17778	178	9941	233	8476
69	16261	124	11191	179	6682	234	14741
70	17232	125	5522	180	8470	235	11322
71	20347	126	14012	181	8255	236	16019
72	6955	127	8857	182	17068	237	7304
73	10983	128	15438	183	7338	238	11215
74	12835	129	18882	184	12792	239	14410
75	12367	130	17257	185	12074	240	16269
76	13398	131	11795	186	11559	241	14976
77	14228	132	10249	187	10501	242	13432
78	11154	133	13841	188	15399	243	6953
79	10800	134	9958	189	16433	244	18468
80	6646	135	9480	190	13812	245	12116
81	12354	136	9753	191	15804	246	22369
82	18389	137	12125	192	16843	247	12451
83	7884	138	9258	193	19699	248	9885
84	17903	139	12285	194	15018	249	7689
85	9960	140	13323	195	9326	250	14324
86	13024	141	16196	196	13116	251	20709
87	10507	142	15886	197	8844	252	16432
88	14335	143	16765	198	16318	253	13780
89	8872	144	12858	199	11781	254	7372
90	12401	145	16565	200	14258	255	6994
91	10016	146	16366	201	18752	256	9777

TABLE DB5-3 *(Continued)*

CUSTOMER NUMBER	PURCHASES (IN $)	CUSTOMER NUMBER	PURCHASES (IN $)	CUSTOMER NUMBER	PURCHASES (IN $)	CUSTOMER NUMBER	PURCHASES (IN $)
257	10599	313	14034	369	12961	425	16180
258	13929	314	16586	370	17653	426	11005
259	17806	315	17533	371	10868	427	13531
260	6547	316	18630	372	8547	428	23604
261	10911	317	8652	373	15578	429	9001
262	11338	318	14347	374	11124	430	15661
263	13316	319	14904	375	8759	431	9036
264	6176	320	15311	376	13657	432	19434
265	6425	321	5104	377	11872	433	11695
266	13191	322	14300	378	10550	434	14098
267	3879	323	11347	379	11748	435	16584
268	17461	324	11642	380	12512	436	16639
269	13235	325	14573	381	15211	437	11651
270	13567	326	20372	382	9415	438	16932
271	11263	327	14272	383	16923	439	10622
272	14224	328	12847	384	15552	440	6150
273	11137	329	10364	385	15618	441	20618
274	4535	330	17481	386	15219	442	8270
275	10984	331	7933	387	9393	443	10520
276	20936	332	12634	388	13958	444	4425
277	15934	333	2484	389	11934	445	19048
278	15758	334	8570	390	10946	446	8174
279	4326	335	12024	391	15407	447	9649
280	13498	336	4535	392	10788	448	13913
281	21579	337	14236	393	7677	449	15358
282	7018	338	9478	394	10505	450	13499
283	10700	339	12560	395	14407	451	5734
284	14837	340	18604	396	7847	452	7889
285	13553	341	15066	397	17238	453	17051
286	10065	342	6877	398	13662	454	3393
287	16853	343	13176	399	16176	455	14166
288	10245	344	13950	400	17284	456	12268
289	14671	345	11520	401	8244	457	15549
290	7438	346	11975	402	14098	458	17189
291	6279	347	8086	403	12535	459	19895
292	13822	348	16219	404	8741	460	14026
293	14473	349	15577	405	11079	461	19816
294	6285	350	7438	406	13786	462	12529
295	8799	351	10543	407	15778	463	11658
296	10598	352	12264	408	2958	464	12815
297	17136	353	7509	409	17919	465	15619
298	9265	354	16812	410	15357	466	16547
299	12262	355	15105	411	13070	467	16577
300	7269	356	13386	412	8972	468	9394
301	6813	357	15225	413	6122	469	16780
302	10345	358	10150	414	17021	470	16224
303	15122	359	14444	415	5478	471	10786
304	7014	360	11033	416	15000	472	12229
305	15148	361	13261	417	12418	473	30832
306	16514	362	15383	418	9968	474	10293
307	13876	363	11772	419	18269	475	20074
308	17023	364	8906	420	12723	476	12621
309	4952	365	16779	421	13348	477	21135
310	15826	366	7767	422	10657	478	6851
311	7623	367	14342	423	12666	479	14606
312	12997	368	13429	424	12030	480	16128

CUSTOMER NUMBER	PURCHASES (IN $)	CUSTOMER NUMBER	PURCHASES (IN $)	CUSTOMER NUMBER	PURCHASES (IN $)	CUSTOMER NUMBER	PURCHASES (IN $)
481	11765	537	23674	593	14307	649	9049
482	12042	538	12571	594	12126	650	7928
483	15414	539	9207	595	9999	651	8887
484	14111	540	17398	596	19135	652	6938
485	9726	541	7321	597	11565	653	13971
486	8562	542	11015	598	17238	654	11077
487	12462	543	15108	599	9848	655	11893
488	14814	544	12798	600	17943	656	16545
489	13083	545	15304	601	9044	657	11291
490	12204	546	17024	602	8613	658	11052
491	19219	547	10971	603	6811	659	13159
492	13323	548	17714	604	20244	660	8791
493	8860	549	15327	605	18240	661	11708
494	18122	550	14081	606	9765	662	6536
495	14450	551	18683	607	17754	663	12097
496	22201	552	10800	608	10702	664	7805
497	12478	553	9571	609	16104	665	16217
498	10883	554	14180	610	11518	666	14921
499	14416	555	9629	611	16368	667	167
500	11942	556	9415	612	17044	668	12394
501	17691	557	8523	613	10049	669	2450
502	11061	558	9955	614	11303	670	13455
503	13629	559	7264	615	14411	671	12466
504	8787	560	11611	616	9302	672	11362
505	15860	561	8499	617	24560	673	8699
506	5225	562	17912	618	17372	674	17768
507	15025	563	8483	619	11165	675	6789
508	12556	564	13335	620	13839	676	4510
509	10517	565	10913	621	13423	677	6237
510	13798	566	7913	622	12793	678	15432
511	16803	567	13140	623	11437	679	9856
512	11587	568	16765	624	16295	680	15760
513	3158	569	12389	625	17034	681	12978
514	14445	570	9117	626	9588	682	14100
515	6480	571	19482	627	18196	683	10757
516	10402	572	14524	628	9242	684	14475
517	19474	573	3888	629	15408	685	9064
518	13497	574	11187	630	8942	686	9730
519	20886	575	10561	631	10651	687	6200
520	12756	576	10777	632	9601	688	10127
521	15200	577	13032	633	10478	689	14254
522	5458	578	9575	634	12437	690	11374
523	4675	579	16104	635	14731	691	12461
524	5516	580	13676	636	14861	692	15698
525	8798	581	12098	637	10143	693	10756
526	8783	582	12655	638	13110	694	12362
527	10612	583	15554	639	12494	695	11282
528	12535	584	15094	640	19424	696	6193
529	12793	585	13030	641	6426	697	10569
530	12080	586	19459	642	11797	698	10560
531	12928	587	13961	643	12418	699	12310
532	14139	588	12844	644	21318	700	14449
533	14335	589	5060	645	22352	701	19862
534	10241	590	9699	646	12676	702	13130
535	12879	591	226	647	15466	703	20070
536	13910	592	8830	648	3874	704	3868

CUSTOMER NUMBER	PURCHASES (IN $)	CUSTOMER NUMBER	PURCHASES (IN $)	CUSTOMER NUMBER	PURCHASES (IN $)	CUSTOMER NUMBER	PURCHASES (IN $)
705	24132	761	17182	817	12242	873	11662
706	2570	762	17738	818	14450	874	13155
707	9110	763	9338	819	11327	875	13148
708	10997	764	15542	820	16512	876	13456
709	23428	765	16369	821	11577	877	8509
710	9698	766	19701	822	15180	878	13398
711	9204	767	14159	823	9260	879	16822
712	14582	768	9895	824	12377	880	10632
713	9455	769	13772	825	14703	881	15322
714	8088	770	4357	826	13878	882	19596
715	10799	771	15666	827	12204	883	15049
716	12750	772	9894	828	18671	884	16780
717	11038	773	13938	829	9588	885	13598
718	19867	774	16811	830	7208	886	14136
719	21806	775	27206	831	7676	887	18348
720	8288	776	10910	832	12665	888	7096
721	12577	777	21167	833	7480	889	18474
722	9344	778	5741	834	10999	890	8718
723	16340	779	17286	835	13399	891	17464
724	14568	780	11778	836	12009	892	7100
725	8804	781	12855	837	18492	893	7916
726	10977	782	11565	838	17644	894	12108
727	13998	783	12574	839	11514	895	17925
728	11087	784	20275	840	8377	896	8209
729	15995	785	13030	841	15697	897	12192
730	21969	786	7584	842	13523	898	9651
731	16690	787	12818	843	12456	899	15609
732	8390	788	11612	844	12904	900	10254
733	10532	789	19433	845	11215	901	5326
734	14417	790	4273	846	4323	902	13869
735	15692	791	17179	847	10465	903	15431
736	2545	792	12113	848	8953	904	18937
737	8767	793	13659	849	18526	905	4476
738	16945	794	13339	850	10645	906	12527
739	11386	795	15157	851	15093	907	12235
740	11786	796	18117	852	14320	908	9525
741	19360	797	10211	853	12758	909	8209
742	19326	798	18183	854	19933	910	10026
743	14657	799	14156	855	11234	911	16040
744	13480	800	11141	856	8209	912	7244
745	13551	801	10335	857	2342	913	15076
746	10832	802	12819	858	12699	914	12330
747	16733	803	5273	859	12797	915	12260
748	16009	804	10525	860	18687	916	13687
749	13503	805	10522	861	17597	917	9069
750	13740	806	14535	862	9508	918	14268
751	8191	807	6335	863	4472	919	11484
752	13302	808	15180	864	13200	920	12876
753	15157	809	11666	865	12231	921	8029
754	17879	810	12196	866	18821	922	14193
755	16970	811	11717	867	12385	923	12351
756	18879	812	11735	868	13884	924	10553
757	8867	813	12079	869	12196	925	10509
758	9916	814	19534	870	17559	926	5164
759	5833	815	13721	871	1730	927	5697
760	16202	816	14948	872	18133	928	12093

TABLE DB5-3 *(Continued)*

CUSTOMER NUMBER	PURCHASES (IN $)	CUSTOMER NUMBER	PURCHASES (IN $)	CUSTOMER NUMBER	PURCHASES (IN $)	CUSTOMER NUMBER	PURCHASES (IN $)
929	9892	985	14781	1041	17603	1097	8261
930	12813	986	16941	1042	11838	1098	18963
931	13590	987	5607	1043	5905	1099	19300
932	15752	988	13017	1044	10216	1100	15647
933	16741	989	17214	1045	8689	1101	21050
934	26272	990	18429	1046	13496	1102	12018
935	15793	991	15634	1047	17448	1103	14416
936	5437	992	13003	1048	6497	1104	8943
937	17201	993	13071	1049	12899	1105	15042
938	18200	994	8093	1050	58	1106	14577
939	10283	995	16346	1051	19451	1107	13580
940	20712	996	13643	1052	5769	1108	13886
941	19711	997	17273	1053	15004	1109	13706
942	7764	998	19334	1054	13290	1110	11254
943	13486	999	15831	1055	13660	1111	12561
944	13247	1000	10908	1056	6783	1112	12287
945	16087	1001	15774	1057	18668	1113	14300
946	9226	1002	9652	1058	14422	1114	13046
947	10115	1003	15179	1059	12200	1115	4505
948	9529	1004	19337	1060	11908	1116	15481
949	15711	1005	16091	1061	15305	1117	23292
950	8266	1006	7878	1062	16164	1118	12269
951	13664	1007	14161	1063	13811	1119	12299
952	15216	1008	9167	1064	9286	1120	14762
953	21625	1009	14100	1065	15835	1121	8245
954	12235	1010	14124	1066	16004	1122	11892
955	7866	1011	11981	1067	8100	1123	8329
956	18107	1012	11194	1068	6084	1124	11400
957	11871	1013	13845	1069	12487	1125	13080
958	11992	1014	11599	1070	18833	1126	17698
959	13667	1015	21550	1071	13990	1127	12455
960	7251	1016	11400	1072	14755	1128	16170
961	13709	1017	16680	1073	12761	1129	7304
962	6571	1018	17033	1074	19640	1130	8192
963	13124	1019	9048	1075	9784	1131	15793
964	12507	1020	21913	1076	18073	1132	14727
965	19294	1021	21365	1077	10499	1133	0
966	12021	1022	12732	1078	14653	1134	8600
967	9600	1023	6869	1079	8804	1135	13495
968	9917	1024	13231	1080	12757	1136	7794
969	10998	1025	16003	1081	16259	1137	10652
970	16000	1026	16509	1082	12534	1138	9452
971	11649	1027	12551	1083	9570	1139	10537
972	17779	1028	10833	1084	14499	1140	11670
973	18718	1029	19334	1085	13288	1141	18648
974	15331	1030	12233	1086	14834	1142	15009
975	18943	1031	16011	1087	8828	1143	23467
976	3756	1032	7578	1088	8952	1144	18225
977	10843	1033	13558	1089	7779	1145	17342
978	4420	1034	6824	1090	13775	1146	8812
979	13972	1035	18637	1091	12506	1147	4611
980	11601	1036	14914	1092	9594	1148	15602
981	12818	1037	10443	1093	9961	1149	15498
982	10597	1038	17073	1094	14227	1150	14629
983	12250	1039	7402	1095	13479		
984	13030	1040	14901	1096	12863		

5-14
Flow Chart

START

Do you want to know the *theoretical* frequency distribution associated with the *possible* outcomes of an experiment?

Yes

Choose the appropriate probability distribution:

Are the random variables (the experimental outcomes) discrete?

No

Yes

① Does each trial have only two possible outcomes? ② Does the probability of the outcome of any trial remain fixed over time? ③ Are the trials statistically independent?

p. 205

No

Yes

① Can the mean number of arrivals per unit time be estimated from past data? ② Is the probability that exactly 1 arrival will occur in one interval a very small number and constant? ③ Is the probability that 2 or more arrivals will occur in one interval such a small number that we can assign it a zero value? ④ Is the number of arrivals per interval independent of time? ⑤ Is the number of arrivals per interval not dependent on the number of arrivals in any other interval?

p. 214

No

Yes

① Does the curve have a single peak? ② Does the mean lie at the center of the curve? ③ Is the curve symmetrical? ④ Do the two tails of the curve extend infinitely and never touch the horizontal axis?

Yes

Consult a statistician about other possible distributions

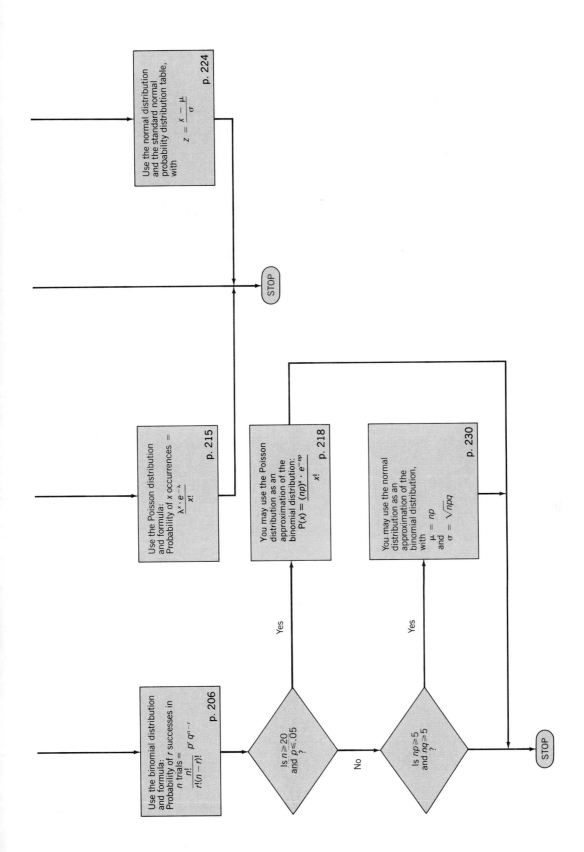

Use the normal distribution and the standard normal probability distribution table, with

$$z = \frac{x - \mu}{\sigma}$$

p. 224

Use the Poisson distribution and formula:
Probability of x occurrences =

$$\frac{\lambda^x \cdot e^{-\lambda}}{x!}$$

p. 215

STOP

You may use the Poisson distribution as an approximation of the binomial distribution:

$$P(x) = \frac{(np)^x \cdot e^{-np}}{x!}$$

p. 218

You may use the normal distribution as an approximation of the binomial distribution, with

$$\mu = np$$
and $\sigma = \sqrt{npq}$

p. 230

Use the binomial distribution and formula:
Probability of r successes in n trials =

$$\frac{n!}{r!(n-r)!} \; p^r \, q^{n-r}$$

p. 206

Is $n \geq 20$ and $p \leq .05$?

Yes

No

Is $np \geq 5$ and $nq \geq 5$?

Yes

STOP

255

Although there are over 200 million TV viewers in the United States and somewhat over half that many TV sets, only about 1,000 of those sets are sampled to determine what programs Americans watch. Why select only about 1,000 sets out of 100 million? Because time and the average cost of an interview prohibit the rating companies from trying to reach millions of people. And since polls are reasonably accurate, interviewing everybody is unnecessary. In this chapter, we examine questions such as these: How many people should be interviewed? How should they be selected? How do we know when our sample accurately reflects the entire population?

6

Sampling and Sampling Distributions

■ **OBJECTIVES**

Statistical sampling, the subject of Chapter 6, is a systematic approach to selecting a few elements (a *sample*) from an entire collection of data (a *population*) in order to make some inferences about the total collection. We shall learn methods that help to ensure that samples represent the entire collection. If you have ever examined a peach on the top of a basket, bought the whole basket on the basis of that peach, and then found the bottom of the basket filled with overripe fruit, you have a good (if somewhat expensive) understanding of statistical sampling and the need for better sampling methods.

6-1
Introduction to Sampling

Reasons for sampling

Shoppers often sample a small piece of cheese before purchasing any. They decide from one piece what the larger chunk will taste like. A chemist does the same thing when he takes a sample of whiskey from a vat, determines that it is 90 proof, and infers that all whiskey in the vat is 90 proof. If the chemist tests all the whiskey or the shoppers taste all the cheese, there will be none to sell. Testing all of the product often destroys it and is unnecessary. To determine the characteristics of the whole, we have to sample only a portion.

Suppose that, as the personnel director of a large bank, you need to write a report describing all the employees who have voluntarily left the company in the last 10 years. You would have a difficult task locating all these thousands of people. They are not easily accessible as a group—many have died, moved from the community, left the country, or acquired a new name by marriage. How do you write the report? The best idea is to locate a representative sample and interview them, in order to generalize about the entire group.

Time is also a factor when managers need information quickly in order to adjust an operation or change a policy. Take an automatic machine that sorts thousands of pieces of mail daily. Why wait for an entire day's output to check whether the machine is working accurately (whether the *population characteristics* are those required by the postal service)? Instead, samples can be taken at specific intervals, and if necessary, the machine can be adjusted right away.

Census or sample

Sometimes it is possible and practical to examine every person or item in the population we wish to describe. We call this a *complete enumeration, or census.* We use sampling when it is not possible to count or measure every item in the population.

Examples of populations and samples

Statisticians use the word *population* to refer not only to people but to all items that have been chosen for study. In the cases we have just mentioned, the populations are all the cheese in the chunk, all the whiskey in the vat, all the employees of the large bank who voluntarily left in the last 10 years, and all mail sorted by the automatic machine since the previous sample check. **Statisticians use the word *sample* to describe a portion chosen from the population.**

STATISTICS AND PARAMETERS

Function of statistics and parameters

Mathematically, we can describe samples and populations by using measures such as the mean, median, mode, and standard deviation, which we introduced in Chapter 3. When these terms describe the characteristics of a sample, they are called *statistics.* When they describe the characteristics of a population, they are called *parameters.* **A statistic is a characteristic of a sample, and a parameter is a characteristic of a population.**

Suppose that the mean height in inches of all tenth graders in the United States is 60 inches. In this case, 60 inches is a characteristic of the population "all tenth graders" and can be called a *population parameter.* On the other hand, if we say that the mean height in Ms. Jones's tenth-grade class in Bennetsville is 60 inches, we are using 60 inches to describe a characteristic of the sample "Ms. Jones's tenth graders." In that case, 60 inches would be a *sample statistic.* If we are convinced that the mean

Using statistics to estimate parameters

height of Ms. Jones's tenth graders is an accurate estimate of the mean height of all tenth graders in the United States, we could use the sample statistic "mean height of

TABLE 6-1 Differences Between Populations and Samples

	POPULATION	SAMPLE
Definition	Collection of items being considered	Part or portion of the population chosen for study
Characteristics	"Parameters"	"Statistics"
Symbols	Population size = N Population mean = μ Population standard deviation = σ	Sample size = n Sample mean = $\bar{x}$ Sample standard deviation = s

Ms. Jones's tenth graders" to estimate the population parameter "mean height of all U.S. tenth-graders" without having to measure all the millions of tenth graders in the United States.

N, μ, σ, and $n, \bar{x}, s$: standard symbols

To be consistent, statisticians use lower case Roman letters to denote sample statistics and Greek or capital letters for population parameters. Table 6-1 lists these symbols and summarizes the definitions we have studied so far in this chapter.

TYPES OF SAMPLING

Judgment and probability sampling

There are two methods of selecting samples from populations: *nonrandom* or *judgment* sampling, and *random* or *probability* sampling. In probability sampling, all the items in the population have a chance of being chosen in the sample. In judgment sampling, personal knowledge and opinion are used to identify those items from the population that are to be included in the sample. A sample selected by judgment sampling is based on someone's expertise about the population. A forest ranger, for example, would have a judgment sample if he decided ahead of time which parts of a large forested area he would walk through to estimate the total board feet of lumber that could be cut. Sometimes a judgment sample is used as a pilot or trial sample to decide how to take a random sample later. Judgment samples avoid the statistical analysis that is necessary to make probability samples. They are more convenient and can be used successfully even though we are unable to measure their validity. But if a study uses judgment sampling and loses a significant degree of "representativeness," it will have purchased convenience at too high a price.

BIASED SAMPLES

Statistics professors often use classroom demonstrations to prove one point or another. One of the most common ones involves tossing a coin to show that the long-run tendency is for the coin (if it's a fair one) to come up heads half the time and tails the other half the time. Suppose our professor tosses a fair coin ten times and it comes up heads on eight of these tosses. What should he do? One explanation for the class is that this coin is biased (not too likely an explanation, since the work involved in biasing a standard coin so that it will behave this way is rather substantial). Another explanation is that he has not tossed the coin a sufficient number of times. The second explanation is more likely to be the one used by the professor. He will more than likely continue to toss the coin until the proportions of heads and tails that appear become more even.

Statistical evidence

But suppose the purpose of such an experiment was to provide "statistical evidence" that was to be used to convince people to change their minds about things other than coins. If you and I interview ten people concerning their political views, we may find that all ten are staunch Democrats. Does this give us the evidence we need to assert publicly, for political purposes, that "all those interviewed support the Democratic platform"? Of course not. But unless the user of this information understands the sampling issue involved, and unless we are given complete information about the sampling process, how are we to react? How can we be sure that the pollster didn't "start out to find a biased coin" and then stop the polling process when an insufficient sample size "uncovered one for him," instead of making sure the sampling procedure was adequate? The answer is that without more complete information or a previous reputation for statistically accurate polling, we cannot be sure. We can, however, be alert to the risks we take when we do not ask for additional information.

Exercises

6-1 What is the major drawback of judgment sampling?

6-2 Are judgment sampling and probability sampling necessarily mutually exclusive? Why or why not?

6-3 List the advantages of sampling over complete enumeration, or census.

6-4 What are some of the disadvantages of probability sampling versus judgment sampling?

6-5 Farlington Savings and Loan is considering a merger with Sentry Bank, but needs shareholder approval before the merger can be accomplished. At its annual meeting, to which all shareholders are invited, the president of FS&L asks the shareholders whether they approve of the deal. Eighty-five percent approve. Is this percentage a sample statistic or a population parameter?

6-6 Jean Mason, who was hired by Former Industries to determine employee attitudes toward the upcoming union vote, met with some difficulty after reporting her findings to management. Mason's study was based on statistical sampling, and from the beginning data it was clear (or so Jean thought) that the employees were favoring a unionized shop. Jean's report was shrugged off with the comment, "This is no good. Nobody can make statements about employee sentiments when she talks to only a little over 15 percent of our employees. Everyone knows you have to check 50 percent to have any idea of what the outcome of the union vote will be. We didn't hire you to make guesses." Is there any defense for Jean's position?

6-7 A consumer protection organization is conducting a census of people who were injured by a particular brand of space heater. Each victim is asked questions about the behavior of the heater just before its malfunction; this information generally is available only from the victim, since the heater in question tends to incinerate itself upon malfunction. Early in the census, it is discovered that several of the victims were elderly and have died. Is any census of the victims now possible? Why or why not?

6-2
Random Sampling

In a random or probability sample, we know what the chances are that an element of the population will or will not be included in the sample. As a result, we can assess objectively the estimates of the population characteristics that result from our sample; that is, we can describe mathematically how objective our estimates are. Let us begin our explanation of this process by introducing four methods of random sampling:

1. Simple random sampling
2. Systematic sampling
3. Stratified sampling
4. Cluster sampling

SIMPLE RANDOM SAMPLING

An example of simple random sampling

Simple random sampling selects samples by methods that allow *each possible sample to have an equal probability of being picked* and *each item in the entire population to have an equal chance of being included in the sample.* We can illustrate these requirements with an example. Suppose we have a population of four students in a seminar and we want samples of two students at a time for interviewing purposes. Table 6-2 illustrates the possible combinations of samples of two students in a population size of four, the probability of each sample being picked, and the probability that each student will be in a sample.

Defining *finite* and *replacement*

Our example illustrated in Table 6-2 uses a *finite* population of four students. By *finite,* we mean that the population has a stated or limited size; that is to say, there is a whole number (N) that tells us how many items there are in the population. Certainly, if we sample without "replacing" the student, we shall soon exhaust our small population group. Notice, too, that if we sample *with replacement* (that is, if we replace the sampled student immediately after he or she is picked and before the second student is chosen), the same person could appear twice in the sample.

An infinite population

We have used this example only to help us think about sampling from an infinite population. An *infinite* population is a population in which it is theoretically impossible to observe all the elements. Although many populations appear to be exceedingly large, no truly infinite population of physical objects actually exists. After all, given unlimited resources and time, we could enumerate any finite population, even the grains of sand on the beaches of North America. As a practical matter, then, we will

TABLE 6-2 **Chances of Selecting Samples of Two Students from a Population of Four Students**

STUDENTS A, B, C, AND D
Possible samples of two persons: *AB, AC, AD, BC, CD, BD*

Probability of drawing this sample of two persons must be:

$AB = \frac{1}{6}$
$AC = \frac{1}{6}$
$AD = \frac{1}{6}$ (There are only six possible samples of two
$BC = \frac{1}{6}$ persons)
$CD = \frac{1}{6}$
$BD = \frac{1}{6}$

Probability of this student being in the sample must be:

$A = \frac{1}{2}$ [In Chapter 4, we saw that the marginal proba-
$B = \frac{1}{2}$ bility is equal to the *sum* of the joint probabili-
$C = \frac{1}{2}$ ties of the events within which the event is
$D = \frac{1}{2}$ contained:
$P(A) = P(AB) + P(AC) + P(AD) = \frac{1}{2}$]

use the term *infinite population* when we are talking about a population that could not be enumerated in a reasonable period of time. In this way, we will use the theoretical concept of infinite population as an approximation of a large finite population, just as we earlier used the theoretical concept of continuous random variable as an approximation of a discrete random variable that could take on many closely spaced values.

How to Do Random Sampling. The easiest way to select a sample randomly is to use random numbers. These numbers can be generated either by a computer programmed to scramble numbers or by a table of random numbers, which should properly be called a *table of random digits.*

Table 6-3 illustrates a portion of such a table. Here we have 1,250 random digits in sets of ten digits. These numbers have been generated by a completely random process. The probability that any one digit from 0 through 9 will appear is the same as that for any other digit, and the probability of one sequence of digits occurring is the same as that for any other sequence of the same length.

Using a table of random digits

To see how to use this table, suppose that we have 100 employees in a company and wish to interview a randomly chosen sample of ten. We could get such a random sample by assigning every employee a number from 00 to 99, consulting Table 6-3, and picking a systematic method of selecting two-digit numbers. In this case, let's do the following:

TABLE 6-3 1,250 Random Digits*

1581922396	2068577984	8262130892	8374856049	4637567488
0928105582	7295088579	9586111652	7055508767	6472382934
4112077556	3440672486	1882412963	0684012006	0933147914
7457477468	5435810788	9670852913	1291265730	4890031305
0099520858	3090908872	2039593181	5973470495	9776135501
7245174840	2275698645	8416549348	4676463101	2229367983
6749420382	4832630032	5670984959	5432114610	2966095680
5503161011	7413686599	1198757695	0414294470	0140121598
7164238934	7666127259	5263097712	5133648980	4011966963
3593969525	0272759769	0385998136	9999089966	7544056852
4192054466	0700014629	5169439659	8408705169	1074373131
9697426117	6488888550	4031652526	8123543276	0927534537
2007950579	9564268448	3457416988	1531027886	7016633739
4584768758	2389278610	3859431781	3643768456	4141314518
3840145867	9120831830	7228567652	1267173884	4020651657
0190453442	4800088084	1165628559	5407921254	3768932478
6766554338	5585265145	5089052204	9780623691	2195448096
6315116284	9172824179	5544814339	0016943666	3828538786
3908771938	4035554324	0840126299	4942059208	1475623997
5570024586	9324732596	1186563397	4425143189	3216653251
2999997185	0135968938	7678931194	1351031403	6002561840
7864375912	8383232768	1892857070	2323673751	3188881718
7065492027	6349104233	3382569662	4579426926	1513082455
0654683246	4765104877	8149224168	5468631609	6474393896
7830555058	5255147182	3519287786	2481675649	8907598697

* Based on first 834 serial numbers of selective service lottery as reported by *The New York Times,* October 30, 1940, p. 12. © 1940 by *The New York Times Company.* Reprinted by permission.

1. Go from the top to the bottom of the columns beginning with the left-hand column, and read only the first two digits in each row. Notice that our first number using this method would be 15, the second 09, the third 41, and so on.

2. If we reach the bottom of the last column on the right and are still short of our desired 10 two-digit numbers of 99 and under, we can go back to the beginning (the top of the left-hand column) and start reading the third and fourth digits of each number. These would begin 81, 28, and 12.

Using slips of paper

Another way to select our employees would be to write the name of each one on a slip of paper and deposit the slips in a box. After mixing them thoroughly, we could draw ten slips at random. This method works well with a small group of people but presents problems if the people in the population number in the thousands. There is the added problem, too, of not being certain that the slips of paper are mixed well. In the draft lottery of 1970, for example, when capsules were drawn from a bowl to determine by birthdays the order of selecting draftees for the armed services, December birthdays appeared more often than the probabilities would have suggested. As it turned out, the December capsules had been placed in the bowl last, and the capsules had not been mixed properly. Thus, December capsules had the highest probability of being drawn.

SYSTEMATIC SAMPLING

In systematic sampling, elements are selected from the population at a uniform interval that is measured in time, order, or space. If we wanted to interview every twentieth student on a college campus, we would choose a random starting point in the first twenty names in the student directory and then pick every twentieth name thereafter.

Characteristics of systematic sampling

Systematic sampling differs from simple random sampling in that each *element* has an equal chance of being selected but each *sample* does *not* have an equal chance of being selected. This would have been the case if, in our earlier example, we had assigned numbers between 00 and 99 to our employees and then had begun to choose a sample of ten by picking every tenth number beginning 1, 11, 21, 31, and so forth. Employees numbered 2, 3, 4, and 5 would have had no chance of being selected.

Shortcomings of the systematic approach

In systematic sampling, there is the problem of introducing an error into the sample process. Suppose we were sampling paper waste produced by households, and we decided to sample 100 households every Monday. Chances are high that our sample would not be representative, because Monday's trash would very likely include the Sunday newspaper. Thus, the amount of waste would be biased upward by our choice of this sampling procedure.

Systematic sampling has advantages too, however. Even though systematic sampling may be inappropriate when the elements lie in a sequential pattern, this method may require less time and sometimes results in lower costs than the simple random sample method.

STRATIFIED SAMPLING

Two ways to take stratified samples

To use stratified sampling, we divide the population into relative homogeneous groups, called *strata.* Then we use one of two approaches. Either we select at random from each stratum a specified number of elements corresponding to the proportion of that stratum in the population as a whole, or we draw an equal number of elements

TABLE 6-4 Composition of Patients by Age

AGE GROUP	PERCENTAGE OF TOTAL
Birth – 19 years	30%
20 – 39 years	40
40 – 59 years	20
60 years and older	10

from each stratum and give weight to the results according to the stratum's proportion of total population. With either approach, stratified sampling guarantees that every element in the population has a chance of being selected.

Stratified sampling is appropriate when the population is already divided into groups of different sizes and we wish to acknowledge this fact. Suppose that a physician's patients are divided into four groups according to age, as shown in Table 6-4. The physician wants to find out how many hours his patients sleep. To obtain an estimate of this characteristic of the population, he could take a random sample from each of the four age groups and give weight to the samples according to the percentage of patients in that group. This would be an example of a stratified sample.

The advantage of stratified samples is that when they are properly designed, they more accurately reflect characteristics of the population from which they were chosen than do other kinds of sampling.

CLUSTER SAMPLING

In cluster sampling, we divide the population into groups, or *clusters,* and then select a random sample of these clusters. We assume that these individual clusters are representative of the population as a whole. If a market research team is attempting to determine by sampling the average number of television sets per household in a large city, they could use a city map to divide the territory into blocks and then choose a certain number of blocks (clusters) for interviewing. Every household in each of these blocks would be interviewed. A well-designed cluster sampling procedure can produce a more precise sample at considerably less cost than that of simple random sampling.

Comparison of stratified and cluster sampling

With both stratified and cluster sampling, the population is divided into well-defined groups. We use *stratified* sampling when each group has small variation within itself but there is a wide variation between the groups. We use *cluster* sampling in the opposite case — when there is considerable variation within each group but the groups are essentially similar to each other.

BASIS OF STATISTICAL INFERENCE: SIMPLE RANDOM SAMPLING

Systematic sampling, stratified sampling, and cluster sampling attempt to approximate simple random sampling. All are methods that have been developed for their precision, economy, or physical ease. Even so, assume for the rest of the examples and problems in this book that we obtain our data using simple random sampling. This is necessary because the principles of simple random sampling are the foundation for *statistical inference,* the process of making inferences about populations from information contained in samples. Once these principles have been developed for simple random sampling, their extension to the other sampling methods is conceptually quite simple but somewhat involved mathematically. If you understand the basic ideas involved in simple random sampling, you will have a good grasp of what is going on in the other cases, even if you must leave the technical details to the professional statistician.

Exercises

6-8   In the example below, probability distributions for three natural subgroups of a larger population are shown. For which situation would you recommend stratified sampling?

| (a) | (b) |

6-9   If we have a population of 10,000 and we wish to sample 20 randomly, use the random digits table (Table 6-3) to select 20 individuals from the 10,000. List the numbers of those elements selected, based on the random digits table.

6-10   Using a calendar, systematically sample every eighteenth day of the year, beginning with January 6.

6-11   A population is made up of groups that have wide variation within each group but little variation from group to group. The appropriate type of sampling for this population is:
(a) Stratified   (b) Systematic   (c) Cluster   (d) Judgment

6-12   A non-profit organization is conducting a door-to-door opinion poll on municipal daycare centers. The organization has devised a scheme for random sampling of houses, and plans to conduct the poll on weekdays from noon to 5 p.m. Will this scheme produce a random sample?

6-13   Bob Peterson, public relations manager for Piedmont Power and Light, has implemented an institutional advertising campaign to promote energy consciousness among its customers. Peterson, anxious to know if the campaign has been effective, plans to conduct a telephone survey of area residents. He plans to look in the telephone book and select random numbers with addresses that correspond to the company's service area. Will Peterson's sample be a random one?

6-14   Consult Table 6-3. What is the probability that a 4 will appear as the leftmost digit in each set of 10 digits? that a 7 will appear? 2? How many times would you expect to see each of these digits in the leftmost position? How many times is each found in that position? Can you explain any differences in the number found and the number expected?

6-15   At the U.S. Mint in Philadelphia, ten machines stamp out pennies in lots of 50. These lots are arranged sequentially on a single conveyor belt which passes an inspection station. An inspector decides to use systematic sampling in inspecting the pennies and is trying to decide whether to inspect every fifth or every seventh lot of pennies. Which is better? Why?

6-16   The state occupational safety board has decided to do a study of work-related accidents within the state, to examine some of the variables involved in the accidents; e.g., the type of job, the cause of the accident, the extent of the injury, the time of day, and whether the employer was negligent. It has been decided that 250 of the 2,500 work-related accidents reported last year in the state will be sampled. The accident reports are filed by date in a filing cabinet. Marsha Gulley, a department employee, has proposed that the study use a systematic sampling technique and select every tenth report in the file for the sample. Would her plan of systematic sampling be appropriate here? Explain.

6-17 Bob Bennett, product manager for Clipper Mowers Company, is interested in looking at the kinds of lawn mowers used throughout the country. Assistant product manager Mary Wilson has recommended a stratified random sampling process in which the cities and communities studied are separated into substrata, depending on the size and nature of the community. Mary Wilson proposes the following classification:

CATEGORY	TYPE OF COMMUNITY
Urban	Inner city (population 100,000+)
Suburban	Outlying areas of cities or smaller communities (pop. 20,000 to 100,000)
Rural	Small communities (fewer than 20,000 residents)

Is stratified random sampling appropriate here?

6-18 A Senate study on the issue of self-rule for the District of Columbia involved surveying 2,000 people from the population of the city regarding their opinions on a number of issues related to self-rule. Washington, D.C., is a city in which many neighborhoods are poor and many neighborhoods are rich, with very few neighborhoods falling between the extremes. The researchers who were administering the survey had reasons to believe that the opinions expressed on the various questions would be highly dependent upon income. Which method was more appropriate, stratified sampling or cluster sampling? Explain briefly.

6-3
Introduction to Sampling Distributions

Statistics differ among samples from the same population

In Chapter 3, we introduced methods by which we can use sample data to calculate statistics such as the mean and the standard deviation. So far in this chapter, we have examined how samples can be taken from populations. If we apply what we have learned and take several samples from a population, the statistics we would compute for each sample need not be the same and most probably would vary from sample to sample.

Sampling distribution defined

Suppose our samples each consist of ten 25-year-old women from a city with a population of 100,000 (an infinite population, according to our usage). By computing the mean height and standard deviation of that height for each of these samples, we would quickly see that the mean of each sample and the standard deviation of each sample would be different. **A probability distribution of all the possible means of the samples is a distribution of the sample means. Statisticians call this a *sampling distribution of the mean.***

We could also have a sampling distribution of a proportion. Assume that we have determined the proportion of beetle-infested pine trees in samples of 100 trees taken from a very large forest. We have taken a large number of those 100-item samples. If we plot a probability distribution of the possible proportions of infested trees in all these samples, we would see a distribution of the sample proportions. In statistics, this is called a *sampling distribution of the proportion.* (Notice that the term *proportion* refers to the proportion that is infested.)

TABLE 6-5 Examples of Populations, Samples, Sample Statistics, and Sampling Distributions

POPULATION	SAMPLE	SAMPLE STATISTIC	SAMPLING DISTRIBUTION
Water in a river	10-gallon containers of water	Mean number of parts of mercury per million parts of water	Sampling distribution of the mean
All professional basketball teams	Groups of 5 players	Median height	Sampling distribution of the median
All parts produced by a manufacturing process	50 parts	Proportion defective	Sampling distribution of the proportion

DESCRIBING SAMPLING DISTRIBUTIONS

Any probability distribution (and, therefore, any sampling distribution) can be partially described by its mean and standard deviation. Table 6-5 illustrates several populations. Beside each, we have indicated the sample taken from that population, the sample statistic we have measured, and the sampling distribution that would be associated with that statistic.

Now, how would we describe each of the sampling distributions in Table 6-5? In the first example, the sampling distribution of the mean can be partially described by its mean and standard deviation. The sampling distribution of the median in the second example can be partially described by the mean and standard deviation of the distribution of the medians. And in the third, the sampling distribution of the proportion can be partially described by the mean and standard deviation of the distribution of the proportions.

CONCEPT OF STANDARD ERROR

Rather than say "standard deviation of the distribution of sample means" to describe a distribution of sample means, statisticians refer to the *standard error of the mean.* Similarly, the "standard deviation of the distribution of sample proportions" is shortened to the *standard error of the proportion.* The term *standard error* is used because it conveys a specific meaning. An example will help explain the reason for the name. Suppose we wish to learn something about the height of freshmen at a large state university. We could take a series of samples and calculate the mean height for each sample. It is highly unlikely that all of these sample means would be the same; we expect to see some variability in our observed means. This variability in the sample statistic results from *sampling error* due to chance; that is, there are differences between each sample and the population, and among the several samples, owing solely to the elements we happened to choose for the samples.

The standard deviation of the distribution of sample means measures the extent to which we expect the means from the different samples to vary because of this chance error in the sampling process. Thus, **the standard deviation of the distribution of a sample statistic is known as the *standard error of the statistic.***

The standard error indicates not only the size of the chance error that has been made but also the accuracy we are likely to get if we use a sample statistic to estimate a

TABLE 6-6 Conventional Terminology Used to Refer to Sample Statistics

WHEN WE WISH TO REFER TO THE:	WE USE THE CONVENTIONAL TERM:
Standard deviation of the distribution of sample means	Standard error of the mean
Standard deviation of the distribution of sample proportions	Standard error of the proportion
Standard deviation of the distribution of sample medians	Standard error of the median
Standard deviation of the distribution of sample ranges	Standard error of the range

population parameter. A distribution of sample means that is less spread out (that has a small standard error) is a better estimator of the population mean than a distribution of sample means that is widely dispersed and has a larger standard error.

Table 6-6 indicates the proper use of the term *standard error.* In Chapter 7, we shall discuss how to *estimate* population parameters using sample statistics.

ONE USE OF THE STANDARD ERROR

A school that trains private pilots for their instrument examination advertised that "our graduates score higher on the instrument written examination than graduates of other schools." To the unsuspecting reader, this seems perfectly clear. If you want to score higher on your instrument written examination, then this school is your best bet.

In fact, however, whenever we are using tests, we have to deal with standard error. Specifically, we need some measure of the precision of the test instrument, usually represented by standard error. This would tell us how large a difference in one school's grades would have to be for it to be statistically significant. Unfortunately, the advertisement did not offer such data; it merely asserted that "our graduates do better."

Exercises

6-19 Suppose you are sampling from a population with a mean of 2.15. What sample size will *guarantee* that:
(a) The sample mean is 2.15?
(b) The standard error of the mean is zero?

6-20 The term *error,* in standard error of the mean, refers to what type of error?

6-21 A machine that fills bottles is known to have a mean filling amount of 125 grams and a standard deviation of 20 grams. A quality control manager took a random sample of filled bottles and found the sample mean to be 130. The quality control manager assumed the sample must not be representative. Is the conclusion correct?

6-22 North Carolina Electric and Gas has determined that the mean cost per 100 sq. ft. for the residential population electrical service is $0.314 with a standard error of $0.07. Two different samples are selected at random, and the means are $0.30 and $0.35, respectively. The assistant in charge of data collection concludes that the second sample is the better one because it is better to overestimate than underestimate the true mean. Comment. Is one of the means "better" in some ways, given the true population mean?

6-23 A woman working for the Nielsen ratings service interviews passersby on a New York street and records each subject's estimate of average time spent viewing prime-time television per night. These interviews continue for 20 days, and at the end of each day the interviewer computes the mean time spent viewing among all those interviewed during the day. At the conclusion of all interviews, she constructs a frequency distribution for these daily means. Is this a sampling distribution of the mean? Explain.

6-24 Charlotte Anne Serrus, a marketing analyst for the Florris Tobacco Company, wants to assess the damage done to FTC's sales by the appearance of a new competitor. Accordingly, she has compiled weekly sales figures from one-year periods before and after the competitor's appearance. Charlotte has graphed the corresponding frequency distributions as follows:

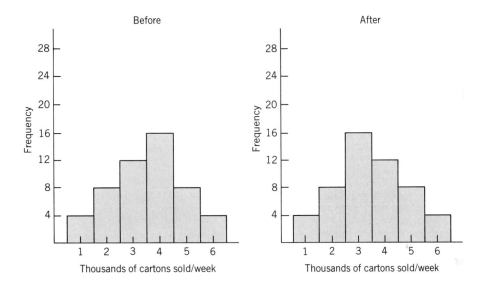

Based on these graphs, what has been the effect of the competitor's appearance on average weekly sales?

6-25 In times of declining SAT scores and problems of functional illiteracy, the admissions committee of a prestigious university is concerned with keeping high standards of admission. Each year, after decisions on acceptance are made, the committee publishes and distributes statistics on students admitted, giving, for example, the average SAT score. On the report containing the statistics are the words, "Standard Error of the Mean." The secretary who types the report knows that for several years, the average SAT score was about 1,200 and has assumed that the standard error of the mean was how much the committee allowed an admitted student's score to deviate from the mean. Is the assumption correct? Explain.

6-26 The president of the American Dental Association wants to determine the average number of times that each dentist's patient flosses per day. Toward this end, he asks each of 100 randomly selected dentists to poll 50 of their patients at random and submit the mean number of flossings per day to the ADA. These numbers are computed, and are submitted to the president. Has he been given a sample from the population of patients or from some other distribution?

6-4
Sampling Distributions in More Detail

In the last section of this chapter, we introduced the idea of a sampling distribution. We examined the reasons why sampling from a population and developing a distribution of these sample statistics would produce a sampling distribution, and we introduced the concept of standard error. Now we will study these concepts further, so that we will not only be able to understand them conceptually but also be able to handle them computationally.

FIGURE 6-1

Conceptual population distribution, sample distributions, and sampling distribution

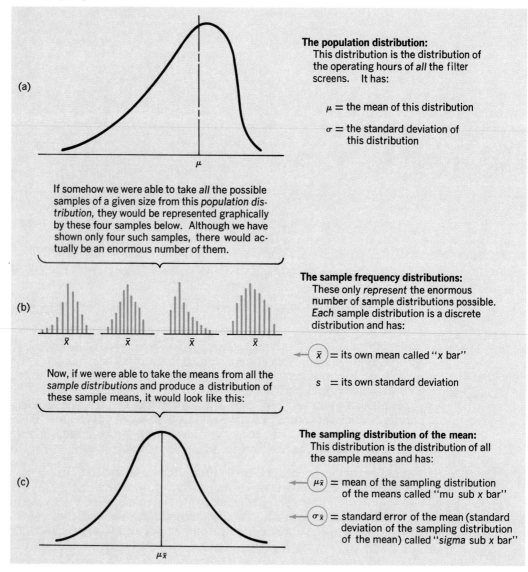

(a)

The population distribution:
This distribution is the distribution of the operating hours of *all* the filter screens. It has:

μ = the mean of this distribution

σ = the standard deviation of this distribution

If somehow we were able to take *all* the possible samples of a given size from this *population distribution*, they would be represented graphically by these four samples below. Although we have shown only four such samples, there would actually be an enormous number of them.

(b)

$\bar{x}$ $\bar{x}$ $\bar{x}$ $\bar{x}$

The sample frequency distributions:
These only *represent* the enormous number of sample distributions possible. *Each* sample distribution is a discrete distribution and has:

$\bar{x}$ = its own mean called "x bar"

s = its own standard deviation

Now, if we were able to take the means from all the *sample distributions* and produce a distribution of these sample means, it would look like this:

(c)

$\mu_{\bar{x}}$

The sampling distribution of the mean:
This distribution is the distribution of all the sample means and has:

$\mu_{\bar{x}}$ = mean of the sampling distribution of the means called "mu sub x bar"

$\sigma_{\bar{x}}$ = standard error of the mean (standard deviation of the sampling distribution of the mean) called "*sigma* sub x bar"

CONCEPTUAL BASIS FOR SAMPLING DISTRIBUTIONS

Deriving the sampling distribution of the mean

Figure 6-1 will help us examine sampling distributions without delving too deeply into statistical theory. We have divided this illustration into three parts. Part *a* of Fig. 6-1 illustrates a *population distribution.* Assume that this population is all the filter screens in a large industrial pollution-control system and that this distribution is the operating hours before a screen becomes clogged. The distribution of operating hours has a mean μ (*mu*) and a standard deviation σ (*sigma*).

Suppose that somehow we are able to take all the possible samples of ten screens from the population distribution (actually, there would be far too many for us to consider). Next we would calculate the mean and the standard deviation for each one of these *samples* as represented in part *b* of Fig. 6-1. As a result, *each* sample would have its own mean, $\bar{x}$ (*x bar*), and its own standard deviation, *s*. All the individual sample means would *not* be the same as the population mean. They would tend to be near the population mean, but only rarely would they be exactly that value.

As a last step, we would produce a distribution of all the means from every sample that could be taken. This distribution, called the *sampling distribution of the mean,* is illustrated in part *c* of Fig. 6-1. This distribution of the sample means (the sampling distribution) would have its own mean $\mu_{\bar{x}}$ (*mu sub x bar*) and its own standard deviation, or standard error, $\sigma_{\bar{x}}$ (*sigma sub x bar*).

Function of theoretical sampling distributions

In statistical terminology, the sampling distribution we would obtain by taking all the samples of a given size is a *theoretical sampling distribution.* Part *c* of Fig. 6-1 describes such an example. In practice, the size and character of most populations prohibit decision makers from taking all the possible samples from a population distribution. Fortunately, statisticians have developed formulas for estimating the characteristics of these theoretical sampling distributions, making it unnecessary for us to collect large numbers of samples. In most cases, decision makers take only one sample from the population, calculate statistics for that sample, and from those statistics infer something about the parameters of the entire population. We shall illustrate this shortly.

Why we use the sampling distribution of the mean

In each example of sampling distributions in the remainder of this chapter, we shall use the sampling distribution of the mean. We could study the sampling distributions of the median, range, or proportion, but we will stay with the mean for the continuity it will add to the explanation. Once you develop an understanding of how to deal computationally with the sampling distribution of the mean, you will be able to apply it to the distribution of any other sample statistic.

SAMPLING FROM NORMAL POPULATIONS

Sampling distribution of the mean from normally distributed populations

Suppose we draw samples from a normally distributed population with a mean of 100 and a standard deviation of 25, and that we start by drawing samples of five items each and by calculating their means. The first mean might be 95, the second 106, the third 101, and so on. Obviously there is just as much chance for the sample mean to be above the population mean of 100 as there is for it to be below 100. Since we are *averaging* five items to get each sample mean, very large values in the sample would be averaged down and very small values up. We would reason that we would get less spread among the sample means than we would among the individual items in the original population. That is the same as saying that the standard error of the mean, or standard deviation of the sampling distribution of the mean, would be less than the standard deviation of the *individual* items in the population. Figure 6-2 illustrates this point graphically.

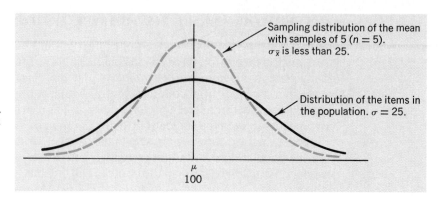

FIGURE 6-2

Relationship between the population distribution and the sampling distribution of the mean for a normal population

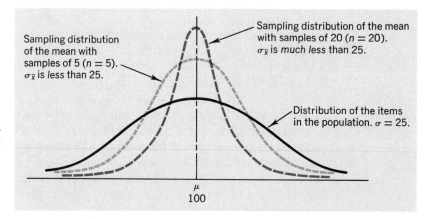

FIGURE 6-3

Relationship between the population distribution and sampling distribution of the mean with increasing n's

Now suppose we increase our sample size from five to 20. This would not change the standard deviation of the items in the original population. But with samples of 20, we have increased the effect of averaging in each sample and would expect even *less* dispersion among the sample means. Figure 6-3 illustrates this point.

Properties of the sampling distribution of the mean

The sampling distribution of a mean of a normally distributed population demonstrates the important properties summarized in Table 6-7. An example will further illustrate these properties. A bank calculates that its individual savings accounts are normally distributed with a mean of $2,000 and a standard deviation of $600. If the bank takes a random sample of 100 accounts, what is the probability that the sample mean will lie between $1,900 and $2,050? This is a question about the sampling distribution of the mean; therefore, we must first calculate the standard error of the

TABLE 6-7 **Properties of the Sampling Distribution of the Mean When the Population Is Normally Distributed**

PROPERTY	ILLUSTRATED SYMBOLICALLY
The sampling distribution has a mean equal to the population mean	$\mu_{\bar{x}} = \mu$
The sampling distribution has a standard deviation (a standard error) equal to the population standard deviation divided by the square root of the sample size	$\sigma_{\bar{x}} = \dfrac{\sigma}{\sqrt{n}}$
The sampling distribution is normally distributed	

mean. In this case, we shall use the equation for the standard error of the mean designed for situations in which the population is infinite (later, we shall introduce an equation for finite populations):

$$\boxed{\text{Standard error of the mean}} \longrightarrow \sigma_{\bar{x}} = \frac{\sigma}{\sqrt{n}} \qquad\qquad [6\text{-}1]$$

where:

Finding the standard error of the mean for infinite populations

- σ = population standard deviation
- n = sample size

Applying this to our example, we get:

$$\sigma_{\bar{x}} = \frac{\$600}{\sqrt{100}}$$

$$= \frac{\$600}{10}$$

$$= \$60 \leftarrow \text{standard error of the mean}$$

Next, we need to use the table of z values (Appendix Table 1) and Equation 5-6, which enables us to use the Standard Normal Probability Distribution Table. With these we can determine the probability that the sample mean will lie between \$1,900 and \$2,050.

$$z = \frac{x - \mu}{\sigma} \qquad\qquad [5\text{-}6]$$

Equation 5-6 tells us that to convert any normal random variable to a standard normal random variable, we must subtract the mean of the variable being standardized and divide by the standard error (the standard deviation of that variable). Thus, in this particular case, Equation 5-6 becomes:

$$\boxed{\text{Sample mean}} \longrightarrow z = \frac{\overline{x} - \mu}{\sigma_{\bar{x}}} \longleftarrow \boxed{\text{Population mean}} \qquad\qquad [6\text{-}2]$$
$$\boxed{\text{Standard error of the mean} = \frac{\sigma}{\sqrt{n}}}$$

Converting the sample mean to a z value

Now we are ready to compute the two z values as follows:

For $\overline{x} = \$1,900$

$$z = \frac{\overline{x} - \mu}{\sigma_{\bar{x}}} \qquad\qquad [6\text{-}2]$$

$$= \frac{\$1,900 - \$2,000}{\$60}$$

$$= -\frac{100}{60}$$

$$= -1.67 \leftarrow \text{standard deviations from the mean of a standard normal probability distribution}$$

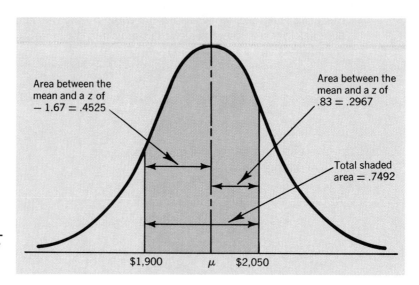

FIGURE 6-4

Probability of sample mean lying between $1,900 and $2,050

Area between the mean and a z of −1.67 = .4525

Area between the mean and a z of .83 = .2967

Total shaded area = .7492

$1,900 μ $2,050$

For $\bar{x} = \$2,050$

$$z = \frac{\bar{x} - \mu}{\sigma_{\bar{x}}}$$ [6-2]

$$= \frac{\$2,050 - \$2,000}{\$60}$$

$$= \frac{50}{60}$$

$= .83 \leftarrow$ standard deviations from the mean of a standard normal probability distribution

Appendix Table 1 gives us an area of .4525 corresponding to a z value of −1.67, and it gives an area of .2967 for a z value of .83. If we add these two together, we get .7492 as the total probability that the sample mean will lie between $1,900 and $2,050. We have shown this problem graphically in Fig. 6-4.

SAMPLING FROM NON-NORMAL POPULATIONS

In the preceding section, we concluded that when the population is normally distributed, the sampling distribution of the mean is also normal. Yet decision makers must deal with many populations that are not normally distributed. How does the sampling distribution of the mean react when the population from which the samples are drawn is *not* normal? An illustration will help us answer this question.

The mean of the sampling distribution of the mean equals the population mean

Consider the data in Table 6-8, concerning five motorcycle owners and the lives of their tires. Since only five people are involved, the population is too small to be approximated by a normal distribution. We'll take all of the possible samples of the owners in groups of three, compute the sample means $(\bar{x})$, list them, and compute the mean of the sampling distribution $(\mu_{\bar{x}})$. We have done this in Table 6-9. These calculations show that even in a case in which the population is not normally distributed, $\mu_{\bar{x}}$, the mean of the sampling distribution, is *still* equal to the population mean, μ.

TABLE 6-8 **Experience of Five Motorcycle Owners with Life of Tires**

Owner	Carl	Debbie	Elizabeth	Frank	George	
Tire life (months)	3	3	7	9	14	**Total: 36 months**

$$\text{Mean} = \frac{36}{5} = 7.2 \text{ months}$$

Now look at Fig. 6-5. Part *a* is the population distribution of tire lives for the five motorcycle owners, a distribution that is anything but normal in shape. In part *b* of Fig. 6-5, we have shown the sampling distribution of the mean for a sample size of three, taking the information from Table 6-9. Notice the difference between the probability distributions in *a* and *b*. In part *b*, the distribution looks a little more like the bell shape of the normal distribution.

TABLE 6-9 **Calculation of sample mean tire life with $n = 3$**

SAMPLES OF THREE	SAMPLE DATA (TIRE LIVES)	SAMPLE MEAN
EFG*	7 + 9 + 14	10
DFG	3 + 9 + 14	8⅔
DEG	3 + 7 + 14	8
DEF	3 + 7 + 9	6⅓
CFG	3 + 9 + 14	8⅔
CEG	3 + 7 + 14	8
CEF	3 + 7 + 9	6⅓
CDF	3 + 3 + 9	5
CDE	3 + 3 + 7	4⅓
CDG	3 + 3 + 14	6⅔
		72 months

$$\mu_{\bar{x}} = \frac{72}{10}$$
$$= 7.2 \text{ months}$$

* Names abbreviated by first initial.

Increase in size of samples leads to a more normal sampling distribution

If we had a long time and much space, we could repeat this example and enlarge the population size to 20. Then we could take samples of *every* size. Next we would plot the sampling distribution of the mean that would occur in *each* case. Doing this

FIGURE 6-5

Population distribution and sampling distribution of the mean tire life

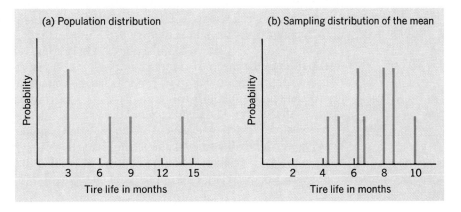

(a) Population distribution — Probability vs. Tire life in months (3, 6, 9, 12, 15)

(b) Sampling distribution of the mean — Probability vs. Tire life in months (2, 4, 6, 8, 10)

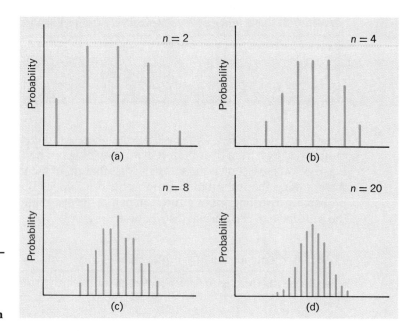

FIGURE 6-6
Simulated effect of increases in the sample size on appearance of sampling distribution

would show quite dramatically how quickly the sampling distribution of the mean approaches normality, regardless of the shape of the population distribution. Figure 6-6 simulates this process graphically without all the calculations.

THE CENTRAL LIMIT THEOREM

Results of increasing sample size

The example in Table 6-9 and the two probability distributions in Fig. 6-5 should suggest several things to you. First, **the mean of the sampling distribution of the mean will equal the population mean** regardless of the sample size, even if the population is not normal. Second, as the sample size increases, **the sampling distribution of the mean will approach normality,** regardless of the shape of the population distribution.

Significance of the central limit theorem

This relationship between the shape of the population distribution and the shape of the sampling distribution of the mean is called the *central limit theorem.* The central limit theorem is perhaps the most important theorem in all of statistical inference. **It assures us that the sampling distribution of the mean approaches normal as the sample size increases.** There are theoretical situations in which the central limit theorem fails to hold, but they are almost never encountered in practical decision making. Actually, a sample does not have to be very large for the sampling distribution of the mean to approach normal. Statisticians use the normal distribution as an approximation to the sampling distribution whenever the sample size is at least 30, but the sampling distribution of the mean can be nearly normal with samples of even half that size. **The significance of the central limit theorem is that it permits us to use sample statistics to make inferences about population parameters without knowing anything about the shape of the frequency distribution of that population other than what we can get from the sample.** Putting this ability to work is the subject of much of the material in the subsequent chapters of this book.

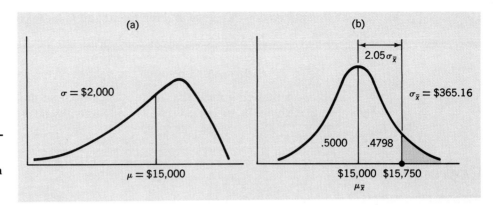

FIGURE 6-7

Population
distribution and
sampling distribution
for bank tellers'
earnings

Using the central limit
theorem

Let's illustrate the use of the central limit theorem. The distribution of annual earnings of all bank tellers with five years' experience is skewed negatively, as shown in part *a* of Fig. 6-7. This distribution has a mean of $15,000 and a standard deviation of $2,000. If we draw a random sample of 30 tellers, what is the probability that their earnings will average more than $15,750 annually? In part *b* of Fig. 6-7, we show the sampling distribution of the mean that would result, and we have colored the area representing "earnings over $15,750."

Our first task is to calculate the standard error of the mean from the population standard deviation, as follows:

$$\sigma_{\bar{x}} = \frac{\sigma}{\sqrt{n}} \qquad [6\text{-}1]$$

$$= \frac{\$2,000}{\sqrt{30}}$$

$$= \frac{\$2,000}{5.477}$$

$$= \$365.16 \leftarrow \text{standard error of the mean}$$

Since we are dealing with a sampling distribution, we must now use Equation 6-2 and the Standard Normal Probability Distribution (Appendix Table 1):

For $\bar{x} = \$15,750$

$$z = \frac{\bar{x} - \mu}{\sigma_{\bar{x}}} \qquad [6\text{-}2]$$

$$= \frac{\$15,750 - \$15,000}{\$365.16}$$

$$= \frac{\$750.00}{\$365.16}$$

$$= 2.05 \leftarrow \text{standard deviations from the mean of a}$$
$$\qquad \text{standard normal probability distribution}$$

This gives us an area of .4798 for a *z* value of 2.05. We show this area in Fig. 6-7 as the area between the mean and $15,750. Since half, or .5000, of the area under the curve lies between the mean and the right-hand tail, the colored area must be:

.5000	Area between the mean and the right-hand tail
−.4798	Area between the mean and $15,750
.0202 ←	Area between the right-hand tail and $15,750

Thus, we have determined that there is slightly more than a 2 percent chance of average earnings being more than $15,750 annually in a group of 30 tellers.

Exercises

6-27 In a sample of sixteen observations from a normal distribution with a mean of 150 and a variance of 256, what is:
(a) $P(\bar{x} < 160)$ (b) $P(\bar{x} > 142)$
If, instead of sixteen observations, nine observations are taken, find:
(c) $P(\bar{x} < 160)$ (d) $P(\bar{x} > 142)$

6-28 In a sample of 25 observations from a normal distribution with mean 98.6 and standard deviation 17.2, what is:
(a) $P(92 < \bar{x} < 102)$
(b) Find the corresponding probability given a sample of 36.

6-29 In a normal distribution with mean 56 and standard deviation 21, how large a sample must be taken so that there will be at least a 90 percent chance that its mean is greater than 52?

6-30 In a normal distribution with mean 375 and standard deviation 48, how large a sample must be taken so that the probability will be at least .95 that the sample mean falls between 370 and 380?

6-31 An astronomer at the Mount Palomar Observatory notes that, during the Geminid meteor shower, an average of 50 meteors appears each hour, with a variance of 9 meteors squared. The Geminid meteor shower will occur next week.
(a) If the astronomer watches the shower for 4 hours, what is the probability that at least 48 meteors per hour will appear?
(b) If the astronomer watches for an additional hour, will this probability rise or fall? Why?

6-32 The average cost of a studio condominium in the Cedar Lakes development is $62,000 with a standard deviation of $4,200.
(a) What is the probability that a condominium in this development will cost at least $65,000?
(b) Is the probability that the average cost of a sample of two condominiums will be at least $65,000 greater or less than the probability of one condominium's costing that much? By how much?

6-33 Robertson Employment Service customarily gives standard intelligence and aptitude tests to all persons who seek employment through the firm. The firm has collected data for several years and has found that the distribution of scores is not normal, but is skewed to the left with a mean of 86 and a standard deviation of 16. What is the probability that in a sample of 75 applicants who take the test, the mean score will be less than 84 or greater than 90?

6-34 An oil refinery has backup monitors to keep track of the refinery flows continuously and to prevent machine malfunctions from disrupting the process. One particular monitor has an average life of 4,300 hours with a standard deviation of 730 hours. In addition to the primary monitor, the refinery has set up two standby units, which are duplicates of the primary one. In the case of malfunction of one of the monitors, another will automatically take over in its place. The operating life of each monitor is independent of the others.
(a) What is the probability that a given set of monitors will last at least 13,000 hours?
(b) At most 12,630 hours?

6-35 Mary Bartel is an auditor for a large credit card company, and knows that, on average, the monthly balance of any given customer is $112, with a standard deviation of $56. If Mary audits 50 randomly selected accounts, what is the probability that the sample average monthly balance is:
(a) Below $100?
(b) Between $100 and $130?

6-36 Calvin Ensor, the president of General Telephone Corp., is upset at the number of telephones produced by GTC that have faulty receivers. On average, 110 telephones per day are being returned because of this problem, with a standard deviation of 64. Mr. Ensor has decided that unless he can be at least 80 percent certain that, on average, no more than 120 phones per day will be returned during the next 48 days, he will order the process overhauled. Will the overhaul be ordered?

6-37 Clara Voyant, whose job is predicting the future for her venture capital company, has just received the statistics describing her company's performance on 1,800 investments last year. Clara knows that, in general, investments generate profits that have a normal distribution with mean $7,500 and standard deviation $3,300. Even before she looked at the specific results from each of the 1,800 investments from last year, Clara was able to make some accurate predictions by using her knowledge of sampling distributions. Follow her analysis by finding the probability that the sample mean of last year's investments:
(a) Exceeded $7,700.
(b) Was less than $7,400.
(c) Was greater than $7,275, but less than $7,650.

6-38 Farmer Braun, who sells grain to West Germany, owns 60 acres of wheat fields. Based on past experience, he knows that the yield from each individual acre is normally distributed with mean 120 bushels and standard deviation 12 bushels. Help Farmer Braun plan for his next year's crop by finding:
(a) The expected mean of the yields from Farmer Braun's 60 acres of wheat.
(b) The standard deviation of the sample mean of the yields from Farmer Braun's 60 acres.
(c) The probability that the mean yield per acre will exceed 123.8 bushels.
(d) The probability that the mean yield per acre will fall between 117 and 122 bushels.

6-39 A ferry carries 25 passengers. The weight of each passenger has a normal distribution with mean 168 pounds and variance 361 pounds squared. Safety regulations state that, for this particular ferry, the total weight of passengers on the boat should not exceed 4,250 pounds more than 5 percent of the time. As a service to the ferry owners, find:
(a) The probability that the total weight of passengers on the ferry will exceed 4,250 pounds.
(b) The 95th percentile of the distribution of the total weight of passengers on the ferry.
Is the ferry complying with safety regulations?

6-5
An Operational Consideration in Sampling: The Relationship Between Sample Size and Standard Error

Precision of the sample mean

We saw earlier in this chapter that the standard error, $\sigma_{\bar{x}}$, is a measure of dispersion of the sample means around the population mean. If the dispersion decreases (if $\sigma_{\bar{x}}$ becomes smaller), then the values taken by the sample mean tend to cluster *more* closely around μ. Conversely, if the dispersion increases (if $\sigma_{\bar{x}}$ becomes larger), the values taken by the sample mean tend to cluster *less* closely around μ. We can think of this relationship this way: **As the standard error decreases, the value of any sample mean will probably be closer to the value of the population mean.** Statisticians describe this phenomenon in another way: As the standard error decreases, the *precision* with which the sample mean can be used to estimate the population mean increases.

If we refer to Equation 6-1, we can see that as *n* increases, $\sigma_{\bar{x}}$ decreases. This happens because in Equation 6-1, a larger denominator on the right side would produce smaller $\sigma_{\bar{x}}$ on the left side. Two examples will show this relationship; both assume the same population standard deviation σ of 100.

$$\sigma_{\bar{x}} = \frac{\sigma}{\sqrt{n}} \qquad [6\text{-}1]$$

When $n = 10$:

$$\sigma_{\bar{x}} = \frac{100}{\sqrt{10}}$$

$$= \frac{100}{3.162}$$

$$= 31.63 \leftarrow \text{standard error of the mean}$$

And when $n = 100$:

$$\sigma_{\bar{x}} = \frac{100}{\sqrt{100}}$$

$$= \frac{100}{10}$$

$$= 10 \leftarrow \text{standard error of the mean}$$

Increasing the sample size: diminishing returns

What have we shown? As we increased our sample size from 10 to 100 (a tenfold increase), the standard error dropped from 31.63 to 10, which is only about one-third of its former value. **Our examples show that, owing to the fact that $\sigma_{\bar{x}}$ varies inversely with the square root of *n*, there is a diminishing return in sampling.**

It is true that sampling more items will decrease the standard error, but this benefit may not be worth the cost. A statistician would say, "The increased precision is not worth the additional sampling cost." In a statistical sense, it seldom pays to take excessively large samples. Managers should always assess *both* the worth and the cost of the additional precision they will obtain from a larger sample before they commit resources to take it.

THE FINITE POPULATION MULTIPLIER

Modifying Equation 6-1

To this point in our discussions of sampling distributions, we have used Equation 6-1 to calculate the standard error of the mean:

$$\sigma_{\bar{x}} = \frac{\sigma}{\sqrt{n}} \qquad [6\text{-}1]$$

This equation is designed for situations in which the population is infinite, or in which we sample from a finite population with replacement (that is to say, after each item is sampled it is put back into the population before the next item is chosen, so that the same item can possibly be chosen more than once). If you will refer back to page 273 where we introduced Equation 6-1, you will recall our parenthesized note, which said, "Later we shall introduce an equation for finite populations." Introducing this new equation is the purpose of this section.

Many of the populations that decision makers examine are finite; that is, of stated or limited size. Examples of these include the employees in a given company, the clients of a city social-services agency, the students in a specific class, and a day's production in a given manufacturing plant. Not one of these populations is infinite, so we need to modify Equation 6-1 to deal with them. The formula designed to find the standard error of the mean when the population is *finite* is:

Finding the standard error of the mean for finite populations

$$\sigma_{\bar{x}} = \frac{\sigma}{\sqrt{n}} \times \sqrt{\frac{N - n}{N - 1}}$$ [6-3]

where:

- N = size of the population
- n = size of the sample

This new term on the right-hand side, which we multiply by our original standard error, is called the *finite population multiplier:*

$$\text{Finite population multiplier} = \sqrt{\frac{N - n}{N - 1}}$$ [6-4]

A few examples will help us become familiar with interpreting and using Equation 6-3. Suppose we are interested in a population of 20 textile companies of the same size, all of which are experiencing excessive labor turnover. Our study indicates that the standard deviation of the distribution of annual turnover is 75 employees. If we sample five of these textile companies and wish to compute the standard error of the mean, we would use Equation 6-3 as follows:

$$\sigma_{\bar{x}} = \frac{\sigma}{\sqrt{n}} \times \sqrt{\frac{N - n}{N - 1}}$$ [6-3]

$$= \frac{75}{\sqrt{5}} \times \sqrt{\frac{20 - 5}{20 - 1}}$$

$$= (33.54)(.888)$$

$$= 29.8 \leftarrow \text{standard error of the mean of a finite population}$$

In this example, a finite population multiplier of .888 reduced the standard error from 33.54 to 29.8.

Sometimes the finite population multiplier is close to 1

In cases in which the population is very large in relation to the size of the sample, this finite population multiplier is close to 1 and has little effect on the calculation of the standard error. Say that we have a population of 1,000 items and that we have taken a sample of 20 items. If we use Equation 6-4 to calculate the finite population multiplier, the result would be:

$$\text{Finite population multiplier} = \sqrt{\frac{N - n}{N - 1}}$$ [6-4]

$$= \sqrt{\frac{1,000 - 20}{1,000 - 1}}$$

$$= \sqrt{.981}$$

$$= .99$$

Using this multiplier of .99 would produce little effect on the calculation of the standard error of the mean.

Sampling fraction defined This last example shows that when we sample a small fraction of the entire population (that is, when the population size N is very large relative to the sample size n), the finite population multiplier takes on a value close to 1.0. Statisticians refer to the fraction n/N as the *sampling fraction,* because it is the fraction of the population N that is contained in the sample.

When the sampling fraction is small, the standard error of the mean for finite populations is so close to the standard error of the mean for infinite populations that we might as well use the same formula for both, namely Equation 6-1: $\sigma_{\bar{x}} = \dfrac{\sigma}{\sqrt{n}}$. The generally accepted rule is: **When the sampling fraction is less than .05, the finite population multiplier need not be used.**

Sample size determines sampling precision When we use Equation 6-1, σ is constant, and so the measure of sampling precision, $\sigma_{\bar{x}}$, depends only on the sample size n and not on the proportion of the population sampled. That is, to make $\sigma_{\bar{x}}$ smaller, it is necessary to make only n larger. **Thus it turns out that it is the absolute size of the sample that determines sampling precision, not the fraction of the population sampled.**

Exercises

6-40 An X-ray technician is taking readings from her machine to ensure that it adheres to federal safety guidelines. She knows that the standard deviation of the amount of radiation emitted by the machine is 150 millirems, but she wants to take readings until the standard error of the sampling distribution is no higher than 25 millirems. How many readings should she take?

6-41 Given a population of size $N = 80$ with a mean of 22 and a standard deviation of 3.2, what is the probability that a sample of 25 will have a mean between 21 and 23.5?

6-42 From a population of 125 items with a mean of 105 and a standard deviation of 17, 64 items were chosen.
(a) What is the standard error of the mean?
(b) What is the $P(107.5 < \bar{x} < 109)$?

6-43 For a population of size $N = 80$ with a mean of 8.2 and a standard deviation of 2.1, find the standard error of the mean for the following sample sizes:
(a) $n = 16$ (b) $n = 25$ (c) $n = 49$

6-44 An underwater salvage team is preparing to explore a site off the coast of Florida where an entire flotilla of 45 Spanish galleons sank. From historical records, the team expects these wrecks to generate an average of $225,000 in revenue when explored, with a standard deviation of $39,000. The team's financier, however, remains skeptical, and has stated that, if the exploration expenses of $2.1 million are not recouped from the first nine wrecks, he will cancel the remainder of the exploration. What is the probability that the exploration continues past the first nine wrecks?

6-45 Jonida Martinez, researcher for the Columbian Coffee Corporation, is interested in determining the rate of coffee usage per household in the United States. She believes that yearly consumption per household is normally distributed with an unknown mean μ and a standard deviation of about 1.25 pounds.
(a) If Martinez takes a sample of 36 households and records their consumption of coffee for 1 year, what is the probability that the sample mean is within one-half pound of the population mean?

(b) How large a sample must she take in order to be 98 percent certain that the sample mean is within one-half pound of the population mean?

6-46 Sara Gordon is heading a fund-raising drive for Milford College. She wishes to concentrate on the current tenth-reunion class, and hopes to get contributions from 36 percent of the 250 members of that class. Past data indicate that those who contribute to the tenth-year reunion gift will donate 4 percent of their annual salaries. Sara believes that the reunion class members have an average annual salary of $32,000 with a standard deviation of $9,600. If her expectations are met (36 percent of the class donate 4 percent of their salaries), what is the probability that the tenth-reunion gift will be between $110,000 and $120,000?

6-47 Davis Aircraft Co. is developing a new wing de-icer system, which it has installed on 30 commercial airliners. The system is designed so that the percentage of ice removed is normally distributed with mean 96 and standard deviation 7. The FAA will do a spot check of six of the airplanes with the new system, and will approve the system if at least 98 percent of the ice is removed on average. What is the probability that the system receives FAA approval?

6-48 Food Place, a chain of 145 supermarkets, has been bought out by a larger nationwide supermarket chain. Before the deal is finalized, the larger chain wants to have some assurance that Food Place will be a consistent moneymaker. The larger chain has decided to look at the financial records for 36 of the Food Place stores. Food Place management claims that each store's profits have an approximately normal distribution with the same mean and a standard deviation of $1,200. If the Food Place management is correct, what is the probability that the sample mean for the 36 stores will fall within $200 of the actual mean?

6-49 Miss Joanne Happ, chief executive officer of Southwestern Life & Surety Corp., wants to undertake a survey of the huge number of insurance policies that her company has underwritten. Miss Happ's firm makes on each policy a yearly profit that is distributed with mean $310 and standard deviation $150. Her personal accuracy requirements dictate that the survey must be large enough to reduce the standard error to no more than 1.5 percent of the population mean. How large should her sample be?

6-6
Design of Experiments

Events and experiments revisited

We have encountered the term *experiment* in Chapter 4, "Probability I." There we defined an *event* as one or more of the possible outcomes of doing something, and an *experiment* as an activity that would produce such events. In a coin-toss experiment, the possible events would be heads and tails.

PLANNING EXPERIMENTS

Sampling is only one part

If we are to conduct experiments that produce meaningful results in the form of usable conclusions, the way in which these experiments are designed is of the utmost importance. A good part of this chapter was taken up with ways of ensuring that random sampling was indeed being done. The way in which sampling is conducted is only a *part* of the total design of an experiment. In fact, the design of experiments is itself the subject of quite a number of books, some of them rather formidable in both scope and volume.

PHASES OF EXPERIMENTAL DESIGN

A claim is made

To get a better feel for the complexity of experimental design without actually getting involved with the complex details, take an example from the many that confront us every day, and follow that example through from beginning to end.

The statement is made that a Crankmaster Battery will start your car's engine better than Battery X. Crankmaster might design its experiment this way:

Objective. This is our beginning point. Crankmaster wants to test its battery against the leading competitor. Although it is possible to design an experiment that would test the two batteries on several characteristics (life, size, cranking power, weight, and cost, to name but a few), Crankmaster has decided to limit this experiment to cranking power.

Objectives are set

What Is to Be Measured. This is often referred to as the response variable. If Crankmaster is to design an experiment that compares the cranking power of its battery to that of another, it must define how cranking power is to be measured. Again, there are quite a few ways in which this can be done. For example, Crankmaster could measure (1) the time it took for the batteries to run down completely while cranking engines, (2) the total number of engine starts it took to run down the batteries, or (3) the number of months in use that the two batteries could be expected to last. Crankmaster decides that the response variable in its experiment will be (1) the time it takes for batteries to run down completely while cranking engines.

The response variable is selected

How Large a Sample Size. Crankmaster wants to be sure that it chooses a sample size large enough to support claims it makes for its battery, without fear of being challenged; however, it knows that the more batteries it tests, the higher the cost of conducting the experiment. As we pointed out in section 5 of this chapter, there is a diminishing return in sampling; and although sampling more items does, in fact, decrease the standard error, the benefit may not be worth the cost. Not wishing to choose a sample size that is too expensive to contend with, Crankmaster decides that comparing ten batteries from each of the two companies (itself and its competitor) will suffice.

How many to test

Conducting the Experiment. Crankmaster must be careful to conduct its experiment under controlled conditions; that is, it has to be sure that it is measuring *cranking power,* and that the other variables (such as temperature, age of engine, and condition of battery cables, to name only a few) are held as nearly constant as practicable. In an effort to accomplish just this, Crankmaster's statistical group uses new cars of the same make and model, conducts the tests at the same outside air temperature, and is careful to be quite precise in measuring the time variable. Crankmaster gathers experimental data on the performance of the twenty batteries in this manner.

Experimental conditions are kept constant

Analyzing the Data. Data on the twenty individual battery tests are subjected to hypothesis testing in the same way that we shall see in Chapter 8, "Testing Hypotheses." Crankmaster is interested in whether there is a significant difference between the cranking power of its battery and that of its competitor. It turns out that the difference between the mean cranking life of Crankmaster's battery and that of its competitor *is* significant. Crankmaster incorporates the result of this experiment into its advertising.

Data are analyzed

REACTING TO EXPERIMENTAL CLAIMS

How should the consumer react?

How should we, as consumers, react to Crankmaster's new battery-life claims in its latest advertising? Should we conclude from the tests it has run that the Crankmaster battery *is* superior to the competitive battery? If we stop for a moment to consider the nature of the experiment, we may not be so quick to come to such a conclusion.

How do we know that the ages and conditions of the cars' engines in the experiment *were* identical? And are we absolutely sure that the battery cables were identical in size and resistance to current? And what about the air temperature during the tests: Was it the same? These are the normal kinds of questions that we should ask.

How should we react to the statement, if it is made, that "we subjected the experimental results to extensive statistical testing"? The answer to that will have to wait until Chapter 8, "Testing Hypotheses," where we can determine if such a difference in battery lives is too large to be attributed to chance. At this point we, as consumers, need to be appropriately skeptical.

OTHER OPTIONS OPEN

Of course, Crankmaster would have had the same concerns we did, and in all likelihood would *not* have made significant advertising claims solely on the basis of the experimental design we have just described. One possible course of action to avoid criticism is to *ensure* that all variables except the one being measured have indeed been controlled. Despite the care taken to produce such controlled conditions, it turns out that these overcontrolled experiments do not really solve our problem. Normally, instead of investing resources in attempts to *eliminate* experimental variations, we choose a *completely different route.* The next few paragraphs show how we can accomplish this.

FACTORIAL EXPERIMENTS

In the Crankmaster situation, we had two batteries (let's refer to them now as A and B) and three test conditions that were of some concern to us: (1) temperature, (2) age of the engine, and (3) condition of the battery cable. Let's introduce the notion of factorial experiments by using this notation:

$$H = \text{Hot temperature} \qquad N = \text{New engine} \qquad G = \text{Good cable}$$
$$C = \text{Cold temperature} \qquad O = \text{Old engine} \qquad W = \text{Worn cable}$$

Of course, in most experiments, we could find more than two temperature conditions and, for that matter, more than two categories for engine condition and battery-cable condition. But it's better to introduce the idea of factorial experiments using a somewhat simplified example.

Now, since there are two batteries, two temperature possibilities, two engine condition possibilities, and two battery-cable possibilities, there are $2 \times 2 \times 2 \times 2 = 16$ possible combinations of factors. If we wanted to write these sixteen possibilities down, they would look like Table 6-10.

Having set up all the possible combinations of factors involved in this experiment, we could now conduct the sixteen tests in the table. If we did this, we would have conducted a complete factorial experiment, because each of the two *levels* of each of the four *factors* would have been used once with each possible combination of other levels of other factors. Designing the experiment this way would permit us to use techniques we shall introduce in Chapter 9, "Chi-Square and Analysis of Variance," to test the effect of each of the factors.

We need to point out, before we leave this section, that in an actual experiment we would hardly conduct the tests in the order in which they appear in the table. They

TABLE 6-10 Sixteen Possible Combinations of Factors for Battery Test

TEST	BATTERY	TEMPERATURE	ENGINE CONDITION	CABLE CONDITION
1	A	H	N	G
2	A	H	N	W
3	A	H	O	G
4	A	H	O	W
5	A	C	N	G
6	A	C	N	W
7	A	C	O	G
8	A	C	O	W
9	B	H	N	G
10	B	H	N	W
11	B	H	O	G
12	B	H	O	W
13	B	C	N	G
14	B	C	N	W
15	B	C	O	G
16	B	C	O	W

were arranged in that order to facilitate your counting the combinations and determining that all possible combinations were indeed represented. In actual practice, we would randomize the order of the tests, perhaps by putting sixteen numbers in a hat and drawing out the order of the experiment in that simple manner.

BEING MORE EFFICIENT IN EXPERIMENTAL DESIGN

A bit of efficiency

As you saw from our four-factor experiment, sixteen tests were required to compare all levels with all factors. If we were to compare the same two batteries, but this time with five levels of temperature, four measures of engine condition, and three measures of battery-cable condition, it would take $2 \times 5 \times 4 \times 3 = 120$ tests for a complete factorial experiment.

Fortunately, statisticians have been able to help us reduce the number of tests in cases like this. To illustrate how this works, look at the consumer-products company that wants to test market a new toothpaste in four different cities with four different kinds of packages and with four different advertising programs. In such a case, a complete factorial experiment would take $4 \times 4 \times 4 = 64$ tests. However, if we do some clever planning, we can actually do it with far fewer tests — sixteen, to be precise.

Let's use the notation:

A = City 1	I = Package 1	1 = Ad program 1
B = City 2	II = Package 2	2 = Ad program 2
C = City 3	III = Package 3	3 = Ad program 3
D = City 4	IV = Package 4	4 = Ad program 4

Now we arrange the cities, packages, and advertising programs in a design called a Latin square (Fig. 6-8).

The statistical analysis

In the experimental design represented by the Latin square, we would need only sixteen tests instead of 64 as originally calculated. Each combination of city, package,

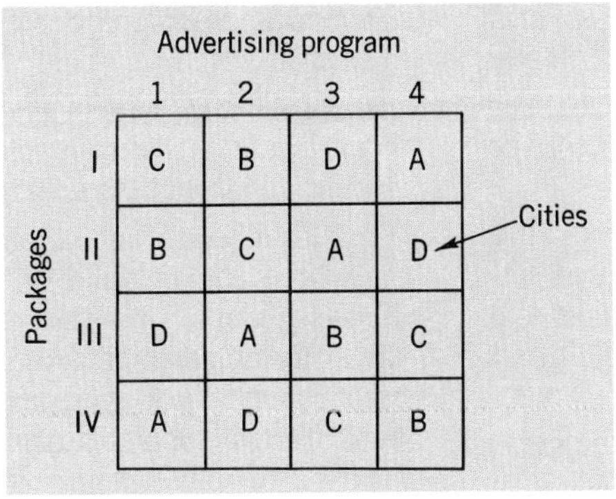

FIGURE 6-8
A Latin square

and advertising program would be represented in the sixteen tests. The actual statistical analysis of the data obtained from such a Latin square experimental design would require a form of analysis of variance a bit beyond the scope of this book.

6-7
Terms Introduced in Chapter 6

Census The measurement or examination of every element in the population.

Central Limit Theorem A rule assuring that the sampling distribution of the mean approaches normal as the sample size increases, regardless of the shape of the population distribution from which the sample is selected.

Clusters Within a population, groups that are essentially similar to each other, although the groups themselves have wide internal variation.

Cluster Sampling A method of random sampling in which the population is divided into groups, or clusters of elements, and then a random sample of these clusters is selected.

Factorial Experiment Experiment in which each factor involved is used once with each other factor. In a complete factorial experiment, every level of each factor is used with each level of every other factor.

Finite Population A population having a stated or limited size

Finite Population Multiplier A factor used to correct the standard error of the mean for studying a population of finite size that is small in relation to the size of the sample.

Infinite Population A population in which it is theoretically impossible to observe all the elements.

Judgment Sampling A method of selecting a sample from a population in which personal knowledge or expertise is used to identify those items from the population that are to be included in the sample.

Latin Square An efficient experimental design that makes it unnecessary to use a complete factorial experiment.

Parameters Values that describe the characteristics of a population.

Precision The degree of accuracy with which the sample mean can estimate the population mean, as revealed by the standard error of the mean.

Random or Probability Sampling A method of selecting a sample from a population in which all the items in the population have an equal chance of being chosen in the sample.

Sample A portion of the elements in a population chosen for direct examination or measurement.

Sampling Distribution of a Statistic For a given population, a probability distribution of all the possible values a statistic may take on for a given sample size.

Sampling Distribution of the Mean A probability distribution of all the possible means of samples of a given size, n, from a population.

Sampling Error Error or variation among sample statistics due to chance; i.e., differences between each sample and the population, and among several samples, which are due solely to the elements we happen to choose for the sample.

Sampling Fraction The fraction or proportion of the population contained in a sample.

Simple Random Sampling Methods of selecting samples that allow each possible sample an equal probability of being picked *and* each item in the entire population an equal chance of being included in the sample.

Standard Error The standard deviation of the sampling distribution of a statistic.

Standard Error of the Mean The standard deviation of the sampling distribution of the mean; a measure of the extent to which we expect the means from different samples to vary from the population mean, owing to the chance error in the sampling process.

Statistical Inference The process of making inferences about populations from information contained in samples.

Statistics Measures describing the characteristics of a sample.

Strata Groups within a population formed in such a way that each group is relatively homogeneous, but wider variability exists among the separate groups.

Stratified Sampling A method of random sampling in which the population is divided into homogeneous groups, or strata and elements within each stratum are selected at random according to one of two rules: (1) A specified number of elements is drawn from each stratum corresponding to the proportion of that stratum in the population, or (2) an equal number of elements is drawn from each stratum, and the results are weighted according to the stratum's proportion of the total population.

Systematic Sampling A method of random sampling used in statistics in which elements to be sampled are selected from the population at a uniform interval that is measured in time, order, or space.

6-8
Equations Introduced in Chapter 6

[6-1]
$$\sigma_{\bar{x}} = \frac{\sigma}{\sqrt{n}}$$
p. 273

Use this formula to derive the *standard error of the mean* when the population is *infinite;* that is, when the elements of the population cannot be enumerated in a reasonable period of time or when we sample with replacement. This equation explains that the sampling distribution has a standard deviation, which we also call a standard error, equal to the population standard deviation divided by the square root of the sample size.

[6-2]
$$z = \frac{\bar{x} - \mu}{\sigma_{\bar{x}}}$$
p. 273

A modified version of Equation 5-6, this formula allows us to determine the distance of the *sample mean* $\bar{x}$ from the population mean μ when we divide the difference by the standard error of the mean $\sigma_{\bar{x}}$. Once we have derived a z value, we can use the Standard Normal Probability Distribution Table and compute the probability that the sample mean will be that distance from the population mean. Because of the central limit theorem, we can use this formula for non-normal distributions if the sample size is at least 30.

[6-3]
$$\sigma_{\bar{x}} = \frac{\sigma}{\sqrt{n}} \times \sqrt{\frac{N - n}{N - 1}}$$
p. 281

where:

$N =$ size of the population

$n =$ size of the sample

This is the formula for finding the *standard error of the mean* when the population is *finite;* that is, of stated or limited size.

[6-4]

$$\text{Finite population multiplier} = \sqrt{\frac{N-n}{N-1}}$$

p. 281

In Equation 6-3, the term $\sqrt{(N-n)/(N-1)}$, which we multiply by the standard error from Equation (6-1), is called the *finite population multiplier.* When the population is small in relation to the size of the sample, the finite population multiplier reduces the size of the standard error. Any decrease in the standard error increases the precision with which the sample mean can be used to estimate the population mean.

6-9
Chapter Review Exercises

6-50 Wayne Nesbitt is an inspector for the Shell Motorcycle Helmet Company. Wayne performs his inspections by selecting a helmet at random from the stream of just-produced helmets. If the helmet's size is sufficiently close to Wayne's hat size, he tests it for defects that would impair fit and/or comfort. If the helmet's size is too small or too large, it is returned to the stream of helmets. Is Wayne's sampling method random or judgmental?

6-51 Jim Ford, advertising manager for a retail department store chain, is responsible for choosing the final advertisements from sample layouts designed by his staff. He has been in the retail advertising business for years and has been responsible for the chain's advertising for quite some time. His assistant, however, having learned the latest advertising effectiveness measurement techniques while at a New York agency, wants to do effectiveness tests for each advertisement considered, using random samples of consumers in the store's retail trading district. These tests will be quite costly. Jim is sure that his experience enables him to decide on appropriate ads, so there has been some disagreement between the two. Can you defend either position?

6-52 Burt Purdue, manager of the Sea Island Development Company, wants to find out residents' feelings toward the development's recreation facilities and the improvements they would like to see implemented. The development includes residents of various ages and income levels, but a large proportion are middle-class residents between the ages of 30 and 50. As yet, Burt is unsure whether there are differences among age groups or income levels in their desire for recreation facilities. Would stratified random sampling be appropriate here?

6-53 A camera manufacturer is attempting to find out what employees feel are the major problems with the company and what improvements are needed. To assess the opinions of the 37 departments, the management is considering a sampling plan. It has been recommended to the personnel director that the management adopt a cluster sampling plan. The management would choose six departments and interview all the employees. Upon collecting and assessing the data gathered from these employees, the company could then make changes and plan for areas of job improvement. Is a cluster sampling plan appropriate in this situation?

6-54 By reviewing sales since opening 6 months ago, a restaurant owner found that the average bill for a couple was $26, with a standard deviation of $5.65. How large would a sample of customers have to be for the probability to be at least 95.44 percent that the mean cost per meal for the sample would fall between $25 and $27?

6-55 Joan Fargo, president of Fargo-Lanna Ltd., wants to offer videotaped courses for employees during the lunch hour, and wants to get some idea of the courses that employees would like to see offered. Accordingly, she has devised a ballot that an employee can fill out in 5 minutes, listing his or her preferences among the possible courses. The ballots, which cost very little to print, will be distributed with paychecks, and the results will be tabulated by the as yet unreassigned clerical staff of a recently dissolved group within the company. Ms. Fargo plans to poll all employees. Are there any reasons to poll a sample of the employees rather than the entire population?

6-56   A drug manufacturer knows that for a certain antibiotic, the average number of doses ordered for a patient is 20. Steve Simmons, a salesman for the company, after looking at 1 day's prescription orders for the drug in his territory, announced that the sample mean for this drug should be lower. He said, "For any sample, the mean should be lower, since the sampling mean always understates the population mean because of sample variation." Is there any truth to what Simmons said?

6-57   Several weeks later at a sales meeting, Steve Simmons again demonstrated his expertise in statistics. He had drawn a graph and presented it to the group, saying, "This is a sampling distribution of means. It is a normal curve and represents a distribution of all observations in each possible sample combination." Is Simmons right? Explain.

6-58   Low-Cal Foods Company uses estimates of the level of activity for various market segments to determine the nutritional composition of its diet food products. Low-Cal is considering the introduction of a liquid diet food for older women, since this segment has special weight problems not met by the competitor's diet foods. To determine the desired calorie content of this new product, Dr. Nell Watson, researcher for the company, conducted tests on a sample of women to determine calorie consumption per day. Her results showed that the average number of calories expended per day for older women is 1,328 with a standard deviation of 275. Dr. Watson estimates that the benefits she obtains with a sample size of 25 are worth $1,720. She expects that reducing the standard error by half its current value will double the benefit. If it costs $16 for every woman in the sample, should Watson reduce her standard error?

6-59   The U.S. Customs Agency routinely checks all passengers arriving from foreign countries as they enter the United States. The department reports that on average, 42 people per day, with a standard deviation of 11, are found to be carrying contraband material as they enter the United States through John F. Kennedy Airport in New York. What is the probability that in 5 days at the airport, the average number of passengers found carrying contraband will exceed 50?

6-60   HAL Corporation manufactures large computer systems and has always prided itself on the reliability of its System 666 central processing units. In fact, past experience has shown that the monthly downtime of System 666 CPUs averages 41 minutes, with a standard deviation of 8 minutes. The computer center at a large state university maintains an installation built around six System 666 CPUs. James Kitchen, the director of the computer center, feels that a satisfactory level of service is provided to the university community if the average downtime of the six CPUs is less than 50 minutes per month. In any given month, what is the probability that Kitchen will be satisfied with the level of service?

6-61   Members of the Organization for Consumer Action send more than 250 volunteers a day all over the state to increase support for a consumer protection bill that is currently before the state legislature. Usually, each volunteer will visit a household and talk briefly with the resident in the hope that the resident will sign a petition to be given to the state legislature. On the average, a volunteer will obtain 5.8 signatures for the petition each day, with a standard deviation of .8. What is the probability a sample of 20 volunteers will result in an average between 5.5 and 6.2 signatures per day?

6-62   Jill Johnson, product manager for Southern Electric's smoke alarm, is concerned over recent complaints from consumer groups about the short life of the device. She has decided to gather evidence to counteract the complaints by testing a sample of the alarms. For the test, it costs $4 per unit in the sample. Since precision is desirable for presenting persuasive statistical evidence to consumer groups, Johnson figures the benefits she will receive for various sample sizes are determined by the formula: Benefits = $5,249/$\sigma_{\bar{x}}$. If Johnson wants to increase her sample until the cost equals the benefit, how many units should she sample? The population standard deviation is 265.

6-63 Ron Blake, a personnel director, wants to study the accuracy level of his company's 70 secretaries. Historically, the number of word processing errors made each day by each secretary has been approximately normal with an average of eighteen, and a standard deviation of four. Mr. Blake monitors fifteen randomly chosen secretaries today. What is the probability that the average number of errors per secretary is:
(a) Fewer than 15.5?
(b) Greater than 20?

6-10
Chapter Concepts Test

Answers are in the back of the book.

T F 1. When the items included in a sample are based upon the judgment of the individual conducting the sample, the sample is said to be nonrandom.

T F 2. A statistic is a characteristic of a population.

T F 3. A sampling plan that selects members from a population at uniform intervals in time, order, or space is called stratified sampling.

T F 4. As a general rule, it is not necessary to include a finite population multiplier in a computation for standard error of the mean when the size of the sample is greater than 50.

T F 5. The probability distribution of all the possible means of samples is known as the sample distribution of the mean.

T F 6. The principles of simple random sampling are the theoretical foundation for statistical inference.

T F 7. The standard error of the mean is the standard deviation of the distribution of sample means.

T F 8. A sampling plan that divides the population into well-defined groups from which random samples are drawn is known as cluster sampling.

T F 9. With increasing sample size, the sampling distribution of the mean approaches normality, regardless of the distribution of the population.

T F 10. The standard error of the mean decreases in direct proportion to sample size.

T F 11. To perform a complete enumeration, one would examine every item in a population.

T F 12. In everyday life, we see many examples of infinite populations of physical objects.

T F 13. To obtain a theoretical sampling distribution, we consider all the samples of a given size.

T F 14. Large samples are always a good idea, since they decrease the standard error.

T F 15. If the mean for a certain population were fifteen, it is likely that most of the samples we could take from that population would have means of fifteen.

T F 16. The precision of a sample is determined by the number of items in the sample and not the proportion of the total population that is sampled.

T F 17. The standard error of a sample statistic is the standard deviation of its sampling distribution.

T F 18. Judgment sampling has the disadvantage that it may lose some representativeness of a sample.

T F 19. The sampling fraction compares the size of a sample to the size of the population.

T F 20. Any sampling distribution can be totally described by its mean and standard deviation.

T F 21. The precision with which the sample mean can be used to estimate the population mean decreases as the standard error increases.

22. Which of the following is a method of selecting samples from a population?
(a) Judgment sampling   (c) Probability sampling   (e) a and b but not c
(b) Random sampling   (d) All of these

23. Choose the pair of symbols that best completes this sentence: _____ is a parameter, whereas _____ is a statistic.
    (a) $N. \ldots \mu$ (c) $N. \ldots n$ (e) b and c but not a
    (b) $\sigma. \ldots s$ (d) All of these

24. In random sampling, we can describe mathematically how objective our estimates are. Why is this?
    (a) We always know the chance that a population element will be included in the sample.
    (b) Every sample always has an equal chance of being selected.
    (c) All the samples are of exactly the same size and can be counted.
    (d) None of these.   (e) a and b but not c.

25. Suppose you are performing stratified sampling on a particular population and have divided the population into strata of different sizes. How can you now make your sample selection?
    (a) Select at random an equal number of elements from each stratum.
    (b) Draw an equal number of elements from each stratum and give weights to the results.
    (c) Draw a number of elements from each stratum proportional to its weight in the population.
    (d) a and b only.   (e) b and c only.

26. In which of the following situations would $\sigma_{\bar{x}} = \dfrac{\sigma}{\sqrt{n}}$ be the correct formula to use for computing $\sigma_{\bar{x}}$?
    (a) Sampling is from an infinite population.
    (b) Sampling is from a finite population with replacement.
    (c) Sampling is from a finite population without replacement.
    (d) a and b only.   (e) b and c only.

27. The dispersion among sample means is less than the dispersion among the sampled items themselves because:
    (a) Each sample is smaller than the population from which it is drawn.
    (b) Very large values are averaged down, and very small values are averaged up.
    (c) The sampled items are all drawn from the same population.
    (d) None of these.   (e) b and c but not a.

28. Suppose that a population with $N = 144$ has $\mu = 24$. What is the mean of the sampling distribution of the mean for samples of size 25?
    (a) 24   (b) 2   (c) 4.8   (d) Cannot be determined from the information given.

29. The central limit theorem assures us that the sampling distribution of the mean:
    (a) Is always normal.   (b) Is always normal for large sample sizes.
    (c) Approaches normality as sample size increases.
    (d) Appears normal only when N is greater than 1,000.

30. Suppose that, for a certain population, $\sigma_{\bar{x}}$ is calculated as 20 when samples of size 25 are taken and as 10 when samples of size 100 are taken. A quadrupling of sample size, then, only halved $\sigma_{\bar{x}}$. We can conclude that increasing sample size is:
    (a) Always cost-effective   (b) Sometimes cost-effective   (c) Never cost-effective

31. Refer again to the data of question 30. What must be the value of σ for this infinite population?
    (a) 1,000   (b) 500   (c) 377.5   (d) 100
    (e) Cannot be determined from the information given

32. The finite population multiplier does not have to be used when the sampling fraction is:
    (a) Greater than .05   (c) Less than .50   (e) None of these
    (b) Greater than .50   (d) Greater than .90

33. The standard error of the mean for a sample size of two or more is:
    (a) Always greater than the standard deviation of the population
    (b) Generally greater than the standard deviation of the population
    (c) Usually less than the standard deviation of the population
    (d) None of these

34. A border patrol checkpoint which stops every passenger van is utilizing:
    (a) Simple random sampling

(b) Systematic sampling
(c) Stratified sampling
(d) Complete enumeration

35. In a normally distributed population, the sampling distribution of the mean:
    (a) Is normally distributed
    (b) Has a mean equal to the population mean
    (c) Has standard deviation equal to the population standard deviation divided by the square root of the simple size
    (d) All of the above
    (e) Both a and b

36. The central limit theorem:
    (a) requires some knowledge of the frequency distribution
    (b) permits us to use sample statistics to make inferences about population parameters
    (c) relates the shape of a sampling distribution of the mean to the mean of the sample
    (d) requires a sample to contain fewer than 30 observations

37. A portion of the elements in a population chosen for direct examination or measurement is a
    _____.

38. The proportion of the population contained in a sample is the _____.

39. _____ _____ is the process by which inferences about a population are made from information about a sample.

40. The _____ _____ _____ is the distribution obtained by finding the sampling distribution of all samples of a given size of a population.

41. _____ sampling should be used when each group considered has small variation within itself but there is wide variation between different groups.

42. A method of random sampling in which elements are selected from the population at uniform intervals is called _____ sampling.

43. _____ is the degree of accuracy with which the sample mean can estimate the population mean.

44. Within a population, groups that are similar to each other (although the groups themselves have wide internal variation) are called _____.

45. A sampling distribution of the proportion is a probability distribution of _____.

6-11
Conceptual Case

(Northern White Metals Company)

Dick looked down at the memo in his hand and frowned. One of Northern's best customers, NES Electronics, had refused to accept an entire shipment of aluminum mounting brackets because of late delivery. A month earlier, a shipment of a similar product had been returned for quality reasons. Lynn Martin had worked for months in developing the NES account and was quite upset at the poor service this valued customer had been getting.

"Something has got to be done, Dick," she said with obvious irritation. "Not only is our company being hurt, but my credibility is being questioned as well. I think we have a real problem here."

"Yes, I agree, Lynn," Dick replied, laying her memo aside. "We do have a problem, and we've got to fix it soon. Can you patch things up with Morty at NES while we work on their next order?" he asked anxiously.

"Probably, but the next foul-up will be the last foul-up as far as they're concerned, I can tell you that much," Lynn grumbled as she turned to leave Dick's office.

Dick sat back in his chair, pondering the problem of disgruntled sales reps and dissatisfied customers. Problems such as those with NES had been occurring more and more frequently. First, the anodizing department had had some difficulty in adjusting to the increasing volume of orders. Now it appeared the fabricating department was having problems as well. Increased demand on this area saw the established, formal quality control procedures becoming increasingly ineffective. Consequently, more and more orders were being shipped that did not meet customer standards.

The first NES quality problem had originated in this way: The mounting brackets NES had ordered were formed in the fabricating area by cutting long lengths of extruded aluminum into small, one-inch sections. An automatic high-speed saw was used in the process, and the lengths of aluminum were fed into the cutting area by continuous conveyor.

For small orders, the saw, once set, did not need to be adjusted. With larger orders, however, the extended use of the machinery would occasionally cause the process to require readjustment. The saw and the conveyor would then have to be shut down and the measuring control recalibrated.

This particular difficulty had first become evident when NES returned the earlier shipment, two-thirds of which was outside of size tolerance limits. To prevent such an egregious error from recurring, Dick had suggested to the fabricating department supervisor that large orders coming through the automatic saw be monitored. The next large order had indeed been moni-

tored, with each individual piece tested for conformance to size specifications. This resulted in continual delays, as the saw was periodically shut down so the testing could catch up with the process.

Similar problems were being observed on other pieces of equipment, and Dick realized that some formal, more sophisticated quality control procedures were needed. He called the New York office.

"Sir," he said as the CEO answered, "we've got a QC situation here that calls for some corporate assistance. Can you spare some technical people for awhile?"

"Sure thing, Lennox," the CEO replied, surprisingly agreeable. "I've got two top people, Jody Wallis and Sarah Porter, just finishing up a big project. I'll send them up on the morning plane." He added, "These two are all business, so be ready to put them to work!"

Increased sales volume has again created some difficulties, this time in the fabricating department. Dick has recognized the need for better quality control procedures and will be receiving some much needed technical assistance in this area. What kind of information will Dick and the fabricating area supervisor need to provide to the technical support staff to aid them in their task? How will Jody and Sarah use this information to help Dick solve the quality control problem?

6-12
Computer Data Base Exercise

One of Hal Rodgers' management initiatives when he took over HH Industries was to introduce competitive procurements. He felt that many of the company's suppliers had been lulled into complacency through years of unchallenged orders. A careful study of the market revealed that a good number of HH's inventoried parts could be purchased from at least two separate manufacturers. Now, three years later, Hal was interested in evaluating the company's progress toward its goal.

Bob Ritchie, Manager of Purchasing, was in charge of the study, which brought him to Laurel's office one sunny afternoon when she was just about to escape to the beach for a few hours. "About this competitive procurement thing," he began. "I'm assuming it's a binomial distribution problem, since any given purchase order was either competitively procured or not. My main question has to do with exactly how to select a truly random sample from our file cabinets full of

POs. Peggy has given me the use of her part-time administrative assistant for a few days next week, and I wanted to get her started."

Laurel brightened when she realized that this particular problem could be handled quickly. Bob, she knew, had the best grasp of statistics of any of the staff, so she wouldn't have to launch into a lecture on sampling distributions, standard error, etc. She quickly summarized the advantages and disadvantages of various methods of sampling and asked Bob what he thought was appropriate.

"As I see it, we could do a couple of different things," he ventured. "We could randomly select a few months and examine every PO in each selected month. That sounds like what you called "cluster sampling." Or we could look at every twentieth PO or so, which is systematic, but sounds like almost as much work as looking at every purchase order. Finally, we could just leaf through the drawers, picking purchase orders at random until we had the sample size we wanted."

1. What method should Bob use for collecting a random sample of purchase orders? Why?

The next day, Stan caught Laurel just as she was heading out to run a few errands on her lunch hour. "Thanks for the information on our customers," he smiled. "But I have a question. I thought this statistics stuff was supposed to work with data *samples*. You used the data from all our active customers to come up with those figures. What gives?"

"Well," Laurel answered, "in this case I was merely taking advantage of the fact that we already had that data in a format that I could use, i.e., on the computer. And obviously, the larger the sample size, the more accurate the results. However, if I had had to punch all that data in, I would definitely have taken a shortcut and used a property called the Central Limit Theorem. If you've got a few minutes this afternoon, I'll stop by and show you how it works."

"That would be terrific," said Stan. "I'll be free after a 2 P.M. meeting—about 3? Great. See you then."

2. Using the customer purchase data from Chapter 5, compute the mean and standard deviation for the purchases of the first 25 customers. Then do the same for the first 50, 100, 250 and 500.

6-13
Flow Chart

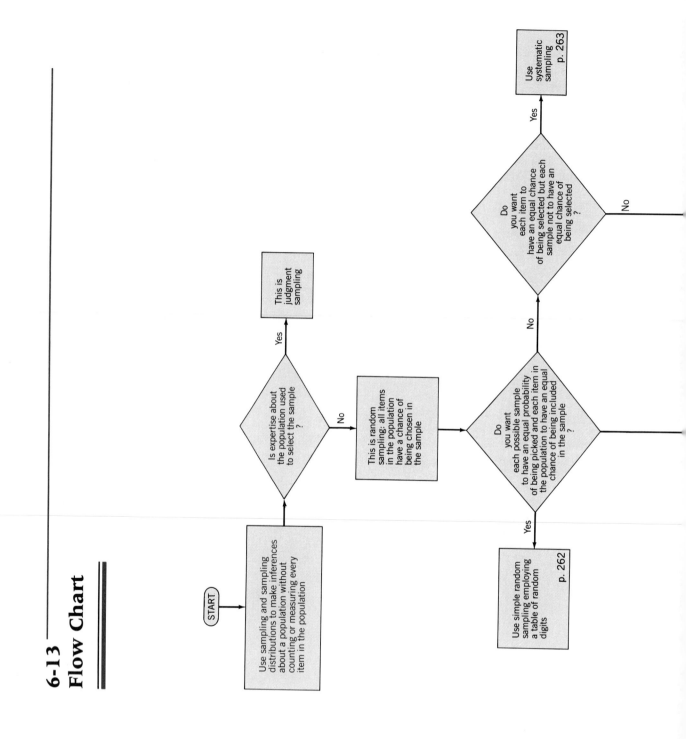

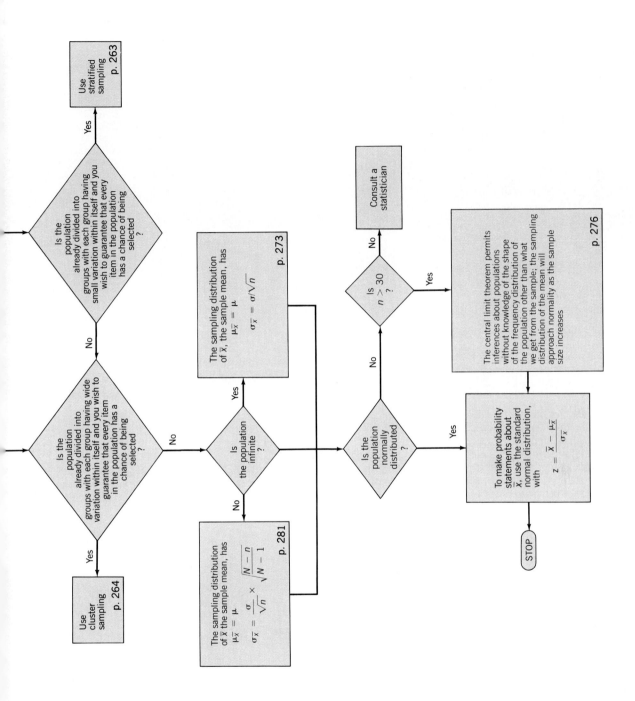

As part of the budgeting process for next year, the manager of the Far Point electric generating plant must estimate the coal he will require for this year. Last year, the plant almost ran out, so he is reluctant to budget for that same amount again. The plant manager, however, does feel that past usage data will help him *estimate* the number of tons of coal to order. A random sample of 10 plant operating weeks chosen over the last 5 years yielded a mean usage of 11,400 tons a week, with a sample standard deviation of 700 tons a week. With the data he has and the methods we shall discuss in this chapter, the plant manager can make a sensible estimate of the amount to order this year, including some idea of the accuracy of the estimate he has made.

7

Estimation

■ OBJECTIVES

Chapters 7 and 8 deal with statistical inference. In Chapter 7, we shall learn to estimate the characteristics of a population by observing the characteristics of a sample. Two characteristics of special interest will be how a population tends to "bunch up" and how it spreads out.

7-1
Introduction

Everyone makes estimates. When you get ready to cross a street, you estimate the speed of any car that is approaching, the distance between you and that car, and your own speed. Having made these quick estimates, you decide whether to wait, walk, or run.

Reasons for estimates

All managers must make quick estimates, too. The outcome of these estimates can affect their organizations as seriously as the outcome of your decision as to whether to cross the street. University department heads make estimates of next fall's enrollment in statistics. Credit managers estimate whether a purchaser will eventually pay his bills. Prospective home buyers make estimates concerning the behavior of interest rates in the mortgage market. All these people make estimates without worry about whether they are scientific but with the hope that the estimates bear a reasonable resemblance to the outcome.

Managers use estimates because in all but the most trivial decisions, they must make rational decisions without complete information and with a great deal of uncertainty about what the future will bring. As educated citizens and professionals, you will be able to make more useful estimates by applying the techniques described in this and subsequent chapters.

Making statistical inferences

The material on probability theory covered in Chapters 4, 5, and 6 forms the foundation for *statistical inference*, the branch of statistics concerned with using probability concepts to deal with uncertainty in decision making. Statistical inference is based on *estimation*, which we shall introduce in this chapter, and *hypothesis testing*, which is the subject of Chapters 8 and 9. In both estimation and hypothesis testing, we shall be making inferences about characteristics of populations from information contained in samples.

Using samples

How do managers use sample statistics to estimate population parameters? The department head attempts to estimate enrollments next fall from current enrollments in the same courses. The credit manager attempts to estimate the creditworthiness of prospective customers from a sample of their past payment habits. The home buyer attempts to estimate the future course of interest rates by observing the current behavior of those rates. In each case, somebody is trying to infer something about a population from information taken from a sample.

Estimating population parameters

This chapter introduces methods that enable us to estimate with reasonable accuracy the *population proportion* (the proportion of the population that possesses a given characteristic) and the *population mean.* To calculate the exact proportion or the exact mean would be an impossible goal. Even so, we will be able to make an estimate, make a statement about the error that will probably accompany this estimate, and implement some controls to avoid as much of the error as possible. As decision makers, we will be forced at times to rely on blind hunches. Yet in other situations, in which information is available and we apply statistical concepts, we can do better than that.

TYPES OF ESTIMATES

Point estimate defined

We can make two types of estimates about a population: a *point* estimate and an *interval* estimate. **A point estimate is a single number that is used to estimate an unknown population parameter.** If, while watching the first members of a football team come onto the field, you say, "Why, I bet their line must weigh 250 pounds," you have made a point estimate. A department chairwoman would make a point estimate if she said, "Our current data indicate that this course will have 350 students in the fall."

Shortcoming of point estimates

A point estimate is often insufficient, because it is either right or wrong. If you are told only that the chairwoman's point estimate of enrollment is wrong, you do not know *how* wrong it is, and you cannot be certain of the estimate's reliability. If you learn that it is off by only ten students, you would accept 350 students as a good estimate of future enrollment. But if the estimate is off by 90 students, you would reject it as an estimate of future enrollment. Therefore, a point estimate is much more useful if it is accompanied by an estimate of the error that might be involved.

Interval estimate defined

An interval estimate is a range of values used to estimate a population parameter. It indicates the error in two ways: by the extent of its range and by the probability of the true population parameter lying within that range. In this case, the department chairwoman would say something like, "I estimate that the true enrollment in this course in the fall will be between 330 and 380 and that it is very likely that the exact enrollment will fall within this interval." The chairwoman has a better idea of the reliability of her estimate. If the course is taught in sections of about 100 students each, and if the chairwoman had tentatively scheduled five sections, then on the basis of her estimate, she can now cancel one of those sections and offer an elective instead.

ESTIMATOR AND ESTIMATES

Estimator defined

Any sample statistic that is used to estimate a population parameter is called an estimator; that is, **an estimator is a sample statistic used to estimate a population parameter.** The sample mean $\bar{x}$ can be an estimator of the population mean μ, and the sample proportion can be used as an estimator of the population proportion. We can also use the sample range as an estimator of the population range.

Estimate defined

When we observe a specific numerical value of our estimator, we call that value an estimate. In other words, **an estimate is a specific observed value of a statistic.** We form an estimate by taking a sample and computing the value taken by our estimator in that sample. Suppose that we calculate the mean odometer reading (mileage) from a sample of used taxis and find it to be 98,000 miles. If we use this specific value to estimate the mileage for a whole fleet of used taxis, the value 98,000 miles would be an estimate. Table 7-1 illustrates several populations, population parameters, estimators, and estimates.

TABLE 7-1 Populations, Population Parameters, Estimators, and Estimates

POPULATION IN WHICH WE ARE INTERESTED	POPULATION PARAMETER WE WISH TO ESTIMATE	SAMPLE STATISTIC WE WILL USE AS AN ESTIMATOR	ESTIMATE WE MAKE
Employees in a furniture factory	Mean turnover per year	Mean turnover for a period of 1 month	8.9% turnover per year
Applicants for town manager of Chapel Hill	Mean formal education (years)	Mean formal education of every 5th applicant	17.9 years of formal education
Teenagers in a given community	Proportion who have criminal records	Proportion of a sample of 50 teenagers who have criminal records	.02, or 2%, have criminal records

CRITERIA OF A GOOD ESTIMATOR

Qualities of a good
estimator

Some statistics are better estimators than are others. Fortunately, we can evaluate the quality of a statistic as an estimator by using four criteria:

1. **Unbiasedness.** This is a desirable property for a good estimator to have. The term *unbiasedness* refers to the fact that a sample mean is an unbiased estimator of a population mean because **the mean of the sampling distribution of sample means taken from the same population is equal to the population mean itself.** We can say that a statistic is an unbiased estimator if, on the average, it tends to assume values that are above the population parameter being estimated as frequently and to the same extent as it tends to assume values that are below the population parameter being estimated.

2. **Efficiency.** Another desirable property of a good estimator is that it be efficient. *Efficiency* refers to the size of the standard error of the statistic. If we compare two statistics from a sample of the same size and try to decide which one is the more efficient estimator, we would pick the statistic that has the smaller standard error, or standard deviation of the sampling distribution. Suppose we choose a sample of a given size and must decide whether to use the sample mean or the sample median to estimate the population mean. If we calculate the standard error of the sample mean and find it to be 1.05 and then calculate the standard error of the sample median and find it to be 1.6, we would say that the sample mean is a *more efficient estimator* of the population mean *because its standard error is smaller.* It makes sense that an estimator with a smaller standard error (with less variation) will have more chance of producing an estimate nearer to the population parameter under consideration.

3. **Consistency.** A statistic is a consistent estimator of a population parameter if *as the sample size increases, it becomes almost certain that the value of the statistic comes very close to the value of the population parameter.* If an estimator is consistent, it becomes more reliable with large samples. Thus, if you are wondering whether to increase the sample size to get more information about a population parameter, find out first whether your statistic is a consistent estimator. If it is not, you will waste time and money by taking larger samples.

4. **Sufficiency.** An estimator is sufficient if it makes so much use of the information in the sample that no other estimator could extract from the sample additional information about the population parameter being estimated. We present these criteria here to make you aware of the care that statisticians must use in picking an estimator.

Finding the best
estimator

A given sample statistic is not always the best estimator of its analogous population parameter. Consider a symmetrically distributed population in which the values of the median and the mean coincide. In this instance, the sample mean would be an *unbiased* estimator of the population median because it would assume values that on the average would equal the population median. Also, the sample mean would be a *consistent* estimator of the population median because, as the sample size increases, the value of the sample mean would tend to come very close to the population median. And the sample mean would be a more *efficient* estimator of the population median than the sample median itself because in large samples, the sample mean has a smaller standard error than the sample median. At the same time, the sample median in a symmetrically distributed population would be an unbiased and consistent estimator of the population mean but *not the most efficient* estimator because in large samples, its standard error is larger than that of the sample mean.

Exercises

7-1 What two basic tools are used in making statistical inferences?

7-2 Why do decision makers often measure samples rather than entire populations? What is the disadvantage?

7-3 Explain a shortcoming that occurs in a point estimate but not in an interval estimate. What measure is included with a point estimate to compensate for this problem?

7-4 What is an estimator? How does an estimate differ from an estimator?

7-5 List and describe briefly the criteria of a good estimator.

7-6 What role does consistency play in determining sample size?

7-2
Point Estimates

Using the sample mean to estimate the population mean

The sample mean $\bar{x}$ is the best estimator of the population mean μ. It is unbiased, consistent, the most efficient estimator, and, as long as the sample is sufficiently large, its sampling distribution can be approximated by the normal distribution.

If we know the sampling distribution of $\bar{x}$, we can make statements about any estimate we may make from sampling information. Let's look at a medical supplies company that produces disposable hypodermic syringes. Each syringe is wrapped in a sterile package and then jumble-packed in a large corrugated carton. Jumble packing causes the cartons to contain differing numbers of syringes. Since the syringes are sold on a per unit basis, the company needs an estimate of the number of syringes per carton for billing purposes. We have taken a sample of 35 cartons at random and recorded the number of syringes in each carton. Table 7-2 illustrates our results.

Finding the sample mean

Using the results of Chapter 3, we can obtain the sample mean $\bar{x}$ by finding the sum of all our results, Σx, and dividing this total by n, the number of cartons we have sampled:

$$\bar{x} = \frac{\Sigma x}{n} \qquad [3\text{-}2]$$

Using this equation to solve our problem, we get:

$$\bar{x} = \frac{3570}{35}$$

$$= 102 \text{ syringes}$$

Thus, using the sample mean $\bar{x}$ as our estimator, the point estimate of the population mean μ is 102 syringes per carton. Since the manufactured price of a disposable

TABLE 7-2 **Results of Sample of 35 Cartons of Hypodermic Syringes (Syringes Per Carton)**

101	103	112	102	98	97	93
105	100	97	107	93	94	97
97	100	110	106	110	103	99
93	98	106	100	112	105	100
114	97	110	102	98	112	99

hypodermic syringe is quite small (about 25¢), both the buyer and seller would accept the use of this point estimate as the basis for billing, and the manufacturer can save the time and expense of counting each syringe that goes into a carton.

POINT ESTIMATE OF THE POPULATION VARIANCE AND STANDARD DEVIATION

Using the sample standard deviation to estimate the population standard deviation

Suppose the management of the medical-supplies company wants to estimate the variance and/or standard deviation of the distribution of the number of packaged syringes per carton. The most frequently used estimator of the population standard deviation σ is the sample standard deviation s. We can calculate the sample standard deviation as in Table 7-3 and discover that the sample standard deviation is 6.01 syringes.

If, instead of considering:

$$s^2 = \frac{\Sigma(x - \bar{x})^2}{n - 1}$$

[3-17]

Why is $n - 1$ the divisor?

as our sample variance, we had considered:

$$s^2 = \frac{\Sigma(x - \bar{x})^2}{n}$$

the result would have some *bias* as an estimator of the population variance; specifically, it would tend to be too low. Using a divisor of $n - 1$ gives us an unbiased estimator of σ^2. Thus, we will use s^2 (as defined in Equation 3-17) and s (as defined in Equation 3-18) to estimate σ^2 and σ.

POINT ESTIMATE OF THE POPULATION PROPORTION

Using the sample proportion to estimate the population proportion

The proportion of units that have a particular characteristic in a given population is symbolized p. If we know the proportion of units in a sample that have that same characteristic (symbolized $\bar{p}$), we can use this $\bar{p}$ as an estimator of p. It can be shown that $\bar{p}$ has all the desirable properties we discussed earlier; it is unbiased, consistent, efficient, and sufficient.

Continuing our example of the manufacturer of medical supplies, we shall try to estimate the population proportion from the sample proportion. Suppose the management wishes to estimate the number of cartons that will arrive damaged, owing to poor handling in shipment after the cartons leave the factory. We can check a sample of 50 cartons from their shipping point to the arrival at their destination and then record the presence or absence of damage. If, in this case, we find that the proportion of damaged cartons in the sample is .08, we would say that:

$$\bar{p} = .08 \leftarrow \text{sample proportion damaged}$$

And since the sample proportion $\bar{p}$ is a convenient estimator of the population proportion p, we can estimate that the proportion of damaged cartons in the population will also be .08.

TABLE 7-3 Calculation of Sample Variance and Standard Deviation for Syringes Per Carton

VALUES OF x (NEEDLES PER CARTON) (1)	x^2 (2)	SAMPLE MEAN $\bar{x}$ (3)	$(x - \bar{x})$ (4) = (1) − (3)	$(x - \bar{x})^2$ (5) = (4)^2
101	10,201	102	−1	1
105	11,025	102	3	9
97	9,409	102	−5	25
93	8,649	102	−9	81
114	12,996	102	12	144
103	10,609	102	1	1
100	10,000	102	−2	4
100	10,000	102	−2	4
98	9,604	102	−4	16
97	9,409	102	−5	25
112	12,544	102	10	100
97	9,409	102	−5	25
110	12,100	102	8	64
106	11,236	102	4	16
110	12,100	102	8	64
102	10,404	102	0	0
107	11,449	102	5	25
106	11,236	102	4	16
100	10,000	102	−2	4
102	10,404	102	0	0
98	9,604	102	−4	16
93	8,649	102	−9	81
110	12,100	102	8	64
112	12,544	102	10	100
98	9,604	102	−4	16
97	9,409	102	−5	25
94	8,836	102	−8	64
103	10,609	102	1	1
105	11,025	102	3	9
112	12,544	102	10	100
93	8,649	102	−9	81
97	9,409	102	−5	25
99	9,801	102	−3	9
100	10,000	102	2	4
99	9,801	102	−3	9
3,570	**365,368**		Sum of all the squared differences $\Sigma(x - \bar{x})^2$	→ **1,228**

[3-17] $s^2 = \dfrac{\Sigma x^2}{n - 1} - \dfrac{n\bar{x}^2}{n - 1}$

$= \dfrac{365{,}368}{34} - \dfrac{35(102)^2}{34}$

$= \dfrac{1228}{34}$ ← or →

$= 36.12$

Sum of the squared differences divided by 34, the number of items in the sample − 1 (sample variance) $\dfrac{\Sigma(x - \bar{x})^2}{n - 1}$ → 36.12

[3-18] $s = \sqrt{s^2}$
$= \sqrt{36.12}$
$= 6.01$ syringes

Sample standard deviation s $\sqrt{\dfrac{\Sigma(x - \bar{x})^2}{n - 1}}$ → 6.01 syringes

Exercises

7-7 Joe Jackson, a meteorologist for the local television station WDUL, would like to report the average rainfall for today on this evening's newscast. Below are the rainfall measurements (in inches) for today's date for sixteen randomly chosen past years. Determine the sample mean rainfall.

| 0.47 | 0.27 | 0.13 | 0.54 | 0.00 | 0.08 | 0.75 | 0.06 |
| 0.00 | 1.05 | 0.34 | 0.26 | 0.17 | 0.42 | 0.50 | 0.86 |

7-8 The Greensboro Coliseum is considering expanding its seating capacity and needs to know both the average number of people who attend events there and the variability in this number. Below are the attendance (in thousands) at nine randomly selected sporting events. Find point estimates of the mean and the variance of the population from which the sample was drawn.

8.8   14.0   21.3   7.9   12.5   20.6   16.3   14.1   13.0

7-9 Electric Pizza was considering national distribution of its regionally successful product and was compiling *pro forma* sales data. Below are listed the average monthly sales figures (in thousands of dollars) from its 30 current distributors. Treating them as (a) a sample and (b) a population, compute the standard deviation.

7.3	5.8	4.5	8.5	5.2	4.1
2.8	3.8	6.5	3.4	9.8	6.5
6.7	7.7	5.8	6.8	8.0	3.9
6.9	3.7	6.6	7.5	8.7	6.9
2.1	5.0	7.5	5.8	6.4	5.2

7-10 In a sample of 400 textile workers, 184 expressed extreme dissatisfaction regarding a prospective plan to modify working conditions. Because this dissatisfaction was vehement enough to allow management to interpret plan reaction as being highly undesirable, they were curious about the proportion of total workers harboring this sentiment. Give a point estimate of this proportion.

7-11 The Pizza Distribution Authority (PDA) has developed quite a business in Carrboro by delivering pizza orders promptly. PDA guarantees that its pizzas will be delivered in 30 minutes or less from the time the order was placed, and if the delivery is late, the pizza is free. The time that it takes to deliver each pizza order that is on time is recorded in the Official Pizza Time Book (OPTB), and the delivery time for those pizzas that are delivered late is recorded as 30 minutes in the OPTB. Below are listed 12 random entries from the OPTB.

| 15.3 | 29.5 | 30 | 10.1 | 30 | 19.6 |
| 10.8 | 12.2 | 14.8 | 30 | 22.1 | 18.3 |

(a) Find the mean for the sample above.
(b) From what population was this sample drawn?
(c) Can this sample be used to estimate the average time that it takes for PDA to deliver a pizza? Explain.

7-3
Interval Estimates: Basic Concepts

The purpose of gathering samples is to learn more about a population. We can compute this information from the samples as either *point* estimates, which we have just discussed, or as *interval* estimates, the subject of the rest of this chapter. *An interval estimate describes a range of values within which a population parameter is likely to lie.*

Start with a point estimate

Suppose the marketing research director needs an estimate in months of the average life of car batteries his company manufactures. We select a random sample of 200 batteries, record the car owners' names and addresses as listed in store records, and interview these owners about the battery life they have experienced. Our sample of 200 users has a mean battery life of 36 months. If we use the point estimate of the sample mean $\bar{x}$ as the best estimator of the population mean μ, we would report that the mean life of the company's batteries is 36 months.

Finding the likely error of this estimate

But the director also asks for a statement about the uncertainty that will be likely to accompany this estimate; that is, a statement about the range within which the unknown population mean is likely to lie. To provide such a statement, we need to find *the standard error of the mean.*

We learned from Chapter 6 that if we select and plot a large number of sample means from a population, the distribution of these means will approximate a normal curve. Furthermore, the mean of the sample means will be the same as the population mean. Our sample size of 200 is large enough so that we can apply the central limit theorem, as we have done graphically in Fig. 7-1. To measure the spread, or dispersion, in our distribution of sample means, we can use the following formula* and calculate the standard error of the mean:

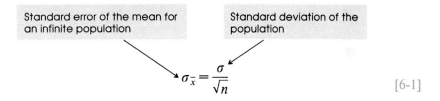

| Standard error of the mean for an infinite population | Standard deviation of the population |

$$\sigma_{\bar{x}} = \frac{\sigma}{\sqrt{n}}$$

[6-1]

FIGURE 7-1

Sampling distribution of the mean for samples of 200 batteries

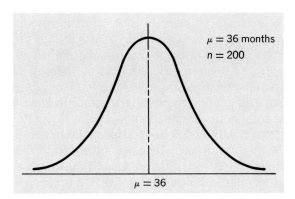

$\mu = 36$ months
$n = 200$

$\mu = 36$

* We have not used the finite population multiplier to calculate the standard error of the mean because the population of batteries is large enough to be considered infinite.

In this case, we have already estimated the standard deviation of the population of the batteries and reported that it is 10 months. Using this standard deviation and the first equation from Chapter 6, we can calculate the standard error of the mean:

$$\sigma_{\bar{x}} = \frac{\sigma}{\sqrt{n}} \qquad\qquad [6\text{-}1]$$

$$= \frac{10}{\sqrt{200}}$$

$$= \frac{10}{14.14}$$

$$= .707 \text{ months} \leftarrow \text{one standard error of the mean}$$

Making an interval estimate

We could now report to the director that our estimate of the life of the company's batteries is 36 months, and the standard error that accompanies this estimate is .707. In other words, the actual mean life for all the batteries *may* lie somewhere in the interval estimate of from 35.293 to 36.707 months. This is helpful but insufficient information for the director. Next, we need to calculate the chance that the actual life will lie in this interval *or* in other intervals of different widths that we might choose, $\pm 2\sigma$ ($2 \times .707$), $\pm 3\sigma$ ($3 \times .707$), and so on.

PROBABILITY OF THE TRUE POPULATION PARAMETER FALLING WITHIN THE INTERVAL ESTIMATE

To begin to solve this problem, we should review relevant parts of Chapter 5. There we worked with the normal probability distribution and learned that specific portions of the area under the normal curve are located between plus and minus any given number of standard deviations from the mean. In Fig. 5-12, we saw how to relate these portions to specific probabilities.

Finding the chance the mean will fall in this interval estimate

Fortunately, we can apply these properties to the standard error of the mean and make the following statement about the range of values in an interval estimate for our battery problem.

The probability is .955 that the mean of a sample size of 200 will be within plus and minus 2 standard errors of the population mean. Stated differently, 95.5 percent of all the sample means are within plus and minus 2 standard errors from μ, and hence **μ is within plus and minus 2 standard errors of 95.5 percent of all the sample means.** Theoretically, if we select 1,000 samples at random from a given population and then construct an interval of plus and minus 2 standard errors around the mean of each of these samples, about 955 of these intervals will include the population mean. Similarly, the probability is .683 that the mean of the sample will be within plus and minus 1 standard error of the population mean, and so forth. This theoretical concept is basic to our study of interval construction and of statistical inference. In Fig. 7-2, we have illustrated the concept graphically, showing five such intervals. Only the interval constructed around the sample mean $\bar{x}_4$ does not contain the population mean. In words, statisticians would describe the interval estimates represented in Fig. 7-2 by saying, "The population mean μ will be located within plus and minus 2 standard errors from the sample mean 95.5 percent of the time."

As far as any particular interval in Fig. 7-2 is concerned, it either contains the population mean or it does not, because the population mean is a fixed parameter and does not vary. Since we know that in 95.5 percent of all samples, the interval will contain the population mean, we say that we are 95.5 percent confident that the interval contains the population mean.

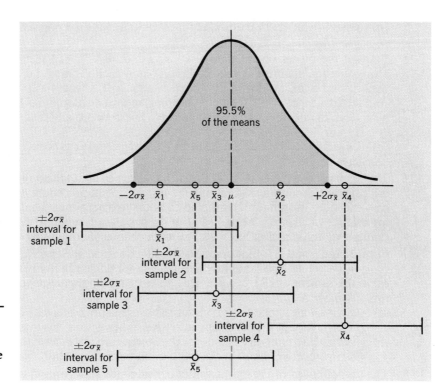

FIGURE 7-2

A number of intervals constructed around sample means; all except one include the population mean

A more useful estimate of battery life

Applying this to the battery example, we can now report to the director. Our best estimate of the life of the company's batteries is 36 months, *and* we are 68.3 percent confident that the life lies in the interval from 35.293 to 36.707 months ($36 \pm 1\sigma_{\bar{x}}$). Similarly, we are 95.5 percent confident that the life falls within the interval of 34.586 to 37.414 months ($36 \pm 2\sigma_{\bar{x}}$), and we are 99.7 percent confident that battery life falls within the interval of 33.879 to 38.121 months ($36 \pm 3\sigma_{\bar{x}}$).

Exercises

7-12 From a population known to have a standard deviation of 1.4, a sample of 60 individuals is taken. The mean for this sample is found to be 6.2.
(a) Find the standard error of the mean.
(b) Establish an interval estimate around the mean, using one standard error of the mean.

7-13 The University of North Carolina is conducting a study on the average weight of the many bricks that comprise the University's walkways. Workers were sent to dig up and weigh a sample of 421 bricks and the average brick weight of this sample was 14.2 lbs. It is a well known fact that the standard deviation of brick weight is .8 lbs.
(a) Find the standard error of the mean.
(b) What is the interval around the sample mean that will include the population mean 95.5 percent of the time?

7-14 For a population with a known variance of 185, a sample of 64 individuals leads to 217 as an estimate of the mean.
(a) Find the standard error of the mean.

(b) Establish an interval estimate that should include the population mean 68.3 percent of the time.

7-15 Because the owner of the Bard's Nook, a recently opened restaurant, has had difficulty estimating the quantity of food to be prepared each evening, he decided to determine the mean number of customers served each night. He selected a sample of 30 nights, which resulted in a mean of 71. The population standard deviation has been established as 3.76.
(a) Give an interval estimate that has a 68.3 percent probability of including the population mean.
(b) Give an interval estimate that has a 99.7 percent chance of including the population mean.

7-16 The manager of the Neuse River Bridge is concerned about the number of cars "running" the toll gates and is considering altering the toll-collection procedure if such alteration would be cost-effective. She randomly sampled 75 hours to determine the rate of violation. The resulting average violations per hour was 7. If the population standard deviation is known to be .9, estimate an interval that has a 95.5 percent chance of containing the true mean.

7-17 Eunice Gunterwal is a money-minded undergraduate at State U. who is interested in purchasing a used car. She randomly selected 125 want ads and found that the average price of a car in this sample was $3,250. Eunice knows that the standard deviation of used-car prices in this city is $615.
(a) Establish an interval estimate for the average price of a car so that Eunice can be 68.3 percent certain that the population mean lies within this interval.
(b) Establish an interval estimate for the average price of a car so that Miss Gunterwal can be 95.5 percent certain that the population mean lies within this interval.

7-18 The school board of Forsight County considers its most important task to be keeping the average class size in Forsight County schools less than the average class size in neighboring Hindsight County. Miss Dee Marks, the school superintendent for Forsight County, has just received reliable information indicating that the average class size in Hindsight County this year is 30.3 students. She does not yet have the figures for all 621 classes in her own school system, so Dee is forced to rely upon the 76 classes that have reported class sizes, yielding an average class size of 29.8 students. Dee knows that the class size of any Forsight County class has a distribution with an unknown mean and standard deviation equal to 8.3 students. Assuming that the sample of 76 that Miss Marks possesses is randomly chosen from the population of all Forsight County class sizes:
(a) Find an interval that Dee can be 95.5 percent certain will contain the true mean.
(b) Do you think that Dee has met her goal?

7-4
Interval Estimates and Confidence Intervals

In using interval estimates, we are not confined to plus and minus 1, 2, and 3 standard errors. According to Appendix Table 1, for example, plus and minus 1.64 standard errors includes about 90 percent of the area under the curve; it includes .4495 of the area on either side of the mean in a normal distribution. Similarly, plus and minus 2.58 standard errors includes about 99 percent of the area, or 49.51 percent on each side of the mean.

Confidence level defined

In statistics, the probability that we associate with an interval estimate is called the confidence level. This probability, then, indicates how confident we are that the interval estimate will include the population parameter. A higher probability means more confidence. In estimation, the most commonly used confidence levels are 90 percent, 95 percent, and 99 percent, but we are free to apply *any* confidence level. In Fig. 7-2, for example, we used a 95.5 percent confidence level.

The confidence interval is the range of the estimate we are making. If we report that we are 90 percent confident that the mean of the population of incomes of persons in a certain community will lie between $8,000 and $24,000, then the range $8,000–$24,000 is our confidence interval. Often, however, we will express the confidence interval in standard errors rather than in numerical values. Thus, we will frequently express confidence intervals like this: $\bar{x} \pm 1.64\sigma_{\bar{x}}$, where:

$$\bar{x} + 1.64\sigma_{\bar{x}} = \text{upper limit of the confidence interval}$$

$$\bar{x} - 1.64\sigma_{\bar{x}} = \text{lower limit of the confidence interval}$$

Thus, confidence limits are the upper and lower limits of the confidence interval. In this case, $\bar{x} + 1.64_{\bar{x}}$ is called the *upper confidence limit,* and $\bar{x} - 1.64\sigma_{\bar{x}}$ is the *lower confidence limit.*

RELATIONSHIP BETWEEN CONFIDENCE LEVEL AND CONFIDENCE INTERVAL

You may think that we should use a high confidence level, such as 99 percent, in all estimation problems. After all, a high confidence level seems to signify a high degree of accuracy in the estimate. In practice, however, high confidence levels will produce large confidence intervals, and such large intervals are not precise; they give very fuzzy estimates.

TABLE 7-4 Illustration of the Relationship Between Confidence Level and Confidence Interval

CUSTOMER'S QUESTION	STORE MANAGER'S RESPONSE	IMPLIED CONFIDENCE LEVEL	IMPLIED CONFIDENCE INTERVAL
Will I get my washing machine within 1 year?	I am absolutely certain of that.	Better than 99%	1 year
Will you deliver the washing machine within 1 month?	I am almost positive it will be delivered this month.	At least 95%	1 month
Will you deliver the washing machine within a week?	I am pretty certain it will go out within this week.	About 80%	1 week
Will I get my washing machine tomorrow?	I am not certain we can get it to you then.	About 40%	1 day
Will my washing machine get home before I do?	There is little chance it will beat you home.	Near 1%	1 hour

Consider an appliance store customer who inquires about the delivery of a new washing machine. In Table 7-4 are several of the questions the customer might ask and the likely responses. This table indicates the direct relationship that exists between the confidence level and the confidence interval for any estimate. As the customer sets a tighter and tighter confidence interval, the store manager agrees to a lower and lower confidence level. Notice, too, that when the confidence interval is too wide, as is the case with a one-year delivery, the estimate may have little real value, even though the store manager attaches a 99 percent confidence level to that estimate. Similarly, if the confidence interval is too narrow ("Will my washing machine get home before I do?"), the estimate is associated with such a low confidence level (1 percent) that we question its value.

USING SAMPLING AND CONFIDENCE INTERVAL ESTIMATION

Estimating from only one sample

In our discussion of the basic concepts of interval estimation, particularly in Fig. 7-2, we described samples being drawn repeatedly from a given population in order to estimate a population parameter. We also mentioned selecting a large number of sample means from a population. In practice, however, it is often difficult or expensive to take more than one sample from a population. Based on just one sample, we estimate the population parameter. We must be careful, then, about interpreting the results of such a process.

Suppose we calculate from one sample in our battery example the following confidence interval and confidence level: "We are 95 percent confident that the mean battery life of the population lies within 30 and 42 months." **This statement does not mean that the chance is .95 that the mean life of all our batteries falls within the interval established from this one sample. Instead, it means that if we select many random samples of this sample size and if we calculate a confidence interval for each of these samples, then in about 95 percent of these cases, the population mean will lie within that interval.**

Exercises

7-19 Define the confidence level for an interval estimate.

7-20 Define the confidence interval.

7-21 Suppose you wish to use a confidence level of 80 percent. Give the upper limit of the confidence interval in terms of sample mean, $\bar{x}$, and the standard error $\sigma_{\bar{x}}$.

7-22 In what way may an estimate be less meaningful because of:
(a) A high confidence level?   (b) A narrow confidence interval?

7-23 Suppose a sample of 50 is taken from a population with standard deviation 27 and that the sample mean is 86.
(a) Establish an interval estimate for the population mean that is 95.5 percent certain to include the true population mean.
(b) Suppose, instead, that the sample size was 5,000. Establish an interval for the population mean that is 95.5 percent certain to include the true population mean.
(c) Why might estimate (a) be preferred to estimate (b)? Why might (b) be preferred to (a)?

7-24 Is the confidence level for an estimate based on the interval constructed from one sample?

7-25 Given the following confidence levels, express the lower and upper limits of the confidence interval for these levels in terms of $\bar{x}$ and $\sigma_{\bar{x}}$.
(a) 54%   (b) 75%   (c) 94%   (d) 98%

7-26 Steve Klippers, the owner of Steve's Barbershop, has built quite a reputation among the residents of Cullowhee. As each customer enters his barbershop, Steve yells out the number of minutes that the customer can expect to wait before getting his haircut. The only statistician in town, after being frustrated by Steve's inaccurate point estimates, has determined that the actual waiting time for any customer is normally distributed with mean equal to Steve's estimate in minutes and standard deviation equal to 5 minutes divided by the customer's position in the waiting line. Help Steve's customers develop 95 percent probability intervals for the following situations:
(a) The customer is second in line, and Steve's estimate is 25 minutes.
(b) The customer is third in line, and Steve's estimate is 15 minutes.
(c) The customer is fifth in line, and Steve's estimate is 38 minutes.
(d) The customer is first in line, and Steve's estimate is 20 minutes.
How are these intervals different from confidence intervals?

7-5
Calculating Interval Estimates of the Mean from Large Samples

Finding a 95 percent confidence interval

A large automotive-parts wholesaler needs an estimate of the mean life it can expect from windshield wiper blades under typical driving conditions. Already, management has determined that the standard deviation of the population life is 6 months. When we select a simple random sample of 100 wiper blades and collect data on their useful lives, we obtain these results:

$n = 100 \leftarrow$ sample size

$\bar{x} = 21$ months $\leftarrow$ sample mean

Population standard deviation is known

$\sigma = 6$ months $\leftarrow$ population standard deviation

---

Since the wholesaler uses tens of thousands of these wiper blades annually, it requests that we find an interval estimate with a confidence level of 95 percent. Since the sample size is greater than 30, we can use the normal distribution as our sampling distribution and calculate the standard error of the mean by using Equation 6-1:

$$\sigma_{\bar{x}} = \frac{\sigma}{\sqrt{n}} \qquad [6\text{-}1]$$

$$= \frac{6 \text{ months}}{\sqrt{100}}$$

$$= \frac{6}{10}$$

$$= .6 \text{ months} \leftarrow \text{standard error of the mean for an infinite population}$$

Next, we consider the confidence level with which we are working. Since a 95 percent confidence level will include 47.5 percent of the area on either side of the mean of the sampling distribution, we can search in the body of Appendix Table 1 for the .475

value. We discover that .475 of the area under the normal curve is contained between the mean and a point 1.96 standard errors to the right of the mean. Therefore, we know that $(2)(.475) = .95$ of the area is located between plus and minus 1.96 standard errors from the mean and that our confidence limits are:

$$\bar{x} + 1.96\sigma_{\bar{x}} \leftarrow \text{upper confidence limit}$$

$$\bar{x} - 1.96\sigma_{\bar{x}} \leftarrow \text{lower confidence limit}$$

Then we substitute numerical values into these two expressions:

$$\bar{x} + 1.96\sigma_{\bar{x}} = 21 \text{ months} + 1.96(.6 \text{ months})$$
$$= 21 + 1.18 \text{ months}$$
$$= 22.18 \text{ months} \leftarrow \text{upper confidence limit}$$

$$\bar{x} - 1.96\sigma_{\bar{x}} = 21 \text{ months} - 1.96(.6 \text{ months})$$
$$= 21 - 1.18 \text{ months}$$
$$= 19.82 \text{ months} \leftarrow \text{lower confidence limit}$$

Our conclusion   We can now report that we estimate the mean life of the population of wiper blades to be between 19.82 and 22.18 months with 95 percent confidence.

WHEN THE POPULATION STANDARD DEVIATION IS UNKNOWN

Finding a 90 percent confidence interval   A more complex interval estimate problem comes from a social-service agency in a local government. It is interested in estimating the mean annual income of 700 families living in a four-square-block section of a community. We take a simple random sample and find these results:

$$n = 50 \leftarrow \text{sample size}$$

$$\bar{x} = \$4{,}800 \leftarrow \text{sample mean}$$

$$s = \$950 \leftarrow \text{sample standard deviation}$$

The agency asks us to calculate an interval estimate of the mean annual income of all 700 families so that it can be 90 percent confident that the population mean falls within that interval. Since the sample size is over 30, we can use the normal distribution as the sampling distribution.

Estimating the population standard deviation.   Notice that one part of this problem differs from our previous examples: we do *not* know the population standard deviation, and so we will use the sample standard deviation to estimate the *population standard deviation:*

$$\boxed{\text{Estimate of the population standard deviation}} \rightarrow \hat{\sigma} = s = \sqrt{\frac{\Sigma(x - \bar{x})^2}{n - 1}} \qquad [7\text{-}1]$$

The value \$950.00 is our estimate of the standard deviation of the population. We can also symbolize this *estimated* value by $\hat{\sigma}$, which is called *sigma hat.*

Now we can estimate the standard error of the mean. Since we have a finite population size of 700, we will use the formula for deriving the standard error of the mean of finite populations:

$$\sigma_{\bar{x}} = \frac{\sigma}{\sqrt{n}} \times \sqrt{\frac{N-n}{N-1}} \qquad [6\text{-}3]$$

Estimating the standard
error of the mean But since we are calculating the standard error of the mean using an *estimate* of the standard deviation of the population, we rewrite this equation so that it is correct symbolically:

Symbol that indicates an
estimated value

Estimate of the population
standard deviation

$$\hat{\sigma}_{\bar{x}} = \frac{\hat{\sigma}}{\sqrt{n}} \times \sqrt{\frac{N-n}{N-1}} \qquad [7\text{-}2]$$

$$= \frac{\$950.00}{\sqrt{50}} \times \sqrt{\frac{700-50}{700-1}}$$

$$= \frac{\$950.00}{7.07} \sqrt{\frac{650}{699}}$$

$$= (\$134.37)(.9643)$$

$$= \$129.57 \leftarrow \text{estimate of the standard error of the mean}$$
of a finite population (derived from an
estimate of the population standard deviation)

Next we consider the 90 percent confidence level, which would include 45 percent of the area on either side of the mean of the sampling distribution. Looking in the body of Appendix Table 1 for the .45 value, we find that about .45 of the area under the normal curve is located between the mean and a point 1.64 standard errors from the mean. Therefore, 90 percent of the area is located between plus *and* minus 1.64 standard errors from the mean, and our confidence limits are:

$$\bar{x} + 1.64\sigma_{\bar{x}} = \$4,800 + 1.64(\$129.57)$$
$$= \$4,800 + \$212.50$$
$$= \$5,012.50 \leftarrow \text{upper confidence limit}$$

$$\bar{x} - 1.64\sigma_{\bar{x}} = \$4,800 - 1.64(\$129.57)$$
$$= \$4,800 - \$212.50$$
$$= \$4,587.50 \leftarrow \text{lower confidence limit}$$

Our conclusion Our report to the social-service agency would be: With 90 percent confidence, we estimate that the average annual income of all 700 families living in this four-square-block section falls between \$4,587.50 and \$5,012.50.

Exercises

7-27 The manager of General Electric's lightbulb division must estimate the average number of hours that a lightbulb made by each lightbulb machine will last. A sample of 40 lightbulbs was selected from machine A and the average burning time was 1416 hours. The standard deviation of burning time is known to be 30 hours.

(a) Compute the standard error of the mean.
(b) Construct a 90 percent confidence interval for the true population mean.

7-28 Upon collecting a sample of 250 from a population with known standard deviation of 13.7, the mean is found to be 112.4.
(a) Find a 95 percent confidence interval for the mean.
(b) Find a 99 percent confidence interval for the mean.

7-29 Jon Jackobsen, an overzealous graduate student, has just completed a first draft of his 700-page dissertation. Jon has typed this paper himself and is interested in knowing the average number of typographical errors per page, but does not want to read the whole paper. Knowing a little bit about business statistics, Jon selected 40 pages at random to read and found that the average number of typos per page was 4.3 while the sample standard deviation was 1.2 typos per page.
(a) Calculate the estimated standard error of the mean.
(b) Construct for Jon a 90 percent confidence interval for the true average number of typos per page in his paper.

7-30 From a population of 540, a sample of 60 individuals is taken. From this sample, the mean is found to be 6.2 and the standard deviation 1.368.
(a) Find the estimated standard of error of the mean.
(b) Construct a 96 percent confidence interval for the mean.

7-31 In an automotive safety test conducted by the North Carolina Highway Safety Research Center, the average tire pressure in a sample of 62 tires was found to be 24 pounds per square inch, and the standard deviation was 2.1 pounds per square inch.
(a) Calculate the estimated population standard deviation for this population. (There are about a million cars registered in North Carolina.)
(b) Calculate the estimated standard error of the mean.
(c) Construct a 95 percent confidence interval for the population mean.

7-32 Joel Friedlander is a broker on the New York Stock Exchange who is curious about the amount of time between the placement and execution of a market order. Joel sampled 45 orders and found that the mean time to execution was 24.3 minutes with a standard deviation of 3.2 minutes. Help Joel by constructing a 95 percent confidence interval for the mean time to execution.

7-33 Oscar T. Grady is the production manager for Citrus Groves Inc., located just north of Ocala, Florida. Oscar is concerned that the last 3 years' late freezes have damaged the 2,500 orange trees that Citrus Groves owns. In order to determine the extent of damage to the trees, Oscar has sampled the number of oranges produced per tree for 42 trees and found that the average production was 525 oranges per tree with a standard deviation of 30 oranges per tree.
(a) Estimate the population standard deviation from the sample standard deviation.
(b) Estimate the standard error of the mean for this finite population.
(c) Construct a 98 percent confidence interval for the mean per-tree output of all 2,500 trees.
(d) If the mean orange output per tree was 600 oranges 5 years ago, what can Oscar say about the possible existence of damage now?

7-34 Chief of Police Kathy Ackert has recently instituted a crackdown on drug dealers in her city. Since the crackdown began, 750 of the 12,368 drug dealers in the city have been caught. The mean dollar value of drugs found on these 750 dealers is $250,000. The standard deviation of the dollar value of drugs for these 750 dealers is $41,000. Construct for Chief Ackert a 90 percent confidence interval for the mean dollar value of drugs possessed by the city's drug dealers.

7-6
Calculating Interval Estimates of the Proportion from Large Samples

Statisticians often use a sample to estimate a *proportion* of occurrences in a population. For example, the government estimates by a sampling procedure the unemployment rate, or the proportion of unemployed persons, in the U.S. work force.

Review of the binomial distribution

In Chapter 5, we introduced the binomial distribution, a distribution of discrete, not continuous, data. Also, we presented the two formulas for deriving the mean and the standard deviation of the binomial distribution:

$$\mu = np \qquad \text{[5-2]}$$

$$\sigma = \sqrt{npq} \qquad \text{[5-3]}$$

where:

- n = number of trials
- p = probability of success
- $q = 1 - p$ = probability of a failure

Theoretically, the binomial distribution is the correct distribution to use in constructing confidence intervals to estimate a population proportion.

Shortcomings of the binomial distribution

Because the computation of binomial probabilities is so tedious (recall that the probability of r successes in n trials is $[n!/r!(n-r)!][p^r q^{n-r}]$), using the binomial distribution to form interval estimates of a population proportion is a complex proposition. Fortunately, as the sample size increases, the binomial can be approximated by an appropriate normal distribution, which we can use to approximate the sampling distribution. Statisticians recommend that in estimation, n be large enough for both np and nq to be at least 5 when you use the normal distribution as a substitute for the binomial.

Finding the mean of the sample proportion

Symbolically, let's express the proportion of successes in a sample by $\bar{p}$ (pronounced *p-bar*). Then modify Equation 5-2, so that we can use it to derive the *mean of the sampling distribution of the proportion of successes*. In words, $\mu = np$ shows that the mean of the binomial distribution is equal to the product of the number of trials, n, and the probability of success, p; that is, np equals the mean number of successes. To change this *number* of successes to the *proportion* of successes, we divide np by n and get p alone. The mean in the left-hand side of the equation becomes $\mu_{\bar{p}}$, or the mean of the sampling distribution of the proportion of successes:

$$\mu_{\bar{p}} = p \qquad \text{[7-3]}$$

Finding the variance of the sample proportion

Similarly, we can modify the formula for the standard deviation of the binomial distribution, $\sqrt{npq}$, which measures the standard deviation in the number of successes. To change number of successes to proportion of successes, we divide $\sqrt{npq}$ by n and get $\sqrt{pq/n}$. In statistical terms, the standard deviation for the proportion of successes in a sample is symbolized:

$$\text{Standard error of the proportion} \longrightarrow \sigma_{\bar{p}} = \sqrt{\frac{pq}{n}}$$

[7-4]

and is called the *standard error of the proportion.*

WHEN THE POPULATION PROPORTION IS UNKNOWN

We can illustrate how to use these formulas if we estimate for a very large organization what proportion of the employees prefer to provide their own retirement benefits in lieu of a company sponsored plan. First, we conduct a simple random sample of 75 employees and find that .4 of them are interested in providing their own retirement plan. Our results are:

$$n = 75 \leftarrow \text{sample size}$$

$$\bar{p} = .4 \leftarrow \text{sample proportion in favor}$$

$$\bar{q} = .6 \leftarrow \text{sample proportion not in favor}$$

Next, management requests that we use this sample to find an interval about which they can be 99 percent confident that it contains the true population proportion.

Estimating a population proportion

But what are p and q for the *population?* We can estimate the population parameters by substituting the corresponding sample statistics $\bar{p}$ and $\bar{q}$ (*p-bar* and *q-bar*) in the formula for the standard error of the proportion.* Doing this, we get:

Symbol indicating that the standard error of the proportion is estimated

Sample statistics

$$\hat{\sigma}_{\bar{p}} = \sqrt{\frac{\bar{p}\,\bar{q}}{n}}$$

[7-5]

$$= \sqrt{\frac{(.4)(.6)}{75}}$$

$$= \sqrt{\frac{.24}{75}}$$

$$= \sqrt{.0032}$$

$$= .057 \leftarrow \text{estimated standard error of the proportion}$$

Computing the confidence limits

Now we can provide the estimate management needs by using the same procedure we have used previously. A 99 percent confidence level would include 49.5 percent of the area on either side of the mean in the sampling distribution. The body of Appendix Table 1 tells us that .495 of the area under the normal curve is located between the mean and a point 2.58 standard errors from the mean. Thus, 99 percent of the area is contained between plus *and* minus 2.58 standard errors from the mean. Our confidence limits then become:

---

* Notice that we do not use the finite population multiplier, because our population is so large compared with the sample size.

$$\bar{p} + 2.58\hat{\sigma}_{\bar{p}} = .4 + 2.58(.057)$$
$$= .4 + .147$$
$$= .547 \leftarrow \text{upper confidence limit}$$

$$\bar{p} - 2.58\hat{\sigma}_{\bar{p}} = .4 - 2.58(.057)$$
$$= .4 - .147$$
$$= .253 \leftarrow \text{lower confidence limit}$$

Our conclusion   Thus, we estimate from our sample of 75 employees that with 99 percent confidence we believe that the proportion of the total population of employees who wish to establish their own retirement plans lies between .253 and .547.

Exercises

7-35   Pascal, Inc., a computer store that buys wholesale, untested computer chips, is considering switching to another supplier who would provide tested and guaranteed chips for a higher price. In order to determine if this is a cost-effective plan, Pascal must determine the proportion of faulty chips that the current supplier provides. A sample of 200 chips was tested and of these, 5 percent were found to be defective.
  (a)   Estimate the standard error of the proportion of defective chips.
  (b)   Construct a 98 percent confidence interval for the proportion of defective chips supplied.

7-36   When a sample of 70 retail executives was surveyed regarding the poor November performance of the retail industry, 65 percent believed that decreased sales were due to unseasonably warm temperatures, resulting in consumers' delaying purchase of cold-weather items.
  (a)   Estimate the standard error of the proportion of retail executives who blame warm weather for low sales.
  (b)   Find the upper and lower confidence limits for this proportion, given a confidence level equal to .95.

7-37   The product manager for the new lemon-lime Clear 'n Light dessert topping was worried about both the product's poor performance and her future with Clear 'n Light. Concerned that her marketing strategy had not properly identified the attributes of the product, she sampled 1,500 consumers and learned that 956 thought that the product was a floor wax.
  (a)   Estimate the standard error of the proportion of people holding this severe misconception about the dessert topping.
  (b)   Construct a 96 percent confidence interval for the true population proportion.

7-38   Michael Jordon, a professional basketball player, shot 200 foul shots and made 174 of them.
  (a)   Estimate the standard error of the proportion of all foul shots that Michael makes.
  (b)   Construct a 98 percent confidence interval for the proportion of all foul shots that Michael makes.

7-39   Dr. Benjamin Shockley, a noted social psychologist, surveyed 150 top executives and found that 42 percent of them were unable to add fractions correctly.
  (a)   Estimate the standard error of the proportion.
  (b)   Construct a 99 percent confidence interval for the true proportion of top executives who cannot correctly add fractions.

7-40   The owner of the Home Loan Company randomly surveyed 150 of the company's 3,000 accounts and determined that 60 percent were in excellent standing.
  (a)   Find a 95 percent confidence interval for the proportion in excellent standing.

(b) Based on part (a), what kind of interval estimate might you give for the absolute number of accounts that meet the requirement of excellence, keeping the same 95 percent confidence level?

7-41 For a year and a half, sales have been falling consistently in all 1,500 franchises of a fast-food chain. A consulting firm has determined that 30 percent of a sample of 95 indicate clear signs of mismanagement. Construct a 98 percent confidence interval for this proportion.

7-42 Student government at the local university sampled 45 textbooks at the University Student Store and determined that of these 45 textbooks, 60 percent had been marked up in price more than 50 percent over wholesale cost. Give an interval for the proportion of books marked up more than 50 percent by the University Student Store that is 96 percent certain to contain the true proportion.

7-43 Barry Turnbull, the noted Wall Street analyst, is interested in knowing the proportion of individual stockholders who plan to sell at least one quarter of all their stock in the next month. Barry has conducted a random survey of 800 individuals who hold stock and has learned that 25 percent of his sample plan to sell at least one quarter of all their stock in the next month. Barry is about to issue his much-anticipated monthly report, "The Wall Street Pulse—the Tape's Ticker," and would like to be able to report a confidence interval to his subscribers. He is more worried about being correct than he is about the width of the interval. Construct a 90 percent confidence interval for the true proportion of individual stockholders who plan to sell at least one quarter of their stock during the next month.

7-7
Interval Estimates Using the *t* Distribution

In our three examples so far, the sample sizes were all larger than 30. We sampled 100 windshield wiper blades, 50 families living in a four-square-block section of a community, and 75 employees of a very large organization. Each time, the normal distribution was the appropriate sampling distribution to use to determine confidence intervals.

Sometimes the normal distribution is not appropriate

However, this is not always the case. How can we handle estimates where the normal distribution is *not* the appropriate sampling distribution; that is, when we are estimating the population standard deviation and the sample size is 30 or less? For example, in our chapter-opening problem of coal usage, we had data from only 10 weeks. Fortunately, another distribution exists that is appropriate in these cases. It is called the *t distribution.*

Background of the t distribution

Early theoretical work on *t* distributions was done by a man named W. S. Gossett in the early 1900s. Gossett was employed by the Guinness Brewery in Dublin, Ireland, which did not permit employees to publish research findings under their own names. So Gossett adopted the pen name "Student" and published under that name. Consequently, the *t* distribution is commonly called *Student's t distribution,* or simply *Student's distribution.*

Conditions for using the t distribution

Since it is used when the sample size is 30 or less, statisticians often associate the *t* distribution with small sample statistics. This is misleading, because the size of the sample is only *one* of the conditions that lead us to use the *t* distribution. The second condition is that the population standard deviation must be unknown. **Use of the *t* distribution for estimating is required whenever the sample size is 30 or less and the population standard deviation is not known. Furthermore, in using the *t* distribution, we assume that the population is normal or approximately normal.**

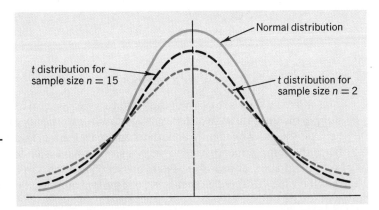

FIGURE 7-3

Normal distribution,
t distribution for
sample size *n* = 15,
and *t* distribution for
sample size *n* = 2

CHARACTERISTICS OF THE *t* DISTRIBUTION

t distribution compared
to normal distribution

Without deriving the *t* distribution mathematically, we can gain an intuitive under-standing of the relationship between the *t* distribution and the *normal* distribution. Both are symmetrical. In general, the *t* distribution is flatter than the normal distri-bution, and there is a different *t* distribution for every possible sample size. Even so, as the sample size gets larger, the shape of the *t* distribution loses its flatness and becomes approximately equal to the normal distribution. In fact, for sample sizes of more than 30, the *t* distribution is so close to the normal distribution that we will use the normal to approximate the *t*.

Figure 7-3 compares one normal distribution with two *t* distributions of different sample sizes. This figure shows two characteristics of *t* distributions: **A *t* distribution is lower at the mean and higher at the tails than a normal distribution.** The figure also demonstrates how the *t* distribution has proportionally more of its area in its tails than the normal does. This is the reason why it will be necessary to go farther out from the mean of a *t* distribution to include the same area under the curve. Interval widths from *t* distributions are, therefore, wider than those based on the normal distribution.

DEGREES OF FREEDOM

Degrees of freedom
defined

We said earlier that there is a separate *t* distribution for each sample size. In proper statistical language, we would say, "There is a different *t* distribution for each of the possible *degrees of freedom*." **What are degrees of freedom? We can define them as the number of values we can choose freely.**

Assume that we are dealing with two sample values, *a* and *b*, and we know that they have a mean of 18. Symbolically, the situation is:

$$\frac{a + b}{2} = 18$$

How can we find what values *a* and *b* can take on in this situation? The answer is that *a* and *b* can be any two values whose sum is 36, because 36 ÷ 2 = 18.

Suppose we learn that *a* has a value of 10. Now *b* is no longer free to take on any value but *must* have the value of 26, because:

$$\text{if} \qquad a = 10$$

$$\text{then} \qquad \frac{10 + b}{2} = 18$$

$$\text{so} \qquad 10 + b = 36$$

$$\text{therefore} \qquad b = 26$$

This example shows that when there are two elements in a sample and we know the sample mean of these two elements, we are free to specify only one of the elements, because the other element will be determined by the fact that the two elements sum to twice the sample mean. Statisticians say, "We have one degree of freedom."

Another example Look at another example. There are seven elements in our sample, and we learn that the mean of these elements is 16. Symbolically, we have this situation:

$$\frac{a + b + c + d + e + f + g}{7} = 16$$

In this case, the degrees of freedom, or the number of variables we can specify freely, are $7 - 1 = 6$. We are free to give values to six variables, and then we are no longer free to specify the seventh variable. It is determined automatically.

With two sample values, we had one degree of freedom ($2 - 1 = 1$), and with seven sample values, we had six degrees of freedom. In each of these two examples, then, we had $n - 1$ degrees of freedom, assuming n is the sample size. Similarly, a sample of 23 would give us 22 degrees of freedom.

Function of degrees of freedom We will use degrees of freedom when we select a t distribution to estimate a population mean, and we will use $n - 1$ degrees of freedom, letting n equal the sample size. If, for example, we use a sample of 20 to estimate a population mean, we will use 19 degrees of freedom in order to select the appropriate t distribution.

USING THE t DISTRIBUTION TABLE

t table compared to z table: 3 differences The table of t distribution values (Appendix Table 2) differs in construction from the z table we have used previously. **The t table is more compact and shows areas and t values for only a few percentages (10, 5, 2, and 1 percent).** Since there is a different t distribution for each number of degrees of freedom, a more complete table would be quite lengthy. Although we can conceive of the need for a more complete table, in fact Appendix Table 2 contains all the commonly used values of the t distribution.

A second difference in the t table is that it does *not* focus on the chance that the population parameter being estimated will fall *within* our confidence interval. Instead, it measures the chance that the population parameter we are estimating will *not* be within our confidence interval (that is, that it will lie *outside* it). If we are making an estimate at the 90 percent confidence level, we would look in the t table under the .10 column (100 percent − 90 percent = 10 percent). This .10 chance of error is symbolized by α, which is the Greek letter *alpha*. We would find the appropriate t values for confidence intervals of 95 percent, 98 percent, and 99 percent under the α columns headed .05, .02, and .01, respectively.

A third difference in using the t table is that we must specify the degrees of freedom with which we are dealing. Suppose we make an estimate at the 90 percent confidence level with a sample size of fourteen, which is thirteen degrees of freedom. Look in Appendix Table 2 under the .10 column until you encounter the row labeled 13 *df* (degrees of freedom). Like a z value, the t value there of 1.771 shows that if we mark off plus and minus 1.771 $\hat{\sigma}_{\bar{x}}$'s (estimated standard errors of $\bar{x}$) on either side of the

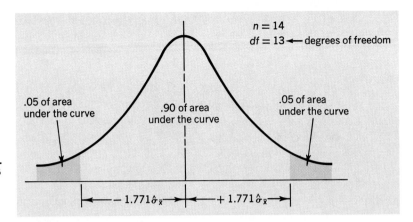

mean, the area under the curve between these two limits will be 90 percent, and the area outside these limits (the chance of error) will be 10 percent (see Fig. 7-4).

Recall that in our chapter-opening problem, the generating plant manager wanted to estimate the coal needed for this year, and he took a sample by measuring coal usage for 10 weeks. The sample data are summarized below:

$$n = 10 \text{ weeks} \leftarrow \text{sample size}$$

$$df = 9 \leftarrow \text{degrees of freedom}$$

$$\bar{x} = 11,400 \text{ tons} \leftarrow \text{sample mean}$$

$$s = 700 \text{ tons} \leftarrow \text{sample standard deviation}$$

Using the *t* table to compute confidence limits

The plant manager wants an interval estimate of the mean coal consumption, and he wants to be 95 percent confident that the mean consumption falls within that interval. **This problem requires the use of a *t* distribution, because the sample size is less than 30 and the population standard deviation is unknown.**

As a first step in solving this problem, recall that we *estimate* the population standard deviation with the sample standard deviation; thus:

$$\hat{\sigma} = s \qquad [7\text{-}1]$$
$$= 700 \text{ tons}$$

Using this estimate of the population standard deviation, we can estimate the standard error of the mean by modifying Equation 7-2 to omit the finite population multiplier (because the population of days is infinite):

$$\hat{\sigma}_{\bar{x}} = \frac{\hat{\sigma}}{\sqrt{n}} \qquad [7\text{-}6]$$
$$= \frac{700}{\sqrt{10}}$$
$$= \frac{700}{3.162}$$

$$= 221.38 \text{ tons} \leftarrow \begin{array}{l} \text{estimated standard error} \\ \text{of the mean of an} \\ \text{infinite population} \end{array}$$

Now we look in Appendix Table 2 down the .05 column (100 percent − 95 percent = 5 percent) until we encounter the row of nine degrees of freedom (10 − 1 = 9). There we see the t value 2.262 and can set our confidence limits accordingly:

$$\bar{x} + 2.262\hat{\sigma}_{\bar{x}} = 11,400 \text{ tons} + 2.262(221.38 \text{ tons})$$
$$= 11,400 + 500.76$$
$$= 11,901 \text{ tons} \leftarrow \text{upper confidence limit}$$

$$\bar{x} - 2.262\hat{\sigma}_{\bar{x}} = 11,400 \text{ tons} - 2.262(221.38 \text{ tons})$$
$$= 11,400 - 500.76$$
$$= 10,899 \text{ tons} \leftarrow \text{lower confidence limit}$$

Our conclusion   We can report to the plant manager with 95 percent confidence that the mean weekly usage of coal lies between 10,899 and 11,901 tons, and we can use the 11,901-ton figure to estimate how much coal to order.

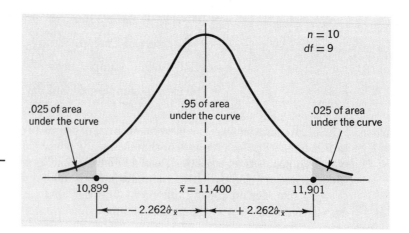

FIGURE 7-5

Coal problem: a *t* distribution with 9 degrees of freedom and a 95 percent confidence interval

The only difference between the process we used to make this coal-usage estimate and the previous estimating problems is the use of the *t* distribution as the appropriate distribution. **Remember that in any estimation problem in which the sample size is 30 or less *and* the standard deviation of the population is unknown *and* the underlying population is normal or approximately normal, we use the *t* distribution.**

SUMMARY OF CONFIDENCE LIMITS UNDER VARIOUS CONDITIONS

Table 7-5 summarizes the various approaches to estimation introduced in this chapter and the confidence limits appropriate for each.

TABLE 7-5 Summary of Formulas for Confidence Limits Estimating Mean and Proportion

	WHEN THE POPULATION IS FINITE	WHEN THE POPULATION IS INFINITE
Estimating μ (the population mean): **When σ (the population standard deviation) is known**	upper limit: $\bar{x} + z\dfrac{\sigma}{\sqrt{n}} \times \sqrt{\dfrac{N-n}{N-1}}$ lower limit: $\bar{x} - z\dfrac{\sigma}{\sqrt{n}} \times \sqrt{\dfrac{N-n}{N-1}}$	$\bar{x} + z\dfrac{\sigma}{\sqrt{n}}$ $\bar{x} - z\dfrac{\sigma}{\sqrt{n}}$
When σ (the population standard deviation) is not known $[\hat{\sigma} = s]$ **When n (the sample size) is larger than 30**	upper limit: $\bar{x} + z\dfrac{\hat{\sigma}}{\sqrt{n}} \times \sqrt{\dfrac{N-n}{N-1}}$ lower limit: $\bar{x} - z\dfrac{\hat{\sigma}}{\sqrt{n}} \times \sqrt{\dfrac{N-n}{N-1}}$	$\bar{x} + z\dfrac{\hat{\sigma}}{\sqrt{n}}$ $\bar{x} - z\dfrac{\hat{\sigma}}{\sqrt{n}}$
When n (the sample size) is 30 or less and the population is normal or approximately normal*	upper limit: $\bar{x} + t\dfrac{\hat{\sigma}}{\sqrt{n}} \times \sqrt{\dfrac{N-n}{N-1}}$ lower limit: $\bar{x} - t\dfrac{\hat{\sigma}}{\sqrt{n}} \times \sqrt{\dfrac{N-n}{N-1}}$	$\bar{x} + t\dfrac{\hat{\sigma}}{\sqrt{n}}$ $\bar{x} - t\dfrac{\hat{\sigma}}{\sqrt{n}}$
Estimating p (the population proportion): **When n (the sample size) is larger than 30** $\left[\hat{\sigma}_{\bar{p}} = \sqrt{\dfrac{\bar{p}\bar{q}}{n}} \right]$	upper limit: $\bar{p} + z\hat{\sigma}_{\bar{p}} \times \sqrt{\dfrac{N-n}{N-1}}$ lower limit: $\bar{p} - z\hat{\sigma}_{\bar{p}} \times \sqrt{\dfrac{N-n}{N-1}}$	$\bar{p} + z\hat{\sigma}_{\bar{p}}$ $\bar{p} - z\hat{\sigma}_{\bar{p}}$

* Remember that the appropriate t distribution to use is the one with $n-1$ degrees of freedom.

Exercises

7-44   For the following sample sizes and confidence levels, find the appropriate t values for constructing confidence intervals:
   (a) $n = 28$; 95%   (c) $n = 13$; 90%   (e) $n = 25$; 99%
   (b) $n = 8$; 98%   (d) $n = 10$; 95%   (f) $n = 10$; 99%

7-45   Given the following sample sizes and t values used to construct confidence intervals, find the corresponding confidence levels:
   (a) $n = 27$; $t = \pm 2.056$
   (b) $n = 5$; $t = \pm 2.132$
   (c) $n = 18$; $t = \pm 2.898$

 7-46   Northern Orange County has found, much to the dismay of the county commissioners, that the population has a severe problem with dental plaque. Every year the local dental board examines a sample of patients and rates each patient's plaque buildup on a scale from 1 to 100 with 1 representing no plaque and 100 representing a great deal of plaque. This year the board examined 21 patients and found that they had an average Plaque Rating Score (PRS) of 72 with a standard deviation of 6.2. Construct for Orange County a 98 percent confidence interval for the mean PRS for Northern Orange County.

7-47 A sample of twelve had a mean of 62 and a standard deviation of 10. Construct a 95 percent confidence interval for the population mean.

7-48 The following sample of eight observations is from an infinite population with normal distribution:

$$75.3 \quad 76.4 \quad 83.2 \quad 91.0 \quad 80.1 \quad 77.5 \quad 84.8 \quad 81.0$$

(a) Find the mean.
(b) Estimate the population standard deviation.
(c) Construct a 98 percent confidence interval for the mean.

7-49 Seven housewives were randomly sampled, and it was determined that they walked an average of 39.2 miles per week in their housework, with a sample standard deviation of 3.2 miles per week. Construct a 95 percent confidence interval for the population mean.

7-50 State Senator Hanna Rowe has ordered an investigation of the large number of boating accidents that have occurred in the state in recent summers. Acting upon her instructions, her aide, Geoff Spencer, has randomly selected 9 summer months within the last few years and has compiled data on the number of boating accidents that occurred during each of these months. The mean number of boating accidents to occur in these 9 months was 31, and the standard deviation in this sample was nine boating accidents per month. Geoff was told to construct a 90 percent confidence interval for the true mean number of boating accidents per month, but he was in such an accident himself recently, so you will have to do this for him.

7-8
Determining the Sample Size in Estimation

In all our discussions so far, we have used for sample size the symbol n instead of a specific number. Now we need to know how to determine what number to use. How large should the sample be? If it is too small, we may fail to achieve the objectives of our analysis. But if it is too large, we waste resources when we gather the sample.

What sample size is adequate?

Some sampling error will arise because we have not studied the whole population. Whenever we sample, we always miss *some* helpful information about the population. If we want a high level of precision (that is, if we want to be quite sure of our estimate), we have to sample enough of the population to provide the required information. Sampling error is controlled by selecting a sample that is adequate in size. In general, the more precision you want, the larger the sample you will need to take. Let us examine some methods that are useful in determining what sample size is necessary for any specified level of precision.

SAMPLE SIZE FOR ESTIMATING A MEAN

Suppose a university is performing a survey of the annual earnings of last year's graduates from its business school. It knows from past experience that the standard deviation of the annual earnings of the entire population (1,000) of these graduates is about $1,500. How large a sample size should the university take in order to estimate the mean annual earnings of last year's class within plus and minus $500 and at a 95 percent confidence level?

Exactly what is this problem asking? The university is going to take a sample of *some* size, determine the mean of the sample, $\bar{x}$, and use it as a point estimate of the population mean. It wants to be 95 percent certain that the true mean annual

TABLE 7-6 Comparison of Two Ways of Expressing the Same Confidence Limits

LOWER CONFIDENCE LIMIT	UPPER CONFIDENCE LIMIT
a. $\bar{x} - \$500$	a. $\bar{x} + \$500$
b. $\bar{x} - z\sigma_{\bar{x}}$	b. $\bar{x} + z\sigma_{\bar{x}}$

Two ways to express a confidence limit

earnings of last year's class are not more than \$500 above or below the point estimate. Row *a* in Table 7-6 summarizes in symbolic terms how the university is defining its confidence limits for us. Row *b* shows symbolically how we normally express confidence limits for an infinite population. When we compare these two sets of confidence limits, we can see that:

$$z\sigma_{\bar{x}} = \$500$$

Thus, the university is actually saying that it wants $z\sigma_{\bar{x}}$ to be equal to \$500. If we look in Appendix Table 1, we find that the necessary z value for a 95 percent confidence level is 1.96. Step by step:

$$\text{If } z\sigma_{\bar{x}} = \$500$$
$$\text{and } z = 1.96$$
$$\text{then } 1.96\ \sigma_{\bar{x}} = \$500$$
$$\text{and } \sigma_{\bar{x}} = \frac{\$500}{1.96}$$
$$= \$255 \leftarrow \text{standard error of the mean}$$

Remember that the formula for the standard error is Equation 6-1:

$$\sigma_{\bar{x}} = \frac{\sigma \longleftarrow \boxed{\text{Population standard deviation}}}{\sqrt{n}} \qquad [6\text{-}1]$$

Finding an adequate sample size

Using Equation 6-1, we can substitute our known population standard deviation value of \$1,500 and our calculated standard error value of \$255 and solve for n:

$$\sigma_{\bar{x}} = \frac{\sigma}{\sqrt{n}} \qquad [6\text{-}1]$$

$$\$255 = \frac{\$1,500}{\sqrt{n}}$$

$$(\sqrt{n})(\$255) = \$1,500$$

$$\sqrt{n} = \frac{\$1,500}{\$255}$$

$$\sqrt{n} = 5.882; \text{ now square both sides}$$

$$n = 34.6 \leftarrow \text{sample size for precision specified}$$

Therefore, since n must be greater than or equal to 34.6, the university should take a sample of 35 business-school graduates to get the precision it wants in estimating the class's mean annual earnings.

FIGURE 7-6

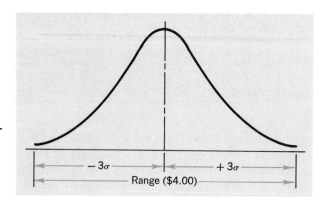

Estimating the standard
deviation from the range

In this example, we knew the standard deviation of the population, but in many cases, the standard deviation of the population is not available. Remember, too, that we have not yet taken the sample, and we are trying to decide how large to make it. We cannot estimate the population standard deviation using methods from the first part of this chapter. If we have a notion about the range of the population, we can use that to get a crude but workable estimate.

Suppose we are estimating hourly manufacturing wage rates in a city and are fairly confident that there is a $4.00 difference between the highest and lowest wage rates. We know that plus and minus 3 standard deviations include 99.7 percent of all the area under the normal curve; that is, plus 3 standard deviations and minus 3 standard deviations include almost all of the distribution. To symbolize this relationship, we have constructed Fig. 7-6, in which $4.00 (the range) equals 6 standard deviations (plus 3 and minus 3). Thus, a rough estimate of the population standard deviation would be:

$$6\hat{\sigma} = \$4.00$$

$$\hat{\sigma} = \frac{\$4.00}{6}$$

Estimate of the population
standard deviation $\longrightarrow \hat{\sigma} = \$0.667$

Our estimate of the population standard deviation using this rough method is not precise, but it may mean the difference between getting a working idea of the required sample size and knowing nothing about that sample size.

SAMPLE SIZE FOR ESTIMATING A PROPORTION

The procedures for determining sample sizes for estimating a population proportion are similar to those for estimating a population mean. Suppose we wish to poll students at a large state university. We want to determine what proportion of them are in favor of a new grading system. We would like a sample size that will enable us to be 90 percent certain of estimating the true proportion that are in favor of the new system within plus and minus .02.

We begin to solve this problem by looking in Appendix Table 1 to find the *z* value for a 90 percent confidence level. That value is plus and minus 1.64 standard errors from the mean. Since we want our estimate to be within .02, we can symbolize the step-by-step process like this:

$$\text{If } z\sigma_{\bar{p}} = .02$$
$$\text{and } z = 1.64$$
$$\text{then } 1.64 \, \sigma_{\bar{p}} = .02$$

If we now substitute the right side of Equation 7-4 for $\sigma_{\bar{p}}$, we get:

$$1.64 \left(\sqrt{\frac{pq}{n}} \right) = .02$$

$$\sqrt{\frac{pq}{n}} = .0122; \text{ now square both sides}$$

$$\frac{pq}{n} = .00014884; \text{ now multiply both sides by } n$$

$$pq = .00014884n$$

$$n = \frac{pq}{.00014884}$$

To find n, we still need an estimate of the population parameters p and q. If we have strong feelings about the actual proportion in favor of the new system, we can use that as our best guess to calculate n. But if we have no idea what p is, then our best strategy is to guess at p in such as way that we choose n in a conservative manner (that is, so that the sample size *is* large enough to supply at least the precision we require no matter what p actually is). At this point in our problem, n is equal to the product of p and q divided by .00014884. The way to get the largest n is to generate the largest possible numerator of that expression, which happens if we pick $p = .5$ and $q = .5$. Then n becomes:

$$n = \frac{pq}{.00014884}$$

$$= \frac{(.5)(.5)}{.00014884}$$

$$= \frac{.25}{.00014884}$$

$$= 1,680 \leftarrow \text{sample size for precision specified}$$

As a result, to be 90 percent certain of estimating the true proportion within .02, we should pick a simple random sample of 1,680 students to interview.

Picking the most conservative proportion

In the problem we have just solved, we picked a value for p that represented the most conservative strategy. The value .5 generated the largest possible sample. We would have used another value of p if we had been able to estimate one *or* if we had a strong feeling about one. Whenever all these solutions are absent, assume the most conservative possible value for p, or .5.

To illustrate that .5 yields the largest possible sample, Table 7-7 solves the grading-system problem using several different values of p. You can see from the sample sizes associated with these different values that for the range of p's from .3 to .7, the change in the appropriate sample size is relatively small. Therefore, even if you knew that the

TABLE 7-7 Sample Size *n* Associated With Different Values of *p* and *q*

CHOOSE THIS VALUE FOR p	VALUE OF q, OR $1-p$	$\left(\dfrac{pq}{.00014884}\right)$	INDICATED SAMPLE SIZE n
.2	.8	$\dfrac{(.2)(.8)}{(.00014884)} =$	1,075
.3	.7	$\dfrac{(.3)(.7)}{.00014884} =$	1,411
.4	.6	$\dfrac{(.4)(.6)}{.00014884} =$	1,613
.5	.5	$\dfrac{(.5)(.5)}{.00014884} =$	1,680 ← most conservative
.6	.4	$\dfrac{(.6)(.4)}{.0014884} =$	1,613
.7	.3	$\dfrac{(.7)(.3)}{.00014884} =$	1,411
.8	.2	$\dfrac{(.8)(.2)}{.0014884} =$	1,075

true population proportion was .3 and you used a value of .5 for *p* anyway, you would have sampled only 269 more people ($1{,}680 - 1{,}411$) than was actually necessary for the desired degree of precision. Obviously, guessing values of *p* in cases like this is not as critical as it seemed at first glance.

Exercises

7-51 If the population standard deviation is 78, find the sample size necessary to estimate the true mean within 50 points for a confidence level of 95 percent.

7-52 For a test market, find the sample size needed to estimate the true proportion of consumers satisfied with a certain new product within ±.04 at the 90 percent confidence level. Assume you have no strong feeling about what the proportion is.

7-53 Given a population with a standard deviation of 8.6, what size sample is needed to estimate the mean of the population within ±.5 with 99 percent confidence?

7-54 We have strong indications that the proportion is around .7. Find the sample size needed to estimate the proportion within ±.02 with confidence level of 90 percent.

7-55 The management of Southern Textiles has recently come under fire regarding the supposedly detrimental effects on health caused by its manufacturing process. A social scientist has advanced a theory that the employees who die from natural causes exhibit remarkable consistency in their life span: The upper and lower limits of their life spans differ by no more than 550 weeks (about 10½ years). For a confidence level of 98 percent, how large a sample should be examined to find the average life span of these employees within ±30 weeks?

7-56 Food Tiger, a local grocery store, sells generic garbage bags and has received quite a few complaints about the strength of these bags. It seems that the generic bags are weaker than the name-brand competitor's bags and, therefore, break more often. John C. Tiger, VP in charge of purchasing, is interested in determining the average maximum weight that can be put into one of the generic bags without its breaking. If the standard deviation of garbage breaking weight is 1.2 lbs, determine the number of bags that must be tested in order for Mr. Tiger to be

95 percent confident that the sample average breaking weight is within .5 lbs of the true average.

✎ 7-57 A speed-reading course guarantees a certain reading rate increase within 2 days. The teacher knows a few people will not be able to achieve this increase, so before stating the guaranteed reading rate increase, he wants to be 98 percent confident that the percentage has been estimated to within ±4 percent of the true value. What is the most conservative sample size needed for this problem?

✎ 7-58 A local store that specializes in candles and clocks, Wicks and Ticks, is interested in obtaining an interval estimate for the mean number of customers that enter the store daily. The owners are reasonably sure that the actual standard deviation of the daily number of customers is fifteen customers. Help Wicks and Ticks out of a fix by determining the sample size it should use in order to develop a 96 percent confidence interval for the true mean that will have a width of only eight customers.

7-9
Terms Introduced in Chapter 7

Confidence Interval A range of values that has some designated probability of including the true population parameter value.

Confidence Level The probability that statisticians associate with an interval estimate of a population parameter indicating how confident they are that the interval estimate will include the population parameter.

Confidence Limits The upper and lower boundaries of a confidence interval.

Consistent Estimator An estimator that yields values more closely approaching the population parameter as the sample size increases.

Degrees of Freedom The number of values in a sample we can specify freely, once we know something about that sample.

Efficient Estimator An estimator with a smaller standard error than some other estimator of the population parameter; i.e., the smaller the standard error of an estimator, the more efficient that estimator is.

Estimate A specific observed value of an estimator.

Estimator A sample statistic used to estimate a population parameter.

Interval Estimate A range of values used to estimate an unknown population parameter.

Point Estimate A single number that is used to estimate an unknown population parameter.

Student's *t* Distribution A family of probability distributions distinguished by their individual degrees of freedom, similar in form to the normal distribution, and used when the population standard deviation is unknown and the sample size is relatively small ($n \leq 30$).

Sufficient Estimator An estimator that uses all the information available in the data concerning a parameter.

Unbiased Estimator An estimator of a population parameter that, on the average, assumes values above the population parameter as often, and to the same extent, as it tends to assume values below the population parameter.

7-10
Equations Introduced in Chapter 7

[7-1]

Estimator of the population standard deviation $\hat{\sigma} = s = \sqrt{\dfrac{\Sigma(x - \bar{x})^2}{n - 1}}$ *p. 314*

This formula indicates that the sample standard deviation can be used as an estimator of the population standard deviation.

$$\hat{\sigma}_{\bar{x}} = \frac{\hat{\sigma}}{\sqrt{n}} \times \sqrt{\frac{N-n}{N-1}}$$

p. 315

This formula enables us to derive an *estimated* standard error of the mean of a *finite* population from an *estimate* of the population standard deviation. The symbol ^, called a hat, indicates that the value is estimated. Equation 7-6 is the corresponding formula for an infinite population.

[7-3]

$$\mu_{\bar{p}} = p$$

p. 317

Use this formula to derive the *mean* of the sampling distribution *of the proportion* of successes. The right-hand side, p, is equal to $(n \times p)/n$, where the numerator is the product of the number of trials and the probability of successes, and the denominator is the number of trials. Symbolically, the proportion of successes *in a sample* is written $\bar{p}$ and is pronounced *p-bar*.

[7-4]

$$\sigma_{\bar{p}} = \sqrt{\frac{pq}{n}}$$

p. 318

To get the *standard error of the proportion,* take the square root of the product of the probabilities of success and failure divided by the number of trials.

[7-5]

$$\hat{\sigma}_{\bar{p}} = \sqrt{\frac{\bar{p}\bar{q}}{n}}$$

p. 318

This is the formula to use to derive an *estimated* standard error of the proportion when the population proportion is unknown and you are forced to use $\bar{p}$ and $\bar{q}$, the sample proportions of successes and failures.

[7-6]

$$\hat{\sigma}_{\bar{x}} = \frac{\hat{\sigma}}{\sqrt{n}}$$

p. 323

This formula enables us to derive an *estimated* standard error of the mean of an *infinite* population from an *estimate* of the population standard deviation. It is exactly like Equation 7-2 except that it lacks the finite population multiplier.

7-11
Chapter Review Exercises

 7-59 From a sample of 42 gasoline stations statewide, the average price of a gallon of unleaded gas was found to be $1.12 with standard deviation $.04 per gallon. In what interval would the true statewide mean per-gallon price of unleaded gasoline fall 99.74 percent of the time?

7-60 What are the advantages of using an interval estimate over a point estimate?

7-61 Why is the size of a statistic's standard error important in its use as an estimator? To which characteristic of estimators does this relate?

 7-62 Suzanne Jones, head registrar for the university system, needs to know what proportion of students have grade-point averages below 2.0. How many students' grades should be looked at in order to determine this proportion to within ±.01 with 95 percent confidence?

7-63 A 95 percent confidence interval for the population mean is given by (94,126) and a 75 percent confidence interval is given by (100.96, 119.04). What are the advantages and disadvantages of each of these interval estimates?

7-64 Fowlers Food Store recently purchased a truckload of 1,500 24-ounce boxes of breakfast cereal. A random sample of 57 of these boxes revealed an average net weight of 23.2 ounces and a standard deviation of .3 ounces.
(a) Estimate the standard deviation of the population from the sample standard deviation.
(b) Estimate the standard error of the mean for this finite population.
(c) What are the upper and lower limits of the confidence interval for the mean net weight given a desired confidence level of .95?

7-65 Given a sample mean of 8, a population standard deviation of 2.6, and a sample size of 32, find the confidence level associated with each of the following intervals:
(a) (7.6136, 8.3864)   (b) (6.85, 9.15)   (c) (7.195, 8.805)

7-66 Based on knowledge about the desirable qualities of estimators, for what reasons might $\bar{x}$ be considered the "best" estimator of the true population mean?

7-67 The president of Offshore Oil has been concerned about the number of fights on his rigs and has been considering various courses of action. In an effort to understand the catalysts of offshore fighting, he randomly sampled 41 days on which a crew had returned from mainland leave. For this sample, the average proportion of workers involved in fisticuffs each day is .032 and the associated standard deviation is .0130.
(a) Give a point estimate for the average proportion of workers involved in fights on any given day that a crew has returned from mainland.
(b) Estimate the population standard deviation associated with this fighting rate.
(c) Find a 90 percent confidence interval for the proportion of returning workers who get involved in fights.

7-68 Given the following expressions for the limits of a confidence interval, find the confidence level associated with the interval:
(a) $\bar{x} - 1.25\sigma_{\bar{x}}$ to $\bar{x} + 1.25\sigma_{\bar{x}}$
(b) $\bar{x} - 2.4\sigma_{\bar{x}}$ to $\bar{x} + 2.4\sigma_{\bar{x}}$
(c) $\bar{x} - 1.68\sigma_{\bar{x}}$ to $\bar{x} + 1.68\sigma_{\bar{x}}$

7-69 Harris Polls Inc., is in the business of surveying households. From previous surveys it is known that the standard deviation of the number of hours of television watched in a week by a household is 1.1 hours. Harris Polls would like to determine the average number of hours of television watched per week per household in the United States. Accuracy is important and, therefore, Harris Polls would like to be 98 percent certain that the sample average number of hours falls within ±.3 hours of the national average. Conservatively, what sample size should Harris Polls use?

7-70 John Bull has just purchased a computer program that claims to pick stocks that will increase in price in the next week with an 85 percent accuracy rate. On how many stocks should John test this program in order to be 98 percent certain that the percentage of stocks that do in fact go up in the next week is within ±.05 of the sample population?

7-71 A ski resort manager in Vermont wants to know the resort's average daily registration. The following table presents the number of guests registered each of 27 randomly selected days. Calculate the sample mean.

61	57	53	60	64	57	54	58	63
59	50	60	60	57	58	62	63	60
61	54	50	54	61	51	53	62	57

7-72 Using the information in exercise 7-71 as a:
(a) Sample, find the sample standard deviation.
(b) Population, find the population standard deviation.

7-73   In evaluating the effectiveness of a federal rehabilitation program, a survey of 52 of a prison's 900 inmates found that 35 percent were repeat offenders.
 (a)   Estimate the standard error of the proportion of repeat offenders.
 (b)   Construct a 90 percent confidence interval for the proportion of repeat offenders among the inmates of this prison.

7-74   During the apple harvest, 105 separate bushels of apples were checked for bad apples (since, as you know, one bad apple can spoil the whole bunch) and it was found that there were an average of 3.2 bad apples per bushel. It is known that the standard deviation of bad apples per bushel is .2 for this type of apple.
 (a)   Calculate the standard error of the mean.
 (b)   Establish an interval estimate around the mean using one standard error of the mean.

7-75   From a random sample of 60 buses, Montreal's mass transit office has calculated the mean number of passengers per kilometer to be 4.1. From previous studies, the population standard deviation is known to be 1.2 passengers per kilometer.
 (a)   Find the standard error of the mean. (Assume that the bus fleet is very large.)
 (b)   Construct a 95 percent confidence interval for the mean number of passengers per kilometer for the population.

7-76   The Internal Revenue Service sampled 200 tax returns recently and found that the sample average income tax refund amounted to $425.39 with sample standard deviation $107.10.
 (a)   Using this information, estimate the population mean tax refund and standard deviation.
 (b)   Using the above estimates, construct an interval in which the population mean is 95 percent certain to fall.

7-77   The Chatham County Rescue Squad is conducting a study to analyze its effectiveness. From a sample of 49 calls, the average response time was 15.2 minutes. The standard deviation of response time is known to be 2.5 minutes from a previous study. Construct a confidence interval for the mean response time with confidence level: (a) 90 percent, (b) 99 percent.

7-78   Bill Wenslaff, an engineer on the staff of a water purification plant, measures the chlorine content in 200 different samples daily. Over a period of years, he has established the population standard deviation to be 1.4 milligrams of chlorine per liter. The latest samples averaged 4.6 milligrams of chlorine per liter.
 (a)   Find the standard error of the mean.
 (b)   Establish the interval around 5.2, the population mean, which will include the sample mean with a probability of 68.7 percent.

7-79   Ellen Harris, an industrial engineer, was accumulating normal times for various tasks on a labor-intensive assembly process. This process included 300 separate job stations, each performing the same assembly task. She sampled seven stations and obtained the following assembly times for each station: 1.9, 2.5, 2.9, 1.3, 2.6, 2.8, and 3.0 minutes.
 (a)   Calculate the mean assembly time and the corresponding standard deviation for the sample.
 (b)   Estimate the population standard deviation.
 (c)   Construct a 98 percent confidence interval for the mean assembly time.

7-80   Larry Culler, the federal grain inspector at a seaport, found spoilage in 40 of 120 randomly selected lots of wheat shipped from the port. Construct a 95 percent confidence interval for him for the actual proportion of lots with spoilage in shipments from that port.

7-81   High Fashion Marketing is considering reintroducing paisley ties. In order to avoid a fashion flop, High Fashion interviewed 90 young executives (their primary market) and found that of the 90 interviewed, 79 believed that paisley ties were fashionable and were interested in purchasing one. Using a confidence level of 98 percent, construct a confidence interval for the proportion of all young executives who find paisley ties fashionable.

7-82   The Department of Transportation has mandated that the average speed of cars on interstate highways must be no more than 67 miles per hour in order for state highway departments to retain their federal funding. North Carolina troopers, in unmarked cars, clocked a sample of

186 cars and found that the average speed was 66.3 miles per hour with a standard deviation of .6 mph.
  (a) Find the standard error of the mean.
  (b) What is the interval around the sample mean that would contain the population mean 95.5 percent of the time?
  (c) Can North Carolina truthfully report that the true mean speed on its highways is 67 mph or less with 95.5% confidence?

7-83 Mark Semmes, owner of the Aurora Restaurant, is considering purchasing new furniture. To help him decide on the amount he can afford to invest in tables and chairs, he wishes to determine the average revenue per customer. He randomly sampled nine customers, whose average check turned out to be $18.30 with a standard deviation of $3.60. Construct a 95 percent confidence interval for the size of the average check per customer.

7-84 John Deer, a horticulturist at Northern Carrboro State University, knows that a certain strain of corn will always produce between 80 and 140 bushels per acre. For a confidence level of 90 percent, how many one-acre samples must be taken in order to estimate the average production per acre to within ±5 bushels per acre?

7-12
Chapter Concepts Test

Answers are in the back of the book.

T F   1. A statistic is said to be an efficient estimator of a population parameter if, with increasing sample size, it becomes almost certain that the value of the statistic comes very close to that of the population parameter.

T F   2. An interval estimate is a range of values used to estimate the shape of a population's distribution.

T F   3. If a statistic tends to assume values higher than the population parameter as frequently as it tends to assume values that are lower, we say that the statistic is an unbiased estimate of the parameter.

T F   4. The probability that a population parameter will lie within a given interval estimate is known as the confidence level.

T F   5. With increasing sample size, the *t* distribution tends to become flatter in shape.

T F   6. We must always use the *t* distribution, rather than the normal, whenever the standard deviation of the population is not known.

T F   7. We may obtain a crude estimate of the standard deviation of some population if we have some information about its range.

T F   8. When using the *t* distribution in estimation, we must assume that the population is approximately normal.

T F   9. Using high confidence levels is not always desirable, because high confidence levels produce large confidence intervals.

T F 10. There is a different *t* distribution for each possible sample size.

T F 11. A point estimate is often insufficient, because it is either right or wrong.

T F 12. A sample mean is said to be an unbiased estimator of a population mean because no other estimator could extract from the sample additional information about the population mean.

T F 13. The most frequently used estimator of σ is s.

T F 14. The standard error of the proportion is calculated as $\sqrt{\dfrac{p(1-p)}{n}}$.

T F 15. The degrees of freedom used in a t-distribution estimation are equal to the sample size.

T F 16. The t distribution is less able to approximate a normal distribution as the sample size increases.

T F 17. The t distribution need not be used in estimating if you know the standard deviation of the population.

T F 18. The sample median is always the best estimator of the population median.

T F 19. As the width of a confidence interval increases, the associated confidence level also increases.

T F 20. Estimating the standard error of the mean of a finite population using an estimate of the population standard deviation requires the use of the t distribution for calculating subsequent confidence intervals.

T F 21. The percentages in the t-distribution table correspond to the chance that the true population parameter will fall outside our confidence interval.

T F 22. In a normal distribution, 100% of the population lies within ± 3 standard deviations of the mean.

23. When choosing an estimator of a population parameter, one should consider:
    (a) Sufficiency   (c) Efficiency   (e) a and c but not b
    (b) Clarity   (d) All of these

24. Suppose that 200 members of a group were asked whether or not they liked a particular product. Fifty said yes; 150 said no. Assuming "yes" means a success, which of the following is correct?
    (a) $\bar{p} = .33$ (b) $\bar{p} = .25$ (c) $p = .33$ (d) $p = .25$ (e) b and d only

25. Assume that you take a sample and calculate $\bar{x}$ as 100. You then calculate the upper limit of a 90 percent confidence interval for μ; its value is 112. What is the lower limit of this confidence interval?
    (a) 88   (c) 100
    (b) 92   (d) Cannot be determined from the information given

26. After taking a sample and computing $\bar{x}$, a statistician says, "I am 88 percent confident that the population mean is between 106 and 122." What does she really mean?
    (a) The probability is .88 that μ is between 106 and 122.
    (b) The probability is .88 that $\mu = 114$, the midpoint of the interval.
    (c) 88 percent of the intervals calculated from samples of this size will contain the population mean.
    (d) All of these.
    (e) a and c but not b.

27. Which of the following is a necessary condition for using a t-distribution table?
    (a) n is small.   (d) All of these.
    (b) s is known but σ is not.   (e) a and b but not c.
    (c) The population is infinite.

28. Which of the following t distributions would be expected to have the most area in its tails?
    (a) $\bar{x} = .83$, degrees of freedom $= 12$ (c) $\bar{x} = 15$, $n = 19$
    (b) $\bar{x} = 15$, degrees of freedom $= 19$ (d) $\bar{x} = 8.3$, $n = 12$

29. Which of the following is a difference between z tables and t tables?
    (a) The t table has values for only a few percentages.
    (b) The t table measures the chance that the population parameter we are estimating will be in our confidence interval.
    (c) We must specify the degrees of freedom with which we are dealing when using a z table.
    (d) All of these.
    (e) a and b but not c.

30. Suppose we are attempting to estimate a population variance by using s^2. It is incorrect to calculate s^2 as $\dfrac{\Sigma(x - \bar{x})^2}{n}$ because the value would be:
    (a) Biased   (b) Inefficient   (c) Inconsistent   (d) Insufficient

31. When considering samples with size greater than 30, we use the normal table, even if the population standard deviation is unknown. Why is this?

336

(a) Calculation of degrees of freedom becomes difficult for large sample sizes.

(b) The number of percentages we need for calculation of confidence intervals exceeds the number contained in the t tables.

(c) It is difficult to calculate $\bar{x}$ (and hence s^2) for large samples.

(d) None of these.

(e) a and c but not b.

32. Assume that, from a population with $N = 50$, a sample of size fifteen is drawn; σ^2 is known to be 36, and s^2 for the sample is 49; $\bar{x}$ for the sample is calculated as 104. Which of the following should be used for calculating a 95 percent confidence interval for μ?

(a) Student's t distribution   (d) a and c but not b

(b) Normal distribution   (e) b and c but not a

(c) Finite population multiplier

33. We can use the normal distribution to represent the sampling distribution of the population when:

(a) The sample size is more than 10   (c) The sample size is more than 5

(b) The sample size is less than 50   (d) None of these

34. If a statistic underestimates a population parameter as much as it overestimates it, we would call it:

(a) Consistent   (c) Efficient   (e) None of these

(b) Sufficient   (d) All of these

35. If population proportion information is unknown, the standard error of the proportion can be estimated by the formula:

(a) $\sqrt{npq}$ (b) $\sqrt{n\bar{p}\bar{q}}$ (c) $\sqrt{pq/n}$ (d) $\sqrt{\bar{p}\bar{q}/n}$

36. The average height of the 25 students in Mr. Stanton's tenth grade math class is known to be 66″. In constructing a 95% confidence interval for the average height of all tenth graders, we would use:

(a) the normal distribution with 24 degrees of freedom.

(b) The t distribution with 24 degrees of freedom.

(c) the t distribution with 65 degrees of freedom.

(d) The t distribution with 25 degrees of freedom.

37. A certain normally distributed population has a known standard deviation of 1.0. What is the total width of a 95% confidence interval for the population mean?

(a) 1.96

(b) 0.98

(c) 3.92

(d) Cannot be determined from the information given.

38. A single number used to estimate an unknown population parameter is a _____ estimate.

39. A range of values used to estimate an unknown population parameter is a _____ estimate.

40. Once we know something about a sample, the number of values in the sample we can specify freely is called _____.

41. The family of probability distributions used when population standard deviation is unknown, sample size is small, and values approximate the normal is the _____.

42. When we give an interval estimate of a population parameter, we show how sure we are that the interval contains the actual population parameter by setting a _____ level.

43. The upper confidence limit and lower confidence limit are the same _____ from the _____.

44. Theoretically, the _____ distribution is the correct distribution to use in constructing confidence intervals to estimate a population proportion.

45. In the absence of additional information, a value of _____ should be used for p when determining a sample size for estimating a population proportion.

7-13

Conceptual Case

(Northern White Metals Company)

Jody Wallis had begun her career in the statistical services department of a large health care insurance company but soon decided to switch to the more glamorous atmosphere of a diversified manufacturing enterprise. Sarah Porter, although less experienced, was highly respected for her technical competence and well liked for her friendly, open manner.

Both had set right to work, as the CEO had said they would, and Dick was very pleased with their progress. A thorough analysis of automated operations in the fabricating department had ultimately resulted in more efficient quality control procedures. Improvements were suggested and effected in the anodizing department as well. Impressed with their dedication and teamwork and the easy way they got along with the employees at Northern, Dick thought what a valuable addition they would be to his staff. His thoughts were interrupted as NWMC's two top sales reps, Bill Hamilton and Lynn Martin, rapped on his half-open office door.

Dick beckoned them in and inquired as to the nature of the unexpected visit.

"We didn't think this should wait until next week's sales meeting," Bill began. "As you know, there have been problems with a few of my accounts, similar to those with NES Electronics."

"I am painfully aware of them," Dick replied, "but I believe our corporate technical staff people have the quality control situation in hand. They've really done a good job," he said enthusiastically.

"That's exactly why we're here," Lynn noted. "Bill and I were hoping that Jody and Sarah could help us

gain back some of the ground we've lost with some important customers." She went on to explain that some of these accounts were displaying a lack of confidence in the quality of NWMC's products and were now reluctant to commit to large volume orders.

At that moment, Jody appeared in the doorway, a stack of paper in hand.

"Sorry to intrude," she started.

"No, not at all," Dick interrupted, "come in."

"Sarah and I have just about finished and I wanted to go over this with you," she said.

"Good," Dick responded. "While you are here, perhaps you can help Lynn and Bill with a sales problem."

Jody answered that she would be happy to try, and Lynn continued where she had left off.

"A few important customers have recently had problems with some of our products. We need something specific, something more than fast talk, to convince them that the situation has improved," Lynn said earnestly. "What kind of assurances can be given about our product quality now?" she asked.

"Well," Jody answered with a smile, "what kind of assurances do you need?"

Lynn and Bill need some technical support for their sales presentations to some customers who have become a bit unsure of NWMC's ability to deliver a product that will conform to specifications. What kind of evidence might be provided that new, more effective quality control procedures are in place? What kind of information will Jody require to provide such evidence?

7-14

Computer Data Base Exercise

 Early the following week, Bob was back in Laurel's office. "Well, we've started pulling our sample," he said. "Could you help me get a feel for exactly how many to examine? I'm interested in a 95% confidence level of being within plus or minus .05 of the actual population proportion. I think you'd agree that, for all practical purposes, we can consider our population to be infinite."

"I think you're right," Laurel agreed. "I've seen your row of filing cabinets! As far as the number to pull, it would help if we had an educated guess for the actual population parameter, but we can at least come up with a range of sample sizes for you."

1. Determine an appropriate sample size for satisfying Bob's conditions if the actual value of p (the proportion of purchase orders competitively bid) is approximately .2, .3, .4, or .5. Which should Bob choose?

About a week later, Bob knocked on Laurel's door. "Here's the raw data. Hal's goal for us at this point is to have at least 60% of the purchase orders competitively bid. Think this will make him happy?"

"Let's calculate our confidence interval and see," Laurel answered.

2. Estimate the proportion and standard error of the proportion for competitively bid purchase

orders using Table DB7-1. Construct a 95% confidence interval for the proportion.

Bob looked skeptically at the results. "Is there any way we can tighten those confidence interval boundaries?" he asked.

"Without any additional sampling effort, you're limited to lowering the confidence level," Laurel explained.

3. Calculate the boundaries of the confidence interval if Bob is willing to settle for a 90% confidence level.

"The other alternative is to try a larger sample," she continued. "Since sampling, in this case, is relatively inexpensive, why not aim for a tighter interval — say, plus or minus .03. We can use our initial proportion as our 'educated guess' about the population's true proportion and maintain our 95% confidence level."

"But how much larger a sample will that require?" asked Bob.

"I can tell you in a second," Laurel replied, pulling out her trusty calculator.

4. Under these new conditions, how many more purchase orders need to be examined?

"Good news!" Bob announced to Laurel several days later. "The new, larger sample showed a proportion of .58. That means I can tell the boss we're between .55 and .61 with 95% confidence. I'm planning on putting a short presentation together for Monday's staff meeting."

"Sounds good," said Laurel. "Just be careful how you throw around your terms. Remember we've got some statistical rookies in there and you don't want to give them the wrong impression."

5. Verify Bob's calculations. What do you think Laurel is concerned about, and how would you focus your presentation if you were Bob?

Bob's presentation went well at Monday's staff meeting. Hal asked a few questions, but was generally pleased with the results. Then he introduced the next order of business.

"As most of you know, we introduced metric parts into our inventory about a year ago. With the influx of mobile hydraulic equipment made overseas by companies like Toyota, Nissan, and Komatsu, the market for metric repair parts seemed to be ripe. And as far as I know, we were the first in our industry to carry several complete lines. At any rate, it's time to see how we're doing and estimate potential sales for the next year. Laurel, I'm afraid we're not giving you much of a break, but you can see that we definitely need you here!"

Back in her office, Laurel reviewed what she knew about HH Industries' metric product lines. Peggy was in the process of running a report which would give Laurel details on sales for the last year. Unfortunately, when metric parts were first incorporated, they weren't given a unique product code designation, which made their sales a little hard to isolate. Nevertheless, she'd do what she could.

6. Based on the data in Table DB7-2, estimate the population mean and standard deviation of weekly metric sales.

7. Estimate the standard error of the mean for this sample.

8. Construct a 95% confidence interval for mean weekly sales of metric parts.

TABLE DB7-1

PURCHASE ORDER DATA (Y — Competitively Bid, N — Sole Source)

```
Y N Y Y Y N N Y Y Y N N N Y N Y Y N N Y Y N N Y N N Y N N Y
N N N Y Y Y Y N N N Y N N Y Y Y N Y Y Y N Y N N N Y Y Y N Y
N N N Y Y Y Y N N Y Y N Y N Y N Y Y N Y Y Y Y N Y N Y N N Y N
Y Y Y N N N Y N Y Y N N Y N Y N Y Y N N Y Y N N N Y N Y
N Y N Y N Y Y N Y Y N Y N Y N N Y N Y Y N N Y Y Y N N Y Y
N N N Y N Y Y Y N Y Y Y Y Y N Y N Y N Y N Y Y Y Y Y Y Y
Y Y N N Y Y Y N Y N Y N Y Y Y N N Y N Y Y Y N Y N N N Y Y
Y Y N N N Y N Y Y Y Y Y N Y N N N N Y Y Y Y N Y N Y Y N N
N Y N N Y Y N Y N Y N Y N Y N Y N Y Y N Y N Y N Y
Y Y Y N Y N Y Y N N Y N N N N Y Y N N N Y Y Y N N N Y Y
Y N Y N Y Y N N N Y Y Y Y N N N Y Y Y Y Y Y N N N Y N Y
N N Y N Y N N N Y Y Y N Y Y Y Y Y N Y N Y Y Y Y Y N N N Y N
Y N N Y Y N N Y N Y Y N Y N Y Y Y N Y Y Y N N N Y N
```

9. Should HH Industries continue to carry metric parts if Hal wants to be 95% certain the next year's sales will be at least $300,000? Assume there will be 50 sales weeks in the coming year.

10. Stan argued that using all 12 months of metric sales data resulted in an unreasonably low estimate, since it included those months when metric parts were first introduced. He is convinced that using the second 6 months of data will show a more accurate prediction, as sales will have leveled off. Laurel agrees. Repeat the above calculations using just the second 25 weeks of data in Table DB7-2.

TABLE DB7-2

METRIC SALES (Weekly sales dollars)				
Jan	2020	3260	2800	3190	
Feb	3450	2930	3060	3260	
Mar	3710	4100	3130	4620	
Apr	6840	8920	10610	8140	7940
May	7490	5660	6380	6120	
Jun	5530	7360	4950	4750	
Jul	9200	8830	6490	4520	
Aug	3780	9290	6110	7240	
Sep	8730	6730	4380	8050	5580
Oct	4360	8290	9890	7970	
Nov	3580	5370	9640	8460	
Dec	7050	5630	2910	4960	

7-15
From the Textbook to the Real World

The Berkeley Engineering Fund

Established in 1979, the Berkeley Engineering Fund solicits contributions to support the College of Engineering at the University of California, Berkeley. Administrators use information about past numbers of donors, gifts, and dollar contributions as input to a mathematical model for predicting monthly and end-of-year contributions. Then they adjust fund-raising efforts accordingly. The model uses a binomial distribution for the numbers of donors and gifts, and a compound Poisson distribution for total dollars contributed. Since 1982, data on donor counts, timing, size of donations, and matching gifts have been recorded for parents, faculty, alumni, and friends of the College.

Parameter Estimation. Forecasts are based on data from previous campaigns. Since identical mailings were used from 1982 to 1984, monthly proportions of total giving have been stable from year to year. For each mailing date, the forecasters determined distributions for the number of gifts from each of the four subgroups, as well as estimates of the mean and variance of gift size.

Mark Britto and Robert M. Oliver, "Forecasting Donors and Donations," *Journal of Forecasting*, vol. 5, pp. 39–55, 1986.

Evaluating the Model. Parent data from 1982–3 and 1983–4 were used to test the Poisson assumption on which the model is based. Using both Poisson tables and a normal approximation, 95% confidence intervals were computed for the monthly numbers of parent donors. Figures RW7.1 and RW7.2 show these intervals for 1982–3 and 1983–4. Only in September of both years did the actual donor counts fall outside the 95% confidence intervals. This supports the assumption of a Poisson distribution.

Results. The model performed well in forecasting year-end totals, but less well on a month-to-month basis. Predictions of donor counts, gift counts, and total donations were more accurate for the parent, faculty, and friend groups than they were for alumni. Administrators gained a better understanding of the effects of personal contacts and mailings. Because the model provided a way to predict the effects of changes in fund-raising techniques, it encouraged administrators to design strategies targetted to specific constituencies.

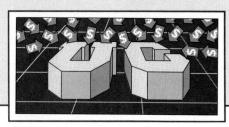

**1982–1983 fitting
monthly parent
donor counts**

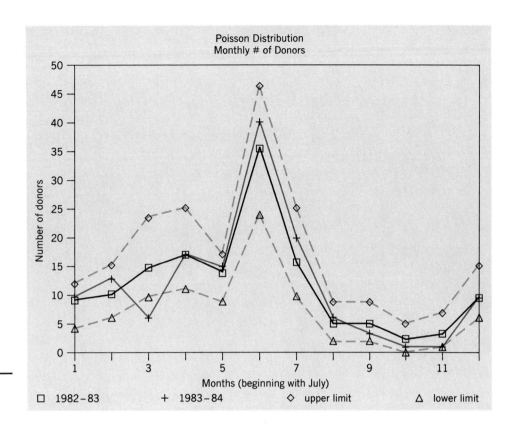

**1983–1984 fitting
monthly parent
donor counts**

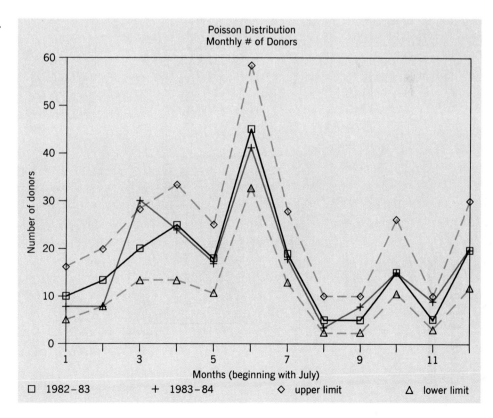

7-16
Flow Chart

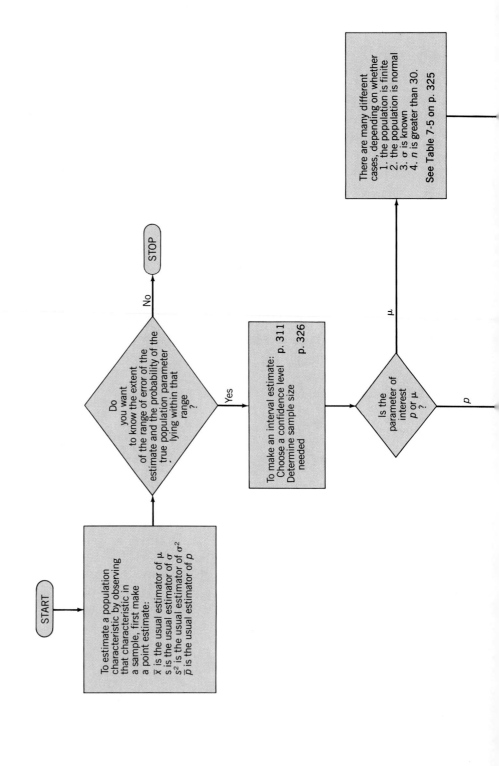

START

To estimate a population characteristic by observing that characteristic in a sample, first make a point estimate:

$\bar{x}$ is the usual estimator of μ
s is the usual estimator of σ
s^2 is the usual estimator of σ^2
$\bar{p}$ is the usual estimator of p

Do you want to know the extent of the range of error of the estimate and the probability of the true population parameter lying within that range?

No → **STOP**

Yes ↓

To make an interval estimate:
Choose a confidence level   p. 311
Determine sample size   p. 326
needed

Is the parameter of interest p or μ?

μ ↑

p →

There are many different cases, depending on whether
1. the population is finite
2. the population is normal
3. σ is known
4. n is greater than 30.

See Table 7-5 on p. 325

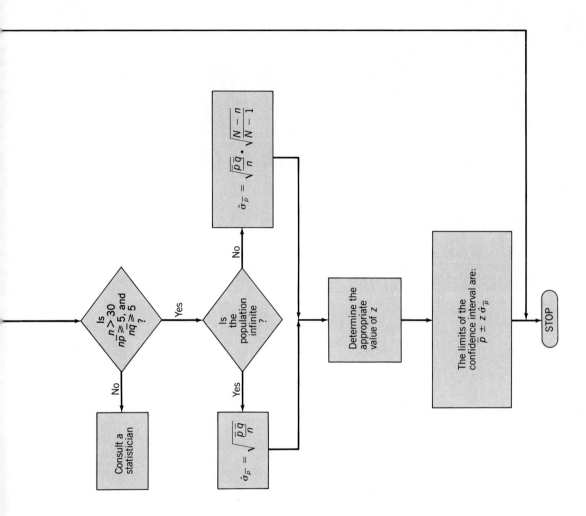

The roofing contract for a new sports complex in San Francisco has been awarded to Parkhill Associates, a large building contractor. Building specifications call for a movable roof covered by approximately 10,000 sheets of .04-inch-thick aluminum. The aluminum sheets cannot be appreciably thicker than .04 inches because the structure could not support the additional weight. Nor can the sheets be appreciably thinner than .04 inches because the strength of the roof would be inadequate. Because of this restriction on thickness, Parkhill carefully checks the aluminum sheets from its supplier. Of course, Parkhill does not want to measure each sheet, so it randomly samples 100. The sheets in the sample have a mean thickness of .0408 inches. From past experience with this supplier, Parkhill believes that these sheets come from a thickness population with a standard deviation of .004 inches. On the basis of this data, Parkhill must decide whether the 10,000 sheets meet specifications. In Chapter 7, we used sample statistics to estimate population parameters. Now, to solve problems like Parkhill's, we shall learn how to use characteristics of samples to test an assumption we have about the population from which that sample came. Our test for Parkhill, later in the chapter, may lead Parkhill to accept the shipment, or it may indicate that Parkhill should reject the aluminum sheets sent by the supplier because they do not meet the architectural specifications.

8

Testing Hypotheses

■ **OBJECTIVES**

The subject of Chapter 8 is *hypothesis testing.* Here we are trying to determine when it is reasonable to conclude, from analysis of a sample, that the entire population possesses a certain property, and when it is not reasonable to reach such a conclusion. Suppose a student purchases a $500 second-hand car from a dealer who advertises, "Our cars are the finest, most dependable in town." If the car's repair bills during the first month are $600, that one-car sample may cause the student to conclude that the dealer's population of used cars is probably not as advertised. Chapter 8 will allow us to test and evaluate larger samples than those available to the buyer of the used car.

Hypothesis testing begins with an assumption, called a *hypothesis,* that we make about a population parameter. Then we collect sample data, produce sample statistics, and use this information to decide how likely it is that our hypothesized population parameter is correct. Say that we assume a certain value for a population mean. To test the validity of our assumption, we gather sample data and determine the difference between the hypothesized value and the actual value of the sample mean. Then we judge whether the difference is significant. The smaller the difference, the greater the likelihood that our hypothesized value for the mean is correct. The larger the difference, the smaller the likelihood.

Unfortunately, the difference between the hypothesized population parameter and the actual sample statistic is more often neither so large that we automatically reject our hypothesis nor so small that we just as quickly accept it. So in hypothesis testing as in most significant real-life decisions, clear-cut solutions are the exception, not the rule.

Suppose a manager of a large shopping mall tells us that the average work efficiency of her employees is 90 percent. How can we test the validity of her hypothesis? Using the sampling methods we learned in Chapter 6, we could calculate the efficiency of a *sample* of her employees. If we did this and the sample statistic came out to be 93 percent, we would readily accept the manager's statement. However, if the sample statistic were 46 percent, we would reject her assumption as untrue. We can interpret both these outcomes, 93 percent and 46 percent, using our common sense.

The basic problem will
be dealing with
uncertainty

Now suppose that our sample statistic reveals an efficiency of 81 percent. This value is relatively close to 90 percent. But is it close enough for us to accept the manager's hypothesis? Whether we accept or reject the manager's hypothesis, we cannot be absolutely certain that our decision is correct; therefore we will have to learn to deal with uncertainty in our decision making. **We cannot accept or reject a hypothesis about a population parameter simply by intuition. Instead, we need to learn how to decide objectively, on the basis of sample information, whether to accept or reject a hunch.**

MAKING BIG JUMPS

College students often see ads for learning aids. One very popular such aid is a combination outline, study guide, and question set for various courses. Advertisements about such items often claim better examination scores with less studying time. Suppose a "study guide" for a basic statistics course is available through an organization that produces such guides for 50 different courses. If this study guide for basic statistics has been tested (and let us assume properly), the firm may advertise that "our study guides have been statistically proven to raise grades and lower study time." Of course this assertion is quite true, but only as it applies to the basic statistics experience. There may be no evidence of statistical significance that establishes the same kind of results for the other 49 guides.

Another product may be advertised as being beneficial in removing crab grass from your lawn and may assert that the product has been "thoroughly tested" on real lawns. Even if we assume that the proper statistical procedures were, in fact, used during the tests, such claims still involve "big jumps." Suppose that the test plot was in Florida, and your lawn problems are in Utah. Differences in rainfall, soil fertility, airborne pollutants, temperature, dormancy hours, and germination conditions may vary widely between these two locations. Claiming results for a statistically valid test under a completely different set of test conditions is invalid. One such test cannot measure effectiveness under a wide variety of environmental conditions.

Exercises

8-1 Why must we be required to deal with uncertainty in our decisions, even when using statistical techniques?

8-2 Theoretically speaking, how might one go about testing the hypothesis that a coin is fair? that a die is fair?

8-3 Is it possible that a false hypothesis will be accepted? How would you explain this?

8-4 Describe the hypothesis-testing process.

8-5 How would you explain a large difference between a hypothesized population parameter and a sample statistic, if, in fact, the hypothesis is true?

8-2
Concepts Basic to the Hypothesis-Testing Procedure

Sports-complex problem

Before we introduce the formal statistical terms and procedures, we'll work our chapter-opening sports-complex problem all the way through. Recall that the aluminum roofing sheets have a claimed average thickness of .04 inches and that they will be unsatisfactory if they are too thick *or* too thin. The contractor takes a sample of 100 sheets and determines that the sample mean thickness is .0408 inches. On the basis of past experience, he knows that the population standard deviation is .004 inches. Does this sample evidence indicate that the batch of 10,000 sheets of aluminum is suitable for constructing the roof of the new sports complex?

Formulating the hypothesis

If we assume that the true mean thickness is .04 inches, and we know that the population standard deviation is .004 inches, how likely is it that we would get a sample mean of .0408 or more from that population? In other words, **if the true mean is .04 inches, and the standard deviation is .004 inches, what are the chances of getting a sample mean that differs from .04 inches by .0008 inches or more?**

These questions show that **to determine whether the population mean is actually .04 inches, we must calculate the probability that a random sample with a mean of .0408 inches will be selected from a population with a μ of .04 inches and a σ of .004 inches. This probability will indicate whether it is *reasonable* to observe a sample like this if the population mean is actually .04 inches.** If this probability is far too low, we must conclude that the aluminum company's statement is false and that the mean thickness of the aluminum sheets is not .04 inches.

To answer the question illustrated in Fig. 8-1: If the hypothesized population mean is .04 inches and the population standard deviation is .004 inches, what are the

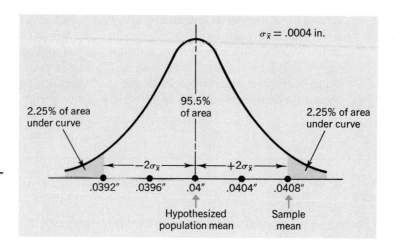

FIGURE 8-1

Probability that $\bar{x}$ will differ from hypothesized μ by 2 standard errors or more

chances of getting a sample mean (.0408 inches) that differs from .04 inches by .0008 inches? First we calculate the standard error of the mean from the population standard deviation:

Calculating the standard error of the mean

$$\sigma_{\bar{x}} = \frac{\sigma}{\sqrt{n}}$$ [6-1]

$$= \frac{.004 \text{ in.}}{\sqrt{100}}$$

$$= \frac{.004 \text{ in.}}{10}$$

$$= .0004 \text{ in.}$$

Next we use Equation 6-2 to discover that the mean of our sample (.0408 inches) lies 2 standard errors to the right of the hypothesized population mean:

$$z = \frac{\bar{x} - \mu}{\sigma_{\bar{x}}}$$ [6-2]

$$= \frac{.0408 - .04}{.0004}$$

$$= 2 \leftarrow \text{standard errors of the mean}$$

Interpreting the probability associated with this difference

Using Appendix Table 1, we learn that 4.5 percent is the *total chance* of our sample mean differing from the population mean by 2 or more standard errors; that is, the chances that the sample mean would be .0408 inches or larger or .0392 inches or smaller are only 4.5 percent ($P(z \geq 2 \text{ or } z \leq -2) = 2(.5 - .4722) = .0456$, or about 4.5 percent). **With this low a chance, Parkhill could conclude that a population with a true mean of .04 inches would not be likely to produce a sample like this.** The project supervisor would reject the aluminum company's statement about the mean thickness of the sheets.

The decision maker's
role in formulating
hypotheses

In this case, the difference between the sample mean and the hypothesized population mean is too large, and the chance that the population would produce such a random sample is far too low. Why this probability of 4.5 percent is too low, or wrong, is a judgment for decision makers to make. Certain situations demand that decision makers be very sure about the characteristics of the items being tested, and then even 20 percent is too high to be attributable to chance. Other processes allow for a wider latitude or variation, and a decision maker might accept a hypothesis with a 4.5 percent probability of chance variation. In each situation, we must try to determine the costs resulting from an incorrect decision and the precise level of risk we are willing to assume.

Risk of rejection

In our example, we rejected the aluminum company's contention that the population mean is .04 inches. But suppose for a moment that the population mean is *actually* .04 inches. If we then stuck to our rejection rule of 2 standard errors or more (the 4.5 percent probability or less in the tails of Fig. 8-1), we would reject a perfectly good lot of aluminum sheets 4.5 percent of the time. Therefore, **our minimum standard for an acceptable probability, 4.5 percent is** *also* **the** *risk* **we take of** *rejecting* **a** *hypothesis that is true.* **In this or any decision making, there can be no risk-free tradeoff.**

Exercises

8-6   What do we mean when we reject a hypothesis on the basis of a sample?

8-7   Explain why there is no single level of probability used to reject or accept in hypothesis testing.

8-8   If we reject a hypothesized value because it differs from a sample statistic by more than 1.75 standard errors, what is the probability that we have rejected a hypothesis that is in fact true?

8-9   How many standard errors around the hypothesized value should we use to be 99.44 percent certain that we accept the hypothesis when it is true?

8-10   Sports and media magnate Ned Sterner is interested in purchasing the Atlanta Stalwarts, if he can be reasonably certain that operating the team will not be too costly. He figures that average attendance would have to be about 28,500 fans per game to make the purchase attractive to him. Ned randomly chooses 64 home games over the past 4 years and finds from figures reported in *Sporting Reviews* that average attendance at these games was 26,100. A study he commissioned the last time he purchased a team showed that the population standard deviation for attendance at similar events had been quite stable for the past 10 years at about 6,000 fans. Using 2 standard errors as the decision criterion, should Ned purchase the Stalwarts? Can you think of any reason(s) why your conclusion might not be valid?

8-11   *Computing World* has asserted that the average owner of a personal computer spends 23.9 hours per week using his or her machine, with a standard deviation of 12.6 hours per week. A random sampling of 81 of its subscribers revealed a sample mean usage of 27.2 hours per week. On the basis of this sample, is it reasonable to conclude (using 2 standard errors as the decision criterion) that *Computing World*'s subscribers are different from average personal computer owners?

8-12   An automobile manufacturer claims that a particular model gets 28 miles to the gallon. The Environmental Protection Agency, using a sample of 49 automobiles of this model, finds the sample mean to be 26.8 miles per gallon. From previous studies, the population standard deviation is known to be five miles per gallon. Could we reasonably expect (within 2 standard errors) that we could select such a sample if indeed the population mean is actually 28 miles per gallon?

8-3
Testing Hypotheses

Making a formal
statement of the null
hypothesis

In hypothesis testing, we must state the assumed or hypothesized value of the population parameter *before* we begin sampling. The assumption we wish to test is called the *null hypothesis* and is symbolized H_0, or "H sub-zero."

Suppose we want to test the hypothesis that the population mean is equal to 500. We would symbolize it as follows and read it, "The null hypothesis is that the population mean is equal to 500":

$$H_0 : \mu = 500$$

The term *null hypothesis* arises from earlier agricultural and medical applications of statistics. In order to test the effectiveness of a new fertilizer or drug, the tested hypothesis (the null hypothesis) was that it had *no effect;* that is, there was no difference between treated and untreated samples.

If we use a hypothesized value of a population mean in a problem, we would represent it symbolically as:

$$\mu_{H_0}$$

This is read, "The hypothesized value of the population mean."

If our sample results fail to support the null hypothesis, we must conclude that something else is true. **Whenever we reject the null hypothesis, the conclusion we do accept is called the *alternative hypothesis* and is symbolized H_1 ("H sub-one").** For the null hypothesis:

$$H_0 : \mu = 200 \text{ (Read: "The null hypothesis is that}$$
$$\text{the population mean is equal to 200.")}$$

Making a formal
statement of the
alternative hypothesis

we will consider three possible alternative hypotheses:

- $H_1 : \mu \neq 200 \leftarrow$ "The alternative hypothesis is that the population mean is *not equal* to 200."
- $H_1 : \mu > 200 \leftarrow$ "The alternative hypothesis is that the population mean is *greater than* 200."
- $H_1 : \mu < 200 \leftarrow$ "The alternative hypothesis is that the population mean is *less than* 200."

INTERPRETING THE SIGNIFICANCE LEVEL

The purpose of hypothesis testing is not to question the computed value of the sample statistic but to make a judgment about the *difference* between that sample statistic and a hypothesized population parameter. The next step after stating the null and alternative hypotheses, then, is to decide what criterion to use for deciding whether to accept or reject the null hypothesis.

In our sports-complex example, we decided that a difference observed between the sample mean $\bar{x}$ and the hypothesized population mean μ_{H_0} had only a 4.5 percent, or .045, chance of occurring. Therefore, we rejected the null hypothesis that the population mean was .04 inches ($H_0 : \mu = .04$ inches). In statistical terms, the value .045 is called the *significance level.*

What if we test a hypothesis at the 5 percent level of significance? This means that we will reject the null hypothesis if the difference between the sample statistic and the hypothesized population parameter is so large that it or a larger difference would occur, on the average, only five or fewer times in every 100 samples when the hypothesized population parameter is correct. **If we assume the hypothesis is correct, then, the significance level will indicate the percentage of sample means that is outside certain limits.** (In estimation, you remember, the confidence level indicated the percentage of sample means that fell *within* the defined confidence limits.)

Figure 8-2 illustrates how to interpret a 5 percent level of significance. Notice that 2.5 percent of the area under the curve is located in each tail. From Appendix Table 1, we can determine that 95 percent of all the area under the curve is included in an interval extending $1.96\sigma_{\bar{x}}$ on either side of the hypothesized mean. In 95 percent of the area, then, there is no significant difference between the sample statistic and the hypothesized population parameter. In the remaining 5 percent (the colored regions in Fig. 8-2), a significant difference does exist.

Also called the area
where we accept the
null hypothesis

Figure 8-3 examines this same example in a different way. Here, the .95 of the area under the curve is where we would accept the null hypothesis. The two colored parts under the curve, representing a total of 5 percent of the area, are where we would reject the null hypothesis.

A word of caution is appropriate here. Even if our sample statistic in Fig. 8-3 does fall in the nonshaded region (that region comprising 95 percent of the area under the curve), this *does not prove* that our null hypothesis (H_0) is true; it simply does not provide statistical evidence to reject it. Why? Because the only way in which the hypothesis can be accepted with certainty is for us to know the population parameter, and unfortunately, this is not possible. Therefore, whenever we say that we accept the null hypothesis, we actually mean that there is not sufficient statistical evidence to reject it. **Use of the term *accept,* instead of *do not reject,* has become standard. It means simply that when sample data do not cause us to reject a null hypothesis, we behave as though that hypothesis is true.**

FIGURE 8-2

Regions of significant difference and of no significant difference at a 5 percent level of significance

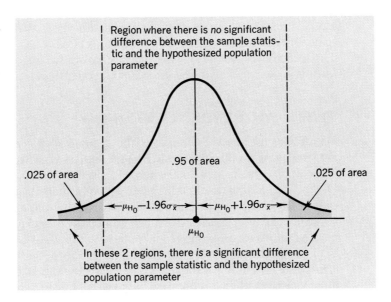

Region where there is *no* significant difference between the sample statistic and the hypothesized population parameter

.95 of area

.025 of area

.025 of area

$\mu_{H_0} - 1.96\sigma_{\bar{x}}$ $\mu_{H_0} + 1.96\sigma_{\bar{x}}$

μ_{H_0}

In these 2 regions, there *is* a significant difference between the sample statistic and the hypothesized population parameter

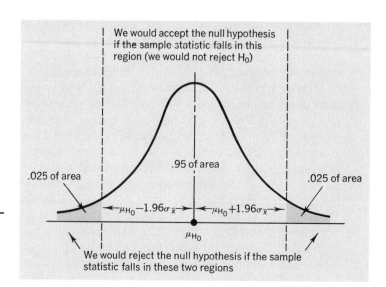

We would accept the null hypothesis if the sample statistic falls in this region (we would not reject H_0)

.95 of area

.025 of area

.025 of area

$\leftarrow \mu_{H_0} - 1.96\sigma_{\bar{x}} \rightarrow \leftarrow \mu_{H_0} + 1.96\sigma_{\bar{x}} \rightarrow$

μ_{H_0}

We would reject the null hypothesis if the sample statistic falls in these two regions

FIGURE 8-3

A 5 percent level of significance, with acceptance and rejection regions designated

SELECTING A SIGNIFICANCE LEVEL

Tradeoffs when choosing a significance level

There is no single standard or universal level of significance for testing hypotheses. In some instances, a 5 percent level of significance is used. Published research results often test hypotheses at the 1 percent level of significance. It is possible to test a hypothesis at *any* level of significance. But remember that our choice of the minimum standard for an acceptable probability, or the significance level, is also the risk we assume of rejecting a null hypothesis when it is true. **The higher the significance level we use for testing a hypothesis, the higher the probability of rejecting a null hypothesis when it is true.**

Examining this concept, we refer to Fig. 8-4. Here we have illustrated a hypothesis test at three different significance levels: .01, .10, and .50. Also, we have indicated the location of the same sample mean $\bar{x}$ on each distribution. In parts *a* and *b*, we would accept the null hypothesis that the population mean is equal to the hypothesized value. But notice that in part *c*, we would reject this same null hypothesis. Why? Our significance level there of .50 is so high that we would rarely accept the null hypothesis when it is *not* true but, at the same time, frequently reject it when it *is* true.

TYPE I AND TYPE II ERRORS

Type I and Type II errors defined

Statisticians use specific definitions and symbols for the concept illustrated in Fig. 8-4. **Rejecting a null hypothesis when it is true is called a Type I error,** and its probability (which, as we have seen, is also the significance level of the test) is symbolized α (alpha). Alternately, **accepting a null hypothesis when it is false is called a Type II error,** and its probability is symbolized β (beta). There is a tradeoff between these two types of errors: The probability of making one type of error can be reduced only if we are willing to increase the probability of making the other type of error. Notice in part *c*, Fig. 8-4, that our acceptance region is quite small (.50 of the area under the curve). With an acceptance region this small, we will rarely accept a null hypothesis when it is not true, but as a cost of being this sure, we will frequently reject a null hypothesis when it is true. Put another way, in order to get a low β, we will

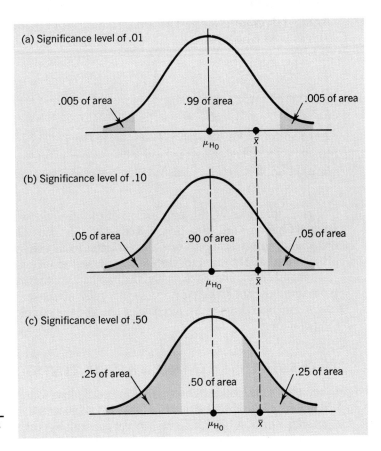

FIGURE 8-4
Three different levels of significance

have to put up with a high α. To deal with this tradeoff in personal and professional situations, decision makers decide the appropriate level of significance by examining the costs or penalties attached to both types of errors.

Preference for a Type I error

Suppose that making a Type I error (rejecting a null hypothesis when it is true) involves the time and trouble of reworking a batch of chemicals that should have been accepted. At the same time, making a Type II error (accepting a null hypothesis when it is false) means taking a chance that an entire group of users of this chemical compound will be poisoned. Obviously, the management of this company will prefer a Type I error to a Type II error and, as a result, will set very high levels of significance in its testing to get low βs.

Preference for a Type II error

Suppose, on the other hand, that making a Type I error involves disassembling an entire engine at the factory, but making a Type II error involves relatively inexpensive warranty repairs by the dealers. Then the manufacturer is more likely to prefer a Type II error and will set low significance levels in its testing.

DECIDING WHICH DISTRIBUTION TO USE IN HYPOTHESIS TESTING

Selecting the correct distribution prior to the test

After deciding what level of significance to use, our next task in hypothesis testing is to determine the appropriate probability distribution. We have a choice between the normal distribution, Appendix Table 1, and the *t* distribution, Appendix Table 2.

TABLE 8-1 Conditions for Using the Normal and *t* Distributions in Testing Hypotheses About Means

	WHEN THE POPULATION STANDARD DEVIATION IS KNOWN	WHEN THE POPULATION STANDARD DEVIATION IS *NOT* KNOWN
Sample size *n* is larger than 30	Normal distribution, z table	Normal distribution, z table
Sample size *n* is 30 or less and we assume the population is normal or approximately so	Normal distribution, z table	*t* distribution, *t* table

The rules for choosing the appropriate distribution are similar to those we encountered in Chapter 7 on estimation. Table 8-1 summarizes when to use the normal and *t* distributions in making tests of means. Later in this chapter, we shall examine the distributions appropriate for testing hypotheses about proportions.

Remember one more rule when testing the hypothesized value of a mean. As in estimation, use the *finite population multiplier* whenever the population is finite in size, sampling is done without replacement, and the sample is more than 5 percent of the population.

TWO-TAILED AND ONE-TAILED TESTS OF HYPOTHESES

Description of a two-tailed hypothesis test

In the tests of hypothesized population means that follow, we shall illustrate two-tailed tests and one-tailed tests. These new terms need a word of explanation. A *two-tailed test* of a hypothesis will reject the null hypothesis if the sample mean is significantly higher than *or* lower than the hypothesized population mean. Thus, in a two-tailed test, there are *two* rejection regions. This is illustrated in Fig. 8-5.

A two-tailed test is appropriate when the null hypothesis is $\mu = \mu_{H_0}$ (μ_{H_0} being some specified value) and the alternative hypothesis is $\mu \neq \mu_{H_0}$. Assume that a manufacturer of light bulbs wants to produce bulbs with a mean life of $\mu = \mu_{H_0} = 1,000$ hours.

FIGURE 8-5

Two-tailed test of a hypothesis, showing the two rejection regions

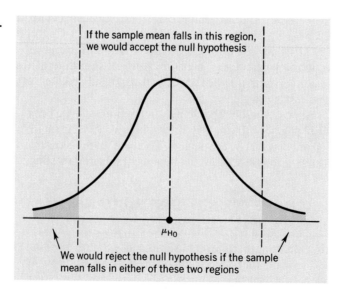

If the sample mean falls in this region, we would accept the null hypothesis

μ_{H_0}

We would reject the null hypothesis if the sample mean falls in either of these two regions

If the lifetime is shorter, he will lose customers to his competition; if the lifetime is longer, he will have a very high production cost because the filaments will be excessively thick. In order to see if his production process is working properly, he takes a sample of the output to test the hypothesis $H_0: \mu = 1,000$. Since he does not want to deviate significantly from 1,000 hours *in either direction,* the appropriate alternative hypothesis is $H_1: \mu \neq 1,000$, and he uses a two-tailed test. That is, he rejects the null hypothesis if the mean life of bulbs in the sample is *either too far above* 1,000 hours *or too far below* 1,000 hours.

Sometimes a one-tailed test is appropriate

However, there are situations in which a two-tailed test is not appropriate, and we must use a one-tailed test. Consider the case of a wholesaler that buys light bulbs from the manufacturer discussed above. The wholesaler buys bulbs in large lots and does not want to accept a lot of bulbs unless their mean life is 1,000 hours. As each shipment arrives, the wholesaler tests a sample to decide whether it should accept the shipment. The company will reject the shipment only if it feels that the mean life is below 1,000 hours. If it feels that the bulbs are *better* than expected (with a mean life above 1,000 hours), it certainly will not reject the shipment, because the longer life comes at no extra cost. So the wholesaler's hypotheses are: $H_0: \mu = 1,000$ hours and $H_1: \mu < 1,000$ hours. It rejects H_0 only if the mean life of the sampled bulbs is significantly *below* 1,000 hours. This situation is illustrated in Fig. 8-6. From this figure we can see why this test is called a *left-tailed test* (or a *lower-tailed test*).

In general, a left-tailed (lower-tailed) test is used if the hypotheses are $H_0: \mu = \mu_{H_0}$ and $H_1: \mu < \mu_{H_0}$. In such a situation, it is sample evidence with the sample mean significantly below the hypothesized population mean that leads us to reject the null hypothesis in favor of the alternative hypothesis. Stated differently, the rejection region is in the lower tail (left tail) of the distribution of the sample mean, and that is why we call this a lower-tailed test.

Left-tailed tests and right-tailed tests

A left-tailed test is one of the two kinds of one-tailed tests. As you have probably guessed by now, the other kind of one-tailed test is a *right-tailed test* (or an *upper-tailed test*). An upper-tailed test is used when the hypotheses are $H_0: \mu = \mu_{H_0}$ and $H_1: \mu > \mu_{H_0}$. Only values of the sample mean that are *significantly* above the hypothesized population mean will cause us to reject the null hypothesis in favor of the

FIGURE 8-6

Left-tailed test (a lower-tailed test) with the rejection region on the left side (lower side)

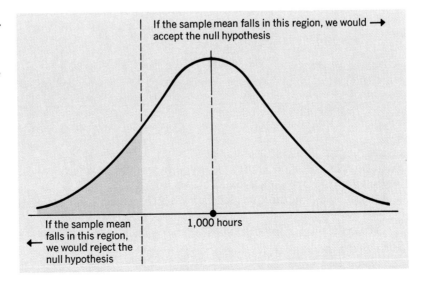

If the sample mean falls in this region, we would → accept the null hypothesis

If the sample mean falls in this region, we would reject the null hypothesis ←

1,000 hours

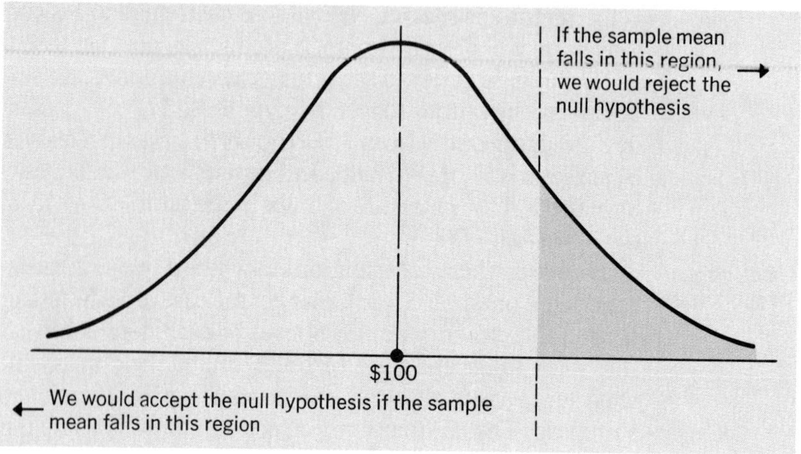
If the sample mean falls in this region, we would reject the null hypothesis
$100
We would accept the null hypothesis if the sample mean falls in this region

FIGURE 8-7
Right-tailed (upper-tailed) test

alternative hypothesis. This is called an upper-tailed test because the rejection region is in the upper tail of the distribution of the sample mean.

The following situation is illustrated in Fig. 8-7; it calls for the use of an upper-tailed test. A sales manager has asked her salespeople to observe a limit on traveling expenses. The manager hopes to keep expenses to an average of $100 per salesperson per day. One month after the limit is imposed, a sample of submitted daily expenses is taken to see if the limit is being observed. The null hypothesis is $H_0: \mu = \$100.00$, but the manager is concerned only with excessively high expenses. Thus, the appropriate alternative hypothesis is $H_1: \mu > \$100.00$, and an upper-tailed test is used. The null hypothesis is rejected (and corrective measures taken) only if the sample mean is significantly higher than $100.00.

Accepting H_0 doesn't guarantee that H_0 is true

Finally, we should remind you again that in each example of hypothesis testing, when we accept a null hypothesis on the basis of sample information we are really saying that there is no statistical evidence to reject it. We are not saying that the null hypothesis is true. The only way to prove a null hypothesis is to know what the population parameter is, and that is not possible with sampling. Thus, we accept the null hypothesis and behave as though it is true simply because we can find no evidence to reject it.

Exercises

8-13 Formulate null and alternative hypotheses to test whether the mean annual snowfall in Buffalo, New York, exceeds 45 inches.

8-14 Describe what the null and alternative hypotheses typically represent in the hypothesis-testing process.

8-15 Define the term *significance level.*

8-16 Define Type I and Type II errors.

8-17 In a trial, the null hypothesis is that an individual is innocent of a certain crime. Would the legal system prefer to commit a Type I or a Type II error with this hypothesis?

8-18 What is the relationship between the significance level of a test and Type I error?

8-19 If our goal is to accept a null hypothesis that $\mu = 36.5$ with 96 percent certainty when it's true, and our sample size is 50, diagram the acceptance and rejection regions for the following alternative hypotheses:
(a) $\mu \neq 36.5$ (b) $\mu > 36.5$ (c) $\mu < 36.5$

8-20 For the following cases, specify which probability distribution to use in a hypothesis test:
(a) $H_0: \mu = 27$, $H_1: \mu \neq 27$, $\bar{x} = 33$, $\hat{\sigma} = 4$, $n = 25$
(b) $H_0: \mu = 98.6$, $H_1: \mu > 98.6$, $\bar{x} = 99.1$, $\sigma = 1.5$, $n = 50$
(c) $H_0: \mu = 3.5$, $H_1: \mu < 3.5$, $\bar{x} = 2.8$, $\hat{\sigma} = 0.6$, $n = 18$
(d) $H_0: \mu = 382$, $H_1: \mu \neq 382$, $\bar{x} = 363$, $\sigma = 68$, $n = 12$
(e) $H_0: \mu = 57$, $H_1: \mu > 57$, $\bar{x} = 65$, $\hat{\sigma} = 12$, $n = 42$

8-21 Your null hypothesis is that the battery for a heart pacemaker has an average life of 300 days, with the alternative hypothesis being that the battery life is more than 300 days. If you are the quality control engineer for the battery manufacturer:
(a) Would you rather make a Type I or a Type II error?
(b) Based on your answer to part (a), should you use a high or a low significance level?

8-22 Under what conditions is it appropriate to use a one-tailed test? a two-tailed test?

8-23 If you have decided that a one-tailed test is the appropriate test to use, how do you decide whether it should be a lower-tailed test or an upper-tailed test?

8-24 Martha Inman, a highway safety engineer, decides to test the load-bearing capacity of a bridge that is 20 years old. Considerable data are available from similar tests on the same type of bridge. Which is appropriate, a one-tailed or a two-tailed test? If the minimum load-bearing capacity of this bridge must be 10 tons, what are the null and alternative hypothesis?

8-25 Dr. Ross Darrow believes that nicotine in cigarettes causes cigarette smokers to have higher daytime heart rates on average than do nonsmokers. He also believes that smokers crave the nicotine in cigarettes rather than just smoking for the physical satisfaction of the act and, accordingly, that the average smoker will smoke more cigarettes per day if he switches from a brand with a high nicotine content to one with a low level of nicotine.
(a) Suppose Ross knows that nonsmokers have an average daytime heart rate of 78 beats per minute. What are the appropriate null and alternative hypotheses for testing his first belief?
(b) For the past 3 months, he has been observing a sample of 48 individuals who smoke an average of 15 high-nicotine cigarettes per day. He has just switched them to a brand with a low nicotine content. State null and alternative hypotheses for testing his second belief.

8-4
Hypothesis Testing of Means — Samples with Population Standard Deviations Known

TWO-TAILED TESTS OF MEANS

A manufacturer supplies the rear axles for U.S. Postal Service mail trucks. These axles must be able to withstand 80,000 pounds per square inch in stress tests, but an excessively strong axle raises production costs significantly. Long experience indicates that the standard deviation of the strength of its axles is 4,000 pounds per square inch. The manufacturer selects a sample of 100 axles from the latest production run, tests them, and finds that the mean stress capacity of the sample is 79,600 pounds per square inch. Written symbolically, the data in this case are:

Setting up the problem
symbolically

$\mu_{H_0} = 80{,}000 \leftarrow$ hypothesized values of the population mean

$\sigma = 4{,}000 \leftarrow$ population standard deviation

$n = 100 \leftarrow$ sample size

$\bar{x} = 79{,}600 \leftarrow$ sample mean

If the axle manufacturer uses a significance level (α) of .05 in testing, will the axles meet his stress requirements? Symbolically, we can state the problem:

$H_0 : \mu = 80{,}000 \leftarrow$ null hypothesis: The true mean is 80,000 pounds per square inch.

$H_1 : \mu \neq 80{,}000 \leftarrow$ alternative hypothesis: The true mean is not 80,000 pounds per square inch.

$\alpha = .05 \leftarrow$ level of significance for testing this hypothesis

Calculating the
standard error of
the mean

Since we know the population standard deviation, and since the size of the population is large enough to be treated as infinite, we can use the normal distribution in our testing. First, we calculate the standard error of the mean using Equation 6-1:

$$\sigma_{\bar{x}} = \frac{\sigma}{\sqrt{n}} \qquad [6\text{-}1]$$

$$= \frac{4{,}000}{\sqrt{100}}$$

$$= \frac{4{,}000}{10}$$

$$= 400 \text{ pounds per square inch} \leftarrow \text{standard error of the mean}$$

Illustrating the problem   Figure 8-8 illustrates this problem, showing the significance level of .05 as the two shaded regions that each contain .025 of the area. The .95 acceptance region contains

FIGURE 8-8

**Two-tailed
hypothesis test at the
.05 significance level**

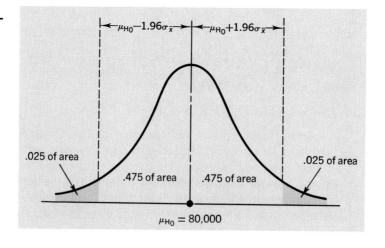

8 TESTING HYPOTHESES

Determining the limits of the acceptance region	two equal areas of .475 each. From the normal distribution table (Appendix Table 1), we can see that the appropriate z value for .475 of the area under the curve is 1.96. Now we can determine the limits of the acceptance region:

$$\mu_{H_0} + 1.96\sigma_{\bar{x}} = 80{,}000 + 1.96(400)$$
$$= 80{,}000 + 784$$
$$= 80{,}784 \text{ pounds per square inch} \leftarrow \text{upper limit}$$

and:

$$\mu_{H_0} - 1.96\sigma_{\bar{x}} = 80{,}000 - 1.96(400)$$
$$= 80{,}000 - 784$$
$$= 79{,}216 \text{ pounds per square inch} \leftarrow \text{lower limit}$$

Interpreting the results   These two limits of the acceptance region (80,784 and 79,216) are shown in Fig. 8-9. Also, we have indicated the sample mean (79,600 pounds per square inch). Obviously, the sample mean lies within the acceptance region; the manufacturer should accept the null hypothesis, because there is no significant difference between the hypothesized mean of 80,000 and the observed mean of the sample axles. On the basis of this sample, the manufacturer should accept the production run as meeting the stress requirements.

FIGURE 8-9

Two-tailed hypothesis test at the .05 significance level, showing acceptance region and sample mean

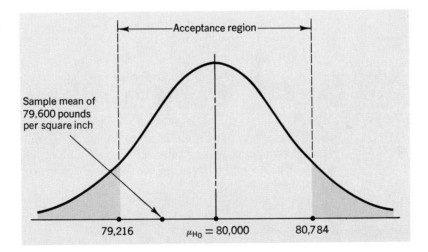

ONE-TAILED TESTS OF MEANS

For a one-tailed test of a mean, suppose a hospital uses large quantities of packaged doses of a particular drug. The individual dose of this drug is 100 cubic centimeters (100 cc). The action of the drug is such that the body will harmlessly pass off excessive doses. On the other hand, insufficient doses do not produce the desired medical effect, and they interfere with patient treatment. The hospital has purchased its requirements of this drug from the same manufacturer for a number of years and knows that the population standard deviation is 2 cc. The hospital inspects 50 doses of this drug at random from a very large shipment and finds the mean of these doses to be 99.75 cc.

$\mu_{H_0} = 100 \leftarrow$ hypothesized value of the population mean

$\sigma = 2 \leftarrow$ population standard deviation

$n = 50 \leftarrow$ sample size

$\bar{x} = 99.75 \leftarrow$ sample mean

If the hospital sets a .10 significance level and asks us whether the dosages in this shipment are too small, how can we find the answer:

To begin, we can state the problem symbolically:

$H_0 : \mu = 100 \leftarrow$ null hypothesis: The mean of the shipments' dosages is 100 cc.

$H_1 : \mu < 100 \leftarrow$ alternative hypothesis: The mean is less than 100 cc.

$\alpha = .10 \leftarrow$ level of significance for testing this hypothesis

Then we can calculate the standard error of the mean, using the known population standard deviation and Equation 6-1 (because the population size is large enough to be considered infinite):

$$\sigma_{\bar{x}} = \frac{\sigma}{\sqrt{n}}$$ [6-1]

$$= \frac{2}{\sqrt{50}}$$

$$= \frac{2}{7.07}$$

$$= .2829 \text{ cc} \leftarrow \text{standard error of the mean}$$

The hospital wishes to know whether the actual dosages are 100 cc or whether, in fact, the dosages are too small. The hospital must determine that the dosages are *more* than a certain amount, or it must reject the shipment. This is a *left-tailed* test, which we have shown graphically in Fig. 8-10. Notice that the colored region corresponds to the .10 significance level. Also notice that the acceptance region consists of 40 percent

FIGURE 8-10

Left-tailed hypothesis test at the .10 significance level

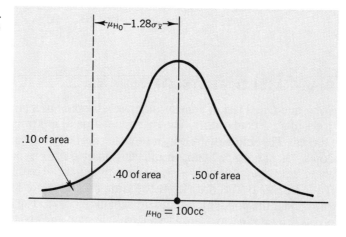

8 TESTING HYPOTHESES

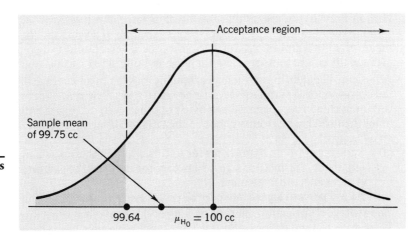

FIGURE 8-11

Left-tailed hypothesis test at the .10 significance level, showing acceptance region and the sample mean

on the left side of the distribution *plus* the entire right side (50 percent), for a total area of 90 percent. Since we know the population standard deviation, and n is larger than 30, we can use the normal distribution. For Appendix Table 1, we can determine that

Determining the limit of the acceptance region

the appropriate z value for 40 percent of the area under the curve is 1.28. Using this information, we can calculate the acceptance region's *lower* limit:

$$\mu_{H_0} - 1.28\sigma_{\bar{x}} = 100 - 1.28(.2829)$$
$$= 100 - .36$$
$$= 99.64 \text{ cc} \leftarrow \text{lower limit}$$

Interpreting the results

This lower limit of the acceptance region, 99.64 cc, and the sample mean, 99.75, are both shown in Fig. 8-11. In this figure, we can see that the sample mean lies within the acceptance region. Therefore, the hospital should accept the null hypothesis, because the observed mean of the sample is not significantly lower than our hypothesized mean of 100 cc. On the basis of this sample of 50 doses, the hospital should accept the doses in the shipment as being sufficient.

Exercises

8-26 Atlas Sporting Goods has implemented a special trade promotion for its propane stove and feels that the promotion should result in a price change for the consumer. Atlas knows that before the promotion began, the average retail price of the stove was $44.95, with a standard deviation of $5.75. Atlas samples 25 of its retailers after the promotion begins and finds the mean price for the stoves is now $42.95. At a .02 significance level, does Atlas have reason to believe that the average retail price to the consumer has decreased?

8-27 From 1980 until 1985, the mean price/earnings ratio of the approximately 1,800 stocks listed on the New York Stock Exchange was 14.35, with a standard deviation of 9.73. In a sample of 30 randomly chosen NYSE stocks, the mean P/E ratio in 1986 was 11.77. Does this sample present sufficient evidence to conclude (at the .05 level of significance) that in 1986 the mean P/E ratio for NYSE stocks had changed from its earlier value?

8-28   Hinton Press hypothesizes that the life of its largest web press is 14,500 hours, with a known standard deviation of 2,100 hours. From a sample of 25 presses, thc company finds a sample mean of 13,000 hours. At a .01 significance level, should the company conclude that the average life of the presses is less than the hypothesized 14,500 hours?

8-29   American Theaters knows that a certain hit movie ran an average of 84 days in each city, and the corresponding standard deviation was 10 days. The manager of the southeastern district was interested in comparing the movie's popularity in his region with that in all of American's other theaters. He randomly chose 75 theaters in his region and found that they ran the movie an average of 81.5 days.

(a)   State appropriate hypotheses for testing whether there was a significant difference in the length of the picture's run between theaters in the southeastern district and all of American's other theaters.

(b)   At a 1 percent significance level, test these hypotheses.

8-30   The average commission charged by full-service brokerage firms on a sale of common stock is $144, with a standard deviation of $52. Joel Freelander has taken a random sample of 121 trades by his clients and determined that they paid an average commission of $151. At a .10 significance level, can Joel conclude that his client's commissions are higher than the industry average?

8-31   Each day, the United States Customs Service has historically intercepted about $28 million in contraband goods being smuggled into the country, with a standard deviation of $16 million per day. On 64 randomly chosen days in 1986, the US Customs Service intercepted an average of $30.3 million in contraband goods. Does this sample indicate (at a 5 percent level of significance) that the Customs Commissioner should be concerned that smuggling has increased above its historic level?

8-32   Prior to the 1973 oil embargo and subsequent increases in the price of crude oil, gasoline usage in the United States had grown at a seasonally-adjusted rate of .57% per month, with a standard deviation of .10% per month. In fifteen randomly chosen months between 1975 and 1985, gasoline usage grew at an average rate of only .33% per month. At a .01 level of significance, can you conclude that the growth in the use of gasoline had decreased as a result of the embargo and its consequences?

8-33   The Bay City Bigleaguers, a semiprofessional baseball team, have the player who led the league in batting average for many years. For the past several years, Joe Carver has compiled a mean batting average of .343, with a standard deviation of .018. This year, however, Joe's average was only .306. Joe is renegotiating his contract for next year, and the salary he will be able to obtain is highly dependent upon his ability to convince the team's owner that his batting average this year was not significantly worse than in previous years. If the owner is willing to use a .02 significance level, will Joe's salary be cut next year?

8-5

Measuring the Power of a Hypothesis Test

What should a good hypothesis test do?

Now that we have considered two examples of hypothesis testing, a step back is appropriate, to discuss what a good hypothesis test *should do*. Ideally, α and β (the probabilities of Type I and Type II errors) should both be small. Recall that a Type I error occurs when we reject a null hypothesis that is true, and that α (the significance level of the test) *is* the probability of making a Type I error. In other words, once we decide upon the significance level, there is nothing else we can do about α. A Type II error occurs when we accept a null hypothesis that is false; the probability of a Type II error is β. What can we say about β?

Meaning of β and $1 - \beta$

Suppose the null hypothesis *is* false. Then managers would like the hypothesis test to reject it all the time. Unfortunately, hypothesis tests cannot be foolproof; sometimes when the null hypothesis is false, a test does not reject it, and thus a Type II error is made. When the null hypothesis is false, μ (the *true* population mean) does not equal μ_{H_0} (the hypothesized population mean); instead, μ equals some other value. For each possible value of μ for which the alternative hypothesis is true, there is a different probability (β) of incorrectly accepting the null hypothesis. Of course, we would like this β (the probability of accepting a null hypothesis when it is false) to be as small as possible, or equivalently, we would like $1 - \beta$ (the probability of rejecting a null hypothesis when it is false) to be as large as possible.

Interpreting the values of $1 - \beta$

Since rejecting a null hypothesis when it is false is exactly what a good test ought to do, a high value of $1 - \beta$ (something near 1.0) means the test is working quite well (it is rejecting the null hypothesis when it is false); a low value of $1 - \beta$ (something near 0.0) means that the test is working very poorly (it's not rejecting the null hypothesis when it is false). Since the value of $1 - \beta$ is the measure of how well the test is working, it is known as the *power of the test*. If we plot the values of $1 - \beta$ for each value of μ for which the alternative hypothesis is true, the resulting curve is known as a *power curve.*

Computing the values of $1 - \beta$

In part *a* of Fig. 8-12, we have reproduced the left-tailed test first introduced in Fig. 8-10. In part *b* of Fig. 8-12, we show the power curve that is associated with this test.

FIGURE 8-12

Left-tailed hypothesis test, associated power curve, and three values of μ

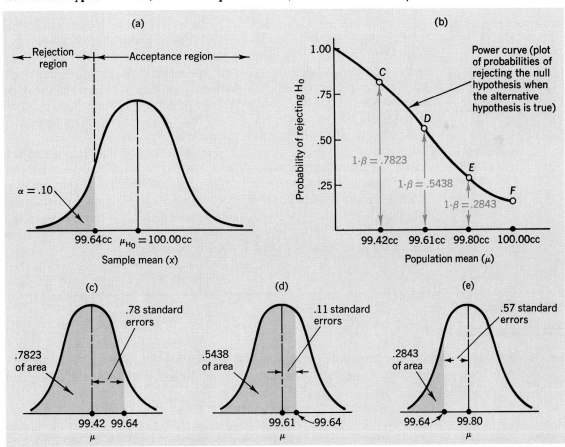

Computing the values of $1 - \beta$ to plot the power curve is not difficult; three such points are shown in b, Fig. 8-12. Recall that with this test we were deciding whether or not to accept a drug shipment. Our test dictated that we should reject the null hypothesis if the sample mean dosage is less than 99.64 cc.

Consider point C on the power curve in b, Fig. 8-12. The population mean dosage is 99.42 cc. Given that the population mean is 99.42 cc, we must compute the probability that the mean of a random sample of 50 doses from this population will be less than 99.64 cc (the point below which we decided to reject the null hypothesis). Now look at c, Fig. 8-12. Earlier we computed the standard error of the mean to be .2829 cc, so 99.64 cc is $(99.64 - 99.42)/.2829$, or .78 standard errors above 99.42 cc. Using Appendix Table 1, we can see that the probability of observing a sample mean less than 99.64 cc and thus rejecting the null hypothesis is .7823, the colored area in c, Fig. 8-12. Thus, the power of the test $(1 - \beta)$ at $\mu = 99.42$ is .7823. This simply means that at $\mu = 99.42$, the probability that this test will reject the null hypothesis when it is false is .7823.

Interpreting a point on the power curve

Now look at point D in b, Fig. 8-12. For this population mean dosage of 99.61 cc, what is the probability that the mean of a random sample of 50 doses from this population will be less than 99.64 cc and thus cause the test to reject the null hypothesis? Look at d, Fig. 8-12. Here we see that 99.64 is $(99.64 - 99.61)/.2829$, or .11 standard errors above 99.61 cc. Using Appendix Table 1 again, we can see that the probability of observing a sample mean less than 99.64 cc and thus rejecting the null hypothesis is .5438, the colored area in d, Fig. 8-12. Thus, the power of the test $(1 - \beta)$ at $\mu = 99.61$ cc is .5438.

Termination point of the power curve

Using the same procedure at point E, we find the power of the test at $\mu = 99.80$ cc is .2843; this is illustrated as the colored area in e, Fig. 8-12. The values of $1 - \beta$ continue to decrease to the right of point E. How low do they get? As the population mean gets closer and closer to 100.00 cc, the power of the test $(1 - \beta)$ must get closer and closer to the probability of rejecting the null hypothesis when the population mean is exactly 100.00 cc. And we know *that* probability is nothing but the significance level of the test — in this case, .10. Thus, the curve terminates at point F, which lies at a height of .10 directly over the population mean.

Interpreting the power curve

What does our power curve in b, Fig. 8-12, tell us? Just that as the shipment becomes less satisfactory (as the doses in the shipment become smaller), our test is more powerful (it has a greater probability of recognizing that the shipment is unsatisfactory). It also shows us, however, that because of sampling error, when the dosage is only slightly less than 100.00 cc, the power of the test to recognize this situation is quite low. Thus, if having *any* dosage below 100.00 cc is completely unsatisfactory, the test we have been discussing is not appropriate.

Exercises

8-34 See exercise 8-31. Compute the power of the test for $\mu = \$28$, $\$29$, and $\$30$ million.

8-35 See exercise 8-32. Compute the power of the test for $\mu = 0.50$, 0.45, and 0.40 percent per month.

8-36 In exercise 8-31, what happens to the power of the test for $\mu = \$28$, $\$29$, and $\$30$ million if the significance level is changed to .02?

8-37 In exercise 8-32, what happens to the power of the test for $\mu = 0.50$, 0.45, and 0.40 percent per month if the significance level is changed to .04?

Hypothesis Testing of Proportions — Large Samples

TWO-TAILED TESTS OF PROPORTIONS

Dealing with proportions

In this section, we'll apply what we have learned about tests concerning means to tests for *proportions* (that is, the proportion of occurrences in a population). But before we apply it, we'll review the important conclusions we made about proportions in Chapter 7. First, remember that the binomial is the theoretically correct distribution to use in dealing with proportions, since the data are discrete, not continuous. As the sample size increases, the binomial distribution approaches the normal in its characteristics, and we can use the normal distribution to approximate the sampling distribution. Specifically, *np and nq each need to be at least 5* before we can use the normal distribution as a substitute for the binomial.

Consider, as an example, a company that is evaluating the promotability of its employees; that is, determining the proportion of them whose ability, training, and supervisory experience qualify them for promotion to the next higher level of management. The human resources director tells the president that 80 percent, or .8, of the employees in the company are "promotable." The president assembles a special committee to assess the promotability of all the employees. This committee conducts in-depth interviews with 150 employees and finds that in its judgment, only 70 percent of the sample are qualified for promotion.

Setting up the problem symbolically

$p_{H_0} = .8 \leftarrow$ hypothesized value of the population proportion of successes (judged promotable, in this case)

$q_{H_0} = .2 \leftarrow$ hypothesized value of the population proportion of failures (judged not promotable)

$n = 150 \leftarrow$ sample size

$\bar{p} = .7 \leftarrow$ sample proportion of promotables

$\bar{q} = .3 \leftarrow$ sample proportion judged not promotable

The president wants to test at the .05 significance level the hypothesis that .8 of the employees are promotable:

$H_0: p = .8 \leftarrow$ null hypothesis: 80 percent of the employees are promotable.

$H_1: p \neq .8 \leftarrow$ alternative hypothesis: The proportion of promotable employees is not 80 percent.

$\alpha = .05 \leftarrow$ level of significance for testing the hypothesis

Calculating the standard error of the proportion

To begin, we can calculate the standard error of the proportion, using the hypothesized values of p_{H_0} and q_{H_0} in Equation 7-4:

$$\sigma_{\bar{p}} = \sqrt{\frac{p_{H_0} q_{H_0}}{n}} \qquad [7\text{-}4]$$

$$= \sqrt{\frac{(.8)(.2)}{150}}$$

$$= \sqrt{.0010666}$$

$$= .0327 \leftarrow \text{standard error of the proportion}$$

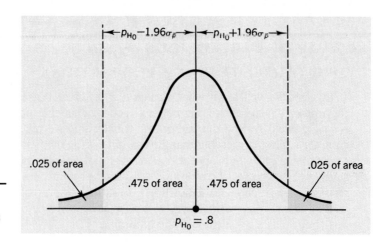

FIGURE 8-13

Two-tailed hypothesis test of a proportion at the .05 level of significance

Illustrating the problem

In this instance, the company wants to know whether the true proportion is larger or smaller than the hypothesized proportion. Thus, a two-tailed test of a proportion is appropriate, and we have shown it graphically in Fig. 8-13. The significance level corresponds to the two colored regions, each containing .025 of the area. The acceptance region of .95 is illustrated as two areas of .475 each. Since np and nq are each larger than 5, we can use the normal approximation of the binomial distribution. From Appendix Table 1, we can determine that the appropriate z value for .475 of the area under the curve is 1.96. Thus, the limits of the acceptance region are:

$$p_{H_0} + 1.96\sigma_{\bar{p}} = .8 + 1.96(.0327)$$
$$= .8 + .0641$$
$$= .8641 \leftarrow \text{upper limit}$$

$$p_{H_0} - 1.96\sigma_{\bar{p}} = .8 - 1.96(.0327)$$
$$= .8 - .0641$$
$$= .7359 \leftarrow \text{lower limit}$$

Interpreting the results

Figure 8-14 illustrates these two limits of the acceptance region, .8641 and .7359, as well as our sample proportion, .7. We can see that our sample proportion does *not* lie

FIGURE 8-14

Two-tailed hypothesis test of a proportion at the .05 significance level, showing acceptance region and sample proportion

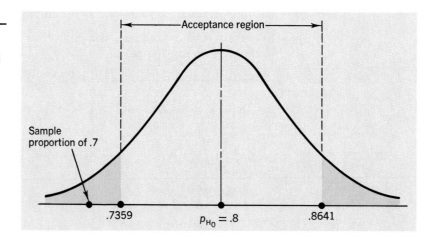

within the acceptance region. Therefore, in this case, the president should reject the null hypothesis and conclude that there *is* a significant difference between the director of human resources' hypothesized proportion of promotable employees (.8) and the observed proportion of promotable employees in the sample. From this, he should infer that the true proportion of promotable employees in the entire company is not 80 percent.

ONE-TAILED TESTS OF PROPORTIONS

A one-tailed test of a proportion is conceptually equivalent to a one-tailed test of a mean, as can be illustrated with this example. A member of a public interest group concerned with environmental pollution asserts at a public hearing that "fewer than 60 percent of the industrial plants in this area are complying with air pollution standards." Attending this meeting is an official of the Environmental Protection Agency who believes that 60 percent of the plants *are* complying with the standards; she decides to test that hypothesis at the .02 significance level.

$H_0 : p = .6 \leftarrow$ null hypothesis: The proportion of plants complying with air pollution standards is .6.

$H_1 : p < .6 \leftarrow$ alternative hypothesis: The proportion complying with the standards is less than .6.

$\alpha = .02 \leftarrow$ level of significance for testing the hypothesis

The official makes a thorough search of the records in her office. She samples 60 plants from a population of over 10,000 plants and finds that 33 are complying with air pollution standards. Is the assertion by the member of the public interest group a valid one?

We begin by summarizing the case symbolically:

Setting up the problem
symbolically

$p_{H_0} = .6 \leftarrow$ hypothesized value of the population proportion that is complying with air pollution standards

$q_{H_0} = .4 \leftarrow$ hypothesized value of the population proportion that is not complying and thus polluting

$n = 60 \leftarrow$ sample size

$\bar{p} = 33/60$ or $.55 \leftarrow$ sample proportion complying

$\bar{q} = 27/60$ or $.45 \leftarrow$ sample proportion polluting

Calculating the
standard error of the
proportion

Next, we can calculate the standard error of the proportion using the hypothesized population proportion as follows:

$$\sigma_{\bar{p}} = \sqrt{\frac{p_{H_0} q_{H_0}}{n}} \qquad [7\text{-}4]$$

$$= \sqrt{\frac{(.6)(.4)}{60}}$$

$$= \sqrt{.004}$$

$$= .0632 \leftarrow \text{standard error of the proportion}$$

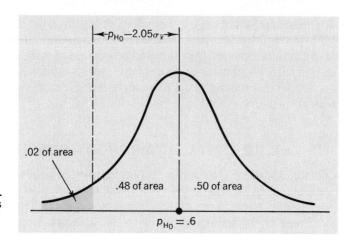

FIGURE 8-15

One-tailed hypothesis
test at the .02 level of
significance

This is a one-tailed test: The EPA official wonders only whether the actual proportion is less than .6. Specifically, this is a left-tailed test. In order to reject the null hypothesis that the true proportion of plants in compliance is 60 percent, the EPA

Illustrating the problem

representative must accept the alternative hypothesis that fewer than .6 have complied. In Fig. 8-15, we have shown this hypothesis test graphically.

Determining the limit of
the acceptance region

Since np and nq are each over 5, we can use the normal approximation of the binomial distribution. The appropriate z value from Appendix Table 1 for .48 of the area under the curve is 2.05. Thus, we can calculate the limit of the acceptance region as follows:

$$p_{H_0} - 2.05\sigma_{\bar{p}} = .6 - 2.05(.0632)$$
$$= .6 - .13$$
$$= .47 \leftarrow \text{lower limit}$$

Interpreting the results

Figure 8-16 illustrates the limit of the acceptance region, .47, and the sample proportion, .55, (33/60). Looking at this figure, we can see that the sample proportion lies within the acceptance region. Therefore, the EPA official should accept the null hypothesis that the true proportion of complying plants is .6. **Although the observed sample proportion is below .6, *it is not significantly below* .6; that is, it is not far enough below .6 to make us accept the assertion by the member of the public interest group.**

FIGURE 8-16

One-tailed (left-
tailed) hypothesis
test at .02
significance level,
showing acceptance
region and sample
proportion

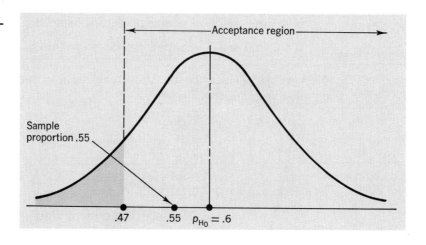

8 TESTING HYPOTHESES

Exercises

8-38 Grant, Inc., a manufacturer of women's dress blouses, knows that its brand is carried in 19 percent of the women's clothing stores east of the Mississippi River. Grant recently sampled 85 women's clothing stores on the West Coast and found that 14.12 percent of the stores carried the brand. At the .04 level of significance, is there evidence that Grant has poorer distribution on the West Coast than it does east of the Mississippi?

8-39 From a total of 10,200 loans made by a state's employees' credit union in the most recent 5-year period, 350 were sampled to determine what proportion was made to women. This sample showed that 39 percent of the loans were made to women employees. A similar study made 5 years ago showed that 41 percent of the borrowers then were women. At a significance level of .02, can you conclude that the proportion of loans made to women has changed significantly in the past 5 years?

8-40 Feronetics specializes in the use of gene-splicing techniques to produce new pharmaceutical compounds. It has recently developed a nasal spray containing interferon, which it believes will limit the transmission of the common cold within families. In the general population 15.1 percent of all individuals will catch a rhinovirus-caused cold once another family member contracts such a cold. The interferon spray was tested on 180 people, one of whose family members subsequently contracted a rhinovirus-caused cold. Only seventeen of the test subjects developed similar colds.

(a) At a significance level of .05, should Feronetics conclude that the new spray effectively reduces transmission of colds?
(b) What should it conclude at $\alpha = .02$?
(c) On the basis of these results, do you think Feronetics should be allowed to market the new spray? Explain.

8-41 Some financial theoreticians believe that the stock market's daily prices constitute a "random walk with positive drift." If this is accurate, then the Dow Jones Industrial Average should show a gain on more than 50 percent of all trading days. If the average increased on 101 of 175 randomly chosen days, what do you think about the suggested theory? Use a .01 level of significance.

8-42 A ketchup manufacturer is in the process of deciding whether to produce a new extra-spicy brand. The company's marketing-research department used a national telephone survey of 6,000 households and found that the extra-spicy ketchup would be purchased by 335 of them. A much more extensive study made 2 years ago showed that 5 percent of the households would purchase the brand then. At a 2 percent significance level, should the company conclude that there is an increased interest in the extra-spicy flavor?

8-43 Steve Cutter sells Big Blade lawn mowers in his hardware store, and he is interested in comparing the reliability of the mowers he sells with the reliability of Big Blade mowers sold nationwide. Steve knows that only 15 percent of all Big Blade mowers sold nationwide require repairs during the first year of ownership. A sample of 120 of Steve's customers revealed that exactly 22 of them required mower repairs in the first year of ownership. At the .02 level of significance, is there evidence that Steve's Big Blade mowers differ in reliability from those sold nationwide?

8-7
Hypothesis Testing of Means Under Different Conditions

When to use the t distribution

When we estimated confidence intervals in Chapter 7, we learned that the difference in size between large and small samples is important when the population standard deviation σ is unknown and must be estimated from the sample standard deviation. If the sample size n is 30 or less and σ is not known, we should use the t distribution. The appropriate t distribution has $n - 1$ degrees of freedom. These rules apply to hypothesis testing, too.

TWO-TAILED TESTS OF MEANS USING THE t DISTRIBUTION

A personnel specialist of a major corporation is recruiting a large number of employees for an overseas assignment. During the testing process, management asks how things are going, and she replies, "Fine. I think the average score on the aptitude test will be 90." When management reviews 20 of the test results compiled, it finds that the mean score is 84, and the standard deviation of this score is 11.

Setting up the problem symbolically

$\mu_{H_0} = 90 \leftarrow$ hypothesized value of the population mean

$n = 20 \leftarrow$ sample size

$\bar{x} = 84 \leftarrow$ sample mean

$s = 11 \leftarrow$ sample standard deviation

If management wants to test her hypothesis at the .10 level of significance, what is the procedure?

$H_0: \mu = 90 \leftarrow$ null hypothesis: the true population mean score is 90

$H_1: \mu \neq 90 \leftarrow$ alternative hypothesis: the mean score is not 90

$\alpha = .10 \leftarrow$ level of significance for testing this hypothesis

Calculating the standard error of the mean

Since the population standard deviation is not known, we must estimate it using the sample standard deviation and Equation 7-1:

$$\hat{\sigma} = s \qquad [7\text{-}1]$$
$$= 11$$

Now we can compute the standard error of the mean. Since we are using $\hat{\sigma}$, an estimate of the population standard deviation, the standard error of the mean will also be an estimate. We can use Equation 7-6, as follows:

$$\hat{\sigma}_{\bar{x}} = \frac{\hat{\sigma}}{\sqrt{n}} \qquad [7\text{-}6]$$

$$= \frac{11}{\sqrt{20}}$$

$$= \frac{11}{4.47}$$

$$= 2.46 \leftarrow \text{estimated standard error of the mean}$$

Illustrating the problem

Figure 8-17 illustrates this problem graphically. Since management is interested in knowing whether the true mean score is *larger* or *smaller* than the hypothesized score, a *two-tailed test* is the appropriate one to use. The significance level of .10 is shown in Fig. 8-17 as the two colored areas, each containing .05 of the area under the t distribution. Since the sample size is 20, the appropriate number of degrees of free-

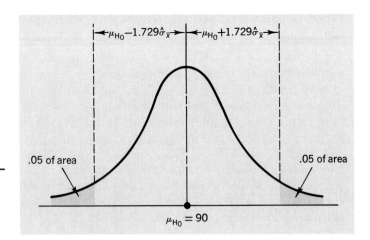

FIGURE 8-17

Two-tailed test of hypothesis at the .10 level of significance using the *t* distribution

.05 of area   .05 of area

$\mu_{H_0} = 90$

dom is 19; that is, $20 - 1$. Therefore, we look in the *t* distribution table, Appendix Table 2, under the .10 column until we reach the 19 degrees of freedom row. There we find the *t* value of 1.729.

This value is the appropriate one to use in calculating the limits of the acceptance region:

Determining the limits of the acceptance region

$$\mu_{H_0} + 1.729\hat{\sigma}_{\bar{x}} = 90 + 1.729(2.46)$$
$$= 90 + 4.25$$
$$= 94.25 \leftarrow \text{upper limit}$$

$$\mu_{H_0} - 1.729\hat{\sigma}_{\bar{x}} = 90 - 1.729(2.46)$$
$$= 90 - 4.25$$
$$= 85.75 \leftarrow \text{lower limit}$$

Interpreting the results   Figure 8-18 illustrates these two limits of the acceptance region, 94.25 and 85.75, and the sample mean, 84. From this figure, we can see that the sample mean lies outside the acceptance region. Therefore, management should reject the null hypothesis (the personnel specialist's assertion that the true mean score of the employees being tested is 90).

FIGURE 8-18

Two-tailed hypothesis test at the .10 level of significance, showing acceptance region and the sample mean

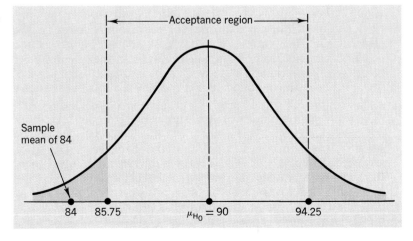

Acceptance region

Sample mean of 84

84   85.75 $\mu_{H_0} = 90$ 94.25

ONE-TAILED TESTS OF MEANS USING THE *t* DISTRIBUTION

One difference from the z tables

The procedure for a one-tailed hypothesis test using the *t* distribution is the same conceptually as for a one-tailed test using the normal distribution and the *z* table. Performing such one-tailed tests may cause some difficulty, however. Notice that the column headings in Appendix Table 2 represent the *area in both tails combined*. Thus, they are appropriate to use in a two-tailed test with *two* rejection regions.

Using the t tables for one-tailed tests

If we use the *t* distribution for a one-tailed test, we need to determine the area located in only one tail. So to find the appropriate *t* value for a one-tailed test at a significance level of .05 with 12 degrees of freedom, we would look in Appendix Table 2 under the .10 column opposite the 12 degrees of freedom row. The answer in this case is 1.782. **This is true because the .10 column represents .10 of the area under the curve contained in *both tails combined,* and so it also represents .05 of the area under the curve contained in each of the tails separately.**

Exercises

8-44 Given a sample mean of 83, a sample standard deviation of 12.5, and a sample size of 22, test the hypothesis that the value of the population mean is 70, against the alternative that it is more than 70. Use the .025 significance level.

8-45 If a sample of 25 observations reveals a sample mean of 52 and a sample variance of 4.2, test the hypothesis that the population mean is 65, against the alternative that it is some other value. Use the .01 significance level.

8-46 Realtor Elaine Snyderman took a random sample of twelve homes in a prestigious suburb of Chicago and found the average appraised market value to be $780,000, with a standard deviation of $49,000. Test the hypothesis that for all homes in the area, the mean appraised value is $825,000, against the alternative that it is less than $825,000. Use the .05 level of significance.

8-47 For a sample of 60 women taken from a population of over 5,000 enrolled in a weight-reducing program at a nationwide chain of health spas, the sample mean diastolic blood pressure is 101 and the sample standard deviation is 42. At a significance level of .02, can you conclude that, on average, the women enrolled in the program have diastolic blood pressure which exceeds the value of 75 recommended by various medical societies?

8-48 The data-processing department at a large life insurance company has installed new color video display terminals to replace the monochrome units it previously used. The 95 operators trained to use the new machines averaged 7.2 hours before achieving a satisfactory level of performance. Their sample variance was 16.2 squared hours. Long experience with operators on the old monochrome terminals showed that they averaged 8.1 hours on the machines before their performances were satisfactory. At the .01 significance level, should the supervisor of the department conclude that the new terminals are easier to learn to operate?

8-49 As the bottom fell out of the oil market in early 1986, educators in Texas worried about how the resulting loss of state revenues (estimated to be about $100 million for each $1 decrease in the price of a barrel of oil) would affect their budgets. The state board of education felt the situation would not be critical so long as they could be reasonably certain that the price would stay above $18 per barrel. They surveyed thirteen randomly chosen oil economists and asked them to predict how low the price would fall before it bottomed out. The thirteen predictions averaged $21.60, with a sample standard deviation of $4.65. At $\alpha = .01$, is the average prediction significantly higher than $18.00? Should the board of education conclude that a budget crisis is unlikely? Explain.

8-50 A television documentary on overeating claimed that Americans are about 10 pounds overweight on average. To test this claim, eighteen randomly selected individuals were examined, and their average excess weight was found to be 12.4 pounds, with a sample standard deviation of 2.7 pounds. At a significance level of .01, is there any reason to doubt the validity of the claimed 10 pound value?

8-51 Picosoft, Ltd., a supplier of operating system software for personal computers, was planning the initial public offering of its stock in order to raise sufficient working capital to finance the development of a radically new, seventh-generation integrated system. With current earnings of $1.61 a share, Picosoft and its underwriters were contemplating an offering price of $21, or about 13 times earnings. In order to check the appropriateness of this price, they randomly chose seven publicly traded software firms and found that their average price/earnings ratio was 11.6, with a sample standard deviation of 1.3. At $\alpha = .02$, can Picosoft conclude that the stocks of publicly traded software firms have an average P/E ratio which is significantly different from 13?

8-8
Hypothesis Testing for Differences Between Means and Proportions

Comparing two populations

In many decision-making situations, people need to determine whether the parameters of two populations are alike or different. A company may want to test, for example, whether its female employees receive lower salaries than its male employees for the same work. A training director may wish to determine whether the proportion of promotable employees at one government installation is different from that at another. A drug manufacturer may need to know whether a new drug causes one reaction in one group of experimental animals but a different reaction in another group.

In each of these examples, decision makers are concerned with the parameters of two populations. In these situations, they are not as interested in the actual value of the parameters as they are in the *relation between* the values of the two parameters — that is, how these parameters differ. *Do* female employees earn less than male employees for the same work? *Is* the proportion of promotable employees at one installation different from that at another? *Did* one group of experimental animals react differently from the other? In this section, we shall introduce methods by which these questions can be answered, using hypothesis-testing procedures.

SAMPLING DISTRIBUTION FOR THE DIFFERENCE BETWEEN TWO POPULATION PARAMETERS — BASIC CONCEPTS

A new way to generate a sampling distribution

In Chapter 6, we introduced the concept of the sampling distribution of the mean as the foundation for the work we would do in estimation and hypothesis testing. For a quick review of the sampling distribution of the mean, you may refer to Fig. 6-1.

Deriving the sampling distribution of the difference between sample means

Since we now wish to study two populations, not just one, the sampling distribution of interest is the *sampling distribution of the difference between sample means*. Figure 8-19 may help us conceptualize this particular sampling distribution. At the top of this figure, we have drawn two populations, identified as Population 1 and Population 2. These two have means of μ_1 and μ_2 and standard deviations of σ_1 and

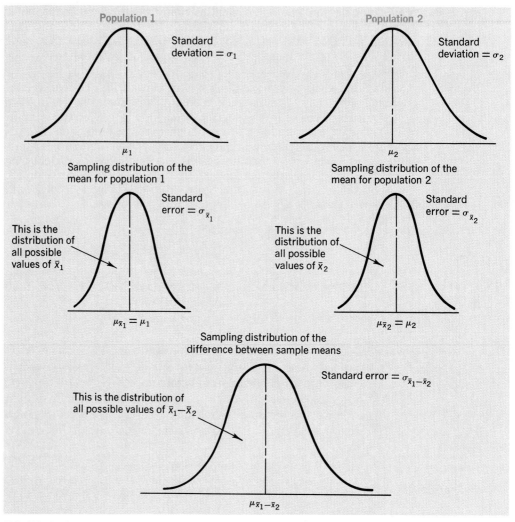

FIGURE 8-19

Basic concepts of population distributions, sampling distributions of the mean, and the sampling distribution of the difference between sample means

σ_2, respectively. Beneath each population, we show the sampling distribution of the mean for that population. At the bottom of the figure is the sampling distribution of the difference between the sample means.

The two theoretical sampling distributions of the mean in Fig. 8-19 are each made up of all the possible samples of a given size that can be drawn from the corresponding population distribution. Now, suppose we take a random sample from the distribution of Population 1 and another random sample from the distribution of Population 2. If we then subtract the two sample means, we get:

$$\bar{x}_1 - \bar{x}_2 \leftarrow \text{difference between sample means}$$

This difference will be positive if $\bar{x}_1$ is larger than $\bar{x}_2$, and negative if $\bar{x}_2$ is greater than $\bar{x}_1$. By constructing a distribution of *all* the possible sample differences of $\bar{x}_1 - \bar{x}_2$, we end up with the sampling distribution of the difference between sample means, which is shown at the bottom of Fig. 8-19.

The *mean of the sampling distribution of the difference between sample means* is symbolized $\mu_{\bar{x}_1 - \bar{x}_2}$ and is equal to $\mu_{\bar{x}_1} - \mu_{\bar{x}_2}$, which as we saw in Chapter 6, is the same as $\mu_1 - \mu_2$. If $\mu_1 = \mu_2$, then $\mu_{\bar{x}_1} - \mu_{\bar{x}_2} = 0$.

The standard deviation of the distribution of the difference between the sample means is called the *standard error of the difference between two means* and is calculated using this formula:

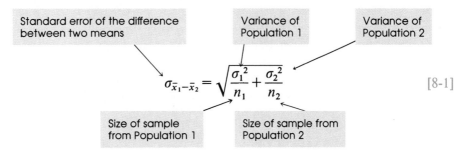

$$\sigma_{\bar{x}_1 - \bar{x}_2} = \sqrt{\frac{\sigma_1^2}{n_1} + \frac{\sigma_2^2}{n_2}}$$ [8-1]

How to estimate the
standard error of this
sampling distribution

If the two population standard deviations are *not* known, we can *estimate* the standard error of the difference between two means. We can use the same method of estimating the standard error that we have used before by letting sample standard deviations estimate the population standard deviations as follows:

$$\hat{\sigma} = s \longleftarrow \text{Sample standard deviation}$$ [7-1]

Therefore, the formula for the estimated standard error of the difference between two means becomes:

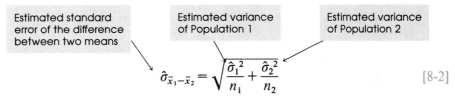

$$\hat{\sigma}_{\bar{x}_1 - \bar{x}_2} = \sqrt{\frac{\hat{\sigma}_1^2}{n_1} + \frac{\hat{\sigma}_2^2}{n_2}}$$ [8-2]

As the following examples show, depending on the sample sizes, we shall use different estimates for $\hat{\sigma}_1$ and $\hat{\sigma}_2$ in Equation 8-2.

TWO-TAILED TESTS FOR DIFFERENCES BETWEEN MEANS (LARGE SAMPLE SIZES)

When both sample sizes are greater than 30, this example illustrates how to do a two-tailed test of a hypothesis about the difference between two means. A man-power-development statistician is asked to determine whether the hourly wages of semiskilled workers are the same in two cities. The statistician takes simple random samples of hourly earnings in both cities. The results of this survey are presented in Table 8-2. Suppose the company wants to test the hypothesis at the .05 level that there is no difference between hourly wages for semiskilled workers in the two cities:

$H_0 : \mu_1 = \mu_2 \longleftarrow$ null hypothesis: there is no difference

$H_1 : \mu_1 \neq \mu_2 \longleftarrow$ alternative hypothesis: a difference exists

$\alpha = .05 \longleftarrow$ level of significance for testing this hypothesis

TABLE 8-2 Data From Sample Survey of Hourly Wages

CITY	MEAN HOURLY EARNINGS FROM SAMPLE	STANDARD DEVIATION OF SAMPLE	SIZE OF SAMPLE
Apex	$8.95	$.40	200
Eden	9.10	.60	175

Calculating the standard error of the difference between two means

Since the company is interested only in whether the means are *or* are not equal, this is a two-tailed test.

The standard deviations of the two populations are not known. Therefore, our first step is to estimate them, as follows:

$$\hat{\sigma}_1 = s_1 \qquad \hat{\sigma}_2 = s_2 \qquad\qquad [7\text{-}1]$$
$$\qquad = \$.40 \qquad\quad = \$.60$$

Now the estimated standard error of the difference between the two means can be determined by:

$$\hat{\sigma}_{\bar{x}_1 - \bar{x}_2} = \sqrt{\frac{\hat{\sigma}_1^2}{n_1} + \frac{\hat{\sigma}_2^2}{n_2}} \qquad\qquad [8\text{-}2]$$

$$= \sqrt{\frac{(.40)^2}{200} + \frac{(.60)^2}{175}}$$

$$= \sqrt{.0028}$$

$$= \$.053 \leftarrow \text{estimated standard error}$$

Illustrating the problem

We can illustrate this hypothesis test graphically. In Fig. 8-20, the significance level of .05 corresponds to the two colored areas, each of which contains .025 of the area. The acceptance region contains two equal areas of .475 each. Since both samples are large, we can use the normal distribution. From Appendix Table 1, we can deter-

FIGURE 8-20

Two-tailed hypothesis test of the difference between two means at the .05 level of significance

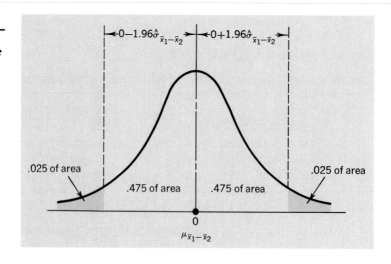

8 TESTING HYPOTHESES

FIGURE 8-21

Two-tailed
hypothesis test of the
difference between
two means at the .05
level of significance,
showing acceptance
region and difference
between sample
means

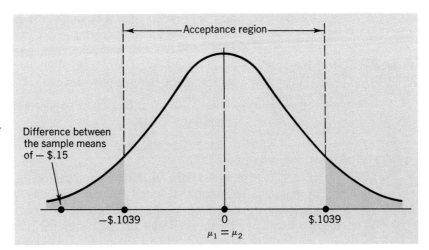

Determining the limits of
the acceptance region

mine the appropriate z value for .475 of the area under the curve to be 1.96. Now we can calculate the limits of the acceptance region:

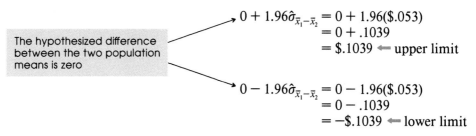

$$0 + 1.96\hat{\sigma}_{\bar{x}_1 - \bar{x}_2} = 0 + 1.96(\$.053)$$
$$= 0 + .1039$$
$$= \$.1039 \leftarrow \text{upper limit}$$

The hypothesized difference between the two population means is zero

$$0 - 1.96\hat{\sigma}_{\bar{x}_1 - \bar{x}_2} = 0 - 1.96(\$.053)$$
$$= 0 - .1039$$
$$= -\$.1039 \leftarrow \text{lower limit}$$

Interpreting the results

Figure 8-21 illustrates these two limits of the acceptance region ($.1039 and $-$.1039) and indicates the difference between the sample means. It is calculated:

$$\text{Difference} = \bar{x}_1 - \bar{x}_2 \text{ (from Table 8-2)}$$
$$= \$8.95 - \$9.10$$
$$= -\$0.15$$

Figure 8-21 demonstrates that the difference between the two sample means lies outside the acceptance region. Thus, we reject the null hypothesis of no difference and conclude that the population means (the average semiskilled wages in these two cities) differ.

ONE-TAILED TESTS FOR DIFFERENCES BETWEEN MEANS (SMALL SAMPLE SIZES)

The procedure for a one-tailed test of the difference between means is conceptually like that for the one-tailed tests of means we have already discussed. The only major difference will be in how we compute the estimated standard error of the difference between the two means. Suppose that a company has been investigating two education programs for increasing the sensitivity of its managers to the needs of its Spanish-speaking employees. The original program consisted of several informal question-and-answer sessions with leaders of the Spanish-speaking community. Over the past few years, a program involving formal classroom contact with professional psychologists and sociologists has been developed. The new program is considerably more expensive, and the president wants to know at the .05 level of significance whether this expenditure has resulted in greater sensitivity. Let's test the following:

Setting up the problem symbolically

$H_0: \mu_1 = \mu_2 \leftarrow$ null hypothesis: There is no difference in sensitivity levels achieved by the two programs.

$H_1: \mu_1 > \mu_2 \leftarrow$ alternative hypothesis: The new program results in higher sensitivity levels.

$\alpha = .05 \leftarrow$ level of significance for testing this hypothesis

Table 8-3 contains the data resulting from a sample of the managers trained in both programs. Because only limited data are available for the two programs, the population standard deviations are estimated from the data. The sensitivity level is measured as a percentage on a standard psychometric scale.

TABLE 8-3 Data From Sample of Two Sensitivity Programs

PROGRAM SAMPLED	MEAN SENSITIVITY AFTER THIS PROGRAM	NUMBER OF MANAGERS OBSERVED	ESTIMATED STANDARD DEVIATION OF SENSITIVITY AFTER THIS PROGRAM
Formal	92%	12	15%
Informal	84%	15	19%

The company wishes to test whether the sensitivity achieved by the new program is *significantly higher* than that achieved under the older, more informal program. To reject the null hypothesis (a result that the company desires), the observed difference of sample means would need to fall sufficiently high in the *right* tail of the distribution. Then we would accept the alternative hypothesis that the new program leads to higher sensitivity levels and that the extra expenditures on this program are justified.

Our first task in performing the test is to calculate the standard error of the difference between the two means. Since the population standard deviations are not known, we must use Equation 8-2:

$$\hat{\sigma}_{\bar{x}_1 - \bar{x}_2} = \sqrt{\frac{\hat{\sigma}_1{}^2}{n_1} + \frac{\hat{\sigma}_2{}^2}{n_2}} \qquad [8\text{-}2]$$

In the previous example, where the sample sizes were large (both greater than 30), we used Equation 7-1 and estimated $\hat{\sigma}_1{}^2$ by $s_1{}^2$, and $\hat{\sigma}_2{}^2$ by $s_2{}^2$. Now, with small sample sizes, that procedure is not appropriate. If we can assume that the unknown population variances are equal (and this assumption can be tested using a method discussed in Section 6 of the next chapter), we can continue. If we cannot assume that $\sigma_1{}^2 = \sigma_2{}^2$, then the problem is beyond the scope of this text.

Estimating σ^2, with small sample sizes

Assuming for the moment that $\sigma_1{}^2 = \sigma_2{}^2$, how can we estimate the common variance σ^2? If we use either $s_1{}^2$ or $s_2{}^2$, we get an unbiased estimator of σ^2, but we don't use all the information available to us, since we ignore one of the samples. Instead we used a weighted average of $s_1{}^2$ and $s_2{}^2$, and the weights are the numbers of degrees of freedom in each sample. This weighted average is called a "pooled estimate" of σ^2. It is given by:

Pooled estimate of σ^2 $\longrightarrow$
$$s_p{}^2 = \frac{(n_1 - 1)s_1{}^2 + (n_2 - 1)s_2{}^2}{n_1 + n_2 - 2} \qquad [8\text{-}3]$$

Plugging this into Equation 8-2 and simplifying gives us:

$$\hat{\sigma}_{\bar{x}_1 - \bar{x}_2} = s_p \sqrt{\frac{1}{n_1} + \frac{1}{n_2}} \qquad [8\text{-}4]$$

When we want to test hypotheses about differences of population means, and we have small samples but equal population variances, we use Equation 8-4 to estimate the standard error of the difference between the two means. Then, as you might have guessed, the test is based on the t distribution. The appropriate number of degrees of freedom is $(n_1 - 1) + (n_2 - 1)$, or $n_1 + n_2 - 2$, which is the denominator in Equation 8-3.

Applying these results to our sensitivity example:

$$s_p^2 = \frac{(n_1 - 1)s_1{}^2 + (n_2 - 1)s_2{}^2}{n_1 + n_2 - 2} \qquad [8\text{-}3]$$

$$= \frac{(12 - 1)(15)^2 + (15 - 1)(19)^2}{12 + 15 - 2}$$

$$= \frac{11(225) + 14(361)}{25}$$

$$= 301.160$$

Taking square roots on both sides, we get $s_p = \sqrt{301.160}$, or 17.354, and so:

$$\hat{\sigma}_{\bar{x}_1 - \bar{x}_2} = s_p \sqrt{\frac{1}{n_1} + \frac{1}{n_2}} \qquad [8\text{-}4]$$

$$= 17.354 \sqrt{\frac{1}{12} + \frac{1}{15}}$$

$$= 17.354(.387)$$

$$= 6.721$$

Illustrating the problem

In Fig. 8-22, a graphic illustration of this hypothesis test, the significance level of .05 is represented by the colored region at the right of the distribution. Since both sample sizes are less than 30, the t distribution with $12 + 15 - 2 = 25$ degrees of freedom is the appropriate sampling distribution. The t value for .05 of the area under the curve is 1.708, according to Appendix Table 2. The hypothesized value of $\mu_{\bar{x}_1 - \bar{x}_2}$,

FIGURE 8-22

Right-tailed hypothesis test of the difference between two means at the .05 level of significance

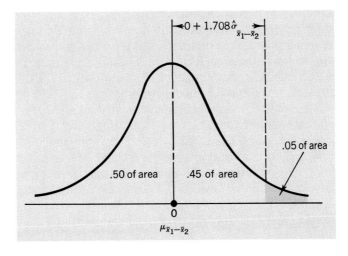

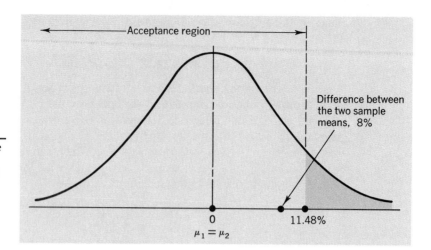

FIGURE 8-23

One-tailed test of the difference between two means at the .05 level of significance, showing acceptance region and the difference between the sample means

Determining the limit of the acceptance region

the mean of the sampling distribution of the difference between the two sensitivity means, is equal to zero. Thus, the calculation for determining the limit of the acceptance region is:

$$0 + 1.708\hat{\sigma}_{\bar{x}_1 - \bar{x}_2} = 0 + 1.708(6.721)$$
$$= 0 + 11.48$$
$$= 11.48\% \leftarrow \text{upper limit}$$

Interpreting the results

In Fig. 8-23, we have illustrated this limit of the acceptance region and the difference between the two sample sensitivities (92% − 84% = 8%). We can see in Fig. 8-23 that the difference between the two sample means lies within the acceptance region. Thus, we accept the null hypothesis that there is no difference between the sensitivities achieved by the two programs. The company's expenditures on the formal instructional program have not produced significantly higher sensitivities among its managers.

TESTING DIFFERENCES BETWEEN MEANS WITH DEPENDENT SAMPLES

Conditions under which paired samples aid analysis

In the last two examples, our samples were chosen *independently* of each other. In the wage example, the samples were taken in two different cities. In the sensitivity example, samples were taken of managers who had gone through two different training programs. Sometimes, however, it will make sense to take samples that are not independent of each other. Often the use of such *dependent* (or *paired*) samples will enable us to perform a more precise analysis, because they will allow us to control for extraneous factors. With dependent samples, we still follow the same basic procedure we have followed in all our hypothesis testing. The only differences are that we will use a different formula for the estimated standard error of the sample differences and that we will require that both samples be of the same size.

A health spa has advertised a weight-reducing program and has claimed that the average participant in the program loses at least seventeen pounds. A somewhat overweight executive is interested in the program but is skeptical about the claims and asks for some hard evidence. The spa allows him to select randomly the records of ten participants and record their weights before and after the program. These data are recorded in Table 8-4. Here we have two samples (a *before* sample and an *after*

TABLE 8-4 Weights Before and After a Reducing Program

Before	189	202	220	207	194	177	193	202	208	233
After	170	179	203	192	172	161	174	187	186	204

sample) that are clearly dependent on each other, since the same ten people have been observed twice.

The overweight executive wants to test at the 5 percent significance level the claimed average weight loss of at least seventeen pounds. Formally, we may state this problem:

$H_0: \mu_1 - \mu_2 = 17 \leftarrow$ null hypothesis: Average weight loss is only 17 pounds.

$H_1: \mu_1 - \mu_2 > 17 \leftarrow$ alternative hypothesis: Average weight loss exceeds 17 pounds.

$\alpha = .05 \leftarrow$ level of significance

Conceptual understanding of differences

What we are really interested in is not the weights before and after but only their *differences*. **Conceptually, what we have is *not two samples* of before and after weights, but rather *one sample* of weight losses.** If the population of weight losses has a mean μ_l, we can restate our hypotheses as:

$H_0: \mu_l = 17$

$H_1: \mu_l > 17$

Now we compute the individual losses, their mean and standard deviation, and proceed exactly as we did when testing hypotheses about a single mean. The computations are done in Table 8-5.

TABLE 8-5 Finding the Mean Weight Loss and Its Standard Deviation

BEFORE	AFTER	LOSS x	LOSS SQUARED x^2
189	170	19	361
202	179	23	529
220	203	17	289
207	192	15	225
194	172	22	484
177	161	16	256
193	174	19	361
202	187	15	225
208	186	22	484
233	204	29	841
		$\Sigma x = $ **197**	$\Sigma x^2 = $ **4,055**

$$\bar{x} = \frac{\Sigma x}{n} \quad [3\text{-}2] \qquad s = \sqrt{\frac{\Sigma x^2}{n-1} - \frac{n\bar{x}^2}{n-1}} \quad [3\text{-}18]$$

$$= \frac{197}{10} \qquad\qquad = \sqrt{\frac{4,055}{9} - \frac{10(19.7)^2}{9}}$$

$$= 19.7 \qquad\qquad = \sqrt{19.34}$$

$$\qquad\qquad\qquad = 4.40$$

We use Equation 7-1 to estimate the unknown population standard deviation:

$$\hat{\sigma} = s$$ [7-1]
$$= 4.40$$

and now we can estimate the standard error of the mean:

$$\hat{\sigma}_{\bar{x}} = \frac{\hat{\sigma}}{\sqrt{n}}$$ [7-6]

$$= \frac{4.40}{\sqrt{10}}$$

$$= \frac{4.40}{3.16}$$

$$= 1.39 \leftarrow \text{estimated standard error of the mean}$$

Figure 8-24 illustrates this problem graphically. Since we want to know if the mean weight loss *exceeds* seventeen pounds, an upper-tailed test is appropriate. The .05 significance level is shown in Fig. 8-24 as the colored area under the *t* distribution. We use the *t* distribution because the sample size is only ten: the appropriate number of degrees of freedom is 9, (10 − 1). Appendix Table 2 gives the *t* value of 1.833.

Determining the limit of the acceptance region

We use this *t* value to calculate the upper limit of the acceptance region:

$$\mu_{H_0} + 1.833\hat{\sigma}_{\bar{x}} = 17 + 1.833(1.39)$$
$$= 17 + 2.55$$
$$= 19.55 \text{ pounds} \leftarrow \text{upper limit}$$

Interpreting the results

Figure 8-25 illustrates the acceptance region and the sample mean, 19.7. We see that the sample mean lies outside the acceptance region, so the executive can reject the null hypothesis and conclude that the claimed weight loss in the program is legitimate.

How does the paired difference test differ?

Let's see how this *paired difference* test differs from a test of the difference of means of *two independent* samples. Suppose that the data in Table 8-4 represent two independent samples of ten individuals *entering* the program and *another* ten randomly

FIGURE 8-24

One-tailed hypothesis test at the .05 level of significance

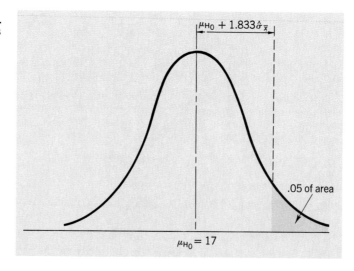

$\mu_{H_0} + 1.833\hat{\sigma}_{\bar{x}}$

.05 of area

$\mu_{H_0} = 17$

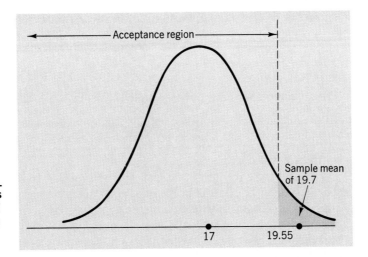

FIGURE 8-25
One-tailed hypothesis test at the .05 level of significance, showing acceptance region and sample mean

selected individuals *leaving* the program. The means and variances of the two samples are given in Table 8-6.

TABLE 8-6 Before and After Means and Variances

SAMPLE	SIZE	MEAN	VARIANCE
Before	10	202.5	253.61
After	10	182.8	201.96

A pooled estimate of σ^2

Since the sample sizes are small, we use Equation 8-3 to get a pooled estimate of σ^2 and Equation 8-4 to estimate $\hat{\sigma}_{\bar{x}_1 - \bar{x}_2}$:

$$s_p^2 = \frac{(n_1 - 1)s_1^2 + (n_2 - 1)s_2^2}{n_1 + n_2 - 2} \qquad [8\text{-}3]$$

$$= \frac{(10 - 1)(253.61) + (10 - 1)(201.96)}{10 + 10 - 2}$$

$$= \frac{2282.49 + 1817.64}{18}$$

$$= 227.79 \leftarrow \text{estimate of common population variance}$$

$$\hat{\sigma}_{\bar{x}_1 - \bar{x}_2} = s_p \sqrt{\frac{1}{n_1} + \frac{1}{n_2}} \qquad [8\text{-}4]$$

$$= \sqrt{227.79} \sqrt{\frac{1}{10} + \frac{1}{10}}$$

$$= 15.09(0.45)$$

$$= 6.79 \leftarrow \text{estimate of } \hat{\sigma}_{\bar{x}_1 - \bar{x}_2}$$

The appropriate test is now based on the t distribution with 18 degrees of freedom $(10 + 10 - 2)$. With a significance level of .05, the appropriate t value from Appendix

Table 2 is 1.734, so the upper limit of the acceptance region is:

$$17 + 1.734\hat{\sigma}_{\bar{x}_1 - \bar{x}_2} = 17 + 1.734(6.79)$$
$$= 17 + 11.77$$
$$= 28.77 \text{ pounds}$$

The observed difference of the sample means is:

$$\bar{x}_1 - \bar{x}_2 = 202.5 - 182.8$$
$$= 19.7 \text{ pounds}$$

so this test will *not* reject H_0.

Explaining differing results   Why did these two tests give such different results? In the paired sample test, the sample standard deviation of the individual differences was relatively small, so 19.7 pounds was significantly larger than the hypothesized weight loss of 17 pounds. With independent samples, however, the estimated standard deviation of the difference between the means depended on the standard deviations of the before weights and the after weights. Since both of these were relatively large, $\hat{\sigma}_{\bar{x}_1 - \bar{x}_2}$ was also large, and thus 19.7 was not significantly larger than 17. The paired sample test controlled this initial and final variability in weights by looking only at the individual changes in weights. Because of this, it was better able to detect the significance of the weight loss.

We conclude this section with two examples showing when to treat two samples of equal size as dependent or independent:

Should we treat samples as dependent or independent?

1. An agricultural extension service wishes to determine whether a new hybrid seed corn has a greater yield than an old standard variety. If the service asks ten farmers to record the yield of an acre planted with the new variety and asks another ten farmers to record the yield of an acre planted with the old variety, the two samples are independent. If, however, it asks ten farmers to plant one acre with each variety and record the results, then the samples are dependent, and the paired difference test is appropriate. In the latter case, differences due to fertilizer, insecticide, rainfall, and so on are controlled, because each farmer treats his two acres identically. Thus, any differences in yield can be attributed solely to the variety planted.

2. The director of the secretarial pool at a large legal office wants to determine whether typing speed depends upon the word-processing software used by a secretary. If she tests seven secretaries using PicosoftWrite and seven using Write-Perfect, she should treat her samples as independent. If she tests the same seven secretaries twice (once on each word processor), then the two samples are dependent. In the paired difference test, differences among the secretaries are eliminated as a contributing factor, and the differences in typing speeds can be attributed to the different word processors.

TWO-TAILED TESTS FOR DIFFERENCES BETWEEN PROPORTIONS

Consider the case of a pharmaceutical manufacturing company testing two new compounds intended to reduce blood-pressure levels. The compounds are administered to two different sets of laboratory animals. In group one, 71 of 100 animals tested respond to drug 1 with lower blood-pressure levels. In group two, 58 of 90 animals tested respond to drug 2 with lower blood-pressure levels. The company wants to test at the .05 level whether there is a difference between the efficacies of these two drugs. How should we proceed with this problem?

$$\bar{p}_1 = .71 \leftarrow \text{sample proportion of successes with drug 1}$$

$$\bar{q}_1 = .29 \leftarrow \text{sample proportion of failures with drug 1}$$

$$n_1 = 100 \leftarrow \text{sample size for testing drug 1}$$

$$\bar{p}_2 = .644 \leftarrow \text{sample proportion of successes with drug 2}$$

$$\bar{q}_2 = .356 \leftarrow \text{sample proportion of failures with drug 2}$$

$$n_2 = 90 \leftarrow \text{sample size for testing drug 2}$$

$\mathrm{H}_0 : p_1 = p_2 \leftarrow$ null hypothesis: There is no difference between these two drugs.

$\mathrm{H}_1 : p_1 \neq p_2 \leftarrow$ alternative hypothesis: There is a difference between them.

$\alpha = .05 \leftarrow$ level of significance for testing this hypothesis

As in our previous examples, we can begin by calculating the standard deviation of the sampling distribution we are using in our hypothesis test. In this example, the binomial distribution is the correct sampling distribution.

We want to find the *standard error of the difference between two proportions;* therefore, we should recall the formula for the *standard error of the proportion:*

$$\sigma_{\bar{p}} = \sqrt{\frac{pq}{n}} \qquad [7\text{-}4]$$

Using this formula and the same form we previously used in Equation 8-1 for the standard error of the difference between two *means,* we get:

$$\sigma_{\bar{p}_1 - \bar{p}_2} = \sqrt{\frac{p_1 q_1}{n_1} + \frac{p_2 q_2}{n_2}} \qquad [8\text{-}5]$$

To test the two compounds, we do not know the population parameters $p_1, p_2, q_1,$ and q_2, and thus we need to estimate them from the sample statistics $\bar{p}_1, \bar{p}_2, \bar{q}_1,$ and $\bar{q}_2$. In this case, we might suppose that the practical formula to use would be:

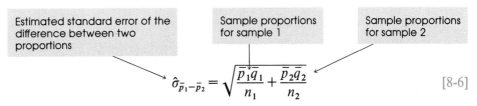

Estimated standard error of the difference between two proportions

Sample proportions for sample 1

Sample proportions for sample 2

$$\hat{\sigma}_{\bar{p}_1 - \bar{p}_2} = \sqrt{\frac{\bar{p}_1 \bar{q}_1}{n_1} + \frac{\bar{p}_2 \bar{q}_2}{n_2}} \qquad [8\text{-}6]$$

But think about this a bit more. After all, if we hypothesize that there is *no difference* between the two population proportions, then our best estimate of the overall population proportion of successes is probably the *combined* proportion of successes in both samples; that is:

Best estimate of the overall proportion of successes in the population if the two proportions are hypothesized to be equal

$=$

$\dfrac{\text{Number of successes} + \text{Number of successes}}{\text{Total size of both samples}}$

in sample 1   in sample 2

And in the case of the two compounds, we use this equation with symbols rather than words:

$$\hat{p} = \frac{(n_1)(\bar{p}_1) + (n_2)(\bar{p}_2)}{n_1 + n_2} \qquad [8\text{-}7]$$

$$= \frac{(100)(.71) + (90)(.644)}{100 + 90}$$

$$= \frac{71 + 58}{190}$$

$$= .6789 \leftarrow \text{estimate of the overall proportion of successes in the combined populations using combined proportions from both samples ($\hat{q}$ would be $1 - .6789 = .3211$)}$$

Now we can appropriately modify Equation 8-6 using the values $\hat{p}$ and $\hat{q}$ from Equation 8-7:

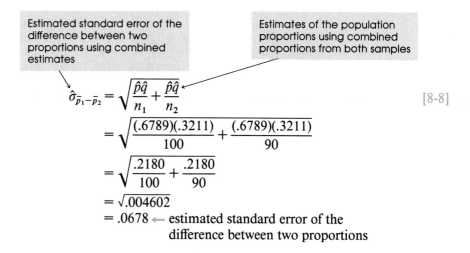

Estimated standard error of the difference between two proportions using combined estimates

Estimates of the population proportions using combined proportions from both samples

$$\hat{\sigma}_{\bar{p}_1 - \bar{p}_2} = \sqrt{\frac{\hat{p}\hat{q}}{n_1} + \frac{\hat{p}\hat{q}}{n_2}} \qquad [8\text{-}8]$$

$$= \sqrt{\frac{(.6789)(.3211)}{100} + \frac{(.6789)(.3211)}{90}}$$

$$= \sqrt{\frac{.2180}{100} + \frac{.2180}{90}}$$

$$= \sqrt{.004602}$$

$$= .0678 \leftarrow \text{estimated standard error of the difference between two proportions}$$

FIGURE 8-26

Two-tailed hypothesis test of the difference between two proportions at the .05 level of significance

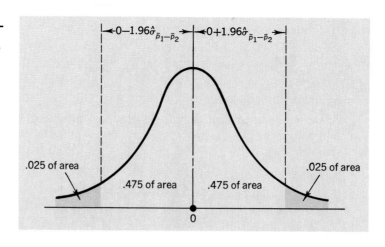

8 TESTING HYPOTHESES

What did we save by using Equation 8-8 instead of Equation 8-6? In Equation 8-8, we needed only *one* value for $\hat{p}$ and *one* value for $\hat{q}$; thus we avoided some of the calculations involved in the use of Equation 8-6.

Illustrating the problem

Figure 8-26 illustrates this hypothesis test graphically. Since the management of the pharmaceutical company wants to know whether there is a difference between the two compounds, this is a two-tailed test. The significance level of .05 corresponds to the colored regions in the figure. Both samples are large enough to justify using the normal distribution to approximate the binomial. From Appendix Table 1, we can determine that the approximate z value for .475 of the area under the curve is 1.96. We can calculate the two limits of the acceptance region as follows:

Determining the limits of the acceptance region

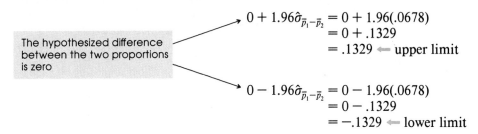

The hypothesized difference between the two proportions is zero

$$0 + 1.96\hat{\sigma}_{\bar{p}_1 - \bar{p}_2} = 0 + 1.96(.0678)$$
$$= 0 + .1329$$
$$= .1329 \leftarrow \text{upper limit}$$

$$0 - 1.96\hat{\sigma}_{\bar{p}_1 - \bar{p}_2} = 0 - 1.96(.0678)$$
$$= 0 - .1329$$
$$= -.1329 \leftarrow \text{lower limit}$$

Figure 8-27 illustrates these two limits of the acceptance region, .1329 and −.1329. It also indicates the difference between the sample proportions, calculated as:

$$\text{Difference} = \bar{p}_1 - \bar{p}_2$$
$$= .71 - .644$$
$$= .066$$

Interpreting the results

We can see in Fig. 8-27 that the difference between the two sample proportions lies within the acceptance region. Thus, we accept the null hypothesis and conclude that these two compounds produce effects on blood pressure that are *not* significantly different.

FIGURE 8-27

Two-tailed hypothesis test of the difference between two proportions at the .05 level of significance, showing acceptance region and the difference between sample proportions

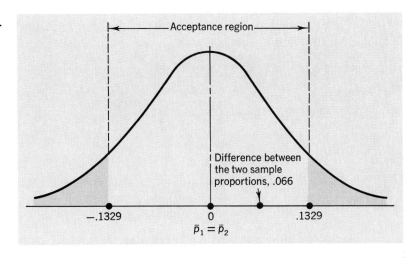

ONE-TAILED TESTS FOR DIFFERENCES BETWEEN PROPORTIONS

Conceptually, the one-tailed test for the difference between two population proportions is similar to a one-tailed test for the difference between two means. Suppose that for tax purposes, a city government has been using two methods of listing property. The first requires the property owner to appear in person before a tax lister, but the second permits the property owner to mail in a tax form. The city manager thinks the personal-appearance method produces far fewer mistakes than the mail-in method. She authorizes an examination of 50 personal-appearance listings and 75 mail-in listings. Ten percent of the personal-appearance forms contain errors; 13.3 percent of the mail-in forms contain them. The results of her sample can be summarized:

Setting up the problem symbolically

$\bar{p}_1 = .10 \leftarrow$ proportion of personal-appearance forms with errors

$\bar{q}_1 = .90 \leftarrow$ proportion of personal-appearance forms without errors

$n_1 = 50 \leftarrow$ sample size of personal-appearance forms

$\bar{p}_2 = .133 \leftarrow$ proportion of mail-in forms with errors

$\bar{q}_2 = .867 \leftarrow$ proportion of mail-in forms without errors

$n_2 = 75 \leftarrow$ sample size of mail-in forms

The city manager wants to test at the .15 level of significance the hypothesis that the personal-appearance method produces a lower proportion of errors. What should she do?

$H_0 : p_1 = p_2 \leftarrow$ null hypothesis: There is no difference between the two methods.

$H_1 : p_1 < p_2 \leftarrow$ alternative hypothesis: The personal-appearance method has a lower proportion of errors than the mail-in method.

$\alpha = .15 \leftarrow$ level of significance for testing the hypothesis

Calculating the standard error of the difference between two proportions

To estimate the *standard error of the difference between two proportions,* we first use the combined proportions from both samples to estimate the overall proportion of successes:

$$\hat{p} = \frac{(n_1)(\bar{p}_1) + (n_2)(\bar{p}_2)}{n_1 + n_2} \qquad [8\text{-}7]$$

$$= \frac{(50)(.10) + (75)(.133)}{50 + 75}$$

$$= \frac{5 + 10}{125}$$

$= .12 \leftarrow$ estimate of the overall proportion of successes in the population using combined proportions from both samples

Now this answer can be used to calculate the standard error of the difference between the two proportions, using Equation 8-8:

$$\hat{\sigma}_{\bar{p}_1 - \bar{p}_2} = \sqrt{\frac{\hat{p}\hat{q}}{n_1} + \frac{\hat{p}\hat{q}}{n_2}} \qquad [8\text{-}8]$$

$$= \sqrt{\frac{(.12)(.88)}{50} + \frac{(.12)(.88)}{75}}$$

$$= \sqrt{\frac{.10560}{50} + \frac{.10560}{75}}$$

$$= \sqrt{.00352}$$

$$= .0593 \leftarrow \text{estimated standard error of the}$$
difference between two proportions
using combined estimates

Illustrating the problem   Figure 8-28 illustrates this hypothesis test. Since the city manager wishes to test whether the personal-appearance listing is better than the mailed-in listing, the appropriate test is a one-tailed test. Specifically, it is a *left-tailed* test, because to reject the null hypothesis, the test result must fall in the colored portion of the left tail, indicating that *significantly fewer errors* exist in the personal-appearance forms. This colored region in Fig. 8-28 corresponds to the .15 significance level.

Determining the limit of   With samples of this size, we can use the standard normal distribution and Appenthe acceptance region   dix Table 1 to determine the appropriate z value for .35 of the area under the curve. We can use this value, 1.04, to calculate the lower limit of the acceptance region:

> The hypothesized difference between the 2 population proportions is zero

$$0 - 1.04\hat{\sigma}_{\bar{p}_1 - \bar{p}_2} = 0 - 1.04(.0593)$$
$$= 0 - .0617$$
$$= -.0617 \leftarrow \text{lower limit}$$

Interpreting the results   We have illustrated this limit to the acceptance region and the difference between the two sample proportions $(.10 - .133 = -.033)$ in Fig. 8-29. This figure shows us that the difference between the two sample proportions lies well within the acceptance region, and the city manager should accept the null hypothesis that there is no difference between the two methods of tax listing. Therefore, if mailed-in listing is considerably less expensive to the city, the city manager should consider increasing the use of this method.

FIGURE 8-28

One-tailed hypothesis test of the difference between two proportions at the .15 level of significance

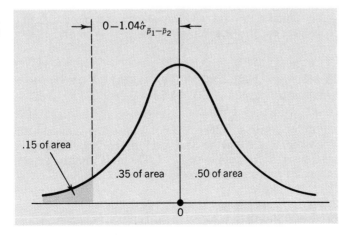

8-8 Hypothesis Testing for Differences Between Means and Proportions   **389**

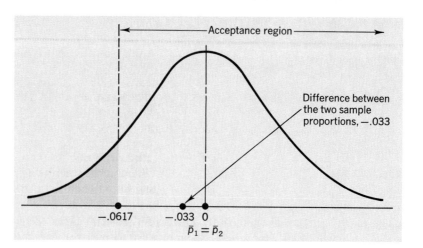

FIGURE 8-29

FIGURE 8-29

One-tailed hypothesis test of the difference between two proportions at the .15 level of significance, showing acceptance region and the difference between the sample proportions

In the figure: Acceptance region. Difference between the two sample proportions, −.033. −.0617   −.033 0 $\bar{p}_1 = \bar{p}_2$

Exercises

8-52 Two independent samples of observations were collected. For the first sample of 60 elements, the mean was 86 and the standard deviation 6. The second sample of 75 elements had a mean of 82 and a standard deviation of 9.
(a) Compute the standard error of the difference between the two means.
(b) Using $\alpha = .01$, test whether the two samples can reasonably be considered to have come from populations with the same mean.

8-53 To celebrate their first anniversary, Randy Nelson decided to buy a pair of diamond earrings for his wife Debbie. He was shown nine pairs with marquise gems weighing approximately 2 carats per pair. Because of differences in the colors and qualities of the stones, the prices varied from set to set. The average price was $2,990, with a sample standard deviation of $370. He also looked at six pairs with pear-shaped stones of the same two-carat approximate weight. These earrings had an average price of $3,065, with a standard deviation of $805. On the basis of this evidence, can Randy conclude (at a significance level of .05) that pear-shaped diamonds cost more, on average, than marquise diamonds?

8-54 The data below are a random sample of nine firms chosen from the "Digest of Earnings Reports" in *The Wall Street Journal* on February 6, 1989:
(a) Find the mean change in earnings per share between 1988 and 1989.
(b) Find the standard deviation of the change and the standard error of the mean.
(c) Were average earnings per share different in 1988 and 1989? Test at $\alpha = .02$.

Firm	1	2	3	4	5	6	7	8	9
1988 earnings	1.38	1.26	3.64	3.50	2.47	3.21	1.05	1.98	2.72
1989 earnings	2.48	1.50	4.59	3.06	2.11	2.80	1.59	0.92	0.47

8-55 In preparation for contract renewal negotiations, the United Manufacturing Workers surveyed its members to see whether they preferred a large increase in retirement benefits or a smaller increase in salary. In a group of 1,000 male members who were polled, 743 were in favor of increased retirement benefits. Of 500 female members surveyed, 405 favored the increase in retirement benefits.
(a) Calculate $\hat{p}$.
(b) Compute the standard error of the difference between the two proportions.

(c) Test the hypothesis that equal proportions of men and women are in favor of increased retirement benefits. Use the .05 level of significance.

8-56 A sample of 32 money-market mutual funds was chosen on January 1, 1989; the average annual rate of return over the past 30 days was found to be 7.23%, with a sample standard deviation of .51%. A year earlier, a sample of 38 money-market funds showed an average rate of return of 8.36%, with a sample standard deviation of .84%. Is it reasonable to conclude (at $\alpha = .05$) that money-market interest rates declined during 1988?

8-57 Two research laboratories have independently produced drugs that provide relief to arthritis sufferers. The first drug was tested on a group of 90 arthritis victims and produced an average of 8.5 hours of relief, with a standard deviation of 1.8 hours. The second drug was tested on 80 arthritis victims, producing an average of 7.9 hours of relief, with a standard deviation of 2.1 hours. At the .05 level of significance, does the second drug provide a significantly shorter period of relief?

8-58 Two different areas of a large eastern city are being considered as sites for day-care centers. Of 200 households surveyed in one section, the proportion in which the mother worked full-time was .52. In the other section, 40 percent of the 150 households surveyed had mothers working at full-time jobs. At the .04 level of significance, is there a significant difference in the proportions of working mothers in the two areas of the city?

8-59 In September, 1989, the Automobile Confederation of the Carolinas surveyed 75 randomly chosen service stations in North and South Carolina and determined that the average price for regular unleaded gasoline at self-service pumps was $1.059, with a standard deviation of 3.9¢. Three months later, another survey of 50 service stations found an average price of $1.189, with a standard deviation of 6.8¢. At $\alpha = .02$, had the Carolinas' average price of self-service regular unleaded gasoline changed significantly in this 3-month period?

8-60 A coal-fired power plant is considering two different systems for pollution abatement. The first system has reduced the emission of pollutants to acceptable levels 68 percent of the time, as determined from 200 air samples. The second, more expensive system has reduced the emission of pollutants to acceptable levels 76 percent of the time, as determined from 250 air samples. If the expensive system is significantly more effective than the inexpensive system in reducing pollutants to acceptable levels, then the management of the power plant will install the former system. Which system will be installed if management uses a significance level of .02 in making its decision?

8-61 A large stock-brokerage firm wants to determine how successful its new account executives have been at recruiting clients. After completing their training, new account execs spend several weeks calling prospective clients, trying to get the prospects to open accounts with the firm. The data below give the numbers of new accounts opened in their first 2 weeks by ten randomly chosen female account execs and by eight randomly chosen male account execs. At $\alpha = .05$, does it appear that the women are more effective at generating new accounts than the men are?

NUMBER OF NEW ACCOUNTS

Female account execs	12	11	14	13	13	14	13	12	14	12
Male account execs	13	10	11	12	13	12	10	12		

8-62 A consumer-research organization routinely selects several car models each year and evaluates their fuel efficiency. In this year's study of two similar subcompact models from two different automakers, the average gas mileage for twelve cars of brand A was 27.2 miles per gallon, with a standard deviation of 3.8 mpg. The nine brand B cars that were tested averaged 32.1 mpg, with a standard deviation of 4.3 mpg. At $\alpha = .01$, should it conclude that brand B cars have higher average gas mileage than do brand A cars?

8-63 Is the perceived level of responsibility for an action related to the severity of its consequences? That question was the basis of a study of responsibility in which the subjects read a description of an accident on an interstate highway. The consequences, in terms of cost and injury, were described as either very minor or serious. A questionnaire was used to rate the degree of responsibility that the subjects believed should be placed on the main figure in the story. Below are the ratings for both the mild-consequences and the severe-consequences groups. High ratings correspond to higher responsibility attributed to the main figure. If a .025 significance level was used, did the study conclude that severe consequences lead to a greater attribution of responsibility?

CONSEQUENCES	DEGREE OF RESPONSIBILITY							
Mild	4	5	3	3	4	1	2	6
Severe	4	5	4	6	7	8	6	5

8-64 Nine computer-components dealers in major metropolitan areas were asked for their prices on two similar dot-matrix printers with standard widths and near-letter-quality fonts. The results of this survey are given below. At $\alpha = .05$, is it reasonable to assert that, on average, the Apson printer is less expensive than the Okaydata printer?

Dealer	1	2	3	4	5	6	7	8	9
Apson price	$350	419	385	360	405	395	389	409	375
Okaydata price	$370	425	369	375	389	385	395	425	400

8-65 Sherri Welch is a quality control engineer with the windshield wiper manufacturing division of Emsco, Inc. Emsco is currently considering two new synthetic rubbers for its wiper blades, and Sherri was charged with seeing if blades made with the two new compounds wear equally well. She equipped twelve cars belonging to other Emsco employees with one blade made of each of the two compounds. On six of the cars the right blade was made of compound A, and the left blade was made of compound B; on the other six cars, compound A was used for the left blade. The cars were driven under normal operating conditions until the blades no longer did a satisfactory job of clearing the windshield of rain. The data below give the usable life (in days) of the blades. At $\alpha = .05$, do the two compounds wear equally well?

Car	1	2	3	4	5	6	7	8	9	10	11	12
Left blade	162	323	220	274	165	271	233	156	238	211	241	154
Right blade	183	347	247	269	189	257	224	178	263	199	263	148

8-66 Donna Rose is a production supervisor on the disk-drive assembly line at Winchester Technologies. Winchester recently subscribed to an easy-listening music service at its factory, hoping that this would relax the workers and lead to greater productivity. Donna is skeptical about this hypothesis and fears the music will be distracting, leading to lower productivity. She sampled weekly production for the same six workers before the music was installed and after it was installed. Her data are given below. At $\alpha = .02$, has average production changed at all?

EMPLOYEE	1	2	3	4	5	6
Week without music	219	205	226	198	209	216
Week with music	235	186	240	203	221	205

8-67 Block Enterprises, a manufacturer of RAM chips for computers, is in the process of deciding whether to replace its current semiautomated assembly line with a fully automated assembly line. Block has gathered some preliminary test data about hourly chip production, which is summarized in the following table, and it would like to know if it should upgrade its assembly line. State (and test at $\alpha = .02$) appropriate hypotheses to help Block decide.

	$\bar{x}$	s	n
Semiautomatic line	198	32	150
Automatic line	206	29	200

8-68 Aquarius Health Club has been advertising a rigorous program for body conditioning. The club claims that after 1 month in the program, the average participant should be able to do eight more push-ups in 2 minutes than he or she could do at the start. Does the random sample of ten program participants given below support the club's claim? Use the .025 level of significance.

Participant	1	2	3	4	5	6	7	8	9	10
Before	38	11	34	25	17	38	12	27	32	29
After	45	24	41	39	30	44	30	39	40	41

8-69 A group of clinical physicians is performing tests on patients to determine the effectiveness of a new antihypertensive drug. Patients with high blood pressure were randomly chosen and then randomly assigned to either the control group (which received a well established antihypertensive) or the treatment group (which received the new drug). The doctors noted the percentage of patients whose blood pressure was reduced to a normal level within 1 year. At the .01 level of significance, test appropriate hypotheses to determine if the new drug is significantly more effective than the older drug in reducing high blood pressure.

GROUP	PROPORTION THAT IMPROVED	NUMBER OF PATIENTS
Treatment	.45	120
Control	.36	150

8-9
Prob Values—Another Way to Look at Testing Hypotheses

In all the work we've done so far on hypothesis testing, one of the first things we had to do was choose a level of significance, α, for the test. It has been traditional to choose a significance level of $\alpha = 10$ percent, 5 percent, 2 percent, or 1 percent, and almost all our examples have been done at these levels. But why use only these few values?

How do we choose a significance level?

When we discussed Type I and Type II errors on page 352, we saw that the choice of the significance level depended on a tradeoff between the costs of each of these two kinds of errors. If the cost of a Type I error (incorrectly rejecting H_0) is relatively high, we want to avoid making this kind of error, so we choose a small value of α. On the other hand, if a Type II error (incorrectly accepting H_0) is relatively more expensive, we are more willing to make a Type I error, and we choose a high value of α. **However, understanding the nature of the tradeoff still doesn't tell us how to choose a significance level.**

Deciding before we take a sample

When we test the hypotheses:

$$H_0 : \mu = \mu_{H_0}$$
$$H_1 : \mu \neq \mu_{H_0}$$
$$\alpha = .05$$

we take a sample, compute $\bar{x}$, and reject H_0 if $\bar{x}$ is so far from μ_{H_0} that the probability of seeing a value of $\bar{x}$ this far (or farther) from μ_{H_0} is less than .05. In other words, **before we take the sample,** we specify how unlikely the observed results will have to be in order for us to reject H_0. There is another way to approach this decision about rejecting or accepting H_0 that doesn't require that we specify the significance level before taking the sample. Let's see how it works.

Prob values

Suppose we take our sample, compute $\bar{x}$, and then ask the question. "Supposing H_0 were true, what's the probability of getting a value of $\bar{x}$ this far or farther from μ_{H_0}?" This probability is called a *prob value* or a *p-value*. **Whereas before we asked, "Is the probability of what we've observed less than α?" now we are merely asking, "How unlikely is the result we have observed?" Once the prob value for the test is reported, *then* the decision maker can weigh all the relevant factors and decide whether to accept or reject H_0, without being bound by a prespecified significance level.**

Another advantage

Another benefit of using prob values is that they provide more information. If you know that I rejected H_0 at $\alpha = .05$, you only know that $\bar{x}$ was *at least* 1.96 standard errors away from μ_{H_0}. However, a prob value of .05 tells you that $\bar{x}$ was *exactly* 1.96 standard errors away from μ_{H_0}. Let's look at an example.

TWO-TAILED PROB VALUES WHEN σ IS KNOWN

A machine is used to cut wheels of Swiss cheese into blocks of specified weight. On the basis of long experience, it has been observed that the weight of the blocks is normally distributed with a standard deviation of .3 ounce. The machine is currently set to cut blocks that weigh 12 ounces. A sample of nine blocks is found to have an average weight of 12.25 ounces. Should we conclude that the cutting machine needs to be recalibrated?

Written symbolically, the data in our problem are:

Setting up the problem symbolically

$\mu_{H_0} = 12 \leftarrow$ hypothesized value of the population mean

$\sigma = .3 \leftarrow$ population standard deviation

$n = 9 \leftarrow$ sample size

$\bar{x} = 12.25 \leftarrow$ sample mean

The hypotheses we wish to test are:

$H_0 : \mu = 12 \leftarrow$ null hypothesis: The true population mean weight is 12 ounces.

$H_1 : \mu \neq 12 \leftarrow$ alternative hypothesis: The true population mean weight is not 12 ounces.

Since this is a two-tailed test, our prob value is the probability of observing a value of $\bar{x}$ at least as far away (on either side) from 12 as 12.25, if H_0 is true. In other words, the prob value is the probability of getting $\bar{x} \geq 12.25$ or $\bar{x} \leq 11.75$ if H_0 is true. To find this probability, we first use Equation 6-1 to calculate the standard error of the mean:

8 TESTING HYPOTHESES

Calculating the standard error of the mean

$$\sigma_{\bar{x}} = \frac{\sigma}{\sqrt{n}} \qquad [6\text{-}1]$$

$$= \frac{.3}{\sqrt{9}}$$

$$= \frac{.3}{3}$$

$$= .1 \text{ ounce} \leftarrow \text{standard error of the mean}$$

Then we use this to convert $\bar{x}$ to a standard z score:

Finding the z score and the prob value

$$z = \frac{\bar{x} - \mu}{\sigma_{\bar{x}}} \qquad [6\text{-}2]$$

$$= \frac{12.25 - 12}{.1}$$

$$= \frac{.25}{.1}$$

$$= 2.5$$

From Appendix Table 1, we see that the probability that z is greater than 2.5 is .5000 − .4938 = .0062. Hence, since this is a two-tailed hypothesis test, the prob value is 2(.0062) = .0124. Our results are illustrated in Fig. 8-30. Given this information, our cheese packer can now decide whether to recalibrate the machine (reject H_0) or not (accept H_0).

Relationship between prob values and significance levels

How is this related to what we did before, when we specified a significance level? If a significance level of $\alpha = .05$ were adopted, we would reject H_0. You can easily see this by looking at Fig. 8-30. At a significance level of $\alpha = .05$, we reject H_0 if $\bar{x}$ is so far from μ_{H_0} that less than .05 of the area under the curve is left in the two tails. Since our observed value of $\bar{x} = 12.25$ leaves only .0124 of the total area in the tails, we would reject H_0 at a significance level of $\alpha = .05$. (You can also verify this result by noting

FIGURE 8-30

Two-tailed hypothesis test, showing prob value of .0124

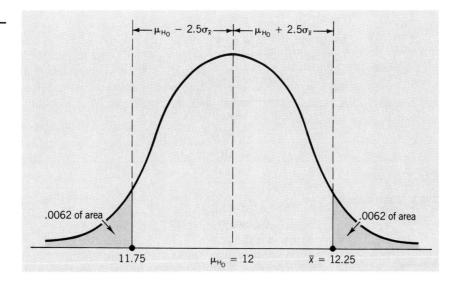

that the upper limit of the acceptance region is $\mu_{H_0} + 1.96\sigma_{\bar{x}} = 12 + 1.96(.1) = 12.20$, so our observed value of $\bar{x} = 12.25$ is *outside* the acceptance region.)

Similarly, we can see that at a significance level of $\alpha = .01$, we would accept H_0, because $\bar{x} = 12.25$ leaves more than .01 of the total area in the tails. (In this case, the upper limit of the acceptance region would be $\mu_{H_0} + 2.57\sigma_{\bar{x}} = 12 + 2.57(.1) = 12.26$, so our observed value of $\bar{x} = 12.25$ is *inside* the acceptance region.) In fact, at any level of α above .0124, we would reject H_0. **Thus we see that the prob value is precisely the largest significance level at which we would accept H_0.**

PROB VALUES UNDER OTHER CONDITIONS

In our example, we did a two-tailed hypothesis test using the normal distribution. How would we proceed in other circumstances?

One-tailed prob values

1. If σ was known, and we were doing a one-tailed test, we would compute the prob value in exactly the same way except that we would not multiply the probability that we got from Appendix Table 1 by 2, since that table gives one-tailed probabilities directly.

Using the *t* distribution

2. If σ was not known, we would use the *t* distribution with $n - 1$ degrees of freedom and Appendix Table 2. This table gives two-tailed probabilities, but only a few of them, so we can't get exact prob values from it. For example, for a two-tailed test, if $\mu_{H_0} = 50$, $\bar{x} = 49.2$, $s = 1.4$, and $n = 16$, we find that:

$$\hat{\sigma}_{\bar{x}} = \frac{\hat{\sigma}}{\sqrt{n}} \qquad [7\text{-}6]$$

$$= \frac{1.4}{\sqrt{16}}$$

$$= .35$$

and that $\bar{x}$ is 2.286 estimated standard errors below μ_{H_0} $[(49.2 - 50)/.35 = -2.286]$. Looking at the 15 degrees of freedom row in Appendix Table 2, we see that 2.286 is between 2.131 ($\alpha = .05$) and 2.602 ($\alpha = .02$). Our prob value is therefore something between .02 and .05, but we can't be more specific.

Prob values in other contexts

Most computer statistics packages report exact prob values, not only for tests about means based on the normal distribution, but for other tests such as chi-square and analysis of variance (which we will discuss in Chapter 9) and tests in the context of linear regression (which we will discuss in Chapters 10 and 11). The discussion we have provided in this section will enable you to understand prob values in those contexts too. Although different statistics and distributions will be involved, the ideas are the same.

Exercises

 8-70   A car retailer thinks that a 40,000 mile claim for tire life by the manufacturer is too high. She carefully records the mileage obtained from a sample of 64 such tires. The mean turns out to be 38,500 miles. The standard deviation of the life of all tires of this type has previously been calculated by the manufacturer to be 7,600 miles. Assuming that the mileage is normally distributed, determine the largest significance level at which we would accept the manufacturer's mileage claim, that is, at which we would not conclude the mileage is significantly less than 40,000 miles.

8-71 The Coffee Institute has claimed that at least 40 percent of American adults regularly have a cup of coffee with breakfast. A random sample of 450 individuals revealed that 200 of them were regular coffee drinkers at breakfast. What is the prob value for a test of hypotheses seeking to show that the Coffee Institute's claim was correct? (Hint: Test $H_0: p = .4$, versus $H_1: p > .4$.)

8-72 Kelly's machine shop uses a machine-controlled metal saw to cut sections of tubing used in pressure measuring devices. The length of the sections is normally distributed with a standard deviation of .06″. Twenty-five pieces have been cut with the machine set to cut sections 5.00″ long. When these pieces were measured, their mean length was found to be 4.97″. Use prob values to determine whether the machine should be recalibrated because the mean length is significantly different fom 5.00″.

8-73 SAT Services advertises that 80 percent of the time its preparatory course will increase an individual's score on the college board exams by at least 50 points on the combined verbal and quantitative total score. Lisle Johns, SAT's marketing director, wants to see if this is a reasonable claim. He has reviewed the records of 125 students who took the course and found that 94 of them did, indeed, increase their scores by at least 50 points. Use prob values to determine if SAT's ads should be changed because the percentage of students whose scores increase by 50 or more points is significantly different from 80 percent.

8-10
Using the Computer to Test Hypotheses

When the final exam for our Fall 1989 statistics course was designed, we expected that the average grade would be about 75% (56.25 points out of a maximum possible score of 75). Let's test (at $\alpha = .05$) whether our expectation was met.

Setting up the problem symbolically

$$H_0: \mu = 56.25 \leftarrow \text{the exam achieved the desired difficulty}$$

$$H_1: \mu \neq 56.25 \leftarrow \text{the desired difficulty was not achieved}$$

$$\alpha = .05 \leftarrow \text{level of significance for this test}$$

Interpreting the results

In Fig. 8-31, we have again used SAS to analyze the data in Appendix 9. The observed t-value for this test is -15.45, with an associated (two-tailed) prob value of 0.0001. Since this prob value is less than our significance level of $\alpha = .05$, we must reject H_0 and conclude that the test did not achieve the desired level of difficulty. (In fact, the test turned out to be much more difficult than we had intended.)

The University had been receiving many complaints about the caliber of teaching being done by the graduate-student teaching assistants. As a result, we wondered whether the students in sections taught by the graduate TAs really did do worse on the

---

FIGURE 8-31

Using SAS to test hypotheses about a population mean

```
                                    SAS
                      1989 GRADES IN BUSINESS STATISTICS
                     MEASURING THE DIFFICULTY OF THE FINAL EXAM
               WAS THE AVERAGE SCORE SIGNIFICANTLY DIFFERENT FROM 56.25?
```

VARIABLE	N	MEAN	STANDARD DEVIATION	VARIANCE	STD ERROR OF MEAN	T	PR>|T|
FINAL	199	45.28140704	10.01419225	100.284046	0.70988727	-15.45	0.0001

```
                              SAS
                  1989 GRADES IN BUSINESS STATISTICS
                 DID TA'S STUDENTS DO WORSE ON THE FINAL?

                          TTEST PROCEDURE

    VARIABLE: FINAL

    INSTRUCT       N              MEAN           STD DEV        STD ERROR

    PR            110        45.56363636      10.24876567      0.97718146
    TA             89        44.93258427       9.76286768      1.03486190

    VARIANCES        T        DF      PROB > |T|

    UNEQUAL       0.4434    191.8      0.6580
    EQUAL         0.4411    197.0      0.6596

    FOR H0:  VARIANCES ARE EQUAL,  F'=    1.10 WITH 109 AND 88 DF
             PROB > F'= 0.6383
```

FIGURE 8-32

Using SAS to test hypotheses about the difference between two means

exam than those students in sections taught by the faculty. If we let the faculty's sections be sample 1 and the TAs' sections be sample 2, then the appropriate hypotheses for testing this concern are:

Setting up the problem symbolically

$$H_0: \mu_1 = \mu_2 \leftarrow \text{the concern is not supported by the data}$$

$$H_1: \mu_1 > \mu_2 \leftarrow \text{the concern is supported by the data}$$

The SAS output for doing this test is given in Fig. 8-32. Notice that test results are reported for two different sets of assumptions: First, that the two population variances are unequal and second, that they are equal. Since our sample sizes are both quite large ($n_1 = 110$ and $n_2 = 89$), the results for the two cases are quite similar (the two-tailed prob values are 0.6580 and 0.6596). However, when the sample sizes are small, the two can be considerably different. If we can assume that the two variances are equal, then the test reported by SAS, is the test we discussed on pages 377–380, where we found a pooled estimate for σ^2. Without this assumption, we couldn't do the test by hand, but SAS gives the results for this test, too. The output also gives the results of a test of whether the two variances are equal or not, and this would enable you to decide which of the two prob values to use in testing the differences of the two means.

Interpreting the results

What should we conclude about whether or not students in sections taught by TAs are at a disadvantage? Since this is a one-tailed test, we must divide the reported two-tailed prob value by two to get a one-tailed prob value. The resulting value (about 0.33) is quite large relative to the typical significance levels we have been using (0.10, 0.05, 0.01, etc.), so we cannot reject H_0. The data do not support the concern expressed in the complaints received by the University.

USING MINITAB AND MYSTAT TO TEST HYPOTHESES

The earnings data in Appendix 10 contain the 1988 last-quarter earnings for 224 companies, in addition to containing the 1989 last-quarter earnings. Since the United States economy had not suffered a recession since 1982, by 1989 many economists were expecting the economy to start slowing down. Let's check (at $\alpha = .10$) whether

398   8 TESTING HYPOTHESES

FIGURE 8-33

Using Minitab to do a
paired-difference test
of means

```
TEST OF MU = 0.0000 VS MU L.T. 0.0000

              N     MEAN   STDEV  SE MEAN      T  P VALUE
CHANGE      224  -0.0354  0.8967   0.0599  -0.59     0.28
```

the year-to-year change in last-quarter earnings gave evidence that their expectation had come to pass. In Fig. 8-33, we have used Minitab to test this.

Setting up the problem
symbolically

$$H_0 : \mu_{1989} = \mu_{1988} \leftarrow \text{the economy didn't slow down}$$

$$H_1 : \mu_{1989} < \mu_{1988} \leftarrow \text{the economy did slow down}$$

$$\alpha = .10 \leftarrow \text{level of significance for this test}$$

To perform this paired-difference test, we first subtracted the 1988 last-quarter earnings from the 1989 last-quarter earnings and stored the results in a variable named "CHANGE." Looking at CHANGE, our hypotheses become:

$$H_0 : \mu = 0 \leftarrow \text{the economy didn't slow down}$$

$$H_1 : \mu < 0 \leftarrow \text{the economy did slow down}$$

$$\alpha = .10 \leftarrow \text{level of significance for this test}$$

Interpreting the results

In Fig. 8-33, we see that the reported prob value for our one-tailed test is 0.28. Since this prob value is greater than our significance level of $\alpha = .10$, we cannot reject H_0. Last-quarter earnings did not decline significantly from year to year, so they don't provide evidence of a slowing economy.

In the test we just did, all 224 companies were used. However, maybe earnings changes for the relatively large companies whose stock is listed on the New York Stock Exchange are different from earnings changes for the smaller companies listed on the American Stock Exchange or traded "over-the-counter." If they differ, perhaps one is a better indicator of the direction in which the economy is heading. To check this out, we can divide the 224 companies into two groups (NYSE and OTHER) and do an independent-samples test of the difference in the mean values of CHANGE in the two groups. Let's test this at $\alpha = .02$.

Setting up the problem
symbolically

$$H_0 : \mu_{NYSE} = \mu_{OTHER} \leftarrow \text{both mean changes are the same}$$

$$H_1 : \mu_{NYSE} \neq \mu_{OTHER} \leftarrow \text{the two mean changes differ}$$

$$\alpha = .02 \leftarrow \text{level of significance for this test}$$

In Fig. 8-34, we have used MYSTAT to perform this test. (Our data set contained a variable named NYORNO\$ (meaning "NYSE or not") with values of NYSE or OTHER for each company's observation. In MYSTAT, the names of variables with alphabetic values must end with a \$.) Just as in the test we did with SAS in Fig. 8-32, MYSTAT also reports two sets of results for independent-samples tests of the difference of two means. However, MYSTAT does not provide a test of the equality of the variances of the two populations. (You will learn how to perform such a test in the

FIGURE 8-34

Using MYSTAT to do
an independent-
samples test of means

```
INDEPENDENT SAMPLES T-TEST ON     CHANGE     GROUPED BY    NYORNO$

         GROUP           N        MEAN          SD
         OTHER          149      -0.061        0.645
         NYSE            75       0.016        1.260

 SEPARATE VARIANCES T =    .495   DF =  94.0   PROB = .621
   POOLED VARIANCES T =    .603   DF =  222    PROB = .547
```

Interpreting the results next chapter.) In this particular case, whether the variances are the same or different, the prob value for the test of the difference of the NYSE and OTHER mean changes is much larger than our significance level of $\alpha = .02$, so we cannot reject H_0. There is not enough evidence to warrant further investigation of using the year-to-year change in last-quarter earnings as evidence of the direction in which the economy was heading.

8-11
Terms Introduced in Chapter 8

Alpha (α) The probability of a Type I error.

Alternative Hypothesis The conclusion we accept when the data fail to support the null hypothesis.

Beta (β) The probability of a Type II error.

Dependent Samples Samples drawn from two populations in such a way that the elements were not chosen independently of one another, in order to allow a more precise analysis or to control for some extraneous factors.

Hypothesis An assumption or speculation we make about a population parameter.

Lower-Tailed Test A one-tailed hypothesis test in which a sample value significantly below the hypothesized population value will lead us to reject the null hypothesis.

Null Hypothesis The hypothesis, or assumption, about a population parameter we wish to test, usually an assumption of the status quo.

One-Tailed Test A hypothesis test in which there is only one rejection region; i.e., we are concerned only with whether the observed value deviates from the hypothesized value in one direction.

Paired Difference Test A hypothesis test of the difference between the sample means of two dependent samples.

Power Curve A graph of the values of the power of a test for each value of μ, or other population parameter, for which the alternative hypothesis is true.

Power of the Hypothesis Test The probability of rejecting the null hypothesis when it is false; i.e., a measure of how well the hypothesis test is working.

Prob Value The largest significance level at which we would accept the null hypothesis. It enables us to test hypotheses without first specifying a value for α.

Significance Level A value indicating the percentage of sample values that is outside certain limits, assuming the null hypothesis is correct; i.e., the probability of rejecting the null hypothesis when it is true.

Two-Tailed Test A hypothesis test in which the null hypothesis is rejected if the sample value is significantly higher or lower than the hypothesized value of the population parameter; a test involving two rejection regions.

Type I Error Rejecting a null hypothesis when it is true.

Type II Error Accepting a null hypothesis when it is false.

Upper-Tailed Test A one-tailed hypothesis test in which a sample value significantly above the hypothesized population value will lead us to reject the null hypothesis.

[8-1]

$$\sigma_{\bar{x}_1 - \bar{x}_2} = \sqrt{\frac{\sigma_1^2}{n_1} + \frac{\sigma_2^2}{n_2}}$$

p. 375

This formula enables us to derive the standard deviation of the distribution of the difference between two sample means; that is, *the standard error of the difference between two means.* To do this, we take the square root of the sum of Population 1's variance divided by its sample size and of Population 2's variance divided by its sample size.

[8-2]

$$\hat{\sigma}_{\bar{x}_1 - \bar{x}_2} = \sqrt{\frac{\hat{\sigma}_1^2}{n_1} + \frac{\hat{\sigma}_2^2}{n_2}}$$

p. 375

If the two population standard deviations are unknown, we can use this formula to derive the *estimated* standard error of the difference between two means. We can use this equation after we have used the two sample standard deviations and Equation 7-1 to determine the estimated standard deviations of Population 1 and Population 2 ($\hat{\sigma} = s$).

[8-3]

$$s_p^2 = \frac{(n_1 - 1)s_1^2 + (n_2 - 1)s_2^2}{n_1 + n_2 - 2}$$

p. 378

With this formula we can get a "pooled estimate" of σ^2. It uses a weighted average of s_1^2 and s_2^2, where the weights are the numbers of degrees of freedom in each sample. Use of this formula assumes that $\sigma_1^2 = \sigma_2^2$ (that the unknown population variances are equal). We use this formula when testing for the differences between means in situations with small sample sizes (less than 30).

[8-4]

$$\hat{\sigma}_{\bar{x}_1 - \bar{x}_2} = s_p \sqrt{\frac{1}{n_1} + \frac{1}{n_2}}$$

p. 379

Given the "pooled estimate" of σ^2 obtained from Equation 8-3, we put this value into Equation 8-2 and simplify the expression. This gives us a formula to estimate the standard error of the difference between sample means when we have small samples (less than 30) but equal population variances.

[8-5]

$$\sigma_{\bar{p}_1 - \bar{p}_2} = \sqrt{\frac{p_1 q_1}{n_1} + \frac{p_2 q_2}{n_2}}$$

p. 385

This is the formula to use to derive the standard error of the difference between two *proportions.* The symbols p_1 and p_2 represent the proportion of successes in Population 1 and Population 2, respectively, and q_1 and q_2 are the proportion of failures in Populations 1 and 2, respectively.

[8-6]

$$\hat{\sigma}_{\bar{p}_1 - \bar{p}_2} = \sqrt{\frac{\bar{p}_1 \bar{q}_1}{n_1} + \frac{\bar{p}_2 \bar{q}_2}{n_2}}$$

p. 385

If the population parameters p and q are unknown, we can use the sample statistics $\bar{p}$ and $\bar{q}$ and this formula to *estimate* the standard error of the difference between two proportions.

$$\hat{p} = \frac{(n_1)(\bar{p}_1) + (n_2)(\bar{p}_2)}{n_1 + n_2}$$

p. 386

Because the null hypothesis assumes that there is *no difference* between the two population proportions, it would be more appropriate to modify Equation 8-6 and to use the combined proportions from both samples to estimate the overall proportion of successes in the combined populations. Equation 8-7 combines the proportions from both samples. Note that the value of $\hat{q}$ is equal to $1 - \hat{p}$.

$$\hat{\sigma}_{\bar{p}_1 - \bar{p}_2} = \sqrt{\frac{\hat{p}\hat{q}}{n_1} + \frac{\hat{p}\hat{q}}{n_2}}$$

p. 386

Now we can substitute the results of Equation 8-7, both $\hat{p}$ and $\hat{q}$, into Equation 8-6 and get a more correct version of Equation 8-6. This new equation, 8-8, gives us the *estimated* standard error of the difference between the two proportions using combined estimates from both samples.

8-13
Chapter Review Exercises

8-74   For the following situations, state appropriate null and alternative hypotheses.
   (a)   The Census Bureau wants to determine if the percentage of homeless people in New York City is the same as it is in Washington, D.C.
   (b)   A local hardware store owner wants to determine if sales of garden supplies are better than usual after a spring promotion.
   (c)   The Weather Channel wants to know if average annual snowfall in the 1980's is significantly different from the average recorded over the past 100 years.
   (d)   A consumer-products investigative magazine wonders whether the fuel efficiency of a new subcompact car is significantly less than the 34 miles per gallon stated on the window sticker.

8-75   Health Electronics, Inc., a manufacturer of pacemaker batteries, specifies that the life of each battery is equal to or greater than 28 months. If scheduling for replacement surgery for the batteries is to be based upon this claim, explain to the management of this company the consequences of Type I and Type II errors.

8-76   A manufacturer of petite women's sportswear has hypothesized that the average weight of the women buying its clothing is 110 pounds. The company takes two samples of its customers and finds one sample's estimate of the population mean is 98 pounds, and the other sample produces a mean weight of 122 pounds. In the test of the company's hypothesis that the population mean is 110 pounds versus the hypothesis that the mean does not equal 110 pounds, is one of these sample values more likely to lead us to accept the null hypothesis? Why or why not?

8-77   Clic Pens has tested two types of point-of-purchase displays for its new erasable pen. A shelf display was placed in a random sample of 40 stores in the test market, and a floor display was placed in 40 other stores in the area. The mean number of pens sold per store in one month with the shelf display was 42, with a standard deviation of 8. With the floor display, the mean number of pens sold per store in the same month was 45, with a standard deviation of 7. At $\alpha = .02$, was there a significant difference between sales with the two types of displays?

8-78   A university librarian suspects that the average number of books checked out to each student per visit has changed recently. In the past, an average of 3.4 books was checked out. However, a recent sample of 23 students averaged 4.3 books per visit, with a standard deviation of 1.5 books. At the .01 level of significance, has the average checkout changed?

8-79 In 1986, a survey of 50 municipal hospitals revealed an average occupancy rate of 73.6 percent, with a standard deviation of 18.2 percent. Another survey of 75 municipal hospitals in 1989 found an average occupancy rate of 68.9 percent, with a standard deviation of 19.7 percent. At $\alpha = .10$, can we conclude that the average occupancy rate changed significantly during the 3 years between surveys?

8-80 On an average day, about 5 percent of the stocks on the New York Stock Exchange set a new high for the year. On Thursday, February 11, 1986, the Dow Jones Industrial Average closed at 1645.07 on a robust volume of over 136 million shares traded. A random sample of 120 stocks determined that sixteen of them had set new annual highs that day. Using a significance level of .01, should we conclude that more stocks than usual set new highs on that day?

8-81 In response to criticism concerning lost mail, the U.S. Postal Service initiated new procedures to alleviate this problem. The postmaster general had been assured that this change would reduce losses to below the historic loss rate of 0.3 percent. After the new procedures had been in effect for 2 months, the USPS sponsored an investigation in which a total of 8,000 pieces of mail were mailed from various parts of the country. Eighteen of the test pieces failed to reach their destinations. At a significance level of .10, can the postmaster general conclude that the new procedures achieved their goal?

8-82 What is the probability that we are rejecting a true null hypothesis when we reject the hypothesized value because:
(a) The sample statistic differs from it by more than 2.15 standard errors in either direction?
(b) The value of the sample statistic is more than 1.6 standard errors above it?
(c) The value of the sample statistic is more than 2.33 standard errors below it?

8-83 If we wish to accept the null hypothesis 85 percent of the time when it is correct, within how many standard errors around the hypothesized mean should the sample mean fall, in order to be in the acceptance region? What if we want to be 98 percent certain of accepting the null hypothesis when it is true?

8-84 Federal environmental statutes applying to a particular nuclear power plant specify that recycled water must, on average, be no warmer than 84° F (28.9° C) before it can be released into the river beside the plant. From 70 samples, the average temperature of recycled water was found to be 86.3° F (30.2° C). If the population standard deviation is 13.5° F (7.5° C), should the plant be cited for exceeding the limitations of the statute? State and test appropriate hypotheses at $\alpha = .05$.

8-85 State inspectors, investigating charges that a Louisiana soft-drink bottling company underfills its product, have sampled 200 bottles and found the average contents to be 31.7 fluid ounces. The bottles are advertised to contain 32 fluid ounces. The population standard deviation is known to be 1.5 fluid ounces. Should the inspectors conclude, at the 2 percent significance level, that the bottles are being underfilled?

8-86 General Cereals has just concluded a new advertising campaign for Fruit Crunch, its all-natural breakfast cereal with nuts, grains, and dried fruits. To test the effectiveness of the campaign, brand manager Alan Neebe surveyed eleven customers before the campaign and another eleven customers after the campaign. Given below are the customers' reported weekly consumption (in ounces) of Fruit Crunch:

Before	14	5	18	18	30	10	8	26	13	29	24
After	23	14	13	29	33	11	12	25	21	26	34

(a) At $\alpha = .05$, can Alan conclude that the campaign has succeeded in increasing demand for Fruit Crunch?
(b) Given Alan's initial survey before the campaign, can you suggest a better sampling procedure for him to follow after the campaign?

8-87 In 1989, the average 2-week-advance-purchase airfare between Raleigh-Durham, North Carolina, and New York City was $235. The population standard deviation was $68. A 1990 survey of 90 randomly chosen travelers between these two cities found that they had paid $218.77, on average, for their tickets. Did the average airfare on this route change significantly between 1989 and 1990? What is the largest prob value at which you would conclude that the observed average fare is not significantly different from $235?

8-88 A company is trying to improve distribution of its brand of frozen desserts. To accomplish this, it has expanded its sales force to push the product into new outlets. Prior to expanding the sales force, the company sampled 150 grocery stores and found that 44 percent carried at least one of its products. After hiring the new salespeople, a sample of 200 grocery stores found 52 percent carrying the brand. At $\alpha = .04$, can the company conclude that distribution has improved?

8-89 Audio Sounds runs a chain of stores selling stereo systems and components. It has been very successful in many university towns, but it has had some failures. Analysis of its failures has led it to adopt a policy of not opening a store unless it can be reasonably certain that at least 15 percent of the students in town own stereo systems costing $1,100 or more. A survey of 300 of the 2,400 students at a small, liberal arts college in the Midwest has discovered that 57 of them own stereo systems costing at least $1,100. If Audio Sounds is willing to run a 5 percent risk of failure, should it open a store in this town?

8-90 Allen Distributing Company hypothesizes that a phone call is more effective than a letter in speeding up collection of slow accounts. Two groups of slow accounts were contacted, one by each method, and the length of time between mailing the letter or making the call and the receipt of payment was recorded:

METHOD USED	DAYS TO COLLECTION						
Letter	10	8	9	11	11	14	10
Phone call	7	4	5	4	8	6	9

(a) At $\alpha = .025$, should Allen conclude that slow accounts are collected more quickly with calls than with letters?
(b) Can Allen conclude that slow accounts respond more quickly to calls than to letters?

8-91 In the second week of February 1985, the average number of units produced per week for all models of automobiles manufactured in the United States was 2,221. A sample of manufacturers' planned production in the second week of February 1986 gave the following results:

Model	Camaro	Sunbird	Century	Topaz	Lynx	Reliant	LeBaron
Units	5004	2931	3773	1313	1292	3600	2600

Do these data indicate that planned production was significantly different from actual production in the previous year? Use the .10 level of significance.

8-92 A buffered aspirin recently lost some of its market share to a new competitor. The competitor advertised that its brand enters the bloodstream faster than the buffered aspirin does and, as a result, it relieves pain sooner. The buffered-aspirin company would like to prove that there is no significant difference between the two products and, hence, that the competitor's claim is false. As a preliminary test, nine subjects were given buffered aspirin once a day for 3 weeks. For another 3 weeks, the same subjects were given the competitive product. For each medication, the average number of minutes it took to reach each subject's bloodstream was recorded:

Subject	1	2	3	4	5	6	7	8	9
Buffered aspirin	16.5	25.5	23.0	14.5	28.0	10.0	21.5	18.5	15.5
Competitor	12.0	20.5	25.0	16.5	24.0	11.5	17.0	15.0	13.0

At $\alpha = .10$, is there any significant difference in the times the two medications take to reach the bloodstream?

8-93 In 1986, it was estimated that about 52 percent of all U.S. households were cable TV subscribers. *Newstime* magazine's editors were sure that their readers subscribed to cable TV at a higher rate than the general population and wanted to use this fact to help sell advertising space for premium cable channels. To verify this belief, they sampled 250 of *Newstime's* subscribers and found that 146 subscribed to cable TV. At a significance level of 2 percent, do the survey data support the editors' belief?

8-94 A chemist developing insect repellents wishes to know if a newly developed formula gives greater protection from insect bites than that given by the leading product on the market. In an experiment, fourteen volunteers each had one arm sprayed with the old product and the other sprayed with the new formula. Then each subject placed his arms into two chambers filled with equal numbers of mosquitoes, gnats, and other biting insects. The numbers of bites received on each arm are given below. At $\alpha = .01$, should the chemist conclude that the new formula is, indeed, more effective than the current market leader?

Subject	1	2	3	4	5	6	7	8	9	10	11	12	13	14
Old Formula	5	2	5	4	3	6	2	4	2	6	5	7	1	3
New formula	3	1	5	1	1	4	4	2	5	2	3	3	1	2

8-95 A company, recently criticized for not paying women as much as men working in the same positions, claims that its average salary paid to all employees is $23,500. From a random sample of 29 women in the company, the average salary was calculated to be $23,000. If the population standard deviation is known to be $1,250 for these jobs, determine whether or not we could reasonably (within 2 standard errors) expect to find $23,000 as the sample mean if, in fact, the company's claim is true.

8-96 A regional grocery chain has installed new computerized checkout centers to reduce customer waiting and labor costs, as well as to aid in inventory control. The 36 employees trained on the new machines averaged 12.4 trials before making an error-free transaction. Long experience with training cashiers to run the old registers showed that they averaged 11.6 trials before a perfect transaction, with a standard deviation of 2.7 trials. At $\alpha = .01$, should the chain conclude that the new, computerized registers are harder to learn to operate?

8-97 Drive-a-Lemon rents cars that are mechanically sound, but older than those rented by the large national rent-a-car chains. As a result, it advertises that its rates are considerably lower than rates at its larger competitors. An industry survey has established that the average total charge per rental at one of the major firms is $77.38. A random sample of eighteen completed transactions at Drive-a-Lemon showed an average total charge of $87.61, with a sample standard deviation of $19.48. Verify that at $\alpha = .025$, Drive-a-Lemon's average total charge is significantly *higher* than that of the major firms. Does this result indicate that Drive-a-Lemon's rates, in fact, are not lower than the rates charged by the major national chains? Explain.

8-98 A machine shop has changed some of its welders from a straight salary to piece work. To see if this resulted in a change in worker productivity, the foreman was asked to keep a record of one day's output (number of pieces completed) for each employee. Using the data below, test at a significance level of 10 percent whether there are significant productivity differences with the two forms of compensation.

COMPENSATION					OUTPUT							
Salary	118	115	122	99	106	125	102	100	92	103	113	129
Piece work	115	126	113	110	135	102	124	137	108	128		

8-99 Refer to exercise 8-26. Compute the power of the test for $\mu = \$41.95$, $\$42.95$, and $\$43.95$.

8-100 A personnel manager believed that 18 percent of the company's employees work overtime every week. If the observed proportion this week is 13 percent in a sample of 250 of the 2,500 employees, can we accept her belief as reasonable or must we conclude that some other value is more appropriate? Use $\alpha = .05$.

8-101 Refer to exercise 8-28. Compute the power of the test for $\mu = 14{,}000$, $13{,}500$, and $13{,}000$.

8-102 A stockbroker claims that she can predict with 85 percent accuracy whether a stock's market value will rise or fall during the coming month. As a test, she predicts the outcome of 60 stocks and is correct in 45 of the predictions. Do these data present conclusive evidence (at $\alpha = .04$) that her prediction accuracy is significantly less than the asserted 85 percent?

8-103 In exercise 8-26, what would be the power of the test for $\mu = \$41.95$, $\$42.95$, and $\$43.95$ if the significance level were changed to .05?

8-104 A manufacturer of a vitamin supplement for newborns inserts a coupon for a free sample of its product in a package which is distributed at hospitals to new parents. Historically, about 18 percent of the coupons have been redeemed. Given current trends for having fewer children and starting families later, the firm suspects that today's new parents are better educated, on average, and, as a result, more likely to use a vitamin supplement for their infants. A sample of 1,500 new parents redeemed 295 coupons. Does this support, at a significance level of 2 percent, the firm's belief about today's new parents?

8-105 An innovator in the motor-drive industry felt that its new electric motor drive would capture 48 percent of the regional market within 1 year, because of the product's low price and superior performance. There are 5,000 users of motor drives in the region. After sampling 10 percent of these users a year later, the company found that 43 percent of them were using the new drives. At $\alpha = .01$, should we conclude that the company failed to reach its market-share goal?

8-106 In exercise 8-28, what would be the power of the test for $\mu = 14{,}000$, $13{,}500$, and $13{,}000$ if the significance level were changed to .10?

8-14
Chapter Concepts Test

Answers are in the back of the book.

T F 1. In hypothesis testing, we assume that some population parameter takes on a particular value before we sample. This assumption to be tested is called an alternative hypothesis.

T F 2. Assuming that a given hypothesis about a population mean is correct, then the percentage of sample means that could fall outside certain limits from this hypothesized mean is called the significance level.

T F 3. In hypothesis testing, the appropriate probability distribution to use is always the normal distribution.

T F 4. If we were to make a Type I error, we would be rejecting a null hypothesis when it is really true.

T F 5. A paired difference test is appropriate when the two samples being tested are dependent samples.

T F 6. A one-tailed test for the difference between means may be undertaken when the sample sizes are either large or small and the procedures are similar. The only difference is that when sample sizes are large, we employ a normal distribution, whereas the t distribution is used when sample sizes are small.

T F 7. If our null and alternative hypotheses are $H_0 : \mu = 80$ and $H_1 : \mu < 80$, it is appropriate to use a left-tailed test.

T F 8. Suppose a hypothesis test is to be made regarding the difference in means between two populations, and our sample sizes are large. If we do not know the actual standard deviations of the two populations, we can use the sample standard deviations as estimates.

T F 9. The value $1 - \beta$ is known as the power of the test.

T F 10. If we took two independent samples and performed a hypothesis test to evaluate significant differences in their means, we would find the results very similar to a paired difference test performed on the same two samples.

T F 11. It is often, but not always, possible to set the value of α so that we obtain a risk-free tradeoff in hypothesis testing.

T F 12. You are performing a two-tailed hypothesis test on a population mean and have set $\alpha = .05$. If the sample statistic falls within the .95 of area around μ_{H_0}, you have proved that the null hypothesis is true.

T F 13. If hypothesis tests were done with a significance level of .60, the null hypothesis would usually be accepted when it was not true.

T F 14. If $\mu_{H_0} = 50$ and $\alpha = .05$, then $1 - \beta$ must be equal to .95 when $\mu = 50$.

T F 15. When performing a two-tailed test for the difference between means, with a null hypothesis of $\mu_1 = \mu_2$, the hypothesized difference between the two population means is zero.

T F 16. Selecting the appropriate significance level is easier than selecting the proper test to use.

T F 17. Mathematical methods exist that guarantee that the significance level chosen will be appropriate.

T F 18. Hypothesis testing helps us draw conclusions about estimated parameters.

T F 19. A hypothesis test will be useful in determining if a population mean is 45 or if it is 60 (i.e., $H_0 : \mu = 45$; $H_1 : \mu = 60$).

T F 20. Hypothesis testing cannot unequivocally prove the "truth" about a population parameter.

T F 21. The power of a hypothesis test is only appropriate for use with one-tailed tests.

T F 22. For hypothesis testing of proportions with small samples, the t distribution is used.

T F 23. The same column of the t-distribution table is appropriate for a one-tailed test at a significance level "α" and for a two-tailed test at a significance level "2α."

T F 24. Exact prob values can't be determined (from the table) when using the t distribution in a hypothesis test.

25. If we say that $\alpha = .10$ for a particular hypothesis test, then we are saying that:
    (a) 10 percent is our minimum standard for acceptable probability.
    (b) 10 percent is the risk we take of rejecting a hypothesis that is true.
    (c) 10 percent is the risk we take of accepting a hypothesis that is false.
    (d) a and b only.
    (e) a and c only.

26. Suppose we wish to test whether a population mean is significantly larger or smaller than 10. We take a sample and find $\bar{x}$ to be 8. What should our alternative hypothesis be?
    (a) $\mu < 10$ (c) $\mu > 10$
    (b) $\mu \neq 10$ (d) Cannot be determined from information given

27. Suppose that a hypothesis test is being performed for a process in which a Type I error will be very costly, but a Type II error will be relatively inexpensive and unimportant. Which of the following would be the best choice for α in this test?
    (a) .01   (b) .10   (c) .25   (d) .50

28. You are performing a right-tailed test of a population mean and σ is not known. A sample of size 26 is taken, and $\bar{x}$ and s are computed. At a significance level of .01, where would you look for a value from a distribution?
    (a) z table where .99 of the area is to the left of the z value.
    (b) z table where .98 of the area is to the left of the z value.
    (c) t table where, with 25 degrees of freedom, the column heading is .02.
    (d) t table where, with 25 degrees of freedom, the column heading is .01.

29. Suppose you are going to test the difference between two sample means, which you have calculated as $\bar{x}_1 - 22$ and $\bar{x}_2 - 27$. You wish to test whether the difference is significant. What is the value of $\mu_{\bar{x}_1 - \bar{x}_2}$ which you will use?
   (a) 5   (b) -5 (c) 0   (d) Cannot be determined from information given

30. Why do we sometimes use paired, as opposed to independent, samples?
   (a) The cost of taking paired samples is always less than the cost of independent sampling.
   (b) Paired samples allow us to control for extraneous factors.
   (c) The sample sizes must be the same for paired samples.
   (d) All of these.
   (e) b and c but not a.

31. A set of two dependent samples of size fifteen was taken and a hypothesis test was performed. A t value with 14 degrees of freedom was used. If the two sets of samples had been treated as independent, how many degrees of freedom would have been used?
   (a) 14   (b) 28   (c) 29   (d) 30

32. A farmer has twelve fields of corn in different parts of a certain county. Testing for significantly different yields from year to year, he checks his records for the past 2 years and is able to gather information about production in eleven of the fields for the first year and second year. Should he treat these samples as:
   (a) Dependent?   (c) Cannot be determined from information given.
   (b) Independent?

33. In a test of difference between proportions, two samples are under consideration. In the first, a sample of size 100 shows 20 successes; in the second, a sample of size 50 shows thirteen successes. What is the value of $\hat{p}$ for this situation?
   (a) $\dfrac{20 + 13}{150}$ (b) $\dfrac{20}{100} + \dfrac{13}{50}$ (c) $\dfrac{33}{150} \times \dfrac{117}{150}$ (d) None of these

34. What is the major assumption we made when performing one-tailed tests for differences between means with small samples?
   (a) Unknown population variances were equal.
   (b) Sampling fractions were quite small.
   (c) The samples were chosen using judgmental sampling techniques.
   (d) None of these.

35. With a lower significance level, the probability of rejecting a null hypothesis that is actually true:
   (a) Decreases.   (c) Increases.
   (b) Remains the same.   (d) All of these.

36. Decision makers make decisions on the appropriate significance level by examining the cost of:
   (a) Performing the test   (c) A type II error   (e) a and c
   (b) A type I error   (d) a and b   (f) b and c

37. Airline A and Airline B boast successful baggage routing rates of 95 and 98 percent, respectively. From this information we can determine:
   (a) Airline A has better baggage service.
   (b) Airline B has better baggage service.
   (c) the baggage services are equally accurate.
   (d) nothing; we need more information.

38. A major auto manufacturer has had to recall several models from its 1990 line due to quality control problems that were not discovered with their random final inspection procedures. This is an example of:
   (a) Type I error.
   (b) Type II error.
   (c) both Type I and Type II error.
   (d) neither type of error.

39. To be assured that a hypothesis test is working correctly, we would like the value of $1 - \beta$ to be as close to _____ as possible.

40. The power of a test refers to the test's ability to _____ the _____ hypothesis when it is _____.

41. An assumption or speculation made about a population parameter is a _____.

42. Accepting a null hypothesis when it is false is a Type _____ error. Its probability is denoted by _____.

43. The assumption about a population parameter that we wish to test is the _____ hypothesis. The conclusion we accept when the data fail to support this assumption is the _____ hypothesis.

44. A hypothesis test of the difference between the sample means of two dependent samples is a _____ difference test.

45. A hypothesis test involving two rejection regions is called a two-_____ test.

46. If the null hypothesis is $\mu = 10$ and the alternative hypothesis is $\mu > 10$, the appropriate test to use is a _____ test.

8-15
Conceptual Case

(Northern White Metals Company)

Dick was so pleased with the work that Sarah and Jody had done that he called the CEO to ask if they could be reassigned from corporate headquarters to Northern for the next few months.

"No way, Lennox!" the CEO growled. "We've got plenty of problems right here that require their attention." Then he softened and added, "Maybe they'll be able to help out from time to time on an ad hoc basis. We'll have to play it by ear."

"Thanks, sir," Dick replied. "I'll check back with them when problems arise."

Although Dick was disappointed that the CEO had turned down his request to have Sarah and Jody transferred from corporate headquarters to Northern, he was pleased that the product quality situation was now under control. Customer problems had been smoothed over, and the sales force's outlook was once again refreshingly optimistic.

The original president of Northern had by now retired, and Dick formally assumed the role of president and general manager. With production running smoothly and sales still growing, Dick decided to turn his attention to improving other phases of Northern's operations. The shipping department first came to mind, as Dick noticed activity in this area becoming increasingly hectic and a bit disorganized. Making the department more efficient, thought Dick, would surely enable the company to serve its customers better.

The shipping department comprised two separate operations, packing and loading. In the packing process, long sections of aluminum extrusions were stacked, forming a sort of bundle. This was then wrapped with heavy-duty cardboard and secured with a series of steel bands. The cardboard served mainly to protect the metal, and the banding actually held the stacked bundle together. The entire process was performed manually, with two employees working at each of the packing stations. The number of stations could be increased or decreased, depending on demand. Wrapped and banded bundles were taken from the packing stations by an overhead hoist, weighed, and then stacked in a holding area to await loading onto trucks. The shipping department was always a flurry of activity; occasionally it became chaotic.

Dick had noted, by observation and by frequent discussions with the chief shipping coordinator, that problems tended to arise most frequently in the packing area. The number of stations was near capacity. Even so, the packers, although good workers, frequently had difficulty in keeping up with the volume of material coming off the production line. Dick was particularly interested in this problem as he had recently been approached by Rich Gochnauer, a sales representative from a packing-materials company, about a new, automatic banding machine the firm had developed.

The new equipment would offer little in the way of packing-material cost savings, but the sales rep claimed it would greatly reduce the time it took to wrap and band a bundle. It would not only make packing operations more efficient, he stated, but would substantially reduce labor costs as well.

Dick was skeptical, although he was anxious to improve the packing area. Mr. Gochnauer agreed that, to convince Dick of the equipment's benefits, a sample unit could be installed at NWMC for a 30-day trial period. Dick felt this would be more than enough time to evaluate the machine, and arrangements were made to set up the trial.

Dick decided that if the new automatic bander provided a significant improvement over current methods, he would have several installed in the packing area. What troubled him now was how to decide if the new equipment was truly superior to manual banding—that is, would it really do the same job in less time? He decided to confer with his new-found "consultants" at corporate technical services.

"Would you be free to come up here and help us out with this?" Dick asked Jody after explaining the situation.

"There is really no need for us to come up there,

Dick," Jody replied calmly. "The problem seems to be rather clear-cut. Just send me the data at the end of the trial period and we'll try to give you an answer straightaway."

What kind of data and general information will Dick need to provide technical services? How will technical services make use of these data, and what sort of "answer" might Jody give Dick about the new equipment?

8-16
Computer Data Base Exercise

Hal dropped in to see Laurel the day after the staff meeting. "I've got a question," he began, "about the study you and Bob did on the competitive bidding of purchase orders. I know I'm a statistical rookie, and I'm trying hard to understand confidence intervals and such things, but isn't there any way just to get a yes-or-no answer to a question like we asked?" He paused, then went on. "I didn't want to ask dumb questions in the meeting yesterday, because I really feel as if it's my lack of knowledge which is making me question the results. Try to see it from my perspective: The figure I want, 60 percent, is *in* the confidence interval, but let's face it—most of the interval is *below* .6. Do you see what I'm getting at?"

Laurel nodded and smiled. "I see exactly what you mean," she said. "You're not as much of a rookie as you think, and it's not a dumb question. Confidence intervals are, by nature, somewhat confusing. I've got a textbook which you may want to borrow which will give you a little more background. And as for the yes-or-no answer—let me introduce you to hypothesis testing." Laurel went on to explain one- and two-tailed tests, illustrating with the situation at hand.

1. Perform a one-tailed hypothesis test to determine if the proportion of competitively bid purchase orders is actually below .6, using $\bar{p} = .58$ and $n = 1052$ from Chapter 8. Test at the .01 significance level.

Gary held the door for Laurel one morning. "I haven't seen you in a while except at our weekly staff meetings," he said, smiling. "In fact, I think

it's been since you helped me with that zip code study shortly after you got here. I hear they're keeping you busy!"

"It has been rather hectic," Laurel agreed. "But I'm having a good time. Being busy is better than being bored! Recently, though, it's let up a little, which is nice. And my skiing vacation in the Rockies is coming up soon, which will be a nice break."

"Sounds like fun! Think you'd have enough time before you go to help me with a little problem?" When Laurel nodded, Gary continued. "We've been seeing some poor quality-control indications from one of our O-ring suppliers. The fit of this particular type of seal is crucial, as you may know. Consequently, when Stan tells me that one or two of our customers have complained, we need to do some careful checking."

"Do you have any incoming inspection procedures?" asked Laurel, turning in to her office.

"Good question," grimaced Gary. "We do what we can, and on larger items shipped in small quantities we'll inspect each and every one. But on something like seals, we get thousands in at a time and inspecting a handful is often all we can manage. I'd really like to set up more rigorous procedures as a long-term goal."

"Sounds like this O-ring problem is a good place to start. I'll walk you through the data we need and the analysis steps, and maybe you can take it from there to evaluate other items." Laurel knew she was slowly gaining the staff's confidence, not only concerning her capabilities, but especially about the validity and usefulness of statistical analysis. "I'll swing by later this morning to get more details."

Later, Laurel found Gary in the warehouse.

"Good timing," he said. "This is the latest batch coming in right now. See this dimension?" Gary scooped an O-ring from the box and indicated the innermost gap. "The required average is .140 inches. Historically, we've had a standard deviation of .003 inches. We've got a calibration instrument to measure these. What if I have my guys record the data from this batch and deliver it to your office tomorrow?"

"That's fine," answered Laurel. "Just for my own information, is too tight as bad as too loose?"

"Yep. Either way can be disastrous for the user," explained Gary.

2. At a significance level of .05, should Laurel conclude that the O-rings are out of tolerance? Use the data in Table DB8-1.

TABLE DB8-1 O-ring data table*

140	142	145	145	144	137	145	145	149	146
143	141	137	148	146	137	142	141	149	138
137	144	138	144	144	142	139	142	145	144
134	146	141	143	144	143	137	140	144	145
135	145	142	144	145	141	134	145	146	146
138	147	147	147	149	137	147	141	148	141
143	145	140	146	146	142	143	146	149	137
143	145	140	137	145	142	141	143	140	137
145	147	142	147	148	145	142	135	145	146
146	145	137	142	147	143	138	142	143	141
139	145	145	137	149	142	145	141	144	136
133	146	140	135	146	142	141	140	138	142
147	146	132	137	148	143	137	141	145	144
148	147	143	146	147	140	141	140	145	147
139	145	144	142	146	135	143	140	137	137
143	146	144	142	149	136	141	139	138	141
141	145	143	140	145	142	139	141	140	137
137	144	146	142	149	140	137	147	137	146
138	146	145	142	147	139	141	142	145	139
140	136	143	139	148	137	143	139	139	144
142	144	142	141	149	142	143	139	142	138
142	143	144	142	146	144	139	143	142	142
145	136	148	137	148	140	141	141	140	140
135	137	144	145	147	138	145	146	142	140
136	142	143	144	147	143	142	148	145	145
145	147	144	137	147	139	135	148	145	141
146	137	149	140	140	145	138	144	144	141
145	142	147	144	132	143	146	147	141	136
143	138	146	142	144	140	142	146	144	146
147	143	144	143	145	139	141	146	146	141
141	137	143	135	141	140	135	148	147	145

* Table entries are in thousandths of an inch.

8-17
From the Textbook to the Real World

TESTING HYPOTHESES
Impact of Deregulation on Railroad Management
Times of change in business often stimulate statistical studies. This was the case in the railroad industry during the 1980s when the Staggers Act, and the deregulation that followed, increased competition in a previously stagnant, protected industry. In 1987, analysts tested the general

hypothesis that observable characteristics and the structure of railroad management had begun to change in conjunction with recent regulatory reform. Management characteristics were analyzed for both 1977 and 1983. The study indicated that managers had become significantly younger and better educated, with fewer years of company and industry service. These results showed that deregulation was successful in rejuvenating a declining industry by challenging it to attract managers who could adapt to a changing environment.

Background: Since the 1900s, employment levels and railroad's percentage of U.S. intercity freight traffic have fallen dramatically. Because highly restrictive federal regulation allowed the management structure of U.S. railroads to become static and bureaucratic, the industry had low levels of profitability and competitiveness. Historically, few railroad managers came from outside the industry. To improve the financial prospects for U.S. railroads, the industry was deregulated during the 1980s.

Testing Hypotheses: Curtis Grimm, James Kling, and Ken Smith from the University of Maryland tested the hypothesis that deregulation would force a modernization of managerial attitudes. Several specific hypotheses were tested to determine the validity of the government's claim that deregulation improved competitiveness. Some of the hypotheses tested included the following:

1. It was hypothesized that the average age of managers in 1983 was significantly lower than in 1977. A competitive environment requires railroads to recruit younger managers, who are likely to be more innovative and aggressive. Age was said to be an indicator of one's flexibility and risk-taking propensity.
2. The second hypothesis concerning managers was that the average number of years of employment with their current railroad employer should be significantly less in 1983 than in 1977. Years of experience may act as a roadblock to organizational change in a newly deregulated industry.
3. It was also hypothesized that the average manager would have fewer years of employment in the railroad industry in 1983 than in 1977. Deregulation would require railroads to seek managers with experience in competitive environments.

Results: The results of the Maryland study demonstrated that railroad management had changed in response to regulatory reform. The average age of railroad managers declined by over 1 full year, from 51.68 years in 1977 to 50.66 years in 1983. This trend towards younger management supported the first hypothesis. The average tenure for managers was found to be 25 years in 1977 and 21.33 years in 1983. This drop of 3.77 years was highly significant ($p < .001$) and supported the second hypothesis. The comparatively larger drop in service time versus age indicated that the influx of younger managers alone was not responsible for the decline in years of company service. Railroads were evidently bringing in managers from outside the firm with more frequency than in the past. Strong support was also revealed for the third hypothesis. The average number of years in the industry declined from 27.23 years in 1977 to 24.88 years in 1983, statistically significant at the 0.001 level. Clearly, the results supported the hypothesis that railroad management would be younger and more mobile after deregulation.

Conclusions: Railroads, airlines, and motor carriers have undergone substantial deregulation during the last decade, which created an impetus for managerial change within these industries. Hypothesis testing and other statistical methods provide a means of determining the effects of regulatory reform on industries. This research can be beneficial in developing successful managerial structures for companies in all industries as they strive for prosperity in highly competitive environments.

Curtis M. Grimm, James A. Kling, and Ken G. Smith, "The Impact of U.S. Rail Regulatory Reform on Railroad Management and Organizational Structure," *Transportation Research-A,* vol. 21A, no. 2, pp. 87–94, 1987.

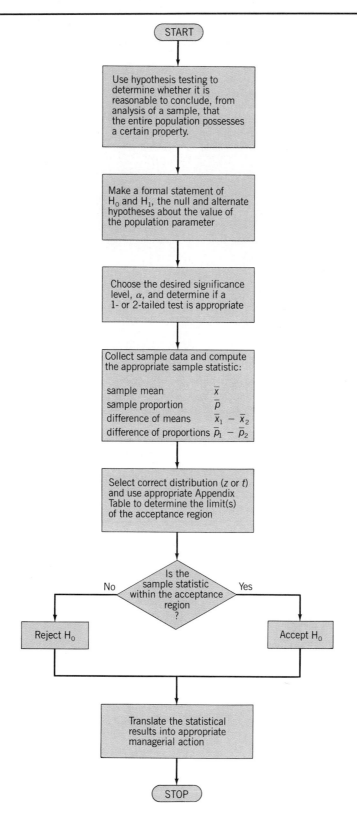

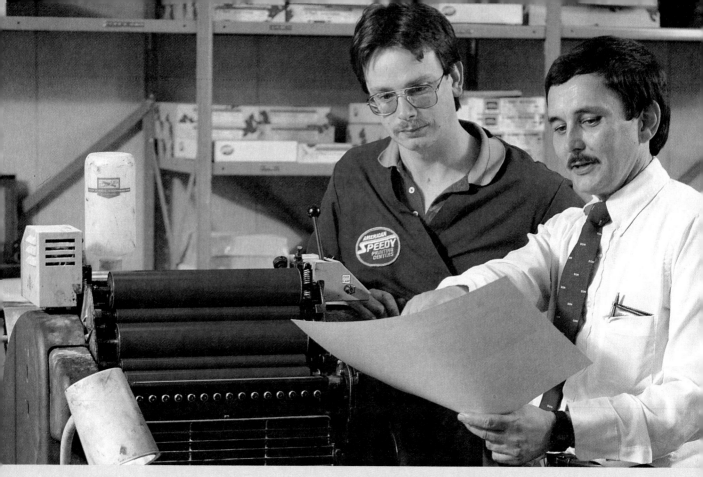

The training director of a company is trying to evaluate three different methods of training new employees. The first method assigns each to an experienced employee for individual help in the factory. The second method puts all new employees in a training room separate from the factory, and the third method uses training films and programmed learning materials. The training director chooses sixteen new employees assigned at random to the three training methods and records their daily production after they complete the programs:

Method 1	15	18	19	22	11	
Method 2	22	27	18	21	17	
Method 3	18	24	19	16	22	15

The director wonders if there are differences in effectiveness among the methods. Using techniques learned in this chapter, we can help answer that question.

9

Chi-Square and Analysis of Variance

■ **OBJECTIVES**

Chapter 9 discusses three statistical techniques: chi-square tests, analysis of variance, and making inferences about population variances. *Chi-square tests* are useful in analyzing more than two populations. They can be helpful in marketing data — for example, to test whether preference for a certain product differs from state to state or region to region. Chi-square tests also enable us to determine whether a group of data that we think could be described by the normal distribution actually does conform to that pattern. *Analysis of variance,* the second subject of Chapter 9, is used to test for differences among several sample means. It is a method an automobile manufacturer might use to evaluate five series of tests on the same model. This method can help in answering the question, "Are the mile-per-gallon results really the same, or do they only appear to be?" The last sections of the chapter show us how to make inferences about the variability present in one or two populations.

9-1
Introduction

Uses of the chi-square test

In the last chapter, we learned how to test hypotheses using data from either one or two samples. We used one-sample tests to determine whether a mean or a proportion was significantly different from a hypothesized value. In the two-sample tests, we examined the difference between either two means or two proportions, and we tried to learn whether this difference was significant.

Suppose we have proportions from five populations instead of only two. In this case, the methods for comparing proportions described in Chapter 8 do *not* apply; we must use the *chi-square test,* the subject of the first portion of this chapter. Chi-square tests enable us to test whether *more* than two population proportions can be considered equal.

Actually, chi-square tests allow us to do a lot more than just test for the equality of several proportions. If we classify a population into several categories with respect to two attributes (for example, age and job performance), we can then use a chi-square test to determine if the two attributes are independent of each other.

Function of analysis of variance

Managers also encounter situations in which it is useful to test for the equality of more than two population means. Again, we cannot apply the methods introduced in Chapter 8, because they are limited to testing for the equality of only two means. The *analysis of variance,* discussed in the fourth section of this chapter, will enable us to test whether *more* than two population means can be considered equal.

Inferences about population variances

It is clear that we will not always be interested in means and proportions. There are many managerial situations where we will be concerned about the variability in a population. Section 5 of this chapter shows how to use the chi-square distribution to form confidence intervals and test hypotheses about a population variance. In Section 6, we show that hypotheses comparing the variances of two populations can be tested using the F distribution.

Exercises

9-1 Why do we use a chi-square test?

9-2 Why do we use analysis of variance?

9-3 In each of the following situations, state whether a chi-square test, analysis of variance, or inference about population variances should be done.
   (a) We want to see if the variance in spring temperatures is the same on the east and west coasts.
   (b) We want to see if the average speed on Interstate 95 differs, depending on the day of the week.
   (c) We want to see if long-term stock performance on Wall Street (classified as good, average or poor) is independent of the size of the company (classified as small, medium or large).
   (d) Before testing whether $\mu_1 = \mu_2$, we want to test if the assumption that $\sigma_1^2 = \sigma_2^2$ is reasonable.

9-4 Answer true or false and explain your answers.
   (a) After reading this chapter, you should know how to make inferences about two or more population variances.
   (b) After reading this chapter, you should know how to make inferences about two or more population means.
   (c) After reading this chapter, you should know how to make inferences about two or more population proportions.

9-5 To help remember which distribution or technique is used, complete the following table with either the name of a distribution or the technique involved. The row classification refers to the number of parameters involved in a test, and the column classification refers to the type of parameter involved. Some cells may not have an entry; others may have more than one possible entry.

NUMBER OF PARAMETERS INVOLVED	TYPE OF PARAMETER		
	μ	σ	p
1			
2			
3 or more			

9-2
Chi-Square as a Test of Independence

Sample differences among proportions: significant or not?

Many times, managers need to know whether the differences they observe among several sample proportions are significant or only due to chance. Suppose the campaign manager for a presidential candidate studies three geographically different regions and finds that 35 percent, 42 percent, and 51 percent of those voters surveyed in the three regions, respectively, recognize the candidate's name. If this difference is significant, the manager may conclude that location will affect the way the candidate should act. But if the difference is not significant (that is, if the manager concludes that the difference is solely due to chance), then he may decide that the place chosen to make a particular policy-making speech will have no effect on its reception. To run the campaign successfully, then, the manager needs to determine whether location and name recognition are dependent or independent.

CONTINGENCY TABLES

Describing a contingency table

Suppose that in four regions, the National Health Care Company samples its hospital employees' attitudes toward job performance reviews. Respondents are given a choice between the present method (two reviews a year) and a proposed new method (quarterly reviews). Table 9-1, which illustrates the response to this question from the sample polled, is called a *contingency table.* A table such as this is made up of rows and

TABLE 9-1 Sample Response Concerning Review Schedules for National Health Care Hospital Employees

	NORTHEAST	SOUTHEAST	CENTRAL	WEST COAST	TOTAL
Number who prefer present method	68	75	57	79	**279**
Number who prefer new method	32	45	33	31	**141**
Total employees sampled in each region	**100**	**120**	**90**	**110**	**420**

columns; rows run horizontally, columns vertically. Notice that the four columns in Table 9-1 provide one basis of classification — geographical regions — and that the two rows classify the information another way: preference for review methods. Table 9-1 is called a "2 × 4 contingency table," because it consists of two rows and four columns. We describe the dimensions of a contingency table by first stating the number of rows and then the number of columns. The "total" column and the "total" row are not counted as part of the dimensions.

OBSERVED AND EXPECTED FREQUENCIES

Setting up the problem symbolically Suppose we now symbolize the true proportions of the total population of employees who prefer the present plan as:

- $p_N \leftarrow$ proportion in Northeast who prefer present plan
- $p_S \leftarrow$ proportion in Southeast who prefer present plan
- $p_C \leftarrow$ proportion in Central region who prefer present plan
- $p_W \leftarrow$ proportion in West Coast region who prefer present plan

Using these symbols, we can state the null and alternative hypotheses as follows:

$H_0: p_N = p_S = p_C = p_W \leftarrow$ null hypothesis

$H_1: p_N, p_S, p_C,$ and p_W are not all equal $\leftarrow$ alternative hypothesis

If the null hypothesis is true, we can combine the data from the four samples and then estimate the proportion of the total work force (the total population) that prefers the present review method:

$$\text{Combined proportion who prefer present method assuming the null hypothesis of no difference is true} = \frac{68 + 75 + 57 + 79}{100 + 120 + 90 + 110}$$

$$= \frac{279}{420}$$

$$= .6643$$

Determining expected frequencies Obviously, if the value .6643 estimates the population proportion expected to prefer the present compensation method, then $.3357 (= 1 - .6643)$ is the estimate of the population proportion expected to prefer the proposed new method. Using .6643 as the *estimate* of the population proportion who prefer the present review method, and .3357 as the *estimate* of the population proportion who prefer the new method, we can estimate the number of sampled employees in each region whom we would expect to prefer each of the review methods. These calculations are done in Table 9-2.

Comparing expected and observed frequencies Table 9-3 combines all the information from Tables 9-1 and 9-2. It illustrates both the actual, or observed, frequency of the employees sampled who prefer each type of job-review method and the theoretical, or expected, frequency of sampled employees preferring each type of method. Remember that the expected frequencies, those in color, were estimated from our combined proportion estimate.

Reasoning intuitively about chi-square tests To test the null hypothesis, $p_N = p_S = p_C = p_W$, we must compare the frequencies that were observed (the black ones in Table 9-3) with the frequencies we would expect if the null hypothesis is true (those in color). If the sets of observed and expected

418

TABLE 9-2 Proportion of Sampled Employees in Each Region Expected to Prefer the Two Review Methods

	NORTHEAST	SOUTHEAST	CENTRAL	WEST COAST
Total number sampled	100	120	90	110
Estimated proportion who prefer present method	×.6643	×.6643	×.6643	×.6643
Number *expected* to prefer present method	66.43	79.72	59.79	73.07
Total number sampled	100	120	90	110
Estimated proportion who prefer new method	×.3357	×.3357	×.3357	×.3357
Number *expected* to prefer new method	33.57	40.28	30.21	36.93

frequencies are nearly alike, we can reason intuitively that we will accept the null hypothesis. If there is a large difference between these frequencies, we may intuitively reject the null hypothesis and conclude that there are significant differences in the proportions of employees in the four regions preferring the new method.

TABLE 9-3 Comparison of Observed and Expected Frequencies of Sampled Employees

	NORTHEAST	SOUTHEAST	CENTRAL	WEST COAST
FREQUENCY PREFERRING PRESENT METHOD:				
Observed (actual) frequency	68	75	57	79
Expected (theoretical) frequency	66.43	79.72	59.79	73.07
FREQUENCY PREFERRING NEW METHOD:				
Observed (actual) frequency	32	45	33	31
Expected (theoretical) frequency	33.57	40.28	30.21	36.93

THE CHI-SQUARE STATISTIC

To go beyond our intuitive feelings about the observed and expected frequencies, we can use the chi-square statistic, which is calculated this way:

Calculating the chi-square statistic

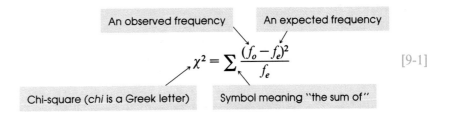

An observed frequency   An expected frequency

$$\chi^2 = \sum \frac{(f_o - f_e)^2}{f_e}$$

[9-1]

Chi-square (*chi* is a Greek letter)   Symbol meaning "the sum of"

TABLE 9-4 Calculation of χ^2 (Chi-Square) Statistic from Data in Table 9-3

f_0	f_e	Step 1 $f_0 - f_e$	Step 2 $(f_0 - f_e)^2$	Step 3 $\dfrac{(f_0 - f_e)^2}{f_e}$
68	66.43	1.57	2.46	.0370
75	79.72	−4.72	22.28	.2795
57	59.79	−2.79	7.78	.1301
79	73.07	5.93	35.16	.4812
32	33.57	−1.57	2.46	.0733
45	40.28	4.72	22.28	.5531
33	30.21	2.79	7.78	.2575
31	36.93	−5.93	35.16	.9521
				2.7638

Step 4 $\sum \dfrac{(f_0 - f_e)^2}{f_e} = 2.764 \leftarrow \chi^2$ (chi-square)

This formula says that chi-square, or χ^2, is the sum we will get if we:

1. Subtract f_e from f_o for each of the eight boxes, or cells, of Table 9-3
2. Square each of the differences
3. Divide each squared difference by f_e
4. Sum all eight of the answers

Numerically, the calculations are easy to do using a table such as Table 9-4, which shows the steps.

Interpreting the chi-square statistic

The answer of 2.764 is the value for chi-square in our problem comparing preferences for review methods. If this value were as large as, say, 20, it would indicate a substantial difference between our observed values and our expected values. A chi-square of zero, on the other hand, indicates that the observed frequencies exactly match the expected frequencies. The value of chi-square can never be negative, since the differences between the observed and expected frequencies are always *squared*.

THE CHI-SQUARE DISTRIBUTION

Describing a chi-square distribution

If the null hypothesis is true, then the sampling distribution of the chi-square statistic, χ^2, can be closely approximated by a continuous curve known as a *chi-square distribution*. As in the case of the t distribution, there is a different chi-square distribution for each different number of degrees of freedom. Figure 9-1 indicates the three different chi-square distributions that would correspond to 1, 5, and 10 degrees of freedom. For very small numbers of degrees of freedom, the chi-square distribution is severely skewed to the right. As the number of degrees of freedom increases, the curve rapidly becomes more symmetrical until the number reaches large values, at which point the distribution can be approximated by the normal.

Finding probabilities when using a chi-square distribution

The chi-square distribution is a probability distribution. Therefore, the total area under the curve in each chi-square distribution is 1.0. Like the t distribution, so many different chi-square distributions are possible that it is not practical to construct a

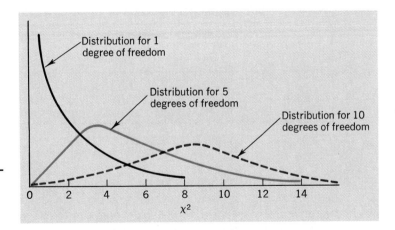

FIGURE 9-1

Chi-square
distributions with 1,
5, and 10 degrees of
freedom

table that illustrates the areas under the curve for all possible values of the area. Appendix Table 5 illustrates only the areas in the tail most commonly used in significance tests using the chi-square distribution.

DETERMINING DEGREES OF FREEDOM

Calculating degrees of freedom

To use the chi-square test, we must calculate the number of degrees of freedom in the contingency table by applying Equation 9-2:

$$\text{Number of degrees of freedom} = (\text{Number of rows} - 1)(\text{Number of columns} - 1) \qquad [9\text{-}2]$$

Let's examine the appropriateness of this equation. Suppose we have a 3×4 contingency table like the one in Fig. 9-2. We know the row and column totals that are designated RT_1, RT_2, RT_3, and CT_1, CT_2, CT_3, CT_4. As we discussed in Chapter 7, the number of degrees of freedom is equal to the number of values that we can freely specify.

Look now at the first row of the contingency table in Fig. 9-2. Once we specify the first three values in that row (denoted by checks in the figure), the fourth value in that row (denoted by a circle) is already determined; we are not free to specify it, because we know the row total.

FIGURE 9-2

A 3×4 contingency
table illustrating
determination of the
number of degrees
of freedom

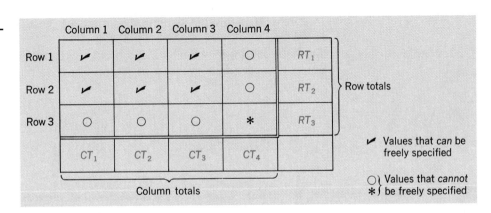

TABLE 9-5 Determination of Degrees of Freedom in Three Contingency Tables

CONTINGENCY TABLE	NUMBER OF ROWS (r)	NUMBER OF COLUMNS (c)	$(r-1)$	$(c-1)$	DEGREES OF FREEDOM $(r-1)(c-1)$
A	3	4	$3-1=2$	$4-1=3$	$(2)(3)=6$
B	5	7	$5-1=4$	$7-1=6$	$(4)(6)=24$
C	6	9	$6-1=5$	$9-1=8$	$(5)(8)=40$

Likewise, in the second row of the contingency table in Fig. 9-2, once we specify the first three values (denoted again by checks), the fourth value is determined and cannot be freely specified. We have denoted this fourth value by a circle.

Turning now to the third row, we see that its first entry is determined, *because we already know the first two entries in the first column and the column total;* again we have denoted this entry with a circle. We can apply this same reasoning to the second and third entries in the third row, both of which have been denoted by a circle too.

Turning finally to the last entry in the third row (denoted by an asterisk), we see that we cannot freely specify its value, because we have already determined the first two entries in the fourth column. By counting the number of checks in the contingency table in Fig. 9-2, you can see that the number of values we are free to specify is six (the number of checks). This is equal to 2×3, or (the number of rows -1) times (the number of columns -1).

This is exactly what we have in Equation 9-2. Table 9-5 illustrates the row-and-column dimensions of three more contingency tables and indicates the appropriate degrees of freedom in each case.

USING THE CHI-SQUARE TEST

Stating the problem symbolically

Returning to our example of job-review preferences of National Health Care hospital employees, we use the chi-square test to determine whether attitude about reviews is independent of geographical region. If the company wants to test the null hypothesis at the .10 level of significance, our problem can be summarized:

H_0: $p_N = p_S = p_C = p_W$ ← null hypothesis

H_1: $p_N, p_S, p_C,$ and p_W are *not* all equal ← alternative hypothesis

$\alpha = .10$ ← level of significance for testing these hypotheses

Calculating degrees of freedom

Since our contingency table for this problem (Table 9-1) has two rows and four columns, the appropriate number of degrees of freedom is:

Number of rows   Number of columns

$$
\begin{aligned}
\text{Number of degrees of freedom} &= (r-1)(c-1) \\
&= (2-1)(4-1) \\
&= (1)(3) \\
&= 3 \leftarrow \text{degrees of freedom}
\end{aligned}
$$

[9-2]

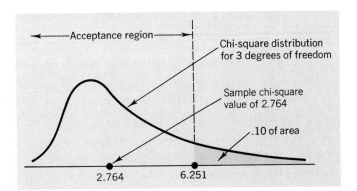

FIGURE 9-3

Chi-square
hypothesis test at
the .10 level of
significance, showing
acceptance region
and sample chi-
square value of 2.764

Illustrating the
hypothesis test

Figure 9-3 illustrates a chi-square distribution for 3 degrees of freedom, showing the significance level in color. In Appendix Table 5, we can look under the .10 column and move down to the 3 degrees of freedom row. There we find the value of the chi-square statistic, 6.251. We can interpret this to mean that with 3 degrees of freedom, the region to the right of a chi-square value of 6.251 contains .10 of the area under the curve. Thus, the acceptance region for the null hypothesis in Fig. 9-3 goes from the left tail of the curve to the chi-square value of 6.251.

Interpreting the results

As we can see from Fig. 9-3, the sample chi-square value of 2.764 which we calculated in Table 9-4, falls within the acceptance region. Therefore, we accept the null hypothesis that there is no difference between the attitudes about job interviews in the four geographical regions. In other words, we conclude that attitude about performance reviews is independent of geography.

CONTINGENCY TABLES WITH MORE THAN TWO ROWS

Are hospital stay and
insurance coverage
independent?

Mr. George McMahon, president of National General Health Insurance Company, is opposed to national health insurance. He argues that it would be too costly to implement, particularly since the existence of such a system would, among other effects, tend to encourage people to spend more time in hospitals. George believes that lengths of stays in hospitals are dependent on the types of health insurance that people have. He asked Donna McClish, his staff statistician, to check the matter out. Donna collected data on a random sample of 660 hospital stays and summarized it in Table 9-6.

Table 9-6 gives observed frequencies in the nine different length-of-stay and type-

TABLE 9-6 Hospital-Stay Data Classified by the Type of Insurance Coverage and Length of Stay

| | | Days in hospital | | | |
		<5	5–10	>10	**TOTAL**
Fraction of costs	<25%	40	75	65	**180**
covered by	25–50%	30	45	75	**150**
insurance	>50%	40	100	190	**330**
	TOTAL	**110**	**220**	**330**	**660**

of-insurance categories (or "cells") into which we have divided the sample. Donna wishcs to tcst thc hypotheses:

Stating the hypotheses

H_0: length of stay and type of insurance are independent

H_1: length of stay depends on type of insurance

$\alpha = .01 \leftarrow$ level of significance for testing these hypotheses

Finding expected frequencies

We will use a chi-square test, so we first have to find the expected frequencies for each of the nine cells. Let's demonstrate how to find them by looking at the cell that corresponds to stays of less than 5 days and insurance covering less than 25 percent of costs.

Estimating the proportions in the cells

A total of 180 of the 660 stays in Table 9-6 had insurance covering less than 25 percent of costs. So we can use the figure 180/660 to *estimate* the proportion in the population having insurance covering less than 25 percent of the costs. Similarly, 110/660 *estimates* the proportion of all hospital stays that last fewer than 5 days. If length of stay and type of insurance really are independent, we can use Equation 4-4 to *estimate* the proportion in the first cell (less than 5 days and less than 25 percent coverage).

We let:

A = the event "a stay corresponds to someone whose insurance covers less than 25 percent of the costs," and

B = the event "a stay lasts less than 5 days."

Then,

$$\text{P(first cell)} = \text{P}(A \text{ and } B)$$
$$= \text{P}(A) \times \text{P}(B) \qquad [4\text{-}4]$$
$$= \left(\frac{180}{660}\right)\left(\frac{110}{660}\right)$$
$$= 1/22$$

Since 1/22 is the expected *proportion* in the first cell, the expected *frequency* in that cell is:

$$(1/22)(660) = 30 \text{ observations}$$

Calculating the expected frequencies for the cells

In general, we can calculate the expected frequency for any cell with Equation 9-3:

$$f_e = \frac{RT \times CT}{n} \qquad [9\text{-}3]$$

where:

- f_e = the expected frequency in a given cell
- RT = the row total for the row containing that cell
- CT = the column total for the column containing that cell
- n = the total number of observations

Now we can use Equations 9-3 and 9-1 to compute all of the expected frequencies and the value of the chi-square statistic. The computations are done in Table 9-7.

Figure 9-4 illustrates a chi-square distribution with 4 degrees of freedom (number of rows $- 1 = 2$) $\times$ (number of columns $- 1 = 2$), showing the .01 significance level

TABLE 9-7 Calculation of Expected Frequencies and Chi-Square from Data in Table 9-6

ROW	COLUMN	f_o	f_e	$= \dfrac{RT \times CT}{n}$	$f_o - f_e$	$(f_o - f_e)^2$	$\dfrac{(f_o - f_e)^2}{f_e}$
1	1	40	30	$\dfrac{180 \times 110}{660}$	10	100	3.333
1	2	75	60	$\dfrac{180 \times 220}{660}$	15	225	3.750
1	3	65	90	$\dfrac{180 \times 330}{660}$	-25	625	6.944
2	1	30	25	$\dfrac{150 \times 110}{660}$	5	25	1.000
2	2	45	50	$\dfrac{150 \times 220}{660}$	-5	25	0.500
2	3	75	75	$\dfrac{150 \times 330}{660}$	0	0	0.000
3	1	40	55	$\dfrac{330 \times 110}{660}$	-15	225	4.091
3	2	100	110	$\dfrac{330 \times 220}{660}$	-10	100	0.909
3	3	190	165	$\dfrac{330 \times 330}{660}$	25	625	3.788

$$[9\text{-}1] \quad \sum \frac{(f_o - f_e)^2}{f_e} = 24.315 \leftarrow \chi^2 \text{ chi-square}$$

FIGURE 9-4

Chi-square hypothesis test at the .01 level of significance, showing acceptance region and sample chi-square value of 24.315

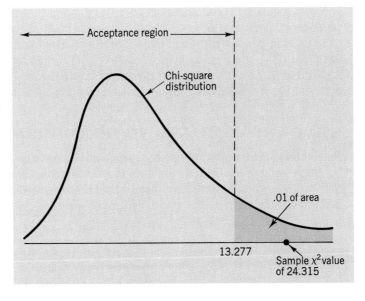

9-2 Chi-Square as a Test of Independence

in color. Appendix Table 5 (in the .01 column and the 4 degrees of freedom row) tells Donna that for her problem, the region to the right of a chi-square value of 13.277 contains .01 of the area under the curve. Thus, the acceptance region for the null hypothesis in Fig. 9-4 goes from the left tail of the curve to the chi-square value of 13.277.

Interpreting the results of the test

As Fig. 9-4 shows Donna, the sample chi-square value of 24.315 she calculated in Table 9-7 is not within the acceptance region. Thus Donna must reject the null hypothesis and inform Mr. McMahon that the evidence supports his belief that length of hospital stay and insurance coverage *are* dependent on each other.

PRECAUTIONS ABOUT USING THE CHI-SQUARE TEST

Use large sample sizes

To use a chi-square hypothesis test, we must have a sample size large enough to guarantee the similarity between the theoretically correct distribution and our sampling distribution of χ^2, the chi-square statistic. When the expected frequencies are too small, the value of χ^2 will be overestimated and will result in too many rejections of the null hypothesis. **To avoid making incorrect inferences from χ^2 hypothesis tests, follow the general rule that an expected frequency of less than 5 in one cell of a contingency table is too small to use.*** When the table contains more than one cell with an expected frequency of less than 5, we can combine these in order to get an expected frequency of 5 or more. But in doing this, we reduce the number of categories of data and will gain less information from the contingency table.

Use carefully collected data

This rule will enable us to use the chi-square hypothesis test properly, but unfortunately, each test can only reflect (and not improve) the quality of the data we feed into it. So far, we have rejected the null hypothesis if the difference between the observed and expected frequencies — that is, the computed chi-square value — is too large. In the case of the job-review preferences, we would reject the null hypothesis at a .10 level of significance if our chi-square value was 6.251 or more. **But if the chi-square value was zero, we should be careful to question whether *absolutely no difference* exists between observed and expected frequencies.** If we have strong feelings that some difference *ought* to exist, we should examine either the way the data were collected or the manner in which measurements were taken, or both, to be certain that existing differences had not been obscured or missed in collecting sample data.

Mendel's pea data

Experiments with the characteristics of peas led the monk Gregor Mendel to propose the existence of genes. Mendel's experimental results were astoundingly close to those predicted by his theory. Some time later, statisticians looked at Mendel's "pea data," performed a chi-square test, and concluded that chi-square was too small; that is, Mendel's reported experimental data were so close to what was expected that they could only conclude that he had fudged the data.

USING THE COMPUTER TO DO CHI-SQUARE TESTS

Using SAS for a chi-square test

Even though the computations necessary to do a chi-square test of independence are relatively simple, for large sets of data they can become rather tedious. Most commonly used computer statistics packages contain routines for doing these tests. In Fig. 9-5, we see the output that results when we use the SAS package to analyze the

---

* Statisticians have developed correction factors that, in some cases, allow us to use cells with expected frequencies of less than 5. The derivation and use of these correction factors are beyond the scope of this book.

```
        ILLUSTRATING THE USE OF SAS FOR A TEST OF INDEPENDENCE

                        DAYS = LENGTH OF STAY
              COVERAGE = % OF COSTS COVERED BY INSURANCE

                    TABLE OF DAYS BY COVERAGE

        DAYS              COVERAGE

        FREQUENCY      |
        EXPECTED       |
        CELL CHI2      | UNDER  |          |  OVER  |
                       |  25%   | 25%-50%  |  50%   |  TOTAL
        ---------------+--------+--------+--------+
        LESS THAN 5    |    40  |    30  |    40  |   110
                       |  30.0  |  25.0  |  55.0  |
                       | 3.33333|     1  | 4.09091|
        ---------------+--------+--------+--------+
        5 TO 10        |    75  |    45  |   100  |   220
                       |  60.0  |  50.0  | 110.0  |
                       |  3.75  |   0.5  | .909091|
        ---------------+--------+--------+--------+
        MORE THAN 10   |    65  |    75  |   190  |   330
                       |  90.0  |  75.0  | 165.0  |
                       | 6.94444|     0  | 3.78788|
        ---------------+--------+--------+--------+
        TOTAL             180      150      330      660

             STATISTICS FOR TABLE OF DAYS BY COVERAGE

        STATISTIC                 DF      VALUE      PROB
        ---------------------------------------------------
        CHI-SQUARE                 4      24.316    0.0001
```

FIGURE 9-5

Output from SAS for the hospital-stay problem

hospital-stay data of Table 9-6. Let's compare the computer output with the analysis we did by hand on pages 423–426.

Comparing computer and hand-computed outputs

In each cell of Fig. 9-5, SAS prints out the observed frequency (f_o), the expected frequency (f_e), and the contribution of that cell to the χ^2 statistic $[(f_o - f_e)^2/f_e]$. Then, at the bottom of the table, SAS prints out the sample chi-square value, the number of degrees of freedom, and a prob value. The last of these (the prob value) is the probability of getting an observed chi-square value as large (or larger) than the sample chi-square value if the hypothesis of independence is valid.

Interpreting the results

Recalling our discussion of prob values in Chapter 8, we know that we will reject H_0 if the prob value is less than α, the significance level of the test. In our example, $\alpha = .01$ and the prob value reported by SAS is .0001, so again we reject H_0 and conclude that length of stay and insurance coverage are not independent.

Using MYSTAT for a chi-square test

As a second computer-based example of a chi-square test, let's return to the earnings data in Appendix 10. We used MYSTAT to categorize the year-to-year change in last-quarter earnings in five groups:

Large decreases:	CHANGE < −$0.20
Moderate decreases:	−$0.20 ≤ CHANGE < −$0.05
Small changes:	−$0.05 ≤ CHANGE < $0.05
Moderate increases:	$0.05 ≤ CHANGE < $0.20
Large increases:	$0.20 ≤ CHANGE

Now, let's test, at $\alpha = .01$, whether the year-to-year change in last-quarter earnings depends on where the company's stock is traded.

```
TABLE OF  CHANGES (ROWS)  BY  EXCHANGES (COLUMNS)
FREQUENCIES
                      A        N        O       TOTAL

    (-10, -.20)       8        17       24       49

    [-.20, -.05)      7        10       14       31

    [-.05, .05)       11       11       41       63

    [.05, .20)        6        17       23       46

    [.20, 10)         6        20       9        35

    TOTAL             38       75       111      224


TEST STATISTIC                   VALUE    DF      PROB
     PEARSON CHI-SQUARE          19.103   8       .014
```

FIGURE 9-6

Using MYSTAT to do a test of independence

Stating the hypotheses

H_0: change in earnings and stock exchange are independent

H_1: change in earnings depends on stock exchange

$\alpha = .01 \leftarrow$ level of significance for testing these hypotheses

Interpreting the results

In Fig. 9-6, we have used MYSTAT to perform this test of independence. In each cell of Fig. 9-6, MYSTAT prints out the observed frequencies (f_o); it also gives the row and column totals. At the bottom of the table, MYSTAT gives the sample chi-square value (identified as "PEARSON CHI-SQUARE"), the degrees of freedom, and the prob value for the test of independence. Since the prob value reported by MYSTAT (.014) is greater than α (.01), we cannot reject H_0. We conclude that change in earnings and stock exchange are independent.

Exercises

9-6 Given the following dimensions for contingency tables, how many degrees of freedom will the chi-square statistic for each have?
(a) 5 rows, 4 columns   (c) 3 rows, 7 columns
(b) 6 rows, 2 columns   (d) 4 rows, 4 columns

 9-7 A brand manager is concerned that her brand's share may be unevenly distributed throughout the country. In a survey in which the country was divided into four geographic regions, a random sampling of 100 consumers in each region was surveyed, with the following results:

| | REGION | | | | |
	NE	NW	SE	SW	TOTAL
Purchase the brand	40	55	45	50	190
Do not purchase	60	45	55	50	210
TOTAL	100	100	100	100	400

Develop a table of observed and expected frequencies for this problem.

9-8 For exercise 9-7:
  (a) Calculate the sample χ^2 value.
  (b) State the null and alternative hypotheses.
  (c) Using the .05 level of significance, should the null hypothesis be rejected?

9-9 To see if silicon chip sales are independent of where the U.S. economy is in the business cycle, data have been collected on the weekly sales of Zippy Chippy, an earthquake valley firm, and on whether the U.S. economy was rising to a cycle peak, at a cycle peak, falling to a cycle trough, or at a cycle trough. The results are:

	WEEKLY CHIP SALES			
Economy	High	Medium	Low	TOTAL
at peak	20	7	3	30
at trough	30	40	30	100
rising	20	8	2	30
falling	30	5	5	40
TOTAL	100	60	40	200

Calculate a table of observed and expected frequencies for this problem.

9-10 For exercise 9-9:
  (a) State the null and alternative hypotheses.
  (b) Calculate the sample χ^2 value.
  (c) At the .10 significance level, what is your conclusion?

9-11 A financial consultant is interested in the differences in capital structure within different firm sizes in a certain industry. The consultant surveys a group of firms with assets of different amounts and divides the firms into three groups. Each firm is classified according to whether its total debt is greater than stockholders' equity or whether its total debt is less than stockholders' equity. The results of the survey are:

	FIRM ASSET SIZE (IN THOUSANDS)			
	<$500	$500–$2,000	$2,000+	TOTAL
Debt less than equity	7	10	8	25
Debt greater than equity	10	18	9	37
Total	17	28	17	62

Do the three firm sizes have the same capital structure? Use the .10 significance level.

9-12 A newspaper publisher, trying to pinpoint his market's characteristics, wondered whether newspaper readership in the community is related to readers' educational achievement. A survey questioned adults in the area on their level of education and their frequency of readership. The results are shown in the following table.

FREQUENCY OF READERSHIP	LEVEL OF EDUCATIONAL ACHIEVEMENT				
	Professional or postgraduate	College graduate	High school grad	Did not complete high school	TOTAL
Never	10	17	11	21	59
Sometimes	12	23	8	5	48
Morning or evening	35	38	16	7	96
Both editions	28	19	6	13	66
TOTAL	85	97	41	46	269

At the .10 significance level, does the frequency of newspaper readership in the community differ according to the readers' level of education?

9-13 An educator has the opinion that the grades high school students make are dependent on the amount of time they spend listening to music. To test this theory, he has randomly given 400 students a questionnaire. Within the questionnaire are the two questions: "How many hours per week do you listen to music?" and "What is the average grade for all your classes?" The data from the survey are in the table below. Using a 5 percent significance level, test whether these factors are independent or dependent.

HOURS SPENT LISTENING TO MUSIC	AVERAGE GRADE A	B	C	D	F	TOTAL
<5 hrs.	13	10	11	16	5	55
5–10 hrs.	20	27	27	19	2	95
11–20 hrs.	9	27	71	16	32	155
>20 hrs.	8	11	41	24	11	95
TOTAL	50	75	150	75	50	400

9-3
Chi-Square as a Test of Goodness of Fit: Testing the Appropriateness of a Distribution

In the preceding section of this chapter, we used the chi-square test to decide whether to accept a null hypothesis that was a hypothesis of independence between two variables. In our example, these two variables were (1) attitude toward job performance reviews and (2) geographical region.

Function of a goodness-of-fit test

The chi-square test can also be used to decide whether a particular probability distribution, such as the binomial, Poisson, or normal, is the *appropriate* distribution. This is an important ability, because as decision makers using statistics, we will need to choose a certain probability distribution to represent the distribution of the data we happen to be considering. We will need the ability to question how far we can go from the assumptions that underlie a particular distribution before we must conclude that this distribution is no longer applicable. **The chi-square test enables us to ask this question and to test whether there is a significant difference between an observed frequency distribution and a theoretical frequency distribution.** In this manner, we can determine the *goodness of fit* of a theoretical distribution (that is, how well it fits the distribution of data that we have actually observed). Thus, we can determine whether we should believe that the observed data constitute a sample drawn from the hypothesized theoretical distribution.

CALCULATING OBSERVED AND EXPECTED FREQUENCIES

Suppose that the Gordon Company requires that college seniors who are seeking positions with it be interviewed by three different executives. This enables the company to obtain a consensus evaluation of each candidate. Each executive gives the candidate either a positive or a negative rating. Table 9-8 contains the interview results of the last 100 candidates.

TABLE 9-8 Interview Results of 100 Candidates

POSSIBLE POSITIVE RATINGS FROM 3 INTERVIEWS	NUMBER OF CANDIDATES RECEIVING EACH OF THESE RATINGS
0	18
1	47
2	24
3	11
	100

For manpower planning purposes, the director of recruitment for this company thinks that the interview process can be approximated by a binomial distribution with $p = .40$; that is, with a 40 percent chance of any candidate receiving a positive rating on any one interview. If the director wants to test this hypothesis at the .20 level of significance, how should he proceed?

Stating the problem symbolically

H_0: A binomial distribution with
 $p = .40$ is a good description
 of the interview process ← null hypothesis

H_1: A binomial distribution with
 $p = .40$ is *not* a good description
 of the interview process ← alternative hypothesis

$\alpha = .20$ ← level of significance for testing these hypotheses

Calculating the binomial probabilities

To solve this problem, we must determine whether the discrepancies between the observed frequencies and those we would expect (if the binomial distribution *is* the proper model to use) are actually due to chance. We can begin by determining what the binomial probabilities would be for this interview situation. For three interviews, we would find the probability of success in the Cumulative Binomial Distribution Table (Appendix Table 3) by looking for the column labeled $n = 3$ and $p = .40$. The results are summarized in Table 9-9.

Now we can use the theoretical binomial probabilities of the outcomes to compute the expected frequencies. By comparing these expected frequencies with our observed frequencies using the χ^2 test, we can examine the extent of the difference between them. Table 9-10 lists the observed frequencies, the appropriate binomial probabilities from Table 9-9, and the expected frequencies for the sample of 100 interviews.

TABLE 9-9 Binomial Probabilities for Interview Problem

POSSIBLE POSITIVE RATINGS FROM 3 INTERVIEWS	BINOMIAL PROBABILITIES OF THESE OUTCOMES
0	$1.0000 - .7840 = .2160$
1	$.7840 - .3520 = .4320$
2	$.3520 - .0640 = .2880$
3	$.0640$
	1.0000

TABLE 9-10 Observed Frequencies, Appropriate Binomial Probabilities, and Expected Frequencies for Interview Problem

POSSIBLE POSITIVE RATINGS FROM 3 INTERVIEWS	OBSERVED FREQUENCY OF CANDIDATES RECEIVING THESE RATINGS	BINOMIAL PROBABILITY OF POSSIBLE OUTCOMES		NUMBER OF CANDIDATES INTERVIEWED		EXPECTED FREQUENCY OF CANDIDATES RECEIVING THESE RATINGS
0	18	.2160	×	100	=	21.6
1	47	.4320	×	100	=	43.2
2	24	.2880	×	100	=	28.8
3	11	.0640	×	100	=	6.4
	100	1.0000				100.0

CALCULATING THE CHI-SQUARE STATISTIC

To compute the chi-square statistic for this problem, we can use Equation 9-1:

$$\chi^2 = \sum \frac{(f_o - f_e)^2}{f_e}$$

[9-1]

and the format we introduced in Table 9-4. This process is illustrated in Table 9-11.

TABLE 9-11 Calculation of χ^2 Statistic from Interview Data Listed in Table 9-10

OBSERVED FREQUENCY f_o	EXPECTED FREQUENCY f_e	$f_o - f_e$	$(f_o - f_e)^2$	$\dfrac{(f_o - f_e)^2}{f_e}$
18	21.6	−3.6	12.96	.6000
47	43.2	3.8	14.44	.3343
24	28.8	−4.8	23.04	.8000
11	6.4	4.6	21.16	3.3063
	$\sum \dfrac{(f_o - f_e)^2}{f_e} = 5.0406 \leftarrow \chi^2$			5.0406

DETERMINING DEGREES OF FREEDOM IN A GOODNESS-OF-FIT TEST

First count the number of classes

Before we can calculate the appropriate number of degrees of freedom for a chi-square goodness-of-fit test, we must count the number of classes (symbolized k) for which we have compared the observed and expected frequencies. Our interview problem contains four such classes: 0, 1, 2, and 3 positive ratings. Thus we begin with 4 degrees of freedom. Yet since the four observed frequencies must sum to 100, the total number of observed frequencies we can freely specify is only $k - 1$, or 3. The fourth is determined, because the total of the four has to be 100.

Then subtract degrees of freedom lost from estimating population parameters

To solve a goodness-of-fit problem, we may be forced to impose additional restrictions on the calculations of the degrees of freedom. Suppose we are using the chi-square test as a goodness-of-fit test to determine whether a normal distribution fits a set of observed frequencies. If we have six classes of observed frequencies ($k = 6$), then we would conclude that we have only $k - 1$, or 5 degrees of freedom. If, however, we also have to use the sample mean as an estimate of the population mean, we will have to subtract an additional degree of freedom, which leaves us with only 4. And third, if we have to use the sample standard deviation to estimate the population standard deviation, we will have to subtract *one more* degree of freedom, leaving us with 3. Our general rule in these cases is, **first employ the $(k-1)$ rule and then subtract an additional degree of freedom for each population parameter that has to be estimated from the sample data.**

In the interview example, we have four classes of observed frequencies. As a result, $k = 4$, and the appropriate number of degrees of freedom is $k - 1$, or 3. We are not required to estimate any population parameter, so we need not reduce this number further.

USING THE CHI-SQUARE GOODNESS-OF-FIT TEST

Calculating the limit of the acceptance region

In the interview problem, the company desires to test the hypothesis of goodness of fit at the .20 level of significance. In Appendix Table 5, then, we must look under the .20 column and move down to the row labeled 3 degrees of freedom. There we find that the value of the chi-square statistic is 4.642. We can interpret this value as follows: With 3 degrees of freedom, the region to the right of a chi-square value of 4.642 contains .20 of the area under the curve.

Illustrating the problem

Figure 9-7 illustrates a chi-square distribution for 3 degrees of freedom, showing in color a .20 level of significance. Notice that the acceptance region for the null hypothesis (the hypothesis that the sample data came from a binomial distribution with

Interpreting the results

$p = .4$) extends from the left tail to the chi-square value of 4.642. Obviously, the sample chi-square value of 5.0406 falls outside this acceptance region. Therefore, we reject the null hypotheses and conclude that the binomial distribution with $p = .4$ fails to provide a good description of our observed frequencies.

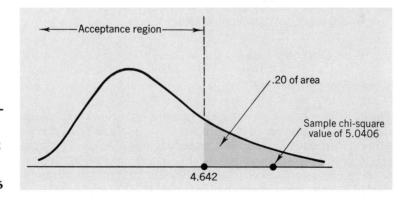

FIGURE 9-7

Goodness-of-fit test at the .20 level of significance, showing acceptance region and sample chi-square value of 5.0406

Exercises

9-14 Louis Armstrong, salesman for the Dillard Paper Company, has five accounts to visit per day. It is suggested that the variable, sales by Mr. Armstrong, may be described by the binomial distribution, with the probability of selling each account being .4. Given the following frequency distribution of Armstrong's number of sales per day, can we conclude that the data does in fact follow the suggested distribution? Use the .05 significance level.

Number of sales per day	0	1	2	3	4	5
Frequency of the number of sales	10	41	60	20	6	3

9-15 At the .10 level of significance, can we conclude that the following data follows a Poisson distribution with $\lambda = 3$?

Number of arrivals per hour	0	1	2	3	4	5 or more
Number of hours	20	57	98	85	78	62

9-16 In order to plan how much cash to keep on hand in the vault, a bank is interested in seeing if the average deposit of a customer is normally distributed. A newly hired employee hoping for a raise has collected the following information:

Deposit	$0–$999	$1,000–$1,999	$2,000 and more
Observed frequency	20	65	25

(a) Compute the expected frequencies if the data are normally distributed with mean $1,500 and standard deviation $600.
(b) Compute the chi-square statistic.
(c) State explicit null and alternative hypotheses.
(d) Test your hypotheses at the .10 level, and state an explicit conclusion.

9-17 Below is an observed frequency distribution. Using a normal distribution with $\mu = 5$ and $\sigma = 1.5$:
(a) Find the probability of falling in each class.
(b) From part (a), compute the expected frequency of each category.
(c) Calculate the chi-square statistic.
(d) At the .10 level of significance, does this frequency distribution seem to be well described by the suggested normal distribution?

Observed value of the variable	<2.6	2.6–3.79	3.8–4.99	5–6.19	6.2–7.39	≥7.4
Observed frequency	6	30	41	52	12	9

9-18 The post office is interested in modeling the "mangled letter" problem. It has been suggested that any letter sent to a certain area has a .15 chance of being mangled. Since the post office is so big, it can be assumed that two letters' chances of being mangled are independent. A sample of 310 people was selected, and two test letters were mailed to each of them. The number of people receiving zero, one, or two mangled letters was 260, 40, and 10, respectively. At the .10 level of significance, is it reasonable to conclude that the number of mangled letters received by people follows a binomial distribution with $p = .15$?

9-19 A state lottery commission claims that for a new lottery game, there is a 10 percent chance of getting a $1 prize, a 5 percent chance of $100, and an 85 percent chance of getting nothing. To test if this claim is correct, a winner from the last lottery went out and bought 1,000 tickets for the new lottery. He had 87 one dollar prizes, 48 one-hundred dollar prizes, and 865 worthless tickets. At the .05 significance level, is the state's claim reasonable?

9-20 Dennis Barry, a hospital administrator, has examined past records from 210 randomly selected 8-hour shifts to determine the frequency with which the hospital treats fractures. The number of days in which zero, one, two, three, four, or five or more patients with broken bones were treated was 25, 55, 65, 35, 20, and 10, respectively. At the .05 level of significance, can we reasonably believe that the incidence of broken bone cases follows a Poisson distribution with $\lambda = 2$?

9-21 A large city fire department calculates that for any given precinct, during any given 8-hour shift, there is a 30 percent chance of receiving at least one fire alarm. Here is a random sampling of 60 days:

Number of shifts during which alarms were received	1	2	3
Number of days	27	11	6

At the .05 level of significance, do these fire alarms follow a binomial distribution? (*Hint:* Combine the last two groups so that all expected frequencies will be greater than 5.)

9-22 A diligent statistics student wants to see if it is reasonable to assume that some sales data have been sampled from a normal population before performing a hypothesis test on the mean sales. She collected some sales data, computed $\bar{x} = 78$ and $s = 9$, and tabulated the data as follows:

Sales	$\leqslant 65$	66–70	71–75	76–80	81–85	$\geqslant 86$
Number of observations in each group	10	20	40	50	40	40

(a) Is it important for the statistics student to check if the data are normally distributed?
(b) State explicit null and alternative hypotheses for checking if the data are normally distributed.
(c) What is the probability (using a normal distribution with $\mu = 78$ and $\sigma = 9$) that sales will be less than or equal to 65; between 66 and 70; between 71 and 75; between 76 and 80; between 81 and 85; greater than or equal to 86?
(d) At the .05 level of significance, does the observed frequency distribution follow a normal distribution?

9-23 A supermarket manager is keeping track of the arrival of customers at checkout counters to see how many cashiers are needed to handle the flow. In a sample of 500 five-minute time periods, there were 22, 74, 115, 95, 94, 80, and 20 periods in which zero, one, two, three, four, five, or six or more customers, respectively, arrived at a checkout counter. Are these data consistent at the .05 level of significance with a Poisson distribution with $\lambda = 3$?

9-24 After years of working at a weighing station for trucks, Jeff Simpson feels that the weight per truck (in 1,000's of pounds) follows a normal distribution with $\mu = 71$ and $\sigma = 15$. In order to test this assumption, Jeff collected the data below one Monday, recording the weight of each truck that entered his station.

85	57	60	81	89	63	52	65	77	64
89	86	90	60	57	61	95	78	66	92
50	56	95	60	82	55	61	81	61	53
63	75	50	98	63	77	50	62	79	69
76	66	97	67	54	93	70	80	67	73

If Jeff used a chi-square goodness-of-fit test on these data, what would he conclude about the trucks' weight distribution? (Use a .10 significance level and be sure to state the hypothesis of interest.) (*Hint:* Use five equally probable intervals.)

9-25 A professional baseball player, Lon Dakestraw, was at bat five times in each of 100 games. Lon claims that he has a probability of .4 of getting a hit each time he goes to bat. Test his claim at the .05 level by seeing if the following data are distributed binomially ($p = .4$). (*Note:* Combine classes if the expected number of observations is less than 5).

Number of hits per game	Number of games with that number of hits
0	12
1	38
2	27
3	17
4	5
5	1

9-4
Analysis of Variance

Function of analysis of variance

Earlier in this chapter, we used the chi-square test to examine the differences among more than two sample proportions and to make inferences about whether such samples are drawn from populations each having the same proportion. In this section, we will learn a technique known as **analysis of variance (often abbreviated ANOVA), which will enable us to test for the significance of the differences among more than two sample means.** Using analysis of variance, we will be able to make inferences about whether our samples are drawn from populations having the same mean.

Situations where we can use ANOVA

Analysis of variance will be useful in such situations as comparing the mileage achieved by five different brands of gasoline, testing which of four different training methods produces the fastest learning record, or comparing the first-year earnings of the graduates of half a dozen different business schools. In each of these cases, we would compare the means of *more* than two samples.

STATEMENT OF THE PROBLEM

In the training director's problem that opened this chapter, she wanted to evaluate three different training methods to determine whether there were any differences in effectiveness.

Calculating the grand mean

After completion of the training period, the company's statistical staff chose sixteen new employees assigned at random to the three training methods.* Counting the production output by these sixteen trainees, the staff has summarized the data and calculated the mean production of the trainees (see Table 9-12). Now if we wish to determine the *grand mean,* or $\overline{\overline{x}}$ (the mean for the entire group of sixteen trainees), we can use one of two methods:

$$1.\ \overline{\overline{x}} = \frac{15+18+19+22+11+22+27+18+21+17+18+24+19+16+22+15}{16}$$

$$= \frac{304}{16}$$

$$= 19 \leftarrow \text{grand mean using all the data}$$

---

* Although in real practice, sixteen trainees would not constitute an adequate statistical sample, we have limited the number here to be able to demonstrate the basic techniques of analysis of variance and to avoid tedious calculations.

TABLE 9-12 Daily Production of 16 New Employees

METHOD 1	METHOD 2	METHOD 3	
		18	
15	22	24	
18	27	19	
19	18	16	
22	21	22	
11	17	15	
85	105	114	
÷5	÷5	÷6	
$17 = \bar{x}_1$	$21 = \bar{x}_2$	$19 = \bar{x}_3$	← sample means
$n_1 = 5$	$n_2 = 5$	$n_3 = 6$	← sample sizes

2. $\bar{\bar{x}} = (5/16)(17) + (5/16)(21) + (6/16)(19)$

$$= \frac{304}{16}$$

$= 19 \leftarrow$ grand mean as a weighted average of the sample means, using the relative sample sizes as the weights

STATEMENT OF THE HYPOTHESES

In this case, our reason for using analysis of variance is to decide whether these three samples (a *sample* is the small group of employees trained by any one method) were drawn from populations (a *population* is the total number of employees who could be trained by that method) having the same means. Because we are testing the effectiveness of the three training methods, we must determine whether the three samples, represented by the sample means $\bar{x}_1 = 17$, $\bar{x}_2 = 21$, and $\bar{x}_3 = 19$, could have been

Stating the problem symbolically drawn from populations having the same mean, μ. A formal statement of the null and alternative hypotheses we wish to test would be:

$H_0: \mu_1 = \mu_2 = \mu_3 \leftarrow$ null hypothesis

$H_1: \mu_1, \mu_2,$ and μ_3 are *not* all equal $\leftarrow$ alternative hypothesis

Interpreting the results   If we can conclude from our test that the sample means do not differ significantly, we can infer that the choice of training method does not influence the productivity of the employee. On the other hand, if we find differences among the sample means that are too large to attribute to chance sampling error, we can infer that the method used in training *does* influence the productivity of the employee. In that case, we would adjust our training program accordingly.

ANALYSIS OF VARIANCE: BASIC CONCEPTS

Assumptions made in analysis of variance In order to use analysis of variance, we must assume that each of the samples is drawn from a normal population and that each of these populations has the same variance, σ^2. If, however, the sample sizes are large enough, we do not need the assumption of normality.

In our training-methods problem, our null hypothesis states that the three populations have the same mean. If this hypothesis is true, classifying the data into three columns in Table 9-12 is unnecessary, and the entire set of sixteen measurements of productivity can be thought of as a sample from one population. This overall population also has a variance of σ^2.

Analysis of variance is based on a comparison of two different estimates of the variance, σ^2, of our overall population. In this case, we can calculate one of these estimates by examining **the variance among the three sample means,** which are 17, 21, and 19. The other estimate of the population variance is determined by **the variation within the three samples** themselves; that is, (15, 18, 19, 22, 11), (22, 17, 18, 21, 17), and (18, 24, 19, 16, 22, 15). Then we compare these two estimates of the population variance. Since both are estimates of σ^2, they should be approximately equal in value *when the null hypothesis is true.* If the null hypothesis is *not* true, these two estimates will differ considerably. The three steps in analysis of variance, then, are:

Steps in analysis of variance

1. Determine one estimate of the population variance from the variance *among the sample means.*
2. Determine a second estimate of the population variance from the variance *within the samples.*
3. Compare these two estimates. If they are approximately equal in value, *accept* the null hypothesis.

In the remainder of this section, we shall learn how to calculate these two estimates of the population variance, how to compare these two estimates, and how to perform a hypothesis test and interpret the results. As we learn how to do these computations, however, keep in mind that all are based on the above three steps.

CALCULATING THE VARIANCE AMONG THE SAMPLE MEANS

Finding the first estimate of the population variance

Step 1 in analysis of variance indicates that we must obtain one estimate of the population variance from the variance among the three sample means. In statistical language, this estimate is called the *between-column variance.*

In Chapter 3, we used Equation 3-17 to calculate the sample variance:

$$\text{Sample variance} \longrightarrow s^2 = \frac{\Sigma(x - \overline{x})^2}{n - 1} \qquad [3\text{-}17]$$

First find the variance among sample means

Now, because we are working with three sample means and a grand mean, let's substitute $\overline{x}$ for x, $\overline{\overline{x}}$ for $\overline{x}$, and k (the number of samples) for n to get a formula for the variance among the sample means:

$$\text{Variance among sample means} \longrightarrow s_{\overline{x}}^2 = \frac{\Sigma(\overline{x} - \overline{\overline{x}})^2}{k - 1} \qquad [9\text{-}4]$$

Then find the population variance using this variance among sample means

Next, we can return for a moment to Chapter 6, where we defined the standard error of the mean as the standard deviation of all possible samples of a given size. The formula to derive the standard error of the mean is Equation 6-1:

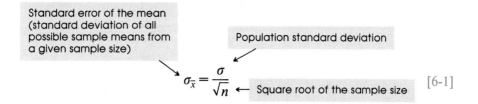

Standard error of the mean (standard deviation of all possible sample means from a given sample size)

Population standard deviation

$$\sigma_{\bar{x}} = \frac{\sigma}{\sqrt{n}}$$ ← Square root of the sample size

[6-1]

We can simplify this equation by cross-multiplying the terms and then squaring both sides in order to change the population standard deviation, σ, into the population variance, σ^2:

Population variance → $$\sigma^2 = \sigma_{\bar{x}}^2 \times n$$

[9-5]

Standard error squared (this is the variance among the sample means)

For our training-method problem, we do not have all the information we need to use this equation to find σ^2. Specifically, we do not know $\sigma_{\bar{x}}^2$. We could, however, calculate the variance among the three sample means, $s_{\bar{x}}^2$, using Equation 9-4. So why not substitute $s_{\bar{x}}^2$ for $\sigma_{\bar{x}}^2$ in Equation 9-5 and calculate an estimate of the population variance? This will give us:

$$\hat{\sigma}^2 = s_{\bar{x}}^2 \times n = \frac{\Sigma n(\bar{x} - \bar{\bar{x}})^2}{k - 1}$$

Which sample size to use
There is a slight difficulty in using this equation as it stands. In Equation 6-1, n represents the sample size, but *which* sample size should we use when the different samples have different sizes? We solve this problem with Equation 9-6, where each $(\bar{x}_j - \bar{\bar{x}})^2$ is multiplied by its own appropriate n_j.

First estimate of the population variance → $$\hat{\sigma}^2 = \frac{\Sigma n_j(\bar{x}_j - \bar{\bar{x}})^2}{k - 1}$$

[9-6]

where:

- $\hat{\sigma}^2$ = our first estimate of the population variance based on the variance among the sample means (the *between-column variance*)
- n_j = the size of the jth sample
- $\bar{x}_j$ = the sample mean of the jth sample
- $\bar{\bar{x}}$ = the grand mean
- k = the number of samples

Now we can use Equation 9-6 and the data from Table 9-12 to calculate the between-column variance. Table 9-13 shows how to make these calculations.

TABLE 9-13 Calculation of the Between-Column Variance

n	$\bar{x}$	$\bar{\bar{x}}$	$\bar{x} - \bar{\bar{x}}$	$(x - \bar{x})^2$	$n(\bar{x} - \bar{\bar{x}})^2$
5	17	19	$17 - 19 = -2$	$(-2)^2 = 4$	$5 \times 4 = 20$
5	21	19	$21 - 19 = 2$	$(2)^2 = 4$	$5 \times 4 = 20$
6	19	19	$19 - 19 = 0$	$(0)^2 = 0$	$6 \times 0 = \underline{0}$

$$\Sigma n_j (\bar{x}_j - \bar{\bar{x}})^2 \rightarrow \textbf{40}$$

$$\hat{\sigma}^2 = \frac{\Sigma n_j (\bar{x}_j - \bar{\bar{x}})^2}{k - 1} = \frac{40}{3 - 1} \qquad \text{[9-6]}$$

$$= \frac{40}{2}$$

$$= 20 \leftarrow \text{the between-column variance}$$

CALCULATING THE VARIANCE WITHIN THE SAMPLES

Finding the second estimate of the population variance

Step 2 in ANOVA requires a second estimate of the population variance based on the variance within the samples. In statistical terms, this can be called the *within-column variance.* Our employee training problem has three samples of five or six items each. We can calculate the variance within each of these three samples using Equation 3-17:

$$\text{Sample variance} \longrightarrow s^2 = \frac{\Sigma(x - \bar{x})^2}{n - 1} \qquad \text{[3-17]}$$

Since we have assumed that the variances of our three populations are the same, we could use any one of the three sample variances (s_1^2 or s_2^2 or s_3^2) as the second estimate of the population variance. Statistically, we can get a better estimate of the population variance by using a weighted average of all three sample variances. The general formula for this second estimate of σ^2 is:

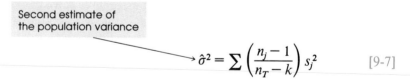

$$\text{Second estimate of the population variance} \longrightarrow \hat{\sigma}^2 = \Sigma \left(\frac{n_j - 1}{n_T - k} \right) s_j^2 \qquad \text{[9-7]}$$

where:

- $\hat{\sigma}^2$ = our second estimate of the population variance based on the variances within the samples (the *within-column variance*)
- n_j = the size of the jth sample
- s_j^2 = the sample variance of the jth sample
- k = the number of samples
- $n_T = \Sigma n_j$ = the total sample size

Using all the information at our disposal

This formula uses all the information that we have at our disposal, not just a portion of it. Had there been seven samples instead of three, we would have taken a weighted average of all seven. The weights used in Equation 9-7 will be explained shortly. Table 9-14 illustrates how to calculate this second estimate of the population variance using the variances within all three of our samples.

TABLE 9-14 Calculation of Variances Within the Samples and the Within-Column Variance

Training method 1 Sample mean: $\bar{x} = 17$		Training method 2 Sample mean: $\bar{x} = 21$		Training method 3 Sample mean: $\bar{x} = 19$	
$x - \bar{x}$	$(x - \bar{x})^2$	$x - \bar{x}$	$(x - \bar{x})^2$	$x - \bar{x}$	$(x - \bar{x})^2$
$15 - 17 = -2$	$(-2)^2 = 4$	$22 - 21 = 1$	$(1)^2 = 1$	$18 - 19 = -1$	$(-1)^2 = 1$
$18 - 17 = 1$	$(1)^2 = 1$	$27 - 21 = 6$	$(6)^2 = 36$	$24 - 19 = 5$	$(5)^2 = 25$
$19 - 17 = 2$	$(2)^2 = 4$	$18 - 21 = -3$	$(-3)^2 = 9$	$19 - 19 = 0$	$(0)^2 = 0$
$22 - 17 = 5$	$(5)^2 = 25$	$21 - 21 = 0$	$(0)^2 = 0$	$16 - 19 = -3$	$(-3)^2 = 9$
$11 - 17 = -6$	$(-6)^2 = 36$	$17 - 21 = -4$	$(-4)^2 = 16$	$22 - 19 = 3$	$(3)^2 = 9$
	$\Sigma(x - \bar{x})^2 = \mathbf{70}$		$\Sigma(x - \bar{x})^2 = \mathbf{62}$	$15 - 19 = -4$	$(-4)^2 = 16$
					$\Sigma(x - \bar{x})^2 = \mathbf{60}$
	$\dfrac{\Sigma(x - \bar{x})^2}{n - 1} = \dfrac{70}{5 - 1}$		$\dfrac{\Sigma(x - \bar{x})^2}{n - 1} = \dfrac{62}{5 - 1}$		$\dfrac{\Sigma(x - \bar{x})^2}{n - 1} = \dfrac{60}{6 - 1}$
	$= \dfrac{70}{4}$		$= \dfrac{62}{4}$		$= \dfrac{60}{5}$
sample variance $\to s_1^2 = 17.5$		sample variance $\to s_2^2 = 15.5$		sample variance $\to s_3^2 = 12.0$	

And:

$$\hat{\sigma}^2 = \Sigma\left(\frac{n_j - 1}{n_T - k}\right)s_j^2 = (4/13)(17.5) + (4/13)(15.5) + (5/13)(12.0) \qquad [9\text{-}7]$$

$$= \frac{192}{13}$$

Second estimate of the population variance based on the variances within

$= 14.769 \leftarrow$ the samples (the within-column variance)

THE F HYPOTHESIS TEST: COMPUTING AND INTERPRETING THE F STATISTIC

Finding the F ratio

Step 3 in ANOVA compares these two estimates of the population variance by computing their ratio, called F, as follows:

$$F = \frac{\text{First estimate of the population variance based on the variance among the sample means}}{\text{Second estimate of the population variance based on the variances within the samples}} \qquad [9\text{-}8]$$

If we substitute the statistical shorthand for the numerator and denominator of this ratio, Equation 9-8 becomes:

$$F = \frac{\text{Between-column variance}}{\text{Within-column variance}} \qquad [9\text{-}9]$$

Now we can find the F ratio for the training-method problem with which we have been working:

$$F = \frac{\text{Between-column variance}}{\text{Within-column variance}} \qquad [9\text{-}9]$$

$$= \frac{20}{14.769}$$

$$= 1.354 \leftarrow F \text{ ratio}$$

Having found this F ratio of 1.354, how can we interpret it? First, examine the denominator, which is based on the variance within the samples. The denominator is a good estimator of σ^2 (the population variance) whether the null hypothesis is true or not. What about the numerator? If the null hypothesis that the three methods of training have equal effects is true, then the numerator, or the variation among the sample means of the three methods, is also a good estimate of σ^2 (the population variance). As a result, **the denominator and numerator should be about equal if the null hypothesis is true.** The nearer the F ratio comes to 1, then the more we are inclined to accept the null hypothesis. Conversely, as the F ratio becomes larger, we will be more inclined to reject the null hypothesis and accept the alternative (that a difference does exist in the effects of the three training methods).

Shortly, we shall learn a more formal way of deciding when to accept or reject the null hypothesis. But even now, you should understand the basic logic behind the F *statistic.* **When populations are not the same, the between-column variance (which was derived from the variance among the sample means) will tend to be larger than the within-column variance (which was derived from the variances within the samples), and the value of F will tend to be large. This will lead us to reject the null hypothesis.**

THE F DISTRIBUTION

Like other statistics we have studied, if the null hypothesis is true, then the F statistic has a particular sampling distribution. Like the t and chi-square distributions, this F distribution is actually a whole family of distributions, three of which are shown in Fig. 9-8. Notice that each is identified by a *pair* of degrees of freedom, unlike the t and chi-square distributions, which have only one value for the number of degrees of freedom. **The first number refers to the number of degrees of freedom in the numerator of the F ratio; the second, to the degrees of freedom in the denominator.**

As we can see in Fig. 9-8, the F distribution has a single mode. The specific shape of an F distribution depends upon the number of degrees of freedom in both the numerator and the denominator of the F ratio. But in general, the F distribution is

FIGURE 9-8

Three F distributions (first value in parentheses equals number of degrees of freedom in the numerator of the F ratio; second equals number of degrees of freedom in the denominator)

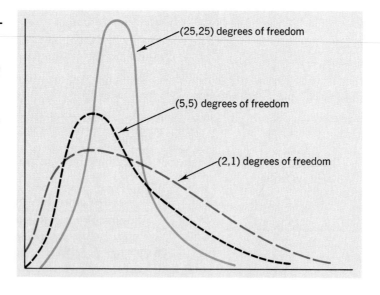

(25,25) degrees of freedom

(5,5) degrees of freedom

(2,1) degrees of freedom

skewed to the right and tends to get more symmetrical as the number of degrees of freedom in the numerator and denominator increase.

USING THE F DISTRIBUTION: DEGREES OF FREEDOM

Calculating degrees of freedom As we have mentioned, each F distribution has a pair of degrees of freedom, one for the numerator of the F ratio and the other for the denominator. How can we calculate both of these?

Finding the numerator degrees of freedom First, think about the numerator, the between-column variance. In Table 9-13, we used three values of $(\bar{x} - \bar{\bar{x}})^2$, one for each sample, to calculate $\Sigma(\bar{x} - \bar{\bar{x}})^2$. Once we knew two of these $(\bar{x} - \bar{\bar{x}})^2$ values, the third was *automatically determined* and could not be freely specified. Thus, one degree of freedom is lost when we calculate the between-column variance, and the number of degrees of freedom for the numerator of the F ratio is always one fewer than the number of samples. The rule, then, is:

$$\text{Number of degrees of freedom in \textit{numerator} of the } F \text{ ratio} = (\text{Number of samples} - 1) \qquad [9\text{-}10]$$

Finding the denominator degrees of freedom Now, what of the denominator? Look at Table 9-14 for a moment. There we calculated the variances within the samples, and we used all three samples. For the jth sample, we used n_j values of $(x - \bar{x})$ to calculate the $\Sigma(x - \bar{x})^2$ for that sample. Once we knew all but one of these $(x - \bar{x})$ values, the last was *automatically determined* and could not be freely specified. Thus, we lost 1 degree of freedom in the calculations for *each* sample, leaving us with 4, 4, and 5 degrees of freedom in the samples. Since we had three samples, we were left with $4 + 4 + 5 = 13$ degrees of freedom (which could also be calculated as $5 + 5 + 6 - 3 = 13$). We can state the rule like this:

$$\text{Number of degrees of freedom in \textit{denominator} of the } F \text{ ratio} = \Sigma(n_j - 1) = n_T - k \qquad [9\text{-}11]$$

where:

- n_j = the size of the jth sample
- k = the number of samples
- $n_T = \Sigma n_j$ = the total sample size

Now we can see that the weight assigned to s_j^2 in Equation 9-7 was just its fraction of the total number of degrees of freedom in the denominator of the F ratio.

USING THE F TABLE

To do F hypothesis tests, we shall use an F table in which the columns represent the number of degrees of freedom for the numerator and the rows represent the degrees of freedom for the denominator. Separate tables exist for each level of significance.

Suppose we are testing a hypothesis at the .01 level of significance, using the F distribution. Our degrees of freedom are 8 for the numerator and 11 for the denominator. In this instance, we would turn to Appendix Table 6. In the body of that table, the appropriate value for 8 and 11 degrees of freedom is 4.74. If our calculated value of F exceeds this table value of 4.74, we would reject the null hypothesis. If not, we would accept it.

TESTING THE HYPOTHESIS

Finding the F statistic and the degrees of freedom

We can now test our hypothesis that the three different training methods produce identical results, using the material we have developed to this point. Let's begin by reviewing how we calculated the F ratio:

$$F = \frac{\text{First estimate of the population variance based on the variance within the samples means}}{\text{Second estimate of the population variance based on the variances within the samples}} \qquad [9\text{-}8]$$

$$= \frac{20}{14.769}$$

$$= 1.354 \leftarrow F \text{ statistic}$$

Next, calculate the number of degrees of freedom in the numerator of the F ratio, using Equation 9-10 as follows:

$$\boxed{\begin{array}{l}\text{Number of degrees of freedom}\\ \text{in } \textit{numerator} \text{ of the } F \text{ ratio}\end{array}} = (\text{Number of samples} - 1) \qquad [9\text{-}10]$$
$$= 3 - 1$$
$$= 2 \leftarrow \text{degrees of freedom}$$
$$\qquad\text{in the numerator}$$

And we can calculate the number of degrees of freedom in the denominator of the F ratio by use of Equation 9-11:

$$\boxed{\begin{array}{l}\text{Number of degrees of freedom}\\ \text{in } \textit{denominator} \text{ of the } F \text{ ratio}\end{array}} = \Sigma(n_j - 1) = n_T - k \qquad [9\text{-}11]$$
$$= (5 - 1) + (5 - 1) + (6 - 1)$$
$$= 16 - 3$$
$$= 13 \leftarrow \text{degrees of freedom}$$
$$\qquad\text{in the denominator}$$

FIGURE 9-9

Hypothesis test at the .05 level of significance, using the F distribution and showing the acceptance region and the calculated F value

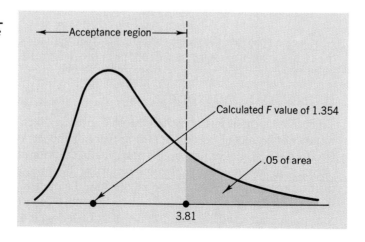

9 CHI-SQUARE AND ANALYSIS OF VARIANCE

Suppose the director of training wants to test at the .05 level the hypothesis that there are no differences among the three training methods. We can look in Appendix Table 6 for 2 degrees of freedom in the numerator and 13 in the denominator. The value we find there is 3.81. Figure 9-9 shows this hypothesis test graphically. The colored region represents the level of significance. The table value of 3.81 sets the upper limit of the acceptance region. Since the calculated value for F of 1.354 lies within the acceptance region, we would accept the null hypothesis and conclude that, according to the sample information we have, there are no differences in the effects of the three training methods on employee productivity.

PRECAUTIONS ABOUT USING THE *F* TEST

As we stated earlier, our sample sizes in this problem are too small for us to be able to draw valid inferences about the effectiveness of the various training methods. We chose small samples so that we could explain the logic of analysis of variance without tedious calculations. In actual practice, our methodology would be the same, but our samples would be larger.

In our example, we have assumed the absence of many factors that might have affected our conclusions. We accepted as given, for example, the fact that all the new employees we sampled had the same demonstrated aptitude for learning—which may or may not be true. We assumed that all the instructors of the three training methods had the same ability to teach and to manage, which may not be true. And we assumed that the company's statistical staff collected the data on productivity during work periods that were similar in terms of time of day, day of the week, time of the year, and so on. To be able to make significant decisions based on analysis of variance, we need to be certain that all these factors are effectively controlled.

Finally, notice that we have discussed only *one-way,* or one-factor, analysis of variance. Our problem examined the effect of the type of training method on employee productivity, nothing else. Had we wished to measure the effect of two factors, such as the training program and the age of the employee, we would need the ability to use two-way analysis of variance, a statistical method best saved for more advanced textbooks.

USING THE COMPUTER FOR ANALYSIS OF VARIANCE

Once again, let us repeat that we used small sample sizes in our ANOVA example so we could explain the logic of the method without getting bogged down in tedious calculations. For a realistic problem, it would be very convenient to use the ANOVA routines that can be found in all the commonly used statistical packages. So that you can compare one of these with the analysis that we did by hand, Figure 9-10 gives the output when SAS is used to analyze the data in our training-method problem.

Let's look at the column of SAS's "ANOVA table" headed "MEAN SQUARE." In the row labeled "MODEL," this column contains the value 20.000, which we recognize as the between-column variance we calculated in Figure 9-10. In the row labeled "ERROR," we find the value 14.769, which is the within-column variance we calculated in Table 9-14. Notice also the column headed "DF" (meaning degrees of freedom). It tells us that the MODEL MEAN SQUARE (the between-column variance) has 2 degrees of freedom and the ERROR MEAN SQUARE (the within-column variance) has 13 degrees of freedom.

FIGURE 9-10

Output from SAS for
the employee
training problem

```
                ILLUSTRATING THE USE OF SAS FOR ANOVA
                DOES PRODUCTIVITY DEPEND ON TRAINING METHOD?

                      ANALYSIS OF VARIANCE PROCEDURE

  DEPENDENT VARIABLE: UNITS        UNITS PRODUCED BY TRAINEE

  SOURCE                    DF      SUM OF SQUARES        MEAN SQUARE

  MODEL                      2        40.00000000        20.00000000

  ERROR                     13       192.00000000        14.76923077

  CORRECTED TOTAL           15       232.00000000

  MODEL F =              1.35                        PR > F = 0.2923
```

The last line of the output gives the value of the F statistic, $F = 1.35$, and the prob value .2923, which is the probability of getting an F statistic as large or larger than 1.35 if H_0 is true. Since the prob value is larger than our significance level of $\alpha = .05$, we again conclude that we cannot reject H_0. On the basis of the sample evidence, these three training methods do not appear to have different effects on employee productivity.

Now that we've seen how to interpret the ANOVA output from SAS, let's analyze a much more realistic example. Despite the conclusion we reached on pages 397–398 that students in the faculty-taught sections of our statistics course didn't do significantly better on the final exam than students who were taught by TAs, we still received complaints. "I'm in Mr. Jackson's class, and my friends in Professor Rubin's class are learning much more than I am" was typical of what we were hearing. We began to wonder if perhaps there were *significant differences among the individual sections of the course,* even if the TAs *as a group* were not significantly different from the faculty *as a group.*

We used the ANOVA procedure in SAS to check this out. The formal statement of our hypotheses was:

H_0: All six μ_i are the same (no differences among sections)

H_1: The six μ_i are not the same (sections differ significantly)

Conclusion about
student complaints

The output from this analysis is shown in Figure 9-11. The calculated value of the F statistic is 1.75, and the probability of observing such a large value of F if H_0 is true (the prob value for this test) is 0.1248. With such a large prob value, we must accept H_0 and conclude that there were no significant differences in the six sections' performances on the final exam.

Using Minitab
for ANOVA

Let's see how Minitab reports the results of an analysis of variance. Recall that on pages 399–400, we used MYSTAT to test whether the year-to-year changes in last-quarter earnings for New York Stock Exchange stocks had a different mean than the year-to-year changes in last-quarter earnings for American Stock Exchange and "over-the-counter" stocks. We grouped the latter two together, since at that point we didn't yet know how to compare more than two means. Now let's look at all three groups separately and use analysis of variance to see if the three means differ significantly.

FIGURE 9-11

Output from SAS for
ANOVA of final
exam scores

```
                                SAS
                  1989 GRADES IN BUSINESS STATISTICS
            DID ALL SECTIONS PERFORM EQUALLY ON THE FINAL EXAM?

                    ANALYSIS OF VARIANCE PROCEDURE

  DEPENDENT VARIABLE: FINAL

    SOURCE                  DF      SUM OF SQUARES         MEAN SQUARE

    MODEL                    5        859.41687836        171.88337567

    ERROR                  193      18996.82432767         98.42914159

    CORRECTED TOTAL        198      19856.24120603


    MODEL F =              1.75                       PR > F = 0.1248
```

Stating the hypotheses

$H_0: \mu_{OTC} = \mu_{ASE} = \mu_{NYSE}$ (no differences by exchange)

$H_1:$ the μ's are not equal (exchanges differ significantly)

Interpreting the results

We used the ONEWAY command in Minitab to perform this analysis of variance. The results are given in Fig. 9-12. Minitab's output for analysis of variance is quite similar to the SAS output we have just seen. The calculated value of the F statistic is 0.88, and the prob value for testing our hypotheses is 0.415. Since this prob value is larger than all of our customary levels of significance ($\alpha = .10, .05, .01$, etc.), we cannot reject H_0; we conclude that the mean values of year-to-year changes in last-quarter earnings on the three exchanges are not significantly different from each other.

FIGURE 9-12

Using Minitab for
ANOVA

```
  ANALYSIS OF VARIANCE ON CHANGE

    SOURCE      DF      SS        MS        F        p

    EXCHANGE     2    1.421     0.711     0.88     0.415
    ERROR      221  177.906     0.805
    TOTAL      223  179.327
```

Exercises

 9-26 A study compared the effects of four 1-month point-of-purchase promotions on sales. Below are the unit sales for five stores using all four promotions in different months.

Free sample	78	87	81	89	85
One-pack gift	94	91	87	90	88
Cents off	73	78	69	83	76
Refund by mail	79	83	78	69	81

(a) Compute the mean unit sales for each promotion and then determine the grand mean.
(b) Estimate the population variance using the between-column variance (Equation 9-6).
(c) Estimate the population variance using the within-column variance computed from the variance within the samples.
(d) Calculate the F ratio. At the .01 level of significance, do the promotions produce different effects on sales?

9-27 Three training methods were compared to see if they led to greater productivity after training. Below are productivity measures for individuals trained by each method.

Method 1	45	40	50	39	53	44
Method 2	59	43	47	51	39	49
Method 3	41	37	43	40	52	37

At the .05 level of significance, do the three training methods lead to different levels of productivity?

9-28 The following data show the number of claims processed per day for a group of four insurance company employees observed for a number of days. Test the hypothesis that the employees' mean claims per day are all the same. Use the .05 level of significance.

Employee 1	15	17	14	12		
Employee 2	12	10	13	17		
Employee 3	11	14	13	15	12	
Employee 4	13	12	12	14	10	9

9-29 Given the measurements on the four samples below, can we conclude that they come from populations having the same mean value? Use the .01 level of significance.

Sample 1	16	21	24	28	29	
Sample 2	29	18	20	19	30	21
Sample 3	14	15	21	19	28	17
Sample 4	21	28	20	22	18	

9-30 The manager of an assembly line in a clock manufacturing plant decided to study how different speeds of the conveyor belt affect the rate of defective units produced in an 8-hour shift. To examine this, he ran the belt at four different speeds for five 8-hour shifts each and measured the number of defective units found at the end of each shift. The results of the study follow:

DEFECTIVE UNITS PER SHIFT

Speed 1	Speed 2	Speed 3	Speed 4
37	27	32	35
35	32	36	27
38	32	33	33
36	34	34	31
34	30	40	29

(a) Calculate the mean number of defective units, $\bar{x}$, for each speed; then determine the grand mean, $\bar{\bar{x}}$.
(b) Using Equation 9-6, estimate the population variance (the between-column variance).
(c) Calculate the variances *within* the samples and estimate the population variance based upon these variances (the within-column variance).

9 CHI-SQUARE AND ANALYSIS OF VARIANCE

(d) Calculate the *F* ratio. At the .05 level of significance, do the four conveyor-belt speeds produce the same mean rate of defective clocks per shift?

9-31 We are interested in testing for differences in the palatability of three products: "C," "liquid H," and "solid H." For each product, a sample of 25 men was chosen. Each rated the product from -3 (terrible) to $+3$ (excellent). The SAS output given below was produced.

```
            ANALYSIS OF VARIANCE PROCEDURE

DEPENDENT VARIABLE:  SCORE  (-3 TO +3)

SOURCE              DF        SUM OF SQUARES      MEAN SQUARE

MODEL                2            15.68              7.84

ERROR               72            94.4               1.31111111

CORRECTED TOTAL     74           110.08

MODEL F =           5.98                      PR > F = 0.004
```

(a) State explicit null and alternative hypotheses.
(b) Test your hypotheses with the SAS output. Use $\alpha = .05$.
(c) State an explicit conclusion.

9-32 The supervisor of security at a large department store would like to know if the store apprehends relatively more shoplifters during the Christmas holiday season than in the weeks before or after the holiday. He gathered data on the number of shoplifters apprehended in the store during the months of November, December, and January over the past 6 years. The information is shown in the table below:

NUMBER OF SHOPLIFTERS

November	43	37	59	55	38	48
December	54	41	48	35	50	49
January	36	28	34	41	30	32

At the .05 level of significance, is the mean number of apprehended shoplifters the same during these 3 months?

9-33 A research company has designed three different systems to clean up oil spills. The following table contains the results, measured by how much surface area (in meters^2) is cleared in 1 hour. The data were found by testing each method in several trials. Are the three systems equally effective? Use the .05 level of significance.

System A	55	60	63	56	59	55
System B	57	53	64	49	62	
System C	66	52	61	57		

9-34 The manufacturer of silicon chips requires so-called "clean rooms," where the air is specially filtered to keep the number of dust particles at a minimum. The Outel Corporation wants to make sure that each of its five clean rooms has the same number of dust particles. Five air samples have been taken in each room. The "dust score," on a scale of 1 (low) to 10 (high), was measured. At the .05 level of significance, do the rooms have the same average dust score?

DUST SCORE (1 to 10)

Room 1	5	6.5	4	7	6
Room 2	3	6	4	4.5	3
Room 3	1	1.5	3	2.5	4
Room 4	8	9.5	7	6	7.5
Room 5	1	2	3.5	1.5	3

9-35 A lumber company is concerned about how rising interest rates are affecting the new housing starts in the area. To explore this question, the company has gathered data on new housing starts during the past 3 quarters for five surrounding counties. This information is presented in the following table. At the .05 level of significance, are there any differences in the number of new housing starts during the 3 quarters?

Quarter 1	41	53	54	55	43
Quarter 2	45	51	48	43	39
Quarter 3	34	44	46	45	51

9-36 Genes-and-Jeans, Inc., offers clones of such popular jeans as Generic, DNA, RNA, and Oops. The store wants to see if there are differences in the number of pairs sold of different brands. The manager has counted the number of pairs sold for each brand on several different days. At the .05 significance level, are the sales of the four brands the same?

PAIRS OF JEANS SOLD

Generic	17	21	13	27	12	
DNA	27	13	29	9		
RNA	13	15	17	23	10	21
Oops	18	25	15	27	12	

9-37 The Government Accounting Office (GAO) is interested in seeing if similar sized offices spend similar amounts on personnel and equipment. (Offices spending more are targeted for special auditing.) Monthly expenses for three offices have been examined, one office in the Agriculture Department, one in the State Department, and one in the Interior Department. The data are given below. At the .01 significance level, are there differences in expenses for the different offices?

MONTHLY OFFICE EXPENSES (in thousands of dollars) FOR SOME PAST MONTHS

Agriculture	10	8	11	9	12	
State	15	9	8	10	13	13
Interior	8	16	12			

9-38 In Bigville, a fast-food chain feels it is gaining a bad reputation because it takes too long to serve the customers. Since the chain has four restaurants in this town, it is concerned with whether all four restaurants have the same average service time. One of the owners of the fast-food chain has decided to visit each of the stores and monitor the service time for five randomly selected customers. At his four noontime visits, he records the following service times in minutes:

Restaurant 1	3	4	5.5	3.5	4
Restaurant 2	3	3.5	4.5	4	5.5
Restaurant 3	2	3.5	5	6.5	6
Restaurant 4	3	4	5.5	2.5	3

(a) Using a 5 percent significance level, do all the restaurants have the same mean service time?

(b) Based on his results, should the owner make any policy recommendations to any of the restaurant managers?

9-5
Inferences About a Population Variance

In Chapters 7 and 8, we learned how to form confidence intervals and test hypotheses about one or two population means or proportions. Earlier in this chapter, we used chi-square and F tests to make inferences about more than two means or proportions. But we are not always interested in means and proportions. In many situations, responsible decision makers have to make inferences about the variability in a population. In order to schedule the labor force at harvest time, a peach grower needs to know not only the mean time to maturity of the peaches, but also their variance around that mean. A sociologist investigating the effect of education on earning power wants to know if the incomes of college graduates are more variable than those of high school graduates. Precision instruments used in laboratory work must be quite accurate on the average; but in addition, repeated measurements should show very little variation. In this section, we shall see how to make inferences about a single population variance. The next section looks at problems involving the variances of two populations.

THE DISTRIBUTION OF THE SAMPLE VARIANCE

In response to a number of complaints about slow mail delivery, the Postmaster General initiates a preliminary investigation. An investigator follows nine letters from New York to Chicago, to estimate the standard deviation in time of delivery. Table 9-15 gives the data and computes $\bar{x}$, s^2, and s. As we saw in Chapter 7, we use s to estimate σ.

We can tell the Postmaster General that the *population* standard deviation, as estimated by the *sample* standard deviation, is approximately 23 hours. But he also wants to know how accurate that estimate is and what uncertainty is associated with it. In other words, he wants a confidence interval, not just a point estimate of σ. In

TABLE 9-15 Delivery Time (in Hours) for Letters Going between New York and Chicago

TIME x	$\bar{x}$	$x - \bar{x}$	$(x - \bar{x})^2$
50	59	−9	81
45	59	−14	196
27	59	−32	1,024
66	59	7	49
43	59	−16	256
96	59	37	1,369
45	59	−14	196
90	59	31	961
69	59	10	100
$\Sigma x = 531$			$\Sigma(x - \bar{x})^2 = 4{,}232$

$$\bar{x} = \frac{\Sigma x}{n} = \frac{531}{9} \quad \text{[3-2]}$$
$$= 59 \text{ hours}$$

$$s^2 = \frac{\Sigma(x - \bar{x})^2}{n - 1} = \frac{4{,}232}{8} \quad \text{[3-17]}$$
$$= 529 \text{ hours squared}$$
$$s = \sqrt{s^2} = \sqrt{529} \quad \text{[3-18]}$$
$$= 23 \text{ hours}$$

order to find such an interval, we must know the sampling distribution of s. It is traditional to talk about s^2 rather than s, but this will cause us no trouble, since we can always go from s^2 and σ^2 to s and σ by taking square roots; and we can go in the other direction by squaring.

If the population variance is σ^2, then the statistic

$$\chi^2 = \frac{(n-1)s^2}{\sigma^2}$$
[9-12]

has a chi-square distribution with $n - 1$ degrees of freedom. This result is exact if the population is normal; but even for samples from nonnormal populations, it is frequently a good approximation. We can now use the chi-square distribution to form confidence intervals and test hypotheses about σ^2.

CONFIDENCE INTERVALS FOR THE POPULATION VARIANCE

Constructing a confidence interval for a variance

Suppose we want a 95 percent confidence interval for the variance in our mail-delivery problem. Figure 9-13 shows how to begin constructing this interval.

We locate two points on the χ^2 distribution: χ_U^2 cuts off .025 of the area in the upper tail of the distribution, and χ_L^2 cuts off .025 of the area in the lower tail. (For a 99 percent confidence interval, we would put .005 of the area in each tail, and similarly for other confidence levels.) The values of χ_L^2 and χ_U^2 can be found in Appendix Table 5. In our mail problem, with $9 - 1 = 8$ degrees of freedom, $\chi_L^2 = 2.180$, and $\chi_U^2 = 17.535$.

Now Equation 9-12 gives χ^2 in terms of s^2, n, and σ^2. To get a confidence interval for σ^2, we solve Equation 9-12 for σ^2:

$$\sigma^2 = \frac{(n-1)s^2}{\chi^2}$$
[9-13]

and then our confidence interval is given by:

Upper and lower limits for the confidence interval

$$\sigma_L^2 = \frac{(n-1)s^2}{\chi_U^2} \leftarrow \text{lower confidence limit}$$

$$\sigma_U^2 = \frac{(n-1)s^2}{\chi_L^2} \leftarrow \text{upper confidence limit}$$
[9-14]

FIGURE 9-13

Constructing a confidence interval for σ^2

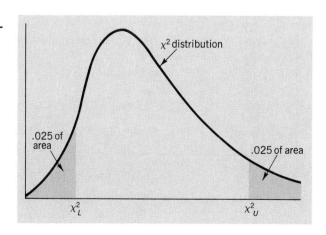

Notice that since χ^2 appears in the denominator in Equation 9-13, we can use χ_U^2 to find σ_L^2 and χ_L^2 to find σ_U^2. Continuing with the Postmaster General's problem, we see he can be 95 percent confident that the population variance lies between 241.35 and 1,941.28 hours squared:

$$\sigma_L^2 = \frac{(n-1)s^2}{\chi_U^2} = \frac{8(529)}{17.535} = 241.35$$

$$\sigma_U^2 = \frac{(n-1)s^2}{\chi_L^2} = \frac{8(529)}{2.180} = 1,941.28$$

[9-14]

So a 95 percent confidence interval for σ would be from $\sqrt{241.35}$ to $\sqrt{1,941.28}$ hours; that is, from 15.54 to 44.06 hours.

A TWO-TAILED TEST OF A VARIANCE

Testing hypotheses about a variance: two-tailed tests

A management professor has given careful thought to the design of examinations. In order for him to be reasonably certain that an exam does a good job of distinguishing the differences in achievement shown by the students, the standard deviation in scores on the examination cannot be too small. On the other hand, if the standard deviation is too large, there will tend to be a lot of very low scores, which is bad for student morale. Past experience has led the professor to believe that a standard deviation of about thirteen points on a 100-point exam indicates that the exam does a good job of balancing these two objectives.

The professor just gave an examination to his class of 31 freshmen and sophomores. The mean score was 72.7, and the sample standard deviation was 15.9. Does this exam meet his goodness criterion? We can summarize the data:

Stating the problem symbolically

$\sigma_{H_0} = 13$ ← hypothesized value of the population standard deviation

$s = 15.9$ ← sample standard deviation

$n = 31$ ← sample size

If the professor uses a significance level of .10 in testing his hypothesis, we can symbolically state the problem:

$H_0: \sigma = 13$ ← null hypothesis: The true standard deviation is 13 points.

$H_1: \sigma \neq 13$ ← alternative hypothesis: The true standard deviation is not 13 points.

$\alpha = .10$ ← level of significance for testing these hypotheses

The first thing we do is to use Equation 9-12 to calculate the χ^2 statistic:

Calculating the χ^2 statistic

$$\chi^2 = \frac{(n-1)s^2}{\sigma^2}$$

[9-12]

$$= \frac{30(15.9)^2}{(13)^2}$$

$$= 44.88$$

This statistic has a χ^2 distribution with $n - 1$ ($= 30$ in this case) degrees of freedom. We will accept the null hypothesis if χ^2 is neither too big nor too small. From the χ^2

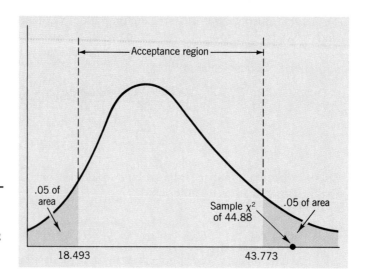

FIGURE 9-14

Two-tailed hypothesis test at the .05 level of significance, showing acceptance region and sample χ^2

distribution table (Appendix Table 5), we can see that the appropriate χ^2 values for .05 of the area to lie in each tail of the curve are 18.493 and 43.773. These two limits of the acceptance region and the observed sample statistic ($\chi^2 = 44.88$) are shown in Fig. 9-14. We see that the sample value of χ^2 is not in the acceptance region, so the professor should reject the null hypothesis; this exam does not meet his goodness criterion.

Interpreting the results

A ONE-TAILED TEST OF A VARIANCE

Testing hypotheses about a variance: one-tailed tests

Precision Analytics manufactures a wide line of precision instruments and has a fine reputation in the field for quality of its instruments. In order to preserve that reputation, it maintains strict quality control on all of its output. It will not release an analytic balance for sale, for example, unless that balance shows a variability significantly below one microgram (at $\alpha = .01$) when weighing quantities of about 500 grams. A new balance has just been delivered to the quality control division from the production line.

The new balance is tested by using it to weigh the same 500-gram standard weight thirty different times. The sample standard deviation turns out to be 0.73 micrograms. Should this balance be sold? We summarize the data:

Stating the problem symbolically

$\sigma_{H_0} = 1$ ← hypothesized value of the population standard deviation

$s = 0.73$ ← sample standard deviation

$n = 30$ ← sample size

and state the problem:

$H_0: \sigma = 1$ ← null hypothesis: The true standard deviation is 1 microgram.

$H_1: \sigma < 1$ ← alternative hypothesis: The true standard deviation is less than 1 microgram.

$\alpha = .01$ ← level of significance for testing these hypotheses

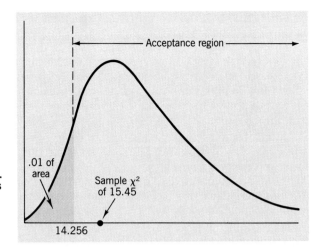

FIGURE 9-15

One-tailed hypothesis test at the .01 significance level, showing acceptance region and sample χ^2

Calculating the χ^2 statistic

We begin by using Equation 9-12 to calculate the χ^2 statistic:

$$\chi^2 = \frac{(n-1)s^2}{\sigma^2} \qquad\qquad [9\text{-}12]$$

$$= \frac{29(.73)^2}{(1)^2}$$

$$= 15.45$$

Interpreting the results

We will reject the null hypothesis and release the balance for sale if this statistic is sufficiently small. From Appendix Table 5, we see that with 29 degrees of freedom $(30 - 1)$, the value of χ^2 that leaves an area of .01 in the lower tail of the curve is 14.256. The acceptance region and the observed value of χ^2 are shown in Fig. 9-15. We see that we cannot reject the null hypothesis. The balance will have to be returned to the production line for adjusting.

Exercises

9-39   A sample of 20 observations from a normal distribution has a mean of 37 and a variance of 12.2. Construct a 90 percent confidence interval for the true population variance.

9-40   The standard deviation of a distribution is hypothesized to be 50. If an observed sample of 30 yields a sample standard deviation of 57, should we reject the null hypothesis that the true standard deviation is 50? Use the .05 level of significance.

9-41   A telescope manufacturer wants its telescopes to have standard deviations in resolution to be significantly below 2 when focusing on objects 500 light-years away. When a new telescope is used to focus on an object 500 light-years away 30 times, the sample standard deviation turns out to be 1.46. Should this telescope be sold?
   (a)   State explicit null and alternative hypotheses.
   (b)   Test your hypotheses at the $\alpha = .01$ level.
   (c)   State an explicit conclusion.

9-42   Given a sample variance of 127 from a set of nine observations, construct a 95 percent confidence interval for the population variance.

9-43 A production manager feels that the output rate of experienced employees is surely greater than that of new employees, but he does not expect the variability in output rates to differ for the two groups. In previous output studies, it has been shown that the average unit output per hour for new employees at this particular type of work is 20 units per hour with a variance of 56 units squared. For a group of 20 employees with 5 years' experience, the average output for this same type of work is 30 units per hour, with a sample variance of 28 units squared. Does the variability in output appear to differ at the two experience levels? Test the hypotheses at the .05 significance level.

9-44 A psychologist is aware of studies showing that the variability of attention spans of 5-year-olds can be summarized by $\sigma^2 = 64$ minutes^2. She wonders if the attention span of 6-year-olds is different. A sample of twenty 6-year-olds gives $s^2 = 28$ minutes^2.
(a) State explicit null and alternative hypotheses.
(b) Test your hypotheses at the $\alpha = .05$ level.
(c) State an explicit conclusion.

9-45 In checking its cars for adherence to emissions standards set by the government, an automaker measured emissions of 30 cars. The average number of particles of pollutants emitted was found to be within the required levels, but the sample variance was 50. Find a 90 percent confidence interval for the variance in emission particles for these cars.

9-46 A bank is considering ways to reduce the costs associated with passbook savings accounts. The bank has found that the variance in the number of days between account transactions for passbook accounts is 80 days squared. The bank wants to reduce the variance by discouraging the present use of accounts for short-term storage of cash. Therefore, after implementing a new policy that penalizes the customer with a service charge for withdrawals more than once a month, the bank decides to test for a change in the variance of days between account transactions. From a sample of 25 savings accounts, the bank finds the variance between transactions to be 28 days squared. Is the bank justified in claiming that the new policy reduces the variance of days between transactions? Test the hypotheses at the .05 level of significance.

9-47 Sam Bogart, the owner of the Play-It-Again Stereo Company, offers 1-year warranties on all the stereos his company sells. For those 30 stereos that were serviced under the warranty last year, the average cost to fix a stereo was $75 and sample standard deviation was $15. Calculate a 95 percent confidence interval for the true standard deviation of the cost of repair. Sam has decided that unless the true standard deviation is less than $20, he will buy his stereos from a different retailer. Help Sam test the appropriate hypotheses, using a significance level of .01. Should he switch retailers?

9-6
Inferences About Two Population Variances

Comparing the variances of two populations

In Chapter 8, we saw several situations in which we wanted to compare the means of two different populations. Recall that we did this by looking at the *difference* of the means of two samples drawn from those populations. Here, we want to compare the variances of two populations. However, rather than looking at the *difference* of the two sample variances, it turns out to be more convenient if we look at their *ratio*. The next two examples show how this is done.

A ONE-TAILED TEST OF TWO VARIANCES

A prominent sociologist at a large midwestern university believes that incomes earned by college graduates show much greater variability than the earnings of those who did not attend college. In order to test out this theory, she dispatches two research assistants to Chicago to look at the earnings of these two populations. The first assistant takes a random sample of 21 college graduates and finds that their earnings have a sample standard deviation of $s_1 = \$17,000$. The second assistant samples 25 nongraduates and obtains a standard deviation in earnings of $s_2 = \$7,500$. The data of our problem can be summarized as follows:

Data for the problem

$s_1 = 17,000 \leftarrow$ standard deviation of first sample

$n_1 = 21 \quad \leftarrow$ size of first sample

$s_2 = 7,500 \leftarrow$ standard deviation of second sample

$n_2 = 25 \quad \leftarrow$ size of second sample

Why a one-tailed test is appropriate

Since the sociologist theorizes that the earnings of college graduates are *more* variable than those of people not attending college, a one-tailed test is appropriate. She wishes to verify her theory at the .01 level of significance. We can formally state her hypotheses:

Statement of the hypotheses

$H_0: \sigma_1^2 = \sigma_2^2$ (or $\sigma_1^2/\sigma_2^2 = 1$) $\leftarrow$ null hypothesis: the two variances are the same

$H_1: \sigma_1^2 > \sigma_2^2$ (or $\sigma_1^2/\sigma_2^2 > 1$) $\leftarrow$ alternative hypothesis: earnings of college graduates have more variance

$\alpha = .01 \leftarrow$ level of significance for testing these hypotheses

We know that s_1^2 can be used to estimate σ_1^2, and s_2^2 can be used to estimate σ_2^2. If the alternative hypothesis is true, we would expect that s_1^2 will be greater than s_2^2 (or, equivalently, that s_1^2/s_2^2 will be greater than 1). But how much greater must s_1^2 be in order for us to be able to reject the null hypothesis? To answer this question, we must know the distribution of s_1^2/s_2^2. If we assume that the two populations are reasonably well described by normal distributions, then the ratio:

Description of the F statistic

$$F = s_1^2/s_2^2 \qquad [9\text{-}15]$$

has an F distribution with $n_1 - 1$ degrees of freedom in the numerator and $n_2 - 1$ degrees of freedom in the denominator.

In the earnings problem, we calculate the sample F statistic:

$$
\begin{aligned}
F &= s_1^2/s_2^2 \qquad\qquad [9\text{-}15]\\
&= \frac{(17,000)^2}{(7,500)^2}\\
&= \frac{289,000,000}{56,250,000}\\
&= 5.14
\end{aligned}
$$

Interpreting the results

For 20 degrees of freedom $(21 - 1)$ in the numerator and 24 degrees of freedom $(25 - 1)$ in the denominator, Appendix Table 6 tells us that the critical value that separates the acceptance and rejection regions is 2.74. Figure 9-16 shows the acceptance region and the observed F statistic of 5.14. Our sociologist rejects the null hypothesis, and the sample data support her theory.

Handling lower-tailed tests in Appendix Table 6

A word of caution about the use of Appendix Table 6 is necessary at this point. You will notice that the table gives values of the F statistic that are appropriate for only *upper-tailed* tests. Contrast this with Appendix Table 5, which gives values

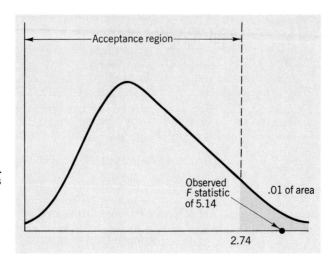

FIGURE 9-16

One-tailed hypothesis test at the .01 level of significance, showing the acceptance region and the sample F statistic

appropriate for both upper- and lower-tailed tests. How can we handle alternative hypotheses of the form $\sigma_1^2 < \sigma_2^2$ (or $\sigma_1^2/\sigma_2^2 < 1$)? This is easily done if we notice that $\sigma_1^2/\sigma_2^2 < 1$ is equivalent to $\sigma_2^2/\sigma_1^2 > 1$. Thus, all we need to do is calculate the ratio s_2^2/s_1^2, which also has an F distribution (but with $n_2 - 1$ numerator degrees of freedom and $n_1 - 1$ denominator degrees of freedom), and then we can use Appendix Table 6. There is another way to say the same thing: **Whenever you are doing a one-tailed test of two variances, number the populations so that the alternative hypothesis has the form:**

$$H_1: \sigma_1^2 > \sigma_2^2 \text{ (or } \sigma_1^2/\sigma_2^2 > 1)$$

and then proceed as we did in the earnings example.

A TWO-TAILED TEST OF TWO VARIANCES

Finding the critical value in a two-tailed test

This procedure for a two-tailed test of two variances is similar to that for a one-tailed test. The only problem arises in finding the critical value in the lower tail. This is related to the problem about lower-tailed tests discussed in the last paragraph, and we will resolve it in a similar way.

One criterion in evaluating oral anesthetics for use in general dentistry is the variability in the length of time between injection and complete loss of sensation in the patient. (This is called the effect delay time.) A large pharmaceutical firm has just developed two new oral anesthetics, which it will market under the names Oralcaine and Novasthetic. From similarities in the chemical structure of the two compounds, it has been predicted that they should show the same variance in effect delay time.

TABLE 9-16 **Effect Delay Times for Two Anesthetics**

ANESTHETIC	SAMPLE SIZE n	SAMPLE VARIANCE (SECONDS SQUARED) s^2
Oralcaine	31	1,296
Novasthetic	41	784

Sample data from tests of the two compounds (which controlled other variables such as age and weight) are given in Table 9-16.

The company wants to test at a 2 percent significance level whether the two compounds have the same variance in effect delay time. Symbolically, the hypotheses are:

Statement of the hypotheses

H_0: $\sigma_1{}^2 = \sigma_2{}^2$ (or $\sigma_1{}^2/\sigma_2{}^2 = 1$) $\leftarrow$ null hypothesis: the two variances are the same

H_1: $\sigma_1{}^2 \neq \sigma_2{}^2$ (or $\sigma_1{}^2/\sigma_2{}^2 \neq 1$) $\leftarrow$ alternative hypothesis: the two variances are different

$\alpha = .02$ $\leftarrow$ significance level of the test

Calculating the F statistic

To test these hypotheses, we again use Equation 9-15:

$$F = s_1{}^2/s_2{}^2 \qquad\qquad [9\text{-}15]$$
$$= 1{,}296/784$$
$$= 1.65$$

This statistic comes from an F distribution with $n_1 - 1$ degrees of freedom in the numerator (30, in this case) and $n_2 - 1$ degrees of freedom in the denominator (40, in this case). Let us use the notation:

Some useful notation for the test

$$F(n, d, \alpha)$$

to denote that value of F with n numerator degrees of freedom, d denominator degrees of freedom, and an area of α in the upper tail. In our problem, the acceptance region extends from $F(30, 40, .99)$ to $F(30, 40, .01)$, as illustrated in Fig. 9-17.

We can get the value of $F(30, 40, .01)$ directly from Appendix Table 6; it is 2.20. However, the value of $F(30, 40, .99)$ is not in the table. Now $F(30, 40, .99)$ will correspond to a *small* value of $s_1{}^2/s_2{}^2$, but to a *large* value of $s_2{}^2/s_1{}^2$, which is just the reciprocal of $s_1{}^2/s_2{}^2$. Given the discussion on pages 457–458 about lower-tailed tests, we might suspect that:

$$F(n, d, \alpha) = \frac{1}{F(d, n, 1 - \alpha)} \qquad\qquad [9\text{-}16]$$

FIGURE 9-17

Two-tailed test of hypotheses at the .02 significance level

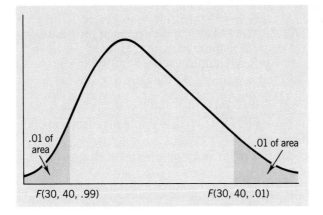

.01 of area

.01 of area

$F(30, 40, .99)$

$F(30, 40, .01)$

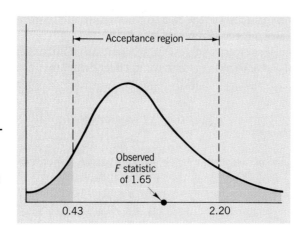

FIGURE 9-18

Two-tailed hypothesis test at the .02 level of significance, showing acceptance region and the sample F statistic

and this turns out to be true. We can use this equation to find $F(30, 40, .99)$:

$$F(30, 40, .99) = \frac{1}{F(40, 30, .01)} \qquad [9\text{-}16]$$

$$= \frac{1}{2.30}$$

$$= 0.43$$

Interpreting the results   In Fig. 9-18 we have illustrated the acceptance region for this hypothesis test and the observed value of F. We see there that the null hypothesis is accepted, so we conclude that the observed difference in the sample variances of effect delay times for the two anesthetics is not statistically significant.

Exercises

9-48   The Raj, an Indian guru with some money to invest, has narrowed his search for a mutual fund down to the Oppy fund or the MLPFS fund. Oppy's rate of return is lower, but seems to be more stable than MLPFS's. If Oppy's variability in rate of return is, indeed, significantly lower than MLPFS's, then he will invest his money there. If there is no significant difference in variability, he'll go with MLPFS. To make a decision, Raj has taken a sample of 21 monthly rates of return for both firms. For Oppy, the *standard deviation* was 2, and for MLPFS the standard deviation was 3. Which firm should the Raj invest in? Test at the $\alpha = .05$ level.

9-49   From a sample of 25 observations, the estimate of the standard deviation of the population was found to be 15.0. From another sample of 14 observations, the estimate was found to be 9.7. Can we accept the hypothesis that the two samples come from populations with equal variances, or must we conclude that the variance of the second population is smaller? Use the .01 level of significance.

9-50   A quality control supervisor for an automobile manufacturer is concerned with uniformity in the number of defects in cars coming off the assembly line. If one assembly line has significantly more variability in the number of defects, then changes have to be made. The supervisor has collected the following data:

NUMBER OF DEFECTS		
	Assembly Line A	Assembly Line B
Mean	10	11
Variance	9	25
Sample size	20	16

Does assembly line B have significantly more variability in the number of defects? Test at the .05 significance level.

9-51 For two populations thought to have the same variance, the following information was found. A sample of sixteen from population 1 exhibited a sample variance of 3.75, while a sample of ten from population 2 had a variance of 5.38.
   (a) Calculate the F ratio for the test of equality of variances.
   (b) Find the critical F value for the upper tail, using the .10 significance level.
   (c) Find the corresponding F value for the lower tail.
   (d) State the conclusion of your test.

9-52 In our study of comparisons between the means of two groups, it was noted that the most common form of the two-group t-test for the difference between two means assumes that the population variances for the two groups are the same. One experimenter, using a control condition and an experimental condition in his study of drug reaction, wished to verify that this assumption held, i.e., that the treatment administered affected only the mean, not the variance of the variable under study. From his data, he calculated the variance of the experimental group to be 25.8 and that of the control group to be 20.6. The experimental group had 25 subjects, and the control group had 31. Can he proceed to use the t-test, which assumes equal variances for the two groups? Use $\alpha = .10$.

9-53 Techgene, Inc., is concerned about variability in the number of bacteria produced by different cultures. If the cultures have significantly different variability in the number of bacteria produced, then experiments are messed up and some strange things get produced. (The management of the company gets understandably anxious when the scientists produce strange things.) The following data have been collected:

NUMBER OF BACTERIA (IN THOUSANDS)										
Culture Type A	91	89	83	101	93	98	144	118	108	125	138
Culture Type B	62	76	90	75	88	99	110	140	145	130	110

   (a) Compute s_A^2 and s_B^2.
   (b) State explicit null and alternative hypotheses and then test at the .02 significance level.

9-54 The HAL Corporation is about to unveil a new, faster personal computer, PAL, to replace its old model CAL. While PAL is faster than CAL on average, PAL's processing speed seems more variable. (Processing speed depends on the program being run, the amount of input, and the amount of output.) Two samples of 25 runs, covering the range of jobs expected, were submitted to PAL and CAL (one sample to each). The results were as follows:

	PROCESSING TIME (in hundredths of seconds)	
	PAL	CAL
Mean	50	75
Standard deviation	20	10

At the .05 level of significance, is PAL's processing speed significantly more variable than CAL's?

9-55 Two brand managers were in disagreement over the issue of whether urban homemakers had greater variability in grocery shopping patterns than did rural homemakers. To test their conflicting ideas, they took random samples of 70 homemakers from urban areas and 60 homemakers from rural areas. They found that the variance in days squared between shopping visits for urban homemakers was 14, while the sample variance for the rural homemakers was 3.5. Is the difference between the variances in days between shopping visits significant at the .01 level?

9-56 Two competing ice cream stores, Yum-Yum and Goody, both advertise ¼ lb. scoops of ice cream. There is some concern about the variability in the serving sizes, so two members of a local consumer group have sampled 25 scoops of Yum-Yum's ice cream and 11 scoops of Goody's. Of course, both members now have stomach aches, so you must help them out. Is there a difference in the variance of ice cream weights between Yum-Yum and Goody? The following data have been collected. Test at the .10 level.

| | SCOOP WEIGHT (in hundredths of pounds) | |
	Yum-Yum	Goody
Mean	25	25
Variance	16	10

9-7
Terms Introduced in Chapter 9

Analysis of Variance (ANOVA) A statistical technique used to test the equality of three or more sample means and thus make inferences as to whether the samples come from populations having the same mean.

Between-Column Variance An estimate of the population variance derived from the variance among the sample means.

Chi-Square Distribution A family of probability distributions, differentiated by their degrees of freedom, used to test a number of different hypotheses about variances, proportions, and distributional goodness of fit.

Contingency Table A table having R rows and C columns. Each row corresponds to a level of one variable; each column, to a level of another variable. Entries in the body of the tables are the frequencies with which each variable combination occurred.

Expected Frequencies The frequencies we would expect to see in a contingency table or frequency distribution if the null hypothesis is true.

F Distribution A family of distributions differentiated by two parameters (df-numerator, df-denominator), used primarily to test hypotheses regarding variances.

F Ratio A ratio used in the analysis of variance, among other tests, to compare the magnitude of two estimates of the population variance to determine if the two estimates are approximately equal; in ANOVA, the ratio of between-column variance to within-column variance is used.

Goodness-of-Fit Test A statistical test for determining whether there is a significant difference between an observed frequency distribution and a theoretical probability distribution hypothesized to describe the observed distribution.

Grand Mean The mean for the entire group of subjects from all the samples in the experiment.

Test of Independence A statistical test of proportions of frequencies, to determine if membership in categories of one variable is different as a function of membership in the categories of a second variable.

Within-Column Variance An estimate of the population variance based on the variances within the k samples, using a weighted average of the k sample variances.

Equations Introduced in Chapter 9

[9-1]
$$\chi^2 = \Sum \frac{(f_o - f_e)^2}{f_e}$$
p. 419

This formula says that the *chi-square statistic* (χ^2) is equal to the sum (Σ) we will get if we:

1. Subtract the expected frequencies, f_e, from the observed frequencies, f_o, for each category of our contingency table.
2. Square each of the differences.
3. Divide each squared difference by f_e.
4. Sum all the results of step 3.

[9-2]
$$\frac{\text{Number of degrees}}{\text{of freedom}} = (\text{Number of rows} - 1)(\text{Number of columns} - 1)$$
p. 421

To calculate number of *degrees of freedom in a chi-square test of independence,* multiply the number of rows (less 1) times the number of columns (less 1).

[9-3]
$$f_e = \frac{RT \times CT}{n}$$
p. 424

With this formula, we can calculate the expected frequency for any cell within a contingency table. RT is the row total for the row containing the cell, CT is the column total for the column containing the cell, and n is the total number of observations.

[9-4]
$$s_{\bar{x}}^2 = \frac{\Sigma(\bar{x} - \bar{\bar{x}})^2}{k - 1}$$
p. 438

To calculate the *variance among the sample means,* use this formula.

[9-5]
$$\sigma^2 = \sigma_{\bar{x}}^2 \times n$$
p. 439

The *population variance* is equal to the product of the square of the standard error of the mean and the sample size.

[9-6]
$$\hat{\sigma}^2 = \frac{\Sigma n_j(\bar{x}_j - \bar{\bar{x}})^2}{k - 1}$$
p. 439

One estimate of the population variance (the between-column variance) can be obtained by using this equation. We obtain this equation by first substituting $s_{\bar{x}}^2$ for $\sigma_{\bar{x}}^2$ in Equation 9-5, and then by weighting each $(\bar{x}_j - \bar{\bar{x}})^2$ by its own appropriate sample size (n_j).

[9-7]
$$\hat{\sigma}^2 = \Sigma \left(\frac{n_j - 1}{n_T - k}\right) s_j^2$$
p. 440

A second estimate of the population variance (the within-column variance) can be obtained from this equation. This equation uses a weighted average of all the sample variances. In this formulation, $n_T = \Sigma n_j$, the total sample size.

$$F = \frac{\text{First estimate of the population variance based on the variance among the sample means}}{\text{Second estimate of the population variance based on the variances within the samples}}$$

p. 441

This ratio is the way we can compare the two estimates of the population variance, which we calculated in Equations 9-6 and 9-7. In a hypothesis test based on an F distribution, we are more likely to accept the null hypothesis if this F *ratio* or F *statistic* is near to the value of 1. As the F ratio increases, the more likely it is that we will reject the null hypothesis.

[9-9]

$$F = \frac{\text{Between-column variance}}{\text{Within-column variance}}$$

p. 441

This restates Equation 9-8, using statistical shorthand for the numerator and the denominator of the F ratio.

[9-10]

$$\frac{\text{Number of degrees of freedom}}{\text{in numerator of the } F \text{ ratio}} = (\text{Number of samples} - 1)$$

p. 443

To do an analysis of variance, we calculate the number of *degrees of freedom in the between-column variance* (the numerator of the F ratio) by subtracting one from the number of samples collected.

[9-11]

$$\frac{\text{Number of degrees of freedom in}}{\text{denominator of the } F \text{ ratio}} = \sum (n_j - 1) = n_T - k$$

p. 443

We use this equation to calculate the number of degrees of freedom in the denominator of the F ratio. This turns out to be the total sample size, n_T, minus the number of samples, k.

[9-12]

$$\chi^2 = \frac{(n-1)s^2}{\sigma^2}$$

p. 452

With a population variance of σ^2, the χ^2 statistic given by this equation has a chi-square distribution with $n-1$ degrees of freedom. This result is exact if the population is normal, but even in samples from non-normal populations, it is frequently a good approximation.

[9-13]

$$\sigma^2 = \frac{(n-1)s^2}{\chi^2}$$

p. 452

To get a confidence interval for σ^2, we solve Equation 9-12 for σ^2.

[9-14]

$$\sigma_L^2 = \frac{(n-1)s^2}{\chi_U^2} \leftarrow \text{lower confidence limit}$$

$$\sigma_U^2 = \frac{(n-1)s^2}{\chi_L^2} \leftarrow \text{upper confidence limit}$$

p. 452

These formulas give the lower and upper confidence limit for a confidence interval for σ^2. (Notice that since χ^2 appears in the denominator, we use χ_U^2 to find σ_L^2 and χ_L^2 to find σ_U^2.)

[9-15]

$$F = \frac{s_1^2}{s_2^2}$$

p. 457

This ratio has an F distribution with $n_1 - 1$ degrees of freedom in the numerator and $n_2 - 1$ degrees of freedom in the denominator. (This assumes that the two populations are reasonably well described by normal distributions.) It is used to test hypotheses about two population variances.

[9-16]

$$F(n, d, \alpha) = \frac{1}{F(d, n, 1 - \alpha)}$$

p. 459

Appendix Table 6 gives values of F for upper-tailed tests only, but this equation enables us to find appropriate values of F for lower-tailed and two-tailed tests.

9-9
Chapter Review Exercises

 9-57 The post office is concerned about the variability in the number of days it takes a letter to go from the east coast to the west coast. A sample of letters was mailed from the east coast, and the time taken for the letters to arrive at their address on the west coast was recorded. The following data were collected:

MAILING TIME (in days)									
2.2	1.7	3.0	2.9	1.9	3.1	4.2	1.5	4.0	2.5

Find a 90 percent confidence interval for the variance in mailing times.

 9-58 For the contingency table below, calculate the observed and expected frequencies and the chi-square statistic. State and test the appropriate hypotheses at the .05 significance level.

	ATTITUDE TOWARD SOCIAL LEGISLATION		
OCCUPATION	Favor	Neutral	Oppose
Blue-collar	19	16	37
White-collar	15	22	46
Professional	24	11	32

 9-59 A pre-election Gallup poll on voting patterns in the presidential race resulted in the following contingency table:

FAVORED CANDIDATE	REGION OF COUNTRY			
	Northeast	Southeast	Northwest	Southwest
Democrat	105	120	105	70
Republican	120	100	130	150
Undecided	25	30	15	30

Political pundits all over the country were eager to find out whether "region of country" had any bearing on which candidate was favored. In order to help them decide:

(a) State the appropriate null and alternative hypotheses.
(b) Show all necessary calculations.
(c) At a significance level of $\alpha = .05$, what should the pundits conclude? What about at $\alpha = .20$?

9-60 What probability distribution is used in each of these types of statistical tests?
(a) Comparing two population proportions
(b) Value of a single population variance
(c) Comparing three or more population means
(d) Comparing two population means from small, dependent samples

9-61 What probability distribution is used in each of these types of statistical tests?
(a) Comparing the means of two small samples from populations with unknown variances
(b) Comparing two population variances
(c) Value of a single population mean based on large samples
(d) Comparing three or more population proportions

9-62 An impoverished business statistics student surveyed several grocery stores to determine if yogurt prices vary considerably from brand to brand. Her survey results follow. At $\alpha = .05$, should she conclude that prices do vary significantly from brand to brand?

PRICE (in cents)

Brand A	Brand B	Brand C	Brand D
61	52	47	67
55	58	52	63
57	54	49	68
60	55	49	59
58	57		65
62			

9-63 An outdoor advertising company must know whether significantly different traffic volumes pass three billboard locations in Newark since the company charges different rates for different traffic volumes. The company measures the volume of traffic at the three locations during randomly selected 5-minute intervals. The table below shows the data gathered. At the .05 level of significance, are the volumes of traffic passing the three billboards the same?

VOLUME OF TRAFFIC

Billboard 1	30	45	26	44	18	38	42	29	
Billboard 2	29	38	36	21	36	18	17	30	32
Billboard 3	32	44	40	43	24	28	18		

9-64 An investor is interested in seeing if there are significant differences in the rates of return on stocks, bonds, and mutual funds. He has taken random samples of each type of investment and has recorded the data below.

RATE OF RETURN (percent)

Stocks	2.0	6.0	2.0	2.1	6.2	2.9
Bonds	4.0	3.1	2.2	5.3	5.9	
Mutual Funds	3.5	3.1	2.9	6.0		

(a) State null and alternative hypotheses.
(b) Test your hypotheses at the .05 significance level.
(c) State an explicit conclusion.

9-65 For the following contingency table:
    (a) Construct a table of observed and expected frequencies.
    (b) Calculate the chi-square statistic.
    (c) State the null and alternative hypotheses.
    (d) Using a .05 level of significance, should the null hypothesis be rejected?

| CHURCH | INCOME LEVEL | | |
ATTENDANCE	Low	Middle	High
Never	27	48	15
Occasional	25	63	14
Regular	22	74	12

9-66 For the following contingency table:
    (a) Construct a table of observed and expected frequencies.
    (b) Calculate the chi-square statistic.
    (c) State the null and alternative hypotheses.
    (d) Using a .01 level of significance, should the null hypothesis be rejected?

| | AGE GROUP | | | |
TYPE OF CAR DRIVEN	16–21	22–30	31–45	46+
4 × 4 Off Road	19	23	15	2
Sports Car	9	14	11	7
Compact	6	8	7	9
Midsize	11	13	19	24
Full size	9	13	22	26

9-67 Swami Zhami claims to be psychic. He says he can correctly guess the suit (diamonds, clubs, hearts, spades) of a randomly chosen card with probability 0.5. Since the cards are chosen randomly from a big pile, we can assume that Zhami's guesses are independent. On 100 randomly chosen days, Zhami made ten guesses, and the number of correct guesses was recorded. We want to see if the number of correct guesses is binomially distributed with $n = 10$, $p = 0.5$. The following data have been collected:

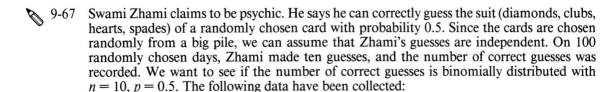

Number of correct guesses per day	0–2	3–5	6–8	9–10
Frequency of number of correct guesses	50	47	2	1

    (a) State explicit null and alternative hypotheses.
    (b) Test your hypotheses. Use $\alpha = .10$.
    (c) If Zhami has no psychic power, then he should have a probability of 0.25 of guessing a card correctly. (Why?) See if the number of correct guesses is distributed binomially with $n = 10$, $p = 0.25$.

9-68 There has been some sociological evidence that women as a group are more variable than men in their attitudes and beliefs. A large private research organization has conducted a survey of men's attitudes on a certain issue and found the standard deviation on this attitude scale to be 16 points. A sociologist gave the same scale to a group of 30 women and found that the sample variance was 400 points squared. At the 0.01 significance level, is there reason to believe that women do indeed show greater variability on this attitude scale?

9-69 Jim Greek makes predictions about the number of baskets that will be made by his favorite basketball team. We are interested in testing if his errors are normally distributed with mean 0 and variance 16. Using the following data, state explicit null and alternative hypotheses and test them at the $\alpha - 0.05$ level.

Error	$\leqslant-7$	-6 to 0	1 to 6	$\geqslant 7$
Number of predictions in each group	5	45	45	5

9-70 Psychologists have often wondered about the effects of stress and anxiety on test performance. An aptitude test was given to two randomly chosen groups of eighteen college students, one group in a nonstressful situation and the other in a stressful situation. The experimenter expects the stress treatment to increase the variance of scores on the test, because he feels some students perform better under stress while others experience adverse reactions to stress. The variances computed for the two groups are $s_1^2 = 23.9$ for the nonstress group and $s_2^2 = 81.2$ for the stress group. Was his hypothesis confirmed? Use the .05 level of significance to test the hypotheses.

9-71 In order to determine how professional women respond to fashion brands, Southern Belle, an area boutique, asked women their occupation (teller, secretary, entrepreneur, socialite) and what fashion style they wore most often (A, B, C, D). The following data were collected:

PROFESSION	STYLE A	B	C	D
Teller	5	7	6	8
Secretary	10	15	12	8
Entrepreneur	8	12	21	25
Socialite	12	14	20	25

At the .10 level of significance, test if the style professional women prefer depends on their occupation.

9-72 In the development of new drugs for the treatment of anxiety, it is important to check the drugs' effects on various motor functions, one of which is driving. The Confab Pharmaceutical Company is testing four different tranquilizing drugs for their effects on driving skill. Subjects take a simulated driving test, and their scores reflect their errors. The more severe errors lead to higher scores. The results of these tests produced the following table:

Drug 1	245	258	239	241	
Drug 2	277	276	263	274	
Drug 3	215	232	225	247	226
Drug 4	241	253	237	246	240

At the .05 level of significance, do the four drugs affect driving skill differently?

9-73 James Clark has just purchased two paper mills and is concerned that they have significantly different variability in output, even though both plants produce about the same average amount of paper each day. The information below was gathered to see if Mr. Clark's concerns are justified. At the $\alpha = .02$ level of significance, do the two plants show the same variance in output?

PLANT	n	s^2
Number 1	31	984 tons squared
Number 2	41	1,136 tons squared

9-74 A trucking firm has three types of trucks. It wishes to determine the effect of the type of truck on operating costs in cents per mile. The data are as follows:

Type A	7.3	8.3	7.6	6.8	8.0	
Type B	5.6	7.6	7.2			
Type C	7.9	9.5	8.7	8.3	9.4	8.4

At the 0.01 level of significance, can we conclude that all three types of trucks have the same operating costs per mile?

9-10
Chapter Concepts Test

Answers are in the back of the book.

T F 1. Analysis of variance may be used to test whether the means of more than two populations can be considered equal.

T F 2. Analysis of variance is based upon a comparison of two estimates of the variance of the overall population that contains all samples.

T F 3. When comparing the variances of two populations, it is convenient to look at the difference in the sample variances, just as we looked at the difference in sample means to make inferences about population means.

T F 4. When the chi-square distribution is used as a test of independence, the number of degrees of freedom is related to both the number of rows and the number of columns in the contingency table.

T F 5. Chi-square may be used as a test to decide whether a particular distribution closely approximates a sample from some population. We refer to such tests as goodness-of-fit tests.

T F 6. If samples are taken from two populations that are both nearly normal, then the ratio of all possible sets of the two sample variances is also normally distributed.

T F 7. When using a chi-square test, we must ensure an adequate sample size, so that we can avoid any tendency for the value of the chi-square statistic to be overestimated.

T F 8. When testing hypotheses about a population's variance, we may form confidence intervals by using the chi-square distribution.

T F 9. The specific shape of an F distribution depends on the number of degrees of freedom in both the numerator and denominator of the F ratio.

T F 10. One convenient aspect of hypothesis testing using the F statistic is that all such tests are upper-tailed tests.

T F 11. Chi-square tests enable us to test whether more than two population proportions can be considered equal.

T F 12. A "3 × 5 contingency table" has three columns and five rows.

T F 13. The total area under the curve of a chi-square distribution, like that of other distributions, is 1.

T F 14. The expected frequency for any cell in a contingency table can be immediately calculated, once we know only the row and column totals for that cell.

T F 15. If the chi-square value for an observation is zero, we know that there will never be any difference between observed and expected frequencies.

T F 16. Sample sizes in analysis of variance need not be equal.

T F 17. The smaller the value of the F statistic, the more we tend to believe there is a difference among the various samples.

T F 18. The accuracy and usefulness of a chi-square test are highly dependent upon the quality of data put into the test.

T F 19. The F table in Appendix Table 6 gives values for upper-tailed tests only, but appropriate values for lower-tailed and two-tailed tests can be calculated from the table entries.

T F 20. In determining the number of degrees of freedom for a chi-square goodness-of-fit test, estimating population parameters from sample data has no impact.

T F 21. For both chi-square and F tests, we reject H_0 if the prob value is less than α, the significance level of the test.

22. Suppose you have observed proportions for three different geographic regions. You wish to test whether the regions have significantly different proportions. Assuming p_1, p_2, p_3 are the true proportions, which of the following would be your null hypothesis?
    (a) $p_1 \neq p_2 \neq p_3$ (c) p_1, p_2, p_3 are not all equal
    (b) $p_1 = p_2 = p_3$ (d) None of these

23. A chi-square value can never be negative because:
    (a) Differences between expected and observed frequencies are squared.
    (b) A negative value would mean that the observed frequencies were negative.
    (c) The absolute value of the differences is computed.
    (d) None of these.
    (e) a and b but not c.

24. Suppose that there are eight possible classes under consideration for a goodness-of-fit test. How many degrees of freedom should be used?
    (a) 8   (c) 6
    (b) 7   (d) Cannot be determined from the information given

25. Which of the following is a step in performing analysis of variance?
    (a) Determine an estimate of population variance from within the samples.
    (b) Determine an estimate of population variance from among the sample means.
    (c) Determine the difference between expected and observed frequency for each class.
    (d) All of these.
    (e) a and b but not c.

26. Suppose you calculated the following variances for several different groups of samples, and all the groups had the same degrees of freedom. For which ratio would you be most likely to accept the null hypothesis of equal means, at a given significance level?
    (a) Between-column variance = 8, within-column variance = 3
    (b) Between-column variance = 6, within-column variance = 3
    (c) Between-column variance = 4, within-column variance = 3
    (d) Between-column variance = 30, within-column variance = 20

27. Suppose σ^2 for a certain population is hypothesized to be 25. You take a sample of size sixteen and find s^2 to be 15. To perform a two-tailed test of variance, you would:
    (a) Compare $\chi^2 = 9$ with values from a chi-square distribution with 16 degrees of freedom.
    (b) Compare $\chi^2 = 9$ with values from a chi-square distribution with 15 degrees of freedom.
    (c) Compare $\chi^2 = 25$ with values from a chi-square distribution with 15 degrees of freedom.
    (d) Compare $\chi^2 = 25$ with values from a chi-square distribution with 16 degrees of freedom.

28. A two-tailed test of two variances is to be performed for samples 1 and 2 with $n_1 = 15$ and $n_2 = 12$. If $\alpha = .10$, which of the following represents the upper value to which s_1^2/s_2^2 should be compared?
    (a) $\dfrac{1}{F(14, 11, .05)}$ (c) $F(11, 14, .05)$ (e) None of these

    (b) $\dfrac{1}{F(14, 11, .95)}$ (d) $F(14, 11, .05)$

29. Assume that a chi-square test is to be performed on a contingency table with four rows and four columns. How many degrees of freedom should be used?
    (a) 16   (b) 8   (c) 9   (d) 6

30. The chi-square and the t distribution are both:
    (a) always symmetrical distributions.   (d) all of the above.
    (b) used for hypothesis testing.   (e) b and c but not a.
    (c) dependent on the number of degrees of freedom. (f) none of the above.

31. The expected frequency in a chi-square contingency table cell can be calculated from the expected proportion for that cell by:
    (a) multiplying by that column's total.
    (b) multiplying by that row's total.
    (c) multiplying by the total sample size.
    (d) using the proportion; the expected frequency and expected proportion are the same.
    (e) none of the above.

32. The F ratio contains:
    (a) two estimates of the population variance.
    (b) two estimates of the population mean.
    (c) one estimate of the population mean and one estimate of the population variance.
    (d) both a and b.
    (e) none of the above.

33. If we have large enough sample sizes, we can discard which of the assumptions associated with ANOVA testing?
    (a) The samples are drawn from a normal population.
    (b) Each population has the same variance.
    (c) both a and b.
    (d) None of the above.

34. When performing a chi-square hypothesis test, what happens when expected frequencies in several cells are too small?
    (a) The value of χ^2 will be overestimated.
    (b) The null hypothesis will be more likely to be rejected than it should be.
    (c) The degrees of freedom are greatly reduced.
    (d) None of these.
    (e) a and b but not c.

35. Suppose you are comparing five groups exposed to different methods of treatment and have taken a sample of size ten from each group. You have calculated $\bar{x}$ for each sample. How could you now calculate the grand mean?
    (a) Multiply each sample mean by $\frac{1}{5}$ and add these values. Then divide this sum by 50.
    (b) Add the 5 sample means and divide by 50.
    (c) Add the 5 sample means and multiply by $\frac{1}{5}$.
    (d) Add the 5 sample means.
    (e) None of these.

36. If we want to test whether the proportions of more than two populations are equal, we use:
    (a) Analysis of variance   (c) The variance   (e) None of these
    (b) Estimation   (d) Interval estimates

37. Which of these distributions has a pair of degrees of freedom:
    (a) Poisson   (c) Chi-square   (e) All of these
    (b) Normal   (d) Binomial   (f) None of these

38. The mean for the entire group of subjects from all the samples in an experiment is called the _____ mean.

39. A statistical technique used to test the equality of three or more population means is called _____ .

40. A test of _____ is used to determine if membership in categories of one variable is different as a function of membership in the categories of a second variable.

41. A family of distributions differentiated by two parameters and used primarily to test hypotheses regarding variances is called the _____ distribution.

42. The _____ test determines whether there is a significant difference between the observed and hypothesized distributions for a sample.

43. Analysis of variance compares the _____ with the _____ to get the _____ statistic.

44. The acceptance region for a null hypothesis in a chi-square test goes from the _____ tail of the curve to the chi-square value. This region contains _____ percent of the area under the curve.

45. The number of degrees of freedom in the denominator of the F ratio is calculated by subtracting the _____ from the _____ .

9-11
Conceptual Case   (Northern White Metals Company)

Very soon after the agreement was reached to test the new automatic banding machine, Dick was visited by Chip Yamaguchi, another packing-equipment sales representative. His company, too, was introducing a new automatic banding machine. This machine, however, was mounted on heavy steel casters, so that, despite its rather large size, it was actually portable. This feature intrigued Dick, for movable equipment could give the shipping department greater flexibility. Still, he thought, as Mr. Yamaguchi continued extolling the wonders of this new machine, what was really needed was equipment that would speed up routine packing operations. Dick explained this to the sales rep and mentioned the upcoming trial that had been arranged with the Bondurant Band and Strap Company's new banding machine.

Mr. Yamaguchi eagerly assured Dick that his banding machine was every bit as efficient as his competitor's, and that he would welcome any comparison.

"Would a three-way test be possible?" he asked.

"I don't see why not," Dick replied after considering the matter for a moment. "Talk to Jan Hazel, my shipping supervisor, about the details."

They shook hands and the sales rep was barely out of the office before Dick was calling technical services at corporate headquarters.

Sarah Porter answered and, after exchanging pleasantries, replied that yes, she was familiar with the pending banding-machine trial in NWMC's shipping department. Dick told her of the addition of another machine to the trial and anxiously asked if this would pose any analytical difficulties.

"Not at all, Dick," Sarah responded, cheerfully amused at his concern. "You deliver the information, as Jody suggested, and we'll handle the rest."

There are now three alternative processes that might be used in the packing area of the shipping department, the manual banding method and two new automatic banding machines. Since Dick is still interested in determining if different methods will speed up packing operations, should the new test situation have data requirements different from the two-method test? How might Sarah and Jody proceed to analyze the data to determine which method offers the fastest banding time?

9-12
Computer Data Base Exercise

Stan Hutchings, VP of Sales, stuck his head into Laurel's office one morning a couple of weeks after the sales meeting. "Have you got a minute? I've been meaning to ask you about something."

"Sure," Laurel answered, sliding aside a stack of data. "What can I do for you?"

"For quite some time now, we've been toying with the idea of instituting an 'inside sales' commission program. As it stands now, only our

two outside sales reps work on a salary-plus-commission basis. However, the folks who work the phones inside actually account for nearly 75 percent of total sales, and they've been itching for a little incentive—in the form of commission. It came up again at the recent sales meeting, and some good ideas were proposed. I have to mention that we tried this kind of program once and it didn't quite work out. The tricky thing is that the calls come in randomly and are answered by the next available sales representative. Some people are just calling for information, some to actually place an order. As it happens, a customer often calls more than once and will probably speak to several reps, resulting in complications in awarding the sale to a single person. The solution that has been proposed is actually quite innovative."

"Each month we have a sales goal, as you know," Stan continued. "The proposed plan involves keeping things as they currently are until we reach 95 percent of our monthly target. Beyond that, a percentage of the sales dollars will be pooled and distributed evenly at the end of the month. Our goal is to encourage a team spirit of sorts, keeping away from the cut-throat competition that commission programs usually foster."

"Sounds great," Laurel agreed, "but how can I help?"

"Well, in the interest of fairness, we need to be sure that sales are actually following a random trend. That is, if I'm assuming correctly, each salesperson's daily average should be about the same over time."

"Ah," said Laurel, "I see what you need. If you can get me some sales data for the different inside sales people, I can do some checking to see what the likelihood is that they actually come from the same distribution."

"Bingo. I thought you might be able to help. I'll get you the data right away. Thanks, Laurel." Stan headed out the door.

Table DB9-1 (p. 474) shows 6 months of daily sales data for the four fulltime inside sales representatives.

1. Do the sampled data come from populations with the same mean? Test this assumption at the 1 percent significance level.

Stan looked at Laurel's results. "Hmm. Seems like Mike's in a class by himself. Well, he has been here longer than the others and there are certain customers that ask specifically for him. What if we worked up a separate commission program for him and created a pool for the other three? Any validity to that?"

"I'll have to make another run to be sure," Laurel replied, "but I think you've got a better chance that way."

2. Verify Stan's conclusion about Mike by looking at the means and standard deviations by salesperson. Test whether the data for Debbie, Jeff, and Barry seem to indicate populations with the same mean. (Use the 1 percent significance level.)

Later, with a few minutes of free time, Laurel decided to go back and verify her assumptions on the staffing study she had done for Stan (see Chapter 5). She knew the recommendations were based heavily on assuming Poisson arrivals of phone calls.

3. Check the phone call data in Table DB5-2 on page 248 to see if they appear to be Poisson distributed. Use the intervals $0-20$, $21-25$, $26-30$, $31-35$, ≥ 36. Test at the 5 percent significance level.

"Darn," muttered Laurel. "I hope I haven't screwed them up too badly with that assumption. If by any chance I'm lucky and the data are actually normally distributed, I can check. At the very least, I've got to let Stan and Hal know." Laurel was never thrilled about admitting mistakes.

4. Check the assumption that the data follow a normal distribution. Test at the .05 significance level.

5. If the assumption of normality appears reasonable, reestimate the number of salespeople needed to staff the phones (ignore the information on page 247, question 7).

Stan looked at Laurel's data with interest. "I knew something wasn't quite right with our original conclusions, but I couldn't quite put my finger on it. Good thing I kept our six sales people," he winked.

Laurel breathed a sigh of relief.

"However," he went on, "this brings up a new question. These data seem to indicate, and I know from experience, that there are definitely some peak hours. I wonder if we could come up with a more cost-effective solution by using a combination of part-time and full-time sales reps. What do you think?"

"You're probably right," Laurel agreed. "Let me put a few more figures together, and we'll take this back to Hal for his opinion."

6. Calculate the average and standard deviation of the number of calls received during each hour. Assuming that during each hour the number of calls received is normally distributed, figure the associated recommended staffing levels in order to be 98% certain that a sales rep only has to deal with eight calls an hour. What combination of full-time and part-time reps seems to be appropriate?

TABLE DB9-1 Daily sales data

	DEBBIE	JEFF	MIKE	BARRY		DEBBIE	JEFF	MIKE	BARRY
1	230	2,343	2,241	2,471	58	2,498	1,579	3,968	3,403
2	370	3,786	2,904	5,458	59	4,016	2,996	2,627	2,126
3	1,392	1,464	4,777	2,414	60	552	213	2,030	780
4	2,891	2,429	4,248	2,332	61	2,798	242	5,129	4,005
5	1,220	2,719	2,894	2,908	62	1,660	769	3,786	4,609
6	4,471	4,589	2,815	1,250	63	1,823	202	2,602	1,844
7	3,288	1,493	6,020	2,392	64	2,589	779	5,791	2,367
8	1,345	2,155	3,559	2,176	65	965	586	1,986	1,752
9	3,192	3,338	6,803	810	66	861	536	4,336	1,608
10	1,323	2,752	3,396	1,273	67	1,953	402	4,082	1,460
11	2,457	2,219	2,680	3,032	68	8,597	915	5,577	1,609
12	1,331	2,046	3,510	4,047	69	1,601	191	4,210	1,130
13	3,003	1,484	4,460	3,209	70	1,207	358	1,848	1,684
14	915	692	1,495	608	71	1,887	2,922	3,041	3,473
15	2,517	761	2,846	1,984	72	4,374	927	3,146	1,989
16	2,520	1,716	2,999	1,814	73	4,082	831	6,809	1,803
17	3,113	4,082	1,892	2,231	74	3,018	1,035	1,991	1,503
18	4,508	1,827	4,445	3,102	75	1,881	2,355	4,035	2,562
19	2,514	2,332	4,209	3,159	76	2,195	841	2,995	1,285
20	1,681	557	4,424	1,417	77	1,302	1,635	1,045	903
21	1,988	2,101	2,728	3,020	78	953	1,124	2,118	2,964
22	2,134	1,606	3,968	3,108	79	2,045	677	3,278	2,105
23	1,981	1,598	5,280	1,679	80	5,642	1,168	6,084	2,985
24	3,841	3,018	1,571	2,650	81	3,171	956	5,266	1,861
25	5,825	6,259	5,778	5,326	82	3,048	293	2,257	2,381
26	2,272	1,663	3,180	6,522	83	2,874	1,527	5,504	3,846
27	2,573	3,580	4,250	2,527	84	5,806	1,735	7,095	160
28	1,799	1,455	5,014	2,069	85	1,432	2,211	4,519	3,556
29	1,169	3,173	5,880	893	86	1,772	1,870	2,124	1,636
30	2,765	2,534	9,498	1,692	87	4,642	1,739	3,325	1,997
31	2,784	3,177	2,756	660	88	2,808	870	3,092	2,860
32	4,428	2,689	6,332	1,704	89	4,179	587	2,463	1,286
33	2,413	1,773	4,090	6,881	90	1,066	2,056	3,344	1,220
34	1,409	1,995	3,853	2,029	91	1,788	1,171	1,744	2,894
35	3,211	2,542	2,481	1,268	92	3,628	5,565	3,941	8,498
36	1,149	2,873	1,521	2,878	93	2,378	3,167	2,902	1,686
37	2,499	1,211	3,166	1,454	94	2,105	1,837	3,858	1,548
38	2,980	3,433	3,762	1,057	95	2,589	825	9,570	1,425
39	1,592	3,334	1,905	1,214	96	3,298	433	2,876	1,802
40	2,905	2,159	4,050	1,473	97	1,929	1,252	3,427	2,255
41	6,882	3,131	1,901	1,171	98	1,580	1,511	2,575	2,696
42	3,411	6,100	6,080	2,789	99	493	1,781	2,999	3,269
43	1,231	1,752	2,882	2,250	100	4,187	1,275	1,422	2,451
44	1,447	2,229	2,663	3,306	101	3,514	2,513	3,546	4,238
45	3,304	2,080	2,533	1,511	102	4,066	1,780	1,221	3,760
46	979	5,435	3,116	2,064	103	2,944	2,656	6,277	2,742
47	5,555	2,428	866	1,545	104	1,559	1,816	2,871	2,745
48	1,000	4,921	2,540	1,145	105	2,063	3,398	4,839	1,653
49	2,724	3,045	1,135	6,074	106	2,395	1,119	2,764	1,358
50	1,405	2,094	2,541	2,172	107	1,069	1,038	2,556	1,467
51	2,719	809	1,440	1,788	108	2,827	2,700	6,841	4,220
52	4,311	1,621	4,398	1,403	109	3,120	5,825	4,307	4,965
53	1,127	2,496	1,468	517	110	2,671	2,441	3,539	516
54	3,356	2,775	2,896	1,777	111	10,561	5,210	11,774	7,716
55	2,333	372	4,022	1,269	112	4,131	3,396	3,732	6,860
56	7,903	4,048	6,553	3,188	113	10,099	7,634	9,413	8,446
57	2,461	1,009	1,413	1,766	114	4,829	2,977	9,501	2,074

9-13
From the Textbook to the Real World

Stimulating Response to Mail Surveys

Marketing professionals use statistics to analyze data and determine the effectiveness of various marketing techniques. Marketing research agencies can collect commercial data through labor-intensive telephone or personnel interviews. In addition, mail surveys can provide a relatively low cost alternative for gathering information from widely scattered populations. One major drawback of mail surveys is that their response rates are generally lower than those of face-to-face or telephone interviews; thus their nonresponse bias is more acute.

In 1987, an experiment was done in London to see if the response rate to mail surveys could be improved by enclosing a small monetary incentive and/or an informational booklet with the survey. Prior to 1987, English research agencies usually chose telephone surveys, and only 4% of companies in the UK had used monetary incentives with their mail surveys. The experiment was designed to test the following null hypotheses:

H_1: Response to a commercial mail survey is independent of the use of a monetary incentive.

H_2: Response to a commercial mail survey is independent of the use of an informational booklet.

The Experiment: The sample consisted of 159 chief executives of building societies. Questionnaires were randomly assigned with either:
1) monetary incentive/ no booklet
2) monetary incentive/booklet
3) no monetary incentive/booklet
4) no monetary incentive/no booklet

A letter enclosed with the 20-pence coin used as a monetary incentive suggested that it could be used to purchase a cup of coffee to ease the task of completing the questionnaire. The letter enclosed with the booklet indicated that it explained the importance of the survey to the research.

David Jobber, Karl Birro, Stuart Sanderson, "A Factorial Investigation of Methods of Stimulating Response to a Mail Survey," *European Journal of Operational Research,* vol. 37 (1988), pp. 158–63.

TABLE RW9-1 ANOVA results for response rates

SOURCE OF VARIATION	SUM OF SQUARES	DF	MEAN SQUARE	F
Main effects	1.04	2	.052	2.26
Monetary Incentive	0.87	1	0.87	3.76*
Booklet	0.16	1	0.16	0.71

* Denotes significance at 0.05 level.

The Results: Analysis of variance was used to test the effects of treatments on the response rates. As a check, the chi-square test was also used to test association for the main effects on response rate. The overall response rate to the mailing was 36.5%. However, response rates associated with the 20-pence coin were 44.2% (versus 29.3% with no coin) and for the booklet 33.3% (versus 40.0% for no booklet). Table RW9-1 presents the ANOVA results. The 14.9% increase in the response rate with the coin was significant at $\alpha = .05$. The booklet/no booklet difference was not significant. The chi-square test confirmed the ANOVA results.

Practical Significance: Practitioners in the UK had voiced skepticism about mail surveys because of nonresponse bias. The experiment indicated that a small monetary incentive could improve response rates to mail surveys without affecting response quality. Expensive booklets had no significant effect on response rate; in fact, response rates were higher without booklets. This evidence suggests that mail surveys are a viable means of obtaining market information and that the time and effort involved in producing a booklet might be better spent more directly on monetary incentives.

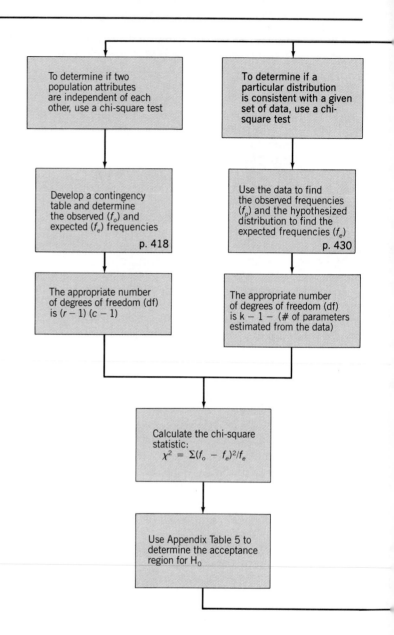

To determine if two population attributes are independent of each other, use a chi-square test

To determine if a particular distribution is consistent with a given set of data, use a chi-square test

Develop a contingency table and determine the observed (f_o) and expected (f_e) frequencies
p. 418

Use the data to find the observed frequencies (f_o) and the hypothesized distribution to find the expected frequencies (f_e)
p. 430

The appropriate number of degrees of freedom (df) is $(r-1)(c-1)$

The appropriate number of degrees of freedom (df) is $k - 1 - $ (# of parameters estimated from the data)

Calculate the chi-square statistic:
$\chi^2 = \Sigma(f_o - f_e)^2/f_e$

Use Appendix Table 5 to determine the acceptance region for H_0

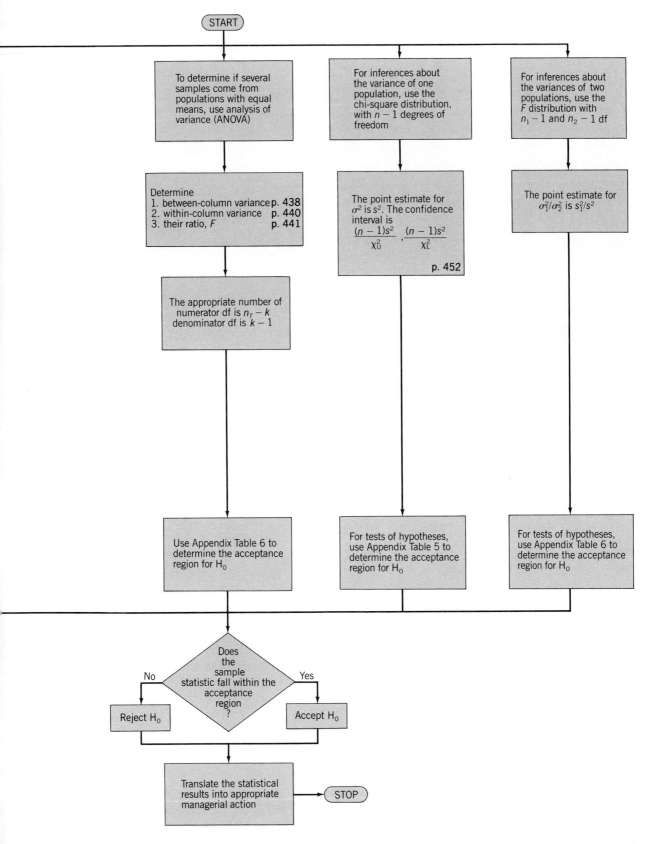

START

To determine if several samples come from populations with equal means, use analysis of variance (ANOVA)

For inferences about the variance of one population, use the chi-square distribution, with $n - 1$ degrees of freedom

For inferences about the variances of two populations, use the F distribution with $n_1 - 1$ and $n_2 - 1$ df

Determine
1. between-column variance   p. 438
2. within-column variance   p. 440
3. their ratio, F p. 441

The point estimate for σ^2 is s^2. The confidence interval is
$$\frac{(n - 1)s^2}{\chi_U^2}, \frac{(n - 1)s^2}{\chi_L^2}$$
p. 452

The point estimate for σ_1^2/σ_2^2 is s_1^2/s_2^2

The appropriate number of numerator df is $n_T - k$ denominator df is $k - 1$

Use Appendix Table 6 to determine the acceptance region for H_0

For tests of hypotheses, use Appendix Table 5 to determine the acceptance region for H_0

For tests of hypotheses, use Appendix Table 6 to determine the acceptance region for H_0

Does the sample statistic fall within the acceptance region ?

No — Reject H_0

Yes — Accept H_0

Translate the statistical results into appropriate managerial action

STOP

The vice-president for research and development of a large chemical and fiber manufacturing company believes that the firm's annual profits depend on the amount spent on R&D. The new chief executive officer does not agree and has asked for evidence. Here are data for 6 years:

YEAR	MILLIONS SPENT ON RESEARCH AND DEVELOPMENT	ANNUAL PROFIT (MILLIONS)
1984	2	20
1985	3	25
1986	5	34
1987	4	30
1988	11	40
1989	5	31

The vice-president for R&D wants an equation for predicting annual profits from the amount budgeted for R&D. With methods in this chapter, we can supply such a decision-making tool and tell him something about the accuracy he can expect in using it to make decisions.

10

Simple Regression and Correlation

■ OBJECTIVES

If your university used your high school grade-point average to predict your college grade-point average, it may have used the technique of *regression analysis,* one of the subjects of Chapter 10. And if you have heard the statement that there is a high correlation between smoking and lung cancer, then the word *correlation* (another topic in Chapter 10) is not strange to you. *Correlation analysis* is used to measure the degree of association between two variables.

10-1
Introduction

Relationship between variables

Every day, managers make personal and professional decisions that are based upon predictions of future events. To make these forecasts, they rely upon the relationship (intuitive and calculated) between what is already known and what is to be estimated. If decision makers can determine how the known is related to the future event, they can aid the decision-making process considerably. That is the subject of this chapter: how to determine the *relationship between variables.*

Difference between chi-square and topics in this chapter

In Chapter 9, we used chi-square tests of independence to determine whether a statistical relationship existed between two variables. The chi-square test tells us *if* there is such a relationship, but it does not tell us *what* that relationship is. **Regression and correlation analyses will show us how to determine both the nature and the strength of a relationship between two variables.** We will learn to predict, with some accuracy, the value of an unknown variable based on past observations of that variable and others.

Origin of terms *regression* and *multiple regression*

The term *regression* was first used as a statistical concept in 1877 by Sir Francis Galton. Galton made a study that showed that the height of children born to tall parents will tend to move back, or "regress," toward the mean height of the population. He designated the word *regression* as the name of the general process of predicting one variable (the height of the children) from another (the height of the parent). Later, statisticians coined the term *multiple regression* to describe the process by which several variables are used to predict another.

Development of an estimating equation

In *regression analysis,* we shall develop an *estimating equation*—that is, a mathematical formula that relates the known variables to the unknown variable. Then, after we have learned the pattern of this relationship, we can apply *correlation analysis* to determine the degree to which the variables are related. Correlation analysis, then, tells us how well the estimating equation actually describes the relationship.

TYPES OF RELATIONSHIPS

Independent and dependent variables

Regression and correlation analyses are based on the relationship, or association, between two (or more) variables. The known variable (or variables) is called the *independent* variable(s). The variable we are trying to predict is the *dependent* variable.

Scientists know, for example, that there is a relationship between the annual sales of aerosol spray cans and the quantity of fluorocarbons released into the atmosphere each year. If we studied this relationship, "the number of aerosol cans sold each year" would be the independent variable, and "the quantity of fluorocarbons released annually" would be the dependent variable.

Let's take another example. Economists might base their predictions of the annual gross national product, or GNP, on the final consumption spending within the economy. Thus, "the final consumption spending" is the independent variable, and "the GNP" would be the dependent variable.

In regression, we can have only one dependent variable in our estimating equation. However, we can use more than one independent variable. Often when we add independent variables, we improve the accuracy of our prediction. Economists, for example, frequently add a second independent variable, "the level of investment spending," to improve their estimate of the nation's GNP.

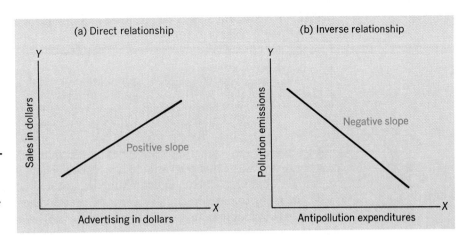

FIGURE 10-1

Direct and inverse relationships between independent variable X and dependent variable Y

Figure content labels: (a) Direct relationship — Y, Sales in dollars, Positive slope, Advertising in dollars, X. (b) Inverse relationship — Y, Pollution emissions, Negative slope, Antipollution expenditures, X.

Direct relationship between X and Y

Our two examples of fluorocarbons and GNP are illustrations of direct associations between independent and dependent variables. As the independent variable increases, the dependent variable also increases. In like manner, we expect the sales of a company to increase as the advertising budget increases. We can graph such a *direct relationship,* plotting the independent variable of the X-axis and the dependent variable on the Y-axis. We have done this in *a,* Fig. 10-1. Notice how the line slopes up as X takes on larger and larger values. The slope of this line is said to be *positive,* because Y increases as X increases.

Inverse relationship between X and Y

Relationships can also be *inverse* rather than direct. In these cases, the dependent variable decreases as the independent variable increases. The government assumes that such an inverse association exists between a company's increased annual expenditures for pollution-abatement devices and decreased pollution emissions. This type of relationship is illustrated in *b,* Fig. 10-1, and is characterized by a *negative* slope (the dependent variable Y decreases as the independent variable X increases).

Frequently, we find a *causal* relationship between variables; that is, the independent variable "causes" the dependent variable to change. This is true in the antipollution example above. But in many cases, some other factor causes the changes in both the dependent and the independent variables. We might be able to predict the sales of diamond earrings from the sales of new Cadillacs, but we could not say that one is caused by the other. Instead, we realize that the sales levels of both Cadillacs and diamond earrings are caused by another factor, such as the level of disposable income.

Relationships of association, not cause and effect

For this reason, it is important that you consider the relationships found by regression to be relationships of association but *not* necessarily of cause and effect. Unless you have specific reasons for believing that the values of the dependent variable are caused by the values of the independent variable(s), do not infer causality from the relationships you find by regression.

SCATTER DIAGRAMS

Scatter diagram

The first step in determining whether there is a relationship between two variables is to examine the graph of the observed (or known) data. This graph, or chart, is called a *scatter diagram.*

TABLE 10-1 Student Scores on Entrance Examinations and Cumulative Grade-Point Averages at Graduation

Student	A	B	C	D	E	F	G	H
Entrance examination scores (100 = maximum possible score)	74	69	85	63	82	60	79	91
Cumulative GPA (4.0 = A)	2.6	2.2	3.4	2.3	3.1	2.1	3.2	3.8

A scatter diagram can give us two types of information. Visually, we can look for patterns that indicate that the variables are related. Then, if the variables are related, we can see what kind of line, or estimating equation, describes this relationship.

We are going to develop and use a specific scatter diagram. Suppose a university admissions director asks us to determine whether any relationship exists between a student's scores on an entrance examination and that student's cumulative grade-point average (GPA) upon graduation. The administrator has accumulated a random sample of data from the records of the university. This information is recorded in Table 10-1.

Transfer tabular information to a graph

To begin, we should transfer the information in Table 10-1 to a graph. Since the director wishes to use examination scores to predict success in college, we have placed the cumulative GPA (the dependent variable) on the vertical or Y-axis and the entrance examination score (the independent variable) on the horizontal or X-axis. Figure 10-2 shows the completed scatter diagram.

At first glance we can see why we call this a scatter diagram. The pattern of points results from the fact that each pair of data from Table 10-1 has been recorded as a single point. When we view all these points together, we can visualize the relationship that exists between the two variables. As a result, we can draw, or "fit," a straight line through our scatter diagram to represent the relationship. We have done this in Fig. 10-3. It is common to try to draw these lines so that an equal number of points lie on either side of the line.

Drawing, or "fitting," a straight line through a scatter diagram

In this case, the line drawn through our data points represents a direct relationship, because Y increases as X increases. Because the data points are relatively close to this line, we can say that there is a high degree of association between the examination scores and the cumulative GPA. In Fig. 10-3, we can see that the relationship described by the data points is well described by a straight line. Thus, we can say that it is a *linear* relationship.

Interpreting our straight line

FIGURE 10-2

Scatter diagram of student scores on entrance examinations plotted against cumulative grade-point averages

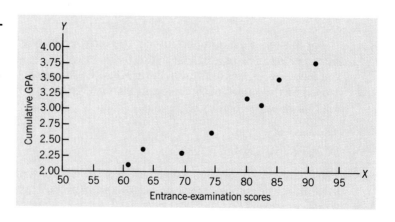

10 SIMPLE REGRESSION AND CORRELATION

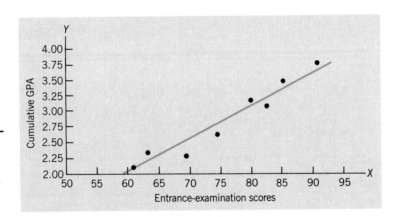

FIGURE 10-3

Scatter diagram with straight line representing the relationship between X and Y "fitted" through it

Curvilinear relationships

The relationship between X and Y variables can also take the form of a curve. Statisticians call such a relationship *curvilinear.* The employees of many industries, for example, experience what is called a "learning curve"; that is, as they produce a new product, the time required to produce one unit is reduced by some fixed proportion as the total number of units doubles. One such industry is aviation. Manufacturing time per unit for a new aircraft tends to decrease by 20 percent each time the total number of completed new planes doubles. Figure 10-4 illustrates the curvilinear relationship of this "learning curve" phenomenon.

The direction of the curve can indicate whether the curvilinear relationship is direct or inverse. The curve in Fig. 10-4 describes an inverse relationship, because Y decreases as X increases.

Review of possible relationships

To review the relationships possible in a scatter diagram, examine the graphs in Fig. 10-5. Graphs *a* and *b* show direct and inverse linear relationships. Graphs *c* and *d* are examples of curvilinear relationships that demonstrate direct and inverse associations between variables, respectively. Graph *e* illustrates an inverse linear relationship with a widely scattered pattern of points. This wider scattering indicates that there is a lower degree of association between the independent and dependent variables than there is in graph *b*. The pattern of points in graph *f* seems to indicate that there is no relationship between the two variables; therefore, knowledge of the past concerning one variable will not allow us to predict future occurrences of the other.

FIGURE 10-4

Curvilinear relationship between new-aircraft construction time and number of units produced

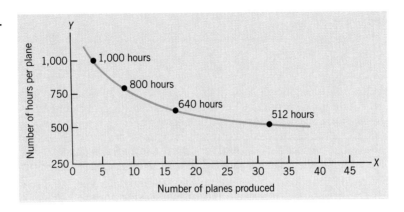

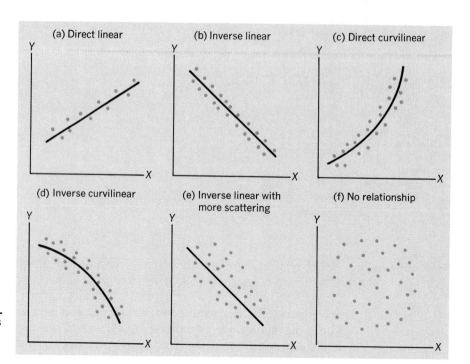

FIGURE 10-5
Possible relationships between X and Y in scatter diagrams

Exercises

10-1   What is regression analysis?

10-2   In regression analysis, what is an estimating equation?

10-3   What is the purpose of correlation analysis?

10-4   Define direct and inverse relationships.

10-5   To what does the term *causal relationship* refer?

10-6   Explain the difference between linear and curvilinear relationships.

10-7   Explain why and how we construct a scatter diagram.

10-8   What is multiple regression analysis?

10-9   An instructor is interested in finding out how the number of students absent on a given day is related to the mean temperature that day. A random sample of 10 days was used for the study. The following data indicate the number of students absent (ABS) and the mean temperature (TEMP) for each day.

ABS	8	7	5	4	2	3	5	6	8	9
TEMP	10	20	25	30	40	45	50	55	59	60

(a)   State the dependent (Y) variable and the independent (X) variable.
(b)   Draw a scatter diagram of the above data.
(c)   Does the relationship between the variables appear to be linear or curvilinear?
(d)   What type of curve could you draw through the data?
(e)   What is the logical explanation for the observed relationship?

10-10   For each of the following scatter diagrams, indicate whether a relationship exists and, if so, whether it is direct or inverse and linear or curvilinear.

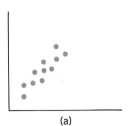

(a)

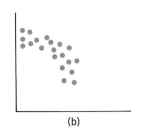

(b)

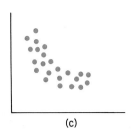

(c)

10-11 William Hawkins, VP of personnel for International Motors, is working on the relationship between a worker's salary and absentee rate. Hawkins divided the salary range of International into twelve grades or levels (1 being the lowest grade, 12 the highest) and then randomly sampled a group of workers. He determined the salary grade for each worker and the number of days that employee had missed over the last 3 years.

Salary ranking	11	10	8	5	9	9	7	3	11	8	7	2	9	8	6	3
Absences	18	17	29	36	11	26	28	35	14	20	32	39	16	26	31	40

Construct a scatter diagram for the data above and indicate the type of relationship.

10-12 The National Institute of Environmental Health Sciences (NIEHS) has been studying the statistical relationships between many different variables and the common cold. One of the variables being examined is the use of facial tissues (X) and the number of days that cold symptoms were exhibited (Y) by seven people over a 12-month period. What relationship, if any, seems to hold between the two variables? Does this indicate any causal effect?

X	2,000	1,500	500	750	600	900	1,000
Y	60	40	10	15	5	25	30

10-2
Estimation Using the Regression Line

Calculating the regression line using an equation

In the scatter diagrams we have used to this point, the *regression lines* were put in place by fitting the lines visually among the data points. In this section, we shall learn how to calculate the regression line somewhat more precisely, using an equation that relates the two variables mathematically. Here, we examine only linear relationships involving two variables. We shall deal with relationships among more than two variables in the next chapter.

Equation for a straight line

The equation for a straight line where the dependent variable Y is determined by the independent variance X is:

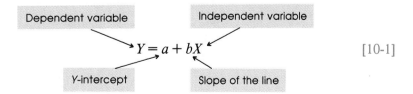

$$Y = a + bX \qquad [10\text{-}1]$$

Interpreting the equation

Using this equation, we can take a given value of X and compute the value of Y. The a is called the "Y-intercept" because its value is the point at which the regression line crosses the Y-axis—that is, the vertical axis. The b in Equation 10-1 is the "slope" of the line. It represents how much each unit change of the independent variable X changes the dependent variable Y. Both a and b are numerical *constants,* since, for any given straight line, their values do not change.

Calculating Y from X using the equation for a straight line
Suppose we know that a is 3 and b is 2. Let us determine what Y would be for an X equal to 5. When we substitute the values of a, b, and X in Equation 10-1, we find the corresponding value of Y to be:

$$Y = a + bX \qquad\qquad\qquad \text{[10-1]}$$
$$= 3 + 2(5)$$
$$= 3 + 10$$
$$= 13 \leftarrow \text{value for } Y \text{ given } X = 5$$

USING THE ESTIMATION EQUATION FOR A STRAIGHT LINE

Finding the values for a and b
How can we find the values of the numerical constants, a and b? To illustrate this process, let's use the straight line in Fig. 10-6.

Visually, we can find a (the Y-intercept) by locating the point where the line crosses the Y-axis. In Fig. 10-6, this happens where $a = 3$.

To find the slope of the line, b, we must determine how the dependent variable, Y, changes as the independent variable, X, changes. We can begin by picking two points on the line in Fig. 10-6. Now, we must find the values of X and Y (the *coordinates*) of both points. We can call the coordinates of our first point (X_1, Y_1) and those of the second point (X_2, Y_2). By examining Fig. 10-6, we can see that $(X_1, Y_1) = (1,5)$ and $(X_2, Y_2) = (2,7)$. At this point, then, we can calculate the value of b, using this equation:

$$b = \frac{Y_2 - Y_1}{X_2 - X_1} \qquad\qquad\qquad \text{[10-2]}$$
$$= \frac{7 - 5}{2 - 1}$$
$$= \frac{2}{1}$$
$$= 2 \leftarrow \text{slope of the line}$$

Writing and using the equation for a straight line
In this manner, we can learn the values of the numerical constants, a and b, and write the equation for a straight line. The line in Fig. 10-6 can be described by Equation 10-1, where $a = 3$ and $b = 2$. Thus:

$$Y = a + bX \qquad\qquad\qquad \text{[10-1]}$$

and:

$$Y = 3 + 2X$$

Using this equation, we can determine the corresponding value of the dependent variable for any value of X. Suppose we wish to find the value of Y when $X = 7$. The answer would be:

$$Y = a + bX \qquad\qquad\qquad \text{[10-1]}$$
$$= 3 + 2(7)$$
$$= 3 + 14$$
$$= 17$$

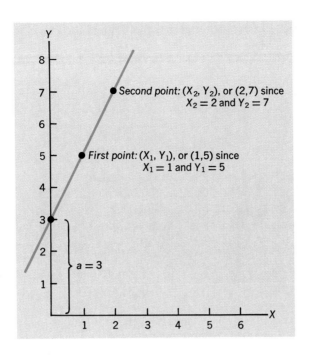

FIGURE 10-6
Straight line with a positive slope, with Y-intercept and two points on the line designated

Figure 10-6 labels:
Second point: (X_2, Y_2), or $(2,7)$ since $X_2 = 2$ and $Y_2 = 7$
First point: (X_1, Y_1), or $(1,5)$ since $X_1 = 1$ and $Y_1 = 5$
$a = 3$

Direct relationship; positive slope

If you substitute more values for X into the equation, you will notice that Y increases as X increases. Thus, the relationship between the variables is *direct,* and the slope is *positive.*

Now consider the line in Fig. 10-7. We see that it crosses the Y-axis at 6. Therefore, we know that $a = 6$. If we select the two points where $(X_1, Y_1) = (0,6)$ and

FIGURE 10-7
Straight line with negative slope

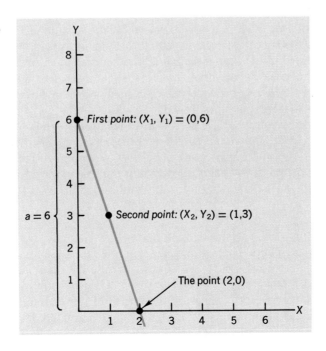

Figure 10-7 labels:
First point: $(X_1, Y_1) = (0,6)$
$a = 6$
Second point: $(X_2, Y_2) = (1,3)$
The point $(2,0)$

$(X_2, Y_2) = (1,3)$, we will find that the slope of the line is

$$b = \frac{Y_2 - Y_1}{X_2 - X_1} \qquad \text{[10-2]}$$
$$= \frac{3 - 6}{1 - 0}$$
$$= -\frac{3}{1}$$
$$= -3$$

Inverse relationship; negative slope
Notice that when b is negative, the line represents an *inverse* relationship, and the slope is *negative* (Y decreases as X increases). Now, with the numerical values of a and b determined, we can substitute them into the general equation for a straight line:

$$Y = a + bX \qquad \text{[10-1]}$$
$$Y = 6 + (-3)X$$
$$Y = 6 - 3X$$

Finding Y given X
Assume that we wish to find the value of the dependent variable that corresponds to $X = 2$. Substituting into the equation above, we get:

$$Y = 6 - (3)(2)$$
$$= 6 - 6$$
$$= 0$$

Thus, when $X = 2$, Y must equal 0. If we refer to the line in Fig. 10-7, we can see that the point (2,0) does lie on the line.

THE METHOD OF LEAST SQUARES

Fitting a regression line mathematically
Now that we have seen how to determine the equation for a straight line, let's think about how we can calculate an equation for a line that is drawn through the middle of a set of points in a scatter diagram. How can we "fit" a line mathematically if none of the points lie on the line? To a statistician, the line will have a "good fit" if it *minimizes the error* between the estimated points on the line and the actual observed points that were used to draw it.

Introduction of Ŷ
Before we proceed, we need to introduce a new symbol. So far, we have used Y to represent the individual values of the observed points measured along the Y-axis. Now we should begin to use $\hat{Y}$ (*Y-hat*) to symbolize the individual values of the *estimated* points—that is, those points that lie on the estimating line. Accordingly, we shall write the equation for the estimating line as:

$$\hat{Y} = a + bX \qquad \text{[10-3]}$$

Which line fits best?
In Fig. 10-8, we have two estimating lines that have been fitted to the same set of three data points. These three given, or observed, data points are shown in black. Two very different lines have been drawn to describe the relationship between the two variables. Obviously, we need a way to decide which of these lines gives us a better fit.

Using total error to determine best fit
One way we can "measure the error" of our estimating line is to *sum* all the individual differences, or errors, between the estimated points shown in color and the

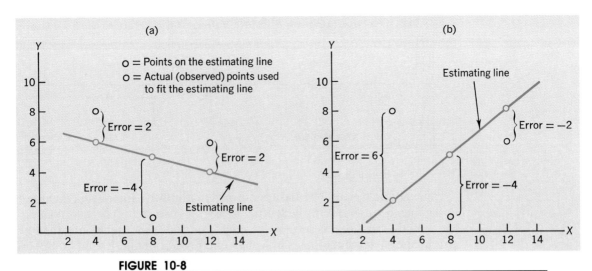

FIGURE 10-8

Two different estimating lines fitted to the same three observed data points, showing errors in both cases

observed points shown in black. In Table 10-2, we have calculated the individual differences between the corresponding Y and $\hat{Y}$, and then we have found the sum of these differences.

A quick visual examination of the two estimating lines in Fig. 10-8 reveals that the line in graph a fits the three data points better than the line in graph b.* However, our process of summing the individual differences in Table 10-2 indicates that both lines describe the data equally well (the total error in both cases is zero). Thus, we must conclude that the process of summing individual differences for calculating the error is not a reliable way to judge the goodness of fit of an estimating line.

Using absolute value of error to measure best fit

The problem with adding the individual errors is the canceling effect of the positive and negative values. From this, we might deduce that the proper criterion for judging the goodness of fit would be to add the *absolute values* (the values without their algebraic signs) of each error. We have done this in Table 10-3. (The symbol for absolute value is two parallel vertical lines, $||$.) Since the absolute error in graph a is smaller than the absolute error in graph b, and since we are looking for the "mini-

---

* We can reason that this is so by noticing that whereas both estimating lines miss the second and third points (reading from left to right) by an equal distance, the line in graph a misses the first point by considerably less than the line in graph b.

TABLE 10-2 Summing the Errors of the Two Estimating Lines in Fig. 10-8

GRAPH a $Y - \hat{Y}$	GRAPH b $Y - \hat{Y}$
$8 - 6 = 2$	$8 - 2 = 6$
$1 - 5 = -4$	$1 - 5 = -4$
$6 - 4 = 2$	$6 - 8 = -2$
$0 \leftarrow$ total error	$0 \leftarrow$ total error

TABLE 10-3 Summing the Absolute Values of the Errors of the Two Estimating Lines in Fig. 10-8

GRAPH a $\|Y - \hat{Y}\|$	GRAPH b $\|Y - \hat{Y}\|$
$\|8 - 6\| = 2$	$\|8 - 2\| = 6$
$\|1 - 5\| = 4$	$\|1 - 5\| = 4$
$\|6 - 4\| = \underline{2}$	$\|6 - 8\| = \underline{2}$
8 ← total absolute error	12 ← total absolute error

mum absolute error," we have confirmed our intuitive impression that the estimating line in graph *a* is the better fit.

On the basis of this success, we might conclude that minimizing the sum of the absolute values of the errors is the best criterion for finding a good fit. But before we feel too comfortable with it, we should examine a different situation.

In Fig. 10-9, we again have two identical scatter diagrams with two different estimating lines fitted to the three data points. In Table 10-4, we have added the absolute values of the errors and found that the estimating line in graph *a* is a better fit than the line in graph *b*. Intuitively, however, it appears that the line in graph *b* is the better fit line, because it has been moved vertically to take the middle point into consideration. Graph *a*, on the other hand, seems to ignore the middle point completely. So we would probably discard this second criterion for finding the best fit. Why? **The sum of the absolute values does not stress the *magnitude* of the error.**

Giving more weight to farther points; squaring the error

It seems reasonable that the farther away a point is from the estimating line, the more serious is the error. We would rather have several small absolute errors than one large one, as we saw in the last example. **In effect, we want to find a way to "penalize" large absolute errors, so that we can avoid them. We can accomplish this if we *square* the individual errors before we add them.** Squaring each term accomplishes two goals:

FIGURE 10-9

Two different estimating lines fitted to the same three observed data points, showing errors in both cases

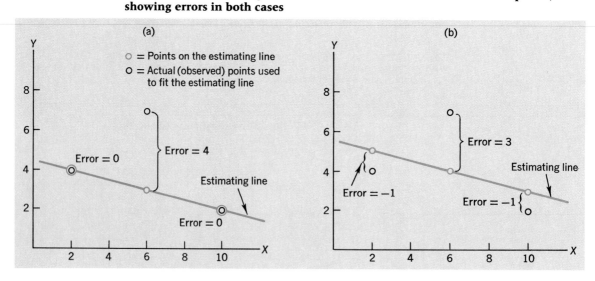

10 SIMPLE REGRESSION AND CORRELATION

TABLE 10-4 Summing the Absolute Values of the Errors of the Two Estimating Lines in Fig. 10-9

GRAPH a $|Y - \hat{Y}|$	GRAPH b $|Y - \hat{Y}|$
$\|4 - 4\| = 0$	$\|4 - 5\| = 1$
$\|7 - 3\| = 4$	$\|7 - 4\| = 3$
$\|2 - 2\| = \underline{0}$	$\|2 - 3\| = \underline{1}$
$\quad\quad 4 \leftarrow$ total absolute error	$\quad\quad 5 \leftarrow$ total absolute error

1. It magnifies, or penalizes, the larger errors.
2. It cancels the effect of the positive and negative values (a negative error squared is still positive).

Using least squares as a measure of best fit

Since we are looking for the estimating line that minimizes the sum of the squares of the errors, we call this the *least squares method.*

Let's apply the least squares criterion to the problem in Fig. 10-9. After we have organized the data and summed the squares in Table 10-5, we can see that, as we thought, the estimating line in graph b is the better fit.

Finding the best-fitting least squares line mathematically

Using the criterion of least squares, we can now determine whether one estimating line is a better fit than another. But for a set of data points through which we could draw an infinite number of estimating lines, how can we tell when we have found *the best-fitting line?*

Statisticians have derived two equations we can use to find the slope and the Y-intercept of the best-fitting regression line. The first formula calculates the slope:

Slope of the least squares regression line

Slope of best-fitting estimating line

$$b = \frac{\Sigma XY - n\overline{X}\,\overline{Y}}{\Sigma X^2 - n\overline{X}^2} \qquad [10\text{-}4]$$

where:

- $b =$ slope of the best-fitting estimate line
- $X =$ values of the independent variable
- $Y =$ values of the dependent variable
- $\overline{X} =$ mean of the values of the independent variable
- $\overline{Y} =$ mean of the values of the dependent variable
- $n =$ number of data points (that is, the number of the pairs of values for the independent and dependent variables)

TABLE 10-5 Applying the Least Squares Criterion to the Estimating Lines

GRAPH a $(Y - \hat{Y})^2$	GRAPH b $(Y - \hat{Y})^2$
$(4 - 4)^2 = (0)^2 = 0$	$(4 - 5)^2 = (-1)^2 = 1$
$(7 - 3)^2 = (4)^2 = 16$	$(7 - 4)^2 = (3)^2 = 9$
$(2 - 2)^2 = (0)^2 = \underline{0}$	$(2 - 3)^2 = (-1)^2 = \underline{1}$
$\quad\quad 16 \leftarrow$ sum of the squares	$\quad\quad 11 \leftarrow$ sum of the squares

The second formula calculates the Y-intercept of the line whose slope we calculated using Equation 10-4:

Intercept of the least squares regression line

$$\text{Y-intercept} \longrightarrow a = \overline{Y} - b\overline{X} \qquad [10\text{-}5]$$

where:

- $a = Y$-intercept
- $b = $ slope from Equation 10-4
- $\overline{Y} = $ mean of the values of the dependent variable
- $\overline{X} = $ mean of the values of the independent variable

With these two equations, we can find the best-fitting regression line for any two-variable set of data points.

USING THE LEAST SQUARES METHOD IN TWO PROBLEMS

Suppose the director of the Chapel Hill Sanitation Department is interested in the relationship between the age of a garbage truck and the annual repair expense he should expect to incur. In order to determine this relationship, the director has accumulated information concerning four of the trucks the city currently owns (Table 10-6).

Example of the least squares method

The first step in calculating the regression line for this problem is to organize the data as outlined in Table 10-7. This allows us to substitute directly into Equations 10-4 and 10-5 in order to find the slope and the Y-intercept of the best-fitting regression line.

With the information in Table 10-7, we can now use the equations for the slope (Equation 10-4) and the Y-intercept (Equation 10-5) to find the numerical constants for our regression line. The slope is:

Finding the value of b

$$b = \frac{\Sigma XY - n\overline{X}\,\overline{Y}}{\Sigma X^2 - n\overline{X}^2} \qquad [10\text{-}4]$$

$$= \frac{78 - (4)(3)(6)}{44 - (4)(3)^2}$$

$$= \frac{78 - 72}{44 - 36}$$

$$= \frac{6}{8}$$

$$= .75 \leftarrow \text{the slope of the line}$$

TABLE 10-6 Annual Truck-Repair Expenses

TRUCK NUMBER	AGE OF TRUCK IN YEARS (X)	REPAIR EXPENSE DURING LAST YEAR IN HUNDREDS OF $ (Y)
101	5	7
102	3	7
103	3	6
104	1	4

TABLE 10-7 Calculation of Inputs for Equations 10-4 and 10-5

TRUCKS (n = 4) (1)	AGE (X) (2)	REPAIR EXPENSE (Y) (3)	XY (2) × (3)	X² (2)²
101	5	7	35	25
102	3	7	21	9
103	3	6	18	9
104	1	4	4	1
	$\Sigma X = 12$	$\Sigma Y = 24$	$\Sigma XY = 78$	$\Sigma X^2 = 44$

$$\overline{X} = \frac{\Sigma X}{n} \qquad [3\text{-}2]$$

$$= \frac{12}{4}$$

$= 3 \leftarrow$ mean of the values of the independent variable

$$\overline{Y} = \frac{\Sigma Y}{n} \qquad [3\text{-}2]$$

$$= \frac{24}{4}$$

$= 6 \leftarrow$ mean of the values of the dependent variable

And the Y-intercept is:

Finding the value of a

$$a = \overline{Y} - b\overline{X} \qquad [10\text{-}5]$$
$$= 6 - (.75)(3)$$
$$= 6 - 2.25$$
$$= 3.75 \leftarrow \text{the } Y\text{-intercept}$$

Determining the estimating equation

Now, to get the estimating equation that describes the relationship between the age of a truck and its annual repair expense, we can substitute the values of a and b in the general equation for a straight line:

$$\hat{Y} = a + bX \qquad [10\text{-}3]$$

$$\hat{Y} = 3.75 + .75X$$

Using the estimating equation

Using this estimating equation (which we could plot as a regression line if we wished), the Sanitation Department director can estimate the annual repair expense, given the age of his equipment. If, for example, the city has a truck that is four years old, the director could use the equation to predict the annual repair expense for this truck as follows:

$$\hat{Y} = 3.75 + .75(4)$$
$$= 3.75 + 3$$
$$= 6.75 \leftarrow \text{expected annual repair expense of \$675.00}$$

Thus, the city might expect to spend about $675 annually in repairs on a 4-year-old truck.

Another example

Now we can solve the chapter-opening problem concerning the relationship between money spent on research and development and the chemical firm's annual profits. Table 10-8 presents the information for the preceding 6 years. With this, we can determine the regression equation describing the relationship.

TABLE 10-8 Annual Relationship Between Research and Development and Profits

YEAR	MILLIONS SPENT ON RESEARCH AND DEVELOPMENT (X)	ANNUAL PROFIT ($ MILLION) (Y)
1989	$ 5	$31
1988	11	40
1987	4	30
1986	5	34
1985	3	25
1984	2	20

Again, we can facilitate the collection of the necessary information if we perform the calculations in a table such as Table 10-9.

With this information, we are ready to find the numerical constants a and b for the estimating equation. The value of b is:

Finding b

$$b = \frac{\Sigma XY - n\overline{X}\,\overline{Y}}{\Sigma X^2 - n\overline{X}^2} \qquad [10\text{-}4]$$

$$= \frac{1,000 - (6)(5)(30)}{200 - (6)(5)^2}$$

$$= \frac{1,000 - 900}{200 - 150}$$

$$= \frac{100}{50}$$

$$= 2 \leftarrow \text{the slope of the line}$$

And the value for a is:

Finding a

$$a = \overline{Y} - b\overline{X} \qquad [10\text{-}5]$$
$$= 30 - (2)(5)$$
$$= 30 - 10$$
$$= 20 \leftarrow \text{the } Y\text{-intercept}$$

Determining the estimating equation

So we can substitute these values a and b into Equation 10-3 and get:

$$\hat{Y} = a + bX \qquad [10\text{-}3]$$
$$\hat{Y} = 20 + 2X$$

Using the estimating equation to predict

Using this estimating equation, the vice-president for research and development can predict what the annual profits will be from the amount budgeted for R&D. If the firm spends $8 million for R&D in 1990, it can expect to earn approximately $36 million in profits during that year:

$$\hat{Y} = 20 + 2(8)$$
$$= 20 + 16$$
$$= 36 \leftarrow \text{expected annual profit (millions)}$$

Shortcoming of the estimating equation

Estimating equations are not perfect predictors. In Fig. 10-10, which plots the points found in Table 10-8, the $36 million estimate of profit for 1990 is only that—an estimate. Even so, the regression does give us an idea of what to expect for the coming year.

TABLE 10-9 Calculation of Inputs for Equations 10-4 and 10-5

YEAR ($n = 6$)	EXPENDITURES FOR R&D (X)	ANNUAL PROFITS (Y)	XY	X^2
1989	5	31	155	25
1988	11	40	440	121
1987	4	30	120	16
1986	5	34	170	25
1985	3	25	75	9
1984	2	20	40	4
	$\Sigma X = 30$	$\Sigma Y = 180$	$\Sigma XY = 1{,}000$	$\Sigma X^2 = 200$

$$\bar{X} = \frac{\Sigma X}{n} \quad \text{[3-2]}$$

$$= \frac{30}{6}$$

$$= 5 \leftarrow \text{mean of the values of the independent variable}$$

$$\bar{Y} = \frac{\Sigma Y}{n} \quad \text{[3-2]}$$

$$= \frac{180}{6}$$

$$= 30 \leftarrow \text{mean of the values of the dependent variable}$$

CHECKING THE ESTIMATING EQUATION

Checking the estimating equation: one way

Now that we know how to calculate the regression line, we can learn how to check our work. A crude way to verify the accuracy of the estimating equation is to examine the graph of the sample points. As we can see from the previous problem, the regression line in Fig. 10-10 does appear to follow the path described by the sample points.

Another way to check the estimating equation

A more sophisticated method comes from one of the mathematical properties of a line fitted by the method of least squares; that is, the individual positive and negative

FIGURE 10-10

Scattering of points around regression line

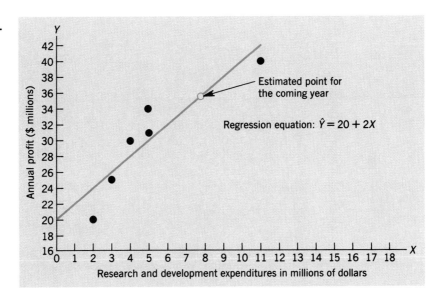

Regression equation: $\hat{Y} = 20 + 2X$

TABLE 10-10 Calculating the Sum of the Individual Errors in Table 10-9

Y	$\hat{Y}$ (THAT IS, 20 + 2X)		INDIVIDUAL ERROR
31	− [20 + (2)(5)]	=	1
40	− [20 + (2)(11)]	=	−2
30	− [20 + (2)(4)]	=	2
34	− [20 + (2)(5)]	=	4
25	− [20 + (2)(3)]	=	−1
20	− [20 + (2)(2)]	=	−4
			0 ← total error

errors must sum to zero. Using the information from Table 10-9, check to see whether the sum of the errors in the last problem is equal to zero. This is done in Table 10-10.

Since the sum of the errors in Table 10-10 does equal zero, and since the regression line appears to "fit" the points in Fig. 10-10, we can be reasonably certain that we have not committed any serious mathematical mistakes in determining the estimating equation for this problem.

THE STANDARD ERROR OF ESTIMATE

Measuring the reliability of the estimating equation

The next process we need to learn in our study of regression analysis is how to measure the reliability of the estimating equation that we have developed. We alluded to this topic when we introduced scatter diagrams. There, we realized intuitively that a line will be more accurate as an estimator when the data points lie close to the line (as in graph *a* of Fig. 10-11) than when the points are farther away from the line (as graph *b* of Fig. 10-11).

FIGURE 10-11

Contrasting degrees of scattering of data points and the resulting effect on accuracy of the regression line

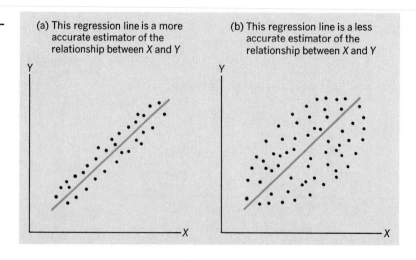

(a) This regression line is a more accurate estimator of the relationship between X and Y

(b) This regression line is a less accurate estimator of the relationship between X and Y

Definition and use of
standard error of
estimate

To measure the reliability of the estimating equation, statisticians have developed the *standard error of estimate.* This standard error is symbolized s_e and is similar to the standard deviation (which we first examined in Chapter 3), in that both are measures of dispersion. You will recall that the standard deviation is used to measure the dispersion of a set of observations about the mean. **The standard error of estimate, on the other hand, measures the variability, or scatter, of the observed values around the regression line.** Even so, you will see the similarity between the standard error of estimate and the standard deviation if you compare Equation 10-6, which defines the standard error of estimate, with Equation 3-18, which defines the standard deviation:

Equation for calculation
of standard error of
estimate

Standard error of estimate

$$s_e = \sqrt{\frac{\Sigma(Y - \hat{Y})^2}{n - 2}} \qquad [10\text{-}6]$$

where:

- Y = values of the dependent variable
- $\hat{Y}$ = estimated values from the estimating equation that correspond to each Y value
- n = number of data points used to fit the regression line

Notice that in Equation 10-6, the sum of the squared deviations is divided by $n - 2$ and not by n. This happens because we have lost 2 degrees of freedom in estimating the regression line. We can reason that since the values of a and b were obtained from a sample of data points, we lose 2 degrees of freedom when we use these points to estimate the regression line.

Now let's refer again to our earlier example of the Sanitation Department director who related the age of his trucks to the amount of annual repairs. We found the estimating equation in that situation to be:

$$\hat{Y} = 3.75 + .75X$$

where X is the age of the truck and $\hat{Y}$ is the estimated amount of annual repairs (in hundreds of dollars).

To calculate s_e for this problem, we must first determine the value of $\Sigma(Y - \hat{Y})^2$; that is, the numerator of Equation 10-6. We have done this in Table 10-11, using $(3.75 + .75X)$ for $\hat{Y}$ whenever it was necessary. Since $\Sigma(Y - \hat{Y})^2$ is equal to 1.50, we can now use Equation 10-6 to find the standard error of estimate:

$$s_e = \sqrt{\frac{\Sigma(Y - \hat{Y})^2}{n - 2}} \qquad [10\text{-}6]$$

$$= \sqrt{\frac{1.50}{4 - 2}}$$

$$= \sqrt{.75}$$

$$= .866 \leftarrow \text{standard error of estimate of } \$86.60$$

TABLE 10-11 Calculating the Numerator of the Fraction in Equation 10-6

X (1)	Y (2)	$\hat{Y}$ (THAT IS, 3.75 + .75X) (3)	INDIVIDUAL ERROR $(Y - \hat{Y})$ (2) − (3)	$(Y - \hat{Y})^2$ [(2) − (3)]^2
5	7	3.75 + (.75)(5)	7 − 7.5 = −.5	.25
3	7	3.75 + (.75)(3)	7 − 6.0 = 1.0	1.00
3	6	3.75 + (.75)(3)	6 − 6.0 = 0.0	.00
1	4	3.75 + (.75)(1)	4 − 4.5 = −.5	.25
			$\Sigma(Y - \hat{Y})^2 = $ **1.50**	← sum of squared errors

USING A SHORT-CUT METHOD TO CALCULATE THE STANDARD ERROR OF ESTIMATE

To use Equation 10-6, we must do the tedious series of calculations outlined in Table 10-11. For every value of Y, we must compute the corresponding value of $\hat{Y}$. Then we must substitute these values into the expression $\Sigma(Y - \hat{Y})^2$.

Fortunately, we can eliminate some of the steps in this task by using the short cut provided by Equation 10-7; that is:

A quicker way to calculate s_e

$$s_e = \sqrt{\frac{\Sigma Y^2 - a\Sigma Y - b\Sigma XY}{n - 2}} \qquad [10\text{-}7]$$

where:

- $X =$ values of the independent variable
- $Y =$ values of the dependent variable
- $a =$ Y-intercept from Equation 10-5
- $b =$ slope of the estimating equation from Equation 10-4
- $n =$ number of data points

This equation is a short cut because, when we first organized the data in this problem so that we could calculate the slope and the Y-intercept (Table 10-7), we determined every value we will need for Equation 10-7 except one—the value of ΣY^2. Table 10-12 is a repeat of Table 10-7 with the Y^2 column added.

Now we can refer to Table 10-12 and our previous calculations of a and b in order to calculate s_e using the short-cut method:

$$s_e = \sqrt{\frac{\Sigma Y^2 - a\Sigma Y - b\Sigma XY}{n - 2}} \qquad [10\text{-}7]$$

$$= \sqrt{\frac{150 - (3.75)(24) - (.75)(78)}{4 - 2}}$$

$$= \sqrt{\frac{150 - 90 - 58.5}{2}}$$

$$= \sqrt{.75}$$

$$= .866 \leftarrow \text{standard error of \$86.60}$$

This is the same result as the one we obtained using Equation 10-6, but think of how many steps we saved!

TABLE 10-12 Calculation of Inputs for Equation 10-7

TRUCKS $n = 4$ (1)	AGE X (2)	REPAIR EXPENSE Y (3)	XY (2) $\times$ (3)	X^2 $(2)^2$	Y^2 $(3)^2$
101	5	7	35	25	49
102	3	7	21	9	49
103	3	6	18	9	36
104	1	4	4	1	16
	$\Sigma X = 12$	$\Sigma Y = 24$	$\Sigma XY = 78$	$\Sigma X^2 = 44$	$\Sigma Y^2 = 150$

INTERPRETING THE STANDARD ERROR OF ESTIMATE

Interpreting and using the standard error of estimate

As was true of the standard deviation, the larger the standard error of estimate, the greater the scattering (or dispersion) of points around the regression line. Conversely, if $s_e = 0$, we expect the estimating equation to be a "perfect" estimator of the dependent variable. In that case, all the data points would lie directly on the regression line, and no points would be scattered around it.

Using s_e to form bounds around the regression line

We shall use the standard error of estimate as a tool in the same way that we can use the standard deviation. That is to say, assuming that the observed points are normally distributed around the regression line, we can expect to find 68 percent of the points within $\pm 1s_e$ (or plus and minus 1 standard error of estimate), 95.5 percent of the points within $\pm 2s_e$, and 99.7 percent of the points within $\pm 3s_e$. Figure 10-12 illustrates these "bounds" around the regression line. Another thing to notice in Fig.

FIGURE 10-12

$\pm 1s_e$, $\pm 2s_e$, and $\pm 3s_e$ bounds around the regression line

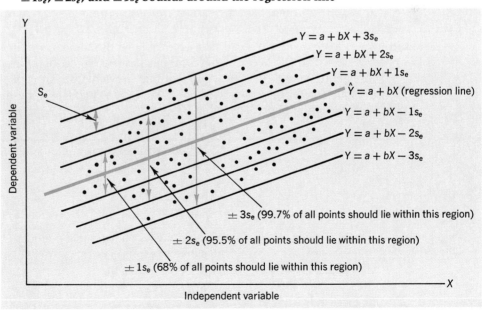

10-12 is that the standard error of estimate is measured along the Y-axis, rather than perpendicularly from the regression line.

Assumptions we make
in use of s_e

At this point, we should state the assumptions we are making, because shortly, we shall make some probability statements based on these assumptions. Specifically, we have assumed that:

1. The observed values for Y are normally distributed around each estimated value of $\hat{Y}$.
2. The variance of the distributions around each possible value of $\hat{Y}$ is the same.

If this second assumption were not true, then the standard error at one point on the regression line could differ from the standard error at another point on the line.

APPROXIMATE PREDICTION INTERVALS

Using s_e to generate
prediction intervals

One way to view the standard error of estimate is to think of it as the statistical tool we can use to make a probability statement about the interval around an estimated value of $\hat{Y}$, within which the actual value of Y lies. We can see, for instance, in Fig. 10-12 that we can be 95.5 percent certain that the actual value of Y will lie within 2 standard errors of the estimated value of $\hat{Y}$. We call these intervals around the estimated $\hat{Y}$ *approximate prediction intervals.* They serve the same function as the confidence intervals did in Chapter 7.

Now, applying the concept of approximate prediction intervals to the Sanitation Department director's repair expenses, we know that the estimating equation used to predict the annual repair expense is:

$$\hat{Y} = 3.75 + .75X$$

Applying prediction
intervals

And we know that if the department has a 4-year-old truck, we predict it will have an annual repair expense of $675:

$$\hat{Y} = 3.75 + .75(4)$$
$$= 3.75 + 3.00$$
$$= 6.75 \leftarrow \text{expected annual repair expense of } \$675$$

One standard error
prediction interval

Finally, you will recall that we calculated the standard error of estimate to be $s_e = .866$ ($86.60). We can now combine these two pieces of information and say that we are roughly 68 percent confident that the actual repair expense will be within ± 1 standard error of estimate from $\hat{Y}$. We can calculate the upper and lower limits of this prediction interval as follows:

$$\hat{Y} + 1s_e = \$675 + (1)(\$86.60)$$
$$= \$761.60 \leftarrow \text{upper limit of prediction interval}$$

and:

$$\hat{Y} - 1s_e = \$675 - (1)(\$86.60)$$
$$= \$588.40 \leftarrow \text{lower limit of prediction interval}$$

Two standard error
prediction interval

If, instead, we say that we are roughly 95.5 percent confident that the actual repair expense will be within ± 2 standard errors of estimate from $\hat{Y}$, we would calculate the limits of this new prediction interval like this:

$$\hat{Y} + 2s_e = \$675 + (2)(\$86.60)$$
$$= \$848.20 \leftarrow \text{upper limit}$$

10 SIMPLE REGRESSION AND CORRELATION

and:

$$\hat{Y} - 2s_e = \$675 - (2)(\$86.60)$$
$$= \$501.80 \leftarrow \text{lower limit}$$

n is too small to use the
normal distribution

Keep in mind that statisticians apply prediction intervals based on the normal distribution (68 percent for $1s_e$, 95.5 percent for $2s_e$, and 99.7 percent for $3s_e$) *only* to large samples; that is, where $n > 30$. In this problem, our sample size is too small ($n = 4$). Thus, *our conclusions are inaccurate.* But the method we have used nevertheless demonstrates the principle involved in prediction intervals.

Using the *t* distribution
for prediction intervals

If we wish to avoid the inaccuracies caused by the size of the sample, we need to use the *t* distribution. Recall that the *t* distribution is appropriate when *n* is less than 30 and the population standard deviation is unknown. We meet both these conditions, since $n = 4$, and s_e is an estimate rather than the known population standard deviation.

An example using the *t*
distribution to calculate
prediction intervals

Now suppose the Sanitation Department director wants to be roughly 90 percent certain that the annual truck-repair expense will lie within the prediction interval. How should we calculate this interval? Since the *t* distribution table focuses on the probability that the parameter we are estimating will lie *outside* the prediction interval, we need to look in Appendix Table 2 under the $100\% - 90\% = 10\%$ value column. Once we locate that column, we look for the row representing 2 degrees of freedom; since $n = 4$ and since we know we lose 2 degrees of freedom (in estimating the values of *a* and *b*), then $n - 2 = 2$. Here we find the appropriate *t* value to be 2.920.

Now we can make a more accurate calculation of our prediction interval limits, as follows:

$$\hat{Y} + t(s_e) = \$675 + (2.920)(\$86.60)$$
$$= \$675 + \$252.87$$
$$= \$927.87 \leftarrow \text{upper limit}$$

and:

$$\hat{Y} - t(s_e) = \$675 - (2.920)(\$86.60)$$
$$= \$675 - \$252.87$$
$$= \$422.13 \leftarrow \text{lower limit}$$

So the director can be 90 percent certain that the annual repair expense on a 4-year-old truck will lie between $422.13 and $927.87.

We stress again that the prediction intervals above are only *approximate*. In fact, statisticians can calculate the exact standard error for the prediction, s_p, using this formula:

$$s_p = s_e \sqrt{1 + \frac{1}{n} + \frac{(\overline{X} - X_0)^2}{\Sigma X^2 - n\overline{X}^2}}$$

where $X_0 =$ the specific value of X at which we want to predict the value of Y.

Notice that if we use this formula, s_p will be different for each value of X_0. In particular, if X_0 is *far* from $\overline{X}$, then s_p will be large, because $(\overline{X} - X_0)^2$ will be large. If, on the other hand, X_0 is close to X, and *n* is moderately large (greater than 10), then s_p will be close to s_e. This happens because $1/n$ will be small and $(\overline{X} - X_0)^2$ will be small. Therefore, the value under the square-root sign will be close to 1, the square root will be even closer to 1, and s_p will be very close to s_e. This justifies our use of s_e to compute approximate prediction intervals.

Exercises

 10-13 For the following set of data:
  (a) Plot the scatter diagram.
  (b) Develop the estimating equation that best describes the data.
  (c) Predict Y for $X = 10, 15, 20$.

X	13	16	14	11	17	9	13	17	18	12
Y	6.2	8.6	7.2	4.5	9.0	3.5	6.5	9.3	9.5	5.7

 10-14 Using the data given below:
  (a) Plot the scatter diagram.
  (b) Develop the estimating equation that best describes the data.
  (c) Predict Y for $X = 5, 6, 7$.

X	16	6	10	5	12	14
Y	−4.4	8.0	2.1	8.7	0.1	−2.9

 10-15 Given the following set of data:
  (a) Find the best-fitting line.
  (b) Compute the standard error of estimate.
  (c) Find a prediction interval (with a 95 percent confidence level) for the dependent variable given that X is 44.

X	56	48	42	58	40	39	50
Y	45	38.5	34.5	46.1	33.3	32.1	40.4

 10-16 Assume that you are in charge of money for the country of Piedmont. You are given the following historical data on the money supply and gross national product (both in millions of dollars; Piedmont is a small country):

MONEY SUPPLY	GROSS NATIONAL PRODUCT
2.0	5.0
2.5	5.5
3.2	6.0
3.6	7.0
3.3	7.2
4.0	7.7
4.2	8.4
4.6	9.0
4.8	9.7
5.0	10.0

  (a) Develop the estimating equation to predict gross national product Y from money supply X.
  (b) How do you interpret the slope of the regression line?
  (c) Compute and interpret the standard error of estimate.
  (d) Compute an approximate 90 percent prediction interval for gross national product when the money supply is 8.0.

10-17 During recent tennis matches, Diane has noticed that her lobs have been less than totally effective because her opponents have been returning some of them. Since some of the people she plays are quite tall, she was wondering if the height of her opponent could be used to explain the number of lobs which are not returned during a match. The following data were collected from five recent matches.

OPPONENT'S HEIGHT (H)	UNRETURNED LOBS (L)
5.0	9
5.5	6
6.0	3
6.5	0
5.0	7

(a) Which variable is the dependent variable?
(b) What is the least squares estimating equation for these data?
(c) What is your best estimate of the number of unreturned lobs in her match tomorrow with an opponent who is 5.9 feet tall?

10-18 A study by the Atlanta, Georgia, Department of Transportation on the effect of bus-ticket prices upon the number of passengers produced the following results:

Ticket Price (cents)	25	30	35	40	45	50	55	60
Passengers per 100 miles	800	780	780	660	640	600	620	620

(a) Plot these data.
(b) Develop the estimating equation that best describes these data.
(c) Predict the number of passengers per 100 miles if the ticket price were 50 cents. Use a 95 percent approximate prediction interval.

10-19 William C. Andrews, an organizational-behavior consultant for Victory Motorcycles, has designed a test to show the company's foremen the dangers of oversupervising their workers. A worker from the assembly line is given a series of complicated tasks to perform. During the worker's performance, a foreman constantly interrupts the worker to assist him in completing the tasks. The worker, upon completion of the tasks, is then given a psychological test designed to measure the worker's hostility toward authority (a high score equals low hostility). Eight different workers were assigned the tasks and then interrupted for the purpose of instructional assistance varying numbers of times (line X). Their corresponding scores on the hostility test are revealed in line Y.

X (number of times worker interrupted)	5	10	10	15	15	20	20	25
Y (worker's score on hostility test)	58	41	45	27	26	12	16	3

(a) Plot these data.
(b) Develop the equation that best describes the relationship between number of times interrupted and test score.
(c) Predict the expected test score if the worker is interrupted eighteen times.

10-20 The editor-in-chief of a major metropolitan newspaper has been trying to convince the paper's owner to improve the working conditions in the pressroom. He is convinced that the noise level when the presses are running creates unhealthy levels of tension and anxiety. He recently had a psychologist conduct a test during which pressmen were placed in rooms with varying levels of noise and then given a test to measure mood and anxiety levels. The following table shows the index of their degree of arousal or nervousness and the level of noise to which they were exposed. (1.0 is low and 10.0 is high).

Noise level	4	3	1	2	6	7	2	3
Degree of arousal	39	38	16	18	41	45	25	38

(a) Plot these data.
(b) Develop an estimating equation that describes these data.
(c) Predict the degree of arousal that we might expect when the noise level is five.

10-21 A firm administers a test to sales trainees before they go into the field. The management of the firm is interested in determining the relationship between the test scores and the sales made by the trainees at the end of one year in the field. The following data were collected for ten sales personnel who have been in the field one year.

SALESPERSON NUMBER	TEST SCORE (T)	NUMBER OF UNITS SOLD (S)
1	2.6	95
2	3.7	140
3	2.4	85
4	4.5	180
5	2.6	100
6	5.0	195
7	2.8	115
8	3.0	136
9	4.0	175
10	3.4	150

(a) Find the least squares regression line which could be used to predict sales from trainee test scores.
(b) How much does the expected number of units sold increase for each one point increase in a trainee's test score?
(c) Use the least squares regression line to predict the number of units which would be sold by a trainee who received an average test score.

10-22 The city council of Bowie, Maryland, has gathered data on the number of minor traffic accidents and the number of youth soccer games that occur in town over a weekend.

X (soccer games)	20	30	10	12	15	25	34
Y (minor accidents)	6	9	4	5	7	8	9

(a) Plot these data.
(b) Develop the estimating equation that best describes these data.
(c) Predict the number of minor traffic accidents that will occur on a weekend during which 33 soccer games take place in Bowie.
(d) Calculate the standard error of estimate.

10-23 In economics, the demand function for a product is often estimated by regressing the quantity sold (Q) on the price (P). The Bamsy Company is trying to estimate the demand function for its new doll "Ma'am," and has collected the following data:

P	20.0	17.5	16.0	14.0	12.5	10.0	8.0	6.5
Q	125	156	183	190	212	238	250	276

(a) Plot these data.
(b) Calculate the least squares regression line.
(c) Draw the fitted regression line on your plot from part (a).

10-24 Cost accountants often estimate overhead based on the level of production. The doll people from problem 10-23 have collected information on overhead expenses and units produced at different plants, and want to estimate a regression equation to predict future overhead.

Overhead	191	170	272	155	280	173	234	116	153	178
Units	40	42	53	35	56	39	48	30	37	40

(a) Develop the regression equation for the cost accountants.
(b) Predict overhead when 50 units are produced.
(c) Calculate the standard error of estimate.

10-3
Correlation Analysis

What correlation analysis does

Correlation analysis is the statistical tool that we can use to describe *the degree to which one variable is linearly related to another.* Frequently, correlation analysis is used in conjunction with regression analysis to measure how well the regression line explains the variation of the dependent variable, Y. Correlation can also be used by itself, however, to measure the degree of association between two variables.

Two measures that describe correlation

Statisticians have developed two measures for describing the correlation between two variables: the *coefficient of determination* and the *coefficient of correlation*. Introducing these two measures of association is the purpose of this section.

THE COEFFICIENT OF DETERMINATION

Developing the sample coefficient of determination

The coefficient of determination is the primary way we can measure the extent, or strength, of the association that exists between two variables, X and Y. Since we have used a sample of points to develop regression lines, we refer to this measure as the *sample coefficient of determination.*

The sample coefficient of determination is developed from the relationship between two kinds of variation: the variation of the Y values in a data set around:

1. The fitted regression line
2. Their own mean

The term *variation* in both these cases is used in its usual statistical sense to mean "the sum of a group of squared deviations." Using this definition, then, it is reasonable to express the variation of the Y values around the regression line with this equation:

$$\text{Variation of the } Y \text{ values around the regression line} = \Sigma(Y - \hat{Y})^2 \qquad [10\text{-}8]$$

The second variation, that of the Y values around their own mean, is determined by:

$$\text{Variation of the } Y \text{ values around their own mean} = \Sigma(Y - \overline{Y})^2 \qquad [10\text{-}9]$$

One minus the ratio between these two variations is the sample coefficient of determination, which is symbolized r^2:

$$\text{Sample coefficient of determination} \longrightarrow r^2 = 1 - \frac{\Sigma(Y - \hat{Y})^2}{\Sigma(Y - \overline{Y})^2} \qquad [10\text{-}10]$$

TABLE 10-13 Illustration of Perfect Correlation Between Two Variables, X and Y

DATA POINT	VALUE OF X	VALUE OF Y
1st	1	4
2nd	2	8
3rd	3	12
4th	4	16
5th	5	20
6th	6	24
7th	7	28
8th	8	32

$$\bar{Y} = \frac{144}{8} = 18 \;\leftarrow\; \text{mean of the values of } Y$$

$$\Sigma Y = 144$$

The next two sections will show you that r^2, as defined by Equation 10-10, is a measure of the degree of linear association between X and Y.

AN INTUITIVE INTERPRETATION OF r^2

Consider the two extreme ways in which the variables X and Y can be related. In Table 10-13, every observed value of Y lies on the estimating line, as can be proven visually by Fig. 10-13. This is *perfect correlation.*

Estimating equation appropriate for perfect correlation example

The estimating equation appropriate for these data is easy to determine. Since the regression line passes through the origin, we know that the Y-intercept is zero; and since Y increases by 4 every time X increases by 1, the slope must equal 4. Thus, the regression line is:

$$\hat{Y} = 4X$$

Determining sample coefficient of determination for perfect correlation example

Now, to determine the sample coefficient of determination for the regression line in Fig. 10-13, we first calculate the numerator of the fraction in Equation 10-10:

$$\begin{aligned} \text{Variation of the } Y \text{ values} \\ \text{around the regression line} \end{aligned} \begin{aligned} &= \Sigma(Y - \hat{Y})^2 \\ &= \Sigma(0)^2 \\ &= 0 \end{aligned} \qquad \text{[10-8]}$$

Since every Y value is on the regression line, the difference between Y and $\hat{Y}$ is zero in each case.

Then we can find the denominator of the fraction:

$$\begin{aligned} \text{Variation of the } Y \text{ values} \\ \text{around their own mean} \end{aligned} = \Sigma(Y - \bar{Y})^2 \qquad \text{[10-9]}$$

$$
\begin{aligned}
&= (\ 4 - 18)^2 = (-14)^2 = 196 \\
&+ (\ 8 - 18)^2 = (-10)^2 = 100 \\
&+ (12 - 18)^2 = (-\ 6)^2 = \ \ 36 \\
&+ (16 - 18)^2 = (-\ 2)^2 = \ \ \ 4 \\
&+ (20 - 18)^2 = (\ \ \ 2)^2 = \ \ \ 4 \\
&+ (24 - 18)^2 = (\ \ \ 6)^2 = \ \ 36 \\
&+ (28 - 18)^2 = (\ \ 10)^2 = 100 \\
&+ (32 - 18)^2 = (\ \ 14)^2 = \underline{196} \\
& \ \ 672 \;\leftarrow\; \Sigma(Y - \bar{Y})^2
\end{aligned}
$$

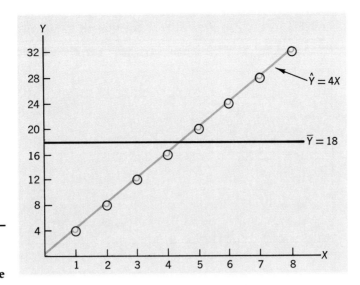

FIGURE 10-13

Perfect correlation between X and Y: Every data point lies on the regression line

With these values to substitute into Equation 10-10, we can find that the sample coefficient of determination is equal to $+1$:

$$r^2 = 1 - \frac{\Sigma(Y - \hat{Y})^2}{\Sigma(Y - \overline{Y})^2}$$ [10-10]

$$= 1 - \frac{0}{672}$$

$$= 1 - 0$$

$$= 1 \leftarrow \text{sample coefficient of determination when there is perfect correlation}$$

In fact, r^2 is equal to $+1$ whenever the regression line is a perfect estimator.

A second extreme way in which the variables X and Y can be related is that the points could lie at equal distances on both sides of a horizontal regression line, as is pictured in Fig. 10-14. The data set here consists of eight points, all of which have been recorded in Table 10-14.

FIGURE 10-14

Zero correlation between X and Y: Same values of Y appear for different values of X

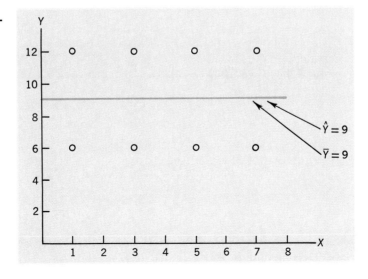

TABLE 10-14 Illustration of Zero Correlation Between Two Variables, X and Y

DATA POINT	VALUE OF X	VALUE OF Y
1st	1	6
2nd	1	12
3rd	3	6
4th	3	12
5th	5	6
6th	5	12
7th	7	6
8th	7	12

$$\Sigma Y = 72$$
$$\bar{Y} = \frac{72}{8}$$
$$= 9 \leftarrow \text{mean of the values of } Y$$

From Fig. 10-14, we can see that the least-squares regression line appropriate for these data is of the form $\hat{Y} = 9$. The slope of the line is *zero,* because the same values of Y appear for all the different values of X. Both the Y-intercept and the mean of the Y values are equal to 9.

Determining sample coefficient of determination for zero correlation Now we'll compute the two variations using Equations 10-8 and 10-9, so that we can calculate the sample coefficient of determination for this regression line. First, the variation of the Y values around the estimating line $\hat{Y} = 9$:

$$\text{Variation of the } Y \text{ values around the regression line} = \Sigma(Y - \hat{Y})^2 \quad\quad [10\text{-}8]$$

$$
\begin{aligned}
&= (\ 6 - 9)^2 = (-3)^2 = \ \ 9 \\
&+ (12 - 9)^2 = (\ \ 3)^2 = \ \ 9 \\
&+ (\ 6 - 9)^2 = (-3)^2 = \ \ 9 \\
&+ (12 - 9)^2 = (\ \ 3)^2 = \ \ 9 \\
&+ (\ 6 - 9)^2 = (-3)^2 = \ \ 9 \\
&+ (12 - 9)^2 = (\ \ 3)^2 = \ \ 9 \\
&+ (\ 6 - 9)^2 = (-3)^2 = \ \ 9 \\
&+ (12 - 9)^2 = (\ \ 3)^2 = \underline{\ \ 9} \\
&\ 72 \leftarrow \Sigma(Y - \hat{Y})^2
\end{aligned}
$$

$$\text{Variation of the } Y \text{ values around their own mean} = \Sigma(Y - \bar{Y})^2 \quad\quad [10\text{-}9]$$

$$
\begin{aligned}
&= (\ 6 - 9)^2 = (-3)^2 = \ \ 9 \\
&+ (12 - 9)^2 = (\ \ 3)^2 = \ \ 9 \\
&+ (\ 6 - 9)^2 = (-3)^2 = \ \ 9 \\
&+ (12 - 9)^2 = (\ \ 3)^2 = \ \ 9 \\
&+ (\ 6 - 9)^2 = (-3)^2 = \ \ 9 \\
&+ (12 - 9)^2 = (\ \ 3)^2 = \ \ 9 \\
&+ (\ 6 - 9)^2 = (-3)^2 = \ \ 9 \\
&+ (12 - 9)^2 = (\ \ 3)^2 = \underline{\ \ 9} \\
&\ 72 \leftarrow \Sigma(Y - \bar{Y})^2
\end{aligned}
$$

Substituting these two values into Equation 10-10, we see that the sample coefficient of determination is 0:

10 SIMPLE REGRESSION AND CORRELATION

$$r^2 = 1 - \frac{\Sigma(Y - \hat{Y})^2}{\Sigma(Y - \overline{Y})^2} \qquad \text{[10-10]}$$

$$= 1 - \frac{72}{72}$$

$$= 1 - 1$$

$$= 0 \leftarrow \text{sample coefficient of determination}$$
$$\text{when there is no correlation}$$

Thus, the value of r^2 is zero when there is no correlation.

Interpreting r^2 valuesIn the problems most decision makers encounter, r^2 will lie somewhere between these two extremes of 1 and 0. Keep in mind, however, that an r^2 close to 1 indicates a strong correlation between X and Y, while an r^2 near 0 means there is little correlation between these two variables.

One point that we must emphasize strongly is that r^2 measures only the strength of a *linear* relationship between two variables. For example, if we had a lot of X, Y points that all fell on the circumference of a circle but at randomly scattered places, clearly there would be a relationship among these points (they all lie on the same circle). But in this instance, if we computed r^2, it would turn out in fact to be close to zero, because the points do not have a *linear* relationship with each other.

INTERPRETING r^2 ANOTHER WAY

Another way to interpret the sample coefficient of determinationStatisticians also interpret the sample coefficient of determination by looking at the *amount of the variation in Y that is explained by the regression line.* To understand this meaning of r^2, consider the regression line (shown in color) in Fig. 10-15. Here, we have singled out one observed value of Y, shown as the upper black circle. If we use the mean of the Y values, $\overline{Y}$, to estimate this black-circled value of Y, then the *total deviation* of this Y from its mean would be $(Y - \overline{Y})$. Notice that if we used the regression line to estimate this black-circled value of Y we would get a better estimate.

Explained and unexplained deviationHowever, even though the regression line accounts for, or explains $(\hat{Y} - \overline{Y})$ of the total deviation, the remaining portion of the total deviation, $(Y - \hat{Y})$, is still *unexplained.*

FIGURE 10-15

Total deviation, explained deviation, and unexplained deviation for one observed value of Y

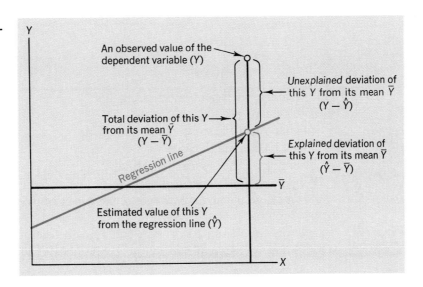

But consider a whole set of observed Y values instead of only one value. The total variation — that is, the sum of the squared total deviations — of these points from their mean would be:

$$\Sigma(Y - \overline{Y})^2 \qquad [10\text{-}9]$$

and the *explained* portion of the total variation, or the sum of the squared explained deviations of these points from their mean, would be:

$$\Sigma(\hat{Y} - \overline{Y})^2$$

The *unexplained* portion of the total variation (the sum of the squared unexplained deviations) of these points from the regression line would be:

$$\Sigma(Y - \hat{Y})^2 \qquad [10\text{-}8]$$

If we want to express the fraction of the total variation that remains *unexplained,* we would divide the unexplained variation, $\Sigma(Y - \hat{Y})^2$, by the total variation, $\Sigma(Y - \overline{Y})^2$, as follows:

$$\frac{\Sigma(Y - \hat{Y})^2}{\Sigma(Y - \overline{Y})^2} \leftarrow \text{fraction of the total variation that is unexplained}$$

and finally, if we subtract the fraction of the total variation that remains unexplained from 1, we will have the formula for finding that fraction of the total variation of Y that *is* explained by the regression line. That formula is:

$$r^2 = 1 - \frac{\Sigma(Y - \hat{Y})^2}{\Sigma(Y - \overline{Y})^2} \qquad [10\text{-}10]$$

the same equation that we have previously used to calculate r^2. It is in this sense, then, that r^2 measures how well X explains Y; that is, the degree of association between X and Y.

One final word about calculating r^2. To obtain r^2 using Equations 10-8, 10-9, and 10-10 requires a series of tedious calculations. To bypass these calculations, statisticians have developed a short-cut version, using values we would have determined already in the regression analysis. The formula is:

$$r^2 \text{ calculated by short-cut method} \longrightarrow r^2 = \frac{a\Sigma Y + b\Sigma XY - n\overline{Y}^2}{\Sigma Y^2 - n\overline{Y}^2} \qquad [10\text{-}11]$$

where:

- $r^2 =$ sample coefficient of determination
- $a = Y$-intercept
- $b =$ slope of the best-fitting estimating line
- $n =$ number of data points
- $X =$ values of the independent variable
- $Y =$ values of the dependent variable
- $\overline{Y} =$ mean of the observed values of the dependent variable

To see why this formula is a short cut, apply it to our earlier regression relating research and development expenditures to profits. In Table 10-15, we have repeated

TABLE 10-15 Calculations of Inputs for Equation 10-11

YEAR $n = 6$ (1)	RESEARCH AND DEVELOPMENT EXPENSE X (2)	ANNUAL PROFIT Y (3)	XY $(2) \times (3)$	X^2 $(2)^2$	Y^2 $(3)^2$
1989	5	31	155	25	961
1988	11	40	440	121	1,600
1987	4	30	120	16	900
1986	5	34	170	25	1,156
1985	3	25	75	9	625
1984	2	20	40	4	400
	$\Sigma X = 30$	$\Sigma Y = 180$	$\Sigma XY = 1,000$	$\Sigma X^2 = 200$	$\Sigma Y^2 = 5,642$

$$\overline{Y} = \frac{180}{6}$$

$$= 30 \leftarrow \text{mean of the values of the dependent variable}$$

the columns from Table 10-9, adding a Y^2 column. Recall that when we found the values for a and b, the regression line for this problem was:

$$\hat{Y} = 20 + 2X$$

Using this line and the information in Table 10-15, we can solve for r^2 as follows:

$$r^2 = \frac{a\Sigma Y + b\Sigma XY - n\overline{Y}^2}{\Sigma Y^2 - n\overline{Y}^2} \qquad [10\text{-}11]$$

$$= \frac{(20)(180) + (2)(1,000) - (6)(30)^2}{5,642 - (6)(30)^2}$$

$$= \frac{3,600 + 2,000 - 5,400}{5,642 - 5,400}$$

$$= \frac{200}{242}$$

$$= .826 \leftarrow \text{sample coefficient of determination}$$

Interpreting r^2 Thus, we can conclude that the variation in the research and development expenditures (the independent variable X) explains 82.6 percent of the variation in the annual profits (the dependent variable Y).

THE COEFFICIENT OF CORRELATION

Sample coefficient of correlation The coefficient of correlation is the second measure that we can use to describe how well one variable is explained by another. When we are dealing with samples, the *sample coefficient of correlation* is denoted by r and is the square root of the sample coefficient of determination:

$$r = \sqrt{r^2} \qquad [10\text{-}12]$$

When the slope of the estimating equation is positive, r is the positive square root, but if b is negative, r is the negative square root. Thus, **the sign of r indicates the direction of the relationship between the two variables X and Y.** If an inverse relationship exists—that is, if Y decreases as X increases—then r will fall between 0 and -1.

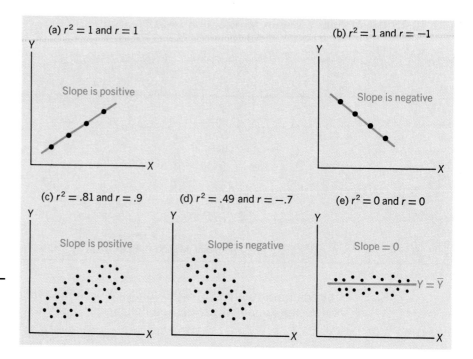

FIGURE 10-16

Various characteristics of r, the sample coefficient of correlation

Likewise, if there is a direct relationship (if Y increases as X increases), then r will be a value within the range of 0 to 1. Figure 10-16 illustrates these various characteristics of r.

Interpreting r
The coefficient of correlation is more difficult to interpret than r^2. What does $r = .9$ mean? To answer that question, we must remember that $r = .9$ is the same as $r^2 = .81$. The latter tells us that 81 percent of the variation in Y is explained by the regression line. So we see that r is nothing more than the square root of r^2, and we cannot interpret its meaning directly.

Calculating r for the research and development problem
Now let's find the coefficient of correlation of our problem relating research and development expenditures and annual profits. Since, in the previous section, we found that the sample coefficient of determination is $r^2 = .826$, we can substitute this value into Equation 10-12 and find that:

$$r = \sqrt{r^2}$$

$$= \sqrt{.826}$$

$$= .909 \leftarrow \text{sample coefficient of correlation}$$

[10-12]

The relation between the two variables is direct and the slope is positive; therefore, the sign for r is positive.

Exercises

In the following exercises, calculate the sample coefficient of determination and the sample coefficient of correlation for the problems specified.

10-25   Calculate the sample coefficient of determination and the sample coefficient of correlation for the data in exercise 10-17.

10-26 Calculate the sample coefficient of determination and the sample coefficient of correlation for the data in exercise 10-18.

10-27 Calculate the sample coefficient of determination and the sample coefficient of correlation for the data in exercise 10-19.

10-28 Calculate the sample coefficient of determination and the sample coefficient of correlation for the data in exercise 10-20.

10-29 Calculate the sample coefficient of determination and the sample coefficient of correlation for the data in exercise 10-21.

10-30 What type of correlation (positive, negative, or zero) should we expect from these variables?
(a) Ability of supervisors and output of their subordinates
(b) Age at first full-time job and number of years of education
(c) Weight and blood pressure
(d) College grade-point average and student's height

10-31 Campus Stores has been selling the *Believe It or Not: Wonders of Statistics Study Guide* for twelve semesters and would like to estimate the relationship between sales and number of sections of elementary statistics taught in each semester. The data below have been collected:

Sales (units)	33	38	24	61	52	45	65	82	29	63	50	79
Number of sections	3	7	6	6	10	12	12	13	12	13	14	15

(a) Develop the estimating equation that best fits the data.
(b) Calculate the sample coefficient of determination and the sample coefficient of correlation.

10-32 Zippy Cola is studying the effect of its latest advertising campaign. People chosen at random were called and asked how many cans of Zippy Cola they had bought in the past week and how many Zippy Cola advertisements they had either read or seen in the past week.

X (number of ads)	3	7	4	2	0	4	1	2
Y (cans purchased)	11	18	9	4	7	6	3	8

(a) Develop the estimating equation that best fits the data.
(b) Calculate the sample coefficient of determination and the sample coefficient of correlation.

10-4
Making Inferences About Population Parameters

Relationship of sample regression line and population regression line

So far, we have used regression and correlation analyses to relate two variables on the basis of sample information. But data from a sample represent only part of the total population. Because of this, we may think of our estimated sample regression line as an estimate of a true, but unknown population regression line of the form:

$$Y = A + BX \qquad [10\text{-}13]$$

Recall our discussion of the Sanitation Department director who tried to use the age of a truck to explain the annual repair expense on it. That expense will probably consist of two parts:

1. Regular maintenance that does not depend on the age of the truck: tune-ups, oil changes, and lubrication. This expense is captured in the intercept term A in Equation 10-13.

2. Expenses for repairs due to aging: relining brakes, engine and transmission overhauls, and painting. Such expenses will tend to increase with the age of the truck, and they are captured in the BX term of the population regression line $Y = A + BX$ in Equation 10-13.

Why data points do not lie exactly on the regression line

Of course, all the brakes of all the trucks will not wear out at the same time, and some of the trucks will run years without engine overhauls. Because of this, the individual data points will probably not lie exactly on the population regression line. Some will be above it; some will fall below it. So, instead of satisfying:

$$Y = A + BX \qquad\qquad [10\text{-}13]$$

the individual data points will satisfy the formula:

$$Y = A + BX + e \qquad\qquad [10\text{-}13a]$$

Random disturbance e and its behavior

where e is a random disturbance from the population regression line. On the average, e equals zero, because disturbances above the population regression line are canceled out by disturbances below the line. We can denote the standard deviation of these individual disturbances by σ_e. The standard error of estimate s_e, then, is an estimate of σ_e, the standard deviation of the disturbances.

Let us look more carefully at Equations 10-13 and 10-13a. Equation 10-13a expresses the individual values of Y (in this case, annual repair expense) in terms of (1) the individual values of X (the age of the truck), and (2) the random disturbance (e). Since disturbances above the population regression line are canceled out by those below the line, we know that the expected value of e is zero, and we see that if we had several trucks of the same age, X, we would expect the average annual repair expense on these trucks to be $Y = A + BX$. This shows us that the population regression line (Equation 10-13) gives the mean value of Y associated with each value of X.

Making inferences about B from b

Since our *sample* regression line, $\hat{Y} = a + bX$ (Equation 10-3), estimates the *population* regression line, $Y = A + BX$ (Equation 10-13), we should be able to use it to make inferences about the population regression line. In this section then, we shall make inferences about the slope B of the "true" regression equation (the one for the entire population) that are based upon the slope b of the regression equation estimated from a sample of values.

SLOPE OF THE POPULATION REGRESSION LINE

Difference between true regression equation and one estimated from sample observations

The regression line is derived from a sample and not from the entire population. As a result, we cannot expect the true regression equation, $Y = A + BX$ (the one for the entire population), to be exactly the same as the equation estimated from the sample observations, or $\hat{Y} = a + bX$. Even so, we can use the value of b, the slope we calculate from a sample, to test hypotheses about the value of the B, the slope of the regression line for the entire population.

Testing a hypothesis about B

The procedure for testing a hypothesis about B is similar to procedures discussed in Chapter 8, on hypothesis testing. To understand this process, return to the problem that related annual expenditures for research and development to profits. On page 494, we pointed out that $b = 2$. The first step is to find some value for B to compare with $b = 2$.

Suppose that over an extended past period of time, the slope of the relationship between X and Y was 2.1. To test if this were still the case, we could define the hypotheses as:

$$H_0: B = 2.1 \leftarrow \text{null hypothesis}$$

$$H_1: B \neq 2.1 \leftarrow \text{alternative hypothesis}$$

In effect, then, we are testing to learn whether current data indicate that B has changed from its historical value of 2.1.

Standard error of the regression coefficient

To find the test statistic for B, it is necessary first to find the *standard error of the regression coefficient*. Here, the regression coefficient we are working with is b, so the standard error of this coefficient is denoted s_b. Equation 10-14 presents the mathematical formula for s_b:

Standard error of the regression coefficient

$$s_b = \frac{s_e}{\sqrt{\Sigma X^2 - n\overline{X}^2}} \qquad [10\text{-}14]$$

where:

- s_b = standard error of the regression coefficient
- s_e = standard error of estimate
- X = values of the independent variable
- $\overline{X}$ = mean of the values of the independent variable
- n = number of data points

Finding upper and lower limits of the acceptance region for our hypothesis test

Once we have calculated s_b, we can use the t distribution with $n - 2$ degrees of freedom and the following equation to calculate the upper and lower limits of the acceptance region:

$$\left. \begin{array}{l} \text{Upper limit of acceptance region} = B + t(s_b) \\ \text{Lower limit of acceptance region} = B - t(s_b) \end{array} \right\} \qquad [10\text{-}15]$$

where:

- t = appropriate t value (with $n - 2$ degrees of freedom) for the significance level of the test
- B = actual slope hypothesized for the population
- s_b = standard error of the regression coefficient

Of course, for a one-tailed test, you would calculate only an upper or lower limit as appropriate.

A glance at Table 10-15 on page 511 enables us to calculate the values of ΣX^2 and $n\bar{X}^2$. To obtain s_e, we can take the short-cut method, as follows:

Calculating s_e

$$s_e = \sqrt{\frac{\Sigma Y^2 - a\Sigma Y - b\Sigma XY}{n - 2}} \qquad [10\text{-}7]$$

$$= \sqrt{\frac{5{,}642 - (20)(180) - (2)(1{,}000)}{6 - 2}}$$

$$= \sqrt{\frac{42}{4}}$$

$$= \sqrt{10.5}$$

$$= 3.24 \leftarrow \text{standard error of estimate}$$

Now we can determine the standard error of the regression coefficient:

Calculating s_b

$$s_b = \frac{s_e}{\sqrt{\Sigma X^2 - n\bar{X}^2}} \qquad [10\text{-}14]$$

$$= \frac{3.24}{\sqrt{200 - (6)(5)^2}}$$

$$= \frac{3.24}{\sqrt{50}}$$

$$= \frac{3.24}{7.07}$$

$$= .46 \leftarrow \text{standard error of the regression coefficient}$$

Conducting the
hypothesis test

Suppose we have reason to test our hypothesis at the 10 percent level of signifi-cance. Since we have six observations in our sample data, we know that we have $n - 2$ or $6 - 2 = 4$ degress of freedom. We look in Appendix Table 2 under the 10 percent column and come down until we find the 4-degrees-of-freedom row. There, we see that the appropriate t value is 2.132. Since we are concerned whether b (the slope of the sample regression line) is significantly *different* from B (the hypothesized slope of the population regression line), this is a two-tailed test, and the limits of the accept-ance region are found using Equation 10-15:

$$B + t(s_b) = 2.1 + 2.132(0.46)$$
$$= 3.081 \leftarrow \text{upper limit of acceptance region}$$

$$B - t(s_b) = 2.1 - 2.132(0.46)$$
$$= 1.119 \leftarrow \text{lower limit of acceptance region}$$

The slope of our regression line (b) is 2.0, which is *inside* the acceptance region. Therefore, we accept the null hypothesis that B still equals 2.1. In other words, there is not enough difference between b and 2.1 for us to conclude that B has changed from its historical value. Because of this, we feel that each additional million dollars spent on research and development still increases annual profits by about $2.1 million, as it has in the past.

In addition to hypothesis testing, we can also construct a *confidence interval* for the value of B. In the same way that b is a point estimate of B, such confidence intervals are interval estimates of B. The problem we just completed, and for which we did a hypothesis test, will illustrate the process of constructing a confidence interval. There, we found that:

$$b = 2.0$$

$$s_b = 0.46$$

$$t = 2.132 \leftarrow \text{10\% level of significance and 4 degrees of freedom}$$

Confidence interval for B   With this information, we can calculate confidence intervals like this:

$$b + t(s_b) = 2 + (2.132)(.46)$$
$$= 2 + .981$$
$$= 2.981 \leftarrow \text{upper limit}$$

$$b - t(s_b) = 2 - (2.132)(.46)$$
$$= 2 - .981$$
$$= 1.019 \leftarrow \text{lower limit}$$

Interpreting the confidence interval   In this situation, then, we are 90 percent confident that the true value of B lies between 1.019 and 2.981; that is, each additional million dollars spent on research and development increases annual profits by some amount between \$1.02 million and \$2.98 million.

Exercises

10-33   In finance, it is of interest to look at the relationship between Y, a stock's average return, and X, the overall market return. The slope coefficient computed by linear regression is called the stock's *beta* by investment analysts. A beta greater than 1 indicates that the stock is relatively sensitive to changes in the market, while a beta less than 1 indicates that the stock is relatively insensitive. For the data below, compute the beta and test to see if it is significantly less than 1. Use $\alpha = .05$.

Y (%)	10	12	8	15	9	11	8	10	13	11
X (%)	11	15	3	18	10	12	6	7	18	13

10-34   In a regression problem with a sample size of 17, the slope was found to be 3.73 and the standard error of estimate 28.654. The quantity $(\Sigma X^2 - n\overline{X}^2) = 871.56$.
(a)   Find the standard error of the regression slope coefficient.
(b)   Construct a 98 percent confidence interval for the population slope.
(c)   Interpret the above confidence interval.

10-35   A broker for a local investment firm has been studying the relationship between increases in the price of gold (X) and her customers' requests to liquidate stocks (Y). From a data set based on fifteen observations, the sample slope was found to be 2.9. If the standard error of the regression slope coefficient is 0.18, is there reason to believe (at the .05 significance level) that the slope has changed from its past value of 3.2?

10-36   For a sample of 25, the slope was found to be 1.685 and the standard error of the regression coefficient was .11. Is there reason to believe that the slope has changed from its past value of 1.50? Use the .05 significance level.

10-37 Realtors are often interested in seeing how the appraised value of a home varies according to the size of the home. Below are some data on area (in thousands of square feet) and appraised value (in thousands of dollars) for a sample of eleven homes.

Area	1.1	1.5	1.6	1.6	1.4	1.3	1.1	1.7	1.9	1.5	1.3
Value	75	95	110	102	95	87	82	115	122	98	90

(a) Estimate the least squares regression to predict appraised value from size.
(b) Generally, realtors feel that a home's value goes up by $50,000 (= 50 thousands of dollars) for every additional 1,000 square feet in area. For this sample, does this relationship seem to hold? Use $\alpha = .10$.

10-38 In 1969, a government health agency found that in a number of counties, the relationship between smokers and heart disease fatalities per 100,000 population had a slope of .08. A recent study of eighteen counties produced a slope of .147 and a standard error of the regression slope coefficient of 0.032.
(a) Construct a 90 percent confidence interval estimate of the slope of the true regression line. Does the result from this study indicate that the true slope has changed?
(b) Construct a 99 percent confidence interval estimate of the slope of the true regression line. Does the result from this study indicate that the true slope has changed?

10-39 The local phone company has always assumed that the average number of daily phone calls goes up by 1.5 for each additional person in a household. It has been suggested that people are more talkative than this. A sample of 64 households was taken, and the slope of the regression of Y (average number of daily phone calls) on X (size of household) was computed to be 1.8 with a standard error of the regression slope coefficient of 0.2. Test if significantly more calls per additional person are being made than the phone company assumes, using $\alpha = .05$. State explicit hypotheses and an explicit conclusion.

10-40 College admissions officers are constantly seeking variables with which to predict grade-point averages for applicants. One commonly used variable is high school grade-point average. For one college, past data indicated that the slope was 0.85. A recent small study of 20 students found that the sample slope was 0.70 and the standard error of estimate was 0.60. The quantity $(\Sigma X^2 - n\overline{X}^2)$ was equal to 0.25. At the .01 level of significance, should the college conclude that the slope has changed?

10-5

Using Regression and Correlation Analyses: Limitations, Errors, and Caveats

Misuse of regression and correlation

Regression and correlation analyses are statistical tools that, when properly used, can significantly help people make decisions. Unfortunately, they are frequently misused. As a result, decision makers often make inaccurate forecasts and less-than-desirable decisions. We'll mention the most common errors made in the use of regression and correlation in the hope that you will avoid them.

EXTRAPOLATION BEYOND THE RANGE OF THE OBSERVED DATA

Specific limited range over which regression equation holds

A common mistake is to assume that the estimating line can be applied over any range of values. Hospital administrators can properly use regression analysis to predict the relationship between costs per bed and occupancy levels at various occupancy levels. Some administrators, however, incorrectly use the same regression equation to predict the costs per bed for occupancy levels that are significantly higher than those that were used to estimate the regression line. Although one relationship holds over the range of sample points, an entirely different relationship may exist for a different range. As a result, these people make decisions on one set of costs and find that the costs change drastically as occupancy increases (owing to things such as overtime costs and capacity constraints). Remember that **an estimating equation is valid only over the same range as the one from which the sample was taken initially.**

CAUSE AND EFFECT

Regression and correlation analyses do not determine cause and effect

Another mistake we can make when we use regression analysis is to assume that a change in one variable is "caused" by a change in the other variable. As we discussed earlier, **regression and correlation analyses can in no way determine cause and effect.** If we say that there is a correlation between students' grades in college and their annual earnings 5 years after graduation, we are *not* saying that one causes the other. Rather, both may be caused by other factors, such as sociological background, parental attitudes, quality of teachers, effectiveness of the job-interviewing process, and economic status of parents—to name only a few potential factors.

We have extensively used the example about research and development expenses and annual profits to illustrate various aspects of regression analysis. But it is really highly unlikely that profits in a given year are *caused* by R&D expenditures in that year. Certainly it would be foolhardy for the VP for R&D to suggest to the chief executive that profits could immediately be increased merely by increasing R&D expenditures. Particularly in high-technology industries, the R&D activity can be used to explain profits, but a better way to do so would be to predict current profits in terms of past research and development expenditures as well as in terms of economic conditions, dollars spent on advertising, and other variables. This can be done by using the multiple regression techniques to be discussed in the next chapter.

USING PAST TRENDS TO ESTIMATE FUTURE TRENDS

Conditions change and invalidate the regression equation

We must take care to reappraise the historical data we use to estimate the regression equation. Conditions can change and violate one or more of the assumptions on which our regression analysis depends. Earlier in this chapter, we made the point that we assume that the variance of the disturbance e around the mean is constant. In many situations, however, this variance changes from year to year.

Values of variables change over time

Another error that can arise from the use of historical data concerns the dependence of some variables on time. Suppose a firm uses regression analysis to determine the relationship between the number of employees and the production volume. If the observations used in the analysis extend back for several years, the resulting regression line may be too steep, because it may fail to recognize the effect of changing technology.

MISINTERPRETING THE COEFFICIENTS OF CORRELATION AND DETERMINATION

Misinterpreting r and r^2

The coefficient of correlation is occasionally misinterpreted as a percentage. If $r = .6$, it is incorrect to state that the regression equation "explains" 60 percent of the total variation in Y. Instead, if $r = .6$, then r^2 must be $.6 \times .6 = .36$. Only 36 percent of the total variation is explained by the regression line.

The coefficient of determination is misinterpreted if we use r^2 to describe the percentage of the change in the dependent variable that is *caused* by a change in the independent variable. This is wrong because r^2 is a measure only of how well one variable describes another, *not* of how much of the change in one variable is caused by the other variable.

FINDING RELATIONSHIPS WHEN THEY DO NOT EXIST

Relationships that have no common bond

When applying regression analysis, people sometimes find a relationship between two variables that, in fact, have no common bond. Even though one variable does not "cause" a change in the other, they think that there must be some factor common to both variables. It might be possible, for example, to find a statistical relationship between a random sample of the number of miles per gallon consumed by eight different cars and the distance from earth to each of the other eight planets. But since there is absolutely no common bond between gas mileage and the distance to other planets, this "relationship" would be meaningless.

Finding things that do not exist

In this regard, if one were to run a large number of regressions between many pairs of variables, it would probably be possible to get some rather interesting suggested "relationships." It might be possible, for example, to find a high statistical relationship between your income and the amount of beer that is consumed in the United States, or even between the length of a freight train (in cars) and the weather. But in neither case is there a factor common to both variables; hence, such "relationships" are meaningless. As in most other statistical situations, it takes *both* knowledge of the inherent limitations of the technique that is used *and* a large dose of common sense to avoid coming to unwarranted conclusions.

Exercises

10-41 Explain why an estimating equation is valid over only the range of values used for its development.

10-42 Explain the difference between the coefficient of determination and the coefficient of correlation.

10-43 Why should we be cautious in using past data to predict future trends?

10-44 Why must we not attribute causality in a relationship even when there is strong correlation between the variables or events?

10-6
Terms Introduced in Chapter 10

Coefficient of Correlation The square root of the coefficient of determination. Its sign indicates the direction of the relationship between two variables, direct or inverse.

Coefficient of Determination A measure of the proportion of variation in Y, the dependent variable,

that is explained by the regression line; i.e., by Y's relationship with the independent variable.

Correlation Analysis A technique to determine the degree to which variables are linearly related.

Curvilinear Relationship An association between two variables that is described by a curved line.

Dependent Variable The variable we are trying to predict in regression analysis.

Direct Relationship A relationship between two variables in which, as the independent variable's value increases, so does the value of the dependent variable.

Estimating Equation A mathematical formula that relates the unknown variable to the known variables in regression analysis.

Independent Variables The known variable, or variables, in regression analysis.

Inverse Relationship A relationship between two variables in which, as the independent variable increases, the dependent variable decreases.

Least Squares Method A technique for fitting a straight line through a set of points in such a way that the sum of the squared vertical distances from the n points to the line is minimized.

Linear Relationship A particular type of association between two variables that can be described mathematically by a straight line.

Multiple Regression The statistical process by which several variables are used to predict another variable.

Regression The general process of predicting one variable from another by statistical means, using previous data.

Regression Line A line fitted to a set of data points to estimate the relationship between two variables.

Scatter Diagram A graph of points on a rectangular grid; the X and Y coordinates of each point correspond to the two measurements made on some particular sample element, and the pattern of points illustrates the relationship between the two variables.

Slope A constant for any given straight line, whose value represents how much each unit change of the independent variable changes the dependent variable.

Standard Error of Estimate A measure of the reliability of the estimating equation, indicating the variability of the observed points around the regression line; i.e., the extent to which observed values differ from their predicted values on the regression line.

Standard Error of the Regression Coefficient A measure of the variability of sample regression coefficients around the true population regression coefficient.

Y-Intercept A constant for any given straight line, whose value represents the value of the Y variable when the X variable has a value of 0.

10-7
Equations Introduced in Chapter 10

[10-1]
$$Y = a + bX$$
p. 485

This is the equation for a *straight line* where the dependent variable Y is "determined" by the independent variable X. The a is called the *Y-intercept* because its value is the point at which the line crosses the Y-axis (the vertical axis). The b is the *slope* of the line; that is, it tells how much each unit change of the independent variable X changes the dependent variable Y. Both a and b are numerical constants, since for any given straight line, their values do not change.

[10-2]
$$b = \frac{Y_2 - Y_1}{X_2 - X_1}$$
p. 486

To calculate the numerical constant b for any given line, find the value of the coordinates, X and Y, for two points that lie on the line. The coordinates of the first point are (X_1, Y_1) and the second point (X_2, Y_2). Remember that b is the slope of the line.

[10-3]
$$\hat{Y} = a + bX$$
p. 488

In regression analysis, $\hat{Y}$ (*Y-hat*) symbolizes the individual Y values of the *estimated* points; that is, those points that lie on the estimating line. Accordingly, Equation 10-3 is the equation for the estimating line.

[10-4]

$$b = \frac{\Sigma XY - n\overline{X}\,\overline{Y}}{\Sigma X^2 - n\overline{Y}^2}$$

p. 491

The equation enables us to calculate the *slope of the best-fitting regression line* for any two-variable set of data points. We introduce two new symbols in this equation, $\overline{X}$ and $\overline{Y}$, which represent the means of the values of the independent variable and the dependent variable, respectively. In addition, this equation contains n, which, in this case, represents the number of data points to which we are fitting the regression line.

[10-5]

$$a = \overline{Y} - b\overline{X}$$

p. 492

Using this formula, we can compute the *Y-intercept of the best-fitting regression line* for any two-variable set of data points.

[10-6]

$$s_e = \sqrt{\frac{\Sigma(Y - \hat{Y})^2}{n - 2}}$$

p. 497

The *standard error of estimate, s_e,* measures the variability or scatter of the observed values around the regression line. In effect it indicates the reliability of the estimating equation. The denominator is $n - 2$ because we lose 2 degrees of freedom (for the values a and b) in estimating the regression line.

[10-7]

$$s_e = \sqrt{\frac{\Sigma Y^2 - a\Sigma Y - b\Sigma XY}{n - 2}}$$

p. 498

Since Equation 10-6 requires tedious calculations, statisticians have devised this *short-cut method for finding the standard error of estimate.* In calculating the values for b and a, we have already calculated every quantity in Equation 10-7 except ΣY^2, which we can do easily.

[10-8]

Variation of the Y values around the regression line $= \Sigma(Y - \hat{Y})^2$ *p. 505*

The variation of the Y values in a data set around the fitted regression line is one of two quantities from which the sample coefficient of determination is developed. Equation 10-8 shows how to measure this particular dispersion, which is the *unexplained* portion of the total variation.

[10-9]

Variation of the Y values around their own mean $= \Sigma(Y - \overline{Y})^2$ *p. 505*

This formula measures the *total variation* of a whole set of Y values; that is, the dispersion of these Y values around their own mean.

[10-10]

$$r^2 = 1 - \frac{\Sigma(Y - \hat{Y})^2}{\Sigma(Y - \overline{Y})^2}$$

p. 505

The *sample coefficient of determination, r^2,* gives the fraction of the total variation of Y that is explained by the regression line. It is an important measure of the degree of association between X and Y. If the value of r^2 is $+1$, then the regression line is a perfect estimator. If $r^2 = 0$, there is no correlation between X and Y.

[10-11]

$$r^2 = \frac{a\Sigma Y + b\Sigma XY - n\overline{Y}^2}{\Sigma Y^2 - n\overline{Y}^2}$$

p. 510

This is a short-cut equation for calculating r^2.

[10-12]
$$r = \sqrt{r^2}$$
p. 511

The *sample coefficient of correlation* is denoted by r and is found by taking the square root of the sample coefficient of determination. It is a second measure (in addition to r^2) we can use to describe how well one variable is explained by another. The sign of r is the same as the sign of b; it indicates the direction of the relationship between the two variables X and Y.

[10-13]
$$Y = A + BX$$
p. 513

Each *population regression line* is of the form in Equation 10-13, where A is the Y-intercept for the population, and B is the slope.

[10-13a]
$$Y = A + BX + e$$
p. 514

Because all the individual points in a population do not lie on the population regression line, the *individual* data points will satisfy Formula 10-13a, where e is a random disturbance from the population regression line. On the average, e equals zero, because disturbances above the population regression line are canceled out by disturbances below it.

[10-14]
$$s_b = \frac{s_e}{\sqrt{\Sigma X^2 - n\overline{X}^2}}$$
p. 515

When we are dealing with a sample, we can use this formula to find the *standard error of the regression coefficient, b.*

[10-15]
$$\text{Upper limit of acceptance region} = B + t(s_b)$$
$$\text{Lower limit of acceptance region} = B - t(s_b)$$
p. 515

Once we have calculated s_b using Equation 10-14, we can determine the upper and lower limits of the acceptance region for a hypothesis test using this pair of equations.

10-8
Chapter Review Exercises

 10-45 A consultant is interested in seeing how accurately a new job performance index measures what is important for a corporation. One way to check is to look at the relationship between the job evaluation index and an employee's salary. A sample of eight employees was taken, and information about salary (in thousands of dollars) and job performance index (1 – 10; 10 is best) was collected.

Job Performance Index (X)	9	7	8	4	7	5	5	6
Salary (Y)	36	25	33	15	28	19	20	22

(a) Develop an estimating equation that best describes these data.
(b) Calculate the standard error of estimate, s_e, for these data.
(c) Calculate the sample coefficient of determination, r^2, for these data.

10-46 The Stork Foundation wishes to show that, contrary to popular belief, storks *do* bring babies. They would like to prove their point with statistics. Thus, they have collected data on the number of storks and the number of babies (both in thousands) in several large cities in central Europe.

Storks	27	38	13	24	6	19	15
Babies	35	46	19	32	15	31	20

(a) Compute the sample coefficient of determination and sample correlation coefficient.
(b) Has statistical science disproved popular belief?

10-47 (Fill in the blanks.) Regression and correlation analyses deal with the _____ between variables. Regression analysis, through _____ equations, enables us to _____ an unknown variable from a set of known variables. The unknown variable is called the _____ variable; known variables are referred to as _____ variables. The correlation between two variables indicates the _____ of the linear relationship between them and thus gives an idea of how well the _____ _____ in regression describes the relationship between the variables.

10-48 Calculate the sample coefficient of determination and the sample correlation coefficient for exercise 10-14.

10-49 The president of Wonx Computers is interested in studying the relationship between the size of the annual raise and the performance of a sales representative over the subsequent year. He sampled twelve sales representatives and determined the sizes of their respective raises (given as a percentage of their individual salaries) and the number of sales made by each one during the 12 months following raises.

Size of raise	7.8	6.9	6.7	6.0	6.9	5.2	6.3	8.4	7.2	10.1	10.8	7.7
Number of sales	64	73	42	49	71	46	32	88	53	84	85	93

(a) Develop the best-fitting estimating equation that describes these data.
(b) Calculate the standard error of estimate for this relationship.
(c) Develop an approximate 90 percent confidence interval for the number of sales made by a salesperson after receiving a 9.6 percent raise.

10-50 For each of the following pairs of plots, state which has a higher value of r, the correlation coefficient, and what the sign of r is:

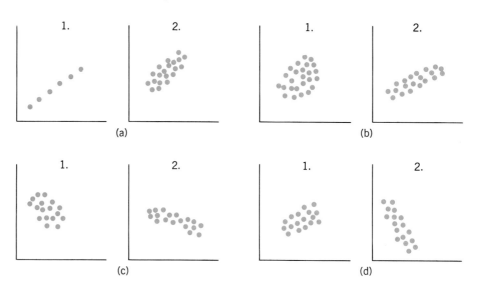

10-51 An operations manager is interested in predicting costs C (in thousands of dollars) based on the amount of raw material input R (in hundreds of pounds) for a jeans manufacturer. If the slope is significantly greater than 0.5 in the sample data below, then there is something wrong with the production process and the assembly line machinery should be adjusted. At the .05 significance level, should the machinery be adjusted? State explicit hypotheses and an explicit conclusion.

C	10	7	5	6	7	6
R	25	20	16	17	19	18

10-52 Calculate the sample coefficient of determination and the sample correlation coefficient for exercise 10-13.

10-53 We should not extrapolate to predict values outside the range of data used in constructing the regression line. The reason (choose one):
(a) The relationship between the variables may not be the same for different values of the variables.
(b) The independent variable may not have the causal effect on the dependent variable for these values.
(c) The variables' values may change over time.
(d) There may be no common bond to explain the relationship.

10-54 Economists are often interested in estimating consumption functions. This is done by regressing consumption Y on income X. (For this regression, economists call the slope the *marginal propensity to consume.*) For a sample of 25 families, a slope of .87 and a standard error of the regression slope coefficient of .035 were computed. For this sample, has the marginal propensity to consume decreased below the standard of .94? Use $\alpha = .05$. State explicit hypotheses and an explicit conclusion.

10-55 Unlike the coefficient of determination, the coefficient of correlation (choose one):
(a) Indicates whether the slope of the regression line is positive or negative.
(b) Measures the strength of association between the two variables more exactly.
(c) Can never have an absolute value greater than 1.
(d) Measures the percentage of variance explained by the regression line.

10-56 Are good grades in college important for earning a good salary? A business statistics student has taken a random sample of starting salaries and college grade-point averages for some recently graduated friends of his. The data are below:

Starting salary (thousands)	36	30	30	24	27	33	21	27
Grade-point average	4.0	3.0	3.5	2.0	3.0	3.5	2.5	2.5

(a) Plot these data.
(b) Develop the estimating equation that best describes these data.
(c) Plot the estimating equation on the scatter plot of part (a).

10-57 A landlord is interested in seeing if his apartment rents are typical. Thus, he has taken a random sample of eleven rents and apartment sizes of similar apartment complexes. The data are below.

Rent	230	190	450	310	218	185	340	245	125	350	280
Number of bedrooms	2	1	3	2	2	2	2	1	1	2	2

(a) Develop an estimating equation that best describes these data.
(b) Calculate the coefficient of determination.
(c) Predict the rent for a two-bedroom apartment.

10-58 The Dipit Donut chain has experienced large fluctuations in revenue over the last several years. Numerous specials, new products, and advertising techniques have been employed during this time, so it is difficult to determine which devices have had the strongest influence on sales. The marketing department has studied a variety of relationships and believes that the monthly expenditures on billboards may be significant. It sampled 7 months and determined the following:

Monthly expenditure on billboards (×$1,000)	25	16	42	34	10	21	19
Monthly sales revenue (×$100,000)	34	14	48	32	26	29	20

(a) Develop an estimating equation that best describes these data.
(b) Calculate the standard error of estimate for this relationship.
(c) For a month with a billboard expenditure of $28,000, develop an approximate 95 percent confidence interval for the expected monthly sales for that month.

10-59 In a CAB study of airline operations, a survey of eighteen companies disclosed that the relationship between the number of pilots employed and the number of planes in service has a slope of 4.3. Previous studies indicated that the slope of this relationship was 4.0. If the standard error of the regression slope coefficient has been calculated to be .17, is there reason to believe, at the .05 level of significance, that the true slope has changed?

10-60 Dave Proffitt, a second year MBA student, is doing a study of companies going public for the first time. He is curious to see whether or not there is a significant relationship between the size of the offering (in millions of dollars) and the price-per-share.
(a) Given the following data, develop the estimating equation that best fits the data.

SIZE ($MILLIONS)	PRICE
108.00	12.00
4.40	4.00
3.50	5.00
3.60	6.00
39.00	13.00
68.40	19.00
7.50	8.50
5.50	5.00
375.00	15.00
12.00	6.00
51.00	12.00
66.00	12.00
10.40	6.50
4.00	3.00

(b) Calculate the sample coefficient of determination. Should Dave use this regression equation for predictive purposes, or search elsewhere for additional explanatory variables?

10-61 Electronic Widgets, Inc. is test-marketing a new product — a battery-operated radar detector. Their testing laboratories have performed limited testing on the units and have collected the following data.

HOURS OF DAILY USE	APPROXIMATE LIFE (MONTHS) LITHIUM	ALKALINE
2.0	3.1	1.3
1.5	4.2	1.6
1.0	5.1	1.8
0.5	6.3	2.2

(a) Develop two linear estimating equations, one to predict product life based on daily use with lithium batteries, one for alkaline batteries.

(b) Predict an approximate 90 percent confidence interval of the life (in months) for 1.25 hours of daily use, for each battery type. Can the company make any claims about which battery will provide a longer life based on these numbers?

10-62 A study has been proposed to investigate the relationship between the birthweight of male babies and their adult height. Using the following data, develop the least squares estimating equation. What percentage of variation is explained by this regression line?

BIRTHWEIGHT	ADULT HEIGHT
5 lb 8 oz	5′ 9″
7 lb	6′
6 lb 4 oz	5′ 6″
7 lb 8 oz	5′ 11″
8 lb 2 oz	6′ 1″
6 lb 12 oz	5′ 10″

10-63 Many college students transfer in the summers before their junior years. To aid in evaluating the academic potential of these junior transfers, Barbara Hoopes, the Dean of Admissions at Piedmont College, is conducting an analysis that compares students' grade point averages (GPAs) during their first two years of college with their GPAs during their final two years, after transferring. Using the data below

Freshman/sophomore GPA	1.7	3.5	2.3	2.6	3.0	2.8	2.4	1.9	2.0	3.1
Junior/senior GPA	2.4	3.7	2.0	2.5	3.2	3.0	2.5	1.8	2.7	3.7

(a) Calculate the least squares estimating equation Hoopes should use to predict junior/senior GPAs for students transferring to Piedmont College.

(b) Hoopes will not admit junior-transfer applicants unless approximate 90 percent prediction intervals for their junior/senior GPAs fall entirely above 2.0. Will she admit a transfer applicant with a 2.5 freshman/sophomore GPA?

10-9
Chapter Concepts Test

Answers are in the back of the book.

T F   1. Regression analysis is used to describe how well an estimating equation describes the relationship being studied.

T F   2. Given that the equation for a line is $Y = 26 - 24X$, we may say that the relationship of Y to X is direct linear.

T F   3. An r^2 value close to zero indicates a strong correlation between X and Y.

T F   4. Regression and correlation analyses are used to determine cause-and-effect relationships.

T F   5. The sample coefficient of correlation, r, is nothing more than $\sqrt{r^2}$, and we cannot interpret its meaning directly as a percentage of some kind.

T F   6. The standard error of estimate measures the variability of the observed values around the regression equation.

T F   7. The regression line is derived from a sample and not the entire population.

T F   8. We may interpret the sample coefficient of determination as the amount of the variation in Y that is explained by the regression line.

T F 9. Lines drawn on either side of the regression line at ± 1, ± 2 and ± 3 times the value of the standard error of estimate are called confidence lines.

T F 10. The estimating equation is valid over only the same range as that given by the original sample data upon which it was developed.

T F 11. In the equation $Y = a + bX$ for dependent variable Y and independent variable X, the Y-intercept is b.

T F 12. If a line is fitted to a set of points by the method of least squares, the individual positive and negative errors from the line sum to zero.

T F 13. If $s_e = 0$ for an estimating equation, it must perfectly estimate the dependent variable at the observed points.

T F 14. Suppose the slope of an estimating equation is positive. Then the value of r must be the positive square root of r^2.

T F 15. If $r = .8$, then the regression equation explains 80 percent of the total variation in the dependent variable.

T F 16. The coefficient of correlation is the percentage of the total variation of the dependent variable that is explained by the regression.

T F 17. The standard error of estimate is measured perpendicularly from the regression line rather than on the Y-axis.

T F 18. By squaring individual errors, the least squares method magnifies all deviations from the estimated regression line.

T F 19. A regression equation may not be valid when extended outside the sample range of the independent variable.

T F 20. An r^2 value measures only the strength of a linear relationship between the two variables X and Y.

T F 21. A small value of r^2 implies that there is not a significant cause-effect relationship between X and Y.

22. Suppose that we know the height of a student but do not know her weight. We use an estimating equation to determine an estimate of her weight based upon her height. We can therefore surmise that:
    (a) Weight is the independent variable.
    (b) Height is the dependent variable.
    (c) The relationship between weight and height is an inverse one.
    (d) None of these.
    (e) b and c but not a.

23. Suppose you are told that there is a direct relationship between the price of artichokes and the amount of rain that fell during the growing season. It can be concluded that:
    (a) Prices tend to be high when rainfall is high.
    (b) Prices tend to be low when rainfall is high.
    (c) A large amount of rain causes prices to rise.
    (d) A lack of rain causes prices to rise.

24. Suppose it is calculated that a is 4 and b is 2 for a particular estimating line with one independent variable. If the independent variable has a value of 2, what value should be expected for the dependent variable?
    (a) 8   (b) 10   (c) -1 (d) 0

25. Suppose the estimating equation $\hat{Y} = 5 - 2X$ has been calculated for a set of data. Which of the following is true for this situation?
    (a) The Y-intercept of the line is 2.
    (b) The slope of the line is negative.
    (c) The line represents an inverse relationship.
    (d) All of these.   (e) b and c but not a.

26. We know that the standard error is the same at all points on a regression line because we assumed that:
    (a) Observed values for Y are normally distributed around each estimated value of $\hat{Y}$.
    (b) The variance of the distributions around each possible value of $\hat{Y}$ is the same.
    (c) All available data were taken into account when the regression line was calculated.
    (d) None of these.

27. The variation of the Y values around the regression line is best expressed as:
    (a) $\Sigma(Y + \overline{Y})^2$ (b) $\Sigma(Y - \overline{Y})^2$ (c) $\Sigma(Y - \hat{Y})^2$ (d) $\Sigma(Y + \hat{Y})^2$

28. The value of r^2 for a particular situation is .49. What is the coefficient of correlation in this situation?
    (a) .49   (c) .07
    (b) .7   (d) Cannot be determined from information given

29. The fraction $\dfrac{\Sigma(Y - \hat{Y})^2}{\Sigma(Y - \overline{Y})^2}$ represents:
    (a) Fraction of total variation in Y that is unexplained
    (b) Fraction of total variation in Y that is explained
    (c) Fraction of total variation in Y that was caused by changes in X
    (d) None of these

30. In the equation $Y = A + BX + e$, the e represents:
    (a) The X-intercept of the observed data
    (b) The value of Y to which others are compared to determine the "best fit"
    (c) Random disturbances from the population regression line
    (d) None of these

31. Suppose you wish to compare the hypothesized value of B to a sample value of b that has been calculated. Which of the following *must* be calculated before the others?
    (a) s_b (c) s_p
    (b) s_e (d) Calculations can be made in any order.

31. For the estimating equation to be a perfect estimator of the dependent variable, which of these would have to be true?
    (a) The standard error of the estimate is zero.
    (b) All the data points are on the regression line.
    (c) The coefficient of determination is -1.
    (d) a and b but not c.
    (e) All of these.

33. If the dependent variable increases as the independent variable increases in an estimating equation, the coefficient of correlation will be in the range:
    (a) 0 to -1 (b) 0 to $-.5$ (c) 0 to -2 (d) None of these

34. Suppose the fraction of variation in Y that is unexplained by the independent variable X is ¼. Then r^2 is:
    (a) ¼
    (b) ¾
    (c) $15/16$
    (d) none of the above

35. The sample coefficient of determination is developed from the variation of the observed Y values around:
    (a) the mean of the observed independent variables
    (b) the mean of the observed dependent variables
    (c) the fitted regression line
    (d) b and c but not a
    (e) a, b, and c

36. If $Y = a + bX$, the sample regression line, and $Y = A + BX$, the true unknown population regression equation, are equivalent, then the following must be true:

(a) the estimating equation is a perfect estimator of the dependent variable
(b) all the data points are on the regression line
(c) $r^2 = 1$
(d) all of the above
(e) none of the above

37. If the dependent variable in a relationship decreases as the independent variable increases, the relationship is _____.

38. An association between two variables that is described by a curved line is a _____ one.

39. Every straight line has a _____, which represents how much each change of the independent variable changes the dependent variable.

40. The extent to which observed values differ from their predicted values on the regression line is measured by the _____.

41. _____ is a measure of the proportion of variation in the dependent variable that is explained by the regression line.

42. If 75 percent of the variation in the dependent variable is explained by the regression line, then the value of r will be about _____.

43. _____ is used to measure how well the regression line explains the variation of the dependent variable.

44. The sign of r indicates the _____ of the relationship between the two variables X and Y.

45. The method of least squares finds the "best fit" line through a set of points, that is the line which _____ the error between the observed points and the estimated points on the line.

10-10
Conceptual Case

(Northern White Metals Company)

By December 1982, Dick felt that most of Northern's immediate difficulties had been taken care of. Except for an occasional problem, production and shipping operations were running quite smoothly. Sales had continued to climb steadily, and costs seemed to be under control. The end of Dick's first full year at Northern saw the company achieve record profits.

The company began 1983 with employee morale high. The past year's success and the bonus reward that went along with it generated an enthusiasm the firm had not seen in years. It was with this spirit that the January production meeting started. Goals and manufacturing improvements were discussed and an overall production plan established.

A small, but potentially very profitable, component of this plan was the introduction of an idea suggested by Northern's production supervisor, M. J. Sabeau. M. J. had been approached a week earlier by Tar Reid, the stooped and wizened proprietor of Reid's Recycling, Inc. Reid, a scrap hauler of some renown, had suggested that his company purchase all of Northern's scrap aluminum.

Although much had been done to improve the quality of manufacturing operations at Northern, large amounts of scrap metal still resulted as a natural by-product of the production process. This waste material was at present discarded, and Northern incurred significant disposal costs, since the metal had to be trucked more than 70 miles to a dumping facility.

Dick was anxious to take advantage of this opportunity to sell Northern's scrap aluminum. Not only would transport costs and dumping fees be eliminated, but a handsome compensation would be received as well. A favorable price per pound was negotiated, and Reid agreed to pick up the scrap metal every Friday afternoon. His only requirement was 1 week's advance notice of the total scrap poundage to be hauled. This was necessary so that the recycler could schedule his trucks and compacting equipment.

From experience, Dick knew that waste was directly related to production volume. The greater the poundage of aluminum coming out of the extrusion press, the more scrap would result. The following week's production was always scheduled—based on customer orders—each Friday morning at the weekly production meeting. Production volume was known a week in advance, therefore, and Dick felt it would be a small matter to forecast the amount of scrap that could be expected as well.

He was uncertain as to how an accurate forecast should be made, however, and he pondered the problem as he picked up the phone.

"Hi, Dick," Sarah said happily. "What can we do for you today?"

Dick explained his situation and requested Sarah's help in developing a means to predict weekly scrap volume.

"Sure thing, Dick," Sarah replied. She was eager to try out a new statistical software package she had recently ordered. "I can run that through on my per-

sonal computer with no problem at all. One thing, though. Do you have much in the way of past data on finished output and scrap poundage?" she asked.

"Yes," Dick responded. "We have readily available weekly records going back at least three years."

"Excellent," Sarah responded. "Now here's the information that I'm going to need . . ."

Sarah will assist Dick in developing the ability to predict the amount of scrap aluminum that will result from a week's expected production. What data will Sarah require to conduct her analysis? What kind of analytical procedures will she have her computer perform on these data? What cautions should Sarah offer to Dick in using whatever conclusions might be drawn from the analysis?

10-11
Computer Data Base Exercise

Hal tracked Laurel down shortly after her return from the Rockies. "You certainly look well rested," he commented. "I could probably use a vacation myself, but I'm afraid it'll have to wait a while. Our busiest time of year is about to set in! Speaking of which, I'd like you to look into something for me. We're in a position to hire some additional warehouse help, both here and at our satellites, mostly for "unskilled" tasks like shipping, receiving, packing, order pulling, etc. What I'd like to know is if there's some 'formula' that the statistics might show is better than others. We've had mixed results in the past. It's expensive these days to hire and train people, and it keeps our personnel costs down considerably when we reduce turnover. Think you can help?"

"Sounds like a little regression analysis is in order," said Laurel. "I'll hunt down Gary, since these are his people we're talking about, and see what I can come up with for you."

Hal smiled. "Great. My secretary, Mary, has all the personnel files on current and past employees. I know we're not a huge company, but we've at least got *some* data points for you to consider."

Laurel headed out into the warehouse to find Gary. "I'll let you know what I come up with," she called over her shoulder.

Gary, busy with a rather large incoming shipment, didn't have much time to talk. After setting up an appointment for the following

afternoon, he managed to come up with one idea for Laurel to start with. "We've had pretty good success with our retiree-hiring program. They're steady workers, happy for a little something to keep them busy, and in plentiful supply here in Florida! Maybe age would be the type of characteristic you're looking for. I promise that before tomorrow I'll give it some more thought, though."

"Thanks," Laurel said. "And sorry to have interrupted you."

"No problem at all." Gary flashed her a quick grin and turned back to his task at hand.

After collecting the appropriate data from Mary, Laurel headed to her terminal. To accurately evaluate the "length of employment" factor, she knew she'd most likely have to use the data for terminated employees. However, there were a few current warehouse employees who had been with the company several years, and she felt they were important enough to include. After a short study of the information available to her, she decided to include current employees with 5 or more years of service.

1. Perform a least-squares linear regression on the data given in Table DB 10-1. What is the standard error of the estimate? Assuming normal distributions around each estimated value and equal variances at each point, calculate an approximate 95.5 percent prediction interval (± 2 standard errors) for the length of employment of a 25-year-old

prospective employee. Do the same calculation for a 65-year-old prospective employee. Given just this information, can we make any recommendations as to which person to hire?

2. What are the coefficient of determination and coefficient of correlation for length of employment (in months) vs. age when hired (in years)?

3. Gary has always felt that (all other factors being equal) each additional year of age of a prospective employee corresponds to one more month of employment at HH Industries. Test the hypothesis that the slope of the population regression line is 1.0 at the 10% significance level.

TABLE DB10-1

AGE WHEN HIRED	LENGTH OF EMPLOYMENT	AGE WHEN HIRED	LENGTH OF EMPLOYMENT
78	72	38	20
44	20	47	54
44	18	37	25
37	29	30	11
30	8	30	28
32	22	25	36
23	12	36	24
46	34	54	31
60	50	48	22
22	19	68	65
20	6	51	40
39	26	35	23
32	18	50	38
17	23	79	48
32	12	27	10
24	18	29	18
28	29	37	33
49	32	76	45
39	24	32	15
25	17	24	6

10-12
From the Textbook to the Real World

Applications of Statistical Methods to Football

Although statistical methods are most commonly used in business settings, they also serve an important function in the world of sports. To the uninitiated, American football features heavily armored opponents ramming each other at full speed and attempting to bash each other into the ground. Beneath this Neanderthal veneer lies a game of remarkable complexity wherein statistics play a major role. Statistics are used by coaches to devise strategies for specific plays and by sports writers to rank teams and predict outcomes of games.

Strategic Implications: Because every play in American football begins with a restart, offensive and defensive players have an opportunity to align themselves against their opponents; hence, strategic planning is essential. Typical statistics include the average distance gained per run, the percentage of passes caught, the average distance gained per successfully caught pass, average distance when kicking the ball, the number of times the ball is fumbled, and the number of interceptions. These statistics are kept by individual and by team. In the 1960s the NFL Dallas Cowboys began using individual play data to identify tendencies exhibited by the opposing offensive teams and to eliminate visible trends in its own offensive plays. As one might suspect, the Cowboys were one of the most successful teams over that period. In reviewing statistics, the coaching staff hopes to locate trends in which the opposing team consistently calls a particular play or uses a particular formation. Once spotted, the defensive players can be aligned to stop the expected play. Today, all 28 teams of the NFL use statistical methods to set defensive plays and establish offensive strategies. Individual statistics also play an important role in the drafting procedure for players.

Ranking and Predictions: Automated predictions have been associated with American football for over 50 years. The Williamsen "system" was

Raymond T. Stefani, "Applications of Statistical Methods to American Football," *Journal of Applied Statistics,* vol. 14, no. 1, 1987.

widely published in newspapers during the 1930s. Williamsen used a least-squares technique to rank college teams and to predict outcomes. Nationally-syndicated wire service polls began in 1936 after Williamsen's data became popular. These polls, which rank the top 20 college teams, are still in use today. Raymond Stefani, Professor of Electrical Engineering at California State University, provided weekly predictions of over 11,000 games beginning with the 1970–71 season and ending with the 1980–81 season, using a least-squares procedure. The use of least squares enabled Stefani to predict the correct winning team in 70% of those games.

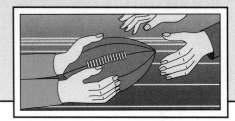

10-13
Flow Chart

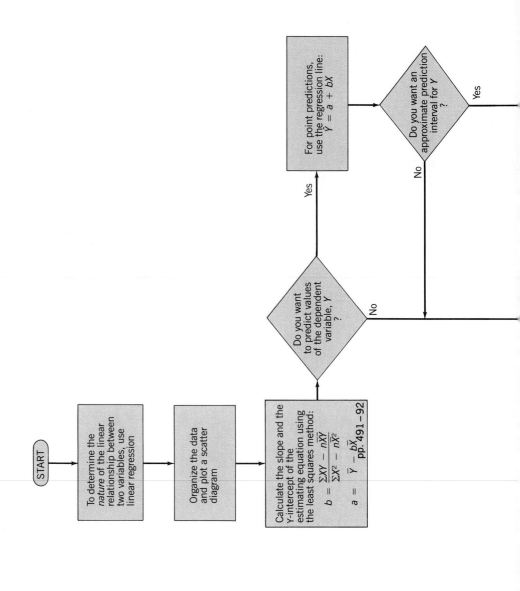

START

To determine the *nature* of the linear relationship between two variables, use linear regression

Organize the data and plot a scatter diagram

Calculate the slope and the Y-intercept of the estimating equation using the least squares method:

$$b = \frac{\Sigma XY - n\overline{X}\overline{Y}}{\Sigma X^2 - n\overline{X}^2}$$

$$a = \overline{Y} - b\overline{X}$$

pp. 491–92

Do you want to predict values of the dependent variable, Y ?

Yes

For point predictions, use the regression line:
$\hat{Y} = a + bX$

No

Do you want an approximate prediction interval for Y ?

No

Yes

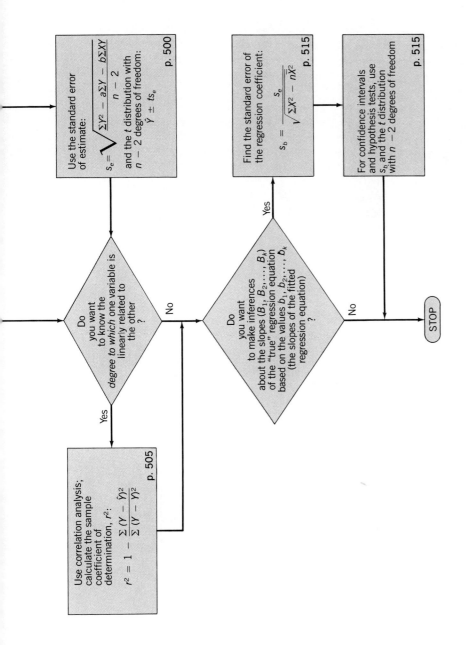

A manufacturer of small office copiers and word-processing machinery pays its salespeople a small base salary plus a commission equal to a fixed percent of the person's sales. One of the salespeople charges that this salary structure discriminates against women. Current base salaries for the firm's nine salespeople are as follows:

Salesmen		Saleswomen	
MONTHS EMPLOYED	BASE SALARY ($1,000s)	MONTHS EMPLOYED	BASE SALARY ($1,000s)
6	7.5	5	6.2
10	8.6	13	8.7
12	9.1	15	9.4
18	10.3	21	9.8
30	13.0		

The director of personnel sees that base salary depends on length of service, but she does not know how to use the data to learn if it also depends on sex and if there is discrimination against women. Methods in this chapter will enable her to find out.

11

Multiple Regression and Modeling Techniques

■ **OBJECTIVES**

Chapter 11 is a continuation of some of the regression ideas introduced in Chapter 10. Here we shall examine how to use regression when we feel that more than one factor is involved in something we are trying to predict. For example, if your university used your high school grade-point average as well as your college board scores to predict your college grade-point average, chances are they were using multiple regression. Also in Chapter 11, we'll try a bit of modeling with regression; that is, we'll get a bit deeper into how we can predict some things by looking at others, and what those others ought to be.

Multiple Regression and Correlation Analysis

Using more than one
independent variable to
estimate the dependent
variable

As we mentioned in Chapter 10, we can use more than one independent variable to estimate the dependent variable and, in this way, attempt to increase the accuracy of the estimate. This process is called multiple regression and correlation analysis. It is based on the same assumptions and procedures we have encountered using simple regression.

Consider the real estate agent who wishes to relate the number of houses the firm sells in a month to the amount of her monthly advertising. Certainly we can find a simple estimating equation that relates these two variables. Could we also improve the accuracy of our equation by including in the estimating process the number of salespeople she employs each month? The answer is probably yes. And now, since we want to use both the number of sales agents and the advertising expenditures to predict monthly house sales, we must use *multiple,* not simple, regression to determine the relationship.

The principal advantage of multiple regression is that it allows us to utilize more of the information available to us to estimate the dependent variable. Sometimes the correlation between two variables may be insufficient to determine a reliable estimating equation. Yet, if we add the data from more independent variables, we may be able to determine an estimating equation that describes the relationship with greater accuracy.

Multiple regression and correlation analysis involve a three-step process such as the one we used in simple regression. In this process, we:

1. Describe the multiple regression equation.
2. Examine the multiple regression standard error of estimate.
3. Use multiple correlation analysis to determine how well the regression equation describes the observed data.

In addition, in multiple regression, we can look at each of the individual independent variables and test whether it contributes significantly to the way the regression describes the data.

In this chapter, we shall see how to find the best-fitting regression equation for a given set of data and how to analyze the equation that we get. Although we shall show how to do multiple regression by hand or on a hand-held calculator, it will quickly become obvious to you that you would not want to do even a modest-size real-life problem by hand. Fortunately, there are available many computer "packages" for doing multiple regressions and other statistical analyses. These packages do the "number crunching" for you and leave you free to concentrate on analyzing the significance of the resulting estimating equation. We shall discuss the regression output from three such packages: SAS, Minitab, and MYSTAT.

Multiple regression will also enable us to fit curves as well as lines. Using the techniques of "dummy variables," we can even include qualitative factors such as sex in our multiple regression. This technique will enable us to analyze the discrimination problem which opened this chapter. Dummy variables and fitting curves are only two of the many *modeling techniques* that can be used in multiple regression to increase the accuracy of our estimating equations.

Exercises

11-1   Why would we use multiple regression instead of simple regression in estimating a dependent variable?

11-2   How will dummy variables be used in our study of multiple regression?

11-3   To what does the word *multiple* refer in the phrase *multiple regression?*

11-4   The owner of a chain of stores would like to predict monthly sales from the size of city in which a store is located. After fitting a simple regression model, she decides that she wants to include the effect of season of the year in the model. Can this be done using the techniques in this chapter?

11-5   Describe the three steps in the process of multiple regression and correlation analysis.

11-6   Will the procedures used in multiple regression differ greatly from those we used in simple regression? Why, or why not?

11-2
Finding the Multiple Regression Equation

A problem to demonstrate multiple regression

Let's see how we can compute the multiple regression equation. For convenience, we shall use only two independent variables in the problem we work in this section. Keep in mind, however, that the same sort of technique is, in principle, applicable to any number of independent variables.

The Internal Revenue Service is trying to estimate the monthly amount of unpaid taxes discovered by its auditing division. In the past, the IRS estimated this figure on the basis of the expected number of field-audit labor hours. In recent years, however, field-audit labor hours have become an erratic predictor of the actual unpaid taxes. As a result, the IRS is looking for another factor with which it can improve the estimating equation.

The auditing division does keep a record of the number of hours its computers are used to detect unpaid taxes. Could we combine this information with the data on field-audit labor hours and come up with a more accurate estimating equation for the unpaid taxes discovered each month? Table 11-1 presents these data for the last 10 months.

TABLE 11-1 Data from IRS Auditing Records During Last 10 Months

MONTH	X_1 FIELD-AUDIT LABOR HOURS (00s OMITTED)	X_2 COMPUTER HOURS (00s OMITTED)	Y ACTUAL UNPAID TAXES DISCOVERED (MILLIONS OF DOLLARS)
January	45	16	$29
February	42	14	24
March	44	15	27
April	45	13	25
May	43	13	26
June	46	14	28
July	44	16	30
August	45	16	28
September	44	15	28
October	43	15	27

In simple regression, X is the symbol used for the values of the independent variable. In multiple regression, we have more than one independent variable. So we shall continue to use X, but we shall add a subscript (for example, X_1, X_2) to distinguish between the independent variables we are using.

In this problem, X_1 will represent the number of field-audit labor hours and X_2 the number of computer hours. The dependent variable, Y, will be the actual unpaid taxes discovered.

Recall that in simple regression, the estimating equation $\hat{Y} = a + bX$ describes the relationship between the two variables X and Y. In multiple regression, we must extend that equation, adding one term for each new variable. In symbolic form, Equation 11-1 is the formula we can use when we have two independent variables:

$$\hat{Y} = a + b_1 X_1 + b_2 X_2 \qquad [11\text{-}1]$$

where:

- $\hat{Y}$ = estimated value corresponding to the dependent variable
- a = Y-intercept
- X_1 and X_2 = values of the two independent variables
- b_1 and b_2 = slopes associated with X_1 and X_2, respectively

We can visualize the simple estimating equation as a line on a graph; similarly, we can picture a two-variable multiple regression equation as a plane, such as the one shown in Fig. 11-1. Here we have a three-dimensional shape that possesses depth,

FIGURE 11-1

Multiple regression plane for 10 data points

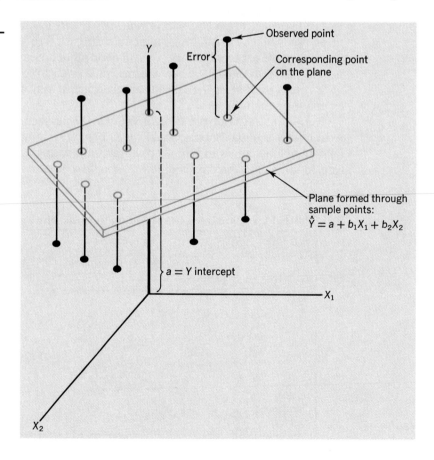

length, and width. To get an intuitive feel for this three-dimensional shape, visualize the intersection of the axes, Y, X_1, and X_2 as one corner of a room.

Figure 11-1 is a graph of the ten sample points from Table 11-1 and the plane about which these points seem to cluster. Some points lie above the plane, and some fall below it—just as points lie above and below the simple regression line.

Using the least squares criterion to fit a regression plane

Our problem is to decide which of the possible planes that we could draw will be the best fit. To do this, we shall again use the least squares criterion and locate the plane that minimizes the sum of the squares of the errors; that is, the distances from the points around the plane to the corresponding points *on* the plane. We use our data and the following three equations to determine the values of the numerical constants, a, b_1, and b_2.

$$\Sigma Y = na + b_1\Sigma X_1 + b_2\Sigma X_2 \qquad [11\text{-}2]$$

$$\Sigma X_1 Y = a\Sigma X_1 + b_1\Sigma X_1^2 + b_2\Sigma X_1 X_2 \qquad [11\text{-}3]$$

$$\Sigma X_2 Y = a\Sigma X_2 + b_1\Sigma X_1 X_2 + b_2\Sigma X_2^2 \qquad [11\text{-}4]$$

Solving Equations 11-2, 11-3, and 11-4 for a, b_1, and b_2 will give us the coefficients for the regression plane. Obviously, the best way to compute all the sums in these three equations is to use a table to collect and organize the necessary information, just as we did in simple regression. This we have done for the IRS problem in Table 11-2.

Equations 11-2, 11-3, and 11-4 used to solve for a, b₁, and b₂

Now, using the information from Table 11-2 in Equations 11-2, 11-3, and 11-4, we get three equations in the three unknown constants (a, b_1, and b_2), which we denote below as ①, ②, and ③.

$$272 = 10a + 441b_1 + 147b_2 \qquad ①$$

$$12{,}005 = 441a + 19{,}461b_1 + 6{,}485b_2 \qquad ②$$

$$4{,}013 = 147a + 6{,}485b_1 + 2{,}173b_2 \qquad ③$$

TABLE 11-2 Values for Fitting Least Squares Plane, Where $n = 10$

Y (1)	X_1 (2)	X_2 (3)	X_1Y (2) × (1)	X_2Y (3) × (1)	X_1X_2 (2) × (3)	X_1^2 (2)²	X_2^2 (3)²	Y^2 (1)²
29	45	16	1,305	464	720	2,025	256	841
24	42	14	1,008	336	588	1,764	196	576
27	44	15	1,188	405	660	1,936	225	729
25	45	13	1,125	325	585	2,025	169	625
26	43	13	1,118	338	559	1,849	169	676
28	46	14	1,288	392	644	2,116	196	784
30	44	16	1,320	480	704	1,936	256	900
28	45	16	1,260	448	720	2,025	256	784
28	44	15	1,232	420	660	1,936	225	784
27	43	15	1,161	405	645	1,849	225	729
272	441	147	12,005	4,013	6,485	19,461	2,173	7,428
↑	↑	↑	↑	↑	↑	↑	↑	↑
ΣY	ΣX_1	ΣX_2	$\Sigma X_1 Y$	$\Sigma X_2 Y$	$\Sigma X_1 X_2$	ΣX_1^2	ΣX_2^2	ΣY^2

$\overline{Y} = 27.2$
$\overline{X}_1 = 44.1$
$\overline{X}_2 = 14.7$

We can find the values for the three numerical constants by solving these three equations simultaneously, as follows:

Step 1. Multiply equation ① by -441. Multiply Equation ② by 10. Add ① to ②. This eliminates a and produces Equation ④.

$$① \times (-441): -119{,}952 = -4410a - 194{,}481b_1 - 64{,}827b_2$$
$$② \times (10) \quad: \quad \underline{120{,}050 = \quad 4410a + 194{,}610b_1 + 64{,}850b_2}$$
$$④: \qquad 98 = \qquad\qquad\qquad 129b_1 + \quad 23b_2$$

Step 2. Multiply Equation ① by -147 and Equation ③ by 10. Add ① to ③. This eliminates a and produces Equation ⑤.

$$① \times (-147): -39{,}984 = -1470a - 64{,}827b_1 - 21{,}609b_2$$
$$③ \times 10 \quad: \quad \underline{40{,}130 = \quad 1470a + 64{,}850b_1 + 21{,}730b_2}$$
$$⑤: \qquad 146 = \qquad\qquad\qquad 23b_1 + \quad 121b_2$$

Step 3. Multiply Equation ④ by -23 and Equation ⑤ by 129. Add ④ to ⑤ to eliminate b_1. This produces Equation ⑥, which can be solved for b_2:

$$④ \times (-23): \quad -2{,}254 = -2{,}967b_1 - \quad 529b_2$$
$$⑤ \times (129): \quad \underline{18{,}834 = \quad 2{,}967b_1 + 15{,}609b_2}$$
$$⑥: \quad 16{,}580 = \qquad\qquad 15{,}080b_2$$

$$b_2 = 1.099$$

Step 4. Find the value of b_1 by substituting the value for b_2 into Equation ④:

$$④: 98 = 129b_1 + 23b_2$$
$$98 = 129b_1 + (23)(1.099)$$
$$98 = 129b_1 + 25.277$$
$$72.723 = 129b_1$$

$$b_1 = .564$$

Step 5. Substitute the values of b_1 and b_2 into Equation ① to determine the value of a:

$$①: 272 = 10a + 441b_1 + 147b_2$$
$$272 = 10a + (441)(.564) + (147)(1.099)$$
$$272 = 10a + 248.724 + 161.553$$
$$-138.277 = 10a$$

$$a = -13.828$$

Step 6. Substitute the values of a, b_1, and b_2 into the general two-variable regression equation (Equation 11-1). The resulting Equation ⑦ describes the relationship among the number of field-audit labor hours, the number of computer hours, and the unpaid taxes discovered by the auditing division.

$$\hat{Y} = a + b_1 X_1 + b_2 X_2 \qquad\qquad\text{[11-1]}$$

$$\text{⑦: } \hat{Y} = -13.828 + .564X_1 + 1.099X_2$$

The auditing division can use this equation monthly to estimate the amount of unpaid taxes it will discover.

Using the multiple
regression equation to
estimate

Suppose the IRS wants to increase its discoveries in the coming month. Since trained auditors are scarce, the IRS does not intend to hire additional personnel. The number of field-audit labor hours, then, will remain at October's level of about 4,300 hours. But in order to increase its discoveries of unpaid taxes, the IRS expects to increase the number of computer hours to about 1,600. As a result:

$$X_1 = 43 \leftarrow 4{,}300 \text{ hours of field-audit labor}$$

$$X_2 = 16 \leftarrow 1{,}600 \text{ hours of computer time}$$

Substituting these values into Equation ⑦, we get:

$$\begin{aligned}
\hat{Y} &= -13.828 + .564X_1 + 1.099X_2 \qquad\qquad\text{⑦}\\
&= -13.828 + (.564)(43) + (1.099)(16)\\
&= -13.828 + 24.252 + 17.584\\
&= 28.008 \leftarrow \text{estimated discoveries of \$28,008,000}
\end{aligned}$$

Interpreting our estimate

Therefore, in the November forecast, the audit division can indicate that it expects about $28 million of discoveries for this combination of factors.

a, b_1, and b_2 are the estimated regression coefficients

So far, we have referred to a as the Y-intercept and to b_1 and b_2 as the slopes of the multiple regression plane. But to be more precise, we should say that these numerical constants are the *estimated regression coefficients.* The constant a is the value of $\hat{Y}$ (in this case, the estimated unpaid taxes) *if* both X_1 and X_2 happen to be zero. The coefficients b_1 and b_2 describe how changes in X_1 and X_2 affect the value of $\hat{Y}$. In Equation ⑦, for example, we can hold the number of field-audit labor hours, X_1, constant and change the number of computer hours, X_2. When we do, the value of $\hat{Y}$ will increase $1,099,000 for every additional 100 hours of computer time. Likewise, we can hold X_2 constant and find that, for every 100-hour increase in the number of field-audit labor hours, $\hat{Y}$ increases by $564,000.

Exercises

11-7 Given the following set of data:
(a) Calculate the multiple regression plane.
(b) Predict Y when $X_1 = 3.0$ and $X_2 = 2.7$.

Y	X₁	X₂
25	3.5	5.0
30	6.7	4.2
11	1.5	8.5
22	0.3	1.4
27	4.6	3.6
19	2.0	1.3

11-8   For the following set of data:
(a)   Calculate the multiple regression plane.
(b)   Predict Y for $X_1 = 38$ and $X_2 = 10$.

Y	X_1	X_2
10	8	4
17	21	9
18	14	11
26	17	20
35	36	13
8	9	28

11-9   Sam Spade, owner and general manager of the Campus Stationery Store, is concerned about the sales behavior of a compact cassette tape recorder sold at the store. He realizes that there are many factors which might help explain sales, but believes that advertising and price are major determinants. Sam has collected the data given below.

Sales (Units sold)	Advertising (Number of ads)	Price ($)
33	3	125
61	6	115
70	10	140
82	13	130
17	9	145
24	6	140

(a)   Calculate the least squares equation to predict sales from advertising and price.
(b)   If advertising is 7 and price is $132, what sales would you predict?

11-10   A developer of food for pigs would like to determine what relationship exists among the age of a pig when it starts receiving a newly developed food supplement, the initial weight of the pig, and the amount of weight it gains in a 1-week period with the food supplement. The following information is the result of a study of eight piglets:

Piglet Number	X_1 Initial Weight (pounds)	X_2 Initial Age (weeks)	Y Weight Gain
1	39	8	7
2	52	6	6
3	49	7	8
4	46	12	10
5	61	9	9
6	35	6	5
7	25	7	3
8	55	4	4

(a)   Calculate the least squares equation that best describes these three variables.
(b)   How much might we expect a pig to gain in a week with the food supplement if it were 9 weeks old and weighed 48 pounds?

11-11   Given the following set of data:
(a)   Calculate the multiple regression plane.
(b)   Predict Y when $X_1 = -1$ and $X_2 = 4$.

11 MULTIPLE REGRESSION AND MODELING TECHNIQUES

Y	X_1	X_2
6	1	3
10	3	−1
9	2	4
14	−2	7
7	3	2
5	6	−4

11-12 The information below has been gathered from a random sample of apartment renters in a city. We are trying to predict rent (in dollars per month) based on the size of the apartment (number of rooms) and the distance from downtown (in miles).

RENT ($)	NUMBER OF ROOMS	DISTANCE FROM DOWNTOWN
360	2	1
1000	6	1
450	3	2
525	4	3
350	2	10
300	1	4

(a) Calculate the least squares equation that best relates these three variables.
(b) If someone is looking for a 2-bedroom apartment two miles from downtown, what rent should he expect to pay?

11-13 The Federal Reserve is performing a preliminary study to determine the relationship between certain economic indicators and annual percentage change in the gross national product (GNP). Two such indicators being examined are the amount of the federal government's deficit (in billions of dollars) and the Dow Jones Industrial Average (the mean value over the year). Data for 6 years are given below:

Y CHANGE IN GNP	X_1 FEDERAL DEFICIT	X_2 DOW JONES
2.5	50	950
−1.0	200	700
4.0	60	1,100
1.0	100	800
1.5	90	850
3.0	40	900

(a) Calculate the least squares equation that best describes the data.
(b) What percentage change in GNP would be expected in a year in which the federal deficit was $120 billion and the mean Dow Jones value was 1,000?

11-3
The Computer and Multiple Regression

Impracticality of computing regressions by hand

In Chapter 10, and so far in this chapter, we have presented simplified problems and samples of small sizes. After the example in the last section, you have probably concluded that you are not interested in regression if you have to do the computations by hand. In fact, as sample size gets larger and the number of independent

TABLE 11-3 Factors Related to the Discovery of Unpaid Taxes

MONTH	FIELD-AUDIT LABOR HOURS (00s OMITTED) X_1	COMPUTER HOURS (00s OMITTED) X_2	REWARDS TO INFORMANTS (000s OMITTED) X_3	ACTUAL UNPAID TAXES DISCOVERED (000,000s OMITTED) Y
January	45	16	71	29
February	42	14	70	24
March	44	15	72	27
April	45	13	71	25
May	43	13	75	26
June	46	14	74	28
July	44	16	76	30
August	45	16	69	28
September	44	15	74	28
October	43	15	73	27

variables in the regression increases, it quickly becomes impractical to do the computations even on a hand-held calculator.

As managers, however, we will have to deal with complex problems requiring larger samples and additional independent variables. To assist us in solving these more detailed problems, we will make use of a computer, which allows us to perform a large number of computations in a very small period of time.

Suppose that we have not one or two independent variables but rather that we have k of them: $X_1, X_2, \ldots, X_k$. As before, we will let n denote the number of data points that we have. The regression equation we are trying to estimate is:

$$\hat{Y} = a + b_1 X_1 + b_2 X_2 + \cdots + b_k X_k \qquad [11\text{-}5]$$

Now we'll see how we can use a computer to estimate the regression coefficients.

Demonstration of multiple regression using the computer

To demonstrate how a computer handles multiple regression analysis, take our IRS problem from the preceding section. Suppose the auditing division adds to its model the information concerning rewards to informants. The IRS wishes to include this third independent variable, X_3, because it feels certain that there is some relationship between these payments and the unpaid taxes discovered. Information for the last 10 months is recorded in Table 11-3.

Using SAS to solve multiple regression problems

To solve this problem, the auditing division has used the multiple regression procedure in the SAS system. Of course, we don't yet know how to interpret the solution provided by SAS, but as we shall see, most of the numbers given in the solution correspond fairly closely to things we have already discussed in the context of simple regression.

SAS OUTPUT

Output from the SAS program

Once all the data have been entered and the independent and dependent variables chosen, SAS computes the regression coefficients and several statistics associated with the regression equation. Let's look at the output for the IRS problem and see what all the numbers mean. The first part of the output is given in Figure 11-2.

1. *The regression equation.* From the numbers given in the "parameter estimate" column, we can read the estimating equation:

FIGURE 11-2

SAS output

VARIABLE	DF	PARAMETER ESTIMATE	STANDARD ERROR	T FOR H0: PARAMETER=0	PROB > |T|
ROOT MSE		0.2861281	R-SQUARE	0.9834	
INTERCEP	1	-45.79634767	4.87765079	-9.389	0.0001
AUDIT	1	0.59697180	0.08112429	7.359	0.0003
COMPUTER	1	1.17683773	0.08407418	13.998	0.0001
REWARDS	1	0.40510865	0.04223359	9.592	0.0001

$$\hat{Y} = a + b_1 X_1 + b_2 X_2 + b_3 X_3 \qquad [11\text{-}5]$$
$$\hat{Y} = -45.796 + .597X_1 + 1.177X_2 + .405X_3$$

Finding and interpreting the regression equation

We can interpret this equation in much the same way that we interpreted the two-variable regression equation on page 543. If we hold the number of field-audit labor hours, X_1, and the number of computer hours, X_2, constant and change the rewards to informants, X_3, then the value of $\hat{Y}$ will increase \$405,000 for each additional \$1,000 paid to informants. Similarly, holding X_1 and X_3 constant, we see that each additional 100 hours of computer time used will increase $\hat{Y}$ by \$1,177,000. Finally, if X_2 and X_3 are held constant, we estimate that an additional 100 hours spent in the field audits will uncover an additional \$597,000 in unpaid taxes.

Suppose that in November, the IRS intends to leave the field-audit labor hours and computer hours at their October levels (4,300 and 1,500) but to increase the rewards paid to informants to \$75,000. How much unpaid taxes do they expect to discover in November? Substituting these values into the estimated regression equation, we get:

$$\begin{aligned}
\hat{Y} &= -45.796 + .597X_1 + 1.177X_2 + .405X_3 \\
&= -45.796 + .597(43) + 1.177(15) + .405(75) \\
&= -45.796 + 25.671 + 17.655 + 30.375 \\
&= 27.905 \leftarrow \text{estimated discoveries of } \$27,905,000
\end{aligned}$$

So the audit division expects to discover about \$28 million in unpaid taxes in November.

Measuring dispersion around the multiple regression plane; using the standard error of estimate

2. *A measure of dispersion, the standard error of estimate for multiple regression.* Now that we have determined the equation that relates our three variables, we need some measure of the dispersion around this multiple regression plane. In simple regression, the estimation becomes more accurate as the degree of dispersion around the regression gets smaller. The same is true of the sample points around the multiple regression plane. To measure this variation, we shall again use the measure called the standard error of estimate:

$$s_e = \sqrt{\frac{\Sigma (Y - \hat{Y})^2}{n - k - 1}} \qquad [11\text{-}6]$$

where:

- Y = sample values of the dependent variable
- $\hat{Y}$ = corresponding estimated values from the regression equation
- n = number of data points in the sample
- k = number of independent variables ($= 3$ in our example)

The denominator of this equation indicates that in multiple regression with k independent variables, the standard error has $n - k - 1$ degrees of freedom. This occurs because the degrees of freedom are reduced from n by the $k + 1$ numerical constants, $a, b_1, b_2, \ldots, b_k$ that have all been estimated from the same sample.

To compute s_e, we look at the individual *errors* $(Y - \hat{Y})$ in the fitted regression plane, *square* them, compute their *mean* (dividing by $n - k - 1$ instead of n), and take the square *root* of the result. Because of the way it is computed, s_e is sometimes called the *root mean square error* (or *root mse* for short). From the SAS output, we see that the root mse in our IRS problem is .286; that is to say, $286,000.

Confidence intervals for $\hat{Y}$

As was the case in simple regression, we can use the standard error of estimate and the t distribution to form an *approximate confidence interval* around our estimated value $\hat{Y}$. In the unpaid tax problem, for 4,300 field-audit labor hours, 1,500 computer hours, and $75,000 paid to informants, our $\hat{Y}$ is $27,905,000 estimated unpaid taxes discovered, and our s_e is $286,000. If we want to construct a 95 percent confidence interval around this estimate of $27,905,000, we look in Appendix Table 2 under the 5 percent column until we locate the $n - k - 1 = 10 - 3 - 1 = 6$ degrees of freedom row. The appropriate t value for our interval estimate is 2.447. Therefore, we can calculate the limits of our confidence interval like this:

$$\hat{Y} + t(s_e) = 27,905,000 + (2.447)(286,000)$$
$$= 27,905,000 + 699,800$$
$$= 28,604,800 \leftarrow \text{upper limit}$$

$$\hat{Y} - t(s_e) = 27,905,000 - (2.447)(286,000)$$
$$= 27,905,000 - 699,800$$
$$= 27,205,200 \leftarrow \text{lower limit}$$

Interpreting the confidence interval

With a confidence level as high as 95 percent, the auditing division can feel certain that the actual discoveries will lie in this large interval from $27,205,200 to $28,604,800. If the IRS wishes to use a lower confidence level, such as 90 percent, it can narrow the range of values in estimating the unpaid taxes discovered. As was true with simple regression, we can use the standard normal distribution, Appendix Table 1, to approximate the t distribution whenever our degrees of freedom (n minus the number of estimated regression coefficients) are greater than 30.

Value of additional variables

Did adding the third independent variable (rewards to informants) make our regression better? Since s_e measures the dispersion of the data points around the regression plane, smaller values of s_e should indicate better regressions. For the two-variable regression done earlier in this chapter, s_e turns out to be 1.076. Since the addition of the third variable reduced s_e to .286, we see that adding the third variable *did* improve the fit of the regression in this example. **It is not true in general, however, that adding variables always reduces s_e.**

Meaning of the coefficient of determination

3. *The coefficient of multiple determination.* In our discussion of simple correlation analysis, we measured the strength of the relation between two variables using the sample coefficient of determination, r^2. This coefficient of determination is the fraction of the total variation of the dependent variable Y that is explained by the estimating equation.

Using the coefficient of multiple determination

Similarly, in multiple correlation, we shall measure the strength of the relationship among three variables using the *coefficient of multiple determination, R^2,* or its square root, R (the coefficient of multiple correlation). **This coefficient of multiple determination is also the fraction that represents the proportion of the total variation of Y that is "explained" by the regression plane.**

Notice that the SAS output gives the value of R^2 as .9834. This tells us that 98.34 percent of the total variation in unpaid taxes discovered is explained by the three independent variables. For the two-variable regression done earlier, R^2 is only .7289, so 72.89 percent of the variation is explained by field-audit labor hours and computer hours. Adding in rewards to informants explains another 25.45 percent of the variation.

We still have not explained the numbers in the columns headed "standard error," "t for H_0: parameter $= 0$," or "prob $> |t|$." These numbers will be used to make inferences about the population regression plane, the topic of Section 11-4.

MINITAB OUTPUT

In Fig. 11-3, we have the first part of the output when Minitab is used to do the auditing division's multiple regression. Minitab presents essentially the same information that SAS provides. It explicitly lists the estimating equation as well as giving a table of the coefficients. The principal differences between the two outputs in Figs. 11-2 and 11-3 are found in the number of decimal places reported and in the column headings in the table of coefficients. In addition, Minitab calls the standard error of estimate s.

FIGURE 11-3
Minitab output

```
The regression equation is
DISCOVER = - 45.8 + 0.597 AUDIT + 1.18 COMPUTER + 0.405 REWARDS


Predictor        Coef        Stdev      t-ratio        p

Constant      -45.796        4.878        -9.39      0.000
AUDIT         0.59697      0.08112         7.36      0.000
COMPUTER      1.17684      0.08407        14.00      0.000
REWARDS       0.40511      0.04223         9.59      0.000


s = 0.2861      R-sq = 98.3%
```

MYSTAT OUTPUT

In Fig. 11-4, we show MYSTAT output for the same problem. Once again, we see essentially the same information. This will be true for almost all widely used software packages for statistical analysis. Their layouts for the output from multiple regressions may differ somewhat, and they may use different names for some of the statistics they report, but they will report essentially the same information.

FIGURE 11-4
MYSTAT output

```
DEP VAR:DISCOVER      N: 10     MULTIPLE R: .992    SQUARED MULTIPLE R: .983
                                       STANDARD ERROR OF ESTIMATE:  0.286


            VARIABLE      COEFFICIENT    STD ERROR      T     P(2 TAIL)

            CONSTANT         -45.796        4.878     -9.389    0.000
               AUDIT           0.597        0.081      7.359    0.000
            COMPUTER           1.177        0.084     13.998    0.000
             REWARDS           0.405        0.042      9.592    0.000
```

Exercises

11-14 Given the following set of data, use whatever computer package is available to find the best-fitting regression equation and answer the following:
  (a) What is the regression equation?
  (b) What is the standard error of estimate?
  (c) What is R^2 for this regression?
  (d) What is the predicted value for Y when $X_1 = 5.8$, $X_2 = 4.2$, and $X_3 = 5.1$?

Y	X_1	X_2	X_3
64.7	3.5	5.3	8.5
80.9	7.4	1.6	2.6
24.6	2.5	6.3	4.5
43.9	3.7	9.4	8.8
77.7	5.5	1.4	3.6
20.6	8.3	9.2	2.5
66.9	6.7	2.5	2.7
34.3	1.2	2.2	1.3

11-15 Given the following set of data, use whatever computer package is available to find the best-fitting regression equation and answer the following:
  (a) What is the regression equation?
  (b) What is the standard error of estimate?
  (c) What is R^2 for this regression?
  (d) Give an approximate 95 percent confidence interval for the value of Y when the values of X_1, X_2, X_3, and X_4 are 52.4, 41.6, 35.8, and 3, respectively.

X_1	X_2	X_3	X_4	Y
21.4	62.9	21.9	−2	22.8
51.7	40.7	42.9	5	93.7
41.8	81.8	69.8	2	64.9
11.8	41.0	90.9	−4	19.2
71.6	22.6	12.9	8	55.8
91.9	61.5	30.9	1	23.1

11-16 Pam Schneider owns and operates an accounting firm in Ithaca, New York. Pam feels that it would be useful to be able to predict in advance the number of rush income tax returns during the busy March 1 to April 15 period so that she can better plan her personnel needs during this time. She has hypothesized that several factors may be useful in her prediction. Data for these factors and number of rush returns for past years are:

X_1 Economic Index	X_2 Population Within 1 Mile of Office	X_3 Average Income in Ithaca	Y Number of Rush Returns March 1 to April 15
99	10,188	21,465	2,306
106	8,566	22,228	1,266
100	10,557	27,665	1,422
129	10,219	25,200	1,721
179	9,662	26,300	2,544

(a) Using whatever computer package is available, determine the best-fitting regression equation for these data.

(b) What percentage of the total variation in the number of rush returns is explained by this equation?

(c) For 1987, the economic index is 169, the population within one mile of the office is 10,212, and the average income in Ithaca is $26,925. How many rush returns should Pam expect to process between March 1 and April 15?

11-17 We are trying to predict the annual demand for widgets (DEMAND), using the following independent variables.

PRICE	= price of widgets	(in $)
INCOME	= consumer income	(in $)
SUB	= price of a substitute commodity	(in $)

(*Note:* A substitute commodity is one which can be substituted for another commodity. For example, margarine is a substitute commodity for butter.)

Data have been collected from 1975 to 1989, as given below:

YEAR	DEMAND	PRICE ($)	INCOME ($)	SUB ($)
1975	40	9	400	10
1976	45	8	500	14
1977	50	9	600	12
1978	55	8	700	13
1979	60	7	800	11
1980	70	6	900	15
1981	65	6	1,000	16
1982	65	8	1,100	17
1983	75	5	1,200	22
1984	75	5	1,300	19
1985	80	5	1,400	20
1986	100	3	1,500	23
1987	90	4	1,600	18
1988	95	3	1,700	24
1989	85	4	1,800	21

(a) Using whatever computer package is available, determine the best-fitting regression equation for these data.

(b) Are the signs (+ or −) of the regression coefficients of the independent variables as one would expect? Explain briefly. (*Note:* This is not a statistical question; you just need to think about what the regression coefficients mean.)

(c) State and interpret the coefficient of multiple determination for this problem.

(d) State and interpret the standard error of estimate for this problem.

(e) Using the equation, what would you predict for DEMAND if the price of widgets was $6, consumer income was $1,200, and the price of the substitute commodity was $17?

11-18 Bill Buxton, a statistics professor in a leading business school, has a keen interest in factors affecting students' performance on exams. The midterm exam for the past semester had a wide distribution of grades, but Bill feels certain that several factors explain the distribution: He allowed his students to study from as many different books as they liked, their IQs vary, they are of different ages, and they study varying amounts of time for exams. To develop a predicting formula for exam grades, Bill asked each student to answer, at the end of the exam, questions regarding study time and number of books used. Bill's teaching records already contained the IQs and ages for the students, so he compiled the data for the class and ran a multiple regression with SAS. The output from Bill's computer run was as follows:

VARIABLE	DF	PARAMETER ESTIMATE	STANDARD ERROR	T FOR H0: PARAMETER=0	PROB > |T|
ROOT MSE		11.657308	R-SQUARE	0.7672	
INTERCEP	1	-49.947647	41.549391	-1.202	0.2684
HOURS	1	1.069316	0.981632	1.089	0.3121
IQ	1	1.364595	0.376270	3.627	0.0084
BOOKS	1	2.039817	1.507990	1.353	0.2182
AGE	1	-1.798903	0.673319	-2.672	0.0319

(a) What is the best-fitting regression equation for these data?
(b) What percentage of the variation in grades is explained by this equation?
(c) What grade would you expect for a 21-year-old student with an IQ of 113, who studied 5 hours and used 3 different books?

11-19 Fourteen Twenty-Two Food Stores, Inc., is planning to expand its convenience store chain. To aid in selecting locations for the new stores, it has collected weekly sales data from each of its 23 stores. To help explain the variability in weekly sales, it has also collected information describing four variables which it believes are related to sales. The data which were collected are listed below. The variables are defined as follows:

SALES   : average weekly sales for each store in thousands of dollars
AUTOS   : average weekly auto traffic volume in thousands of cars
ENTRY   : ease of entry/exit measured on a scale of 1 to 100
ANNINC   : average annual household income for the area in thousands of dollars
DISTANCE: distance in miles from the store to the nearest supermarket

The data were analyzed using SAS and the output is given below.

VARIABLE	DF	PARAMETER ESTIMATE	STANDARD ERROR	T FOR H0: PARAMETER=0	PROB > |T|
ROOT MSE		85.5865	R-SQUARE	0.9579	
INTERCEP	1	175.371	92.624	1.893	0.0745
AUTOS	1	-0.028	0.315	-0.090	0.9293
ENTRY	1	3.775	1.272	2.966	0.0082
ANNINC	1	1.990	4.510	0.441	0.6643
DISTANCE	1	212.407	28.090	7.562	0.0001

(a) What is the best-fitting regression equation, as given by SAS?
(b) What is the standard error of estimate for this equation?
(c) What fraction of the variation in sales is explained by this regression?
(d) What sales would you predict for a store located in a neighborhood which had an average annual household income of $20,000, was 2 miles from the nearest supermarket, was on a road with weekly traffic volume of 100,000 autos, and had an ease of entry of 50?

11-20 Rick Blackburn is thinking about selling his house. In order to decide what price to ask, he has collected the data below for twelve recent closings. He has recorded sales price (in $1,000's), the number of square feet in the house (in 100's of sq. ft.), the number of stories, the number of bathrooms, and the age of the house (in years).

Sales Price	Square Feet	Stories	Bathrooms	Age
49.65	8.9	1	1.0	2
67.95	9.5	1	1.0	6
81.15	12.6	2	1.5	11
81.60	12.9	2	1.5	8
91.50	19.0	2	1.0	22
95.25	17.6	1	1.0	17
100.35	20.0	2	1.5	12
104.25	20.6	2	1.5	11
112.65	20.5	1	2.0	9
149.70	25.1	2	2.0	8
160.65	22.7	2	2.0	18
232.50	40.8	3	4.0	12

(a) Using whatever computer package is available, determine the best fitting regression equation for these data.

(b) What is R^2 for this equation? What does this number measure?

(c) If Rick's house has 1,800 square feet ($=18.0$ hundreds of square feet), 1 story, 1.5 bathrooms, and is 6 years old, what sales price can Rick expect?

11-21 Allegheny Steel Corporation has been looking into the factors that influence how many millions of tons of steel it is able to sell each year. The management suspects that the following are major factors: the annual national inflation rate, the average price per ton by which imported steel undercuts Allegheny's prices (in dollars), and the number of cars (in millions) that U.S. automakers are planning to produce in that year. Data for the past 7 years have been collected:

Year	Y Millions of Tons Sold	X_1 Inflation Rate	X_2 Imported Undercut	X_3 Number of Cars
1985	4.2	3.1	3.10	6.2
1984	3.1	3.9	5.00	5.1
1983	4.0	7.5	2.20	5.7
1982	4.7	10.7	4.50	7.1
1981	4.3	15.5	4.35	6.5
1980	3.7	13.0	2.60	6.1
1979	3.5	11.0	3.05	5.9

(a) Using whatever computer package is available, determine the best-fitting regression equation for these data.

(b) What percentage of the total variation in the number of millions of tons of steel sold by Allegheny each year is explained by this equation?

(c) How many tons of steel should Allegheny expect to sell in a year in which the inflation rate is 7.1, American automakers are planning to produce 6.0 million cars, and the average imported price undercut per ton is $3.50?

11-4
Making Inferences About Population Parameters

In the preceding chapter, we noted that the *sample* regression line, $\hat{Y} = a + bX$ (Equation 10-3), estimates the *population* regression line, $Y = A + BX$ (Equation 10-13). The reason we could only estimate the population regression line rather than find it exactly was that the data points didn't fall exactly on the population regression line. Because of random disturbances, the data points satisfied $Y = A + BX + e$ (Equation 10-13a) rather than $Y = A + BX$.

Population regression plane

Exactly the same sort of thing happens in multiple regression. Our estimated regression plane:

$$\hat{Y} = a + b_1 X_1 + b_2 X_2 + \cdots + b_k X_k \qquad [11\text{-}5]$$

is an estimate of a true but unknown population regression plane of the form:

$$Y = A + B_1 X_1 + B_2 X_2 + \cdots + B_k X_k \qquad [11\text{-}7]$$

Once again, the individual data points usually won't lie exactly on the population regression plane. Consider our IRS problem to see why this is so. Not all payments to informants will be equally effective. Some of the computer hours may be used for collecting and organizing data; others may be used for analyzing those data to seek errors and fraud. The success of the computer in discovering unpaid taxes may depend on how much time is devoted to each of these activities. For these and other reasons, some of the data points will be above the regression plane and some will be below it. Instead of satisfying:

Random disturbances move points off the regression plane

$$Y = A + B_1 X_1 + B_2 X_2 + \cdots + B_k X_k \qquad [11\text{-}7]$$

the individual data points will satisfy:

$$Y = A + B_1 X_1 + B_2 X_2 + \cdots + B_k X_k + e \qquad [11\text{-}7a]$$

The quantity e in Equation 11-7a is a random disturbance, which equals zero on the average. The standard deviation of the individual disturbances is σ_e, and the standard error of estimate, s_e, which we looked at in the last section, is an estimate of σ_e.

Since our *sample* regression plane, $\hat{Y} = a + b_1 X_1 + b_2 X_2 + \cdots + b_k X_k$ (Equation 11-5), estimates the unknown population regression plane, $Y = A + B_1 X_1 + B_2 X_2 + \cdots + B_k X_k$ (Equation 11-7), we should be able to use it to make inferences about the population regression plane. In this section, we shall make inferences about the slopes $(B_1, B_2, \ldots, B_k)$ of the "true" regression equation (the one for the entire population) that are based on the slopes $(b_1, b_2, \ldots, b_k)$ of the regression equation estimated from the sample of data points.

INFERENCES ABOUT AN INDIVIDUAL SLOPE B_i

Difference between true regression equation and one estimated from sample observations

The regression plane is derived from a sample and not from the entire population. As a result, we cannot expect the true regression equation, $Y = A + B_1 X_1 + B_2 X_2 + \cdots + B_k X_k$ (the one for the entire population) to be exactly the same as the equation estimated from the sample observations, $\hat{Y} = a + b_1 X_1 + b_2 X_2 + \cdots + b_k X_k$. Even so, we can use the value of b_i, one of the slopes we calculate from a sample, to test hypotheses about the value of B_i, one of the slopes of the regression plane for the entire population.

Testing a hypothesis about B_i

The procedure for testing a hypothesis about B_i is similar to procedures discussed in Chapter 8 on hypothesis testing. To understand this process, return to the problem that related unpaid taxes discovered to field-audit labor hours, computer hours, and rewards to informants. On page 547, we pointed out that $b_1 = .597$. The first step is to find some value for B_1 to compare with $b_1 = .597$.

Suppose that over an extended past period of time, the slope of the relationship between Y and X_1 was .400. To test if this were still the case, we could define the hypotheses as:

$$H_0: B_1 = .400 \leftarrow \text{null hypothesis}$$

$$H_1: B_1 \neq .400 \leftarrow \text{alternative hypothesis}$$

In effect, then, we are testing to learn whether current data indicate that B_1 has changed from its historical value of .400.

Standard error of the regression coefficient

To find the test statistic for B_1, it is necessary first to find the *standard error of the regression coefficient*. Here, the regression coefficient we are working with is b_1, so the standard error of this coefficient is denoted s_{b_1}.

It is too difficult to compute s_{b_1} by hand, but fortunately, SAS computes the standard errors of all the regression coefficients for us. For convenience, Figure 11-2 is repeated.

VARIABLE	DF	ROOT MSE	0.2861281	R-SQUARE	0.9834

VARIABLE	DF	PARAMETER ESTIMATE	STANDARD ERROR	T FOR H0: PARAMETER=0	PROB > |T|
INTERCEP	1	-45.79634767	4.87765079	-9.389	0.0001
AUDIT	1	0.59697180	0.08112429	7.359	0.0003
COMPUTER	1	1.17683773	0.08407418	13.998	0.0001
REWARDS	1	0.40510865	0.04223359	9.592	0.0001

FIGURE 11-2

SAS output (repeated)

Finding upper and lower limits of the acceptance region for our hypothesis test

From the output, we see that s_{b_1} is 0.0811. (Similarly, if we want to test a hypothesis about B_2, we see that the appropriate standard error to use is $s_{b_2} = 0.0841$.) Once we have found s_{b_1} we can use the t distribution with $n - k - 1$ degrees of freedom and the following equation to calculate the upper and lower limits of the acceptance region.

$$\left. \begin{array}{l} \text{Upper limit of acceptance region} = B_i + t(s_{b_i}) \\ \text{Lower limit of acceptance region} = B_i - t(s_{b_i}) \end{array} \right\} \qquad [11\text{-}8]$$

where:

- t = appropriate t value (with $n - k - 1$ degrees of freedom) for the signficance level of the test
- B_i = actual slope hypothesized for the population
- s_{b_i} = standard error of the regression coefficient

Conducting the hypothesis test

Suppose we are interested in testing our hypothesis at the 10 percent level of significance. Since we have ten observations in our sample data, and three independent variables, we know that we have $n - k - 1$ or $10 - 3 - 1 = 6$ degrees of freedom. We look in Appendix Table 2 under the 10 percent column and come down until we find the 6 degrees of freedom row. There, we see that the appropriate t value is 1.943. Since we are concerned whether b_1 (the slope of the sample regression plane) is significantly different from B_1 (the hypothesized slope of the population regression plane), this is a two-tailed test, and the limits of the acceptance region are found using Equation 11-8, with $i = 1$, since we are testing hypotheses about B_1.

$$B_1 + t(s_{b_1}) = .400 + 1.943(0.0811)$$
$$= .558 \leftarrow \text{upper limit of acceptance region}$$

$$B_1 - t(s_{b_1}) = .400 - 1.943(0.0811)$$
$$= .242 \leftarrow \text{lower limit of acceptance region}$$

The slope of our regression plane (b_1) is .597, which is *not* inside the acceptance region. Therefore, we reject the null hypothesis that B_1 still equals .400. In other words, there *is* enough difference between b_1 and .400 for us to conclude that B_1 has changed from its historical value. Because of this, we feel that each additional 100 hours of field-audit labor no longer increases unpaid taxes discovered by $400,000 as it did in the past.

Confidence interval for B_i

In addition to hypothesis testing, we can also construct a *confidence interval* for any one of the values of B_i. In the same way that b_i is a point estimate of B_i, such confidence intervals are interval estimates of B_i. To illustrate the process of constructing a confidence interval, let's find a 95 percent confidence interval for B_3 in our IRS problem. The relevant data are:

$$\left.\begin{array}{l} b_3 = 0.405 \\ s_{b_3} = 0.0422 \end{array}\right\} \text{ from Fig. 11.2}$$

$$t = 2.447 \leftarrow \text{5 percent level of significance and} $$
$$\text{6 degrees of freedom}$$

With this information, we can calculate confidence intervals like this:

$$b_3 + t(s_{b_3}) = 0.405 + 2.447(0.0422)$$
$$= .508 \leftarrow \text{upper limit}$$

$$b_3 - t(s_{b_3}) = 0.405 - 2.447(0.0422)$$
$$= .302 \leftarrow \text{lower limit}$$

We see that we can be 95 percent confident that each additional $1,000 paid to informants increases the unpaid taxes discovered by some amount between $302,000 and $508,000.

Is an explanatory variable significant?

We will often be interested in questions of the form: Does Y really depend on X_i? For example, we could ask whether unpaid taxes discovered really depend on computer hours. Frequently this question is phrased as, "Is X_i a significant explanatory variable for Y?" A bit of thought should convince you that Y depends on X_i (that is, Y varies when X_i varies) if $B_i \neq 0$, and it doesn't depend on X_i if $B_i = 0$.

We see that our question leads to hypotheses of the form:

$H_0: B_i = 0 \leftarrow$ null hypothesis: X_i is not a significant explanatory variable.

$H_1: B_i \neq 0 \leftarrow$ alternative hypothesis: X_i is a significant explanatory variable.

We can test these hypotheses using Equation 11-8 just as we did when we tested our hypotheses about whether B_1 still equaled .400. However, there is an easier way to do this, using the column on the output in Figure 11-2 headed "t for H_0: parameter $= 0$." Look at Equation 11-8 again:

$$\left.\begin{array}{l} \text{Upper limit of acceptance region} = B_i + t(s_{b_i}) \\ \text{Lower limit of acceptance region} = B_i - t(s_{b_i}) \end{array}\right\} \qquad \text{[11-8]}$$

If we let U denote the upper limit and L the lower limit, and note that $B_i = 0$ in the hypothesis test, Equation 11-8 becomes:

$$U = B_i + t(s_{b_i}) = 0 + t(s_{b_i}) = t(s_{b_i})$$
$$L = B_i - t(s_{b_i}) = 0 - t(s_{b_i}) = -t(s_{b_i})$$

and we accept H_0 if:

$$-t(s_{b_i}) \leq b_i \leq t(s_{b_i})$$

which is the same as saying, accept H_0 if:

$$-t \leq \frac{b_i}{s_{b_i}} \leq t$$

Now the t value in this last expression is the "critical" t value that we look up in Appendix Table 2. Let's call this t_c. The ratio b_i/s_{b_i} is called the "observed" or "computed" t value, denoted t_o. This is the number that appears in the column headed "t for H_0: parameter $= 0$" in Figure 11-2. So, to test hypotheses about whether X_i is a significant explanatory variable, we need only check whether:

$$-t_c \leq t_o \leq t_c \qquad \text{[11-9]}$$

where:

-      t_c = appropriate t value (with $n - k - 1$ degrees of freedom) for the significance level of the test
-   $t_o = b_i/s_{b_i}$ = observed (or computed) t value obtained from the computer output

If t_o falls between $-t_c$ and t_c, we accept H_0 and conclude X_i is not a significant explanatory variable. Otherwise, we reject H_0 and conclude that X_i is a significant explanatory variable.

Testing the significance of computer hours in the IRS problem   Let's test, at the .01 significance level, whether computer hours is a significant explanatory variable for unpaid taxes discovered. From Appendix Table 2, with $n - k - 1 = 10 - 3 - 1 = 6$ degrees of freedom and $\alpha = .01$, we see that $t_c = 3.707$. From Fig. 11-2, we see that $t_o = 13.998$. Since $t_o > t_c$, we conclude that computer hours *is* a significant explanatory variable. In fact, looking at the computed t values for the other two independent variables (field-audit labor hours $t_o = 7.359$ and rewards to informants, $t_o = 9.592$), we see that each of them is also a significant explanatory variable.

We can also use the column headed "prob $> |t|$" to test if X_i is a significant explanatory variable. In fact, using that information, we don't even need to use Appendix Table 2. The entries in this column are *prob values* for the hypotheses:

$$\overline{}$$
$$H_0: B_i = 0$$
$$H_1: B_i \neq 0$$
$$\overline{}$$

Recall from the discussion of section 9 in Chapter 8 that these prob values are the probabilities that each b_i would be as far (or farther) away from zero than the observed

11-4 Making Inferences About Population Parameters   **557**

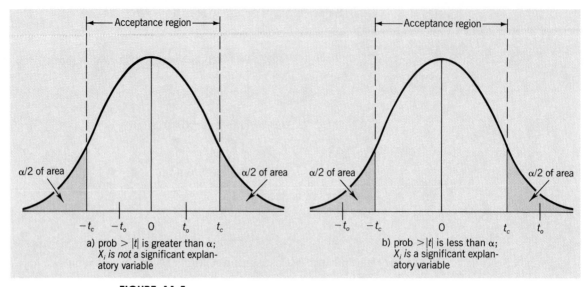

FIGURE 11-5

Using "prob > |t|" to see if X_i is a significant explanatory variable

value obtained from our regression, *if H_0 is true*. As Fig. 11-5 illustrates, we need only compare these prob values with α, the significance level of the test, to determine whether or not X_i is a significant explanatory variable for Y.

The absolute-value sign is included in "prob > |t|" because testing the significance of an explanatory variable is a two-tailed test. The independent variable X_i is a significant explanatory variable if b_i is significantly *different* from zero: that is, if t_c is a large positive or a large negative number.

In the IRS example, let's repeat our tests at $\alpha = .01$. For each of the three independent variables, prob > |t| is less than .01, so we again conclude that each one is a significant explanatory variable.

USING MINITAB AND MYSTAT

Output from Minitab and MYSTAT

Look back at Figs. 11-3 and 11-4 on p. 549. Both Minitab and MYSTAT also provide us with the standard errors of the regression coefficients, the observed t values for testing the significance of the explanatory variables, and the prob values for those two-tailed tests of significance. Minitab calls them "Stdev," "t-ratio," and "p," respectively. MYSTAT calls them "STD ERROR," "T," and "P(2 TAIL)." You should be able to find these quantities in the outputs of any statistical software package you use.

INFERENCES ABOUT THE REGRESSION AS A WHOLE

Suppose you put a piece of graph paper over a dartboard and randomly tossed a bunch of darts at it. After you took the darts out, you would have something that looked very much like a scatter diagram. Suppose you then fit a simple regression line to this set of "observed data points" and calculated r^2. Because the darts were randomly tossed, you would expect to get a low value of r^2, since in this case, X really doesn't explain Y. However, if you did this many times, occasionally you would observe a high value of r^2, just by pure chance.

Well, then, given any simple (or multiple) regression, **it's natural to ask whether the value of r^2 (or R^2) really indicates that the independent variables explain Y, or might this have happened just by chance?** This question is often phrased, Is the regression as a whole significant? In the last section, we looked at how to tell whether an individual X_i was a significant explanatory variable; now we see how to tell whether all the X_i's taken together significantly explain the variability observed in Y. Our hypotheses are:

$H_0: B_1 = B_2 \cdots = B_k = 0 \leftarrow$ null hypothesis: Y doesn't depend on the X_i's.

$H_1:$ at least one $B_i \neq 0 \leftarrow$ alternative hypothesis: Y depends on at least one of the X_i's.

When we discussed r^2 in Chapter 10, we looked at the total variation in Y, $\Sigma(Y - \overline{Y})^2$, the part of that variation which is explained by the regression $\Sigma(\hat{Y} - \overline{Y})^2$, and the unexplained part of the variation, $\Sigma(Y - \hat{Y})^2$. Figure 11-6 is a duplicate of Fig. 10-15. It reviews the relationship between total deviation, explained deviation, and unexplained deviation for a single data point in a simple regression. Although we can't draw a similar picture for a multiple regression, we are doing the same thing conceptually.

In discussing the variation in Y, then, we look at three different terms, each of which is a sum of squares. We denote these by:

$$\left.\begin{array}{ll} \text{SST} = \text{the total sum of squares} & = \Sigma(Y - \overline{Y})^2 \\ \text{SSR} = \text{the regression sum of squares} = \Sigma(\hat{Y} - \overline{Y})^2 \\ \qquad \text{(i.e., the explained part)} \\ \text{SSE} = \text{the error sum of squares} & = \Sigma(Y - \hat{Y})^2 \\ \qquad \text{(i.e., the unexplained part)} \end{array}\right\} \quad [11\text{-}10]$$

FIGURE 11-6

Total deviation, explained deviation, and unexplained deviation for *one* observed value of Y

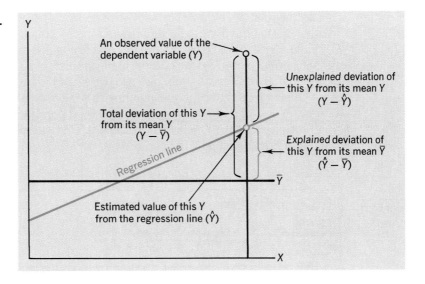

FIGURE 11-7

More SAS output: the
analysis of variance

```
DEP VARIABLE: DISCOVER    UNPAID TAXES DISCOVERED ($MILLIONS)
                        ANALYSIS OF VARIANCE

                      SUM OF           MEAN
SOURCE       DF      SQUARES          SQUARE     F VALUE      PROB>F

MODEL         3    29.10878410     9.70292803    118.517     0.0001
ERROR         6     0.49121590     0.08186932
C TOTAL       9    29.60000000
```

These are related by the equation

$$SST = SSR + SSE \qquad [11\text{-}11]$$

which says that the total variation in Y can be broken down into two parts, the explained part and the unexplained part.

Each of these sums of squares has an associated number of degrees of freedom. SST has $n - 1$ degrees of freedom (n observations, but we lose a degree of freedom because the sample mean is fixed). SSR has k degrees of freedom, because there are k independent variables being used to explain Y. Finally, SSE has $n - k - 1$ degrees of freedom, because we used our n observations to estimate $k + 1$ constants, $a, b_1, b_2, \ldots, b_k$. If the null hypothesis is true, the ratio:

$$F = \frac{SSR/k}{SSE/(n - k - 1)} \qquad [11\text{-}12]$$

F test on the regression as a whole

has an F distribution with k numerator degrees of freedom and $n - k - 1$ denominator degrees of freedom. If the null hypothesis is false, then the F ratio tends to be larger than it is when the null hypothesis is true. So if the F ratio is too high (as determined by the significance level of the test and the appropriate value from Appendix Table 6), we reject H_0 and conclude that the regression as a whole *is* significant.

Analysis of variance for the regression

Fig. 11-7 gives more of the SAS output for the IRS problem. (The corresponding parts of the Minitab and MYSTAT outputs are given in Figs. 11-8 and 11-9.) This part of the output includes the computed F ratio for the regression, and is sometimes called "the analysis of variance for the regression." You are probably wondering whether this has anything to do with the analysis of variance we discussed in Chapter 9. Yes, it does. Although we did not do so, it is possible to show that the analysis of variance in Chapter 9 also looks at the total variation of all of the observations about the grand mean and breaks it up into two parts: one part explained by the differences among the several groups (corresponding to what we called the "between-column variance") and the other part unexplained by those differences (corresponding to what we called the "within-column variance"). This is precisely analogous to what we just did in Equation 11-11.

FIGURE 11-8

Minitab's output for
analysis of variance

```
Analysis of Variance

SOURCE       DF        SS          MS       F         p
Regression    3    29.1088     9.7029   118.52    0.000
Error         6     0.4912     0.0819
Total         9    29.6000
```

FIGURE 11-9

MYSTAT's output for
analysis of variance

```
                         ANALYSIS OF VARIANCE

    SOURCE    SUM-OF-SQUARES   DF   MEAN-SQUARE    F-RATIO     P

    REGRESSION       29.109     3        9.703    118.517     0.000
    RESIDUAL          0.491     6        0.082
```

For the IRS problem, we see that SSR = 29.109 (with $k = 3$ degrees of freedom), SSE = 0.491 (with $n - k - 1 = 10 - 3 - 1 = 6$ degrees of freedom) and that:

Testing the significance of the IRS regression

$$F = \frac{29.109/3}{0.491/6} = \frac{9.703}{0.082} = 118.517$$

The entries in the "mean square" (or "ms") column are just the sums of squares divided by their degrees of freedom. For 3 numerator degrees of freedom and 6 denominator degrees of freedom, Appendix Table 6 tells us that 9.78 is the upper limit of the acceptance region for a significance level of $\alpha = .01$. Our calculated F value of 118.517 is far above 9.78, so we see that the regression as a whole is highly significant. We can also reach the same conclusion by noting that the outputs tell us that "prob $> F$" is .0001 (or that "P" is 0.000). Since this prob value is less than our significance level of $\alpha = .01$, we conclude that the regression as a whole is significant. Using "prob $> F$" analogously to the way we used "prob $> |t|$" in testing the significance of the individual explanatory variables, we see that we can do the test without having to use Appendix Table 6.

MULTICOLLINEARITY IN MULTIPLE REGRESSION

Definition and effect of multicollinearity

In multiple regression analysis, the regression coefficients often become less reliable as the degree of correlation between the independent variables increases. If there is a high level of correlation between them, we have a problem that statisticians call *multicollinearity.*

Multicollinearity might occur if we wished to estimate a firm's sales revenue and we used both the number of salespersons employed and their total salaries. Since the values associated with these two independent variables are highly correlated, we need to use only one set of them to make our estimate. In fact, adding a second variable that is correlated with the first distorts the values of the regression coefficients. Nevertheless, we can often predict Y well, even when multicollinearity is present.

An example of multicollinearity

Let's look at an example in which multicollinearity is present to see how it affects the regression. For the past 12 months, the manager of Pizza Shack has been running a series of advertisements in the local newspaper. The ads are scheduled and paid for in the month before they appear. Each of the ads contains a two-for-one coupon, which entitles the bearer to receive two Pizza Shack pizzas while paying for only the more expensive of the two. The manager has collected the data in Table 11-4 and would like to use it to predict pizza sales.

Two simple regressions

In Figures 11-10 and 11-11, we have given the SAS outputs for the regressions of total sales on number of ads and cost of ads respectively.

For the regression on number of ads, we see that the observed t value is 3.952. With 10 degrees of freedom and a significance level of $\alpha = .01$, the critical t value (from

TABLE 11-4 Pizza Shack Sales and Advertising Data

MONTH	X_1 NUMBER OF ADS APPEARING	X_2 COST OF ADS APPEARING (00s OF DOLLARS)	Y TOTAL PIZZA SALES (000s OF DOLLARS)
May	12	$13.9	$43.6
June	11	12.0	38.0
July	9	9.3	30.1
Aug.	7	9.7	35.3
Sept.	12	12.3	46.4
Oct.	8	11.4	34.2
Nov.	6	9.3	30.2
Dec.	13	14.3	40.7
Jan.	8	10.2	38.5
Feb.	6	8.4	22.6
March	8	11.2	37.6
April	10	11.1	35.2

Appendix Table 2) is found to be 3.169. Since $t_o > t_c$ (or equivalently, since prob $> |t|$ is less than .01), we conclude that the number of ads is a highly significant explanatory variable for total sales. Note also that $r^2 = .6097$, so that the number of ads explains about 61 percent of the variation in pizza sales.

For the regression on cost of ads, the observed t value is 4.538, so that cost of ads is even more significant as an explanatory variable for total sales than was number of ads (for which the observed t value was only 3.952). In this regression, $r^2 = .6731$, so about 67 percent of the variation in pizza sales is explained by the cost of ads.

Using both explanatory variables in a multiple regression

Since both explanatory variables are highly significant by themselves, we try to use both of them in a multiple regression. The output is in Figure 11-12.

The multiple regression is highly significant as a whole, since prob $> F$ is 0.0056.

The multiple coefficient of determination is $R^2 = .6840$, so the two variables together explain about 68 percent of the variation in total sales.

Loss of individual significance

However, if we look at the prob $> |t|$ values for the variables in the multiple regression, we see that even at $\alpha = .1$, neither variable is a significant explanatory variable.

FIGURE 11-10

Regression of sales on number of ads

```
MODEL: ADS
DEP VARIABLE: SALES        TOTAL PIZZA SALES (THOUSANDS OF $)
                            ANALYSIS OF VARIANCE

                    SUM OF          MEAN
    SOURCE    DF    SQUARES         SQUARE      F VALUE     PROB>F

    MODEL      1    276.30787       276.30787    15.621     0.0027
    ERROR     10    176.87880       17.68787958
    C TOTAL   11    453.18667
        ROOT MSE    4.205696        R-SQUARE    0.6097


                PARAMETER       STANDARD     T FOR H0:
VARIABLE   DF   ESTIMATE        ERROR        PARAMETER=0    PROB > |T|

INTERCEP   1    16.93691099     4.98182652    3.400         0.0068
ADS        1     2.08324607     0.52708642    3.952         0.0027
```

FIGURE 11-11

Regression of sales on cost of ads

```
MODEL: COST
DEP VARIABLE: SALES    TOTAL PIZZA SALES (THOUSANDS OF $)
                           ANALYSIS OF VARIANCE

                          SUM OF         MEAN
          SOURCE    DF    SQUARES       SQUARE      F VALUE      PROB>F

          MODEL      1   305.03863    305.03863     20.590      0.0011
          ERROR     10   148.14803   14.81480342
          C TOTAL   11   453.18667
               ROOT MSE      3.849      R-SQUARE      0.6731


                        PARAMETER      STANDARD     T FOR H0:
VARIABLE    DF          ESTIMATE        ERROR      PARAMETER=0    PROB > |T|

INTERCEP     1         4.17270022    7.10879031      0.587        0.5702
COST         1         2.87248383    0.63303557      4.538        0.0011
```

What has happened here? In the simple regression, each variable is highly significant, and in the multiple regression, they are collectively very significant, but individually not significant.

This apparent contradiction is explained once we notice that the number of ads is highly correlated with the cost of ads. In fact, the correlation between these two variables is $r = .8949$, so we have a problem with multicollinearity in our data. You might wonder why these two variables are not perfectly correlated. This is because the cost of an ad varies slightly, depending on where it appears in the newspaper. For instance, in the Sunday paper, ads in the TV section cost more than ads in the news section, and the manager of Pizza Shack has placed Sunday ads in each of these sections on different occasions.

Since X_1 and X_2 are closely related to each other, in effect they each explain the same part of the variability in Y. That's why we get $r^2 = .6097$ in the first simple regression, $r^2 = .6731$ in the second simple regression, but an r^2 of only .6840 in the multiple regression: Adding numbers of ads as a second explanatory variable to cost of ads explains only about 1 percent more of the variation in total sales.

Correlation between the two explanatory variables

Both variables explain the same thing

FIGURE 11-12

Regression of sales on number and cost of ads

```
MODEL: BOTH
DEP VARIABLE: SALES    TOTAL PIZZA SALES (THOUSANDS OF $)
                           ANALYSIS OF VARIANCE

                          SUM OF         MEAN
          SOURCE    DF    SQUARES       SQUARE      F VALUE      PROB>F

          MODEL      2   309.98585    154.99292      9.741       0.0056
          ERROR      9   143.20082   15.91120195
          C TOTAL   11   453.18667
               ROOT MSE   3.988885     R-SQUARE      0.6840


                        PARAMETER      STANDARD     T FOR H0:
VARIABLE    DF          ESTIMATE        ERROR      PARAMETER=0    PROB > |T|

INTERCEP     1         6.58357840    8.54215539      0.771        0.4606
ADS          1         0.62467534    1.12027693      0.558        0.5907
COST         1         2.13886380    1.47014990      1.455        0.1797
```

Individual contributions
can't be separated out

At this point, it is fair to ask, "Which variable is really explaining the variation in total sales in the multiple regression?" The answer is that both are, but **we cannot separate out their individual contributions, because they are so highly correlated with each other. As a result of this, their coefficients in the multiple regression have high standard errors, relatively small computed t values, and relatively large prob $> |t|$ values.**

How does this multicollinearity affect us? We are still able to make relatively precise predictions when it is present: Note that for the multiple regression (output in Figure 11-12), the standard error of estimate, which determines the width of confidence intervals for predictions, is 3.99, while for the simple regression with cost of ads as the explanatory variable (output in Figure 11-11), we have $s_e = 3.85$. What we can't do is tell with much precision how sales will change if we increase the number of ads by one. The multiple regression says $b_1 = .625$ (that is, each ad increases total pizza sales by about \$625), but the standard error of this coefficient is 1.12 (that is, about \$1,120).

Exercises

 11-22 Mark Lowtown publishes the *Mosquito Junction Enquirer* and is having difficulty predicting the amount of newsprint needed each day. He has randomly selected 27 days over the past year and recorded the following information:

$$POUNDS \quad = \text{pounds of newsprint used for that day's newspaper}$$

$$CLASFIED = \text{number of classified advertisements}$$

$$DISPLAY \quad = \text{number of display advertisements}$$

$$FULLPAGE = \text{number of full-page advertisements}$$

Using SAS to regress POUNDS on the other variables, Mark got the output which follows.

VARIABLE	DF	PARAMETER ESTIMATE	STANDARD ERROR	T FOR H0: PARAMETER=0	PROB > ITI
INTERCEP	1	1072.953	872.433	1.230	0.2317
CLASFIED	1	0.251	0.126	1.988	0.0595
DISPLAY	1	1.250	0.884	1.414	0.1715
FULLPAGE	1	250.659	67.915	3.691	0.0013

(a) Mark had always felt that each display advertisement used at least three pounds of newsprint. Does the regression give him significant reason to doubt this belief at the 5 percent level?

(b) Similarly, Mark had always felt that each classified advertisement used roughly half a pound of newsprint. Does he now have significant reason to doubt this belief at the 5 percent level?

(c) Mark sells full-page advertising space to the local merchants for \$30 per page. Should he consider adjusting his rates if newsprint costs him 9¢ per pound? Assume other costs are negligible. State explicit hypotheses and an explicit conclusion. (Hint: Holding all else constant, each additional full-page ad uses 250.659 pounds of paper $\times$ \$0.09 per pound = \$22.56 cost. Breakeven is at 333.333 pounds. Why? Thus, if the slope coefficient for FULLPAGE is significantly above 333.333, Mark is not making a profit and his rates should be changed.)

11-23 Refer to exercise 11-18. At a significance level of .10, which variables are significant explanatory variables for exam scores? (There were twelve students in the sample.)

11-24 Refer to exercise 11-18. The following additional output was provided by SAS when Bill ran the multiple regression:

```
DEP VARIABLE: SCORE    EXAM SCORE
                    ANALYSIS OF VARIANCE

                   SUM OF       MEAN
SOURCE     DF     SQUARES      SQUARE     F VALUE
MODEL       4     3134.417     783.604
ERROR       7      951.250     135.893
C TOTAL    11     4085.667
```

(a) What is the observed value of F?

(b) At a significance level of .05, what is the appropriate critical value of F to use in determining if the regression as a whole is significant?

(c) Based on your answers to (a) and (b), is the regression significant as a whole?

11-25 Refer to exercise 11-19. At a significance level of .01, is DISTANCE a significant explanatory variable for SALES?

11-26 Refer to exercise 11-19. The following additional output was provided by SAS when the multiple regression was run:

```
DEP VARIABLE: SALES    AVERAGE WEEKLY SALES (THOUSANDS OF $)
                    ANALYSIS OF VARIANCE

                   SUM OF       MEAN
SOURCE     DF     SQUARES      SQUARE     F VALUE    PROB>F
MODEL       4     2861495      715374     102.39     0.0001
ERROR      18      125761     6986.701
C TOTAL    22     2987256
```

At the .05 level of significance, is the regression significant as a whole?

11-27 Henry Lander is director of production for the Alecos Corporation of Caracas, Venezuela. Henry has asked you to help him determine a formula for predicting absenteeism in a meat-packing facility. He hypothesizes that percentage absenteeism can be explained by average daily temperature. Data are gathered for several months, you run the simple regression, and you find that temperature explains 66 percent of the variation in absenteeism. But Henry is not convinced that this is a satisfactory predictor. He suggests that daily rainfall may also have something to do with absenteeism. So you gather data, run a regression of absenteeism during rainfall, and get an R^2 of .59. "Eureka!" you cry, "I've got it! With one predictor that explains 66 percent and another that explains 59 percent, all I have to do is run a multiple regression using both predictors, and I'll surely have an almost perfect predictor!" To your dismay, however, the multiple regression has an R^2 of only 68 percent, which is just slightly better than the temperature variable alone. How can you account for this apparent discrepancy?

11-28 Juan Armenlegg, manager of Rocky's Diamond and Jewelry Store, is interested in developing a model to estimate consumer demand for his rather expensive merchandise. Since most customers buy diamonds and jewelry on credit, Juan is sure that two factors that must influence consumer demand are the current annual inflation rate and the current prime lending rate at the leading banks in the country. Explain some of the problems that Juan might encounter if he were to set up a regression model based on his two predictor variables.

11-29 Edith Pratt is a busy executive in a nationwide trucking company. Edith is late for a meeting because she has been unable to locate the multiple regression output that a subordinate produced for her. If the total regression was significant at the .05 level, then she wanted to use the computer output as evidence to support some of her ideas at the meeting. The subordinate, however, is sick today and Edith has been unable to locate his work. As a matter of fact, all the information she possesses concerning the multiple regression is a piece of scrap paper with the following on it:

REGRESSION FOR
E. PRATT

SSR	872.4, with		df
SSE		, with	17 df
SST	1023.6, with		24 df

Since the scrap paper doesn't even have a complete set of numbers on it, Edith has concluded that it must be useless. You, however, should know better. Should Edith go directly to the meeting, or continue looking for the computer output?

11-30 A New England-based commuter airline has taken a survey of its fifteen offices and has obtained the following data for the month of February, where:

SALES = total revenue based on number of tickets sold (in thousands of dollars)

PROMOT = amount spent on promoting the airline in the area (in thousands of dollars)

COMP = number of competing airlines in the area

FREE = the percentage of passengers who flew free (for various reasons)

SALES ($)	PROMOT ($)	COMP	FREE
79.3	2.5	10	3
200.1	5.5	8	6
163.2	6.0	12	9
200.1	7.9	7	16
146.0	5.2	8	15
177.7	7.6	12	9
30.9	2.0	12	8
291.9	9.0	5	10
160.0	4.0	8	4
339.4	9.6	5	16
159.6	5.5	11	7
86.3	3.0	12	6
237.5	6.0	6	10
107.2	5.0	10	4
155.0	3.5	10	4

(a) Using whatever computer package is available, determine the best-fitting regression equation for the airline.
(b) Do the passengers who fly free cause sales to decrease significantly? State and test appropriate hypotheses. Use $\alpha = .05$.
(c) Does an increase in promotions by $1,000 change sales by $28,000, or is the change significantly different from $28,000? State and test appropriate hypotheses. Use $\alpha = .10$.
(d) Give a 90 percent confidence interval for the slope coefficient of COMP.

11 MULTIPLE REGRESSION AND MODELING TECHNIQUES

11-5
Modeling Techniques

Looking at different
models

Given a variable we want to explain and a bunch of potential explanatory variables, there may be several different regression equations we can look at, depending on which explanatory variables we include and how we include them. Each such regression equation is called a *model*. *Modeling techniques* are the various ways in which we can include the explanatory variables and check the appropriateness of our regression models. There are many different modeling techniques, but we shall look at only two of the most commonly used devices.

QUALITATIVE DATA AND DUMMY VARIABLES

In all the regression examples we have looked at so far, the data have been numerical, or *quantitative*. But occasionally we will be faced with a variable that is categorical, or *qualitative*. In our chapter-opening problem, the director of personnel wanted to see if the base salary of a salesperson depended on the person's sex. Table 11-5 repeats the data of that problem.

Reviewing a previous
way to approach the
problem

For the moment, ignore the length of employment and use the technique developed in Chapter 8 for testing the difference between means of two populations, to see if men earn more than women. Test this at $\alpha = .01$. If we let the men be population 1 and the women be population 2, we are testing:

$H_0: \mu_1 = \mu_2 \leftarrow$ null hypothesis: There is no sex discrimination in base salaries.

$H_1: \mu_1 > \mu_2 \leftarrow$ alternative hypothesis: Women are discriminated against in base salary.

$\alpha = .01 \leftarrow$ level of significance

We sketch the analysis below. If you have any trouble following it, you should review briefly pages 377–380.

$$n_1 = 5 \qquad n_2 = 4$$
$$\bar{x}_1 = 9.7 \qquad \bar{x}_2 = 8.525$$
$$s_1^2 = 4.415 \qquad s_2^2 = 2.609$$

TABLE 11-5 Data for Sex-Discrimination Problem

Salesmen		Saleswomen	
MONTHS EMPLOYED	BASE SALARY ($1,000s)	MONTHS EMPLOYED	BASE SALARY ($1,000s)
6	7.5	5	6.2
10	8.6	13	8.7
12	9.1	15	9.4
18	10.3	21	9.8
30	13.0		

$$s_p{}^2 = \frac{(n_1 - 1)s_1{}^2 + (n_2 - 1)s_2{}^2}{n_1 + n_2 - 2} \qquad [8\text{-}3]$$

$$= \frac{4(4.415) + 3(2.609)}{5 + 4 - 2}$$

$$= 3.641$$

$$\hat{\sigma}_{\bar{x}_1 - \bar{x}_2} = s_p \sqrt{\frac{1}{n_1} + \frac{1}{n_2}} \qquad [8\text{-}4]$$

$$= 1.28$$

With 7 degrees of freedom, the upper limit of the acceptance region is $0 +$ $1.28(2.998) = 3.84$. The observed value of $\bar{x}_1 - \bar{x}_2 = 1.175$, which we see is less than 3.84, so we cannot reject H_0.

The old approach doesn't detect any discrimination

Our analysis therefore concludes that there does not appear to be any sex discrimination in base salaries. But recall that we have ignored the length-of-employment data thus far in the analysis.

"Eyeballing" the data

Before we go any farther, look at a scatter diagram of the data. In Fig. 11-13, the black points correspond to men and the colored circles correspond to women. The scatter diagram clearly shows that base salary increases with length of service; but if you try to "eyeball" the regression line, you'll note that the black points tend to be above it, and the colored circles tend to be below it.

Figure 11-14 gives the output from a regression of base salary on months employed. From that output we see that months employed is a very highly significant explanatory variable.

Also, $r^2 = .9260$, indicating that months employed explains about 93 percent of the variation in base salary. Figure 11-14 contains part of the output that we haven't seen before, a table of *residuals*. For each data point, the residual is just $Y - \hat{Y}$, which we recognize as the error in the fit of the regression line at that point.

FIGURE 11-13

Scatter diagram of base salaries plotted against months employed

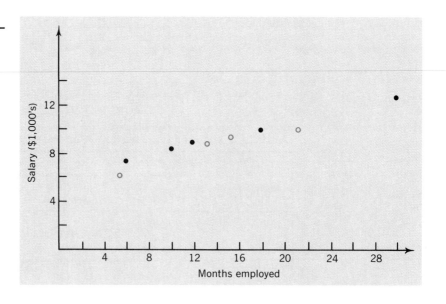

```
MODEL: MONTHS
DEP VARIABLE: SALARY    BASE SALARY (THOUSANDS OF $)
                          ANALYSIS OF VARIANCE

                      SUM OF           MEAN
        SOURCE    DF   SQUARES        SQUARE      F VALUE      PROB>F

        MODEL     1   26.44272420   26.44272420   87.607      0.0001
        ERROR     7    2.11283135    0.30183305
        C TOTAL   8   28.55555556
            ROOT MSE    0.5493933    R-SQUARE     0.9260


                    PARAMETER       STANDARD     T FOR H0:
    VARIABLE   DF    ESTIMATE         ERROR     PARAMETER=0    PROB > |T|

    INTERCEP   1    5.80927788     0.40380201     14.386       0.0001
    MONTHS     1    0.23320384     0.02491529      9.360       0.0001

                                     PREDICT
                    OBS    ACTUAL     VALUE     RESIDUAL

                     1    7.5000     7.2085     0.2915
                     2    8.6000     8.1413     0.4587
                     3    9.1000     8.6077     0.4923
                     4   10.3000    10.0069     0.2931
                     5   13.0000    12.8054     0.1946
                     6    6.2000     6.9753    -0.7753
                     7    8.7000     8.8409    -0.1409
                     8    9.4000     9.3073     0.0927
                     9    9.8000    10.7066    -0.9066
```

FIGURE 11-14

Regression of base salary on months employed

"Squeezing the residuals"

Perhaps the most important part of analyzing a regression output is looking at the residuals. If the regression includes all the relevant explanatory factors, these residuals ought to be random. Looking at this in another way, if the residuals show any nonrandom patterns, this indicates that there is something systematic going on that we have failed to take into account. So we look for patterns in the residuals; or to put it somewhat more picturesquely, we "squeeze the residuals until they talk."

Noticing a pattern in the residuals

As we look at the residuals in Figure 11-14, we note that the first five residuals are positive. So for the salesmen, we have $Y - \hat{Y} > 0$, or $Y > \hat{Y}$; that is to say, the regression line falls below these five data points. Three of the last four residuals are negative. And thus for the saleswomen, we have $Y - \hat{Y} < 0$, or $Y < \hat{Y}$, so the regression line lies above three of the four data points. This confirms the observation we made when we looked at the scatter diagram in Fig. 11-13. This nonrandom pattern in the residuals suggests that sex *is* a factor in determining base salary.

Using dummy variables

How can we incorporate the salesperson's sex *into* the regression model? We do this by using a device called a *dummy variable* (or an *indicator variable*). For the points representing salesmen, this variable is given the value 0, and for the points representing saleswomen, it is given the value 1. The input data for our regression using dummy variables are given in Table 11-6.

To the data in Table 11-6, we fit a regression of the form:

$$\hat{Y} = a + b_1 X_1 + b_2 X_2 \qquad [11\text{-}5]$$

Let's see what happens if we use this regression to predict the base salary of an individual with X_1 months of service:

Salesman: $\hat{Y} = a + b_1 X_1 + b_2(0) = a + b_1 X_1$

Saleswoman: $\hat{Y} = a + b_1 X_1 + b_2(1) = a + b_1 X_1 + b_2$

For salesmen and saleswomen with the same length of employment, we predict a base salary difference of b_2 thousands of dollars. Now, b_2 is just our estimate of B_2 in the population regression:

$$Y = A + B_1 X_1 + B_2 X_2 \qquad [11\text{-}7]$$

If there really is discrimination against women, they should earn less than men with the same length of service. In other words, B_2 should be negative. We can test this at the .01 level of significance.

$H_0: B_2 = 0 \leftarrow$ null hypothesis: There is no sex discrimination in base salaries.

$H_1: B_2 < 0 \leftarrow$ alternative hypothesis: Women are discriminated against.

$\alpha = .01 \leftarrow$ level of significance

In order to test these hypotheses, we run a regression on the data in Table 11-6. The results of that regression are given in Figure 11-15.

Our hypothesis test is based on the t distribution with $n - k - 1 = 9 - 2 - 1 = 6$ degrees of freedom. The appropriate t value from Appendix Table 2 is 3.143. The lower limit of the acceptance region is:

$$\begin{aligned} \text{Lower limit of acceptance region} &= B_2 - t(s_{b_2}) \qquad [11\text{-}8]\\ &= 0 - 3.143(.238)\\ &= -0.748 \end{aligned}$$

Figure 11-16 illustrates this limit of the acceptance region and the observed value of $b_2 = -0.789$. **We see that the observed b_2 lies outside the acceptance region, so we reject the null hypothesis and conclude that the firm does discriminate against its saleswomen.** We also note, in passing, that the computed t value for b_1 in this regression is 14.089, so including sex as an explanatory variable makes months employed even more significant an explanatory variable than it was before. Finally, we note that the residuals for this regression don't seem to show any nonrandom pattern.

Now to review how we handled the qualitative variable in this problem. We set up a dummy variable, which we gave the value 0 for the men and the value 1 for the women. Then the coefficient of the dummy variable can be interpreted as the difference between a woman's base salary and the base salary for a man. Suppose we had set

TABLE 11-6 Input Data for Sex-Discrimination Regression

X_1 MONTHS EMPLOYED		X_2 SEX	Y BASE SALARY ($1,000s)
Men	6	0	7.5
	10	0	8.6
	12	0	9.1
	18	0	10.3
	30	0	13.0
Women	5	1	6.2
	13	1	8.7
	15	1	9.4
	21	1	9.8

```
MODEL: BOTH
DEP VARIABLE: SALARY    BASE SALARY (THOUSANDS OF $)
                          ANALYSIS OF VARIANCE

                         SUM OF          MEAN
        SOURCE     DF     SQUARES        SQUARE       F VALUE      PROB>F

        MODEL      2    27.80774397    13.90387198    111.556      0.0001
        ERROR      6     0.74781159     0.12463526
        C TOTAL    8    28.55555556
              ROOT MSE    0.3530372    R-SQUARE        0.9738


                      PARAMETER       STANDARD      T FOR H0:
        VARIABLE   DF   ESTIMATE        ERROR      PARAMETER=0    PROB > |T|

        INTERCEP   1    6.24847853    0.29145011     21.439        0.0001
        MONTHS     1    0.22707378    0.01611723     14.089        0.0001
        SEX        1   -0.78897457    0.23840426     -3.309        0.0162


                                       PREDICT
                    OBS    ACTUAL        VALUE      RESIDUAL

                     1     7.5000       7.6109      -0.1109
                     2     8.6000       8.5192       0.0808
                     3     9.1000       8.9734       0.1266
                     4    10.3000      10.3358      -0.0358
                     5    13.0000      13.0607      -0.0607
                     6     6.2000       6.5949      -0.3949
                     7     8.7000       8.4115       0.2885
                     8     9.4000       8.8656       0.5344
                     9     9.8000      10.2281      -0.4281
```

FIGURE 11-15

Output from sex-discrimination regression

the dummy variable to 0 for women and 1 for men. Then its coefficient would be the difference between a man's base salary and the base salary for a woman. Can you guess what the regression would have been in this case? It shouldn't surprise you to learn that it would have been:

$$\hat{Y} = 5.459504 + 0.227074X_1 + .788975X_2$$

The choice of which category is given the value 0 and which the value 1 is totally arbitrary and affects only the sign, not the numerical value of the coefficient of the dummy variable.

FIGURE 11-16

Left-tailed hypothesis test at the .01 significance level, showing acceptance region and the observed regression coefficient

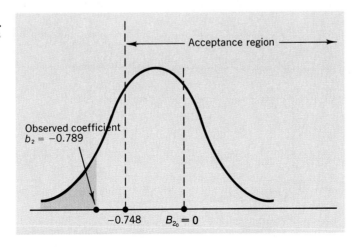

TABLE 11-7 **Number of Defective Shafts Per Batch**

BATCH SIZE	NUMBER DEFECTIVE	BATCH SIZE	NUMBER DEFECTIVE
100	5	250	37
125	10	250	41
125	6	250	34
125	7	275	49
150	6	300	53
150	7	300	54
175	17	325	69
175	15	350	82
200	24	350	81
200	21	350	84
200	22	375	92
225	26	375	96
225	29	375	97
225	25	400	109
250	34	400	112

Extensions of dummy variable techniques

Our example had only one qualitative variable (sex), and that variable had only two possible categories (male and female). Although we won't pursue the details here, dummy variable techniques can also be used in problems with several qualitative variables, and those variables can have more than two possible categories.

TRANSFORMING VARIABLES AND FITTING CURVES

A manufacturer of small electric motors uses an automatic milling machine to produce the slots in the shafts of the motors. A batch of shafts is run and then checked.

FIGURE 11-17

Scatter diagram of defective shafts plotted against size of batch

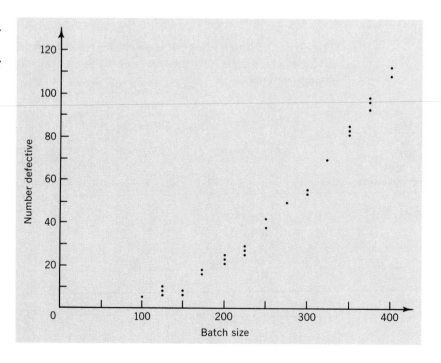

11 MULTIPLE REGRESSION AND MODELING TECHNIQUES

All shafts in the batch that do not meet required dimensional tolerances are discarded. At the beginning of each new batch, the milling machine is readjusted, since its cutter head wears slightly during the production of the batch. The manufacturer is trying to pick an optimal batch size; but in order to do this, he must know how the size of a batch affects the number of defective shafts in the batch. Table 11-7 gives data for a sample of 30 batches, arranged by ascending size of batch.

Noticing a pattern in the residuals

Figure 11-17 is a scatter diagram for these data. Since there are two batches of size 250 with 34 defective shafts, two of the points in the scatter diagram coincide (this is indicated by a colored data point in Fig. 11-17).

We are going to run a regression of number of defective shafts on the batch size. The output from the regression is in Figure 11-18. What does this output tell us? First of all, we note that batch size does a fantastic job of explaining the number of defective shafts: The computed t value is 23.935 and $r^2 = .9534$. However, despite the

FIGURE 11-18

Regression of number of defects on batch size

```
MODEL: LINE
DEP VARIABLE: DEFECTS   DEFECTIVE PIECES IN BATCH
                       ANALYSIS OF VARIANCE

                    SUM OF          MEAN
        SOURCE   DF  SQUARES        SQUARE       F VALUE    PROB>F

        MODEL     1  32744.45526   32744.45526   572.905    0.0001
        ERROR    28   1600.34474      57.15516925
        C TOTAL  29  34344.80000
             ROOT MSE    7.560104      R-SQUARE     0.9534


                    PARAMETER      STANDARD      T FOR H0:
VARIABLE   DF       ESTIMATE       ERROR      PARAMETER=0    PROB > |T|

INTERCEP    1      -47.90069462   4.11155834    -11.650       0.0001
BATCHSIZ    1        0.36713146   0.01533841     23.935       0.0001


                                   PREDICT
                OBS    ACTUAL        VALUE      RESIDUAL

                 1      5.0000     -11.1875      16.1875
                 2     10.0000      -2.0093      12.0093
                 3      6.0000      -2.0093       8.0093
                 4      7.0000      -2.0093       9.0093
                 5      6.0000       7.1690      -1.1690
                 6      7.0000       7.1690      -0.1690
                 7     17.0000      16.3473       0.6527
                 8     15.0000      16.3473      -1.3473
                 9     24.0000      25.5256      -1.5256
                10     21.0000      25.5256      -4.5256
                11     22.0000      25.5256      -3.5256
                12     26.0000      34.7039      -8.7039
                13     29.0000      34.7039      -5.7039
                14     25.0000      34.7039      -9.7039
                15     34.0000      43.8822      -9.8822
                16     37.0000      43.8822      -6.8822
                17     41.0000      43.8822      -2.8822
                18     34.0000      43.8822      -9.8822
                19     49.0000      53.0605      -4.0605
                20     53.0000      62.2387      -9.2387
                21     54.0000      62.2387      -8.2387
                22     69.0000      71.4170      -2.4170
                23     82.0000      80.5953       1.4047
                24     81.0000      80.5953       0.4047
                25     84.0000      80.5953       3.4047
                26     92.0000      89.7736       2.2264
                27     96.0000      89.7736       6.2264
                28     97.0000      89.7736       7.2264
                29    109.0000      98.9519      10.0481
                30    112.0000      98.9519      13.0481
```

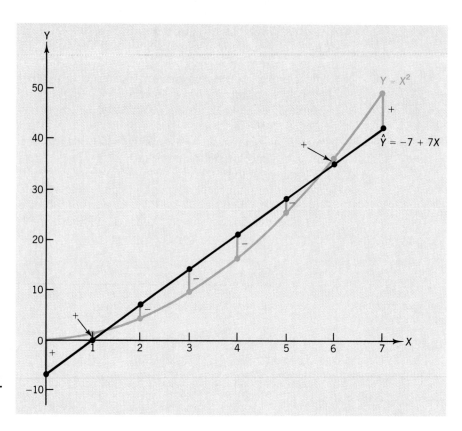

FIGURE 11-19

Fitting a straight line to points on a curve

incredibly high *t* value, and despite the fact that batch size explains 95 percent of the variation in number of defectives, the residuals in this regression are far from random. Notice how they start out as large positive values, become smaller, then go negative, then become more negative, and then turn around again, finishing up with large positive values.

TABLE 11-8 Input for Fitting a Curve to the Motor-Shaft Data

X_1 BATCH SIZE	X_2 (BATCH SIZE)^2	Y NUMBER DEFECTIVE	X_1 BATCH SIZE	X_2 (BATCH SIZE)^2	Y NUMBER DEFECTIVE
100	10,000	5	250	62,500	37
125	15,625	10	250	62,500	41
125	15,625	6	250	62,500	34
125	15,625	7	275	75,625	49
150	22,500	6	300	90,000	53
150	22,500	7	300	90,000	54
175	30,625	17	325	105,625	69
175	30,625	15	350	122,500	82
200	40,000	24	350	122,500	81
200	40,000	21	350	122,500	84
200	40,000	22	375	140,625	92
225	50,625	26	375	140,625	96
225	50,625	29	375	140,625	97
225	50,625	25	400	160,000	109
250	62,500	34	400	160,000	112

What the pattern suggests

What does this indicate? Look at Fig. 11-19, where we have fit a black regression line ($\hat{Y} = -7 + 7X$) to the eight points $(X,Y) = (0,0), (1,1), (2,4), (3,9), \ldots, (7,49)$, all of which lie on the colored curve ($Y = X^2$). The figure also shows the residuals and their signs.

The pattern of residuals that we got in our motor-shaft problem is quite similar to the pattern seen in Fig. 11-19. Maybe the shaft data are better approximated by a curve than a straight line. Look back at Fig. 11-19. What do you think?

Fitting a curve to the data

But we've fitted only straight lines before. How do we go about fitting a curve? It's simple; all we do is introduce another variable, $X_2 =$ (batch size)^2, and then run a multiple regression. The input data are in Table 11-8, and the results are in Figure 11-20 below.

The curve is much better than the line

Looking at Figure 11-20, we see that batch size and (batch size)^2 are *both* significant explanatory variables, since their t values are -3.815 and 15.671 respectively. The multiple coefficient of determination is $R^2 = .9954$; so together, our two vari-

FIGURE 11-20
Regression on batch size and (batch size)²

MODEL: CURVE
DEP VARIABLE: DEFECTS DEFECTIVE PIECES IN BATCH

ANALYSIS OF VARIANCE

SOURCE	DF	SUM OF SQUARES	MEAN SQUARE	F VALUE	PROB>F
MODEL	2	34186.27736	17093.13868	2911.349	0.0001
ERROR	27	158.52264	5.87120890		
C TOTAL	29	34344.80000			
ROOT MSE		2.423058	R-SQUARE	0.9954	

VARIABLE	DF	PARAMETER ESTIMATE	STANDARD ERROR	T FOR H0: PARAMETER=0	PROB > |T|
INTERCEP	1	6.89758532	3.73689436	1.846	0.0759
BATCHSIZ	1	-0.12010256	0.03147803	-3.815	0.0007
SIZESQ	1	0.000949539	0.000060593	15.671	0.0001

OBS	ACTUAL	PREDICT VALUE	RESIDUAL
1	5.0000	4.3827	0.6173
2	10.0000	6.7213	3.2787
3	6.0000	6.7213	-0.7213
4	7.0000	6.7213	0.2787
5	6.0000	10.2468	-4.2468
6	7.0000	10.2468	-3.2468
7	17.0000	14.9593	2.0407
8	15.0000	14.9593	0.0407
9	24.0000	20.8586	3.1414
10	21.0000	20.8586	0.1414
11	22.0000	20.8586	1.1414
12	26.0000	27.9449	-1.9449
13	29.0000	27.9449	1.0551
14	25.0000	27.9449	-2.9449
15	34.0000	36.2181	-2.2181
16	37.0000	36.2181	0.7819
17	41.0000	36.2181	4.7819
18	34.0000	36.2181	-2.2181
19	49.0000	45.6782	3.3218
20	53.0000	56.3253	-3.3253
21	54.0000	56.3253	-2.3253
22	69.0000	68.1593	0.8407
23	82.0000	81.1802	0.8198
24	81.0000	81.1802	-0.1802
25	84.0000	81.1802	2.8198
26	92.0000	95.3880	-3.3880
27	96.0000	95.3880	0.6120
28	97.0000	95.3880	1.6120
29	109.0000	110.7828	-1.7828
30	112.0000	110.7828	1.2172

ables explain 99.5 percent of the variation in the number of defective motor shafts. As a final comparison of our two regressions, notice that the standard error of estimate, which measures the dispersion of the sample points around the fitted model, is 7.560 for the straight-line model but only 2.423 for the curved model. **The curved model is far superior to the straight-line model, even though the latter explained 95 percent of the variation! And remember, it was the pattern that we observed in the residuals for the straight-line model that suggested to us that a curved model would be more appropriate.**

Transforming variables

In our curved model, we got our second variable, (batch size)^2, by doing a *mathematical transformation* of our first variable, batch size. Because we squared a variable, the resulting curved model is known as a *second-degree* (or *quadratic*) regression model. There are many other ways in which we can transform variables to get new variables, and most computer regression packages have these transformations built into them. You do not have to compute the transformed variables by hand as we did in Table 11-8. SAS and other packages have the capability to compute all sorts of transformations of one or more variables: sums, differences, products, quotients, roots, powers, logarithms, exponentials, trigonometric functions, and many more.

Exercises

11-31 Describe three situations in everyday life in which dummy variables could be used in regression models.

11-32 A restaurant owner with restaurants in two cities believes that revenue can be predicted from traffic flow in front of the restaurant with a quadratic model.
(a) Describe a quadratic model to predict revenue from traffic flow. State the form of the regression equation.
(b) It has been suggested that the city the restaurant is in has an effect on revenue. Extend your model above by using a dummy variable to incorporate the suggestion. Again, state the form of the regression model.

11-33 Cindy's, a popular fast food chain, has recently experienced a marked change in its sales as a result of a very successful advertising campaign. As a result, management is now looking for a new regression model for its sales. The data below have been collected in the 12 weeks since the advertising campaign began.

TIME	SALES (in thousands)	TIME	SALES (in thousands)
1	4,618	7	19,746
2	311	8	34,215
3	7,119	9	50,306
4	4,367	10	65,717
5	5,118	11	86,434
6	8,887	12	105,464

(a) Using any available computer package, fit a linear model with TIME as the independent variable and SALES as the dependent variable.

(b) Are you satisfied with your model as a predictor for SALES? Explain.

(c) Fit a quadratic model for the data. Is this model better? Explain.

11-34 Dr. Linda Frazer runs a medical clinic in Philadelphia. She collected data on age, reaction to penicillin, and systolic blood pressure for thirty patients. She established systolic blood pressure as the dependent variable, age as X_1 (independent variable), and reaction to penicillin as X_2 (independent variable). Letting 0 stand for a positive reaction to penicillin, and 1 stand for a negative reaction, she ran a multiple regression on her desktop PC. The predicting equation was: $\hat{Y} = 6.7 + 3.5X_1 + .489X_2$.

(a) After the regression had already been run, Dr. Frazer discovered that she had meant to code a positive reaction as 1 and a negative reaction as 0. Does she have to rerun the regression? If so, why? If not, give her the equation she would have gotten if the variable had been coded as she had originally intended.

(b) If s_{b_2} has a value of .09, is there evidence at a significance level of .05 that the reaction to penicillin is a significant explanatory variable for systolic blood pressure?

11-35 A statistician collected a set of 20 pairs of data points. He called the independent variable X_1 and the dependent variable Y. He ran a linear regression of Y on X_1, and he was dissatisfied with the results. Because of some nonrandom patterns he observed in the residuals, he decided to square the values of X_1; he called these squared values X_2. The statistician then ran a multiple regression of Y on X_1 and X_2. The resulting equation was:

$$\hat{Y} = 200.4 + 2.79X_1 - 3.92X_2.$$

The value of s_{b_1} was 3.245 and the value of s_{b_2} was 1.53. At a .05 level of significance, determine if:

(a) The set of unsquared values of X_1 is a significant explanatory variable for Y.

(b) The set of squared values of X_1 is a significant explanatory variable for Y.

11-36 Suppose you have a set of data points to which you have fitted a linear regression equation. Even though the R^2 for the line is very high, you wonder whether it would be a good idea to fit a second-degree equation to the data. Describe how you would make your decision based on:

(a) A scattergram of the data

(b) A table of residuals from the linear regression

11-37 Below are some data on consumption expenditures, CONSUMP; disposable income, INCOME; and sex of the head of household, SEX, of $n = 12$ randomly chosen families. The variable GENDER has been coded:

$$\text{GENDER} = \begin{cases} 1 \text{ if SEX} = \text{'M' (male)} \\ 0 \text{ if SEX} = \text{'F' (female)} \end{cases}$$

CONSUMP	INCOME ($)	SEX	GENDER
18,535	22,550	M	1
11,350	14,035	M	1
12,130	13,040	F	0
15,210	17,500	M	1
8,680	9,430	F	0
16,760	20,635	M	1
13,480	16,470	M	1
9,680	10,720	F	0
17,840	22,350	M	1
11,180	12,200	F	0
14,320	16,810	F	0
19,860	23,000	M	1

(a) Using any available computer package, fit a regression model to predict CONSUMP from INCOME and GENDER.

(b) State the fitted regression equation.

(c) Holding disposable income constant, is there a significant difference in consumption between households headed by a male versus those where the head of household is female? State explicit hypotheses, test them at the .10 level, and state an explicit conclusion.

(d) Give an approximate 95 percent confidence interval for consumption for a household with disposable income of $23,000 headed by a male.

11-6
Terms Introduced in Chapter 11

Analysis of Variance for Regression The procedure for computing the F-ratio used to test the significance of the regression as a whole. It is related to the analysis of variance discussed in Chapter 9.

Coefficient of Multiple Correlation, R The positive square root of R^2.

Coefficient of Multiple Determination, R^2 The fraction of the variation of dependent variable that is explained by the regression. R^2 measures how well the multiple regression fits the data.

Computed F Ratio A statistic used to test the significance of the regression as a whole.

Computed t A statistic used for testing the significance of an individual explanatory variable.

Dummy Variable A variable taking the value 0 or 1, enabling us to include in a regression model qualitative factors such as sex, marital status, and education level.

Modeling Techniques Methods for deciding which

variables to include in a regression model and the different ways in which they can be included.

Multicollinearity A statistical problem sometimes present in multiple regression analysis in which the reliability of the regression coefficients is reduced, owing to a high level of correlation between the independent variables.

Multiple Regression The statistical process by which several variables are used to predict another variable.

SAS A computer program for doing regression and other statistical analyses. Other commonly available packages include Minitab and SYSTAT.

Standard Error of a Regression Coefficient A measure of our uncertainty about the exact value of a regression coefficient.

Transformations Mathematical manipulations for converting one variable into a different form, so we can fit curves as well as lines by regression.

11-7
Equations Introduced in Chapter 11

[11-1]
$$\hat{Y} = a + b_1 X_1 + b_2 X_2 \qquad \text{p. 540}$$

In multiple regression, this is the formula for the estimating equation that describes the relationship between three variables: Y, X_1, and X_2. Picture a two-variable multiple regression equation as a plane, rather than a line.

[11-2]
$$\Sigma Y = na + b_1 \Sigma X_1 + b_2 \Sigma X_2$$

[11-3]
$$\Sigma X_1 Y = a\Sigma X_1 + b_1 \Sigma X_1^2 + b_2 \Sigma X_1 X_2 \qquad \text{p. 541}$$

[11-4]
$$\Sigma X_2 Y = a\Sigma X_2 + b_1 \Sigma X_1 X_2 + b_2 \Sigma X_2^2$$

Solving these three equations determines the values of the numerical constants a, b_1, and b_2 and thus the best-fitting multiple regression plane in a two-variable multiple regression.

$$\hat{Y} = a + b_1 X_1 + b_2 X_2 + \cdots + b_k X_k$$

[11-5]   p. 546

This is the formula for the estimating equation describing the relationship between Y and the k independent variables, $X_1, X_2, \ldots, X_k$. Equation 11-1 is the special case of this equation for $k = 2$.

$$s_e = \sqrt{\frac{\Sigma(Y - \hat{Y})^2}{n - k - 1}}$$

[11-6]   p. 547

To measure the variation around a multiple regression equation when there are k independent variables, use this equation to find the *standard error of estimate*. The standard error, in this case, has $n - k - 1$ degrees of freedom, owing to the $k + 1$ numerical constants that must be calculated from the data (a, b_1, . . . , b_k).

$$Y = A + B_1 X_1 + B_2 X_2 + \cdots + B_k X_k$$

[11-7]   p. 554

This is the *population regression equation* for the multiple regression. Its Y intercept is A, and it has k slope coefficients, one for each of the independent variables.

$$Y = A + B_1 X_1 + B_2 X_2 + \cdots + B_k X_k + e$$

[11-7a]   p. 554

Because all the individual points in a population do not lie on the population regression equation, the *individual* data points will satisfy this equation, where e is a random disturbance from the population regression equation. On the average, e equals zero, because disturbances above the population regression equation are canceled out by disturbances below it.

$$\text{Upper limit of acceptance region} = B_i + t(s_{b_i})$$
$$\text{Lower limit of acceptance region} = B_i - t(s_{b_i})$$

[11-8]   p. 555

To test hypotheses about the slopes of multiple regression equations, we use this pair of equations to find the limits of the acceptance region. The standard error of the coefficient (s_{b_i}) is obtained from the computer package we are using, and the t value is taken from the t distribution with $n - k - 1$ degrees of freedom.

$$-t_c \leqq t_o \leqq t_c$$

[11-9]   p. 557

To test whether a given independent variable is significant, we use this formula to see if the observed t value (taken from the computer output) lies between plus and minus the critical t value (taken from the t distribution with $n - k - 1$ degrees of freedom). The variable *is* significant when t_o is *not* in the indicated range. If your computer package gives you "prob $> |t|$" values, the variable *is* significant when this value is *less than* α, the significance level of the test.

[11-10]

$$\left.\begin{array}{lll} \text{SST} = \text{Total sum of squares} & = \Sigma(Y - \overline{Y})^2 \\ \text{SSR} = \text{Regression sum of squares} & = \Sigma(\hat{Y} - \overline{Y})^2 \\ \qquad \text{(the explained part of SST)} \\ \text{SSE} = \text{Error sum of squares} & = \Sigma(Y - \hat{Y})^2 \\ \qquad \text{(the unexplained part of SST)} \end{array}\right\}$$

p. 559

[11-11] $$SST = SSR + SSE$$ p. 560

These two equations enable us to break down the variability of the dependent variable into two parts (one explained by the regression and the other unexplained) so we can test for the significance of the regression as a whole.

[11-12] $$F = \frac{SSR/k}{SSE/(n - k - 1)}$$ p. 560

This F ratio, which has k numerator degrees of freedom and $n - k - 1$ denominator degrees of freedom, is used to test the significance of the regression as a whole. If F is *bigger* than the critical value, then we conclude that the regression as a whole *is* significant. The same conclusion holds if the "prob F" value (from the computer output) is *less than* α, the significance level of the test.

11-8
Chapter Review Exercises

11-38 Homero Martinez is a judge in Barcelona, Spain. He has recently called you in as a statistical consultant to investigate what purports to be a significant finding. He claims that the number of days a case is in court can be used to estimate the amount of damages that should be awarded. He has gathered data from his court and from the courts of several of his fellow judges. For each of the numbers 1 to 9, he has located a case that took that many days in court, and he has determined the amount (in millions of pesetas) of damages awarded in that case. The following SAS results were generated when damages awarded were regressed on days in court.

```
DEP VARIABLE: DAMAGES     DAMAGES AWARDED (MILLIONS OF PESETAS)
                         ANALYSIS OF VARIANCE

                    SUM OF          MEAN
SOURCE      DF      SQUARES        SQUARE      F VALUE      PROB>F
MODEL       1      16.094260      16.094260    102.765      0.0001
ERROR       7       1.096290       0.156613
C TOTAL     8      17.190550
     ROOT MSE       0.395743      R-SQUARE      0.9362


                  PARAMETER     STANDARD    T FOR H0:
VARIABLE    DF    ESTIMATE       ERROR     PARAMETER=0    PROB > |T|

INTERCEP    1    -0.406250      0.287501     -1.413        0.2005
DAYS        1     0.517917      0.051090     10.137        0.0001


                                  PREDICT
                 OBS    ACTUAL      VALUE      RESIDUAL
                  1     0.645     0.111667     0.533333
                  2     0.750     0.629583     0.120417
                  3     1.000     1.147500    -0.147500
                  4     1.300     1.665417    -0.365417
                  5     1.750     2.183333    -0.433333
                  6     2.205     2.701250    -0.496250
                  7     3.500     3.219167     0.280833
                  8     4.000     3.737083     0.262917
                  9     4.500     4.255000     0.245000
```

Of course, you are quite pleased with these results, since the value R^2 is very high. But the judge is not convinced that you are right. He says, "This is the worst job I've ever seen! I don't care if this line *does* fit the data I gave you. I can tell by looking at the output that it won't work for other data! If you can't do any better, just let me know, and I'll hire a *smart* statistician!"

(a) Why is the judge upset?

(b) Suggest a better model that will calm the judge.

11-39 Jon Grant, supervisor of the Carven Manufacturing Facility, is examining the relationship among an employee's score on an aptitude test, prior work experience, and success on the job. An employee's prior work experience is studied and weighted, yielding a rating between 2 and 12. The measure of on-the-job success is based on a point system involving total output and efficiency, with a maximum possible value of 50. Grant sampled 6 first-year employees and obtained the following:

X_1 Aptitude Test Score	X_2 Prior Experience	Y Performance Evaluation
74	5	28
87	11	33
69	4	21
93	9	40
81	7	38
97	10	46

(a) Develop the estimating equation best describing these data.

(b) If an employee scored 83 on the aptitude test and had a prior work experience of 7, what performance evaluation would be expected?

11-40 Jay Footclamper is the president and chief executive officer of Fiber Shoes, Inc., a company that manufactures wooden clogs for clogging competitions. Jay is concerned about hiring better salespeople. One effort to make better choices of salespeople has been based on an analysis of the performance of the current sales force on four aptitude tests that those people took when they were hired. Jay has collected sales growth data for each of 25 salespeople, along with scores on four aptitude tests (creativity, mechanical ability, abstract thinking, and mathematical calculation). A multiple regression was fit, with the output given below:

```
DEP VARIABLE: GROWTH
                        ANALYSIS OF VARIANCE

                    SUM OF        MEAN
    SOURCE    DF    SQUARES      SQUARE     F VALUE    PROB>F
    MODEL      4   1050.786     262.697     62.640     0.0001
    ERROR     20     83.875250    4.193763
    C TOTAL   24   1134.662
        ROOT MSE    2.047868     R-SQUARE    0.9261


                    PARAMETER    STANDARD    T FOR H0:
    VARIABLE   DF   ESTIMATE      ERROR     PARAMETER=0   PROB > |T|

    INTERCEP    1   70.065659    2.130314     32.890      0.0001
    CREAT       1    0.421601    0.171915      2.452      0.0235
    MECH        1    0.271403    0.218402      1.243      0.2284
    ABST        1    0.745042    0.289818      2.571      0.0182
    MATH        1    0.419545    0.068712      6.106      0.0001
```

(a) Give the regression equation for Jay to predict a salesperson's sales growth.

(b) How much of the variation in sales growth is explained by the four aptitude tests?

(c) At a significance level of .05, which of the aptitude tests are significant explanatory variables for sales growth?

(d) Is the overall model significant as a whole?

(e) Paul had scores as follows on the four tests: CREAT = 12, MECH = 14, ABST = 18, and MATH = 30. What is his predicted sales growth?

11-41 The Money Bank desires to open new checking accounts for customers who will write at least 30 checks per month. To assist in selecting new customers, the bank has studied the relationship between the number of checks written and the age and annual income of eight of their present customers. AGE was recorded to the nearest year, and annual INCOME was recorded in thousands of dollars. The data are given below:

CHECKS	AGE	INCOME
29	37	16.2
42	34	25.4
9	48	12.4
56	38	25.0
2	43	8.0
10	25	18.3
48	33	24.2
4	45	7.9

(a) Develop an estimating equation to use age and income to predict the number of checks written per month.
(b) How many checks per month would be expected from a 35-year-old with annual income of $22,500?

11-42 Dr. Harden Ricci is a veterinarian in Sacramento, California. Recently, he has been trying to develop a predicting equation for the amount of anesthesia (measured in milliliters) to be used in operations. He feels that the amount used will depend on the weight of the animal (in pounds), length of the operation (in hours), and whether the animal is a cat (coded 0) or a dog (coded 1). He used SAS to run a regression on his data from thirteen recent operations, and got these results:

DEP VARIABLE: ANESTHES   MILLILITERS OF ANESTHETIC USED
ANALYSIS OF VARIANCE

SOURCE	DF	SUM OF SQUARES	MEAN SQUARE	F VALUE	PROB>F
MODEL	3	590880	196960	60.474	0.0001
ERROR	9	29312.398	3256.933		
C TOTAL	12	620192			
ROOT MSE		57.069547	R-SQUARE	0.9527	

VARIABLE	DF	PARAMETER ESTIMATE	STANDARD ERROR	T FOR H0: PARAMETER=0	PROB > |T|
INTERCEP	1	90.032476	56.842294	1.584	0.1477
TYPE	1	99.485929	42.373539	2.348	0.0435
WEIGHT	1	21.536329	2.668117	8.072	0.0001
HOURS	1	-34.460982	28.606709	-1.205	0.2591

(a) What is the predicting equation for amounts of anesthesia, as given by SAS?
(b) Give an approximate 95 percent confidence interval for the amount of anesthesia to be used in a 90-minute operation on a 25-pound dog.
(c) At a significance level of 10 percent, is the amount of anesthesia needed significantly different for dogs and cats?
(d) At a significance level of 5 percent, is this regression significant as a whole?

11-43 James Black is considering moving to another part of town and would like to predict the selling price of his home. He has decided to use TAXVALUE (in $1,000's) and CORNER (= 1 for corner lots and 0 otherwise) as explanatory variables. To fit his model, he collected the data below on nine randomly chosen sales, with PRICE measured in $1,000's. He decided to use TAXVALUE, (TAXVALUE)^2, and CORNER as explanatory variables, since he felt a quadratic relationship existed.

PRICE	TAXVALUE	TAXSQ = (TAXVALUE)²	CORNER
56.2	17.5	306.25	1
42.5	12.5	156.25	1
67.5	20.0	400.00	1
39.0	11.5	132.25	1
33.3	12.5	156.25	0
29.0	10.0	100.00	0
30.0	10.8	116.64	0
48.0	17.0	289.00	0
44.3	16.0	256.00	0

(a) Use any available computer package to calculate the best-fitting regression equation for these data.

(b) What fraction of the variation in PRICE is explained by this equation?

(c) Give a 90 percent confidence interval for the increase in selling price attributable to having a corner lot.

(d) Was it a good idea to include $(TAXVALUE)^2$ in the regression? Explain.

11-44 Camping-R-Us, a newcomer to the outdoor equipment field, plans to market a two-person, three-season tent for weekend campers. To set a fair price, they look at eight comparable tents currently on the market, in terms of weight and square footage. The data are given below.

	WEIGHT (OZ.)	SQ. FT.	PRICE
Kelty Nautilus	94	37	$225
North Face Salamander	90	36	240
REI Mountain Hut	112	35	225
Sierra Designs Meteor Light	92	40	220
Eureka! Cirrus 3	93	48	167
Sierra Designs Clip 3	98	40	212
Eureka! Timberline Deluxe	114	40	217
Diamond Brand Free Spirit	108	35	200

(a) Calculate the least squares equation to predict price from weight and square footage.

(b) If Camping-R-Us' tent weighs 100 ounces and has 46 square feet of space, how much should they charge?

11-45 The Carolina Athletic Association is interested in organizing the First Annual Tarheel Triathlon. To attract top competitors, they wish to establish cash incentives for the top finishers by setting times for both men and women overall winners. Because this course has never been run before, the CAA has chosen ten races of varying lengths that they consider comparable in weather and course conditions.

	MILES			WINNING TIMES (HR:MIN:SEC)	
TRIATHLON	SWIM	BIKE	RUN	MEN	WOMEN
Bud Light Ironman	2.4	112	26.2	8:09:15	9:00:56
World's Toughest	2.0	100	18.6	8:25:09	9:49:04
Muncie Endurathon	1.2	55.3	13.1	4:05:30	4:40:06
Texas Hill Country	1.5	48	10.0	3:24:24	3:55:02
Leon's Q.E.M.	0.93	24.8	6.2	1:54:32	2:07:10
Sacramento International	0.93	24.8	6.2	1:48:16	2:00:45
Malibu	0.50	18	5.0	1:19:25	1:30:19
Bud Light Endurance	2.4	112	26.2	9:26:30	11:00:29
Wendy's	0.5	20	4.0	1:14:59	1:23:09
Mammoth/Snowcreek	0.6	25	6.2	1:56:07	2:11:49

(a) Determine the regression equations to predict men's and women's winning times, in terms of the length of each individual race segment. (Convert the times to minutes for use in calculations.)

(b) Predict the winning times if the Tarheel Triathlon comprises a 1 mile swim, 50 mile bike ride and a 12.5 mile run.

(c) If the CAA wants to use the lower limit of an approximate 90 percent confidence interval for the incentive times for men and women, what would these times be?

11-46 Peoria, Illinois, is in the process of modifying its tax structure. Twelve cities of comparable size and economic structure were surveyed as to specific taxes and the associated total tax revenue.

(a) Use the following data to determine the least squares equation relating revenue to the three tax rates.

TAX RATES			TAX REVENUE
PROPERTY	SALES	GASOLINE	(IN 000s)
1.639%	2.021%	3.300 ¢/gal	28,867.5
1.686	1.972	3.300	28,850.2
1.639	2.041	3.300	29,011.5
1.639	2.363	0.131	28,806.5
1.639	2.200	2.540	28,821.7
1.639	2.201	1.560	28,774.6
1.654	2.363	0.000	28,803.2
2.643	1.000	3.300	28,685.7
2.584	1.091	2.998	28,671.8
2.048	1.752	1.826	28,671.0
2.176	1.648	1.555	28,627.4
1.925	1.991	0.757	28,670.7

(b) Two proposals have been submitted for Peoria. Estimate total tax revenues if the tax rates are:

	PROPERTY	SALES	GASOLINE
Proposal A	2.763%	1.000%	1.0 ¢/gal
Proposal B	1.639	2.021	3.3

Determine which proposal the city should adopt.

11-47 The National Cranberry Cooperative, an organization formed and owned by growers of cranberries to process and market their berries, is trying to establish a relationship between average price per barrel received in any given year, and the total number of barrels sold in the previous year (divided into fresh sales and berries sold for processing).

(a) Calculate the least squares equation to predict price from these sales figures.

SALES (IN THOUSANDS OF BARRELS)		FOLLOWING YEAR'S
Fresh	Process	PRICE
844	256	15.50
965	335	17.15
470	672	11.71
320	460	9.79
528	860	10.90
340	761	15.88

11 MULTIPLE REGRESSION AND MODELING TECHNIQUES

(b) Predict next year's price per barrel if this year's sales are 980 (fresh) and 360 (process).

11-48 Cellular phones were introduced in Europe in 1980, and since then, their growth in popularity has been phenomenal. The number of subscribers in subsequent years is contained in the following table.

1981	3,510
1982	34,520
1983	80,180
1984	143,300
1985	288,420
1986	507,930
1987	877,850
1988	1,471,200
1989	2,342,080

Using the number of years since the introduction of cellular phones as the independent variable (i.e., 1981 = 1, etc.), find the least squares linear equation relating these two variables. Look at the residuals—do they have a noticeable pattern? Find the least squares quadratic equation. Which appears to be a better fit?

11-49 While shopping for a new down sleeping bag, Fred Montana is curious about what features of a bag are most important in determining the bag's price. He picks six Gore-Tex sleeping bags and decides to run a linear regression analysis to find out.

	DOWN FILL (OZ.)	TOTAL WEIGHT (LBS.)	LOFT (IN.)	TEMP. RATING (°F)	PRICE ($)
Swallow	14.0	2.00	5.5	20	255
Snow Bunting	18.0	2.25	6.5	10	285
Puffin	24.0	3.13	6.5	10	329
Widgeon	25.5	3.25	7.5	-10	395
Tern	32.5	3.63	9.0	-30	459
Snow Goose	41.0	4.25	10.0	-40	509

(a) Regress price on ounces of down fill, total weight, loft and temperature rating. Using the prob $> |t|$ values, determine which of these variables are significant at the $\alpha = .01$ level.

(b) What about the regression as a whole? Use the prob $> F$ value, again at the $\alpha = .01$ level, to determine if the regression as a whole is significant.

(c) What problem might there be in using all these variables together? Do the answers to (a) and (b) seem to indicate this problem might be present?

11-9
Chapter Concepts Test

Answers are in the back of the book.

T F 1. The principal advantage of multiple regression over simple regression is that it allows us to use more of the information available to us to estimate the dependent variable.

T F 2. Suppose, in the multiple regression equation $\hat{Y} = 24.4 + 5.6X_1 + 6.8X_2$, $\hat{Y}$ stands for weight (in pounds) and X_2 stands for age (in years). For each additional year of age, then, it can be expected that weight will increase by 24.4 pounds.

T F   3. Although it is theoretically possible to do multiple regression calculations by hand, we seldom do so.

T F   4. Suppose you are attempting to form a confidence interval for a value of Y from a multiple regression equation. If there are 20 elements in the sample and 4 independent variables are used in the regression, you should use 16 degrees of freedom when you get a value from the t table.

T F   5. The standard error of the coefficient b_2 in a multiple regression is denoted s_2.

T F   6. Suppose we wish to test whether the values of Y in a multiple regression really depend upon the values of X_1. The null hypothesis for our test would be: $B_1 = 0$.

T F   7. To determine whether a regression is significant as a whole, an observed value of F is calculated and compared to a value from a table.

T F   8. If one knows the total sum of squares and regression sum of squares for a multiple regression, the error sum of squares can always be quickly calculated.

T F   9. If a multiple regression includes all the relevant explanatory factors for the dependent variable, the residuals are usually nonrandom.

T F 10. Simple regressions of Y on X_1 and Y on X_2 show that X_1 and X_2 are both significant explanatory variables for Y. But a multiple regression of Y on X_1 and X_2 says that neither X_1 nor X_2 is a significant explanatory variable for Y. Clearly, this is a case of multicollinearity.

T F 11. Dummy variables are often used to incorporate qualitative data into multiple regressions.

T F 12. When using a dummy variable with values of 0 and 1, it is very important to make sure that the 0's and 1's are used according to standard practice. Reversing the coding will completely destroy the results of the multiple regression.

T F 13. We can form a second-degree regression model by multiplying observed values of an independent variable by 2.

T F 14. Adding additional variables to a multiple regression will always reduce the standard error of estimate.

T F 15. Suppose a multiple regression yielded this equation: $\hat{Y} = 5.6 + 2.8X_1 - 3.9X_2 + 5.6X_3$. If X_1, X_2, and X_3 all had values of zero, then Y could be expected to have a value of 5.6.

T F 16. The analysis of the residuals in a straight-line regression model is done to determine the correct value for s_e.

T F 17. Although it is possible to make inferences about the regression as a whole, it is not possible to make inferences about the estimated regression coefficients.

T F 18. If there is a high level of correlation between explanatory variables, it is usually possible to disentangle the separate contributions of these variables in a regression.

T F 19. The standard error of the population data points is denoted s_e.

T F 20. If a regression includes all relevant explanatory factors, the residuals should be random.

T F 21. A linear relationship between explanatory variables will assuredly produce multicollinearity in the regression model.

22. Suppose that a multiple regression yielded this equation: $\hat{Y} = 51.21 + 6.88X_1 + 7.06X_2 - 3.71X_3$. The value of b_2 for this equation is:
(a) 51.21 (d) -3.71
(b) 6.88 (e) Cannot be determined from information given
(c) 7.06

23. We have said that the standard error of estimate has $n - k - 1$ degrees of freedom. What does the k stand for in this expression?
(a) Number of elements in the sample
(b) Number of independent variables in the multiple regression
(c) Mean of the sample values of the dependent variable
(d) None of these

24. Suppose that you have run a multiple regression and have found that the value of b_1 is 1.66. Historical data, however, indicate that the value of B_1 should be 1.34. You wish to test, at a

.05 level of significance, the null hypothesis that B_1 is still 1.34. Assuming that you have access to any tables you may need, what other information is required for you to perform your test?

(a) Degrees of freedom   (d) a and b but not c

(b) s_{b_1} (e) a and c but not b

(c) s_e

25. Suppose that a toy manufacturer wishes to determine if his red toys sell better than his blue toys. He gathered data regarding sales levels, color, price, and average age levels for which the toys are intended. He entered these into a computer run. The resulting multiple regression equation was: $\hat{Y} = 70{,}663 - 713X_1 - 59.6X_2 + 66.4X_3$, where $\hat{Y}$ refers to sales levels in units, X_1 refers to color (0 = blue, 1 = red), X_2 refers to retail price (in dollars), and X_3 refers to average age level (in years). Which of the following is true if factors of price and age level are held constant?

(a) Red toys should sell 713 more units than blue toys.

(b) Red toys should sell 713 fewer units than blue toys.

(c) Children will always choose a blue toy over a red one.

(d) b and c but not a.

Questions 26 through 31 deal with a director of personnel who is trying to determine a predicting equation for longevity in his plant. He has used SAS to regress months employed for several employees on their education levels (years of schooling), age when hired, score on the company's psychological maturity test, and number of dependents (including the employee). Here are his results:

```
DEP VARIABLE: LONGEV    LENGTH OF EMPLOYMENT (MONTHS)
                        ANALYSIS OF VARIANCE

                    SUM OF        MEAN
SOURCE     DF       SQUARES       SQUARE     F VALUE     PROB>F
MODEL      4        7325.325      1831.331   10.194      0.0127
ERROR      5        898.275       179.655
C TOTAL    9        8223.600
    ROOT MSE        13.403541     R-SQUARE   0.8908


                    PARAMETER     STANDARD   T FOR H0:
VARIABLE   DF       ESTIMATE      ERROR      PARAMETER=0   PROB > |T|

INTERCEP   1        82.237454     81.737817  1.006         0.3605
SCHOOL     1        -1.552644     4.362058   -0.356        0.7364
AGE        1        -1.685367     1.252534   -1.346        0.2362
SCORE      1        0.110216      0.290813   0.379         0.7203
DEPENDEN   1        6.875539      7.657836   0.898         0.4104
```

26. The regression equation for these data is:

(a) $\hat{Y} = 82.24 - 1.55X_1 - 1.69X_2 + 0.11X_3 + 6.88X_4$

(b) $\hat{Y} = 13.40 - 1.55X_1 - 1.69X_2 + 0.11X_3 + 6.88X_4$

(c) $\hat{Y} = 81.74 + 4.36X_1 + 1.25X_2 + 0.29X_3 + 7.66X_4$

(d) $\hat{Y} = 82.24 - 0.36X_1 - 1.35X_2 + 0.38X_3 + 0.90X_4$

27. How much of the variation in length of employment is explained by the regression?

(a) 94%   (b) 82%   (c) 89%   (d) 13%

28. Suppose you wish to test whether years of school is a significant explanatory variable for longevity. The degrees of freedom you would use would be:

(a) 4   (b) 10   (c) 6   (d) 5

29. What is the value of s_{b_3}?

(a) 13.4   (b) .29   (c) .38   (d) .11

30. How many denominator degrees of freedom would there be for an F test to determine if this regression was significant as a whole?

(a) 5   (b) 4   (c) 9   (d) 10

31. How many data points did the director enter?
    (a) 9   (b) 10   (c) 18   (d) 19

32. In the equation $Y = A + B_1 X_1 + B_2 X_2$, Y is independent of X_1 if:
    (a) $B_2 = 0$ (c) $B_1 = 1$
    (b) $B_2 = -1$ (d) None of these

33. A normal distribution can be used to approximate the t distribution for multiple regression whenever the degrees of freedom (n minus the number of estimated regression coefficients) are:
    (a) Less than 40   (c) Equal to 5   (e) None of these
    (b) More than 10   (d) More than 50

34. Since $r^2 = 1 - \dfrac{(Y - \hat{Y})^2}{(Y - \bar{Y})^2}$, r^2 is equivalent to:
    (a) $1 - \text{SSR/SST}$ (c) $1 - \text{SSE/SSR}$ (e) $1 - \text{SST/SSE}$
    (b) $1 - \text{SSE/SST}$ (d) $1 - \text{SST/SSR}$

35. For the multiple regression $\hat{Y} = a + b_1 X_1 + b_2 X_2$ used to estimate $Y = A + B_1 X_1 + B_2 X_2$, the form of a plausible confidence interval for B_1 is:
    (a) $B_1 - ts_{b_1}, B_1 + ts_{b_1}$ (c) $b_1 - ts_{b_1}, b_1 + ts_{b_1}$
    (b) $B_1 - ts_e, B_1 + ts_e$ (d) $b_1 - ts_e, b_1 + ts_e$

36. Signs of the possible presence of multicollinearity in a multiple regression are:
    (a) significant t values for the coefficients
    (b) low standard errors for the coefficients
    (c) a sharp increase in a t value for the coefficient of an explanatory variable when another variable is removed from the model
    (d) all of the above

37. _____ are methods for deciding which variables to include in a regression model and the different ways in which they can be included.

38. Mathematical manipulations for converting a variable into a different form so that we can fit regression curves are called _____.

39. The _____ is a statistic used to test the significance of a regression as a whole.

40. A _____ variable takes on the values 0 and 1 to describe qualitative data.

41. A measure of our uncertainty about the exact value of a multiple regression coefficient is the _____ of the coefficient.

42. The coefficient of multiple determination in multiple regression measures the _____.

43. The significance of a multiple regression can be tested with the null hypothesis _____ which indicates that Y does not depend on the X_i's.

44. The standard error s_e is also called the _____.

45. Alternating strings of consecutive _____ with like sign in a linear regression model indicate that the data might better fit a curve than a straight line.

11-10
Conceptual Case   (Northern White Metals Company)

Dick's predecessor at NWMC had often remarked that the company was "adrift in a sea of unpredictable circumstance. Sales go up, sales go down," he would say, "and that's all there is to it." This cavalier, some- what fatalistic attitude had struck Dick as strange, and he was determined to provide a little more insight and direction into the planning process at Northern than had existed previously.

On his next trip to corporate headquarters in New York, he made it a point to arrange a short meeting with Sarah and Jody. Looking out their office window at the cold, cloudy October afternoon, Dick thought how well the weather matched his mood.

Despite some indications from an earlier analysis that Northern's advertising program was perhaps not a very significant factor in explaining sales, Dick had proceeded to accelerate advertising efforts throughout the third quarter. A subsequent analysis revealed little difference from the first one. Expenses were up considerably, and Dick finally decided to scrap the project.

"Probably a wise choice," offered Sarah as Dick related his plight.

"Dick, you're interested in getting a better understanding of the behavior of sales so you can improve your planning capabilities," Jody said. "Why don't we look at some other factors that might explain sales volume? We should be able to draw some useful conclusions for you," she stated confidently.

"That would be great," Dick said as his eyes brightened a bit. "You know, one of my top sales reps thought the number of people out making calls was more important than advertising; and sales did grow rather briskly as I expanded the sales force last year."

"There you go," said Jody. "Sales force size might be a factor."

"We would probably want to segregate building-products and high-tech-applications products sales," Dick said, "since these are probably affected differently by general economic conditions."

"We could check it out," Sarah offered. "Why don't you talk with your sales reps, decide what you think are the major determinants of sales, and we'll take it from there."

Dick left, grateful for their counsel and convinced that the planning process at Northern was soon to be improved considerably.

After Dick and the sales force decide upon some principal determinants of sales volume, what information will they need to provide to Jody and Sarah? What analyses can they be expected to perform? What results might they obtain that would be useful to Dick in a decision-making or planning capacity?

11-11
Computer Data Base Exercise

 The next day, Laurel explained her findings to Gary. "Age very well may play a role," she concluded, "but it's definitely not the *only* factor. Come up with any additional ideas?"

"I don't know how much they'll help, but I've got a couple of suggestions," Gary answered. "For starters, gender may have something to do with it. Without having any specific data to support my hunch, it appears to me that the women workers tend to stay around longer than the men. In addition, years of education may be a factor. The folks who tend to stay with us, it seems, are usually those who don't have a college degree tempting them on to bigger and better things. Sound reasonable?"

"Both of those ideas are good," nodded Laurel, jotting down notes. "I'll let you know what I come up with—if anything!"

1. Do a simple regression of length of employment in Table DB10-1, on p. 532 vs. gender in Table DB11-1, (use 1 for male, 0 for female).

TABLE DB11-1

SEX	YEARS OF EDUCATION	SEX	YEARS OF EDUCATION
F	10	F	12
M	16	F	10
F	12	M	12
M	14	M	15
M	16	M	12
F	14	F	11
M	12	M	14
F	11	M	12
F	10	M	14
M	12	F	9
M	14	F	10
M	11	M	12
M	16	M	11
M	12	F	9
M	13	M	16
F	15	M	14
M	12	M	11
F	12	F	10
M	13	M	16
M	16	M	14

What are the coefficients of determination and correlation? Repeat the same analysis for length of employment vs. years of education.

2. Now run a multiple regression using all three independent variables (age when hired, gender, and years of education). Is this equa-tion better or worse than the simple regressions?

3. If you had to pick just two explanatory factors, which two seem most appropriate? (Use the prob $> |t|$ values, if available.) Perform this multiple regression and compare it to the three-variable regression.

11-12
From the Textbook to the Real World

Repairable Part Management at American Airlines

To support its fleet of over 400 aircraft, American Airlines maintains an inventory of spare repairable aircraft parts. This inventory contains over 5,000 different types of units ranging in price from several hundred dollars to over $500,000. A PC-based decision support system, the Rotables Allocation and Planning System (RAPS), was developed to provide forecasts of rotable (i.e., re-pairable) part demand and to recommend least-cost allocations of parts to airports. The system uses linear regression in forecasting and other statistical methods to determine expected demand and cost allocations. The bottom line: a one-time savings of $7 million and recurring annual savings of nearly $1 million.

Business Problem and Data. Prior to departure, the entire complement of parts on an aircraft is expected to be fully operational. If a rotable part is defective, the part will be removed, and, ideally, it will be replaced by a serviceable part from the station stock room. The defective part is shipped out to be repaired, and another serviceable unit is ordered for the stockroom. One of the roles of American Airline's Materials Management department is to distribute parts to stations in a cost-effective manner, balancing the cost of part ownership against the cost of part shortage, while maintaining an acceptable level of availability. The problem is to find an allocation method which provides the least total cost.

Development of RAPS. American had been using a Rotable Forecasting and Availability Control System (ROFACS) based on time-series methodology to support decisions on repairable part distribution. ROFACS was a valuable indica-tor of appropriate allocation levels, but Decision Technologies and Materials Management recog-nized deficiencies in the system. Sensitivity analysis was difficult and time-consuming, system documentation was nonexistent, and some of the critical data elements were thought to be inaccu-rate. Also, the forecasts were slow to respond to moderate changes in aircraft utilization and fleet expansion. Decision Technologies developed the Rotables Allocation and Planning System (RAPS) with the approval, cooperation and involvement of Materials Management. The purpose of RAPS is to recommend allocations of spare parts and to assist inventory managers in analyzing rotable part control.

Forecasting. The ultimate result of a RAPS run is a least-cost allocation of rotable parts derived from a two-phase forecasting process: (1) calculat-ing total system demand for the part and (2) distributing demand among individual stations. To calculate total expected system demand, RAPS uses linear regression to establish a relationship between monthly part removals and various functions of monthly flying hours. The system updates rolling 18-month histories of removals and flying hours monthly. Then, a module calculates the coefficients corresponding to the best regression and examines many possible forecasts based upon flying hours or functions of flying hours. Evaluations of regressions are based on fit and statistical significance. The process of generating monthly demand forecasts for more than 5,000 parts using regression is completely au-tomated. Prior to RAPS, it took days to produce the forecasts and to verify their accuracy. It now takes only a few hours. To distribute system demand among the individual stations, RAPS assigns weights to each station which reflect its ex-pected activity based on data collected from flight and maintenance schedules. Once actual demand is established, the total cost of allocation can be determined by assigning costs to inventory ownership and to the expected shortage costs. Together, the modules of RAPS permit Materials Management personnel to make informed decisions about the number and locations of required parts and to examine consequences of changes in basic allocation assumptions.

Benefits. In strictly economic terms, RAPS was a huge success because it produced multimillion dollar savings. It also provided indirect benefits. RAPS increased the productivity of analysts by enabling them to analyze many more parts in a single day. It also provided an audit trail that recorded dates and times of part analyses. Because the process was simplified, the time between analyses of the same part was shortened, which means that allocations are based on more current data. Finally, the use of regression in RAPS has heightened the analysts' awareness of the sensitivity of an allocation to all input parameters, both independently and in combination. RAPS' extensive sensitivity analysis capability created a more future-oriented system, able to analyze changing conditions and behavior.

Mark J. Tedone, "Repairable Part Management," *Interfaces,* vol. 19, no. 4 (July–August 1989), pp. 61–68.

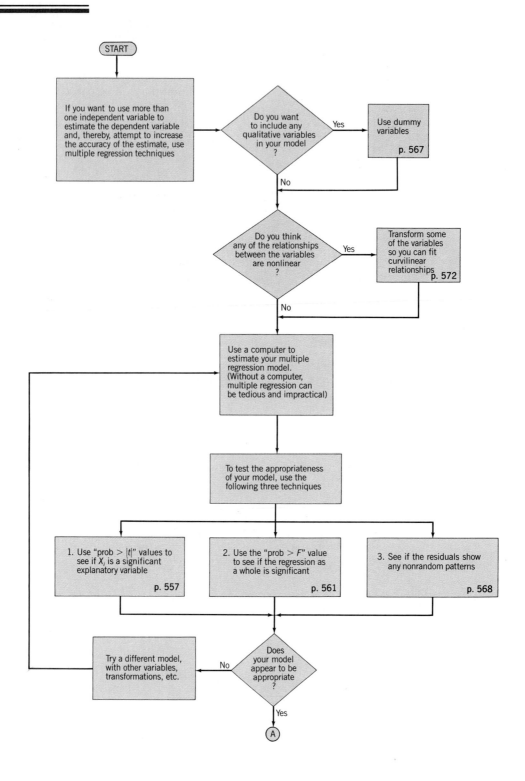

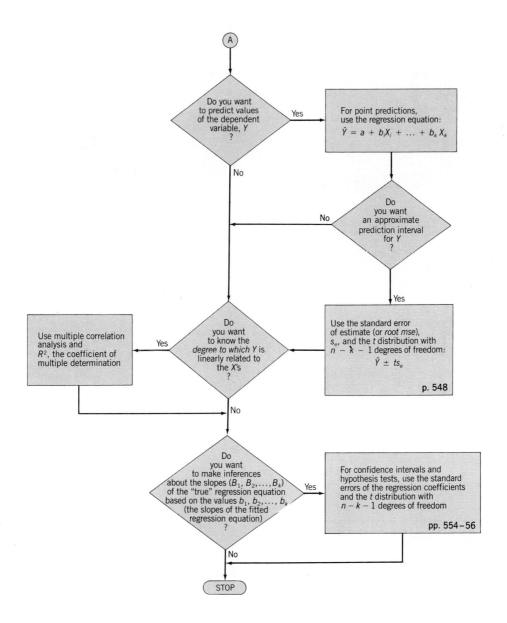

Although the effect of air pollution on health is a complex problem, an international organization has decided to make a preliminary investigation of (1) average year-round quality of air, and (2) the incidence of pulmonary-related diseases. A preliminary study ranked eleven of the world's major cities from 1 (worst) to 11 (best) in these two variables.

	CITY										
	A	B	C	D	E	F	G	H	I	J	K
Air-quality rank	4	7	9	1	2	10	3	5	6	8	11
Pulmonary-disease rank	5	4	7	3	1	11	2	10	8	6	9

The health organization's data are different from any we have seen so far in this book: They do not give us the *variable* used to determine these ranks. (We don't know if the rank of pulmonary disease is a result of pneumonia, emphysema, or other illnesses per 100,000 population.) Nor do we know the values (whether City D has twice as much pollution as city K or 20 times as much). If we knew the variables and their values, we could use the regression techniques of Chapter 10. Unfortunately, that is not the case, but even without any knowledge of either variables or values, we can use the techniques in this chapter to help the health organization with its problem.

12

Nonparametric Methods

■ OBJECTIVES

In Chapters 6 to 11, we learned how statisticians take samples from populations and attempt to reach conclusions from those samples. But how can we handle cases in which we do not know what kind of population we are sampling—that is, when we do not know the shape of the population distribution? In these cases, we can often apply the techniques of *nonparametric statistics* discussed in this chapter.

Parametric statistics	The majority of hypothesis tests discussed so far have made inferences about

Parametric statistics

The majority of hypothesis tests discussed so far have made inferences about population *parameters,* such as the mean and the proportion. These parametric tests have used the parametric statistics of samples that came from the population being tested. To formulate these tests, we made restrictive assumptions about the populations from which we drew our samples. In each case in Chapter 8, for example, we assumed that our samples either were large or came from *normally distributed* populations. But populations are not always normal. And even if a goodness-of-fit test (Chapter 9) indicates that a population *is* approximately normal, we cannot always be sure we're right, because the test is not 100 percent reliable. Clearly, there are certain situations in which the use of the normal curve is not appropriate. For these cases, we need alternatives to the parametric statistics and the specific hypothesis tests we've been using so far.

Shortcomings of parametric statistics

12-1
Introduction to Nonparametric Statistics

Nonparametric statistics

Fortunately, in recent times statisticians have developed useful techniques that do not make restrictive assumptions about the shape of population distributions. **These are known as *distribution-free* or, more commonly, *nonparametric* tests.** The hypotheses of a nonparametric test are concerned with something other than the value of a population parameter. A large number of these tests exist, but this chapter will examine only a few of the better known and more widely used ones:

1. The sign test for paired data, where positive or negative signs are substituted for quantitative values.
2. A rank sum test, often called the Mann-Whitney *U* Test, which can be used to determine whether two independent samples have been drawn from the same population. It uses more information than the sign test.
3. Another rank sum test, the Kruskal-Wallis Test, which generalizes the analysis of variance discussed in Chapter 9 to enable us to dispense with the assumption that the populations are normally distributed.
4. The one-sample runs test, a method for determining the randomness with which sampled items have been selected.
5. Rank correlation, a method for doing correlation analysis when the data are not available to use in numerical form, but when information is sufficient to rank the data first, second, third, and so forth.
6. The Kolmogorov-Smirnov Test, another method for determining the goodness of fit between an observed sample and a theoretical probability distribution.

ADVANTAGES OF NONPARAMETRIC METHODS

Advantages of nonparametric methods

Nonparametric methods have a number of clear advantages over parametric methods:

1. **They do not require us to make the assumption that a population is distributed in the shape of a normal curve or another specific shape.**
2. **Generally, they are easier to do and to understand.** Most nonparametric tests do not demand the kind of laborious computations often required, for example, to calculate a standard deviation. A nonparametric test may ask us to replace

TABLE 12-1 Converting Parametric Values to Nonparametric Ranks

Parametric value	113.45	189.42	76.50	13.33	101.79
Nonparametric value	4	5	2	1	3

numerical values with the order in which those values occur in a list, as has been done in Table 12-1. Obviously, dealing computationally with 1, 2, 3, 4, and 5 takes less effort than working with 13.33, 76.50, 101.79, 113.45, and 189.42.

3. **Sometimes even formal ordering or ranking is not required.** Often, all we can do is describe one outcome as "better" than another. When this is the case, or when our measurements are not as accurate as is necessary for parametric tests, we can use nonparametric methods.

DISADVANTAGES OF NONPARAMETRIC METHODS

Shortcomings of
nonparametric methods

Two disadvantages accompany the use of nonparametric tests:

1. **They ignore a certain amount of information.** We have demonstrated how the values 1, 2, 3, 4, and 5 can replace the numbers 13.33, 76.50, 101.79, 113.45, and 189.42. Yet if we represent "189.42" by "5," we lose information that is contained in the value of 189.42. Notice that in our ordering of the values 13.33, 76.50, 101.79, 113.45, and 189.42, the value 189.42 can become 1,189.42 and still be the fifth, or largest, value in the list. But if this list is a data set, we can learn more knowing that the highest value is 1,189.42 instead of 189.42 than we can by representing both these numbers by the value 5.

2. **They are often not as efficient or "sharp" as parametric tests.** The estimate of an interval at the 95 percent confidence level using a nonparametric test may be twice as large as the estimate using a parametric test such as those in Chapter 7. When we use nonparametric tests, we make a tradeoff: We lose sharpness in estimating intervals, but we gain the ability to use less information and to calculate faster.

Exercises

12-1 What is the difference between the kinds of questions answered by parametric tests and those answered by nonparametric tests?

12-2 The null hypothesis most often examined in nonparametric tests:
  (a) Includes specification of a population's parameters.
  (b) Is used to evaluate some general population aspect.
  (c) Is very similar to that used in regression analysis.
  (d) Simultaneously tests more than two population parameters.

12-3 What are the major advantages of nonparametric methods over parametric methods?

12-4 What are the primary shortcomings of nonparametric tests?

12-5 George Shoaf is an interviewer with a large insurance company. George works in the company's home office, and to make the best use of his time, the company requires the receptionist to schedule his interviews according to a precise schedule. There is no 5-minute period unaccounted for, including telephone calls. Unfortunately, the receptionist has been underestimating the amount of time interviews will take, and she has been scheduling too many prospective employees, resulting in long waits in the lobby. Although waiting periods may be short in the morning, as the day progresses and the interviewer gets further behind, the waits become longer. In assessing the problem, should the interviewer assume that the successive waiting times are normally distributed?

12-6 International Communications Corporation is planning to change the benefits package offered to employees. The company is considering different combinations of profit-sharing, health-care, and retirement benefits. Samples of a broad range of benefit combinations were described in a pamphlet and distributed among employees, whose preferences were then recorded. The results follow:

RANK	1	2	3	4	5	6	7	8	9	10	11	12	13	14	15	16	17	18	19
PROFIT-SHARING – HEALTH-CARE – RETIREMENT COMBINATION	15	5	14	4	6	16	7	8	13	3	17	18	12	2	9	1	11	19	10
NUMBER OF PREFERENCES	52	49	39	38	37	36	32	29	26	25	24	18	15	15	14	10	10	10	9

Will the company sacrifice any real information by using the ranking test as its decision criterion? (*Hint:* You might graph the data.)

12-2
The Sign Test for Paired Data

Use the sign test for paired data

One of the easiest nonparametric tests to use is the sign test. Its name comes from the fact that it is based on the direction (or signs for pluses or minuses) of a pair of observations and not on their numerical magnitude.

Consider the result of a test panel of 40 college juniors evaluating the effectiveness of two types of classes: large lectures by full professors or small sections by graduate assistants. Table 12-2 lists the responses to this request: "Indicate how you rate the effectiveness in transmitting knowledge of these two types of classes by giving them a number from 4 to 1. A rating of 4 is excellent, and 1 is poor." In this case, the sign test can help us determine whether students feel there is a difference between the effectiveness of the two types of classes.

Converting values to signs

We can begin, as we have in Table 12-2, by converting the evaluations of the two teaching methods into signs. Here a plus sign means the student prefers large lectures; a minus sign indicates a preference for small sections; and a zero represents a tie (no preference). If we count the bottom row of Table 12-2, we get these results:

Number of + signs	19
Number of − signs	11
Number of 0s	10
Total sample size	**40**

TABLE 12-2 Evaluation by 40 Students of 2 Types of Classes

Panel-member number	1	2	3	4	5	6	7	8	9	10	11	12	13	14	15	16
Score for large lectures (1)	2	1	4	4	3	3	4	2	4	1	3	3	4	4	4	1
Score for small sections (2)	3	2	2	3	4	2	2	1	3	1	2	3	4	4	3	2
Sign of score 1 minus score 2	−	−	+	+	−	+	+	+	+	0	+	0	0	0	+	−

STATING THE HYPOTHESES

Finding the sample size

We are using the sign test to determine whether our panel can discern a real difference between the two types of classes. Since we are testing perceived differences, we shall exclude tie evaluations (0s). We can see that we have nineteen plus signs and eleven minus signs, for a total of 30 usable responses. If there is no difference between the two types of classes, p (the probability that the first score exceeds the second score) would be .5, and we would expect to get about fifteen plus signs and fifteen minus signs. We would set up our hypotheses like this:

$H_0: p = .5 \leftarrow$ null hypothesis: There is no difference between the 2 types of classes.

$H_1: p \neq .5 \leftarrow$ alternative hypothesis: There is a difference between the 2 types of classes.

Choosing the distribution

If you look carefully at the hypotheses, you will see that the situation is similar to the fair-coin toss that we discussed in Chapter 4. If we tossed a fair coin 30 times, p would be .5, and we would expect about fifteen heads and fifteen tails. In that case, we would use the binomial distribution as the appropriate sampling distribution. You may also remember that when np and nq are each at least 5, we can use the normal distribution to approximate the binomial. This is just the case with the results from our panel of college juniors. Thus, we can apply the normal distribution to our test of the two teaching methods.

Setting up the problem symbolically

$p_{H_0} = .5 \leftarrow$ hypothesized proportion of the population who feels that both types of classes are the same

$q_{H_0} = .5 \leftarrow$ hypothesized proportion of the population who feels the 2 types of classes are different ($q_{H_0} = 1 - p_{H_0}$)

$n = 30 \leftarrow$ sample size

$\bar{p} = .633 \leftarrow$ proportion of successes in the sample (19/30)

$\bar{q} = .367 \leftarrow$ proportion of failures in the sample (11/30)

TESTING A HYPOTHESIS OF NO DIFFERENCE

Calculating the standard error

Suppose the chancellor's office wants to test the hypothesis that there is no difference between student perception of the two types of classes at the .05 level of significance. We shall conduct this test using the methods we introduced in Chapter 8. The first step is to calculate the standard error of the proportion:

17	18	19	20	21	22	23	24	25	26	27	28	29	30	31	32	33	34	35	36	37	38	39	40
1	2	2	4	4	4	4	3	3	2	3	4	3	4	3	1	4	3	2	2	2	1	3	3
3	2	3	3	1	4	3	3	2	2	1	1	1	3	2	2	4	4	3	3	1	1	4	2
−	0	−	+	+	0	+	0	+	0	+	+	+	+	+	−	0	−	−	−	+	0	−	+

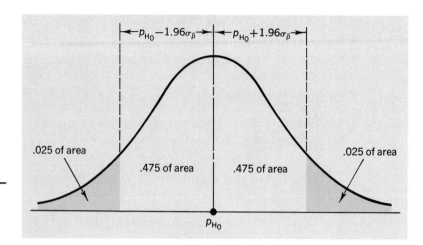

FIGURE 12-1

Two-tailed
hypothesis test of a
proportion at the .05
level of significance

$$\sigma_{\bar{p}} = \sqrt{\frac{pq}{n}} \qquad [7\text{-}4]$$

$$= \sqrt{\frac{(.5)(.5)}{30}}$$

$$= \sqrt{.00833}$$

$$= .091 \leftarrow \text{standard error of the proportion}$$

Illustrating the test
graphically

Since we want to know whether the true proportion is larger *or* smaller than the hypothesized proportion, this is a two-tailed test. Figure 12-1 illustrates this hypothesis test graphically. The two colored regions represent the .05 level of significance.

Finding the limits of the
acceptance region

Because we are using the normal distribution in our test, we can determine from Appendix Table 1 that the z value for .475 of the area under the curve is 1.96. Thus, we can calculate the limits of the acceptance region for the null hypothesis as follows:

$$p_{H_0} + 1.96\sigma_{\bar{p}} = .5 + (1.96)(.091)$$
$$= .5 + .178$$
$$= .678 \leftarrow \text{upper limit}$$

and:

$$p_{H_0} - 1.96\sigma_{\bar{p}} = .5 - (1.96)(.091)$$
$$= .5 - .178$$
$$= .322 \leftarrow \text{lower limit}$$

Interpreting the results

Figure 12-2 illustrates these two limits of the acceptance region, .322 and .678, and the sample proportion, .633. We can see that the sample proportion falls within the acceptance region for this hypothesis test. Therefore, the chancellor should accept the null hypothesis that students perceive no difference between the two types of classes.

A final word about
the sign test

A sign test such as this is quite simple to do and applies to both one-tailed and two-tailed tests. It is usually based on the binomial distribution. Remember, however, that we were able to use the normal approximation to the binomial as our sampling distribution because np and nq were both greater than 5. If these conditions are not met, we must use the binomial instead.

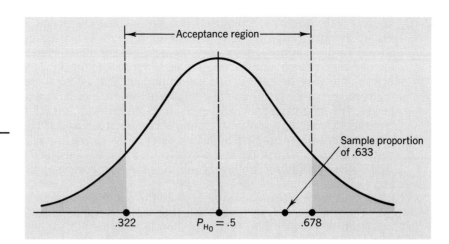

FIGURE 12-2
Two-tailed hypothesis test at the .05 level of significance, illustrating the acceptance region and the sample proportion.

Acceptance region

Sample proportion of .633

.322 $P_{H_0} = .5$ .678

Exercises

12-7 The following data show employees' rates of defective work before and after a change in the wage incentive plan. Compare the two sets of data below to see if the change lowered the defective units produced. Use the .10 level of significance.

Before	8	7	6	9	7	10	8	6	5	8	10	8
After	6	5	8	6	9	8	10	7	5	6	9	5

12-8 Use the sign test to see if there is a difference between the number of days required to collect an account receivable before and after a new collection policy. Use the .05 significance level.

Before	33	36	41	32	39	47	34	29	32	34	40	42	33	36	29
After	35	29	38	34	37	47	36	32	30	34	41	38	37	35	28

12-9 A light-aircraft engine repair shop switched the payment method it used from hourly wage to hourly wage plus a bonus computed on the time required to disassemble, repair, and reassemble an engine. Below are data collected for 25 engines before the change and 25 after the change. At a .10 significance level, did the new plan increase productivity?

HOURS REQUIRED		HOURS REQUIRED	
Before	After	Before	After
29	32	25	34
34	19	42	27
32	22	20	26
19	21	25	25
31	20	33	31
22	24	34	19
28	25	20	22
31	31	21	32
32	18	22	31
44	22	45	30
41	24	43	29
23	26	31	20
34	41		

12-10 Because of the severity of recent winters, there has been talk that the earth is slowly progressing toward another ice age. Some scientists hold different views, however, because the summers have brought extreme temperatures as well. One scientist suggested looking at the mean temperature for each month to see if it was lower than in the previous year. Another meteorologist at the government weather service argued that perhaps they should look as well at temperatures in the spring and fall months of the last 2 years, so that their conclusions would be based on other than extreme temperatures. In this way, he said, they could detect whether there appeared to be a general warming or cooling trend or just extreme temperatures in the summer and winter months. So fifteen dates in the spring and fall were randomly selected, and the temperatures in the last 2 years were noted for a particular location with generally moderate temperatures. Following are the dates and corresponding temperatures for 1988 and 1989.

(a) Is the meteorologist's reasoning as to the method of evaluation sound? Explain.

(b) Using a sign test, determine whether the meteorologist can conclude at $\alpha = .05$ that 1989 was cooler than 1988, based on these data.

	TEMPERATURE	(FAHRENHEIT)			
DATE	1988	1989	DATE	1988	1989
Mar. 29	58°	57°	Oct. 12	54°	48°
Apr. 4	45	70	May 31	74	79
Apr. 13	56	46	Sept. 28	69	60
May 22	75	67	June 5	80	74
Oct. 1	52	60	June 17	82	79
Mar. 23	49	47	Oct. 5	59	72
Nov. 12	48	45	Nov. 28	50	50
Sept. 30	67	71			

12-11 With the concern over radiation exposure and its relationship to the incidence of cancer, city environmental specialists keep a close eye on the types of industry coming into the area and the degree to which they employ radiation in their production. An index of exposure to radioactive contamination has been developed and is used daily to determine if the levels are increasing or are higher under certain atmospheric conditions.

Environmentalists claim that radioactive contamination has increased in the last year because of new industry in the city. City administrators, however, claim that new, more stringent regulations on industry in the area have made levels lower than last year, even with new industry using radiation. To test their claim, records for 11 randomly selected days of the year have been checked, and the index of exposure to radioactive contamination has been noted. The following results were obtained:

INDEX OF RADIATION EXPOSURE

1988	1.402	1.401	1.400	1.404	1.395	1.402	1.406	1.401	1.404	1.406	1.397
1989	1.440	1.395	1.398	1.404	1.393	1.400	1.401	1.402	1.400	1.403	1.402

Can the administrators conclude at $\alpha = .15$ that the levels of radioactive contamination have changed—or more specifically, that they have been reduced?

12-12 As part of the recent interest in population growth and the sizes of families, a population researcher examined a number of hypotheses concerning the family size that various people look upon as ideal. She suspected that variables of race, sex, age, and background might account for some of the different views. In one pilot sample, the researcher tested the hypothesis that women today think of an ideal family as being smaller than the ideal held by their mothers. She asked each of the participants in the pilot study to state the number of children she would choose to have or that she considered ideal. Responses were anonymous, to guard against the possibility that people would feel obligated to give a socially desirable answer. In addition, people of different backgrounds were included in the sample. Below are the responses of the mother-daughter pairs.

	IDEAL FAMILY SIZE												
SAMPLE PAIR	A	B	C	D	E	F	G	H	I	J	K	L	M
Daughter	3	4	2	1	5	4	2	2	3	3	1	4	2
Mother	4	4	4	3	5	3	3	5	3	2	2	3	1

(a) Can the researcher conclude at $\alpha = .03$ that the mothers and daughters do not have essentially the same ideal of family size? Use the binomial distribution.

(b) Determine if the researcher could conclude that the mothers do not have essentially the same family-size preferences as their daughters by using the normal approximation to the binomial.

(c) Assume that for each pair listed, there were ten more pairs who responded in an identical manner. Calculate the range of the proportion for which the researcher would conclude that there is no difference in the mothers and daughters. Is your conclusion different?

(d) Explain any differences in conclusions obtained in parts (a), (b), and (c).

12-13 After collecting data on the amount of air pollution in Los Angeles, the Environmental Protection Agency decided to issue strict new rules to govern the amount of hydrocarbons in the air. For the next year, it took monthly measurements of this pollutant and compared them to the preceding year's measurements for corresponding months. Based on the following data, does the EPA have enough evidence to conclude with 98 percent confidence that the new rules were effective in lowering the amount of hydrocarbons in the air? To justify these laws for another year, it must conclude at $\alpha = .05$ that they are effective. Will these laws still be in effect next year?

	LAST YEAR*	THIS YEAR
Jan.	7.0	5.3
Feb.	6.0	6.0
Mar.	5.4	5.6
April	5.9	5.7
May	3.9	3.7
June	5.7	4.7
July	6.9	6.1
Aug.	7.6	7.2
Sept.	6.3	6.4
Oct.	5.8	5.7
Nov.	5.1	4.9
Dec.	5.9	5.8

* Measured in parts per million.

12-3
Rank Sum Tests: The Mann-Whitney U Test and the Kruskal-Wallis Test

In Chapter 9 we showed how to use analysis of variance to test the hypothesis that several population means are equal. We assumed in such tests that the populations were normally distributed with equal variances. Many times these assumptions cannot be met, and in such cases we can use two nonparametric tests, neither of which depends on the normality assumptions. Both of these tests are called rank sum tests because the test depends on the ranks of the sample observations.

Rank sum tests are a whole family of tests. We shall concentrate on just two members of this family, the Mann-Whitney U test and the Kruskal-Wallis test. We'll use the Mann-Whitney test when only two populations are used and the Kruskal-Wallis test when more than two populations are involved. Use of these tests will enable us to determine whether independent samples have been drawn from the same population (or from different populations having the same distribution). The use of *ranking* information rather than pluses and minuses is less wasteful of data than the sign test.

Use based on the number of populations involved

APPROACHING A PROBLEM USING THE MANN-WHITNEY U TEST

Suppose that the board of regents of a large eastern state university wants to test the hypothesis that the mean SAT scores of students at two branches of the state university are equal. The board keeps statistics on all students at all branches of the system. A random sample of fifteen students from each branch has produced the data shown in Table 12-3.

Ranking the items to be tested

To apply the Mann-Whitney U test to this problem, we begin by ranking all the scores in order from lowest to highest, indicating beside each the symbol of the branch. Table 12-4 accomplishes this.

Next, let's learn the symbols used in a Mann-Whitney U test in the context of this problem:

Symbols for expressing the problem

$n_1 =$ number of items in sample 1; that is, the number of students at Branch A

$n_2 =$ number of items in sample 2; that is, the number of students at Branch S

$R_1 =$ sum of the ranks of the items in sample 1: the sum from Table 12-5 of the ranks of all the Branch A scores

$R_2 =$ sum of the ranks of the items in sample 2: the sum from Table 12-5 of the ranks of all the Branch S scores

---

In this case, both n_1 and n_2 are equal to 15, but it is *not* necessary for both samples to be of the same size. Now in Table 12-5, we can reproduce the data from Table 12-3, adding the ranks from Table 12-4. Then we can total the ranks for each branch. As a result, we have all the values we need to solve this problem, because we know that:

$$n_1 = 15$$
$$n_2 = 15$$
$$R_1 = 247$$
$$R_2 = 218$$

TABLE 12-3 SAT Scores for Students at Two State University Branches

| Branch A | 1,000 | 1,100 | 800 | 750 | 1,300 | 950 | 1,050 | 1,250 | 1,400 | 850 | 1,150 | 1,200 | 1,500 | 600 | 775 |
| Branch S | 920 | 1,120 | 830 | 1,360 | 650 | 725 | 890 | 1,600 | 900 | 1,140 | 1,550 | 550 | 1,240 | 925 | 500 |

TABLE 12-4 SAT Scores Ranked From Lowest to Highest

RANK	SCORE	BRANCH	RANK	SCORE	BRANCH
1	500	S	16	1,000	A
2	550	S	17	1,050	A
3	600	A	18	1,100	A
4	650	S	19	1,120	S
5	725	S	20	1,140	S
6	750	A	21	1,150	A
7	775	A	22	1,200	A
8	800	A	23	1,240	S
9	830	S	24	1,250	A
10	850	A	25	1,300	A
11	890	S	26	1,360	S
12	900	S	27	1,400	A
13	920	S	28	1,500	A
14	925	S	29	1,550	S
15	950	A	30	1,600	S

CALCULATING THE *U* STATISTIC

U statistic defined

Using the values for n_1 and n_2 and the rank sums R_1 and R_2, we can determine the *U statistic*, a measure of the difference between the ranked observations of the two samples of SAT scores:

Computing the *U* statistic

$$U = n_1 n_2 + \frac{n_1(n_1 + 1)}{2} - R_1 \qquad [12\text{-}1]$$

$$= (15)(15) + \frac{(15)(16)}{2} - 247$$

$$= 225 + 120 - 247$$

$$= 98 \leftarrow U \; statistic$$

TABLE 12-5 Raw Data and Rank for SAT Scores

BRANCH A	RANK	BRANCH S	RANK
1,000	16	920	13
1,100	18	1,120	19
800	8	830	9
750	6	1,360	26
1,300	25	650	4
950	15	725	5
1,050	17	890	11
1,250	24	1,600	30
1,400	27	900	12
850	10	1,140	20
1,150	21	1,550	29
1,200	22	550	2
1,500	28	1,240	23
600	3	925	14
775	7	500	1
	247 ← total ranks		218 ← total ranks

If the null hypothesis that the $n_1 + n_2$ observations came from identical populations is true, then this U statistic has a sampling distribution with a mean of:

Mean of the U statistic $\longrightarrow$

$$\mu_U = \frac{n_1 n_2}{2} \qquad\qquad [12\text{-}2]$$

$$= \frac{(15)(15)}{2}$$

$$= 112.5 \longleftarrow \text{mean of the } U \text{ statistic}$$

and a standard error of:

Standard error of the U statistic $\longrightarrow$

$$\sigma_U = \sqrt{\frac{n_1 n_2 (n_1 + n_2 + 1)}{12}} \qquad\qquad [12\text{-}3]$$

$$= \sqrt{\frac{(15)(15)(15 + 15 + 1)}{12}}$$

$$= \sqrt{\frac{6,975}{12}}$$

$$= \sqrt{581.25}$$

$$= 24.1 \longleftarrow \text{standard error of the } U \text{ statistic}$$

TESTING THE HYPOTHESES

The sampling distribution of the U statistic can be approximated by the normal distribution when both n_1 and n_2 are larger than 10. Because our problem meets this condition, we can use the standard normal probability distribution table to make our test. The board of regents wishes to test at the .15 level of significance the hypothesis that these samples were drawn from identical populations.

Stating the hypotheses

$\mathrm{H}_0 : \mu_1 = \mu_2 \longleftarrow$ null hypothesis: There is no difference between the two populations, and so they have the same mean.

$\mathrm{H}_1 : \mu_1 \neq \mu_2 \longleftarrow$ alternative hypothesis: There is a difference between the two populations; in particular, they have different means.

$\alpha = .15 \longleftarrow$ level of significance for testing these hypotheses

Illustrating the test graphically

Finding the limits of the acceptance region

The board of regents wants to know whether the mean SAT score for students at either of the two schools is better or worse than the other. Therefore, this is a two-tailed hypothesis test. Figure 12-3 illustrates this test graphically. The two colored areas represent the .15 level of significance. Since we are using the normal distribution as our sampling distribution in this test, we can determine from Appendix Table 1 that the appropriate z value for an area of .425 is 1.44. The two limits of the acceptance region can be calculated like this:

$$\mu_U + 1.44\sigma_U = 112.5 + (1.44)(24.1)$$

$$= 112.5 + 34.7$$

$$= 147.2 \longleftarrow \text{upper limit}$$

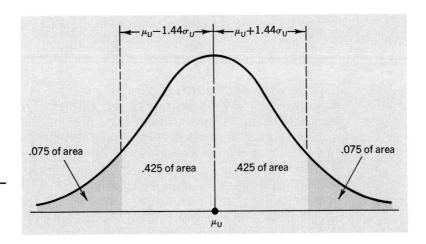

FIGURE 12-3

Two-tailed
hypothesis test at
the .15 level of
significance

.075 of area

.425 of area

.425 of area

.075 of area

$\mu_U - 1.44\sigma_U$

$\mu_U + 1.44\sigma_U$

μ_U

and:

$$\mu_U - 1.44\sigma_U = 112.5 - (1.44)(24.1)$$
$$= 112.5 - 34.7$$
$$= 77.8 \leftarrow \text{lower limit}$$

Interpreting the results

Figure 12-4 illustrates the limits of the acceptance region, 77.8 and 147.2, and the U value calculated earlier, 98. We can see that the sample U statistic does lie within the acceptance region. Thus, we would accept the null hypothesis of no difference and conclude that the distributions, and hence the mean SAT scores at the two schools, are the same.

SPECIAL PROPERTIES OF THE U TEST

Another way to
compute the U statistic

The U statistic has a feature that enables users to save calculating time when the two samples under observation are of unequal size. We just computed the value of U using Equation 12-1:

$$U = n_1 n_2 + \frac{n_1(n_1 + 1)}{2} - R_1 \qquad [12\text{-}1]$$

FIGURE 12-4

Two-tailed
hypothesis test at
the .15 level of
significance, showing
the acceptance
region and the
sample U statistic

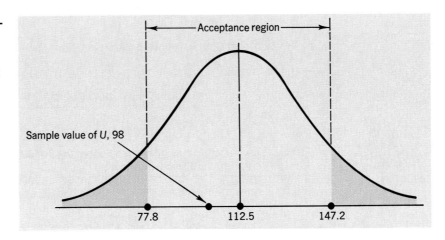

Acceptance region

Sample value of U, 98

77.8   112.5   147.2

But just as easily, we could have computed the U statistic using the R_2 value, like this:

$$U = n_1 n_2 + \frac{n_2(n_2 + 1)}{2} - R_2 \qquad [12\text{-}4]$$

The answer would have been 127 (which is just as far *above* the mean of 112.5 as 98 was *below* it). In this problem, we would have spent the same amount of time calculating the value of the U statistic using either Equation 12-1 or Equation 12-4. In other cases, when the number of items is larger in one sample than in the other, choose the equation that will require less work. Regardless of whether you calculate U using Equation 12-1 or 12-4, you will come to the same conclusion. Notice that in this example, the answer 127 falls in the acceptance region just as 98 did.

Handling ties in the data
What about *ties* that may happen when we rank the items for this test? For example, what if the two scores ranked 13 and 14 in Table 12-4 both had the value 920? In this case, we would find the average of their ranks $(13 + 14)/2 = 13.5$, and assign the result to both of them. If there were a three-way tie among the scores ranked 13, 14, and 15, we would average these ranks $(13 + 14 + 15)/3 = 14$, and use that value for all three items.

SOLVING A PROBLEM USING THE KRUSKAL-WALLIS TEST

Testing for differences when more than 2 populations are involved
As we noted earlier in this section, the Kruskal-Wallis test is an extension of the Mann-Whitney test to situations where more than two populations are involved. This test, too, depends upon the ranks of the sample observations.

In Table 12-6, we have shown the scores of a sample of 20 student pilots on their Federal Aviation Agency written examination, arranged according to which method was used in their training: video cassette, audio cassette, or classroom training.

The FAA is interested in evaluating the effectiveness of these three training methods. Specifically, it wants to test at the .10 level of significance the hypothesis that the mean written examination scores of student pilots trained by each of these three methods are equal. Since we have more than two populations involved, the Kruskal-Wallis test is appropriate in this instance. To apply the Kruskal-Wallis test to this problem, we begin in Table 12-7 by ranking all the scores in order, from lowest to highest, indicating beside each the symbol of the training method that was used. Ties are handled by averaging ranks, exactly as we did with the Mann-Whitney test.

Ranking the items to be tested

Next, let's learn the symbols used in a Kruskal-Wallis test:

Symbols used for a Kruskal-Wallis test

$n_j = $ the number of items in sample j

$R_j = $ the sum of the ranks of all the items in sample j

$k = $ the number of samples

$n = n_1 + n_2 + \cdots + n_k$, the total number of observations in all the samples

TABLE 12-6 Written Examination Scores for 20 Student Pilots Trained by Three Different Methods

Video cassette	74	88	82	93	55	70			
Audio cassette	78	80	65	57	89				
Classroom	68	83	50	91	84	77	94	81	92

TABLE 12-7 Written Examination Scores Ranked From Lowest to Highest

RANK	SCORE	TRAINING METHOD	RANK	SCORE	TRAINING METHOD
1	50	C	11	81	C
2	55	VC	12	82	VC
3	57	AC	13	83	C
4	65	AC	14	84	C
5	68	C	15	88	VC
6	70	VC	16	89	AC
7	74	VC	17	91	C
8	77	C	18	92	C
9	78	AC	19	93	VC
10	80	AC	20	94	C

Rearranging data to compute sums of ranks

Table 12-8 rearranges the data from Table 12-7 so that we can easily compute the sums of the ranks for each training method. Then we can use Equation 12-5 to compute the K statistic, a measure of the differences among the ranked observations in the three samples.

Computing the K statistic

$$K = \frac{12}{n(n+1)} \sum \frac{R_j^2}{n_j} - 3(n+1) \qquad [12\text{-}5]$$

$$= \frac{12}{20(20+1)} \left[\frac{(61)^2}{6} + \frac{(42)^2}{5} + \frac{(107)^2}{9} \right] - 3(20+1)$$

$$= (.02857)(620.2 + 352.8 + 1272.1) - 63$$

$$= 1.143$$

TESTING THE HYPOTHESES

The sampling distribution of the K statistic can be approximated by a chi-square distribution *when all the sample sizes are at least 5.* Because our problem meets this condition, we can use the chi-square distribution and Appendix Table 5 for this test. In a Kruskal-Wallis test, the approximate number of degrees of freedom is $k - 1$,

TABLE 12-8 Data and Rank Arranged by Training Method

VIDEO CASSETTE	RANK	AUDIO CASSETTE	RANK	CLASSROOM	RANK
74	7	78	9	68	5
88	15	80	10	83	13
82	12	65	4	50	1
93	19	57	3	91	17
55	2	89	16	84	14
70	6		42 ← sum of ranks	77	8
	61 ← sum of ranks			94	20
				81	11
				92	18
					107 ← sum of ranks

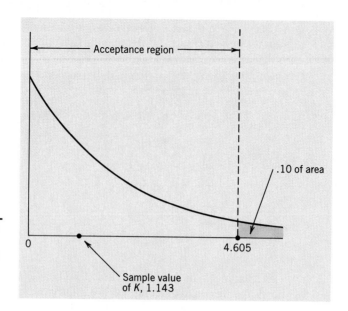

FIGURE 12-5

Kruskal-Wallis test at the .10 level of significance, showing the acceptance region and the sample K statistic

which in this problem is $(3 - 1)$ or 2, since we are dealing with three samples. The hypotheses can be stated as follows:

Stating the hypotheses

$H_0: \mu_1 = \mu_2 = \mu_3$ ← null hypothesis: There are no differences among the three populations, and so they have the same mean

$H_1: \mu_1, \mu_2,$ and μ_3 ← alternative hypothesis: There are differences among are not all equal the three populations; in particular, they have different means

$\alpha = .10$ ← level of significance for testing these hypotheses

Illustrating the test graphically

Interpreting the results

Figure 12-5 illustrates a chi-square distribution with 2 degrees of freedom. The colored area represents the .10 level of significance. Notice that the acceptance region for the null hypothesis (the hypothesis that there are no differences among the three populations) extends from zero to a chi-square value of 4.605. Obviously, the sample K value of 1.143 is within this acceptance region; therefore the FAA should accept the null hypothesis and conclude that there are no differences in the results obtained by using the three training methods.

Exercises

12-14   Test the hypothesis of no difference between the ages of male and female employees of a certain company, using the Mann-Whitney U test for the sample data below. Use the .10 level of significance.

Males	31	25	38	33	42	40	44	26	43	35
Females	44	30	34	47	35	32	35	47	48	34

12-15   The following table shows sample retail prices for three brands of shoes. Use the Kruskal-Wallis test to determine if there is any difference among the retail prices of the brands throughout the country. Use the .01 level of significance.

Brand A	$89	90	92	81	76	88	85	95	97	86	100
Brand B	$78	93	81	87	89	71	90	96	82	85	
Brand C	$80	88	86	85	79	80	84	85	90	92	

12-16   A mail-order gift company has the following sample data on dollar sales, separated according to how the order was paid for. Test the hypothesis that there is no difference in the dollar amount of orders paid for by cash, by check, or by credit card. Use the Kruskal-Wallis test with a level of significance of .05.

Credit-card orders	78	64	75	45	82	69	60
Check orders	110	70	53	51	61	68	
Cash orders	90	68	70	54	74	65	59

12-17   The following data show annual hours missed due to illness for the 24 men and women at the Northern Packing Company, Inc. At the .10 level of significance, is there any difference attributable to gender? Use a Mann-Whitney U test.

Men	31	44	25	30	70	63	54	42	36	22	25	50
Women	38	34	33	47	58	83	18	36	41	37	24	48

12-18   A manufacturer of toys changed the type of plastic molding machines it was using, because a new one gave evidence of being more economical. As the Christmas season began, however, productivity seemed somewhat lower than last year. Since production records for the past years were readily available, the production manager decided to compare the monthly output for the 15 months when the old machines were used and the 11 months of production so far this year. Records show these output amounts with the old and new machines.

	MONTHLY OUTPUT IN UNITS		
OLD MACHINES	NEW MACHINES	OLD MACHINES	NEW MACHINES
992	965	966	956
945	1,054	889	900
938	912	972	938
1,027	850	940	
892	796	873	
983	911	1,016	
1,014	877	897	
1,258	902		

Can the company conclude at $\alpha = .10$ that the change in machines has reduced output?

12-19   Melisa's Boutique has three mall locations. Melisa keeps a daily record for each location of the number of customers who actually make a purchase. A sample of those data are shown below. Using the Kruskal-Wallis test, can you say at the .05 level of significance that her stores have the same number of customers who buy?

Eastowne Mall	99	64	101	85	79	88	97	95	90	100
Craborchard Mall	83	102	125	61	91	96	94	89	93	75
Fairforest Mall	89	98	56	105	87	90	87	101	76	89

12-20 To increase sales during heavy shopping days, a chain of stores selling cheese in shopping malls gives away samples at the stores' entrances. The chain's management defines the heavy shopping days and randomly selects the days for sampling. From a sample of days that were considered heavy shopping days, the data below give one store's sales on days when cheese sampling was done and on days when it was not done.

SALES (in hundreds)

Promotion days	18	21	23	15	19	26	17	18	22	20	18	21	27
Regular days	22	17	15	23	25	20	26	24	16	17	23	21	

Use a Mann-Whitney U test and a 5 percent level of significance to decide whether the storefront sampling produced greater sales.

12-21 A company is interested in knowing whether there is a difference in the output rate for men and women employees in the molding department. Judy Johnson, production manager, was asked to conduct a study in which male and female workers' output was measured for 1 week. Somehow, one of the office clerks misplaced a portion of the data, and Judy was able to locate only the following information from the records of the tests:

$$\sigma_U = 176.4275$$
$$\mu_U = 1,624$$
$$R_1 = 3,255$$

Judy also remembered that the sample size for men, n_2, had been two units larger than n_1.

Reconstruct a z value for the test and determine if the weekly output can be assumed, with a five percent level of significance, to be the same for both men and women. Indicate also the values for n_1, n_2, and R_2.

12-22 A large hospital hires most of its nurses from the two major universities in the area. Over the last year, they have been giving a test to the newly graduated nurses entering the hospital to determine which school, if either, seems to educate its nurses better. Based on the following scores (out of 100 possible points), help the personnel office of the hospital determine whether the schools differ in quality. Use the Mann-Whitney U test with a 6 percent level of significance.

TEST SCORES

School A	97	69	73	84	76	92	90	88	84	87	93		
School B	88	99	65	69	97	84	85	89	91	90	87	91	72

12-23 Twenty salespersons of Henley Paper Company have received sales training during the past year. Some were sent to a national program conducted by Salesmasters. The others received training at the company office conducted by the Henley sales manager. Percents of selling quotas realized by both groups during last year are shown below. Mr. Boyden Henley, president, believes that the backgrounds, sales aptitudes, and motivation of both groups are comparable. At the .10 level of significance, has either method of training been better? Use the Mann-Whitney U test.

PERCENT OF QUOTA REALIZED

Salesmasters	90	95	105	110	100	75	80	90	105	120
Company	80	90	100	120	95	95	90	100	95	105

12-4
One-Sample Runs Test

Concept of randomness

So far, we have assumed that the samples in our problems were randomly selected—that is, chosen without preference or bias. What if you were to notice recurrent patterns in a sample chosen by someone else? Suppose that applicants for advanced job training were to be selected without regard to gender from a large population. Using the notation W = woman and M = man, you find that the first group enters in this order:

W, W, W, W, M, M, M, M, W, W, W, W, M, M, M, M

By inspection, you would conclude that although the total number of applicants is equally divided between the sexes, the order is not random. A random process would rarely list two items in alternating groups of four. Suppose now that the applicants begin to arrive in this order:

W, M, W, M, W, M, W, M, W, M, W, M, W, M, W, M

It is just as unreasonable to think that a random selection process would produce such an orderly pattern of men and women. In this case, too, the *proportion* of women to men is right, but you would be suspicious about the *order* in which they are arriving.

To allow us to test samples for the randomness of their order, statisticians have developed the *theory of runs*. **A run is a sequence of identical occurrences preceded and followed by different occurrences or by none at all.** If men and women enter as follows, the sequence will contain three runs:

$$\underbrace{W,}_{\text{1st}} \underbrace{M, M, M, M,}_{\text{2nd}} \underbrace{W}_{\text{3rd}}$$

And this sequence contains six runs:

$$\underbrace{W, W, W,}_{\text{1st}} \underbrace{M, M,}_{\text{2nd}} \underbrace{W,}_{\text{3rd}} \underbrace{M, M, M, M,}_{\text{4th}} \underbrace{W, W, W, W,}_{\text{5th}} \underbrace{M}_{\text{6th}}$$

A *test of runs* would use the following symbols if it contained just two kinds of occurrences:

Symbols used for a runs test

n_1 = number of occurrences of type 1

n_2 = number of occurrences of type 2

r = number of runs

Let's apply these symbols to a different pattern for the arrival of applicants:

M, W, W, M, M, M, M, W, W, W, M, M, W, M, W, W, M

In this case, the values of n_1, n_2, and r would be:

$n_1 = 8 \leftarrow$ number of women

$n_2 = 9 \leftarrow$ number of men

$r = 9 \leftarrow$ number of runs

A PROBLEM ILLUSTRATING A ONE-SAMPLE RUNS TEST

A manufacturer of breakfast cereal uses a machine to insert randomly one of two types of toys in each box. The company wants randomness so that every child in the neighborhood does not get the same toy. Testers choose samples of 60 successive boxes to see if the machine is properly mixing the two types of toys. Using the symbols A and B to represent the two types of toys, a tester reported that one such batch looked like this:

B, A, B, B, B, A, A, A, B, B, A, B, B, B, B, A, A, A, A, B,
A, B, A, A, B, B, B, A, A, B, A, A, A, A, B, B, A, B, B, A,
A, A, A, B, B, A, B, B, B, B, A, A, B, B, A, B, A, A, B, B

Stating the problem symbolically

The values in our test will be:

$$n_1 = 29 \leftarrow \text{number of boxes containing toy A}$$

$$n_2 = 31 \leftarrow \text{number of boxes containing toy B}$$

$$r = 29 \leftarrow \text{number of runs}$$

THE SAMPLING DISTRIBUTION OF THE r STATISTIC

The r statistic, the basis of a one-sample runs test

The *number of runs,* or r, is a statistic with its own special sampling distribution and its own test. Obviously, runs may be of differing lengths, and various numbers of runs can occur in one sample. Statisticians can prove that too many or too few runs in a sample indicate that something other than chance was at work when the items were selected. **A *one-sample runs test,* then, is based on the idea that *too few* or *too many* runs show that the items were not chosen randomly.**

To derive the mean of the sampling distribution of the r statistic, use the following formula:

Mean and standard error of the r statistic

Mean of the r statistic $\longrightarrow \mu_r = \dfrac{2n_1 n_2}{n_1 + n_2} + 1$ [12-6]

Applying this to be cereal company, the mean of the r statistic would be:

$$\mu_r = \frac{(2)(29)(31)}{29 + 31} + 1$$

$$= \frac{1{,}798}{60} + 1$$

$$= 29.97 + 1$$

$$= 30.97 \leftarrow \text{mean of the } r \text{ statistic}$$

The standard error of the r statistic can be calculated with this formidable-looking formula:

Standard error of the r statistic $\longrightarrow \sigma_r = \sqrt{\dfrac{2n_1 n_2 (2n_1 n_2 - n_1 - n_2)}{(n_1 + n_2)^2 (n_1 + n_2 - 1)}}$ [12-7]

For our problem, the standard error of the r statistic becomes:

$$\sigma_r = \sqrt{\frac{(2)(29)(31)(2 \times 29 \times 31 - 29 - 31)}{(29 + 31)^2(29 + 31 - 1)}}$$

$$= \sqrt{\frac{(1,798)(1,738)}{(60)^2(59)}}$$

$$= \sqrt{14.71}$$

$$= 3.84 \leftarrow \text{standard error of the } r \text{ statistic}$$

TESTING THE HYPOTHESES

In the one-sample runs test, the sampling distribution of r can be closely approximated by the normal distribution if *either n_1 or n_2* is larger than 20. Since our cereal company has a sample of 60 boxes, we can use the normal approximation. Management is interested in testing at the .20 level the hypothesis that the toys are randomly mixed, so the test becomes:

Stating the hypotheses

H_0: In a one-sample runs $\leftarrow$ null hypothesis: The toys are randomly
test, a symbolic state- mixed.
H_1: ment of the hypotheses $\leftarrow$ alternative hypothesis: The toys are
is not appropriate. not randomly mixed.

$\sigma = .20 \leftarrow$ level of significance for testing these
hypotheses

Illustrating the test graphically

Since too many *or* too few runs would indicate that the process by which the toys are inserted is not random, a two-tailed test is appropriate. Figure 12-6 illustrates this test graphically.

Because we can use the normal distribution, we can turn to Appendix Table 1 to find the appropriate z value for .40 of the area under the curve. We can then use this

FIGURE 12-6

Two-tailed hypothesis test at the .20 level of significance

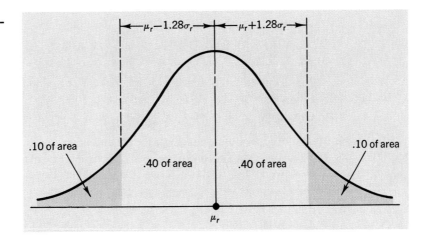

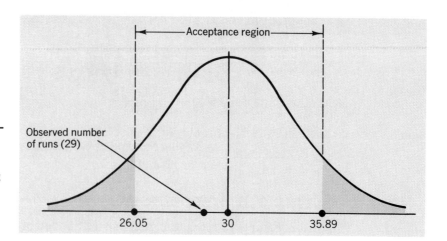

FIGURE 12-7

Two-tailed hypothesis test at the .20 level of significance, showing the acceptance region and the observed number of runs

value, 1.28, to calculate the limits of the acceptance region:

Finding the limits of the acceptance region

$$\mu_r + 1.28\sigma_r = 30.97 + (1.28)(3.84)$$
$$= 30.97 + 4.92$$
$$= 35.89 \leftarrow \text{upper limit}$$

and:

$$\mu_r - 1.28\sigma_r = 30.97 - (1.28)(3.84)$$
$$= 30.97 - 4.92$$
$$= 26.05 \leftarrow \text{lower limit}$$

Interpreting the results

Both these limits to the acceptance region, 26.05 and 35.89, and the number of runs in the sample, 29, are shown in Fig. 12-7. There, we can see that the observed number of runs, 29, falls within the acceptance region. Therefore, management should accept the null hypothesis and conclude from this test that the toys are being inserted in the boxes in random order.

Exercises

12-24 Test for the randomness of the following sample, using the .05 significance level:

A, B, A, A, A, B, B, A, B, B, A, A, B, A, B, A, A, B, B, B, B, A, B, B,
A, A, A, B, A, B, A, A, B, B, A, B, B, A, A, A, B, B, A, A, B, A, A, A

12-25 A sequence of small glass sculptures was inspected for shipping damage. The sequence of acceptable and damaged pieces was as follows:

D, A, A, A, D, D, D, D, D, A, A, D, D, A, A, A, A, D, A, A, D, D, D, D, D

Test for the randomness of the damage to the shipment, using the .05 significance level.

12-26 The *News and Clarion* kept a record of the sex of people who called the circulation office to complain about delivery problems with the Sunday paper. For a recent Sunday these data were as follows:

M, F, F, F, M, M, F, M, F, F, F, F, M, M, M, F, M, F, M, F, F, F, F, M, M, M, M, M

Using the .05 level of significance, test this sequence for randomness. Is there anything about the nature of this problem that would cause you to believe that such a sequence would not be random?

12-27 Kerwin County Social Services Agency kept this record of the daily number of applicants for marriage counseling in the order in which they appeared at the agency office in 30 working days.

3, 4, 6, 8, 4, 6, 7, 2, 5, 7, 4, 8, 4, 7, 9, 5, 9, 10,
5, 7, 4, 9, 8, 9, 11, 6, 7, 5, 9, 12

Test the randomness of this sequence by seeing if values above and below the mean occur in random order. Use the .10 level of significance. Can you think of any characteristic of the environment of this problem that would support the statistical finding you reached?

12-28 A restaurant owner has noticed over the years that older couples appear to eat earlier than young couples at his quiet, romantic restaurant. He suspects that perhaps it is because of children having to be left with babysitters and also because the older couples may retire earlier at night. One night he decided to keep a record of couples' arrivals at the restaurant. He noted whether each couple was over or under 30. His notes are reproduced below. (A = 30 and older; B = younger than 30.)

(5:30 P.M.) A, A, A, A, A, A, B, A, A, A, A, A, A, A, B, B,
B, A, B, B, B, B, B, B, A, B, B, B, A, B, B, B, (10 P.M.)

At a 5 percent level of significance, was the restaurant owner correct in his thought that the age of his customers at different dining hours is less than random?

12-29 Kathy Phillips is in charge of production scheduling for a printing company. The company has six large presses, which frequently break down, and one of Kathy's biggest problems is meeting deadlines when there are unexpected breakdowns in presses. She suspects that the older presses break down earlier in the week than the new presses, since all presses are checked and repaired over the weekend. To test her hypothesis, Kathy recorded the number of all the presses as they broke down during the week. Presses numbered 1, 2, and 3 are the older ones.

NUMBER OF PRESS IN ORDER OF BREAKDOWN

1, 2, 3, 1, 4, 5, 3, 1, 2, 5, 1, 3, 6, 2, 3, 6, 2, 2, 3, 5, 4,
6, 4, 2, 1, 3, 4, 5, 5, 1, 4, 5, 2, 3, 5, 6, 4, 3, 2, 5, 4, 3

(a) At a 5 percent level of significance, does Kathy have a valid hypothesis that the breakdowns of presses are not random?
(b) Is her hypothesis appropriate for the decision she wishes to make about rescheduling more work earlier in the week on the newer presses?

12-30 Martha Bowen, a department manager working in a large marketing-research firm, is in charge of all the research data analyses done in the firm. Accuracy and thoroughness are her responsibility. The department employs a number of research assistants to do some analyses and uses a computer to do other analyses. Typically, each week Martha randomly chooses completed analyses before they are reported and conducts tests to ensure that they have been done correctly and thoroughly. Martha's assistant, Kim Tadlock, randomly chooses 49 analyses per week from those completed and filed each day, and Martha does the re-analyses. Martha wanted to make certain that the selection process was a random one, so she could provide assurances that the computer analyses and those done by hand were both periodically checked. She arranged to have the research assistants place a special mark on the back of the records, so that they could be identified. Since Kim was unaware of the mark, the randomness of the test would not be affected. Kim completed her sample with the following data:

1, 1, 1, 1, 1, 1, 1, 1, 1, 2, 1, 1, 1, 1, 1, 1, 1, 1, 1, 2, 1, 1, 1, 1, 1,
1, 1, 1, 1, 2, 1, 1, 1, 1, 1, 1, 1, 1, 1, 2, 1, 1, 1, 1, 1, 1, 1, 1, 1

(a) At a 1 percent significance level, can you conclude that the sample was random?
(b) If the sample were distributed as follows, would the sample be random?

1, 1, 1, 1, 1, 1, 1, 1, 1, 1, 1, 1, 1, 1, 1, 1, 1, 1, 1, 1, 1, 1, 1, 1, 1,
1, 1, 1, 1, 1, 1, 1, 1, 1, 1, 1, 1, 1, 1, 1, 1, 1, 1, 1, 1, 2, 2, 2, 2

(c) Since computer analyses are much faster than those done by hand, and since a number of the analyses are possible to do by computer, there are about three times as many computer analyses per week as hand analyses. Is there statistical evidence in part (a) to support the belief that somewhere in the sampling process there is something less than randomness occurring? If so, what is the evidence?
(d) Does the conclusion you reached in part (c) lead you to any new conclusions about the one-sample runs test, particularly in reference to your answer in part (a)?

12-31 Prof. Ike Newton is interested in determining if his brightest students (those making the best grades) tend to turn in their tests earlier (because they can recall the material faster) or later (because they take longer to write down all they know) than the others in the class. For a particular physics test, he observes that the students make the following grades in order of turning their tests in:

ORDER	GRADES									
1–10	94	70	85	89	92	98	63	88	74	85
11–20	69	90	57	86	79	72	80	93	66	74
21–30	50	55	47	59	68	63	89	51	90	88

(a) If Professor Newton counts those making a grade of 90 and above as his brightest students, then at a 5 percent level of significance, can he conclude the brightest students turned their tests in randomly?
(b) If 60 and above is passing in Professor Newton's class, then did those students passing versus those not passing turn their tests in randomly? (Also use the 5 percent significance level.)

12-32 The First National Bank of Smithville recorded the sex of the first 40 customers who appeared last Tuesday with this notation:

M, F, M, M, M, M, F, F, M, M, M, F, M, M, M, M, M, F, F, M,
F, M, M, M, F, M, M, M, M, M, M, F, M, M, M, M, M, F, F, M

At the .05 level of significance, test the randomness of this sequence. Is there anything in banking or in the nature of this problem that would lead you to accept intuitively what you have found statistically?

12-5
Rank Correlation

Function of the rank
correlation coefficient

Chapters 10 and 11 introduced us to the notion of correlation and to the correlation coefficient, a measure of the closeness of association between two variables. Often in correlation analysis, information is not available in the form of numerical values like those we used in the problems of those chapters. But if we can assign rankings to the items in each of the two variables we are studying, a *rank correlation coefficient* can be calculated. **This is a measure of the correlation that exists between the two sets of ranks, a measure of the degree of association between the variables that we would not have been able to calculate otherwise.**

Another advantage of
using rank correlation

A second reason for learning the method of rank correlation is to be able to simplify the process of computing a correlation coefficient from a very large set of data for each of two variables. To prove how tedious this can be, try expanding one of the correlation problems in Chapter 10 by a factor of 10 and performing the necessary calculations. Instead of having to do these calculations, we can compute a measure of association that is based on the *ranks* of the observations, *not the numerical values* of the data. This measure is called the Spearman rank correlation coefficient, in honor of the statistician who developed it in the early 1900s.

THE COEFFICIENT OF RANK CORRELATION

Listing the ranked
variables

By working a couple of examples, we can learn how to calculate and interpret this measure of the association between two ranked variables. First, consider Table 12-9, which lists five persons and compares the academic rank they achieved in college with the level they have attained in a certain company 10 years after graduation. The value of 5 represents the highest rank in the group; the rank of 1, the lowest.

Calculating the rank
correlation coefficient

Using the information in Table 12-9, we can calculate a coefficient of rank correlation between success in college and company level achieved 10 years later. All we need is Equation 12-8 and a few computations.

Coefficient of
rank correlation

$$r_s = 1 - \frac{6 \Sigma d^2}{n(n^2 - 1)} \qquad [12\text{-}8]$$

where:

- r_s = coefficient of rank correlation (Notice that the subscript s, from Spearman, distinguishes this r from the one we calculated in Chapter 10.)
- n = number of paired observations
- Σ = notation meaning "the sum of"
- d = difference between the ranks for each pair of observations

The computations are easily done in tabular form, as we show in Table 12-10.

**TABLE 12-9 Comparison of the Ranks
of 5 Students**

STUDENT	COLLEGE RANK	COMPANY RANK 10 YEARS LATER
John	4	4
Margaret	3	3
Debbie	1	1
Steve	2	2
Lisa	5	5

TABLE 12-10 Generating Information to Compute the Rank Correlation Coefficient

STUDENT	COLLEGE RANK (1)	COMPANY RANK (2)	DIFFERENCE BETWEEN THE 2 RANKS (1) − (2)	DIFFERENCE SQUARED [(1) − (2)]²
John	4	4	0	0
Margaret	3	3	0	0
Debbie	1	1	0	0
Steve	2	2	0	0
Lisa	5	5	0	0
				$\Sigma d^2 = 0$ ← sum of the squared differences

Therefore, we have all the information we need to find the rank correlation coefficient for this problem:

$$r_s = 1 - \frac{6\Sigma d^2}{n(n^2 - 1)} \qquad [12\text{-}8]$$

$$= 1 - \frac{6(0)}{5(25 - 1)}$$

$$= 1 - \frac{0}{120}$$

$$= 1 \leftarrow \text{rank correlation coefficient}$$

Explaining values of the rank correlation coefficient

Computing another rank correlation coefficient

As we learned in Chapter 10, this correlation coefficient of 1 shows that there is a perfect association or *perfect correlation* between the two variables. This verifies the fact that the college and company ranks for each person were identical.

One more example should make us feel comfortable with the coefficient of rank correlation. Table 12-11 illustrates five more people, but this time, the ranks in college and in a company 10 years later seem to be extreme opposites. We can compute the difference between the ranks for each pair of observations, find d^2, and

TABLE 12-11 Generating Data to Compute the Rank Correlation Coefficient

STUDENT	COLLEGE RANK (1)	COMPANY RANK (2)	DIFFERENCE BETWEEN THE 2 RANKS (1) − (2)	DIFFERENCE SQUARED [(1) − (2)]²
Roy	5	1	4	16
David	1	5	−4	16
Jay	3	3	0	0
Charlotte	2	4	−2	4
Kathy	4	2	2	4
				$\Sigma d^2 = 40$ ← sum of the squared differences

then take the sum of all the d^2s. Substituting these values into Equation 12-8, we find a rank correlation coefficient of -1:

$$r_s = 1 - \frac{6\Sigma d^2}{n(n^2 - 1)} \qquad [12\text{-}8]$$

$$= 1 - \frac{6(40)}{5(25 - 1)}$$

$$= 1 - \frac{240}{120}$$

$$= 1 - 2$$

$$= -1 \leftarrow \text{rank correlation coefficient}$$

Interpreting the results In Chapter 10, we learned that a correlation coefficient of -1 represents *perfect inverse correlation.* And that is just what happened in our case: The people who did the best in college wound up 10 years later in the lowest ranks of an organization. Now let's apply these ideas.

SOLVING A PROBLEM USING RANK CORRELATION

Rank correlation is a useful technique for looking at the connection between air quality and the evidence of pulmonary-related diseases that we discussed in our chapter-opening problem. Table 12-12 reproduces the data found by the health organization studying the problem. In the same table, we also do some of the calculations needed to find r_s.

Finding the rank correlation coefficient Using the data in Table 12-12 and Equation 12-8, we can find the rank correlation coefficient for this problem:

$$r_s = 1 - \frac{6\Sigma d^2}{n(n^2 - 1)} \qquad [12\text{-}8]$$

$$= 1 - \frac{6(58)}{11(121 - 1)}$$

$$= 1 - \frac{348}{1,320}$$

$$= 1 - .264$$

$$= .736 \leftarrow \text{rank correlation coefficient}$$

Interpreting the results A correlation coefficient of .736 suggests a substantial positive association between average air quality and the occurrence of pulmonary disease, at least in the eleven cities sampled; that is, high levels of pollution go with high incidence of pulmonary disease.

How can we test this value of .736? We can apply the same methods we used to test hypotheses in Chapter 8. In performing such tests on r_s, we are trying to avoid the error of concluding that an association exists between two variables if, in fact, no such association exists in the population from which these two samples were drawn; that is, if the *population* rank correlation coefficient, ρ_s *(rho-sub-s),* is really equal to zero.

Testing hypotheses about rank correlation **For small values of *n* (*n* less than or equal to 30), the distribution of r_s is not normal, and unlike other small sample statistics we have encountered, it is not appropriate to**

TABLE 12-12 Ranking of Eleven Cities

CITY	AIR-QUALITY RANK (1)	PULMONARY-DISEASE RANK (2)	DIFFERENCE BETWEEN THE 2 RANKS (1) − (2)	DIFFERENCE SQUARED [(1) − (2)]²
A	4	5	−1	1
B	7	4	3	9
C	9	7	2	4
D	1	3	−2	4
E	2	1	1	1
F	10	11	−1	1
G	3	2	1	1
H	5	10	−5	25
I	6	8	−2	4
J	8	6	2	4
K	11	9	2	4

Best rank = 11
Worst rank = 1

$\Sigma d^2 = 58 \leftarrow$ sum of the squared differences

use the *t* distribution for testing hypotheses about the rank correlation coefficient. Instead, we use Appendix Table 7 to determine the acceptance and rejection regions for such hypotheses. In our current problem, suppose that the health organization wants to test, at the .05 level of significance, the null hypothesis that there is zero correlation in the ranked data of *all* cities in the world. Our problem then becomes:

$H_0 : \rho_s = 0$ ← null hypothesis: There is no correlation in the ranked data of the population.

$H_1 : \rho_s \neq 0$ ← alternative hypothesis: There is a correlation in the ranked data of the population

$\alpha = .05$ ← level of significance for testing these hypotheses

A two-tailed test is appropriate, so we look at Appendix Table 7 in the row for $n = 11$ (the number of cities) and the column for a significance level of .05. There we find that the critical values for r_s are ± .6091; that is, the upper limit of the acceptance region is .6091, and the lower limit of the acceptance region is − .6091.

Figure 12-8 shows the limits of the acceptance region and the rank correlation coefficient we calculated from the air-quality sample. From this figure, we can see that the rank correlation coefficient lies outside the acceptance region. Therefore, we would reject the null hypothesis of no correlation and conclude that there *is* an association between air-quality levels and the incidence of pulmonary disease in the world's cities.

The appropriate distribution for values of n greater than 30

If the sample size is greater than 30, we can no longer use Appendix Table 7. However, when n is greater than 30, the sampling distribution of r_s is approximately normal, with a mean of zero and a standard deviation of $1/\sqrt{n-1}$. Thus, the standard error of r_s is:

Standard error of r_s $\longrightarrow$
$$\sigma_{r_s} = \frac{1}{\sqrt{n-1}}$$

[12-9]

622   12 NONPARAMETRIC METHODS

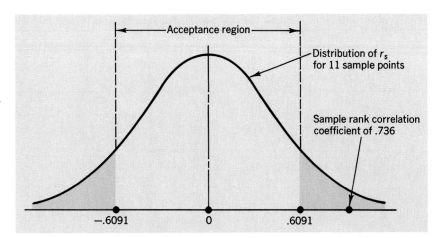

FIGURE 12-8

Two-tailed
hypothesis test, using
Appendix Table 7 at
the .05 level of
significance, showing
the acceptance
region and the
sample rank
correlation
coefficient

and we can use Appendix Table 1 to find the appropriate z values for testing hypotheses about the population rank correlation.

Example with n greater than 30

As an example of hypothesis testing of rank correlation coefficients when n is greater than 30, consider the case of a social scientist who tries to determine whether bright people tend to choose spouses who are also bright. He randomly chooses 32 couples and tests to see if there is a significant rank correlation in the IQs of the couples. His data and computations are given in Table 12-13.

Using the data in Table 12-13 and Equation 12-8, we can find the rank correlation coefficient for this problem:

$$r_s = 1 - \frac{6\Sigma d^2}{n(n^2 - 1)} \qquad [12\text{-}8]$$

$$= 1 - \frac{6(1,043.5)}{32(1,024 - 1)}$$

$$= 1 - \frac{6,261}{32,736}$$

$$= 1 - .191$$

$$= .809 \leftarrow \text{rank correlation coefficient}$$

If the social scientist wishes to test his hypothesis at the .01 level of significance, his problem can be stated:

Stating the hypotheses

$H_0: \rho_s = 0$ ← null hypothesis: There is no rank correlation in the population; that is, husband's and wife's intelligence is randomly mixed.

$H_1: \rho_s > 0$ ← alternative hypothesis: The population rank correlation is positive; that is, bright people choose bright spouses.

$\alpha = .01$ ← level of significance for testing these hypotheses

An upper-tailed test is appropriate. From Appendix Table 1, we find that the appropriate z value for the .01 level of significance is 2.33. Figure 12-9 illustrates this hypothesis test graphically; we show there the colored region in the upper tail of the distribution that corresponds to the .01 level of significance.

TABLE 12-13 Computation of Rank Correlation of Husbands' and Wives' IQs

COUPLE (1)	HUSBAND'S IQ (2)	WIFE'S IQ (3)	HUSBAND'S RANK (4)	WIFE'S RANK (5)	DIFFERENCE BETWEEN RANKS (4) − (5)	DIFFERENCE SQUARED $[(4) - (5)]^2$
1	95	95	8	4.5	3.5	12.25
2	103	98	20	8.5	11.5	132.25
3	111	110	26	23	3	9.00
4	92	88	4	2	2	4.00
5	150	106	32	18	14	196.00
6	107	109	24	21.5	2.5	6.25
7	90	96	3	6	−3	9.00
8	108	131	25	32	−7	49.00
9	100	112	17.5	25.5	−8	64.00
10	93	95	5.5	4.5	1	1.00
11	119	112	29	25.5	3.5	12.25
12	115	117	28	30	−2	4.00
13	87	94	1	3	−2	4.00
14	105	109	21	21.5	−0.5	0.25
15	135	114	31	27	4	16.00
16	89	83	2	1	1	1.00
17	99	105	14.5	16.5	−2	4.00
18	106	115	22.5	28	−5.5	30.25
19	126	116	30	29	1	1.00
20	100	107	17.5	19	−1.5	2.25
21	93	111	5.5	24	−18.5	342.25
22	94	98	7	8.5	−1.5	2.25
23	100	105	17.5	16.5	1	1.00
24	96	103	10	15	−5	25.00
25	99	101	14.5	13	1.5	2.25
26	112	123	27	31	−4	16.00
27	106	108	22.5	20	2.5	6.25
28	98	97	12.5	7	5.5	30.25
29	96	100	10	11.5	−1.5	2.25
30	98	99	12.5	10	2.5	6.25
31	100	100	17.5	11.5	6	36.00
32	96	102	10	14	−4	16.00

Sum of the squared differences → $\Sigma d^2 = \underline{\mathbf{1{,}043.50}}$

FIGURE 12-9

Upper-tailed hypothesis test at the .01 level of significance

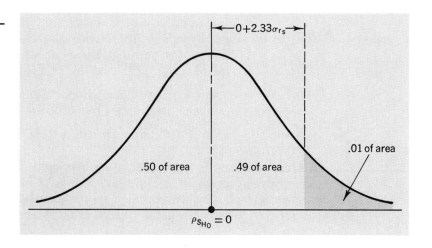

We can now calculate the limit of our acceptance region:

$$p_{s_{H_0}} + 2.33\sigma_{r_s} = 0 + 2.33\left(\frac{1}{\sqrt{n-1}}\right)$$

$$= 0 + \frac{2.33}{\sqrt{31}}$$

$$= 0 + \frac{2.33}{5.568}$$

$$= 0.42 \leftarrow \text{upper limit of acceptance region}$$

Figure 12-10 shows the limit of the acceptance region and the rank correlation coefficient we calculated from the IQ data. In Fig. 12-10, we can see that the rank correlation coefficient of .809 lies far outside the acceptance region. Therefore, we would reject the null hypothesis of no correlation and conclude that bright people tend to choose bright spouses.

A SPECIAL PROPERTY OF RANK CORRELATION

Rank correlation has a useful advantage over the correlation method we discussed in Chapter 10. Suppose we have cases in which one or several very extreme observations exist in the original data. By the use of numerical values as was done in Chapter 10, the correlation coefficient may not be a good description of the association that exists between two variables. Yet extreme observations in a *rank* correlation test will never produce a large rank difference.

Consider the following data array of two variables, X and Y:

$$\begin{array}{llllll} X & 10 & 13 & 16 & 19 & 25 \\ Y & 34 & 40 & 45 & 51 & 117 \end{array}$$

Because of the large value of the fifth Y term, we would get two significantly different answers for r using the conventional and the rank correlation methods. In this case, the rank correlation method would be less sensitive to the extreme value. We would assign a rank order of 5 to the numerical value of 117 and avoid the unduly large effect on the value of the correlation coefficient.

FIGURE 12-10

Upper-tailed hypothesis test at the .01 level of significance, showing the acceptance region and the sample rank correlation coefficient

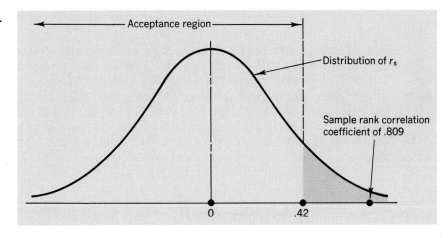

Exercises

 12-33 Below are ratings of aggressiveness *(X)* and amount of sales in the last year *(Y)* for eight salespeople. Is there a significant rank correlation between the two measures? Use the .10 significance level.

X	30	17	35	28	42	25	19	29
Y	35	31	43	46	50	32	33	42

 12-34 A plant supervisor ranked a sample of eight workers on the number of hours worked overtime and length of employment. Is the rank correlation between the two measures significant at the .01 level?

Amount of overtime	5.0	8.0	2.0	4.0	3.0	7.0	1.0	6.0
Years employed	1.0	6.0	4.5	2.0	7.0	8.0	4.5	3.0

 12-35 Most people believe that managerial experience produces better interpersonal relationships between a manager and her employees. The Quill Corporation has the following data matching years of experience on the part of the manager with the number of grievances filed last year by the employees reporting to that manager. At the .05 level of significance, does the rank correlation between these two suggest that experience improves relationships?

Age of manager	32	43	42	29	56	62	45	39	40	35
Number of grievances	5	2	4	4	3	2	4	5	4	6

 12-36 The Occupational Safety and Health Administration (OSHA) was conducting a study of the relationship of expenditures for plant safety and the accident rate in the plants. OSHA had confined its studies to the synthetic chemical industry. To adjust for the size differential that existed among some of the plants, OSHA had converted its data into expenditures per production employee. The results of the data are listed below.

EXPENDITURE BY CHEMICAL COMPANIES PER PRODUCTION EMPLOYEE
IN RELATION TO ACCIDENTS PER YEAR

Company	A	B	C	D	E	F	G	H	I	J	K
Expenditure	$60	$37	$30	$20	$24	$42	$39	$54	$48	$58	$26
Accidents	2	7	6	9	7	4	8	2	4	3	8

Is there a significant correlation between expenditures and accidents in the chemical-company plants? Use a rank correlation (with 1 representing highest expenditure and accident rate) to support your conclusion. Test at the 1 percent significance level.

 12-37 Two business school professors were discussing how difficult it is to predict the success of graduates based on grades alone. One professor thought that the number of years of experience M.B.A.s had before returning for their degrees was probably a better predictor. Using the data below, at the .02 level of significance, which rank correlation is a better predictor of career success?

Years experience	4	3	4	3	6	7	1	5	5	2
Grade-point average	3.4	3.2	3.5	3.0	2.9	3.4	2.5	3.9	3.6	3.0
Success rank (10 = top)	4	2	6	5	7	9	1	8	10	3

12-38 The Carolina Lighting Company has two trained interviewers to recruit manager trainees for new sales outlets. Although each of the interviewers has a unique style, both are thought to be good preliminary judges of managerial potential. The personnel manager wondered how closely the interviewers would agree, so she had both of them independently evaluate fourteen applicants. They ranked the applicants in terms of their degree of potential contribution to the company. The results are given below. Use a rank correlation and a 2 percent significance level to determine if there is a significant positive correlation between the two interviewers' rankings.

Applicant	1	2	3	4	5	6	7	8	9	10	11	12	13	14
Interviewer 1	1	11	13	2	12	10	3	4	14	5	6	9	7	8
Interviewer 2	4	12	11	2	14	10	1	3	13	8	6	7	9	5

12-39 Nancy McKenzie, foreman for a lithographic camera assembly process, feels that the longer a group of employees work together, the higher the daily output rate. She has gathered the following data for a group of employees who worked together for 10 days.

Daily output	4.0	7.0	5.0	6.0	8.0	2.0	3.0	0.5	9.0	6.0
Days worked together	1	2	3	4	5	6	7	8	9	10

Can Nancy conclude at a 5 percent significance level that there is no correlation between the number of days worked together and the daily output?

12-40 An electronics firm, which recruits many engineers, wonders if the cost of extensive recruiting efforts is worth it. If the firm could be confident (using a 1 percent significance level) that the population rank correlation between applicants' résumés scored by the personnel department and interview scores is positive, it would feel justified in discontinuing interviews and relying on résumé scores in hiring. The firm has drawn a sample of 35 engineer applicants in the last two years. On the basis of this sample, shown below, should the firm discontinue interviews and use résumé scores to hire?

INDIVIDUAL	INTERVIEW SCORE	RÉSUMÉ SCORE	INDIVIDUAL	INTERVIEW SCORE	RÉSUMÉ SCORE
1	81	113	19	81	111
2	88	88	20	84	121
3	55	76	21	82	83
4	83	129	22	90	79
5	78	99	23	63	71
6	93	142	24	78	108
7	65	93	25	73	68
8	87	136	26	79	121
9	95	82	27	72	109
10	76	91	28	95	121
11	60	83	29	81	140
12	85	96	30	87	132
13	93	126	31	93	135
14	66	108	32	85	143
15	90	95	33	91	118
16	69	65	34	94	147
17	87	96	35	94	138
18	68	101			

12-41 Below are salary and age data for the ten Ph.D. candidates graduating this year from the School of Accounting at Northwest University. At the .05 level of significance, does the rank correlation of age and salary suggest that older candidates get higher starting salaries?

SALARY	AGE
$67,000	29
60,000	25
57,500	30
59,500	35
50,000	27
55,000	31
59,500	32
63,000	38
69,500	28
72,000	34

 12-42 Dee Boone operates a repair facility for light-aircraft engines. He is interested in improving his estimates of repair time required and believes that the best predictor is the number of operating hours on the engine since its last major repair. Below are data on ten engines Dee worked on recently. At the .10 level of significance, does the rank correlation suggest a strong relationship?

ENGINE	HOURS SINCE LAST MAJOR REPAIR	HOURS REQUIRED TO REPAIR
1	1,000	40
2	1,200	54
3	900	41
4	1,450	60
5	2,000	65
6	1,300	50
7	1,650	42
8	1,700	65
9	500	43
10	2,100	66

12-6
The Kolmogorov-Smirnov Test

The K-S test and its advantages

The Kolmogorov-Smirnov test, named for the statisticians A. N. Kolmogorov and N. V. Smirnov who developed it, is a simple nonparametric method for testing whether there is a significant difference between an observed frequency distribution and a theoretical frequency distribution. The K-S test is therefore another measure of the *goodness of fit* of a theoretical frequency distribution, as was the chi-square test we studied in Chapter 9. However, the K-S test has several advantages over the χ^2 test: It is a more powerful test, and it is easier to use, since it does not require that data be grouped in any way.

A special advantage

The K-S statistic, D_n, is particularly useful for judging how close the observed frequency distribution is to the expected frequency distribution, because the probability distribution of D_n depends on the sample size n but is independent of the expected frequency distribution (D_n is a "distribution-free" statistic).

A PROBLEM ILLUSTRATING THE K-S TEST

Suppose that the Orange County Telephone Exchange has been keeping track of the number of "senders" (a type of automatic equipment used in telephone exchanges) that were in use at a given instant. Observations were made on 3,754 different occasions. For capital-investment planning purposes, the budget officer of this company thinks that the pattern of usage follows a Poisson distribution with a mean of 8.5. If he wants to test this hypothesis at the .01 level of significance, he can employ the K-S test.

We would set up our hypotheses like this:

Stating the hypothesis

H_0: A Poisson distribution with $\lambda = 8.5$ is a good description of the pattern of usage. ← null hypothesis

H_1: A Poisson distribution with $\lambda = 8.5$ is not a good description of the pattern of usage. ← alternative hypothesis

$\alpha = .01$ ← level of significance for testing these hypotheses

---

Next, we would list the data that we observed. Table 12-14 lists the observed frequencies and transforms them into observed relative cumulative frequencies.

Computing and comparing expected frequencies

Now we can use the Poisson formula to compute the expected frequencies. From Equation 5-4, this is $e^{-\lambda} \cdot \lambda^x / x!$. By comparing these expected frequencies with our observed frequencies, we can examine the extent of the difference between them: the absolute deviation. Table 12-15 lists the observed relative cumulative frequencies F_o, the expected relative cumulative frequencies F_e, and the absolute deviations for $x = 0$ to 22.

TABLE 12-14 Observed and Relative Cumulative Frequencies

NUMBER BUSY	OBSERVED FREQUENCY	OBSERVED CUMULATIVE FREQUENCY	OBSERVED RELATIVE CUMULATIVE FREQUENCY
0	0	0	.0000
1	5	5	.0013
2	14	19	.0051
3	24	43	.0115
4	57	100	.0266
5	111	211	.0562
6	197	408	.1087
7	278	686	.1827
8	378	1,064	.2834
9	418	1,482	.3948
10	461	1,943	.5176
11	433	2,376	.6329
12	413	2,789	.7429
13	358	3,147	.8383
14	219	3,366	.8966
15	145	3,511	.9353
16	109	3,620	.9643
17	57	3,677	.9795
18	43	3,720	.9909
19	16	3,736	.9952
20	7	3,743	.9971
21	8	3,751	.9992
22	3	3,754	1.0000

TABLE 12-15 Relative Observed Cumulative Frequencies, Expected Relative Cumulative Frequencies, and Absolute Deviations

NUMBER BUSY	OBSERVED FREQUENCY	OBSERVED CUMULATIVE FREQUENCY	OBSERVED RELATIVE CUMULATIVE FREQUENCY	EXPECTED RELATIVE CUMULATIVE FREQUENCY	$\|F_e - F_o\|$ ABSOLUTE DEVIATION
0	0	0	.0000	.0002	.0002
1	5	5	.0013	.0019	.0006
2	14	19	.0051	.0093	.0042
3	24	43	.0115	.0301	.0186
4	57	100	.0266	.0744	.0478
5	111	211	.0562	.1496	.0934
6	197	408	.1087	.2562	.1475
7	278	686	.1827	.3856	.2029
8	378	1,064	.2834	.5231	.2397
9	418	1,482	.3948	.6530	.2582
10	461	1,943	.5176	.7634	.2458
11	433	2,376	.6329	.8487	.2158
12	413	2,789	.7429	.9091	.1662
13	358	3,147	.8383	.9486	.1103
14	219	3,366	.8966	.9726	.0760
15	145	3,511	.9353	.9862	.0509
16	109	3,620	.9643	.9934	.0291
17	57	3,677	.9795	.9970	.0175
18	43	3,720	.9909	.9987	.0078
19	16	3,736	.9952	.9995	.0043
20	7	3,743	.9971	.9998	.0027
21	8	3,751	.9992	.9999	.0007
22	3	3,754	1.0000	1.0000	.0000

CALCULATING THE K-S STATISTIC

To compute the K-S statistic for this problem, you simply pick out D_n, the maximum absolute deviation of F_e from F_o.

Computing the K-S statistic

$$\text{K-S statistic} \longrightarrow D_n = \max |F_e - F_o| \qquad [12\text{-}10]$$

In this problem, $D_n = .2582$ at $x = 9$.

Computing the critical value

A K-S test must always be a one-tailed test. The critical values for D_n have been tabulated and can be found in Appendix Table 8. By looking in the row for $n = 3,754$ (the sample size) and the column for a significance level of .01, we find that the critical value of D_n must be computed using the formula:

$$\frac{1.63}{\sqrt{n}} = \frac{1.63}{\sqrt{3,754}} = \frac{1.63}{61.27} = .0266$$

Our conclusion

The next step is to compare the calculated value of D_n with the critical value of D_n from the table. If the table value for the chosen significance level is greater than the calculated value of D_n, then we will accept the null hypothesis. Obviously, .0266 < .2582, so we reject H_0 and conclude that a Poisson distribution with a mean of 8.5 is *not* a good description of the pattern of sender usage at the Orange County Telephone Exchange.

Exercises

12-43   At the .05 level of significance, can we conclude that the following distribution follows a Poisson distribution with $\lambda = 3$?

Number of arrivals per day	0	1	2	3	4	5	6 or more
Number of days	6	18	30	24	11	2	9

12-44   Randall Nelson, salesman for the V-Star company, has seven accounts to visit per week. It is thought that the sales by Mr. Nelson may be described by the binomial distribution, with the probability of selling each account being .45. Examining the observed frequency distribution of Mr. Nelson's number of sales per week, determine whether the distribution does in fact correspond to the suggested distribution. Use the .05 significance level.

Number of sales per week	0	1	2	3	4	5	6	7
Frequency of the number of sales	25	32	61	47	39	21	18	12

12-45   Below is a table of observed frequencies, along with the frequencies to be expected under a normal distribution.
(a)   Calculate the K-S statistic.
(b)   Can we conclude that this distribution does in fact follow a normal distribution? Use the .10 level of significance.

	TEST SCORE				
	51–60	61–70	71–80	81–90	91–100
Observed frequency	30	100	440	500	130
Expected frequency	40	170	500	390	100

12-46   Kevin Morgan, national sales manager of an electronics firm, has collected the following salary statistics on his field salesforce earnings. He has both observed frequencies and frequencies expected if the distribution of salaries is normal. At the .10 level of significance, can Kevin conclude that the distribution of salesforce earnings is normal?

	EARNINGS IN THOUSANDS						
	25–30	31–36	37–42	43–48	49–54	55–60	61–66
Observed frequency	9	22	25	30	21	12	6
Expected frequency	6	17	32	35	18	13	4

12-47   Below is an observed frequency distribution. Using a normal distribution with $\mu = 6.80$ and $\sigma = 1.24$:
(a)   Find the probability of falling into each class.
(b)   From part (a), compute the expected frequency of each category.
(c)   Calculate D_n.
(d)   At the .15 level of significance, does this distribution seem to be well described by the suggested normal distribution:

Value of the variable	≤4.009	4.010–5.869	5.870–7.729	7.730–9.589	≥9.590
Observed frequency	13	158	437	122	20

✎ 12-48 Jackie Denn, an airline food-service administrator, has examined past records from 200 randomly selected cross-country flights to determine the frequency with which low-sodium meals were requested. The number of flights in which 0, 1, 2, 3, or 4 or more low-sodium meals were requested was 25, 45, 67, 43, and 20, respectively. At the .05 level of significance, can she reasonably conclude that these requests follow a Poisson distribution with $\lambda = 1$?

12-7
Terms Introduced in Chapter 12

Kolmogorov-Smirnov Test A nonparametric test, which does not require that data be grouped in any way, for determining whether there is a significant difference between an observed frequency distribution and a theoretical frequency distribution.

Kruskal-Wallis Test A nonparametric method for testing whether three or more independent samples have been drawn from populations with the same distribution. It is a nonparametric version of ANOVA, which we studied in Chapter 9.

Mann-Whitney U Test A nonparametric method used to determine whether two independent samples have been drawn from populations with the same distribution.

Nonparametric Tests Statistical techniques that do not make restrictive assumptions about the shape of a population distribution when performing a hypothesis test.

One-Sample Runs Test A nonparametric method for determining the randomness with which sampled items have been selected.

Rank Correlation A method for doing correlation analysis when the data are not available to use in numerical form, but when information is sufficient to rank the data.

Rank Correlation Coefficient A measure of the degree of association between two variables that is based on the ranks of observations, not their numerical values.

Rank Sum Tests A family of nonparametric tests that make use of the order information in a set of data.

Run A sequence of identical occurrences preceded and followed by different occurrences or by none at all.

Sign Test A test for the difference between paired observations where $+$ and $-$ signs are substituted for quantitative values.

Theory of Runs A theory developed to allow us to test samples for the randomness of their order.

12-8
Equations Introduced in Chapter 12

[12-1]
$$U = n_1 n_2 + \frac{n_1(n_1 + 1)}{2} - R_1$$
p. 605

To apply the Mann-Whitney U test, you need this formula to derive the U statistic, a measure of the difference between the ranked observations of the two variables. R_1 is the sum of the ranks of the observations of variable 1; n_1 and n_2 are the numbers of items in samples 1 and 2 respectively. Both samples need not be of the same size.

[12-2]
$$\mu_U = \frac{n_1 n_2}{2}$$
p. 606

If the null hypothesis of a Mann-Whitney U test is that $n_1 + n_2$ observations came from identical populations, then the U statistic has a sampling distribution with a mean equal to the product of n_1 and n_2 divided by 2.

[12-3]
$$\sigma_U = \sqrt{\frac{n_1 n_2 (n_1 + n_2 + 1)}{12}}$$
p. 606

This formula enables us to derive the *standard error of the U statistic* of a Mann-Whitney U test.

[12-4]
$$U = n_1 n_2 + \frac{n_2(n_2 + 1)}{2} - R_2$$
p. 608

This formula and Equation 12-1 can be used interchangeably to derive the U statistic in a Mann-Whitney U test. To save time, use this formula if the number of observations in sample 2 is significantly smaller than the number of observations in sample 1.

[12-5]
$$K = \frac{12}{n(n + 1)} \sum_{j=1}^{k} \frac{R_j^2}{n_j} - 3(n + 1)$$
p. 609

The formula computes the K statistic used in a Kruskal-Wallis Test for different means among three or more populations. The appropriate sampling distribution for K is chi-square with $k - 1$ degrees of freedom, when each sample contains at least five observations.

[12-6]
$$\mu_r = \frac{2n_1 n_2}{n_1 + n_2} + 1$$
p. 614

When doing a one-sample runs test, use this formula to derive the mean of the sampling distribution of the r *statistic*. This r statistic is equal to the *number of runs* in the sample being tested.

[12-7]
$$\sigma_r = \sqrt{\frac{2n_1 n_2 (2n_1 n_2 - n_1 - n_2)}{(n_1 + n_2)^2 (n_1 + n_2 - 1)}}$$
p. 614

This formula enables us to derive the *standard error of the r statistic* in a one-sample runs test.

[12-8]
$$r_s = 1 - \frac{6 \Sigma d^2}{n(n^2 - 1)}$$
p. 619

The *coefficient of rank correlation, r_s*, is a measure of the closeness of association between two ranked variables.

[12-9]
$$\sigma_{r_s} = \frac{1}{\sqrt{n - 1}}$$
p. 622

This formula enables us to calculate the *standard error of r_s* in a hypothesis test on the coefficient of rank correlation.

[12-10]
$$D_n = \max|F_e - F_o|$$
p. 630

If we compare this computed value to a critical value of D_n in the K-S table, we can test distributional goodness of fit.

Chapter Review Exercises

 12-49 A college football coach has a theory that in athletics, success feeds on itself. In other words, he feels that winning a championship one year increases the team's motivation to win it the next year. He expressed his theory to a student of statistics, who asked him for the records of the team's wins and losses over the last several years. The coach gave him a list, specifying whether the team had won (W) or lost (L) the championship that year. The results of this tally are presented below.

W, W, W, W, W, W, L, W, W, W, W, W, L, W, W, W, W, L, L, W, W, W, W, W, W

(a) At a 10 percent significance level, is the occurrence of wins and losses a random one?
(b) Does your answer to question (a), combined with a sight inspection of the data, tell you anything about the one-sample runs test?

 12-50 A small metropolitan airport recently opened a new runway, creating a new flight path over an upper-income residential area. Complaints of excessive noise had deluged the airport authority to the point that the two major airlines servicing the city had installed special engine baffles on the turbines of the jets to reduce noise and help ease the pressure on the authority. Both airlines wanted to see if the baffles had helped to reduce the number of complaints that had been brought against the airport. If they had not, the baffles would be removed, because they increased fuel consumption. Based on the following random samples of 13 days before the baffles were installed and another 13 days after installation, can it be said at the .02 level of significance that installing the baffles has reduced the number of complaints?

COMPLAINTS BEFORE AND AFTER BAFFLES WERE INSTALLED

Before	27	15	20	24	13	18	30	46	15	29	17	21	18
After	26	23	19	12	25	9	16	12	28	20	16	14	11

 12-51 The American Broadcasting System (ABS) has invested a sizable amount of money into a new program for television, *High Times*. *High Times* was ABS's entry into the situation-comedy market and featured the happy-go-lucky life in a college dormitory. Unfortunately, the program had not done as well as expected, and the sponsor was considering canceling. To beef up the ratings, ABS introduced coed dormitories into the series. Presented below are the results of telephone surveys before and after the change in the series. Surveys were conducted in several major metropolitan areas, so the results are a composite from the cities.
(a) Using a *U* test, can you infer at the .10 significance level that the change in the series format helped the ratings?
(b) Do the results of your test say anything about the effect of sex on TV program ratings?

SHARE OF AUDIENCE BEFORE AND AFTER CHANGE TO CO-ED DORMITORIES

Before	22	18	19	20	31	22	25	19	22	24	18	16	14	28	23	15	16
After	25	28	18	30	33	25	29	32	19	16	30	33	17	25			

 12-52 The director of human resources suspects that more lenient standards are being used in giving performance ratings in the operations department than in the accounting department. Data for the last ten such ratings in each department are given below. At the .05 level of significance, test the hypothesis of no difference.

Operations department	72	80	86	90	95	92	88	96	91	82
Accounting department	80	79	90	82	81	84	78	74	85	71

12-53 The Ways and Means Committee of the U.S. House of Representatives was attempting to evaluate the results of a tax cut given to individuals during the preceding year. The intended purpose had been to stimulate the economy, the theory being that with a tax reduction, the consumer would spend the tax savings. The committee had employed an independent consumer-research group to select a sample of households and maintain records of consumer spending both before and after the legislation was put into effect. A portion of the data from the research group is listed below.

SCHEDULE OF CONSUMER SPENDING

HOUSE-HOLD	BEFORE LEGISLATION	AFTER LEGISLATION	HOUSE-HOLD	BEFORE LEGISLATION	AFTER LEGISLATION
1	$ 3,578	$ 4,296	17	$11,597	$12,093
2	10,856	9,000	18	9,612	9,675
3	7,450	8,200	19	3,461	3,740
4	9,200	9,200	20	4,500	4,500
5	8,760	8,840	21	8,341	8,500
6	4,500	4,620	22	7,589	7,609
7	15,000	14,500	23	25,750	24,321
8	22,350	22,500	24	14,673	13,500
9	7,346	7,250	25	5,003	6,072
10	10,345	10,673	26	10,940	11,398
11	5,298	5,349	27	8,000	9,007
12	6,950	7,000	28	14,256	14,500
13	34,782	33,892	29	4,322	4,258
14	12,837	14,297	30	6,828	7,204
15	7,926	8,437	31	7,549	7,678
16	5,789	6,006	32	8,129	8,125

At a significance level of 3 percent, determine if the tax-reduction policy has achieved its desired goals.

12-54 John Adams, estimator for an air-conditioning installation service, must be concerned about the weather, since poor weather conditions can cause unnecessary delays and increase labor costs on a job. When establishing bids for installation jobs, should Adams consider inclement weather (rain, snow, too cold, too hot) as a random event?

12-55 Two television weather forecasters got into a discussion one day about whether years with heavy rainfall tended to occur in spurts. One of them said he thought that there were patterns of annual rainfall amounts, and that several wet years were often followed by a number of drier-than-average years. The other forecaster was skeptical and said she thought that the amount of rainfall for consecutive years was fairly random. To investigate the question, they decided to look at the annual rainfall for several years back. They found the median amount and classified the rainfall as below (B) or above (A) the median annual rainfall. A summary of their results follows:

A, A, A, B, B, B, A, B, A, A, B, B, A, B, A, B, A, B, A, A, B, B, A, A, A, B, A, A,
A, A, A, B, B, B, A, B, B, B, A, B, A, A, A, A, B, A, A, A, A, B, A, B, B, A, B, B,

If the forecasters test at a 5 percent significance level, will they conclude that the annual rainfall amounts do not occur in patterns?

12-9 Chapter Review Exercises   **635**

12-56 Anne J. Montgomery, administrative director of executive education at Southern University, uses two kinds of promotional material to announce seminars: personal letters and brochures. She feels quite strongly that brochures are the more effective method. She has collected data on numbers of people attending each of the last ten seminars promoted with each method. At the .15 level of significance, is her hunch right?

NUMBER ATTENDING

| Personal letter | 35 | 85 | 90 | 92 | 88 | 46 | 78 | 57 | 85 | 67 |
| Brochure | 42 | 74 | 82 | 87 | 45 | 73 | 89 | 75 | 60 | 94 |

12-57 The National Association of Better Advertising for Children (NABAC), a consumer group for improving children's television, was conducting a study on the effect of Saturday morning advertising. Specifically, the group wanted to know if a significant degree of purchasing was stimulated by advertising directed at children, and if there was a positive correlation between Saturday morning TV advertising time and product sales.

NABAC chose the children's breakfast-cereal market as a sample group. It selected products whose advertising message was aimed entirely at children. The results of the study are presented below. (The highest-selling cereal has sales rank 1.)

COMPARISON OF TV ADVERTISING TIME AND
PRODUCT SALES

Product	Advertising time In minutes	Sales rank
Captain Grumbles	0.50	10
Obnoxious Berries	3.00	1
Fruity Hoops	1.25	9
OO La Granola	2.00	5
Sweet Tweets	3.50	2
Chocolate Chumps	1.00	11
Sugar Spots	4.00	3
County Cavity	2.50	8
Crunchy Munchies	1.75	6
Karamel Kooks	2.25	4
Flakey Flakes	1.50	7

Can the group conclude that there is a *positive* rank correlation between the amount of Saturday morning advertising time and sales volume of breakfast cereals? Test at a 5 percent significance level.

12-58 *American Motoring Magazine* recently tested two brake-disk materials for stopping effectiveness. Data representing stopping distances for both kinds of materials are given below. At the .05 level of significance, test the hypothesis that there is no difference in the effectiveness of the materials.

STOPPING DISTANCE (FEET)

| Graphite bonded | 110 | 120 | 130 | 110 | 100 | 105 | 110 | 130 | 145 | 125 |
| Sintered bronze | 100 | 110 | 135 | 105 | 105 | 100 | 100 | 115 | 135 | 120 |

12-59 As part of a survey on restaurant quality, a local magazine asked area residents to rank two steak houses. On a scale of 1 to 10, subjects were to rate characteristics such as food quality, atmosphere, service, and price. After data were collected, one of the restaurant owners proposed that various statistical tests be performed. He specifically mentioned that he would like to see a mean and standard deviation for the responses to each question about each restaurant, in order to see which one had scored better. Several of the magazine workers argued against his suggestions, noting that the quality of input data would not justify a detailed statistical analysis. They argued that what was important was the residents' rankings of the two restaurants. Evaluate the arguments presented by the restaurant owner and the magazine employees.

 12-60 Senior business students interviewed by Ohio Insurance Company were asked not to discuss their interviews with others in the school until the recruiter left. The recruiter, however, suspected that the later applicants knew more about what she was looking for. Were her suspicions correct? To find out, rank the interview scores received by subjects given in the table below. Then test the significance of the rank correlation coefficient between the scores and interview number. Use the .02 significance level.

INTERVIEW NUMBER	SCORE	INTERVIEW NUMBER	SCORE	INTERVIEW NUMBER	SCORE	INTERVIEW NUMBER	SCORE
1	63	6	57	11	77	16	70
2	59	7	76	12	61	17	75
3	50	8	81	13	53	18	90
4	60	9	58	14	74	19	80
5	66	10	65	15	82	20	89

12-61 More than 3 years ago, the Occupational Safety and Health Administration (OSHA) required a number of safety measures to be implemented in the Northbridge Aluminum plant. Now OSHA would like to see whether the changes have resulted in fewer accidents in the plant. It has collected these data:

ACCIDENTS AT THE NORTHBRIDGE PLANT

	JAN.	FEB.	MAR.	APR.	MAY	JUNE	JULY	AUG.	SEPT.	OCT.	NOV.	DEC.
1986	5	3	4	2	6	4	3	3	2	4	5	3
1987	4	4	3	3	3	4	0	5	4	2	0	1
1988	3	2	1	1	0	2	4	3	2	1	1	2
1989	2	1	0	0	1	2						

(a) Determine the median number of accidents per month. If the safety measures have been effective, we should find early months falling above the median and later months below the median. Accordingly, there will be a small number of runs above and below the median. Conduct a test at the .03 level of significance to see if the accidents are randomly distributed.

(b) What can you conclude about the effectiveness of the safety measures?

12-62 A large countywide ambulance service calculates that for any given township it serves, during any given 6-hour shift, there is a 35 percent chance of receiving at least one call for assistance. The following is a random sampling of 90 days:

Number of shifts during which calls were received	1	2	3	4
Number of days	35	30	13	7

At the .05 level of significance, do these calls for assistance follow a binomial distribution?

 12-63 Steve Townsend, owner of Crow's Nest Marina, believes that the number of hours a boat engine has been run in salt water and not the age of the boat itself is the best predictor of engine failure. His service manager, James, has collected the data below from his repair records on failed engines. At the .05 level of significance, is Steve's hunch right?

ENGINE	HOURS IN SALT WATER	AGE OF ENGINE (YEARS)	COST OF REPAIR (DOLLARS)
1	300	4	625
2	150	6	350
3	200	3	390
4	250	6	530
5	100	4	200
6	400	5	1,000
7	275	6	550
8	350	6	800
9	325	3	700
10	375	2	600

 12-64 SavEnergy, an international activist group concerned about the gross domination of the "western" areas in energy usage, has claimed that population size and energy consumption are negatively correlated. Their opponents claim no correlation is present. Using the following data, test the hypothesis that no rank correlation exists between population and energy consumption, versus SavEnergy's negative correlation claim. Use the .10 level of significance.

	1989 POPULATION (000,000 OMITTED)	TOTAL ENERGY CONSUMPTION
United States	249	68×10^{15} joules
Latin America	438	16
Africa	646	11
Europe	499	65
Soviet Union	289	54
India	835	9
China	1,100	24

 12-65 Highway crashes killed more than 75,000 occupants of passenger cars during 1986–1988. Using that grim statistic as a starting point, researchers at the Insurance Institute for Highway Safety computed death rates for the 103 largest-selling vehicle series. Vehicles were categorized as Station Wagons & Vans, Four-Door Cars, Two-Door Cars or Sports & Specialty Cars. Further stratification in each category labelled vehicles as large, midsize or small. Looking at the rates (deaths per 10,000 registered vehicles) for Four-Door Cars, the figures are as follows:

Large	1.2	1.3	1.4	1.5	1.5	1.5	1.6	1.8		
Midsize	1.1	1.2	1.2	1.2	1.3	1.3	1.3	1.3	1.4	1.4
	1.5	1.6	1.6	1.6	1.7	1.7	1.8	1.9	2.0	2.3
	2.3	2.4	2.5	2.6	2.9					
Small	1.1	1.5	1.6	1.7	1.8	2.0	2.0	2.0	2.3	2.5
	2.6	2.8	3.2	4.1						

Use the Kruskal-Wallis test to test whether the three population means are, in fact, equal. Test at the .05 level of significance.

12-66 1989 was a particularly bad year for injuries to professional baseball players. From the data below, does a sign test for paired data indicate that American League players suffered significantly more injuries than their National League counterparts? Use a .05 level of significance.

INJURY LOCATION	AL	NL
Shoulder	46	22
Neck	3	0
Rib	7	5
Elbow	21	19
Back	10	7
Wrist	10	2
Hip	1	1
Hand	6	4
Finger	7	5
Thigh	17	14
Groin	7	3
Knee	16	18
Ankle	6	4
Foot	1	4
Toe	0	1
Other	10	4

 12-67 In continuing research about what weather patterns may be correlated with such solar activity as sunspots, recent efforts have focused on polar temperature (the average temperature in the stratosphere above the North Pole) during periods when certain equatorial winds are blowing. When these winds are from the west, the polar temperature appears to rise and fall with solar activity. When the winds are easterly, the temperature appears to do the opposite of what the sun is doing. From the data below, calculate the coefficients of rank correlation between these variables and test, at the .05 level of significance, if the hypothesized relationships hold (i.e., positive correlation for westerly winds, negative correlation for easterly winds).

	POLAR TEMPERATURE (°F)	
SOLAR ACTIVITY	East winds	West winds
230	−85	−76
160	−97	−86
95	−88	−100
75	−85	−110
100	−90	−108
165	−96	−85
155	−91	−70
120	−76	−100
75	−80	−110
65	−86	−112
125	−90	−99
195	−104	−91
190	−95	−93
125	−99	−99
75	−73	−103

12-68 Guards monitoring a security gate entrance to a military base are having trouble with long lines developing during peak traffic hours. Before they continue their analysis of the problem, they need to know the approximate distribution of the arrival of cars. They collected the following data every minute between 7:10 and 8:00.

12-9 Chapter Review Exercises   **639**

NUMBER OF ARRIVALS	1	2	3	4	5	6	7	8	9	10	11
FREQUENCY	5	3	2	6	6	2	6	10	4	4	2

Test whether a Poisson distribution with a mean of 6 adequately describes these data. Use a .05 level of significance.

12-69 The results of the Carolina Athletic Association's first 10K run showed the following order of male and female finishers:

```
M M M M M M M M M M M M M W M M M M M M W M M M M
M W M M M M M M M M M W M W M M M M W M M M M W M
M W M M M M M M W M M W M M M W W W W M W M W W W
W M M M W M W W M W W W W W M M M W M M
```

Did the women finish randomly throughout? Use a .20 level of significance.

12-70 Several groups were given a list of 30 activities and technological advances and were asked to rank them, considering the risk of dying as a consequence of each. The results are in the following table. Calculate the rank correlation coefficient of each group relative to the experts' ranking. Which group seemed to have the most accurate perception of the risks involved?

A Experts
B League of Women Voters
C College Students
D Civic Club Members

RISK	A	B	C	D
Motor vehicles	1	2	5	3
Smoking	2	4	3	4
Alcoholic beverages	3	6	7	5
Handguns	4	3	2	1
Surgery	5	10	11	9
Motorcycles	6	5	6	2
X-rays	7	22	17	24
Pesticides	8	9	4	15
Electric power (non-nuclear)	9	18	19	19
Swimming	10	19	30	17
Contraceptives	11	20	9	22
General (private) aviation	12	7	15	11
Large construction	13	12	14	13
Food preservatives	14	25	12	28
Bicycles	15	16	24	14
Commercial aviation	16	17	16	18
Police work	17	8	8	7
Fire fighting	18	11	10	6
Railroads	19	24	23	20
Nuclear power	20	1	1	8
Food coloring	21	26	20	30
Home appliances	22	29	27	27
Hunting	23	13	18	10
Prescription antibiotics	24	28	21	26
Vaccinations	25	30	29	29
Spray cans	26	14	13	23
High school & College football	27	23	26	21
Power mowers	28	27	28	25
Mountain climbing	29	15	22	12
Skiing	30	21	25	16

12-71 In testing a new hayfever medication, researchers measured the incidence of adverse side effects of the drug by administering it to a large number of patients and evaluating them against a control group. The percentage of patients reporting thirteen types of side effects was recorded. Using a sign test for paired data, can you determine if, on the whole, either group experienced more adverse side effects? Use a .10 significance level.

SIDE EFFECT	DRUG	CONTROL
A	9.0	18.1
B	6.3	3.8
C	2.9	5.8
D	1.4	1.0
E	0.9	0.6
F	0.9	0.2
G	0.6	0.0
H	4.6	2.7
I	2.3	3.5
J	0.9	0.5
K	0.5	0.5
L	0.0	0.2
M	1.0	1.4

12-10
Chapter Concepts Test

Answers are in the back of the book.

T F 1. One advantage of nonparametric methods is that some of the tests do not require us even to rank the observations.

T F 2. The Mann-Whitney U test is one of a family of tests known as rank difference tests.

T F 3. A sign test for paired data is based upon the binomial distribution but can often be approximated by the normal distribution.

T F 4. One disadvantage of nonparametric methods is that they tend to ignore a certain amount of information.

T F 5. In the Mann-Whitney U test, two samples, of sizes n_1 and n_2, are taken to determine the U statistic. The sampling distribution of the U statistic can be approximated by the normal distribution when either n_1 or n_2 is greater than 10.

T F 6. The Mann-Whitney U test tends to waste less data than the sign test.

T F 7. Assume that in a rank test, two elements are tied for the tenth rank position. We assign each of them a rank of 10.5 and the next element after these two receives a rank of 11.

T F 8. In contrast to regression analysis, where one may compute a coefficient of correlation, an equivalent measure may be determined in a ranking of two variables in nonparametric testing. This equivalent measure is called a rank correlation coefficient.

T F 9. In a one-sample runs test, the number of runs is a statistic having its own sampling distribution.

T F 10. One disadvantage in using the rank correlation coefficient is that it is very sensitive to extreme observations in the data set.

T F 11. The Kolmogorov-Smirnov test is a measure of the goodness of fit of a theoretical distribution.

T F 12. Nonparametric methods are more efficient than parametric methods.

T F 13. The one-sample runs test enables us to determine whether two independent samples have been drawn from populations with the same distributions.

T F 14. The sequence A, A, B, A, B, contains four runs.

T F 15. A rank correlation coefficient of -1 represents perfect inverse rank correlation.

T F 16. In a one-sample runs test, the alternative hypothesis is that the sequence of observations is not random.

T F 17. In the Mann-Whitney U test, it is not necessary that the two samples be of the same size.

T F 18. The K-S test statistic is simply the minimum absolute deviation between the observed relative cumulative frequencies and the expected relative cumulative frequencies.

T F 19. The rank sum tests test the hypothesis that several population means are equal, provided the populations are normally distributed with equal variances.

T F 20. The Kruskal-Wallis test is a nonparametric version of ANOVA.

T F 21. The sampling distribution of the Kruskal-Wallis K statistic can be approximated by a chi-square distribution only if all sample sizes are at least 5.

22. In a sign test for paired data, 800 students were asked to give ranks (on a scale of 0 to 10) for their attitudes toward true-false and multiple-choice tests. When signs were calculated for the two sets of paired data, 138 of the 800 paired responses received a value of 0. Does this mean that 138 students:
   (a) Did not like either type of test?
   (b) Did not answer the survey?
   (c) Ranked the types equally?
   (d) Thought one of the types was perfect and the other was awful?

23. Suppose that, in question 22, the administration felt that true-false tests were liked 3 times as well as multiple-choice tests. Assuming that a preference for true-false tests is a "success," what is the null hypothesis for the administration's sign test for paired data?
   (a) $p = .25$ (b) $p = .75$ (c) $p \neq .25$ (d) $p \neq .75$

Questions 24 and 25 refer to the following situation. Five former patients are selected at random from Ward A at Trinity Hospital, and four former patients are selected at random from Ward B. The patients stayed the following number of days:

$$\begin{array}{lccccc} \text{Ward A:} & 13 & 4 & 2 & 10 & 6 \\ \text{Ward B:} & 10 & 9 & 7 & 8 \end{array}$$

24. A Mann-Whitney U test is to be performed to determine if there is a significant difference between the lengths of the hospital stays for the two wards. If the lengths of stay are ranked from shortest to longest, what is the ranking for the 13-day stay in Ward A?
   (a) 9 (b) 8 (c) 9½ (d) 7½

25. If the lengths of stay are ranked from shortest to longest, what is the value of $(R_1 - R_2)$?
   (a) $-\frac{1}{2}$ (b) 0 (c) ½ (d) 2½

26. What is the maximum number of runs possible in a sequence of length 5 using two symbols?
   (a) 6 (b) 4 (c) 3 (d) 5

27. The sequence of C, D, C, D, C, D, C, D, C, D would probably be rejected by a test of runs as not being truly random because:
   (a) The pattern C, D occurs only 5 times; this is not often enough to guarantee randomness.
   (b) The sequence contains too many runs.
   (c) The sequence contains too few runs.
   (d) The sequence contains only two symbols.
   (e) None of these.

28. In a Mann-Whitney U test, a particular sampling distribution for U has a mean of 15. One value of U is calculated as $n_1 n_2 + \dfrac{n_1(n_1 + 1)}{2} - R_1$, which equals 22.5. Can we immediately

conclude that the value of $n_1 n_2 + \dfrac{n_2(n_2 + 1)}{2} - R_2$ in this situation is:

(a) 10?   (c) 7.5?
(b) 12.5?   (d) Cannot be determined from information given

Questions 29 to 31 refer to the following situation: Seven executives (denoted A–G) were ranked from 1 to 7 on a scale of yearly salary level, with 1 being highest. The results were:

A	B	C	D	E	F	G
2	6	4	1	3	5	7

29. Which of the following is correct?
    (a) E earned more than four others.
    (b) C and F earned the same amount.
    (c) C's earnings are less than those of four others.
    (d) All of these.
    (e) a and c but not b.

30. Suppose that, as the second part of this study, the seven executives are ranked according to how happy they seem to be, with 1 being the happiest. If salaries and happiness are perfectly correlated, what must be the happiness ranking for businessman A?
    (a) 1   (b) 2   (c) 3   (d) 6

31. If, in the happiness ranking of question 30, salaries and happiness were perfectly inversely correlated, what must be the happiness ranking of executive F?
    (a) 7   (b) 2   (c) 5   (d) 3

32. When compared to parametric methods, nonparametric methods:
    (a) Are less accurate   (e) All of these
    (b) Are less efficient   (f) b, c, and d, but not a
    (c) Are computationally easier (g) None of these
    (d) Require less information

33. For a perfect inverse correlation, the coefficient of rank correlation r_s would be:
    (a) equal to 1   (c) equal to 0
    (b) between 0 and -1 (d) none of these

34. For samples of size greater than 30 the sampling distribution of the rank correlation coefficient is approximately that of which distribution:
    (a) t (b) binomial   (c) chi-square   (d) normal

35. In the Kruskal-Wallis test of k samples the approximate number of degrees of freedom is:
    (a) k (b) $k - 1$ (c) $n_k - 1$ (d) $n - k$

36. Choose the sample with the largest rank sum if elements are ranked from largest to smallest:

Sample A:	1	3	9
Sample B:	5	1	8
Sample C:	9	4	2

    (a) C with rank sum 15   (c) A with rank sum 16
    (b) C with rank sum 20.5   (d) B with rank sum 14.5

37. A sequence of identical occurrences preceded and followed by different occurrences or none at all is a _____.

38. A nonparametric method used to determine whether two independent samples have been drawn from populations with the same distribution is the _____.

39. A nonparametric technique for determining the randomness with which sampled items have been selected is the _____.

40. A _____ test tests for the difference between paired observations by substituting $+$, $-$, and 0 for quantitative values.

41. A _____ coefficient measures the degree of association between two variables and is based on the ranks of the observations.

42. The U statistic has a special property that enables us to save computational time when _____ .

43. To distinguish it from the coefficient of correlation, the rank coefficient of correlation is denoted _____ .

44. The K-S statistic D_n is a _____ statistic in that it is independent of the expected frequency distribution.

45. The _____ test has advantages over the chi-square test for goodness of fit because the data need not be grouped in any way.

12-11
Conceptual Case

(Northern White Metals Company)

Winston Allen, Northern's grizzled chief shipping coordinator, walked briskly across the plant, his rapid pace and the spring in his step belying his advanced years. He was on his way to meet with Norma Hasselman, the company's financial officer, to discuss which trucking firm Northern should use as its primary shipper in the coming year.

Northern actually owned only one tractor-trailer truck, and this was used for specialty deliveries, primarily those to other Segue subsidiary companies. All other shipments of Northern products were made by independent trucking firms, with trucks hired on an as-needed basis. The company usually shipped orders that comprised an entire truckload, although occasionally smaller shipments were made. In either case, transportation arrangements were made at least 3 days in advance, and all freight charges were prepaid by Northern.

Using common carriers, as these truck-for-hire firms are called, had served Northern well for many years. As the size and number of orders grew, however, the system became increasingly cumbersome and difficult to coordinate. Convinced of the need for a change in the company's shipping methods, Norma had undertaken a comprehensive financial study to evaluate the feasibility of running a fleet of company-owned trucks. She had decided that, based on Northern's current requirements, this system would prove too costly and should not be considered further. It was at this point that Winston, who had first worked as a dispatcher for a local trucking firm, suggested using a contract carrier to serve Northern's shipping needs.

Under a contract-carrier arrangement, an agreement is reached with a trucking company whereby the firm provides exclusive service to the hirer but maintains control and management of all trucking equipment and personnel. In Northern's case, this method would cost a bit more than using common carriers but would offer the company a much greater degree of shipping department flexibility.

Under Winston's recommendation, two firms were selected as possible candidates. Each had served many of Northern's customers at one time or another over the years and preliminary negotiations indicated that the contract fees would be nearly identical with either firm.

Norma, with her usual penchant for complexity, suggested that in order to make the proper selection, she would need data about delivery-time comparisons, annual dollar losses from damage, accidents per driver-mile and resultant delay-time figures, and numerous other factors. These would be subjected to rigorous analysis, and only then could an intelligent decision be made.

"Hold it, Norma," Winston grumbled. "Even if we could get all these data, which we can't, I don't see that we really need it. Look, these two firms are basically the same," he continued, "and all we want is to provide our customers with the best service we possibly can."

"And . . .?" Norma prompted him.

"And all we really need to do is simply ask a group of our customers who have experience with both firms which one provides the better service," Winston responded, more patient now. "Then we just choose one."

"Well, I don't believe it's quite as simple as that," she exclaimed, "but I think you may be on to something there, Win!"

Smiling, Winston left the office and hurried back to the loading docks.

Assuming that good service means things like prompt delivery, driver courtesy, neat paperwork, and so forth, how might Northern survey its customers to determine preference between the two trucking firms?

What analytical procedures might be employed to determine if one firm is superior to the other? If no difference were detected, how might Norma decide which company to contract with?

12-12
Computer Data Base Exercise

 Still sensitive about what the Poisson assumption had done for the phone call study, Laurel reflected on the sales commission questions she had recently answered for Stan. The assumption of normal populations with the same standard deviation was critical to the conclusions she had drawn. "Just to be on the safe side," she thought, "I think I'll verify my results with some rank sum analysis."

1. Using the sales data from Chapter 9, test the assumption that these samples come from populations with the same mean. What if Mike is excluded as before? Test at the .05 significance level.

At lunch the following week, Gary and Laurel discussed the results of the hiring-criteria study they had just completed. "As it turns out," Gary said, "that study is even more timely than we initially thought. It appears that Hal's got plans in the works to establish another satellite warehouse—this time in the Midwest region. I guess our business is so solid there that we're advancing on this pretty quickly. This will sure make my staffing job a lot easier."

"By the way," he continued, "remember when we were talking about the UPS study that resulted in our Pennsylvania warehouse? It was shortly after you arrived, and you did a terrific analysis on our success in reaching the targeted geographic area."

"Uh oh," Laurel teased. "I know when praise comes from you, you've got more work for me up your sleeve! Yes, I remember our conversations. What about it?"

"At the time," Gary went on, "you may recall that I made some cryptic comments about what I felt *should have been,* versus what actually *was,* included in the study. At any rate, it's been bugging me and I'd like to know your opinion."

"Go on," Laurel sighed, feigning irritation. "I think I've created a statistical monster!"

Gary laughed. "You sure know how to make a guy feel bad! Seriously, I don't think this will be much trouble—I'm just curious about something. When UPS did that study, it only took into account packages we *shipped.* As it turns out, *receiving* costs are also fairly significant. And, as you could probably guess, here in Florida we pay an extra "penalty" for being at the end of the shipping line. Most of the trucks that deliver to us end up leaving the state empty, unable to find freight that needs delivering back to other areas of the country.

"I'm formulating a proposal that would essentially suggest that our new Midwest site become our *main* warehouse. We would maintain all our administrative functions here in Florida, but from an inventory standpoint, we'd act purely as a satellite. That's a long explanation for a short question: Would it be possible to rank all the states we ship to and receive from, just to see if there's any correlation at all there? That would give me some preliminary information for my proposal."

Laurel realized she had been holding her breath. "Whew," she managed. "That's a much easier question than I had anticipated! The whole study sounds interesting, *and* time-consuming. But in answer to *today's* question—yes, that should be relatively simple. I could probably have it for you by the end of this week. And thanks for the warning. I know you'll be back with more requests for help, and next time they won't be so easy! I'm going to start gathering some data I think might be useful. Be sure and let me know how things are going."

"Somehow I figured I could count on you. Thanks, Laurel." Gary smiled. "Lunch is on me."

2. Using the following data, calculate the rank correlation coefficient between the states which HH Industries shipped to and those it received shipments from. At the .01 significance level, can we conclude there is a relationship between these two?

TABLE DB12-1

OBS	STATE	RCVING	SHIPPING	OBS	STATE	RCVING	SHIPPING
1	NH	188	36,112	26	WA	5,227	24,565
2	NJ	42	33,266	27	SD	0	555
3	NY	36,491	83,239	28	ND	30	3,836
4	PA	30,969	62,239	29	CO	100	33,604
5	WV	11,654	23,887	30	WY	0	1,131
6	NC	511	65,360	31	ID	0	5,821
7	SC	10,888	62,848	32	UT	0	1,345
8	GA	237,933	109,965	33	NM	205	20,393
9	FL	7,081	946,862	34	NV	90	10,233
10	TN	3,391	51,814	35	HI	0	4,742
11	MS	8,504	37,600	36	OR	50	12,270
12	KY	17,580	13,348	37	MA	400	23,174
13	OH	441,829	91,402	38	RI	0	1,247
14	IN	27,187	51,007	39	ME	0	5,653
15	MI	199,379	23,899	40	CT	340	30,896
16	IA	54,554	26,163	41	DE	0	3,005
17	WI	58,011	24,415	42	MD	120	16,884
18	MN	3,365	44,826	43	VA	560	34,565
19	MT	33	8,696	44	LA	930	59,072
20	IL	153,552	60,656	45	MO	40	20,734
21	KS	202	5,811	46	AL	450	47,455
22	NE	67,487	14,292	47	AR	190	29,468
23	TX	47,005	164,163	48	OK	0	6,966
24	AZ	1,725	146,367	49	AK	0	4,913
25	CA	158,610	130,826	50	VT	330	100

12-13
From the Textbook to the Real World

Statistics in Medicine

Statistical methods are often employed in researching the origin, treatment, and control of various diseases. Because much of the data found in medical research does not conform to the normal distribution, nonparametric methods are particularly useful. Charles H. Kirkpatrick, M.D., and David W. Alling, M.D., PhD., applied the Mann-Whitney test in a clever way to assess the results of a randomized clinical trial involving the treatment of chronic oral candidiasis, a disease characterized by recurrent infections of the skin, nails, and mucous membranes. Results of their tests indicated that clotrimazole, which had been used successfully on similar disorders, was a highly effective treatment for chronic oral candidiasis.

The Clinical Trial: Twenty patients suffering from persistent oral candidiasis were admitted to the study and assigned by random allocation to treatment with either clotrimazole lozenges or a placebo. Subject's responses to the treatment were assessed 2 to 7 days after treatment, as shown in Table RW12-1. This format captures two kinds of outcomes and combines them so that the larger of any two scores connotes the less favorable out-

TABLE RW12-1 Scoring System for Outcomes of Treatment for Chronic Oral Candidiasis

SCORE	CLINICAL FINDINGS	LABORATORY FINDINGS
1	Absent	Negative
2	Improved	Negative
3	Improved	Positive
4	Unimproved	Positive

come; these scores define an ordered classification. The results of the clotrimazole and placebo treatments are summarized in Table RW12-2. All ten patients on the clotrimazole lozenges appeared to have no symptoms by the fifth day of treat-

TABLE RW12-2 Outcomes After 2 to 7 Days of Treatment in 20 Patients

TREATMENT GROUP	RESULT SCORE				TOTAL PATIENTS
	1	2	3	4	
Clotrimazole	6	3	1	0	10
Placebo	1	0	0	9	10

Kirkpatrick, C. H., Alling, D. W., "Treatment of Chronic Oral Candidiasis with Clotrimazole Troches: A Controlled Clinical Trial," *The New England Journal of Medicine,* vol. 299 (1978), p. 1201–3.

ment. This visual observation was confirmed by a Mann-Whitney test which offered strong statistical support.

The Bottom Line: Successful treatments for diseases are found only through research. In this case, although clotrimazole is known to cause adverse side effects when administered over a prolonged period, preliminary studies employing oral clotrimazole on an intermittent schedule have shown clinical benefits. The use of statistical methods enables clinical researchers to quantify results of medical treatments which lends credibility to their findings.

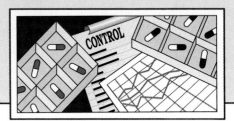

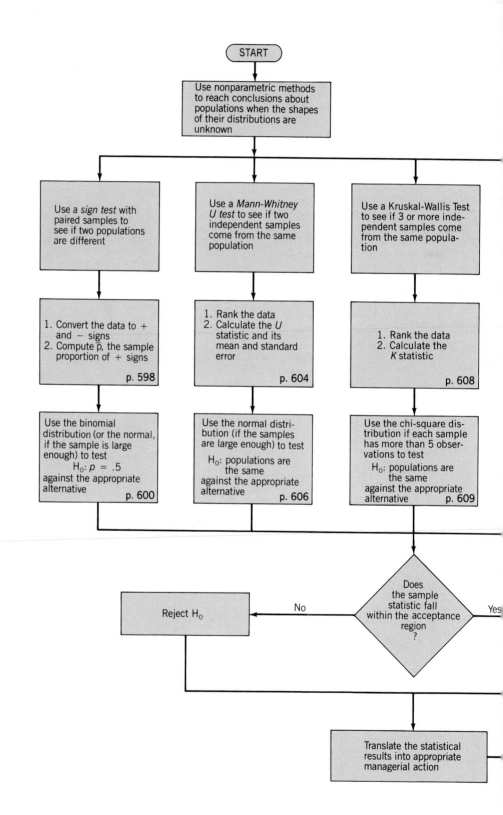

START

Use nonparametric methods to reach conclusions about populations when the shapes of their distributions are unknown

Use a *sign test* with paired samples to see if two populations are different

Use a *Mann-Whitney U test* to see if two independent samples come from the same population

Use a Kruskal-Wallis Test to see if 3 or more independent samples come from the same population

1. Convert the data to + and − signs
2. Compute p̄, the sample proportion of + signs
   p. 598

1. Rank the data
2. Calculate the U statistic and its mean and standard error
   p. 604

1. Rank the data
2. Calculate the K statistic
   p. 608

Use the binomial distribution (or the normal, if the sample is large enough) to test
$H_0: p = .5$
against the appropriate alternative   **p. 600**

Use the normal distribution (if the samples are large enough) to test
H_0: populations are the same
against the appropriate alternative   **p. 606**

Use the chi-square distribution if each sample has more than 5 observations to test
H_0: populations are the same
against the appropriate alternative   **p. 609**

Reject H_0

No

Does the sample statistic fall within the acceptance region ?

Yes

Translate the statistical results into appropriate managerial action

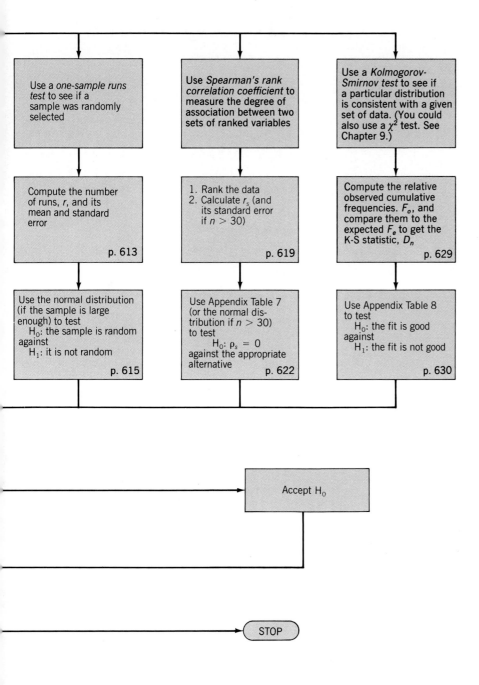

Use a *one-sample runs test* to see if a sample was randomly selected

Compute the number of runs, r, and its mean and standard error

p. 613

Use the normal distribution (if the sample is large enough) to test
   H_0: the sample is random against
   H_1: it is not random

p. 615

Use *Spearman's rank correlation coefficient* to measure the degree of association between two sets of ranked variables

1. Rank the data
2. Calculate r_s (and its standard error if $n > 30$)

p. 619

Use Appendix Table 7 (or the normal distribution if $n > 30$) to test
   H_0: $\rho_s = 0$
against the appropriate alternative

p. 622

Use a *Kolmogorov-Smirnov test* to see if a particular distribution is consistent with a given set of data. (You could also use a χ^2 test. See Chapter 9.)

Compute the relative observed cumulative frequencies. F_o, and compare them to the expected F_e to get the K-S statistic, D_n

p. 629

Use Appendix Table 8 to test
   H_0: the fit is good against
   H_1: the fit is not good

p. 630

Accept H_0

STOP

The management of a ski resort has these quarterly occupancy data over a 5-year period:

YEAR	1ST QTR.	2ND QTR.	3RD QTR.	4TH QTR.
1985	1,861	2,203	2,415	1,908
1986	1,921	2,343	2,514	1,986
1987	1,834	2,154	2,098	1,799
1988	1,837	2,025	2,304	1,965
1989	2,073	2,414	2,339	1,967

To improve service, management must establish the seasonal pattern of demand for rooms. Using methods covered in this chapter, we shall help the hotel discern such a seasonal pattern, if it exists, and use it to forecast demand for rooms.

13

Time Series

■ OBJECTIVES

In Chapter 13, we shall study the behavior of *time series,* data collected over a period of time. Our purpose will be to see what changes take place over time in the event we are observing. Often we may try to predict what the future behavior of that event will be. If you have ever been asked, "Why isn't your grade-point average higher for the last 3 years?" and you have countered with, "But look what I did last semester," you have invited your questioner to examine the time series of your grades, hoping that the recent behavior of this series will overshadow earlier behavior.

13-1
Introduction

Forecasting, or predicting, is an essential tool in any decision-making process. Its uses vary from determining inventory requirements for a local shoe store to estimating the annual sales of video games. The quality of the forecasts management can make is strongly related to the information that can be extracted and used from past data. *Time series analysis* is one quantitative method we use to determine patterns in data collected over time. Table 13-1 is an example of time series data.

TABLE 13-1 Time Series for the Number of Ships Loaded at Morehead City, N.C.

Year	1982	1983	1984	1985	1986	1987	1988	1989
Number	98	105	116	119	135	156	177	208

Use of time series analysis

Time series analysis is used to detect patterns of change in statistical information over regular intervals of time. We *project* these patterns to arrive at an estimate for the future. Thus, time series analysis helps us cope with uncertainty about the future.

Exercises

13-1 Of what value are forecasts in the decision-making process?

13-2 For what purpose do we apply time series analysis to data collected over a period of time?

13-3 How can one benefit from determining past patterns?

13-4 How would errors in forecasts affect a city government?

13-2
Variations in Time Series

Four kinds of variation in time series

We use the term *time series* to refer to any group of statistical information accumulated at regular intervals. There are four kinds of change, or variation, involved in time series analysis. They are:

1. Secular trend
2. Cyclical fluctuation
3. Seasonal variation
4. Irregular variation

Secular trend

With the first type of change, secular trend, the value of the variable tends to increase or decrease over a long period of time. The steady increase in the cost of living recorded by the Consumer Price Index is an example of secular trend. From year to individual year, the cost of living varies a great deal, but if we examine a long-term period, we see that the trend is toward a steady increase. Figure 13-1(a) shows a secular trend in an increasing but fluctuating time series.

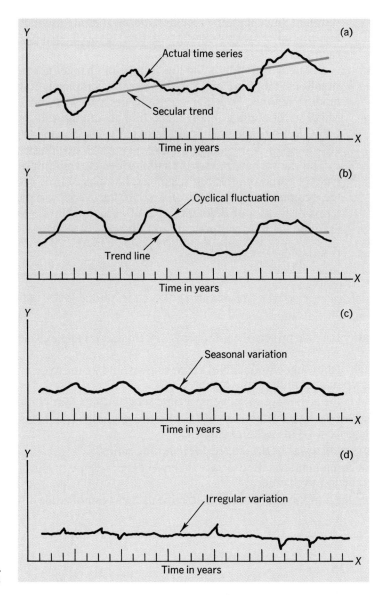

FIGURE 13-1
Time series variations

Cyclical fluctuation

The second type of variation seen in a time series is cyclical fluctuation. The most common example of cyclical fluctuation is the business cycle. Over time, there are years when the business cycle hits a peak above the trend line. At other times, business activity is likely to slump, hitting a low point below the trend line. The time between hitting peaks or falling to low points is at least 1 year, and it can be as many as 15 or 20 years. Figure 13-1(b) illustrates a typical pattern of cyclical fluctuation above and below a secular trend line. Note that the cyclical movements do not follow any regular pattern but move in a somewhat unpredictable manner.

Seasonal variation

The third kind of change in time series data is seasonal variation. As we might expect from the name, seasonal variation involves patterns of change within a year that tend to be repeated from year to year. For example, a physician can expect a substantial increase in the number of flu cases every winter and of poison ivy every summer. Since these are regular patterns, they are useful in forecasting the future. In Fig. 13-1(c), we see a seasonal variation. Notice how it peaks in the fourth quarter of each year.

Irregular variation

Irregular variation is the fourth type of change in time series analysis. In many situations, the value of a variable may be completely unpredictable, changing in a random manner. Irregular variations describe such movements. The effects of the Middle East conflict in 1973, the Iranian situation in 1979–1981, the collapse of OPEC in 1986, and the Iraqi situation in 1990 on gasoline prices in the United States are examples of irregular variation. Figure 13-1(d) illustrates irregular variation.

Thus far we have referred to a time series as exhibiting one or another of these four types of variation. In most instances, however, a time series will contain several of these components. Thus we can describe the overall variation in a single time series in terms of these four different kinds of variation. In the following sections, we will examine the four components and the ways in which we measure each.

Exercises

13-5 Identify the four principal components of a time series and explain the kind of change, over time, to which each applies.

13-6 Which of the four components of a time series would we use to describe the effect of Christmas sales upon a retail department store?

13-7 What is the advantage of reducing a time series into its four components?

13-8 Which of the four components of a time series might the U.S. Department of Agriculture use to describe a 7-year weather pattern?

13-9 How would a war be accounted for in a time series?

13-10 What component of a time series explains the general growth and decline of the steel industry over the last two centuries?

13-11 Using the four kinds of variation, describe the behavior of crude oil prices from 1970 to 1987.

13-3
Trend Analysis

Two methods of fitting a trend line

Of the four components of a time series, secular trend represents the long-term direction of the series. One way to describe the trend component is to fit a line visually to a set of points on a graph. Any given graph, however, is subject to slightly different interpretations by different individuals. We can also fit a trend line by the method of least squares, which we examined in Chapter 10. In our discussion, we will concentrate on the method of least squares, since visually fitting a line to a time series is not a completely dependable process.

REASONS FOR STUDYING TRENDS

There are three reasons why it is useful to study secular trends:

Three reasons for studying secular trends

1. The study of secular trends allows us to describe a historical pattern. There are many instances when we can use a past trend to evaluate the success of a previous

654 13 TIME SERIES

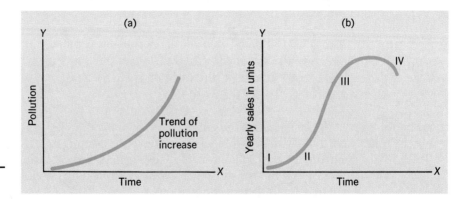

FIGURE 13-2
Curvilinear trend relationships

policy. For example, a university may evaluate the effectiveness of a recruiting program by examining its past enrollment trends.

2. **Studying secular trends permits us to project past patterns, or trends, into the future.** Knowledge of the past can tell us a great deal about the future. Examining the growth rate of the world's population, for example, can help us estimate the population for some future time.

3. **In many situations, studying the secular trend of a time series allows us to eliminate the trend component from the series.** This makes it easier for us to study the other three components of the time series. If we want to determine the seasonal variation in ski sales, for example, eliminating the trend component gives us a more accurate idea of the seasonal component.

Trend lines take different forms

Trends can be linear, or they can be curvilinear. Before we examine the linear, or straight-line, method of describing trends, we should remember that some relationships do not take that form. The increase of pollutants in the environment follows an upward sloping curve similar to that in Fig. 13-2(a). Another common example of a curvilinear relationship is the life cycle of a new business product, illustrated in Fig. 13-2(b). When a new product is introduced, its sales volume is low (I). As the product gains recognition and success, unit sales grow at an increasingly rapid rate (II). After the product is firmly established, its unit sales grow at a stable rate (III). Finally, as the product reaches the end of its life cycle, unit sales begin to decrease (IV).

FITTING THE LINEAR TREND BY THE LEAST SQUARES METHOD

Besides those trends that can be described by a curved line, there are others that are described by a straight line. These are called linear trends. Before developing the equation for a linear trend, we need to review the general equation for estimating a straight line (Equation 10-3):

Equation for estimating a straight line $\longrightarrow \hat{Y} = a + bX$ [10-3]

where:

- $\hat{Y}$ is the estimated value of the dependent variable
- X is the independent variable (*time* in trend analysis)
- a is the Y-intercept (the value of Y when $X = 0$)
- b is the slope of the trend line

Finding the best-fitting trend line
We can describe the general trend of many time series using a straight line. But we are faced with the problem of finding the best-fitting line. As we did in Chapter 10, we can use the least squares method to calculate the best-fitting line, or equation. There we saw that the best-fitting line was determined by Equations 10-4 and 10-5, which are now renumbered as Equations 13-1 and 13-2.

$$b = \frac{\Sigma XY - n\overline{X}\,\overline{Y}}{\Sigma X^2 - n\overline{X}^2} \qquad [13\text{-}1]$$

$$a = \overline{Y} - b\overline{X} \qquad [13\text{-}2]$$

where:

- Y represents the values of the dependent variable.
- X represents the values of the independent variable.
- $\overline{Y}$ is the mean of the values of the dependent variable.
- $\overline{X}$ is the mean of the values of the independent variable.
- n is the number of data points in the time series.
- a is the Y-intercept.
- b is the slope.

With Equations 13-1 and 13-2, we can establish the best-fitting line to describe time series data. However, the regularity of time series data allows us to simplify the calculations in Equations 13-1 and 13-2 through the process we shall now describe.

TRANSLATING OR CODING TIME

Coding the time variable to simplify computation
Normally, we measure the independent variable *time* in terms such as *weeks, months,* and *years.* Fortunately, we can convert these traditional measures of time to a form that simplifies the computation. In Chapter 3, we called this process *coding.* To use coding here, we find the mean time and then subtract that value from each of the sample times. Suppose our time series consists of only three points, 1986, 1987, and 1988. If we had to place these numbers in Equations 13-1 and 13-2, we would find the resultant calculations tedious. Instead, we can transform the values 1986, 1987, and 1988 into corresponding values of -1, 0, and 1, where 0 represents the mean (1987), -1 represents the first year ($1986 - 1987 = -1$), and 1 represents the last year ($1988 - 1987 = 1$).

Treating odd and even numbers of elements
We need to consider two cases when we are coding time values. The first is a time series with an *odd number of elements,* as in the previous example. The second is a series with an *even number of elements.* Consider Table 13-2. In part *a*, on the left, we have an odd number of years. Thus, the process is the same as the one we just described, using the years 1986, 1987, and 1988. In part *b*, on the right, we have an *even* number of elements. In cases like this, when we find the mean and subtract it from each element, the fraction ½ becomes part of the answer. To simplify the coding

TABLE 13-2 Translating, or Coding, Time Values

(a) When there is an *odd* number of elements in the time series			(b) When there is an *even* number of elements in the time series			
X (1)	$X - \bar{X}$ (2)	TRANSLATED OR CODED TIME (3)	X (1)	$X - \bar{X}$ (2)	$(X - \bar{X}) \times 2$ (3)	TRANSLATED OR CODED TIME (4)
1983	1983 − 1986 =	−3	1984	1984 − 1986½ = −2½ × 2 =		−5
1984	1984 − 1986 =	−2	1985	1985 − 1986½ = −1½ × 2 =		−3
1985	1985 − 1986 =	−1	1986	1986 − 1986½ = − ½ × 2 =		−1
1986	1986 − 1986 =	0	1987	1987 − 1986½ = ½ × 2 =		1
1987	1987 − 1986 =	1	1988	1988 − 1986½ = 1½ × 2 =		3
1988	1988 − 1986 =	2	1989	1989 − 1986½ = 2½ × 2 =		5
1989	1989 − 1986 =	3				

$\Sigma X = 13,902 \qquad$ $\bar{x}$ (the mean year) = 0 $\qquad \Sigma X = 11,919 \qquad$ $\bar{x}$ (the mean year) = 0

$$\bar{X} = \frac{\Sigma X}{n} \qquad\qquad\qquad \bar{X} = \frac{\Sigma X}{n}$$

$$= \frac{13,902}{7} \qquad\qquad\qquad = \frac{11,919}{6}$$

$$= 1986 \qquad\qquad\qquad\qquad = 1986½$$

process and to remove the ½, we multiply each time element by 2. We will denote the "coded," or translated, time with a lowercase x.

Why use coding?

We have two reasons for this translation of time. First, it eliminates the need to square numbers as large as 1983, 1984, 1985, and so on. This method also sets the mean year, $\bar{x}$, equal to zero and allows us to simplify Equations 13-1 and 13-2.

Simplifying the calculation of a and b

Now we can return to our calculations of the slope (Equation 13-1) and the Y-intercept (Equation 13-2) to determine the best fitting line. Since we are using the coded variable x, we replace X and $\bar{X}$ by x and $\bar{x}$ in Equations 13-1 and 13-2. Then, since the mean of our coded time variable $\bar{x}$ is zero, we can substitute 0 for $\bar{x}$ in Equations 13-1 and 13-2, as follows:

$$b = \frac{\Sigma XY - n\bar{X}\bar{Y}}{\Sigma X^2 - n\bar{X}^2} \qquad\qquad [13\text{-}1]$$

$$= \frac{\Sigma xY - n\bar{x}\bar{Y}}{\Sigma x^2 - n\bar{x}^2} \leftarrow \begin{cases} \bar{x} \text{ (the coded variable) substituted for } \bar{X} \\ \text{and } x \text{ substituted for } X \end{cases}$$

$$= \frac{\Sigma xY - n0\bar{Y}}{\Sigma x^2 - n0^2} \leftarrow \{ \bar{x} \text{ replaced by 0}$$

$$= \frac{\Sigma xY}{\Sigma x^2} \qquad\qquad [13\text{-}3]$$

Equation 13-2 changes as follows:

$$a = \bar{Y} - b\bar{X} \qquad\qquad [13\text{-}2]$$

$$= \bar{Y} - b\bar{x} \leftarrow \{ \bar{x} \text{ substituted for } \bar{X}$$

$$= \bar{Y} - b0 \leftarrow \{ \bar{x} \text{ replaced by 0}$$

$$= \bar{Y} \qquad\qquad [13\text{-}4]$$

Equations 13-3 and 13-4 represent a substantial improvement over Equations 13-1 and 13-2.

A PROBLEM USING THE LEAST SQUARES METHOD IN A TIME SERIES (EVEN NUMBER OF ELEMENTS)

Using the least squares method

Consider the data in Table 13-1, illustrating the number of ships loaded at Morehead City between 1982 and 1989. In this problem, we want to find the equation that will describe the secular trend of loadings. To calculate the necessary values for Equations 13-3 and 13-4, let us look at Table 13-3.

Finding the slope and Y-intercept

With these values, we can now substitute into Equations 13-3 and 13-4 to find the slope and the Y-intercept for the line describing the trend in ship loadings:

$$b = \frac{\Sigma xY}{\Sigma x^2} \tag{13-3}$$

$$= \frac{1,266}{168}$$

$$= 7.536$$

and:

$$a = \overline{Y} \tag{13-4}$$

$$= 139.25$$

Thus, the general linear equation describing the secular trend in ship loadings is:

$$\hat{Y} = a + bx \tag{10-3}$$

$$= 139.25 + 7.536x$$

where:

- $\hat{Y}$ is the estimated annual number of ships loaded.
- x is the coded time value representing the number of *half-year* intervals. (A minus sign indicates half-year intervals before 1985½; a plus sign indicates half-year intervals after 1985½.)

TABLE 13-3 Intermediate Calculations for Computing the Trend

X (1)	Y† (2)	X − X̄ (3)	x (4)	xY (4) × (2)	x² (4)²
1982	98	1982 − 1985½‡ = −3½ × 2 = −7		−686	49
1983	105	1983 − 1985½ = −2½ × 2 = −5		−525	25
1984	116	1984 − 1985½ = −1½ × 2 = −3		−348	9
1985	119	1985 − 1985½ = − ½ × 2 = −1		−119	1
1986	135	1986 − 1985½ = ½ × 2 = 1		135	1
1987	156	1987 − 1985½ = 1½ × 2 = 3		468	9
1988	177	1988 − 1985½ = 2½ × 2 = 5		885	25
1989	208	1989 − 1985½ = 3½ × 2 = 7		1,456	49
ΣX = 15,884	ΣY = 1,114			ΣxY = 1,266	Σx² = 168

$$\overline{X} = \frac{\Sigma X}{n} = \frac{15,884}{8} = 1,985\tfrac{1}{2}$$

$$\overline{Y} = \frac{\Sigma Y}{n} = \frac{1,114}{8} = 139.25$$

† Y is in number of ships.
‡ 1,985½ corresponds to $x = 0$.

PROJECTING WITH THE TREND EQUATION

Once we have developed the trend equation, we can project it to forecast the variable in question. In the problem of finding the secular trend in ship loadings, for instance, we determined that the appropriate secular trend equation was:

$$\hat{Y} = 139.25 + 7.536x$$

Using our trend line to predict

Now, suppose we want to estimate ship loadings for 1990. First, we must convert 1990 to the value of the coded time (in half-year intervals).

$$x = 1990 - 1985\frac{1}{2}$$
$$= 4.5 \text{ years}$$
$$= 9 \text{ } half\text{-year intervals}$$

Substituting this value into the equation for the secular trend, we get:

$$\hat{Y} = 139.25 + 7.536(9)$$
$$= 139.25 + 67.82$$
$$= 207 \text{ ships loaded}$$

Therefore, we have estimated 207 ships will be loaded in 1990. If the number of elements in our time series had been odd, not even, our procedure would have been the same except that we would have dealt with one-year intervals, not half-year intervals.

USE OF THE SECOND-DEGREE EQUATION IN A TIME SERIES

Handling time series that are described by curves

So far, we have described the method of fitting a straight line to a time series. But many time series are best described by curves, not straight lines. In these instances, the linear model does not adequately describe the change in the variable as time changes. To overcome this problem, we often use a parabolic curve, which is described mathematically by a second-degree equation. Such a curve is illustrated in Fig. 13-3. The general form for an estimated second-degree equation is:

$$\hat{Y} = a + bx + cx^2 \qquad \text{[13-5]}$$

FIGURE 13-3

Form and equation for a parabolic curve

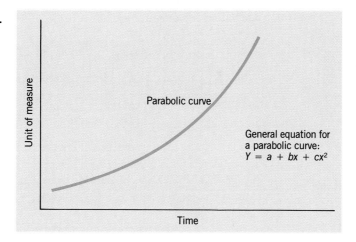

where:

- $\hat{Y}$ is the estimate of the dependent variable.
- a, b, and c are numerical constants.
- x represents the coded values of the time variables.

Finding the values for
a, b, and c

Again we use the least squares method to determine the second-degree equation to describe the best fit. The derivation of the second-degree equation is beyond the scope of this text. However, we can determine the value of the numerical constants (a, b, and c) from the following three equations:

Equations to find
a, b, and c to fit
a parabolic curve

$$\Sigma Y = an + c\Sigma x^2 \qquad \text{[13-6]}$$

$$\Sigma x^2 Y = a\Sigma x^2 + c\Sigma x^4 \qquad \text{[13-7]}$$

$$b = \frac{\Sigma xY}{\Sigma x^2} \qquad \text{[13-3]}$$

When we find the values of a, b, and c by solving Equations 13-6, 13-7, and 13-3, simultaneously, we substitute these values into the second-degree equation, Equation 13-5.

As in describing a linear relationship, we transform the independent variable, time (X), into a coded form (x) to simplify the calculation. We'll now work through a problem in which we fit a parabola to a time series.

A PROBLEM INVOLVING A PARABOLIC TREND (ODD NUMBER OF ELEMENTS IN THE TIME SERIES)

In recent years, the sale of electric quartz watches has increased at a significant rate. Table 13-4 contains sales information that will help us determine the parabolic trend describing watch sales.

Coding the time variable

We organize the necessary calculations in Table 13-5. The first step in this process is to translate the independent variable X into a coded time variable x. Note that the coded variable x is listed in one-year intervals because there is an odd number of elements in our time series. Thus, it is not necessary to multiply the variable by 2.

Calculating a, b, and c
by substitution

Substituting the values from Table 13-5 into equations 13-6, 13-7, and 13-3, we get:

$$247 = 5a + 10c \quad \text{①} \qquad \text{[13-6]}$$

$$565 = 10a + 34c \quad \text{②} \qquad \text{[13-7]}$$

$$b = \frac{227}{10} \quad \text{③} \qquad \text{[13-3]}$$

TABLE 13-4 Annual Sales of Electric Quartz Watches

X (year)	1985	1986	1987	1988	1989
Y (unit sales in millions)	13	24	39	65	106

TABLE 13-5 Intermediate Calculations for Computing the Trend

Y (1)	X (2)	$X - \bar{X} = x$ (3)	x^2 $(3)^2$	x^4 $(3)^4$	xY $(3) \times (1)$	x^2Y $(3)^2 \times (1)$
13	1985	$1985 - 1987 = -2$	4	16	-26	52
24	1986	$1986 - 1987 = -1$	1	1	-24	24
39	1987	$1987 - 1987 = 0$	0	0	0	0
65	1988	$1988 - 1987 = 1$	1	1	65	65
106	1989	$1989 - 1987 = 2$	4	16	212	424
$\Sigma Y = 247$	$\Sigma X = 9{,}935$		$\Sigma x^2 = 10$	$\Sigma x^4 = 34$	$\Sigma xY = 227$	$\Sigma x^2Y = 565$

$$\bar{X} = \frac{\Sigma X}{n} = \frac{9{,}935}{5} = 1987$$

From ③ we see that:

$$b = 22.7$$

Now we must find a and c by solving equations ① and ②.

1. Multiply equation ① by 2 and subtract equation ② from equation ①.

$$
\begin{array}{rlrl}
① \times (2): & 494 = & 10a + 20c \\
-②: & -565 = & -10a - 34c \\
\hline
④: & -71 = & -14c
\end{array}
$$

From equation ④ we readily find c:

$$-14c = -71$$

$$c = \frac{-71}{-14}$$

$$= 5.07$$

2. Substitute the value for c into equation ①:

$$247 = 5a + 10c$$

$$247 = 5a + 10(5.07)$$

$$247 = 5a + 50.7$$

$$196.3 = 5a$$

$$a = 39.3$$

This gives us the appropriate values of a, b, and c to describe the time series presented in Table 13-4 by the following equation:

$$
\begin{aligned}
\hat{Y} &= a + bx + cx^2 \qquad\qquad [13\text{-}5] \\
&= 39.3 + 22.7x + 5.07x^2
\end{aligned}
$$

Does our curve fit the data?   Let's graph the watch data to see how well the parabola we just derived fits the time series. We've done this in Fig. 13-4.

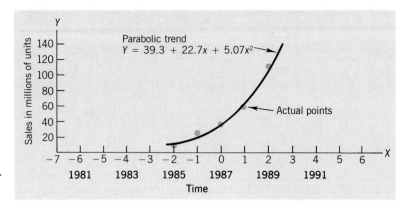

FIGURE 13-4

Parabolic trend fitted to data in Table 13-4

FORECASTS BASED ON A SECOND-DEGREE EQUATION

Making the forecast

Suppose we want to forecast watch sales for 1994. To make a prediction, we must first translate 1994 into a coded variable x by subtracting the mean year, 1987:

$$X - \overline{X} = x$$
$$1994 - 1987 = 7$$

This value ($x = 7$) is then substituted into the second-degree equation describing watch sales:

$$\hat{Y} = 39.3 + 22.7x + 5.07x^2$$
$$= 39.3 + 22.7(7) + 5.07(7)^2$$
$$= 39.3 + 158.9 + 248.4$$
$$= 446.6$$

We conclude, based on the past secular trend, that watch sales should be approximately 446,600,000 units by 1994. This extraordinarily large forecast suggests, however, that we must be more careful in forecasting with a parabolic curve than we are when using a linear trend. The slope of the second-degree equation in Fig. 13-4 is continually increasing. Therefore, the parabolic curve may become a poor estimator as we attempt to predict farther into the future. In using the second-degree-equation method, we must also take into consideration factors that may be slowing or reversing the growth rate of the variable.

Being careful in interpreting the forecast

In our watch example, we can assume that during the time period under consideration, the product is at a very rapid growth stage in its life cycle. But we must realize that as the cycle approaches a mature stage, sales will probably decelerate and no longer be predicted accurately by our parabolic curve. When we calculate predictions for the future, we need to consider the possibility that the trend line may *change*. Such a situation could cause considerable error. It is therefore necessary to exercise particular care when using a second-degree equation as a forecasting tool.

Exercises

13-12 Robin Zill and Stewart Griffiths own a small company that manufactures portable massage tables in Hillsborough, North Carolina. Since they started the company, the number of tables they have sold is represented by this time series:

Year	1981	1982	1983	1984	1985	1986	1987	1988	1989	1990
Tables sold	42	50	61	75	92	111	120	127	140	138

(a) Find the linear equation that describes the trend in the number of tables sold by Robin and Stewart.
(b) Estimate their sales of tables in 1992.

13-13 The owner of Progressive Builders is examining the number of solar homes started in the region in each of the last 7 months:

Month	June	July	Aug.	Sept.	Oct.	Nov.	Dec.
Number of homes	16	17	25	28	32	43	50

(a) Plot these data.
(b) Develop the linear estimating equation that best describes these data, and plot the line on the graph from part (a) (let x units equal one month).
(c) Develop the second-degree estimating equation that best describes these data and plot this curve on the graph from part (a).
(d) Estimate March sales using both curves you have plotted.

13-14 The number of faculty-owned personal computers at the University of Ohio has increased dramatically over the last 6 years:

Year	1984	1985	1986	1987	1988	1989
Number of PCs	50	110	350	1,020	1,950	3,710

(a) Develop a linear estimating equation that best describes these data.
(b) Develop a second-degree estimating equation that best describes these data.
(c) Estimate the number of PCs that will be in use at the university in 1993 using both equations.
(d) If there are 8,000 faculty members at the university, which equation is the better predictor? Why?

13-15 Mike Godfrey, the auditor of a state public school system, has reviewed the inventory records to determine if the current inventory holdings of textbooks are typical. The following inventory amounts are from the previous 5 years:

Year	1985	1986	1987	1988	1989
Inventory ($\times$$1,000)	$4,620	$4,910	$5,490	$5,730	$5,990

(a) Find the linear equation that describes the trend in the inventory holdings.
(b) Estimate for him the value of the inventory for the year 1990.

13-16 The following table describes first-class postal rates from 1968 to 1988

Year	1968	1970	1972	1974	1976	1978	1980	1982	1984	1986	1988
Rate (¢)	5	5	8	8	10	13	15	18	20	22	25

(a) Develop the linear estimating equation that best describes these data.
(b) Develop the second-degree estimating equation that best describes these data.
(c) Is there anything in the economic or political environment that would suggest that one or the other of these two equations is likely to be the better predictor of postal rates?

13-17 Environtech Engineering, a company that specializes in the construction of antipollution filtration devices, has recorded the following sales record over the last 9 years:

Year	1981	1982	1983	1984	1985	1986	1987	1988	1989
Sales (×$100,000)	13	15	19	21	27	35	47	49	57

(a) Plot these data.
(b) Develop the linear estimating equation that best describes these data, and plot this line on the graph from part (a).
(c) Develop the second-degree estimating equation that best describes these data, and plot this curve on the graph from part (a).
(d) Does the market to the best of your knowledge favor (b) or (c) as the more accurate estimating method?

13-18 Here are data describing the air pollution rate (in ppm of particles in the air) in a western city:

Year	1974	1979	1984	1989
Pollution rate	220	350	800	2450

(a) Would a linear or a second-degree estimating equation provide the better prediction of future pollution in that city?
(b) Considering the economic, social, and political environment, would you change your answer to part (a)?
(c) Describe how political and social action could change the effectiveness of either of the estimating equations in part (a).

13-19 The State Department of Motor Vehicles is studying the number of traffic fatalities in the state resulting from drunk driving for each of the last 9 years.

Year	1981	1982	1983	1984	1985	1986	1987	1988	1989
Deaths	175	190	185	195	180	200	185	190	205

(a) Find the linear equation that describes the trend in the number of traffic fatalities in the state resulting from drunk driving.
(b) Estimate the number of traffic fatalities resulting from drunk driving that the state can expect in 1990.

13-4
Cyclical Variation

Cyclical variation is the component of a time series that tends to oscillate above and below the secular trend line for periods longer than 1 year. The procedure used to identify cyclical variation is the residual method.

Cyclical variation defined

RESIDUAL METHOD

When we look at a time series consisting of annual data, only the secular-trend, cyclical, and irregular components are considered. (This is true because seasonal variation makes a complete, regular cycle within each year and thus does not affect one year any more than another.) Since we can describe secular trend using a trend line, we can isolate the remaining cyclical and irregular components from the trend. We will assume that the cyclical component explains most of the variation left unexplained by the trend component. (Many real-life time series do not satisfy this assumption. Methods such as Fourier analysis and spectral analysis can analyze the cyclical component for such time series. These, however, are beyond the scope of this book.)

Expressing cyclical variation as a percent of trend

If we use a time series composed of annual data, we can find the fraction of the trend by dividing the actual value (Y) by the corresponding trend value ($\hat{Y}$) for each value in the time series. We then multiply the result of this calculation by 100. This gives us the measure of cyclical variation as a *percent of trend*. We express this process in Equation 13-8:

$$\text{Percent of trend} = \frac{Y}{\hat{Y}} \times 100 \qquad [13\text{-}8]$$

where:

- Y is the actual time series value.
- $\hat{Y}$ is the estimated trend value from the same point in the time series.

Now let's apply this procedure.

Measuring variation

A farmers' marketing cooperative wants to measure the variations in its members' wheat harvest over an 8-year period. Table 13-6 shows the volume harvested in each of the 8 years. Column $\hat{Y}$ contains the values of the linear trend for each time period. The trend line has been generated using the methods illustrated in section 3 of this chapter. Note that when we graph the actual (Y) and the trend ($\hat{Y}$) values for the 8 years in Fig. 13-5, the actual values move above and below the trend line.

Interpreting cyclical variations

Now we can determine the percent of trend for each of the years in the sample (column 4 in Table 13-7). From this column we can see the variation in actual harvests around the estimated trend (98.7 to 102.5). We can attribute these cyclical variations to factors such as rainfall and temperature. However, since these factors

TABLE 13-6 Grain Received by Farmers' Cooperative Over 8 Years

X YEAR	Y ACTUAL BUSHELS ($\times$10,000)	$\hat{Y}$ ESTIMATED BUSHELS ($\times$10,000)
1982	7.5	7.6
1983	7.8	7.8
1984	8.2	8.0
1985	8.2	8.2
1986	8.4	8.4
1987	8.5	8.6
1988	8.7	8.8
1989	9.1	9.0

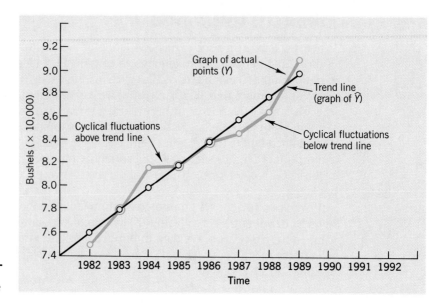

FIGURE 13-5
Cyclical fluctuations around the trend line

are relatively unpredictable, we cannot forecast any specific patterns of variation using the method of residuals.

Expressing cyclical variations in terms of relative cyclical residual

The *relative cyclical residual* is another measure of cyclical variation. In this method, the *percentage deviation* from the trend is found for each value. Equation 13-9 presents the mathematical formula for determining the relative cyclical residuals. As with percents of trend, this measure is also a percentage.

$$\text{Relative cyclical residual} = \frac{Y - \hat{Y}}{\hat{Y}} \times 100 \qquad [13\text{-}9]$$

where:

- Y is the actual time series value.
- $\hat{Y}$ is the estimated trend value from the same point in the time series.

TABLE 13-7 Calculation of Percent of Trend

X YEAR (1)	Y ACTUAL BUSHELS (×10,000) (2)	$\hat{Y}$ ESTIMATED BUSHELS (×10,000) (3)	$\frac{Y}{\hat{Y}} \times 100$ PERCENT OF TREND $(4) = \frac{(2)}{(3)} \times 100$
1982	7.5	7.6	98.7
1983	7.8	7.8	100.0
1984	8.2	8.0	102.5
1985	8.2	8.2	100.0
1986	8.4	8.4	100.0
1987	8.5	8.6	98.8
1988	8.7	8.8	98.9
1989	9.1	9.0	101.1

TABLE 13-8 Calculation of Relative Cyclical Residuals

YEAR (1)	Y ACTUAL BUSHELS (×10,000) (2)	Ŷ ESTIMATED BUSHELS (×10,000) (3)	$\frac{Y}{\hat{Y}} \times 100$ PERCENT OF TREND $(4) = \frac{(2)}{(3)} \times 100$	$\frac{Y - \hat{Y}}{\hat{Y}} \times 100$ RELATIVE CYCLICAL RESIDUAL $(5) = (4) - 100$
1982	7.5	7.6	98.7	−1.3
1983	7.8	7.8	100.0	0.0
1984	8.2	8.0	102.5	2.5
1985	8.2	8.2	100.0	0.0
1986	8.4	8.4	100.0	0.0
1987	8.5	8.6	98.8	−1.2
1988	8.7	8.8	98.9	−1.1
1989	9.1	9.0	101.1	1.1

Table 13-8 shows the calculation of the relative cyclical residual for the farmers' cooperative problem. Note that the easy way to compute the relative cyclical residual (column 5) is to subtract 100 from the percent of trend (column 4).

Comparing the two measures of cyclical variation

These two measures of cyclical variation, percent of trend and relative cyclical residual, are percentages of the trend. For example, in 1987, the *percent of trend* indicated that the actual harvest was 98.8 percent of the expected harvest for that year. For the same year, the *relative cyclical residual* indicated that the actual harvest was 1.2 percent short of the expected harvest (a relative cyclical residual of −1.2).

Graphing cyclical variation

Frequently, we graph cyclical variation as the percent of trend. Figure 13-6 illustrates how this process eliminates the trend line and isolates the cyclical component

FIGURE 13-6

Graph of percent of trend around trend line for data in Table 13-7

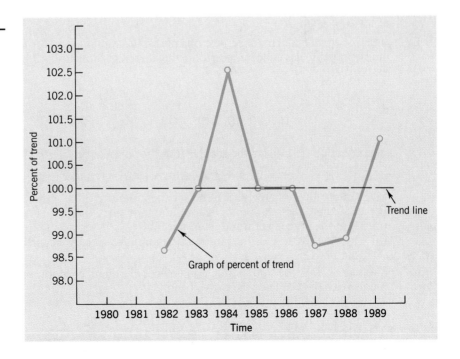

of the time series. It must be emphasized that the procedures discussed in this section can be used only for describing past cyclical variations and not for predicting future cyclical variations. Predicting cyclical variation requires the use of techniques beyond the scope of this book.

Exercises

13-20 Microprocessing, a computer firm specializing in software engineering, has compiled the following revenue records for the years 1983 to 1989.

Year	1983	1984	1985	1986	1987	1988	1989
Revenue ($\times$ $100,000)	1.1	1.5	1.9	2.1	2.4	2.9	3.5

The second-degree equation that best describes the secular trend for these data is:

$$\hat{Y} = 2.086 + .375x + .025x^2, \text{ where } 1986 = 0 \text{ and } x \text{ units} = 1 \text{ year}$$

(a) Calculate the percent of trend for these data.
(b) Calculate the relative cyclical residual for these data.
(c) Plot the percent of trend from part (a).
(d) In which year does the largest fluctuation from trend occur, and is it the same for both methods?

13-21 The Western Natural Gas Company has supplied 18, 20, 21, 25, and 26 billion cubic feet of gas, respectively, for the years 1985 to 1989.
(a) Find the linear estimating equation that best describes these data.
(b) Calculate the percent of trend for these data.
(c) Calculate the relative cyclical residual for these data.
(d) In which years does the largest fluctuation from trend occur, and is it the same for both methods?

13-22 Joe Honeg, the sales manager responsible for the appliance division of a large consumer-products company, has collected the following data regarding unit sales for his division during the last 5 years:

Year	1985	1986	1987	1988	1989
Units ($\times$ 10,000)	32	46	50	66	68

The equation describing the secular trend for appliance sales is:

$$\hat{Y} = 52.4 + 9.2x, \text{ where } 1987 = 0 \text{ and } x \text{ units} = 1 \text{ year}$$

(a) Calculate the percent of trend for these data.
(b) Calculate the relative cyclical residual for these data.
(c) Plot the percent of trend from part (a).
(d) In which year does the largest fluctuation from trend occur, and is it the same for both methods?

13-23 Suppose you are the capital budgeting officer of a small corporation whose financing requirements over the last few years have been:

Year	1983	1984	1985	1986	1987	1988	1989
Millions of dollars required	2.2	2.1	2.4	2.6	2.7	2.9	2.8

The trend equation that best describes these data is:

$$\hat{Y} = 2.53 + .13x, \text{ where } 1986 = 0 \text{ and } x \text{ units} = 1 \text{ year}$$

(a) Calculate the percent of trend for these data.
(b) Calculate the relative cyclical residual for these data.
(c) In which year does the largest fluctuation from trend occur and is it the same for both methods?
(d) As the capital budgeting officer, what would this fluctuation mean for you and the activities you perform?

13-24 Parallel Breakfast Foods has data on the number of boxes of cereal it has sold in each of the last 7 years.

Year	1983	1984	1985	1986	1987	1988	1989
Boxes ($\times$10,000)	21.0	19.4	22.6	28.2	30.4	24.0	25.0

(a) Find the linear estimating equation that best describes these data.
(b) Calculate the percent of trend for these data.
(c) Calculate the relative cyclical residual for these data.
(d) In which year does the biggest fluctuation from the trend occur under each measure of cyclical variation? Is this year the same for both measures? Why, or why not?

13-25 Wombat Airlines, an Australian company, has gathered data on the number of passengers who have flown on its planes during each of the last 5 years.

Year	1985	1986	1987	1988	1989
Passengers (in tens of thousands)	3.5	4.2	3.9	3.8	3.6

(a) Find the linear estimating equation that best describes these data.
(b) Calculate the percent of trend for these data.
(c) Calculate the relative cyclical residual for these data.
(d) Based on the data and your calculations above, give a one-sentence summary of the position that Wombat Airlines is in.

13-5
Seasonal Variation

Seasonal variation defined

Besides secular trend and cyclical variation, time series also include seasonal variation. Seasonal variation is defined as repetitive and predictable movement around the trend line in *one year or less*. In order to detect seasonal variation, time intervals need to be measured in small units, such as days, weeks, months, or quarters.

We have three main reasons for studying seasonal variation:

Three reasons for studying seasonal variation

1. **We can establish the pattern of past changes.** This gives us a way to compare two time intervals that would otherwise be too dissimilar. If a flight training school wants to know if a slump in business during December is normal, it can examine the seasonal pattern in previous years and find the information it needs.

2. **It is useful to project past patterns into the future.** In the case of long-range decisions, secular trend analysis may be adequate. But for short-run decisions, the ability to predict seasonal fluctuations is often essential. Consider a wholesale food chain that wants to maintain a minimum adequate stock of all items. The ability to predict short-range patterns, such as the demand for turkeys at Thanks-

giving, candy at Christmas, or peaches in the summer, is useful to the management of the chain.

3. **Once we have established the seasonal pattern that exists, we can eliminate its effects from the time series.** This adjustment allows us to calculate the cyclical variation that takes place each year. When we eliminate the effect of seasonal variation from a time series, we have *deseasonalized* the time series.

RATIO-TO-MOVING-AVERAGE METHOD

Using the ratio-to-moving-average method of measuring seasonal variation

In order to measure seasonal variation, we typically use the ratio-to-moving-average method. This technique provides an *index* that describes the degree of seasonal variation. The index is based on a mean of 100, with the degree of seasonality measured by variations away from the base. For example, if we examine the seasonality of canoe rentals at a summer resort, we might find that the spring-quarter index is 142. The value 142 indicates that 142 percent of the average quarterly rentals occur in the spring. If management recorded 2,000 canoe rentals for all of last year, then the average quarterly rental would be 2,000/4 = 500. Since the spring-quarter index is 142, we estimate the number of spring rentals as follows:

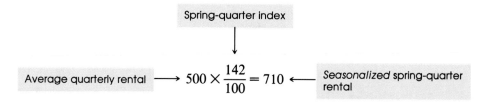

An example of the ratio-to-moving-average method

Our chapter-opening example can illustrate the ratio-to-moving-average method. The resort hotel wanted to establish the seasonal pattern of room demand by its clientele. Hotel management wants to improve customer service and is considering several plans to employ personnel during peak periods to achieve this goal. Table 13-9 contains the quarterly occupancy, that is, the average number of guests during each quarter of the last five years.

We will refer to Table 13-9 to demonstrate the six steps required to compute a seasonal index.

Step 1: Calculate 4-quarter moving total

1. **The first step in computing a seasonal index is to calculate the 4-quarter moving total for the time series.** To do this, we total the values for the quarters during the first year, 1985, in Table 13-9; 1,861 + 2,203 + 2,415 + 1,908 = 8,387. A moving total is associated with the middle data point in the set of values from which it

TABLE 13-9 Time Series for Hotel Occupancy

| YEAR | Number of guests per quarter | | | |
	I	II	III	IV
1985	1,861	2,203	2,415	1,908
1986	1,921	2,343	2,514	1,986
1987	1,834	2,154	2,098	1,799
1988	1,837	2,025	2,304	1,965
1989	2,073	2,414	2,339	1,967

was calculated. Since our first total of 8,387 was calculated from four data points, we place it opposite the midpoint of those quarters, so it falls in column 4 of Table 13-10, between the rows for the 1985-II and 1985-III quarters.

We find the next moving total by dropping the 1985-I value, 1,861, and adding the 1986-I value, 1,921. By dropping the first value and adding the fifth, we keep four quarters in the total. The four values added now are $2,203 + 2,415 + 1,908 + 1,921 = 8,447$. This total is entered in Table 13-10 directly below the first quarterly total of 8,387. We continue the process of "sliding" the 4-quarter total over the time series until we have included the last value in the series. In this example, it is the 1,967 rooms in the fourth quarter of 1989, the last number in column 3 of Table 13-10. The last entry in the moving total column is 8,793. It is between the rows for the 1989-II and 1989-III quarters, since it was calculated from the data for the 4 quarters of 1989.

Step 2: Compute the 4-quarter moving average	**2. In the second step, we compute the 4-quarter moving average by dividing each of the 4-quarter totals by 4.** In Table 13-10, we divided the values in column 4 by 4, to arrive at the values for column 5.
Step 3: Center the 4-quarter moving average	**3. In the third step, we** *center* **the 4-quarter moving average.** The moving averages in column 5 all fall halfway between the quarters. We would like to have moving averages associated with each quarter. In order to *center* our moving averages, we

TABLE 13-10 Calculating the 4-Quarter Centered Moving Average

YEAR (1)	QUARTER (2)	OCCUPANCY (3)	STEP 1: 4-QUARTER MOVING TOTAL (4)	STEP 2: 4-QUARTER MOVING AVERAGE (5) = (4) ÷ 4	STEP 3: 4-QUARTER CENTERED MOVING AVERAGE (6)	STEP 4: PERCENTAGE OF ACTUAL TO MOVING AVERAGE VALUES $(7) = \frac{(3)}{(6)} \times 100$
1985	I	1,861				
	II	2,203	8,387	2,096.75		
	III	2,415	8,447	2,111.75	2,104.250	114.8
	IV	1,908			2,129.250	89.6
1986	I	1,921	8,587	2,146.75	2,159.125	89.0
	II	2,343	8,686	2,171.50	2,181.250	107.4
	III	2,514	8,764	2,191.00	2,180.125	115.3
	IV	1,986	8,677	2,169.25	2,145.625	92.6
1987	I	1,834	8,488	2,122.00	2,070.000	88.6
	II	2,154	8,072	2,018.00	1,994.625	108.0
	III	2,098	7,885	1,971.25	1,971.625	106.4
	IV	1,799	7,888	1,972.00	1,955.875	92.0
1988	I	1,837	7,759	1,939.75	1,965.500	93.5
	II	2,025	7,965	1,991.25	2,012.000	100.6
	III	2,304	8,131	2,032.75	2,062.250	111.7
	IV	1,965	8,367	2,091.75	2,140.375	91.8
1989	I	2,073	8,756	2,189.00	2,193.375	94.5
	II	2,414	8,791	2,197.75	2,198.000	109.8
	III	2,339	8,793	2,198.25		
	IV	1,967				

associate with each quarter the average of the two 4-quarter moving averages falling just above and just below it. For the 1985-III quarter, the resulting **4-quarter centered moving average** is 2104.25, that is, (2096.75 + 2111.75)/2. The other entries in column 6 are calculated the same way. Figure 13-7 illustrates how the moving average has smoothed the peaks and troughs of the original time series. The seasonal and irregular components have been smoothed, and the resulting dotted colored line represents the cyclical and trend components.

Sometimes step 3 can be skipped

Suppose we were working with the admissions data for a hospital emergency room, and we wanted to compute *daily* indices. In steps 1 and 2, we would compute 7-day moving totals and moving averages, **and the moving averages would already be centered** (because the middle of a 7-day period is the fourth of those 7 days). In this case, step 3 is unnecessary. Whenever the number of periods for which we want indices is odd (7 days in a week, three shifts in a day), we can skip step 3. However, when the number of periods is even (4 quarters, 12 months, 24 hours), then we must use step 3 to center the moving averages we get with step 2.

Step 4: Calculate percentage of actual value to moving average value

4. **Next, we calculate the percentage of the actual value to the moving average value for each quarter in the time series having a 4-quarter moving average entry.** This step allows us to recover the seasonal component for the quarters. We determine this percentage by dividing each of the actual quarter values in column 3 of Table 13-10 by the corresponding 4-quarter centered moving-average values in column 6 and then multiplying the result by 100. For example, we find the percentage for 1985-III as follows:

$$\frac{\text{Actual}}{\text{Moving average}} \times 100 = \frac{2,415}{2,104.250} \times 100$$
$$= 114.8$$

Step 5: Collect answers from step 4 and calculate modified mean

5. **To collect all the percentage of actual to moving-average values in column 7 of Table 13-10, arrange them by quarter.** Then calculate the "modified mean" for each quarter. The modified mean is calculated by discarding the highest and lowest values for each quarter and averaging the remaining values. In Table 13-11, we present the fifth step and show the process for finding the modified mean.

FIGURE 13-7

Using a moving average to smooth the original time series

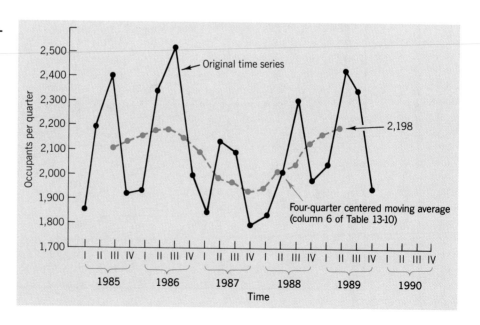

TABLE 13-11 Demonstration of Step 5 in Computing a Seasonal Index*

YEAR	QUARTER I	QUARTER II	QUARTER III	QUARTER IV
1985	—	—	114.8	~~89.6~~
1986	89.0	107.4	~~115.3~~	~~92.6~~
1987	~~88.6~~	108.0	~~106.4~~	92.0
1988	93.5	~~100.6~~	111.7	91.8
1989	~~94.5~~	~~109.8~~	—	—
	182.5	**215.4**	**226.5**	**183.8**

Modified mean:

Quarter I: $\dfrac{182.5}{2} = 91.25$

Quarter II: $\dfrac{215.4}{2} = 107.70$

Quarter III: $\dfrac{226.5}{2} = 113.25$

Quarter IV: $\dfrac{183.8}{2} = 91.90$

Total of indices = **404.1**

* Eliminated values are indicated by a colored slash.

Reducing extreme cyclical and irregular variations

The seasonal values that we recovered for the quarters in column 7 of Table 13-10 still contain the cyclical and irregular components of variation in the time series. By eliminating the highest and lowest values from each quarter, we *reduce* the extreme cyclical and irregular variations. When we average the remaining values, we further smooth the cyclical and irregular components. Since cyclical and irregular variations tend to be removed by this process, the modified mean is an index of the seasonality component. (Some statisticians prefer to use the median value instead of computing the modified mean to achieve the same outcome.)

Step 6: Adjust the modified mean

6. **The final step, demonstrated in Table 13-12, adjusts the modified mean slightly.** Notice that the four indices in Table 13-11 total 404.1. However, the base for an index is 100. Thus, the four quarterly indices should total 400, and their mean should be 100. To correct for this error, we multiply each of the quarterly indices in Table 13-11 by an adjusting constant. This number is found by dividing the desired sum of the indices (400) by the actual sum (404.1). In this case, the result is .9899. Table 13-12 shows that multiplying the indices by the adjusting constant

---

TABLE 13-12 Demonstration of Step 6

QUARTER	UNADJUSTED INDICES	×	ADJUSTING CONSTANT	=	SEASONAL INDEX
I	91.25	×	.9899	=	90.3
II	107.70	×	.9899	=	106.6
III	113.25	×	.9899	=	112.1
IV	91.90	×	.9899	=	91.0
			Total of seasonal indices =		**400.0**

Mean of seasonal indices $= \dfrac{400}{4}$

$= 100.0$

brings the quarterly indices to a total of 400. (Sometimes even after this adjustment, the mean of the seasonal indices is not exactly 100 because of accumulated rounding errors. In this case, however, it is exactly 100.)

USES OF THE SEASONAL INDEX

Deseasonalizing the time series

The ratio-to-moving-average method just explained allows us to identify seasonal variation in a time series. The seasonal indices are used to remove the effects of seasonality from a time series. This is called *deseasonalizing* a time series. Before we can identify either the trend or cyclical components of a time series, we must eliminate seasonal variation. To deseasonalize a time series, we divide each of the actual values in the series by the appropriate seasonal index (expressed as a percent). To demonstrate, we shall deseasonalize the value of the first four quarters in Table 13-9. In Table 13-13, we show the deseasonalizing process using the values for the seasonal indices from Table 13-12. Once the seasonal effect has been eliminated, the deseasonalized values that remain reflect only the trend, cyclical, and irregular components of the time series.

Using seasonality in forecasts

Once we have removed the seasonal variation, we can compute a deseasonalized trend line, which we can then project into the future. Suppose the hotel management in our example estimates from a deseasonalized trend line that the deseasonalized average occupancy for the fourth quarter of the *next* year will be 2,121. When this prediction has been obtained, management must then take the seasonality into account. To do this, it multiplies the deseasonalized predicted average occupancy of 2,121 by the fourth-quarter seasonal index (expressed as a percent) to obtain a seasonalized estimate of 1,930 rooms for the fourth-quarter average occupancy. Here are the calculations:

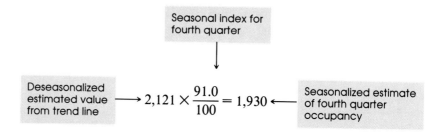

TABLE 13-13 Demonstration of Deseasonalizing Data

YEAR (1)	QUARTER (2)	ACTUAL OCCUPANCY (3)		$\left(\dfrac{\text{SEASONAL INDEX}}{100}\right)$ (4)		DESEASONALIZED OCCUPANCY (5) = (3) ÷ (4)
1985	I	1,861	÷	$\left(\dfrac{90.3}{100}\right)$	=	2,061
1985	II	2,203	÷	$\left(\dfrac{106.6}{100}\right)$	=	2,067
1985	III	2,415	÷	$\left(\dfrac{112.1}{100}\right)$	=	2,154
1985	IV	1,908	÷	$\left(\dfrac{91.0}{100}\right)$	=	2,097

Exercises

13-26 The owner of The Pleasure-Glide Boat Company has compiled the following quarterly figures regarding the company's level of accounts receivable over the last 5 years ($\times$ $1,000):

	SPRING	SUMMER	FALL	WINTER
1985	102	120	90	78
1986	110	126	95	83
1987	111	128	97	86
1988	115	135	103	91
1989	122	144	110	98

(a) Calculate a 4-quarter centered moving average.
(b) Find the percentage of actual to moving average for each period.
(c) Determine the modified seasonal indices and the seasonal indices.

13-27 Marie Wiggs, personnel director for a pharmaceutical company, recorded these percentage absentee rates for each quarter over a four-year period:

	SPRING	SUMMER	FALL	WINTER
1986	5.6	6.8	6.3	5.2
1987	5.7	6.7	6.4	5.4
1988	5.3	6.6	6.1	5.1
1989	5.4	6.9	6.2	5.3

(a) Construct a 4-quarter centered moving average and plot it on a graph along with the original data.
(b) What can you conclude about absenteeism from part (a)?

13-28 The Federal Reserve released the following percentages of actual to moving average describing the quarterly amount of cash in circulation over a 4-year period:

	SPRING	SUMMER	FALL	WINTER
1986	87	106	86	125
1987	85	110	83	127
1988	84	105	87	128
1989	88	104	88	124

Calculate the seasonal index for each quarter.

13-29 A large manufacturer of automobile springs has determined the following percentages of actual to moving average describing the firm's quarterly cash needs for the last 6 years:

	SPRING	SUMMER	FALL	WINTER
1984	108	128	94	70
1985	112	132	88	68
1986	109	134	84	73
1987	110	131	90	69
1988	108	135	89	68
1989	106	129	93	72

Calculate the seasonal index for each quarter. Comment on how it compares to the indices you calculated for exercise 13-26.

13-30 A university's dean of admissions has compiled the following quarterly enrollment figures for the previous 5 years (×100):

	FALL	WINTER	SPRING	SUMMER
1985	220	203	193	84
1986	235	208	206	76
1987	236	206	209	73
1988	241	215	206	92
1989	239	221	213	115

(a) Calculate a 4-quarter centered moving average.
(b) Find the percentage of actual to moving average for each period.
(c) Determine the modified seasonal indices and the seasonal indices.

 13-31 The Ski and Putt Resort, a combination of ski slopes and golf courses, has just recently tabulated its data on the number of customers it has had during each season of the last 5 years. Calculate the seasonal index for each quarter. If fifteen people are employed in the summer, what should winter employment be, assuming both sports have equal labor requirements?

	SPRING	SUMMER	FALL	WINTER
1985	200	300	125	325
1986	175	250	150	375
1987	225	300	200	450
1988	200	350	225	375
1989	175	300	200	350

(The table entries are in thousands of customers.)

 13-32 David Curl Builders has collected quarterly data on the number of homes it has started during the last 5 years.

	SPRING	SUMMER	FALL	WINTER
1985	8	10	7	5
1986	9	10	7	6
1987	10	11	7	6
1988	10	12	8	7
1989	11	13	9	8

(a) Calculate the seasonal index for each quarter.
(b) If David's working capital needs are related directly to the number of starts, by what percentage should his working capital need decrease between summer and winter?

13-6
Irregular Variation

The final component of a time series is irregular variation. After we have eliminated trend, cyclical, and seasonal variations from a time series, we still have an unpredictable factor left. Typically, irregular variation occurs over short intervals and follows a random pattern.

Difficulty of dealing with
irregular variation

Because of the unpredictability of irregular variation, we do not attempt to explain it mathematically. However, we can often isolate its causes. New York City's finan-

676 13 TIME SERIES

cial crisis of 1975, for example, was an irregular factor that severely depressed the municipal bond market. In 1984, the unusually cold temperatures in late December in the southern states were an irregular factor that significantly increased electricity and fuel oil consumption. Not all causes of irregular variation can be identified so easily, however. One factor that allows managers to cope with irregular variation is that over time, these random movements tend to counteract each other.

Exercises

13-33 Why don't we project irregular variations into the future?

13-34 Which of the following illustrate irregular variations?
  (a) An extended drought leading to higher food prices.
  (b) The effect of snow on ski slope business.
  (c) A one-time federal tax rebate provision for the purchase of new houses.
  (d) The collapse of crude oil prices in early 1986.
  (e) The energy use reduction after the 1973 oil embargo.

13-35 Make a list of five irregular variations in time series that you deal with as a part of your daily routine.

13-36 What allows management to cope with irregular variation in time series?

13-7
A Problem Involving All Four Components of a Time Series

For a problem that involves all four components of a time series, we turn to a firm that specializes in producing recreational equipment. To forecast future sales based on an analysis of its past pattern of sales, the firm has collected the information in Table 13-14. Our procedure for describing this time series will consist of three stages:

1. Deseasonalizing the time series
2. Developing the trend line
3. Finding the cyclical variation around the trend line

Step 1: Computing seasonal indices

Since the data are available on a quarterly basis, we must first deseasonalize the time series. The steps to do this are shown in Table 13-15 and 13-16. These steps are the same as those originally introduced in section 5 of this chapter.

In Table 13-15, we have tabulated the first four steps in computing the seasonal index. In Table 13-16, we complete the process.

TABLE 13-14 Quarterly Sales

| YEAR | Sales per quarter ($\times$ $10,000) | | | |
	I	II	III	IV
1985	16	21	9	18
1986	15	20	10	18
1987	17	24	13	22
1988	17	25	11	21
1989	18	26	14	25

TABLE 13-15 Calculation of the First 4 Steps to Compute the Seasonal Index

YEAR (1)	QUARTER (2)	ACTUAL SALES (3)	STEP 1 4-QUARTER MOVING TOTAL (4)	STEP 2 4-QUARTER MOVING AVERAGE $(5)=\frac{(4)}{4}$	STEP 3 4-QUARTER CENTERED MOVING AVERAGE (6)	STEP 4 PERCENTAGE OF ACTUAL TO MOVING AVERAGE $(7)=\frac{(3)}{(6)}\times 100$
1985	I	16				
	II	21				
			64	16.00		
	III	9			15.825	56.7
			63	15.75		
	IV	18			15.625	115.2
			62	15.50		
1986	I	15			15.625	96.0
			63	15.75		
	II	20			15.750	127.0
			63	15.75		
	III	10			16.000	62.5
			65	16.25		
	IV	18			16.750	107.5
			69	17.25		
1987	I	17			17.625	96.5
			72	18.00		
	II	24			18.500	129.7
			76	19.00		
	III	13			19.000	68.4
			76	19.00		
	IV	22			19.125	115.0
			77	19.25		
1988	I	17			19.000	89.5
			75	18.75		
	II	25			18.625	134.2
			74	18.50		
	III	11			18.625	59.1
			75	18.75		
	IV	21			18.875	111.3
			76	19.00		
1989	I	18			19.375	92.9
			79	19.75		
	II	26			20.250	128.4
			83	20.75		
	III	14				
	IV	25				

Finding the deseasonalized values

Once we have computed the quarterly seasonal indices, we can find the deseasonalized values of the time series by dividing the actual sales (in Table 13-14) by the seasonal indices. Table 13-17 (on page 680) shows the calculation of the deseasonalized time series values.

Step 2: Developing the trend line using the least squares method

The second step in describing the components of the time series is to develop the trend line. We accomplish this by applying the least squares method to the deseasonalized time series (after we have translated the time variable). Table 13-18 presents the calculations to identify the trend component (see page 681).

With the values from Table 13-18, we can now find the equation for the trend. From Equations 13-3 and 13-4 we find the slope and Y-intercept for the trend line as follows:

$$b = \frac{\Sigma xY}{\Sigma x^2} \qquad [13\text{-}3]$$

$$= \frac{420.3}{2,660}$$

$$= .16$$

$$a = \overline{Y} \qquad [13\text{-}4]$$

$$= 18.0$$

TABLE 13-16 Steps 5 and 6 in Computing the Seasonal Index

		Step 5*		
YEAR	I	II	III	IV
1985	—	—	56.7	115.2
1986	96.0	127.0	62.5	107.5
1987	96.5	129.7	68.4	115.0
1988	89.5	134.2	59.1	111.3
1989	92.9	128.4	—	—
Modified sum =	**188.9**	**258.1**	**121.6**	**226.3**

Modified mean: Quarter $I \dfrac{188.9}{2} = 94.45$

$II \dfrac{258.1}{2} = 129.05$

$III \dfrac{121.6}{2} = 60.80$

$IV \dfrac{226.3}{2} = \underline{113.15}$
$\phantom{IV \dfrac{226.3}{2} = }\textbf{397.45}$

* Arrange percentages from column 7, Table 13-15, by quarter and find the modified mean.

Step 6†

Adjusting factor $= \dfrac{400}{397.45} = 1.0064$

QUARTER	INDICES	×	ADJUSTING FACTOR	=	SEASONAL INDICES
I	94.45	×	1.0064	=	95.1
II	129.05	×	1.0064	=	129.9
III	60.80	×	1.0064	=	61.2
IV	113.15	×	1.0064	=	113.9
			Sum of seasonal indices	=	**400.1**

† Correcting the indices in step 5.

The appropriate trend line is described using the straight-line equation (Equation 10-3), with X replaced by x:

$$\hat{Y} = a + bx \qquad\qquad [10\text{-}3]$$
$$= 18 + .16x$$

Step 3: Finding the cyclical variation

We have now identified the seasonal and trend components of the time series. Next we find the cyclical variation around the trend line. This component is identified by measuring deseasonalized variation around the trend line. In this problem, we will calculate cyclical variation in Table 13-19, using the residual method. (See page 682.)

Assumptions about irregular variation

If we assume that irregular variation is generally short-term and relatively insignificant, we have completely described the time series in this problem using the trend, cyclical, and seasonal components. Figure 13-8 (on page 683) illustrates the original time series, its moving average (containing both the trend and cyclical components), and the trend line.

Predictions using time series

Now suppose that the management of the recreation company we have been using as an example wants to estimate the sales volume for the third quarter of 1990. What should the management do?

TABLE 13-17 Calculation of Deseasonalized Time Series Values

YEAR (1)	QUARTER (2)	ACTUAL SALES (3)	SEASONAL INDEX 100 (4)	DESEASONALIZED SALES (5) = (3) ÷ (4)
1985	I	16	.951	16.8
	II	21	1.299	16.2
	III	9	.612	14.7
	IV	18	1.139	15.8
1986	I	15	.951	15.8
	II	20	1.299	15.4
	III	10	.612	16.3
	IV	18	1.139	15.8
1987	I	17	.951	17.9
	II	24	1.299	18.5
	III	13	.612	21.2
	IV	22	1.139	19.3
1988	I	17	.951	17.9
	II	25	1.299	19.2
	III	11	.612	18.0
	IV	21	1.139	18.4
1989	I	18	.951	18.9
	II	26	1.299	20.0
	III	14	.612	22.9
	IV	25	1.139	21.9

Step 1: Determining the deseasonalized value for sales for the period desired

1. It has to determine the deseasonalized value for sales in the third quarter of 1990 by using the trend equation, $\hat{Y} = 18 + .16x$. This requires it to code the time, 1990-III. That quarter (1990-III) is three quarters past 1989-IV, which, we see in Table 13-18, has a coded time value of 19. Adding 2 for each quarter, management finds $x = 19 + 2(3) = 25$. Substituting this value ($x = 25$) into the trend equation produces the following result:

$$\hat{Y} = a + bx \qquad\qquad [10\text{-}3]$$
$$= 18 + .16(25)$$
$$= 18 + 4$$
$$= 22$$

Thus, the deseasonalized sales estimate for 1990-III is $220,000. This point is shown on the trend line in Fig. 13-8.

Step 2: Seasonalizing the initial estimate

2. Now management must seasonalize this estimate by multiplying it by the third-quarter seasonal index, expressed as a percent:

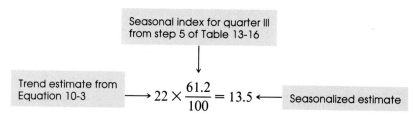

Caution in using the forecast

On the basis of this analysis, the firm estimates that sales for 1990-III will be $135,000. We must stress, however, that this value is only an estimate and does not take into account the cyclical and irregular components. As we noted earlier,

TABLE 13-18 Identifying the Trend Component

YEAR (1)	QUARTER (2)	Y DESEASONALIZED SALES (COLUMN 5 OF TABLE 13-17) (×\$10,000) (3)	(½x) TRANSLATING OR CODING THE TIME VARIABLE (4)	x (5) = (4) × 2	xY (6) = (5) × (3)	x^2 (7) = (5)²
1985	I	16.8	$-9\frac{1}{2}$	-19	-319.2	361
	II	16.2	$-8\frac{1}{2}$	-17	-275.4	289
	III	14.7	$-7\frac{1}{2}$	-15	-220.5	225
	IV	15.8	$-6\frac{1}{2}$	-13	-205.4	169
1986	I	15.8	$-5\frac{1}{2}$	-11	-173.8	121
	II	15.4	$-4\frac{1}{2}$	-9	-138.6	81
	III	16.3	$-3\frac{1}{2}$	-7	-114.1	49
	IV	15.8	$-2\frac{1}{2}$	-5	-79.0	25
1987	I	17.9	$-1\frac{1}{2}$	-3	-53.7	9
	II	18.5	$-\frac{1}{2}$	-1	-18.5	1
Mean			0*			
	III	21.2	$\frac{1}{2}$	1	21.2	1
	IV	19.3	$1\frac{1}{2}$	3	57.9	9
1988	I	17.9	$2\frac{1}{2}$	5	89.5	25
	II	19.2	$3\frac{1}{2}$	7	134.4	49
	III	18.0	$4\frac{1}{2}$	9	162.0	81
	IV	18.4	$5\frac{1}{2}$	11	202.4	121
1989	I	18.9	$6\frac{1}{2}$	13	245.7	169
	II	20.0	$7\frac{1}{2}$	15	300.0	225
	III	22.9	$8\frac{1}{2}$	17	389.3	289
	IV	21.9	$9\frac{1}{2}$	19	416.1	361
		$\Sigma Y = 360.9$			$\Sigma xY = 420.3$	$\Sigma x^2 = 2{,}660$

$$\bar{Y} = \frac{\Sigma Y}{n}$$

$$= \frac{360.9}{20}$$

$$= 18.0$$

* We assign the mean of 0 to the middle of the data (1987-II½) and then measure the translated time, x by ½ quarters because we have an even number of periods.

the irregular variation cannot be predicted mathematically. Also, remember that our earlier treatment of cyclical variation was descriptive of past behavior and not predictive of future behavior.

Exercises

 13-37 A state commission designed to monitor energy consumption assembled the following seasonal data regarding natural gas consumption, in millions of cubic feet:

	WINTER	SPRING	SUMMER	FALL
1986	293	246	231	282
1987	301	252	227	291
1988	304	259	239	296
1989	306	265	240	300

TABLE 13-19 Identifying the Cyclical Variation

YEAR (1)	QUARTER (2)	Y DESEASONALIZED SALES (COLUMN 5, TABLE 13-17) (3)	$a + bx = \hat{Y}*$ (4)	$\dfrac{Y}{\hat{Y}} \times 100$ PERCENT OF TREND $(15) = \dfrac{(3)}{(4)} \times 100$
1985	I	16.8	$18 + .16(-19) = 14.96$	112.3
	II	16.2	$18 + .16(-17) = 15.28$	106.0
	III	14.7	$18 + .16(-15) = 15.60$	94.2
	IV	15.8	$18 + .16(-13) = 15.92$	99.2
1986	I	15.8	$18 + .16(-11) = 16.24$	97.3
	II	15.4	$18 + .16(-9) = 16.56$	93.0
	III	16.3	$18 + .16(-7) = 16.88$	96.6
	IV	15.8	$18 + .16(-5) = 17.20$	91.9
1987	I	17.9	$18 + .16(-3) = 17.52$	102.2
	II	18.5	$18 + .16(-1) = 17.84$	103.7
	III	21.2	$18 + .16(1) = 18.16$	116.7
	IV	19.3	$18 + .16(3) = 18.48$	104.4
1988	I	17.9	$18 + .16(5) = 18.80$	95.2
	II	19.2	$18 + .16(7) = 19.12$	100.4
	III	18.0	$18 + .16(9) = 19.44$	92.6
	IV	18.4	$18 + .16(11) = 19.76$	93.1
1989	I	18.9	$18 + .16(13) = 20.08$	94.1
	II	20.0	$18 + .16(15) = 20.40$	98.0
	III	22.9	$18 + .16(17) = 20.72$	110.5
	IV	21.9	$18 + .16(19) = 21.04$	104.1

* The appropriate value for *x* in this equation is obtained from column 5 of Table 13-18.

(a) Determine the seasonal indices and deseasonalize these data (using a 4-quarter centered moving average).
(b) Calculate the least squares line that best describes these data.
(c) Identify the cyclical variation in these data by the relative cyclical residual method.
(d) Plot the original data, the deseasonalized data, and the trend.

13-38 The following data describe the marketing performance of a regional beer producer:

SALES BY QUARTER (×$100,000)

YEAR	I	II	III	IV
1985	19	24	38	25
1986	21	28	44	23
1987	23	31	41	23
1988	24	35	48	21

(a) Calculate the seasonal indices for these data. (Use a 4-quarter centered moving average.)
(b) Deseasonalize these data using the indices from part (a).

13-39 For exercise 13-38:
(a) Find the least squares line that best describes the trend in deseasonalized beer sales.
(b) Identify the cyclical component in this time series by computing the percent of trend.

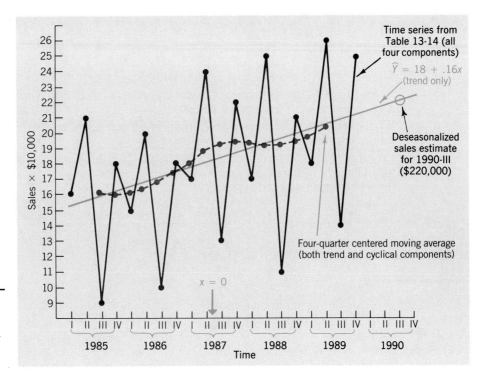

FIGURE 13-8

Time series, trend line, and 4-quarter centered moving average for quarterly sales data in Table 13-14

13-8
Time Series Analysis in Forecasting

In this chapter, we have examined all four components of a time series. We have described the process of projecting past trend and seasonal variation into the future, while taking into consideration the inherent inaccuracies of this analysis. In addition, we noted that although the irregular and cyclical components do affect the future, they are erratic and difficult to use in forecasting.

Recognizing limitations of time series analysis

We must realize that the mechanical approach of time series analysis is subject to considerable error and change. It is necessary for management to combine these simple procedures with knowledge of other factors in order to develop workable forecasts. Analysts are constantly revising, updating, and discarding their forecasts. If we wish to cope successfully with the future, we must do the same.

When using the procedures described in this chapter, we should pay attention particularly to the two following problems:

1. In forecasting, we project past trend and seasonal variation into the future. We must ask, "How regular and lasting were the past trends? What are the chances that these patterns are changing?"

2. How accurate are the historical data we use in series analysis? If a company has changed from a FIFO (first-in, first-out) to a LIFO (last-in, first-out) inventory accounting system in a period during the time under consideration, the data (such as quarterly profits) before and after the change are not comparable and not very useful for forecasting.

Exercises

13-40 List 4 errors that can affect forecasting with time series.

13-41 When using time series to predict the future, what assurances do we need about the historical data on which our forecasts are based?

13-42 What problems would you see developing if we used past college enrollments to predict future college enrollments?

13-43 How would forecasts using time series analysis handle things such as:
   (a) Changes in the federal tax laws?
   (b) Changes in accounting systems?

13-9
Terms Introduced in Chapter 13

Coding A method of converting traditional measures of time to a form that simplifies computation (often called translating).

Cyclical Fluctuation A type of variation in time series, in which the value of the variable fluctuates above and below a secular trend line.

Deseasonalization A statistical process used to remove the effects of seasonality from a time series.

Irregular Variation A condition in time series when the value of a variable is completely unpredictable.

Modified Mean A statistical method used in time series. Discards the highest and lowest values when computing a mean.

Ratio-to-Moving-Average Method A statistical method used to measure seasonal variation. Employs an index describing the degree of that variation.

Relative Cyclical Residual A measure of cyclical variation, it uses the percentage deviation from the trend for each value in the series.

Residual Method A method of describing the cyclical component of a time series. It assumes that most of the variation in the series not explained by the secular trend is cyclical variation.

Seasonal Variation Patterns of change in a time series within a year; patterns that tend to be repeated from year to year.

Second-Degree Equation A mathematical form used to describe a parabolic curve that may be used in time series trend analysis.

Secular Trend A type of variation in time series, the value of the variable tending to increase or decrease over a long period of time.

Time Series Information accumulated at regular intervals and the statistical methods used to determine patterns in such data.

13-10
Equations Introduced in Chapter 13

[13-1]

$$b = \frac{\Sigma XY - n\overline{X}\,\overline{Y}}{\Sigma X^2 - n\overline{X}^2}$$

p. 656

This formula, originally introduced in Chapter 10 as Equation 10-4, enables us to calculate the *slope of the best-fitting regression line* for any two-variable set of data points. The symbols $\overline{X}$ and $\overline{Y}$ represent the means of the value of the independent variable and dependent variable respectively; n represents the number of data points with which we are fitting the line.

[13-2]

$$a = \overline{Y} - b\overline{X}$$

p. 656

We met this formula as Equation 10-5. It enables us to compute the *Y-intercept of the best-fitting regression line* for any 2-variable set of data points.

[13-3]
$$b = \frac{\Sigma xY}{\Sigma x^2}$$
p. 657

When the individual years (X) are changed to coded time values (x) by subtracting out the mean ($x = X - \overline{X}$), Equation 13-1 for the slope of the trend line is simplified and becomes Equation 13-3.

[13-4]
$$a = \overline{Y}$$
p. 657

In a similar fashion, using coded time values also allows us to simplify Equation 13-2 for the intercept of the trend line.

[13-5]
$$\hat{Y} = a + bx + cx^2$$
p. 659

Sometimes we wish to fit a trend with a parabolic (or second-degree) curve instead of a straight line ($\hat{Y} = a + bx$). The general form for a fitted second-degree curve is obtained by including the second-degree term (cx^2) in the equation for $\hat{Y}$.

[13-6]
$$\Sigma Y = an + c\Sigma x^2$$
p. 660

[13-7]
$$\Sigma x^2 Y = a\Sigma x^2 + c\Sigma x^4$$
p. 660

In order to find the least squares second-degree fitted curve, we must solve Equations 13-6 and 13-7 simultaneously for the values of a and c. The value for b is obtained from Equation 13-3.

[13-8]
$$\text{Percent of trend} = \frac{Y}{\hat{Y}} \times 100$$
p. 665

We can measure cyclical variation as a *percent of trend* by dividing the actual value (Y) by the trend value ($\hat{Y}$) and then multiplying by 100.

[13-9]
$$\text{Relative cyclical residual} = \frac{Y - \hat{Y}}{\hat{Y}} \times 100$$
p. 666

Another measure of cyclical variation is the *relative cyclical residual,* obtained by dividing the deviation from the trend ($Y - \hat{Y}$) by the trend value, and multiplying the result by 100. The relative cyclical residual can easily be obtained by subtracting 100 from the percent of trend.

13-11
Chapter Review Exercises

13-44   The owner of an air-conditioning and heating company is examining data regarding quarterly revenue (in thousands of dollars). He wants to determine the trend in his business.

	SPRING	SUMMER	FALL	WINTER
1986	29	30	41	43
1987	27	34	45	48
1988	33	36	46	51
1989	34	40	47	53

(a) Calculate the seasonal indices for these data (use a 4-quarter centered moving average).
(b) Deseasonalize these data, using the indices from part (a).
(c) Find the least squares line that best describes these data.

13-45 Wheeler Airline, a regional carrier, has estimated the number of passengers to be 595,000 (deseasonalized) for the month of December. How many passengers should the company anticipate if the December seasonal index is 128?

13-46 An EPA research group has measured the level of mercury contamination in the ocean at a certain point off the East Coast. The following percentages of mercury were found in the water:

	JAN.	FEB.	MAR.	APR.	MAY	JUNE	JULY	AUG.	SEPT.	OCT.	NOV.	DEC.
1987	.3	.7	.8	.8	.7	.7	.6	.6	.4	.7	.2	.5
1988	.4	.9	.7	.9	.5	.8	.7	.7	.4	.6	.3	.4
1989	.2	.6	.6	.9	.7	.7	.8	.8	.5	.6	.3	.5

Construct a 4-month centered moving average, and plot it on a graph along with the original data.

13-47 A production manager for a Canadian paper mill has accumulated the following information describing the millions of pounds processed quarterly:

	WINTER	SPRING	SUMMER	FALL
1986	3.1	5.1	5.6	3.6
1987	3.3	5.1	5.8	3.7
1988	3.4	5.3	6.0	3.8
1989	3.7	5.4	6.1	3.9

(a) Calculate the seasonal indices for these data (percentage of actual to centered moving average)
(b) Deseasonalize these data, using the seasonal indices from part (a).
(c) Find the least squares line that best describes these data.
(d) Estimate the number of pounds that will be processed during the spring of 1990.

13-48 Describe some of the difficulties in using a linear estimating equation to describe these data:
(a) Gasoline mileage achieved by U.S. automobiles.
(b) Fatalities in commercial aviation.
(c) The grain exports of a single country.
(d) The price of gasoline.

13-49 Comment on the difficulties you would have using a second-degree estimating equation to predict the future behavior of the process which generated these data:
(a) Sales of personal computers in the U.S.
(b) Use of video games in the U.S.
(c) Premiums for medical malpractice insurance.
(d) The number of M.B.A.s graduated from U.S. universities.

13-50 John Barry, a hospital administrator planning for a new emergency-room facility, has examined the number of patients who have visited the present facility during each of the last 6 years.

Year	1984	1985	1986	1987	1988	1989
Number of patients (×100)	596	688	740	812	857	935

(a) Find the linear equation that describes the trend in the number of patients visiting the emergency room.
(b) Estimate for him the number of patients the hospital's emergency room should be prepared to accommodate in 1991.

13-51 An assistant undersecretary in the U.S. Commerce Department has the following data describing the value of grain exported during the last 15 quarters (in billions of dollars):

	I	II	III	IV
1986	1	3	6	4
1987	2	2	7	5
1988	2	4	8	5
1989	1	3	8	6

(a) Determine the seasonal indices and deseasonalize these data (using a 4-quarter centered moving average).
(b) Calculate the least squares line that best describes these data.
(c) Identify the cyclical variation in these data by the relative cyclical residual method.
(d) Plot the original data, the deseasonalized data, and the trend.

13-52 Richie Bell's College Bicycle Shop has determined from a previous trend analysis that spring sales should be 165 bicycles (deseasonalized). If the spring seasonal index is 143, how many bicycles should the shop sell this spring?

13-53 With the U.S. Interstate Highway program nearly finished, of what use are old data to the manufacturers of heavy earth-moving equipment as they attempt to forecast sales? What new data would you suggest they utilize in their forecasting?

13-54 R. B. Fitch Builders has completed these numbers of homes in the 8 years it has been in business:

Year	1982	1983	1984	1985	1986	1987	1988	1989
Completions	12	11	19	17	19	18	20	23

(a) Develop the linear estimating equation which best describes the trend of completions.
(b) How many completions should R. B. plan on for 1993?
(c) Along with the answer to part (b), what advice would you give R. B. about using this forecasting technique?

13-55 As part of an investigation being done by a federal agency into the psychology of criminal activity, a survey of the number of homicides and assaults over the course of a year produced the following results:

SEASON	SPRING	SUMMER	FALL	WINTER
Number of homicides and assaults	31,000	52,000	39,000	29,000

(a) If the corresponding seasonal indices are 84, 134, 103, and 79, respectively, what are the deseasonalized values for each season?
(b) What is the meaning of the seasonal index of 79 for the winter season?

13-56 A state's quarterly deseasonalized unemployment percentage figures for years 1985–89 are as follows:

	I	II	III	IV
1985	7.3	7.2	7.3	8.1
1986	8.7	9.2	9.8	10.5
1987	10.2	9.9	9.2	8.3
1988	7.6	7.4	7.5	7.6
1989	7.4	7.0	6.8	6.5

(a) Find the linear equation that describes this unemployment trend.
(b) Calculate the percent of trend for these data.
(c) Plot the cyclical variation in the unemployment rates from the percent of trend figures.

13-57 The number of confirmed AIDS cases reported at a local health clinic during the five years from 1985 to 1989 were 2, 4, 7, 13, and 21 respectively.
(a) Develop the linear regression line for these data.
(b) Find the least squares second-degree curve for these data.
(c) Construct a table of each year's actual cases, the linear estimates from the regression in part (a), and the second-degree values from the curve in part (b).
(d) Which regression appears to be the better estimator?

13-58 The manager of Pizza Pizzaz Pizza Parlor wishes to estimate the future sales of a new menu item based on the first seven weeks of sales data. The weekly sales volumes are as follows:

Week	1	2	3	4	5	6	7
Sales	41	52	79	76	72	59	41

(a) Find the linear regression line that best fits these data.
(b) Estimate the expected number of sales for week 8.
(c) Based on the estimate in part (b) and the available data, does the regression accurately describe the sales trend for this item?

13-59 The College Town busing system has collected the following count of passengers per season during 1988 and 1989. The deseasonalized data (in thousands of passengers) are:

	SPRING	SUMMER	FALL	WINTER
1988	593	545	610	575
1989	640	560	600	555

(a) If the seasonal indices used to deseasonalize these data were 110, 73, 113, and 104, respectively, find the actual passenger counts (in thousands) for these eight seasons.
(b) Which season in 1989 saw the fewest passengers? The most?
(c) If the linear estimating equation for these deseasonalized data is $\hat{Y} = 584.75 - .45x$ (with x measured in ½ quarters and $x = 0$ between the winter 1988 and spring 1989 quarters), what is the expected number of actual riders (in thousands) for the fall 1990 season?

13-60 Ferris Wheeler, director of the Whirly World amusement park, has provided the following attendance data (in thousands of admissions) for the park's open seasons:

	SPRING	SUMMER	FALL
1986	750	1,150	680
1987	780	1,100	580
1988	800	1,225	610
1989	640	1,050	600

(a) Calculate the seasonal indices for these data using a 3-period moving average.
(b) Deseasonalize these data, using the seasonal indices from part (a).

13-61 A restaurant manager wishes to improve customer service and employee scheduling based on the daily levels of customers in the past four weeks. The numbers of customers served in the restaurant during that period were:

		MON	TUE	WED	THU	FRI	SAT	SUN
	1	345	310	385	416	597	706	653
Week	2	418	333	400	515	664	761	702
	3	393	387	311	535	625	711	598
	4	406	412	377	444	650	803	822

Determine the seasonal (daily) indices for these data. (Use a 7-day moving average.)

13-62 Suppose television sales by a small appliance chain for the years 1985 – 1989 were as follows:

Year	1985	1986	1987	1988	1989
Sales	230	250	265	300	310

(a) Develop the second-degree estimating equation for these data.
(b) What do the magnitudes of the coefficients a, b, and c tell you about the choice of a second-degree equation for these data?

13-63 The Zapit Company has recorded the following numbers (in hundreds of thousands) of total sales of its line of microwave ovens over the last five years:

Year	1985	1986	1987	1988	1989
Sales	3.5	3.8	4.0	3.7	3.9

The equation describing the trend for these sales volumes is:

$$\hat{Y} = 3.78 + .07x, \text{ where } 1987 = 0 \text{ and } x \text{ units} = 1 \text{ year}$$

(a) Which year had the largest percent of trend?
(b) Which year was closest to the trend line?

13-12
Chapter Concepts Test

Answers are in the back of the book.

T F 1. Time series analysis is used to detect patterns of change in statistical information over regular intervals of time.

T F 2. Secular trends represent the long-term direction of a time series.

T F 3. When coding time values, we subtract from each value the smallest time value in the series; hence, the code of the smallest value is zero.

T F 4. When using the least squares method to determine a second-degree equation of best fit, the values of four numerical constants must be determined.

T F 5. Time series analysis helps us to analyze past trends, but it cannot aid us in future uncertainties.

T F 6. When we are predicting far into the future, a second-degree equation usually gives more accurate predictions than a linear equation.

T F 7. When using the residual method, we assume that the cyclical component explains most of the variation left unexplained by the trend component.

T F 8. The relative cyclical residual can be computed for an entry in a time series by subtracting 10 from the percent of trend for that entry.

T F 9. The repetitive movement around a trend line in a 2-year period is best described as seasonal.

T F 10. Once seasonal indices are computed for a time series, the series can be deseasonalized so that only the trend component remains.

T F 11. The percent of trend should not be used for predicting future cyclical variations.

T F 12. Over time, random movements tend to counteract one another in irregular variation in a time series.

T F 13. Before percent of trend can be calculated, a trend line (graph of $\hat{Y}$) must first be calculated.

T F 14. If a time series contains an odd number of elements, then the coding for some of the entries will be in half-units.

T F 15. To be considered a time series, a group of statistical information must have been accumulated at *regular* intervals.

T F 16. Of the four types of variation, cyclical is the most difficult to predict.

T F 17. Seasonal variation is a repetitive and predictable variation around the trend line within a year.

T F 18. To picture the isolated cyclical component of a time series, we may graph either the percent of trend values or the relative cyclical residual values.

T F 19. The adjusted seasonal indices must always sum to 400.

T F 20. A time series should be deseasonalized after the trend or cyclical components of the time series have been identified.

T F 21. Removing the highest and lowest actual-to-moving-average values from each period when computing a seasonal index reduces the extreme cyclical and irregular variations.

22. A time series of annual data can contain which of the following components?
(a) Secular trend   (c) Seasonal variation   (e) a and b but not c
(b) Cyclical fluctuation   (d) All of these

23. Suppose you were considering a time series of data for the quarters of 1989 and 1990. The third quarter of 1990 would be coded as:
(a) 2   (b) 3   (c) 5   (d) 6

24. Suppose that a particular time series should be fitted with a parabolic curve. The general form for this second-degree equation is $\hat{Y} = a + bx + cx^2$. What do the x's represent in this formula?
(a) Coded values of the time variables
(b) A numerical constant that is determined by a formula
(c) Estimates of the dependent variable
(d) None of these

25. Assume that a time series with annual data for the years 1982–1990 is described well by the second-degree equation $\hat{Y} = 5 + 3x + 9x^2$. Based only upon this secular trend, what is the forecast value for 1991?
(a) 161   (b) 245   (c) 347   (d) 293.75   (e) 200.75

26. Suppose that the linear equation $\hat{Y} = 10 + 3x$ describes well an annual time series for 1984–1990. If the actual value of Y for 1987 is 8, what is the percent of trend for 1987?
(a) 125%   (b) 112.5%   (c) 90%   (d) 80%

27. A time series for the years 1979–1990 had the following relative cyclical residuals, in chronological order: −1%, −2%, 1%, 2%, −1%, −2%, 1%, 2%, −1%, −2%, 1%, 2%. The relative cyclical residual for 1991 should be:
(a) 3%   (c) −2%
(b) −1%   (d) Cannot be determined from information given

28. Assume that you have been given quarterly sales data for a 5-year period. To use the ratio-to-moving-average method of computing a seasonal index, your first step would be:
(a) Compute the 4-quarter moving average.
(b) Discard highest and lowest values for each quarter.
(c) Calculate the 4-quarter moving total.
(d) None of these.

Questions 29 through 31 deal with a seasonal index being computed, using the ratio-to-moving-average method for quarterly data from 1986–1990. The percentages of actual to moving average for the third quarter of each year are:

1986: 109.0; 1987: 112.8; 1988: 110.0; 1989: 108.0; 1990: 104.6

29. What is the *unadjusted* index for the third quarter?
    (a) 108.88   (b) 109.0   (c) 110.23   (d) 110.96   (e) None of these

30. Assume that the total of the unadjusted indices for the four quarters is 404.04. If the unadjusted index for the first quarter is 97.0, what is the adjusted seasonal index for the first quarter?
    (a) 96.03   (c) 24.01   (e) Cannot be determined from information given
    (b) 97.98   (d) 99.00

31. The adjusted seasonal index for the fourth quarter is 95.0. If the deseasonalized trend line that was calculated to estimate quarterly sales is $\hat{Y} = 400 + 9x$, what would be the seasonalized sales estimate for the fourth quarter of 1991?
    (a) 499.7   (b) 643.0   (c) 610.85   (d) 676.8

32. If a time series has an even number of years, and we use coding, then each coded interval is equal to:
    (a) 1 year   (c) 1 month   (e) None of these
    (b) 2 years   (d) 6 months

33. A method used to deal with cyclical variation when the cyclical component does not explain most of the variation left unexplained by the trend component is:
    (a) Spearman analysis   (c) Second-degree analysis   (e) All of these
    (b) Specific analysis   (d) Relative cyclical residual   (f) None of these

34. For a given year, if an adjusted seasonal index for some period is greater than 100, then the following must be true:
    (a) The adjusted index for some other period is > 100.
    (b) The adjusted index for some other period is < 100.
    (c) The adjusted index for some other period is $= 100$.
    (d) a and b but not c.
    (e) None of the above.

35. If the percent of trend for a particular year in a time series is greater than 100% then for this year:
    (a) The actual time series value lies below the trend line, and the relative cyclical residual is negative.
    (b) The actual time series value lies below the trend line, and the relative cyclical residual is positive.
    (c) The actual time series value lies above the trend line, and the relative cyclical residual is negative.
    (d) The actual time series value lies above the trend line, and the relative cyclical residual is positive.

36. Which of the following are common reasons for studying both secular trends and seasonal variation:
    (a) to allow the elimination of the component from the series
    (b) to describe past patterns
    (c) to project past patterns into the future
    (d) all of the above
    (e) none of the above

37. Dividing each actual value in a time series by the corresponding trend value, and multiplying by 100, gives the _____.

38. Repetitive and predictable movement around the trend line in one year or less is _____ variation.

39. _____ variation in time series is characterized by unpredictable, random movement and usually occurs over short intervals.

40. _____ variation is the time series component that oscillates above and below the trend line for periods longer than one year.

41. Using seasonal indices to remove effects of seasonality from a time series is known as _____ the time series.

42. The first step in computing a seasonal index is to calculate the _____.

43. The steady increase in the cost of living recorded by the CPI (Consumer Price Index) is an example of a _____.

44. The result of discarding the highest and lowest values before averaging is called a _____.

45. A _____ is a projection of past patterns into the future.

13-13
Conceptual Case

(Northern White Metals Company)

"I just wanted to let you know we appreciated your help on that trucking decision," Dick said into the phone.

"Well, thank you, but it was nothing," replied Jody. "How did everything turn out?"

"Turned out fine," Dick answered. "Don Wills and Dave Lillich negotiated a great deal for us. They're a shrewd pair, even for flashy New York lawyers," he chuckled.

"So I hear," Jody replied. "By the way, what did you think of that sales analysis Sarah ran for you? Was it helpful?"

Dick replied that it was indeed helpful and that he especially appreciated the brief explanatory discourse on regression analysis that accompanied it. He further noted that he had nearly completed Northern's 1984 sales plan and was about to begin work formulating his general 5-year business plan. This would be submitted to Segue corporate management and would include anticipated new equipment requirements, cost estimates, and financing needs as well as long-run sales projections.

"Which brings to mind a question," he continued. "I think it's safe to state that high-tech applications sales, which we're still rather new in, will continue to increase at the present rate. It's a booming business, and I don't see it fluctuating like building products sales do. The point is, I'm having trouble trying to forecast sales in construction-related products, in spite of our long history of selling to this industry. You've seen the data, Jody; what do you think?" Dick asked.

"I see your problem," Jody replied, thinking. "I agree with your conclusions about high-tech products, at least from what I've seen so far. I'll need some more information on Northern's past building-product sales, but I think we can help you out."

"I also need some idea about trends in aluminum raw material prices," Dick added. "I think they tend to move with the business cycle, a lot like construction does, but I need a better idea of where they might be heading so I can forecast production costs, too."

"No problem, Dick," Jody said reassuringly. "Look forward to hearing from you."

Dick needs some assistance in analyzing historical data to help him make inferences about the future— that is, to aid him in developing a workable 5-year plan. What information does he have to provide to Jody, and how will she analyze this information to help Dick formulate his projections? What words of advice about interpreting the analysis should she pass to Dick so he can make the best use of it?

13-14
Computer Data Base Exercise

 The following week, Stan approached Laurel about some data for his upcoming quarterly sales meeting. "If you remember those first talks we had about the company's history," he said, "you'll remember my telling you how seals and seal kits, our most extensive product line, are the cornerstone of our sales. In fact, it's the product line Mr. Douglas basically started the business with. As it turns out, it's also the product line which generates our largest gross margin percentage. Is there anything you could do in the way of charts or graphs which would illustrate the behavior of seal sales over the last 10 years or so? I've got either daily or monthly data you could work with."

"What if I deseasonalize the data, to show a more accurate rate of growth?" Laurel suggested. "I could use the monthly sales figures and generate some graphs showing the trends. By calculating a least-squares estimate, I could also give you a rough predictive tool for anticipating seal sales, deseasonalized that is, for the next few years. How does that sound?"

"You lost me on the least-squares part," Stan admitted, "but that sounds exactly like the type of thing I'm looking for. It will be interesting to see how sales look without seasonal trends. Can you

have a rough draft of the figures by the first part of next week?"

"You bet," answered Laurel. "I'll bring it all by your office Monday or Tuesday."

1. Do a time-series analysis of seal sales over the last 10 years. Deseasonalize sales by month, using the ratio-to-moving-average method. (Use a 12-month centered moving average.) Then find the least-squares linear equation that best describes the deseasonalized data.
2. Use your results to forecast sales for each month of 1991.
3. Look at the residuals associated with the linear regression equation. Is there any pattern that might cause you to be suspicious that a straight line is not the best fit?

TABLE DB13-1 Monthly Seal Sales (1981–1990)

	J	F	M	A	M	J	J	A	S	O	N	D
1981	1,421	1,434	1,952	1,533	1,853	1,516	1,663	1,969	1,304	1,465	1,369	979
1982	1,535	1,549	2,108	1,656	2,001	1,637	1,796	2,127	1,408	1,582	1,478	1,057
1983	1,381	1,395	1,897	1,490	1,801	1,473	1,619	1,914	1,347	1,424	1,330	1,360
1984	1,561	1,576	2,144	1,684	2,035	1,665	1,829	2,163	1,522	1,609	1,503	1,511
1985	1,734	1,751	2,382	1,871	2,261	1,850	2,029	2,403	1,591	1,788	1,670	1,194
1986	2,232	1,704	1,733	2,017	2,258	1,914	1,895	2,429	2,028	2,371	1,557	1,381
1987	1,867	1,873	2,053	1,906	2,465	2,094	2,691	2,331	2,233	2,828	2,008	1,901
1988	2,365	2,060	2,242	2,820	2,409	2,191	2,871	2,414	2,890	2,380	2,730	2,157
1989	2,662	2,590	2,799	2,605	2,907	2,513	3,230	3,171	3,126	3,676	2,610	2,804
1990	3,328	3,237	3,500	3,256	3,630	3,141	4,037	3,964	3,910	4,595	3,263	3,505

13-15
From the Textbook to the Real World

Icelandic Fisheries

A model has been developed for the Ministry of Fisheries in Iceland to facilitate decision making in fisheries management. It is used primarily for short-term management of quota systems and long-term investment planning. With this model, predictions can be made about catches of cod and other demersal species several years ahead. Earnings and cost information can also be calculated. Analysts collect data on a number of variables, including the size of the fish stocks in the beginning of the planning period and the size and classification of the fishing fleet. Recent studies indicate that the fishing fleet is far too

large, and unless adequate measures can be taken to limit fishing off the Icelandic coast, the backbone of the Icelandic economy may be threatened.

BACKGROUND: Fishing is the dominant industry in Iceland's economy, with fish and fish products representing approximately 70% of the country's exports. The demersal species is the most important species of fish in Iceland, and cod accounts for 55% of the demersal catch. Until 1976, when Iceland gained full sovereignty over her fishing grounds, foreign vessels accounted for about half of the total catch. Icelandic fishing companies began modernizing their fleets as early as 1970, in anticipation of the removal of foreign competition. As the fleet grew in size and became more efficient, concerns about stock protection arose. Stock size estimations prepared in 1975 indicated that the cod stock was down to less than half of its average size for the post-war period. Furthermore, the age and structure of the catch was not favorable. Despite the removal of foreign fishing vessels, the total fishing effort hardly decreased due to modern fishing techniques and equipment. By 1983, the cod catch reached an all-time low. Authorities and the fishing industry realized the fishing fleet, and hence the effort expended, was too large. Expansion of the fleet must be contained. Initially, the fishing period was restricted by enforcing extended Christmas and Easter vacations for fishermen and also by setting ceilings on the allowable annual operating time of each trawler. In 1984, general quota systems were introduced.

FISHING MODELS: In 1979, the Ministry of Fisheries established a working group consisting of members from the University of Iceland, the Marine Research Institute and other groups, to develop a model of demersal fisheries. The model would be a decision support tool for long- and short-term management. Short-term planning involves closing areas for fishing, mesh size regulations, and quota systems. In the long run, fleet size and its composition can be managed through the government's control over banking and the investment in new vessels.

DATA ON FISHERIES: Over the last few decades, extensive data on fishing in Iceland have been collected. The government's involvement in transactions between fishermen and the fish processing industry has made it beneficial for both partners to report catches and other data properly,

so the data are found to be very reliable. Although the data are accurate, randomness exists due to the impact which harsh and unstable weather has on the fishing grounds. There are four groups of data: landings, stock sizes, fishing power and selectivity, and economic data. From this information, trends can be extrapolated regarding the expected catch for a given fishing unit, the expected profits or losses for the fleet, and other statistics, year by year. The year 1983 is used as a base year by the government committee to compare sustainable yield for different fleet size and types. Sustainable yield refers to the equilibrium catch for a given constant effort and standard environmental factors.

RESULTS: The main conclusion from the study was that the fleet is too large, and the stock of future fish is being jeopardized by the fishing efforts of so many vessels. Although the problems associated with renewable natural resources involve uncertainty and are often unpredictable, the time-series model used by the Ministry of Fisheries in Iceland provided a tool for determining the nature and severity of the problem. It also allowed policymakers to concentrate on comparisons of different policies through sensitivity analysis, rather than to seek predictions of absolute values. By observing trends in stock size and other variables, politicians can determine the effects of different governmental policies. In Iceland, decision makers found that early strategies were unsuccessful in decreasing the size of the catch, so quota systems and investment limitations were imposed to preserve the country's fishing industry.

Thorkell Helgason and Snojolfur Olafsson, "An Icelandic Fisheries Model," *European Journal of Operational Research,* vol. 33 (1988), pp. 191–199, North-Holland.

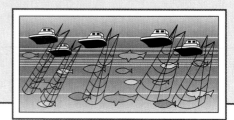

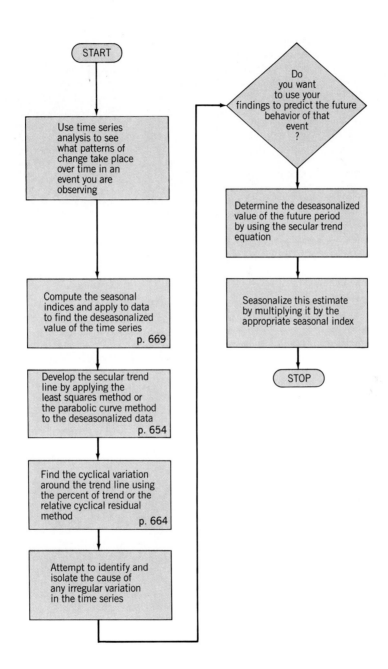

Precision Metal Products manufactures high-quality fabrications for use in the production of machinery for heavy industry. The company's three principal materials are coal, iron ore, and nickel ore. Management has the following data showing prices of these materials in 1969 and 1989 and quantity data for 1982, a year when purchasing patterns were characteristic of the entire 20-year period.

RAW MATERIAL	QTY. USED 1982 (000 TONS)	PRICE/TON 1969	PRICE/TON 1989
Coal	158	$ 7.56	$19.50
Iron ore	12	9.20	21.40
Nickel ore	5	12.30	36.10

Management would like help in constructing some measure of the change in material prices in the 20-year period. Using the methods in this chapter, we can supply it with such a figure to use in its planning.

14

Index Numbers

■ OBJECTIVES

Index numbers are shorthand for describing economic variables. Suppose you hear that the cost-of-living index is now 120 when compared with the base year of 1986. This number is a statistician's quick way of saying that the cost of living has risen 20 percent since 1986. We can also use index numbers to measure changes in productivity, unemployment, and wage rates.

At some time, everyone faces the question of how much something has changed over a period of time. We may want to know how much the price of groceries has increased, so we can adjust our budgets accordingly. A factory manager may wish to compare this month's per-unit production cost with that of the past 6 months. Or a medical research team may wish to compare the number of flu cases reported this year with the number reported in previous years. In each of these situations, the degree of change needs to be determined and defined. Typically, we use *index numbers* to measure such differences.

14-1
Defining an Index Number

What is an
index number?

An index number measures how much a variable changes over time. We calculate an index number by finding the ratio of the current value to a base value. Then we multiply the resulting number by 100 to express the index as a percentage. This final value is the *percentage relative*. Note that the index number for the base point in time is always 100.

Computing a simple
index

The Secretary of State of North Carolina has data indicating the number of new businesses incorporated. The data he collects show that 9,300 were started in 1974, 6,500 in 1979, 9,600 in 1984, and 10,100 in 1989. If 1974 is the base year, he can calculate the index numbers reflecting volume changes using the process presented in Table 14-1.

Using these calculations, the secretary of state finds that incorporations in 1979 had an index of 70 relative to 1974. Another way to state this is to say that the number of incorporations in 1979 was 70 percent of the number of incorporations in 1974.

TYPES OF INDEX NUMBERS

Price index

There are three principal types of indices: the price index, the quantity index, and the value index. A *price index* is the one most frequently used. It compares levels of prices from one period to another. The familiar Consumer Price Index, tabulated by the Bureau of Labor Statistics, measures overall price changes of a variety of consumer goods and services and is used to define the cost of living.

TABLE 14-1 Calculation of Index Numbers (Base Year = 1974)

YEAR (1)	NUMBER OF NEW INCORPORATIONS (000) (2)	RATIO (3) = (2) ÷ (9.3)	INDEX OR PERCENTAGE RELATIVE (4) = (3) × 100
1974	9.3	$\frac{9.3}{9.3} = 1.00$	$1.00 \times 100 = 100$
1979	6.5	$\frac{6.5}{9.3} = 0.70$	$0.70 \times 100 = 70$
1984	9.6	$\frac{9.6}{9.3} = 1.03$	$1.03 \times 100 = 103$
1989	10.1	$\frac{10.1}{9.3} = 1.09$	$1.09 \times 100 = 109$

TABLE 14-2 Computing a Value Index (Base Year = 1974)

YEAR (1)	INCORPORATED VALUE (MILLIONS) (2)	RATIO (3) = (2) ÷ (18.4)	INDEX OR PERCENTAGE RELATIVE (4) = (3) × 100
1974	$18.4	$\frac{18.4}{18.4} = 1.00$	1.00 × 100 = 100
1979	14.6	$\frac{14.6}{18.4} = 0.79$	0.79 × 100 = 79
1984	26.2	$\frac{26.2}{18.4} = 1.42$	1.42 × 100 = 142
1989	29.4	$\frac{29.4}{18.4} = 1.60$	1.60 × 100 = 160

Quantity index

A *quantity index* measures how much the number or quantity of a variable changes over time. Our example using incorporations determined a quantity index relating the numbers in 1979, 1984, and 1989 to that in 1974.

Value index

The last type of index, the *value index,* measures changes in total monetary worth. That is, it measures changes in the dollar value of a variable. In effect, the value index combines price and quantity changes to present a more informative index. In our example, we determined only a quantity index. However, we could have included the dollar effect by computing the total capitalized value for the years under consideration. Table 14-2 presents the corresponding value indices for 1979, 1984, and 1989. From this computation, we can say that the *value index* of incorporations in 1989 was 160. Or we can say that the incorporated value of 1989 increased 60 percent relative to the incorporated value of 1974.

Usually an index measures change in a variable over a period of time, such as in a time series. However, it can also be used to measure differences in a given variable in different locations. This is done by simultaneously collecting data in different locations and then comparing the data. The comparative cost-of-living index, for example, shows that in terms of the cost of goods and services, it is cheaper to live in Austin, Texas, than in New York City.

Composite index numbers

A single index may reflect a composite, or group, of changing variables. The Consumer Price Index measures the general price level for specific goods and services in the economy. It combines the individual prices of the goods and services to form a composite price index number.

USES OF INDEX NUMBERS

Index numbers can be used in several ways. It is most common to use them by themselves, as an end result. Index numbers such as the Consumer Price Index are often cited in news reports as general indicators of the nation's economic condition.

One use of the Consumer Price index

Management uses index numbers as part of an intermediate computation to understand other information better. In the chapter on time series, seasonal indices were used to modify and improve estimates of the future. The use of the Consumer Price Index to determine the "real" buying power of money is another example of how index numbers help increase knowledge of other factors. Table 14-3 shows the weekly salary paid to a secretary over a period of years, the corresponding Consumer

TABLE 14-3 Computation of Real Wages

YEAR (1)	WEEKLY SALARY PAID (2)	CONSUMER PRICE INDEX (3)	$(4) = \dfrac{(2) \times 100}{(3)}$	REAL OR ADJUSTED SALARY
1973	$114.75	100	$114.75 \times \dfrac{100}{100} =$	$114.75
1979	145.50	123	$145.50 \times \dfrac{100}{123} =$	$118.29
1989	472.98	200	$472.98 \times \dfrac{100}{200} =$	$236.44

Price Index values, and computation of the secretary's real salary. The secretary's dollar salary increased substantially, but the actual buying power of her income increased less rapidly. This can be attributed to the simultaneous rise in the cost-of-living index from 100 to 200.

PROBLEMS RELATED TO INDEX NUMBERS

Several things can distort index numbers. The four common causes of distortion are discussed below:

Limited data

1. Sometimes there is **difficulty in finding suitable data** to compute an index. Suppose the sales manager of Colonial Aircraft is interested in computing an index describing seasonal variation in the sale of the company's small planes. If sales are reported only on an annual basis, he would be unable to determine the seasonal sales pattern.

Incomparability

2. **Incomparability of indices** occurs when attempts are made to compare one index with another after there has been a basic change in what is being measured. If Citizens for Reasonable Transportation compare price indices of automobiles from 1979 to 1989, they find that prices have increased substantially. However, this comparison does not take into consideration technological advances in the quality of automobiles achieved over the time period in consideration.

Inappropriate weighting

3. **Inappropriate weighting of factors** can also distort an index. In developing a composite index, such as the Consumer Price Index, we must consider changes in some variables to be more important than changes in others. The effect on the economy of a 50-cent-per-gallon increase in the price of gasoline cannot be counterbalanced by a 50-cent decrease in the price of cars. It must be realized that the 50-cent per gallon increase in gas cost has a much greater effect on consumers. Thus, greater weight has to be assigned to the increased gas price than to the decrease in the cost of cars.

Use of an improper base

4. Distortion of index numbers also occurs when **selection of an improper base** occurs. Sometimes a firm selects a base that automatically leads to a result that is in its own interest and proves its initial assumption. If Consumers Against Oil Waste wants to portray oil companies in a bad light, it might measure this year's profits with a recession year as its base for oil profits. This would produce an index that shows oil profits have increased substantially. On the other hand, if Consumers for Unlimited Oil Use wishes to show that this year's profits are minimal, it might select a year with high profits for its base year. Using high profit as a base would probably result in an index indicating a small increase, or maybe even a decline, in oil profits this year. Therefore, we must always consider how

and why the base period was selected before we accept a claim based on the result of comparing index numbers.

SOURCES OF INDEX NUMBERS

Sources of data for index numbers

When managers apply index numbers to everyday problems, they use many sources to obtain the necessary information. The source depends on their information requirements. A firm can use monthly sales reports to determine its seasonal sales pattern. In dealing with broad areas of national economy and the general level of business activity, publications such as the *Federal Reserve Bulletin, Moody's, Monthly Labor Review,* and the *Consumer Price Index* provide a wealth of data. Many federal and state publications are listed in the U.S. Department of Commerce pamphlet, *Measuring Markets.* Almost all government agencies distribute data about their activities, from which index numbers can be computed. Many financial newspapers and magazines provide information from which index numbers can be computed. When you read these sources, you will find that many of them use index numbers themselves.

Exercises

14-1 What is the index for a base year?

14-2 Explain the differences among the three principal types of indices: *price, quantity,* and *value.*

14-3 What does the Consumer Price index measure? Is this based on a single variable or a composite of variables?

14-4 What are two basic ways of using index numbers?

14-5 What does an index number measure?

14-6 How is a percentage relative (index) found?

14-2
Unweighted Aggregates Index

The simplest form of a composite index is an unweighted aggregates index. *Unweighted* means that all the values considered in calculating the index are of equal importance. *Aggregate* means that we add, or sum, all the values. The principal advantage of an unweighted aggregates index is its simplicity.

Computing an unweighted aggregates index

An unweighted aggregates index is calculated by adding all the elements in the composite for the given time period and then dividing this result by the sum of the same elements during the base period. Equation 14-1 presents the mathematical formula for computing an unweighted aggregates quantity index.

$$\text{Unweighted aggregates quantity index} = \frac{\Sigma Q_1}{\Sigma Q_0} \times 100 \qquad [14\text{-}1]$$

where:

- Q_1 = quantity of each element in the composite for the current year
- Q_0 = quantity of each element in the composite for the base year

TABLE 14-4 Computation of an Unweighted Index

	Prices	
ELEMENTS IN THE COMPOSITE	1984 P_0	1989 P_1
Milk (1 gallon)	$1.92	$3.40
Eggs (1 dozen)	.81	1.00
Hamburger (1 pound)	1.49	2.00
Gasoline (1 gallon)	1.00	1.17
	$\Sigma P_0 = 5.22$	$\Sigma P_1 = 7.57$

$$\text{Unweighted aggregates price index} = \frac{\Sigma P_1}{\Sigma P_0} \times 100 \qquad [14\text{-}1]$$

$$= \frac{7.57}{5.22} \times 100$$

$$= 1.45 \times 100$$

$$= 145$$

Note that we can substitute *either* prices or values for quantities in Equation 14-1 to find the general equation for a price index or a value index. Since the ratio is multiplied by 100, the resulting index is technically a percentage. However, it is customary to refer only to the value and to omit the percent sign when discussing index numbers.

Using an unweighted index   The example in Table 14-4 demonstrates how we apply an unweighted index. In this case, we want to measure changes in general price levels on the basis of changes in prices of a few items. The 1984 prices are the base values to which we compare the 1989 prices.

Interpreting the index   From these calculations, we determine that the price index describing the change in these items from 1984 to 1989 is 145. If the elements in this composite are

TABLE 14-5 Computation of an Unweighted Index

	Prices	
ELEMENTS IN THE COMPOSITE	1984 P_0	1989 P_1
Milk (1 gallon)	$ 1.92	$ 3.40
Eggs (1 dozen)	.81	1.00
Hamburger (1 pound)	1.49	2.00
Gasoline (1 gallon)	1.00	1.17
Hand-held electronic calculator (1)	15.00	11.00
	$\Sigma P_0 = 20.22$	$\Sigma P_1 = 18.57$

$$\text{Unweighted aggregates price index} = \frac{\Sigma P_1}{\Sigma P_0} \times 100 \qquad [14\text{-}1]$$

$$= \frac{18.57}{20.22} \times 100$$

$$= .92 \times 100$$

$$= 92$$

representative of the general price level, we can say that prices rose 45 percent from 1984 to 1989. We cannot, however, expect a sample of four items to reflect accurate price changes for all goods and services. Thus, this calculation provides us with only a very rough estimate.

Suppose we now add the change in price of hand-held electronic calculators from 1984 to 1989 to our composite (Table 14-5). Again, 1984 is the base period against which we compare the 1989 prices.

Limitations of an unweighted index

Intuitively we know that the previous index of 145 is a more accurate estimate of general price behavior than 92, since more prices rose than fell between 1984 and 1989. Thus we see **the major disadvantage of an unweighted index. It does not attach greater importance, or weight, to the price change of a high-use item than it does to a low-volume item.** (A family may purchase 50 dozen eggs a year, but it would be unusual for a family to own more than one or two calculators.) A substantial price change for slow-moving items can completely distort an index. For this reason, it is not common to use a simple unweighted index in important analyses.

The deficiencies of an unweighted index suggest that we use a weighted index. There are two ways to calculate more sophisticated indices. Each of these will be discussed in detail in the following sections.

Exercises

14-7   In an effort to get a measure of economic hardship, the IMF collected data on the price behavior of five major products imported by a group of less-developed countries. Using 1986 as the base period, express the 1989 prices in terms of an unweighted aggregates index.

PRODUCT	A	B	C	D	E
1986 price	$127	$532	$2,290	$60	$221
1989 price	$152	$651	$2,314	$76	$286

14-8   With union negotiations pending, representatives of the management of a large manufacturing facility are compiling data on wage levels. The following data concern base pay for the different classes of labor within the facility over a 4-year period.

	WAGES PER HOUR			
	1986	1987	1988	1989
Class A	$8.48	$9.32	$10.34	$11.16
Class B	6.90	7.52	8.19	8.76
Class C	4.50	4.99	5.48	5.86
Class D	3.10	3.47	3.85	4.11

Using 1986 as the base period, calculate the unweighted aggregates wage index for 1987, 1988, and 1989.

14-9   The VP of sales for Xenon Computer Corporation is examining the commission rate employed for the last 3 years. Below are the commission earnings of the company's top five sales personnel.

	1987	1988	1989
Guy Howell	$48,500	$55,100	$63,800
Skip Ford	41,900	46,200	60,150
Nelson Price	38,750	43,500	46,700
Nina Williams	36,300	45,400	39,900
Ken Johnson	33,850	38,300	50,200

Using 1987 as the base period, express the commission earnings in 1988 and 1989 in terms of an unweighted aggregates index.

14-10 Bill Ivey, the administrator of a small rural hospital, has compiled the information shown below regarding food purchased for the hospital kitchen. For the commodities listed, the corresponding price indicates the average price for that year. Using 1988 as the base period, express the prices in 1987 and 1989 in terms of an unweighted aggregates index.

COMMODITY	1987	1988	1989
Dairy products	$2.34	$2.38	$2.60
Meat products	3.19	3.41	3.36
Vegetable products	.85	.89	.94
Fruit products	1.11	1.19	1.18

14-11 A chemical processing plant utilized five materials in the manufacture of an industrial cleaning agent. The following data indicate the final inventory levels for these materials for the years 1987 and 1989.

MATERIAL	A	B	C	D	E
Inventory (tons) 1987	86	395	1,308	430	113
Inventory (tons) 1989	95	380	1,466	469	108

Using 1987 as the base period, express the 1989 inventory levels in terms of an unweighted aggregates index.

14-12 John Dykstra, a management trainee in a bank, has collected information on the bank's transactions for the years 1988 and 1989:

TYPE OF TRANSACTION	WITHDRAWALS SAVINGS	WITHDRAWALS CHECKING	DEPOSITS SAVINGS	DEPOSITS CHECKING
Number of transactions 1988	169,000	21,843,000	293,000	2,684,000
Number of transactions 1989	158,000	23,241,000	303,000	3,361,000

Using 1988 as the base period, express the number of banking transactions in 1989 in terms of an unweighted aggregates index.

14-13 The Bookster Publishing Company began its business of publishing college textbooks in 1986. It is interested in determining how its sales have changed compared to its first year. A summary of the company's records shows how many new books it published in each year in the following areas:

	1987	1988	1989
Biology	48	53	50
Mathematics	32	37	35
History	19	15	22
English	16	20	21
Sociology	24	18	26
Physics	10	26	32
Chemistry	27	26	30
Philosophy	11	8	15

Using 1987 as the base year, calculate the unweighted aggregates quantity index for 1988 and 1989. Interpret the results for the publishing company.

14-3
Weighted Aggregates Index

Advantages of weighting in an index

As we have said, often we have to attach greater importance to changes in some variables than to others when we compute an index. This weighting allows us to include more information than just the change in price over time. It also lets us improve the accuracy of the general price level estimate based on our sample. The problem is to decide how much weight to attach to each of the variables in the sample.

Computing a weighted aggregates index

The general formula for computing a weighted aggregates price index is:

$$\text{Weighted aggregates price index} = \frac{\Sigma P_1 Q}{\Sigma P_0 Q} \times 100 \qquad [14\text{-}2]$$

where:

- P_1 = price of each element in the composite in the current year
- P_0 = price of each element in the composite in the base year
- Q = quantity weighting factor chosen

Consider the sample in Table 14-6. Each of the elements in the composite is taken from Table 14-5 and is weighted according to the volume of sales. The process of weighted aggregates confirms our earlier intuitive impression from page 703 that the general price level had risen (index = 129).

Typically, management uses the quantity of an item consumed as the measure of its importance in computing a weighted aggregates index. This leads to an important question in applying the process: Which quantities are used?

Three ways to weight an index

In general, there are three ways to weight an index. The first involves using quantities consumed during the base period in computing each index number. This is called the *Laspeyres method,* after the statistician who developed it. The second uses quantities consumed during the period in question for each index. This is the *Paasche method,* in honor of the person who devised it. The third way is called the *fixed weight aggregates method.* With this method, one period is chosen, and its quantities are used to find *all* indices. (Note that if the chosen period is the base period, the fixed weight aggregates method is the same as the Laspeyres method.)

TABLE 14-6 Computation of a Weighted Aggregates Index

ELEMENTS IN THE COMPOSITE	Q VOLUME (BILLIONS) (1)	P_0 1984 PRICES (2)	P_1 1989 PRICES (3)	P_0Q WEIGHTED SALES (4) = (2) × (1)	P_1Q WEIGHTED SALES (5) = (3) × (1)
Milk	20.000 (gal.)	$ 1.92	$ 3.40	1.92 × 20.0 = 38.40	3.40 × 20.00 = 68.00
Eggs	3.500 (doz.)	.81	1.00	.81 × 3.5 = 2.84	1.00 × 3.5 = 3.50
Hamburger	11.000 (lbs.)	1.49	2.00	1.49 × 11.0 = 16.39	2.00 × 11.00 = 22.00
Gasoline	154.000 (gal.)	1.00	1.17	1.00 × 154.0 = 154.00	1.17 × 154.00 = 180.18
Calculators	0.002 (units)	15.00	11.00	15.00 × 0.002 = .03	11.00 × 0.002 = .02
				$\Sigma P_0Q = $ **211.66**	$\Sigma P_1Q = $ **273.70**

$$\text{Weighted aggregates index} = \frac{\Sigma P_1Q}{\Sigma P_0Q} \times 100 \qquad [14\text{-}2]$$

$$= \frac{273.70}{211.66} \times 100$$

$$= 1.29 \times 100$$

$$= 129$$

LASPEYRES METHOD

The Laspeyres method

The Laspeyres method, which uses quantities consumed during the base period, is the method most commonly used, because it requires quantity measures for only one period. Since each index number depends upon the same base price and quantity, management can compare the index of one period directly with the index of another. Suppose a steel manufacturer's price index is 103 in 1986 and 125 in 1989, using 1983 base prices and quantities. The company concludes that the general price level has

Computing a Laspeyres index

increased 22 percent from 1986 to 1989. To calculate the Laspeyres index, the company first multiplies the current period price by the base period quantity for each element in the composite, then it sums each of the resulting values. Next it multiplies the base period price by the base period quantity for each element, and again it sums the resulting values. By dividing the first sum by the second and multiplying the result by 100, management can convert this value to a percentage relative. Equation 14-3 presents the formula used to determine the Laspeyres index.

$$\text{Laspeyres index} = \frac{\Sigma P_1Q_0}{\Sigma P_0Q_0} \times 100 \qquad [14\text{-}3]$$

where:

- P_1 = prices in the current year
- P_0 = prices in the base year
- Q_0 = quantities sold in the base year

Example using the Laspeyres method

Let's work an example to demonstrate how the Laspeyres method is used. Suppose we want to determine changes in price level between 1985 and 1989. Table 14-7 contains the pertinent data for 1985 and 1989.

Drawing conclusions from the calculated index

If we have selected a representative sample of goods, we can conclude that the general price index for 1989 is 121 based on the 1985 index of 100. Alternatively, we can say that prices have increased by 21 percent. Notice that we have used the average

TABLE 14-7 Calculation of a Laspeyres Index

ELEMENTS IN THE COMPOSITE (1)	P_0 BASE PRICE 1985 (2)	P_1 CURRENT PRICE 1989 (3)	Q_0 AVERAGE QUANTITY CONSUMED IN 1985 BY A FAMILY (4)	P_0Q_0 (5) = (2) × (4)	P_1Q_0 (6) = (3) × (4)
Bread (1 loaf)	$ .91	$1.19	200 loaves	$182	$238
Potatoes (1 lb.)	.79	.99	300 lbs.	237	297
Chicken (3-lb. fryer)	3.92	4.50	100 chickens	392	450
				$\Sigma P_0Q_0 = 811$	$\Sigma P_1Q_0 = \overline{985}$

$$\text{Laspeyres price index} = \frac{\Sigma P_1Q_0}{\Sigma P_0Q_0} \times 100 \quad [14\text{-}3]$$

$$= \frac{985}{811} \times 100$$

$$= 1.21 \times 100$$

$$= 121$$

quantity consumed in 1985 rather than the total quantity consumed. Actually, it does not matter which is used, as long as we apply the same quantity measure throughout the problem. Typically, we select the quantity measure that is easiest to find.

Advantages of the Laspeyres method

One advantage of the Laspeyres method is the comparability of one index with another. If we had the 1986 prices for the previous example, we would be able to find a value for the 1986 general price index. This index could be compared directly with the 1989 index. Using the same base period quantity allows us to make a direct comparison.

Another advantage is that many commonly used quantity measures are not tabulated every year. A firm might be interested in some variable whose quantity measure is computed once every 10 years. Since the Laspeyres method uses only one quantity measure, that of the base year, the firm does not need yearly tabulations to measure quantities consumed.

Disadvantage of the Laspeyres method

The primary disadvantage of the Laspeyres method is that it does not take into consideration changes in consumption patterns. Items purchased in large quantities just a few years ago may be relatively unimportant today. Suppose the base quantity of an item differs greatly from the quantity for the period in question. Then the change in that item's price indicates very little about the change in the general price level.

PAASCHE METHOD

Difference between Paasche and Laspeyres methods

The second way to compute a weighted aggregates price index is the Paasche method. Finding a Paasche index is similar to finding a Laspeyres index. The difference is that the Paasche method uses quantity measure for the *current* period rather than for the *base* period.

Computing a Paasche index

The Paasche index is calculated by multiplying the current period price by the current period quantity for each item in the composite and summing these products. Then the base period price is multiplied by the current period quantity for each item, and the results are summed. The first sum is divided by the second sum, and the resulting value is multiplied by 100 to convert the value into a percentage relative. Equation 14-4 defines the method for calculating a Paasche index.

$$\text{Paasche index} = \frac{\Sigma P_1 Q_1}{\Sigma P_0 Q_1} \times 100 \qquad [14\text{-}4]$$

where:

- P_1 = current period prices
- P_0 = base period prices
- Q_1 = current period quantities

With this equation, we can rework the problem in Table 14-7. Notice that we have discarded the quantities consumed in 1985. They have been replaced by the quantities consumed in 1989. Table 14-8 presents the information necessary for this modified problem.

Interpreting the difference between the two methods

In this analysis, we find that the price index for 1989 is 117. As you see from Table 14-7 on page 707, the price index calculated by the Laspeyres method is 121. The difference between these indices reflects the change in consumption patterns of the three variables in the composite.

Advantage of the Paasche method

The Paasche method is particularly helpful because it combines the effects of changes in price and consumption patterns. Thus, it is a better indicator of general changes in the economy than the Laspeyres method. In our examples, the Paasche index shows a trend toward less expensive goods and services, since it indicates a price level increase of 17 percent instead of the 21 percent increase calculated using the Laspeyres method.

Disadvantages of the Paasche method

One of the principal disadvantages of the Paasche method is the need to tabulate quantity measures for each period examined. Frequently, quantity information for each period is either expensive to gather or unavailable. It would be hard, for example, to find reliable sources of data to determine quantity measures of 100 food products consumed in different countries for each of several years.

TABLE 14-8 Calculation of a Paasche Index

ELEMENTS IN THE COMPOSITE (1)	P_1 CURRENT PRICE 1989 (2)	P_0 BASE PRICE 1985 (3)	Q_1 AVERAGE QUANTITY CONSUMED IN 1989 BY A FAMILY (4)	$P_1 Q_1$ (5) = (2) × (4)	$P_0 Q_1$ (6) = (3) × (4)
Bread (1 loaf)	$1.19	$ .91	200 loaves	$ 238	$ 182
Potatoes (1 lb.)	.99	.79	100 lbs.	99	79
Chicken (3-lb. fryer)	4.50	3.92	300 chickens	1,350	1,176
				$\Sigma P_1 Q_1 =$ 1,687	$\Sigma P_0 Q_1 =$ 1,437

$$[14\text{-}4] \quad \text{Paasche price index} = \frac{\Sigma P_1 Q_1}{\Sigma P_0 Q_1} \times 100$$

$$= \frac{1,687}{1,437} \times 100$$

$$= 1.17 \times 100$$

$$= 117$$

Each value for a Paasche price index is the result of both price and quantity changes from the base period. **Since the quantity measures used for one index period are usually different from the quantity measures for another index period, it is impossible to attribute the difference between the two indices to price changes only.** Thus, it is difficult to compare indices from different periods as calculated by the Paasche method.

FIXED WEIGHT AGGREGATES METHOD

Fixed weight aggregates index

The third technique used to assign weights to elements in a composite is the fixed weight aggregates method. It is similar to both the Laspeyres and Paasche methods. However, instead of using base period or current period weights (quantities), it uses weights from a representative period. The representative weights are referred to as fixed weights. The fixed weights and the base prices do not have to come from the same period.

Computing a fixed weight aggregates index

We calculate a fixed weight aggregates price index by multiplying the current period prices by the fixed weights and summing the results. Then we multiply the base period prices by the fixed weights and sum them. Finally, we divide the first sum by the second and multiply by 100 to convert the ratio to a percentage relative. The formula used to calculate a fixed weight aggregates price index is presented in Equation 14-5.

$$\text{Fixed weight aggregates price index } = \frac{\Sigma P_1 Q_2}{\Sigma P_0 Q_2} \times 100 \qquad [14\text{-}5]$$

where:

- P_1 = current period prices
- P_0 = base period prices
- Q_2 = fixed weights

TABLE 14-9 Computation of a Fixed Weight Aggregate Index

RAW MATERIALS (1)	Q_2 QUANTITY CONSUMED 1982 (THOUSANDS OF TONS) (2)	P_0 AVERAGE PRICE 1969 ($ PER TON) (3)	P_1 AVERAGE PRICE 1989 ($ PER TON) (4)	WEIGHTED AGGREGATE 1969 (5) = (3) × (2)	WEIGHTED AGGREGATE 1989 (6) = (4) × (2)
Coal	158	$ 7.56	$19.50	$1,194.48	$3,081.00
Iron ore	12	9.20	21.40	110.40	256.80
Nickel ore	5	12.30	36.10	61.50	180.50
				$\Sigma P_0 Q_2$ = **1,366.38**	$\Sigma P_1 Q_2$ = **3,518.30**

$$\text{Fixed weight aggregates price index } = \frac{\Sigma P_1 Q_2}{\Sigma P_0 Q_2} \times 100 \qquad [14\text{-}5]$$

$$= \frac{3{,}518.30}{1{,}366.38} \times 100$$

$$= 2.57 \times 100$$

$$= 257$$

We can demonstrate the process used to calculate a fixed weight aggregates price index by solving our chapter-opening example. Recall that management wants to determine the price level changes of raw materials consumed by the company between 1969 and 1989. It has accumulated the information in Table 14-9. From examination of past purchasing records, management has decided that the quantities purchased in 1982 were characteristic of the purchasing patterns during the 20-year period. The 1969 price level is the base price in this analysis. Calculation of the fixed weight aggregates index is shown in Table 14-9. The company management concludes from this analysis that the general price level has increased 157 percent over the 20-year period.

The primary advantage of a fixed weight aggregates price index is the flexibility in selecting the base price and the fixed weight (quantity). In many cases, the period that a company wishes to use as the base price level may have an uncharacteristic consumption level. Therefore, by being able to select a different period for the fixed weight, the company can improve the accuracy of the index. This index also allows a company to change the price base without changing the fixed weight. This is useful because quantity measures are often expensive or impossible to obtain for certain periods.

Exercises

14-14 Bill Simpson, owner of a California vineyard has collected the following information describing the prices and quantities of harvested crops for the years 1986, 1987, 1988, and 1989.

TYPE OF GRAPE	PRICE (PER TON)				QUANTITY HARVESTED (TONS)			
	1986	1987	1988	1989	1986	1987	1988	1989
Ruby Cabernet	$108	$109	$113	$111	1,280	1,150	1,330	1,360
Barber	93	96	96	101	830	860	850	890
Chenin Blanc	97	99	106	107	1,640	1,760	1,630	1,660

Construct a Laspeyres index for each of these 4 years, using 1986 as the base period.

14-15 Use the data from exercise 14-14 to calculate a fixed weight index for each year, using 1986 prices as the base and the 1989 quantities as the fixed weights.

14-16 Use the data from exercise 14-14 to calculate a Paasche index for each year, using 1987 as the base period.

14-17 Julie Pristash, the marketing manager of Mod-Stereo, a manufacturer of blank cassette tapes, has compiled the following information regarding unit sales for 1987, 1988, and 1989. Using the average quantities sold from 1987 to 1989 as the fixed weights, calculate the fixed weight index for each of the years 1987 to 1989 based on 1987.

LENGTH OF TAPE	RETAIL PRICE			AVERAGE QUANTITY (× 100,000) 1987–1989
	1987	1988	1989	
30 minutes	$2.20	$2.60	$2.85	32
60 minutes	2.60	2.90	3.15	119
90 minutes	3.10	3.20	3.25	75
120 minutes	3.30	3.35	3.40	16

14-18 Gray P. Saeurs owns the corner fruitstand in a small town. After hearing many complaints that his prices constantly change during the summer, he has decided to see if this is true. Based on the following data, help Mr. Saeurs calculate the appropriate weighted aggregate price indices for each month. Use June as the base period. Is your result a Laspeyres index or a Paasche index?

| | PRICE PER POUND | | | NO. OF POUNDS SOLD |
FRUIT	JUNE	JULY	AUG.	JUNE
Apples	$ .59	$ .64	$ .69	150
Oranges	.75	.65	.70	200
Peaches	.87	.90	.85	125
Watermelons	1.00	1.10	.95	350
Canteloupes	.95	.89	.90	150

14-19 Charles Widget is in charge of keeping in stock certain items that his company needs in repairing its machines. Since he started this job 3 years ago, he has been observing the changes in the prices for the items he keeps in stock. He arranged the data in the following table in order to calculate a fixed weight aggregate price index. Perform the calculations Mr. Widget would do using 1987 as the base year.

| | PRICE PER ITEM | | | AVERAGE NO. USED |
ITEM	1987	1988	1989	DURING 3-YEAR PERIOD
W-gadget	$1.25	$1.50	$2.00	900
X-gadget	6.50	7.00	6.25	50
Y-gadget	5.25	5.90	6.40	175
Z-gadget	.50	.80	1.00	200

14-4
Average of Relatives Methods

UNWEIGHTED AVERAGE OF RELATIVES METHOD

As an alternative to the aggregates methods, we can use the average of relatives method to construct an index. Once again, we will use a price index to introduce the process.

Actually, we used a form of the average of relatives method in calculating the simple index in Table 14-1 on page 698. In that one-product example, we calculated the percentage relative by dividing the number of incorporations in the current year, Q_1, by the number in the base year, Q_0, and multiplying the result by 100.

Computing an unweighted average of relatives index

With more than one product (or activity), we first find the ratio of the current price to the base price for each product and multiply each ratio by 100. We then add the resulting percentage relatives and divide by the number of products. (Notice that the aggregates methods discussed in section 14-3 differ from this method. They sum all the prices *before* finding the ratio.) Equation 14-6 presents the general form for the unweighted average of relatives method.

$$\text{Unweighted average of relatives index} = \frac{\Sigma \left(\dfrac{P_1}{P_0} \times 100 \right)}{n} \qquad [14\text{-}6]$$

TABLE 14-10 Computation of an Unweighted Average of Relatives Index

PRODUCT (1)	1984 PRICES (2)	1989 PRICES (3)	RATIO $\times$ 100 $(4) = \frac{(3)}{(2)} \times 100$
Milk (1 gal.)	$1.92	$3.40	$\frac{3.40}{1.92} \times 100 = 1.77 \times 100 = 177$
Eggs (1 doz.)	.81	1.00	$\frac{1.00}{.81} \times 100 = 1.23 \times 100 = 123$
Hamburger (1 lb.)	1.49	2.00	$\frac{2.00}{1.49} \times 100 = 1.34 \times 100 = 134$
Gasoline (1 gal.)	1.00	1.17	$\frac{1.17}{1.00} \times 100 = 1.17 \times 100 = \underline{117}$

$$\sum \left(\frac{P_1}{P_0} \times 100 \right) = 551$$

$$\text{Unweighted average of relatives index} = \frac{\sum \left(\frac{P_1}{P_0} \times 100 \right)}{n} \qquad [14\text{-}6]$$

$$= \frac{551}{4}$$

$$= 138$$

where:

- P_1 = current period prices
- P_0 = base period prices
- n = number of elements (or products) in the composite

Comparing the unweighted aggregates index and the unweighted average of relatives index

In Table 14-10, we rework the problem in Table 14-4 on page 702 using the unweighted average of relatives method rather than the unweighted aggregates method.

Based on this analysis, the general price level index for 1989 is 138. In Table 14-4, the unweighted aggregates index for the same problem is 145. Obviously, there is a difference between these two indices. With the unweighted average of relatives method, we compute the average of the ratios of the prices for each product. With the unweighted aggregates method, we compute the ratio of the sums of the prices of each product. Notice that this is not the same as assigning some items more weight than others. Rather, the average of relatives method converts each element to a relative scale where each element is represented as a *percentage* rather than as an *amount*. Because of this, each of the elements in the composite is measured against a base of 100.

WEIGHTED AVERAGE OF RELATIVES METHOD

Most problems management has to deal with require weighting by *importance*. Thus, it is more common to use the weighted average of relatives method than the unweighted method. When we computed a weighted aggregates price index in section 3 of this chapter, we used the quantity consumed to weight the elements in the composite. To assign weights using the weighted average of relatives, we use the value of each element in the composite. (The value is the total dollar volume obtained by multiplying price by quantity.)

With the weighted average of relatives methods, there are several ways to determine weighted value. As in the Laspeyres method, we can use the base value found by multiplying the base quantity by the base price. Using the base value will produce exactly the same result as calculating the index using the Laspeyres method. Since the result is the same, the decision to use the Laspeyres method or the weighted average of relatives method often depends on the availability of data. If value data are more readily available, the weighted average of relatives method is used. We use the Laspeyres method when quantity data are more readily obtained.

Computing a weighted
average of relatives
index

Equation 14-7 is used to compute a weighted average of relatives price index. This is a general equation into which we can substitute values from the base period, the current period, or any fixed period.

$$\text{Weighted average of relatives price index (general form)} = \frac{\Sigma\left[\left(\frac{P_1}{P_0}\times 100\right)(P_nQ_n)\right]}{\Sigma P_nQ_n} \qquad [14\text{-}7]$$

where:

- P_nQ_n = the value
- P_0 = prices in the base period
- P_1 = prices in the current period
- P_n and Q_n = quantities and prices that determine values we use for weights. In particular, $n = 0$ for the base period, $n = 1$ for the current period, and $n = 2$ for a fixed period that is not a base or current period.

If we wish to compute a weighted average of relatives index using base values, P_0Q_0, the equation would be:

$$\text{Weighted average of relatives price index (using base values)} = \frac{\Sigma\left[\left(\frac{P_1}{P_0}\times 100\right)(P_0Q_0)\right]}{\Sigma P_0Q_0} \qquad [14\text{-}8]$$

Relation of weighted
average of relatives to
Laspeyres method

Equation 14-8 is equivalent to the Laspeyres method for any given problem.

In addition to the specific cases of the general form of the weighted average of relatives method, we can use values determined by multiplying the price from one period by the quantity from a different period. Usually, however, we find Equations 14-7 and 14-8 adequate.

Example of weighted
average of relatives
index

Here is an example. The information in Table 14-11 comes from Table 14-7 on page 707. Since we have base quantities and base prices, we will use Equation 14-8. The price index of 122 differs slightly from the 121 calculated in Table 14-7 using the Laspeyres method, but only because of intermediate rounding.

As was the case for weighted aggregates, when we use base values, P_0Q_0, or fixed values, P_2Q_2, for weighted averages, we can readily compare the price level of one period with that of another. However, when we use current values, P_1Q_1, in computing a weighted average of relatives price index, we *cannot* directly compare values from different periods, since both the prices and the quantities may have changed. Thus, we usually use either base values or fixed values when computing a weighted average of relatives index.

TABLE 14-11 Computing a Weighted Average of Relatives Index

ELEMENTS IN THE COMPOSITE (1)	PRICES 1985 P_0 (2)	PRICES 1989 P_1 (3)	QUANTITY 1985 Q_0 (4)	PERCENTAGE PRICE RELATIVE $\frac{P_1}{P_0} \times 100$ $(5) = \frac{(3)}{(2)} \times 100$	BASE VALUE $P_0 Q_0$ $(6) = (2) \times (4)$	WEIGHTED PERCENTAGE RELATIVE $(7) = (5) \times (6)$
Bread (1 loaf)	$ .91	$1.19	200 loaves	$\frac{1.19}{.91} \times 100 = 131$	$182	23,842
Potatoes (1 lb.)	.79	.99	300 lbs.	$\frac{.99}{.79} \times 100 = 125$	237	29,625
Chicken (3-lb. fryer)	3.92	4.50	100 fryers	$\frac{4.50}{3.92} \times 100 = 115$	392	45,080

$$\Sigma P_0 Q_0 = 811$$

$$\Sigma \left[\left(\frac{P_1}{P_0} \times 100 \right) (P_0 Q_0) \right] = 98{,}547$$

$$\text{Weighted average of relatives index} = \frac{\Sigma \left[\left(\frac{P_1}{P_0} \times 100 \right) (P_0 Q_0) \right]}{\Sigma P_0 Q_0} \qquad [14\text{-}8]$$

$$= \frac{98{,}547}{811}$$

$$= 122$$

Exercises

 14-20 F. C. Linley, owner of the San Mateo Seals, collected information regarding the ticket prices and volume for his franchise over the last 4 years.

| | AVERAGE ANNUAL PRICE | | | | TICKETS SOLD ($\times$ 10,000) | | | |
	1986	1987	1988	1989	1986	1987	1988	1989
Box seats	$6.50	$7.25	$7.50	$8.10	26	27	31	28
General admission	3.50	3.85	4.30	4.35	71	80	89	90

Calculate a weighted average of relatives price index for each of the years 1986 through 1988, using 1987 as the base year and for weighting.

14-21 The following table contains information from the raw-material purchase records of a tire manufacturer for the years 1987, 1988, and 1989.

MATERIAL	AVERAGE ANNUAL PURCHASE PRICE/TON 1987	1988	1989	VALUE OF PURCHASE (THOUSANDS) 1989
Butadiene	$ 17	$ 15	$ 11	$ 50
Styrene	85	89	95	210
Rayon cord	348	358	331	1,640
Carbon black	62	58	67	630
Sodium pyrophosphate	49	56	67	90

Calculate a weighted average of relatives price index for each of those 3 years, using 1989 for weighting and for the base year.

14-22 A Tennessee public interest group has surveyed the cost of automobile repairs in three major Tennessee cities (Knoxville, Memphis, and Nashville). With the following information, construct an unweighted average of relatives price index using the 1985 prices as a base.

TYPE OF REPAIR	1985	1987	1989
Replacement of water pump	$ 35	$ 37	$ 41
Regrinding of engine valves (6 cyl.)	189	205	216
Wheel balancing	26	29	30
Tune-up (minor)	16	16	18

14-23 Garret Cage, president of a local bank, is interested in the average levels of total savings and checking accounts for each of the last 3 years. He sampled days from each of these years; using the levels on those days, he determined the following yearly averages:

	1987	1988	1989
Savings accounts	$1,845,000	$2,320,000	$2,089,000
Checking accounts	385,000	447,000	491,000

Calculate an unweighted average of relatives index for each year, using 1987 as the base period.

14-24 As a part of the evaluation of a possible acquisition, a New York City conglomerate has collected this sales information:

	AVERAGE ANNUAL PRICE		TOTAL DOLLAR VALUE (THOUSANDS)
PRODUCT	1987	1989	1987
Calculators	$ 27	$ 20	$ 150
Radios	30	42	900
Portable TVs	157	145	1,370

(a) Calculate the unweighted average of relatives price index, using 1987 as the base period.
(b) Calculate the weighted average of relatives price index, using the dollar value for each product in 1987 as the appropriate set of weights and 1987 as the base year.

14-25 A survey of transatlantic passenger rates for flights from New York to various European cities produced these results:

	AVERAGE ANNUAL PASSENGER RATES					PASSENGERS (×1,000)
DESTINATION	1985	1986	1987	1988	1989	1989
Paris	$690	$714	$732	$777	$783	2,835
London	648	654	675	696	744	5,175
Munich	702	723	753	768	798	2,505
Rome	840	867	903	939	975	2,145

Calculate the weighted average of relatives index for each of the years 1985 through 1988, using 1989 as the base year and for weighting.

14-26 In a study of group health insurance policies, commissioned by the Rhode Island Medical Care Association, the following sample of average individual rates was collected. Using 1988 as the base period, calculate an unweighted average of relatives price index for each year.

INSURANCE GROUP	1986	1987	1988	1989
Physicians	$54	$65	$86	$103
Students	39	41	55	76
Government employees	48	61	76	93
Teachers	46	58	75	96

14-27 A new motel chain hopes to place its first motel in Boomingville, but before it makes a commitment to start construction, it wants to check out the room prices charged nightly by the other motels and hotels. After sending an employee to investigate the prices, the motel chain received data in the following form:

| HOTEL | PRICE PER ROOM PER NIGHT | | | NO. ROOMS RENTED |
	1987	1988	1989	1987
Happy Hotel	$35	$37	$42	1,250
Room Service Rooms	25	26	28	950
Executive Motel	45	45	51	1,000
Country Inn	37	38	44	600
Family Fun Motel	26	30	31	2,075

Help the company determine the relative prices, using 1987 as the base year, and using an unweighted average of relatives index.

14-28 The Quick-Stop Gas Station has been selling road maps to its customers for the past 3 years. The maps that are sold are of the nearest city, the county the gas station is in, the state it is in, and the entire United States. From the following table, calculate the weighted average of relatives price indices for 1988 and 1989, using 1987 as the base year.

| MAPS | PRICE PER MAP | | | QUANTITY SOLD |
	1987	1988	1989	1987
City	$ .75	$ .90	$1.10	1,000
County	.75	.90	1.00	400
State	1.00	1.50	1.50	1,000
United States	2.50	2.75	2.75	220

14-5
Quantity and Value Indices

QUANTITY INDICES

Using a quantity index

Our discussion of index numbers up to now has concentrated on price indices so that it would be easier to understand the general concepts. However, we can also use index numbers to describe quantity and value changes. Of these two, we more frequently use quantity indices. The Federal Reserve Board calculates quarterly indices in its monthly publication, *The Index of Industrial Production* (IIP). The IIP measures the quantity of production in the areas of manufacturing, mining, and utilities. It is computed using a weighted average of relatives quantity index in which the fixed weights (prices) and the base quantities are measured from 1977.

Advantages of a quantity index

In times of inflation, a quantity index provides a more reliable measure of actual output of raw materials and finished goods than a corresponding value index does. Similarly, agricultural production is best measured using a quantity index, because it eliminates misleading effects from fluctuating prices. We frequently use a quantity index to measure commodities that are subject to considerable price variation.

Any of the methods discussed in previous sections of this chapter to determine price indices can be used to calculate quantity indices. When we computed price indices, we used quantities or values as weights. Now that we want to compute quantity indices, we use prices or values as weights. Let's consider the construction of a weighted average of relatives quantity index.

Computing a weighted average of relatives quantity index

The general process for computing a weighted average of relatives quantity index is the same as that used to compute a price index. Equation 14-9 describes the formula for this type of quantity index. In this equation, value is determined by multiplying quantity by price. The value associated with each quantity is used to weight the elements in the composite.

$$\text{Weighted average of relatives quantity index} = \frac{\Sigma\left[\left(\frac{Q_1}{Q_0} \times 100\right)(Q_n P_n)\right]}{\Sigma Q_n P_n} \quad [14\text{-}9]$$

where:

- Q_1 = quantities for the current period
- Q_0 = quantities for the base period
- P_n and Q_n = quantities and prices that determine values we use for weights. In particular, $n = 0$ for the base period, $n = 1$ for the current period, and $n = 2$ for a fixed period that is not a base or current period.

Consider the problem in Table 14-12. We use Equation 14-9 to compute a weighted average of relatives quantity index. The value, $Q_n P_n$, is determined from the base period and is therefore symbolized $Q_0 P_0$.

TABLE 14-12 Computation of a Weighted Average of Relatives Quantity Index

ELEMENTS IN THE COMPOSITE (1)	QUANTITIES (BILLIONS OF BUSHELS) 1985 Q_0 (2)	1989 Q_1 (3)	PRICE (PER BUSHEL) 1985 P_0 (4)	$\frac{Q_1}{Q_0} \times 100$ PERCENTAGE RELATIVES $(5) = \frac{(3)}{(2)} \times 100$	BASE VALUE $Q_0 P_0$ $(6) = (2) \times (4)$	$\frac{Q_1}{Q_0} \times 100 \times Q_0 P_0$ WEIGHTED RELATIVES $(7) = (5) \times (6)$
Wheat	29	24	$3.80	$\frac{24.0}{29.0} \times 100 = 83$	$29 \times 3.80 = 110.20$	9,146.60
Corn	3	2.5	2.91	$\frac{2.5}{3} \times 100 = 83$	$3 \times 2.91 = 8.73$	724.59
Soybeans	12	14	6.50	$\frac{14.0}{12.0} \times 100 = 117$	$12 \times 6.50 = 78.00$ $\Sigma Q_0 P_0 = 196.93$	9,126.00

$$\Sigma\left[\left(\frac{Q_1}{Q_0} \times 100\right)(Q_0 P_0)\right] = 18,997.19$$

$$\text{Weighted average of relatives quantity index} = \frac{\Sigma\left[\left(\frac{Q_1}{Q_0} \times 100\right)(Q_0 P_0)\right]}{\Sigma Q_0 P_0} \quad [14\text{-}9]$$

$$= \frac{18,997.19}{196.93}$$

$$= 96$$

VALUE INDICES

A disadvantage of a value index

A value index measures general changes in the total value of some variable. Since value is determined both by price and quantity, a value index actually measures the combined effects of price and quantity changes. The principal disadvantage of a value index is that it does not distinguish between the effects of these two components.

Advantages of a value index

Nevertheless, a value index is useful in measuring overall changes. Medical insurance companies, for example, often cite the sharp increase in the *value* of payments awarded in medical malpractice suits as the primary reason for discontinuing malpractice insurance. In this situation, value involves both a greater number of payments and larger cash amounts awarded.

Exercises

 14-29 The financial VP of the American division of Banshee Camera Company is examining the company's cash and credit sales over the last 5 years.

	VALUE OF SALES (× $100,000)				
	1985	1986	1987	1988	1989
Credit	$5.66	$6.32	$6.53	$6.98	$7.62
Cash	2.18	2.51	2.48	2.41	2.33

Calculate an unweighted average of relatives value index for each year, using 1985 as the base period.

14-30 A Georgia firm manufacturing heavy equipment has collected the following production information about the company's principal products. Calculate a weighted aggregates quantity index using the quantities and prices from 1989 as the bases and the weights.

	QUANTITIES PRODUCED			COST OF PRODUCTION/UNIT (THOUSANDS)
PRODUCT	1987	1988	1989	1989
River barges	92	118	85	$ 33
Railroad gondola cars	456	475	480	56
Off-the-road trucks	52	56	59	116

 14-31 Arkansas Electronics has marketed three basic types of calculators: for the business sector, the scientific sector, and a simple model capable of basic computational functions. The following information describes unit sales for the past 3 years:

	NUMBER SOLD (× 100,000)			PRICE
MODEL	1987	1988	1989	1989
Business	11.85	13.32	15.75	$34.00
Scientific	10.32	11.09	10.18	69.00
Basic	7.12	7.48	7.89	13.00

Calculate the weighted average of relatives quantity indices using the prices and quantities from 1989 to compute the value weights, with 1987 as the base year.

14-32 Explain the principal disadvantage in using value indices.

14-33   What is the major difference between a weighted aggregates index and a weighted average of relatives index?

14-34   In preparation for an appropriations hearing, the police commissioner of a Maryland town has collected the following information:

TYPE OF CRIME	1986	1987	1988	1989
Assault and rape	110	128	134	129
Murder	30	45	40	48
Robbery	610	720	770	830
Larceny	2,450	2,630	2,910	2,890

Calculate the unweighted average of relatives quantity index for each of these years, using 1989 as the base period.

14-35   William Olsen, owner of a real estate office, has collected the following sales information for each of the firm's sales personnel:

| SALESPERSON | VALUE OF SALES (× 1,000) | | | |
	1986	1987	1988	1989
Thompson	$490	$560	$530	$590
Alfred	630	590	540	680
Jackson	760	790	810	840
Blockard	230	250	240	360

Calculate an unweighted average of relatives value index for each year, using 1986 as the base period.

14-36   After encouraging a chemical company to make its employees handle certain dangerous chemicals with protective gloves, the Public Health Agency is now interested in seeing if this ruling has had its effect in curbing the number of cancer deaths in that area. Before this rule went into effect, cancer was widespread not only among the workers at the company but also among their families, close friends, and neighbors. The following data shows what these numbers were in 1960 before the ruling and what they were after the ruling in 1980.

AGE GROUP	NO. IN POPULATION FOR 1960	DEATHS IN 1960	DEATHS IN 1980
<4 yrs.	5,000	400	125
4–15 yrs.	4,000	295	200
16–35 yrs.	24,000	1,230	1,000
36–60 yrs.	19,000	700	450
>60 yrs.	7,000	1,100	935

Use a weighted aggregates index of the number of deaths, using the 1960 population size as the weights to help the Public Health Agency understand what has happened to the cancer rate.

14-37   A veterinarian has noticed she has treated a large number of pets this past winter. She wonders whether this amount was spread across the 3 winter months evenly or whether she treated more pets in any certain month. Using December as the base period, calculate the weighted average of relatives quantity indices for January and February.

| | NUMBER TREATED | | | PRICE PER VISIT |
	DEC.	JAN.	FEB.	AVERAGE FOR 3 MONTHS
Cats	100	200	95	$ 55
Dogs	125	75	200	65
Parrots	15	20	15	85
Snakes	10	5	5	100

Issues in Constructing and Using Index Numbers

In this chapter, we have used examples with small samples and short time spans. Actually, index numbers are computed for composites with many elements, and they cover long periods of time. This produces relatively accurate measures of changes. However, even the best index numbers are imperfect.

PROBLEMS IN CONSTRUCTION

Although there are many problems in constructing an index number, there are three principal areas of difficulty:

1. **Selecting an item to be included in a composite.** Almost all indices are constructed to answer a particular question. Thus, the items included in the composite depend upon the question. The Consumer Price Index asks, "How much has the price of a certain group of items purchased by moderate-income urban Americans changed from one period to another?" From this question, we know that only those items that reflect the purchases of moderate-income urban families should be included in the composite. We must realize that the Consumer Price Index will less accurately reflect price changes of goods purchased by low- or high-income rural families than by moderate-income urban families.

2. **Selecting the appropriate weights.** In the previous sections of this chapter, we emphasized that the weights selected should represent the relative importance of the various elements. Unfortunately, what is appropriate in one period may become inappropriate in a short period of time. This must be kept in mind when comparing values of indices computed at different times.

3. **Selecting the base period.** Typically, the base period selected should be a normal period, preferably a fairly recent period. "Normal" means that the period should not be at either the peak or the trough of a fluctuation. One technique to avoid using an irregular period is to average the values of several consecutive periods to determine a normal value. The U.S. Bureau of Labor Statistics uses the average of 1982, 1983, and 1984 consumption patterns to compute the Consumer Price Index. Frequently, management tries to select a base period that coincides with the base period for one or more of the major indices, such as the Index of Industrial Production. Use of a common base allows management to relate its index to the major indices.

CAVEATS IN INTERPRETING AN INDEX

In addition to these problems in constructing indices, there are several common errors made in interpreting indices:

1. **Generalization from a specific index.** One of the most common misinterpretations of an index is generalization of the results. The Consumer Price Index measures how prices of a particular combination of goods purchased by moderate-income urban Americans has changed. Despite its specific definition, the Consumer Price Index is frequently described as reflecting the cost of living for all Americans. Although it is related to the cost of living to some degree, to say that it measures the change in the cost of living is incorrect.

2. **Lack of general knowledge regarding published indices.** Part of the problem leading to the error above is lack of knowledge of what the various published

indices measure. All the well-known indices are accompanied by detailed statements concerning measurement. Management should become familiar with exactly what each index measures.

Time affects an index

3. Effect of time span on an index. Factors related to an index tend to change with time. In particular, the appropriate weights tend to change. Thus, unless the weights are changed accordingly, the index becomes less reliable.

Lack of measurement of quality

4. Quality changes. One frequent criticism of index numbers is that they do not reflect changes in the quality of the items they measure. If the quality has indeed changed, then the index either understates or overstates the price level changes. For example, if we construct an index number to describe price changes in pocket calculators over the last decade, the resulting index would understate the actual change that is due to rapid technological improvements in calculators.

Exercises

14-38   What is the effect of time upon the weighting of a composite index?

14-39   List several preferences for the choice of base period.

14-40   Describe a technique used to avoid the use of an irregular period for a base.

14-41   Is it correct to say that the Consumer Price Index measures the "cost of living"?

14-42   What problems exist with index numbers if the quality of an item changes?

14-7
Terms Introduced in Chapter 14

Consumer Price Index The U.S. government prepares this index, which measures changes in the prices of a representative set of consumer items.

Fixed Weight Aggregates Method To weight an aggregates index, this method uses as weights quantities consumed during some representative period.

Index Number A ratio that measures how much a variable changes over time.

Index of Industrial Production Prepared monthly by the Federal Reserve Board, the IIP measures the quantity of production in the areas of manufacturing, mining, and utilities.

Laspeyres Method To weight an aggregates index, this method uses as weights the quantities consumed during the base period.

Paasche Method In weighting an aggregates index, the Paasche method uses as weights the quantities consumed during the current period.

Percentage Relative Ratio of a current value to a base value with the result multiplied by 100.

Price Index Compares levels of prices from one period to another.

Quantity Index A measure of how much the number or quantity of a variable changes over time.

Unweighted Aggregates Index Uses all the values considered, and assigns equal importance to each of these values.

Unweighted Average of Relatives Method To construct an index number, this method first finds the ratio of the current price to the base price for each product, adds the resulting percentage relatives, and then divides by the number of products.

Weighted Aggregates Index Using all the values considered, this index assigns weights to these values.

Weighted Average of Relatives Method To construct an index number, this method weights by importance and uses the value of each element in the composite.

Equations Introduced in Chapter 14

[14-1] $$\text{Unweighted aggregates quantity index} = \frac{\Sigma Q_1}{\Sigma Q_0} \times 100$$ *p. 701*

To compute an unweighted aggregates index, divide the sum of the current year quantities of the elements in the index by the sum of the base year quantities, and multiply the result by 100.

[14-2] $$\text{Weighted aggregates price index} = \frac{\Sigma P_1 Q}{\Sigma P_0 Q} \times 100$$ *p. 705*

For a weighted aggregates price index using quantities as weights, obtain the weighted sum of the current year prices by multiplying each price in the index by its associated quantity and summing the results. Then divide this weighted sum by the weighted sum of the base year prices, and multiply the result by 100.

[14-3] $$\text{Laspeyres index} = \frac{\Sigma P_1 Q_0}{\Sigma P_0 Q_0} \times 100$$ *p. 706*

The Laspeyres price index is a weighted aggregates price index using the base year quantities as weights.

[14-4] $$\text{Paasche index} = \frac{\Sigma P_1 Q_1}{\Sigma P_0 Q_1} \times 100$$ *p. 708*

To get the Paasche price index, we compute a weighted aggregates price index using the current year quantities for weights.

[14-5] $$\text{Fixed weight aggregates price index} = \frac{\Sigma P_1 Q_2}{\Sigma P_0 Q_2} \times 100$$ *p. 709*

The fixed weight aggregates price index is a weighted aggregates price index whose weights are the quantities from a representative year, not necessarily either the base year or the current year.

[14-6] $$\text{Unweighted average of relatives price index} = \frac{\Sigma \left(\frac{P_1}{P_0} \times 100 \right)}{n}$$ *p. 711*

We compute an unweighted average of relatives price index by multiplying the ratios of current prices to base prices by 100, summing the results, and then dividing by the number of elements used in the index.

[14-7] $$\text{Weighted average of relatives price index} = \frac{\Sigma \left[\left(\frac{P_1}{P_0} \times 100 \right) (P_n Q_n) \right]}{\Sigma P_n Q_n}$$ *p. 713*

With this index, we weight the relative prices by the values for a fixed reference period and divide the weighted sum of relative prices by the sum of the weights. If we use the base year values as weights, we get:

[14-8]

$$\frac{\sum\left[\left(\frac{P_1}{P_0}\times 100\right)(P_0 Q_0)\right]}{\sum P_0 Q_0}$$

p. 713

which is the same as the Laspeyres price index.

[14-9]

$$\text{Weighted average of relatives quantity index} = \frac{\sum\left[\left(\frac{Q_1}{Q_0}\times 100\right)(Q_n P_n)\right]}{\sum Q_n P_n}$$

p. 717

In this quantity index, we weight the relative quantities by the values for a fixed reference period and divide the weighted sum by the sum of the weights.

14-9
Chapter Review Exercises

14-43   Kamischika Motorcycles began producing three models of mopeds in 1987. For the 3 years 1987 through 1989, sales were as follows:

MODEL	AVERAGE ANNUAL PRICE			UNITS SOLD (× 10,000)		
	1987	1988	1989	1987	1988	1989
I	$139	$155	$149	3.7	4.1	7.6
II	169	189	189	2.3	4.6	8.1
III	199	205	219	1.6	2.1	3.4

(a)   Calculate the weighted average of relatives price indices using the prices and quantities from 1989 as the bases and weights.
(b)   Calculate the weighted average of relatives price indices using the total dollar values for each year as the weights and 1989 as the base year.

14-44   These data indicate the value (in millions of dollars) of the principal products exported by a developing country. Determine unweighted aggregate value indices for 1987 and 1989 based on 1985.

COMMODITY	1985	1987	1989
Coffee	$834	$1,436	$1,321
Sugar	96	118	122
Copper	241	258	269
Zinc	142	125	106

14-45   In a survey of U.S. coal production for 4 years, the information below was collected. Using the value of the 1986 production for weighting and 1986 as the base year, calculate the weighted average of relatives quantity index for each of the 4 years.

TYPE OF COAL	PRODUCTION (MILLIONS OF TONS)				VALUE (MILLIONS) 1986
	1983	1984	1985	1986	
Anthracite	7.4	6.8	7.1	7.2	$ 90
Bituminous	595	580	601	625	5,050

14-46 A survey by the National Dairy Products Association produced the following information. Construct a Laspeyres index with 1985 as the base period.

PRODUCT	AVERAGE PRICE PER UNIT		TOTAL QUANTITY (BILLIONS) 1985
	1985	1989	
Cheese (lbs.)	$1.45	$1.49	2.6
Milk (gals.)	1.60	1.61	47.6
Butter (lbs.)	70	80	3.1

14-47 Robert Barry, Ltd., a garment consulting firm, has examined the pricing trends of clothing items for a client. This table contains the results of the survey (shown in unit prices):

PRODUCTS	1986	1987	1988	1989
Jeans	$13.00	$13.00	$15.00	$15.00
Jackets	19.00	19.50	22.00	24.00
Shirts	12.00	11.00	12.00	13.00

Calculate an unweighted average of relatives index for each year, using 1986 as the base period.

14-48 What problem would exist in comparing price indices describing computer sales over the past few decades?

14-49 The VP of sales for the National Hospital Supply Company conducted a survey of travel expenses incurred by selected salespeople. Of particular interest were the following data regarding expenditures for gasoline and the price paid per gallon.

SALESPEOPLE	EXPENDITURES ON GASOLINE			AVERAGE PRICE/GALLON 1985
	1985	1986	1987	
A	$704	$ 985	$1,391	.52
B	635	875	1,306	.55
C	752	1,023	1,523	.59
D	503	696	1,106	.56
E	593	781	1,215	.55

Calculate an unweighted average of relatives index for each year, using 1987 as the base period.

14-50 This information describes the unit sales of a bicycle shop for 3 years:

MODEL	NUMBER SOLD			PRICE 1987
	1987	1988	1989	
Sport	45	48	56	$ 89
Touring	64	67	71	104
Cross-country	28	35	27	138
Sprint	21	16	28	245

Calculate the weighted average of relatives quantity indices, using the prices and quantities from 1987 to compute the value weights, with 1987 as the base year.

14-51 Denise Alford, accountant for a mass-transit system, has recorded the following per-vehicle expenses for the years 1985, 1987, and 1989. Using 1987 as the base period, express the expenses of 1985 and 1989 in terms of an unweighted aggregates index.

COSTS	1985	1987	1989
Fuel	$24,378	$36,421	$37,613
Wages	1,816	2,019	2,136
Maintenance	638	681	701

14-52 An Ohio consumer protection agency has surveyed the price changes of a meat-packing company. The following table contains the average annual per-pound prices for a sample of the firm's products. Construct an unweighted average of relatives price index using the prices from 1987 as the base period.

PRODUCTS	1987	1988	1989
Sirloin	$1.69	$1.81	$1.85
Chuck	.91	1.15	1.24
Bologna	1.45	1.58	1.53
Hot dogs	.99	1.03	1.01
Rib eyes	2.39	2.61	2.56

14-53 Why must one exercise caution in selecting a base period?

14-54 Harry Wada, a purchasing agent, has compiled the price information presented below. Using 1986 as the base period, calculate the unweighted aggregates price index for 1987, 1988, and 1989.

MATERIAL	1986	1987	1988	1989
Aluminum	$ .96	$ .99	$1.03	$1.06
Steel	1.48	1.54	1.55	1.59
Brass tubing	.21	.25	.26	.31
Copper wire	.06	.08	.07	.09

14-55 A USDA survey of grain production for selected areas in the U.S. yielded this information:

PRODUCT	QUANTITIES PRODUCED (MILLIONS OF BUSHELS)					PRICE PER BUSHEL 1985
	1985	1986	1987	1988	1989	
Wheat	610	620	640	630	650	$ 4.40
Corn	390	390	410	440	440	3.60
Oats	100	90	120	130	150	1.20
Rye	10	20	10	10	20	24.00
Barley	160	150	120	190	180	2.10
Soybeans	130	140	160	120	130	5.60

Using the prices from 1985 for weights, calculate the weighted aggregates quantity indices for each year.

14-56 John Pringle, an international mineral trader, has collected the following information on prices and quantities of minerals exported by an African country for the years 1988 and 1989. Calculate a Paasche index for 1989, using 1988 as the base period.

MINERAL	QUANTITY (MILLION TONS) 1989	PRICE (PER LB.) 1988	1989
Copper	38.1	$.59	$.63
Lead	53.5	.17	.16
Zinc	86.4	.21	.23

14-57 A European automobile manufacturer has compiled the following information on car sales of one U.S. manufacturer:

SIZE	AVERAGE ANNUAL PRICE (HUNDREDS) 1985	1987	1989	UNITS SOLD (×1,000) 1985	1987	1989
Subcompact	$62	$68	$70	32	65	86
Compact	76	78	80	45	68	73
Sedan	90	98	106	462	325	386

(a) Calculate the weighted average of relatives price indices using the prices and quantities from 1987 as the bases and weights.
(b) Calculate the weighted average of relatives price indices using the total dollar values for each year as the weights and 1987 as the base year.

14-58 Sylvia Jensen, cost analyst for a major appliance firm, has compiled price data for four of the company's products. The figures (given in unit prices) for 1987 through 1990 are shown in the table below:

PRODUCTS	1987	1988	1989	1990
Dishwasher	$219	$241	$272	$306
Washing machine	362	385	397	413
Dryer	229	241	261	275
Refrigerator	562	580	598	625

Using 1987 as the base period, express the prices in 1988, 1989, and 1990 in terms of an unweighted aggregates index.

14-59 The budget director for a New England college wants to keep track of the budget that each engineering department requires to recruit new graduate students. He has received the following data from four departments.

DEPARTMENT	TOTAL EXPENDITURES 1988	1989	1990
Mechanical	$3,642	$3,891	$4,253
Chemical	3,888	4,052	4,425
Biomedical	4,251	4,537	4,724
Electrical	3,764	4,305	4,297

Calculate an unweighted average of relatives index for each year using 1988 as the base period.

14-60 In 1985, the average weekly wage for a certain group of households was $422.60. In 1990, the average weekly wage for the same group was $521.35. The Consumer Price Index in 1990, using 1985 as a base, was 152. Calculate the "real" average weekly wage for this group in 1990.

14-61 A national shopping survey was conducted to study the average weekly buying habits of a typical family in 1986 and 1990. The data collected are as follows:

ITEMS	1986 UNIT PRICE	1986 QUANTITY	1990 UNIT PRICE	1990 QUANTITY
Cheese (8 oz.)	$1.19	2	$2.09	1
Bread (1 loaf)	.79	3	1.09	3
Eggs (1 doz.)	.84	2	1.35	1
Milk (1 gal.)	1.36	2	2.39	2

Calculate a Paasche index for 1990 using 1986 as the base period.

14-62 A recent survey by the American Association of Colleges for Teacher Education indicates that there has been a jump in interest in teaching. Average enrollment figures for 90 teaching programs (broken down by subject areas) are given in the table below.

	1987	1988	1989	1990
Math	73	76	112	107
Science	101	129	163	162
English	163	189	271	268
History	183	210	303	298

Calculate the unweighted average of relatives quantity index for each of these years, using 1990 as the base period.

14-63 Francis Hill, president of an agricultural trade consulting company, has obtained the following information on grain (prices and sales) exported by the United States.

PRODUCT	AMOUNT EXPORTED (IN MILLIONS OF TONS) 1986	1987	1988	1989	PRICE PER TON 1988
Wheat	4.6	6.7	4.0	5.2	$2,680
Feed Grains	4.9	6.2	1.8	1.2	2,270
Soybeans	4.7	5.7	1.2	1.8	3,430

Compute the weighted aggregates quantity indices for each year, using the prices for 1988 as weights, and 1988 as the base year.

14-64 Andrea Graham, a budget analyst for a long-distance phone company, has collected price and sales volume data for phone calls from New York to Boston. The data for each of the three rate schedules are given below.

RATE (TIMES)	PRICE PER CALL (PER MINUTE) 1985	1990	TOTAL # CALLS (MILLIONS) 1985
Day (8am–5pm)	$.17	$.19	5.2
Evening (5pm–11pm)	.13	.16	8.7
Night (11pm–8am)	.09	.12	10.3

Construct a Laspeyres price index using 1985 as the base period.

14-65 The Reliable Bus Company provides transportation for its own town, and in addition, it sells buses to neighboring towns. The company has collected the following data in order to analyze its sales for years 1986, 1988, and 1990.

| TOWN | AVERAGE SELLING PRICE PER BUS | | | NUMBER OF BUSES SOLD |
	1986	1988	1990	1988
Greenville	$21,206	$24,210	$26,235	17
Hampton	17,129	19,722	22,109	14
Middletown	25,723	28,657	32,481	21

Construct a Laspeyres index using 1988 as the base period.

14-66 A local fast-food restaurant wants to examine how sales are changing for each of its four most popular menu items. The data for the years 1987 through 1990 are listed in the table below.

| MENU ITEM | UNIT PRICE | | | | QUANTITY SOLD (MILLIONS) | | | |
	1987	1988	1989	1990	1987	1988	1989	1990
Hamburger	$.58	$.62	$.69	$.79	2.1	2.5	2.0	1.8
Chicken Sandwich	1.89	2.09	2.18	2.25	1.5	1.2	1.8	2.1
French Fries	.84	.89	.99	.99	2.9	2.7	2.3	2.4
Onion Rings	.91	.99	1.14	1.19	3.1	2.4	2.0	1.6

Calculate a fixed weight aggregates index for each year, using 1987 prices as the base and the 1990 prices as the fixed weights.

14-67 Use the data from Problem 14-66 to calculate a Paasche index for each year, using 1989 as the base period.

14-10
Chapter Concepts Test

Answers are in the back of the book.

T F 1. The index number for a base year is always zero.

T F 2. Index numbers can be used to measure differences in a given variable in several locations.

T F 3. The simplest form of a composite index is an unweighted aggregates index.

T F 4. A disadvantage of the Laspeyres method is that indices are not comparable to one another.

T F 5. If the fixed weight aggregates method is used, with the chosen value period being the base period, this is the same as the Paasche method.

T F 6. The average of relatives method sums percentages, not amounts.

T F 7. A substantial price change for a slow-moving item can completely distort an unweighted index.

T F 8. In times of inflation, a quantity index provides a better measure of actual output than a corresponding value index.

T F 9. A value index measures the combined effects of price and quantity changes.

T F 10. When using the weighted average of relatives price index, indices from different periods are always comparable.

T F 11. The Laspeyres method is most commonly used because it requires quantity measures for only one period.

T F 12. An index number is always found by taking the ratio of a current value to a base value and multiplying by 100.

T F 13. A chief advantage of index numbers is that selection of an improper base does not distort them.

T F 14. While often used as measurements in and of themselves, index numbers can also be used as parts of intermediate computations.

T F 15. Whenever we use the symbol P_1 in one of our index formulas, we are referring to the price in the base year.

T F 16. With the aggregates or average of relatives index, it is more common to weight the elements making up the index.

T F 17. The major disadvantage of an unweighted aggregates index is that it does not allow for changes in price.

T F 18. The Consumer Price Index and the Index of Industrial Production are both examples of a value index.

T F 19. The weighted average of relatives method divides the weighted sum by the sum of the weights.

T F 20. Index numbers are inherently confusing and thus are seldom used in the real world.

T F 21. The Consumer Price Index measure is based on a single variable.

22. If an index number calculation over 8 years with a base value of 100 gave an index for 1976 of 110, what would be the percentage relative for 1976?
    (a) 110 (d) 880
    (b) 90.9 (e) Cannot be determined from information given
    (c) 13.75

23. To measure changes in total monetary worth, one should calculate:
    (a) A price index (c) A value index
    (b) A quantity index (d) None of these

24. Suppose that the composite price index for 1 gallon of milk, 2 loaves of bread, and 1 pound of hamburger was 110 in 1989 and 119 in 1990. If both these indices were computed from a 1988 base of 100, how much did the general price level rise between 1989 and 1990?
    (a) 9% (d) 7.56%
    (b) 8.18% (e) Cannot be determined from information given
    (c) 19%

25. Which of the following describes an advantage of using the Laspeyres method?
    (a) Many commonly used quantity measures are not tabulated for every period.
    (b) Changes in consumption patterns are taken into account.
    (c) One index can be easily compared with another.
    (d) All of these.
    (e) a and c but not b.

26. Suppose that the weighted aggregates price index for a set of prices was calculated as 106 using the Laspeyres method and as 112 using the Paasche method. What can be concluded from this?
    (a) The Paasche index is incorrect.
    (b) There is a trend toward less expensive goods.
    (c) There is a trend toward more expensive goods.
    (d) The difference between the two indices can be attributed to a poor estimation of consumer attitudes.
    (e) a and d only.

27. When computing a weighted average of relatives index, we would be best able to compare indices from various periods if:
    (a) Base values were used as $P_n Q_n$.
    (b) Current values were used as $P_n Q_n$.
    (c) Fixed values were used as $P_n Q_n$.
    (d) Either base or fixed values were used as $P_n Q_n$.
    (e) Either current values or fixed values were used as $P_n Q_n$.

28. Commodities that are subject to considerable price variations could best be measured by a:
    (a) Price index (c) Value index
    (b) Quantity index (d) None of these

29. A base period can be described as a "normal" period if:
   (a) It is at neither the peak nor the trough of a fluctuation.
   (b) It is the most recent period for which we have data.
   (c) There was no inflation or deflation of prices during the period.
   (d) It is the average of several consecutive periods.

30. The weights used in a quantity index are:
   (a) Percentages of total quantity   (c) Average of quantities
   (b) Prices   (d) None of these

31. In the unweighted average of relatives method, $\frac{P_1}{P_0} \times 100$ should be calculated for each product in the composite. What is then done with these values to finish the calculation?
   (a) The values are multiplied together.
   (b) The largest value is found.
   (c) The values are averaged.
   (d) The average difference from the median of the values is found and then squared.

32. If you wanted to measure how much the cost of a particular variable changes over time, you would use:
   (a) A value index   (d) All of these
   (b) An inflation index   (e) None of these
   (c) A quantity index

33. It is possible to change the base year without changing the quantities used for weights when using the:
   (a) Paasche method   (c) Weighted aggregates method
   (b) Laspeyres method   (d) None of these

34. When the base year values are used as weights, the weighted average of relatives price index is the same as
   (a) the Paasche index.
   (b) the Laspeyres index.
   (c) the unweighted average of relatives price index.
   (d) none of the above.

35. One primary difference between average of relatives methods and aggregates methods is that
   (a) aggregates methods sum all prices before finding the ratio.
   (b) average of relatives methods sum all prices before finding the ratio.
   (c) aggregates methods are only useful for price indices.
   (d) a and c but not b.
   (e) none of the above.

36. Comparing price indices of military airplanes from 1970 to 1990
   (a) would be a great way of proving how defense spending has skyrocketed in the last 20 years.
   (b) would best be accomplished using the Paasche method.
   (c) should use the average of 1971 and 1972 for the base period.
   (d) would make little sense, given the significant technological differences in the items being compared.

37. If the organizers of the 1989 Ironman Triathlon wished to evaluate the winning times each year, relative to the winning time in 1977 (the first year of the competition), they might use
   (a) an unweighted aggregates index, with 1977 as the base.
   (b) a weighted aggregates index with 1977 as the base, using the number of competitors each year as the weights.
   (c) the Paasche method.
   (d) any of the above.
   (e) a or b but not c.

38. If all the values considered in calculating an index are of equal importance, the index is
   _____.

39. The weighted index method in which quantities consumed during the base period are used as weights is the _____ method.

40. If we sum all the values in calculating an index, the index is called _____.

41. Using weights from a representative period (which is not necessarily the base or current period) to compute a weighted aggregates price index is the _____ aggregates method.

42. The _____ method uses quantities consumed in the current period in question when computing a weighted index.

43. We must realize that the mechanical approach of index numbers is subject to considerable _____ and _____.

44. The three principal types of indices are the _____ index, the _____ index and the _____ index.

45. The _____ is calculated by taking a ratio of the current value to a base value and multiplying by 100.

14-11
Conceptual Case

(Northern White Metals Company)

Dick sat in his office early one cold December evening. "Jody has done her usual thorough job," he thought, as he reviewed the large volume of information that had arrived in the afternoon mail. The analysis was complete, but it was also rather complex. Bleary-eyed at the end of a long day, Dick decided to postpone any further work until the morning.

At 7:30 A.M. the following day, a hot cup of coffee in hand, Dick again began to review the analysis of building-products sales and raw-material price trends Jody had provided. Primary aluminum prices were currently a bit depressed but had been heading upward for many years. Dick knew the industry had undergone several overcapacity–undercapacity cycles during these years, which led to alternating high and low raw-material prices. Nevertheless, the data seemed to reveal generally increasing costs to NWMC. Turning to the next section of Jody's report, Dick was surprised at what he found. She had compiled some additional data, information he had not requested, with a brief note of explanation. Dick picked up the phone and called New York.

"I knew you'd be calling," Jody answered. "What did you think of the little bonus analysis?"

"I'm not quite sure," Dick replied. "I know you did a lot of work on this, but all I expected was sales and materials cost trends. It's a little hard to relate all these other factors, how they've changed, and whatnot. What prompted you to check all these things out, anyway?"

Impatient that Dick had not yet perceived the full significance of the analysis, Jody explained. "Actually, it was Sarah's idea. We noticed the trends in materials cost, and then she decided to do a little research. We checked out the price trends of raw aluminum production equipment, and they've been moving in a different direction—that is, down!"

"Wait a minute," Dick interrupted. "If you're suggesting we start manufacturing our own primary aluminum . . ."

"I know, I know," Jody responded. "That requires a huge investment in mining and other production equipment that Northern could never afford."

"You bet it does," Dick said.

"But," Jody added with emphasis, "you could afford recycling equipment to melt down scrap and waste aluminum. We checked out scrap resale prices and, with the way high-tech applications products are growing," she continued enthusiastically, "well, we think you should add some scrap-melting capacity."

Dick sat back, amazed.

"You guys don't kid around, do you?" he said with admiration. "I want to review all this in detail, as there are some pretty obvious implications for my long-term planning. But honestly, Jody, isn't there some way you can arrange all this information to make it a little easier to understand *and* present? We have all these variables, and they're all changing in all different directions, and . . ."

"Easy Dick," Jody reassured him. "Sarah has already taken care of that. We sent out the information last night, so you can expect it before noon. Call me if you have any other questions or need any more work done. Things are a little slow around here."

Dick, appreciative of the scope of the analysis Jody and Sarah conducted for him, nevertheless wanted additional help in understanding how these many variables have changed over time. Furthermore, he hopes the implications of these changes, which so interested Sarah and Jody, will be made clearer. Anticipating this in advance, Jody has assured Dick that Sarah has taken the appropriate action. What would Sarah have done to measure and relate the changes in materials prices, equipment costs, scrap prices, and so on, to enable Dick to better understand and utilize the information? What difficulties might she have encountered, and what qualifications might she wish to provide Dick for interpreting the data?

14-12
Computer Data Base Exercise

Laurel knocked on Hal's door. "You wanted to see me?" she asked.

"Yes, please come in Laurel, and close the door behind you," Hal said, looking up from the stack of papers on his desk. "Thanks for coming by. I've got some decision making to do which, unfortunately, won't be a lot of fun, and I could use your help."

"Sure," Laurel nodded. "I'll be glad to do what I can." Hal looked unusually troubled, and Laurel wondered what was up.

"It's about our employee benefits," Hal began. "I don't know if you're aware of how health insurance costs have skyrocketed in recent years, but it's getting incredibly expensive for us to carry policies for our employees. Several small business owners I know have stopped providing health insurance altogether, but I just can't do that. I've always tried to do the best by my employees, but I need help with some justification for my next move, which may seem rather drastic to the people on my staff. I think if I have some information about previous trends and how the current situation fits in, it will be easier to convince them of its necessity."

"Let me give you some background," he continued. "Until a few years ago, we could expect a 10–12 percent yearly increase in insurance costs. More recently, however, the increase has been closer to 20 percent per year, and our agent is predicting as high as 30 percent increases in the near future. The company policy has always been to pay at least 75 percent of the premium, with the rest being covered by paycheck deductions.

Family coverage costs us 2.5 times that for individuals, so that's what is reflected in the deductions the employees see. For a long time, we managed to get by without increasing the rates to employees, but it became necessary to implement yearly increases several years ago. In my efforts to give employees the best deal possible, I'm afraid the deductions haven't kept pace with what is required. I don't mind the company bearing a *little* more of the cost, but we can't survive at this rate that much longer. What I need from you is an idea of what's reasonable, based on past history. What do you think?"

"I'll see what I can do," answered Laurel. "I think I can generate some index numbers which capture past trends, and come up with some recommendations for you."

"Great," smiled Hal, "here are some historical figures. You know, I hate being caught between being a nice guy and running a business!"

1. Compute a weighted aggregates price index of employee contribution to health insurance using the number of "individual" and "family" employees covered each year from 1971 to 1991, as shown in Table DB14-1. Use 1971 as the base year. Compare this to an index of the total company insurance cost per year.

2. The anticipated insurance policy cost for 1992 is $270,000, and there are 20 "individual" and 45 "family" employees to be insured. If Hal doesn't mind the total-cost-index to employee-contribution-index ratio running as high as 1.2, what must the individual and family deductions be for 1992?

TABLE DB14-1

YEAR	INDIVIDUAL	YEARLY DEDUCTION	FAMILY	YEARLY DEDUCTION	TOTAL COMPANY INSURANCE COST
1971	3	$180	7	$450	$ 15,000
1972	4	180	8	450	17,600
1973	5	150	10	375	19,500
1974	4	150	11	375	22,000
1975	6	150	13	375	24,300
1976	8	150	14	375	27,300
1977	7	150	17	375	31,000
1978	10	150	18	375	34,500
1979	12	150	20	375	38,800
1980	13	150	24	375	44,100
1981	14	150	26	375	49,000
1982	12	160	28	400	55,200
1983	15	170	28	425	61,300
1984	15	180	30	450	68,100
1985	18	200	33	500	79,400
1986	19	210	35	525	92,800
1987	17	230	35	575	108,000
1988	18	250	37	625	126,400
1989	18	270	39	675	150,000
1990	17	300	40	750	180,000
1991	18	320	43	800	219,000

14-13
From the Textbook to the Real World

Index of Leading Economic Indicators

For businesses suffering through cycles of economic prosperity and depression, the composite index of leading economic indicators provides a means of attaining advance information about the future direction of the economy. Although not infallible, this index number provides a tool economists have used for more than 50 years to divine future trends. The system of leading, coincident, and lagging indicators was originally developed by Arthur F. Burns, Wesley C. Mitchell, and their colleagues at the National Bureau of Economic Research (NBER) during the Great Depression. It is currently maintained by the U.S. Department of Commerce and updated on a monthly basis.

Composition and History: The index is a weighted average consisting of eleven components (Table RW14-1), each of which has historically moved ahead of periods of general business expansion and decline. The data are combined into an index which measures the change from the base year (1982) value of 100. The index tends to foreshadow movements in the general economy and was first used to determine when the U.S. would come out of the depression of the 1930s. From 1923 to 1969, the NBER predicted seven major economic contractions. Analysis of the leading indicators during this period shows that on average, 75 percent of the indicators turned down prior to the peak of the economic cycle. Periodically, the index is tested and recalibrated to ensure its continued accuracy. For example, in 1975 it was modified to reflect the influence of rampant price inflation which had begun to distort its forecasts.

Benefit and Limitations: The importance of the index of leading economic indicators is demonstrated in its use as the government's chief economic forecasting tool. Although it sometimes signals turning points which never materialize, it has generally been successful in signaling those that

TABLE RW-1 Components of the Leading Indicator Index

- Average weekly hours of production or nonsupervisory workers, manufacturing.
- Average weekly initial claims for unemployment insurance, state programs.
- Manufacturers' new orders in 1982 dollars, consumer goods and materials industries.
- Index of stock prices, 500 common stocks.
- Contracts and orders for plant and equipment in 1982 dollars.
- Index of new private housing units authorized by local building permits.
- Vendor performance, slower deliveries diffusion index.
- Index of consumer expectations.
- Change in manufacturers' unfilled orders in 1982 dollars, durable goods industries.
- Change in sensitive material prices.
- Money supply M2 in 1982 dollars.

have occurred. A rule of thumb among economists is that 3 successive months of decline in the index are a sign of an impending recession. The index may sometimes be misleading in that indicators may exhibit random fluctuations due to events such as strikes or severe weather. Reporting lags create another deficiency in the index. Regardless of the frequency of reporting, data are reported with lags and are subject to revision weeks, months, or years later. The index is only one tool that provides information which is more qualitative than quantitative. An analysis of underlying economic factors using the index of leading economic indicators in conjunction with other forecasting devices benefits businesses by providing a broad picture of economic activity which can be translated into effective data for policy and strategic decisions.

Flow Chart

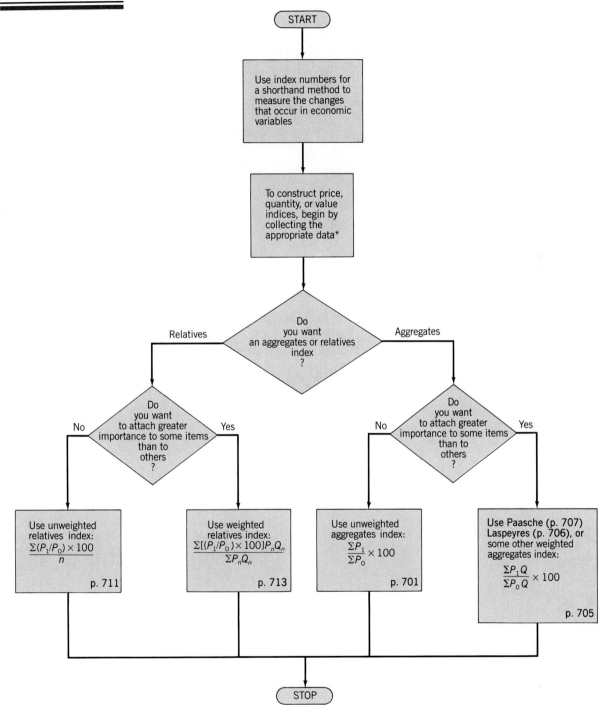

START

Use index numbers for a shorthand method to measure the changes that occur in economic variables

To construct price, quantity, or value indices, begin by collecting the appropriate data*

Do you want an aggregates or relatives index?

Relatives   Aggregates

Do you want to attach greater importance to some items than to others?

No   Yes

Do you want to attach greater importance to some items than to others?

No   Yes

Use unweighted relatives index:
$$\frac{\Sigma(P_1/P_0) \times 100}{n}$$
p. 711

Use weighted relatives index:
$$\frac{\Sigma[(P_1/P_0) \times 100]P_nQ_n}{\Sigma P_nQ_n}$$
p. 713

Use unweighted aggregates index:
$$\frac{\Sigma P_1}{\Sigma P_0} \times 100$$
p. 701

Use Paasche (p. 707) Laspeyres (p. 706), or some other weighted aggregates index:
$$\frac{\Sigma P_1 Q}{\Sigma P_0 Q} \times 100$$
p. 705

STOP

*All formulas in this flow chart are for price indices. Those for quantity or value indices are similar, and many of them are included in the chapter

Acme Fruit and Produce Wholesalers buys blueberries, then sells them to retailers. Acme currently pays $20 a case. Berries sold on the same day bring $32 a case. Extremely perishable, berries not sold on the first day are worth only $2 a case. Acme has calculated that the mean past daily sales is 60 cases and that the standard deviation of past daily sales is 10 cases. Using the techniques introduced in this chapter, we can tell Acme how many cases to order each day to maximize profits.

15

Decision Theory

■ **OBJECTIVES**

Most consequential managerial decisions must be made under conditions of uncertainty, because managers seldom have complete information about what the future will bring. In our final chapter, we shall learn methods that are useful when we must decide among alternatives despite uncertain conditions. We shall also investigate how to determine the worth of additional information. As a student, you make complex decisions about which questions are apt to appear on examinations and what study times will be required to earn certain grades in a course. When you do this, you demonstrate intuitive use of some techniques we shall introduce here.

In section 3 of Chapter 5 (beginning on page 201) we introduced you to the idea of using expected value in decision making. There we worked through a simple problem involving the purchase of strawberries for resale. That kind of problem is part of a set of problems that can be solved using the techniques developed in this chapter.

What is decision theory?

In the last 30 years, managers have used newly developed statistical techniques to solve problems for which information was incomplete, uncertain, or in some cases almost completely lacking. This new area of statistics has a variety of names: *statistical decision theory, Bayesian decision theory* (after the Reverend Thomas Bayes, whom we introduced in Chapter 4), or simply *decision theory.* These names are used interchangeably.

When we did hypothesis testing, we had to decide whether to accept or to reject the stated hypothesis. In decision theory, we must decide among alternatives by taking into account the *monetary* repercussions of our actions. A manager who must select from among a number of available investments should consider the profit or loss that might result from each alternative. Applying decision theory involves selecting an alternative and having a reasonable idea of the economic consequences of choosing that action.

15-1
The Decision Environment

Decision theory can be applied to problems whether the time span is 5 years or 1 day, whether they involve financial management or a plant assembly line, and whether they are in the public or private sector. Regardless of the environment, most of these problems have common characteristics. As a result, decision makers approach their solutions in fairly consistent ways. The elements common to most decision-theory problems are these:

Elements common to decision-theory problems

1. **An objective the decision maker is trying to reach.** If the objective is to minimize downtime of expensive machinery, the manager may try to find the optimal number of spare motors to be kept on hand for quick repairs. Success in finding that number can be measured by counting downtime each month.

2. **Several courses of action.** The decision should involve a choice among alternatives (called *acts*). In our example involving spare motors, the various acts open to the decision maker include stocking one, two, three, four, or five spare motors or choosing not to stock any spare motors.

3. **A calculable measure of the benefit or worth of the various alternatives.** In general, these costs can be negative or positive and are called *payoffs.* Cost accountants should be able to determine the cost of lost production time resulting from a motor burnout both when a spare is on hand and when one is not available. But sometimes the payoffs involve consequences that are more than solely financial. Imagine trying to decide the optimal number of spare generators a hospital might require in the event of a power failure. Not having enough could cost lives as well as money.

4. **Events beyond the control of the decision maker.** These uncontrollable occurrences are often called *outcomes* or *states of nature,* and their existence creates difficulties as well as interest in decision making under uncertainty. Such events could be the number of motors in our expensive production machinery that will burn out in a given month. Preventive maintenance will reduce motor burnouts, but they will still happen.

5. **Uncertainty concerning which outcome or state of nature will actually happen.** In our example, we are uncertain about how many motors will burn out. This uncertainty is generally handled by the use of probabilities assigned to the various events that might take place, say a .1 chance of losing five motors a month.

Exercises

15-1 Wholesale Lamps has been in contact with Leerie's, a local retail lamp shop, about supplying it with a special chrome tree lamp, which the shop wants to use as a drawing card in an upcoming sale. Wholesale Lamps must order the lamps in 2 days to deliver them by the sale date. Wholesale's cost is $49 for the lamps; it will sell them to Leerie's for $54. Wholesale is uncertain about the number Leerie's desires but guesses that it will be between 15 and 20. One of the managers has assigned probabilities to the various numbers that Leerie's might order. The manager of Wholesale Lamps does not foresee a market for the lamps it does not sell to Leerie's. Leerie's is expected to submit the order tomorrow. Should the manager of Wholesale Lamps use decision theory to order the lamps for Leerie's?

15-2 Adventures, Inc., is a source of capital for entrepreneurs starting new firms in the field of genetic engineering. Lisa Levin, a partner in Adventures, has been examining several business proposals that have recently been made to her. Each proposal describes a new venture, outlines its potential market, and solicits investment by Adventures. Lisa has just finished reading the chapter on decision theory in her father's statistics text. She thinks it provides a methodology which can help her decide which ventures to support and at what level. Is Lisa correct? If so, what information does she need in order to apply decision theory to her problem? If not, why not?

15-3 The 8th Avenue Book Store relied on the Grambler News Service to supply it with several well-known magazines. Each week, Grambler would deliver a predetermined number of *Today's Romances,* among others, and pick up any unsold copies of the previous week's magazines. The number of copies that the bookstore would sell was never known for sure, but the manager did have past sales data. Grambler charged its bookstands 38¢ for magazines that sold for 50¢. Management of the bookstore wanted to get maximum profitability from the sale of its magazines and was considering the optimal number of *Today's Romances* to order. Should the manager of the bookstore use decision theory to decide the number of magazines to stock?

15-2
Expected Profit under Uncertainty: Assigning Probability Values

Buying decision under conditions of uncertainty

Buying and selling strawberries, as in our example in Chapter 5, is only one case in which decisions have to be made under uncertainty. Another involves a newspaper dealer who buys newspapers for 6¢ each and sells them for 10¢ each. Any papers not sold by the end of the day are completely worthless to him. The dealer's problem is to determine the optimal number he should order each day. On days when he stocks more than he sells, his profits are reduced by the cost of the unsold papers. On days when buyers request more copies than he has in stock, he loses sales and makes smaller profits than he could have.

The dealer has kept a record of his sales for the past 100 days (Table 15-1). This information is a distribution of the dealer's past sales. Because sales volume can take

TABLE 15-1 Distribution of Newspaper Sales

DAILY SALES	NUMBER OF DAYS SOLD	PROBABILITY OF EACH NUMBER BEING SOLD
300	15	.15
400	20	.20
500	45	.45
600	15	.15
700	5	.05
	100	**1.00**

on only a limited number of values, the distribution is discrete. We will assume, for purposes of discussion, that the dealer will sell only the numbers of papers listed — not, say, 412, 525, or 637. Furthermore, the dealer has no reason to believe that sales volume will take on any other value in the future.

Computing probabilities of sales levels This information tells the dealer something about the historical pattern of his sales. Although it does not tell him what quantity the buyers will request tomorrow, it does tell him that there are 45 chances in 100 that the quantity will be 500 papers. Therefore, a probability of .45 is assigned to the sales figure of 500 papers. The probability column in Table 15-1 shows the relationship between the total observations of sales (100 days) and the number of times each possible value of daily sales appeared in the 100 observations. The probability of each sales level occurring is thus derived by dividing the total number of times each value has appeared in the 100 observations by the total number of observations, that is, 15/100, 20/100, 45/100, 15/100, and 5/100.

MAXIMIZING PROFITS INSTEAD OF MINIMIZING LOSSES

Back in section 3 of Chapter 5, when we first introduced you to using expected value in decision making, we used an approach that minimized losses and led us to an optimal stocking pattern for our strawberry dealer. It is just as easy to find the optimal stocking pattern by *maximizing profits,* and that's just what we'll do at this point.

A Chapter 5 problem worked another way Recall that our fruit and vegetable wholesaler in Chapter 5 bought strawberries at $20 a case and resold them at $50 a case. There we assumed that the product had no value if not sold on the first day (a restriction we shall soon lift). If buyers call for more cases tomorrow than the wholesaler has in stock, profits suffer by $30 (selling price minus cost) for each case he cannot sell. On the other hand, costs also result from stocking *too many* units on a given day. If the wholesaler has thirteen cases in stock but sells only ten, he makes a profit of $300, or $30 a case on ten cases. But this profit must be reduced by $60, the cost of the three cases not sold and of no value.

A 100-day observation of past sales gives the information shown in Table 15-2. The probability values there are obtained just as they were in Table 5-6.

Notice that there are only four discrete values for sales volume, and as far as we know, there is no discernible pattern in the sequence in which these four values occur. We assume that the retailer has no reason to believe sales volume will behave differently in the future.

TABLE 15-2 Cases Sold During 100 Days

DAILY SALES	NUMBER OF DAYS SOLD	PROBABILITY OF EACH NUMBER BEING SOLD
10	15	.15
11	20	.20
12	40	.40
13	25	.25
	100	1.00

CALCULATING CONDITIONAL PROFITS

To illustrate this retailer's problem, we can construct a table showing the results in dollars of all possible combinations of purchases and sales. The only values for purchases and for sales that have meaning to us are ten, eleven, twelve, and thirteen cases, because the retailer has no reason to consider buying fewer than ten or more than thirteen cases.

Conditional profit table

Table 15-3, called a *conditional profit table,* shows the profit resulting from any possible combination of supply and demand. The profits could be either positive or negative (although they are all positive in this example) and are conditional in that a certain profit results from taking a specific stocking action (ordering ten, eleven, twelve, or thirteen cases) and selling a specific number of cases (ten, eleven, twelve, or thirteen cases).

Table 15-3 reflects the losses that occur when stock remains unsold at the end of a day. Notice, too, that the retailer forgoes potential additional profit when customers demand more cases than he has stocked.

Explaining elements in the conditional profit table

Observe that the stocking of ten cases each day will always result in a profit of $300. Even on those days when buyers want thirteen cases, the retailer can sell only ten. When the retailer stocks eleven cases, his profit will be $330 on days when buyers request eleven, twelve, or thirteen cases. But on days when he has eleven cases in stock and buyers buy only ten cases, profit drops to $280. The $300 profit on the ten cases sold must be reduced by $20, the cost of the unsold case. A stock of twelve cases will increase daily profits to $360, but only on those days when buyers want twelve or thirteen cases. Should buyers want only ten cases, profit is reduced to $260; the $300 profit on the sale of ten cases is reduced by $40, the cost of two unsold cases. Stocking thirteen cases will result in a profit of $390 (a $30 profit on each case sold, with no

TABLE 15-3 Conditional Profit Table

POSSIBLE DEMAND (SALES) IN CASES	Possible stock action			
	10 CASES	11 CASES	12 CASES	13 CASES
10	$300	$280	$260	$240
11	300	330	310	290
12	300	330	360	340
13	300	330	360	390

unsold cases) when there is a market for thirteen cases. When buyers purchase fewer than thirteen cases, such a stock action results in profits of less than $390. For example, with a stock of thirteen cases and sale of only eleven cases, the profit is $290; the profit on eleven cases, $330, is reduced by the cost of two unsold cases ($40).

Function of the
conditional profit table

Such a conditional profit table does *not* show the retailer how many cases he should stock each day in order to maximize profits. It reveals the outcome only if a specific number of cases is stocked and a specific number of cases is sold. Under conditions of uncertainty, the retailer does not know in advance the size of any day's market. However, he must still decide which number of cases, stocked consistently, will maximize profits over a long period of time.

CALCULATING EXPECTED PROFITS

The next step in determining the best number of cases to stock is assigning probabilities to the possible outcomes or profits. We saw in Table 15-2 that the probabilities of the possible values for the retailer's sales are as follows:

Cases	10	11	12	13
Probability	.15	.20	.40	.25

Using these probabilities and the information contained in Table 15-3, we can now compute the expected profit of each possible stock action.

Computing expected
profit

We stated in Chapter 5 that **we can compute the expected value of a random variable by weighting each possible value the variable can take by the probability of its taking on that value.** Using this procedure, we can compute the expected daily profit from stocking ten cases each day. See Table 15-4. The figures in column 4 of Table 15-4 are obtained by weighting the conditional profit of each possible sales volume (column 2) by the probability of that conditional profit occurring (column 3).

For 10 units

The sum in the last column is the expected daily profit resulting from stocking ten cases each day. It is not surprising that this expected profit is $300, since we saw in Table 15-3 that stocking ten cases each day would always result in a daily profit of $300, regardless of whether buyers wanted ten, eleven, twelve, or thirteen cases.

For 11 units

The same computation for a daily stock of eleven units can be made, as we have done in Table 15-5. This tells us that if the retailer stocks eleven cases each day, his expected daily profit over time will be $322.50. Eighty-five percent of the time the daily profit will be $330; on these days, buyers ask for eleven, twelve, or thirteen cases.

TABLE 15-4 Expected Profit from Stocking 10 Cases

MARKET SIZE IN CASES (1)	CONDITIONAL PROFIT (2)		PROBABILITY OF MARKET SIZE (3)		EXPECTED PROFIT (4)
10	$300	×	.15	=	$ 45.00
11	300	×	.20	=	60.00
12	300	×	.40	=	120.00
13	300	×	.25	=	75.00
			1.00		$300.00

TABLE 15-5 Expected Profit from Stocking 11 Cases

MARKET SIZE IN CASES	CONDITIONAL PROFIT		PROBABILITY OF MARKET SIZE		EXPECTED PROFIT
10	$280	×	.15	=	$ 42.00
11	330	×	.20	=	66.00
12	330	×	.40	=	132.00
13	330	×	.25	=	82.50
			1.00		**$332.50**

For 12 and 13 units

However, column 3 tells us that 15 percent of the time the market will take only ten cases, resulting in a profit of only $280. It is this fact that reduces the daily expected profit to $322.50.

For twelve and thirteen units, the expected daily profit is computed as shown in Tables 15-6 and 15-7 respectively.

We have now computed the expected profit of each of the four stock actions open to the retailer. These expected profits are:

- If 10 cases are stocked each day, expected daily profit is $300.00.
- If 11 cases are stocked each day, expected daily profit is $322.50.
- If 12 cases are stocked each day, expected daily profit is $335.00.
- If 13 cases are stocked each day, expected daily profit is $327.50.

Optimal solution The *optimal stock action* is the one that results in the greatest expected profit—the largest daily average profits and thus the maximum total profits over a period of time. In this illustration, the proper number to stock each day is twelve cases, since that

TABLE 15-6 Expected Profit from Stocking 12 Cases

MARKET SIZE IN CASES	CONDITIONAL PROFIT		PROBABILITY OF MARKET SIZE		EXPECTED PROFIT	
10	$260	×	.15	=	$ 39.00	
11	310	×	.20	=	62.00	
12	360	×	.40	=	144.00	optimal
13	360	×	.25	=	90.00	stock
			1.00		**$335.00**	← action

TABLE 15-7 Expected Profit from Stocking 13 Cases

MARKET SIZE IN CASES	CONDITIONAL PROFIT		PROBABILITY OF MARKET SIZE		EXPECTED PROFIT
10	$240	×	.15	=	$ 36.00
11	290	×	.20	=	58.00
12	340	×	.40	=	136.00
13	390	×	.25	=	97.50
			1.00		**$327.50**

quantity will give the highest possible average daily profits under the conditions given.

What the solution means

We have *not* reduced uncertainty in the problem facing the retailer. Rather, we have used his past experience to determine the best stock action open to him. He still does not know how many cases will be requested on any given day. There is no guarantee that he will make a profit of $335.00 tomorrow. However, if he stocks twelve cases each day under the conditions given, he will have *average* profits of $335.00 per day. This is the *best* he can do, because the choice of any one of the other three possible stock actions will result in a lower expected daily profit.

EXPECTED PROFIT WITH PERFECT INFORMATION

Definition of perfect information

Now suppose that the retailer in our illustration could remove all uncertainty from his problem by obtaining complete and accurate information about the future, referred to as *perfect* information. This does not mean that sales would not vary from ten to thirteen cases per day. Sales would still be ten cases per day 15 percent of the time, eleven cases 20 percent of the time, twelve cases 40 percent of the time, and thirteen cases 25 percent of the time. However, with perfect information, the retailer would know in advance how many cases were going to be called for each day.

Use of perfect information

Under these circumstances, the retailer would stock today the exact number of cases buyers will want tomorrow. For sales of ten cases, the retailer would stock ten cases and realize a profit of $300. When sales were going to be eleven cases, he would stock exactly eleven cases, thus realizing a profit of $330.00.

Table 15-8 shows the conditional profit values that are applicable to the retailer's problem if he has perfect information. Knowing the size of the market in advance for a particular day, the retailer chooses the stock action that will maximize his profits. This means he buys and stocks quantities that avoid *all* losses from obsolete stock as well as *all* losses that reflect lost profits on unfilled requests for strawberries.

Expected profit under certainty

We can now compute the expected profit under certainty. This is shown in Table 15-9. The procedure is the same as that already used, but you will notice that the conditional profit figures in column 2 of Table 15-9 are the maximum profits possible for each sales volume. When buyers buy twelve cases, for example, the retailer will always make a profit of $360 under certainty, because he will have stocked exactly 12 cases. With perfect information, then, our retailer could count on making an average profit of $352.50 a day. This is a significant figure because it is the *maximum expected profit* possible.

TABLE 15-8 Conditional Profit Table Under Certainty

POSSIBLE SALES IN CASES	Possible stock actions			
	10 CASES	11 CASES	12 CASES	13 CASES
10	$300	—	—	—
11	—	$330	—	—
12	—	—	$360	—
13	—	—	—	$390

15 DECISION THEORY

TABLE 15-9 Expected Profit Under Certainty

MARKET SIZE IN CASES	CONDITIONAL PROFIT UNDER CERTAINTY		PROBABILITY OF MARKET SIZE		EXPECTED PROFIT UNDER CERTAINTY
10	$300	×	.15	=	$ 45.00
11	330	×	.20	=	66.00
12	360	×	.40	=	144.00
13	390	×	.25	=	97.50
			1.00		**$352.50**

EXPECTED VALUE OF PERFECT INFORMATION

Value of certainty

Assuming that a retailer could obtain a perfect predictor about the future, what would be its value to him? He must compare the cost of that information with the additional profit he would realize as a result of having the information.

Why do we need the value of certainty?

The retailer in our example can earn average daily profits of $352.50 if he has perfect information about the future (see Table 15-9). His best expected daily profit without the predictor is only $335.00 (see Tables 15-4 to 15-7). The difference of $17.50 is the maximum amount the retailer would be willing to pay, per day, for a perfect predictor, because that is the maximum amount by which he can increase his expected daily profit. The difference is the *expected value of perfect information* and is referred to as EVPI. There is no sense in paying more than $17.50 for the predictor; to do so would cost more than the knowledge is worth.

Calculating the value of additional information in the decision-making process is a serious problem for managers. In our illustration, we found that our retailer would pay $17.50 a day for a perfect predictor. Only infrequently, however, can we secure a perfect predictor. In most decision-making situations, managers are really attempting to evaluate the worth of information that will enable them to make better, rather than perfect, decisions.

Exercises

 15-4 Center City Motor Sales has recently incorporated. Its chief asset is a franchise to sell automobiles of a major American manufacturer. CCMS's general manager is planning the staffing of the dealership's garage facilities. From information provided by the manufacturer and from other nearby dealerships, he has estimated the number of annual mechanic hours that the garage will be likely to need.

Hours	10,000	12,000	14,000	16,000
Probability	.2	.3	.4	.1

The manager plans to pay each mechanic $9.00 per hour and to charge his customer $16.00. Mechanics will work a 40-hour week and get an annual 2-week vacation.
(a) Determine how many mechanics Center City should hire.
(b) How much should Center City pay to get perfect information about the number of mechanics it needs?

15-5 Airport Rent-A-Car is a locally operated business in competition with several major firms. ARC is planning a new deal for customers who want to rent a car for only one day and return it to the airport. For $24.95, the company will rent a small economy car to a customer, whose only other expense is to fill the car with gas at the day's end. ARC is planning to buy a number of small cars from the manufacturer at a reduced price of $6,750. The big question is how many to buy. Company executives have decided on the following estimated probability distribution of the number of cars rented per day:

Number of cars rented	10	11	12	13	14	15
Probability	.18	.19	.21	.15	.14	.13

The company intends to offer the plan 6 days a week (312 days per year) and anticipates that its variable cost per car per day will be $2.25. After using the cars for 1 year, ARC expects to sell them and recapture 45 percent of the original cost. Ignoring the time value of money and any noncash expenses, determine the optimal number of cars for ARC to buy.

15-6 For several years, the Madison Rhodes Department Store had featured personalized pencils as a Christmas special. Madison Rhodes purchased the pencils from its supplier, who provided the embossing machine. The personalizing was done on the department store premises. Despite the success of the pencil sales, Madison Rhodes had received comments that the quality of the lead in the pencils was poor, and the store had found a different supplier. The new supplier would, however, be unable to begin servicing the department store until after the first of January. Madison Rhodes was forced to purchase its pencils one final time from its original supplier, to meet Christmas demand. It was, therefore, important that pencils not be overstocked, and yet the manager was adamant about not losing too many customers because of stockouts. The pencils came packed fifteen to the box, 72 boxes to the case. Madison Rhodes paid $60 per case and sold the pencils for $1.50 per box. Labor costs are 37.5¢ per box sold. Based on previous years' sales, management constructed the following schedule:

Expected sales (cases)	15	16	17	18	19	20
Probability	.05	.20	.30	.25	.10	.10

(a) How many cases should Madison Rhodes order?
(b) What's the expected profit?

15-7 Emily Scott, head of a small business consulting firm, must decide how many M.B.A.s to hire as full-time consultants for the next year. (Emily has decided that she will not bother with any part-time employees.) Emily knows from experience that the probability distribution on the number of consulting jobs her firm will get each year is represented by the numbers below:

Consulting jobs	24	27	30	33
Probability	.3	.2	.4	.1

Emily also knows that each M.B.A. hired will be able to handle exactly three consulting jobs per year. The salary of each M.B.A. is $60,000. Each consulting job is worth $30,000 to Emily's firm. Each consulting job that the firm is awarded but cannot complete costs the firm $10,000 in future business lost.
(a) How many M.B.A.s should Emily hire?
(b) What is the expected value of perfect information to Emily?

15-8 The Writer's Workbench operates a chain of word-processing franchises in college towns. For an hourly fee of $8.00, Writer's Workbench provides access to a personal computer, word-processing software, and a printer to students who need to prepare papers for their classes. Paper is provided at no additional cost. The firm estimates that its hourly variable cost per machine (principally due to paper, ribbons, electricity, and wear and tear on the computers and printers) is about 85¢. Deborah Rubin is considering opening a Writer's Workbench franchise in Ames, Iowa. A preliminary market survey has resulted in the following probability distribution of the number of machines demanded per hour during the hours she plans to operate:

Number of machines	22	23	24	25	26	27
Probability	.12	.16	.22	.27	.18	.05

If she wishes to maximize her profit contribution, how many machines should Deborah plan to have? What is the hourly expected value of perfect information in this situation? Even if Deborah could obtain a perfectly accurate forecast of the demand for each and every hour, why wouldn't she be willing to pay up to the EVPI for that information in this situation?

15-9 Manfred Baum, merchandise manager for the Grant Shoe Company, is planning production decisions for the coming year's summer line of shoes. His chief concern is estimating the sales of a new design of fashion sandals. These sandals have posed problems in the past for two reasons: (1) The limited selling season does not provide enough time for the company to produce a second run of a popular item, and (2) the styles change dramatically from year to year, and unsold sandals become worthless. Manfred has discussed the newest design with salespeople and has formulated the following estimates of how the item will sell:

Pairs (thousands)	45	50	55	60	65
Probability	.25	.30	.20	.15	.10

Information from the production department reveals that the sandal will cost $15.25 per pair to manufacture, and marketing has informed Manfred that the wholesale price will be $31.35 a pair. Using the expected value decision criterion, calculate the number of pairs that Manfred should recommend the company produce.

15-3
Using Continuous Distributions in Decision Theory: Marginal Analysis

Limitations of the tabular approach

In many inventory problems, the number of computations required makes the use of conditional profit and expected profit tables difficult. Our previous illustration contained only four possible stock actions and four possible sales levels, resulting in a conditional profit table containing sixteen possibilities for conditional profits. If we had 300 possible values for sales volume and an equal number of calculations for determining conditional and expected profit, we would have to do a great many computations. The marginal approach avoids this problem.

Marginal analysis is based on the fact that when an additional unit of an item is bought, two fates are possible: The unit will be sold, or it will not be sold. The sum of the probabilities of these two events must be 1. (For example, if the probability of selling the additional unit is .6, then the probability of not selling it must be .4).

Derivation of marginal profit

If we let p represent the probability of selling one additional unit, then $1 - p$ must be the probability of not selling it. If the additional unit is sold, we shall realize an increase in our conditional profits as a result of the profit from the additional unit. We refer to this as *marginal profit*, or *MP*. In our previous illustration about the retailer, the marginal profit resulting from the sale of an additional unit is $30, the selling price ($50) minus the cost ($20).

TABLE 15-10 Conditional Profit Table

POSSIBLE DEMAND (SALES) IN CASES	PROBABILITY OF MARKET SIZE	Possible stock actions			
		10 CASES	11 CASES	12 CASES	13 CASES
10	.15	$300	$280	$260	$240
11	.20	300	330	310	290
12	.40	300	330	360	340
13	.25	300	330	360	390

Table 15-10 illustrates this point. If we stock ten units each day and daily demand is for ten or more units, our conditional profit is $300 per day. Now we decide to stock eleven units each day. If the eleventh unit is sold (and this is the case when demand is for eleven, twelve, or thirteen units), our conditional profit is increased to $330 per day. Notice that the increase in conditional profit does not follow merely from *stocking* the eleventh unit. Under the conditions assumed in the problem, this increase in profit will result only when demand is for eleven or more units. This will be the case 85 percent of the time.

Marginal loss

We must also consider how profits would be affected by stocking an additional unit and not selling it. This reduces our conditional profit. The amount of the reduction is referred to as the *marginal loss (ML)* resulting from the stocking of an item that is not sold. In our previous example, the marginal loss was $20 per unit, the cost of the item.

Table 15-10 also illustrates marginal loss. Once more we decide to stock eleven units. If the eleventh unit (the marginal unit) is not sold, the conditional profit is $280. The $300 conditional profit when ten units were stocked and ten were sold is reduced by $20, the cost of the unsold unit.

Derivation of stocking rule

Additional units should be stocked as long as the expected marginal profit from stocking each of them is greater than the expected marginal loss from stocking each. **The size of each day's order should be increased up to the point where the expected marginal profit from stocking one more unit if it sells is just equal to the expected marginal loss from stocking that unit if it remains unsold.**

In our illustration, the probability distribution of demand is:

MARKET SIZE	PROBABILITY OF MARKET SIZE
10	.15
11	.20
12	.40
13	.25
	1.00

This distribution tells us that as we increase our stock, the probability of selling one additional unit (this is p) decreases. If we increase our stock from ten to eleven units, the probability of selling all eleven is .85. This is the probability that demand will be for eleven units or more. Here is the computation:

Probability that demand will be for 11	.20
Probability that demand will be for 12	.40
Probability that demand will be for 13	.25
Probability that demand will be for 11 or more units	**.85**

If we add a twelfth unit, the probability of selling all twelve units is reduced to .65 (the sum of the probabilities of demand for twelve or thirteen units). Finally, the addition of a thirteenth unit carries with it only a .25 probability of our selling all thirteen units, because demand will be for thirteen units only 25 percent of the time.

DERIVING THE MINIMUM PROBABILITY EQUATION

Expected marginal profit and loss defined

The *expected marginal profit* from stocking and selling an additional unit is the marginal profit of the unit multiplied by the probability that the unit will be sold; this is $p(MP)$. The *expected marginal loss* from stocking and not selling an additional unit is the marginal loss incurred if the unit is unsold multiplied by the probability that the unit will not be sold; this is $(1 - p)(ML)$. We can generalize that the retailer in this situation would stock up to the point at which:

$$p(MP) = (1 - p)(ML) \qquad [15\text{-}1]$$

This equation describes the point at which the expected marginal profit from stocking and selling an additional unit, $p(MP)$, is equal to the expected marginal loss from stocking and not selling the unit, $(1 - p)(ML)$. As long as $p(MP)$ is larger than $(1 - p)(ML)$, additional units should be stocked, because the expected profit from such a decision is greater than the expected loss.

Optimal inventory stock action

In any given inventory problem, there will be only *one* value of p for which the maximizing equation will be true. We must determine that value in order to know the optimal stock action to take. We can do this by taking our maximizing equation and solving it for p in the following manner:

$$p(MP) = (1 - p)(ML) \qquad [15\text{-}1]$$

Multiplying the two terms on the right side of the equation, we get:

$$p(MP) = ML - p(ML)$$

Collecting terms containing p, we have:

$$p(MP) + p(ML) = ML$$

or:

$$p(MP + ML) = ML$$

Dividing both sides of the equation by $MP + ML$ gives:

Minimum probability equation

Minimum required probability $\longrightarrow$
$$p^* = \frac{ML}{MP + ML} \qquad [15\text{-}2]$$

The symbol p^* represents the minimum required probability of selling at least one additional unit to justify the stocking of that additional unit. The retailer should stock

TABLE 15-11 Cumulative Probabilities of Sales

SALES UNITS	PROBABILITY OF THIS SALES LEVEL	CUMULATIVE PROBABILITY THAT SALES WILL BE AT THIS LEVEL OR GREATER
10	.15	1.00
11	.20	.85
12	.40	.65
13	.25	.25

additional units as long as the probability of selling at least an additional unit is greater than p^*.

We can now compute p^* for our illustration. The marginal profit per unit is \$30 (the selling price minus the cost); the marginal loss per unit is \$20 (the cost of each unit); thus:

$$p^* = \frac{ML}{MP + ML} = \frac{\$20}{\$30 + \$20} = \frac{\$20}{\$50} = .40$$

This value of .40 for p^* means that in order to make the stocking of an additional unit justifiable, we must have at least a .40 *cumulative* probability of selling that unit or more. In order to determine the probability of selling each additional unit we consider stocking, we must compute a series of cumulative probabilities as we have done in Table 15-11.

Calculation of cumulative probabilities The cumulative probabilities in the right-hand column of Table 15-11 represent the probabilities that sales will reach or exceed each of the four sales levels. For example, the 1.00 that appears beside the 10-unit sales level means that we are 100 percent certain of selling ten or more units. This must be true because our problem assumes that one of the four sales levels will *always* occur.

The .85 probability value beside the eleven-unit sales figure means that we are only 85 percent sure of selling eleven or more units. This can be calculated in two ways. First, we could add the chances of selling eleven, twelve, or thirteen units:

11 units	.20
12 units	.40
13 units	+.25
	.85 = probability of selling 11 or more

Or we could reason that sales of eleven or more units include all possible outcomes except sales of ten units, which has a probability of .15.

All possible outcomes	1.00
Probability of selling 10	−.15
	.85 = probability of selling 11 or more

The cumulative probability value of .65 assigned to sales of twelve units or more can be established in similar fashion. Sales of twelve or more must mean sales of twelve or of thirteen units; so:

Probability of selling 12	.40
Probability of selling 13	+ .25
	.65 = probability of selling 12 or more

And, of course, the cumulative probability of selling thirteen units is still .25, because we have assumed that sales will never exceed thirteen.

As we mentioned previously, the value of p decreases as the level of stock increases. This causes the expected marginal profit to decrease and the expected marginal loss to increase until, at some point, our stocking of an additional unit would not be profitable.

Stocking rule   We have said that additional units should be stocked as long as the probability of selling at least an additional unit is greater than p^*. We can now apply this rule to our probability distribution of sales and determine how many units should be stocked.

In this case, the probability of selling eleven or more units is .85, a figure clearly greater than our p^* of .40; thus, we should stock an eleventh unit. The expected marginal profit from stocking this unit is greater than the expected marginal loss from stocking it. We can verify this as follows:

$$p(MP) = .85(\$30) = \$25.50 \text{ expected marginal profit}$$

$$(1 - p)(ML) = .15(\$20) = \$3.00 \text{ expected marginal loss}$$

A twelfth unit should be stocked because the probability of selling twelve or more units (.65) is greater than the required p^* of .40. Such action will result in the following expected marginal profit and expected marginal loss:

$$p(MP) = .65(\$30) = \$19.50 \text{ expected marginal profit}$$

$$(1 - p)(ML) = .35(\$20) = \$7.00 \text{ expected marginal loss}$$

Optimal stocking level for this problem   Twelve is the *optimal* number of units to stock, because the addition of a thirteenth unit carried with it only a .25 probability that it will be sold, and that is less than our required p^* of .40. The following figures reveal why the thirteenth unit should not be stocked:

$$p(MP) = .25(\$30) = \$7.50 \text{ expected marginal profit}$$

$$(1 - p)(ML) = .75(\$20) = \$15.00 \text{ expected marginal loss}$$

If we stock a thirteenth unit, we add more to expected loss than we add to expected profit.

Notice that the use of marginal analysis leads us to the same conclusion that we reached with the use of conditional profit and expected profit tables. Both methods of analysis suggest that the retailer should stock twelve units each period.

Adjusting the optimal stocking level   Our strategy, to stock twelve cases every day, assumes that daily sales is a random variable. In actual practice, however, daily sales often take on recognizable patterns depending upon the particular day of the week. In retail sales, Saturday is generally recognized as being a higher-volume day than, say, Tuesday. Similarly, Monday retail sales are typically less than those on Friday. In situations with recognizable patterns in daily sales, we can apply the techniques we have learned by computing an optimal stocking level for *each* day of the week. For Saturday, we would use as our input data past sales experience for Saturdays only. Each of the other 6 days could be treated in the same fashion. Essentially, this approach represents nothing more than recognition of, and reaction to, discernible patterns in what may at first appear to be a completely random environment.

USING THE STANDARD NORMAL PROBABILITY DISTRIBUTION

We first learned the concept of the standard normal probability distribution in Chapter 5. We can now use this idea to help us solve a decision theory problem employing a continuous distribution.

Solving a problem using marginal analysis

Assume that a manager sells an article having normally distributed sales with a mean of 50 units daily and a standard deviation in daily sales of 15 units. The manager purchases this article for $4 per unit and sells it for $9 per unit. If the article is not sold on the selling day, it is worth nothing. Using the marginal method of calculating optimal inventory purchase levels, we can calculate our required $p*$:

$$p* = \frac{ML}{MP + ML} \qquad [15\text{-}2]$$

$$= \frac{\$4}{\$5 + \$4} = .44$$

This means that the manager must be .44 sure of selling at least an additional unit before it would pay to stock that unit. Let us reproduce the curve of past sales and determine how to incorporate the marginal method with continuous distributions of past daily sales.

Using the standard normal probability distribution in marginal analysis

Now refer to Fig. 15-1. If we erect a vertical line b at 50 units, the area under the curve to the right of this line is one-half the total area. This tells us that the probability of selling 50 or more units is .5. *The area to the right of any such vertical line represents the probability of selling that quantity or more.* As the area to the right of any vertical line decreases, so does the probability that we will sell that quantity or more.

Suppose the manager considers stocking 25 units, line a. Most of the entire area under the curve lies to the right of the vertical line drawn at 25; thus, the probability is

FIGURE 15-1

Normal distribution of past daily sales

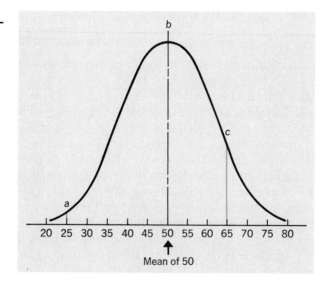

15 DECISION THEORY

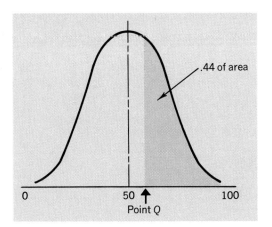

FIGURE 15-2

Normal probability distribution, with .44 of the area under the curve shaded

.44 of area

0	50	100

Point Q

great that the manager will sell 25 units or more. If he considers stocking 50 units (the mean), one-half the entire area under the curve lies to the right of vertical line *b*; thus he is .5 sure of selling the 50 units or more. Now, say he considers stocking 65 units. Only a small portion of the entire area under the curve lies to the right of line *c*; thus the probability of selling 65 or more units is quite small.

Figure 15-2 illustrates the .44 probability that must exist before it pays our manager to stock another unit. He will stock additional units until he reaches point *Q*. If he stocks a larger quantity, the shaded area under the curve drops below .44 and the probability of selling another unit or more falls below the required .44. How can we locate point *Q*? As we saw in Chapter 5, we can use Appendix Table 1 to determine how many standard deviations it takes to include any portion of the area under the curve measuring from the mean to any points such as *Q*. In this particular case, since we know that the shaded area must be .44 of the total area, then the area from the mean to point *Q* must be .06 (the total area from the mean to the right tail is .50). Looking in the body of the table, we find that .06 of the area under the curve is located between the mean and a point .15 standard deviations to the right of the mean. Thus we know that point *Q* is .15 standard deviations to the right of the mean (50).

Optimal solution for this problem

We have been given the information that 1 standard deviation for this distribution is 15 units; so .15 times this would be 2.25 units. Since point *Q* is 2.25 units to the right of the mean (50), it must be at about 52 units. This is the optimal order for the manager to place: 52 units per day.

Now that we have been through one problem using a continuous probability distribution, we can work our chapter-opening problem involving these data for a normally distributed daily sales record:

Mean of past daily sales	60 cases
Standard deviation of past daily sales distribution	10 cases
Cost per case	$20
Selling price per case	$32
Value if not sold on first day	$ 2

As we did in the previous problem, we first calculate the *p** that is required to justify the stocking of an additional case. In this instance:

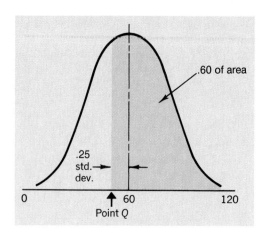

Minimum required
probability

$$p^* = \frac{ML}{MP + ML}$$

[15-2]

$$= \frac{\$20 - \$2}{\$12 + (\$20 - \$2)}$$

Notice that a salvage value of \$2
is deducted from the cost of \$20
to obtain the *ML*.

$$= \frac{\$18}{\$12 + \$18}$$

$$= \frac{\$18}{\$30} = .60$$

We can now illustrate the probability on a normal curve by marking off .60 of the
area under the curve, starting from the right-hand end of the curve, as in Fig. 15-3.

The manager wants to increase his order size until it reaches point *Q*. Now point *Q*
lies to the *left* of the mean, whereas in the preceding problem it lay to the *right*. How
can we locate point *Q*? Since .5 of the area under the curve is located between the
mean and the right-hand tail, .10 of the shaded area must be to the left of the mean,
(.60 − .5 = .10). In the body of Appendix Table 1, the nearest value to .10 is .0987, so
we want to find a point *Q* with .0987 of the area under the curve contained between
the mean and point *Q*. The table indicates point *Q* is .25 standard deviations from the
mean. We now solve for point *Q* as follows:

Optimal solution for
chapter opening
problem

$$.25 \times \text{standard deviation} = .25 \times 10 \text{ cases} = 2.5 \text{ cases}$$

$$\text{Point } Q = \text{mean less 2.5 cases}$$
$$= 60 - 2.5 \text{ cases} = 57.5, \text{ or } 57 \text{ cases}$$

Since *p* decreases as the stock level increases, we *always round fractional values of Q
down to the next whole number*.

Exercises

 15-10 Highway construction in North Carolina is concentrated in the months from May through
September. To provide some protection to the crews at work on the highways, the Department of Transportation (DOT) requires that large, orange MEN WORKING signs be placed

in advance of any construction. Because of vandalism, wear and tear, and theft, DOT purchases new signs each year. Although the signs are made under the auspices of the Department of Correction, DOT is charged a price equivalent to one it would pay were it to buy the signs from an outside source. The interdepartmental charge for the signs is $21 if more than 35 of the same kind are ordered. Otherwise, the cost per sign is $29. Because of budget pressures, DOT attempts to minimize its costs both by not buying too many signs and by attempting to buy in sufficiently large quantity to get the $21 price. In recent years, the department has averaged purchases of 78 signs per year, with a standard deviation of 15. Determine the number of signs DOT should purchase.

15-11 The town of Green Lake, Wisconsin, is preparing for the celebration of the seventy-ninth Annual Milk and Dairy Day. As a fund-raising device, the city council once again plans to sell souvenir T-shirts. The T-shirts, printed in six colors, will have a picture of a cow and the words, "79th Annual Milk and Dairy Day," on the front. The city council purchases heat transfer patches from a supplier for $.75 and plain white cotton T-shirts for $1.50. A local merchant supplies the appropriate heating device and also purchases all unsold white cotton T-shirts. The council plans to set up a booth on Main Street and sell the shirts for $3.25. The transfer of the color to the shirt will be completed when the sale is made. In the past year, similar shirt sales have averaged 200 with a standard deviation of 34. The council knows that there will be no market for the patches after the celebration. How many patches should the city council buy?

15-12 Floyd Guild operates a newsstand near the 53rd Street station of the IC South Shore and Suburban line. The *City Herald* is the most popular of the newspapers which Floyd stocks. Over many years, he has observed that daily demand for the Herald is well described by a normal distribution with mean $\mu = 165$ and standard deviation $\sigma = 40$. Copies of the *Herald* sell for 25¢, but the publisher charges Floyd only 10¢ for each copy he orders. If any *Heralds* are left over at the end of the evening commuting hours, Floyd sells them to Jesselman's Fish Market down the street for a nickel each. If Floyd wishes to maximize his expected daily profit, how many copies of the *Herald* should he order?

15-13 Bike Wholesale Parts was established in the early 1980s in response to demands of several small and newly established bicycle shops that needed access to a wide variety of inventory but were not able to finance it themselves. The company carries a wide variety of replacement parts and accessories but does not maintain any stock of completed bicycles. Management is preparing to order 27″ × 1¼″ rims from the Flexspin Company in anticipation of a business upturn expected in about 2 months. Flexspin makes a superior product, but the lead time required necessitates that wholesalers make only one order, which must last through the critical summer months. In the past, Bike Wholesale Parts has sold an average of 120 rims per summer with a standard deviation of 28. The company expects that its stock of rims will be depleted by the time the new order arrives. Bike Wholesale Parts has been quite successful and plans to move its operations to a larger plant during the winter. Management feels that the combined cost of moving some items such as rims and the existing cost of financing them is at least equal to the firm's purchase cost of $7.30. Accepting management's hypothesis that any unsold rims at the end of the summer season are permanently unsold, determine the number of rims the company should order if the selling price is $8.10.

15-14 The B&G Cafeteria features barbecued chicken each Thursday, and Priscilla Alden, the cafeteria manager, wants to ensure that the cafeteria will make money on this dish. Including labor and other costs of preparation, each portion of chicken costs $1.35. The $2.15 selling price per portion is such a bargain that the barbecued chicken special has become a very popular item. Data taken from the last year indicate that demand for the special is normally distributed with mean $\mu = 190$ portions and standard deviation $\sigma = 32$ portions. If B&G Cafeteria prepares two portions of barbecued chicken from each whole chicken it cooks, how many chickens should Priscilla order each Thursday?

15-15 Paige's Tire Service stocks two types of radial tires: polyester-belted and steel-belted. The polyester-belted radials cost the company $30 each and sell for $35. The steel-belted radials cost the company $45 and sell for $60. For various reasons, Paige's Tire Service will not be able to reorder any radials from the factory this year, so it must order just once to satisfy customers' demand for the entire year. At the end of the year, owing to new tire models, Paige will have to sell all its inventory of radials for scrap rubber at $5 each. The annual sales of both types of radial tires are normally distributed with means and standard deviations indicated below.

	ANNUAL MEAN SALES	STANDARD DEVIATION
Polyester-belted	300	50
Steel-belted	200	20

(a) How many polyester-belted radials should be ordered?
(b) How many steel-belted radials should be ordered?

15-4
Utility as a Decision Criterion

Different decision criteria

So far in this chapter, we have used expected value (expected profit, for example) as our decision criterion. We assumed that if the expected profit of alternative A was better than that of alternative B, then the decision maker would certainly choose alternative A. Conversely, if the expected loss of alternative C was greater than the expected loss of alternative D, then we assumed that the decision maker would surely choose D as the better course of action.

SHORTCOMINGS OF EXPECTED VALUE AS A DECISION CRITERION

Expected value is sometimes inappropriate

There are situations, however, in which the use of expected value as the decision criterion would get a manager into serious trouble. Suppose an entrepreneur owns a new factory worth $2 million. Suppose further that there is only one chance in 1,000 (.001) that it will burn down this year. From these two figures we can compute the expected loss:

$$.001 \times \$2,000,000 = \$2,000 = \text{expected loss by fire}$$

An insurance representative offers to insure the building for $2,250 this year. If the entrepreneur applies the notion of minimizing expected losses, he will refuse to insure the building. The expected loss of insuring ($2,250) is higher than the expected loss by fire. If, however, the businessman feels that a $2 million uninsured loss would wipe him out, he will probably discard expected value as his decision criterion and buy the insurance at the extra cost of $250 per year per policy ($2,250 − 2,000). He would choose *not* to minimize expected loss in this case.

A personal example

Take an example closer, perhaps, to student life. You are a student with just enough money to get through the semester. A friend offers to sell you a .9 chance of winning $10 for just $1. You would most likely think of the problem in terms of expected values and reason as follows: "Is .9 × $10 greater than $1?" Because $9 (the expected value of the bet) is nine times greater than the cost of the bet ($1), you might feel inclined to take your friend up on this offer. Even if you lose, the loss of $1 will not affect your situation materially.

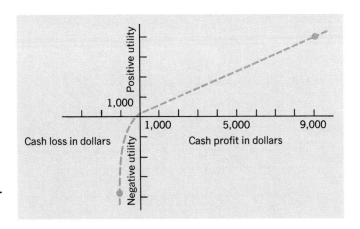

FIGURE 15-4

Utility of various profits and losses

Now your friend offers to sell you a .9 chance of winning $1,000 for $100. The question you would now ponder is, "Is .9 × $1,000 greater than $100?" Of course, $900 (the expected value of the bet) is still nine times the cost of the bet ($100), but you would more than likely think twice before putting up your money. Why? Because even though the pleasure of winning $1,000 would be high, the pain of losing your hard-earned $100 might be more than you care to experience.

Say, finally, that your friend offers to sell you a .9 chance at winning $10,000 for your total assets, which happen to be $1,000. If you use expected value as your decision criterion, you would ask the question, "Is .9 × $10,000 greater than $1,000?" You would get the same answer as before — yes. The expected value of the bet ($9,000) is still nine times greater than the cost of the bet ($1,000), but now you would probably refuse your friend, not because the expected value of the bet is unattractive, but because the thought of losing all your assets is completely unacceptable as an outcome.

Function of utility   In this example, you changed the decision criterion away from expected value when the thought of losing $1,000 was too painful, despite the pleasure to be gained from $10,000. At this point, you no longer considered the expected value; you thought solely of *utility*. In this sense, utility refers to the pleasure or displeasure one would derive from certain outcomes. Your utility curve in Fig. 15-4 is linear around the origin ($1 of gain is as pleasurable as $1 of loss is painful in this region), but it turns down rapidly when the potential loss rises to levels near $1,000. Specifically, this utility curve shows us that from your point of view, the displeasure from losing $1,000 is about equal to the pleasure from winning nine times that amount. The shape of one's utility curve is a product of one's psychological makeup, one's expectations about the future, and the particular decision or act being evaluated. A person can have one utility curve for one situation and quite a different one for the next situation.

DIFFERENT UTILITIES

Attitudes toward risk   The utility curves of three different managers' decision are shown on the graph in Fig. 15-5. We have arbitrarily named these managers David, Ann, and Jim. Their attitudes are readily apparent from analysis of their utility curves. David is a cautious and conservative businessman. A move to the right of the zero profit point increases his utility only very slightly, whereas a move to the left of the zero profit point decreases his utility rapidly. In terms of numerical values, David's utility curve indicates that

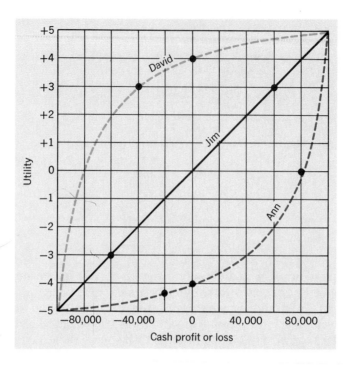

FIGURE 15-5
Three utility curves

going from $0 to $100,000 profit increases his utility by a value of 1 on the vertical scale, while moving into the loss range by only $40,000 decreases his utility by the same value of 1, on the vertical scale. David will avoid situations in which high losses might occur; he is said to be averse to risk.

Ann is quite another story. We see from her utility curve that a profit increases her utility by much more than a loss of the same amount decreases it. Specifically, increasing her profits $20,000 (from $80,000 to $100,000) raises her utility from 0 to +5 on the vertical scale, but lowering her profits $20,000 (from $0 to −$20,000) decreases her utility by only .25, from −4 to −4.25. Ann is a player of long shots; she feels strongly that a large loss would not make things much worse than they are now, but that a big profit would be quite rewarding. She will take large risks to earn even larger gains.

Who would use expected value?

Jim, fairly well-off financially, is the kind of businessman who would not suffer greatly from a $60,000 loss nor increase his wealth significantly with a $60,000 gain. Pleasure from making an additional $60,000 or pain from losing it would be of about equal intensity. **Because his utility curve is linear, he can effectively use expected value as his decision criterion, whereas David and Ann must use utility. Jim will act when the expected value is positive, David will demand a high expected value for the outcome, and Ann may act when the expected value is negative.**

Exercises

15-16 Bill Johnson's income places him in the 50 percent bracket for federal income tax purposes. Johnson often supplies venture capital to small start-up firms in return for some type of equity position in the firm. Recently, Bill has been approached by Circutronics, a small firm entering the microcircuitry industry. Circutronics has requested $1,600,000 backing. Because of his tax position, Bill invests in tax-exempt municipal securities when he cannot find any attractive ventures to back. Currently he has a large position in North Carolina Eastern Municipal Power Agency bonds, which are yielding a return of 9.43 percent. Bill considers this 9.43 percent after-tax return to be his utility breakeven point. Above that point, his utility rises very rapidly; below, it drops slightly, since he can well afford to lose the money.

(a) What dollar return must Circutronics promise before Bill will consider financing it?

(b) Graph Bill's utility curve.

15-17 The Enduro Manufacturing Company is a partnership producing structural-steel building components. Financial manager and partner William Flaherty is examining potential projects that the firm might undertake in the coming fiscal year. The company has a target rate of return of 10 percent on its investment, but because there is no outside financing and interference, the partners have accepted projects with rates of return between 0 and 100 percent. Above 10 percent, the partners' utility rises very rapidly; between 0 and 10 percent, it rises only slightly above 0; below 0, it falls very rapidly. Flaherty is considering several projects that will cause Enduro to invest $250,000. Plot the firm's utility curve.

15-18 An investor is convinced that the price of a share of PDQ stock will rise in the near future. PDQ stock is currently selling for $57 a share. Upon inspecting the latest quotes on the options market, the investor finds that she can purchase an option at a cost of $5 per share, allowing her to buy PDQ for $55 per share within the next 2 months. She can also purchase an option to buy the stock within a 4-month period; this option, which costs $10 per share, also has an exercise price of $55 per share. She has estimated the following probability distributions for the stock price on the days the options expire:

Price	50	55	60	65	70	75
Probability at 2 Months	.05	.15	.15	.25	.35	.05
Probability at 4 Months	0	.05	.05	.20	.30	.40

The investor plans to exercise her option just prior to its expiration if PDQ stock is selling for more than $55 and immediately sell the stock at that market price. Of course, if the stock is selling for $55 or less when the option expires, she will lose the entire purchase cost of the option. The investor is relatively conservative, with the following utility values for changes in her dollar assets:

Change	+1,500	+1,000	+500	0	−500	−1,000
Utility	1.0	0.9	0.8	0.7	0.1	0.0

She is considering one of three alternatives:

1) To buy a 2-month option on 100 shares
2) To buy a 4-month option on 100 shares
3) Not to buy at all

Which of these alternatives will maximize her expected utility?

15-5
Helping Decision Makers Supply the Right Probabilities

Missing information

The two problems we worked using the normal probability distribution (pp. 752–54) required us to know both the mean (μ) and the standard deviation (σ). But how can we make use of a probability distribution when past data are missing or incomplete? By working through a problem, we shall see how we can often generate the required values by using an *intuitive* approach.

AN INTUITIVE APPROACH TO ESTIMATING THE MEAN AND STANDARD DEVIATION

Assume that you are thinking about purchasing a machine to replace hand labor on an operation. The machine will cost $10,000 per year to operate and will save $8 for each hour it operates. To break even, then, it must operate at least $10,000/$8 = 1,250 hours annually. If you are interested in the probability that it will run more than 1,250 hours, you must know something about the distribution of running times, specifically the mean and standard deviation of this distribution. But since you do not have a history of the machine's operation, where would you find these figures?

Estimating the mean

We could ask the foreman of this operation, who has been closely involved with the process, to guess the mean running time of the machine. Let us say that his best estimate is 1,400 hours. But how would he react if you asked him to give you the standard deviation of the distribution? This term may not be meaningful to him, and yet he probably has some intuitive notion of the dispersion of the distribution of running times. Since most people understand betting odds, let us approach him on that basis.

Estimating the standard deviation

We begin by counting off an equal distance on each side of his mean, say 200 hours. This gives us an interval from 1,200 to 1,600 hours. Then we can ask, "What are the odds the number of hours will lie between 1,200 and 1,600 hours?" If he has had any experience with betting, he should be able to reply. Suppose he says, "I think the odds it will run between 1,200 and 1,600 hours are 4 to 3." We show his answer on a probability distribution in Fig. 15-6.

Figure 15-6 illustrates the foreman's reply that the odds are 4 to 3 the machine will run between 1,200 and 1,600 hours rather than outside those limits. What should we do next? First, we label the 1,600-hour point on the distribution in Fig. 15-6 point Q. Then we can see that the area under the curve between the mean and point Q according to the foreman's estimates is 4/7 of *half* the area under the entire curve, or $4/14 = (.2857)$ of the *total* area under the curve.

Look at Fig. 15-7. If we turn to Appendix Table 1 for the value .2857, we find that point Q is .79 standard deviation to the right of the mean. Since we know that the distance from the mean to Q is 200 hours, we see that:

$$.79 \text{ standard deviations} = 200 \text{ hours}$$

FIGURE 15-6

Foreman's odds intervals for operating times of proposed machines

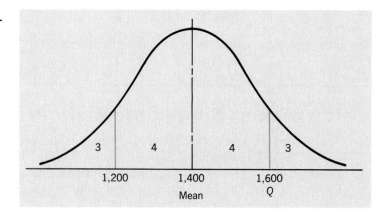

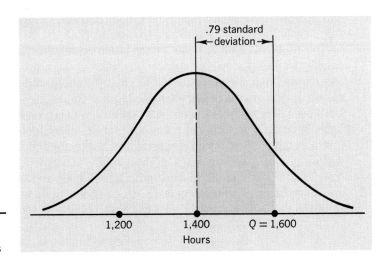

FIGURE 15-7

Determination of standard deviation from foreman's odds

and thus:

$$1 \text{ standard deviation} = 200/.79$$
$$= 253 \text{ hours}$$

Calculating the breakeven probability

Now that we know the mean and standard deviation of the distribution of running times, we can calculate the probability of the machine's running fewer than its break-even point of 1,250 hours:

$$\frac{1,400 - 1,250}{253} = \frac{150}{253}$$
$$= .59 \text{ standard deviations}$$

Figure 15-8 illustrates this situation. In Appendix Table 1, we find that the area between the mean of the distribution and a point .59 standard deviation below the mean (1,250 hours) is .2224 of the total area under the curve. To .2224, we add .5, the area from the mean to the right-hand tail. This gives us .7224. Because .7224 is the probability that the machine will operate *more* than 1,250 hours, the chances that it

FIGURE 15-8

Probability the machine will operate between 1,250 and 1,400 hours

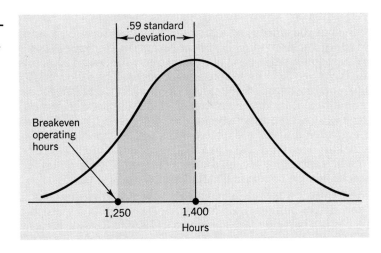

will operate fewer than 1,250 hours (its breakeven point) are $1 - .7224$, or $.2776$. Apparently, this is not too risky a situation.

This problem illustrates how we can make use of other people's knowledge about a situation without requiring them to understand the intricacies of various statistical techniques. Had we expected the foreman to comprehend the theory behind our calculations, or had we even attempted to explain the theory to him, we might never have been able to benefit from his practical wisdom concerning the situation. By using language and terms of reference that he understood, we were able to get the foreman to give us workable estimates of the mean and standard deviation of the distribution of operating times for the machine we contemplated purchasing. In this case (and for that matter, in most others, too), it is wiser to accommodate the ideas and knowledge of other people in your models than to search until you find a situation that will fit a model that has already been developed.

Exercises

15-19 Northwestern Industrial Pipe Company is considering the purchase of a new electric arc welder for $2,100. The welder is expected to save the firm $5 an hour when it can be used in place of the present, less efficient welder. Before making the decision, Northwestern's production manager noted there were only about 185 hours a year of welding on which the new arc welder could be substituted for the present one. He gave 7 to 3 odds that the actual outcome would be within 25 hours of this estimate. In addition, he felt secure in assuming that the number of hours was well described by a normal distribution. Can Northwestern be 98 percent sure that the new electric arc welder will pay for itself over a 3-year period?

15-20 Relman Electric Battery Company has felt the effects of a recovering economy as demand for its products has risen in recent months. The company is considering hiring six new people for its assembly operation. Plant production manager Mike Casey, whose performance is evaluated in part by cost efficiency, does not want to hire additional employees unless they can be expected to have jobs for at least 6 months. If the employees are terminated involuntarily before that time, the company is forced by union rules to pay a substantial termination bonus. Additionally, if employees are laid off within 6 months after hiring, the company's unemployment insurance rate is raised. Relman's corporate economist expects that the upswing in the economy will last at least 8 months and gives 7 to 2 odds that the length of the upswing will be within a 1-month range of that figure. Casey wants to be 95 percent sure that he will not have to lay off any newly hired employees. Should he hire six new people at this time?

15-21 John Stein is the scheduling director of SATPlus Services, a firm which guarantees that its preparatory course for the college board exams will increase a student's combined score on the verbal and quantitative parts of those exams by at least 120 points. Each student taking the course is charged $275 in tuition, and it costs SATPlus about $3,300 in salaries, supplies, and facility rental costs to teach the course. John will not schedule the course in any location where he cannot be at least 90 percent certain that SATPlus will earn no less than $2,200 in profit. Reviewing a marketing survey that he just received from Charlottesville, Virginia, he has decided that, if the course is offered there, he can expect about 30 students to enroll. He also feels that the odds are about 8 to 5 that actual enrollment will be between 25 and 35 students and that it is appropriate to use the normal distribution to describe course enrollment. Should John schedule the course in Charlottesville?

15-22 Natalie Larsen, a traveling sales representative for Nova Products, is considering the purchase of a new car for business use. The car she has in mind has a sticker price of $7,497, but she thinks she can bargain the dealer down to $6,650. Because her car is used solely for business purposes, Natalie can deduct 25¢ a mile for operating expenses. She will buy the car only if the resulting tax savings will pay for the car over its lifetime. Natalie has been in a combined federal and state 34 percent tax bracket for some years, and it appears she will remain there for the foreseeable future. A reputable automotive magazine states that the average life of the car she is considering is 90,000 miles. The article further states that the odds are 4 to 3 that the actual life of the car will be within 12,000 miles of 90,000. What is the probability that the car will go long enough for Natalie to break even?

15-23 The Newton Pines Police Force is considering purchasing a VASCAR radar unit to be installed on the town's single police cruiser. The town council has balked at the idea, because it is not certain that the unit is worth its price of $2,000. Police Chief Buren Hubbs has stated that he is sure that the unit will pay for itself through the increased number of $20 citations that he and his deputy will give. Buren has been overheard to say that he will give 9 to 1 odds that the increase in citations in the first year will be between 95 and 135 if the unit is purchased. He expects that there will be 115 more tickets given if the cruiser is equipped with VASCAR. Can the town council be 99 percent sure that the unit will be paid for by the increase in revenue from citations in the first year?

15-24 You are planning to invest $15,000 in Infometrics common stock if you can be reasonably certain that its price will rise to $60 a share within 6 months. You ask two knowledgeable brokers the following questions:
(a) What is your best estimate of the highest price at which Infometrics will sell in the next 6 months?
(b) What odds will you give that your estimate will be off by no more than $5?
Their responses are as follows:

BROKER	BEST ESTIMATE	ODDS
A	68	2 to 1
B	65	5 to 1

If you had decided that you would buy the stock only if each broker was at least 80 percent certain that it would be selling for at least $60 sometime within the next 6 months, what should you do?

15-6
Decision-Tree Analysis

Decision-tree fundamentals

A *decision tree* is a graphic model of a decision process. With it, we can introduce probabilities into the analysis of complex decisions involving (1) many alternatives and (2) future conditions that are not known but that can be specified in terms of a set of discrete probabilities or a continuous probability distribution. Decision-tree analysis is a useful tool in making decisions concerning investments, the acquisition or disposal of physical property, project management, personnel, and new-product strategies.

The term *decision tree* is derived from the physical appearance of the usual graphic representation of this technique. A decision tree is like the probability trees we introduced in Chapter 4. But a decision tree contains *not only* the probabilities of outcomes *but also* the conditional monetary (or utility) values attached to those outcomes. Because of this, we can use these trees to indicate the expected values of different actions that we can take. Decision trees have standard symbols:

Squares symbolize *decision points,* where the decision maker must choose among several possible actions. From these decision *nodes* we draw one *branch* for each of the possible actions.

- Squares symbolize *decision points,* where the decision maker must choose among several possible actions. From these decision *nodes* we draw one *branch* for each of the possible actions.
- Circles represent *chance events,* where some state of nature is realized. These chance events are not under the decision maker's control. From these chance nodes, we draw one branch for each possible outcome.

Decision-tree example: running a ski resort

Let's use a decision tree to help Christie Stem, the owner and general manager of the Snow Fun Ski Resort, decide how the hotel should be run in the coming season. Christie's profits for this year's skiing season will depend on how much snowfall occurs during the winter months. On the basis of previous experience, she believes the probability distribution of snowfall and the resulting profit can be summarized by Table 15-12.

Christie has recently received an offer from a large hotel chain to operate the resort for the winter, guaranteeing her a $45,000 profit for the season. She has also been considering leasing snowmaking equipment for the season. If the equipment is leased, the resort will be able to operate full time, regardless of the amount of natural snowfall. If she decides to use man-made snow to supplement the natural snowfall, her profit for the season will be $120,000 minus the cost of leasing and operating the snowmaking equipment. The leasing cost will be about $12,000 per season, regardless of how much it is used. The operating cost will be $10,000 if the natural snowfall is more than 40 inches, $50,000 if it is between 20 and 40 inches, and $90,000 if it is less than 20 inches.

Christie's decision tree

Figure 15-9 illustrates Christie's problem as a decision tree. The three branches emanating from the decision node represent her three possible ways to operate the resort this winter: hiring the hotel chain, running it herself without snow-making equipment, and running it by herself with the snowmakers. Each of the last two branches terminates in a chance node representing the amount of snow that will fall during the season. Each of these nodes has three branches emanating from it, one for each possible value of snowfall, and the probabilities of that much snow are indicated on each branch. **Notice that time flows from left to right in the tree; that is, nodes at the left represent actions or chance events which occur before nodes which fall farther to the right. It is very important to maintain the proper time sequence when constructing decision trees.**

At the end of each right-most branch is the net profit that Christie will earn if a path is followed from the root of the tree (at the decision node) to the top of the tree. For example, if she operates the resort herself with the snowmaker and the snowfall is between 20 and 40 inches, her profit will be $58,000 ($120,000 less $12,000 to lease the snowmaker and $50,000 to operate it). The other net profits are calculated similarly.

Rules for analyzing a decision tree

We can now begin to analyze Christie's decision tree. **(The process starts from the right (at the top of the tree) and works back to the left (to the root of the tree). In this**

TABLE 15-12 Distribution of Snowfall and Profit for Snow Fun Ski Resort

AMOUNT OF SNOW	PROFIT	PROBABILITY OF OCCURRENCE
More than 40 inches	$120,000	0.4
20 to 40 inches	40,000	0.2
Less than 20 inches	−40,000	0.4

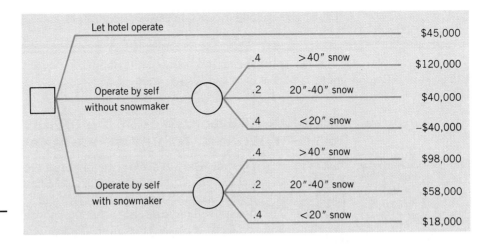

FIGURE 15-9
Christie Stem's decision tree

rollback **process, by working from right to left, we make the future decisions first and then roll them back to become part of earlier decisions.) We have two rules directing this process:**

1. If we are analyzing a *chance node (circle),* we calculate the expected value at that node by multiplying the probability on each branch emanating from the node by the profit at the end of that branch and then summing the products for all of the branches emanating from the node.
2. If we are analyzing a *decision node (square),* we let the expected value at that node be the maximum of the expected values for all of the branches emanating from the node. In this way, we choose the action with the largest expected value and we *prune* the branches corresponding to the less profitable actions. We mark those branches with a double slash to indicate that they have been pruned.

Christie's optimal decision

For Christie's decision, which is illustrated in Fig. 15-10, the expected value of hiring the hotel chain to manage the resort is $45,000. If she operates the resort herself and doesn't use the snowmaking equipment, her expected profit is

$$\$40,000 = \$120,000(0.4) + \$40,000(0.2) - \$40,000(0.4)$$

FIGURE 15-10
Christie Stem's analyzed decision tree

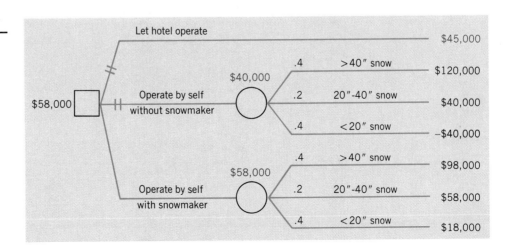

If she uses the snowmakers, her expected profit is

$$\$58,000 = \$98,000(0.4) + \$58,000(0.2) + \$18,000(0.4)$$

Thus her optimal decision is to operate Snow Fun herself with snowmaking equipment.

DECISION TREES AND NEW INFORMATION: USING BAYES' THEOREM TO REVISE PROBABILITIES

Cost and value of new information

Just as Christie is getting ready to decide whether to let the hotel chain operate Snow Fun or to operate it herself, she receives a call from Meteorological Associates offering to sell her a forecast of snowfall in the coming season. The price of the forecast will be $2,000. The forecast will indicate either that the snowfall will be above normal or else that it will be below normal. After doing a bit of research, Christie learns that Meteorological Associates is a reputable firm whose forecasts have been quite good in the past, although, of course, they haven't been absolutely reliable. In the past, the firm has forecast above normal snowfall in 90 percent of all years when the natural snowfall has been above 40 inches, in 60 percent of all years when it has been between 20 and 40 inches, and in 30 percent of those years in which it has been below 20 inches.

Incorporating new information

In order to incorporate this new information and decide whether she should purchase the snowfall forecast, Christie has to use Bayes' Theorem (which we discussed in Chapter 4) to see how the results of the forecast will cause her to revise the snowfall probabilities that she is using to make her decision. The forecast will have some value to her if it will cause her to change her decision and avoid taking a less-than-optimal action. However, before doing the calculations necessary to apply Bayes' Theorem, she decides to see first how much an absolutely reliable forecast of the snowfall would be worth. The calculation of this EVPI can be done with the tree given in Fig. 15-11. In this figure, we have reversed the time sequence of Christie's

FIGURE 15-11

Christie's tree with a perfectly reliable forecast

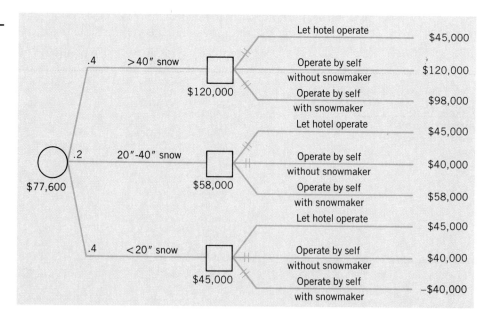

decision and when she learns the season's level of snowfall. In Fig. 15-9, she had to decide how to operate the resort, and she then learned the amount of snowfall by actually experiencing it. Now, were a perfectly reliable forecast available, she would learn how much snow would fall *before she had to decide how to operate the resort.*

Expected value of perfect information

Let's examine Fig. 15-11 carefully. Even though Christie is trying to determine the worth of an absolutely reliable forecast, she can't know beforehand what the result of the forecast will be. Forty percent of the time, there will over 40 inches of snow in a skiing season. So, the probability is .4 that the forecast will be for over 40 inches of snow. When the snowfall is at that level, Christie's best course of action is to operate the resort herself, without using snow-making equipment, and her profit will be $120,000. In another 20 percent of all seasons, when snowfall is between 20 and 40 inches, Christie will earn $58,000 by operating the resort herself and using snow-makers to supplement the meager natural snowfall. Finally, in those years with less than 20 inches of natural snowfall (and this happens 40 percent of the time), she should take the $45,000 profit available by letting the hotel chain operate Snow Fun. With a perfectly reliable forecast, we thus see that Christie's expected profit would be

$$\$77,600 = \$120,000(0.4) + \$58,000(0.2) + \$45,000(0.4)$$

Since her best course of action without the forecast (operating Snow Fun herself with the snowmaking equipment), has an expected profit of only $58,000, her EVPI is $19,600 ($77,600 − $58,000).

Because the forecast from Meteorological Associates is not absolutely reliable, it will be worth less than $19,600. Nevertheless, Christie sees that additional information about the amount of snowfall can be quite valuable. Will the Meteorological Associates forecast be worth its $2,000 cost? The answer to this question can be found in Table 15-13 and Fig. 15-12. Table 15-13 uses the same format we used in Chapter 4 to do the calculations for using Bayes' theorem to update the snowfall probabilities, given the results of the forecast.

Notice how the probabilities change. If the forecast is for above normal snowfall, Christie's probability that there will be more than 40 inches of snow increases to .6 from its initial value of .4. With a forecast for below normal snowfall, she revises her probability downward to .1.

Figure 15-12 gives the entire tree, including the option to buy the forecast from Meteorological Associates. Let's review the rollback procedure for this tree. The top of the tree (from node 3 on) is the same as Fig. 15-10. The bottom of the tree (from node 2 on) analyzes Christie's options if she buys the forecast. At the chance nodes 8,

TABLE 15-13 Christie's Posterior Probabilities

FORECAST	EVENT (SNOWFALL)	P(EVENT)	P(FORECAST |EVENT)	P(FORECAST & EVENT)	P(EVENT| FORECAST)
Above normal	Over 40″	0.4	0.9	.4 × .9 = .36	.36/.60 = .6
	20″–40″	0.2	0.6	.2 × .6 = .12	.12/.60 = .2
	Under 20″	0.4	0.3	.4 × .3 = .12	.12/.60 = .2
				P(above normal) = .60	
Below normal	Over 40″	0.4	0.1	.4 × .1 = .04	.04/.40 = .1
	20″–40″	0.2	0.4	.2 × .4 = .08	.08/.40 = .2
	Under 20″	0.4	0.7	.4 × .7 = .28	.28/.40 = .7
				P(below normal) = .40	

15-6 Decision-Tree Analysis   **767**

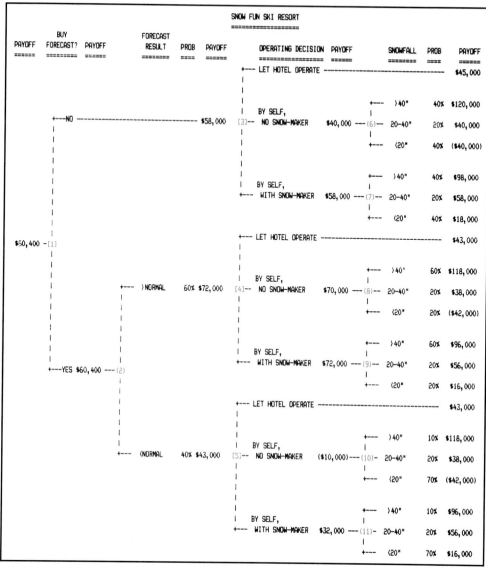

FIGURE 15-12
Christie Stem's complete decision tree

9, 10, and 11, she has calculated expected values using rule 1 on p. 765. Using rule 2, she decides at node 4 that she will run the resort by herself (but hedges her bets by using the snowmaking equipment) if the forecast is for above normal snowfall. She decides at node 5, on the other hand, that she will accept the hotel chain's offer to operate Snow Fun if the forecast is for below normal snowfall.

Continuing to work her way back through the tree, at node 2 she finds that the expected value of buying the forecast is $60,400. Finally, at node 1, Christie decides that she should pay Meteorological Associates the $2,000 that it is charging for its forecast, since the resulting expected profit of $60,400 is more than the $58,000 she expects to earn without the forecast.

Christie's optimal decision

In summary, we see that Christie's optimal decision is to buy the forecast. Then, if the forecast is for above normal snowfall, she should operate the resort by herself, but hedge her bets by using the snowmaking equipment. However, if the forecast is for below normal snowfall, she should accept the hotel chain's offer to operate Snow Fun for her. If she follows this course of action, she expects her profit for the season to be $60,400. Even after paying $2,000 for the forecast, she is $2,400 better off than she would be if she didn't use it. What is the maximum amount she would be willing to pay for the forecast? She would pay up to an additional $2,400 for it and still expect to earn at least as much as she could earn without buying it. Thus, the expected value of the forecast (sometimes called *the expected value of sample information,* or EVSI) is $4,400, and this is the maximum amount that Christie would be willing to pay for it.

Decision trees on the personal computer

You probably noticed that Fig. 15-12 (Christie's expanded decision tree) was output from a computer. In fact, we constructed the tree and did the Bayes' Theorem calculations and the rollback procedure using the Lotus 1-2-3 spreadsheet program on a personal computer. (Figure 15-13 gives the input data and the Bayes' computations from our spreadsheet.) Similar analysis can be done with many other spreadsheet programs. A discussion of how to do this kind of analysis is given by J. Morgan Jones in "Decision Analysis Using Spreadsheets," *The European Journal of Operations Research,* XXVI, No. 3 (1986), pp. 385–400. There is also some special purpose software that is designed specifically for analyzing decision trees. See the survey article, "Software for Decision Analysis" by Max Herion in *OR/MS Today,* XII, No. 12 (1985), pp. 24–29.

Changing some input data

Christie is pleased with the results of this analysis, but she still isn't sure that she should go ahead and implement the optimal policy. Her uncertainty stems from the fact that she doesn't know for sure that leasing the snowmaking equipment will cost $12,000 for the season. That was the amount that her friend, Deborah Rubin, had paid last year for snowmakers at her place, The Quaking Aspen Lodge. But there are many differences, among them the fact that Snow Fun's slopes are longer than Quaking Aspen's and that there are several more firms renting snowmakers this year. Christie is reasonably certain that the cost of leasing the equipment will be somewhere between $5,000 and $20,000.

Reasonable strategies

She has realized that there are only three reasonable courses of action *(strategies)* to take:

1. Don't buy the forecast and operate Snow Fun herself using the snowmakers.
2. Buy the forecast and operate Snow Fun herself without snowmakers if the predicted snowfall is above normal, but accept the hotel chain's offer if below normal snowfall is predicted.

FIGURE 15-13

Spreadsheet with Christie's input and Bayes' theorem calculations

INPUT DATA AND BAYES' REVISIONS FOR CHRISTIE STEM AND THE SNOW FUN SKI RESORT

SNOWFALL STATE	PRIOR PROB	PROFIT WITHOUT SNOW-MAKER	SNOW-MAKER OPERATING COST	PROFIT WITH SNOW-MAKER	FORECAST RESULT PROBABILITIES)NORMAL	(NORMAL	JOINT PROBABILITIES)NORMAL	(NORMAL	REVISED PROBABILITIES)NORMAL	(NORMAL
)40"	40%	$120,000	$10,000	$98,000	90%	10%	36%	4%	60%	10%
20-40"	20%	$40,000	$50,000	$58,000	60%	40%	12%	8%	20%	20%
(20"	40%	($40,000)	$90,000	$18,000	30%	70%	12%	28%	20%	70%
							60%	40%	(=PROBABILITY OF FORECAST RESULTS	

PROFIT FROM=) $45,000 HOTEL LEASE

$120,000 (=REVENUE WITH SNOW-MAKER

$12,000 (=COST OF SNOW-MAKER LEASE

$2,000 (=COST OF FORECAST

3. Buy the forecast and operate Snow Fun herself with snowmakers if the predicted snowfall is above normal, but accept the hotel chain's offer if below normal snowfall is predicted.

Sensitivity analysis

With her original $12,000 "guesstimate" of the leasing cost, Christie's optimal decision is to follow the third strategy. She wonders how other possible leasing costs between $5,000 and $20,000 will affect her optimal strategy and expected profit, if at all. Although such a *sensitivity analysis* is tedious to do by hand, it is quite easy to do in Lotus 1-2-3, and Fig. 15-14 shows Christie what to do as the cost of leasing the snowmaking equipment varies from $5,000 to $20,000. If the cost is between $5,000 and $6,000, she should adopt the first strategy. (At exactly $6,000, she is indifferent between the first and third strategies.) For costs between $6,000 and $14,000, strategy three is optimal. (At exactly $14,000, she is indifferent between the second and third strategies.) Finally, if the cost is above $14,000, she should adopt strategy two.

The last column in Fig. 15-14 gives the maximum amount that Christie will be willing to pay for the snowfall forecast. She is including this calculation in her analysis because she has heard a rumor that Meteorological Associates has gotten so much business that they are considering increasing their fees. These figures will be useful to her if she has to negotiate the fee for the forecast.

Other sensitivities

We have just seen a sensitivity analysis with respect to a cost. In a similar fashion, it is possible to see how optimal decisions and profits change when payoffs or probabilities vary. This capability is especially important when you are using subjective probability estimates in your decision making, and it can be done in a quite straightforward fashion on a personal computer. The ability to perform such sensitivity analyses greatly enhances the value of decision trees in helping us to make important decisions.

FIGURE 15-14

Sensitivity analysis on the cost of leasing the snowmaking equipment

```
SENSITIVITY ANALYSIS ON SNOWMAKER LEASE COST
===================================================
STRATEGY 1: OPERATE BY SELF WITH SNOWMAKERS
STRATEGY 2: BUY FORECAST AND
            OPERATE BY SELF W/O SNOWMAKERS IF >NORMAL
            LET HOTEL CHAIN OPERATE IF <NORMAL
STRATEGY 3: BUY FORECAST AND
            OPERATE BY SELF WITH SNOWMAKERS IF >NORMAL
            LET HOTEL CHAIN OPERATE IF <NORMAL
```

COST OF SNOW-MAKERS	STRATEGY/EXPECTED PROFIT 1	2	3	OPTIMAL STRATEGY	EXPECTED VALUE	MAXIMUM TO PAY FOR FORECAST
$5,000	$65,000	$59,200	$64,600	1	$65,000	$1,600
$6,000	$64,000	$59,200	$64,000	1 or 3	$64,000	$2,000
$7,000	$63,000	$59,200	$63,400	3	$63,400	$2,400
$8,000	$62,000	$59,200	$62,800	3	$62,800	$2,800
$9,000	$61,000	$59,200	$62,200	3	$62,200	$3,200
$10,000	$60,000	$59,200	$61,600	3	$61,600	$3,600
$11,000	$59,000	$59,200	$61,000	3	$61,000	$4,000
$12,000	$58,000	$59,200	$60,400	3	$60,400	$4,400
$13,000	$57,000	$59,200	$59,800	3	$59,800	$4,800
$14,000	$56,000	$59,200	$59,200	2 or 3	$59,200	$5,200
$15,000	$55,000	$59,200	$58,600	2	$59,200	$6,200
$16,000	$54,000	$59,200	$58,000	2	$59,200	$7,200
$17,000	$53,000	$59,200	$57,400	2	$59,200	$8,200
$18,000	$52,000	$59,200	$56,800	2	$59,200	$9,200
$19,000	$51,000	$59,200	$56,200	2	$59,200	$10,200
$20,000	$50,000	$59,200	$55,600	2	$59,200	$11,200

USING DECISION-TREE ANALYSIS

Solving Christie Stem's problem was easy, because the tree had only eleven nodes in it. But real-world decision analysis problems can be much more complex. There can be many more alternatives to consider at each decision node and many more possible outcomes at each chance node. In addition, more realistic problems often involve longer sequences of decisions and chance events. (The trees get taller and bushier!) When solving a problem with a decision tree, remember to stop at a level of complexity that allows you to consider major consequences of future alternatives without becoming bogged down in too much detail.

Generally, decision-tree analysis requires the decision maker to proceed through the following six steps:

Decision-tree steps

1. **Define the problem in structured terms.** First determine which factors are relevant to the solution. Then estimate probability distributions that are appropriate to describe future behavior of those factors. Collect financial data concerning conditional outcomes.

2. **Model the decision process;** that is, construct a decision tree that illustrates all the alternatives involved in the problem. This step *structures* the problem, in that it allows the entire decision process to be presented schematically and in an organized, step-by-step fashion. In this step, the decision maker chooses the number of periods into which the future is to be divided.

3. **Apply the appropriate probability values and financial data** to each of the branches and subbranches of the decision tree. This will enable you to distinguish the probability value and conditional monetary value associated with each outcome.

4. **"Solve" the decision tree.** Using the methodology we have illustrated, proceed to locate that particular branch of the tree that has the largest expected value or that maximizes the decision criterion, whatever it is.

5. **Perform sensitivity analysis;** that is, determine how the solution reacts to changes in the inputs. Changing probability values and conditional financial values allows the decision maker to test both the magnitude and the direction of the reaction. This step allows experiment without real commitments or real mistakes and without disrupting operations.

6. **List the underlying assumptions.** Explain the estimating techniques used to arrive at the probability distributions. What kinds of accounting and cost-finding assumptions underlie the conditional financial values used to arrive at a solution? Why has the future been divided into a certain number of periods? By making these assumptions explicit, you enable others to know what risks they are taking when they use the results of your decision-tree analysis. Use this step to specify limits under which the results obtained will be valid, and especially the conditions under which the decision will not be valid.

Advantages of the decision-tree approach

Decision-tree analysis is a technique managers use to structure and display alternatives and decision processes. It is popular because it:

- Structures the decision process, guiding managers to approach decision making in an orderly, sequential fashion
- Requires the decision maker to examine all possible outcomes, desirable and undesirable

- Communicates the decision-making process to others, illustrating each assumption about the future
- Allows a group to discuss alternatives by focusing on each financial figure, probability value, and underlying assumption — one at a time; thus, a group can move in orderly steps toward a consensus decision, instead of debating a decision in its entirety
- Can be used with a computer, so that many different sets of assumptions can be simulated and their effects on the final outcome observed

Exercises

 15-25 The Motor City Auto Company is planning to introduce a new automobile that features a radically new pollution-control system. It has two options. The first option is to build a new plant, anticipating full production in 3 years. The second option is to rebuild a small existing pilot plant for limited production for the coming model year. If the results of the limited production show promise at the end of the first year, full-scale production in a newly constructed plant would still be possible 3 years from now. If they decide to proceed with the pilot plant, and later analysis shows that it is unattractive to go into full production, the pilot plant can still be operated by itself at a small profit. The expected annual profits for various alternatives are as follows:

PRODUCTION FACILITY	CONSUMER ACCEPTANCE	ANNUAL PROFIT (MILLION)
New plant	High	14
New plant	Low	−6
Pilot plant	High	2
Pilot plant	Low	1

Motor City's marketing-research division has estimated that there is a 50 percent probability that consumer acceptance will be high and 50 percent that it will be low. If the pilot plant is put into production, with a correspondingly low-keyed advertising program, the researchers feel that the probabilities are 45 percent for high consumer acceptance and 55 percent for low acceptance. Further, they have estimated that if the pilot plant is built and consumer acceptance is found to be high, there is a 90 percent probability of high acceptance with full production. If consumer acceptance with the pilot models is found to be low, however, there is only a 10 percent probability of high eventual acceptance with full production. Which plant should be built?

 15-26 Refer to Christie Stem's problem on p. 764 and in Fig. 15-9.
(a) Suppose that the operating cost of the snowmaking equipment is actually 30 percent higher than Christie had estimated, that is, $13,000 if the snowfall is heavy, $65,000 if it is moderate, and $117,000 if it is light. How will this affect Christie's optimal decision and expected profit?
(b) Answer the same questions if the actual operating cost is 20 percent higher than Christie's original estimate.
(c) At what percentage increase of the operating cost will Christie be indifferent between the optimal decisions in (a) and (b)? At this point, what will be her expected profit?

 15-27 International Pictures is trying to decide how to distribute its new movie *Claws. Claws* is the story of an animal husbandry experiment at North Carolina State University that goes astray, with tragicomic results. An effort to breed meatier turkeys somehow produces an intelligent, 1,000-pound turkey that escapes from the lab and terrorizes the campus. In a surprise ending, the turkey is befriended by Coach Tim Galvano, who teaches it how to play basketball, and State goes on to win the NCAA championship. Because of the movie's controversial nature, it has the potential to be either a smash hit, a modest success, or a total bomb. International is trying to decide whether to release the picture for general distribution initially or to start out with a "limited first-run release" at a few selected theaters, followed by general distribution after 3 months. The company has estimated the following probabilities and conditional profits for *Claws*:

LEVEL OF SUCCESS	PROBABILITY	PROFITS (MILLIONS OF $)	
		Limited release	General distribution
Smash	.3	22	12
Modest	.4	9	8
Bomb	.3	−10	−2

(a) Construct a decision tree to help International decide how to release *Claws*.
(b) Which decision will maximize the expected profit.
(c) How much would International pay for an absolutely reliable forecast of the movie's level of success?
(d) International can run several sneak previews of *Claws* to get a better idea of the movie's ultimate level of success. Preview audiences rate movies as either good or excellent, but their opinions are not completely reliable. On the basis of past experience with previews, International has found that 90 percent of all smash successes were rated excellent (with 10 percent of them being rated good), 65 percent of all modest success were rated excellent (with 35 percent of them being rated good), and 40 percent of all bombs were rated excellent (with 60 percent of them being rated good). If the cost of sneak previews would be about $750,000, should *Claws* be previewed? How should International respond to the preview results? What is the maximum amount International should be willing to pay for the previews?

15-28 Sam Crawford, a junior business major, lives off campus and has just missed the bus that would have taken him to campus for his 9 A.M. test. It is now 8:45 A.M. and Sam has several options available to get him to campus: waiting for the next bus, walking, riding his bike, or driving his car. The bus is scheduled to arrive in 10 minutes, and it will take Sam exactly 20 minutes to get to his test from the time he gets on the bus. However, there is a .2 chance that the bus will be five minutes early, and a .3 chance that the bus will be 5 minutes late. If Sam walks, there is a .8 chance he will get to his test in 30 minutes, and a .2 chance he will get there in 35 minutes. If Sam rides his bike, he will get to the test in 25 minutes with probability .5, 30 minutes with probability .4, and there is a .1 chance of a flat tire, causing him to take 45 minutes. If Sam drives his car to campus, he will take 15 minutes to get to campus, but the time needed to park his car and get to his test is given by the following table:

Time to park & arrive (minutes)	10	15	20	25
Probability	.30	.45	.15	.10

(a) Assuming that Sam wants to minimize his expected late time in getting to his test, draw the decision tree and determine his best option.
(b) Suppose instead that Sam wants to maximize his expected utility as measured by the projected test score given below. Use the same decision tree to determine his optional decision now.

Arrival time	9:10	9:15	9:20	9:25	9:30
Projected test score	95	85	70	60	45

15-29 Evelyn Parkhill is considering three possible ways to invest the $200,000 she has just inherited.

   (1)   Some of her friends are considering financing a combined laundromat, video-game arcade, and pizzeria, where the young singles in the area can meet and play while doing their laundry. This venture is highly risky, and could result in either a major loss or a substantial gain within a year. Evelyn estimates that with probability .6, she will lose all of her money. However, with probability .4, she will make a $200,000 profit.

   (2)   She can invest in some new apartments that are being built in town. Within 1 year, this fairly conservative project will produce a profit of at least $10,000, but it might yield $15,000, $20,000, $25,000, or possibly even $30,000. Evelyn estimates the probabilities of these five returns at .20, .30, .25, .20, and .05, respectively.

   (3)   She can invest in some government securities which have a current yield of 8.25 percent.

   (a)   Construct a decision tree to help Evelyn decide how to invest her money.

   (b)   Which investment will maximize her expected 1-year profit?

   (c)   How high would the yield on the government bonds have to be before she would decide to invest in them?

   (d)   How much would she be willing to pay for perfect information about the success of the laundromat?

   (e)   How much would she be willing to pay for perfect information about the success of the apartments?

15-7
Terms Introduced in Chapter 15

Certainty The decision environment in which only one state of nature exists.

Conditional Profit The profit that would result from a given combination of decision alternative and state of nature.

Decision point Branching point that requires a decision.

Decision Tree Graphic display of the decision environment, indicating decision alternatives, states of nature, probabilities attached to those states of nature, and conditional benefits and losses.

Expected Marginal Loss The marginal loss multiplied by the probability of not selling that unit.

Expected Marginal Profit The marginal profit multiplied by the probability of selling that unit.

Expected Profit The sum of the conditional profits for a given decision alternative, each weighted by the probability that it will happen.

Expected Profit with Perfect Information The expected value of profit with perfect certainty about the occurrence of the states of nature.

Expected Value Criterion A criterion requiring the decision maker to calculate the expected value for each decision alternative (the sum of the weighted payoffs for that alternative in which the weights are the probability values assigned by the decision maker to the states of nature that can happen).

Expected Value of Perfect Information The difference between expected profit (under conditions of risk) and expected profit with perfect information.

Marginal Loss The loss incurred from stocking a unit that is not sold.

Marginal Profit The profit earned from selling one additional unit.

Minimum Probability The probability of selling at least an additional unit that must exist to justify stocking that unit.

Node Point at which a chance event or a decision takes place on a decision tree.

Obsolescence Loss The loss occasioned by stocking too many units and having to dispose of unsold units.

Opportunity Loss The profit that could have been earned if stock had been sufficient to supply a unit that was demanded.

Payoff The benefit that accrues from a given combination of decision alternative and state of nature.

Rollback Also called foldback; method of using decision trees to find optimal alternatives. Involves working from right to left in the tree.

Salvage Value The value of an item after the initial selling period.

State of Nature Future event not under the control of the decision maker.

Utility The value of a certain outcome or payoff to someone; the pleasure or displeasure someone derives from an outcome.

15-8
Equations Introduced in Chapter 15

[15-1]
$$p(MP) = (1 - p)(ML)$$
p. 749

This equation describes the point at which the *expected marginal profit* from stocking and selling an additional unit, $p(MP)$, is equal to the *expected marginal loss* from stocking and not selling the unit, $(1 - p)(ML)$. As long as $p(MP)$ is larger than $(1 - p)(ML)$, additional units should be stocked, because the expected marginal profit from such a decision is greater than the expected marginal loss.

[15-2]
$$p^* = \frac{ML}{MP + ML}$$
p. 749

This is the *minimum probability equation.* The symbol p^* represents the minimum required probability of selling at least an additional unit to justify the stocking of that additional unit. As long as the probability of selling one additional unit is greater than p^*, the retailer should stock that unit. This equation is Equation 15-1 solved for p^*.

15-9
Chapter Review Exercises

 15-30 The Mountain Manufacturing Company is planning to produce dot-matrix printers for use with microcomputers. One problem it faces is a make-or-buy decision for the print heads. It can buy these units from a Japanese manufacturer for $35 each or it can produce them at its own plant with variable costs of $24 a unit. If it elects to produce the print heads itself, it will incur fixed costs of $28,000 each year. Because of defective units, each printer requires 1.15 print heads. The company foresees annual demand for its printers to be normally distributed with mean $\mu = 3,000$ units and standard deviation $\sigma = 700$ units. What is the probability that the required usage of print heads will be sufficiently large to justify producing them rather than buying them? If it is company policy to make components only when there is better than a 60 percent chance that usage is 1.5 standard deviations above the make-or-buy breakeven point, what should the decision be on this matter?

15-31 Sarah Peterson is going to open a health-food store, the Boysenberry Farms Organic Food Emporium. In planning for her initial stock, Sarah is trying to decide how many jars of Mrs. Mile's Currant Jelly to purchase. Mrs. Miles makes her currant jelly only once every 2 months, so it is necessary for Sarah to plan in advance how much she will need (there is no chance of reorder in the interim period). Sarah is torn between satisfying her customers and friends and losing money because of spoilage, since the jelly has only a 2-month shelf life. Sarah is sure that she will sell at least ten jars during the period, and eighteen different friends have promised that they will buy the jelly when it comes into stock. Sarah knows that the probability of selling more than eighteen jars is practically nil and feels that sales will fall somewhere between ten and eighteen jars—despite what her friends have promised. Sarah has all the cost data and is planning a 50 percent markup on cost. As the problem stands now, can Sarah reach a solution to her problem by using decision theory?

15-32 For the price of $26.95, La Langouste offers an entrée consisting of two broiled spiny-lobster tails with drawn-butter garlic sauce. Because of federal health regulations, the lobsters, which are imported from the Yucatan Peninsula, cannot enter the United States if they are still alive. Accordingly, only refrigerated or frozen tails can be imported. The chef at La Langouste refuses to use frozen lobster tails and, to maintain his establishment's reputation for serving only *haute cuisine*, he employs an agent to place freshly refrigerated lobster tails on a plane leaving the peninsula each day. Any tail not served the day it is shipped must be discarded. The chef wants to know how many tails the agent should ship each day. He wants to be able to satisfy his customers, but he realizes that always ordering enough to meet potential demand could involve substantial waste on days with low demand. He has calculated the cost of a single lobster tail at $7.35, including transportation charges. Past records show the following distribution of daily demand for the lobster-tail entrée:

Number	18	19	20	21	22	23	24	25
Probability	.07	.09	.11	.16	.20	.15	.14	.08

(a) If he wishes to maximize his daily expected profits on spiny-lobster tails, how many tails should the chef order?
(b) If La Langouste adopted a policy that required customers to order spiny lobster a day in advance, how much increase in profit could it expect to see?

15-33 Bay Lakes Lawn and Garden Care Company provides services for homeowners and small businesses. The firm is considering the purchase of a new fertilizer spreader at a cost of $43.50. The spreader is estimated to save 8 minutes labor for every hour it is in use. Head lawn-care specialist Ralph Medlin estimates that the expected life of the spreader is only 48 hours due to corrosion and the odds are 7 to 5 that its life will be between 42 and 54 hours. If the company pays its gardening help $12.50 an hour, what is the probability that the spreader will pay for itself before it is scrapped?

15-34 The luggage department of Madison Rhodes Department Store featured a special Day-After-Christmas Sale of Luggage on unsold Christmas merchandise. The luggage brand on sale was Imagemaker. The manager of the luggage department was planning his order. Because the store did not carry Imagemaker during the year, the manager wanted to avoid overstocking; yet, because of a special price the manufacturer offered on the line, he also wanted to minimize stockouts. He was currently attempting to decide the number of women's tote bags to purchase. His estimate of the probable sales, based in part on past performance, is shown below.

Bags	32	33	34	35	36	37	38
Probability	.10	.14	.15	.20	.17	.13	.11

The store is planning to sell the tote bag for $42.75. The wholesale cost is $26.00. How many bags should be ordered for the sale?

15-35 Archdale Stores, a chain of retailers specializing in men's fashions, is considering purchasing a batch of 5,700 neckties from Beau Charm Company. The batch of ties will cost Archdale $16,500, and each tie will sell for $3.50. Archdale's vice-president of sales has stated that he

thinks the chain could sell 5,000 ties, and the odds are 2 to 3 that the actual sales will be within 200 of his estimate. Leftover ties are worthless.
(a) What is the probability that Archdale will at least break even on the necktie sales?
(b) What is the probability that Archdale can earn 10 percent on its inventory investment?

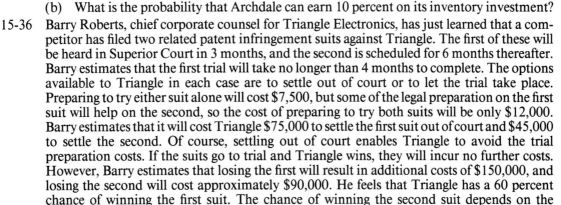

15-36 Barry Roberts, chief corporate counsel for Triangle Electronics, has just learned that a competitor has filed two related patent infringement suits against Triangle. The first of these will be heard in Superior Court in 3 months, and the second is scheduled for 6 months thereafter. Barry estimates that the first trial will take no longer than 4 months to complete. The options available to Triangle in each case are to settle out of court or to let the trial take place. Preparing to try either suit alone will cost $7,500, but some of the legal preparation on the first suit will help on the second, so the cost of preparing to try both suits will be only $12,000. Barry estimates that it will cost Triangle $75,000 to settle the first suit out of court and $45,000 to settle the second. Of course, settling out of court enables Triangle to avoid the trial preparation costs. If the suits go to trial and Triangle wins, they will incur no further costs. However, Barry estimates that losing the first will result in additional costs of $150,000, and losing the second will cost approximately $90,000. He feels that Triangle has a 60 percent chance of winning the first suit. The chance of winning the second suit depends on the resolution of the first: 40 percent if it is settled out of court, 80 percent if it is tried and won, and 10 percent if it is tried and lost.
(a) Construct Barry's decision tree for deciding how to proceed.
(b) What should Barry do to minimize Triangle's expected cost?
(c) Barry could run a mock trial to get a better idea of the probability of winning the first suit. How much should Triangle be willing to pay if Barry can arrange for an absolutely reliable mock trial?
(d) How would Barry's decision in (b) change if the cost of settling the second suit were only $20,000? What if that cost were $90,000?

15-37 The policy of the Newland Company is not to undertake new business ventures unless annual return on investment has a 60 percent probability of being 13 percent or higher. The managers are contemplating a new venture, the production of dentures. This venture will require an investment of $500,000. They estimate that a set will cost them $80 in variable costs, and their annual fixed costs are expected to be $125,000. Their marketing specialists have analyzed the potential demand for dentures and have found that at a selling price of $130 per set, the expected annual sales would be 4,000 sets, and the standard deviation is estimated to be 450 sets. They further determined that at a price of $140 per set, expected annual demand would be 3,200 sets with a standard deviation of 300 sets annually. Should they proceed with this venture? If so, which selling price would allow a higher probability of returning 13 percent on their investment annually?

15-38 At the Campus Set, a clothing store for stylish young moderns, manager Judy Sommers is ordering the season's bathing suits from Jamaican Swimwear. As in past years, she is ordering mostly two-piece suits, but she does plan to carry some one-piece suits. From past experience, she estimates demand for the latter as follows:

Units demanded	19	20	21	22	23	24	25
Probability	.05	.18	.21	.22	.16	.10	.08

The one-piece suits will retail for $43.95; Judy's cost is $21.50. Any suits left at the end of the season go on sale for $19.95 and are certain to sell at that price. Use marginal analysis to determine the number of one-piece suits Judy should order.

15-39 Flint City Appliance Sales is planning for its big Founder's Day Weekend Sale. As a special offer, the store is selling a Royalty washer-and-dryer combination for only $600. Royalty has recently informed its distributors that a product innovation will make existing washer-dryer combinations virtually obsolete, and therefore it is offering stores its current first-line washer-dryer combination for only $325. Although the manager of Flint City does not believe all of

Royalty's talk of obsolescence, he does know that any new gadget that Royalty puts on its newer machines will make his older machines very difficult to sell. He wants, therefore, to be very careful about the number of machines he orders for the Founder's Day Sale. His estimate of the demand for the washer-dryer combinations during the sale is given below.

Units demanded	6	7	8	9	10	11
Probability	.04	.12	.30	.24	.18	.12

Use marginal analysis to determine how many more washer-dryer combinations should be ordered for the sale if Flint City already has two in stock.

15-40 Steel-fab Manufacturing is a competitor of the Enduro Company (problem 15-17) in the structural steel components market. Unlike Enduro, Steel-fab is publicly held and is also financed in part by a bond issue. Accordingly, the company has adopted a 9 percent cutoff rate of return. Below the 9 percent level, the firm's utility curve steepens as the return moves farther away. Above the 9 percent level, the firm's utility grows at a slower rate because of the accompanying risk involved with higher rates of return. The utility for 15 percent is only slightly higher than for 14 percent. Steel-fab is considering a $300,000 project. Plot the firm's utility curve.

15-41 A textile mill must decide whether to extend $150,000 credit to a new customer that manufactures dresses. The mill's prior experience with a number of dress manufacturers has led it to classify such customers as follows: 25 percent are poor risks; 45 percent are average risks; and 30 percent are good risks. Expected profits on this order (if credit is extended to the dress manufacturer) are −$20,000 if it turns out to be a poor risk; $18,000 if it turns out to be an average risk, and $25,000 if it turns out to be a good risk. Draw a decision tree to determine whether the mill should extend credit to this manufacturer.

15-42 For $750, the textile mill in exercise 15-41 can purchase a comprehensive credit analysis and rating of the manufacturer. The rating, in increasing order of creditworthiness, will be C, B, or A. The credit agency's reliability is summed up in the following table, whose entries are the probabilities (from past experience) of the agency's rating of the dress manufacturer, given the true credit category in which the manufacturer belongs.

	TRUE CATEGORY		
AGENCY RATING	Poor	Average	Good
A	.1	.1	.6
B	.2	.8	.3
C	.7	.1	.1

(a) Use Bayes' Theorem and a decision tree to determine if the mill should purchase the credit rating.
(b) If it does purchase the rating, how will this affect the decision to grant credit to the dress manufacturer?
(c) What is the maximum amount the mill will be willing to pay for the credit report?
(d) What would the mill pay for an absolutely reliable credit rating of the manufacturer?

15-43 John Silver can use his boat, the *Jolly Roger*, for either commercial tuna fishing or else for sport fishing. For the latter, he rents it out at a daily charge of $500. In a fishing season with good weather, he averages 150 rental days. However, if the weather is bad, he averages only 105 rental days. For each day the boat is rented, John estimates he incurs variable costs of about $135. When the weather is good, the revenues from fishing for tuna exceed the variable costs of that operation by $50,000, whereas in seasons with bad weather the profit contribution from tuna fishing is only $43,000. At the beginning of the 1990 season, John feels that the odds are about 7 to 3 in favor of good weather for the season.

(a) Use a decision tree to help John decide how to use the *Jolly Roger* during the 1990 fishing season.

(b) How much would John pay for a perfectly reliable long-range weather forecast for the season?

John's good friend, Jim Hawkins, runs a private weather forecasting service that has been 90 percent accurate in the past. In 90 percent of all seasons that had good weather, Jim had forecast good weather, and likewise in 90 percent of all seasons when the weather proved to be bad, Jim's forecast had been for bad weather. Jim usually sells his forecast for $1,000, but since John is a good friend, Jim is willing to sell it to him for only $400.

(c) Expand your decision tree to help John decide if he should buy Jim's forecast. How will the forecast affect his use of the boat during the 1990 season?

(d) Would John buy Jim's forecast if they weren't friends? Explain. What is the maximum amount John would be willing to pay for the forecast?

15-44 Robert Ingersoll of Tungsten Products has approached both the Enduro Manufacturing Company and Steel-fab Manufacturing about the possibility of a joint venture with one of them. In this venture, a tungsten alloy is used in place of certain steel alloys. Tungsten Products has the technological expertise but not the production capabilities. The joint venture will be a 50-50 split and will cost each company $500,000 in capital investment.

(a) If the expected first-year profit on the project is $80,000, would either or both firms accept the offer?

(b) Superimpose the graphs from questions 15-17 and 15-40, adjusting the coordinates, and show the area where Enduro would accept a project and Steel-fab would not.

(c) If the expected first-year profit on the project was $110,000, would either of the firms accept it? How much would Steel-fab bid for a 50 percent share of the $110,000?

15-45 The Sporty Sneaker Company is deciding whether or not to market its newest basketball sneaker, the High Jump. The company's management believes that either 15 percent, 30 percent, or 45 percent of its customers will purchase the High Jump if it is put on the market. Based on its knowledge and past experience, the management has assigned certain payoffs and probabilities, as given in the table below. Based on these data alone, what should the company do?

| | PAYOFFS | | |
EVENT	MARKET	DO NOT MARKET	PROBABILITY
15% purchase	−$42,000	$0	.50
30% purchase	26,000	$0	.30
45% purchase	71,000	$0	.20

15-46 Stanley Glass, the owner of a chain of family amusement centers in Ohio, plans to open another center in Cincinnati. He must decide whether it should have 20, 25, or 35 video games. He expects that the demand may be either high, medium, or low, and he has determined probabilities associated with each level. The probabilities and payoffs are as follows:

EVENT	PROBABILITY	20 GAMES	25 GAMES	35 GAMES
High Demand	.55	$12,600	$18,000	$23,000
Medium Demand	.30	11,000	16,200	15,000
Low Demand	.15	10,600	8,500	7,100

(a) Without further information about demand, what should Mr. Glass choose to do?

(b) What is the maximum amount he would be willing to pay for perfect information?

15-47 The new engineering school at a small southern university is currently deciding which textbooks to use in its undergraduate courses. The department chairpersons want to know whether to use textbooks written by professors within the university ("university textbooks") or those written by professors from other institutions ("outside textbooks"). It has been rumored that the school's administrators are pushing for more support for the university and may require that departments use university textbooks whenever possible. If this requirement is passed, and if the department has decided to purchase outside textbooks, the switch to university textbooks will prove to be quite costly. The university's preliminary payoff table is given below (payoffs are in thousands of dollars).

EVENT	PROBABILITY	USE UNIVERSITY TEXTS	USE OUTSIDE TEXTS
Requirement passed	.70	$ 8	$13
Requirement not passed	.30	16	13

(a) Compute the expected payoff for each of the two decisions.
(b) Which decision should the engineering school choose?

15-48 Allyson Smith, assistant manager of Records and Tapes Unlimited, plans to sell a weekly music magazine. She is aware that if the magazine does not sell within the week of publication, it is considered to be worthless to the store. Allyson speculates, based on past sales data, about how well the magazine would sell; her weekly sales and probability estimates are as follows:

No. of magazines	500	600	700	800	900
Probability	.10	.12	.15	.33	.30

The magazine has a production cost of $.70 each, but Records and Tapes Unlimited plans to sell it for $1.50 each. Determine the optimal number of magazines that the store should order, using the expected value decision criterion.

15-49 The women of Alpha Zeta sorority at a small midwestern college are getting ready to participate in the school's annual 3-day spring celebration. As in previous years, the sorority will run a soda booth, selling drinks for $.75 a cup. When initial set-up and material costs are deducted, the sorority incurs a cost of $.35 for each (8 oz.) cup of soda. Data collected from last year's celebration indicate that total soda sales are normally distributed with mean 960 and standard deviation of 140. Determine the amount of soda (in ounces) that the women should purchase.

15-50 The chief administrator of a chain of convalescent homes wants to open a new facility in southern California. His decision to build a 50-, 75-, or 150-bed facility will be based on whether expected demand is low, medium, or high. Based on past experience, he constructs the following table of short-range profits:

EVENT	PROBABILITY	50-BED	75-BED	150-BED
Low demand	0.2	$41,000	−$12,000	−$53,000
Medium demand	0.3	52,000	68,000	−24,000
High demand	0.5	65,000	80,000	117,000

(a) What size facility should the administrator decide to build?
(b) Calculate the expected profit with perfect information.
(c) Use your answer to part (b) to calculate the expected value of perfect information.

15-51 University Gear Sweatshop is a clothing store that caters to the students of a college well-known for its fantastic football record. Janet Sawyer, the store's manager, is deciding whether to order more sweatshirts printed with the team's name and mascot. If the team loses the championship this year, the extra sweatshirts won't sell very well, but if the team wins, she expects to be able to make a high profit on the shirts. The local paper is predicting a 65 percent chance that the team will win the championship. Sawyer has constructed the following payoff table (for the additional sweatshirts):

EVENT	STOCK ADDITIONAL SHIRTS	DON'T STOCK SHIRTS
Team wins	$6,110	$0
Team loses	$1,500	$0

What course of action should Ms. Sawyer take?

15-52 A local telephone distributor, Phones and More, plans to offer a special deal this week on its remote-activated answering machine. The store needs to decide how many "standard" and how many "remote" answering machines to order from the manufacturer. Based on prior experience, the management estimates the sales of the remote machine as given in the table below.

Sales	15	16	17	18	19	20	21
Probability	.12	.17	.26	.23	.15	.05	.02

The retail price of the remote machine is $89.95, but Phones and More's cost will be $75.50. Use marginal analysis to determine the number of remote machines that the distributor should order.

15-10
Chapter Concepts Test

Answers are in the back of the book.

T F   1. Decision theory assumes that no events are beyond the control of the decision maker.
T F   2. A conditional profit table does not reflect the profit denied a retailer because of inability to fill all buyers' requests.
T F   3. An obsolescence loss occurs when a retailer is out of stock and buyers want to buy.
T F   4. In most stocking actions, several values of p will solve the equation $p(MP) = (1 - p)(ML)$, but only one is the best solution.
T F   5. If stocking nineteen units of a good yields an expected daily profit of $51.50, a retailer stocking nineteen units can expect average profits of $51.50 per day.
T F   6. A person can have one utility curve for one situation and quite a different one for the next situation.
T F   7. It is always difficult to make use of other people's knowledge about a situation without explaining statistical techniques to them.
T F   8. With perfect information, a retailer would consistently make the maximum profit possible.
T F   9. One advantage of using decision trees is that every outcome, desirable or undesirable, must be investigated.
T F 10. On a decision tree, a circle represents a decision point.
T F 11. If a retailer can earn $100 per day with perfect information, then EVPI = $100.
T F 12. The loss that results from stocking an item that is not sold is denoted *ML*.
T F 13. When rolling back a decision tree, the process moves from right to left.

T F 14. Business executives with a linear utility curve can effectively use expected monetary value as their decision criterion.

T F 15. On the graph of a normal distribution of sales, the area to the right of a vertical line represents the probability of selling that quantity or less.

T F 16. A decision that maximizes expected profits will also minimize expected losses.

T F 17. An individual's utility curve is based on mathematical, not behavioral considerations.

T F 18. The expected marginal loss is equal to the marginal loss multiplied by 1 minus the probability of selling that unit.

T F 19. Payoffs refer only to the positive benefits of various alternatives.

T F 20. Perfect information, in reality, is rarely available; information to help make better, not perfect, decisions is more often the case.

T F 21. The expected value of a random variable weights each possible value of the variable by 1 minus the probability of taking on that value.

22. From which of the following can retailers immediately determine how many cases they should stock each day to maximize profits?
   (a) Expected profit from each stocking action   (d) a, b, and c
   (b) Expected loss from each stocking action   (e) a and b but not c
   (c) Conditional profit table

23. Consider a conditional loss table with possible sales levels listed vertically in the first column and possible stock actions listed horizontally in the first row. Any value in a column below a zero indicates:
   (a) An opportunity loss   (c) A profit
   (b) An obsolescence loss   (d) None of these

24. Suppose that the only two possible stocking actions for a particular product are ten and fifteen bottles. Expected profits are $3.35 for ten bottles and $3.50 for fifteen bottles. If expected loss for ten bottles is $1.10 and fifteen bottles are stocked, we may conclude that expected loss is:
   (a) Higher than $1.10   (c) Higher than $2.25
   (b) Lower than $1.10   (d) Undeterminable from information given

25. A businessman who is said to be averse to risk:
   (a) Prefers to take large risks to earn large gains
   (b) Prefers to act anytime expected monetary value is positive
   (c) Avoids all situations but those with very high expected values
   (d) None of these

26. Suppose that the actual standard deviation of a normal distribution is unknown but that you are told, "The odds are 5 to 3 that a random observation is between 500 and 900." You know that the mean is 700. The area under the normal curve between the values 700 and 900 is:
   (a) $8/16$ (b) $3/8$ (c) $5/8$ (d) $5/16$

27. A certain product sells for $25 and is purchased by the retailer for $17. If it is not sold within 2 weeks, the retailer will recoup only $8 of his original $17 investment because of spoilage. The value of MP for this situation is:
   (a) $9   (b) $17   (c) $8   (d) $25

28. Assume that for a particular stocking operation, $ML = \$10$ and $MP = \$30$. Then, $p = .25$. For which of the following situations would you stock the unit in question?
   (a) The fifth unit when P(requests for 5 or more units) $= .50$
   (b) The third unit when P(requests for fewer than 3 units) $= .10$ and P(requests for exactly 3 units) $= .09$
   (c) The ninth unit when P(requests for more than 9 units) $= .16$ and P(requests for exactly 9 units) $= .05$
   (d) All of these
   (e) a and b but not c

29. A manager is deciding whether to buy a new building or to rent it. If he buys, the cost for the next year will be $5,500, which will include mortgage payments, insurance, and other usual expenses. If he rents, the comparable expense for the next year will be either $6,000, $5,300, or $4,200, depending upon market fluctuations. The manager wishes to make his choice based upon expected monetary values for the next year. The decision tree for this situation would have:
    (a) 1 decision point and no chance events   (c) 2 decision points and 3 chance events
    (b) 1 chance event and 1 decision point   (d) 1 decision point and 3 chance events

30. For a particular decision, the total benefit of a new plant is $18,200,000. If the expected net benefit of this plant is $11,500,000, what is the cost of the plant?
    (a) $6,700,000   (d) $11,500,000
    (b) $8,400,000   (e) Cannot be determined from information given
    (c) $29,700,000

31. Assume that three businesswomen are questioned regarding their utilities in risk situations. It is found that Laura is averse to risk, Lisa plays long shots, and Leslie is so well-off financially that the amounts of money in question are negligible when compared to her wealth. For the situations in question, utility could be used as the decision criterion for:
    (a) Laura   (c) Leslie   (e) a and b but not c
    (b) Lisa   (d) All three

32. A person who is attempting to maximize his expected utility would use the expected value criterion if:
    (a) He is risk-averse   (c) He has a nonlinear utility curve
    (b) He is a risk seeker   (d) None of these

33. When a problem has a large number of possible actions, we would normally use a:
    (a) Conditional table   (c) Utility table   (e) None of these
    (b) Marginal table   (d) Marginal analysis

34. Decision theory deals with
    (a) Making decisions under conditions of uncertainty.
    (b) Quantity-oriented decision, ignoring financial repercussions.
    (c) The worth of additional information to the decision maker.
    (d) a and b but not c.
    (e) a and c but not b.

35. Once a decision tree is "solved," the analyst should
    (a) Immediately go out and make the decision.
    (b) Specify underlying assumptions to point out, among other things, the limits under which the decision tree is valid.
    (c) Perform sensitivity analysis to determine how the solution reacts to changes in the inputs.
    (d) b and c but not a.
    (e) All of the above.

36. An item costs the retailer $3.25 and can be sold for a price of $5.75. If unsold, the item can be sold for a salvage value of $1.50. Which of the following statements are true?
    (a) $ML = \$4.25$
    (b) $p^* = \dfrac{(\$3.25 - \$1.50)}{(\$5.75 - \$1.50)}$
    (c) In order to justify the stocking of an additional item, the cumulative probability of selling that unit or more must be 50%.
    (d) None of the above.

37. Events beyond the control of the decision maker are called _____ or _____ of nature.

38. The maximum amount that a retailer will be willing to pay for a perfect predictor is called the _____ .

39. There are two types of losses in a stocking operation: _____ losses and _____ losses.

40. The pleasure or displeasure one receives from certain outcomes is one's _____.

41. The act of calculating expected benefits for each circle and square of a decision tree is called _____.

42. If a profit increases a person's utility by much more than a loss of the same size would decrease it, that person will often act when the expected value is _____.

43. The loss incurred from stocking an item that is not sold is called _____.

44. Observing how optimal decisions and profits change when payoffs or probabilities vary is called _____.

45. Time sequencing in a decision tree occurs from _____ to _____; rollback is accomplished from _____ to _____.

15-11
Conceptual Case   (Northern White Metals Company)

Dick was hopeful as he completed the presentation of his 5-year plan at the December 1983 division presidents' meeting. He had made three principal recommendations, all of which he felt were vital to the long-term success of NWMC.

First, he recommended the purchase of some small-scale scrap-smelting equipment, so that scrap aluminum and waste by-products could be recycled into reusable raw materials. Even if open-market raw-materials prices declined more than 75 percent (a very unlikely event), the smelter would still provide lower costs and thereby improve Northern's profitability. Segue management had given its unanimous approval for this subject.

Dick's second recommendation was to expand Northern's customer base outside the northeastern United States. The company had nearly doubled sales in 2 years, he had asserted proudly, but growth was now slowing because of market saturation. Corporate management could see the advisability of this recommendation, and Dick appeared to have a well-conceived sales extension plan. His final recommendation, though, left the CEO strangely reticent.

Dick pointed out that, even without a sales extension program, Northern's plant would reach its capacity limit within 18 months. He therefore recommended that an additional plant be built, or an aluminum manufacturing company acquired, to serve new markets.

"That's not a whole lot of lead time, Dick," the CEO said with concern," and it seems as though there is little point in expanding your market if we don't add more manufacturing facilities, wouldn't you agree?"

"Unfortunately, sir, I can't do one without the other," Dick replied with confidence.

"Well, I'll think about it and let you know my decision next week," the CEO said as he got up to leave.

Dick decided not to stay in New York that evening and caught an afternoon flight back to Boston. On his way home, he stopped off at his office to finish some paperwork. He found, though, that the disappointment of an unenthusiastic response to his expansion plans made it difficult to concentrate. As he got up to leave, the telephone rang.

"I thought you'd be there," the CEO barked. "Listen, Lennox, I'm not entirely in favor of your southern expansion scheme, but everyone else seems to think your plan is rock solid. At any rate, they recommend giving you carte blanche on expanding your operations, and I've decided to go along with it. You find a good deal and we'll do it!" he exclaimed. "Keep me advised along the way, that's all," he added, and hung up. Dick was ecstatic. Not only had his recommendations been approved, he had been given full authority to implement them as well.

The next morning Dick and Norma, the chief financial officer, discussed the available options. Northern's expansion could be brought about by building a new plant or by acquisition. After a quick analysis they determined that, given current construction prices and the small amount of time he had, building a new factory should not be considered a viable option. That afternoon, Dick was on the phone to Segue's investment bankers, the prestigious Wall Street firm of Specker, Stathis, Mallinson & Co. He explained the situation, and a meeting was arranged to discuss plans to acquire an aluminum manufacturing company located in the southern part of the country.

Within two months, the firm had identified three possible acquisition candidates. Each was a different-size operation, offering different levels of production capacity, and all were favorably located.

Dick decided that selection should be based on cost,

of course, but more important on the sales volume that could be expected within 5 years in the new geographic region. If the large plant were purchased, Dick thought, and sales were flat, as in a recession, the company would face tremendous extra costs from the excess capacity. On the other hand, if the small plant were purchased and demand grew rapidly, Northern would lose valuable sales to competitors.

Dick knew that many intermediate situations could occur, and laughed when he realized he had initially imagined two negative scenarios. In any event, the difficulty of this acquisition-based expansion decision was clear, and he thought he knew where he might turn for help.

"Jody," Dick began as she answered the phone, "NWMC is about to begin its pincer-like movement southward, and once again, we require your expert assistance." He proceeded to relate his dilemma. Before long, Jody interrupted him.

"Dick, this is a pretty big problem, and we'll need to talk about a few things in more detail," she explained. "Sarah and I will be on the 8:00 shuttle to Boston on Friday. Have someone meet us at the airport," she requested, "and, by the way, make sure the car has a ski rack on it, ok?"

Before Sarah and Jody enjoy a well-deserved ski weekend in New England, they will endeavor to aid Dick in his rather complex decision problem. What steps will Sarah and Jody take to establish a usable framework for the problem? What information will they require of Dick? How can they assist Dick in providing the most useful information possible? What analysis should Jody and Sarah perform? What qualifications and cautions should they offer Dick in utilizing the results of their analysis?

15-12
From the Textbook to the Real World

(1) Flanking in a Price War

In March of 1983, a small Canadian grocery chain used the results from a study on pricing strategies to compete successfully during a price war. The study indicated that the price sensitivity of stock-up grocery goods is different from that of nonstock-up goods. A Bayesian decision framework was used to determine the optimal price treatment strategy, as well as the dollar risk associated with this strategy. It also provided an optimal stopping rule for the experiment. Rather than responding to the competition with across-the-board price cuts, the chain implemented a precise, profit-preserving strategy. As a result, the chain substantially increased market share during the price war, at the cost of only 1.2 percent of its gross margin. Its competition suffered margin decreases of about 5 percent.

The Quebec Grocery Market. Until 1980, Quebec's grocery retailing industry was dominated by Steinberg, Inc. Steinberg's use of a cost-squeezing, price-cutting strategy kept competition to a minimum and made it Canada's twenty-fourth largest firm (in terms of sales). The retail grocery industry began to consolidate to better compete with Steinberg. By 1982, the industry was an oligopoly dominated by Provigo, Metro-Richelieu, Steinberg, and Hudon and Deaudelin (IGA), with market shares of 31, 25, 20, and 8.5 percent, respectively. Ironically, Steinberg, which caused the consolidation, became the most vulnerable to it. It had higher labor costs and was subject to regulations limiting its operating hours and restricting the sale of beer and wine.

The Pricing Experiment. As the fourth largest firm in the oligopoly, Hudon and Deaudelin would have to respond to competitive moves by the other major players, yet the management knew that across-the-board price cuts would cause heavy losses. To prepare the firm for an impending price war, Hudon and Deaudelin's president hired consultants to perform a pricing experiment. The study indicated that very little difference in sales level occurred when the price of fresh fruit was changed, while a greater change occurred when the price of canned vegetables was altered. The experiment investigated this difference in price sensitivity in stock-up goods and nonstock-up goods. Stock-up items are those items that can be purchased in large quantities, are used frequently, and are nonperishable. Conversely, nonstock-up items may be perishable, are sold only in large containers, or are used infrequently. The study used a Bayesian decision framework because:

(1) The price strategy yielding the highest profitability could be selected, and the dollar risk associated with this strategy could be estimated. This would indicate the optimal strategy to use during a price war.

(2) This design indicates when to stop the experiment, which is very important due to the expense involved in price experimentation.

The model represents sales of each product as a function of product type (stock-up or nonstock-up) and price level (regular price and 20 percent above or below regular price). Six possible price treatments could be evaluated: raising prices of stock-up or nonstock-up goods, lowering prices of stock-up or nonstock-up goods, or maintaining regular prices on either type of good. Measuring changes in sales was important, but the perceived utility associated with each treatment was also needed. After each week, a value of expected loss of immediate decision was obtained. Continuing the experiment was justified only if new information reduced this expected loss of immediate decision by an amount greater than the cost of the new information.

Results: After 2 weeks it became apparent that consumers were highly sensitive to price changes in the stock-up items, but could not take advantage of fluctuations in the price of nonstock-up goods by stockpiling (see Table RW15-1). The results suggest that across-the-board cuts may hurt revenues unnecessarily. If price cuts become necessary, Hudon and Deaudelin (IGA) should cut prices only on stock-up items, while the prices on nonstock-up items could be raised or kept constant. In early March 1983, Steinberg announced its new promotion, "5% back on your bill." Within hours, Metro-Richelieu and Provigo followed suit. IGA carried out price reductions on hundreds of stock-up items, but it did not lower prices across-the-board. As a result, it experienced the smallest decline in overall margin. The price war lasted only 14 weeks and caused both Steinberg and Metro-Richelieu to lose gross margin and market share. By planning ahead and using statistical methods, IGA not only saved millions of dollars by preserving its margin, but it actually increased its market share from 8.5 to 9.5 percent.

Roger J. Calantone, Cornelia Droge, David S. Litvack, C. Anthony Di Benedetto, "Flanking in a Price War," *Interfaces,* vol. 19, no. 2 (1989), pp. 1–12.

TABLE RW15-1 Price Manipulation

PRODUCT TYPE	LOWERED 20%	UNCHANGED	RAISED 20%
Stock-up	54.95	1.75	−24.10
Nonstock-up	10.55	6.95	−7.60

Percent change in standardized unit sales after price manipulation. Sales of stock-up goods increase sharply in response to a price cut and decrease sharply in reponse to a price increase. Changes in sales of nonstock-up goods are much less dramatic.

(2) US Postal Automation

In 1984, the U.S. Postal Service decided to continue using the nine-digit zip code (ZIP + 4) for first-class business mailers and to purchase additional capital equipment as part of its continuing movement toward automation. Prior to this decision, the Office of Technology Assessment (OTA) and its contractors were asked to perform technical and economic analyses to evaluate the options available to the U.S. Congress and the Postal Service. Automation options involved capital investments of over $350 million and annual maintenance and other costs that could escalate to over $300 million a year, but they afforded potential annual savings of about $1.5 billion from reduced labor requirements. In the face of uncertainty about possible savings, the OTA used decision theory to determine the best option for the U.S. Postal Service (USPS).

Postal Automation-Costs and Benefits. Since October 1983, the USPS had encouraged business mailers to use the nine-digit ZIP code by offering a discount rate for large-volume first-class mail using ZIP + 4. Concurrently, the USPS began Phase I of its automation program. By 1984, it had purchased 252 optical character readers (OCRs) and 248 bar code sorters (BCSs) at a cost of approximately $234 million. OTA was asked to review the system before Phase II of the operation began. Reducing the number of mail clerks involved in intermediate addressing would provide the greatest area of savings because labor represents about 85 percent of total postal costs. Big gains would come from automation in conjunction with ZIP + 4, which allows sorting to a more advanced level than five-digit ZIP codes. OCRs read the ZIP + 4 code, translate it into a bar code, and print the bar code on the envelope. BCSs then sort the letter automatically to the level of carrier routes, eliminating all intermediate sorting. The USPS allocated $450 million for Phase II. It had just received bids on 403 more OCRs and was planning to solicit bids on an additional 452 BCSs.

Decision Setting. Before proceeding with the automation plan, the OTA was asked to investigate the advisability of the strategy on both technical and economic grounds. Its study judged the strategy to be technically feasible, but several implementation options warranted further analysis to determine economic viability. The USPS originally purchased single-line OCRs which read the last line of an address. Multi-line OCRs were also available with capability to read up to four lines of an address. Multi-line OCRs had equivalent performance reading ZIP + 4 codes but were better than single-line OCRs at reading five-digit ZIP codes. Several vendors were identified for procuring these OCRs. The outlook was further complicated because large savings were contingent on reduced sorting, which, at least with single-line OCRs, required high-volume first-class mailers to use ZIP + 4. To address this complex and uncertain situation, Decision Science Consortium, Inc., was contracted in February 1984 to perform a decision analysis of postal automation alternatives. The basic model involved six steps: (1) identify decision options, (2) develop a probabilistic cash-flow model for each option, (3) analyze results, (4) discuss the model at a public workshop, (5) refine the model based on information exchanged at the workshop, and (6) present the analyses and evaluations to Congress.

The Decision Analysis Model—Structure, Options, and Valuation. Six options were identified: (A) Single-Line OCR, (B) Multi-Line with ZIP + 4, (C) Multi-line without ZIP + 4,

Jacob W. Ulivila, "Postal Automation," *Interfaces,* vol. 17, no. 2 (March-April 1987), pp. 1–12.

(D) Convert to multi-lines later, (E) Hedge (convert only if ZIP + 4 use were low), (F) Cancel Phase II and ZIP + 4. Each option was evaluated on the basis of internal rate of return and net present value of cash flows. A discount rate of 15 percent was used, and the time horizon was 1985 through 1998. Annual net cash flow was calculated as savings minus investment, maintenance, and rate reduction. Three major uncertainties affecting the savings from postal automation were modeled: ZIP + 4 usage, savings percentage, and usage savings. Historically, the USPS tended to overestimate both mailers' usage of new programs and the savings potential of new equipment. Under conditions of high ZIP + 4 usage and high savings, option D (convert) had an internal rate of return of 111 percent and a Net Present Value (NPV) of $2.7 billion, making it a very attractive alternative. From the trees, the expected incremental NPVs were calculated as follows:

Option A: $1.3 billion   Option B: $1.2 billion
Option C: $0.9 billion   Option D: $1.5 billion
Option E: $1.4 billion

Thus on an expected value basis, option D (convert) was preferred, and any Phase II was better than canceling.

Conclusions. The decision tree analysis was used as a basis for OTA's report to Congress in June 1984. It provided detailed, quantitative assessments of the economic implications of the strategy options that reflected uncertainties. It also helped OTA to think creatively about the problem and to generate options. Furthermore, it facilitated the use of multiple or plural analyses to arrive at an overall evaluation.

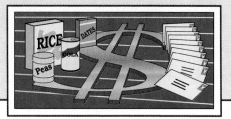

Appendix Tables

APPENDIX TABLE 1 Areas Under the Standard Normal Probability Distribution Between the Mean and Positive Values of z*

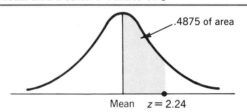

.4875 of area

Mean   z = 2.24

EXAMPLE: To find the area under the curve between the mean and a point 2.24 standard deviations to the right of the mean, look up the value opposite 2.2 and under .04 in the table; .4875 of the area under the curve lies between the mean and a z value of 2.24.

z	.00	.01	.02	.03	.04	.05	.06	.07	.08	.09
0.0	.0000	.0040	.0080	.0120	.0160	.0199	.0239	.0279	.0319	.0359
0.1	.0398	.0438	.0478	.0517	.0557	.0596	.0636	.0675	.0714	.0753
0.2	.0793	.0832	.0871	.0910	.0948	.0987	.1026	.1064	.1103	.1141
0.3	.1179	.1217	.1255	.1293	.1331	.1368	.1406	.1443	.1480	.1517
0.4	.1554	.1591	.1628	.1664	.1700	.1736	.1772	.1808	.1844	.1879
0.5	.1915	.1950	.1985	.2019	.2054	.2088	.2123	.2157	.2190	.2224
0.6	.2257	.2291	.2324	.2357	.2389	.2422	.2454	.2486	.2517	.2549
0.7	.2580	.2611	.2642	.2673	.2704	.2734	.2764	.2794	.2823	.2852
0.8	.2881	.2910	.2939	.2967	.2995	.3023	.3051	.3078	.3106	.3133
0.9	.3159	.3186	.3212	.3238	.3264	.3289	.3315	.3340	.3365	.3389
1.0	.3413	.3438	.3461	.3485	.3508	.3531	.3554	.3577	.3599	.3621
1.1	.3643	.3665	.3686	.3708	.3729	.3749	.3770	.3790	.3810	.3830
1.2	.3849	.3869	.3888	.3907	.3925	.3944	.3962	.3980	.3997	.4015
1.3	.4032	.4049	.4066	.4082	.4099	.4115	.4131	.4147	.4162	.4177
1.4	.4192	.4207	.4222	.4236	.4251	.4265	.4279	.4292	.4306	.4319
1.5	.4332	.4345	.4357	.4370	.4382	.4394	.4406	.4418	.4429	.4441
1.6	.4452	.4463	.4474	.4484	.4495	.4505	.4515	.4525	.4535	.4545
1.7	.4554	.4564	.4573	.4582	.4591	.4599	.4608	.4616	.4625	.4633
1.8	.4641	.4649	.4656	.4664	.4671	.4678	.4686	.4693	.4699	.4706
1.9	.4713	.4719	.4726	.4732	.4738	.4744	.4750	.4756	.4761	.4767
2.0	.4772	.4778	.4783	.4788	.4793	.4798	.4803	.4808	.4812	.4817
2.1	.4821	.4826	.4830	.4834	.4838	.4842	.4846	.4850	.4854	.4857
2.2	.4861	.4864	.4868	.4871	.4875	.4878	.4881	.4884	.4887	.4890
2.3	.4893	.4896	.4898	.4901	.4904	.4906	.4909	.4911	.4913	.4916
2.4	.4918	.4920	.4922	.4925	.4927	.4929	.4931	.4932	.4934	.4936
2.5	.4938	.4940	.4941	.4943	.4945	.4946	.4948	.4949	.4951	.4952
2.6	.4953	.4955	.4956	.4957	.4959	.4960	.4961	.4962	.4963	.4964
2.7	.4965	.4966	.4967	.4968	.4969	.4970	.4971	.4972	.4973	.4974
2.8	.4974	.4975	.4976	.4977	.4977	.4978	.4979	.4979	.4980	.4981
2.9	.4981	.4982	.4982	.4983	.4984	.4984	.4985	.4985	.4986	.4986
3.0	.4987	.4987	.4987	.4988	.4988	.4989	.4989	.4989	.4990	.4990

* From Robert D. Mason, *Essentials of Statistics,* © 1976, p. 307. Reprinted by permission of Prentice-Hall, Inc., Englewood Cliffs, N.J.

APPENDIX TABLE 2 Areas in Both Tails Combined for Student's *t* Distribution.*

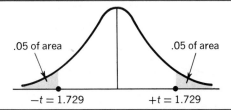

.05 of area   .05 of area

$-t = 1.729$ $+t = 1.729$

EXAMPLE: To find the value of *t* which corresponds to an area of .10 in both tails of the distribution combined, when there are 19 degrees of freedom, look under the .10 column, and proceed down to the 19 degrees of freedom row; the appropriate *t* value there is 1.729.

Degrees of freedom	Area in both tails combined			
	.10	.05	.02	.01
1	6.314	12.706	31.821	63.657
2	2.920	4.303	6.965	9.925
3	2.353	3.182	4.541	5.841
4	2.132	2.776	3.747	4.604
5	2.015	2.571	3.365	4.032
6	1.943	2.447	3.143	3.707
7	1.895	2.365	2.998	3.499
8	1.860	2.306	2.896	3.355
9	1.833	2.262	2.821	3.250
10	1.812	2.228	2.764	3.169
11	1.796	2.201	2.718	3.106
12	1.782	2.179	2.681	3.055
13	1.771	2.160	2.650	3.012
14	1.761	2.145	2.624	2.977
15	1.753	2.131	2.602	2.947
16	1.746	2.120	2.583	2.921
17	1.740	2.110	2.567	2.898
18	1.734	2.101	2.552	2.878
19	1.729	2.093	2.539	2.861
20	1.725	2.086	2.528	2.845
21	1.721	2.080	2.518	2.831
22	1.717	2.074	2.508	2.819
23	1.714	2.069	2.500	2.807
24	1.711	2.064	2.492	2.797
25	1.708	2.060	2.485	2.787
26	1.706	2.056	2.479	2.779
27	1.703	2.052	2.473	2.771
28	1.701	2.048	2.467	2.763
29	1.699	2.045	2.462	2.756
30	1.697	2.042	2.457	2.750
40	1.684	2.021	2.423	2.704
60	1.671	2.000	2.390	2.660
120	1.658	1.980	2.358	2.617
Normal Distribution	1.645	1.960	2.326	2.576

* Taken from Table III of Fisher and Yates, *Statistical Tables for Biological, Agricultural and Medical Research,* published by Longman Group Ltd., London (previously published by Oliver & Boyd, Edinburgh) and by permission of the authors and publishers.

EXAMPLE: These tables describe the cumulative binomial distribution; a sample problem will illustrate how they are used. Suppose that we are grading bar examinations and wish to find the probability of finding 7 or more failures in a batch of 15, when the probability that any one exam is a failure is .20.

In binomial notation, the elements in this example can be represented:

n = 15 (number of exams to be graded)
p = .20 (probability that any one exam will be a failure)
r = 7 (number of failures in question)

Steps for solution:

1. Since the problem involves 15 trials or inspections, first find the table for n = 15.
2. The probability of a failing examination is .20; therefore, we look through the n = 15 table until we find the column where p = 20.
3. We then move down the p = 20 column until we are opposite the r = 7 row.
4. The answer there is found to be 0181; this is interpreted to be a probability of .0181.

This problem asked for the probability of *7 or more* failures. Had it asked for the probability of *more than 7* failures, we would have looked up the probability of *8 or more*.

Note that this table only goes up to p = .50. When p is *larger* than .50, q $(1 - p)$ is *less* than .50. Therefore the problem is worked in terms of q and the number of passing exams $(n - r)$ rather than in terms of p and r (the number of failures). For example, suppose p = .60 and n = 15. What is the probability of more than 12 failures? More than 12 failures (13, 14, or 15 failures) is the same as 2 or fewer successes. The probability of 2 or fewer successes is 1 − the probability of 3 or more successes. We look in the n = 15 table for the p = 40 column and the r = 3 row. There we see the number 9729, which we interpret as a probability of .9729; so the answer is 1 − .9729, or .0271.

					$n = 1$					
P	01	02	03	04	05	06	07	08	09	10
R										
1	0100	0200	0300	0400	0500	0600	0700	0800	0900	1000
P	11	12	13	14	15	16	17	18	19	20
R										
1	1100	1200	1300	1400	1500	1600	1700	1800	1900	2000
P	21	22	23	24	25	26	27	28	29	30
R										
1	2100	2200	2300	2400	2500	2600	2700	2800	2900	3000
P	31	32	33	34	35	36	37	38	39	40
R										
1	3100	3200	3300	3400	3500	3600	3700	3800	3900	4000
P	41	42	43	44	45	46	47	48	49	50
R										
1	4100	4200	4300	4400	4500	4600	4700	4800	4900	5000

* Reproduced from Robert Schlaifer, *Introduction to Statistics for Business Decisions*, published by McGraw-Hill Book Company, 1961, by specific permission from the copyright holder, the President and Fellows of Harvard College.

P	01	02	03	04	05	06	07	08	09	10
R										
1	0199	0396	0591	0784	0975	1164	1351	1536	1719	1900
2	0001	0004	0009	0016	0025	0036	0049	0064	0081	0100
P	11	12	13	14	15	16	17	18	19	20
R										
1	2079	2256	2431	2604	2775	2944	3111	3276	3439	3600
2	0121	0144	0169	0196	0225	0256	0289	0324	0361	0400
P	21	22	23	24	25	26	27	28	29	30
R										
1	3759	3916	4071	4224	4375	4524	4671	4816	4959	5100
2	0441	0484	0529	0576	0625	0676	0729	0784	0841	0900
P	31	32	33	34	35	36	37	38	39	40
R										
1	5239	5376	5511	5644	5775	5904	6031	6156	6279	6400
2	0961	1024	1089	1156	1225	1296	1369	1444	1521	1600
P	41	42	43	44	45	46	47	48	49	50
R										
1	6519	6636	6751	6864	6975	7084	7191	7296	7399	7500
2	1681	1764	1849	1936	2025	2116	2209	2304	2401	2500

P	01	02	03	04	05	06	07	08	09	10
R										
1	0297	0588	0873	1153	1426	1694	1956	2213	2464	2710
2	0003	0012	0026	0047	0073	0104	0140	0182	0228	0280
3				0001	0001	0002	0003	0005	0007	0010
P	11	12	13	14	15	16	17	18	19	20
R										
1	2950	3185	3415	3639	3859	4073	4282	4486	4686	4880
2	0336	0397	0463	0533	0608	0686	0769	0855	0946	1040
3	0013	0017	0022	0027	0034	0041	0049	0058	0069	0080
P	21	22	23	24	25	26	27	28	29	30
R										
1	5070	5254	5435	5610	5781	5948	6110	6268	6421	6570
2	1138	1239	1344	1452	1563	1676	1793	1913	2035	2160
3	0093	0106	0122	0138	0156	0176	0197	0220	0244	0270
P	31	32	33	34	35	36	37	38	39	40
R										
1	6715	6856	6992	7125	7254	7379	7500	7617	7730	7840
2	2287	2417	2548	2682	2818	2955	3094	3235	3377	3520
3	0298	0328	0359	0393	0429	0467	0507	0549	0593	0640
P	41	42	43	44	45	46	47	48	49	50
R										
1	7946	8049	8148	8244	8336	8425	8511	8594	8673	8750
2	3665	3810	3957	4104	4253	4401	4551	4700	4850	5000
3	0689	0741	0795	0852	0911	0973	1038	1106	1176	1250

P	01	02	03	04	05	06	07	08	09	10
R										
1	0394	0776	1147	1507	1855	2193	2519	2836	3143	3439
2	0006	0023	0052	0091	0140	0199	0267	0344	0430	0523
3			0001	0002	0005	0008	0013	0019	0027	0037
4									0001	0001
P	11	12	13	14	15	16	17	18	19	20
R										
1	3726	4003	4271	4530	4780	5021	5254	5479	5695	5904
2	0624	0732	0847	0968	1095	1228	1366	1509	1656	1808
3	0049	0063	0079	0098	0120	0144	0171	0202	0235	0272
4	0001	0002	0003	0004	0005	0007	0008	0010	0013	0016

P	21	22	23	24	25	26	27	28	29	30
R										
1	6105	6298	6485	6664	6836	7001	7160	7313	7459	7599
2	1963	2122	2285	2450	2617	2787	2959	3132	3307	3483
3	0312	0356	0403	0453	0508	0566	0628	0694	0763	0837
4	0019	0023	0028	0033	0039	0046	0053	0061	0071	0081

P	31	32	33	34	35	36	37	38	39	40
R										
1	7733	7862	7985	8103	8215	8322	8425	8522	8615	8704
2	3660	3837	4015	4193	4370	4547	4724	4900	5075	5248
3	0915	0996	1082	1171	1265	1362	1464	1569	1679	1792
4	0092	0105	0119	0134	0150	0168	0187	0209	0231	0256

P	41	42	43	44	45	46	47	48	49	50
R										
1	8788	8868	8944	9017	9085	9150	9211	9269	9323	9375
2	5420	5590	5759	5926	6090	6252	6412	6569	6724	6875
3	1909	2030	2155	2283	2415	2550	2689	2834	2977	3125
4	0283	0311	0342	0375	0410	0448	0488	0531	0576	0625

P	01	02	03	04	05	06	07	08	09	10
R										
1	0490	0961	1413	1846	2262	2661	3043	3409	3760	4095
2	0010	0038	0085	0148	0226	0319	0425	0544	0674	0815
3		0001	0003	0006	0012	0020	0031	0045	0063	0086
4						0001	0001	0002	0003	0005

P	11	12	13	14	15	16	17	18	19	20
R										
1	4416	4723	5016	5296	5563	5818	6061	6293	6513	6723
2	0965	1125	1292	1467	1648	1835	2027	2224	2424	2627
3	0112	0143	0179	0220	0266	0318	0375	0437	0505	0579
4	0007	0009	0013	0017	0022	0029	0036	0045	0055	0067
5				0001	0001	0001	0001	0002	0002	0003

P	21	22	23	24	25	26	27	28	29	30
R										
1	6923	7113	7293	7464	7627	7781	7927	8065	8196	8319
2	2833	3041	3251	3461	3672	3883	4093	4303	4511	4718
3	0659	0744	0836	0933	1035	1143	1257	1376	1501	1631
4	0081	0097	0114	0134	0156	0181	0208	0238	0272	0308
5	0004	0005	0006	0008	0010	0012	0014	0017	0021	0024

P	31	32	33	34	35	36	37	38	39	40
R										
1	8436	8546	8650	8748	8840	8926	9008	9084	9155	9222
2	4923	5125	5325	5522	5716	5906	6093	6276	6455	6630
3	1766	1905	2050	2199	2352	2509	2670	2835	3003	3174
4	0347	0390	0436	0486	0540	0598	0660	0726	0796	0870
5	0029	0034	0039	0045	0053	0060	0069	0079	0090	0102

P	41	42	43	44	45	46	47	48	49	50
R										
1	9285	9344	9398	9449	9497	9541	9582	9620	9655	9688
2	6801	6967	7129	7286	7438	7585	7728	7865	7998	8125
3	3349	3525	3705	3886	4069	4253	4439	4625	4813	5000
4	0949	1033	1121	1214	1312	1415	1522	1635	1753	1875
5	0116	0131	0147	0165	0185	0206	0229	0255	0282	0313

P	01	02	03	04	05	06	07	08	09	10
R										
1	0585	1142	1670	2172	2649	3101	3530	3936	4321	4686
2	0015	0057	0125	0216	0328	0459	0608	0773	0952	1143
3		0002	0005	0012	0022	0038	0058	0085	0118	0159
4					0001	0002	0003	0005	0008	0013
5										0001

P	11	12	13	14	15	16	17	18	19	20
R										
1	5030	5356	5664	5954	6229	6487	6731	6960	7176	7379
2	1345	1556	1776	2003	2235	2472	2713	2956	3201	3446
3	0206	0261	0324	0395	0473	0560	0655	0759	0870	0989
4	0018	0025	0034	0045	0059	0075	0094	0116	0141	0170
5	0001	0001	0002	0003	0004	0005	0007	0010	0013	0016
6										0001

P	21	22	23	24	25	26	27	28	29	30
R										
1	7569	7748	7916	8073	8220	8358	8487	8607	8719	8824
2	3692	3937	4180	4422	4661	4896	5128	5356	5580	5798
3	1115	1250	1391	1539	1694	1856	2023	2196	2374	2557
4	0202	0239	0280	0326	0376	0431	0492	0557	0628	0705
5	0020	0025	0031	0038	0046	0056	0067	0079	0093	0109
6	0001	0001	0001	0002	0002	0003	0004	0005	0006	0007

P	31	32	33	34	35	36	37	38	39	40
R										
1	8921	9011	9095	9173	9246	9313	9375	9432	9485	9533
2	6012	6220	6422	6619	6809	6994	7172	7343	7508	7667
3	2744	2936	3130	3328	3529	3732	3937	4143	4350	4557
4	0787	0875	0969	1069	1174	1286	1404	1527	1657	1792
5	0127	0148	0170	0195	0223	0254	0288	0325	0365	0410
6	0009	0011	0013	0015	0018	0022	0026	0030	0035	0041

P	41	42	43	44	45	46	47	48	49	50
R										
1	9578	9619	9657	9692	9723	9752	9778	9802	9824	9844
2	7819	7965	8105	8238	8364	8485	8599	8707	8810	8906
3	4764	4971	5177	5382	5585	5786	5985	6180	6373	6563
4	1933	2080	2232	2390	2553	2721	2893	3070	3252	3438
5	0458	0510	0566	0627	0692	0762	0837	0917	1003	1094
6	0048	0055	0063	0073	0083	0095	0108	0122	0138	0156

P	01	02	03	04	05	06	07	08	09	10
R										
1	0679	1319	1920	2486	3017	3515	3983	4422	4832	5217
2	0020	0079	0171	0294	0444	0618	0813	1026	1255	1497
3		0003	0009	0020	0038	0063	0097	0140	0193	0257
4				0001	0002	0004	0007	0012	0018	0027
5								0001	0001	0002

P	11	12	13	14	15	16	17	18	19	20
R										
1	5577	5913	6227	6521	6794	7049	7286	7507	7712	7903
2	1750	2012	2281	2556	2834	3115	3396	3677	3956	4233
3	0331	0416	0513	0620	0738	0866	1005	1154	1313	1480
4	0039	0054	0072	0094	0121	0153	0189	0231	0279	0333
5	0003	0004	0006	0009	0012	0017	0022	0029	0037	0047
6					0001	0001	0001	0002	0003	0004

P / R	21	22	23	24	25	26	27	28	29	30
1	8080	8243	8395	8535	8665	8785	8895	8997	9090	9176
2	4506	4775	5040	5298	5551	5796	6035	6266	6490	6706
3	1657	1841	2033	2231	2436	2646	2861	3081	3304	3529
4	0394	0461	0536	0617	0706	0802	0905	1016	1134	1260
5	0058	0072	0088	0107	0129	0153	0181	0213	0248	0288
6	0005	0006	0008	0011	0013	0017	0021	0026	0031	0038
7					0001	0001	0001	0001	0002	0002

P / R	31	32	33	34	35	36	37	38	39	40
1	9255	9328	9394	9454	9510	9560	9606	9648	9686	9720
2	6914	7113	7304	7487	7662	7828	7987	8137	8279	8414
3	3757	3987	4217	4447	4677	4906	5134	5359	5581	5801
4	1394	1534	1682	1837	1998	2167	2341	2521	2707	2898
5	0332	0380	0434	0492	0556	0625	0701	0782	0869	0963
6	0046	0055	0065	0077	0090	0105	0123	0142	0164	0188
7	0003	0003	0004	0005	0006	0008	0009	0011	0014	0016

P / R	41	42	43	44	45	46	47	48	49	50
1	9751	9779	9805	9827	9848	9866	9883	9897	9910	9922
2	8541	8660	8772	8877	8976	9068	9153	9233	9307	9375
3	6017	6229	6436	6638	6836	7027	7213	7393	7567	7734
4	3094	3294	3498	3706	3917	4131	4346	4563	4781	5000
5	1063	1169	1282	1402	1529	1663	1803	1951	2105	2266
6	0216	0246	0279	0316	0357	0402	0451	0504	0562	0625
7	0019	0023	0027	0032	0037	0044	0051	0059	0068	0078

P / R	01	02	03	04	05	06	07	08	09	10
1	0773	1492	2163	2786	3366	3904	4404	4868	5297	5695
2	0027	0103	0223	0381	0572	0792	1035	1298	1577	1869
3	0001	0004	0013	0031	0058	0096	0147	0211	0289	0381
4			0001	0002	0004	0007	0013	0022	0034	0050
5							0001	0001	0003	0004

P / R	11	12	13	14	15	16	17	18	19	20
1	6063	6404	6718	7008	7275	7521	7748	7956	8147	8322
2	2171	2480	2794	3111	3428	3744	4057	4366	4670	4967
3	0487	0608	0743	0891	1052	1226	1412	1608	1815	2031
4	0071	0097	0129	0168	0214	0267	0328	0397	0476	0563
5	0007	0010	0015	0021	0029	0038	0050	0065	0083	0104
6		0001	0001	0002	0002	0003	0005	0007	0009	0012
7									0001	0001

P / R	21	22	23	24	25	26	27	28	29	30
1	8483	8630	8764	8887	8999	9101	9194	9278	9354	9424
2	5257	5538	5811	6075	6329	6573	6807	7031	7244	7447
3	2255	2486	2724	2967	3215	3465	3718	3973	4228	4482
4	0659	0765	0880	1004	1138	1281	1433	1594	1763	1941
5	0129	0158	0191	0230	0273	0322	0377	0438	0505	0580
6	0016	0021	0027	0034	0042	0052	0064	0078	0094	0113
7	0001	0002	0002	0003	0004	0005	0006	0008	0010	0013
8									0001	0001

P	31	32	33	34	35	36	37	38	39	40
R										
1	9486	9543	9594	9640	9681	9719	9752	9782	9808	9832
2	7640	7822	7994	8156	8309	8452	8586	8711	8828	8936
3	4736	4987	5236	5481	5722	5958	6189	6415	6634	6846
4	2126	2319	2519	2724	2936	3153	3374	3599	3828	4059
5	0661	0750	0846	0949	1061	1180	1307	1443	1586	1737
6	0134	0159	0187	0218	0253	0293	0336	0385	0439	0498
7	0016	0020	0024	0030	0036	0043	0051	0061	0072	0085
8	0001	0001	0001	0002	0002	0003	0004	0004	0005	0007

P	41	42	43	44	45	46	47	48	49	50
R										
1	9853	9872	9889	9903	9916	9928	9938	9947	9954	9961
2	9037	9130	9216	9295	9368	9435	9496	9552	9602	9648
3	7052	7250	7440	7624	7799	7966	8125	8276	8419	8555
4	4292	4527	4762	4996	5230	5463	5694	5922	6146	6367
5	1895	2062	2235	2416	2604	2798	2999	3205	3416	3633
6	0563	0634	0711	0794	0885	0982	1086	1198	1318	1445
7	0100	0117	0136	0157	0181	0208	0239	0272	0310	0352
8	0008	0010	0012	0014	0017	0020	0024	0028	0033	0039

P	01	02	03	04	05	06	07	08	09	10
R										
1	0865	1663	2398	3075	3698	4270	4796	5278	5721	6126
2	0034	0131	0282	0478	0712	0978	1271	1583	1912	2252
3	0001	0006	0020	0045	0084	0138	0209	0298	0405	0530
4			0001	0003	0006	0013	0023	0037	0057	0083
5						0001	0002	0003	0005	0009
6										0001

P	11	12	13	14	15	16	17	18	19	20
R										
1	6496	6835	7145	7427	7684	7918	8131	8324	8499	8658
2	2599	2951	3304	3657	4005	4348	4685	5012	5330	5638
3	0672	0833	1009	1202	1409	1629	1861	2105	2357	2618
4	0117	0158	0209	0269	0339	0420	0512	0615	0730	0856
5	0014	0021	0030	0041	0056	0075	0098	0125	0158	0196
6	0001	0002	0003	0004	0006	0009	0013	0017	0023	0031
7						0001	0001	0002	0002	0003

P	21	22	23	24	25	26	27	28	29	30
R										
1	8801	8931	9048	9154	9249	9335	9411	9480	9542	9596
2	5934	6218	6491	6750	6997	7230	7452	7660	7856	8040
3	2885	3158	3434	3713	3993	4273	4552	4829	5102	5372
4	0994	1144	1304	1475	1657	1849	2050	2260	2478	2703
5	0240	0291	0350	0416	0489	0571	0662	0762	0870	0988
6	0040	0051	0065	0081	0100	0122	0149	0179	0213	0253
7	0004	0006	0008	0010	0013	0017	0022	0028	0035	0043
8			0001	0001	0001	0001	0002	0003	0003	0004

P	31	32	33	34	35	36	37	38	39	40
R										
1	9645	9689	9728	9762	9793	9820	9844	9865	9883	9899
2	8212	8372	8522	8661	8789	8908	9017	9118	9210	9295
3	5636	5894	6146	6390	6627	6856	7076	7287	7489	7682
4	2935	3173	3415	3662	3911	4163	4416	4669	4922	5174
5	1115	1252	1398	1553	1717	1890	2072	2262	2460	2666
6	0298	0348	0404	0467	0536	0612	0696	0787	0886	0994
7	0053	0064	0078	0094	0112	0133	0157	0184	0215	0250
8	0006	0007	0009	0011	0014	0017	0021	0026	0031	0038
9				0001	0001	0001	0001	0002	0002	0003

P	41	42	43	44	45	46	47	48	49	50
R										
1	9913	9926	9936	9946	9954	9961	9967	9972	9977	9980
2	9372	9442	9505	9563	9615	9662	9704	9741	9775	9805
3	7866	8039	8204	8359	8505	8642	8769	8889	8999	9102
4	5424	5670	5913	6152	6386	6614	6836	7052	7260	7461
5	2878	3097	3322	3551	3786	4024	4265	4509	4754	5000
6	1109	1233	1366	1508	1658	1817	1985	2161	2346	2539
7	0290	0334	0383	0437	0498	0564	0637	0717	0804	0898
8	0046	0055	0065	0077	0091	0107	0125	0145	0169	0195
9	0003	0004	0005	0006	0008	0009	0011	0014	0016	0020

P	01	02	03	04	05	06	07	08	09	10
R										
1	0956	1829	2626	3352	4013	4614	5160	5656	6106	6513
2	0043	0162	0345	0582	0861	1176	1517	1879	2254	2639
3	0001	0009	0028	0062	0115	0188	0283	0401	0540	0702
4			0001	0004	0010	0020	0036	0058	0088	0128
5					0001	0002	0003	0006	0010	0016
6									0001	0001

P	11	12	13	14	15	16	17	18	19	20
R										
1	6882	7215	7516	7787	8031	8251	8448	8626	8784	8926
2	3028	3417	3804	4184	4557	4920	5270	5608	5932	6242
3	0884	1087	1308	1545	1798	2064	2341	2628	2922	3222
4	0178	0239	0313	0400	0500	0614	0741	0883	1039	1209
5	0025	0037	0053	0073	0099	0130	0168	0213	0266	0328
6	0003	0004	0006	0010	0014	0020	0027	0037	0049	0064
7			0001	0001	0001	0002	0003	0004	0006	0009
8									0001	0001

P	21	22	23	24	25	26	27	28	29	30
R										
1	9053	9166	9267	9357	9437	9508	9570	9626	9674	9718
2	6536	6815	7079	7327	7560	7778	7981	8170	8345	8507
3	3526	3831	4137	4442	4744	5042	5335	5622	5901	6172
4	1391	1587	1794	2012	2241	2479	2726	2979	3239	3504
5	0399	0479	0569	0670	0781	0904	1037	1181	1337	1503
6	0082	0104	0130	0161	0197	0239	0287	0342	0404	0473
7	0012	0016	0021	0027	0035	0045	0056	0070	0087	0106
8	0001	0002	0002	0003	0004	0006	0007	0010	0012	0016
9							0001	0001	0001	0001

P	31	32	33	34	35	36	37	38	39	40
R										
1	9755	9789	9818	9843	9865	9885	9902	9916	9929	9940
2	8656	8794	8920	9035	9140	9236	9323	9402	9473	9536
3	6434	6687	6930	7162	7384	7595	7794	7983	8160	8327
4	3772	4044	4316	4589	4862	5132	5400	5664	5923	6177
5	1679	1867	2064	2270	2485	2708	2939	3177	3420	3669
6	0551	0637	0732	0836	0949	1072	1205	1348	1500	1662
7	0129	0155	0185	0220	0260	0305	0356	0413	0477	0548
8	0020	0025	0032	0039	0048	0059	0071	0086	0103	0123
9	0002	0003	0003	0004	0005	0007	0009	0011	0014	0017
10								0001	0001	0001

P R	41	42	43	44	45	46	47	48	49	50
1	9949	9957	9964	9970	9975	9979	9983	9986	9988	9990
2	9594	9645	9691	9731	9767	9799	9827	9852	9874	9893
3	8483	8628	8764	8889	9004	9111	9209	9298	9379	9453
4	6425	6665	6898	7123	7340	7547	7745	7933	8112	8281
5	3922	4178	4436	4696	4956	5216	5474	5730	5982	6230
6	1834	2016	2207	2407	2616	2832	3057	3288	3526	3770
7	0626	0712	0806	0908	1020	1141	1271	1410	1560	1719
8	0146	0172	0202	0236	0274	0317	0366	0420	0480	0547
9	0021	0025	0031	0037	0045	0054	0065	0077	0091	0107
10	0001	0002	0002	0003	0003	0004	0005	0006	0008	0010

P R	01	02	03	04	05	06	07	08	09	10
1	1047	1993	2847	3618	4312	4937	5499	6004	6456	6862
2	0052	0195	0413	0692	1019	1382	1772	2181	2601	3026
3	0002	0012	0037	0083	0152	0248	0370	0519	0695	0896
4			0002	0007	0016	0030	0053	0085	0129	0185
5					0001	0003	0005	0010	0017	0028
6								0001	0002	0003

P R	11	12	13	14	15	16	17	18	19	20
1	7225	7549	7839	8097	8327	8531	8712	8873	9015	9141
2	3452	3873	4286	4689	5078	5453	5811	6151	6474	6779
3	1120	1366	1632	1915	2212	2521	2839	3164	3494	3826
4	0256	0341	0442	0560	0694	0846	1013	1197	1397	1611
5	0042	0061	0087	0119	0159	0207	0266	0334	0413	0504
6	0005	0008	0012	0018	0027	0037	0051	0068	0090	0117
7		0001	0001	0002	0003	0005	0007	0010	0014	0020
8							0001	0001	0002	0002

P R	21	22	23	24	25	26	27	28	29	30
1	9252	9350	9436	9511	9578	9636	9686	9730	9769	9802
2	7065	7333	7582	7814	8029	8227	8410	8577	8730	8870
3	4158	4488	4814	5134	5448	5753	6049	6335	6610	6873
4	1840	2081	2333	2596	2867	3146	3430	3719	4011	4304
5	0607	0723	0851	0992	1146	1313	1493	1685	1888	2103
6	0148	0186	0231	0283	0343	0412	0490	0577	0674	0782
7	0027	0035	0046	0059	0076	0095	0119	0146	0179	0216
8	0003	0005	0007	0009	0012	0016	0021	0027	0034	0043
9			0001	0001	0001	0002	0002	0003	0004	0006

P R	31	32	33	34	35	36	37	38	39	40
1	9831	9856	9878	9896	9912	9926	9938	9948	9956	9964
2	8997	9112	9216	9310	9394	9470	9537	9597	9650	9698
3	7123	7361	7587	7799	7999	8186	8360	8522	8672	8811
4	4598	4890	5179	5464	5744	6019	6286	6545	6796	7037
5	2328	2563	2807	3059	3317	3581	3850	4122	4397	4672
6	0901	1031	1171	1324	1487	1661	1847	2043	2249	2465
7	0260	0309	0366	0430	0501	0581	0670	0768	0876	0994
8	0054	0067	0082	0101	0122	0148	0177	0210	0249	0293
9	0008	0010	0013	0016	0020	0026	0032	0039	0048	0059
10	0001	0001	0001	0002	0002	0003	0004	0005	0006	0007

P R	41	42	43	44	45	46	47	48	49	50
1	9970	9975	9979	9983	9986	9989	9991	9992	9994	9995
2	9739	9776	9808	9836	9861	9882	9900	9916	9930	9941
3	8938	9055	9162	9260	9348	9428	9499	9564	9622	9673
4	7269	7490	7700	7900	8089	8266	8433	8588	8733	8867
5	4948	5223	5495	5764	6029	6288	6541	6787	7026	7256
6	2690	2924	3166	3414	3669	3929	4193	4460	4729	5000
7	1121	1260	1408	1568	1738	1919	2110	2312	2523	2744
8	0343	0399	0461	0532	0610	0696	0791	0895	1009	1133
9	0072	0087	0104	0125	0148	0175	0206	0241	0282	0327
10	0009	0012	0014	0018	0022	0027	0033	0040	0049	0059
11	0001	0001	0001	0001	0002	0002	0002	0003	0004	0005

P R	01	02	03	04	05	06	07	08	09	10
1	1136	2153	3062	3873	4596	5241	5814	6323	6775	7176
2	0062	0231	0486	0809	1184	1595	2033	2487	2948	3410
3	0002	0015	0048	0107	0196	0316	0468	0652	0866	1109
4		0001	0003	0010	0022	0043	0075	0120	0180	0256
5				0001	0002	0004	0009	0016	0027	0043
6							0001	0002	0003	0005
7										0001

P R	11	12	13	14	15	16	17	18	19	20
1	7530	7843	8120	8363	8578	8766	8931	9076	9202	9313
2	3867	4314	4748	5166	5565	5945	6304	6641	6957	7251
3	1377	1667	1977	2303	2642	2990	3344	3702	4060	4417
4	0351	0464	0597	0750	0922	1114	1324	1552	1795	2054
5	0065	0095	0133	0181	0239	0310	0393	0489	0600	0726
6	0009	0014	0022	0033	0046	0065	0088	0116	0151	0194
7	0001	0002	0003	0004	0007	0010	0015	0021	0029	0039
8					0001	0001	0002	0003	0004	0006
9										0001

P R	21	22	23	24	25	26	27	28	29	30
1	9409	9493	9566	9629	9683	9730	9771	9806	9836	9862
2	7524	7776	8009	8222	8416	8594	8755	8900	9032	9150
3	4768	5114	5450	5778	6093	6397	6687	6963	7225	7472
4	2326	2610	2904	3205	3512	3824	4137	4452	4765	5075
5	0866	1021	1192	1377	1576	1790	2016	2254	2504	2763
6	0245	0304	0374	0453	0544	0646	0760	0887	1026	1178
7	0052	0068	0089	0113	0143	0178	0219	0267	0322	0386
8	0008	0011	0016	0021	0028	0036	0047	0060	0076	0095
9	0001	0001	0002	0003	0004	0005	0007	0010	0013	0017
10						0001	0001	0001	0002	0002

P R	31	32	33	34	35	36	37	38	39	40
1	9884	9902	9918	9932	9943	9953	9961	9968	9973	9978
2	9256	9350	9435	9509	9576	9634	9685	9730	9770	9804
3	7704	7922	8124	8313	8487	8648	8795	8931	9054	9166
4	5381	5681	5973	6258	6533	6799	7053	7296	7528	7747
5	3032	3308	3590	3876	4167	4459	4751	5043	5332	5618
6	1343	1521	1711	1913	2127	2352	2588	2833	3087	3348
7	0458	0540	0632	0734	0846	0970	1106	1253	1411	1582
8	0118	0144	0176	0213	0255	0304	0359	0422	0493	0573
9	0022	0028	0036	0045	0056	0070	0086	0104	0127	0153
10	0003	0004	0005	0007	0008	0011	0014	0018	0022	0028
11				0001	0001	0001	0001	0002	0002	0003

P / R	41	42	43	44	45	46	47	48	49	50
1	9982	9986	9988	9990	9992	9994	9995	9996	9997	9998
2	9834	9860	9882	9901	9917	9931	9943	9953	9961	9968
3	9267	9358	9440	9513	9579	9637	9688	9733	9773	9807
4	7953	8147	8329	8498	8655	8801	8934	9057	9168	9270
5	5899	6175	6443	6704	6956	7198	7430	7652	7862	8062
6	3616	3889	4167	4448	4731	5014	5297	5577	5855	6128
7	1765	1959	2164	2380	2607	2843	3089	3343	3604	3872
8	0662	0760	0869	0988	1117	1258	1411	1575	1751	1938
9	0183	0218	0258	0304	0356	0415	0481	0555	0638	0730
10	0035	0043	0053	0065	0079	0095	0114	0137	0163	0193
11	0004	0005	0007	0009	0011	0014	0017	0021	0026	0032
12				0001	0001	0001	0001	0001	0002	0002

P / R	01	02	03	04	05	06	07	08	09	10
1	1225	2310	3270	4118	4867	5526	6107	6617	7065	7458
2	0072	0270	0564	0932	1354	1814	2298	2794	3293	3787
3	0003	0020	0062	0135	0245	0392	0578	0799	1054	1339
4		0001	0005	0014	0031	0060	0103	0163	0242	0342
5				0001	0003	0007	0013	0024	0041	0065
6						0001	0001	0003	0005	0009
7									0001	0001

P / R	11	12	13	14	15	16	17	18	19	20
1	7802	8102	8364	8592	8791	8963	9113	9242	9354	9450
2	4270	4738	5186	5614	6017	6396	6751	7080	7384	7664
3	1651	1985	2337	2704	3080	3463	3848	4231	4611	4983
4	0464	0609	0776	0967	1180	1414	1667	1939	2226	2527
5	0097	0139	0193	0260	0342	0438	0551	0681	0827	0991
6	0015	0024	0036	0053	0075	0104	0139	0183	0237	0300
7	0002	0003	0005	0008	0013	0019	0027	0038	0052	0070
8			0001	0001	0002	0003	0004	0006	0009	0012
9								0001	0001	0002

P / R	21	22	23	24	25	26	27	28	29	30
1	9533	9604	9666	9718	9762	9800	9833	9860	9883	9903
2	7920	8154	8367	8559	8733	8889	9029	9154	9265	9363
3	5347	5699	6039	6364	6674	6968	7245	7505	7749	7975
4	2839	3161	3489	3822	4157	4493	4826	5155	5478	5794
5	1173	1371	1585	1816	2060	2319	2589	2870	3160	3457
6	0375	0462	0562	0675	0802	0944	1099	1270	1455	1654
7	0093	0120	0154	0195	0243	0299	0365	0440	0527	0624
8	0017	0024	0032	0043	0056	0073	0093	0118	0147	0182
9	0002	0004	0005	0007	0010	0013	0018	0024	0031	0040
10			0001	0001	0001	0002	0003	0004	0005	0007
11									0001	0001

P / R	31	32	33	34	35	36	37	38	39	40
1	9920	9934	9945	9955	9963	9970	9975	9980	9984	9987
2	9450	9527	9594	9653	9704	9749	9787	9821	9849	9874
3	8185	8379	8557	8720	8868	9003	9125	9235	9333	9421
4	6101	6398	6683	6957	7217	7464	7698	7917	8123	8314
5	3760	4067	4376	4686	4995	5301	5603	5899	6188	6470
6	1867	2093	2331	2581	2841	3111	3388	3673	3962	4256
7	0733	0854	0988	1135	1295	1468	1654	1853	2065	2288
8	0223	0271	0326	0390	0462	0544	0635	0738	0851	0977
9	0052	0065	0082	0102	0126	0154	0187	0225	0270	0321
10	0009	0012	0015	0020	0025	0032	0040	0051	0063	0078
11	0001	0001	0002	0003	0003	0005	0006	0008	0010	0013
12							0001	0001	0001	0001

P / R	41	42	43	44	45	46	47	48	49	50
1	9990	9992	9993	9995	9996	9997	9997	9998	9998	9999
2	9895	9912	9928	9940	9951	9960	9967	9974	9979	9983
3	9499	9569	9630	9684	9731	9772	9808	9838	9865	9888
4	8492	8656	8807	8945	9071	9185	9288	9381	9464	9539
5	6742	7003	7254	7493	7721	7935	8137	8326	8502	8666
6	4552	4849	5146	5441	5732	6019	6299	6573	6838	7095
7	2524	2770	3025	3290	3563	3842	4127	4415	4707	5000
8	1114	1264	1426	1600	1788	1988	2200	2424	2659	2905
9	0379	0446	0520	0605	0698	0803	0918	1045	1183	1334
10	0096	0117	0141	0170	0203	0242	0287	0338	0396	0461
11	0017	0021	0027	0033	0041	0051	0063	0077	0093	0112
12	0002	0002	0003	0004	0005	0007	0009	0011	0014	0017
13							0001	0001	0001	0001

P / R	01	02	03	04	05	06	07	08	09	10
1	1313	2464	3472	4353	5123	5795	6380	6888	7330	7712
2	0084	0310	0645	1059	1530	2037	2564	3100	3632	4154
3	0003	0025	0077	0167	0301	0478	0698	0958	1255	1584
4		0001	0006	0019	0042	0080	0136	0214	0315	0441
5				0002	0004	0010	0020	0035	0059	0092
6						0001	0002	0004	0008	0015
7									0001	0002

P / R	11	12	13	14	15	16	17	18	19	20
1	8044	8330	8577	8789	8972	9129	9264	9379	9477	9560
2	4658	5141	5599	6031	6433	6807	7152	7469	7758	8021
3	1939	2315	2708	3111	3521	3932	4341	4744	5138	5519
4	0594	0774	0979	1210	1465	1742	2038	2351	2679	3018
5	0137	0196	0269	0359	0467	0594	0741	0907	1093	1298
6	0024	0038	0057	0082	0115	0157	0209	0273	0349	0439
7	0003	0006	0009	0015	0022	0032	0046	0064	0087	0116
8		0001	0001	0002	0003	0005	0008	0012	0017	0024
9						0001	0001	0002	0003	0004

P / R	21	22	23	24	25	26	27	28	29	30
1	9631	9691	9742	9786	9822	9852	9878	9899	9917	9932
2	8259	8473	8665	8837	8990	9126	9246	9352	9444	9525
3	5887	6239	6574	6891	7189	7467	7727	7967	8188	8392
4	3366	3719	4076	4432	4787	5136	5479	5813	6137	6448
5	1523	1765	2023	2297	2585	2884	3193	3509	3832	4158
6	0543	0662	0797	0949	1117	1301	1502	1718	1949	2195
7	0152	0196	0248	0310	0383	0467	0563	0673	0796	0933
8	0033	0045	0060	0079	0103	0132	0167	0208	0257	0315
9	0006	0008	0011	0016	0022	0029	0038	0050	0065	0083
10	0001	0001	0002	0002	0003	0005	0007	0009	0012	0017
11						0001	0001	0001	0002	0002

$$n = 14$$

P	31	32	33	34	35	36	37	38	39	40
R										
1	9945	9955	9963	9970	9976	9981	9984	9988	9990	9992
2	9596	9657	9710	9756	9795	9828	9857	9881	9902	9919
3	8577	8746	8899	9037	9161	9271	9370	9457	9534	9602
4	6747	7032	7301	7556	7795	8018	8226	8418	8595	8757
5	4486	4813	5138	5458	5773	6080	6378	6666	6943	7207
6	2454	2724	3006	3297	3595	3899	4208	4519	4831	5141
7	1084	1250	1431	1626	1836	2059	2296	2545	2805	3075
8	0381	0458	0545	0643	0753	0876	1012	1162	1325	1501
9	0105	0131	0163	0200	0243	0294	0353	0420	0497	0583
10	0022	0029	0037	0048	0060	0076	0095	0117	0144	0175
11	0003	0005	0006	0008	0011	0014	0019	0024	0031	0039
12		0001	0001	0001	0001	0002	0003	0003	0005	0006
13										0001

P	41	42	43	44	45	46	47	48	49	50
R										
1	9994	9995	9996	9997	9998	9998	9999	9999	9999	9999
2	9934	9946	9956	9964	9971	9977	9981	9985	9988	9991
3	9661	9713	9758	9797	9830	9858	9883	9903	9921	9935
4	8905	9039	9161	9270	9368	9455	9532	9601	9661	9713
5	7459	7697	7922	8132	8328	8510	8678	8833	8974	9102
6	5450	5754	6052	6344	6627	6900	7163	7415	7654	7880
7	3355	3643	3937	4236	4539	4843	5148	5451	5751	6047
8	1692	1896	2113	2344	2586	2840	3105	3380	3663	3953
9	0680	0789	0910	1043	1189	1348	1520	1707	1906	2120
10	0212	0255	0304	0361	0426	0500	0583	0677	0782	0898
11	0049	0061	0076	0093	0114	0139	0168	0202	0241	0287
12	0008	0010	0013	0017	0022	0027	0034	0042	0053	0065
13	0001	0001	0001	0002	0003	0003	0004	0006	0007	0009
14										0001

$$n = 15$$

P	01	02	03	04	05	06	07	08	09	10
R										
1	1399	2614	3667	4579	5367	6047	6633	7137	7570	7941
2	0096	0353	0730	1191	1710	2262	2832	3403	3965	4510
3	0004	0030	0094	0203	0362	0571	0829	1130	1469	1841
4		0002	0008	0024	0055	0104	0175	0273	0399	0556
5			0001	0002	0006	0014	0028	0050	0082	0127
6					0001	0001	0003	0007	0013	0022
7								0001	0002	0003

P	11	12	13	14	15	16	17	18	19	20
R										
1	8259	8530	8762	8959	9126	9269	9389	9490	9576	9648
2	5031	5524	5987	6417	6814	7179	7511	7813	8085	8329
3	2238	2654	3084	3520	3958	4392	4819	5234	5635	6020
4	0742	0959	1204	1476	1773	2092	2429	2782	3146	3518
5	0187	0265	0361	0478	0617	0778	0961	1167	1394	1642
6	0037	0057	0084	0121	0168	0227	0300	0387	0490	0611
7	0006	0010	0015	0024	0036	0052	0074	0102	0137	0181
8	0001	0001	0002	0004	0006	0010	0014	0021	0030	0042
9					0001	0001	0002	0003	0005	0008
10									0001	0001

P \ R	21	22	23	24	25	26	27	28	29	30
1	9709	9759	9802	9837	9866	9891	9911	9928	9941	9953
2	8547	8741	8913	9065	9198	9315	9417	9505	9581	9647
3	6385	6731	7055	7358	7639	7899	8137	8355	8553	8732
4	3895	4274	4650	5022	5387	5742	6086	6416	6732	7031
5	1910	2195	2495	2810	3135	3469	3810	4154	4500	4845
6	0748	0905	1079	1272	1484	1713	1958	2220	2495	2784
7	0234	0298	0374	0463	0566	0684	0817	0965	1130	1311
8	0058	0078	0104	0135	0173	0219	0274	0338	0413	0500
9	0011	0016	0023	0031	0042	0056	0073	0094	0121	0152
10	0002	0003	0004	0006	0008	0011	0015	0021	0028	0037
11			0001	0001	0001	0002	0002	0003	0005	0007
12									0001	0001

P \ R	31	32	33	34	35	36	37	38	39	40
1	9962	9969	9975	9980	9984	9988	9990	9992	9994	9995
2	9704	9752	9794	9829	9858	9883	9904	9922	9936	9948
3	8893	9038	9167	9281	9383	9472	9550	9618	9678	9729
4	7314	7580	7829	8060	8273	8469	8649	8813	8961	9095
5	5187	5523	5852	6171	6481	6778	7062	7332	7587	7827
6	3084	3393	3709	4032	4357	4684	5011	5335	5654	5968
7	1509	1722	1951	2194	2452	2722	3003	3295	3595	3902
8	0599	0711	0837	0977	1132	1302	1487	1687	1902	2131
9	0190	0236	0289	0351	0422	0504	0597	0702	0820	0950
10	0048	0062	0079	0099	0124	0154	0190	0232	0281	0338
11	0009	0012	0016	0022	0028	0037	0047	0059	0075	0093
12	0001	0002	0003	0004	0005	0006	0009	0011	0015	0019
13					0001	0001	0001	0002	0002	0003

P \ R	41	42	43	44	45	46	47	48	49	50
1	9996	9997	9998	9998	9999	9999	9999	9999	10000	10000
2	9958	9966	9973	9979	9983	9987	9990	9992	9994	9995
3	9773	9811	9843	9870	9893	9913	9929	9943	9954	9963
4	9215	9322	9417	9502	9576	9641	9697	9746	9788	9824
5	8052	8261	8454	8633	8796	8945	9080	9201	9310	9408
6	6274	6570	6856	7131	7392	7641	7875	8095	8301	8491
7	4214	4530	4847	5164	5478	5789	6095	6394	6684	6964
8	2374	2630	2898	3176	3465	3762	4065	4374	4686	5000
9	1095	1254	1427	1615	1818	2034	2265	2510	2767	3036
10	0404	0479	0565	0661	0769	0890	1024	1171	1333	1509
11	0116	0143	0174	0211	0255	0305	0363	0430	0506	0592
12	0025	0032	0040	0051	0063	0079	0097	0119	0145	0176
13	0004	0005	0007	0009	0011	0014	0018	0023	0029	0037
14			0001	0001	0001	0002	0002	0003	0004	0005

APPENDIX TABLE 4 Values of $e^{-\lambda}$ (for Computing Poisson Probabilities)

λ	$e^{-\lambda}$	λ	$e^{-\lambda}$	λ	$e^{-\lambda}$	λ	$e^{-\lambda}$
0.1	0.90484	2.6	0.07427	5.1	0.00610	7.6	0.00050
0.2	0.81873	2.7	0.06721	5.2	0.00552	7.7	0.00045
0.3	0.74082	2.8	0.06081	5.3	0.00499	7.8	0.00041
0.4	0.67032	2.9	0.05502	5.4	0.00452	7.9	0.00037
0.5	0.60653	3.0	0.04979	5.5	0.00409	8.0	0.00034
0.6	0.54881	3.1	0.04505	5.6	0.00370	8.1	0.00030
0.7	0.49659	3.2	0.04076	5.7	0.00335	8.2	0.00027
0.8	0.44933	3.3	0.03688	5.8	0.00303	8.3	0.00025
0.9	0.40657	3.4	0.03337	5.9	0.00274	8.4	0.00022
1.0	0.36788	3.5	0.03020	6.0	0.00248	8.5	0.00020
1.1	0.33287	3.6	0.02732	6.1	0.00224	8.6	0.00018
1.2	0.30119	3.7	0.02472	6.2	0.00203	8.7	0.00017
1.3	0.27253	3.8	0.02237	6.3	0.00184	8.8	0.00015
1.4	0.24660	3.9	0.02024	6.4	0.00166	8.9	0.00014
1.5	0.22313	4.0	0.01832	6.5	0.00150	9.0	0.00012
1.6	0.20190	4.1	0.01657	6.6	0.00136	9.1	0.00011
1.7	0.18268	4.2	0.01500	6.7	0.00123	9.2	0.00010
1.8	0.16530	4.3	0.01357	6.8	0.00111	9.3	0.00009
1.9	0.14957	4.4	0.01228	6.9	0.00101	9.4	0.00008
2.0	0.13534	4.5	0.01111	7.0	0.00091	9.5	0.00007
2.1	0.12246	4.6	0.01005	7.1	0.00083	9.6	0.00007
2.2	0.11080	4.7	0.00910	7.2	0.00075	9.7	0.00006
2.3	0.10026	4.8	0.00823	7.3	0.00068	9.8	0.00006
2.4	0.09072	4.9	0.00745	7.4	0.00061	9.9	0.00005
2.5	0.08208	5.0	0.00674	7.5	0.00055	10.0	0.00005

APPENDIX TABLE 5 Area in the Right Tail of a Chi-square (χ^2) Distribution.*

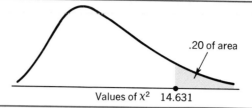

.20 of area

Values of χ^2 14.631

EXAMPLE: In a chi-square distribution with 11 degrees of freedom, if we want to find the appropriate chi-square value for .20 of the area under the curve (the colored area in the right tail) we look under the .20 column in the table and proceed down to the 11 degrees of freedom row; the appropriate chi-square value there is 14.631

Degrees of freedom	Area in right tail				
	.99	.975	.95	.90	.800
1	.00016	.00098	.00398	.0158	.0642
2	.0201	.0506	.103	.211	.446
3	.115	.216	.352	.584	1.005
4	.297	.484	.711	1.064	1.649
5	.554	.831	1.145	1.610	2.343
6	.872	1.237	1.635	2.204	3.070
7	1.239	1.690	2.167	2.833	3.822
8	1.646	2.180	2.733	3.490	4.594
9	2.088	2.700	3.325	4.168	5.380
10	2.558	3.247	3.940	4.865	6.179
11	3.053	3.816	4.575	5.578	6.989
12	3.571	4.404	5.226	6.304	7.807
13	4.107	5.009	5.892	7.042	8.634
14	4.660	5.629	6.571	7.790	9.467
15	5.229	6.262	7.261	8.547	10.307
16	5.812	6.908	7.962	9.312	11.152
17	6.408	7.564	8.672	10.085	12.002
18	7.015	8.231	9.390	10.865	12.857
19	7.633	8.907	10.117	11.651	13.716
20	8.260	9.591	10.851	12.443	14.578
21	8.897	10.283	11.591	13.240	15.445
22	9.542	10.982	12.338	14.041	16.314
23	10.196	11.689	13.091	14.848	17.187
24	10.856	12.401	13.848	15.658	18.062
25	11.524	13.120	14.611	16.473	18.940
26	12.198	13.844	15.379	17.292	19.820
27	12.879	14.573	16.151	18.114	20.703
28	13.565	15.308	16.928	18.939	21.588
29	14.256	16.047	17.708	19.768	22.475
30	14.953	16.791	18.493	20.599	23.364

* Taken from Table IV of Fisher and Yates, *Statistical Tables for Biological, Agricultural and Medical Research*, published by Longman Group Ltd., London (previously published by Oliver & Boyd, Edinburgh) and by permission of the authors and publishers.

Note: If v, the number of degrees of freedom, is greater than 30, we can approximate χ^2_α, the chi-square value leaving α of the area in the right tail, by

$$\chi^2_\alpha = v \left(1 - \frac{2}{9v} + z_\alpha \sqrt{\frac{2}{9v}} \right)^3$$

where z_α is the standard normal value (from Appendix Table 1) that leaves α of the area in the right tail.

		Area in right tail			Degrees of freedom
.20	.10	.05	.025	.01	
1.642	2.706	3.841	5.024	6.635	1
3.219	4.605	5.991	7.378	9.210	2
4.642	6.251	7.815	9.348	11.345	3
5.989	7.779	9.488	11.143	13.277	4
7.289	9.236	11.070	12.833	15.086	5
8.558	10.645	12.592	14.449	16.812	6
9.803	12.017	14.067	16.013	18.475	7
11.030	13.362	15.507	17.535	20.090	8
12.242	14.684	16.919	19.023	21.666	9
13.442	15.987	18.307	20.483	23.209	10
14.631	17.275	19.675	21.920	24.725	11
15.812	18.549	21.026	23.337	26.217	12
16.985	19.812	22.362	24.736	27.688	13
18.151	21.064	23.685	26.119	29.141	14
19.311	22.307	24.996	27.488	30.578	15
20.465	23.542	26.296	28.845	32.000	16
21.615	24.769	27.587	30.191	33.409	17
22.760	25.989	28.869	31.526	34.805	18
23.900	27.204	30.144	32.852	36.191	19
25.038	28.412	31.410	34.170	37.566	20
26.171	29.615	32.671	35.479	38.932	21
27.301	30.813	33.924	36.781	40.289	22
28.429	32.007	35.172	38.076	41.638	23
29.553	33.196	36.415	39.364	42.980	24
30.675	34.382	37.652	40.647	44.314	25
31.795	35.563	38.885	41.923	45.642	26
32.912	36.741	40.113	43.194	46.963	27
34.027	37.916	41.337	44.461	48.278	28
35.139	39.087	42.557	45.722	49.588	29
36.250	40.256	43.773	46.979	50.892	30

APPENDIX TABLE 6 Values of F for F Distributions with .05 of the Area in the Right Tail*

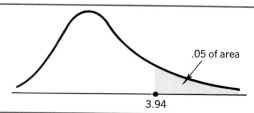

.05 of area

3.94

EXAMPLE: For a test at a significance level of .05 where we have 15 degrees of freedom for the numerator and 6 degrees of freedom for the denominator, the appropriate F value is found by looking under the 15 degrees of freedom column and proceeding down to the 6 degrees of freedom row; there we find the appropriate F value to be 3.94.

Degrees of freedom for numerator

	1	2	3	4	5	6	7	8	9	10	12	15	20	24	30	40	60	120	∞
1	161	200	216	225	230	234	237	239	241	242	244	246	248	249	250	251	252	253	254
2	18.5	19.0	19.2	19.2	19.3	19.3	19.4	19.4	19.4	19.4	19.4	19.4	19.4	19.5	19.5	19.5	19.5	19.5	19.5
3	10.1	9.55	9.28	9.12	9.01	8.94	8.89	8.85	8.81	8.79	8.74	8.70	8.66	8.64	8.62	8.59	8.57	8.55	8.53
4	7.71	6.94	6.59	6.39	6.26	6.16	6.09	6.04	6.00	5.96	5.91	5.86	5.80	5.77	5.75	5.72	5.69	5.66	5.63
5	6.61	5.79	5.41	5.19	5.05	4.95	4.88	4.82	4.77	4.74	4.68	4.62	4.56	4.53	4.50	4.46	4.43	4.40	4.37
6	5.99	5.14	4.76	4.53	4.39	4.28	4.21	4.15	4.10	4.06	4.00	3.94	3.87	3.84	3.81	3.77	3.74	3.70	3.67
7	5.59	4.74	4.35	4.12	3.97	3.87	3.79	3.73	3.68	3.64	3.57	3.51	3.44	3.41	3.38	3.34	3.30	3.27	3.23
8	5.32	4.46	4.07	3.84	3.69	3.58	3.50	3.44	3.39	3.35	3.28	3.22	3.15	3.12	3.08	3.04	3.01	2.97	2.93
9	5.12	4.26	3.86	3.63	3.48	3.37	3.29	3.23	3.18	3.14	3.07	3.01	2.94	2.90	2.86	2.83	2.79	2.75	2.71
10	4.96	4.10	3.71	3.48	3.33	3.22	3.14	3.07	3.02	2.98	2.91	2.85	2.77	2.74	2.70	2.66	2.62	2.58	2.54
11	4.84	3.98	3.59	3.36	3.20	3.09	3.01	2.95	2.90	2.85	2.79	2.72	2.65	2.61	2.57	2.53	2.49	2.45	2.40
12	4.75	3.89	3.49	3.26	3.11	3.00	2.91	2.85	2.80	2.75	2.69	2.62	2.54	2.51	2.47	2.43	2.38	2.34	2.30
13	4.67	3.81	3.41	3.18	3.03	2.92	2.83	2.77	2.71	2.67	2.60	2.53	2.46	2.42	2.38	2.34	2.30	2.25	2.21
14	4.60	3.74	3.34	3.11	2.96	2.85	2.76	2.70	2.65	2.60	2.53	2.46	2.39	2.35	2.31	2.27	2.22	2.18	2.13
15	4.54	3.68	3.29	3.06	2.90	2.79	2.71	2.64	2.59	2.54	2.48	2.40	2.33	2.29	2.25	2.20	2.16	2.11	2.07
16	4.49	3.63	3.24	3.01	2.85	2.74	2.66	2.59	2.54	2.49	2.42	2.35	2.28	2.24	2.19	2.15	2.11	2.06	2.01
17	4.45	3.59	3.20	2.96	2.81	2.70	2.61	2.55	2.49	2.45	2.38	2.31	2.23	2.19	2.15	2.10	2.06	2.01	1.96
18	4.41	3.55	3.16	2.93	2.77	2.66	2.58	2.51	2.46	2.41	2.34	2.27	2.19	2.15	2.11	2.06	2.02	1.97	1.92
19	4.38	3.52	3.13	2.90	2.74	2.63	2.54	2.48	2.42	2.38	2.31	2.23	2.16	2.11	2.07	2.03	1.98	1.93	1.88
20	4.35	3.49	3.10	2.87	2.71	2.60	2.51	2.45	2.39	2.35	2.28	2.20	2.12	2.08	2.04	1.99	1.95	1.90	1.84
21	4.32	3.47	3.07	2.84	2.68	2.57	2.49	2.42	2.37	2.32	2.25	2.18	2.10	2.05	2.01	1.96	1.92	1.87	1.81
22	4.30	3.44	3.05	2.82	2.66	2.55	2.46	2.40	2.34	2.30	2.23	2.15	2.07	2.03	1.98	1.94	1.89	1.84	1.78
23	4.28	3.42	3.03	2.80	2.64	2.53	2.44	2.37	2.32	2.27	2.20	2.13	2.05	2.01	1.96	1.91	1.86	1.81	1.76
24	4.26	3.40	3.01	2.78	2.62	2.51	2.42	2.36	2.30	2.25	2.18	2.11	2.03	1.98	1.94	1.89	1.84	1.79	1.73
25	4.24	3.39	2.99	2.76	2.60	2.49	2.40	2.34	2.28	2.24	2.16	2.09	2.01	1.96	1.92	1.87	1.82	1.77	1.71
30	4.17	3.32	2.92	2.69	2.53	2.42	2.33	2.27	2.21	2.16	2.09	2.01	1.93	1.89	1.84	1.79	1.74	1.68	1.62
40	4.08	3.23	2.84	2.61	2.45	2.34	2.25	2.18	2.12	2.08	2.00	1.92	1.84	1.79	1.74	1.69	1.64	1.58	1.51
60	4.00	3.15	2.76	2.53	2.37	2.25	2.17	2.10	2.04	1.99	1.92	1.84	1.75	1.70	1.65	1.59	1.53	1.47	1.39
120	3.92	3.07	2.68	2.45	2.29	2.18	2.09	2.02	1.96	1.91	1.83	1.75	1.66	1.61	1.55	1.50	1.43	1.35	1.25
∞	3.84	3.00	2.60	2.37	2.21	2.10	2.01	1.94	1.88	1.83	1.75	1.67	1.57	1.52	1.46	1.39	1.32	1.22	1.00

Degrees of freedom for denominator

* Source: M. Merrington and C. M. Thompson, *Biometrika,* vol. 33 (1943).

Values of *F* for *F* Distributions with .01 of the Area in the Right Tail

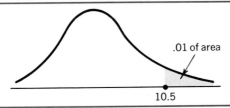

.01 of area

10.5

EXAMPLE: For a test at a significance level of .01 where we have 7 degrees of freedom for the numerator and 5 degrees of freedom for the denominator, the appropriate *F* value is found by looking under the 7 degrees of freedom column and proceeding down to the 5 degrees of freedom row; there we find the appropriate *F* value to be 10.5.

Degrees of freedom for numerator

	1	2	3	4	5	6	7	8	9	10	12	15	20	24	30	40	60	120	∞
1	4,052	5,000	5,403	5,625	5,764	5,859	5,928	5,982	6,023	6,056	6,106	6,157	6,209	6,235	6,261	6,287	6,313	6,339	6,366
2	98.5	99.0	99.2	99.2	99.3	99.3	99.4	99.4	99.4	99.4	99.4	99.4	99.4	99.5	99.5	99.5	99.5	99.5	99.5
3	34.1	30.8	29.5	28.7	28.2	27.9	27.7	27.5	27.3	27.2	27.1	26.9	26.7	26.6	26.5	26.4	26.3	26.2	26.1
4	21.2	18.0	16.7	16.0	15.5	15.2	15.0	14.8	14.7	14.5	14.4	14.2	14.0	13.9	13.8	13.7	13.7	13.6	13.5
5	16.3	13.3	12.1	11.4	11.0	10.7	10.5	10.3	10.2	10.1	9.89	9.72	9.55	9.47	9.38	9.29	9.20	9.11	9.02
6	13.7	10.9	9.78	9.15	8.75	8.47	8.26	8.10	7.98	7.87	7.72	7.56	7.40	7.31	7.23	7.14	7.06	6.97	6.88
7	12.2	9.55	8.45	7.85	7.46	7.19	6.99	6.84	6.72	6.62	6.47	6.31	6.16	6.07	5.99	5.91	5.82	5.74	5.65
8	11.3	8.65	7.59	7.01	6.63	6.37	6.18	6.03	5.91	5.81	5.67	5.52	5.36	5.28	5.20	5.12	5.03	4.95	4.86
9	10.6	8.02	6.99	6.42	6.06	5.80	5.61	5.47	5.35	5.26	5.11	4.96	4.81	4.73	4.65	4.57	4.48	4.40	4.31
10	10.0	7.56	6.55	5.99	5.64	5.39	5.20	5.06	4.94	4.85	4.71	4.56	4.41	4.33	4.25	4.17	4.08	4.00	3.91
11	9.65	7.21	6.22	5.67	5.32	5.07	4.89	4.74	4.63	4.54	4.40	4.25	4.10	4.02	3.94	3.86	3.78	3.69	3.60
12	9.33	6.93	5.95	5.41	5.06	4.82	4.64	4.50	4.39	4.30	4.16	4.01	3.86	3.78	3.70	3.62	3.54	3.45	3.36
13	9.07	6.70	5.74	5.21	4.86	4.62	4.44	4.30	4.19	4.10	3.96	3.82	3.66	3.59	3.51	3.43	3.34	3.25	3.17
14	8.86	6.51	5.56	5.04	4.70	4.46	4.28	4.14	4.03	3.94	3.80	3.66	3.51	3.43	3.35	3.27	3.18	3.09	3.00
15	8.68	6.36	5.42	4.89	4.56	4.32	4.14	4.00	3.89	3.80	3.67	3.52	3.37	3.29	3.21	3.13	3.05	2.96	2.87
16	8.53	6.23	5.29	4.77	4.44	4.20	4.03	3.89	3.78	3.69	3.55	3.41	3.26	3.18	3.10	3.02	2.93	2.84	2.75
17	8.40	6.11	5.19	4.67	4.34	4.10	3.93	3.79	3.68	3.59	3.46	3.31	3.16	3.08	3.00	2.92	2.83	2.75	2.65
18	8.29	6.01	5.09	4.58	4.25	4.01	3.84	3.71	3.60	3.51	3.37	3.23	3.08	3.00	2.92	2.84	2.75	2.66	2.57
19	8.19	5.93	5.01	4.50	4.17	3.94	3.77	3.63	3.52	3.43	3.30	3.15	3.00	2.92	2.84	2.76	2.67	2.58	2.49
20	8.10	5.85	4.94	4.43	4.10	3.87	3.70	3.56	3.46	3.37	3.23	3.09	2.94	2.86	2.78	2.69	2.61	2.52	2.42
21	8.02	5.78	4.87	4.37	4.04	3.81	3.64	3.51	3.40	3.31	3.17	3.03	2.88	2.80	2.72	2.64	2.55	2.46	2.36
22	7.95	5.72	4.82	4.31	3.99	3.76	3.59	3.45	3.35	3.26	3.12	2.98	2.83	2.75	2.67	2.58	2.50	2.40	2.31
23	7.88	5.66	4.76	4.26	3.94	3.71	3.54	3.41	3.30	3.21	3.07	2.93	2.78	2.70	2.62	2.54	2.45	2.35	2.26
24	7.82	5.61	4.72	4.22	3.90	3.67	3.50	3.36	3.26	3.17	3.03	2.89	2.74	2.66	2.58	2.49	2.40	2.31	2.21
25	7.77	5.57	4.68	4.18	3.86	3.63	3.46	3.32	3.22	3.13	2.99	2.85	2.70	2.62	2.53	2.45	2.36	2.27	2.17
30	7.56	5.39	4.51	4.02	3.70	3.47	3.30	3.17	3.07	2.98	2.84	2.70	2.55	2.47	2.39	2.30	2.21	2.11	2.01
40	7.31	5.18	4.31	3.83	3.51	3.29	3.12	2.99	2.89	2.80	2.66	2.52	2.37	2.29	2.20	2.11	2.02	1.92	1.80
60	7.08	4.98	4.13	3.65	3.34	3.12	2.95	2.82	2.72	2.63	2.50	2.35	2.20	2.12	2.03	1.94	1.84	1.73	1.60
120	6.85	4.79	3.95	3.48	3.17	2.96	2.79	2.66	2.56	2.47	2.34	2.19	2.03	1.95	1.86	1.76	1.66	1.53	1.38
∞	6.63	4.61	3.78	3.32	3.02	2.80	2.64	2.51	2.41	2.32	2.18	2.04	1.88	1.79	1.70	1.59	1.47	1.32	1.00

Degrees of freedom for denominator

APPENDIX TABLE 7 Values for Spearman's Rank Correlation (r_s) for Combined Areas in Both Tails*

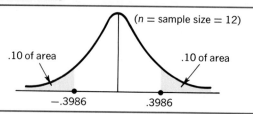

EXAMPLE: For a two-tailed test of significance at the .20 level, with $n = 12$, the appropriate value for r_s can be found by looking under the .20 column and proceeding down to the 12 row; there we find the appropriate r_s value to be .3986.

n	.20	.10	.05	.02	.01	.002
4	.8000	.8000				
5	.7000	.8000	.9000	.9000		
6	.6000	.7714	.8286	.8857	.9429	
7	.5357	.6786	.7450	.8571	.8929	.9643
8	.5000	.6190	.7143	.8095	.8571	.9286
9	.4667	.5833	.6833	.7667	.8167	.9000
10	.4424	.5515	.6364	.7333	.7818	.8667
11	.4182	.5273	.6091	.7000	.7455	.8364
12	.3986	.4965	.5804	.6713	.7273	.8182
13	.3791	.4780	.5549	.6429	.6978	.7912
14	.3626	.4593	.5341	.6220	.6747	.7670
15	.3500	.4429	.5179	.6000	.6536	.7464
16	.3382	.4265	.5000	.5824	.6324	.7265
17	.3260	.4118	.4853	.5637	.6152	.7083
18	.3148	.3994	.4716	.5480	.5975	.6904
19	.3070	.3895	.4579	.5333	.5825	.6737
20	.2977	.3789	.4451	.5203	.5684	.6586
21	.2909	.3688	.4351	.5078	.5545	.6455
22	.2829	.3597	.4241	.4963	.5426	.6318
23	.2767	.3518	.4150	.4852	.5306	.6186
24	.2704	.3435	.4061	.4748	.5200	.6070
25	.2646	.3362	.3977	.4654	.5100	.5962
26	.2588	.3299	.3894	.4564	.5002	.5856
27	.2540	.3236	.3822	.4481	.4915	.5757
28	.2490	.3175	.3749	.4401	.4828	.5660
29	.2443	.3113	.3685	.4320	.4744	.5567
30	.2400	.3059	.3620	.4251	.4665	.5479

* Source: W.J. Conover, *Practical Nonparametric Statistics*, John Wiley & Sons, Inc., New York, 1971.

APPENDIX TABLE 8 Critical Values of D in the Kolmogorov-Smirnov Goodness-of-Fit Test*

Sample size (n)	Level of significance for $D = $ Maximum $|F_e - F_o|$				
	.20	.15	.10	.05	.01
1	.900	.925	.950	.975	.995
2	.684	.726	.776	.842	.929
3	.565	.597	.642	.708	.828
4	.494	.525	.564	.624	.733
5	.446	.474	.510	.565	.669
6	.410	.436	.470	.521	.618
7	.381	.405	.438	.486	.577
8	.358	.381	.411	.457	.543
9	.339	.360	.388	.432	.514
10	.322	.342	.368	.410	.490
11	.307	.326	.352	.391	.468
12	.295	.313	.338	.375	.450
13	.284	.302	.325	.361	.433
14	.274	.292	.314	.349	.418
15	.266	.283	.304	.338	.404
16	.258	.274	.295	.328	.392
17	.250	.266	.286	.318	.381
18	.244	.259	.278	.309	.371
19	.237	.252	.272	.301	.363
20	.231	.246	.264	.294	.356
25	.21	.22	.24	.27	.32
30	.19	.20	.22	.24	.29
35	.18	.19	.21	.23	.27
Over 35	$\dfrac{1.07}{\sqrt{n}}$	$\dfrac{1.14}{\sqrt{n}}$	$\dfrac{1.22}{\sqrt{n}}$	$\dfrac{1.36}{\sqrt{n}}$	$\dfrac{1.63}{\sqrt{n}}$

* Source: Adapted from F. J. Massey, Jr., "The Kolmogorov-Smirnov test for goodness of fit," *J. Am. Stat. Assoc.* 46:68–78, 1951. By permission of the author and publishers.

Note: The values of D given in the table are critical values associated with selected values of n. Any value of D that is greater than or equal to the tabulated value is significant at the indicated level of significance.

Listed below are the records for the 199 students who used this text in our course in the fall semester of 1989. These data are included in the data disk that accompanies the text. Each observation contains the following 9 variables:

STUDENT — the student's position on the roster.
SECTION — which of the six sections of the class the student was enrolled in.
INSTRUCT — the type of instructor (TA or PROF).
EXAM1 — score on first mid-term (75 points possible).
EXAM2 — score on second mid-term (75 points possible).
HOMEWORK — score on homework (137 points possible).
FINAL — score on final exam (75 points possible).
TOTAL — raw score, computed as

20 *(EXAM1 + EXAM2 + 2*FINAL)/75 + 20 *HWK/137

GRADE— letter grade in class determined by

TOTAL	GRADE
0–49	F
50–59	D
60–63	C—
64–69	C
70–73	C+
74–75	B—
76–78	B
79–80	B+
81–85	A—
86–100	A

1989 GRADES IN BUSINESS STATISTICS

STUDENT	SECTION	INSTRUCT	EXAM1	EXAM2	HWK	FINAL	TOTAL	GRADE
1	1	TA	55	61	121	44	72.0642	C+
2	1	TA	49	56	110	44	67.5251	C
3	1	TA	41	54	100	48	65.5319	C
4	1	TA	40	29	76	41	51.3616	D
5	1	TA	47	62	119	50	73.1056	C+
6	1	TA	35	50	112	42	61.4170	C—
7	1	TA	55	60	122	49	74.6102	B—
8	1	TA	49	46	116	45	66.2676	C
9	1	TA	50	49	114	40	64.3757	C
10	1	TA	67	66	129	61	86.8321	A
11	1	TA	45	46	75	41	57.0822	D
12	1	TA	45	63	119	46	70.7056	C+
13	1	TA	45	62	111	41	66.6044	C
14	1	TA	53	52	114	45	68.6423	C
15	1	TA	46	50	111	42	64.2044	C

STUDENT	SECTION	INSTRUCT	EXAM1	EXAM2	HWK	FINAL	TOTAL	GRADE
16	1	TA	69	65	125	62	87.0482	A
17	1	TA	54	64	112	53	76.0837	B
18	1	TA	37	54	125	41	64.3815	C
19	1	TA	35	56	101	27	53.4112	D
20	1	TA	58	65	123	54	79.5562	B+
21	1	TA	21	16	32	14	22.0049	F
22	1	TA	57	68	134	58	83.8287	A−
23	1	TA	40	41	100	50	62.8652	C−
24	1	TA	54	68	106	56	77.8745	B
25	1	TA	57	61	106	64	81.0745	A−
26	1	TA	29	20	111	32	46.3377	F
27	1	TA	40	55	121	45	66.9976	C
28	2	PROF	56	62	97	49	71.7606	C+
29	2	PROF	54	55	108	40	66.1664	C
30	2	PROF	48	61	113	41	67.4297	C
31	2	PROF	52	57	116	42	68.4010	C
32	2	PROF	33	39	132	32	55.5367	D
33	2	PROF	43	69	135	61	82.1080	A−
34	2	PROF	62	69	94	37	68.3893	C
35	2	PROF	43	57	108	43	65.3664	C
36	2	PROF	56	63	113	50	74.8964	B−
37	2	PROF	40	59	126	39	65.5942	C
38	2	PROF	60	70	124	65	87.4355	A
39	2	PROF	52	62	107	47	71.0871	C+
40	2	PROF	65	70	114	60	84.6423	A−
41	2	PROF	50	64	132	30	65.6701	C
42	2	PROF	67	69	130	57	85.6448	A
43	2	PROF	67	69	133	62	88.7494	A
44	2	PROF	50	54	122	57	75.9436	B
45	2	PROF	39	56	66	32	52.0350	D
46	2	PROF	36	39	56	29	43.6418	F
47	2	PROF	45	58	109	40	64.7124	C
48	2	PROF	56	55	111	37	65.5377	C
49	2	PROF	46	24	85	45	55.0754	D
50	2	PROF	44	45	78	34	53.2535	D
51	2	PROF	36	53	120	38	61.5182	C−
52	2	PROF	59	64	117	43	72.8136	C+
53	2	PROF	40	38	101	13	42.4779	F
54	2	PROF	50	69	123	47	74.7562	B−
55	2	PROF	69	72	124	63	89.3022	A
56	2	PROF	67	69	119	49	79.7723	B+
57	2	PROF	50	52	107	35	61.4871	C−
58	2	PROF	42	50	109	32	57.5124	D
59	2	PROF	64	59	122	44	74.0769	B−
60	2	PROF	51	67	127	52	77.7401	B
61	2	PROF	73	73	135	74	98.1080	A
62	2	PROF	49	69	124	53	77.8355	B
63	2	PROF	38	57	110	44	64.8584	C
64	2	PROF	58	62	105	50	73.9951	B−
65	2	PROF	30	33	78	18	37.7869	F
66	2	PROF	53	57	117	38	66.6803	C
67	2	PROF	43	58	116	53	72.1343	C+

STUDENT	SECTION	INSTRUCT	EXAM1	EXAM2	HWK	FINAL	TOTAL	GRADE
68	2	PROF	56	66	126	44	74.3942	B−
69	2	PROF	61	59	127	52	78.2735	B
70	2	PROF	53	64	124	50	75.9689	B
71	2	PROF	47	49	120	54	71.9182	C+
72	2	PROF	54	63	119	43	71.5056	C+
73	2	PROF	31	51	97	41	57.8939	D
74	3	PROF	55	66	114	55	78.2423	B
75	3	PROF	67	68	120	59	84.9849	A−
76	3	PROF	63	66	112	55	80.0837	B+
77	3	PROF	35	50	110	51	66.4584	C
78	3	PROF	36	64	100	53	69.5319	C+
79	3	PROF	57	69	126	54	80.7942	A−
80	3	PROF	48	66	87	55	72.4341	C+
81	3	PROF	55	60	123	47	73.6895	B−
82	3	PROF	61	58	129	59	82.0321	A−
83	3	PROF	55	55	117	49	72.5470	C+
84	3	PROF	53	67	115	49	74.9217	B−
85	3	PROF	49	61	119	43	69.6389	C+
86	3	PROF	57	58	105	49	72.1285	C+
87	3	PROF	66	72	122	63	88.2102	A
88	3	PROF	39	44	109	35	56.7124	D
89	3	PROF	58	66	109	41	70.8457	C+
90	3	PROF	56	57	119	54	76.3056	B
91	3	PROF	56	64	128	51	77.8861	B
92	3	PROF	50	55	106	43	66.4078	C
93	3	PROF	63	56	116	48	74.2676	B−
94	3	PROF	68	65	118	58	83.6263	A−
95	3	PROF	61	62	131	57	82.3241	A−
96	3	PROF	59	71	130	58	84.5781	A−
97	3	PROF	48	62	125	48	73.1815	C+
98	3	PROF	47	66	112	52	74.2170	B−
99	3	PROF	44	48	101	34	57.4112	D
100	3	PROF	38	46	98	40	58.0399	D
101	3	PROF	52	49	35	40	53.3762	D
102	3	PROF	41	49	94	34	55.8560	D
103	3	PROF	60	62	114	49	75.3090	B−
104	3	PROF	60	72	130	55	83.5114	A−
105	3	PROF	54	62	111	45	71.1377	C+
106	3	PROF	51	53	107	47	68.4204	C
107	3	PROF	41	53	111	41	63.1377	C−
108	3	PROF	58	65	98	42	69.5066	C+
109	3	PROF	64	69	122	53	81.5436	A−
110	3	PROF	43	63	113	49	70.8964	C+
111	4	TA	42	56	104	39	62.1158	C−
112	4	TA	57	58	113	36	66.3630	C
113	4	TA	43	66	116	60	78.0010	B
114	4	TA	64	64	115	50	77.5883	B
115	4	TA	53	70	117	54	78.6803	B+
116	4	TA	52	60	109	38	66.0457	C
117	4	TA	47	54	120	37	64.1849	C
118	4	TA	51	59	115	44	69.5883	C+
119	4	TA	58	61	127	43	73.2068	C+

STUDENT	SECTION	INSTRUCT	EXAM1	EXAM2	HWK	FINAL	TOTAL	GRADE
120	4	TA	54	72	108	46	73.8998	B−
121	4	TA	59	68	115	57	81.0550	A−
122	4	TA	43	65	100	45	67.3985	C
123	4	TA	44	58	101	45	65.9445	C
124	4	TA	47	57	112	55	73.4170	C+
125	4	TA	62	54	99	45	69.3859	C
126	4	TA	56	54	108	43	68.0331	C
127	4	TA	31	45	62	37	49.0511	F
128	4	TA	53	51	84	29	55.4628	D
129	4	TA	32	59	72	31	51.3109	D
130	4	TA	48	67	107	51	73.4871	C+
131	4	TA	50	48	88	57	69.3800	C
132	4	TA	54	63	117	45	72.2803	C+
133	4	TA	57	59	107	46	71.0871	C+
134	4	TA	45	57	99	37	61.3859	C−
135	4	TA	68	60	114	52	78.5090	B+
136	4	TA	50	59	90	46	66.7387	C
137	5	TA	60	66	127	59	83.6068	A−
138	5	TA	46	56	93	46	65.3100	C
139	5	TA	41	25	61	27	40.9051	F
140	5	TA	43	54	121	54	72.3309	C+
141	5	TA	47	32	114	39	58.5090	D
142	5	TA	55	65	114	40	69.9757	C+
143	5	TA	36	63	132	39	66.4701	C
144	5	TA	58	65	128	64	85.6195	A
145	5	TA	46	71	128	58	80.8195	A−
146	5	TA	72	72	132	65	92.3367	A
147	5	TA	35	46	115	36	57.5883	D
148	5	TA	54	58	102	49	70.8905	C+
149	5	TA	49	65	97	34	62.6939	C−
150	5	TA	44	64	103	52	71.5698	C+
151	5	TA	65	68	128	44	77.6195	B
152	5	TA	64	70	128	61	86.9528	A
153	5	TA	56	58	113	49	73.0297	C+
154	5	TA	51	53	94	35	60.1226	C−
155	5	TA	49	67	106	46	70.9411	C+
156	5	TA	43	57	117	36	62.9470	C−
157	5	TA	48	46	117	37	61.8803	C−
158	5	TA	44	50	116	43	64.9343	C
159	5	TA	54	46	13	25	41.8978	F
160	5	TA	58	62	124	51	77.3022	B
161	5	TA	45	57	70	34	55.5523	D
162	5	TA	41	51	116	41	63.3343	C−
163	5	TA	45	50	107	44	64.4204	C
164	5	TA	52	55	75	48	65.0822	C
165	5	TA	51	71	133	50	78.6161	B+
166	5	TA	50	65	124	61	81.3022	A−
167	5	TA	44	46	121	35	60.3309	C−
168	5	TA	44	48	114	46	65.7090	C
169	5	TA	56	62	106	47	72.0078	C+
170	5	TA	50	51	96	36	60.1479	C−
171	5	TA	38	32	74	32	46.5363	F

STUDENT	SECTION	INSTRUCT	EXAM1	EXAM2	HWK	FINAL	TOTAL	GRADE
172	5	TA	47	47	106	33	58.1411	D
173	6	PROF	46	63	127	54	76.4068	B
174	6	PROF	41	52	100	44	62.8652	C−
175	6	PROF	53	60	92	40	64.8973	C
176	6	PROF	45	65	90	51	69.6720	C+
177	6	PROF	47	65	83	45	65.9835	C
178	6	PROF	39	52	74	45	59.0696	D
179	6	PROF	59	56	120	51	75.3849	B−
180	6	PROF	50	39	115	39	61.3217	C−
181	6	PROF	54	41	93	55	68.2433	C
182	6	PROF	41	43	83	24	47.3168	F
183	6	PROF	44	35	98	34	53.5066	D
184	6	PROF	63	61	126	46	75.9942	B
185	6	PROF	52	54	107	43	66.8204	C
186	6	PROF	37	46	110	24	50.9917	D
187	6	PROF	61	65	120	48	76.7182	B
188	6	PROF	35	30	105	34	50.7951	D
189	6	PROF	50	62	105	44	68.6618	C
190	6	PROF	47	36	106	42	60.0078	C−
191	6	PROF	54	64	117	50	75.2136	B−
192	6	PROF	50	60	122	42	69.5436	C+
193	6	PROF	47	41	112	47	64.8837	C
194	6	PROF	66	63	125	51	79.8482	B+
195	6	PROF	39	50	76	17	43.8949	F
196	6	PROF	52	61	81	33	59.5582	C−
197	6	PROF	34	49	85	38	54.8088	D
198	6	PROF	50	35	78	46	58.5869	D
199	6	PROF	58	58	120	50	75.1182	B−

APPENDIX TABLE 10 Company Earnings Data for Computer Examples

Listed below are the earnings data for 224 companies whose 1989 last-quarter earnings were published in *The Wall Street Journal* during the week of February 12, 1990. These data are included on the data disk that accompanies the text. Each observation contains the following seven variables:

COMPANY - the name of the company
EXCHANGE - the exchange where the stock is traded (N for New York Stock Exchange, A for American Stock Exchange, O for "over-the-counter"
LQ89 - 1989 last-quarter earnings
LQ88 - 1988 last-quarter earnings
CHANGE - The change in last-quarter earnings (LQ89 – LQ88)
GRPLQ89 - grouped 1989 last-quarter earnings; each earnings value is rounded to the nearest 25¢
GRPLQ88 - grouped 1988 last-quarter earnings; each earnings value is rounded to the nearest 25¢

COMPANY	EXCHANGE	LQ89	LQ88	CHANGE	GRLP89	GRLP88
ADAGE INC	O	0.10	−0.17	0.27	0.00	−0.25
ADAMS RESOURCES & ENERGY	A	0.11	0.09	0.02	0.00	0.00
ADIA SERVICES INC	O	0.36	0.32	0.04	0.25	0.25
AMERICAN TELEV & COMMUN	O	0.24	0.18	0.06	0.25	0.25
AVON PRODUCTS INC	N	−0.61	0.89	−1.50	−0.50	1.00
BIOMAGNETIC TECHNOLOGY	A	−0.29	−0.04	−0.25	−0.25	0.00
BRUNSWICK CORP	N	−0.07	0.20	−0.27	0.00	0.25
CANADA SOUTHERN PETROLEUM	A	−0.02	−0.06	0.04	0.00	0.00
CARLISLE COMPANIES INC	N	0.58	−0.16	0.74	0.50	−0.25
CENTRAL RESERVE LIFE	O	0.22	0.21	0.01	0.25	0.25
CIVIC BANCORP	O	0.30	0.22	0.08	0.25	0.25
COMPUCHEM CORP	O	0.12	0.16	−0.04	0.00	0.25
CONSUMERS' WATER CO	O	0.16	0.42	−0.26	0.25	0.50
COOPER TIRE & RUBBER	N	0.88	0.68	0.20	1.00	0.75
CUTCO INDUSTRIES INC	O	0.20	0.39	−0.19	0.25	0.50
DANA CORP	N	0.49	1.04	−0.55	0.50	1.00
DATA SWITCH CORP	O	0.15	0.13	0.02	0.25	0.25
DIBRELL BROTHERS INC	O	0.48	0.71	−0.23	0.50	0.75
DREXLER TECHNOLOGY CORP	O	−0.23	0.04	−0.27	−0.25	0.00
DURR-FILLAUER MEDICAL	O	0.44	0.45	−0.01	0.50	0.50
EAGLE BANCORP INC	O	0.26	0.55	−0.29	0.25	0.50
FAIRFIELD COUNTY BANC	O	−0.84	0.21	−1.05	−0.75	0.25
FIRST ESSEX BANCORP	O	−0.12	0.21	−0.33	0.00	0.25
FRIEDMAN INDUSTRIES INC	A	0.29	0.42	−0.13	0.25	0.50
FIRST FINANCIAL CORP	O	0.27	0.51	−0.24	0.25	0.50
GENUINE PARTS CO	N	0.70	0.64	0.06	0.75	0.75
GLATFELTER (P.H.) CO	A	0.91	0.96	−0.05	1.00	1.00
GOLDEN VALLEY MICROWAVE	N	0.54	0.40	0.14	0.50	0.50
GRAINGER (W.W) INC	N	1.21	0.94	0.27	1.25	1.00
HASBRO INC	A	0.40	0.36	0.04	0.50	0.25
IEH CORP	O	−0.05	−0.04	−0.01	0.00	0.00
IMAGE RETAILING GROUP	O	0.09	0.11	−0.02	0.00	0.00
IMCO RECYCLING INC	O	0.08	0.16	−0.08	0.00	0.25
INDEPENDENT BANK-MASS	O	−0.07	0.40	−0.47	0.00	0.50
INGLES MARKETS INC	O	0.15	0.17	−0.02	0.25	0.25
INSTRUMENT SYSTEMS	A	0.07	−0.02	0.09	0.00	0.00
INTERMET CORP	O	0.15	0.20	−0.05	0.25	0.25
INTL TOTALIZATOR SYS	O	0.22	0.01	0.21	0.25	0.00
IPCO CORP	N	−0.78	−0.31	−0.47	−0.75	−0.25
INDEX TECHNOLOGY CORP	O	0.10	0.22	−0.12	0.00	0.25

COMPANY	EXCHANGE	LQ89	LQ88	CHANGE	GRLP89	GRLP88
JEFFERSON-PILOT CORP	N	1.09	0.75	0.34	1.00	0.75
K N ENERGY INC	N	0.92	−0.04	0.96	1.00	0.00
KENTUCKY CENTRAL LIFE	O	0.35	0.63	−0.28	0.25	0.75
LINCOLN TELECOMMUNICATION	O	0.40	0.35	0.05	0.50	0.25
LADD FURNITURE INC	O	0.06	0.28	−0.22	0.00	0.25
LANCASTER COLONY CORP	O	0.45	0.40	0.05	0.50	0.50
LUBRIZOL CORP	N	0.43	1.93	−1.50	0.50	2.00
MASS MICROSYSTEMS INC	O	0.05	−0.13	0.18	0.00	−0.25
MAXXAM INC	A	4.74	−0.50	5.24	4.75	−0.50
MONARCH CAPITAL CORP	N	−5.45	0.30	−5.75	−5.50	0.25
NEECO INC	O	0.48	0.34	0.14	0.50	0.25
NEW ENGLAND BANCORP	O	−0.18	0.34	−0.52	−0.25	0.25
NEW LONDON INC	O	0.03	0.03	0.00	0.00	0.00
ONEITA INDUSTRIES	A	0.15	0.04	0.11	0.25	0.00
ORBIT INSTRUMENT CORP	O	0.06	0.03	0.03	0.00	0.00
OREGON STEEL MILLS INC	N	0.66	0.70	−0.04	0.75	0.75
PACIFICORP	N	0.97	0.82	0.15	1.00	0.75
PUGET SOUND POWER & LIGHT	N	0.32	0.57	−0.25	0.25	0.50
PACIFIC SCIENTIFIC CO	N	0.27	−0.74	1.01	0.25	−0.75
PROVIDENT LIFE AND ACCIDENT	O	1.10	0.89	0.21	1.00	1.00
REPUBLIC SAV FINANCIAL	O	0.13	0.11	0.02	0.25	0.00
ROBERT HALF INTL INC	N	0.29	0.26	0.03	0.25	0.25
SAZTEC INTERNATIONAL	O	0.12	0.09	0.03	0.00	0.00
SOUTHERN ELECTRONICS	O	0.38	0.21	0.17	0.50	0.25
SPI PHARMACEUTICALS	A	0.30	0.29	0.01	0.25	0.25
SUNGARD DATA SYSTEMS	O	0.30	0.38	−0.08	0.25	0.50
SYNBIOTICS CORP	O	−0.11	−0.39	0.28	0.00	−0.50
SYNERGEN INC	O	−0.10	−0.21	0.11	0.00	−0.25
THERMAL INDUSTRIES	O	0.10	0.09	0.01	0.00	0.00
TII INDUSTRIES INC	A	−0.23	0.03	−0.26	−0.25	0.00
TIME WARNER INC	N	−3.69	0.97	−4.66	−3.75	1.00
TECHNICAL COMMUNICATIONS	O	0.25	0.90	−0.65	0.25	1.00
TONKA CORP	N	0.13	0.95	−0.82	0.25	1.00
US HOME CORP	N	0.00	0.03	−0.03	0.00	0.00
VENTURA COUNTY NATL BANCORP	O	0.14	0.18	−0.04	0.25	0.25
VALID LOGIC SYSTEMS	O	0.13	0.08	0.05	0.25	0.00
WEDCO TECHNOLOGY INC	A	0.45	0.85	−0.40	0.50	0.75
WESTMARK INTERNATIONAL	O	0.60	0.40	0.20	0.50	0.50
WILLIAMS COMPANIES INC	N	0.53	−0.07	0.60	0.50	0.00
ADAC LABORATORIES	O	0.03	0.09	−0.06	0.00	0.00
AMERICAN COLLOID CO	O	0.32	0.31	0.01	0.25	0.25
ANAREN MICROWAVE INC	O	−0.20	−0.22	0.02	−0.25	−0.25
ANGELES CORP	A	−0.33	0.10	−0.43	−0.25	0.00
ARKLA CORP	N	0.52	0.39	0.13	0.50	0.50
ARROW AUTOMOTIVE INDUSTRIES	A	0.34	−0.10	0.44	0.25	0.00
ASTROTECH INTERNATIONAL	A	0.09	−0.31	0.40	0.00	−0.25
BAYOU STEEL CORP	A	0.06	0.13	−0.07	0.00	0.25
BOSTON CELTICS LIM PARTNERS	N	0.52	0.50	0.02	0.50	0.50
BERNARD CHAUS INC	N	−0.15	0.01	−0.16	−0.25	0.00
BRITISH TELECOMMUNICATIONS	N	0.76	0.66	0.10	0.75	0.75
CAGLE'S INC	A	−0.31	0.20	−0.51	−0.25	0.25
CIRCLE FINE ART CORP	O	0.04	0.17	−0.13	0.00	0.25
COASTAL CORP	N	0.70	−0.02	0.72	0.75	0.00
COOKER RESTAURANT CORP	O	0.04	0.03	0.01	0.00	0.00
DANAHER CORP	N	1.13	0.32	0.81	1.25	0.25
DECOM SYSTEMS INC	O	0.02	0.05	−0.03	0.00	0.00
ENRON CORP	N	1.90	0.34	1.56	2.00	0.25
ENRON OIL & GAS CO	N	0.03	−0.06	0.09	0.00	0.00

COMPANY	EXCHANGE	LQ89	LQ88	CHANGE	GRLP89	GRLP88
FNB ROCHESTER CORP	O	0.34	0.32	0.02	0.25	0.25
GREEN MOUNTAIN POWER	N	0.44	0.52	−0.08	0.50	0.50
GROUP 1 SOFTWARE	O	0.12	0.16	−0.04	0.00	0.25
HEARTLAND EXPRESS INC	O	0.27	0.25	0.02	0.25	0.25
HEMACARE CORP	O	0.04	0.02	0.02	0.00	0.00
HOME BENEFICIAL CORP	O	1.17	1.04	0.13	1.25	1.00
HON INDUSTRIES	O	−0.02	1.01	−1.03	0.00	1.00
HYTEK MICROSYSTEMS INC	O	−0.41	−0.08	−0.33	−0.50	0.00
IDEAL BASIC INDUSTRIES	N	−0.07	−0.04	−0.03	0.00	0.00
INTER-TEL INC	O	0.11	0.03	0.08	0.00	0.00
INTL CONTAINER SYSTEMS	O	−0.05	0.12	−0.17	0.00	0.00
IOWA SOUTHERN INC	O	1.22	0.75	0.47	1.25	0.75
IOWA-ILLINOIS GAS & ELEC	N	0.61	0.52	0.09	0.50	0.50
JORGENSEN (EARLE M.) CO	N	0.57	0.33	0.24	0.50	0.25
KETCHUM & CO	A	−0.56	−0.66	0.10	−0.50	−0.75
LEWIS GALOOB TOYS INC	N	0.44	0.00	0.44	0.50	0.00
LUND INTL HOLDINGS	O	0.08	0.10	−0.02	0.00	0.00
MEDEX INC	O	0.19	0.20	−0.01	0.25	0.25
MIDWEST COMMUNICATIONS	O	0.10	0.11	−0.01	0.00	0.00
MITEL CORP	N	0.03	0.04	−0.01	0.00	0.00
MORRISON KNUDSEN CORP	N	0.93	−2.59	3.52	1.00	−2.50
MOUNTAIN MEDICAL EQUIP	A	−0.38	0.13	−0.51	−0.50	0.25
NATIONAL PIZZA CO	O	0.25	0.15	0.10	0.25	0.25
OHM CORP	N	0.14	0.64	−0.50	0.25	0.75
PARLEX CORP	O	−0.16	−0.65	0.49	−0.25	−0.75
PEOPLES SAVINGS BK BROCKTON	O	0.13	0.83	−0.70	0.25	0.75
PERSONAL DIAGNOSTICS	O	0.10	0.07	0.03	0.00	0.00
PLASTI-LINE INC	O	0.23	0.25	−0.02	0.25	0.25
PROGRESSIVE CORP	N	0.03	0.96	−0.93	0.00	1.00
PROSPECT GROUP INC	O	−0.57	0.91	−1.48	−0.50	1.00
PROVIDENCE ENERGY CORP	A	1.10	0.61	0.49	1.00	0.50
PRUDENTIAL REALTY TRUST	N	0.07	0.08	−0.01	0.00	0.00
ROCHESTER TELEPHONE	N	0.45	0.59	−0.14	0.50	0.50
SERVICE FRACTURING CO	O	−0.02	−0.11	0.09	0.00	0.00
SMITH INTERNATIONAL	N	−0.06	0.00	−0.06	0.00	0.00
TRAVELERS CORP	N	1.42	2.47	−1.05	1.50	2.50
TRISTATE BANCORP	O	0.46	0.52	−0.06	0.50	0.50
UNIVERSITY NATL BANK & TRUST	O	0.64	0.73	−0.09	0.75	0.75
UNUM CORP	N	1.07	0.89	0.18	1.00	1.00
VALLEY INDUSTRIES INC	N	−0.14	0.01	−0.15	−0.25	0.00
VERSAR INC	A	−0.08	0.03	−0.11	0.00	0.00
WEBSTER FINANCIAL CORP	O	−0.22	0.34	−0.56	−0.25	0.25
WISCONSIN PUBLIC SERVICE	N	0.56	0.60	−0.04	0.50	0.50
ABATIX ENVIRONMENTAL	O	0.06	0.01	0.05	0.00	0.00
ACUSON CORP	N	0.44	0.35	0.09	0.50	0.25
AETNA LIFE & CASUALTY	N	1.35	1.85	−0.50	1.25	1.75
AIRGAS INC	N	5.23	1.34	3.89	5.25	1.25
ALDUS CORP	O	0.36	0.34	0.02	0.25	0.25
AMERICAN MEDICAL ELECT	O	0.02	0.07	−0.05	0.00	0.00
AMERICAN TECH CERAMICS	A	−0.10	0.03	−0.13	0.00	0.00
ANDAL CORP	A	−0.08	−0.03	−0.05	0.00	0.00
ATLAS CORP	N	0.22	0.26	−0.04	0.25	0.25
ATMOS ENERGY CORP	N	0.81	0.71	0.10	0.75	0.75
AVONDALE INDUSTRIES	O	−0.11	0.19	−0.30	0.00	0.25
BERKSHIRE GAS	O	−0.55	−0.33	−0.22	−0.50	−0.25
BOWMAR INSTRUMENT CORP	A	−0.03	−0.05	0.02	0.00	0.00
BIO-RAD LABORATORIES	A	0.22	0.24	−0.02	0.25	0.25
BISCAYNE HOLDINGS INC	A	0.04	1.20	−1.16	0.00	1.25

COMPANY	EXCHANGE	LQ89	LQ88	CHANGE	GRLP89	GRLP88
BRITISH AIRWAYS PLC	N	0.64	0.46	0.18	0.75	0.50
CBS INC	N	2.31	1.56	0.75	2.25	1.50
CERNER CORP	O	0.33	0.16	0.17	0.25	0.25
CHANDLER INSURANCE CO	O	0.50	0.35	0.15	0.50	0.25
CNA FINANCIAL CORP	N	0.85	2.29	−1.44	0.75	2.25
CONSOLIDATED FIBRES	N	0.08	0.14	−0.06	0.00	0.25
CONTINENTAL CORP	N	1.30	−2.01	3.31	1.25	−2.00
CSC INDUSTRIES INC	O	−1.60	0.15	−1.75	−1.50	0.25
CURTISS-WRIGHT CORP	N	0.33	1.52	−1.19	0.25	1.50
DOTRONIX INC	O	−0.24	0.08	−0.32	−0.25	0.00
DBA SYSTEMS INC	O	−3.75	0.45	−4.20	−3.75	0.50
DIGITAL SOLUTIONS INC	O	−0.02	−0.03	0.01	0.00	0.00
EASTERN ENVIRONMENTAL SERVICES	O	0.03	0.07	−0.04	0.00	0.00
ELAN CORP	A	0.05	0.03	0.02	0.00	0.00
ELDON INDUSTRIES INC	N	0.25	0.21	0.04	0.25	0.25
ENCLEAN INC	O	0.20	0.19	0.01	0.25	0.25
ENTERGY CORP	N	0.08	0.29	−0.21	0.00	0.25
FAB INDUSTRIES INC	A	0.80	0.75	0.05	0.75	0.75
FEDERAL MOGUL CORP	N	0.04	0.38	−0.34	0.00	0.50
FIRST AMARILLO BANCORP	O	0.15	0.05	0.10	0.25	0.00
FLANIGAN'S ENTERPRISES	A	0.52	0.25	0.27	0.50	0.25
FLEXTRONICS INC	O	−0.58	−0.46	−0.12	−0.50	−0.50
FORUM GROUP INC	O	−0.04	−0.07	0.03	0.00	0.00
FREMONT GENERAL CORP	O	1.12	0.04	1.08	1.00	0.00
FROZEN FOOD EXPRESS INDS	A	0.08	0.23	−0.15	0.00	0.25
GEO INTERNATIONAL CORP	N	0.01	−0.10	0.11	0.00	0.00
GORMAN-RUPP CO	A	0.20	0.01	0.19	0.25	0.00
GUEST SUPPLY INC	O	−0.12	−0.05	−0.07	0.00	0.00
HALIFAX ENGINEERING	A	−0.29	0.17	−0.46	−0.25	0.25
HALL (FRANK B.) & CO	N	−0.28	−0.78	0.50	−0.25	−0.75
HEALTH & REHAB PROP TRUST	N	0.19	0.18	0.01	0.25	0.25
HEALTHSOURCE INC	O	0.28	0.11	0.17	0.25	0.00
HEI CORP	O	0.12	0.07	0.05	0.00	0.00
HERITAGE MEDIA CORP	A	−0.08	−0.23	0.15	0.00	−0.25
INFORMIX CORP	O	0.20	−0.21	0.41	0.25	−0.25
JACKPOT ENTERPRISES	N	0.13	0.29	−0.16	0.25	0.25
JWP INC	N	0.53	0.42	0.11	0.50	0.50
KATY INDUSTRIES INC	N	0.34	0.44	−0.10	0.25	0.50
KINETIC CONCEPTS INC	O	0.12	0.15	−0.03	0.00	0.25
KNOWLEDGE DATA SYSTEMS	O	0.01	0.00	0.01	0.00	0.00
LESLIE FAY COMPANIES	N	0.13	0.24	−0.11	0.25	0.25
MCDERMOTT INTERNATIONAL	N	1.14	−0.86	2.00	1.25	−0.75
MECHANICAL TECHNOLOGY	O	−0.16	0.26	−0.42	−0.25	0.25
MICKELBERRY CORP	N	−0.01	−0.13	0.12	0.00	−0.25
MOSCOM CORP	O	0.17	0.09	0.08	0.25	0.00
NATIONAL HERITAGE INC	N	0.03	0.10	−0.07	0.00	0.00
NORTH AMERICAN NATIONAL	O	0.18	0.15	0.03	0.25	0.25
OPTICAL RADIATION CORP	O	0.35	0.24	0.11	0.25	0.25
PAY-FONE SYSTEMS INC	A	0.01	−0.02	0.03	0.00	0.00
PAYCO AMERICAN CORP	O	0.17	0.11	0.06	0.25	0.00
PRICOR INC	O	0.03	−0.01	0.04	0.00	0.00
QUESTAR CORP	N	0.84	0.72	0.12	0.75	0.75
RENAISSANCE GRX INC	O	−0.17	−0.33	0.16	−0.25	−0.25
ROPAK CORP	O	−0.03	0.14	−0.17	0.00	0.25
SANMARK-STARDUST INC	A	0.02	0.11	−0.09	0.00	0.00
SOMERSET GROUP INC	O	−0.60	0.18	−0.78	−0.50	0.25
SENSOR CONTROL CORP	O	0.07	0.07	0.00	0.00	0.00
SOUTHWESTERN ENERGY CO	N	0.73	0.60	0.13	0.75	0.50

818   APPENDIX TABLES

COMPANY	EXCHANGE	LQ89	LQ88	CHANGE	GRLP89	GRLP88
TRANSAMERICA CORP	N	0.95	0.73	0.22	1.00	0.75
THERMO ELECTRON CORP	N	0.41	0.35	0.06	0.50	0.25
THERMO CARDIOSYSTEMS	A	0.00	0.00	0.00	0.00	0.00
TWO PESOS INC	A	−0.06	−0.52	0.46	0.00	−0.50
VERDIX CORP	O	0.06	0.05	0.01	0.00	0.00
VIACOM INC	A	−0.55	−0.49	−0.06	−0.50	−0.50
VIKONICS INC	O	−0.27	−0.13	−0.14	−0.25	−0.25
WOLOHAN LUMBER	O	0.35	0.45	−0.10	0.25	0.50
WPL HOLDINGS INC	N	0.72	0.47	0.25	0.75	0.50
YORK RESEARCH CORP	O	0.09	0.06	0.03	0.00	0.00

Answers to Chapter Concepts Tests

CHAPTER 2

1. T	16. F	31. c
2. T	17. T	32. e
3. F	18. F	33. e
4. F	19. T	34. e
5. T	20. F	35. e
6. T	21. F	36. b
7. T	22. d	37. incomplete, biased
8. T	23. b	38. representative
9. F	24. a	39. data array, frequency distribution
10. F	25. c	40. population, sample
11. F	26. c	41. frequency
12. F	27. a	42. discrete, continuous
13. T	28. d	43. fractions, percentages
14. T	29. b	44. ogive
15. F	30. e	45. data point

CHAPTER 3

1. F	19. T	37. b	55. f
2. T	20. F	38. a	56. e
3. F	21. T	39. b	57. symmetrical, skewed
4. F	22. T	40. c	58. sample, population
5. F	23. F	41. d	59. coding
6. T	24. T	42. b	60. geometric, arithmetic
7. T	25. F	43. c	61. bimodal
8. F	26. T	44. e	62. dispersion
9. T	27. F	45. f	63. fractile
10. F	28. T	46. e	64. interquartile
11. T	29. T	47. c	65. variance, standard
12. F	30. F	48. c	deviation
13. T	31. T	49. a	66. coefficient of variation
14. F	32. T	50. a	67. standard score
15. F	33. F	51. c	68. percentiles
16. F	34. F	52. d	69. d
17. F	35. c	53. d	70. b
18. T	36. d	54. e	

CHAPTER 4

1. F	16. F	31. d
2. F	17. T	32. c
3. T	18. F	33. c
4. T	19. F	34. e
5. T	20. T	35. e
6. F	21. F	36. d
7. F	22. b	37. event, experiment
8. T	23. d	38. sample space
9. T	24. c	39. Venn diagram
10. T	25. b	40. mutually exclusive
11. F	26. c	41. conditional
12. F	27. b	42. subjective approach
13. F	28. e	43. Bayes's
14. T	29. a	44. collectively exhaustive
15. T	30. d	45. classical, relative frequency, subjective

CHAPTER 5

1. F	16. F	31. c
2. F	17. F	32. e
3. T	18. F	33. 12.7
4. F	19. F	34. c
5. T	20. T	35. d
6. T	21. T	36. f
7. F	22. e	37. expected value
8. F	23. d	38. binomial, Bernoulli
9. F	24. d	39. continuity
10. T	25. e	40. np, $\sqrt{npq}$
11. T	26. b	41. λ (lambda)
12. F	27. a	42. probability distribution
13. T	28. d	43. mean, standard deviation
14. F	29. d	44. random
15. F	30. c	45. discrete, continuous

CHAPTER 6

1. T	16. T	31. d
2. F	17. T	32. e
3. F	18. T	33. d
4. F	19. T	34. d
5. T	20. F	35. d
6. T	21. T	36. b
7. T	22. d	37. sample
8. F	23. b	38. sampling fraction
9. T	24. e	39. statistical inference
10. F	25. e	40. theoretical sampling distribution
11. T	26. d	41. stratified
12. F	27. b	42. systematic
13. T	28. a	43. Precision
14. F	29. c	44. clusters
15. F	30. b	45. sample proportions

CHAPTER 7

1. F	16. F	31. d
2. F	17. T	32. e
3. T	18. F	33. d
4. T	19. T	34. e
5. F	20. F	35. d
6. F	21. T	36. b
7. T	22. F	37. d
8. T	23. e	38. point
9. T	24. b	39. interval
10. T	25. a	40. degrees of freedom
11. T	26. c	41. Student's t-distribution
12. F	27. e	42. confidence
13. T	28. d	43. distance, mean
14. T	29. a	44. binomial
15. F	30. a	45. $p = .5$

CHAPTER 8

1. F	16. F	31. b
2. T	17. F	32. c
3. F	18. T	33. a
4. T	19. F	34. a
5. T	20. T	35. a
6. F	21. F	36. f
7. T	22. F	37. d
8. T	23. T	38. b
9. T	24. T	39. one
10. F	25. d	40. reject, null, false
11. F	26. b	41. hypothesis
12. F	27. a	42. II, β (beta)
13. F	28. c	43. null, alternative
14. F	29. c	44. paired
15. T	30. b	45. tailed
		46. upper-tailed (or right-tailed)

CHAPTER 9

1. T	16. T	31. c
2. T	17. F	32. a
3. F	18. T	33. a
4. T	19. T	34. e
5. T	20. F	35. c
6. F	21. T	36. e
7. T	22. b	37. f
8. T	23. a	38. grand
9. T	24. d	39. analysis of variance (ANOVA)
10. F	25. e	40. independence
11. T	26. c	41. F
12. F	27. b	42. goodness-of-fit
13. T	28. d	43. within-column variance, between-column variance, F
14. F	29. c	44. lower, $100(1 - \alpha)$
15. F	30. e	45. number of samples, total sample size

CHAPTER 10

1. F	16. F	31. b
2. F	17. F	32. d
3. F	18. F	33. d
4. F	19. T	34. b
5. T	20. T	35. d
6. T	21. F	36. e
7. T	22. d	37. inverse
8. T	23. a	38. curvilinear
9. F	24. a	39. slope
10. T	25. e	40. standard error of estimate
11. F	26. b	41. r^2, the coefficient of determination
12. T	27. c	
13. T	28. d	42. ± 0.866
14. T	29. a	43. Correlation analysis
15. F	30. c	44. direction (direct or inverse)
		45. minimizes

CHAPTER 11

1. T	16. F	31. b
2. F	17. F	32. d
3. T	18. F	33. e (or perhaps d)
4. T	19. F	34. b
5. F	20. T	35. c
6. T	21. T	36. c
7. T	22. c	37. modeling techniques
8. T	23. b	38. transformations
9. F	24. d	39. (computed) F-ratio
10. T	25. b	40. dummy
11. T	26. a	41. standard error
12. F	27. c	42. fraction of the variation in Y explained by the regression
13. F	28. d	
14. F	29. b	43. $B_1 = B_2 = \ldots = B_k = 0$
15. T	30. a	44. root-mean-square error
		45. residuals

CHAPTER 12

1. T 16. T 31. d
2. F 17. T 32. f
3. T 18. F 33. d
4. T 19. F 34. d
5. F 20. T 35. b
6. T 21. T 36. c
7. F 22. c 37. run
8. T 23. b 38. Mann-Whitney U-test
9. T 24. a 39. one-sample runs test
10. F 25. b 40. sign
11. T 26. d 41. rank correlation
12. F 27. b 42. the sample sizes are unequal
13. F 28. c 43. r_s
14. T 29. a 44. distribution free
15. T 30. b 45. Kolmogorov-Smirnov

CHAPTER 13

1. T 16. F 31. c
2. T 17. T 32. d
3. F 18. T 33. f
4. F 19. F 34. b
5. F 20. F 35. d
6. F 21. T 36. d
7. T 22. e 37. percent of trend
8. F 23. c 38. seasonal
9. F 24. a 39. irregular
10. F 25. b 40. Cyclical
11. T 26. d 41. deseasonalizing
12. T 27. d 42. four-quarter moving total
13. T 28. c 43. secular trend
14. F 29. b 44. modified mean
15. T 30. a 45. forecast

CHAPTER 14

1. F 16. T 31. c
2. T 17. F 32. e
3. T 18. F 33. d
4. F 19. T 34. b
5. F 20. F 35. a
6. T 21. F 36. d
7. T 22. a 37. a
8. T 23. c 38. unweighted
9. T 24. e 39. Laspeyres
10. F 25. e 40. aggregate
11. T 26. c 41. fixed weight
12. T 27. d 42. Paasche
13. F 28. b 43. error, change
14. T 29. a 44. price, quantity, value
15. F 30. b 45. percentage relative (or index number)

CHAPTER 15

1. F 16. T 31. d
2. T 17. F 32. d
3. F 18. T 33. d
4. F 19. F 34. e
5. T 20. T 35. d
6. T 21. F 36. b
7. F 22. e 37. outcomes, states
8. T 23. a 38. expected value of perfect information or EVPI
9. T 24. b 39. opportunity, obsolescence
10. F 25. c 40. utility
11. F 26. d 41. rollback
12. T 27. c 42. negative
13. T 28. e 43. obsolescence (or marginal)
14. T 29. b 44. sensitivity analysis
15. F 30. a 45. left, right; right, left

Answers to Selected Even-Numbered Exercises

CHAPTER 2

2-2 Since the Department of Commerce keeps statistics on all the cars sold in the U.S., this conclusion is drawn from a *population*.

2-4 On the basis of German history since the end of World War II, and given the bias produced by his own strong belief in the validity of Communism, Ulbricht was unable to foresee the possibility of the changes that resulted from Gorbachev's hands-off policy toward the eastern European satellite nations.

2-6 No conclusions follow easily from the data in their current form. Some rearrangement, such as listing in ascending order or finding the most frequent pair, might help in drawing conclusions.

2-8 No. In this case, the raw data would be a list of sample units indicating which were defective. The quality control section has already done some analysis in calculating the averages contained in the report.

2-10 In addition to the 7 stores with under 475 service actions which are not breaking even, another 6 stores fall on the "store watch list."

2-12

7 INTERVALS:		13 INTERVALS:			
Age	Frequency	Age	Frequency	Age	Frequency
30–39	.02	35–39	.02	70–74	.10
40–49	.06	40–44	.04	75–79	.10
50–59	.16	45–49	.02	80–84	.12
60–69	.32	50–54	.08	85–89	.04
70–79	.20	55–59	.08	90–94	.04
80–89	.16	60–64	.10	95–99	.04
90–99	.08	65–69	.22		1.00
	1.00				

(a) Either distribution shows approximately 90% older than 50; the program is not in compliance.

(b) Both are equally easy to use.

(c) The 13-interval distribution gives a better estimate because it has a class for 45–49, whereas the 7-interval distribution lumps together all observations between 40 and 49.

2-14   From these arrays, we can see that high GPAs at one level tend to go with high GPAs at the other.

2-16   (a)

SPREAD	SAT DIFFERENTIAL	SPREAD	SAT DIFFERENTIAL
1.3	140	0.1	− 20
0.8	150	0.0	10
0.6	60	−0.1	− 10
0.4	60	−0.2	20
0.3	60	−0.2	0
0.3	50	−0.5	− 30
0.2	0	−0.5	− 90
0.1	20	−0.6	− 120
0.1	− 10	−0.7	− 100
0.1	− 10	−1.1	− 120

(b) 0.1
(c) − 10
(d) High (low) spreads and high (low) SAT differentials tend to go together, so the SAT differential appears to be a good indicator of spread.

2-18

PRESSURE (lbs./sq. in.)	RELATIVE FREQUENCY
2,490.0–2,493.9	.150
2,494.0–2,497.9	.175
2,498.0–2,501.9	.325
2,502.0–2,505.9	.225
2,506.0–2,509.9	.125
	1.000

The greatest number of samples (32.5%) fell in class 2,498.0–2,501.9 lbs./sq. in.

2-20   (a) Before:

BOXES BOUGHT	FREQUENCY	RELATIVE FREQUENCY
1–2	5	.25
3–4	6	.30
5–6	7	.35
7–8	2	.10
9–10	0	.00
	20	1.00

(b) After:

BOXES BOUGHT	FREQUENCY	RELATIVE FREQUENCY
1–2	2	.10
3–4	4	.20
5–6	6	.30
7–8	6	.30
9–10	2	.10
	20	1.00

(c) In order to be able to compare the two distributions.

(d)

"CHANGE" CLASS	FREQUENCY	RELATIVE FREQUENCY
-5 to -4	1	.05
-3 to -2	0	.00
-1 to 0	5	.25
1 to 2	8	.40
3 to 4	5	.25
5 to 6	1	.05
	20	1.00

(e) Sales appear to have increased, but the apparent increase could be due to other factors we don't know about, so we can't say for sure that the new slogan has helped.

2-22

Age	<25	25-34	35-44	45-54	≥55
Frequency	6	9	7	3	5
Relative Frequency	.200	.300	.233	.100	.167

(a) Most purchasers are under 45.
(b) About 75% of the purchasers are under 45.

2-24 (a) No, not enough classes in relevant ranges.
(b) Five classes with midpoints at 25, 27, 29, 31, and 33.

2-26 Closed: single, married, divorced, separated, widowed
Open: single, married, other

2-28 The classes are <85, $85 - 114$, $115 - 144$, and ≥ 145 dB. Since the group wants to highlight the noisy flights, this distribution is not adequate because the 115-144 class includes noise levels on both sides of the 140 dB limit.

2-30 (a)

WAITING TIME (DAYS)	FREQUENCY
22-24	3
25-27	3
28-30	6
31-33	12
34-36	8
37-39	6
40-42	5
43-45	4
46-48	2
49-51	1
	50

(b)

WAITING TIME (DAYS)	FREQUENCY
22-27	6
28-33	18
34-39	14
40-45	9
46-51	3
	50

(c) Yes, he wants to know the relative proportions at each level.

2-32 (a) Discrete and closed
(b) Discrete and closed
(c) Flavor is qualitative, amount is quantitative.
(d) Collect data on how often stores run out of each flavor and how much of each is left over.

2-34

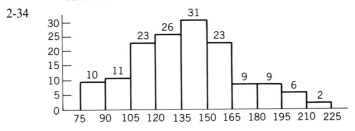

(a) The lower tail of the distribution is fatter than the upper.
(b) Pair each person who appears to be heavy (≥180 pounds) with a lighter person.

2-36

CLASS	FREQUENCY	CUMULATIVE RELATIVE FREQUENCY
2,000–3,999	3	.15
4,000–5,999	7	.50
6,000–7,999	7	.85
8,000–9,999	3	1.00

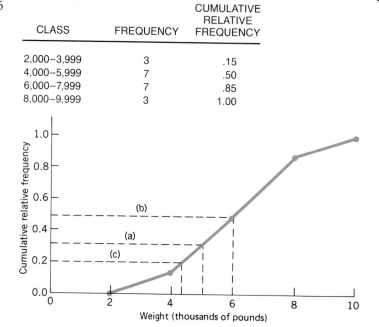

(a) About 65% break even, that is, catch 5000 pounds or more.
(b) Approximately 6,000 pounds
(c) Approximately 4,300 pounds

2-38 (a)

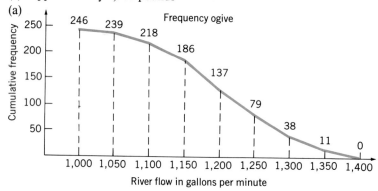

River flow more than	1000	1050	1100	1150	1200	1250	1300	1350	1400
Cumulative frequency	246	239	218	186	137	79	38	11	0

(b)

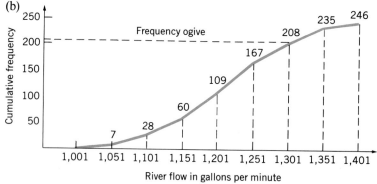

River flow less than	1001	1051	1101	1151	1201	1251	1301	1351	1401
Cumulative frequency	0	7	28	60	109	167	208	235	246

(c) about 85%

2-40   (b)

MINUTES	FREQUENCY	CUMULATIVE FREQUENCY	MINUTES	FREQUENCY	CUMULATIVE FREQUENCY
19.0–19.7	4	4	22.2–22.9	7	30
19.8–20.5	4	8	23.0–23.7	5	35
20.6–21.3	10	18	23.8–24.5	11	46
21.4–22.1	5	23	24.6–25.3	4	50

(c)

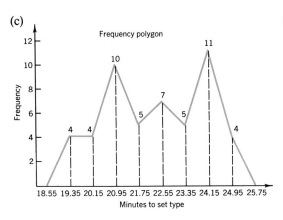

(d)

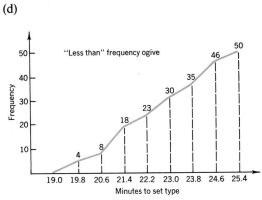

(e) About 78% of the time.

2-42

EARNINGS	FREQUENCY	CUMULATIVE FREQUENCY	EARNINGS	FREQUENCY	CUMULATIVE FREQUENCY
≤$50,000	5	.038	20,001–30,000	37	.731
$ 5,001–10,000	9	.108	30,001–40,000	19	.877
10,001–15,000	11	.192	40,001–50,000	9	.946
15,001–20,000	33	.446	≥50,001	7	1.000
			Total	130	

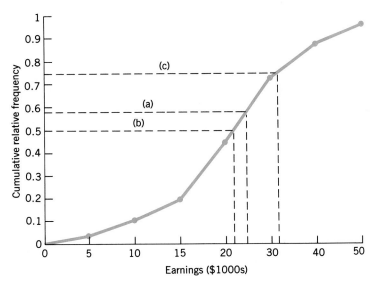

(a) about 42%   (b) about $22,000   (c) about $31,000

2-44　By grouping those of the same educational level together, we can more clearly see group differences associated with educational level:

EDUCATIONAL LEVEL	SALARY RANGE
Did not finish high school	$14,400 – 17,600
High school graduates	17,000 – 30,400
One or two years of college	14,400 – 22,400
College graduates	19,600 – 34,400
Master's degrees	23,200 – 36,200
Ph.D. degrees	29,000 – 64,000
Doctors and lawyers	52,000 –100,000

2-46　(a) 1.9　1.8　1.7　1.6　1.5　1.5　1.5　1.5　1.2　0.9
　　　　　0.9　0.9　0.9　0.8　0.7　0.7　0.5　0.4　0.4　0.3

(b)

GROWTH (inches)	FREQUENCY	RELATIVE FREQUENCY	CUMULATIVE RELATIVE FREQUENCY
0.000–0.249	0	.00	.00
0.250–0.499	3	.15	.15
0.500–0.749	3	.15	.30
0.750–0.999	5	.25	.55
1.000–1.249	1	.05	.60
1.250–1.499	0	.00	.60
1.500–1.749	6	.30	.90
1.750–1.999	2	.10	1.00

(c) The data are distinctly bimodal, with modal classes 0.750–0.999 and 1.500–1.749.

(d)

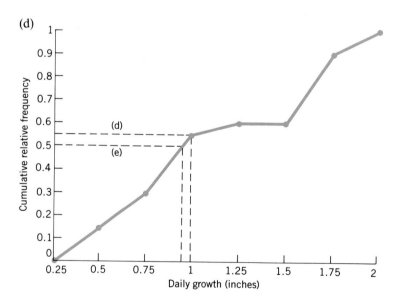

About 45% grew more than 1.0 inches per week.

(e) About .95 inches.

2-48   The 5 classes used are 9,700–9,899 units, 9,900–10,099 units, . . . , 10,500–10,699 units, with cumulative relative frequencies .200, .733, .867, .867, and 1.000.

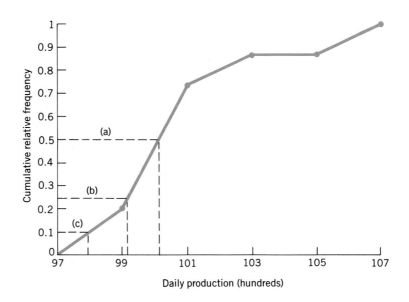

(a) About 50% (7 or 8 items) exceeded the breakeven point.
(b) About 9,900 units.
(c) About 9,800 units.

2-50   It tells you what fraction of the observations fit in each class, making it easier to compare samples or populations of different sizes.

2-52   2,000/(2,000 + 8,000) = .2; .2(250) = 50 women

2-54   Histogram

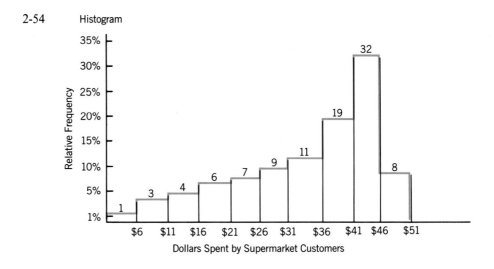

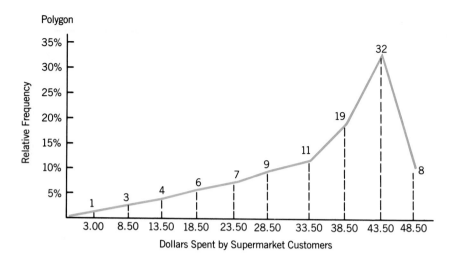

2-56   (a)

MILES/DAY	FREQUENCY	CUM. REL. FREQUENCY
1.00–1.39	32	0.035
1.40–1.79	43	0.081
1.80–2.19	81	0.168
2.20–2.59	122	0.300
2.60–2.99	131	0.441
3.00–3.39	130	0.581
3.40–3.79	111	0.701
3.80–4.19	95	0.804
4.20–4.59	82	0.892
4.60–4.99	47	0.943
5.00 and up	53	1.000

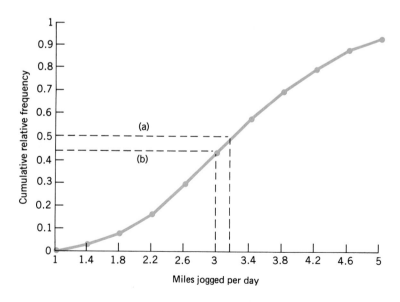

(a) About 3.20 miles per day.   (b) About 56% run at least 3 miles per day.

2-58   510, 930, 810, 630, and 120

2-60   Only 880 of 2,000 questions were returned.
    (a) With only a 44% response rate, the data may be biased. We have no way of telling if those who respond are representative of the population as a whole.
    (b) So far as we know, there is no other evidence available.
    (c) Yes, we are missing the data from the 56% who didn't reply.
    (d) 880; no, they don't represent those individuals who chose not to respond.
    (e) No conclusions are given in the example.

2-62   Rounding to avoid inconvenient values like $2.995, the midpoints for the first nine classes are $3, $8.50, $13.50, $18.50, $23.50, $28.50, $33.50, $38.50, and $43.50. The open uppermost class has no midpoint.

2-64   Yes and no. It is not raw data, because the scores are composites of other values. The raw data would be the individual scores on tests, homework, and papers. However, if someone were interested in doing some analysis on final grades, it would be raw data for that purpose.

2-66   (a) 0–4,999, 5,000–9,999, . . . , 30,000–34,999 is one possible set of intervals to use. Another possibility is 0–5,000, 5,001–10,000, . . . , 30,001–35,000.
    (b) under 10,000, 10,000–14,999, . . . , 25,000–29,999, 30,000 and over is one possibility. Another possibility is 10,000 and under, 10,001–15,000, . . . , 25,001–30,000, over 30,000.

2-68   (b) 16 above the limit, 18 below, 1 exactly at
    (c)

Class (minutes)	60–69	70–79	80–89	90–99	100–109	110–119	120–129	130–139
Frequency	2	2	3	6	6	11	4	1
Relative Frequency	.057	.057	.086	.171	.171	.314	.114	.029

    (d) If 108 minutes is typical, then about half should be above 108 and half below. The data support this. Since we don't know how much downtime per shift is viewed as excessive, we cannot tell if Cline should be concerned or not.

2-70   (b) 92%; 4%
    (c) 64%; stop ordering from the new supplier

2-72   (b) 1.

Class (sales)	1	2	3	4	5	6	7	8	9
Frequency	10	3	4	1	4	2	2	1	1
Relative Frequency	.357	.107	.143	.036	.143	.071	.071	.036	.036

    2.

Class (sales)	1–3	4–6	7–9
Frequency	17	7	4
Relative Frequency	.607	.250	.143

    Both distributions are skewed: many countries have relatively few sales, and then the distribution tails off to the right.

2-74   (a) 4600–5199, 5200–5799, 5800–6399, 6400–6999, 7000–7599, and 7600–8199.
    (b) 0.00–1.39, 1.40–2.79, 2.80–4.19, 4.20–5.59, 5.60–6.99, and 7.00–8.39.

2-76   (a) 13.1%   (b) 47.5%

CHAPTER 3

3-2

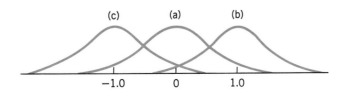

3-4 (a) B (b) A (c) A (d) B (e) B (f) A (g) neither

3-6 $\bar{x} = 9.091$; they don't qualify

3-8 (a)

Age	40–49	50–59	60–69	70–79	80–89
Frequency	4	4	3	2	7

(b) 67 (c) 66.75
(d) As expected, they are close, but not exactly the same.

3-10 $\bar{x} = \$68,967$; it does qualify.

3-12 $\bar{x} = 23.295$ seconds: the manager should be concerned.

3-14 (a) Q1: 20, Q2: 10, Q3: 30, Q4: 25 (all values in thousands of dollars)
(b) Y1: 13.75, Y2: 15, Y3: 35
(c) all three of the averages mentioned are equal to 21.25

3-16 88.55 87.75 89.55 86.65 88.50

3-18 2.021 times

3-20 $0.1162 per ounce

3-22 7.58% per year

3-24 8.98% per year: 22,819 units

3-26 7.24% per week

3-28 4.66% per year; $75.66

3-30 (a) 722.5 miles (b) 709.1 miles (c) both equally good

3-32 (a) 300–349.5 (b) average of 150th and 151st
(c) .6944 (d) 326.7344

3-34 median = 31 minutes; speeds are not excessive

3-36 $877.54

3-38 (a) 6 (b) 5.8 (c) mean is better

3-40 (a) Brunette (b) A (c) Wednesday and Saturday

3-42 $928.57

3-44 (a) $1,000–1,499 (b) $1,240 (c) approximately 628

3-46 a, because the values tend to cluster closer to the mean

3-48 c

3-50 There are many ways that the concept may be involved. Certainly, the FTC would examine the price variability for the industry and compare the result to that of the suspect companies. The agency might examine price distributions for similar products, for the same products in a city, or for the same products in different cities. If the variability was significantly different in any of these cases, this result might constitute evidence of a conspiracy to set prices at the same levels.

3-52 The range is $185–$51 = $134. It is not particularly useful, because all the rest of the data falls between $83 and $157. The range greatly overstates the typical variability, because it is determined by two outliers in the data set.

3-54 29

3-56 range: 1.10 minutes interquartile range: .32 minutes

3-58 range: 16,700 miles interquartile range: 4,600 miles

3-60 (a) 410 (b) 236.5 (c) 276

3-62 The standard deviation of 3.1 boats represents an unacceptable level of variability.

3-64 With a standard deviation of 242.5 checks per day, he should worry.

3-66 (a) $\bar{x} = 7.715$ days, $s = 4.69$ days
(b) 150 expected, something between 182 and 191 observed.
(c) 191 expected

3-68 5 weeks; 1 week

3-70

Product	1	2	3
Standard score	−1.25	−1.67	2.22

Product 3 is farthest from average.

3-72 $390,000 \pm \$20,000$

3-74

Team	Bullets	Trailblazers
CV	8.04%	6.15%

The Bullets' weights have the greater CV.

3-76

Program	Regular	Evening
CV	10.02%	9.46%

There isn't much difference between the two groups.

3-78

Company	1	2
CV	18.93%	12.70%

Company 1 pursued the riskier strategy.

3-80

Retailer	Lee	Forrest	Davis
CV	1.20%	1.49%	1.56%

Lee would be slightly better, but there really isn't much difference.

3-82

Configuration	I	II	III
CV	13.79%	29.41%	10.13%

Configuration III has least relative variation.

3-84   The statement is incorrect, because it completely ignores the variability in yards gained per carry.

3-86   Officer salaries: A, aircraft maintenance: C, food purchases: B

3-88   The company may be hiring less experienced sales reps while its established sales reps are increasing their sales levels. Another possibility is that it is simultaneously hiring inexperienced and highly experienced sales reps.

3-90   The later period has both a higher mean and more variability.

3-92   Range = 128 pounds, s^2 = 1,439.46 pounds squared, s = 37.94 pounds. The data are reasonably well spread out over the entire range, so it's not a bad measure of the variability in this case.

3-94   Interquartile range = $0.08, s^2 = .0056 dollars squared, s = $0.0748. However you measure it, the variability in average heating fuel price across the eight states is quite small.

3-96   (a) $\bar{x}$ = 143, s = 5.28
      (b) 11 or 12 expected, 15 observed

3-98   (a) range = 38,200, s^2 = 100,619,121, s = 10,031
      (b) s is a good measure of the variability.
      (c) In isolation, no other is needed. However, to compare the Eagles with other teams, we could look at the coefficient of variation.
      (d) CV = 37.22%

3-100   (a) 10 days   (b) 7.5 days

3-102   The weekly news magazines would probably have the highest average readerships, the medical journals the smallest average readerships, with the monthly magazines somewhere in the middle.
Monthly magazines and medical journals with many low circulation items and few high circulation items are likely to be skewed to the right. There are only a few weekly news magazines, so it's difficult to assess the skewness of this distribution.

3-104   (a) 5.51 mpg   (b) 5.5325 mpg

Class (mpg)	4.77–5.03	5.04–5.30	5.31–5.57	5.58–5.84	5.85–6.11
Frequency	4	4	0	1	7

       The modal class is 5.85–6.11 mpg.
      (d) It depends. If she is ordering fuel for only one car, she should be cautious and use the modal value. If she is ordering fuel for several cars running in the same race, the mean or median is probably ok.

3-106   (a) mean = 35.4 bulbs, median = 35 bulbs
      (b) Skewed right

3-108   (a) median = 4.32mm; modal class = 4.01–4.50mm
      (b) 3.5mm screen

CHAPTER 4

4-2   Extensive tests with animals indicated (with other factors held as constant as possible) that subjects which consumed saccharin were more likely to develop cancer than those not exposed to saccharin. Extrapolating these results to humans, it was concluded that saccharin consumption produces an increased risk of cancer.

4-4   This decision involves estimates of consumer preference, brand loyalty, competitor response, and numerous other factors, all involving uncertainty. Hence the estimates are based on probabilities.

4-6   (1) b and d   (2) a, b, and d

4-8   0, 1/36, 4/36, 5/36, 6/36, 3/36, and 2/36

4-10   (a) They are collectively exhaustive, but not mutually exclusive.
        (b) There are 17 possible subsets of the set of target segments which can be covered within the $800,000 budget:

M	Bu	W	P	Bl	M, W	M, P
M, Bl	M, W, P	M, P, Bl	Bu, W	Bu, P	Bu, Bl	W, P
W, Bl	W, P, Bl	P, Bl				

        (c) The only subsets for which the entire budget is spent are:
           Bu, W   Bu, Bl   M, W, P   M, P, Bl

4-12   (a) 1/13   (b) 1/2   (c) 2/13   (d) 1/13   (e) 3/26
        These are classical probabilities.

4-14

Interval	.00–.24	.25–.49	.50–.74	.75–.99	1.00
Probability	0.00	0.20	0.50	0.25	0.05

4-16   (a) relative frequency   (b) subjective   (c) classical
        (d) relative frequency (or subjective)   (e) subjective

4-18 $P(A) = .28$, $P(B) = .38$, $P(A \text{ or } B) = .54$

4-20   .013

4-22   (a) .0625   (b) lower (86.25%)

4-24   (a) 1/2   (b) 1/2

4-26   (a) 3/13   (b) 1/13   (c) 1/26

4-28   (a) .02   (b) .07   (c) .0014

4-30   (a) .5576   (b) .1224

4-32   (a) .481545   (b) .015795   (c) .013595   (d) .000585   (e) .013

4-34   .45

4-36 $P(A|C) = 3/7$, $P(C|A) = 2/3$, $P(B \text{ and } C) = 5/63$, $P(C|B) = 10/21$

4-38   (a) .646   (b) .4845

4-40   Not consistent: $P(A|B) \times P(B) = .52$, but $P(B|A) \times P(A) = .5225$. However, they must both have the same value, since each equals $P(A \text{ and } B)$.

4-42   (a) .585   (b) .78

4-44   (a) .739   (b) .169   (c) .092

4-46   .4178

4-48   (a) .336   (b) .5

4-50   (a) .3810   (b) .5

4-52   The difference in life insurance premiums agrees with our common-sense belief that the risk of dying in any given year increases as we get older. Higher automobile insurance rates for younger drivers suggest that they have a higher probability of being involved in accidents.

4-54   They have used data on the past rate of failure for restaurants to predict the current rate.

4-56   (a) 1/7   (b) 2/7   (c) 3/7
        These are classical probabilities.

4-58   (a) No: There are no vice-presidential nominations during mid-term elections.
        (b) No: he could be renominated and reelected. However, winning and losing the nomination are clearly mutually exclusive.
        (c) No: he could be renominated but lose the election.

4-60   (a) .208   (b) .690   (c) .064

4-62   (a) relative frequency   (b) .1290

4-64   Assuming that needing X-rays and having insurance are independent, the probability is .1656.

4-66   (a) 120   (b) 100   (c) 60   (d) 160

4-68   (a) .5746   (b) .2388   (c) .1866

4-70

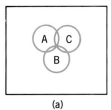 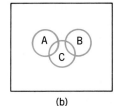 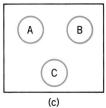 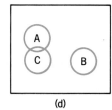

       (a)   (b)   (c)   (d)

4-72   (a) .005   (b) .003   (c) .175

4-74   (a) 3/15, 2/15   (b) 10/45   (c) 15/30

4-76   (a) .8044   (b) .4796   (c) .0039

4-78   (a) A, because .11 < .13   (b) Yes, switch to B, because .02 < .08

4-80   (a) .93   (b) .25

CHAPTER 5

5-2

Value	2	4	5	7	8
Probability	.30	.20	.05	.35	.10

5-4   a, b, and e

5-6

Number sold	2,500	5,000	5,500
Probability	.2	.7	.1

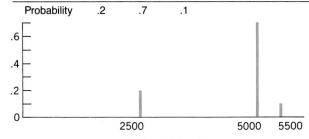

Number of jets sold

5-8

Outcome	8,000	9,000	10,000	11,000	12,000	13,000
Probability	.05	.15	.25	.30	.20	.05

   b) $10,600

5-10

Outcome	0	15	30	45	60	75
Probability	.05	.25	.15	.35	.15	.05

   b) 36.75

5-12   13.29 months

5-14   For the truck and air divisions, respectively, the expected numbers of lost letters per month are 3.083 and 3.167, so he should investigate the air division.

5-16   16 cars

5-18   (a) .0043   (b) .1480   (c) 1   (d) .0333

5-20   (a) $\mu = 6.4, \sigma = 1.960$ (b) $\mu = 7.5, \sigma = 1.369$
        (c) $\mu = 3.3, \sigma = 1.675$ (d) $\mu = 315, \sigma = 5.612$
        (e) $\mu = 3.9, \sigma = 1.925$

5-22 (a) .0009 (b) .8171

5-24 (a) Claim 1 implies that $p = .40$, claim 2 that $p = .467$; so they are not consistent.
(b) No, since they claim that $p = .40$.

5-26 (a) .9953 (b) .7031 (c) .0047 (d) .5155

5-28 (a) .2103 (b) .4101 (c) .0360

5-30 (a) .03414 (b) .99922 (c) 0.00000

5-32 Yes, the probability of resting more than 12 minutes is .5859.

5-34 (a) .323323 (b) .135335

5-36 (a) .00674 (b) .01813 (c) .00016

5-38 (a) .7422 (b) .9484 (c) .0016 (d) .4658

5-40 (a) 11.72 tubes (b) 120 tubes

5-42 .4870

5-44 $P(3.9 < x < 4.1) = .7745$; the standards are not satisfied.

5-46 (a) .2537 (b) .1210 (c) .1489

5-48 .2266

5-50 (a) .3372 (b) .1587 (c) .68 (d) .32

5-52 (a) normal (b) Poisson (c) binomial (d) normal

5-54 A random variable is discrete if it can assume only a limited number of values, continuous if it can assume all values in a given range. The different types of random variables have different probability functions (also called discrete and continuous) associated with them.

5-56 (a) .0413 (b) .1606

5-58 11 interns

5-60 (a) normal (b) binomial (c) Poisson (d) normal

5-62 (a) .01832 (b) .00529

5-64 (a) .2202 (b) .0081 (c) .2811 (d) .1117

5-66 (a) .9943 (b) .0208 (c) .7346

5-68 (a) 3,500 lbs (b) $1,500

5-70 .8944

5-72 (a) $P(mpg_A > 45) = .2266$, $P(mpg_B > 45) = .1587$, so choose A.
(b) $P(mpg_A < 39) = .2266$, $P(mpg_B < 39) = .5557$, so choose A.

5-74 (a) add bike lanes (b) add bike lanes (c) no preference

5-76 (a) .6255 (b) .0015

5-78 (a) .9984 (exact answer is .9943, 0.4% error)
(b) .0146 (exact answer is .0208, 30% error)
(c) .7123 (exact answer is .7346, 3% error)

5-80 25,000 roses

5-82 The probabilities of 0, 1, 2, 3, or 4 towers going dark are .62742, .31019, .05751, .00474, and .00015, respectively.

5-84 (a) $\mu = 1168$, $\sigma = 15.28$ (b) $\mu = 1021.79$, $\sigma = 15.33$

5-86 .0197; the 40% estimate appears to be overly optimistic

CHAPTER 6

6-2 Not necessarily. If there is little information available about the population of interest, the best judgment of the individual conducting the study could suggest that probability sampling be used.

6-4 Probability samples involve more statistical analysis and planning at the beginning of a study and usually take more time and money than judgment samples.

6-6 From what we've been told in the problem, Jean's position is apparently quite defensible. Perhaps what makes statistical sampling unique is that it permits statistical inference to be made about a population and its parameters. This is apparently what Jean has done. There are no hard and fast rules as to the size of the sample that must be drawn before inferences can be made. Specifically, there is nothing magic about the 50 percent mark. Common sense would seem to point out that gathering data from 50 percent of some populations might tend to be just as difficult as gathering data from the entire population—for instance, the population of the United States or the world. The defense for Jean's position lies in empirical evidence and some explanation and reasoning with management, educating them about the abilities of statistical inference.

6-8   b, because there is greater between-group-, and lesser within-group-variance.

6-10   Assuming a non-leap year: 1/6, 1/24, 2/11, 3/1, 3/19, 4/6, 4/24, 5/12, 5/30, 6/17, 7/5, 7/23, 8/10, 8/28, 9/15, 10/3, 10/21, 11/8, 11/26, 12/14.

6-12   No. If both parents work, no one will be at home between noon and 5:00, and some of the heaviest users of daycare will be excluded from the survey.

6-14   .10; 12.5 times; seventeen 4's, fourteen 7's, and eleven 2's; random variation and small sample size.

6-16   Yes. The accident times during the year are probably randomly distributed, making that a good candidate for systematic sampling.

6-18   Stratified sampling is more appropriate in this case, since there appear to be two very dissimilar groups, which probably have smaller variation *within* each group than *between* groups.

6-20   Sampling error

6-22   In general, overestimating the mean is neither better nor worse than underestimating. In his case, the underestimate (30¢) is closer to the true mean (31.4¢) than is the overestimate (35¢).

6-24   Average weekly sales have decreased from slightly below 4,000 cartons to slightly above 3,000 cartons.

6-26   It is a sample from the sampling distribution of the mean of samples of size 50 drawn from the population.

6-28   (a) $P(-1.92 < z < 0.99) = .4726 + .3389 = .8115$
        (b) $P(-2.30 < z < 1.18) = .4893 + .3810 = .8703$

6-30   At least 355

6-32   (a) $P(z \geq 0.71) = .5000 - .2611 = .2389$
        (b) $P(z \geq 1.01) = .5000 - .3438 = .1562$
          It has decreased by .0827.

6-34   (a) $P(z \geq 0.08) = .5000 - .0319 = .4681$
        (b) $P(z \leq -0.21) = .5000 - .0832 = .4168$

6-36 $P(z < 1.08) = .5000 + .3599 = .8599 > .80$
       The overhaul will not be ordered.

6-38   (a) 120 bu   (b) 1.549 bu
        (c) $P(z > 2.45) = .5000 - .4929 = .0071$
        (d) $P(-1.94 < z < 1.29) = .4738 + .4015 = .8753$

6-40   At least 36

6-42   (a) 1.490   (b) $P(1.68 < z < 2.68) = .4963 - .4535 = .0428$

6-44 $P(z \geq 0.71) = .5000 - .2611 = .2389$

6-46 $P(-1.78 < z < 1.64) = .4625 + .4495 = .9120$

6-48 $P(-1.15 \leq z \leq 1.15) = .3749 + .3749 = .7498$

6-50   Judgmental, because a helmet is inspected if its size is sufficiently close to Wayne's hat size.

6-52   Yes.

6-54   At least 128 customers

6-56   No. In general, sample means overestimate population means as often as they underestimate them.

6-58   Yes. Sampling the necessary 75 additional women will cost $1,600, and will increase the benefits by $1,720.

6-60 $P(z < 2.76) = .5000 + .4971 = .9971$

6-62   At least 25 alarms

CHAPTER 7

7-2   Measuring an entire population may not be feasible because of time and cost consider-
       ations. A sample yields only an estimate and is subject to sampling errors.

7-4   An estimator is a sample statistic used to estimate a population parameter. An esti-
       mate is a specific numerical value for an estimator resulting from the particular sample
       which is observed.

7-6   It assures us that the estimator becomes more reliable with larger samples.

7-8 $\bar{x} = 14.278$ thousand people, $s^2 = 21.119$ (thousands of people)^2

7-10   .46

7-12   (a) 0.181   (b) 6.2 ± 0.181

7-14   (a) 1.70   (b) 217 ± 1.70

7-16 7 ± 0.208 cars

7-18   (a) 29.8 ± 1.786 students
       (b) No, we cannot be 95.5% certain that the average class size in Foresight County is
           less than that in Hindsight County.

7-20   The range of an estimate between and including the upper and lower confidence limits

7-22   (a) High confidence levels produce wide intervals, so we sacrifice precision to gain
           confidence.
       (b) Narrow intervals result from low confidence levels, so we sacrifice confidence to
           gain precision.

7-24   No, it is based on the expected results if the sampling process is repeated many times.

7-26   (a) 25 ± 4.9 minutes   (b) 15 ± 3.267 minutes
       (c) 38 ± 1.96 minutes   (d) 20 ± 9.8 minutes
       (e) These are prediction intervals for the next observation rather than confidence
           intervals for the population mean based on a sample which has already been
           taken.

7-28   (a) 112.4 ± 1.697 (b) 112.4 ± 2.234

7-30   (a) 0.167   (b) 6.2 ± 0.342

7-32 24.3 ± 0.935 minutes

7-34 $250,000 \pm \$2,380$

7-36   (a) .0570   (b) $.65 \pm .1117$

7-38   (a) .0238   (b) $.87 \pm .0555$

7-40   (a) $.6 \pm .076$ (b) $1,800 \pm 228$ accounts

7-42 $.6 \pm .1497$

7-44   (a) 2.052   (b) 2.998   (c) 1.782   (d) 2.262   (e) 2.797   (f) 3.250

7-46 72 ± 3.420

7-48   (a) 81.1625   (b) 5.1517   (c) 81.1625 ± 5.4606

7-50 31 ± 5.58 accidents

7-52 $n \geqslant 421$

7-54 $n \geqslant 1413$

7-56 $n \geqslant 23$ bags

7-58 $n \geqslant 60$ days

7-60   An interval estimate gives an indication of possible error through the extent of its
       range and its associated confidence level. A point estimate is only a single number, and
       thus one needs additional information to determine its reliability.

7-62 $n \geqslant 9,604$ grades

7-64   (a) 0.3 ounces   (b) 0.0397 ounces   (c) $23.2 \pm .0778$ ounces.

7-66   It is unbiased, consistent, efficient, and sufficient.

7-68   (a) 78.88%   (b) 98.36%   (c) 90.70%

7-70 $n \geqslant 543$ stocks (using $p = .5$; $p = .85$ gives $n \geqslant 277$).

7-72   (a) 4.11   (b) 4.03

7-74   (a) 0.0195 apples   (b) 3.2 ± 0.0195 apples

7-76   (a) $\bar{x} = \$425.39$, $s = \$107.10$ (b) $\$425.39 \pm \$14.84$

7-78   (a) 0.0990 mg/li   (b) 5.2 ± 0.0990 mg/li

7-80 $.3333 \pm .0843$

7-82   (a) 0.0440 mph   (b) 66.3 ± 0.0880 mph
        (c) Yes, since the entire interval lies below 67 mph.

7-84 $n \geqslant 11$ acres

CHAPTER 8

For the solutions of exercises which require testing specific hypotheses, we give the observed value of the test statistic, the appropriate limit(s) of the acceptance region (denoted by the subscripts L or U), and the conclusion.

8-2   Theoretically, one could toss a coin a large number of times to see if the proportion of heads was very different from .5. Similarly, by recording the outcomes of many dice rolls, one could see if the proportion of any side was very different from 1/6. A large number of trials would be needed for each of these examples.

8-4   (a) Assume a hypothesis about a population.
        (b) Collect sample data.
        (c) Calculate a sample statistic.
        (d) Use the sample statistic to evaluate the hypothesis.

8-6   We mean that we would not have reasonably expected to find that particular sample if in fact the hypothesis had been true.

8-8   .0802

8-10 $\bar{x} = 26{,}100$, $\bar{x}_L = 27{,}000$, $\bar{x}_U = 30{,}000$, so Ned should not purchase the Stalwarts. If σ has increased, the conclusion might not be valid.

8-12 $\bar{x} = 26.8$ mpg, $\bar{x}_L = 26.57$, $\bar{x}_U = 29.43$, so such a sample is not unreasonable.

8-14   A null hypothesis represents the hypothesis you are trying to reject; the alternative hypothesis represents all other possibilities.

8-16   Type I: rejecting a null hypothesis when in fact it is true
        Type II: accepting a null hypothesis when in fact it is false

8-18   The significance level of a test is the probability of a type I error.

8-20   (a) t with 24 df   (b) normal   (c) t with 17 df   (d) normal
        (e) t with 41 df (so we use the normal table)

8-22   A one-tailed test would be used when we are testing whether the population mean is higher (upper-tailed test) or lower (lower-tailed test) than some hypothesized value. We use a two-tailed test to determine if the population mean is different (in either direction) from the hypothesized value.

8-24 $H_0: \mu = 10$ tons $H_1: \mu > 10$ tons

8-26 $\bar{x} = \$42.95$, $\bar{x}_L = \$42.59$ so don't reject H_0. Atlas should not believe the price has decreased.

8-28 $\bar{x} = 13{,}000$ hours, $\bar{x}_L = 13{,}521$ hours, so reject H_0. The average life is significantly less.

8-30 $\bar{x} = \$151$, $\bar{x}_U = \$150$, so reject H_0. Their commissions are significantly higher.

8-32 $\bar{x} = 0.33\%$, $\bar{x}_L = 0.51\%$, so reject H_0. The growth rate has decreased significantly.

8-34   .0505, .1271, .2611

8-36   .0202, .0606, .1469

8-38 $\bar{p} = .1412$, $\bar{p}_L = .1155$, so don't reject H_0. There is not evidence that West Coast distribution is significantly worse.

8-40   (a) $\bar{p} = .0944$, $\bar{p}_L = .1072$, so reject H_0. Yes, they should conclude that transmission is reduced.
        (b) $\bar{p}_L = .0963$, so the conclusion is unchanged.
        (c) Not necessarily: among other reasons, we have been given no information about potential adverse side-effects of the spray.

8-42 $\bar{p} = .05583$, $\bar{p}_U = .05577$, so reject H_0. Interest has increased significantly (although just barely).

8-44 $\bar{x} = 83$, $\bar{x}_0 = 75.54$, so reject H_0.

8-46 $\bar{x} = \$780,000$, $\bar{x}_L = 799,595$, so reject H_0.

8-48 $\bar{x} = 7.2$ hours, $\bar{x}_L = 7.14$ hours, so accept H_0.

8-50 $\bar{x} = 12.4$ pounds, $\bar{x}_L = 8.16$ pounds, $\bar{x}_U = 11.84$ pounds, so reject H_0. There is significant evidence for doubting the claim.

8-52 (a) 1.296
    (b) $\bar{x}_1 - \bar{x}_2 = 4$, the limits of the acceptance region are ± 3.331, so reject H_0. They appear to come from different populations.

8-54 (a) $\bar{x} = \bar{x}_{1989} - \bar{x}_{1988} = -\$0.19$ (b) $s = \$1.05$, $\hat{\sigma}_{\bar{x}} = \$0.35$
    (c) Limits of the acceptance region are $\pm\$1.01$, so accept H_0. They were not significantly different.

8-56 $\bar{x}_1 - \bar{x}_2 = 1.13\%$, $(\bar{x}_1 - \bar{x}_2)_U = 0.27\%$, so reject H_0. Rates did decline significantly.

8-58 $\bar{p}_1 - \bar{p}_2 = .12$, the limits of the acceptance region are $\pm.11$, so reject H_0. The proportions are significantly different.

8-60 $\bar{p}_1 - \bar{p}_2 = -.080$, $(\bar{p}_1 - \bar{p}_2)_L = -.087$, so accept H_0. Install the less expensive system.

8-62 $\bar{x}_A - \bar{x}_B = -4.9$ mpg, $(\bar{x}_A - \bar{x}_B)_L = -4.50$ mpg, so reject H_0. Brand B has significantly higher mileage.

8-64 $\bar{x} = \bar{x}_O - \bar{x}_A = \$5.11$, $\bar{x}_U = \$9.69$, so accept H_0. The Apson is not significantly less expensive.

8-66 $\bar{x} = \bar{x}_{\text{with}} - \bar{x}_{\text{without}} = 2.833$, $\bar{x}_L = -19.95$, $\bar{x}_U = 19.95$, so accept H_0. The music has no significant effect.

8-68 $\bar{x} = \bar{x}_{\text{after}} - \bar{x}_{\text{before}} = 11$ push-ups, $\bar{x}_U = 10.76$ push-ups, so reject H_0. The claim is supported.

8-70 Prob value $= .0571$

8-72 Prob value $= .0124$, so recalibrate if $\alpha > .0124$.

8-74 (a) $H_1 : p_{NY} \neq p_{DC}$
    (b) $H_1 : \mu_A > \mu_B$
    (c) $H_1 : \mu \neq 8$
    (d) $H_1 : \mu < 34$

8-76 No, because each is equally distant from the hypothesized mean and hence equally likely to lead to acceptance in a two-tailed test.

8-78 $\bar{x} = 4.3$ books, $\bar{x}_L = 2.52$ books, $\bar{x}_U = 4.28$ books, so reject H_0. The average has changed significantly.

9-80 $\bar{p} = .1333$, $\bar{p}_U = .0964$, so reject H_0. Significantly more than usual set new highs.

9-82 (a) .0316   (b) .0548   (c) .0099

9-84 $\bar{x} = 86.3°$ F, $\bar{x}_U = 86.65°$ F, so accept H_0. It should not be cited.

8-86 (a) $\bar{x}_{\text{after}} - \bar{x}_{\text{before}} = 4.18$ ounces, $(\bar{x}_{\text{after}} - \bar{x}_{\text{before}})_U = 6.25$ ounces, so accept H_0. The campaign has not increased demand significantly.
    (b) Re-interview the same 11 customers who were interviewed before the campaign.

8-88 $\bar{p}_{\text{after}} - \bar{p}_{\text{before}} = .08$, $(\bar{p}_{\text{after}} - \bar{p}_{\text{before}})_U = .0945$, so accept H_0. It has not improved significantly.

8-90 (a) $\bar{x}_L - \bar{x}_C = 4.29$ days, $(\bar{x}_L - \bar{x}_C)_U = 2.24$ days, so reject H_0. Calls do lead to significantly faster collections.
    (b) No, he cannot. He doesn't know how much of the collection time with letters is due to the interval between the letter's mailing and its receipt by the customer.

8-92 $\bar{x} = \bar{x}_C - \bar{x}_B = -2.06$ minutes, $\bar{x}_L = -1.86$ minutes, $\bar{x}_U = 1.86$ minutes, so reject H_0. There is a significant difference.

8-94 $\bar{x} = \bar{x}_{\text{new}} - \bar{x}_{\text{old}} = -1.29$ bites, $\bar{x}_L = -1.43$ bites, so accept H_0. The new formula is not significantly more effective.

8-96 $\bar{x} = 12.4$ trials, $\bar{x}_U = 12.65$ trials, so accept H_0. They are not significantly harder.

8-98 $\bar{x}_S - \bar{x}_{PR} = -9.47$ pieces, the limits of the acceptance region are ± 8.70 pieces, so reject H_0. There are significant differences in productivity.

8-100 $\bar{p} = .13$, $\bar{p}_L = .1347$, $\bar{p}_U = .2253$, so reject H_0. Her belief is not reasonable.

8-102 $\bar{p} = .75$, $\bar{p}_L = .7693$, so reject H_0. Her accuracy is significantly less than asserted.

8-104 $\bar{p} = .1967, \bar{p}_U = .2003$, so accept H_0. Although the proportion of redeemed coupons has not increased significantly, we can say nothing about the proportion of new parents who use the supplement.

8-106 (a) .4641   (b) .8643   (c) .9890

CHAPTER 9

9-2 To determine whether or not three or more population means can be considered equal.

9-4 (a) False; can do inferences on only one or two variances.
     (b) True; use analysis of variance.
     (c) True; use a chi-square test.

9-6 (a) 12   (b) 5   (c) 12   (d) 9

9-8 (a) $\chi^2 = 5.012$
     (b) There are two possibilities:
         1. H_0: region and purchasing are independent
            H_1: region and purchasing are dependent
         2. H_0: $p_{NE} = p_{NW} = p_{SE} = p_{SW}$
            H_1: not all the proportions are equal
     (c) $\chi^2_U = 7.815$, so we accept H_0

9-10 (a) H_0: sales and economy are independent
          H_1: sales and economy are dependent
      (b) $\chi^2 = 34.597$
      (c) $\chi^2_U = 10.645$, so we reject H_0.

9-12 $\chi^2 = 32.855, \chi^2_U = 14.684$, so we reject H_0. Different levels of education do correspond to different frequencies of readership.

9-14 $\chi^2 = 8.964, \chi^2_U = 9.488$, so we accept H_0. The data are well described by the binomial distribution with $n = 5$ and $p = .4$.

9-16 (a)

Deposit	$0-999	$1,000-1,999	$2,000+
f_e	22.36	65.27	22.36

      (b) $\chi^2 = 0.562$
      (c) H_0: Deposits normally distributed with $\mu = \$1,500, \sigma = \$600$.
          H_1: They are not so distributed.
      (d) $\chi^2_U = 4.605$, so we accept H_0. The data are well described by the normal distribution with $\mu = \$1,500$ and $\sigma = \$600$.

9-18 $\chi^2 = 26.39, \chi^2_U = 4.605$, so we reject H_0. The data are not well described by the binomial distribution with $n = 2$ and $p = .15$.

9-20 $\chi^2 = 2.030, \chi^2_U = 11.070$, so we accept H_0. The data are well described by the Poisson distribution with $\lambda = 2$.

9-22 (a) No: with $n = 200$, the Central Limit Theorem allows us to base a test of μ on the normal distribution even if the population isn't normal.
      (b) H_0: data normally distributed (with some unspecified μ and σ)
          H_1: data not normally distributed
      (c) .0823, .1210, .1864, .2206, .1864, .2033
      (d) $\chi^2 = 4.455, \chi^2_U = 7.815$, so we accept H_0. The data are well described by a normal distribution.

9-24 $\chi^2 = 8.6, \chi^2_U = 7.779$, so we reject H_0. Jeff is wrong.

9-26 (a) Free sample: 84, On-pack gift: 90, Cents off: 75.8, Refund by mail: 78, grand mean: 81.95
      (b) 204.05
      (c) 21.05
      (d) $F = 9.69, F_U = 5.29$, so we reject H_0. The promotions have significantly different effects on sales.

9-28 $F = 1.47, F_U = 3.29$, so we accept H_0. The employees' productivities are not significantly different.

9-30   (a) $\bar{x}_j = 36, 31, 35, 31; \bar{\bar{x}} = 33.25$
       (b) 34.5833
       (c) 7.375
       (d) $F = 4.69$, $F_U = 3.24$, so we reject H_0. The different speeds lead to significantly different numbers of defective clocks.

9-32 $F = 6.67$, $F_U = 3.68$, so we reject H_0. The average numbers of apprehended shoplifters differ significantly during these months.

9-34 $F = 18.17$, $F_U = 2.87$, so we reject H_0. The rooms have significantly different average dust scores.

9-36 $F = 0.23$, $F_U = 3.24$, so we accept H_0. The sales of the four brands are not significantly different.

9-38   (a) $F = 0.51$, $F_U = 3.24$, so we accept H_0. The mean service times are not significantly different.
       (b) Since no restaurant is significantly worse than the others, any recommendations would have to be made to all of the managers.

9-40 $\chi^2 = 37.688$, $\chi_U = 45.722$, so we accept H_0.

9-42   (57.941, 466.055)

9-44   (a) $H_0: \sigma^2 = 64$, $H_1: \sigma^2 \neq 64$
       (b) $\chi^2 = 8.31$, $\chi_L^2 = 8.907$, $\chi_U^2 = 32.852$, so we reject H_0.
       (c) Six-year-olds' attention spans have significantly different variabilities than five-year-olds' attention spans.

9-46 $\chi^2 = 8.4$, $\chi_L^2 = 13.848$, so we reject H_0. The variance has been reduced significantly.

9-48 $F = 2.25$, $F_U = 2.12$, so we reject H_0. Oppy has a significantly lower variance, so he should invest in Oppy.

9-50 $F = 2.78$, $F_U = 2.23$, so we reject H_0. Line B's defect rate is significantly more variable.

9-52 $F = 1.25$, $F_L = 1/1.94 = 0.52$, $F_U = 1.89$, so we accept H_0. It's OK to go ahead with the t-test.

9-54 $F = 4$, $F_U = 1.98$, so we reject H_0. PAL's processing speed is significantly more variable.

9-56 $F = 1.6$, $F_L = 1/2.25 = 0.44$, $F_U = 2.74$, so we accept H_0. The variances are not significantly different.

9-58 H_0: occupation and attitude are independent
       H_1: occupation and attitude are dependent
       $\chi^2 = 6.607$, $\chi_U^2 = 9.488$, so we accept H_0.

9-60   (a) normal   (b) chi-square   (c) F (ANOVA)   (d) t

9-62 $F = 24.00$, $F_U = 3.24$, so we reject H_0. Prices do vary significantly from brand to brand.

9-64   (a) $H_0: \mu_S = \mu_S = \mu_M$
          H_1: the μ_j are not all the same
       (b) $F = 0.15$, $F_U = 3.89$, so we accept H_0.
       (c) The rates of return for the three types of investments are not significantly different.

9-66   (a) Reading across rows, the f_e are: 11.933, 15.689, 16.352, 15.026, 8.292, 10.903, 11.363, 10.442, 6.067, 7.978, 8.315, 7.640, 13.551, 17.816, 18.569, 17.064, 14.157, 18.614, 19.401, and 17.828.
       (b) 33.811
       (c) H_0: car and age are independent; H_1: car and age are dependent
       (d) $\chi_U^2 = 26.217$, so we reject H_0.

9-68 $\chi^2 = 45.313$, $\chi_U^2 = 49.588$, so we accept H_0. Women do not show significantly greater variability.

9-70 $F = 3.4$, $F_U \doteq 2.25$, so we reject H_0. The stress group has significantly higher variability.

9-72 $F = 18.96$, $F_U = 3.34$, so we reject H_0. The drugs have significantly different effects on driving skills.

9-74 $F = 7.72$, $F_U = 7.21$, so we reject H_0. The three types have significantly different operating costs.

CHAPTER 10

Note: Regression results are given from analysis with SAS. Hand calculations will differ slightly because of rounding errors.

10-2 An estimating equation is the formula describing the relationship between a dependent variable and one or more independent variables.

10-4 In a *direct relationship,* the dependent variable increases as the independent variable increases; in an *inverse relationship,* the dependent variable decreases as the independent variable increases.

10-6 In a *linear* relationship, the dependent variable changes a constant amount for equal incremental changes in the independent variable(s); in a *curvilinear* relationship, the dependent variable does not change at a constant rate with equal incremental changes in the independent variable(s).

10-8 Multiple regression is a process which determines the relationship between a dependent variable and more than one independent variable.

10-10 (a) direct and linear   (b) inverse and curvilinear
(c) inverse and curvilinear

10-12 A scatter diagram suggests a direct, linear relationship. Clearly, usage of facial tissues does not cause colds.

10-14 (a)

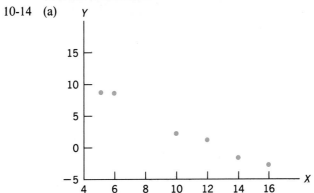

(b) $\hat{Y} = 15.0281 - 1.2471X$
(c) 8.7926, 7.5455, 6.2984

10-16 (a) $\hat{\text{GNP}} = 1.1681 + 1.7156 \cdot \text{MONEY}$
(b) When money supply increases by \$1 million, GNP increases by \$1.7156 million.
(c) $s_e = .3737$. The standard deviation of the data points around the regression line is about \$370,000.
(d) \$14.89 ± \$0.69 (millions)

10-18 (a)

(b) $\hat{\text{PASSENGERS}} = 952.6190 - 6.2381 \cdot \text{PRICE}$
(c) 640.7140 ± 93.1279 passengers

10-20 (a)

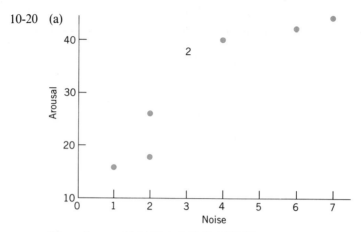

(b) $\widehat{\text{AROUSAL}} = 16.5167 + 4.5667 \cdot \text{NOISE}$
(c) 39.35

10-22 (a)

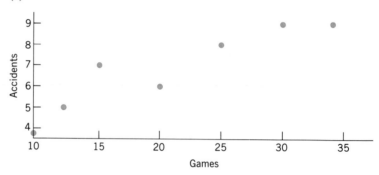

(b) $\widehat{\text{ACCIDENTS}} = 2.7317 + 0.1978 \cdot \text{GAMES}$
(c) 9.3 accidents
(d) 0.7882 accidents

10-24 (a) $\widehat{\text{OVERHEAD}} = -80.4428 + 6.4915 \cdot \text{UNITS}$
(b) 244.1322
(c) 10.2320

10-26 $r^2 = 0.8246$, $r = -0.9081$

10-28 $r^2 = 0.7191$, $r = 0.8480$

10-30 (a) positive   (b) positive   (c) positive   (d) zero

10-32 (a) $\widehat{\text{PURCHASES}} = 3.3308 + 1.7110 \cdot \text{ADS}$
(b) $r^2 = 0.6189$, $r = 0.7867$

10-34 (a) 0.9706   (b) (1.20, 6.26)
(c) In repeated sampling, 98 out of 100 intervals constructed as in (b) would contain the true, but unknown, population slope.

10-36 $b_L = 1.27$ and $b_U = 1.73$, so we accept H_0. The slope has not changed significantly from its past value.

10-38 (a) $b_L = .091$ and $b_U = .203$, so at $\alpha = .10$, we reject H_0 and conclude that the slope has changed since 1969.
(b) $b_L = .054$ and $b_U = .241$, so at $\alpha = .01$, the slope hasn't changed significantly.

10-40 $b_L = -2.6$ and $b_U = 4.3$, so we accept H_0. The slope has not changed significantly.

10-42 The coefficient of determination is the fraction of the variation in Y that is explained by X. Its square root, the coefficient of correlation, indicates whether the relationship is direct or inverse.

10-44 Correlation only measures the strength of the relationship between the values of two variables. In no way does it address the cause of that relationship.

10-46   (a) $r^2 = 0.9581$, $r = 0.9788$

       (b) No, the high correlation is spurious. It simply reflects the fact that both the number of storks and the number of births tend to rise when the population increases. Higher population means more people to have children and more roofs for storks to nest on.

10-48 $r^2 = 0.9938$, $r = -0.9969$

10-50   (a) 1, +   (b) 2, +   (c) 2, −   (d) 2, −

10-52 $r^2 = 0.9888$, $r = 0.9944$

10-54 $H_0: B = .94$, $H_1: B < .94$

       $b = .87$, $b_L = .8800$, so we reject H_0. The marginal propensity to consume has decreased significantly.

10-56   (a, c)

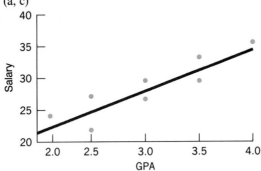

       (b) $\widehat{\text{SALARY}} = 9 + 6.5 \cdot \text{GPA}$

10-58   (a) $\widehat{\text{REVENUE}} = 9.6184 + 0.8124 \cdot \text{EXPENDITURE}$

       (b) \$6.8637 hundred thousand

       (c) \$32.3656 ± \$17.6466 (hundred thousands)

10-60   (a) $\widehat{\text{PRICE}} = 7.5294 + 0.0285 \cdot \text{SIZE}$

       (b) $r^2 = 0.3412$; Dave should search elsewhere.

10-62 $\widehat{\text{HEIGHT}} = 56.4667 + 0.1249 \cdot \text{WEIGHT}$

       $r^2 = 0.5524$; 55% of the variation is explained.

CHAPTER 11

11-2   To include qualitative factors in our regressions.

11-4   Yes. Season is a qualitative factor which can be modeled with *dummy variables.*

11-6   No. Multiple regression is based on the same assumptions and procedures as simple regression.

11-8   (a) $\hat{Y} = 2.5915 + 0.8897X_1 + 0.0592X_2$

     (b) 36.99

11-10 (a) $\widehat{\text{GAIN}} = -4.1917 + 0.1048 \cdot \text{WEIGHT} + 0.8065 \cdot \text{AGE}$

     (b) 8.10 pounds

11-12 (a) $\widehat{\text{RENT}} = 96.4581 + 136.4847 \cdot \text{ROOMS} - 2.4035 \cdot \text{DISTANCE}$

     (b) \$365

11-14 (a) $\hat{Y} = 34.8079 + 5.2618X_1 - 8.0187X_2 + 6.8084X_3$

     (b) 4.0688   (c) .9834   (d) 66.37

11-16 (a) $\widehat{\text{NUMBER}} = -1274.7929 + 17.0588 \cdot \text{INDEX} + 0.5406 \cdot \text{PEOPLE} - 0.1743 \cdot \text{INCOME}$

     (b) 87.25%   (c) 2,436 rush returns

11-18 (a) $\widehat{\text{GRADE}} = -49.95 + 1.07 \cdot \text{HOURS} + 1.36 \cdot \text{IQ} + 2.04 \cdot \text{BOOKS} - 1.80 \cdot \text{AGE}$

     (b) 76.72%   (c) About 77

11-20 (a) $\widehat{\text{PRICE}} = -1.381 + 2.852 \cdot \text{SQFT} - 3.713 \cdot \text{STORIES} + 30.285 \cdot \text{BATHS} + 1.172 \cdot \text{AGE}$

(b) $R^2 = .952$, 95.2% of the variation in sales price is explained by the four explanatory variables.

(c) $98,700

11-22 (a) $H_1: B_2 < 3$, $b_2 = 1.25$, $(b_2)_L = 1.485$, so we reject H_0. The regression does not support Mark's belief.

(b) $H_1: B_1 \neq 0.5$, $b_1 = 0.251$, $(b_1)_L = 0.24$, $(b_1)_U = 0.76$, so we accept H_0. This belief is supported by the regression.

(c) $H_1: B_3 > 333.333$. Since $b_3 = 250.659$, which is less than 333.333, we accept H_0. Mark's rates are OK.

11-24 (a) $F = 5.77$ (b) $F_U = 4.12$ (c) Yes, because we reject H_0.

11-26 Yes, because the PROB>F value (.0001) is less than α (.05). It is significant as a whole.

11-28 Multicollinearity is present because the prime rate at banks is dependent upon the Federal Reserve discount rate, which, for the most part, moves directly with the inflation rate.

11-30 (a) $\hat{\text{SALES}} = 172.340 + 25.950 \cdot \text{PROMOT} - 13.238 \cdot \text{COMP} - 3.041 \cdot \text{FREE}$

(b) $H_1: B_3 < 0$. The (one-tailed) prob value is $.221/2 = .111$, which is greater than α (.05), so we accept H_0. Sales do not decrease significantly with free flights.

(c) $H_1: B_1 \neq 28$. $b_1 = 25.950$, $(b_1)_L = 19.24$, $(b_1)_U = 36.76$, so we accept H_0. The change in sales per $1,000 increase in promotions is not significantly different from $28,000.

(d) $(-19.86, -6.62)$

11-32 (a) $\hat{\text{REVENUE}} = a + b_1 \cdot \text{FLOW} + b_2 \cdot \text{FLOW}^2$

(b) Let CITY be 0 for the first city, 1 for the second.
$\hat{\text{REVENUE}} = a + b_1 \cdot \text{FLOW} + b_2 \cdot \text{FLOW}^2 + b_3 \cdot \text{CITY}$

11-34 (a) With X_2^* as the new dummy variable, the regression equation becomes $\hat{Y} = 7.189 + 3.5X_1 - 0.489X_2^*$.

(b) $H_1: B_2 \neq 0$. The limits of the acceptance region are ± 0.18. Since $b_2 = .489$, we reject H_0. Penicillin reaction is a significant explanatory variable.

11-36 (a) Deviations from the line will not be random.

(b) The residuals would show the same non-random pattern as in (a).

11-38 (a) He has spotted the obvious pattern in the residuals.

(b) Include the square of the number of days in court as an additional explanatory variable.

11-40 (a) $\hat{\text{GROWTH}} = 70.066 + 0.422 \cdot \text{CREAT} + 0.271 \cdot \text{MECH} + 0.745 \cdot \text{ABST} + 0.420 \cdot \text{MATH}$

(b) 92.61%   (c) CREAT, ABST, and MATH

(d) Yes, since PROB>F $= .0001$ (e) 104.93

11-42 (a) $\hat{\text{ANESTHES}} = 90.032 + 99.486 \cdot \text{TYPE} + 21.536 \cdot \text{WEIGHT} - 34.461 \cdot \text{HOURS}$

(b) $(547, 805)$ milliliters

(c) $H_1: B_1 \neq 0$. Since the (two-tailed) prob value (.0435) is less than α (.10), we reject H_0. The amounts of anesthesia needed for dogs and cats are significantly different.

(d) Yes, because the PROB>F value (.0001) is less than α (.05).

11-44 (a) $\hat{\text{PRICE}} = 444.7183 - 0.6124 \cdot \text{WEIGHT} - 4.3769 \cdot \text{SQFT}$ (b) $182

11-46 (a) $\hat{\text{REVENUE}} = 28725.416 - 139.760 \cdot \text{PROPERTY} + 105.176 \cdot \text{SALES} + 56.065 \cdot \text{GASOLINE}$

(b) A: 28500.50, B: 28893.92; they should adopt proposal B.

11-48 $\hat{\text{PHONES}} = -6.6325 + 2.6040 \cdot \text{YEARS}$ (in 100,000's of units), $r^2 = 0.7951$
The residuals show that curvature is present.
$\hat{\text{PHONES}} = 3.6280 - 2.9926 \cdot \text{YEARS} + 0.5597 (\text{YEARS})^2$, $r^2 = 0.9836$
The quadratic equation is a better fit.

CHAPTER 12

12-2 b

12-4 They do not use all the information in the data, since they usually rely on ranks or counts.

12-6 Yes. If the data were examined by graphing the number of preferences against the combination number, it could be seen that there is a very distinct bimodal distribution. In this instance, choice of two packages might well be the better alternative.

12-8 $P(\leq 6$ or $\geq 7 +$'s$) = 1$, so we accept H_0. There has not been a significant change in collection time.

12-10 (a) No. Even if 1989 is significantly cooler than 1988, that alone is not strong evidence of a *long-run trend* toward cooler weather.
      (b) $P(9$ or more $+$'s$) = .2120$, so we accept H_0. 1989 was not significantly cooler than 1988.

12-12 (a) $P(6$ or more $+$'s$) = .3770$, so we accept H_0. Mothers' ideal family sizes are not significantly greater than daughters'.
      (b) $\bar{p} = .6$, $\bar{p}_U = .798$, so again we accept H_0.
      (c) Now $\bar{p}_U = .590$, so we reject H_0. Ideal family size has decreased significantly.
      (d) With larger n, $\sigma_{\bar{p}}$ decreases, so the width of the acceptance region gets smaller. Thus with the larger sample we could be confident that .6 was significantly greater than .5, whereas with the smaller sample we could not draw that conclusion.

12-14 $U = 61.5$, $U_L = 28.30$, $U_U = 71.70$, so we accept H_0. The mean ages are not significantly different.

12-16 $K = 0.341$, $\chi_U^2 = 5.991$, so we accept H_0. The average amounts paid by the three methods are not significantly different.

12-18 $U = 115.5$, $U_U = 107.2$, so we reject H_0. Output has been significantly reduced.

12-20 $U = 73$, $U_U = 108.1$, so we accept H_0. The promotion has not increased sales significantly. (In fact, sales haven't increased at all!)

12-22 $U = 74.5$, $U_L = 39.05$, $U_U = 103.95$, so we accept H_0. There is no significant difference between the two schools.

12-24 $n_1 = 26$, $n_2 = 22$, $r = 27$, $r_L = 18.2$, $r_U = 31.5$, so we accept H_0. The sequence appears to be random.

12-26 $n_1 = 14$, $n_2 = 14$, $r = 13$, $r_L = 9.9$, $r_U = 20.1$, so we accept H_0. The sequence appears to be random, as we would have expected.

12-28 $n_1 = 15$, $n_2 = 16$, $r = 10$, $r_L = 12.0$, so we reject H_0.
      The sequence is not random, as the owner suspected.

12-30 (e) $n_1 = 45$, $n_2 = 4$, $r = 9$, $r_L = 5.80$, $r_U = 10.90$, so we accept H_0. The sample appears to be random.
      (b) With the same acceptance region, r is now 2, so we reject H_0. The sample is not random (which was obvious by inspection).
      (c) The sample proportion of computer analyses should be about .75. $P(45$ or more computer analyses out of $49 | p = .75) = .0033$, so there are many more computer analyses in the sample than we could reasonably expect to see. Even odder is the particular sequence that was reported: nine 1's, one 2, etc.
      (d) The test only looks at the number of runs in the sample and not at other patterns in the data. In addition, it does not check to see if the sample proportion is reasonable.

12-32 $n_1 = 29$, $n_2 = 11$, $r = 17$, $r_L = 12.1$, $r_U = 21.8$, so we accept H_0. The sample appears to be random, as we would have expected.

12-34 $r_s = .185$, the critical values are $\pm.8571$, so we accept H_0. The rank correlation is not significant.

12-36 $r_s = -.86$, the critical values are $\pm.7455$, so we reject H_0. The rank correlation is significant.

12-38 $r_s = .89$, the upper-tail critical value is .6220, so we reject H_0. The rank correlation is significantly positive.

12-40 $r_s = .498$, the upper-tail critical value is .400, so we reject H_0. The rank correlation is significantly positive, so the interviews should no longer be used.

12-42 $r_s = .791$, the critical values are $\pm.5515$, so we reject H_0. The rank correlation is significant.

12-44 $D_n = .1463$, the upper-tail critical value is .0852, so we reject H_0. The suggested distribution is unlikely to be correct.

12-46 $D_n = .064$, the upper-tail critical value is .1091, so we accept H_0. The data are well described by the suggested distribution.

12-48 $D_n = .3858$, the upper-tail critical value is .0962, so we reject H_0. The data are not well described by a Poisson distribution with $\lambda = 1$.

12-50 $U = 113.5$, $U_U = 124.47$, so we accept H_0. The number of complaints has not been significantly reduced.

12-52 $U = 79.5$, $U_U = 71.7$, so we reject H_0. Ratings are significantly higher in the operations department.

12-54 Although historical data enable us to know what sort of weather to expect at any season of the year, the weather conditions that actually occur are quite random.

12-56 $U = 53 > \mu_U = 50$. Since a lower-tail test is appropriate, we accept H_0. The data do not support her hunch.

12-58 $U = 63.5$, $U_L = 24.07$, $U_U = 75.93$, so we accept H_0. The mean stopping distances are not significantly different.

12-60 $r_s = .642$ the critical values are $\pm.5203$, so we reject H_0. The rank correlation is significant, which supports her suspicion.

12-62 $D_n = .1229$, the upper-tail critical value is .1434, so we accept H_0. The data are well described by a binomial distribution with $n = 4$ and $p = .35$.

12-64 $r_s = -.643$, the lower-tail critical value is $-.538$, so we reject H_0. The data support the claim.

12-66 P(12 or more $-$'s) $= .0176$, so we reject H_0. American League players do suffer more injuries.

12-68 $D_n = .1440$, the upper-tail critical value is .1923, so we accept H_0. The data are well described by a Poisson distribution with $\lambda = 6$.

12-70 The rank correlations are .5933, .6374, and .5359 for the three groups. The college students have the most accurate perception. However, we do not know how to test whether the observed differences are significant.

CHAPTER 13

13-2 To determine what patterns exist within the data over the period examined.

13-4 Demands for services such as water and sewer would perhaps not be met. Adjustment of the tax rate to provide for municipal services might lag behind the actual demand for those services. Extra resources would probably be needed to allow a smooth municipal operation in a situation in which forecasting is poor.

13-6 Seasonal variation

13-8 Cyclical fluctuation

13-10 Secular trend

13-12 (a) $\hat{Y} = 95.6 + 5.9939x$ (b) 173.5 tables

13-14 (a) $\hat{Y} = 1198.3333 + 349.8571x$
(b) $\hat{Y} = 611.8750 + 349.8571x + 50.2679x^2$
(c) linear: 5746 PCs, quadratic: 13655 PCs
(d) Neither is very good. The linear trend misses the acceleration in the rate of faculty PC acquisition. The quadratic trend assumes the acceleration will continue, ignoring the fact that there are only 8000 faculty members.

13-16 (a) $\hat{Y} = 13.5455 + 2.0818x$
(b) $\hat{Y} = 12.6946 + 2.0818x + 0.0851x^2$
(c) Political resistance to increased rates makes it unlikely that the quadratic trend would continue to be a good predictor.

13-18 (a) Since the rate of increase in the pollution rating is itself increasing, a second-degree trend would fit the data better than a linear trend.
(b) However, as the air gets more polluted and citizens get more concerned, actions will be taken to control pollution, so the predictions of the second-degree trend will in all likelihood be too dire.

13-20 (a) 92.75, 104.46, 109.45, 100.67, 96.54, 98.77, 101.86
(b) -7.25, 4.46, 9.45, 0.67, -3.46, -1.23, 1.86
(d) Largest fluctuation (by both methods) was in 1985.

13-22 (a) 94.12, 106.48, 95.42, 107.14, 96.05

(b) -5.88, 6.48, -4.58, 7.14, -3.95
(d) Largest fluctuation (by both methods) was in 1988.

13-24 (a) $\hat{Y} = 24.3714 + 1.0357x$
(b) 98.76, 87.00, 96.85, 115.71, 119.65, 90.76, 90.98
(c) -1.24, -13.00, -3.15, 15.71, 19.65, -9.24, -9.02
(d) Largest fluctuation (by both methods) was in 1987.

13-26 (a) 98.5, 100.25, 101.625, 102.875, 103.625, 104, 104.5, 105.125, 106, 107.375, 109, 110.375, 111.875, 113.875, 115.875, 117.625
(b) 91.37, 77.81, 108.24, 122.48, 91.68, 79.81, 106.22, 121.76, 91.51, 80.09, 105.50, 122.31, 92.07, 79.91, 105.29, 122.42
(c) modified indices: 105.86, 122.36, 91.59, 79.86
seasonal indices: 105.95, 122.46, 91.67, 79.93

13-28 85.15, 104.45, 85.64, 124.75

13-30 (a) 176.875, 179.375, 181.625, 182.25, 181.375, 181.25, 181.375, 181.375, 181.625, 183.375, 184.125, 186.125, 188.25, 188.75, 190.375, 194.125
(b) 109.117, 46.829, 129.387, 114.129, 113.577, 41.931, 130.117, 113.577, 115.072, 39.809, 130.889, 115.514, 109.429, 48.742, 125.542, 113.844
(c) modified indices: 129.752, 113.987, 111.503, 44.380
seasonal indices: 129.875, 114.095, 111.609, 44.422

13-32 (a) 114.50, 129.02, 85.81, 70.67 (b) 45.23 percent

13-34 c and d

13-36 They even themselves out over time and they are frequently minor in magnitude.

13-38 (a) 75.886, 105.081, 142.050, 76.984
(b) 25.038, 22.840, 26.751, 32.474, 27.673, 26.646, 30.975, 29.876, 30.309, 29.501, 28.863, 29.876, 31.626, 33.308, 33.791, 27.278

13-40 A large irregular component; a change in the weather which produces a larger or smaller than expected seasonal index; a change in technology which affects the secular trend; an economic change which alters the time scale of the cyclical component.

13-42 The decline in birth rates which has occurred will no doubt affect future college enrollments; we need to be especially careful about the behavior in birth rates seventeen or eighteen years in the past when estimating college enrollments.

13-44 (a) 78.51, 88.88, 113.51, 119.09
(b) 36.938, 33.753, 36.120, 36.107, 34.391, 38.254, 39.644, 40.306, 42.033, 40.504, 40.525, 42.825, 43.307, 45.005, 41.406, 44.504
(c) $\hat{Y} = 39.7263 + 0.3310x$

13-46 $.7000$, $.7500$, $.7250$, $.6750$, $.6125$, $.5750$, $.5250$, $.4625$, $.4500$, $.4750$, $.5625$, $.6750$, $.7375$, $.7375$, $.7250$, $.7000$, $.6625$, $.6250$, $.5500$, $.4625$, $.4000$, $.3750$, $.4125$, $.5125$, $.6375$, $.7125$, $.7500$, $.7625$, $.7250$, $.6875$, $.6125$, $.5125$

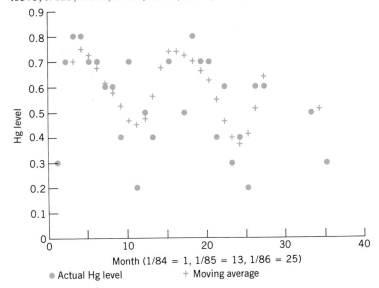

Month (1/84 = 1, 1/85 = 13, 1/86 = 25)
● Actual Hg level   + Moving average

13-48 (a) Gasoline mileage is affected by such things as government responses to the 1973 oil embargo and the resultant mandated fleet mileage standards.
(b) This series is almost entirely irregular variation, because commercial aviation fatalities occur in random batches as the result of unpredictable airplane crashes.
(c) Although total world demand has a long-run increasing trend, there are so many grain growers that each one's exports do not grow smoothly over time but depend instead on political and economic conditions in both importing and exporting nations.
(d) In addition to seasonalities resulting from higher usage in the summer months, gasoline prices are also greatly affected by unpredictable geopolitical events.

13-50 (a) $\hat{Y} = 771.3333 + 32.4857x$
(b) 1064 patients

13-52 236 bicycles

13-54 (a) $\hat{Y} = 17.3750 + 0.7202x$
(b) about 28 completions
(c) He should be very careful about predicting so far in advance, because of the many things that can change in the home-building business in the meantime.

13-56 (a) $\widehat{\text{UNEMPLOYMENT}} = 8.175 - 0.0379x$
(b) 82.1, 81.6, 83.5, 93.5, 101.3, 108.0, 116.1, 125.5, 123.1, 120.5, 113.1, 103.0, 95.2, 93.6, 95.7, 98.0, 96.3, 92.0, 90.3, 87.2
(c)

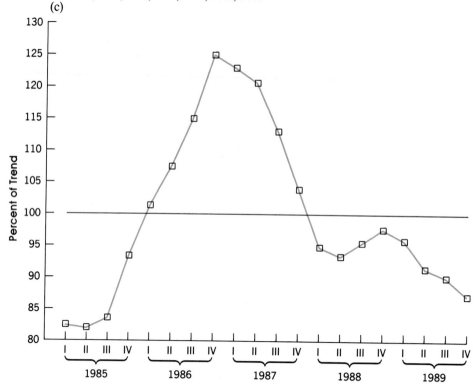

13-58 (a) $\widehat{\text{SALES}} = 60 + 0.25x$
(b) 61
(c) No, a second-degree curve would have been better.

13-60 (a) 91.04, 135.31, 73.65
(b) 823.78, 849.89, 923.34, 856.74, 812.94, 787.55, 878.70, 905.32, 828.29, 702.96, 775.99, 814.71

13-62 (a) $\widehat{\text{SALES}} = 271 + 21x + 0x^2$
(b) The choice of a second degree curve was unnecessary, since the best fitting second-degree equation has c = 0, and hence is a linear equation!

CHAPTER 14

14-2   Price and quantity indices describe the change (usually over time) in a single variable, price and quantity (or number), respectively. Value indices describe the change in the product of price and quantity.

14-4   An index may be used by itself or as part of an intermediate computation, the better to understand some other information.

14-6   Percentage relative $= \dfrac{\text{Current value}}{\text{Base value}} \times 100$

14-8   1987: 110.1; 1988: 121.2; 1989: 130.1

14-10   1987: 95.2; 1989: 102.7

14-12   108.3

14-14   1986: 100.0; 1987: 101.9; 1988: 106.3; 1989: 107.2

14-16   1986: 98.2; 1987: 100.0; 1988: 104.3; 1989: 105.1

14-18   July: 102.1; August: 97.3; these are Laspeyres indices.

14-20   1986: 90.4; 1987: 100.0; 1988: 108.5; 1989: 112.5

14-22   1985: 100.0; 1987: 106.4; 1989: 114.8

14-24   (a) 102.1   (b) 108.9

14-26   1986: 64.5; 1987: 77.0; 1988: 100.0; 1989: 127.0

14-28   1988: 129.4; 1989: 138.7

14-30   1987: 94.7; 1988: 101.3; 1989: 100.0

14-32   Since a value index depends on changes in both prices and quantities, it cannot be identified with either of these variables alone.

14-34   1986: 76.5; 1987: 92.7; 1988: 95.2; 1989: 100.0

14-36   75.5

14-38   Appropriate weighting for one period may become inappropriate in a short time. Unless the weights are changed, the index becomes less informative.

14-40   The values from several adjoining periods are averaged.

14-42   By not reflecting the change in quality, the index may not accurately reflect the change in price level.

14-44   1987: 147.5; 1989: 138.5

14-46   101.1

14-48   The problem of incomparability of indices would be present because computer technology has changed so significantly over the past few decades.

14-50   1987: 100.0; 1988: 101.6; 1989: 116.7

14-52   1987: 100.0; 1988: 111.1; 1989: 112.1

14-54   1987: 105.5; 1988: 107.4; 1989: 112.5

14-56   105.5

14-58   1990: 105.5; 1991: 111.4; 1992: 118.0

14-60 $342.99

14-62   1987: 63.2; 1988: 72.9; 1989: 102.0; 1990: 100.0

14-64   122.9

14-66   1987: 100.0; 1988: 108.7; 1989: 118.1; 1990: 122.9

CHAPTER 15

15-2   Lisa is correct only if she can obtain all of the following information: her objective (presumably Adventures, Inc.'s profit), the available courses of action (which investments to make), the payoffs from these actions, and the probabilities of the various payoffs being realized. The last two of these will, in all likelihood, be difficult to obtain.

15-4   (a) six mechanics
        (b) EVPI = $11,712 (assuming the mechanics get paid vacations)
15-6   (a) 17 cases   (b) $332.70
15-8   (a) 26 machines   (b) hourly EVPI = $1.777
        (c) Since she can't adjust the number of machines available every hour, an hour-by-hour forecast of demand is of little value to her.
15-10 $p^* = .7241$, so order 69 signs
15-12 $p^* = .25$, so order 192 copies
15-14 $p^* = .6279$, so order 90 chickens
15-16   (a) $301,760
        (b)

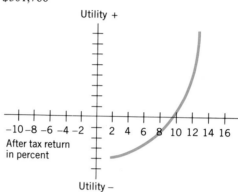

15-18

Alternative	2-month option	4-month option	no purchase
Expected utility	0.685	0.870	0.700

She should purchase the 4-month option

15-20   P(lasting ≥ 6 months) = .9927, so he should hire.
15-22   P(lasting ≥ 78,235 miles) = .7794
15-24 $p_A = .9394$, $p_B = .9162$, so buy the stock
15-26   (a) Payoffs on "operate by self, with snowmaker" branches become 95, 43, −9, with an expected value of 43. She should let the hotel operate the resort.
        (b) Now the payoffs and EV become 96, 48, 0, and 48. She should operate by herself, using the snow-making equipment.
        (c) She is indifferent at a 26% increase in operating cost; her profit from either alternative is $45,000 at this point.

15-28   (a)

Option	bus	walk	bike	car
Expected lateness	15.50	16.00	14.00	15.25

He should ride his bike.

        (b)

Option	bus	walk	bike	car
Expected utility	82.50	82.00	86.00	83.25

He should still ride his bike.

15-30   (a) P(demand ≥ 2213) = .8686
        (b) P(demand ≥ 3263) < .5, so they should buy the modules.
15-32   (a) $p^* = .545$, so order 44 tails
        (b) EVPI = $21.88, the expected increase in profit if the requirement of advance orders doesn't change the demand distribution.
15-34 $p^* = .608$, so order 35 bags.
15-36   (a) The three numbers at some of the nodes are the expected costs for parts b, d.i, and d.ii.

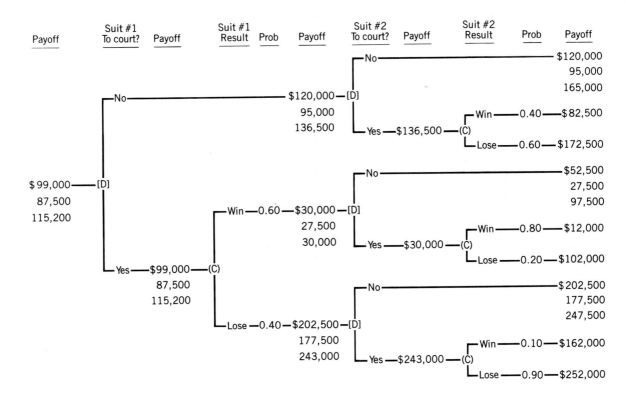

Payoff	Suit #1 To court?	Payoff	Suit #1 Result	Prob	Payoff	Suit #2 To court?	Payoff	Suit #2 Result	Prob	Payoff

(b) Try #1. If he wins, he should try #2; otherwise, he should settle #2.

(c) $99,000 − $66,000 = $33,000

(d) i. Try #1. Settle #2 regardless of the trial #1 outcome.
   ii. Try #1. Try #2 regardless of the trial #1 outcome.

15-38 $p^* = .065$, so stock 25 suits.

15-40

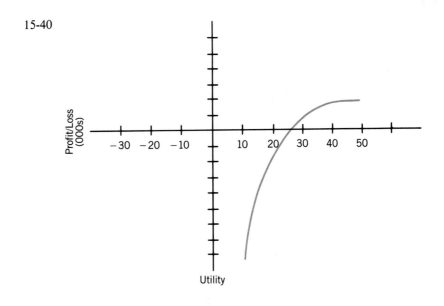

15-42

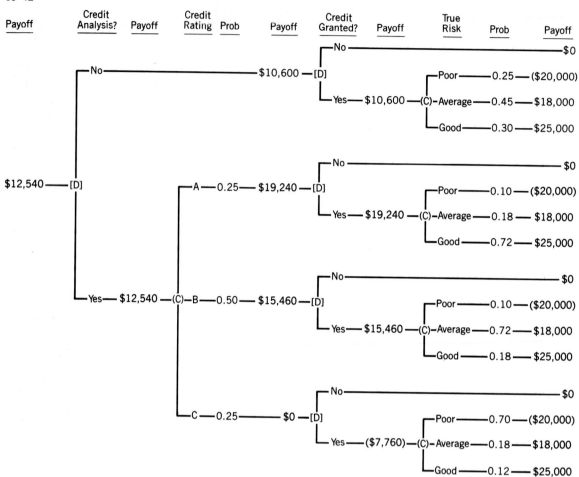

Payoff	Credit Analysis?	Payoff	Credit Rating	Prob	Payoff	Credit Granted?	Payoff	True Risk	Prob	Payoff

(a) Yes, since $12,540 − $10,600 > $750, they should purchase the credit rating.
(b) If the rating is A or B, grant credit.
(c) $12,540 − $10,600 = $1,940
(d) $5,000

15-44 (a) Enduro would accept.
(b)

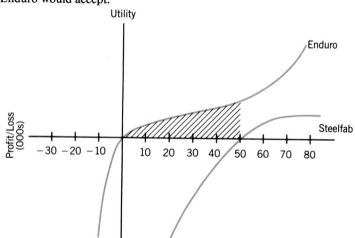

(c) Both would. Steelfab would bid up to $611,111.
15-46 (a) Use 35 games   (b) EVPI = $885
15-48 800
15-50 (a) 75-bed   (b) $87,100   (c) EVPI = $29,100
15-52 16

Bibliography

DATA ANALYSIS AND PRESENTATION:

CLEVELAND, W. S., *The Elements of Graphing Data,* Monterey, CA, Wadsworth Advanced Books and Software, 1985.

EVERITT, B. S., AND G. DUNN, *Advanced Methods of Data Exploration and Modelling,* London, England, Heinemann Education Books, Ltd., 1983.

SCHMID, C. F., *Statistical Graphics: Design Principles and Practices,* New York, NY, John Wiley & Sons, 1983.

TUFTE, E. R., *The Visual Display of Quantitative Information,* Cheshire, CT, Graphics Press, 1983.

TUKEY, J. W., *Understanding Robust and Exploratory Data Analysis,* New York, NY, John Wiley & Sons, 1983.

VELLEMAN, P. F., AND HOAGLIN, D., *Applications, Basics, and Computing of Exploratory Data Analysis,* Boston, MA, Duxbury Press, 1981.

HISTORY OF STATISTICS:

PETERS, W. S., *Counting for Something: Statistical Principles and Personalities,* New York, NY, Springer-Verlag, 1987.

STIGLER, S. M., *The History of Statistics: The Measurement of Uncertainty before 1900,* Cambridge, MA, Belknap Press, 1986.

INTRODUCTORY STATISTICS:

ANDERSON, D. R., D. J. SWEENEY, AND T. A. WILLIAMS, *Statistics for Business and Economics,* 4th ed., Saint Paul, MN, West Publishing Co., 1990.

BERENSON, M. L., AND D. M. LEVINE, *Basic Business Statistics: Concepts and Applications,* 4th ed., Englewood Cliffs, NJ, Prentice Hall, 1989.

FREUND, J. E., F. J. WILLIAMS, AND B. M. PERLES, *Elementary Business Statistics,* 5th ed., Englewood Cliffs, NJ, Prentice Hall, 1988.

IMAN, R. L., AND W. J. CONOVER, *Modern Business Statistics,* 2nd ed., New York, NY, John Wiley & Sons, 1989.

MCCLAVE, J. T., AND P. G. BENSON, *Statistics for Business and Economics,* 4th ed., San Francisco, CA, Dellen Publishing Co., 1988.

MENDENHALL, W., J. E. REINMUTH, AND R. BEAVER, *Statistics for Management and Economics,* 6th ed., Boston, MA, PWS-Kent Publishing Co., 1989.

NONPARAMETRIC STATISTICS:

CONOVER, W. J., *Practical Nonparametric Statistics,* 2nd ed., New York, NY, John Wiley & Sons, 1980.

GIBBONS, J. D., *Nonparametric Statistical Inference,* New York, NY, Marcel Dekker, 1985.

LEHMANN, E. L., *Nonparametrics: Statistical Methods Based on Ranks,* San Francisco, CA, Holden-Day, 1975.

PRATT, J. W., *Concepts of Nonparametric Theory,* New York, NY, Springer-Verlag, 1981.

PROBABILITY:

FELLER, W., *An Introduction to Probability Theory and Its Applications,* Vol. 1, 3rd ed., New York, NY, John Wiley & Sons, 1968.

HOGG, R. V., AND A. ELLIOTT, *Probability and Statistical Inference,* 2nd ed., New York, NY, Macmillan Publishing Co., 1983.

ROWNTREE, D., *Probability,* New York, NY, Charles Scribner's Sons, 1984.

REGRESSION AND ANALYSIS OF VARIANCE:

BERRY, W. D., *Multiple Regression in Practice,* Beverly Hills, CA, Sage Publications, 1985.

COOK, R. D., AND S. WEISBERG, *Residuals and Inference in Regression,* New York, NY, Chapman and Hall, 1982.

KLEINBAUM, D. G., L. L. KUPPER, AND K. E. MULLER, *Applied Regression Analysis and Other Multivariable Methods,* 2nd ed., Boston, MA, PWS-Kent Publishing Co., 1988.

MENDENHALL, W., *A Second Course in Business Statistics: Regression Analysis,* 3rd ed., San Francisco, CA, Dellen Publishing Co., 1989.

NETER, J., W. WASSERMAN, AND M. H. KUTNER, *Applied Linear Statistical Models,* 2nd ed., Homewood, IL, Richard D. Irwin, Inc., 1985.

WEISBERG, S., *Applied Linear Regression,* New York, NY, John Wiley & Sons, 1985.

SAMPLING:

COCHRAN, W. G., *Sampling Techniques,* 3rd ed., New York, NY, John Wiley & Sons, 1977.

GUY, D. M., *Audit Sampling: An Introduction to Statistical Sampling in Auditing,* New York, NY, John Wiley & Sons, 1986.

SCHAEFER, R. L., *Elementary Survey Sampling,* Boston, MA, Duxbury Press, 1986.

SPECIAL TOPICS IN STATISTICS:

BEHN, R. D., AND J. VAUPEL, *Quick Analysis for Busy Decision Makers,* New York, NY, Basic Books, Inc., 1982.

HUFF, D., *How to Lie with Statistics,* New York, NY, W. W. Norton & Co., 1954.

JAFFE, A. J., *Misused Statistics: Straight Talk for Twisted Numbers,* New York, NY, Marcel Dekker, 1987.

MADANSKY, A., *Prescriptions for Working Statisticians,* New York, NY, Springer-Verlag, 1988.

STATISTICAL DECISION THEORY:

BUNN, D. W., *Applied Decision Analysis,* New York, NY, McGraw-Hill Book Co., 1984.

COOK, T. M., AND R. A. RUSSELL, *Introduction to Management Science,* 4th ed., Englewood Cliffs, NJ, Prentice Hall, 1989.

HILLIER, F. S., AND G. J. LIEBERMAN, *Introduction to Operations Research,* 5th ed., New York, NY, McGraw-Hill Book Co., 1990.

LEVIN, R. I., D. S. RUBIN, J. P. STINSON, AND E. S. GARDNER, JR., *Quantitative Approaches to Management,* 7th ed., New York, NY, McGraw-Hill Book Co., 1989.

STATISTICAL SOFTWARE:

NORUSIS, M. J., *SPSS/PC+ Studentware,* Chicago, IL, SPSS Inc., 1988.

RYAN, B. F., B. L. JOINER, AND T. A. RYAN, *MINITAB Handbook,* 2nd ed., Boston, MA, PWS-Kent Publishing Co., 1985.

SAS INSTITUTE, INC., *SAS Introductory Guide for Personal Computers,* Release 6.03 ed., Cary, NC, 1988.

R. L. SCHAEFER, AND R. B. ANDERSON, *The Student Edition of Minitab,* Reading, MA, Addison-Wesley Publishing Co., Inc., 1989.

SYSTAT, INC., *MYSTAT: A Personal Version of SYSTAT,* Evanston, IL, 1989.

SYSTAT, INC., *Business MYSTAT: An Instructional Business Version of SYSTAT,* Evanston, IL, 1989.

TIME SERIES:

ARMSTRONG, J. S., *Long Range Forecasting,* revised ed., New York, NY, John Wiley & Sons, 1985.

BOWERMAN, B. L., *Time Series and Forecasting: Unified Concepts and Computer Implementation,* Boston, MA, Duxbury Press, 1987.

CHATFIELD, C., *The Analysis of Time Series: An Introduction,* New York, NY, Chapman and Hall, 1984.

FARNUM, N. R., AND L. W. STANTON, *Quantitative Forecasting Methods,* Boston, MA, PWS-Kent Publishing Co., 1989.

MILLS, T. C., *Time Series Techniques for Economists,* Cambridge, England, Cambridge University Press, 1990.

Index

INDEX OF APPLICATIONS

Exercise numbers are in three parts. For example, Advertising 3–17, **77** is exercise 17 in chapter 3 found on page **77**. Page numbers are in bold type.